For Reference

Not to be taken from this room

THE FIRESIDE ENCYCLOPÆDIA

OF

POETRY

"STRONG AND FREE, STRONG AND FREE
THE FLOOD-GATES ARE OPEN, AWAY TO THE SEA."
Song of the River.

THE

FIRESIDE ENCYCLOPÆDIA

OF

POETRY.

COMPRISING

THE BEST POEMS OF THE MOST FAMOUS WRITERS,

ENGLISH AND AMERICAN.

COMPILED AND EDITED

BY

HENRY T. COATES.

Granger Index Reprint Series

 BOOKS FOR LIBRARIES PRESS
FREEPORT, NEW YORK

CARNEGIE LIBRARY
LIVINGSTONE COLLEGE
SALISBURY, N. C. 28144

First Published 1878
Reprinted 1971

INTERNATIONAL STANDARD BOOK NUMBER:
0-8369-6266-4

LIBRARY OF CONGRESS CATALOG CARD NUMBER:
79-160903

PRINTED IN THE UNITED STATES OF AMERICA

TO MY

ALMA MATER,

HAVERFORD COLLEGE,

IN REMEMBRANCE OF

THE WARM FRIENDSHIPS FORMED THERE,

THE MANY JOYOUS DAYS SPENT THERE,

AND,

ABOVE ALL,
THE LITERARY ASPIRATIONS WHICH SHE KINDLED AND FOSTERED,
WHICH HAVE SHED A GLADDENED LIGHT OVER THE YEARS
SINCE I LEFT HER HALLOWED PRECINCTS,

THIS VOLUME IS

AFFECTIONATELY DEDICATED.

PREFACE.

NINE years ago this month this work was commenced, principally to while away the long winter evenings, which threatened to hang heavy on the Editor's hands, and, though often laid aside for months at a time, it has been a labor of love ever since; and now it is with feelings akin to those felt at parting with an old and valued friend that he pens these prefatory lines, which mark the completion of his task.

It has been his aim to present a comprehensive collection—an ENCYCLOPÆDIA, in fact—of the poetry of the English language, one that will be a welcome companion at every FIRESIDE; and which, while representing all that is best and brightest in our poetic literature, should contain nothing that would tend to undermine any one's faith or destroy a single virtuous impulse.

Fully aware of the danger of trusting to the caprices or fancies of any individual judgment, the Editor has diligently consulted the works of the best critics and reviewers, and has not hesitated to accept such pieces as have received their united commendation, or such as, through some peculiar power, have touched the popular heart. Each poem has been given complete, and great care has been taken to follow the most authentic and approved editions of the respective authors; and though the quantity of space assigned to each and the selections made may not, and probably will not, satisfy every judgment, it is believed that none of the most famous minor poems of the English language will be found missing from these pages.

At the very outset it was deemed best to discard the chronological arrangement followed by most compilers, and to adopt the plan of classifying each poem according to its subject-matter, originated by Mr. Charles A. Dana in his excellent *Household Book of Poetry*. In many cases this has been found exceedingly difficult; as often, under-currents so run in opposite directions as to threaten the entire foundation upon which the title of a poem is based; and in many poems the "moral" is dwelt on at greater length than the tale itself, so that the Editor has often been sorely tempted to end his perplexity by throwing them into those convenient "olla podridas," "*Poems of Sentiment*" and "*Moral and Didactic Poetry.*" But with all these drawbacks the advantages of the system are so great that there has been no hesitation in adopting it. By it, every taste may be gratified, all moods and humors the better served. Here are "Psalms and Hymns and Spiritual Songs" for Sunday reading, Poems of Home Life and Domestic Bliss for the cold winter nights when the logs are blazing brightly on the cozy hearth, Poems on Nature for the blooming Spring-time and melancholy Autumn, Poems for the lover, and Historical Poems, Old Legends, and Ballads for all.

From the days when
"Adam delved and Eve span"
to the present, human nature has been ever the same. Kingdoms have risen and been forgotten, languages been formed and fallen into disuse, but love, patriotism, sorrow and death, are the same in all ages and climes. The language may be different and the allusions seem strange to our ears, but the same old, old story was told by gallant knight to high-bred dame in the good old days of Queen Bess as is now whispered into the ear of rustic beauty or ball-room belle.

"Each heart recall'd a different name, but all sang 'Annie Laurie.'"

The same impulses animated Horatius as he faced Lars Porsena's army on the banks of the Tiber centuries ago, as actuated the brave boys who flocked to their country's standard during the late civil war; while the parent even now mourns for his erring child in the same language of the heart as did the sweet Singer of Israel for his erring Absalom. For, though long cycles have intervened between Shakespeare and Tennyson, Sir Walter Raleigh and Longfellow, Herrick and Burns, Herbert and Whittier, rare Ben Jonson and Mrs. Browning, one animating purpose breathes alike through the voices of the poets of the past and the present.

As many poems are founded upon some historical fact or some interesting incident or legend, a knowledge of which greatly aids the reader in his appreciation of them, Explanatory and Corroborative Notes have been appended at the end of the volume. This plan has been adopted in preference to placing the notes at the bottom of the page; as many readers, who are familiar with their substance, naturally object to such an arrangement as distracting their attention and marring the continuity of the poem.

The compiler would express his thanks to the various authors and publishers who have so kindly permitted him to use the copyright poems contained in this collection, and especially to Messrs. Houghton, Osgood & Co., who, notwithstanding that they publish excellent works of a similar character, generously granted the use of the various poems by Longfellow, Whittier, Emerson, Lowell, Holmes, Bret Harte, Saxe, Bayard Taylor, Stedman, Stoddard, Trowbridge, Thomas Bailey Aldrich, Parsons, Lucy Larcom, Julia Ward Howe, and Phœbe Cary, the brightest galaxy of names ever collected together by any American publishing-house. He would also acknowledge his obligation to Mr. N. Clemmons Hunt for the assistance rendered in the selection and arrangement of many of the poems in this work.

Originality cannot be claimed for a work of this character, notwithstanding the labor and thought bestowed upon it; *all* the glory, *all* the praise, belongs to the poets themselves. In the words of Montaigne: "Here is a nosegay of culled flowers, to which I have brought nothing of my own *but the thread that ties them.*"

H. T. C.

PHILADELPHIA, October 18th, 1878.

CONTENTS.

	PAGE
INDEX OF THE NAMES OF THE POEMS	ix
INDEX OF AUTHORS	xxv
POEMS OF HOME AND THE FIRESIDE	1
POEMS OF INFANCY AND CHILDHOOD	29
POEMS OF MEMORY AND RETROSPECTION	73
POEMS OF LOVE	97
PERSONAL POEMS	221
HISTORICAL POEMS	283
POEMS OF PATRIOTISM	353
LEGENDARY AND BALLAD POETRY	367
POEMS OF NATURE	423
POEMS OF PLACES	503
"PSALMS AND HYMNS AND SPIRITUAL SONGS"	523
MORAL AND DIDACTIC POETRY	613
POEMS OF LABOR AND SOCIAL QUESTIONS	691
POEMS OF SENTIMENT	723
WEIRD AND FANTASTIC POETRY	793
HUMOROUS AND SATIRICAL POETRY	891
NOTES, EXPLANATORY AND CORROBORATIVE	961
INDEX OF FIRST LINES	989

INDEX OF THE NAMES OF THE POEMS,

ALPHABETICALLY ARRANGED.

	PAGE
ABBOT M'KINNON, The............*James Hogg.*	878
Abide with Me....................*Henry F. Lyte.*	557
Abou Ben Adhem..................*Leigh Hunt.*	664
Abraham Lincoln...................*Tom Taylor.*	280
Absence..................*Frances Anne Kemble.*	101
Absent Wife, To an.........*George D. Prentice.*	14
Addison, To the Earl of Warwick on the Death of.......................*Thomas Tickell.*	242
Address to Certain Gold-Fishes..*H. Coleridge.*	469
Address to the Mummy in Belzoni's Exhibition............................*Horace Smith.*	744
Address to the Soul..............*A. M. Toplady.*	596
Address to the Toothache.........*Robert Burns.*	953
Adelgitha...................... *Thomas Campbell.*	145
Adonais............... *Percy Bysshe Shelley.*	253
Afar in the Desert................*Thomas Pringle.*	490
After Death in Arabia...........*Edwin Arnold.*	681
After the Ball.......................*Nora Perry.*	786
Age and Song.........*Algernon C. Swinburne.*	741
Aged Man-at-Arms, The........... *George Peele.*	751
Aged Oak at Oakley, The............. *H. Alford.*	458
Age of Wisdom, The......... *W. M. Thackeray.*	87
Agincourt, The Ballad of....*Michael Drayton.*	298
Ah, how Sweet it is to Love!....*John Dryden.*	97
A-Hunting We Will Go......*Author Unknown.*	493
Airs of Spring, The............... *Thomas Carew.*	431
Alexander Selkirk, Verses supposed to be Written by .... *Wm. Cowper.*	679
Alexander's Feast....................*John Dryden.*	724
Alice Brand....................*Sir Walter Scott.*	838
Allen-a-Dale.................*Sir Walter Scott.*	186
All Quiet Along the Potomac...*Ethel L. Beers.*	349
Almond-Blossom ....*Edwin Arnold.*	457
Alnwick Castle.............*Fitz-Greene Halleck.*	513
Alonzo the Brave and the Fair Imogine, *Matthew G. Lewis.*	871
Alpine Sheep, The............*Maria W. Lowell.*	638
Althea, To, from Prison.....*Richard Lovelace.*	124
A Man's a Man for a' That......*Robert Burns.*	704
America..........................*Samuel F. Smith.*	354
American Flag, The..........*Joseph R. Drake.*	353
Amynta........................*Sir Gilbert Elliot.*	200
Ancient Mariner, Rime of the.......*Coleridge.*	855
Angel in the House, An............*Leigh Hunt.*	743
Angels of Buena Vista, The....*J. G. Whittier.*	345
Angels' Whisper, The..............*Samuel Lover.*	33

	PAGE
Angler, The.....................*John Chalkhill.*	468
Angler's Trysting-Tree, The..*T. T. Stoddart.*	469
Angler's Wish, The................*Isaak Walton.*	467
Annabel Lee..................... *Edgar A. Poe.*	410
Annie Laurie................*Author Unknown.*	199
Antony and Cleopatra....... *William H. Lytle.*	290
Arab's Farewell to his Horse, The..*C. Norton.*	492
Arethusa................ ......*Percy Bysshe Shelley.*	460
Ariel's Songs............... *William Shakespeare.*	794
Armstrong's Good-Night.....*Author Unknown.*	656
Arsenal at Springfield, The..*H. W. Longfellow.*	521
Art of Book-keeping, The.......*Thomas Hood.*	951
Art thou Weary?.....................*John M. Neale.*	577
As by the Shore at Break of Day ...*T. Moore.*	363
Ask me no More..............*Alfred Tennyson.*	192
Ask me no more where Jove bestows..*T. Carew.*	192
At Dieppe........................... *W. W. Story.*	518
At Sea ....*J. T. Trowbridge.*	465
At Setting Day and Rising Morn..*A. Ramsay.*	195
At the Church-Gate........ *Wm. M. Thackeray.*	211
Auf Wiedersehen................*James R. Lowell.*	217
Auld Lang Syne.....................*Robert Burns.*	81
Auld Robin Gray..........*Lady Anne Barnard.*	137
Autumn, A Dirge.........*Percy Bysshe Shelley.*	436
Autumn, To........................*John Keats.*	435
Aux Italiens.................*Robert B. Lytton.*	180
Awakening of Endymion....*L. E. L. Maclean.*	172
BABE, The...................*Sir William Jones.*	50
Babie, The..........................*J. E. Rankin.*	41
Baby Bell......................... *T. B. Aldrich.*	30
Baby Louise.................*Margaret Eytinge.*	29
Baby May...................... *W. C. Bennett.*	29
Baby's Début, The..................*James Smith.*	940
Bachelor's Dream, The...........*Thomas Hood.*	902
Bachelor's Hall........................*John Finley.*	960
Ballad of Agincourt, The......*Michael Drayton.*	298
Ballad of Bouillabaisse, The..*W.M.Thackeray.*	89
Ballad of Chevy-Chace, The..*Author Unknown.*	299
Ballad of the Tempest.........*James T. Fields.*	38
Banks o' Doon, The.................*Robert Burns.*	170
Bannockburn........................*Robert Burns.*	295
Baptismal Hymn..................*Henry Alford.*	563
Barbara Allen's Cruelty......*Author Unknown.*	417
Barbara Frietchie.............*John G. Whittier.*	350
Bard, The.............................. *Thomas Gray.*	293

ix

INDEX OF THE NAMES OF THE POEMS.

	PAGE
Baron's Last Banquet, The........*A. G. Greene.*	621
Battle-Field, The............*William C. Bryant.*	676
Battle-Hymn of the Republic..*Julia W. Howe.*	354
Battle of Blenheim, The........*Robert Southey.*	677
Battle of Fontenoy, The............*B. Dowling.*	322
Battle of the Baltic, The....*Thomas Campbell.*	341
Baucis and Philemon............*Jonathan Swift.*	899
Beaumont, On my Dear Son, Gervase, *Sir John Beaumont.*	226
Beautiful Snow..................*John W. Watson.*	720
Beauty Fades................*William Drummond.*	741
Bedford, On Lucy, Countess of.....*Ben Jonson.*	233
Bedouin Song ....*Bayard Taylor.*	177
Beggar's Petition, The.............*Thomas Moss.*	717
Behold, I Stand at the Door and Knock, *William W. How.*	550
Believe me, if All those Endearing Young Charms.....................*Thomas Moore.*	162
Bells, The................. ....*Edgar Allan Poe.*	765
Bells of Shandon..*F. Mahony (Father Prout).*	516
Beth Gêlert............ *William Robert Spencer.*	392
Better Land, The.................*Felicia Hemans.*	598
Between the Lights............*Author Unknown.*	683
Bingen on the Rhine ....*Caroline Norton.*	83
Bird, To a, that Haunted the Waters of Laaken ....*Lord Thurlow.*	472
Birth of St. Patrick, The.........*Samuel Lover.*	943
Black Cock, The..................*Joanna Baillie.*	481
Blame not my Lute ....*Sir Thomas Wyatt.*	190
Blessed Damozel, The..*Dante Gabriel Rossetti.*	839
Blest be Thy Love, dear Lord.....*John Austin.*	548
Blind Boy, The ....*Colley Cibber.*	67
Blood Horse, The.......*Bryan Waller Procter.*	488
Blossoms, To.......................*Robert Herrick.*	457
Blow, Blow, thou Winter Wind...*Shakespeare.*	438
Blue-Bird, The ....*Alexander Wilson.*	475
Boatie Rows, The.............. ....*John Ewen.*	701
Boat Song ....*Sir Walter Scott.*	364
Bonnets of Bonnie Dundee, The..*Sir W. Scott.*	316
Bonnie George Campbell.....*Author Unknown.*	419
Bonnie Lesley........................*Robert Burns.*	145
Bonnie Prince Charlie.................*James Hogg.*	326
Border Ballad...................*Sir Walter Scott.*	358
Bound upon th' Accursèd Tree..*H. H. Milman.*	535
Boyhood................ *Washington Allston.*	53
Boys, The................*Oliver Wendell Holmes.*	80
Braes o' Balquhither ....*Robert Tannahill.*	498
Braes of Yarrow, The, *William Hamilton of Bangour.*	382
Braes of Yarrow, The ....*John Logan.*	384
Break, Break, Break.....*Alfred Tennyson.*	88
Bridal of Andalla, The......*John G. Lockhart.*	209
Bridal Song..................*Henry Hart Milman.*	220
Bridge of Sighs, The............... *Thomas Hood.*	719
Briefless Barrister, The..........*John G. Saxe.*	920
Broadswords of Scotland, The..*J. G. Lockhart.*	357
Brookside, The..............*Richard M. Milnes.*	169
Brown of Ossawatomie......*John G. Whittier.*	279

	PAGE
Bugle Song.....................*Alfred Tennyson.*	502
Bull-Fight of Gazul, The...*John G. Lockhart.*	408
Bumboat-Woman's Story ...... *Wm. S. Gilbert.*	894
Burd Helen.......................*Author Unknown.*	412
Burial Hymn ....*Henry Hart Milman.*	595
Burial March of Dundee...... *Wm. E. Aytoun.*	317
Burial of Moses, The......*Cecil F. Alexander.*	580
Burial of Sir John Moore ......*Charles Wolfe.*	252
Burns.......................*Fitz-Greene Halleck.*	249
Burns, Ode on the Centenary of..*Isa C. Knox.*	250
Butterfly, To the ....*Samuel Rogers.*	482
By the Autumn Sea.....*Paul Hamilton Hayne.*	466
CALL, The ....*George Darley.*	178
Canadian Boat-Song, A ....*Thomas Moore.*	735
Captain Reece................ *William S. Gilbert.*	954
Captive Bee, The..................*Robert Herrick.*	209
Carçamon................*Henry Augustin Beers.*	404
Careless Content......................*John Byrom.*	660
Carmen Bellicosum...........*Guy H. McMaster.*	331
Casabianca........................*Felicia Hemans.*	345
Casa Wappy..................*David Macbeth Moir.*	39
Castara.....................*William Habington.*	179
Castles in the Air.............*James Ballantyne.*	37
Cataract of Lodore, The........*Robert Southey.*	508
Cavalier's Song, The...... *William Motherwell.*	311
Cavalry Song.......*Edmund Clarence Stedman.*	366
Celestial Country, The, *Bernard of Cluny (Translation of John Mason Neale).*	604
Celia, To ....*Ben Jonson.*	195
Chambered Nautilus, The...*Oliver W. Holmes.*	470
Chameleon, The....................*James Merrick.*	686
Changed Cross, The......*Mrs. Charles Hobart.*	590
Character of a Happy Life.....*Sir H. Wotton.*	661
Charade—Camp-Bell...... *Winthrop M. Praed.*	264
Charge of the Light Brigade, ...*A. Tennyson.*	348
Charlie is my Darling ....*James Hogg.*	325
Charlotte Pulteney, To........*Ambrose Philips.*	35
Chaucer, Inscription for a Statue of, *Mark Akenside.*	225
Cherry-Ripe........................*Robert Herrick.*	214
Chess-Board, The ....*Robert Bulwer Lytton.*	85
Chevy-Chace, The Ballad of..*Author Unknown.*	299
Child and the Mourners, The........*C. Mackay.*	55
Child and the Watcher, The..*E. B. Browning.*	33
Child embracing his Mother, To a.....*T. Hood.*	35
Child of Elle, The.............*Author Unknown.*	385
Children, The.............*Charles M. Dickinson.*	62
Children......... ....*Walter Savage Landor.*	36
Children in the Wood, The...*Author Unknown.*	53
Children of the Heavenly King....*J. Cennick.*	574
Children's Hour, The........*H. W. Longfellow.*	45
Child's Thought of God, A, *E. B. Browning.*	44
Chimes of England, The.......*Arthur C. Coxe.*	503
Chorus—" Before the beginning of years," *Algernon Charles Swinburne.*	744
Chorus—" When the hounds of spring are on winter's traces"...*Algernon C. Swinburne.*	426

INDEX OF THE NAMES OF THE POEMS.

	PAGE
Chorus of the Flowers............Leigh Hunt.	449
Christabel............Samuel Taylor Coleridge.	841
Christ Crucified............Henry Hart Milman.	534
Christmas...................Nahum Tate.	529
Christmas Carol............Author Unknown.	531
Christmas Carol...............John Byrom.	531
Christmas Carol........Arthur Cleveland Coxe.	530
Christmas Carol............Dinah M. Craik.	533
Christmas Hymn, A............Alfred Domett.	529
Christ Risen............Anna Lætitia Barbauld.	536
Christ will Gather in His Own.Author Unknown.	609
Chronicle of the Drum,The.. W. M. Thackeray.	334
Closing Scene, The............Thomas B. Read.	640
Closing Year, The...........George D. Prentice.	95
Cloud, The............Percy Bysshe Shelley.	444
Colin and Lucy............Thomas Tickell.	197
Cologne............Samuel Taylor Coleridge.	928
Come away, Come away, Death...Shakespeare.	197
Come, Holy Spirit, Heavenly Dove...I. Watts.	542
Come into the Garden, Maud.....A. Tennyson.	177
Come, Rest in this Bosom......Thomas Moore.	147
Come, Thou Fount of Every Blessing,	
Robert Robinson.	585
Come, Ye Lofty............Archer Gurney.	530
Comin' Through the Rye.....Author Unknown.	214
Common Lot, The............James Montgomery.	618
Complaining............George Herbert.	585
Complaints of the Poor, The..Robert Southey.	714
Comus: A Mask............John Milton.	818
Content............Robert Greene.	660
Contented Mind, A............Joshua Sylvester.	660
Contrast, The............Horace Smith.	342
Coral Grove, The........James Gates Percival.	464
Corinna's going a-Maying.....Robert Herrick.	428
Coronach............Sir Walter Scott.	625
Coronation............Helen Hunt.	702
Coronation............Edward Perronet.	536
Cotter's Saturday Night, The...Robert Burns.	3
Courtin', The............James Russell Lowell.	891
Court Lady, A............Elizabeth B. Browning.	361
Covenanters' Battle-Chant............Motherwell.	310
Cowper's Grave............Elizabeth B. Browning.	246
Crabbèd Age and Youth.....Wm. Shakespeare.	756
Cradle Hymn............Isaac Watts.	34
Cradle Song............Elizabeth Prentiss.	32
Crescentius............L. E. L. Maclean.	292
Cromwell, Sonnet to the Lord General...Milton.	234
Crowded Street, The......William C. Bryant.	647
Cruel Sister, The............Author Unknown.	418
Cry of the Children, The......E. B. Browning.	63
Cuckoo, To the............John Logan.	481
Cuckoo, To the............William Wordsworth.	480
Culprit Fay, The........Joseph Rodman Drake.	810
Cumberland, The............Author Unknown.	350
Cumnor Hall............William Julius Mickle.	379
Cupid and Campaspe............John Lyly.	99
Cupid Carrying Provisions......George Croly.	156
Cupid Swallowed............Leigh Hunt.	103

	PAGE
Curfew must not ring To-night.Rosa H. Thorpe.	404
Cynthia, To............Ben Jonson.	446
Cyriac Skinner, Sonnet to.........John Milton.	234
DAFFODILS............William Wordsworth.	452
Daffodils, To............Robert Herrick.	453
Daisy, To the............William Wordsworth.	454
Daisy, To the............William Wordsworth.	453
Dante, On a Bust of..Thomas William Parsons.	221
Day is Done, The........Henry W. Longfellow.	774
Days that are No More, The......A. Tennyson.	91
Deacon's Masterpiece........Oliver W. Holmes.	932
Dead Politician, The............F. Bret Harte.	704
Death-bed, A............James Aldrich.	625
Death-bed, The............Thomas Hood.	625
Death of the Flowers, The....Wm. C. Bryant.	456
Death of the Old Year, The..Alfred Tennyson.	438
Death of the Virtuous,	
Anna Lætitia Barbauld.	618
Death's Final Conquest............James Shirley.	623
Dedication to Idylls of the King.A.Tennyson.	280
Delight in Disorder............Robert Herrick.	740
Delight in God Only............Francis Quarles.	576
Departure of the Nightingale, The...C. Smith.	480
Description of Spring...........Henry Howard.	425
Deserted Village............Oliver Goldsmith.	756
Destruction of Sennacherib, The...Lord Byron.	283
Devil's Thoughts, The....Samuel T. Coleridge.	917
Dianeme, To............Robert Herrick.	210
Dickens in Camp............F. Bret Harte.	282
Dies Iræ............Thomas de Celano.	609
Dies Iræ............Translation of John A. Dix.	611
Dies Iræ...........Translation of Wm. J. Irons.	610
Dies Iræ......Paraphrase of Sir Walter Scott.	610
Differences............Charles Mackay.	705
Different Minds............Richard C. Trench.	658
Dirge for a Soldier............George H. Boker.	279
Dirge from "The White Devil"...J. Webster.	638
Dirge from " Cymbeline"... Wm. Shakespeare.	637
Dirge, in Cymbeline............William Collins.	637
Dirge, "Softly!"............Charles G. Eastman.	638
Disdain Returned............Thomas Carew.	180
Ditty, A—" My true-love hath my heart, and	
I have his"............Sir Philip Sidney.	127
Diverting History of John Gilpin, The,	
William Cowper.	929
Dolcino to Margaret..........Charles Kingsley.	780
Doubting Heart, A.....Adelaide Anne Procter.	684
Dowie Dens of Yarrow, The..Author Unknown.	381
Drake, Epigram on Sir Francis...Ben Jonson.	225
Drake, On the Death of Joseph Rodman,	
Fitz-Greene Halleck.	253
Dream, A............Adelaide Anne Procter.	774
Dream, The............Lord Byron.	790
Dream of Eugene Aram, The...Thomas Hood.	375
Drifting............Thomas Buchanan Read.	465
Drinking............Abraham Cowley.	446
Dryburgh Abbey............Charles Swain.	264

INDEX OF THE NAMES OF THE POEMS.

	PAGE
Dumb Child, The............*Author Unknown.*	41
Dum Vivimus Vivamus..........*P. Doddridge.*	574
Duncan Gray ....*Robert Burns.*	144
Duty, Ode to............*William Wordsworth.*	664
Dying Christian to his Soul, The......*A. Pope.*	596
Dying Man in his Garden, The......*G. Sewell.*	637
EACH AND ALL.........*Ralph Waldo Emerson.*	707
Early Blue-Bird, The..........*L. H. Sigourney.*	475
Early Piety......................*Reginald Heber.*	575
Echo and Silence......*Sir S. Egerton Brydges.*	502
Edinburgh after Flodden..*William E. Aytoun.*	302
Edward, Edward..............*Author Unknown*	380
Elegiac Stanzas...........*William Wordsworth.*	505
Elegy on Captain Matthew Henderson..*Burns.*	247
Elegy on that Glory of her Sex, Mrs. Mary Blaize, An..................*Oliver Goldsmith.*	912
Elegy on the Death of a Mad Dog, *Oliver Goldsmith.*	928
Elegy to the Memory of an Unfortunate Lady.......................*Alexander Pope.*	635
Elegy, Written in a Country Church-yard...............*Thomas Gray.*	630
Elixir, The............................*George Herbert.*	544
Emigrants in the Bermudas, The..*A. Marvell.*	549
End of the Play, The.....*Wm. M. Thackeray.*	673
Endurance...........*Elizabeth Akers Allen.*	617
Epicurean Reminiscences of a Sentimentalist, *Thomas Hood.*	952
Epigram.............*Samuel Taylor Coleridge.*	959
Epigram on Sir Francis Drake....*Ben Jonson.*	225
Epiphany......................*Reginald Heber.*	534
Epitaph Extempore..............*Matthew Prior.*	241
Epitaph on a Living Author..*Abraham Cowley.*	226
Epitaph on Elizabeth L. H.........*Ben Jonson.*	233
Epitaph on Salathiel Pavy.........*Ben Jonson.*	232
Epitaph on the Admirable Dramatic Poet, W. Shakespeare.............*John Milton.*	230
Epitaph on the Countess of Pembroke, *Ben Jonson.*	233
Epitaph on the Tombstone Erected over the Marquis of Anglesea's Leg....*G. Canning.*	948
Epitaph upon Husband and Wife.*R. Crashaw.*	635
Epitaph upon the Right Honourable Sir Philip Sidney.........*Sir Walter Raleigh.*	227
Epithalamium..............*John G. C. Brainard.*	220
Etiquette..................... *William S. Gilbert.*	925
Eton College, On a Distant Prospect of, *Thomas Gray.*	504
Euphrosyne.......................*Matthew Arnold.*	213
Eva, To...............*Ralph Waldo Emerson.*	217
Evelyn Hope..................*Robert Browning.*	196
Evening, Ode to...............*William Collins.*	440
Evening Cloud, The...............*John Wilson.*	442
Evening Contemplation.....*George W. Doane.*	552
Evening Hymn......................*Thomas Ken.*	555
Evening Hymn...............*George Wither.*	556
Evening Hymn....................*John Keble.*	555

	PAGE
Evening Hymn............*Frederick W. Faber.*	556
Evening Hymn............*Sir Thomas Browne.*	556
Evening Hymn of the Alpine Shepherds, *William Beattie.*	552
Evening Star, To the..............*John Leyden.*	447
Evening Star, Song to the.....*Thos. Campbell.*	447
Evening Wind, The........*William C. Bryant.*	442
Eve of Election, The ....*John G. Whittier.*	675
Eve of St. Agnes, The ....*John Keats.*	127
Excelsior...................*Henry W. Longfellow.*	785
Execution, The.......*Richard Harris Barham.*	941
Execution of Montrose, The ...*W. E. Aytoun.*	313
Exile of Erin, The............*Thomas Campbell.*	359
Exile's Song, The.................*Robert Gilfillan.*	362
Exile to his Wife, The............*Joseph Brenan.*	11
FAIR ANNIE of Lochroyan...*Author Unknown.*	394
Fair Helen......................*Author Unknown.*	402
Fairies of the Caldon Low, The..*Mary Howitt.*	809
Fairies, The..................... *Wm. Allingham.*	794
Fair Ines..........................*Thomas Hood.*	102
Fairy Queen...................*Author Unknown.*	793
Fairy Song ....*John Keats.*	793
Faith..........................*Frances Anne Kemble.*	679
Faithless Nelly Gray...............*Thomas Hood.*	896
Faithless Sally Brown ....*Thomas Hood.*	897
Family Meeting, The..........*Charles Sprague.*	17
Fancy ....*John Keats.*	500
Fancy in Nubibus...*Samuel Taylor Coleridge.*	446
Fare Thee Well........................*Lord Byron.*	15
Farewell, A..▲............*Charles Kingsley.*	72
Farewell! but whenever you Welcome the Hour.......................*Thomas Moore.*	85
Farewell to Nancy..................*Robert Burns.*	154
Farewell to Thee, Araby's Daughter....*Moore.*	781
Farewell to the Fairies ....*Richard Corbet.*	833
Farewell to Tobacco, A ....*Charles Lamb.*	919
Fate...............................*F. Bret Harte.*	785
Father, Thy Will be Done...*Sarah F. Adams.*	544
Fear, Ode to.................. *William Collins.*	776
Fireside, The....................*Nathaniel Cotton.*	2
First Snow-Fall, The....*James Russell Lowell.*	437
Fisherman's Song, The..........*Francis Davis.*	696
Florence Vane..........*Philip Pendleton Cooke.*	171
Flower, The..................*George Herbert.*	579
Flowers.........................*H. W. Longfellow.*	448
Flowers................................*John Keble.*	448
Flowers of The Forest, The.........*Jane Elliot.*	306
Flow Gently, Sweet Afton.........*Robert Burns.*	515
Folding the Flocks.......*Beaumont & Fletcher.*	495
Fontenoy.................*Thomas Osborne Davis.*	321
Fontenoy, Battle of....................*B. Dowling.*	322
Footsteps of Angels ....*H. W. Longfellow.*	773
Forced Recruit at Solferino, A, *Elizabeth Barrett Browning.*	364
For ever with the Lord.....*James Montgomery.*	597
Forget me Not.........................*Amelia Opie.*	94
Forging of the Anchor........*Samuel Ferguson.*	693

INDEX OF THE NAMES OF THE POEMS. xiii

	PAGE
For New-Year's Day.........*Philip Doddridge.*	559
Fountain of Mercy! God of Love!	
Anne Flowerdew.	563
Fragment from Sappho, A...*Ambrose Philips.*	192
France: An Ode.....*Samuel Taylor Coleridge.*	333
Friar of Orders Gray, The......*Thomas Percy.*	117
Friend after Friend Departs...*J. Montgomery.*	638
Friend of Humanity and the Knife-Grinder, The........................*George Canning.*	935
Fringed Gentian, To the.......*Wm. C. Bryant.*	455
GAFFER GRAY...............*Thomas Holcroft.*	715
Gambols of Children, The......*George Darley.*	53
Gane were but the Winter Cauld, *Allan Cunningham.*	638
Genevieve..................*Samuel T. Coleridge.*	155
Gethsemane..................*James Montgomery.*	534
Ginevra......................*Samuel Rogers.*	406
Girl of Cadiz, The................*Lord Byron.*	146
Give me the Old............*Robert H. Messinger.*	749
Glenlogie........................*Author Unknown.*	406
Glorying in the Cross..............*Isaac Watts.*	547
Glove and the Lions, The..........*Leigh Hunt.*	411
Glow-Worm, Sonnet to the.........*John Clare.*	483
God......................*John Donne.*	565
God is Love.....................*Sir John Bowring.*	544
God Save the King................*Henry Carey.*	355
God's Judgment on a Wicked Bishop.*Southey.*	409
Golden-tressèd Adelaide.........*B. W. Procter.*	39
Go, Lovely Rose..................*Edmund Waller.*	185
Good-Bye................*Ralph Waldo Emerson.*	657
Good Counseil of Chaucer...*Geoffrey Chaucer.*	688
Good, Great Man, The..........*S. T. Coleridge.*	662
Good Lord Clifford, The....*Wm. Wordsworth.*	223
Good-Morrow Song............*Thomas Heywood.*	215
Good-Night...................*Author Unknown.*	688
Good-Night......................*Robert C. Sands.*	618
Good Time Coming, The........*Charles Mackay.*	750
Go, Pretty Birds..............*Thomas Heywood.*	162
Go where Glory waits Thee....*Thomas Moore.*	95
Grasshopper and Cricket, On the.....*J. Keats.*	482
Grasshopper and Cricket, To the..*Leigh Hunt.*	482
Grave, The..................*James Montgomery.*	641
Grave of Macaura, The.........*Mary Downing.*	221
Graves of a Household, The.........*F. Hemans.*	28
Grecian Urn, Ode on a.............*John Keats.*	746
Grongar Hill.........................*John Dyer.*	506
Groomsman to the Bridesmaid..*T. W. Parsons.*	183
Groves of Blarney, The...........*R. A. Millikin.*	516
Guide me, O Thou Great Jehovah! *William Williams.*	573
Gulf-Weed, The..................*C. G. Fenner.*	463
HAG, The...................*Robert Herrick.*	875
Hail, Thou Once-despisèd Jesus...*J. Bakewell.*	538
Hallo, my Fancy...............*William Cleland.*	884
Hallowed Ground..........*Thomas Campbell.*	633
Hamilton, To Lady Anne.....*Wm. R. Spencer.*	779

	PAGE
Hannah Binding Shoes...........*Lucy Larcom.*	698
Happy Marriage, The...........*Edward Moore.*	2
Hark! how All the Welkin Rings, *Charles Wesley.*	532
Hark, the Glad Sound.......*Philip Doddridge.*	533
Harmosan..............*Richard Chenevix Trench.*	291
Hart-leap Well............*William Wordsworth.*	387
Has Sorrow thy Young Days Shaded? *Thomas Moore.*	742
Haunted House, The..............*Thomas Hood.*	866
Haunted Palace, The.........*Edgar Allan Poe.*	871
Health, A..................*Edward Coate Pinkney.*	178
Hear my Prayer, O Heavenly Father, *Harriet T. Parr.*	564
Heart of the War, The...........*J. G. Holland.*	365
Heart's Song, The................*Arthur C. Coxe.*	575
Heavenly Wisdom..................*John Logan.*	575
He Came too Late.............*Elizabeth Bogart.*	102
Heir of Linne, The.............*Author Unknown.*	368
Helen of Kirkconnell................*John Mayne.*	403
Hellvellyn..................*Sir Walter Scott.*	514
Henderson, Elegy on Captain Matthew, *Robert Burns.*	247
Here's to Thee, my Scottish Lassie, *John Moultrie.*	214
Heritage, The..............*James Russell Lowell.*	705
Her Last Verses..........................*Alice Cary.*	629
Her Letter.........................*F. Bret Harte.*	207
Hermioné......................*Robert Buchanan.*	7
Hermit, The.........................*James Beattie.*	648
Hermit, The.....................*Oliver Goldsmith.*	159
Hermit, The......................*Thomas Parnell.*	666
Hervé Riel........ ....*Robert Browning.*	319
Hester..............................*Charles Lamb.*	741
Highland Girl, To a..........*Wm. Wordsworth.*	65
Highland Mary.................*Robert Burns.*	120
High-mettled Racer, The......*Charles Dibdin.*	488
High Tide on the Coast of Lincolnshire, *Jean Ingelow.*	415
His Last Verses........................*John Clare.*	618
History................*Robert Southey.*	352
Hohenlinden....................*Thomas Campbell.*	340
Holly Tree, The....................*Robert Southey.*	458
Holy Trinity, The...............*Reginald Heber.*	546
Homes of England, The.......*Felicia Hemans.*	1
Home, Sweet Home...............*John H. Payne.*	1
Hope, Sonnet to.........*Helen Maria Williams.*	663
Horatian Ode, An..............*Andrew Marvell.*	238
Horatius...............*Thomas B. Macaulay.*	283
Horse, To my.....................*Author Unknown.*	493
Horseback Ride, The...*Sara Jane Lippincott.*	489
Hour of Death, The.............*Felicia Hemans.*	630
Hour of Prayer, The...........*Felicia Hemans.*	564
Household Woman, The.......*Caroline Gilman.*	24
How Kindly hast Thou Led Me!..*T. Grinfield.*	570
How many Times......*Thomas Lovell Beddoes.*	102
How Sleep the Brave...................*W. Collins.*	363
How's my Boy?.....................*Sydney Dobell.*	67

INDEX OF THE NAMES OF THE POEMS.

How Sweet the Name of Jesus Sounds, *John Newton.* 541
How they Brought the Good News from Ghent to Aix.............*Robert Browning.* 372
Humble-Bee, The...........*Ralph W. Emerson.* 482
Hundred Years to Come, A....*Wm. G. Brown.* 675
Hunter of the Prairies, The...*Wm. C. Bryant.* 494
Hymn before Sunrise in the Vale of Chamouni.............*Samuel Taylor Coleridge.* 518
Hymn, "Drop, drop, slow tears," *Phineas Fletcher.* 544
Hymn for Family Worship.......*H. K. White.* 568
Hymn, "How are Thy servants blest, O Lord!"............*Joseph Addison.* 558
Hymn, "Lord, with glowing heart I'd praise Thee".....................*Francis Scott Key.* 548
Hymn on the Seasons..........*James Thomson.* 423
Hymn to Adversity................*Thomas Gray.* 777
Hymn to Contentment, A.......*Thos. Parnell.* 659
Hymn to Neptune....................*Albert Pike.* 887
Hymn to the Flowers..............*Horace Smith.* 451

I am a Friar of Orders Gray........*J. O'Keefe.* 916
Ianthe, To................ *Walter Savage Landor.* 213
Ichabod..................*John Greenleaf Whittier.* 267
I Give Immortal Praise.............*Isaac Watts.* 546
I Hae Naebody Now................*James Hogg.* 83
I Knew by the Smoke that so Gracefully Curled..........................*Thomas Moore.* 763
I lay in Sorrow deep Distressed...*C. Mackay.* 687
I love Thy Kingdom, Lord...*Timothy Dwight.* 574
I love my Love................*Charles Mackay.* 146
Il Penseroso...........................*John Milton.* 735
I'm Growing Old....................*John G. Saxe.* 751
In a Year........................*Robert Browning.* 211
Inchcape Rock, The..............*Robert Southey.* 378
Incident of the French Camp....*R. Browning.* 341
Indian Gold Coin, Ode to an......*John Leyden.* 87
Indian Names........*Lydia Huntley Sigourney.* 520
Indian Revelry...........*Bartholomew Dowling.* 787
Influence of Music.............. *W. Shakespeare.* 732
Influence of Time on Grief.*Wm. Lisle Bowles.* 686
"In Memoriam," From........*Alfred Tennyson.* 689
Inner Calm, The...............*Horatius Bonar.* 565
In Remembrance of Joseph Sturge, *John Greenleaf Whittier.* 277
Inscription for a Statue of Chaucer at Woodstock......................*Mark Akenside.* 225
In Sorrow.....................*Thomas Hastings.* 543
In the Down-hill of Life..........*John Collins.* 674
Intimations of Immortality from Recollections of Early Childhood..*W. Wordsworth.* 644
Introduction to "Songs of Innocence," *William Blake.* 68
Invitation, The............*Percy Bysshe Shelley.* 499
Invitation to Izaak Walton....*Charles Cotton.* 467
I Prithee send me back my Heart, *Sir John Suckling.* 171

I Remember, I Remember......*Thomas Hood.* 73
Irishman, The...................*William Maginn.* 896
Isabella Markham, Lines on.*John Harrington.* 124
Is it Come?........................*Frances Brown.* 748
Italian Song, An...................*Samuel Rogers.* 498
It came upon the Midnight Clear..*E. H. Sears.* 532
It is Great for our Country to Die, *James Gates Percival.* 365
It's Hame, and it's Hame..*Allan Cunningham.* 357
Ivry................*Thomas Babington Macaulay.* 307
Ivy Green, The..................*Charles Dickens.* 456
I would not Live Alway...*W. A. Muhlenberg.* 593

Jacobite Toast........................*John Byrom.* 310
James Melville's Child...*Mrs. A. S. Menteath.* 43
Jealousy, the Tyrant of the Mind..*J. Dryden.* 213
Jean........................ *Robert Burns.* 126
Jeanie Morrison............ *William Motherwell.* 118
Jenny Kissed Me......................*Leigh Hunt.* 186
Jessie, the Flower o' Dumblane.*R. Tannahill.* 163
Jessy...... ....*Robert Burns.* 166
Jester's Sermon, The..........*G. W. Thornbury.* 916
Jesus, I my Cross have Taken......*H. F. Lyte.* 539
Jesu, Lover of my Soul........*Charles Wesley.* 540
Jesu, my Strength, my Hope..*Charles Wesley.* 579
Jesus Wept....................*Benjamin Beddome.* 535
Jock of Hazeldean.............*Sir Walter Scott.* 134
John Anderson, my Jo............*Robert Burns.* 8
John Gilpin, The Diverting History of, *William Cowper.* 929
Jolly Good Ale and Old..........*John Still.* 917
Jolly Old Pedagogue, The......*George Arnold.* 927
Jovial Beggar, The............*Author Unknown.* 918
Joy and Peace in Believing......*Wm. Cowper.* 573
July....... ....*John Clare.* 432
Just as I am ....*Charlotte Elliott.* 568

Kane............................*Fitz-James O'Brien.* 276
Katharine Janfarie...........*Author Unknown.* 393
Kilmeny...........................*James Hogg.* 833
Kingdom of God, The.....*Richard C. Trench.* 662
King of Brentford's Testament, The, *William Makepeace Thackeray.* 906
King of Denmark's Ride, The ......*C. Norton.* 420
Kisses .... *William Strode.* 156
Kitten, The. ....*Joanna Baillie.* 484
Kitten and the Falling Leaves, The, *William Wordsworth.* 485
Knight's Tomb, The......*Samuel T. Coleridge.* 626
Kubla Khan..........*Samuel Taylor Coleridge.* 848

La Belle Dame sans Merci.......*John Keats.* 865
Laborare est Orare....*Frances Sargent Osgood.* 691
Laborer, The ....*John Clare.* 702
Lachrymatory, The..............*Charles Turner.* 740
Ladder of St. Augustine, The......*Longfellow.* 679
Lady Anne Bothwell's Lament, *Author Unknown.* 32

INDEX OF THE NAMES OF THE POEMS. xv

	PAGE
Lady Clara Vere de Vere....*Alfred Tennyson.*	210
Lady Clare.........................*Alfred Tennyson.*	138
Lady Geraldine's Courtship...*E. B. Browning.*	104
Lady Margaret Ley, To the.......*John Milton.*	235
Lady of Shalott, The.........*Alfred Tennyson.*	888
Lady's Dream, The................*Thomas Hood.*	714
Lady's Yes, The........*Elizabeth B. Browning.*	138
Laird o' Cockpen, The.........*Lady C. Nairne.*	892
Lake of the Dismal Swamp, The....*T. Moore.*	422
L'Allegro................................*John Milton.*	733
Lament, A....................*Percy Bysshe Shelley.*	766
Lamentation for Celin, The....*J. G. Lockhart.*	373
Lamentation of Don Roderick.*J. G. Lockhart.*	290
Lament of the Border Widow.*Author Unknown.*	417
Lament of the Irish Emigrant.*Lady Dufferin.*	86
Lancashire Doxology, A......*Dinah M. Craik.*	583
Landing of the Pilgrim Fathers in New England, The...............*Felicia Hemans.*	308
Land o' the Leal, The.........*Lady C. Nairne.*	636
Langley Lane....................*Robert Buchanan.*	203
Lass of Patie's Mill, The........*Allan Ramsay.*	155
Last Buccaneer, The..........*Charles Kingsley.*	419
Last Conqueror, The...............*James Shirley.*	623
Last Leaf, The..........*Oliver Wendell Holmes.*	755
Last Man, The..................*Thomas Campbell.*	643
La Tricoteuse........*George Walter Thornbury.*	332
Lawyer's Farewell to his Muse, The, *Sir William Blackstone.*	738
Lawyer's Invocation to Spring, The, *Henry Howard Brownell.*	951
Lead, Kindly Light......*John Henry Newman.*	569
Lemuel's Song....................*George Wither.*	24
Leven Water, Ode to............*Tobias Smollett.*	515
Levett, On the Death of Dr..*Samuel Johnson.*	245
Lie, The..........................*Sir Walter Raleigh.*	655
Life....................................*Lord Bacon.*	613
Life................*Anna Lætitia Barbauld.*	613
Life.............................*George Herbert.*	756
Life.............................*Francis Scott Key.*	577
Life.............................*Bryan Waller Procter.*	615
Life on the Ocean Wave, A......*Epes Sargent.*	695
Light.........................*F. W. Bourdillon.*	180
Light Shining out of Darkness...*W. Cowper.*	543
Lilian............................*Alfred Tennyson.*	203
Lines on Isabella Markham.*John Harrington.*	124
Lines on the Mermaid Tavern.....*John Keats.*	504
Lines on the Portrait of Shakespeare. *Jonson.*	230
Lines to an Indian Air........*Percy B. Shelley.*	103
Lines Written in Richmond Churchyard, Yorkshire.............*Herbert Knowles.*	633
Lines Written in the Tower.......*C. Tychborn.*	688
Lines Written on the Night of the 30th of July, 1847............*Thomas B. Macaulay.*	273
Lines Written the Night before his Execution........................*Sir Walter Raleigh.*	230
Lines Written to his Wife.....*Reginald Heber.*	9
Lines Written under the Picture of John Milton...........................*John Dryden.*	240

	PAGE
Litany............................*Sir Robert Grant.*	539
Little Beach-Bird, The......*Richard H. Dana.*	471
Little Bell.....................*Thomas Westwood.*	38
Little Billee............. *William M. Thackeray.*	909
Little Black Boy, The............*William Blake.*	37
Little While, A..................*Horatius Bonar.*	595
Living Lost, The......*William Cullen Bryant.*	682
Lochaber no More................*Allan Ramsay.*	195
Lochiel's Warning............*Thomas Campbell.*	323
Lochinvar...................... *Sir Walter Scott.*	136
Locksley Hall................*Alfred Tennyson.*	149
Lo! He comes, with Clouds Descending, *Thomas Olivers.*	611
Long-Ago, The......*Richard Monckton Milnes.*	749
Long did I Toil..............*Henry Francis Lyte.*	569
Look Out, Bright Eyes...*Beaumont & Fletcher.*	184
Lord, dismiss us with Thy Blessing, *Walter Shirley.*	612
Lord is Risen, The................*Charles Wesley.*	535
Lord Lovel......................*Author Unknown.*	198
Lord of Burleigh, The........*Alfred Tennyson.*	201
Lord of Butrago, The........*John G. Lockhart.*	296
Lord, shall Thy Children come to Thee, *Samuel Hinds.*	582
Lord Ullin's Daughter.......*Thomas Campbell.*	381
Lost Heir, The.....................*Thomas Hood.*	904
Lost Leader, The...............*Robert Browning.*	263
Lot of Thousands, The.............*Anne Hunter.*	685
Louis XV..............................*John Sterling.*	328
Love.............................*Samuel T. Coleridge.*	100
Love and Death......................*John Ford.*	203
Love in the Valley............*George Meredith.*	142
Love is a Sickness...............*Samuel Daniel.*	98
Love-Knot, The.......................*Nora Perry.*	217
Love Lightens Labor.........*Author Unknown.*	24
Loveliness of Love, The......*Author Unknown.*	139
Lovely Mary Donnelly.........*Wm. Allingham.*	122
Love Not......................*Caroline Norton.*	187
Love not me for Comely Grace, *Author Unknown.*	139
Love's Omnipresence...........*Joshua Sylvester.*	99
Love's Philosophy........*Percy Bysshe Shelley.*	97
Love still hath Something of the Sea, *Sir Charles Sedley.*	99
Lovest thou Me...................*William Cowper.*	541
Love will Find out the Way, *Author Unknown.*	97
Low-backed Car, The..............*Samuel Lover.*	165
Loyalty Confined..........*Sir Roger L'Estrange.*	241
Lucasta, To. (On Going beyond the Seas.) *Richard Lovelace.*	125
Lucasta, To. (On Going to the Wars.) *Richard Lovelace.*	124
Lucy..........................*William Wordsworth.*	49
Lucy Gray; or, Solitude....*Wm. Wordsworth.*	56
Lucy's Flittin'...................*William Laidlaw.*	202
Lullaby........................*Thomas Dekker.*	32
Lycidas..............................*John Milton.*	235

INDEX OF THE NAMES OF THE POEMS.

	PAGE
MAIDENHOOD............Henry W. Longfellow.	66
Maiden's Choice, The...............Henry Carey.	210
Maid of Athens.....................Lord Byron.	145
Maid's Lament, The......... Walter S. Landor.	141
Make Way for Liberty.....James Montgomery.	297
Malbrouck...Francis Mahony (Father Prout), (from the French).	948
Man's Mortality..................Simon Wastell.	626
Marching Along...............Robert Browning.	310
March to Moscow.................Robert Southey.	949
Marco Bozzaris...........Fitz-Greene Halleck.	347
Mariner's Dream, The........ William Dimond.	696
Mariner's Wife, The....................Jean Adam.	10
Mary, To..........................Samuel Bishop.	10
Mary, To........................ William Cowper.	245
Mary in Heaven, To.............Robert Burns.	137
Mary Morison......................Robert Burns.	147
Mary of Castle Cary ....Hector Macneill.	164
Massacre of the Macpherson... W. E. Aytoun.	934
Matrimonial Happiness...........John Lapraik.	7
Maude Clare.......Christina Georgina Rossetti.	188
Maud Muller...................John G. Whittier.	167
May, Song to....................Erasmus Darwin.	431
May, Song to..................... Lord Thurlow.	428
May, Sonnet on...................Thomas Watson.	428
May, The Reign of......James Gates Percival.	432
May Morning, Song on..............John Milton.	427
May Queen, The.................Alfred Tennyson.	69
Means to Attain Happy Life..Henry Howard.	616
Meeting of the Waters, The...Thomas Moore.	517
Melancholia......................John Fletcher.	656
Men of England..............Thomas Campbell.	356
Men of Old, The............Richard M. Milnes.	747
Merry Pranks of Robin Good-Fellow, The, Author Unknown.	808
Messiah.............................Alexander Pope.	527
Midnight Hymn.....................Thomas Ken.	557
Milk-Maid's Mother's Answer, Sir Walter Raleigh.	140
Milk-Maid's Song.........Christopher Marlowe.	140
Miller's Daughter, The........Alfred Tennyson.	155
Milton, Lines Written under the Picture of, John Dryden.	240
Milton, Sonnet to.......... William Wordsworth.	240
Milton's Prayer of Patience......E. L. Howell.	235
Minstrel's Song, The........Thomas Chatterton.	147
Missionary Hymn...............Reginald Heber.	580
Mistress Margaret Hussey, To...John Skelton.	225
Mitherless Bairn, The........... William Thom.	46
Modern Belle, The............................Stark.	922
Monody on the Death of an Only Client, London Punch.	921
Monsieur Tonson.....................John Taylor.	945
Monterey................Charles Fenno Hoffman.	348
Moon, Sonnet to the ....Sir Philip Sidney.	118
Moon, Sonnet to the...............Lord Thurlow.	446
Moon, To the..........................P. B. Shelley.	446
Morning..................... William Shakespeare.	439

	PAGE
Morning-Glory, The.......Maria White Lowell.	49
Morning Hymn.........................John Keble.	553
Morning Hymn.........................Thomas Ken.	553
Morning Hymn.......................George Wither.	554
Morning Song...................Joanna Baillie.	499
Morning Street, The.................John J. Piatt.	782
Morton, Tears Wept at the Grave of Sir Albertus.........................Sir H. Wotton.	228
Mother and Poet.......Elizabeth B. Browning.	26
Mother's Hope, The.........Laman Blanchard.	52
Mountain Daisy, To a.............Robert Burns.	454
Mouse, To a ....Robert Burns.	483
Mr. Barney Maguire's Account of the Coronation..............Richard Harris Barham.	956
Mr. Molony's Account of the Ball, William Makepeace Thackeray.	955
Mrs. Unwin, To................. William Cowper.	245
Musical Instrument...Elizabeth B. Browning.	723
Music, when Soft Voices Die....P. B. Shelley.	185
My Ain Fireside ....Elizabeth Hamilton.	1
My Child.........................John Pierpont.	48
My Days among the Dead are Passed, Robert Southey.	737
My Dear and Only Love.,......James Graham.	193
My Faith looks up to Thee........Ray Palmer.	538
My Heart's in the Highlands ...Robert Burns.	358
My Love.....................James Russell Lowell.	208
My Minde to me a Kingdom is... Wm. Byrd.	737
My Only Jo and Dearie, O.......Richard Gall.	202
My Playmate ....John G. Whittier.	82
My Psalm.........................John G. Whittier.	613
My Ship ....Elizabeth Akers Allen.	789
NABOB, The......................Susanna Blamire.	93
Nantucket Skipper, The.......James T. Fields.	927
Napoleon...................John Gibson Lockhart.	268
Napoleon, The Return of, from St. Helena, Lydia H. Sigourney.	268
Naseby.......... Thomas Babington Macaulay.	311
Nearer Home........................Phœbe Cary.	587
Nearer, my God, to Thee....Sarah F. Adams.	564
Neckan, The......................Matthew Arnold.	883
Neglected Call, The......Hannah Lloyd Neale.	684
Never Again..........Richard Henry Stoddard.	764
New Jerusalem ....Author Unknown.	602
New Year's Day, For ....Philip Doddridge.	559
Niagara....................John G. C. Brainard.	520
Night ....James Montgomery.	687
Night..............................Hartley Coleridge.	775
Night....................... William Habington.	775
Night before Christmas, The......C. C. Moore.	67
Nightingale, Ode to a ....John Keats.	478
Nightingale, The........Richard Barnefield.	480
Nightingale, The Departure of the..C. Smith.	480
Nightingale, To a..........William Drummond.	477
Nightingale, To the .... William Drummond.	478
Nightingale, To the...............John Milton.	478
Night Piece, The.................Robert Herrick.	127

INDEX OF THE NAMES OF THE POEMS.

	PAGE
Night, To.....................Percy Bysshe Shelley.	442
Night, To....................Joseph Blanco White.	441
Ninety and Nine........Elizabeth C. Clephane.	581
No Age Content with his Own Estate, Henry Howard.	657
Nocturnal Reverie, A, Anne, Countess of Winchelsea.	434
Nocturnal Sketch, A..............Thomas Hood.	959
Nongtongpaw......................Charles Dibdin.	948
Nothing but Leaves.........Lucy E. Akerman.	578
Nothing to Wear.........William Allen Butler.	708
Not on the Battle-Field...........John Pierpont.	677
Not Ours the Vows.............Bernard Barton.	101
Now and Afterward............Dinah M. Craik.	620
Nun, The..................................Leigh Hunt.	171
Nut-Brown Maid, The........Author Unknown.	112
Nymph Complaining for the Death of her Fawn.........................Andrew Marvell.	501
O'CONNOR'S CHILD.............Thomas Campbell.	395
Ode, An, in Imitation of Alcæus.Sir W. Jones.	363
Ode,—"Bards of passion and of mirth".Keats.	740
Ode, Intimations of Immortality from Recollections of Early Childhood. Wordsworth.	644
Ode on a Grecian Urn.................John Keats.	746
Ode on Solitude...................Alexander Pope.	755
Ode on St. Cecilia's Day......Alexander Pope.	727
Ode on the Centenary of Burns..Isa C. Knox.	250
Ode on the Death of the Duke of Wellington, Alfred Tennyson.	270
Ode on the Death of Mr. Thomson. W. Collins.	244
Ode, On the Spring................Thomas Gray.	427
Ode,—"The spacious firmament on high," Joseph Addison.	545
Ode to a Nightingale...............John Keats.	478
Ode to an Indian Gold Coin......John Leyden.	87
Ode to Duty .... William Wordsworth.	664
Ode to Evening....................William Collins.	440
Ode to Fear ....William Collins.	776
Ode to Himself......................Ben Jonson.	225
Ode to Leven Water.............Tobias Smollett.	515
Ode to my Little Son...............Thomas Hood.	903
Ode to the West Wind...Percy Bysshe Shelley.	436
O Fairest of the Rural Maids!.W. C. Bryant.	779
Of Myself.........................Abraham Cowley.	233
Oft, in the Stilly Night..........Thomas Moore.	77
O God of Bethel, by whose Hand... Variation by John Logan (from Philip Doddridge).	587
O Happy Soul, that Lives on High!.I. Watts.	575
Oh, Breathe not his Name......Thomas Moore.	252
Oh, had we some Bright Little Isle of our Own!................... Thomas Moore.	194
Oh! Snatched away in Beauty's Bloom, Lord Byron.	743
Oh! the Pleasant Days of Old.......F. Brown.	747
Oh why should the Spirit of Mortal be Proud?....................... William Knox.	627
Old and Young Courtier.....Author Unknown.	672

	PAGE
Old Arm-Chair, The.....................Eliza Cook.	73
Old Clock on the Stairs, The......Longfellow.	76
Old Familiar Faces, The.........Charles Lamb.	77
Old Folks at Home.............Stephen C. Foster.	18
Old Grimes........................Albert G. Greene.	912
Old Letters........................Frederick Locker.	88
Old Man Dreams, The ......Oliver W. Holmes.	899
Old Man's Comforts, The........Robert Southey.	674
Old Man's Wish, The................Walter Pope.	754
Old Oaken Bucket, The...Samuel Woodworth.	74
Old St. David's at Radnor...H. W. Longfellow.	522
Omnipotent Decree, The........Charles Wesley.	585
On a Bust of Dante..Thomas William Parsons.	221
On a Contented Mind.....Thomas, Lord Vaux.	658
On a Day, Alack the Day !... W. Shakespeare.	141
On a Distant Prospect of Eton College.T. Gray.	504
On a Distant View of England. W. L. Bowles.	356
On a Girdle..........................Edmund Waller.	185
On an Intaglio Head of Minerva.T. B. Aldrich.	780
O Nanny, wilt Thou go with Me......T. Percy.	161
On Another's Sorrow............ William Blake.	589
On a Prayer-Book, sent to Mrs. M. R., Robert Crashaw.	586
On a Sprig of Heath.................Anne Grant.	447
Once upon a Time.........Caroline B. Southey.	93
One by One...............Adelaide Anne Procter.	683
One Gray Hair, The......... Walter S. Landor.	751
One Word is too often Profaned.P. B. Shelley.	148
On First Looking into Chapman's Homer, John Keats.	739
On his Being Arrived at the Age of Twenty-Three ....John Milton.	226
On his Blindness......................John Milton.	234
On his Divine Poems..........Edmund Waller.	688
On Lending a Punch-Bowl.......O. W. Holmes.	90
On Lucy, Countess of Bedford.....Ben Jonson.	233
Only Waiting..........Francis Laughton Mace.	639
On my Dear Son, Gervase Beaumont, Sir John Beaumont.	226
On Revisiting the River Loddon...T. Warton.	508
On the Death of Dr. Levett...Samuel Johnson.	245
On the Death of Joseph Rodman Drake, Fitz-Greene Halleck.	253
On the Extinction of the Venetian Republic, William Wordsworth.	348
On the Funeral of Charles the First, William Lisle Bowles.	312
On the Grasshopper and Cricket......J. Keats.	482
On the Late Massacre in Piedmont...J. Milton.	313
On the Morning of Christ's Nativity...Milton.	523
On the Prospect of Planting Arts and Learning in America............George Berkeley.	723
On the Receipt of my Mother's Picture, William Cowper.	15
On the Tombs in Westminster Abbey, Francis Beaumont.	504
On this Day I Complete my Thirty-Sixth Year.........................Lord Byron.	88

B

	PAGE
Origin of the Opal............Author Unknown.	459
Orphan Boy's Tale, The...........Amelia Opie.	46
O Thou from whom all Goodness Flows, Thomas Haweis.	584
O Thou, the Contrite Sinner's Friend, Charlotte Elliott.	539
Outlaw, The......................Sir Walter Scott.	176
Over Hill, Over Dale....William Shakespeare.	794
Over the River........Nancy A. W. Wakefield.	629
PAN, To.....................Beaumont & Fletcher.	425
Pan in Wall Street.Edmund Clarence Stedman.	886
Panglory's Wooing Song.........Giles Fletcher.	98
Paradise....................Frederick W. Faber.	601
Paraphrase of Psalm XXIII......J. Addison.	561
Paraphrase of Psalm XXIII......R. Crashaw.	562
Parody on Pope....................Sydney Smith.	923
Passing Away.......................John Pierpont.	628
Passing Under the Rod......Mary S. B. Dana.	589
Passions, The............................W. Collins.	730
Past, The................William Cullen Bryant.	91
Pastoral, A..............................John Byrom.	173
Pastoral, A.........................Nicholas Breton.	182
Pastoral Ballad, A...........William Shenstone.	205
Paul Revere's Ride......Henry W. Longfellow.	329
Pauper's Death-bed, The..........C. B. Southey.	721
Pauper's Drive, The...............Thomas Noel.	722
Pavy, Epitaph on Salathiel.........Ben Jonson.	232
Peal of Bells, A.........Christina G. Rossetti.	764
Pearl-Wearer, The......Bryan Waller Procter.	700
Pembroke, Epitaph on the Countess of, Ben Jonson.	233
Pericles and Aspasia..............George Croly.	289
Per Pacem ad Lucem....Adelaide A. Procter.	537
Petition to Time, A....Bryan Waller Procter.	751
Pet Lamb, The.................W. Wordsworth.	487
Philip, my King..................Dinah M. Craik.	30
Phillida and Corydon..........Nicholas Breton.	145
Philomela..................... Matthew Arnold.	472
Philosopher's Scales, The.........Jane Taylor.	665
Pibroch of Donuil Dhu......Sir Walter Scott.	359
Picture, A....................Charles G. Eastman.	6
Picture of T. C., The, in a Prospect of Flowers....................Andrew Marvell.	240
Pied Piper of Hamelin, The......R. Browning.	851
Pilgrimage, The..............Sir Walter Raleigh.	578
Pilgrims of the Night, The..Fred. W. Faber.	600
Place to Die, The.......Michael Joseph Barry.	680
Plain Language from Truthful James, Bret Harte.	933
Ploughman, The......Oliver Wendell Holmes.	692
Poet's Bridal-Day Song...Allan Cunningham.	18
Poet's Song to his Wife..........B. W. Procter.	14
Pompadour, The..............G. W. Thornbury.	327
Poor Jack........................Charles Dibdin.	698
Pope, Parody on....................Sydney Smith.	923
Portrait, The...............Robert Bulwer Lytton.	199
Power of Love, The.....Beaumont & Fletcher.	169

	PAGE
Praise.................................Edward Osler.	601
Praise of a Countryman's Life.John Chalkhill.	496
Praise of a Solitary Life, The..W. Drummond.	658
Praise of his Love, A............Henry Howard.	154
Praise to God..........Anna Lætitia Barbauld.	548
Praxiteles and Phryne...... William W. Story.	784
Pre-Existence.....................Paul H. Hayne.	783
Present Crisis, The......James Russell Lowell.	343
Priest, The.........................Nicholas Breton.	552
Primrose, The.....................Robert Herrick.	214
Primrose, To an Early........Henry K. White.	452
Primroses Filled with Morning Dew, To, Robert Herrick.	452
Prisoned in Windsor, he Recounteth his Pleasure there Passed......Henry Howard.	222
Prisoner of Chillon...................Lord Byron.	398
Problem, The............Ralph Waldo Emerson.	663
Progress of Poesy, The...........Thomas Gray.	728
Prologue to Mr. Addison's Tragedy of "Cato," Alexander Pope.	242
Proud Maisie is in the Wood..Sir Walter Scott.	890
Psalm of Life, A........Henry W. Longfellow.	615
Psalm XXIII, Paraphrase of.......J. Addison.	561
Psalm XXIII, Paraphrase of......R. Crashaw.	562
Psalm LXXII—"Hail to the Lord's Anointed"........................James Montgomery.	537
Psalm LXXXIV—"Pleasant are Thy courts above".................Henry Francis Lyte.	600
Psalm LXXXVII—"Glorious things of Thee are spoken"....................John Newton.	598
Psalm XC—"Our God, our help in ages past"..............................Isaac Watts.	549
Psalm XCVIII—"Joy to the world! the Lord is come"..................Isaac Watts.	549
Psalm C—"With one consent let all the earth"..............................Tate & Brady.	545
Psalm C—"Before Jehovah's awful throne," Isaac Watts (varied by Charles Wesley).	546
Psalm CXVII—"From all that dwell below the skies".... ....Isaac Watts.	552
Psalm CXXI—"Up to the hills I lift mine eyes"..............................Isaac Watts.	583
Psalm CXLVIII—"Come, oh come! in pious lays"...........................George Wither.	551
Pulley, The...........................George Herbert.	662
QUA CURSUM VENTUS.....Arthur Hugh Clough.	744
Quaker Widow, The..............Bayard Taylor.	22
Question, The...............Percy Bysshe Shelley.	459
Quince............. Winthrop Mackworth Praed.	911
RAINBOW, The......................Henry Vaughan.	443
Rainbow, The............. William Wordsworth.	444
Rainbow, To the..............Thomas Campbell.	444
Rainy Day, The.........Henry W. Longfellow.	775
Randolph of Roanoke........John G. Whittier.	262
Rape of the Lock, The.........Alexander Pope.	795
Raven, The.....................Edgar Allan Poe.	849

INDEX OF THE NAMES OF THE POEMS.

	PAGE
Rebecca's Hymn...............*Sir Walter Scott.*	550
Recipe for Salad, A...............*Sydney Smith.*	959
Reconciliation, The............*Alfred Tennyson.*	39
Re-cured Lover Exulteth in his Freedom, The...........................*Sir Thomas Wyatt.*	191
Redbreast, Sonnet to the......*John Bampfylde.*	477
Red, Red Rose, A.....................*Robert Burns.*	157
Red River Voyageur, The...*John G. Whittier.*	680
Reflective Retrospect, A............*John G. Saxe.*	79
Reign of May, The.......*James Gates Percival.*	432
Renunciation, A....*E. Vere (Earl of Oxford).*	190
Resignation........................*Richard Baxter.*	566
Resignation...................... *Thomas Chatterton.*	565
Resignation.....*Henry Wadsworth Longfellow.*	646
Retirement........ ....*William Cowper.*	582
Retirement, The.....................*Charles Cotton.*	495
Retreat, The......................*Henry Vaughan.*	92
Return of Napoleon from St. Helena, *Lydia H. Sigourney.*	268
Rêve du Midi..................*Rose Terry Cooke.*	433
Rhine, The................*William Lisle Bowles.*	518
Rhodora, The............*Ralph Waldo Emerson.*	455
Right must Win, The....*Frederick W. Faber.*	572
Rime of the Ancient Mariner, The, *Samuel Taylor Coleridge.*	855
Rise, my Soul, and Stretch thy Wings, *Robert Seagrave.*	570
Robin Hood and Allen-a-Dale, *Author Unknown.*	390
Robin Redbreast............ *William Allingham.*	477
Rock me to Sleep........*Elizabeth Akers Allen.*	74
Rock of Ages....*Augustus Montague Toplady.*	540
Romance of the Swan's Nest...*E. B. Browning.*	47
Rory O'More........................*Samuel Lover.*	165
Rosabelle.............................*Sir Walter Scott.*	403
Rosader's Sonetto...................*Thomas Lodge.*	156
Rosalind's Madrigal.............*Thomas Lodge.*	98
Rosaline............................*Thomas Lodge.*	123
Rule, Britannia....................*James Thomson.*	355
Ruth .... *Thomas Hood.*	144
SABBATH CHIMES......................*Charles Swain.*	561
Sabbath Evening.....*George Denison Prentice.*	441
Sabbath Morning, The..............*John Leyden.*	439
Sailor's Wife, The...............*Charles Mackay.*	25
Sally in our Alley....................*Henry Carey.*	120
Sands of Dee, The.............*Charles Kingsley.*	417
Saturday Afternoon..................*N. P. Willis.*	77
Saviour, who Thy Flock art Feeding, *William Augustus Muhlenberg.*	540
School and School-fellows........*W. M. Praed.*	79
Schoolmistress, The.........*William Shenstone.*	57
Sea, The..............................*B. W. Procter.*	462
Sea-Limits, The.........*Dante Gabriel Rossetti.*	462
Seasons, Hymn on the.........*James Thomson.*	423
Seneca Lake, To..........*James Gates Percival.*	521
September..........................*George Arnold.*	434
Serenade, A.......................*Thomas Hood.*	903

	PAGE
Serenade, A.......................*Sir Walter Scott.*	189
Shakespeare, Epitaph on...........*John Milton.*	230
Shakespeare, Lines on the Portrait of...*Jonson.*	230
Shakespeare, To the memory of...*Ben Jonson.*	228
Shall I Tell you Whom I Love?.*Wm. Browne.*	123
She is Far from the Land ......*Thomas Moore.*	275
She is not Fair to Outward View.*H. Coleridge.*	172
Shepherd's Resolution, The....*George Wither.*	169
Shepherd's Wife's Song, The.........*R. Greene.*	142
Sheridan's Ride.......*Thomas Buchanan Read.*	351
She's Gane to Dwell in Heaven.*A. Cunningham.*	218
She Walks in Beauty..................*Lord Byron.*	741
She was a Phantom of Delight....*Wordsworth.*	10
Ships at Sea............................*R. B. Coffin.*	789
Shortness of Life, The..........*Francis Quarles.*	615
Shout the Glad Tidings..*Wm. A. Muhlenberg.*	533
Sic Vita....................................*Henry King.*	688
Sidney, Epitaph upon Sir Philip. *W. Raleigh.*	227
Siege of Belgrade, The.......*Author Unknown.*	960
Sigh no More, Ladies........*Wm. Shakespeare.*	187
Silent Lover, The............*Sir Walter Raleigh.*	182
Siller Croun, The.................*Susanna Blamire.*	147
Sir Marmaduke...*George Colman, the Younger.*	784
Sir Patrick Spens...............*Author Unknown.*	367
Sister Helen....... ....*Dante Gabriel Rossetti.*	875
Sixteen.................... *Walter Savage Landor.*	214
Skeleton, To a .... *Author Unknown.*	642
Skeleton in Armor, The.....*H. W. Longfellow.*	864
Skipper Ireson's Ride........*John G. Whittier.*	371
Skylark, The............................*James Hogg.*	473
Skylark, To a ....*Percy Bysshe Shelley.*	474
Skylark, To a............. *William Wordsworth.*	473
Skylark, To a............. *William Wordsworth.*	473
Sleep, Sonnet on.. ....*Samuel Daniel.*	776
Sleep, Sonnet on..............*Sir Philip Sidney.*	776
Sleep, The................*Elizabeth B. Browning.*	622
Sleeping Babe, The..................*Samuel Hinds.*	45
Smack in School, The... *William Pitt Palmer.*	923
Society upon the Stanislow, The....*Bret Harte.*	944
Soldier, Rest......................*Sir Walter Scott.*	700
Soldier's Dream, The.........*Thomas Campbell.*	83
Solitude, Ode on.................*Alexander Pope.*	755
Somerset, Upon the Sudden Restraint of the Earl of............................*Sir H. Wotton.*	230
Son-Dayes.......................*Henry Vaughan.*	560
Song—" Busy, curious, thirsty fly "..*W. Oldys.*	483
Song—" Day in melting purple dying," *Maria Brooks.*	170
Song—" Follow a Shadow, it still Flies you," *Ben Jonson.*	124
Song for St. Cecilia's Day, A.....*John Dryden.*	726
Song. (From the "Merchant of Venice"), *William Shakespeare.*	838
Song—" Lay a garland on my hearse," *Beaumont & Fletcher.*	212
Song of Fairies.......................*Leigh Hunt.*	794
Song of Margaret...................*Jean Ingelow.*	195
Song of Marion's Men............. *W. C. Bryant.*	331

INDEX OF THE NAMES OF THE POEMS.

	PAGE
Song of the Brook............... *Alfred Tennyson.*	460
Song of the Camp, The......... *Bayard Taylor.*	216
Song of the Fairies........................ *John Lyly.*	793
Song of the Greek Poet............... *Lord Byron.*	360
Song of the North, A............ *Elizabeth Doten.*	421
Song of the River............... *Charles Kingsley.*	461
Song of the Shirt, The............ *Thomas Hood.*	716
Song of the Summer Winds.... *George Darley.*	433
Song, on May Morning............... *John Milton.*	427
Song—"Oh welcome, bat and owlet gray," *Joanna Baillie.*	481
Song—"Rarely, rarely, comest thou," *Percy Bysshe Shelley.*	779
Songs of Birds, The..................... *John Lyly.*	480
Song—"Still to be neat, still to be drest," *Ben Jonson.*	740
Song, sung by Rogero........... *George Canning.*	935
Song—"The lark now leaves his watery nest"................... *Sir William Davenant.*	472
Song—"'Tis sweet to hear the merry lark," *Hartley Coleridge.*	472
Song to May....................... *Erasmus Darwin.*	431
Song to May........................... *Lord Thurlow.*	428
Song, To the Evening Star........ *T. Campbell.*	447
Song—"To thy lover"....... *Richard Crashaw.*	126
Song—"Under the greenwood tree," *William Shakespeare.*	457
Songs of Praise the Angels Sang.*J. Montgomery.*	588
Songs of Seven........................ *Jean Ingelow.*	19
Sonnet—"A good that never satisfies the mind"................ *William Drummond.*	656
Sonnet—"Because I oft in dark abstracted guise"........................ *Sir Philip Sidney.*	781
Sonnet, Composed upon Westminster Bridge, *William Wordsworth.*	503
Sonnet—"Full many a glorious morning have I seen"................ *William Shakespeare.*	439
Sonnet—"Having this day my horse, my hand, my lance"......... *Sir Philip Sidney.*	192
Sonnet—"It is a beauteous evening, calm and free"............ *William Wordsworth.*	441
Sonnet—"Let me not to the marriage of true minds"................. *William Shakespeare.*	218
Sonnet—"Like as the culver, on the barèd bough"........................ *Edmund Spenser.*	190
Sonnet—"Like as the waves make toward the pebbled shore"...... *William Shakespeare.*	753
Sonnet, May....................... *Thomas Watson.*	428
Sonnet—"No longer mourn for me when I am dead"............ *William Shakespeare.*	219
Sonnet—"Not marble, nor the gilded monuments"................ *William Shakespeare.*	752
Sonnet—"O happy Thames that didst my Stella bear!"............... *Sir Philip Sidney.*	191
Sonnet—"Oh, how much more doth beauty beauteous seem"... *William Shakespeare.*	753
Sonnet, On a Distant View of England, *William Lisle Bowles.*	356

	PAGE
Sonnet, On his being Arrived at the Age of Twenty-three............... *John Milton.*	226
Sonnet, On his Blindness........... *John Milton.*	234
Sonnet on Parting with his Books.*W. Roscoe.*	784
Sonnet on Sleep..................... *Samuel Daniel.*	776
Sonnet on Sleep............... *Sir Philip Sidney.*	776
Sonnet, On the Late Massacre in Piedmont, *John Milton.*	313
Sonnet—"Poor soul, the centre of my sinful earth"................. *William Shakespeare.*	753
Sonnet—"Sad is our youth, for it is ever going"...................... *Aubrey de Vere.*	614
Sonnet—"Scorn not the sonnet; critic, you have frown'd"...... *William Wordsworth.*	781
Sonnets from the Portuguese..*E. B. Browning.*	134
Sonnet—"Shall I compare thee to a summer's day?".................... *William Shakespeare.*	220
Sonnet—"Since I did leave the presence of my love"................... *Edmund Spenser.*	190
Sonnet—"Since there's no help, come, let us kiss and part"............. *Michael Drayton.*	170
Sonnet, Summer..................... *Lord Thurlow.*	433
Sonnet—"Sweet is the rose, but grows upon a brere".................. *Edmund Spenser.*	780
Sonnet—"That time of year thou may'st in me behold".......... *William Shakespeare.*	219
Sonnet—"The doubt which ye misdeem, fair love, is vain"............... *Edmund Spenser.*	101
Sonnet—"They that have power to hurt, and will do none"........ *William Shakespeare.*	754
Sonnet—"Time wasteth years, and months, and hours".................... *Thomas Watson.*	172
Sonnet—"Tired with all these, for restful death I cry"........ *William Shakespeare.*	219
Sonnet, To Cyriac Skinner.......... *John Milton.*	234
Sonnet to his Lute......... *William Drummond.*	734
Sonnet to Hope......... *Helen Maria Williams.*	663
Sonnet—"To live in hell, and heaven to behold"........................ *Henry Constable.*	212
Sonnet—"To me, fair friend, you never can be old"............... *William Shakespeare.*	752
Sonnet, To Milton........ *William Wordsworth.*	240
Sonnet—"To one who has been long in city pent"................................. *John Keats.*	499
Sonnet to the Glow-Worm.......... *John Clare.*	483
Sonnet, To the Lord General Cromwell, *John Milton.*	234
Sonnet, To the Moon......... *Sir Philip Sidney.*	118
Sonnet, To the Moon............... *Lord Thurlow.*	446
Sonnet, To the Redbreast.... *John Bampfylde.*	477
Sonnet—"When I do count the clock that tells the time"....... *William Shakespeare.*	752
Sonnet—"When in disgrace with fortune and men's eyes"......... *William Shakespeare.*	219
Sonnet—"When in the chronicle of wasted time"................... *William Shakespeare.*	220
Sonnet, When the Assault was Intended to the City...... .... *John Milton.*	313

INDEX OF THE NAMES OF THE POEMS.

	PAGE
Sonnet—"When to the sessions of sweet silent thought"............. *William Shakespeare.*	753
Sonnet written after seeing Windsor Castle, *Thomas Warton.*	504
Sorrows of Werther, The... *W. M. Thackeray.*	895
Sound the Loud Timbrel........ *Thomas Moore.*	550
Spring.................................... *Thomas Nash.*	427
Spring.................................... *Henry Timrod.*	431
Spring, Ode on the................ *Thomas Gray.*	427
Spring, To..................... *William Drummond.*	425
Squire's Pew, The..................... *Jane Taylor.*	671
St. Agnes' Eve................... *Alfred Tennyson.*	546
Stanzas—"And thou art dead, as young and fair"................................. *Lord Byron.*	742
Stanzas—"Farewell, life! my senses swim," *Thomas Hood.*	637
Stanzas—"My life is like the summer rose," *Richard Henry Wilde.*	616
Stanzas—"Oh, talk not to me of a name great in story"......................... *Lord Byron.*	157
Stanzas on the Death of a Friend... *R. Heber.*	594
Stanzas—"Thought is deeper than all speech," *C. P. Cranch.*	782
Stanzas—"When lovely woman stoops to folly"....................... *Oliver Goldsmith.*	687
Stanzas—"When midnight o'er the moonless skies"............ *William Robert Spencer.*	94
Stanzas for Music—"There be none of Beauty's daughters"............ *Lord Byron.*	157
Stanzas written in Dejection near Naples, *Percy Bysshe Shelley.*	261
St. Anthony's Sermon to the Fishes, *Author Unknown.*	915
Star of Bethlehem, The ...... *Henry K. White.*	577
Star-Spangled Banner, The... *Francis S. Key.*	353
St. Cecilia's Day, Ode on...... *Alexander Pope.*	727
St. Cecilia's Day, Song for....... *John Dryden.*	726
Steadfast Shepherd, The........ *George Wither.*	153
Stolen Kiss, A.................... *George Wither.*	156
Stormy Petrel, The...... *Bryan Waller Procter.*	470
St. Patrick was a Gentleman... *Henry Bennett.*	924
Stranger and his Friend, The... *J. Montgomery.*	541
Stranger on the Sill, The... *T. Buchanan Read.*	75
Stream of Life, The........ *Arthur Hugh Clough.*	614
Sturge, In Remembrance of Joseph. *Whittier.*	277
Summer Longings.......... *Denis F. McCarthy.*	429
Summer, Sonnet on................ *Lord Thurlow.*	433
Sunday.............................. *George Herbert.*	560
Superstition........................ *John Norris.*	179
Supplication, A.................. *Abraham Cowley.*	121
Sweet and Low.................. *Alfred Tennyson.*	31
Sweet-and-Twenty.............. *W. Shakespeare.*	163
Sweet are the Charms............. *Barton Booth.*	154
Sweet Baby, Sleep.................. *George Wither.*	34
Sweet Content..................... *Thomas Dekker.*	660
Sweet Innisfallen.................. *Thomas Moore.*	517
Sweet William's Farewell to Black-Eyed Susan............................... *John Gay.*	119

	PAGE
Take, oh Take those Lips away, *Beaumont & Fletcher.*	184
Take thy Old Cloak about Thee, *Author Unknown.*	901
Tale of Drury Lane, A............ *Horace Smith.*	936
Tam O'Shanter........................ *Robert Burns.*	873
Tears of Scotland, The......... *Tobias Smollett.*	327
Tears Wept at the Grave of Sir Albertus Morton......................... *Sir H. Wotton.*	228
Tell me How to Woo Thee, *Robert Graham of Gartmore.*	161
Tempest, The .... *Sir Humphry Davy.*	462
Ternissa .... *Walter Savage Landor.*	196
Thanatopsis............. *William Cullen Bryant.*	624
Thanksgiving Hymn.............. *Henry Alford.*	558
Thanksgiving to God for His House, A, *Robert Herrick.*	559
Theatre, The........................... *James Smith.*	938
The Child Leans on its Parent's Breast, *Isaac Williams.*	573
The Dule's i' this Bonnet o' Mine.. *E. Waugh.*	166
The God of Abraham Praise......... *T. Olivers.*	583
The Harp that once through Tara's Halls, *Thomas Moore.*	362
The Heath this Night must be my Bed, *Sir Walter Scott.*	186
The House is Dark and Dreary, *R. H. Stoddard.*	785
The Midges Dance aboon the Burn, *Robert Tannahill.*	440
There be Those .... *Bernard Barton.*	617
There is a Dwelling-Place Above..... *R. Mant.*	599
There is a Garden in her Face........ *R. Alison.*	185
There is a Happy Land......... *Andrew Young.*	599
There is a Land of Pure Delight. *Isaac Watts.*	599
There's not a Joy the World can Give, *Lord Byron.*	656
The Sun Rises Bright in France, *Allan Cunningham.*	358
The Wretch, condemned with Life to Part, *Oliver Goldsmith.*	785
They are all Gone.............. *Henry Vaughan.*	597
They come! the Merry Summer Months, *William Motherwell.*	430
They're Dear Fish to Me .... *Author Unknown.*	699
Thomson, Ode on the Death of..... *W. Collins.*	244
Those Evening Bells.............. *Thomas Moore.*	764
Thou art, O God............ ...... *Thomas Moore.*	551
Thought among the Roses, A... *Peter Spencer.*	456
Thoughts in a Garden .... *Andrew Marvell.*	497
Thoughts in a Library........ *Anne C. L. Botta.*	738
Thou hast Sworn by thy God, my Jeanie, *A. Cunningham.*	157
Three Fishers, The .... *Charles Kingsley.*	699
Three Ravens, The............ *Author Unknown.*	411
Three Sons, The........... ...... *John Moultrie.*	50
Three Troopers, The... *George W. Thornbury.*	309
Three Warnings, The... *Hester Thrale Piozzi.*	619

	PAGE		PAGE
Three Years she Grew......Wm. Wordsworth.	49	To Night......................Percy Bysshe Shelley.	442
Thrush's Nest, The........................John Clare.	476	To Night......................Joseph Blanco White.	441
Thy Goodness, Lord, our Souls Confess, Thomas Gibbons.	562	Too Late..........................Dinah M. Craik.	17
Thy Voice is Heard thro' Rolling Drums, Alfred Tennyson.	743	To Pan..........................Beaumont & Fletcher.	425
Thy Will be Done................Charlotte Elliott.	566	To Primroses, filled with Morning Dew, Robert Herrick.	452
Thy Will be Done..............Anna L. Waring.	567	To Q. H. F..........................Austin Dobson.	921
Thy Will be Done..............John G. Whittier.	568	To Seneca Lake............James Gates Percival.	521
Tiger, The...........................William Blake.	494	To Sigh, yet Feel no Pain......Thomas Moore.	182
Times Go by Turns............Robert Southwell.	778	To Spring......................William Drummond.	425
'Tis the Last Rose of Summer........T. Moore.	456	To the Butterfly..................Samuel Rogers.	482
Tithonus........................Alfred Tennyson.	787	To the Cuckoo..........................John Logan.	481
To a Bird that Haunted the Waters of Laaken in the Winter....................Lord Thurlow.	472	To the Cuckoo.............William Wordsworth.	480
To a Child Embracing his Mother...T. Hood.	35	To the Daisy...............William Wordsworth.	453
To a Highland Girl............Wm. Wordsworth.	65	To the Daisy...............William Wordsworth.	454
To Althea, from Prison......Richard Lovelace.	124	To the Earl of Warwick on the Death of Mr. Addison.........................Thomas Tickell.	242
To a Mountain Daisy..............Robert Burns.	454	To the Evening Star..................John Leyden.	447
To a Mouse........................Robert Burns.	483	To the Fringed Gentian...........W C. Bryant.	455
To an Absent Wife..........George D. Prentice.	14	To the Grasshopper and Cricket......L. Hunt.	482
To an Early Primrose........Henry K. White.	452	To the Lady Margaret..........Samuel Daniel.	230
To a Nightingale...........William Drummond.	477	To the Lady Margaret Ley........John Milton.	235
To a Skeleton....................Author Unknown.	642	To the Memory of my Beloved, the Author, Mr. William Shakespeare, and what he hath left us..........................Ben Jonson.	228
To a Skylark...............Percy Bysshe Shelley.	474	To the Moon......Percy Bysshe Shelley.	446
To a Skylark...............William Wordsworth.	473	To the Nightingale.........William Drummond.	478
To a Skylark...............William Wordsworth.	473	To the Nightingale..................John Milton.	478
To Autumn..........................John Keats.	435	To the Rainbow...............Thomas Campbell.	444
To a very Young Lady......Sir Charles Sedley.	189	To the Sister of Elia.........Walter S. Landor.	273
To a Water-Fowl.......William Cullen Bryant.	471	To thy Temple I Repair..........J. Montgomery.	561
To Blossoms.........................Robert Herrick.	457	To T. L. H............................Leigh Hunt.	36
To Celia..............................Ben Jonson.	195	Touchstone, The............William Allingham.	665
To Charlotte Pulteney........Ambrose Philips.	35	Toujours Amour...Edmund Clarence Stedman.	163
To Cynthia............................Ben Jonson.	446	To Vincent Corbet, my Son...Richard Corbet.	233
To Daffodils......................Robert Herrick.	453	To Virgins to make Much of Time...Herrick.	123
To Dianeme......................Robert Herrick.	210	Traveller, The..................Oliver Goldsmith.	767
To Eva...................Ralph Waldo Emerson.	217	Treasures of the Deep, The..........F. Hemans.	463
To his Forsaken Mistress........Sir R. Ayton.	148	Triumph of Charis, The.............Ben Jonson.	160
To his Lute..................William Drummond.	734	Trooper to his Mare, The........C. G. Halpine.	493
To his Mistress, the Queen of Bohemia, Sir Henry Wotton.	185	Twa Corbies, The..............Author Unknown.	412
To Ianthe..................Walter Savage Landor.	213	'Twas when the Seas were Roaring.....J. Gay.	125
To Keep a True Lent............Robert Herrick.	587	Twenty-One..........................Julia C. Dorr.	682
To Lady Anne Hamilton........W. R. Spencer.	779	Twenty Years Ago..............Author Unknown.	78
To Lucasta, On Going beyond the Seas, Richard Lovelace.	125	Twins, The..................Henry S. Leigh.	906
To Lucasta, On Going to the Wars..R.Lovelace.	124	Two Rivers..............Ralph Waldo Emerson.	764
To Mary....................Samuel Bishop.	10	Under my Window................T. Westwood.	53
To Mary....................William Cowper.	245	Unfortunate Miss Bailey....Frederick Locker.	954
To Mary in Heaven..................Robert Burns.	137	Universal Prayer, The..........Alexander Pope.	545
Tom Bowling......................Charles Dibdin.	639	Up-Hill............Christina Georgina Rossetti.	578
Tom Dunstan........................R. Buchanan.	702	Upon the Death of Sir Albertus Morton's Wife...............................Sir H. Wotton.	228
To Mistress Margaret Hussey........J. Skelton.	225	Upon the Sudden Restraint of the Earl of Somerset....................Sir H. Wotton.	230
Tommy's Dead....................Sydney Dobell.	620	Urania......................Matthew Arnold.	216
To Mrs. Unwin..................William Cowper.	245	Useful Plough, The............Author Unknown.	692
To my Horse....................Author Unknown.	493	Use of Flowers, The..................Mary Howitt.	455
To my Picture................Thomas Randolph.	755		
To my Wife...............Thomas Haynes Bayly.	9		

INDEX OF THE NAMES OF THE POEMS. xxiii

	PAGE
VAGABONDS, The..............*J. T. Trowbridge.*	717
Valediction.........................*Richard Baxter.*	592
Vanity of Human Wishes, The....*S. Johnson.*	649
Vanity of the World, The....*Francis Quarles.*	654
Vengeance of Mudara, The....*J. G. Lockhart.*	292
Veni Creator ....*John Dryden.*	543
Veni Creator Spiritus.........*Author Unknown.*	542
Verses in Praise of Angling....*Sir H. Wotton.*	467
Verses, supposed to be Written by Alexander Selkirk..................*William Cowper.*	679
Very Mournful Ballad, A...........*Lord Byron.*	295
Vicar, The.........*Winthrop Mackworth Praed.*	913
Vicar of Bray, The.............*Author Unknown.*	914
Village Blacksmith, The...*H. W. Longfellow.*	693
Vincent Corbet, my Son, To..........*R. Corbet.*	233
Violet, The.............. *William Wetmore Story.*	453
Virtue ....*George Herbert.*	662
Virtuoso, A........................*Austin Dobson.*	958
Vision upon this Conceit of the Faerie Queene, A................*Sir Walter Raleigh.*	739
Voiceless, The ....*Oliver Wendell Holmes.*	626
WAE'S ME FOR PRINCE CHARLIE.....*Wm. Glen.*	326
Walking with God..............*William Cowper.*	564
Waly, Waly, but Love be Bonny, *Author Unknown.*	103
Wandering Jew, The..........*Author Unknown.*	374
Warren's Address.................. *John Pierpont.*	329
Watchman, tell us of the Night, *Sir John Bowring.*	523
Water-Fowl, To a .....*William Cullen Bryant.*	471
We are Brethren a'...................*Robert Nicoll.*	706
We are Seven.............. *William Wordsworth.*	51
Weary............*Christina Georgina Rossetti.*	591
Web of Life, The..................*Clara J. Moore.*	617
Weep no More.......................*John Fletcher.*	786
Welcome, The.................... *William Browne.*	125
Welcome, The ....*Thomas Osborne Davis.*	158
Wellington, Ode on the Death of the Duke of.................................*Alfred Tennyson.*	270
Well of St. Keyne, The.........*Robert Southey.*	898
We Parted in Silence............*Julia Crawford.*	85
We Sing the Praise of Him who Died, *Thomas Kelly.*	535
West Wind, Ode to the........*Percy B. Shelley.*	436
Wet Sheet and a Flowing Sea.*A. Cunningham.*	695
What Ails this Heart o' Mine ....*S. Blamire.*	199
What are These in Bright Array, *James Montgomery.*	598
What is Prayer...............*James Montgomery.*	563
What Mr. Robinson Thinks........*J. R. Lowell.*	922
When all Thy Mercies, O my God.*J. Addison.*	547
When Coldness Wraps this Suffering Clay, *Lord Byron.*	625
When Gathering Clouds around I View, *Sir Robert Grant.*	569
When Icicles Hang by the Wall..*Shakespeare.*	438
When Maggie Gangs Away........*James Hogg.*	161

	PAGE
When our Heads are Bowed with Woe, *Henry Hart Milman.*	582
When Stars are in the Quiet Skies, *Edward Bulwer Lytton.*	218
When the Assault was Intended to the City. *John Milton.*	313
When the Kye comes Hame........*James Hogg.*	167
When we Two Parted ....*Lord Byron.*	86
Where did you Come from?....*G. Macdonald.*	31
Where are you Going, my Pretty Maid? *Author Unknown.*	898
Where lies the Land......*Arthur Hugh Clough.*	466
Where shall the Lover Rest ......*Sir W. Scott.*	176
Which shall it Be?............*Ethel Lynn Beers.*	45
Whilst as Fickle Fortune Smiled, *Richard Barnefield.*	778
Whilst Thee I Seek ...*Helen Maria Williams.*	572
Whiskers, The.................*Samuel Woodworth.*	892
White Rose, The.................*Author Unknown.*	214
Who is Sylvia?............ *William Shakespeare.*	217
Why so Pale?............*Sir John Suckling.*	104
Why thus Longing? ....*Harriet W. Sewall.*	766
Widow and Child, The........*Alfred Tennyson.*	56
Wife, A...................... *William Allingham.*	12
William and Margaret.............*David Mallet.*	175
Willie Winkie..................... *William Miller.*	41
Will of God, The...........*Frederick W. Faber.*	566
Windsor Castle, Sonnet written after seeing, *Thomas Warton.*	504
Winifreda ....*Author Unknown.*	7
Winsome Wee Thing, The ....*Robert Burns.*	9
Wish, A...........................*Samuel Rogers.*	6
Wishes for the Supposed Mistress, *Richard Crashaw.*	121
With a Guitar, to Jane........*Percy B. Shelley.*	732
Without and Within...........*James R. Lowell.*	707
Without and Within ....*Richard H. Stoddard.*	12
Woman's Answer, A.......*Adelaide A. Procter.*	188
Woman's Inconstancy........*Sir Robert Ayton.*	141
Woman's Question, A ....*Adelaide A. Procter.*	187
Wonderfu' Wean, The ....*William Miller.*	42
Woodman, Spare that Tree!......*G. P. Morris.*	75
Wrestling Jacob..................*Charles Wesley.*	571
YARN of the "Nancy Bell," The, *William S. Gilbert.*	910
Yarrow Revisited.........*William Wordsworth.*	511
Yarrow Unvisited........*William Wordsworth.*	510
Yarrow Visited ....*William Wordsworth.*	510
Ye Gentlemen of England.....*Martyn Parker.*	701
Ye Golden Lamps of Heaven, Farewell, *Philip Doddridge.*	588
Ye Mariners of England ....*T. Campbell.*	356
Young Airly....................*Author Unknown.*	325
Young May Moon, The ....*Thomas Moore.*	162
Youth and Age.............*Samuel T. Coleridge.*	94
ZARA'S EAR-RINGS......*John Gibson Lockhart.*	183

INDEX OF AUTHORS.

ADAM, JEAN (b. 1710, d. 1765).
 The Mariner's Wife 10
ADAMS, SARAH FLOWER (b. 1805, d. 1849).
 Father, Thy Will be Done 544
 "Nearer, my God, to Thee" 564
ADDISON, JOSEPH (b. 1672, d. 1719).
 An Ode—"The spacious firmament on high" .. 545
 Hymn—"How are thy servants blest, O Lord!" 558
 Paraphrase of Psalm XXIII 561
 "When all Thy mercies, O my God!" 547
AKENSIDE, MARK (b. 1721, d. 1770).
 Inscription for a Statue of Chaucer 225
AKERMAN, LUCY EVELINA.
 Nothing but Leaves 578
ALDRICH, JAMES (b. 1810, d. 1856).
 A Death-bed 625
ALDRICH, THOMAS BAILEY (b. 1836).
 Baby Bell 30
 On an Intaglio Head of Minerva 780
ALEXANDER, CECIL FRANCES (b. 1823).
 The Burial of Moses 580
ALFORD, HENRY (b. 1810, d. 1871).
 Baptismal Hymn 563
 Thanksgiving Hymn 558
 The Aged Oak 458
ALISON, RICHARD (about 1606).
 "There is a garden in her face" 185
ALLEN, ELIZABETH AKERS (1832).
 Endurance 617
 My Ship 789
 "Rock me to sleep" 74
ALLINGHAM, WILLIAM (b. 1828).
 A Wife 12
 Lovely Mary Donnelly 122
 Robin Redbreast 477
 The Fairies 794
 The Touchstone 665
ALLSTON, WASHINGTON (b. 1779, d. 1843).
 Boyhood 53
ARNOLD, EDWIN (b. 1832).
 After Death in Arabia 681
 Almond-Blossom 457
ARNOLD, GEORGE (b. 1834, d. 1865).
 September 434
 The Jolly Old Pedagogue 927
ARNOLD, MATTHEW (b. 1822).
 Euphrosyne 213
 Philomela 472

 The Neckan 883
 Urania 216
AUSTIN, JOHN (d. 1669).
 "Blest be Thy love, dear Lord" 548
AYTON, SIR ROBERT (b. 1570, d. 1638).
 To his Forsaken Mistress 148
 Woman's Inconstancy 141
AYTOUN, WILLIAM EDMONDSTOUNE (b. 1813, d. 1865).
 Burial-March of Dundee 317
 Edinburgh after Flodden 302
 Execution of Montrose 313
 Massacre of the Macpherson 934
BACON, FRANCIS, BARON VERULAM (b. 1561, d. 1626).
 Life 613
BAILLIE, JOANNA (b. 1762, d. 1851).
 The Black Cock 481
 The Kitten 484
 Morning Song 499
 Song—"Oh welcome, bat and owlet gray" 481
BAKEWELL, JOHN (b. 1721, d. 1819).
 "Hail! Thou once-despisèd Jesus!" 538
BALLANTYNE, JAMES (b. 1808).
 Castles in the Air 37
BAMPFYLDE, JOHN (b. 1754, d. 1796).
 Sonnet to the Redbreast 477
BARBAULD, ANNA LÆTITIA (b. 1743, d. 1825).
 Christ Risen 536
 Death of the Virtuous 618
 Life 613
 Praise to God 548
BARHAM, RICHARD HARRIS (b. 1788, d. 1845).
 Mr. Barney Maguire's account of the Coronation 956
 The Execution 941
BARNARD, LADY ANNE (b. 1750, d. 1825).
 Auld Robin Gray 137
BARNEFIELD, RICHARD (b. 1574, d. 1627).
 The Nightingale 480
 "Whilst as fickle Fortune smiled" 778
BARRY, MICHAEL JOSEPH.
 The Place to Die 680
BARTON, BERNARD (b. 1784, d. 1849).
 Not ours the Vows 101
 "There be Those" 617
BAXTER, RICHARD (b. 1615, d. 1691).
 Resignation 566
 Valediction 592
BAYLY, THOMAS HAYNES (b. 1797, d. 1839).
 To My Wife 9

INDEX OF AUTHORS.

	PAGE
BEATTIE, JAMES (b. 1735, d. 1803).	
The Hermit	648
BEATTIE, WILLIAM (b. about 1797, d. 1875).	
Evening Hymn of the Alpine Shepherds	552
BEAUMONT, FRANCIS (b. 1586, d. 1616).	
On the Tombs in Westminster Abbey	504
BEAUMONT AND FLETCHER.	
Folding the Flocks	495
"Look out, bright eyes"	184
Song—"Lay a garland on my hearse"	212
"Take, oh take, those lips away"	184
The Power of Love	169
To Pan	425
BEAUMONT, SIR JOHN (b. 1582, d. 1628).	
On my Dear Son, Gervase Beaumont	226
BEDDOES, THOMAS LOVELL (b. 1803, d. 1849).	
How Many Times	102
BEDDOME, BENJAMIN (b. 1717, d. 1795).	
Jesus Wept	535
BEERS, ETHEL LYNN (b. 1827, d. 1879).	
All Quiet Along the Potomac	349
Which Shall it Be?	45
BEERS, HENRY AUGUSTIN (b. 1847.)	
Carçamon	404
BENNETT, HENRY.	
St. Patrick was a Gentleman	924
BENNETT, WILLIAM COX (b. 1820).	
Baby May	29
BERKELEY, GEORGE (b. 1684, d. 1753).	
On the Prospect of Planting Arts and Learning in America	723
BERNARD DE MORLAIX, MONK OF CLUNY.	
The Celestial Country	604
BISHOP, SAMUEL (b. 1731, d. 1795).	
To Mary	10
BLACKSTONE, SIR WILLIAM (b. 1723, d. 1780).	
The Lawyer's Farewell to his Muse	738
BLAKE, WILLIAM (b. 1757, d. 1827).	
Introduction to "Songs of Innocence"	68
On Another's Sorrow	589
The Little Black Boy	37
The Tiger	494
BLAMIRE, SUSANNA (b. 1747, d. 1794).	
The Nabob	93
The Siller Croun	147
"What ails this heart o' mine?"	199
BLANCHARD, LAMAN (b. 1803, d. 1865).	
The Mother's Hope	52
BOGART, ELIZABETH.	
He Came too Late	102
BOKER, GEORGE HENRY (b. 1824).	
Dirge for a Soldier	279
BONAR, HORATIUS (b. 1808, d. 1869).	
A Little While	595
The Inner Calm	565
BOOTH, BARTON (b. 1681, d. 1733).	
"Sweet are the charms"	154
BOTTA, ANNE C. LYNCH (b. about 1820).	
Thoughts in a Library	738
BOURDILLON, FRANCIS W. (b. 1852).	
Light	180
BOWLES, WILLIAM LISLE (b. 1762, d. 1850).	
Influence of Time on Grief	686
On the Funeral of Charles I	312
Sonnet on a Distant View of England	356
The Rhine	518
BOWRING, SIR JOHN (b. 1792, d. 1872).	
God is Love	544
"Watchman, tell us of the night"	523
BRADY, NICHOLAS (b. 1659, d. 1726).	
Psalm C	545
BRAINARD, JOHN GARDNER CALKINS (b. 1796, d. 1828).	
Epithalamium	220
Niagara	520
BRENAN, JOSEPH (b. 1829, d. 1857).	
The Exile to his Wife	11
BRETON, NICHOLAS (b. 1555, d. 1624).	
A Pastoral	182
Phillida and Corydon	145
The Priest	552
BROOKS, MARIA (b. 1795, d. 1845).	
Song—"Day in melting purple dying"	170
BROWN, WILLIAM GOLDSMITH.	
A Hundred Years to Come	675
BROWNE, FRANCES (b. 1816, d. 1864).	
Is it Come?	748
"Oh, the pleasant days of old!"	747
BROWNE, SIR THOMAS (b. 1605, d. 1682).	
Evening Hymn	556
BROWNE, WILLIAM (b. 1590, d. 1645).	
"Shall I tell you whom I love?"	123
The Welcome	125
BROWNELL, HENRY HOWARD (b. 1820, d. 1872).	
The Lawyer's Invocation to Spring	951
BROWNING, ELIZABETH BARRETT (b. 1809, d. 1861).	
A Child's Thought of God	44
A Court Lady	361
A Forced Recruit at Solferino	364
A Musical Instrument	723
Cowper's Grave	246
Lady Geraldine's Courtship	104
Mother and Poet	26
Romance of the Swan's Nest	47
Sonnets from the Portuguese—	
"First time he kissed me, he but only kiss'd"	135
"How do I love thee? let me count the ways"	135
"If I leave all for thee, wilt thou exchange"	135
"If thou must love me, let it be for naught"	134
"I never gave a lock of hair away"	134
"My letters! all dead paper,... mute and white"	135
"Say over again, and yet once over again"	134
The Child and the Watcher	33
The Cry of the Children	63
The Lady's Yes	138
The Sleep	622
BROWNING, ROBERT (b. 1812).	
Evelyn Hope	196

INDEX OF AUTHORS.

	Page
Hervé Riel	319
How they Brought the Good News	372
In a Year	211
Incident of the French Camp	341
Marching Along	310
The Lost Leader	263
The Pied Piper of Hamelin	851

BRYANT, WILLIAM CULLEN (b. 1794, d. 1878).

O Fairest of the Rural Maids	779
Song of Marion's Men	331
Thanatopsis	624
The Battle-Field	676
The Crowded Street	647
The Death of the Flowers	456
The Evening Wind	442
The Hunter of the Prairies	494
The Living Lost	682
The Past	91
To a Water-Fowl	471
To the Fringed Gentian	455

BRYDGES, SIR SAMUEL EGERTON (b. 1762, d. 1837).

Sonnet—Echo and Silence	502

BUCHANAN, ROBERT (b. 1841).

Hermione	7
Langley Lane	203
Tom Dunstan	702

BURNS, ROBERT (b. 1759, d. 1796).

Address to the Toothache	953
A Man's a Man for a' That	704
A Red, Red Rose	157
Auld Lang Syne	81
Bannockburn	295
Bonnie Lesley	145
Duncan Gray	144
Elegy on Captain Matthew Henderson	247
Farewell to Nancy	154
"Flow gently, sweet Afton"	515
Highland Mary	120
Jean—"Of a' the airts the wind can blaw"	126
Jessy—"Here's a health to ane I lo'e dear"	166
John Anderson, my Jo	8
Mary Morison	147
"My heart's in the Highlands"	358
Tam O'Shanter	873
The Banks o' Doon	170
The Cotter's Saturday Night	3
The Winsome Wee Thing	9
To a Mountain Daisy	454
To a Mouse	483
To Mary in Heaven	137

BUTLER, WILLIAM ALLEN (b. 1825).

Nothing to Wear	708

BYRD, WILLIAM (b. about 1540, d. 1623).

"My minde to me a kingdom is"	737

BYROM, JOHN (b. 1691, d. 1763).

A Pastoral	173
Careless Content	660
Christmas Carol	531
Jacobite Toast	310

BYRON, GEORGE GORDON NOEL BYRON LORD (b. 1788, d. 1824).

A Very Mournful Ballad	295
Destruction of Sennacherib	283
Fare thee Well	15
Girl of Cadiz	146
Maid of Athens	145
"Oh, snatched away in beauty's bloom"	743
On this Day I Complete my Thirty-sixth Year	88
Prisoner of Chillon	398
"She walks in beauty"	741
Song of the Greek Poet	360
Stanzas—"And thou art dead, as young and fair"	742
Stanzas—"Oh talk not to me of a name great in story"	157
Stanzas for Music	157
The Dream	790
"There's not a joy the world can give"	656
"When coldness wraps this suffering clay"	625
"When we two parted"	86

CAMPBELL, THOMAS (b. 1777, d. 1844).

Adelgitha	145
Battle of the Baltic	341
Hallowed Ground	633
Hohenlinden	340
Lochiel's Warning	323
Lord Ullin's Daughter	381
Men of England	356
O'Connor's Child	395
The Exile of Erin	359
The Last Man	643
The Soldier's Dream	83
To the Evening Star	447
To the Rainbow	444
"Ye mariners of England"	356

CANNING, GEORGE (b. 1770, d. 1827).

Epitaph on the Tombstone Erected over the Marquis of Anglesea's Leg	948
Song by Rogero, in "The Rovers"	935
The Friend of Humanity and the Knife-Grinder	935

CAREW, THOMAS (b. 1589, d. 1639).

"Ask me no more where Jove bestows"	192
Disdain Returned	180
The Airs of Spring	431

CAREY, HENRY (b. about 1663, d. 1743).

God Save the King	355
Sally in our Alley	120
The Maiden's Choice	210

CARY, ALICE (b. 1820, d. 1879).

Her Last Verses	629

CARY, PHŒBE (b. 1824, d. 1871).

Nearer Home	587

CENNICK, JOHN (b. 1717, d. 1755).

"Children of the heavenly King"	574

CHALKHILL, JOHN (b. 1600, d. 1679).

Praise of a Country Man's Life	496
The Angler	468

CHATTERTON, THOMAS (b. 1752, d. 1770).

Minstrel's Song in Aella	147
Resignation	565

CHAUCER, GEOFFREY (b. about 1340, d. 1400).

Good Counseil	688

CIBBER, COLLEY (b. 1671, d. 1757).

The Blind Boy	67

INDEX OF AUTHORS.

CLARE, JOHN (b. 1793, d. 1864).
His Last Verses.. 618
July.. 432
Sonnet—To the Glowworm.............................. 483
The Laborer... 702
The Thrush's Nest.. 476

CLELAND, WILLIAM (b. about 1661, d. 1689).
Hallo, my Fancy... 884

CLEPHANE, ELIZABETH C.
The Ninety and Nine...................................... 581

CLOUGH, ARTHUR HUGH (b. 1819, d. 1861).
Qua Cursum Ventus.. 744
The Stream of Life... 614
Where Lies the Land..................................... 466

COFFIN, ROBERT BARRY (b. 1826).
Ships at Sea.. 789

COLERIDGE, HARTLEY (b. 1796, d. 1849).
Address to Certain Gold-fishes...................... 469
Night.. 775
"She is not fair to outward view"................. 172
Song—"'Tis sweet to hear the merry lark"..... 472

COLERIDGE, SAMUEL TAYLOR (b. 1772, d. 1834).
Christabel.. 841
Cologne... 928
Epigram... 959
Fancy in Nubibus.. 446
France, an Ode... 333
Genevieve.. 155
Hymn before Sunrise in the Vale of Chamouni... 518
Kubla Khan... 848
Love.. 100
Rime of the Ancient Mariner........................ 855
The Devil's Thoughts..................................... 917
The Good, Great Man.................................. 662
The Knight's Tomb.. 626
Youth and Age.. 94

COLLINS, JOHN (18th century).
"In the downhill of life"............................... 674

COLLINS, WILLIAM (b. 1721, d. 1759).
Dirge in Cymbeline....................................... 637
Ode—"How sleep the brave"........................ 363
Ode on the Death of Thomson.................... 244
Ode to Evening.. 440
Ode to Fear.. 776
The Passions.. 730

COLMAN, GEORGE, THE YOUNGER (b. 1762, d. 1836).
Sir Marmaduke... 784

CONSTABLE, HENRY (b. about 1560, d. 1612).
Sonnet—"To live in hell, and heaven to behold".. 212

COOK, ELIZA (b. 1817).
The Old Arm-Chair.. 73

COOKE, PHILIP PENDLETON (b. 1816, d. 1850).
Florence Vane... 171

COOKE, ROSE TERRY (b. 1827).
Rêve du Midi.. 433

CORBET, RICHARD (b. 1582, d. 1635).
Farewell to the Fairies.................................. 833
To Vincent Corbet, my Son........................... 233

COTTON, CHARLES (b. 1630, d. 1687).
Invitation to Izaak Walton............................. 467
The Retirement... 495

COTTON, NATHANIEL (b. 1721, d. 1788).
The Fireside.. 2

COWLEY, ABRAHAM (b. 1618, d. 1667).
A Supplication.. 121
Drinking.. 446
Epitaph upon a Living Author...................... 226
Of Myself.. 233

COWPER, WILLIAM (b. 1731, d. 1800).
Diverting History of John Gilpin.................. 929
Joy and Peace in Believing........................... 573
Light Shining out of Darkness..................... 543
"Lovest thou Me?"... 541
On the Receipt of my Mother's Picture...... 15
Retirement.. 582
To Mary.. 245
To Mrs. Unwin... 245
Verses supposed to be Written by Alexander Selkirk... 679
Walking with God.. 564

COXE, ARTHUR CLEVELAND (b. 1818).
Christmas Carol... 530
The Chimes of England................................ 503
The Heart's Song... 575

CRAIK, DINAH MARIA MULOCK (b. 1826).
A Lancashire Doxology................................. 583
Christmas Carol... 533
Now and Afterwards...................................... 620
Philip, my King.. 30
Too Late... 17

CRANCH, CHRISTOPHER PEARSE (b. 1813).
Stanzas—"Thought is deeper than all speech". 782

CRASHAW, RICHARD (b. about 1613, d. 1650).
Epitaph upon a Husband and Wife............. 635
On a Prayer-Book.. 586
Paraphrase of Psalm XXIII........................... 562
Song—"To thy lover".................................... 126
Wishes for the Supposed Mistress.............. 121

CRAWFORD, JULIA.
We Parted in Silence.................................... 85

CROLY, GEORGE (b. 1780, d. 1860).
Cupid carrying Provisions............................. 156
Pericles and Aspasia..................................... 289

CUNNINGHAM, ALLAN (b. 1784, d. 1842).
"A wet sheet and a flowing sea"................. 695
"Gane were but the winter cauld".............. 638
It's Hame and it's Hame............................... 357
Poet's Bridal-Day Song.................................. 18
She's gane to Dwall in Heaven.................... 218
The Sun rises Bright in France................... 358
"Thou hast sworn by thy God, my Jeanie".... 157

DANA, MARY S. B.
Passing Under the Rod................................. 589

DANA, RICHARD HENRY (b. 1787, d. 1879).
The Little Beach-Bird................................... 471

DANIEL, SAMUEL (b. 1562, d. 1619).
"Love is a sickness"..................................... 98
Sonnet—Sleep.. 776
To the Lady Margaret.................................. 230

DARLEY, GEORGE (b. 1785, d. 1849).
Gambols of Children..................................... 53
Song of the Summer Winds......................... 433
The Call.. 178

INDEX OF AUTHORS.

DARWIN, ERASMUS (b. 1731, d. 1802).
   Song to May.. 431
DAVENANT, SIR WILLIAM (b. 1605, d. 1668).
   Song—"The lark now leaves his watery nest" 472
DAVIS, FRANCIS.
   The Fisherman's Song...................................... 696
DAVIS, THOMAS OSBORNE (b. 1814, d. 1845).
   Fontenoy... 321
   The Welcome... 158
DAVY, SIR HUMPHRY (b. 1778, d. 1829).
   The Tempest.. 462
DE CELANO, THOMAS (d. 1253).
   Dies Iræ.. 609
DEKKER, THOMAS (b. about 1570, d. about 1641).
   A Lullaby.. 32
   Sweet Content... 660
DE VERE, AUBREY THOMAS (b. 1814).
   Sonnet—"Sad is our youth"............................ 614
DIBDIN, CHARLES (b. 1745, d. 1814).
   Nongtongpaw.. 948
   Poor Jack.. 698
   The High-Mettled Racer.................................. 488
   Tom Bowling... 639
DICKENS, CHARLES (b. 1812, d. 1870).
   The Ivy Green.. 456
DICKINSON, CHARLES M.
   The Children... 62
DIMOND, WILLIAM (b. 1800, d. 1837).
   The Mariner's Dream...................................... 696
DIX, JOHN ADAMS (b. 1798, d. 1879).
   Translation of Dies Iræ................................... 611
DOANE, GEORGE WASHINGTON (b. 1799, d. 1859).
   Evening Contemplation.................................. 552
DOBELL, SYDNEY (b. 1824, d. 1874).
   How's my Boy?... 67
   Tommy's Dead.. 620
DOBSON, AUSTIN (b. 1840).
   A Virtuoso.. 958
   To Q. H. F... 921
DODDRIDGE, PHILIP (b. 1702, d. 1751).
   Dum Vivimus, Vivamus................................. 574
   For New Year's Day....................................... 559
   "Hark! the glad sound".................................. 533
   "O God of Bethel, by whose hand".................. 587
   "Ye golden lamps of heaven, farewell"............ 588
DOMETT, ALFRED (b. 1811).
   A Christmas Hymn... 529
DONNE, JOHN (b. 1573, d. 1631).
   God.. 565
DORR, JULIA CAROLINE (b. 1825).
   Twenty-One.. 682
DOTEN, ELIZABETH (b. about 1829).
   Song of the North.. 421
DOWLING, BARTHOLOMEW.
   Battle of Fontenoy.. 322
   Indian Revelry... 787
DOWNING, MARY (b. 1830).
   Grave of Macaura.. 221

DRAKE, JOSEPH RODMAN (b. 1795, d. 1820).
   Culprit Fay... 810
   The American Flag.. 353
DRAYTON, MICHAEL (b. 1563, d. 1631).
   Ballad of Agincourt....................................... 298
   Sonnet—"Since there's no help, come, let us kiss and part"... 170
DRUMMOND, WILLIAM (b. 1585, d. 1649).
   Beauty Fades.. 741
   Praise of a Solitary Life................................. 658
   Sonnet — "A good that never satisfies the mind"... 656
   To a Nightingale... 477
   To his Lute... 734
   To Spring... 425
   To the Nightingale... 478
DRYDEN, JOHN (b. 1631, d. 1700).
   "Ah! how sweet it is to love"............................ 97
   Alexander's Feast.. 724
   Jealousy the Tyrant of the Mind..................... 213
   Lines Written under the Picture of John Milton.. 240
   Song for St. Cecilia's Day............................... 726
   Veni Creator... 543
DUFFERIN, HELEN SELINA SHERIDAN, LADY (b. 1807, d. 1867).
   Lament of the Irish Emigrant.......................... 86
DWIGHT, TIMOTHY (b. 1752, d. 1817).
   "I love Thy kingdom, Lord"............................ 574
DYER, JOHN (b. 1700, d. 1758).
   Grongar Hill... 506
EASTMAN, CHARLES GAMAGE (b. 1816, d. 1861).
   A Picture.. 6
   Dirge... 638
ELLIOT, SIR GILBERT (b. 1722, d. 1777).
   Amynta... 200
ELLIOT, JANE (b. 1727, d. 1805).
   The Flowers of the Forest.............................. 306
ELLIOTT, CHARLOTTE (b. 1789, d. 1871).
   "Just as I am".. 568
   "O Thou, the contrite sinner's friend"............ 539
   Thy Will be Done.. 566
EMERSON, RALPH WALDO (b. 1803, d. 1882).
   Each and All... 707
   Good-Bye.. 657
   The Humble-Bee... 482
   The Problem.. 663
   The Rhodora.. 455
   To Eva... 217
   Two Rivers... 764
EWEN, JOHN (b. 1741, d. 1821).
   The Boatie Rows... 701
EYTINGE, MARGARET.
   Baby Louise... 29
FABER, FREDERICK WILLIAM (b. 1815, d. 1863).
   Evening Hymn.. 556
   Paradise.. 601
   The Pilgrims of the Night............................... 600
   The Right must Win...................................... 572
   The Will of God.. 566
FENNER, CORNELIUS GEORGE (b. 1822, d. 1847).
   Gulf-Weed... 463

INDEX OF AUTHORS.

	Page
FERGUSON, SIR SAMUEL (b. 1810).	
The Forging of the Anchor	693
FIELDS, JAMES TICKNOR (b. 1817, d. 1881).	
Ballad of the Tempest	38
The Nantucket Skipper	927
FINLEY, JOHN (b. 1797, d. 1866).	
Bachelor's Hall	960
FLETCHER, GILES (b. about 1582, d. unknown).	
Panglory's Wooing Song	98
FLETCHER, JOHN (b. 1576, d. 1625).	
Melancholia	656
Weep no More	786
FLETCHER, PHINEAS (b. about 1584, d. about 1650).	
Hymn	544
FLOWERDEW, ANNE.	
"Fountain of mercy! God of love!"	563
FORD, JOHN (b. 1586, d. 1639).	
Love and Death	203
FOSTER, STEPHEN COLLINS (b. 1826, d. 1864).	
Old Folks at Home	18
GALL, RICHARD (b. 1766, d. 1801).	
My only Jo and Dearie, O	202
GAY, JOHN (b. 1688, d. 1732).	
Sweet William's Farewell to Black-Eyed Susan	119
"'Twas when the seas were roaring"	125
GIBBONS, THOMAS (b. 1720, d. 1785).	
Thy Goodness, Lord, our Souls Confess	562
GILBERT, WILLIAM SCHWENCK (b. 1836).	
Captain Reece	954
Etiquette	925
The Bumboat Woman's Story	894
Yarn of the Nancy Bell	910
GILFILLAN, ROBERT (b. 1798, d. 1850).	
The Exile's Song	362
GILMAN, CAROLINE (b. 1794).	
The Household Woman	24
GLEN, WILLIAM (b. 1789, d. 1826).	
"Wae's me for Prince Charlie"	326
GOLDSMITH, OLIVER (b. 1728, d. 1774).	
Elegy on that Glory of her Sex, Mrs. Mary Blaize	912
Elegy on the Death of a Mad Dog	928
Stanzas—"When lovely woman stoops to folly"	687
The Deserted Village	756
The Hermit	159
The Traveller	767
"The wretch condemned with life to part"	785
GRAHAM, JAMES, MARQUIS OF MONTROSE (b. 1612, d. 1650).	
"My dear and only love"	193
GRAHAM, ROBERT, OF GARTMORE (b. 1750, d. 1797).	
"Tell me how to woo thee"	161
GRANT, ANNE (b. 1755, d. 1838).	
On a Sprig of Heath	447
GRANT, SIR ROBERT (b. 1785, d. 1838).	
Litany	539
"When gathering clouds around I view"	569

	Page
GRAY, THOMAS (b. 1716, d. 1771).	
Elegy Written in a Country Churchyard	630
Hymn—To Adversity	777
Ode—On the Spring	427
On a Distant Prospect of Eton College	504
The Bard	293
The Progress of Poesy	728
GREENE, ALBERT G. (b. 1802, d. 1868).	
Old Grimes	912
The Baron's Last Banquet	621
GREENE, ROBERT (b. about 1560, d. 1592).	
Sonnet—Content	660
The Shepherd's Wife's Song	142
GRINFIELD, THOMAS (b. 1788).	
How Kindly Hast Thou Led Me!	570
GURNEY, ARCHER THOMPSON (b. 1820).	
Come, ye Lofty	530
HABINGTON, WILLIAM (b. 1605, d. 1645).	
Castara	179
Night	775
HALLECK, FITZ-GREENE (b. 1790, d. 1867).	
Alnwick Castle	513
Burns	249
Marco Bozzaris	347
On the Death of Joseph Rodman Drake	253
HALPINE, CHARLES G. (b. 1829, d. 1868).	
The Trooper to his Mare	493
HAMILTON, ELIZABETH (b. 1758, d. 1816).	
My Ain Fireside	1
HAMILTON, WILLIAM (OF BANGOUR), (b. 1704, d. 1754).	
The Braes of Yarrow	382
HARRINGTON, JOHN (b. 1534, d. 1582).	
Lines on Isabella Markham	124
HARTE, FRANCIS BRET (b. 1839).	
Dickens in Camp	282
Fate	785
Her Letter	207
Plain Language from Truthful James	933
The Dead Politician	704
The Society upon the Stanislow	944
HASTINGS, THOMAS (b. 1784, d. 1872).	
In Sorrow	543
HAWEIS, THOMAS (b. 1732, d. 1820).	
"O Thou from whom all goodness flows"	584
HAYNE, PAUL HAMILTON (b. 1831).	
By the Autumn Sea	466
Pre-Existence	783
HEBER, REGINALD (b. 1783, d. 1826).	
Early Piety	575
Epiphany	534
Lines Written to his Wife	9
Missionary Hymn	580
Stanzas on the Death of a Friend	594
The Holy Trinity	546
HEMANS, FELICIA DOROTHEA BROWNE (b. 1794, d. 1835).	
Casabianca	345
The Better Land	598
The Graves of a Household	28
The Homes of England	1
The Hour of Death	630
The Hour of Prayer	564

	Page
The Landing of the Pilgrim Fathers	308
The Treasures of the Deep	463

HERBERT, GEORGE (b. 1593, d. 1633).
- Complaining ... 585
- Life ... 756
- Sunday ... 560
- The Elixir ... 544
- The Flower ... 579
- The Pulley ... 662
- Virtue ... 662

HERRICK, ROBERT (b. 1591, d. 1674).
- A Thanksgiving to God for His House ... 559
- Cherry Ripe ... 214
- Corinna's going a-Maying ... 428
- Delight in Disorder ... 740
- The Captive Bee ... 209
- The Hag ... 875
- The Night Piece ... 127
- The Primrose ... 214
- To Blossoms ... 457
- To Daffodils ... 453
- To Dianeme ... 210
- To Keep a True Lent ... 587
- To Primroses filled with Morning Dew ... 452
- To Virgins, to make much of Time ... 123

HEYWOOD, THOMAS (d. about 1640).
- Good-Morrow Song ... 215
- Go, Pretty Birds ... 162

HINDS, SAMUEL (b. 1793, d. 1872).
- "Lord, shall Thy children come to Thee" ... 582
- The Sleeping Babe ... 45

HOBART, MRS. CHARLES.
- The Changed Cross ... 590

HOFFMAN, CHARLES FENNO (b. 1806).
- Monterey ... 348

HOGG, JAMES (b. 1770, d. 1835).
- Abbot M'Kinnon ... 878
- Bonnie Prince Charlie ... 326
- Charlie is my Darling ... 325
- "I hae naebody now" ... 83
- Kilmeny ... 833
- The Skylark ... 473
- When Maggie gangs away ... 161
- When the Kye comes Hame ... 167

HOLCROFT, THOMAS (b. 1744, d. 1809).
- Gaffer Gray ... 715

HOLLAND, JOSIAH GILBERT (b. 1819, d. 1881).
- The Heart of the War ... 365

HOLMES, OLIVER WENDELL (b. 1809).
- On Lending a Punch-Bowl ... 90
- The Boys ... 80
- The Chambered Nautilus ... 470
- The Deacon's Masterpiece ... 932
- The Last Leaf ... 755
- The Old Man Dreams ... 899
- The Ploughman ... 692
- The Voiceless ... 626

HOOD, THOMAS (b. 1798, d. 1845).
- Art of Book-Keeping ... 951
- Dream of Eugene Aram ... 375
- Epicurean Reminiscences of a Sentimentalist. 952
- Fair Ines ... 102
- Faithless Nelly Gray ... 896
- Faithless Sally Brown ... 897

	Page
"I remember, I remember"	73
Nocturnal Sketch	959
Ode to my Little Son	903
Ruth	144
Serenade	903
Stanzas—"Farewell, life"	637
The Bachelor's Dream	902
The Bridge of Sighs	719
The Death-bed	625
The Haunted House	866
The Lady's Dream	714
The Lost Heir	904
The Song of the Shirt	716
To a Child Embracing his Mother	35

HOW, WILLIAM WALSHAM (b. 1823).
- Behold, I Stand at the Door and Knock ... 550

HOWARD, HENRY, EARL OF SURREY (b. 1518, d. 1547).
- Description of Spring ... 425
- Means to attain Happy Life ... 616
- No Age content with his Own Estate ... 657
- Praise of his Love ... 154
- Prisoned in Windsor, he Recounteth his Pleasure there Passed ... 222

HOWE, JULIA WARD (b. 1819).
- Battle Hymn of the Republic ... 354

HOWELL, ELIZABETH LLOYD.
- Milton's Prayer of Patience ... 235

HOWITT, MARY (b. 1804).
- The Fairies of the Caldon Low ... 809
- The Use of Flowers ... 455

HUNT, JAMES HENRY LEIGH (b. 1784, d. 1859).
- Abou Ben Adhem ... 664
- An Angel in the House ... 743
- Chorus of the Flowers ... 449
- Cupid Swallowed ... 103
- Jenny Kissed me ... 186
- Song of the Fairies ... 794
- The Glove and the Lions ... 411
- The Nun ... 171
- To the Grasshopper and Cricket ... 482
- To T. L. H., Six Years Old, during a Sickness.. 36

HUNTER, ANNE HOME (b. 1742, d. 1821).
- The Lot of Thousands ... 685

INGELOW, JEAN (b. 1830).
- Song of Margaret ... 195
- Songs of Seven ... 19
- The High Tide on the Coast of Lincolnshire ... 415

IRONS, WILLIAM JOSIAH (b. 1812).
- Translation of Dies Iræ ... 610

JACKSON, HELEN HUNT, b. (1830).
- Coronation ... 702

JOHNSON, SAMUEL (b. 1709, d. 1784).
- On the Death of Dr. Levett ... 245
- The Vanity of Human Wishes ... 649

JONES, SIR WILLIAM (b. 1746, d. 1794).
- Ode—In Imitation of Alcæus ... 363
- The Babe (translation) ... 50

JONSON, BEN (b. 1574, d. 1637).
- Epigram on Sir Francis Drake ... 225
- Epitaph on Elizabeth L. H ... 233
- Epitaph on Salathiel Pavy ... 232
- Epitaph on the Countess of Pembroke ... 233

INDEX OF AUTHORS.

	PAGE
Lines on the Portrait of Shakespeare	230
Ode—To Himself	225
On Lucy, Countess of Bedford	233
Song—"Follow a shadow, it still flies you"	124
Song—"Still to be neat"	740
The Triumph of Charis	160
To Celia	195
To Cynthia	446
To the Memory of my Beloved Master, William Shakespeare	228

KEATS, JOHN (b. 1795, d. 1821).
Eve of St. Agnes	127
Fairy Song	793
Fancy	500
La Belle Dame sans Merci	865
Lines on the Mermaid Tavern	504
Ode—"Bards of passion and of mirth"	740
Ode on a Grecian Urn	746
Ode to a Nightingale	478
On First Looking into Chapman's Homer	739
On the Grasshopper and Cricket	482
To Autumn	435
"To one who has been long in city pent"	499

KEBLE, JOHN (b. 1792, d. 1866).
Evening Hymn	555
Flowers	448
Morning Hymn	553

KELLY, THOMAS (b. 1769, d. 1855).
"We sing the praise of Him who died"	535

KEMBLE, FRANCES ANNE (b. 1809).
Absence	101
Faith	679

KEN, THOMAS (b. 1637, d. 1711).
Evening Hymn	555
Midnight Hymn	557
Morning Hymn	553

KEY, FRANCIS SCOTT (b. 1779, d. 1843).
Hymn—"Lord, with glowing heart I'd praise Thee"	548
Life	577
The Star-Spangled Banner	353

KING, HENRY (b. 1591, d. 1669).
Sic Vita	688

KINGSLEY, CHARLES (b. 1819, d. 1875).
A Farewell	72
Dolcino to Margaret	780
Song of the River	461
The Last Buccaneer	419
The Sands o' Dee	417
The Three Fishers	699

KNOWLES, HERBERT (b. 1798, d. 1817).
Lines written in Richmond Churchyard, Yorkshire	633

KNOX, ISA CRAIG (b. 1831).
Ode on the Centenary of Burns	250

KNOX, WILLIAM (b. 1789, d. 1825).
"Oh why should the spirit of mortal be proud?"	627

LAIDLAW, WILLIAM (b. 1780, d. 1845).
Lucy's Flittin'	202

LAMB, CHARLES (b. 1775, d. 1834).
Farewell to Tobacco	919
Hester	741
The Old Familiar Faces	77

LANDOR, WALTER SAVAGE (b. 1775, d. 1864).
Children	36
Sixteen	214
Ternissa	196
The Maid's Lament	141
The One Gray Hair	751
To Ianthe	213
To the Sister of Elia	273

LAPRAIK, JOHN (b. 1717, d. 1807).
Matrimonial Happiness	7

LARCOM, LUCY (b. 1826).
Hannah Binding Shoes	698

LEIGH, HENRY S.
The Twins	906

L'ESTRANGE, SIR ROGER (b. 1616, d. 1704).
Loyalty Confined	241

LEWIS, MATTHEW GREGORY (b. 1775, d. 1818).
Alonzo the Brave and the Fair Imogine	871

LEYDEN, JOHN (b. 1775, d. 1811).
Ode to an Indian Gold Coin	87
The Sabbath Morning	439
To the Evening Star	447

LIPPINCOTT, SARA JANE ("GRACE GREENWOOD"), (b. 1823).
The Horseback Ride	489

LOCKER, FREDERICK (b. 1821).
Old Letters	88
Unfortunate Miss Bailey	954

LOCKHART, JOHN GIBSON (b. 1794, d. 1854).
Napoleon	268
The Bridal of Andalla (*Translation*)	209
The Broadswords of Scotland	357
The Bull-Fight of Gazul (*Translation*)	408
The Lamentation for Celin (*Translation*)	373
The Lamentation of Don Roderick (*Translation*)	290
The Lord of Butrago (*Translation*)	296
The Vengeance of Mudara (*Translation*)	292
Zara's Ear-rings (*Translation*)	183

LODGE, THOMAS (b. about 1556, d. 1625).
Rosader's Sonetto	156
Rosalind's Madrigal	98
Rosaline	123

LOGAN, JOHN (b. 1748, d. 1788).
Heavenly Wisdom	575
"O God of Bethel, by whose hand"	587
The Braes of Yarrow	384
To the Cuckoo	481

LONGFELLOW, HENRY WADSWORTH (b. 1807, d. 1882).
Excelsior	785
Flowers	448
Footsteps of Angels	773
Maidenhood	66
Old St. David's at Radnor	522
Paul Revere's Ride	329
Psalm of Life	615
Resignation	646
The Arsenal at Springfield	521
The Children's Hour	45
The Day is Done	774
The Ladder of St. Augustine	679

	PAGE
The Old Clock on the Stairs	76
The Rainy Day	775
The Skeleton in Armor	864
The Village Blacksmith	693

LOVELACE, RICHARD (b. 1618, d. 1658).
To Althea, from Prison	124
To Lucasta, on going beyond the Seas	125
To Lucasta, on going to the Wars	124

LOVER, SAMUEL (b. 1797, d. 1868).
Rory O'More	165
The Angels' Whisper	33
The Birth of St. Patrick	943
The Low-Backed Car	165

LOWELL, MARIA WHITE (b. 1821, d. 1853).
The Alpine Sheep	638
The Morning Glory	49

LOWELL, JAMES RUSSELL (b. 1819).
Auf Wiedersehen	217
My Love	208
The Courtin'	891
The First Snowfall	437
The Heritage	705
The Present Crisis	343
What Mr. Robinson Thinks	922
Without and Within	707

LYLY, JOHN (b. 1553, d. about 1600).
Cupid and Campaspe	99
Song of the Fairies	793
The Songs of Birds	480

LYTE, HENRY FRANCIS (b. 1793, d. 1847).
Abide with Me	557
"Jesus, I my cross have taken"	539
"Long did I toil"	569
Psalm LXXXIV	600

LYTLE, WILLIAM HAINES (b. 1826, d. 1863).
Antony and Cleopatra	290

LYTTON, EDWARD GEORGE EARLE BULWER (LORD LYTTON), (b. 1805, d. 1873).
"When stars are in the quiet skies"	218

LYTTON, EDWARD ROBERT BULWER (LORD LYTTON), ("OWEN MEREDITH"), (b. 1831).
Aux Italiens	180
The Chess-Board	85
The Portrait	199

MACAULAY, THOMAS BABINGTON (b. 1800, d. 1859).
Horatius	283
Ivry	307
Lines Written on the Night of the 30th of July, 1847	273
Naseby	311

MACDONALD, GEORGE (b. 1824).
"Where did you come from?"	31

MACE, FRANCES LAUGHTON (b. 1836).
Only Waiting	639

MACKAY, CHARLES (b. 1814).
Differences	705
"I lay in sorrow, deep distressed"	687
I Love my Love	146
The Child and the Mourners	55
The Good Time Coming	750
The Sailor's Wife	25

C

	PAGE

MACLEAN, LÆTITIA ELIZABETH LANDON ("L. E. L."), (b. 1802, d. 1838).
Crescentius	292
The Awakening of Endymion	172

MACNEILL, HECTOR (b. 1746, d. 1818).
Mary of Castle Cary	164

MAGINN, WILLIAM (b. 1793, d. 1842).
The Irishman	896

MAHONY, FRANCIS ("FATHER PROUT"), (b. about 1805, d. 1866).
Malbrouck (Translation)	948
The Bells of Shandon	516

MALLET, DAVID (b. 1700, d. 1765).
William and Margaret	175

MANT, RICHARD (b. 1776, d. 1848).
"There is a dwelling-place above"	599

MARLOWE, CHRISTOPHER (b. 1564, d. 1593).
The Milkmaid's Song	140

MARVELL, ANDREW (b. 1620, d. 1678).
An Horatian Ode	238
The Emigrants in the Bermudas	549
The Nymph Complaining for the Death of her Fawn	501
The Picture of T. C. in a Prospect of Flowers	240
Thoughts in a Garden	497

MAYNE, JOHN (b. 1761, d. 1836).
Helen of Kirkconnell	403

McCARTHY, DENIS FLORENCE (b. 1817, d. 1882).
Summer Longings	429

McMASTER, GUY HUMPHREY (b. 1829).
Carmen Bellicosum	331

MENTEATH, MRS. A. STUART.
James Melville's Child	43

MEREDITH, GEORGE (b. 1828).
Love in the Valley	142

MERRICK, JAMES (b. 1720, d. 1769).
The Chameleon	686

MESSINGER, ROBERT HINCKLEY (b. 1811, d. 1874).
Give me the Old	749

MICKLE WILLIAM JULIUS (b. 1734, d. 1788).
Cumnor Hall	379

MILLER, WILLIAM (b. 1810, d. 1872).
The Wonderfu' Wean	42
Willie Winkie	41

MILLIKEN, RICHARD ALFRED (b. 1757, d. 1815).
The Groves of Blarney	516

MILMAN, HENRY HART (b. 1791, d. 1868).
"Bound upon th' accursèd tree"	535
Bridal Song	220
Burial Hymn	595
Christ Crucified	534
"When our heads are bowed with woe"	582

MILNES, RICHARD MONCKTON (BARON HOUGHTON), (b. 1809).
The Brookside	169
The Long Ago	749
The Men of Old	747

INDEX OF AUTHORS.

MILTON, JOHN (b. 1608, d. 1674).
  Comus: A Mask 818
  Epitaph on Shakespeare 230
  Il Penseroso 735
  L'Allegro 733
  Lycidas 235
  On the Morning of Christ's Nativity 523
  Song—On May Morning 427
  Sonnet—On his being Arrived to the Age of Twenty-three 226
  Sonnet—On his Blindness 234
  Sonnet—On the Late Massacre in Piedmont 313
  Sonnet—To Cyriac Skinner 234
  Sonnet—To the Lady Margaret Ley 235
  Sonnet—To the Lord General Cromwell 234
  Sonnet—To the Nightingale 478
  Sonnet—When the Assault was Intended to the City 313

MOIR, DAVID MACBETH (b. 1798, d. 1851).
  Casa Wappy 39

MONTGOMERY, JAMES (b. 1771, d. 1854).
  "For ever with the Lord" 597
  "Friend after friend departs" 638
  Gethsemane 534
  Make Way for Liberty 297
  Night 687
  Psalm LXXII 537
  "Songs of praise the angels sang" 588
  The Common Lot 618
  The Grave 641
  The Stranger and his Friend 541
  "To Thy temple I repair" 561
  "What are these in bright array" 598
  What is Prayer? 563

MOORE, CLARA JESSUP.
  The Web of Life 617

MOORE, CLEMENT C. (b. 1779, d. 1863).
  The Night before Christmas 67

MOORE, EDWARD (b. 1712, d. 1757).
  The Happy Marriage 2

MOORE, THOMAS (b. 1779, d. 1852).
  "As by the shore at break of day" 363
  "Believe me, if all those endearing young charms" 162
  Canadian Boat-Song 735
  "Come rest in this bosom" 147
  "Farewell! but whenever you welcome the hour" 85
  Farewell to thee, Araby's Daughter 781
  "Go where glory waits thee" 95
  "Has sorrow thy young days shaded" 742
  "I knew by the smoke that so gracefully curled" 763
  "Oft in the stilly night" 77
  "Oh breathe not his name" 252
  "Oh had we some bright little isle of our own" .. 194
  "She is far from the land" 275
  "Sound the loud timbrel" 550
  Sweet Innisfallen 517
  "The harp that once through Tara's halls" 362
  The Lake of the Dismal Swamp 422
  The Meeting of the Waters 517
  The Young May Moon 162
  Those Evening Bells 764
  "Thou art, O God" 551

"'Tis the last rose of summer" 456
"To sigh, yet feel no pain" 182

MORRIS, GEORGE P. (b. 1802, d. 1864).
  "Woodman, spare that tree" 75

MOSS, THOMAS (b. 1740, d. 1808).
  The Beggar's Petition 717

MOTHERWELL, WILLIAM (b. 1797, d. 1835).
  Cavalier's Song 311
  Covenanters' Battle-Chant 310
  Jeanie Morrison 118
  "They come! the merry summer months" 430

MOULTRIE, JOHN (b. 1799, d. 1874).
  "Here's to thee, my Scottish lassie" 214
  The Three Sons 50

MUHLENBERG, WILLIAM AUGUSTUS (b. 1796, d. 1877).
  "I would not live alway" 593
  "Saviour, who Thy flock art feeding" 540
  "Shout the glad tidings" 533

NAIRNE, CAROLINA, LADY (b. 1766, d. 1845).
  The Laird o' Cockpen 892
  The Land of the Leal 636

NASH, THOMAS (b. about 1564, d. 1604).
  Spring 427

NEALE, HANNAH LLOYD.
  The Neglected Call 684

NEALE, JOHN MASON (b. 1818, d. 1866).
  "Art thou weary?" (*Translation*) 577
  The Celestial Country " 604

NEWMAN, JOHN HENRY (b. 1801).
  Lead, Kindly Light 569

NEWTON, JOHN (b. 1725, d. 1807).
  "How sweet the name of Jesus sounds" 541
  Psalm LXXXVII 598

NICOLL, ROBERT (b. 1814, d. 1837).
  "We are brethren a'" 706

NOEL, THOMAS.
  The Pauper's Drive 722

NORRIS, JOHN (b. 1657, d. 1711).
  Superstition 179

NORTON, CAROLINE ELIZABETH SARAH (b. 1808, d. 1877).
  Bingen on the Rhine 83
  Love Not 187
  The Arab's Farewell to his Horse 492
  The King of Denmark's Ride 420

O'BRIEN, FITZ-JAMES (b. 1829, d. 1862).
  Kane 276

O'KEEFE, JOHN (b. 1747, d. 1833).
  "I am a friar of orders gray" 916

OLDYS, WILLIAM (b. 1696, d. 1761).
  Song—"Busy, curious, thirsty fly" 483

OLIVERS, THOMAS (b. 1725, d. 1799).
  "Lo! He comes with clouds descending" 611
  "The God of Abraham praise" 583

OPIE, AMELIA (b. 1769, d. 1853).
  Forget me Not 94
  The Orphan Boy's Tale 46

INDEX OF AUTHORS.

OSGOOD, FRANCES SARGENT (b. 1812, d. 1850).
   Laborare est Orare... 691

OSLER, EDWARD.
   Praise... 601

PALMER, RAY (b. 1808).
   "My faith looks up to Thee"... 538

PALMER, WILLIAM PITT (b. 1805).
   The Smack in School... 923

PARKER, MARTYN.
   Ye Gentlemen of England... 701

PARNELL, THOMAS (b. 1679, d. 1717).
   Hymn to Contentment... 659
   The Hermit... 666

PARR, HARRIET T.
   "Hear my prayer, O heavenly Father"... 564

PARSONS, THOMAS WILLIAM (b. 1819).
   On a Bust of Dante... 221
   The Groomsman to the Bridesmaid... 183

PAYNE, JOHN HOWARD (b. 1792, d. 1852).
   Home, Sweet Home... 1

PEELE, GEORGE (b. about 1552, d. 1598).
   The Aged Man-at-Arms... 751

PERCIVAL, JAMES GATES (b. 1795, d. 1856).
   It is Great for our Country to Die... 365
   The Coral Grove... 464
   The Reign of May... 432
   To Seneca Lake... 521

PERCY, THOMAS (b. 1728, d. 1811).
   "O Nanny, wilt thou go with me"... 161
   The Friar of Orders Gray... 117

PERRONET, EDWARD (d. 1792).
   Coronation... 536

PERRY, NORA.
   After the Ball... 786
   The Love-Knot... 217

PHILIPS, AMBROSE (b. 1671, d. 1749).
   Fragment from Sappho... 192
   To Charlotte Pulteney... 35

PIATT, JOHN JAMES (b. 1835).
   The Morning Street... 782

PIERPONT, JOHN (b. 1785, d. 1866).
   My Child... 48
   Not on the Battle-Field... 677
   Passing Away... 628
   Warren's Address... 329

PIKE, ALBERT (b. 1809).
   Hymn to Neptune... 887

PINKNEY, EDWARD COATE (b. 1802, d. 1828).
   A Health... 178

PIOZZI, HESTER LYNCH THRALE (b. 1739, d. 1821).
   The Three Warnings... 619

POE, EDGAR ALLAN (b. 1809, d. 1849).
   Annabel Lee... 410
   The Bells... 765
   The Haunted Palace... 871
   The Raven... 849

POPE, ALEXANDER (b. 1688, d. 1744).
   Elegy to the Memory of an Unfortunate Lady. 635
   Messiah... 527
   Ode on St. Cecilia's Day... 727
   Ode on Solitude... 755
   Prologue to Mr. Addison's Tragedy of Cato.... 242
   The Dying Christian to his Soul... 596
   The Rape of the Lock... 795
   The Universal Prayer... 545

POPE, WALTER (b. about 1630, d. 1714).
   The Old Man's Wish... 754

PRAED, WINTHROP MACKWORTH (b. 1802, d. 1839).
   Charade—Camp-Bell... 264
   Quince... 911
   School and Schoolfellows... 79
   The Vicar... 913

PRENTICE, GEORGE DENISON (b. 1802, d. 1870).
   Sabbath Evening... 441
   The Closing Year... 95
   To an Absent Wife... 14

PRENTISS, ELIZABETH.
   Cradle Song (*Translation*)... 32

PRINGLE, THOMAS (b. 1789, d. 1834).
   "Afar in the desert"... 490

PRIOR, MATTHEW (b. 1664, d. 1721).
   Epitaph Extempore... 241

PROCTER, ADELAIDE ANNE (b. 1825, d. 1864).
   A Doubting Heart... 684
   A Dream... 774
   A Woman's Answer... 188
   A Woman's Question... 187
   One by One... 683
   Per Pacem ad Lucem... 537

PROCTER, BRYAN WALLER (b. 1787, d. 1874).
   Golden-tressèd Adelaide... 39
   Life... 615
   Petition to Time... 751
   The Blood Horse... 488
   The Pearl-Wearer... 700
   The Poet's Song to his Wife... 14
   The Sea... 462
   The Stormy Petrel... 470

QUARLES, FRANCIS (b. 1592, d. 1644).
   Delight in God only... 576
   Shortness of Life... 615
   Vanity of the World... 654

RALEIGH, SIR WALTER (b. 1552, d. 1618).
   A Vision upon this Conceit of the Faerie Queene... 739
   Epitaph upon Sir Philip Sidney... 227
   Lines written the Night before his Execution. 230
   The Lie... 655
   The Milkmaid's Mother's Answer... 140
   The Pilgrimage... 578
   The Silent Lover... 182

RAMSAY, ALLAN (b. 1686, d. 1758).
   "At setting day and rising morn"... 195
   Lochaber no More... 195
   The Lass of Patie's Mill... 155

RANDOLPH, THOMAS (b. 1605, d. 1634).
   To my Picture... 755

RANKIN, J. E.
   The Babie... 41

READ, THOMAS BUCHANAN (b. 1822, d. 1872).
   Drifting... 465
   Sheridan's Ride... 351
   The Closing Scene... 640
   The Stranger on the Sill... 75

	Page
ROBINSON, ROBERT (b. 1735, d. 1790).	
"Come, Thou Fount of every blessing".......	585
ROGERS, SAMUEL (b. 1763, d. 1855).	
An Italian Song....................................	498
A Wish..	6
Ginevra...	406
To the Butterfly..................................	482
ROSCOE, WILLIAM (b. 1753, d. 1831).	
Sonnet—On Parting with his Books.......	784
ROSSETTI, CHRISTINA GEORGINA (b. 1830).	
Maude Clare..	188
Peal of Bells.......................................	764
Up-Hill...	578
Weary..	591
ROSSETTI, DANTE GABRIEL (b. 1828, d. 1882).	
Sister Helen..	875
The Blessed Damozel...........................	839
The Sea Limits....................................	462
SANDS, ROBERT C. (b. 1799, d. 1832).	
Good-Night...	618
SARGENT, EPES (b. 1812, d. 1880).	
A Life on the Ocean Wave...................	695
SAXE, JOHN GODFREY (b. 1816).	
"I'm growing old"...............................	751
Reflective Retrospect...........................	79
The Briefless Barrister.........................	920
SCOTT, SIR WALTER (b. 1771, d. 1832).	
Alice Brand...	838
Allen-a-Dale..	186
Boat-Song—"Hail to the chief".............	364
Bonnets of Bonnie Dundee...................	316
Border Ballad.....................................	358
Coronach..	625
Hellvellyn...	514
Jock of Hazeldean................................	134
Lochinvar...	136
Paraphrase of Dies Iræ........................	610
Pibroch of Donuil Dhu.........................	359
"Proud Maisie is in the wood".............	890
Rebecca's Hymn.................................	550
Rosabelle..	403
Serenade..	189
"Soldier, rest".....................................	700
"The heath this night must be my bed"..	186
The Outlaw...	176
"Where shall the lover rest".................	176
SEAGRAVE, ROBERT (b. 1693, d. unknown).	
"Rise, my soul, and stretch thy wings"..	570
SEARS, EDMUND HAMILTON (b. 1810, d. 1876).	
"It came upon the midnight clear"........	532
SEDLEY, SIR CHARLES (b. 1639, d. 1701).	
"Love still hath something of the sea"...	99
To a Very Young Lady.........................	189
SEWALL, HARRIET WINSLOW (b. 1819).	
Why thus Longing..............................	766
SEWELL, GEORGE (d. 1726).	
The Dying Man in his Garden.............	637
SHAKESPEARE, WILLIAM (b. 1564, d. 1616).	
Ariel's Songs in "The Tempest"............	794
"Come unto these yellow sands."	
"Full fathom five thy father lies."	
"Where the bee sucks, there suck I."	
"Blow, blow, thou winter wind"..........	438

	Page
"Come away, come away, Death"........	197
Crabbèd Age and Youth......................	756
Dirge from "Cymbeline"......................	637
Influence of Music..............................	732
Morning...	439
"On a day—alack the day"..................	141
"Over hill, over dale"..........................	794
"Sigh no more, ladies"........................	187
Song—"Tell me where is Fancy bred"..	838
Song—"Under the greenwood tree".....	457
Sonnet—"Full many a glorious morning have I seen"...................................	439
Sonnet—"Let me not to the marriage of true minds"..	218
Sonnet—"Like as the waves make toward the pebbled shore"...................	753
Sonnet—"No longer mourn for me when I am dead"....................................	219
Sonnet—"Not marble nor the gilded monuments".......................................	752
Sonnet—"Oh, how much more doth beauty beauteous seem".....................	753
Sonnet—"Poor Soul, the centre of my sinful earth"...	753
Sonnet—"Shall I compare thee to a summer's day?"....................................	220
Sonnet—"That time of year thou may'st in me behold"...............................	219
Sonnet—"They that have power to hurt, and will do none".........................	754
Sonnet—"Tired with all these, for restful death I cry".................................	219
Sonnet—"To me, fair friend, you never can be old"...................................	752
Sonnet—"When I do count the clock that tells the time".............................	752
Sonnet—"When in disgrace with fortune and men's eyes"...........................	219
Sonnet—"When in the chronicle of wasted time".......................................	220
Sonnet—"When to the sessions of sweet silent thought".............................	753
Sweet-and-Twenty.............................	163
"When icicles hang by the wall"..........	438
Who is Sylvia?...................................	217
SHELLEY, PERCY BYSSHE (b. 1792, d. 1822).	
Adonais..	253
A Lament...	766
Arethusa...	460
Autumn, a Dirge................................	436
Lines to an Indian Air........................	103
Love's Philosophy...............................	97
"Music when soft voices die"..............	185
Ode to the West Wind........................	436
"One word is too often profaned"........	148
Song—"Rarely, rarely comest thou".....	779
Stanzas written in Dejection near Naples........	261
The Cloud..	444
The Invitation....................................	499
The Question.....................................	459
To a Skylark......................................	474
To Night..	442
To the Moon......................................	446
With a Guitar—To Jane......................	732
SHENSTONE, WILLIAM (b. 1714, d. 1763).	
Pastoral Ballad...................................	205
The Schoolmistress.............................	57

INDEX OF AUTHORS.

SHIRLEY, JAMES (b. 1596, d. 1666).
   Death's Final Conquest.................................. 623
   The Last Conqueror...................................... 623

SHIRLEY, WALTER (b. 1725, d. 1786).
   "Lord, dismiss us with Thy blessing"............. 612

SIDNEY, SIR PHILIP (b. 1554, d. 1586).
   A Ditty... 127
   Sonnet—"Because I oft in dark abstracted guise".. 781
   Sonnet—"Having this day my horse, my hand, my lance"... 192
   Sonnet—"O happy Thames, that didst my Stella bear"... 191
   Sonnet—On Sleep.. 776
   Sonnet—To the Moon...................................... 118

SIGOURNEY, LYDIA HUNTLEY (b. 1791, d. 1865).
   Indian Names... 520
   The Early Blue-Bird....................................... 475
   The Return of Napoleon from St. Helena........ 268

SKELTON, JOHN (b. about 1460, d. 1529).
   To Mistress Margaret Hussey.......................... 225

SMITH, CHARLOTTE (b. 1749, d. 1806).
   On the Departure of the Nightingale.............. 480

SMITH, HORACE (b. 1779, d. 1849).
   Address to the Mummy in Belzoni's Exhibition. 744
   Hymn to the Flowers...................................... 451
   Tale of Drury Lane... 936
   The Contrast.. 342

SMITH, JAMES (b. 1775, d. 1839).
   The Baby's Début... 940
   The Theatre.. 938

SMITH, SAMUEL FRANCIS (b. 1808).
   America... 354

SMITH, SYDNEY (b. 1771, d. 1845).
   Parody on Pope... 923
   Recipe for Salad... 959

SMOLLETT, TOBIAS GEORGE (b. 1721, d. 1771).
   Ode to Leven Water.. 515
   The Tears of Scotland 327

SOUTHEY, CAROLINE ANNE BOWLES (b. 1787, d. 1854).
   Once upon a Time... 93
   The Pauper's Death-bed.................................. 721

SOUTHEY, ROBERT (b. 1774, d. 1843).
   Battle of Blenheim.. 677
   Cataract of Lodore.. 508
   Complaints of the Poor.................................... 714
   God's Judgment on a Wicked Bishop.............. 409
   History.. 352
   Inchcape Rock... 378
   "My days among the dead are passed"........... 737
   The Holly Tree.. 458
   The March to Moscow..................................... 949
   The Old Man's Comforts.................................. 674
   Well of St. Keyne... 898

SOUTHWELL, ROBERT (b. 1560, d. 1595).
   Times go by Turns.. 778

SPENCER, PETER.
   A Thought among the Roses........................... 456

SPENCER, WILLIAM ROBERT (b. 1770, d. 1834).
   Beth-Gêlert... 392

Stanzas—"When midnight o'er the moonless skies"... 94
   To Lady Anne Hamilton.................................. 779

SPENSER, EDMUND (b. 1552, d. 1599).
   Sonnet—"Like as the culver on the barèd bough"... 190
   Sonnet—"Since I did leave the presence of my love".. 190
   Sonnet—"Sweet is the rose, but grows upon a brere"... 780
   Sonnet—"The doubt which ye misdeem, fair love, is vain".. 101

SPRAGUE, CHARLES (b. 1791, d. 1875).
   The Family Meeting....................................... 17

STARK.
   Modern Belle.. 922

STEDMAN, EDMUND CLARENCE (b. 1833).
   Cavalry Song.. 366
   Pan in Wall Street.. 886
   Toujours Amour.. 163

STERLING, JOHN (b. 1806, d. 1844).
   Louis XV... 328

STILL, JOHN (b. 1543, d. 1607).
   Jolly Good Ale and Old................................... 917

STODDARD, RICHARD HENRY (b. 1825).
   Never Again.. 764
   "The house is dark and dreary"...................... 785
   Without and Within.. 12

STODDART, THOMAS TOD (b. 1810).
   Angler's Trysting Tree.................................... 469

STORY, WILLIAM WETMORE (b. 1819).
   At Dieppe... 518
   Praxiteles and Phryne.................................... 784
   The Violet.. 453

STRODE, WILLIAM (b. 1600, d. 1644).
   Kisses... 156

SUCKLING, SIR JOHN (b. 1609, d. about 1641).
   "I prithee send me back my heart"................. 171
   "Why so pale".. 104

SWAIN, CHARLES (b. 1803, d. 1874).
   Dryburgh Abbey... 264
   Sabbath Chimes.. 561

SWIFT, JONATHAN (b. 1667, d. 1745).
   Baucis and Philemon...................................... 899

SWINBURNE, ALGERNON CHARLES (b. 1837).
   Age and Song... 741
   Chorus—"Before the beginning of years"....... 744
   Chorus—"When the hounds of spring".......... 426

SYLVESTER, JOSHUA (b. 1563, d. 1618).
   A Contented Mind.. 660
   Love's Omnipresence...................................... 99

TANNAHILL, ROBERT (b. 1774, d. 1810).
   Jessie the Flower of Dumblane....................... 163
   The Braes of Balquhither............................... 498
   "The midges dance aboon the burn".............. 440

TATE, NAHUM (b. 1652, d. 1715).
   Christmas 529

TATE (NAHUM) and BRADY (NICHOLAS), (b. 1659, d. 1726).
   Psalm C.. 545

INDEX OF AUTHORS.

	PAGE
TAYLOR, BAYARD (b. 1825, d. 1878).	
Bedouin Song	177
Quaker Widow	22
Song of the Camp	216
TAYLOR, JANE (b. 1783, d. 1824).	
The Philosopher's Scales	665
The Squire's Pew	671
TAYLOR, JOHN.	
Monsieur Tonson	945
TAYLOR, TOM (b. 1817).	
Abraham Lincoln	280
TENNYSON, ALFRED (b. 1809).	
"Ask me no more"	192
"Break, break, break"	88
Bugle Song	502
Charge of the Light Brigade	348
"Come into the garden, Maud"	177
Death of the Old Year	438
Dedication to "The Idylls of the King"	280
From "In Memoriam"—	
"Again at Christmas did we weave"	689
"Contemplate all this work of Time"	690
"I envy not, in any moods"	689
"I held it truth, with him who sings"	689
"Oh yet we trust that somehow good"	689
"Ring out, wild bells, to the wild sky"	690
"Who loves not Knowledge? Who shall rail"	690
Lady Clara Vere de Vere	210
Lady Clare	138
Lady of Shalott	888
Lilian	203
Locksley Hall	149
Lord of Burleigh	201
May Queen	69
Miller's Daughter	155
Ode on the Death of the Duke of Wellington	270
Reconciliation	39
Song of the Brook	460
St. Agnes' Eve	546
"Sweet and low"	31
The Days that are no More	91
"Thy voice is heard through rolling drums"	743
Tithonus	787
Widow and Child	56
THACKERAY, WILLIAM MAKEPEACE (b. 1811, d. 1863).	
Age of Wisdom	87
At the Church Gate	211
Ballad of Bouillabaisse	89
Chronicle of the Drum	334
End of the Play	673
King of Brentford's Testament	906
Little Billee	909
Mr. Molony's Account of the Ball	955
Sorrows of Werther	895
THOM, WILLIAM (b. 1789, d. 1848).	
The Mitherless Bairn	46
THOMSON, JAMES (b. 1700, d. 1748).	
Hymn—The Seasons	423
Rule, Britannia	355
THORNBURY, GEORGE WALTER (b. 1828, d. 1876).	
La Tricoteuse	332

	PAGE
The Jester's Sermon	916
The Pompadour	327
The Three Troopers	309
THORPE, ROSA HARTWICK (b. 1850).	
Curfew must not Ring to-night	404
THURLOW, EDWARD HOVELL THURLOW, LORD (b. 1781, d. 1829).	
Song to May!	428
Sonnet—Summer	433
Sonnet—To a Bird that Haunted the Waters of Laaken in the Winter	472
Sonnet—To the Moon	446
TICKELL, THOMAS (b. 1686, d. 1740).	
Colin and Lucy	197
To the Earl of Warwick on the Death of Mr. Addison	242
TIMROD, HENRY (b. 1829, d. 1867).	
Spring	431
TOPLADY, AUGUSTUS MONTAGUE (b. 1740, d. 1778).	
Address to the Soul	596
Rock of Ages	540
TRENCH, RICHARD CHENEVIX (b. 1807).	
Different Minds	658
Harmosan	291
The Kingdom of God	662
TROWBRIDGE, JOHN T. (b. 1827).	
At Sea	465
The Vagabonds	717
TURNER, CHARLES (b. 1808, d. 1879.).	
The Lachrymatory	740
TYCHBORN, CHIDIOCK (d. 1586).	
Lines Written by One in the Tower, being Young and Condemned to Die	688
VAUGHAN, HENRY (b. 1621, d. 1695).	
Son-Dayes	560
The Rainbow	443
The Retreat	92
They are all Gone	597
VAUX, THOMAS, LORD (b. 1510, d. 1557).	
On a Contented Mind	658
VERE, EDWARD, EARL OF OXFORD (b. about 1534, d. 1604).	
A Renunciation	190
WAKEFIELD, NANCY A. W. P. (b. 1836, d. 1870).	
Over the River	629
WALLER, EDMUND (b. 1605, d. 1687).	
Go, Lovely Rose	185
On a Girdle	185
On his Divine Poems	688
WALTON, IZAAK (b. 1593, d. 1683).	
The Angler's Wish	467
WARING, ANNA LÆTITIA.	
Thy Will be Done	567
WARTON, THOMAS (b. 1687, d. 1745).	
Sonnet—Written after Seeing Windsor Castle	504
WARTON, THOMAS (b. 1728, d. 1790).	
On Revisiting the River Loddon	508

INDEX OF AUTHORS.

WASTELL, SIMON (b. about 1560, d. about 1630).
Man's Mortality 626

WATSON, JOHN W.
Beautiful Snow 720

WATSON, THOMAS (b. 1560, d. 1592).
Sonnet—May 428
Sonnet—"Time wasteth years, and months, and hours" 172

WATTS, ISAAC (b. 1674, d. 1748).
"Come, Holy Spirit, heavenly Dove" 542
Cradle Hymn 34
Glorying in the Cross 547
"I give immortal praise" 546
"O happy soul that lives on high" 575
Psalm XC 549
Psalm XCVIII 549
Psalm C 546
Psalm CXVII 552
Psalm CXXI 583
"There is a land of pure delight" 599

WAUGH, EDWIN (b. 1818).
"The dule's i' this bonnet o' mine" 166

WEBSTER, JOHN (b. about 1585, d. about 1654).
Dirge from "The White Devil" 638

WESLEY, CHARLES (b. 1708, d. 1788).
"Hark, how all the welkin rings" 532
"Jesu, lover of my soul" 540
"Jesu, my strength, my hope" 579
The Omnipotent Decree 585
The Lord is Risen 535
Wrestling Jacob 571

WESTWOOD, THOMAS (b. 1814).
Little Bell 38
Under my Window 53

WHITE, HENRY KIRKE (b. 1785, d. 1806).
Hymn for Family Worship 568
The Star of Bethlehem 577
To an Early Primrose 452

WHITE, JOSEPH BLANCO (b. 1775, d. 1841).
Sonnet—To Night 441

WHITTIER, JOHN GREENLEAF (b. 1807).
Angels of Buena Vista 345
Barbara Frietchie 350
Brown of Ossawatomie 279
Eve of Election 675
Ichabod 267
In Remembrance of Joseph Sturge 277
Maud Muller 167
My Playmate 82
My Psalm 613
Randolph of Roanoke 262
Red River Voyageur 680
Skipper Ireson's Ride 371
Thy Will be Done 568

WILDE, RICHARD HENRY (b. 1789, d. 1847).
Stanzas—"My life is like the summer rose" 616

WILLIAMS, HELEN MARIA (b. 1762, d. 1827).
Sonnet—To Hope 663
"Whilst Thee I seek" 572

WILLIAMS, ISAAC (b. 1802, d. 1865).
"The child leans on its parent's breast" 573

WILLIAMS, WILLIAM (b. 1717, d. 1791).
"Guide me, O Thou great Jehovah" 579

WILLIS, NATHANIEL PARKER (b. 1807, d. 1867).
Saturday Afternoon 77

WILSON, ALEXANDER (b. 1766, d. 1813).
The Blue Bird 475

WILSON, JOHN (b. 1785, d. 1854).
The Evening Cloud 442

WINCHELSEA, ANNE, COUNTESS OF (b. about 1660, d. 1720).
A Nocturnal Reverie 434

WITHER, GEORGE (b. 1588, d. 1667).
A Stolen Kiss 156
Evening Hymn 556
Lemuel's Song 24
Morning Hymn 554
Psalm CXLVIII 551
"Sweet baby, sleep" 34
The Shepherd's Resolution 169
The Steadfast Shepherd 153

WOLFE, CHARLES (b. 1791, d. 1823).
The Burial of Sir John Moore 252

WOODWORTH, SAMUEL (b. 1785, d. 1842).
The Old Oaken Bucket 74
The Whiskers 892

WORDSWORTH, WILLIAM (b. 1770, d. 1850).
Daffodils 452
Elegiac Stanzas suggested by a Picture of Peele Castle 505
Hart-Leap Well 387
Lucy 49
Lucy Gray; or, Solitude 56
Ode—Intimations of Immortality from Recollections of Early Childhood 644
Ode to Duty 664
"She was a Phantom of delight" 10
Sonnet—Composed upon Westminster Bridge .. 503
Sonnet—"It is a beauteous evening calm and free" 441
Sonnet—On the Extinction of the Venetian Republic 343
Sonnet—"Scorn not the sonnet" 781
Sonnet—To Milton 249
The Good Lord Clifford 223
The Kitten and the Falling Leaves 485
The Pet Lamb 487
The Rainbow 444
"Three years she grew" 49
To a Highland Girl 65
To a Skylark 473
To a Skylark 473
To the Cuckoo 480
To the Daisy 453
To the Daisy 454
We are Seven 51
Yarrow Revisited 511

INDEX OF AUTHORS.

	PAGE
Yarrow Unvisited	510
Yarrow Visited	510

WOTTON, SIR HENRY (b. 1568, d. 1639).

Character of a Happy Life	661
Tears wept at the Grave of Sir Albertus Morton	228
To his Mistress, the Queen of Bohemia	185
Upon the Death of Sir Albertus Morton's Wife	228
Upon the Sudden Restraint of the Earl of Somerset	230
Verses in Praise of Angling	467

WYATT, SIR THOMAS (b. 1503, d. 1542).

Blame not my Lute	190
The Recured Lover Exulteth in his Freedom	191

YOUNG, ANDREW (b. about 1809).

"There is a happy land"	599

AUTHOR UNKNOWN.

A-Hunting we will Go	493
Annie Laurie	199
Armstrong's Good-Night	656
Ballad of Chevy-Chace	299
Barbara Allen's Cruelty	417
Between the Lights	683
Bonnie George Campbell	419
Burd Helen	412
Child of Elle	385
Children in the Wood	53
Christmas Carol	531
"Christ will gather in His own"	609
Comin' through the Rye	214
Cruel Sister	418
Cumberland, The	350
Dowie Dens of Yarrow	381
Dumb Child	41
Edward, Edward	380
Fair Annie of Lochroyan	394
Fair Helen	402

	PAGE
Fairy Queen	793
Glenlogie	406
Good-Night	688
Heir of Linne	368
Jovial Beggar	918
Katharine Janfarie	393
Lady Anne Bothwell's Lament	32
Lament of the Border Widow	417
Lord Lovel	198
Love Lightens Labor	24
Loveliness of Love	139
"Love not me for comely grace"	130
Love will Find out the Way	97
Merry Pranks of Robin Goodfellow	808
Monody on the Death of an Only Client	921
New Jerusalem	602
Nut-Brown Maid	112
Old and Young Courtier	672
Origin of the Opal	459
Robin Hood and Allen-a-Dale	390
Siege of Belgrade	960
Sir Patrick Spens	367
St. Anthony's Sermon to the Fishes	915
Take thy Old Cloak about Thee	901
They're Dear Fish to Me	699
Three Ravens	411
To a Skeleton	642
To my Horse	493
Twa Corbies	412
Twenty Years Ago	78
Useful Plough	692
Veni Creator Spiritus	542
Vicar of Bray	914
Waly, waly, but Love be Bonny	103
Wandering Jew	374
Where are you Going, my Pretty Maid?	898
White Rose	214
Winifreda	7
Young Airly	325

'Mid pleasures & palaces though we may roam
Be it ever so humble, there's no place like Home!
A charm from the sky seems to hallow us there
Which, seek through the world, is ne'er met with elsewhere!

  Home, home! sweet, sweet Home!
  There's no place like Home!
  There's no place like Home!

John Howard Payne.

POETRY

OF

HOME AND THE FIRESIDE.

HOME, SWEET HOME.

'MID pleasures and palaces though we may
  roam,
Be it ever so humble, there's no place like
  home!
A charm from the sky seems to hallow us
  there,
Which, seek through the world, is ne'er
  met with elsewhere.
  Home, home, sweet, sweet, home!
  There's no place like home!

An exile from home, splendor dazzles in
  vain;
Oh! give me my lowly thatch'd cottage
  again!
The birds, singing gayly, that came at my
  call—
Give me them!—and the peace of mind
  dearer than all.
  Home, sweet, sweet, sweet, home!
  There's no place like home!
JOHN HOWARD PAYNE.

THE HOMES OF ENGLAND.

THE stately Homes of England!
  How beautiful they stand,
Amidst their tall, ancestral trees,
  O'er all the pleasant land!
The deer across their greensward bound,
  Through shade and sunny gleam,
And the swan glides past them with the
  sound
  Of some rejoicing stream.

The merry Homes of England!
  Around their hearths by night,
What gladsome looks of household love
  Meet in the ruddy light!
There woman's voice flows forth in song,
  Or childhood's tale is told,
Or lips move tunefully along
  Some glorious page of old.

The blessed Homes of England!
  How softly on their bowers
Is laid the holy quietness
  That breathes from Sabbath hours!
Solemn, yet sweet, the church-bell's chime
  Floats through their woods at morn:
All other sounds, in that still time,
  Of breeze and leaf are born.

The cottage Homes of England!
  By thousands on her plains,
They are smiling o'er the silvery brooks,
  And round the hamlet fanes.
Through glowing orchards forth they peep,
  Each from its nook of leaves,
And fearless there the lowly sleep,
  As the bird beneath their eaves.

The free, fair Homes of England!
  Long, long, in hut and hall,
May hearts of native proof be rear'd
  To guard each hallow'd wall!
And green for ever be the groves,
  And bright the flowery sod,
Where first the child's glad spirit loves
  Its country and its God!
FELICIA DOROTHEA HEMANS.

MY AIN FIRESIDE.

I HAE seen great anes, and sat in great ha's,
'Mang lords and fine ladies a' cover'd wi'
  braws,
At feasts made for princes wi' princes I've
  been,
When the grand shine o' splendor has
  dazzled my een;

But a sight sae delightfu' I trow I ne'er spied
As the bonny blithe blink o' my ain fireside.
My ain fireside, my ain fireside,
Oh cheery's the blink o' my ain fireside;
  My ain fireside, my ain fireside,
  Oh, there's naught to compare wi' ane's ain fireside.

Ance mair, Gude be thankit, round my ain heartsome ingle,
Wi' the friends o' my youth I cordially mingle;
Nae forms to compel me to seem wae or glad,
I may laugh when I'm merry, and sigh when I'm sad.
Nae falsehood to dread, and nae malice to fear,
But truth to delight me, and friendship to cheer;
Of a' roads to happiness ever were tried,
There's nane half so sure as ane's ain fireside.
  My ain fireside, my ain fireside,
  Oh, there's naught to compare wi' ane's ain fireside.

When I draw in my stool on my cozy hearthstane,
My heart loups sae light I scarce ken't for my ain;
Care's down on the wind, it is clean out o' sight,
Past troubles they seem but as dreams o' the night.
I hear but kend voices, kend faces I see,
And mark saft affection glent fond frae ilk ee;
Nae fleechings o' flattery, nae boastings o' pride,
'Tis heart speaks to heart at ane's ain fireside.
  My ain fireside, my ain fireside,
  Oh there's naught to compare wi' ane's ain fireside.
                ELIZABETH HAMILTON.

THE HAPPY MARRIAGE.

How blest has my time been, what joys have I known,
Since wedlock's soft bondage made Jessy my own!
So joyful my heart is, so easy my chain,
That freedom is tasteless, and roving a pain.

Through walks grown with woodbines, as often we stray,
Around us our boys and girls frolic and play:
How pleasing their sport is! The wanton ones see,
And borrow their looks from my Jessy and me.

To try her sweet temper, ofttimes am I seen,
In revels all day, with the nymphs on the green:
Though painful my absence, my doubts she beguiles,
And meets me at night with complacence and smiles.

What though on her cheeks the rose loses its hue,
Her wit and good-humor bloom all the year through;
Time still, as he flies, adds increase to her truth,
And gives to her mind what he steals from her youth.

Ye shepherds so gay, who make love to ensnare
And cheat with false vows the too credulous fair;
In search of true pleasure, how vainly you roam!
To hold it for life, you must find it at home.
                EDWARD MOORE.

THE FIRESIDE.

DEAR CHLOE, while the busy crowd,
  The vain, the wealthy, and the proud,
    In folly's maze advance,
Though singularity and pride
Be call'd our choice, we'll step aside,
    Nor join the giddy dance.

From the gay world we'll oft retire
To our own family and fire,
  Where love our hours employs;
No noisy neighbor enters here,
No intermeddling stranger near,
  To spoil our heartfelt joys.

If solid happiness we prize,
Within our breast this jewel lies,
  And they are fools who roam;

The world hath nothing to bestow—
From our own selves our bliss must flow,
And that dear hut, our home.

Of rest was Noah's dove bereft,
When with impatient wing she left
   That safe retreat, the ark;
Giving her vain excursion o'er,
The disappointed bird once more
   Explored the sacred bark.

Though fools spurn Hymen's gentle powers,
We, who improve his golden hours,
   By sweet experience know
That marriage, rightly understood,
Gives to the tender and the good
   A paradise below.

Our babes shall richest comforts bring;
If tutor'd right, they'll prove a spring
   Whence pleasures ever rise;
We'll form their minds with studious care
To all that's manly, good, and fair,
   And train them for the skies.

While they our wisest hours engage,
They'll joy our youth, support our age,
   And crown our hoary hairs;
They'll grow in virtue every day,
And thus our fondest loves repay,
   And recompense our cares.

No borrow'd joys, they're all our own,
While to the world we live unknown,
   Or by the world forgot;
Monarchs! we envy not your state—
We look with pity on the great,
   And bless our humble lot.

Our portion is not large, indeed;
But then how little do we need,
   For Nature's calls are few!
In this the art of living lies—
To want no more than may suffice,
   And make that little do.

We'll therefore relish with content
Whate'er kind Providence has sent,
   Nor aim beyond our power;
For, if our stock be very small,
'Tis prudence to enjoy it all,
   Nor lose the present hour.

To be resign'd when ills betide,
Patient when favors are denied,
   And pleased with favors given—

Dear Chloe, this is wisdom's part,
This is that incense of the heart
   Whose fragrance smells to heaven.

We'll ask no long-protracted treat,
Since winter-life is seldom sweet;
   But, when our feast is o'er,
Grateful from table we'll arise,
Nor grudge our sons, with envious eyes,
   The relics of our store.

Thus hand in hand through life we'll go;
Its chequer'd paths of joy and woe
   With cautious steps we'll tread;
Quit its vain scenes without a tear,
Without a trouble or a fear,
   And mingle with the dead;

While conscience, like a faithful friend,
Shall through the gloomy vale attend,
   And cheer our dying breath—
Shall, when all other comforts cease,
Like a kind angel whisper peace,
   And smooth the bed of death.
                NATHANIEL COTTON.

THE COTTER'S SATURDAY NIGHT.

INSCRIBED TO ROBERT AIKEN, ESQ.

"Let not Ambition mock their useful toil,
  Their homely joys, and destiny obscure;
Nor Grandeur hear, with a disdainful smile,
  The short and simple annals of the poor."—GRAY.

My lov'd, my honor'd, much-respected
   friend!
No mercenary bard his homage pays;
With honest pride, I scorn each selfish end:
   My dearest meed, a friend's esteem and
     praise;
To you I sing, in simple Scottish lays,
The lowly train in life's sequester'd scene;
   The native feelings strong, the guileless
     ways;
What Aiken in a cottage would have
   been;
Ah! tho' his worth unknown, far happier
   there, I ween!

November chill blaws loud wi' angry sugh;
   The short'ning winter-day is near a close;
The miry beasts retreating frae the pleugh;
   The black'ning trains o' craws to their
     repose:
The toil-worn Cotter frae his labor goes,—

This night his weekly moil is at an end,—
  Collects his spades, his mattocks, and his hoes,
Hoping the morn in ease and rest to spend,
And weary, o'er the moor, his course does hameward bend.

At length his lonely cot appears in view,
  Beneath the shelter of an aged tree;
Th' expectant wee-things, toddlin, stacher through
  To meet their "dad," wi' flichterin' noise an' glee.
His wee bit ingle, blinkin' bonnilie,
His clean hearth-stane, his thriftie wifie's smile,
The lisping infant, prattling on his knee,
Does a' his weary kiaugh and care beguile,
And makes him quite forget his labor and his toil.

Belyve, the elder bairns come drapping in,
  At service out, amang the farmers roun';
Some ca' the pleugh, some herd, some tentie rin
  A cannie errand to a neibor town:
Their eldest hope, their Jenny, woman grown,
In youthfu' bloom—love sparkling in her e'e—
  Comes hame; perhaps, to show a braw new gown,
Or deposite her sair-won penny-fee,
To help her parents dear, if they in hardship be.

With joy unfeign'd, brothers and sisters meet,
  And each for other's welfare kindly spiers:
The social hours, swift-wing'd, unnoticed fleet;
  Each tells the uncos that he sees or hears.
The parents, partial, eye their hopeful years;
Anticipation forward points the view;
  The mother, wi' her needle and her shears,
Gars auld claes look amaist as weel's the new:
The father mixes a' wi' admonition due.

Their master's and their mistress's command,
  The younkers a' are warnèd to obey;
And mind their labors wi' an eydent hand,
  And ne'er, tho' out o' sight, to jauk or play;
"And oh, be sure to fear the Lord alway,
And mind your duty, duly, morn and night;
  Lest in temptation's path ye gang astray,
Implore His counsel and assisting might:
They never sought in vain that sought the Lord aright."

But hark! a rap comes gently to the door;
  Jenny, wha kens the meaning o' the same,
Tells how a neibor lad came o'er the moor,
  To do some errands, and convoy her hame.
The wily mother sees the conscious flame
Sparkle in Jenny's e'e, and flush her cheek;
  With heart-struck anxious care, inquires his name,
While Jenny hafflins is afraid to speak;
Weel pleased the mother hears, it's nae wild, worthless rake.

With kindly welcome, Jenny brings him ben;
  A strappin' youth, he takes the mother's eye;
Blythe Jenny sees the visit's no ill ta'en;
  The father cracks of horses, pleughs, and kye.
The youngster's artless heart o'erflows wi' joy,
But, blate an' laithfu', scarce can weel behave;
  The mother, wi' a woman's wiles, can spy
What makes the youth sae bashfu' an' sae grave;
Weel pleased to think her bairn's respected like the lave.

O happy love! where love like this is found:
  O heartfelt raptures! bliss beyond compare!
I've pacèd much this weary, mortal round,
  And sage experience bids me this declare,—
"If Heaven a draught of heavenly pleasure spare—

One cordial in this melancholy vale,—
  'Tis when a youthful, loving, modest pair
In other's arms breathe out the tender tale,
  Beneath the milk-white thorn that scents the evening gale."

Is there, in human form, that bears a heart,
  A wretch! a villain! lost to love and truth!
That can, with studied, sly, ensnaring art,
  Betray sweet Jenny's unsuspecting youth?
    Curse on his perjured arts! dissembling, smooth!
Are honor, virtue, conscience, all exiled?
  Is there no pity, no relenting ruth,
Points to the parents fondling o'er their child?
Then paints the ruin'd maid, and their distraction wild?

But now the supper crowns their simple board,
  The halesome parritch, chief of Scotia's food;
The sowpe their only hawkie does afford,
  That, 'yont the hallan snugly chows her cood:
    The dame brings forth, in complimental mood,
To grace the lad, her weel-hain'd kebbuck, fell;
  And aft he's prest, and aft he ca's it guid:
The frugal wifie, garrulous, will tell
How 'twas a towmond auld, sin' lint was i' the bell.

The cheerfu' supper done, wi' serious face,
  They, round the ingle, form a circle wide;
The sire turns o'er, with patriarchal grace,
  The big ha' Bible, ance his father's pride:
His bonnet rev'rently is laid aside,
  His lyart haffets wearing thin and bare;
Those strains that once did sweet in Zion glide,
  He wales a portion with judicious care;
And "Let us worship God!" he says with solemn air.

They chant their artless notes in simple guise,
  They tune their hearts, by far the noblest aim:
Perhaps "Dundee's" wild warbling measures rise,
  Or plaintive "Martyrs," worthy of the name;
Or noble "Elgin" beets the heavenward flame,
The sweetest far of Scotia's holy lays:
  Compared with these, Italian trills are tame:
The tickled ears no heartfelt raptures raise;
Nae unison hae they with our Creator's praise.

The priest-like father reads the sacred page,
  How Abram was the friend of God on high;
Or, Moses bade eternal warfare wage
  With Amalek's ungracious progeny;
Or, how the royal bard did groaning lie
Beneath the stroke of Heaven's avenging ire;
  Or Job's pathetic plaint, and wailing cry;
Or rapt Isaiah's wild, seraphic fire;
Or other holy seers that tune the sacred lyre.

Perhaps the Christian volume is the theme,
  How guiltless blood for guilty man was shed;
How He, who bore in Heaven the second name,
  Had not on earth whereon to lay His head;
How His first followers and servants sped;
The precepts sage they wrote to many a land:
  How he, who lone in Patmos banishèd,
Saw in the sun a mighty angel stand,
And heard great Bab'lon's doom pronounced by Heaven's command.

Then kneeling down, to Heaven's Eternal King
  The saint, the father, and the husband prays:
Hope "springs exulting on triumphant wing,"
  That thus they all shall meet in future days,
There, ever bask in uncreated rays,
No more to sigh, or shed the bitter tear,
  Together hymning their Creator's praise

In such society, yet still more dear,
　While circling time moves round in an
　　eternal sphere.

Compared with this, how poor Religion's
　pride,
　In all the pomp of method, and of art,
When men display to congregations wide
　Devotion's ev'ry grace, except the
　　heart!
The Power, incensed, the pageant will
　desert,
The pompous strain, the sacerdotal stole;
　But haply, in some cottage far apart,
May hear, well pleased, the language of
　the soul;
And in His Book of Life the inmates poor
　enroll.

Then homeward all take off their sev'ral
　way;
　The youngling cottagers retire to rest:
The parent pair their secret homage pay,
　And proffer up to Heaven the warm
　　request,
　That He who stills the raven's clam'rous
　　nest,
And decks the lily fair in flow'ry pride,
　Would, in the way His wisdom sees the
　　best,
For them and for their little ones provide;
But chiefly, in their hearts with grace divine
　preside.

From scenes like these old Scotia's grandeur
　springs,
　That makes her loved at home, revered
　　abroad:
Princes and lords are but the breath of kings,
　"An honest man's the noblest work of
　　God;"
　And certes, in fair Virtue's heavenly road,
The cottage leaves the palace far behind;
　What is a lordling's pomp? a cumbrous
　　load,
Disguising oft the wretch of human kind,
Studied in arts of hell, in wickedness refined!

O Scotia! my dear, my native soil!
　For whom my warmest wish to Heaven
　　is sent,
Long may thy hardy sons of rustic toil
　Be blest with health, and peace, and
　　sweet content!

And oh, may Heaven their simple lives
　prevent
From luxury's contagion, weak and vile!
　Then, howe'er crowns and coronets be
　　rent,
A virtuous populace may rise the while,
And stand a wall of fire around their much-
　loved isle.

O Thou! who pour'd the patriotic tide,
　That stream'd thro' Wallace's undaunted
　　heart,
Who dared to nobly stem tyrannic pride,
　Or nobly die, the second glorious part:
(The patriot's God, peculiarly Thou art,
　His friend, inspirer, guardian, and re-
　　ward!)
Oh never, never Scotia's realm desert;
But still the patriot, and the patriot-bard,
　In bright succession raise, her ornament
　　and guard!
　　　　　　　　　　ROBERT BURNS.

A WISH.

MINE be a cot beside the hill;
　A beehive's hum shall soothe my ear;
A willowy brook, that turns a mill,
　With many a fall shall linger near.

The swallow, oft, beneath my thatch,
　Shall twitter from her clay-built nest;
Oft shall the pilgrim lift the latch,
　And share my meal, a welcome guest.

Around my ivied porch shall spring
　Each fragrant flower that drinks the dew;
And Lucy, at her wheel, shall sing
　In russet gown and apron blue.

The village church, among the trees,
　Where first our marriage vows were given,
With merry peals shall swell the breeze,
　And point with taper spire to heaven.
　　　　　　　　　　SAMUEL ROGERS.

A PICTURE.

THE farmer sat in his easy-chair
　Smoking his pipe of clay,
While his hale old wife, with busy care,
　Was clearing the dinner away;
A sweet little girl, with fine blue eyes,
On her grandfather's knee was catching
　flies.

The old man laid his hand on her head,
  With a tear on his wrinkled face;
He thought how often her mother, dead,
  Had sat in the self-same place.
As the tear stole down from his half-shut eye,
"Don't smoke!" said the child; "how it makes you cry!"

The house-dog lay stretch'd out on the floor,
  Where the shade after noon used to steal;
The busy old wife, by the open door,
  Was turning the spinning-wheel;
And the old brass clock on the manteltree
Had plodded along to almost three.

Still the farmer sat in his easy-chair,
  While close to his heaving breast
The moisten'd brow and the cheek so fair
  Of his sweet grandchild were press'd;
His head, bent down, on her soft hair lay:
Fast asleep were they both, that summer day!
            CHARLES G. EASTMAN.

MATRIMONIAL HAPPINESS.

WHEN I upon thy bosom lean,
  And fondly clasp thee a' my ain,
I glory in the sacred ties
  That made us ane wha ance were twain.
A mutual flame inspires us baith,
  The tender look, the meltin' kiss;
Even years shall ne'er destroy our love,
  But only gi'e us change o' bliss.

Hae I a wish? it's a' for thee!
  I ken thy wish is me to please;
Our moments pass sae smooth away
  That numbers on us look and gaze;
Weel pleased they see our happy days,
  Nor envy's sel' finds aught to blame;
And aye when weary cares arise,
  Thy bosom still shall be my hame.

I'll lay me there and tak' my rest;
  And if that aught disturb my dear,
I'll bid her laugh her cares away,
  And beg her not to drop a tear.
Hae I a joy? it's a' her ain!
  United still her heart and mine;
They're like the woodbine round the tree,
  That's twined till death shall them disjoin.
            JOHN LAPRAIK.

WINIFREDA.

AWAY! let naught to love displeasing,
  My Winifreda, move your care;
Let naught delay the heavenly blessing,
  Nor squeamish pride nor gloomy fear.

What though no grants of royal donors
  With pompous titles grace our blood;
We'll shine in more substantial honors,
  And to be noble we'll be good.

Our name, while virtue thus we tender,
  Will sweetly sound where'er 'tis spoke,
And all the great ones, they shall wonder
  How they respect such little folk.

What though from fortune's lavish bounty
  No mighty treasures we possess;
We'll find within our pittance plenty,
  And be content without excess.

Still shall each returning season
  Sufficient for our wishes give;
For we will live a life of reason;
  And that's the only life to live.

Through youth and age, in love excelling,
  We'll hand in hand together tread;
Sweet-smiling peace shall crown our dwelling,
  And babes, sweet-smiling babes, our bed.

How should I love the pretty creatures
  While round my knees they fondly clung,
To see them look their mother's features,
  To hear them lisp their mother's tongue!

And when with envy time, transported,
  Shall think to rob us of our joys,
You'll in your girls again be courted,
  And I'll go a-wooing in my boys.
            AUTHOR UNKNOWN.

HERMIONÉ.

WHEREVER I wander, up and about,
This is the puzzle I can't make out—
Because I care little for books, no doubt:

I have a wife, and she is wise,
  Deep in philosophy, strong in Greek;
Spectacles shadow her pretty eyes,
  Coteries rustle to hear her speak;

She writes a little—for love, not fame;
Has publish'd a book with a dreary name;
   And yet (God bless her!) is mild and
     meek.
And how I happened to woo and wed
   A wife so pretty and wise withal,
Is part of the puzzle that fills my head—
Plagues me at day-time, racks me in bed,
   Haunts me, and makes me appear so
     small.
The only answer that I can see
Is—I could not have married Hermioné
(That is her fine wise name), but she
Stoop'd in her wisdom and married *me*.

For I am a fellow of no degree,
Given to romping and jollity;
The Latin they thrash'd into me at school
   The world and its fights have thrash'd
     away:
At figures alone I am no fool,
   And in city circles I say my say.
But I am a dunce at twenty-nine,
And the kind of study that I think fine
Is a chapter of Dickens, a sheet of the
   Times,
   When I lounge, after work, in my easy-
     chair;
Punch for humor, and Praed for rhymes,
   And the butterfly *mots* blown here and
     there
   By the idle breath of the social air.
A little French is my only gift,
Wherewith at times I can make a shift,
Guessing at meanings, to flutter over
   A filigree tale in a paper cover.

Hermioné, my Hermioné!
What could your wisdom perceive in me?
And, Hermioné, my Hermioné!
How does it happen at all that we
Love one another so utterly?
Well, I have a bright-eyed boy of two,
   A darling who cries with lung and
     tongue about:
As fine a fellow, I swear to you,
   As ever poet of sentiment sung about!
And my lady-wife with the serious eyes
   Brightens and lightens when he is nigh,
And looks, although she is deep and wise,
   As foolish and happy as he or I!
And I have the courage just then, you see,
   To kiss the lips of Hermioné—
Those learnèd lips that the learnèd praise—
   And to clasp her close as in sillier days;
To talk and joke in a frolic vein,
   To tell her my stories of things and men;
And it never strikes me that I'm profane,
For she laughs and blushes, and kisses
     again;
And, presto! fly! goes her wisdom then!
For boy claps hands, and is up on her
     breast,
   Roaring to see her so bright with mirth;
And I know she deems me (oh the jest!)
   The cleverest fellow on all the earth!

And Hermioné, my Hermioné,
Nurses her boy and defers to me;
Does not seem to see I'm small—
Even to think me a dunce at all!
And wherever I wander, up and about,
Here is the puzzle I can't make out:
That Hermioné, my Hermioné,
In spite of her Greek and philosophy,
When sporting at night with her boy and me,
Seems sweeter and wiser, I assever—
Sweeter and wiser, and far more clever,
And makes me feel more foolish than ever,
Through her childish, girlish, joyous grace,
And the silly pride in her learnèd face!

That is the puzzle I can't make out—
Because I care little for books, no doubt;
But the puzzle is pleasant, I know not
   why,
   For, whenever I think of it, night or
     morn,
I thank my God she is wise, and I
   The happiest fool that was ever born!
                      ROBERT BUCHANAN.

JOHN ANDERSON, MY JO.

JOHN ANDERSON, my jo, John,
   When we were first acquent,
Your locks were like the raven,
   Your bonnie brow was brent;
But now your brow is beld, John,
   Your locks are like the snaw;
But blessings on your frosty pow,
   John Anderson, my jo!

John Anderson, my jo, John,
   We clamb the hill thegither,
And mony a cantie day, John,
   We've had wi' ane anither:

Now we maun totter down, John;
  And hand in hand we'll go,
And sleep thegither at the foot,
  John Anderson, my jo.
                    ROBERT BURNS.

LINES WRITTEN TO HIS WIFE,
WHILE ON A VISIT TO UPPER INDIA.

If thou wert by my side, my love,
  How fast would evening fail
In green Bengala's palmy grove,
  Listening the nightingale!

If thou, my love, wert by my side,
  My babies at my knee,
How gaily would our pinnace glide
  O'er Gunga's mimic sea!

I miss thee at the dawning gray,
  When, on our deck reclined,
In careless ease my limbs I lay,
  And woo the cooler wind.

I miss thee when by Gunga's stream
  My twilight steps I guide;
But most beneath the lamp's pale beam
  I miss thee from my side.

I spread my books, my pencil try,
  The lingering noon to cheer,
But miss thy kind, approving eye,
  Thy meek, attentive ear.

But when of morn and eve the star
  Beholds me on my knee,
I feel, though thou art distant far,
  Thy prayers ascend for me.

Then on! then on! where duty leads,
  My course be onward still—
On broad Hindostan's sultry meads,
  O'er black Almorah's hill.

That course nor Delhi's kingly gates
  Nor mild Malwah detain;
For sweet the bliss us both awaits
  By yonder western main.

Thy towers, Bombay, gleam bright, they say,
  Across the dark blue sea;
But never were hearts so light and gay
  As then shall meet in thee!
                    REGINALD HEBER.

TO MY WIFE.

Oh, hadst thou never shared my fate,
  More dark that fate would prove:
My heart were truly desolate
  Without thy soothing love.

But thou hast suffer'd for my sake,
  Whilst this relief I found,
Like fearless lips that strive to take
  The poison from a wound.

My fond affection thou hast seen,
  Then judge of my regret
To think more happy thou hadst been
  If we had never met!

And has that thought been shared by thee?
  Ah, no! that smiling cheek
Proves more unchanging love for me
  Than labor'd words could speak.

But there are true hearts which the sight
  Of sorrow summons forth;
Though known in days of past delight,
  We knew not half their worth.

How unlike some who have profess'd
  So much in Friendship's name,
Yet calmly pause to think how best
  They may evade her claim.

But ah! from them to thee I turn,—
  They'd make me loathe mankind;
Far better lessons I may learn
  From thy more holy mind.

The love that gives a charm to home
  I feel they cannot take:
We'll pray for happier years to come,
  For one another's sake.
                    THOMAS HAYNES BAYLY.

THE WINSOME WEE THING.

She is a winsome wee thing,
She is a handsome wee thing,
She is a lo'esome wee thing,
  This dear wee wife o' mine.

I never saw a fairer,
I never lo'ed a dearer;
And neist my heart I'll wear her,
  For fear my jewel tine.

She is a winsome wee thing,
She is a handsome wee thing,

She is a lo'esome wee thing,
  This dear wee wife o' mine.

The warld's wrack we share o't,
The warstle and the care o't,
Wi' her I'll blythely bear it,
And think my lot divine.
                        ROBERT BURNS.

SHE WAS A PHANTOM OF DELIGHT.

SHE was a Phantom of delight
When first she gleam'd upon my sight;
A lovely Apparition, sent
To be a moment's ornament;
Her eyes as stars of Twilight fair;
Like Twilight's, too, her dusky hair;
But all things else about her drawn
From May-time and the cheerful Dawn;
A dancing Shape, an Image gay,
To hunt, to startle, and waylay.

I saw her, upon nearer view,
A Spirit, yet a Woman too!
Her household motions light and free,
And steps of virgin liberty;
A countenance in which did meet
Sweet records, promises as sweet;
A Creature, not too bright or good
For human nature's daily food—
For transient sorrows, simple wiles,
Praise, blame, love, kisses, tears, and smiles.

And now I see with eye serene
The very pulse of the machine;
A Being breathing thoughtful breath,
A Traveller between life and death;
The reason firm, the temperate will,
Endurance, foresight, strength, and skill;
A perfect Woman, nobly plann'd,
To warn, to comfort, and command;
And yet a Spirit still, and bright
With something of an angel light.
                    WILLIAM WORDSWORTH.

TO MARY.

"THEE, Mary, with this ring I wed"—
So, fourteen years ago, I said.
Behold another ring!—"For what?—
To wed thee o'er again?" Why not?
With that first ring I married youth,
Grace, beauty, innocence, and truth;
Taste long admired, sense long revered,
And all my Molly then appear'd.

If she, by merit since disclosed,
Prove twice the woman I supposed,
I plead that double merit now
To justify a double vow.
Here, then, to-day (with faith as sure,
With ardor as intense, as pure,
As when, amidst the rites divine,
I took thy troth and plighted mine),
To thee, sweet girl, my second ring,
A token and a pledge, I bring:
With this I wed, till death us part,
Thy riper virtues to my heart—
Those virtues which, before untried,
The wife has added to the bride;
Those virtues whose progressive claim,
Endearing wedlock's very name,
My soul enjoys, my song approves,
For conscience' sake as well as love's.
And why? They show me every hour
Honor's high thought, Affection's power,
Discretion's deed, sound Judgment's sentence,
And teach me all things—but repentance.
                        SAMUEL BISHOP.

THE MARINER'S WIFE.

AND are ye sure the news is true?
  And are ye sure he's weel?
Is this a time to think o' wark?
  Ye jauds fling by your wheel!
Is this a time to think o' wark,
  When Colin's at the door?
Rax me my cloak, I'll to the quay
  And see him come ashore.
For there's nae luck about the house,
  There's nae luck at a';
There's little pleasure in the house
  When our gudeman's awa'.

And gie to me my bigonet,
  My bishop's satin gown;
For I maun tell the baillie's wife
  That Colin's come to town.
My Turkey slippers maun gae on,
  My hose o' pearl blue;
It's a' to pleasure my ain gudeman,
  For he's baith leal and true.

Rise up and mak a clean fireside,
  Put on the muckle pot;
Gie little Kate her Sunday gown,
  And Jock his button coat;

And mak their shoon as black as slaes,
  Their hose as white as snaw;
It's a' to please my ain gudeman,
  For he's been long awa'.

There's twa fat hens upo' the bank
  They've fed this month and mair;
Mak haste and thraw their necks about,
  That Colin weel may fare;
And spread the table neat and clean,
  Gar ilka thing look braw;
For wha can tell how Colin fared
  When he was far awa'?

Sae true his heart, sae smooth his speech,
  His breath like caller air;
His very foot has music in't
  As he comes up the stair.
And will I see his face again?
  And will I hear him speak?
I'm downright dizzy wi' the thought,
  In troth I'm like to greet!

Since Colin's weel, I'm weel content,
  I hae nae mair to crave:
Could I but live to mak him blest,
  I'm blest aboon the lave:
And will I see his face again?
  And will I hear him speak?
I'm downright dizzy wi' the thought,
  In troth I'm like to greet.
For there's nae luck about the house,
  There's nae luck at a';
There's little pleasure in the house
  When our gudeman's awa'.
                    JEAN ADAM.

THE EXILE TO HIS WIFE.

COME to me, dearest, I'm lonely without thee,
Day-time and night-time, I'm thinking about thee;
Night-time and day-time, in dreams I behold thee;
Unwelcome the waking which ceases to fold thee.
Come to me, darling, my sorrows to lighten;
Come in thy beauty to bless and to brighten;
Come in thy womanhood, meekly and lowly,
Come in thy lovingness, queenly and holy.

Swallows will flit round the desolate ruin,
Telling of spring and its joyous renewing,
And thoughts of thy love, and its manifold treasure,
Are circling my heart with a promise of pleasure.
O Spring of my spirit! O May of my bosom!
Shine out on my soul, till it bourgeon and blossom;
The waste of my life has a rose-root within it,
And thy fondness alone to the sunshine can win it.

Figure that moves like a song through the even;
Features lit up by a reflex of heaven;
Eyes like the skies of poor Erin, our mother,
Where shadow and sunshine are chasing each other;
Smiles coming seldom, but childlike and simple,
Planting in each rosy cheek a sweet dimple;—
Oh, thanks to the Saviour, that even thy seeming
Is left to the exile to brighten his dreaming!

You have been glad when you knew I was gladden'd;
Dear, are you sad now to hear I am sadden'd?
Our hearts ever answer in tune and in time, love,
As octave to octave, and rhyme unto rhyme, love:
I cannot weep but your tears will be flowing,
You cannot smile but my cheek will be glowing;
I would not die without you at my side, love;
You will not linger when I shall have died, love.

Come to me, dear, ere I die of my sorrow,
Rise on my gloom like the sun of to-morrow;
Strong, swift, and fond as the words which I speak, love,
With a song on your lip and a smile on your cheek, love.

Come, for my heart in your absence is weary,—
Haste, for my spirit is sicken'd and dreary,—
Come to the arms which alone should caress thee,
Come to the heart that is throbbing to press thee!
JOSEPH BRENAN.

A WIFE.

THE wife sat thoughtfully turning over
  A book inscribed with the school-girl's name;
A tear, one tear, fell hot on the cover
  So quickly closed when her husband came.

He came, and he went away, it was nothing;
  With commonplace upon either side;
But, just as the sound of the room-door shutting,
  A dreadful door in her soul stood wide.

Love she had read of in sweet romances,
  Love that could sorrow, but never fail;
Built her own palace of noble fancies,
  All the wide world like a fairy tale.

Bleak and bitter and utterly doleful,
  Spread to this woman her map of life:
Hour after hour she look'd in her soul, full
  Of deep dismay and turbulent strife.

Face in hands, she knelt on the carpet;
  The cloud was loosen'd, the storm-rain fell.
Oh life has so much to wither and warp it,
  One poor heart's day what poet could tell?
WILLIAM ALLINGHAM.

WITHOUT AND WITHIN.

I.

THE night is dark, and the winter winds
  Go stabbing about with their icy spears;
The sharp hail rattles against the panes,
  And melts on my cheeks like tears.

'Tis a terrible night to be out of doors,
  But some of us must be, early and late;
We needn't ask who, for don't we know
  It has all been settled by Fate?

Not woman, but man. Give woman her flowers,
  Her dresses, her jewels, or what she demands:
The work of the world must be done by man,
  Or why has he brawny hands?

As I feel my way in the dark and cold,
  I think of the chambers warm and bright—
The nests where these delicate birds of ours
  Are folding their wings to-night!

Through the luminous windows, above and below,
  I catch a glimpse of the life they lead:
Some sew, some sing, others dress for the ball,
  While others (fair students) read.

There's the little lady who bears my name—
  She sits at my table now, pouring her tea;
Does she think of me as I hurry home,
  Hungry and wet? Not she.

She helps herself to the sugar and cream
  In a thoughtless, dreamy, nonchalant way;
Her hands are white as the virgin rose
  That she wore on her wedding-day.

My stubbèd fingers are stain'd with ink—
  The badge of the ledger, the mark of trade;
But the money I give her is clean enough,
  In spite of the way it is made.

I wear out my life in the counting-room,
  Over day-book and cash-book, Bought and Sold;
My brain is dizzy with anxious thought,
  My skin is as sallow as gold.

How does she keep the roses of youth
  Still fresh in her cheeks? My roses are flown.
It lies in a nutshell: why do I ask?
  A woman's life is her own.

She gives me a kiss when we part for the day,
   Then goes to her music, blithe as a bird;
She reads it at sight, and the language too,
   Though I know never a word.

She sews — a little; makes collars and sleeves;
   Or embroiders me slippers (always too small);
Nets silken purses (for me to fill)—
   Often does nothing at all

But dream in her chamber, holding a flower,
   Or reading my letters (she'd better read me)!
Even now, while I am freezing with cold,
   She is cozily sipping her tea.

If I ever reach home I shall laugh aloud
   At the sight of a roaring fire once more;
She must wait, I think, till I thaw myself,
   For the usual kiss at the door.

I'll have with my dinner a bottle of port,
   To warm up my blood and soothe my mind;
Then a little music, for even I
   Like music—when I have dined.

I'll smoke a pipe in the easy-chair,
   And feel her behind me patting my head;
Or, drawing the little one on my knee,
   Chat till the hour for bed.

II.

Will he never come? I have watch'd for him
   Till the misty panes are roughen'd with sleet;
I can see no more: shall I never hear
   The welcome sound of his feet?

I think of him in the lonesome night,
   Tramping along with a weary tread,
And wish he were here by the cheery fire,
   Or I were there in his stead.

I sit by the grate, and hark for his step,
   And stare in the fire with a troubled mind;
The glow of the coals is bright in my face,
   But my shadow is dark behind.

I think of woman, and think of man,
   The tie that binds, and the wrongs that part,
And long to utter in burning words
   What I feel to-night in my heart.

No weak complaint of the man I love,
   No praise of myself or my sisterhood;
But—something that women understand,
   By men never understood.

Their natures jar in a thousand things;
   Little matter, alas! who is right or wrong.
She goes to the wall. "*She is weak!*" they say;
   It is that that makes them strong.

But grant us weak (as in truth we are
   In our love for them), they should make us strong;
But do they? Will they? "WOMAN IS WEAK!"
   Is the burden still of their song.

Wherein am I weaker than Arthur, pray?
   He has, as he should, a sturdier frame,
And he labors early and late for me:
   But I—I could do the same.

My hands are willing, my brain is clear,
   The world is wide, and the workers few;
But the work of the world belongs to man;
   There is nothing for woman to do.

Yes, she has the holy duties of home,
   A husband to love, and children to bear;
The softer virtues, the social arts—
   In short, a life without care.

So our masters say. But what do they know
   Of our lives and feelings when they are away?
Our household duties, our petty tasks,
   The nothings that waste the day?

Nay, what do they care? 'Tis enough for them
   That their homes are pleasant; they seek their ease:
One takes a wife to flatter his pride;
   Another, to keep his keys.

They say they love us; perhaps they do,
   In a masculine way, as they love their wine;

But the soul of a woman needs something
    more,
      Or it suffers at times like mine.

Not that Arthur is ever unkind
    In word or deed, for he loves me well;
But I fear he thinks me weak as the rest—
    (And I may be: who can tell?)

I should die if he changed or loved me less,
    For I live at best but a restless life;
Yet he may, for they say the kindest men
    Grow tired of a sickly wife.

Oh, love me, Arthur, my lord, my life!
    If not for my love and my womanly
      fears,
At least for your child. But I hear his
    step—
      He must not find me in tears.
              RICHARD HENRY STODDARD.

THE POET'S SONG TO HIS WIFE.

How many summers, love,
    Have I been thine?
How many days, my dove,
    Hast thou been mine?
Time, like the wingèd wind
    When 't bends the flowers,
Hath left no mark behind,
    To count the hours!

Some weight of thought, though loath,
    On thee he leaves;
Some lines of care round both
    Perhaps he weaves;
Some fears,—a soft regret
    For joys scarce known;
Sweet looks we half forget;
    All else is flown!

Ah! with what thankless heart
    I mourn and sing!
Look, where our children start,
    Like sudden spring!
With tongues all sweet and low,
    Like a pleasant rhyme,
They tell how much I owe
    To thee and Time!
            BRYAN WALLER PROCTER
              (BARRY CORNWALL).

TO AN ABSENT WIFE.

WRITTEN AT BILOXI.

'TIS Morn:—the sea-breeze seems to bring
Joy, health, and freshness on its wing;
Bright flowers, to me all strange and new,
Are glittering in the early dew,
And perfumes rise from every grove,
As incense to the clouds that move
Like spirits o'er yon welkin clear:
But I am sad—thou art not here!

'Tis Noon:—a calm, unbroken sleep
Is on the blue waves of the deep;
A soft haze, like a fairy dream,
Is floating over wood and stream;
And many a broad magnolia flower,
Within its shadowy woodland bower,
Is gleaming like a lovely star:
But I am sad—thou art afar!

'Tis Eve:—on earth the sunset skies
Are painting their own Eden dyes;
The stars come down, and trembling glow
Like blossoms on the waves below,
And, like an unseen spirit, the breeze
Seems lingering 'midst these orange trees,
Breathing its music round the spot:
But I am sad—I see thee not!

'Tis Midnight:—with a soothing spell,
The far tones of the ocean swell,
Soft as a mother's cadence mild,
Low bending o'er her sleeping child;
And on each wandering breeze are heard
The rich notes of the mocking-bird,
In many a wild and wondrous lay:
But I am sad—thou art away!

I sink in dreams:—low, sweet, and clear,
Thy own dear voice is in my ear;
Around my neck thy tresses twine—
Thy own loved hand is clasped in mine—
Thy own soft lip to mine is pressed—
Thy head is pillowed on my breast:—
Oh! I have all my heart holds dear,
And I am happy—thou art here!
            GEORGE DENNISON PRENTICE.

FARE THEE WELL!

Fare thee well! and if for ever,
  Still for ever, fare *thee well:*
Even though unforgiving, never
  'Gainst thee shall my heart rebel.

Would that breast were bared before thee
  Where thy head so oft hath lain,
While that placid sleep came o'er thee
  Which thou ne'er canst know again!

Would that breast, by thee glanced over,
  Every inmost thought could show!
Then thou wouldst at last discover
  'Twas not well to spurn it so.

Though the world for this commend thee,—
  Though it smile upon the blow,
Even its praises must offend thee,
  Founded on another's woe:

Though my many faults defaced me,
  Could no other arm be found,
Than the one which once embraced me,
  To inflict a cureless wound?

Yet, oh yet, thyself deceive not:
  Love may sink by slow decay,
But by sudden wrench, believe not
  Hearts can thus be torn away:

Still thine own its life retaineth,—
  Still must mine, though bleeding, beat;
And the undying thought which paineth
  Is—that we no more may meet.

These are words of deeper sorrow
  Than the wail above the dead;
Both shall live, but every morrow
  Wake us from a widowed bed.

And when thou wouldst solace gather,
  When our child's first accents flow,
Wilt thou teach her to say "Father!"
  Though his care she must forego?

When her little hands shall press thee,
  When her lip to thine is pressed,
Think of him whose prayer shall bless thee,
  Think of him thy love had blessed!

Should her lineaments resemble
  Those thou nevermore mayst see,
Then thy heart will softly tremble
  With a pulse yet true to me.

All my faults perchance thou knowest,
  All my madness none can know;
All my hopes, where'er thou goest,
  Wither, yet with *thee* they go.

Every feeling hath been shaken;
  Pride, which not a world could bow,
Bows to thee,—by thee forsaken,
  Even my soul forsakes me now:

But 'tis done: all words are idle,—
  Words from me are vainer still;
But the thoughts we cannot bridle
  Force their way without the will.

Fare thee well!—thus disunited,
  Torn from every nearer tie,
Seared in heart, and lone, and blighted,
  More than this I scarce can die.
                Lord Byron.

ON THE RECEIPT OF MY MOTHER'S PICTURE.

Oh that those lips had language! Life has pass'd
With me but roughly since I heard thee last.
Those lips are thine—thy own sweet smile I see,
The same that oft in childhood solaced me;
Voice only fails, else how distinct they say,
"Grieve not, my child, chase all thy fears away!"
The meek intelligence of those dear eyes
(Blest be the Art that can immortalize,—
The Art that baffles Time's tyrannic claim
To quench it!) here shines on me still the same.
  Faithful remembrancer of one so dear,
O welcome guest, though unexpected, here!
Who bidst me honor with an artless song,
Affectionate, a mother lost so long.
I will obey, not willingly alone,
But gladly, as the precept were her own;
And while that face renews my filial grief,
Fancy shall weave a charm for my relief,—
Shall steep me in Elysian reverie,
A momentary dream, that thou art she.
  My mother! when I learn'd that thou wast dead,
Say, wast thou conscious of the tears I shed?
Hover'd thy spirit o'er thy sorrowing son,
Wretch even then, life's journey just begun?

Perhaps thou gav'st me, though unfelt, a kiss;
Perhaps a tear, if souls can weep in bliss—
Ah, that maternal smile!—it answers—Yes.
I heard the bell toll'd on thy burial-day,
I saw the hearse that bore thee slow away,
And, turning from my nursery window, drew
A long, long sigh, and wept a last adieu!
But was it such?—It was.—Where thou art gone
Adieus and farewells are a sound unknown.
May I but meet thee on that peaceful shore,
The parting words shall pass my lips no more!
Thy maidens, grieved themselves at my concern,
Oft gave me promise of thy quick return.
What ardently I wish'd, I long believed,
And disappointed still, was still deceived;
By expectation every day beguiled,
Dupe of to-morrow even from a child.
Thus many a sad to-morrow came and went,
Till, all my stock of infant sorrows spent,
I learn'd at last submission to my lot,
But, though I less deplored thee, ne'er forgot.
  Where once we dwelt our name is heard no more,
Children not thine have trod my nursery floor;
And where the gardener Robin, day by day,
Drew me to school along the public way,
Delighted with my bauble coach, and wrapt
In scarlet mantle warm, and velvet-capt,
'Tis now become a history little known,
That once we call'd the pastoral house our own.
Short-lived possession! But the record fair,
That memory keeps of all thy kindness there,
Still outlives many a storm, that has effaced
A thousand other themes less deeply traced.
Thy nightly visits to my chamber made,
That thou mightst know me safe and warmly laid;
Thy morning bounties ere I left my home,
The biscuit, or confectionery plum;
The fragrant waters on my cheeks bestow'd
By thy own hand, till fresh they shone and glow'd;
All this, and, more endearing still than all,
Thy constant flow of love, that knew no fall,
Ne'er roughen'd by those cataracts and breaks
That humor interposed too often makes;
All this, still legible in memory's page,
And still to be so to my latest age,
Adds joy to duty, makes me glad to pay
Such honors to thee as my numbers may;
Perhaps a frail memorial, but sincere,
Not scorn'd in heaven, though little noticed here.
  Could Time, his flight reversed, restore the hours,
When playing with thy vesture's tissued flowers,
The violet, the pink, and jessamine,
I prick'd them into paper with a pin
(And thou wast happier than myself the while,
Wouldst softly speak, and stroke my head, and smile),—
Could those few pleasant days again appear,
Might one wish bring them, would I wish them here?
I would not trust my heart; the dear delight
Seems so to be desired, perhaps I might.
But no—what here we call our life is such,
So little to be loved, and thou so much,
That I should ill requite thee to constrain
Thy unbound spirit into bonds again.
  Thou, as a gallant bark from Albion's coast
(The storms all weather'd and the ocean cross'd),
Shoots into port at some well-haven'd isle,
Where spices breathe, and brighter seasons smile,
There sits quiescent on the floods, that show
Her beauteous form reflected clear below,
While airs impregnated with incense play
Around her, fanning light her streamers gay;

So thou, with sails how swift! hast reach'd
  the shore,
"Where tempests never beat nor billows
  roar;"
And thy loved consort on the dangerous
  tide
Of life long since has anchor'd by thy
  side.
But me, scarce hoping to attain that rest,
Always from port withheld, always dis-
  tress'd,—
Me howling blasts drive devious, tempest-
  toss'd,
Sails ripp'd, seams opening wide, and com-
  pass lost,
And day by day some current's thwarting
  force
Sets me more distant from a prosperous
  course.
Yet oh, the thought that thou art safe,
  and he!
That thought is joy, arrive what may to me.
My boast is not that I deduce my birth
From loins enthroned and rulers of the
  earth,
But higher far my proud pretensions
  rise,—
The son of parents pass'd into the skies.
And now, farewell!—Time unrevoked has
  run
His wonted course, yet what I wish'd is
  done.
By contemplation's help, not sought in
  vain,
I seem to have lived my childhood o'er
  again;
To have renew'd the joys that once were
  mine,
Without the sin of violating thine;
And, while the wings of fancy still are
  free,
And I can view this mimic show of thee,
Time has but half succeeded in his theft,—
Thyself removed, thy power to soothe me
  left.
WILLIAM COWPER.

TOO LATE.

"Dowglas, Dowglas, tendir and treu."

COULD ye come back to me, Douglas,
    Douglas,
  In the old likeness that I knew,
I would be so faithful, so loving, Douglas,
  Douglas, Douglas, tender and true.

Never a scornful word should grieve ye,
  I'd smile on ye sweet as the angels do;—
Sweet as your smile on me shone ever,
  Douglas, Douglas, tender and true.

Oh to call back the days that are not!
  My eyes were blinded, your words were
    few;
Do you know the truth now up in heaven,
  Douglas, Douglas, tender and true?

I never was worthy of you, Douglas;
  Not half worthy the like of you;
Now all men beside seem to me like
    shadows—
  I love *you*, Douglas, tender and true.

Stretch out your hand to me, Douglas,
    Douglas,
  Drop forgiveness from heaven like dew;
As I lay my heart on your dead heart,
    Douglas,
  Douglas, Douglas, tender and true.
DINAH MULOCK CRAIK.

THE FAMILY MEETING.

  WE are all here,
    Father, mother,
    Sister, brother,
  All who hold each other dear.
Each chair is fill'd; we're all at home!
To-night let no cold stranger come.
  It is not often thus around
  Our old familiar hearth we're found.
Bless, then, the meeting and the spot;
For once be every care forgot;
Let gentle Peace assert her power,
And kind Affection rule the hour.
  We're all—all here.

  We're not all here!
Some are away,—the dead ones dear,
Who throng'd with us this ancient hearth,
And gave the hour to guileless mirth.
Fate, with a stern, relentless hand,
Look'd in, and thinn'd our little band;
Some like a night-flash pass'd away,
And some sank lingering day by day;
The quiet graveyard,—some lie there.—
And cruel Ocean has his share.
  We're not all here.

We are all here!
Even they,—the dead,—though dead, so
  dear,—
Fond Memory, to her duty true,
Brings back their faded forms to view.
How life-like, through the mist of years,
Each well-remember'd face appears!
We see them, as in times long past;
From each to each kind looks are cast;
We hear their words, their smiles behold;
They're round us, as they were of old.
  We are all here.

  We are all here,
    Father, mother,
    Sister, brother,
You that I love with love so dear.
This may not long of us be said;
Soon must we join the gather'd dead,
And by the hearth we now sit round
Some other circle will be found.
Oh, then, that wisdom may we know,
Which yields a life of peace below!
So, in the world to follow this,
May each repeat in words of bliss,
  We're all—all here!
CHARLES SPRAGUE.

THE POET'S BRIDAL-DAY SONG.

OH, my love's like the steadfast sun,
Or streams that deepen as they run;
Nor hoary hairs, nor forty years,
Nor moments between sighs and tears—
Nor nights of thought, nor days of pain,
Nor dreams of glory dream'd in vain—
Nor mirth, nor sweetest song that flows
To sober joys and soften woes,
Can make my heart or fancy flee
One moment, my sweet wife, from thee.

Even while I muse I see thee sit
In maiden bloom and matron wit—
Fair, gentle as when first I sued,
Ye seem, but of sedater mood;
Yet my heart leaps as fond for thee
As when, beneath Arbigland tree,
We stay'd and woo'd, and thought the
  moon
Set on the sea an hour too soon;
Or linger'd 'mid the falling dew,
When looks were fond and words were
  few.

Though I see smiling at thy feet
Five sons and ae fair daughter sweet;
And time, and care, and birth-time woes
Have dimm'd thine eye and touch'd thy rose;
To thee, and thoughts of thee belong
Whate'er charms me in tale or song;
When words descend like dews unsought
With gleams of deep, enthusiast thought,
And Fancy in her heaven flies free—
They come, my love, they come from thee.

Oh, when more thought we gave of old
To silver than some give to gold,
'Twas sweet to sit and ponder o'er
How we should deck our humble bower!
'Twas sweet to pull in hope with thee
The golden fruit of Fortune's tree;
And sweeter still to choose and twine
A garland for that brow of thine—
A song-wreath which may grace my Jean,
While rivers flow and woods grow green.

At times there come, as come there ought,
Grave moments of sedater thought—
When Fortune frowns, nor lends our night
One gleam of her inconstant light;
And Hope, that decks the peasant's bower,
Shines like a rainbow through the shower—
Oh, then I see, while seated nigh,
A mother's heart shine in thine eye;
And proud resolve and purpose meek,
Speak of thee more than words can speak:
I think this wedded wife of mine
The best of all things not divine.
ALLAN CUNNINGHAM.

OLD FOLKS AT HOME.

'WAY down upon de Swannee Ribber,
  Far, far away,—
Dare's wha my heart is turning ebber,—
  Dare's wha de old folks stay.
All up and down de whole creation
  Sadly I roam;
Still longing for de old plantation,
  And for de old folks at home.
    All de world am sad and dreary
      Eb'rywhere I roam;
    Oh, darkeys, how my heart grows weary,
      Far from de old folks at home!

All 'round de little farm I wander'd
    When I was young;
Den many happy days I squander'd,—
    Many de songs I sung.
When I was playing wid my brudder,
    Happy was I;
Oh, take me to my kind old mudder!
    Dare let me live and die!
      All de world am sad and dreary
        Eb'rywhere I roam;
      Oh, darkeys, how my heart grows weary,
        Far from de old folks at home!

One little hut among de bushes,—
    One dat I love,—
Still sadly to my mem'ry rushes,
    No matter where I rove.
When will I see de bees a-humming
    All round de comb?
When will I hear de banjo tumming
    Down in my good old home?
      All de world am sad and dreary
        Eb'rywhere I roam;
      Oh, darkeys, how my heart grows weary,
        Far from de old folks at home!
            STEPHEN C. FOSTER.

SONGS OF SEVEN.

SEVEN TIMES ONE.

EXULTATION.

THERE'S no dew left on the daisies and
    clover,
    There's no rain left in heaven:
I've said my "seven times" over and over,
    Seven times one are seven.

I am old, so old, I can write a letter;
    My birthday lessons are done;
The lambs play always, they know no
    better;
    They are only one times one.

O moon! in the night I have seen you
    sailing
    And shining so round and low;
You were bright! ah bright! but your
    light is failing,—
    You are nothing now but a bow.

You moon, have you done something
    wrong in heaven
    That God has hidden your face?
I hope if you have you will soon be for-
    given,
    And shine again in your place.

O velvet bee, you're a dusty fellow,
    You've powder'd your legs with gold!
O brave marshmary buds, rich and yellow,
    Give me your money to hold!

O columbine, open your folded wrapper,
    Where two twin turtle-doves dwell!
O cuckoopint, toll me the purple clapper
    That hangs in your clear green bell!

And show me your nest with the young
    ones in it;
    I will not steal them away;
I am old! you may trust me, linnet, lin-
    net,—
    I am seven times one to-day.

SEVEN TIMES TWO.

ROMANCE.

YOU bells in the steeple, ring, ring out
    your changes,
    How many soever they be,
And let the brown meadow-lark's note as
    he ranges
    Come over, come over to me.

Yet bird's clearest carol by fall or by
    swelling
    No magical sense conveys,
And bells have forgotten their old art of
    telling
    The fortune of future days.

"Turn again, turn again," once they rang
    cheerily,
    While a boy listen'd alone;
Made his heart yearn again, musing so
    wearily
    All by himself on a stone.

Poor bells! I forgive you; your good
    days are over,
    And mine, they are yet to be;
No listening, no longing shall aught, aught
    discover:
    You leave the story to me.

The foxglove shoots out of the green mat-
    ted heather,
    Preparing her hoods of snow;

She was idle, and slept till the sunshiny
    weather:
    Oh, children take long to grow.

I wish, and I wish that the spring would
    go faster,
    Nor long summer bide so late;
And I could grow on like the foxglove and
    aster,
    For some things are ill to wait.

I wait for the day when dear hearts shall
    discover,
    While dear hands are laid on my head;
"The child is a woman, the book may
    close over,
    For all the lessons are said."

I wait for my story—the birds cannot sing it,
    Not one, as he sits on the tree;
The bells cannot ring it, but long years, oh
    bring it!
    Such as I wish it to be.

SEVEN TIMES THREE.
LOVE.

I LEAN'D out of window, I smelt the
    white clover,
    Dark, dark was the garden, I saw not
    the gate;
"Now, if there be footsteps, he comes, my
    one lover—
    Hush nightingale, hush! O sweet night-
    ingale, wait
        Till I listen and hear
        If a step draweth near,
    For my love he is late!

"The skies in the darkness stoop nearer
    and nearer,
    A cluster of stars hangs like fruit in the
    tree,
The fall of the water comes sweeter, comes
    clearer:
    To what art thou listening, and what
    dost thou see?
        Let the star-clusters glow,
        Let the sweet waters flow,
    And cross quickly to me.

" You night-moths that hover where honey
    brims over
    From sycamore blossoms, or settle or
    sleep;

You glow-worms, shine out, and the path-
    way discover
    To him that comes darkling along the
    rough steep.
        Ah, my sailor, make haste,
        For the time runs to waste,
    And my love lieth deep—

" Too deep for swift telling; and yet, my
    one lover,
    I've conn'd thee an answer, it waits thee
    to-night."
By the sycamore pass'd he, and through
    the white clover,
    Then all the sweet speech I had fashion'd
    took flight;
        But I'll love him more, more
        Than e'er wife loved before,
    Be the days dark or bright.

SEVEN TIMES FOUR.
MATERNITY.

HEIGH-HO! daisies and buttercups,
    Fair yellow daffodils, stately and tall!
When the wind wakes how they rock in
    the grasses,
    And dance with the cuckoo-buds slender
    and small!
Here's two bonny boys, and here's mother's
    own lasses,
    Eager to gather them all.

Heigh-ho! daisies and buttercups!
    Mother shall thread them a daisy chain;
Sing them a song of the pretty hedge-
    sparrow,
    That loved her brown little ones, loved
    them full fain;
Sing, "Heart, thou art wide, though the
    house be but narrow,"—
    Sing once, and sing it again.

Heigh-ho! daisies and buttercups,
    Sweet wagging cowslips, they bend and
    they bow;
A ship sails afar over warm ocean waters,
    And haply one musing doth stand at her
    prow.
O bonny brown sons, and O sweet little
    daughters,
    Maybe he thinks on you now!

Heigh-ho! daisies and buttercups,
    Fair yellow daffodils, stately and tall—

A sunshiny world full of laughter and
    leisure,
And fresh hearts unconscious of sorrow
    and thrall!
Send down on their pleasure smiles passing
    its measure,
        God that is over us all!

SEVEN TIMES FIVE.
WIDOWHOOD.

I SLEEP and rest, my heart makes moan
    Before I am well awake;
"Let me bleed! oh let me alone,
    Since I must not break!"

For children wake, though fathers sleep
    With a stone at foot and at head;
O sleepless God, for ever keep,
    Keep both living and dead!

I lift mine eyes, and what to see
    But a world happy and fair?
I have not wish'd it to mourn with me—
    Comfort is not there.

Oh, what anear but golden brooms,
    And a waste of reedy rills!
Oh, what afar but the fine glooms
    On the rare blue hills!

I shall not die, but live forlorn;
    How bitter it is to part!
Oh, to meet thee, my love, once more!
    Oh, my heart, my heart!

No more to hear, no more to see;
    Oh, that an echo might wake,
And waft one note of thy psalm to me
    Ere my heart-strings break!

I should know it how faint soe'er,
    And with angel-voices blent;
Oh, once to feel thy spirit anear,
    I could be content!

Or once between the gates of gold,
    While an angel entering trod,
But once—thee sitting to behold
    On the hills of God!

SEVEN TIMES SIX.
GIVING IN MARRIAGE.

To bear, to nurse, to rear,
    To watch, and then to lose:
To see my bright ones disappear,
    Drawn up like morning dews;

To bear, to nurse, to rear,
    To watch, and then to lose:
This have I done when God drew near
    Among his own to choose.

To hear, to heed, to wed,
    And with thy Lord depart
In tears that he, as soon as shed,
    Will let no longer smart;
To hear, to heed, to wed,
    This while thou didst I smiled,
For now it was not God who said,
    "Mother, give ME thy child."

Oh, fond, oh, fool, and blind,
    To God I gave with tears;
But when a man like grace would find,
    My soul put by her fears.
Oh, fond, oh, fool, and blind,
    God guards in happier spheres;
That man will guard where he did bind
    Is hope for unknown years.

To hear, to heed, to wed,
    Fair lot that maidens choose,
Thy mother's tenderest words are said,
    Thy face no more she views;
Thy mother's lot, my dear,
    She doth in naught accuse;
Her lot to bear, to nurse, to rear,
    To love,—and then to lose.

SEVEN TIMES SEVEN.
LONGING FOR HOME.

A SONG of a boat:—
    There was once a boat on a billow:
Lightly she rock'd to her port remote,
And the foam was white in her wake like
    snow,
And her frail mast bow'd when the breeze
    would blow,
    And bent like a wand of willow.

I shaded mine eyes one day when a boat
    Went curtseying over the billow,
I mark'd her course till a dancing mote
She faded out on the moonlit foam,
And I stay'd behind in the dear loved home;
    And my thoughts all day were about the
    boat
    And my dreams upon the pillow.

I pray you hear my song of a boat,
    For it is but short:—
My boat, you shall find none fairer afloat,
    In river or port.
Long I look'd out for the lad she bore,
    On the open desolate sea,
And I think he sail'd to the heavenly
      shore,
    For he came not back to me—
                Ah me!

A song of a nest:—
    There was once a nest in a hollow:
Down in the mosses and knot-grass press'd,
    Soft and warm, and full to the brim.
Vetches lean'd over it purple and dim,
    With buttercup buds to follow.

I pray you hear my song of a nest,
    For it is not long:—
You shall never light, in a summer quest,
    The bushes among—
Shall never light on a prouder sitter,
    A fairer nestful, nor ever know
A softer sound than their tender twitter,
    That wind-like did come and go.

I had a nestful once of my own,
    Ah happy, happy I!
Right dearly I loved them: but when they
      were grown
    They spread out their wings to fly.
Oh, one after one they flew away
    Far up to the heavenly blue,
To the better country, the upper day,
    And—I wish I was going too.

I pray you, what is the nest to me,
    My empty nest?
And what is the shore where I stood to see
    My boat sail down to the west?
Can I call that home where I anchor
      yet,
    Though my good man has sail'd?
Can I call that home where my nest was
      set,
    Now all its hope hath fail'd?
Nay, but the port where my sailor went,
    And the land where my nestlings be,—
There is the home where my thoughts
      are sent,
    The only home for me—
                Ah me!
            JEAN INGELOW.

THE QUAKER WIDOW.

THEE finds me in the garden, Hannah,—
    come in! 'Tis kind of thee
To wait until the Friends were gone, who
    came to comfort me.
The still and quiet company a peace may
    give, indeed,
But blessed is the single heart that comes
    to us at need.

Come, sit thee down! Here is the bench
    where Benjamin would sit
On the First-day afternoons in spring, and
    watch the swallows flit;
He loved to smell the sprouting box, and
    hear the pleasant bees
Go humming round the lilacs and through
    the apple trees.

I think he loved the spring: not that he
    cared for flowers; most men
Think such things foolishness,—but we
    were first acquainted then,
One spring: the next he spoke his mind;
    the third I was his wife,
And in the spring (it happen'd so) our
    children enter'd life.

He was but seventy-five: I did not think
    to lay him yet
In Kennett graveyard, where at Monthly
    Meeting first we met.
The Father's mercy shows in this: 'tis
    better I should be
Pick'd out to bear the heavy cross—alone
    in age—than he.

We've lived together fifty years: it seems
    but one long day,
One quiet Sabbath of the heart, till he was
    call'd away;
And as we bring from Meeting-time a
    sweet contentment home,
So, Hannah, I have store of peace for all
    the days to come.

I mind (for I can tell thee now) how hard
    it was to know
If I had heard the Spirit right, that told
    me I should go;

For father had a deep concern upon his
  mind that day,
But mother spoke for Benjamin,—she knew
  what best to say.

Then she was still: they sat a while: at last
  she spoke again,
"The Lord incline thee to the right!" and
  "Thou shalt have him, Jane!"
My father said. I cried. Indeed, 'twas
  not the least of shocks,
For Benjamin was Hicksite, and father
  Orthodox.

I thought of this ten years ago, when
  daughter Ruth we lost:
Her husband's of the world, and yet I
  could not see her cross'd.
She wears, thee knows, the gayest gowns,
  she hears a hireling priest—
Ah, dear! the cross was ours: her life's a
  happy one, at least.

Perhaps she'll wear a plainer dress when
  she's as old as I,—
Would thee believe it, Hannah? once *I*
  felt temptation nigh!
My wedding-gown was ashen silk, too
  simple for my taste:
I wanted lace around the neck, and a rib-
  bon at the waist.

How strange it seem'd to sit with him
  upon the women's side!
I did not dare to lift my eyes: I felt more
  fear than pride,
Till, "in the presence of the Lord," he
  said, and then there came
A holy strength upon my heart, and I
  could say the same.

I used to blush when he came near, but
  then I show'd no sign;
With all the meeting looking on, I held
  his hand in mine.
It seem'd my bashfulness was gone, now I
  was his for life:
Thee knows the feeling, Hannah,—thee,
  too, hast been a wife.

As home we rode, I saw no fields look
  half so green as ours;
The woods were coming into leaf, the
  meadows full of flowers;

The neighbors met us in the lane, and
  every face was kind,—
'Tis strange how lively everything comes
  back upon my mind.

I see, as plain as thee sits there, the wed-
  ding-dinner spread:
At our own table we were guests, with
  father at the head,
And Dinah Passmore help'd us both—
  'twas she stood up with me,
And Abner Jones with Benjamin,—and
  now they're gone, all three!

It is not right to wish for death; the Lord
  disposes best.
His Spirit comes to quiet hearts, and fits
  them for His rest;
And that He halved our little flock was
  merciful, I see:
For Benjamin has two in heaven, and two
  are left with me.

Eusebius never cared to farm,—'twas not
  his call, in truth,
And I must rent the dear old place, and
  go to daughter Ruth.
Thee'll say her ways are not like mine,—
  young people now-a-days
Have fallen sadly off, I think, from all the
  good old ways.

But Ruth is still a Friend at heart; she
  keeps the simple tongue,
The cheerful, kindly nature we loved when
  she was young;
And it was brought upon my mind, remem-
  bering her, of late,
That we on dress and outward things per-
  haps lay too much weight.

I once heard Jesse Kersey say, a spirit
  clothed with grace,
And pure, almost, as angels are, may have
  a homely face.
And dress may be of less account: the
  Lord will look within:
The soul it is that testifies of righteousness
  or sin.

Thee mustn't be too hard on Ruth: she's
  anxious I should go,
And she will do her duty as a daughter
  should, I know.

'Tis hard to change so late in life, but we
    must be resign'd:
The Lord looks down contentedly upon a
    willing mind.
BAYARD TAYLOR.

LOVE LIGHTENS LABOR.

A GOOD wife rose from her bed one morn,
    And thought, with a nervous dread,
Of the piles of clothes to be washed, and
    more
    Than a dozen mouths to be fed.
"There's the meals to get for the men in
    the field,
    And the children to fix away
To school, and the milk to be skimmed and
    churned;
    And all to be done this day."

It had rained in the night, and all the
    wood
    Was wet as it could be;
There were puddings and pies to bake, be-
    sides
    A loaf of cake for tea.
And the day was hot, and her aching head
    Throbbed wearily as she said,
"If *maidens* but knew what *good wives* know,
    They would not be in haste to *wed!*"

"Jennie, what do you think I told Ben
    Brown?"
    Called the farmer from the well;
And a flush crept up to his bronzèd brow,
    And his eyes half-bashfully fell.
"It was this," he said, and coming near
    He smiled, and stooping down
Kissed her cheek,—"'twas this, that you
    were the best
    And the *dearest* wife in town!"

The farmer went back to the field, and the
    wife,
    In a smiling, absent way,
Sang snatches of tender little songs
    She'd not sung for many a day.
And the pain in her head was gone, and
    the clothes
    Were white as the foam of the sea;
Her bread was light, and her butter was
    sweet,
    And as golden as it could be.

"Just think," the children all called in a
    breath,
    "Tom Wood has run off to sea!
He wouldn't, I know, if he'd only had
    As happy a home as we."
The night came down, and the good wife
    smiled
    To herself, as she softly said,
"'Tis so sweet to labor for those we love!—
    It's *not* strange that *maids will wed!*"
AUTHOR UNKNOWN.

THE HOUSEHOLD WOMAN.

GRACEFUL may seem the fairy form,
With youth, and health, and beauty warm,
Gliding along the airy dance,
Imparting joy at every glance.

And lovely, too, when o'er the strings
Her hand of music woman flings,
While dewy eyes are upward thrown,
As if from heaven to claim the tone.

And fair is she when mental flowers
Engage her soul's devoted powers,
And wreaths, unfading wreaths of mind,
Around her temples are entwined.

But never, in her varied sphere,
Is woman to the heart more dear
Than when her homely task she plies,
With cheerful duty in her eyes;
And, every lowly path well trod,
Looks meekly upward to her God.
CAROLINE GILMAN.

LEMUEL'S SONG.

WHO finds a woman good and wise,
    A gem more worth than pearls hath got;
Her husband's heart on her relies;
    To live by spoil he needeth not.
His comfort all his life is she;
    No wrong she willingly will do;
For wool and flax her searches be,
    And cheerful hands she puts thereto.

The merchant-ship, resembling right,
    Her food she from afar doth fet.
Ere day she wakes, that give she might
    Her maids their task, her household meat.
A field she views, and that she buys;
    Her hand doth plant a vineyard there;

Her loins with courage up she ties;
  Her arms with vigor strengthened are.

If in her work she profit feel,
  By night her candle goes not out:
She puts her finger to the wheel,
  Her hand the spindle turns about.
To such as poor and needy are
  Her hand (yea, both hands) reacheth she.
The winter none of hers doth fear,
  For double clothed her household be.
She mantles maketh, wrought by hand,
  And silk and purple clothing gets.
Among the rulers of the land
  (Known in the gate) her husband sits.
For sale fine linen weaveth she,
  And girdles to the merchant sends.
Renown and strength her clothing be,
  And joy her later time attends.
She speaks discreetly when she talks;
  The law of grace her tongue hath learned;
She heeds the way her household walks,
  And feedeth not on bread unearned.
Her children rise, and blest her call;
  Her husband thus applaudeth her,
"Oh, thou hast far surpassed them all,
  Though many daughters thriving are!"

Deceitful favor quickly wears,
  And beauty suddenly decays;
But, if the Lord she truly fears,
  That woman well deserveth praise,
The fruit her handiwork obtains:
  Without repining grant her that,
And yield her when her labor gains,
  To do her honor in the gate.
                GEORGE WITHER.

THE SAILOR'S WIFE.

PART I.

I'VE a letter from thy sire,
  Baby mine, baby mine;
I can read and never tire,
  Baby mine.
  He is sailing o'er the sea,
  He is coming back to thee,
  He is coming home to me,
    Baby mine.

He's been parted from us long,
  Baby mine, baby mine;
But if hearts be true and strong,
  Baby mine,
They shall brave Misfortune's blast,
  And be overpaid at last
For all pain and sorrow pass'd,
  Baby mine.

Oh, I long to see his face,
  Baby mine, baby mine,
In his old-accustom'd place,
  Baby mine.
  Like the rose of May in bloom,
  Like a star amid the gloom,
  Like the sunshine in the room,
    Baby mine.

Thou wilt see him and rejoice,
  Baby mine, baby mine;
Thou wilt know him by his voice,
  Baby mine,
By his love-looks that endear,
By his laughter ringing clear,
By his eyes that know not fear,
  Baby mine.

I'm so glad—I cannot sleep,
  Baby mine, baby mine.
I'm so happy—I could weep,
  Baby mine.
  He is sailing o'er the sea,
  He is coming home to me,
  He is coming back to thee,
    Baby mine.

PART II.

O'er the blue ocean gleaming
  She sees a distant ship,
    As small to view
    As the white sea-mew
  Whose wings in the billows dip.
"Blow, favoring gales, in her answering sails,
Blow steadily and free!
  Rejoicing, strong,
  Singing a song
  Her rigging and her spars among,
  And waft the vessel in pride along
That bears my love to me."

Nearer, still nearer driving,
  The white sails grow and swell;
    Clear to her eyes
    The pennant flies,
  And the flag she knows so well.

"Blow, favoring gales, in her answering
    sails.
  Waft him, O gentle sea!
  And still, O heart,
    Thy fluttering start!
  Why throb and beat as thou wouldst
    part,
  When all so happy and bless'd thou
    art?
  He comes again to thee!"

The swift ship drops her anchor,
  A boat puts off for shore;
    Against its prow
    The ripples flow
  To the music of the oar.
"And art thou here, mine own, my dear,
  Safe from the perilous sea?
  Safe, safe at home,
  No more to roam!
  Blow, tempests, blow; my love has
    come!
  And sprinkle the clouds with your
    dashing foam!
  He shall part no more from me."
                                CHARLES MACKAY.

MOTHER AND POET.

DEAD! One of them shot by the sea in
    the East,
  And one of them shot in the West by
    the sea.
Dead! both my boys! When you sit at
    the feast
  And are wanting a great song for Italy
    free,
    Let none look at *me!*

Yet I was a poetess only last year,
  And good at my art, for a woman, men
    said;
But *this* woman, — *this*, who is agonized
    here, —
  The east sea and the west sea rhyme on
    in her head
    For ever instead.

What art can a woman be good at? Oh,
    vain!
  What art *is* she good at, but hurting her
    breast
With the milk-teeth of babes, and a smile
    at the pain?

Ah, boys, how you hurt! You were
    strong as you pressed,
  And I proud by that test.

What art's for a woman? To hold on her
    knees
  Both darlings! to feel all their arms
    round her throat,
Cling, strangle a little! to sew by de-
    grees
  And 'broider the long clothes and neat
    little coat;
  To dream and to dote.

To teach them. — It stings there! *I* made
    them, indeed,
  Speak plain the word *country*. *I* taught
    them, no doubt,
That a country's a thing men should die
    for at need.
  I prated of liberty, rights, and about
    The tyrant cast out.

And when their eyes flashed, — oh, my
    beautiful eyes! —
  I exulted; nay, let them go forth at the
    wheels
Of the guns, and denied not. But, then,
    the surprise
  When one sits quite alone! Then one
    weeps, then one kneels!
    God, how the house feels!

At first, happy news came, in gay letters
    mailed
  With my kisses, — of camp-life and glory,
    and how
They both loved me; and, soon coming
    home to be spoiled,
  In return would fan off every fly from
    my brow
    With their green laurel-bough.

Then was triumph at Turin: "Ancona was
    free!"
  And some one came out of the cheers in
    the street,
With a face pale as stone, to say something
    to me.
  My Guido was dead! I fell down at his
    feet,
    While they cheered in the street.

I bore it; friends soothed me; my grief looked sublime
    As the ransom of Italy. One boy remained
To be leant on and walked with, recalling the time
    When the first grew immortal, while both of us strained
To the height he had gained.

And letters still came, shorter, sadder, more strong,
    Writ now but in one hand, "I was not to faint,—
One loved me for two—would be with me ere long:
    And *viva l'Italia!* — *he* died for, our saint,
Who forbids our complaint."

My Nanni would add, "he was safe, and aware
    Of a presence that turned off the balls,—was imprest,
It was Guido himself, who knew what I could bear,
    And how 'twas impossible, quite dispossessed,
To live on for the rest."

On which, without pause, up the telegraph-line
    Swept smoothly the next news from Gaeta:—*Shot;*
Tell his mother. Ah, ah, "his," "their" mother,—not "mine,"
    No voice says, "*My mother*," again to me. What!
You think Guido forgot?

Are souls straight so happy that, dizzy with Heaven,
    They drop earth's affections, conceive not of woe?
I think not. Themselves were too lately forgiven
    Through that love and sorrow which reconciled so
The Above and Below.

O Christ of the seven wounds, who look'dst through the dark
    To the face of Thy mother! consider, I pray,
How we common mothers stand desolate, mark,
    Whose sons, not being Christs, die with eyes turned away,
And no last word to say!

Both boys dead? but that's out of nature. We all
    Have been patriots, yet each house must always keep one.
'Twere imbecile, hewing out roads to a wall;
    And, when Italy's made, for what end is it done
If we have not a son?

Ah, ah, ah! when Gaeta's taken, what then?
    When the fair wicked queen sits no more at her sport
Of the fire-balls of death crashing souls out of men?
    When the guns of Cavalli, with final retort,
Have cut the game short?

When Venice and Rome keep their new jubilee,
    When your flag takes all heaven for its white, green and red,
When *you* have your country from mountain to sea,
    When King Victor has Italy's crown on his head
(And *I* have my Dead)—

What then? Do not mock me. Ah, ring your bells low,
    And burn your lights faintly! *My* country is *there*,
Above the star pricked by the last peak of snow:
    My Italy's THERE, with my brave civic Pair,
To disfranchise despair!

Forgive me. Some women bear children in strength,
    And bite back the cry of their pain in self-scorn;

But the birth-pangs of nations will wring
    us at length
  Into wail such as this—and we sit on forlorn
    When the man-child is born.

Dead! One of them shot by the sea in the
    East,
  And one of them shot in the West by the
    sea.
Both! both my boys! If in keeping the
    feast
  You want a great song for your Italy
    free,
    Let none look at *me!*
            ELIZABETH BARRETT BROWNING.

THE GRAVES OF A HOUSEHOLD.

THEY grew in beauty, side by side,
  They fill'd one home with glee;—
Their graves are sever'd, far and wide,
  By mount, and stream, and sea.

The same fond mother bent at night
  O'er each fair sleeping brow;
She had each folded flower in sight—
  Where are those dreamers now?

One, 'midst the forests of the West
  By a dark stream is laid—
The Indian knows his place of rest
  Far in the cedar shade.

The sea, the blue lone sea, hath one—
  He lies where pearls lie deep;
He was the loved of all, yet none
  O'er his low bed may weep.

One sleeps where southern vines are drest
  Above the noble slain:
He wrapt his colors round his breast
  On a blood-red field of Spain.

And one—o'er *her* the myrtle showers
  Its leaves, by soft winds fann'd;
She faded midst Italian flowers—
  The last of that bright band.

And parted thus they rest, who play'd
  Beneath the same green tree;
Whose voices mingled as they pray'd
  Around one parent knee!

They that with smiles lit up the hall,
  And cheer'd with song the hearth!—
Alas! for love, if *thou* wert all,
  And naught beyond, O earth!
            FELICIA DOROTHEA HEMANS.

We thought her lovely when she came,
But she was holy, saintly now---
Around her pale angelic brow
We saw a slender ring of flame!
    Thomas Bailey Aldrich.

POETRY

OF

INFANCY AND CHILDHOOD.

BABY MAY.

CHEEKS as soft as July peaches;
Lips whose velvet scarlet teaches
Poppies paleness; round large eyes
Ever great with new surprise;
Minutes filled with shadeless gladness;
Minutes just as brimm'd with sadness;
Happy smiles and wailing cries,
Crows and laughs and tearful eyes,
Lights and shadows, swifter born
Than on windswept autumn corn;
Ever some new tiny notion,
Making every limb all motion,
Catchings up of legs and arms,
Throwings back and small alarms,
Clutching fingers—straightening jerks,
Twining feet whose each toe works,
Kickings up and straining risings,
Mother's ever-new surprisings;
Hands all wants, and looks all wonder
At all things the heavens under;
Tiny scorns of smiled reprovings
That have more of love than lovings;
Mischiefs done with such a winning
Archness that we prize such sinning;
Breakings dire of plates and glasses,
Graspings small at all that passes;
Pullings off of all that's able
To be caught from tray or table;
Silences—small meditations
Deep as thoughts of cares for nations—
Breaking into wisest speeches
In a tongue that nothing teaches,
All the thoughts of whose possessing
Must be woo'd to light by guessing;
Slumbers—such sweet angel-seemings
That we'd ever have such dreamings,
Till from sleep we see thee breaking,
And we'd always have thee waking;
Wealth for which we know no measure,
Pleasure high above all pleasure,
Gladness brimming over gladness,
Joy in care—delight in sadness,
Loveliness beyond completeness,
Sweetness distancing all sweetness,
Beauty all that beauty may be,
That's May Bennett; that's my baby.
W. C. BENNETT.

BABY LOUISE.

I'M in love with you, Baby Louise!
With your silken hair and your soft blue eyes,
And the dreamy wisdom that in them lies,
And the faint, sweet smile you brought from the skies;
   God's sunshine, Baby Louise!

When you fold your hands, Baby Louise—
Your hands, like a fairy's, so tiny and fair—
With a pretty, innocent, saint-like air,
Are you trying to think of some angel-taught prayer
   You learned above, Baby Louise?

I'm in love with you, Baby Louise!
Why! you never raise your beautiful head!
Some day, little one, your cheek will grow red
With a flush of delight to hear the words said,
   "I love you," Baby Louise.

Do you hear me, Baby Louise?
I have sung your praises for nearly an hour,

And your lashes keep drooping lower and
    lower,
And you've gone to sleep like a weary
    flower,
        Ungrateful Baby Louise!
                MARGARET EYTINGE.

PHILIP MY KING.

"Who bears upon his baby brow the round
And top of sovereignty."

LOOK at me with thy large brown eyes,
    Philip, my king!
Round whom the enshadowing purple lies
Of babyhood's royal dignities:
Lay on my neck thy tiny hand,
  With Love's invisible sceptre laden;
I am thine Esther to command
    Till thou shalt find a queen-hand-
      maiden,
    Philip, my king!

Oh, the day when thou goest a-wooing,
    Philip, my king!
When those beautiful lips 'gin suing,
And, some gentle heart's bars undoing,
Thou dost enter, love-crown'd, and there
  Sittest, love-glorified!—Rule kindly,
Tenderly, over thy kingdom fair;
  For we that love, ah! we love so blindly,
    Philip, my king!

Up from thy sweet mouth up to thy brow,
    Philip, my king!
The spirit that there lies sleeping now
May rise like a giant, and make men bow
As to one heaven-chosen amongst his peers.
  My Saul, than thy brethren taller and
    fairer
Let me behold thee in future years!
  Yet thy head needeth a circlet rarer,
    Philip, my king—

A wreath, not of gold, but palm. One day,
    Philip, my king!
Thou, too, must tread, as we trod, a way
Thorny, and cruel, and cold, and gray;
Rebels within thee and foes without
  Will snatch at thy crown. But march
    on, glorious,
Martyr, yet monarch! till angels shout,
  As thou sitt'st at the feet of God vic-
    torious,
    "Philip, the king!"
                DINAH MULOCK CRAIK.

BABY BELL.

HAVE you not heard the poets tell
  How came the dainty Baby Bell
    Into this world of ours?
The gates of heaven were left ajar:
With folded hands and dreamy eyes,
  Wandering out of Paradise,
She saw this planet, like a star,
  Hung in the glistening depths of
    even,—
Its bridges, running to and fro,
O'er which the white-wing'd angels go,
  Bearing the holy dead to heaven.
She touch'd a bridge of flowers,—those
    feet,
So light they did not bend the bells
Of the celestial asphodels,
They fell like dew upon the flowers:
Then all the air grew strangely sweet!
And thus came dainty Baby Bell
  Into this world of ours.

She came, and brought delicious May.
  The swallows built beneath the eaves;
  Like sunlight, in and out the leaves
The robins went the livelong day;
The lily swung its noiseless bell;
  And o'er the porch the trembling vine
  Seem'd bursting with its veins of wine.
How sweetly, softly, twilight fell!
Oh, earth was full of singing-birds
  And opening spring-tide flowers,
When the dainty Baby Bell
  Came to this world of ours!

Oh, Baby, dainty Baby Bell,
How fair she grew from day to day!
  What woman-nature fill'd her eyes,
  What poetry within them lay!
Those deep and tender twilight eyes,
  So full of meaning, pure and **bright**
  As if she yet stood in the light
Of those oped gates of Paradise.
And so we loved her more and more:
  Ah, never in our hearts before
    Was love so lovely born:
We felt we had a link between
This real world and that unseen—
    The land beyond the morn;
And for the love of those dear eyes,
For love of her whom God led forth,
(The mother's being ceased on earth
When Baby came from Paradise),—

For love of Him who smote our lives,
    And woke the chords of joy and pain,
We said, *Dear Christ!*—our hearts bent down
    Like violets after rain.

And now the orchards, which were white
And red with blossoms when she came,
Were rich in autumn's mellow prime;
The cluster'd apples burnt like flame,
The soft-cheek'd peaches blush'd and fell,
The ivory chestnut burst its shell,
The grapes hung purpling in the grange;
And time wrought just as rich a change
    In little Baby Bell.
Her lissome form more perfect grew,
    And in her features we could trace,
    In soften'd curves, her mother's face.
Her angel-nature ripen'd too:
We thought her lovely when she came,
But she was holy, saintly now:—
Around her pale angelic brow
We saw a slender ring of flame!

God's hand had taken away the seal
    That held the portals of her speech;
And oft she said a few strange words
    Whose meaning lay beyond our reach.
She never was a child to us,
We never held her being's key;
We could not teach her holy things:
    She was Christ's self in purity.

It came upon us by degrees,
We saw its shadow ere it fell,—
The knowledge that our God had sent
His messenger for Baby Bell.
We shudder'd with unlanguaged pain,
And all our hopes were changed to fears,
And all our thoughts ran into tears
    Like sunshine into rain.
We cried aloud in our belief,
"Oh, smite us gently, gently, God!
Teach us to bend and kiss the rod,
And perfect grow through grief."
Ah, how we loved her, God can tell;
Her heart was folded deep in ours.
    Our hearts are broken, Baby Bell!

At last he came, the messenger,
    The messenger from unseen lands:
And what did dainty Baby Bell?
She only cross'd her little hands,

She only look'd more meek and fair!
We parted back her silken hair,
We wove the roses round her brow,—
White buds, the summer's drifted snow,—
Wrapt her from head to foot in flowers!
And thus went dainty Baby Bell
    Out of this world of ours!
                  THOMAS BAILEY ALDRICH.

WHERE DID YOU COME FROM?

WHERE did you come from, baby dear?
Out of the everywhere into here.

Where did get your eyes so blue?
Out of the sky as I came through.

What makes the light in them sparkle and spin?
Some of the starry spikes left in.

Where did you get that little tear?
I found it waiting when I got here.

What makes your forehead so smooth and high?
A soft hand stroked it as I went by.

What makes your cheek like a warm white rose?
I saw something better than any one knows.

Whence that three-corner'd smile of bliss?
Three angels gave me at once a kiss.

Where did you get this pearly ear?
God spoke, and it came out to hear.

Where did you get those arms and hands?
Love made itself into hooks and bands.

Feet, whence did you come, you darling things?
From the same box as the cherubs' wings.

How did they all come just to be you?
God thought of me, and so I grew.

But how did you come to us, you dear?
God thought of you, and so I am here.
                  GEORGE MACDONALD.

"SWEET AND LOW."

SWEET and low, sweet and low,
    Wind of the western sea,
Low, low, breathe and blow,
    Wind of the western sea!

Over the rolling waters go,
Come from the dying moon, and blow,
Blow him again to me,
While my little one, while my pretty one,
sleeps.

Sleep and rest, sleep and rest,
Father will come to thee soon;
Rest, rest, on mother's breast,
Father will come to thee soon;
Father will come to his babe in the nest,
Silver sails all out of the west
Under the silver moon:
Sleep, my little one, sleep, my pretty one,
sleep.
ALFRED TENNYSON.

LULLABY.

GOLDEN slumbers kiss your eyes,
Smiles awake you when you rise.
Sleep, pretty wantons; do not cry,
And I will sing a lullaby:
Rock them, rock them, lullaby.

Care is heavy, therefore sleep you;
You are care, and care must keep you.
Sleep, pretty wantons; do not cry,
And I will sing a lullaby:
Rock them, rock them, lullaby.
THOMAS DEKKER.

LADY ANNE BOTHWELL'S LAMENT.

BALOW, my babe, lye stil and sleipe!
It grieves me sair to see thee weipe:
If thou'st be silent, I'se be glad,
Thy maining maks my heart ful sad.
Balow, my boy, thy mother's joy,
Thy father breides me great annoy.
    Balow, my babe, ly still and sleipe,
    It grieves me sair to see thee weipe.

Whan he began to court my luve,
And with his sugred wordes to muve,
His faynings fals, and flattering cheire
To me that time did not appeire:
But now I see, most cruell hee
Cares neither for my babe nor mee.
    Balow, my babe, ly stil and sleipe,
    It grieves me sair to see thee weipe.

Ly stil, my darling, sleipe a while,
And when thou wakest, sweitly smile:
But smile not, as thy father did,
To cozen maids: nay, God forbid!
Bot yett I feire, thou wilt gae neire
Thy fatheris hart and face to beire.
    Balow, my babe, ly stil and sleipe,
    It grieves me sair to see thee weipe.

I cannae chuse, but ever will
Be luving to thy father stil:
Whair-eir he gae, whair-eir he ryde,
My luve with him doth stil abyde:
In weil or wae, whair-eir he gae,
Mine hart can neire depart him frae.
    Balow, my babe, ly stil and sleipe,
    It grieves me sair to see thee weipe.

But doe not, doe not, pretty mine,
To faynings fals thine hart incline;
Be loyal to thy luver trew,
And nevir change her for a new:
If gude or faire, of hir have care,
For women's banning's wondrous sair.
    Balow, my babe, ly stil and sleipe,
    It grieves me sair to see thee weipe.

Bairne, sin thy cruel father is gane,
Thy winsome smiles maun eise my paine;
My babe and I'll together live,
He'll comfort me when cares doe grieve:
My babe and I right saft will ly,
And quite forgeit man's cruelty.
    Balow, my babe, ly stil and sleipe,
    It grieves me sair to see thee weipe.

Fareweil, fareweil, thou falsest youth,
That evir kist a woman's mouth!
I wish all maides be warn'd by mee
Nevir to trust man's curtesy;
For if we doe bot chance to bow,
They'll use us than they care not how.
    Balow, my babe, ly stil and sleipe,
    It grieves me sair to see thee weipe.
AUTHOR UNKNOWN.

CRADLE SONG.

[From the German.]

SLEEP, baby, sleep!
Thy father's watching the sheep,
Thy mother's shaking the dreamland tree,
And down drops a little dream for thee.
    Sleep, baby, sleep!

Sleep, baby, sleep!
The large stars are the sheep,

The little stars are the lambs, I guess,
The bright moon is the shepherdess.
    Sleep, baby, sleep.

Sleep, baby, sleep!
And cry not like a sheep.
Else the sheep-dog will bark and whine,
And bite this naughty child of mine.
    Sleep, baby, sleep!

Sleep, baby, sleep!
Thy Saviour loves His sheep;
He is the Lamb of God on high
Who for our sakes came down to die.
    Sleep, baby, sleep!

Sleep, baby, sleep!
Away to tend the sheep,
Away, thou sheep-dog fierce and wild,
And do not harm my sleeping child!
    Sleep, baby, sleep!
        ELIZABETH PRENTISS.

THE ANGELS' WHISPER.

A BABY was sleeping;
  Its mother was weeping;
For her husband was far on the wild raging sea;
  And the tempest was swelling
  Round the fisherman's dwelling;
And she cried, "Dermot, darling, oh come back to me!"

Her beads while she number'd,
  The baby still slumber'd,
And smiled in her face as she bended her knee:
  "Oh, blest be that warning,
  My child, thy sleep adorning,
For I know that the angels are whispering with thee!

"And while they are keeping
  Bright watch o'er thy sleeping,
Oh, pray to them softly, my baby, with me!
  And say thou wouldst rather
  They'd watch o'er thy father!
For I know that the angels are whispering to thee."

The dawn of the morning
Saw Dermot returning,
And the wife wept with joy her babe's father to see;
  And closely caressing
  Her child with a blessing,
Said, "I knew that the angels were whispering with thee."
        SAMUEL LOVER.

THE CHILD AND THE WATCHER.

SLEEP on, baby on the floor,
  Tired of all thy playing—
Sleep with smile the sweeter for
  That you dropped away in;
On your curls, fair roundness stand
  Golden lights serenely;
One cheek, push'd out by the hand
  Folds the dimple inly—
Little head and little foot
  Heavy laid for pleasure;
Underneath the lids half-shut
  Plants the shining azure;
Open-soul'd in noonday sun,
  So, you lie and slumber;
Nothing evil having done,
  Nothing can encumber.

I, who cannot sleep as well,
  Shall I sigh to view you?
Or sigh further to foretell
  All that may undo you?
Nay, keep smiling, little child,
  Ere the fate appeareth!
I smile too; for patience mild
  Pleasure's token weareth.
Nay, keep sleeping before loss;
  I shall sleep, though losing!
As by cradle, so by cross,
  Sweet is the reposing.

And God knows, who sees us twain,
  Child at childish leisure,
I am all as tired of pain
  As you are of pleasure.
Very soon, too, by His grace,
  Gently wrapt around me,
I shall show as calm a face,
  I shall sleep as soundly—
Differing in this, that you
  Clasp your playthings sleeping,
While my hand must drop the few
  Given to my keeping—

Differing in this, that I,
  Sleeping, must be colder,

And, in waking presently,
  Brighter to beholder—
Differing in this, beside
  (Sleeper, have you heard me?)
Do you move and open wide
  Your great eyes toward me?),
That while I you draw withal
  From this slumber solely,
Me, from mine, an angel shall,
  Trumpet-tongued and holy!
          ELIZABETH BARRETT BROWNING.

SWEET BABY, SLEEP.

SWEET baby, sleep! what ails my dear?
  What ails my darling, thus to cry?
Be still, my child, and lend thine ear,
  To hear me sing thy lullaby.
My pretty lamb, forbear to weep;
Be still, my dear; sweet baby, sleep.

Thou blessed soul, what canst thou fear?
  What thing to thee can mischief do?
Thy God is now thy Father dear,
  His holy Spouse thy mother too.
Sweet baby, then forbear to weep;
Be still, my babe; sweet baby, sleep.

Though thy conception was in sin,
  A sacred bathing thou hast had;
And though thy birth unclean hath been,
  A blameless babe thou now art made.
Sweet baby, then forbear to weep;
Be still, my dear; sweet baby, sleep.

While thus thy lullaby I sing,
  For thee great blessings ripening be;
Thine eldest brother is a King,
  And hath a kingdom bought for thee.
Sweet baby, then forbear to weep;
Be still, my babe; sweet baby, sleep.

Sweet baby, sleep, and nothing fear;
  For whosoever thee offends
By thy Protector threaten'd are,
  And God and angels are thy friends.
Sweet baby, then forbear to weep;
Be still, my babe; sweet baby, sleep.

When God with us was dwelling here,
  In little babes He took delight;
Such innocents as thou, my dear,
  Are ever precious in His sight.
Sweet baby, then forbear to weep;
Be still, my babe; sweet baby, sleep.

A little infant once was He;
  And strength in weakness then was laid
Upon His virgin mother's knee,
  That power to thee might be convey'd.
Sweet baby, then forbear to weep;
Be still, my babe; sweet baby, sleep.

In this thy frailty and thy need
  He friends and helpers doth prepare,
Which thee shall cherish, clothe, and feed,
  For of thy weal they tender are.
Sweet baby, then forbear to weep;
Be still, my babe; sweet baby, sleep.

The King of kings, when He was born,
  Had not so much for outward ease;
By Him such dressings were not worn,
  Nor such-like swaddling-clothes as these.
Sweet baby, then forbear to weep;
Be still, my babe; sweet baby, sleep.

Within a manger lodged thy Lord,
  Where oxen lay and asses fed:
Warm rooms we do to thee afford,
  An easy cradle or a bed.
Sweet baby, then forbear to weep;
Be still, my babe; sweet baby, sleep.

The wants that He did then sustain
  Have purchased wealth, my babe, for thee;
And by His torments and His pain
  Thy rest and ease securèd be.
My baby, then forbear to weep;
Be still, my babe; sweet baby, sleep.

Thou hast, yet more to perfect this,
  A promise and an earnest got
Of gaining everlasting bliss,
  Though thou, my babe, perceiv'st it not:
Sweet baby, then forbear to weep;
Be still, my babe; sweet baby, sleep.
              GEORGE WITHER.

CRADLE HYMN.

HUSH, my dear! Lie still and slumber!
  Holy angels guard thy bed!
Heavenly blessings without number,
  Gently falling on thy head.

Sleep, my babe! thy food and raiment,
　House and home, thy friends provide;
All without thy care or payment,
　All thy wants are well supplied.

How much better thou'rt attended
　Than the Son of God could be,
When from heaven He descended,
　And became a child like thee!

Soft and easy is thy cradle:
　Coarse and hard thy Saviour lay,
When His birthplace was a stable
　And His softest bed was hay.

Blessed Babe! what glorious features,—
　Spotless fair, divinely bright!
Must He dwell with brutal creatures?
　How could angels bear the sight?

Was there nothing but a manger
　Cursed sinners could afford,
To receive the heavenly stranger?
　Did they thus affront the Lord?

Soft, my child! I did not chide thee,
　Though my song might sound too hard:
'Tis thy mother sits beside thee,
　And her arm shall be thy guard.

Yet to read the shameful story,
　How the Jews abused their King,
How they served the Lord of glory,
　Makes me angry while I sing.

See the kinder shepherds round Him,
　Telling wonders from the sky!
Where they sought Him, there they found Him,
　With His virgin mother by.

See the lovely Babe a-dressing;
　Lovely Infant, how He smiled!
When He wept, His mother's blessing
　Sooth'd and hush'd the holy Child.

Lo, He slumbers in a manger,
　Where the hornèd oxen fed:—
Peace, my darling, here's no danger:
　There's no ox a-near thy bed.

'Twas to save thee, child, from dying,
　Save my dear from burning flame,
Bitter groans and endless crying,
　That thy blest Redeemer came.

May'st thou live to know and fear Him,
　Trust and love Him all thy days,
Then go dwell for ever near Him:
　See His face, and sing His praise!

I could give thee thousand kisses!
　Hoping what I most desire,
Not a mother's fondest wishes
　Can to greater joys aspire!
　　　　　　　　　ISAAC WATTS.

TO A CHILD
EMBRACING HIS MOTHER.

LOVE thy mother, little one!
　Kiss and clasp her neck again,—
Hereafter she may have a son
　Will kiss and clasp her neck in vain.
　Love thy mother, little one!

Gaze upon her living eyes,
　And mirror back her love for thee,—
Hereafter thou may'st shudder sighs
　To meet them when they cannot see.
　Gaze upon her living eyes!

Press her lips the while they glow
　With love that they have often told,—
Hereafter thou may'st press in woe,
　And kiss them till thine own are cold.
　Press her lips the while they glow!

Oh, revere her raven hair!
　Although it be not silver-gray—
Too early Death, led on by Care,
　May snatch save one dear lock away.
　Oh, revere her raven hair!

Pray for her at eve and morn,
　That Heaven may long the stroke defer—
For thou may'st live the hour forlorn
　When thou wilt ask to die with her.
　Pray for her at eve and morn!
　　　　　　　　　THOMAS HOOD.

TO CHARLOTTE PULTENEY.

TIMELY blossom, infant fair,
Fondling of a happy pair,
Every morn and every night
Their solicitous delight;
Sleeping, waking, still at ease,
Pleasing, without skill to please;
Little gossip, blithe and hale,
Tattling many a broken tale;

Singing many a tuneless song,
Lavish of a heedless tongue;
Simple maiden, void of art,
Babbling out the very heart,
Yet abandon'd to thy will,
Yet imagining no ill,
Yet too innocent to blush;
Like the linnet in the bush
To the mother-linnet's note
Moduling her slender throat,
Chirping forth thy petty joys,
Wanton in the change of toys;
Like the linnet green in May
Flitting to each bloomy spray;
Wearied then and glad of rest,
Like the linnet in the nest;—
This thy present happy lot
This, in time will be forgot:
Other pleasures, other cares,
Ever-busy Time prepares;
And thou shalt in thy daughter see
This picture, once, resembled thee.
AMBROSE PHILIPS.

TO T. L. H.

SIX YEARS OLD, DURING A SICKNESS.

SLEEP breathes at last from out thee,
  My little, patient boy;
And balmy rest about thee
  Smooths off the day's annoy.
    I sit me down, and think
    Of all thy winning ways;
Yet almost wish, with sudden shrink,
    That I had less to praise.

Thy sidelong pillowed meekness,
  Thy thanks to all that aid,
Thy heart, in pain and weakness,
  Of fancied faults afraid;
    The little trembling hand
    That wipes thy quiet tears:
These, these are things that may demand
    Dread memories for years.

Sorrows I've had, severe ones,
  I will not think of now;
And calmly, midst my dear ones,
  Have wasted with dry brow;
    But when thy fingers press
    And pat my stooping head,
I cannot bear the gentleness—
    The tears are in their bed.

Ah, first-born of thy mother,
  When life and hope were new;
Kind playmate of thy brother,
  Thy sister, father too;
    My light, where'er I go;
    My bird, when prison-bound;
My hand-in-hand companion—No,
    My prayers shall hold thee round.

To say " He has departed "—
  " His voice "—" his face "—is gone,
To feel impatient-hearted,
  Yet feel we must bear on—
    Ah, I could not endure
    To whisper of such woe,
Unless I felt this sleep ensure
    That it will not be so.

Yes, still he's fixed, and sleeping!
  This silence too the while—
Its very hush and creeping
  Seem whispering us a smile;
    Something divine and dim
    Seems going by one's ear,
Like parting wings of cherubim,
    Who say, " We've finished here."
LEIGH HUNT.

CHILDREN.

CHILDREN are what the mothers are.
No fondest father's fondest care
Can fashion so the infant heart
As those creative beams that dart,
With all their hopes and fears, upon
The cradle of a sleeping son.

His startled eyes with wonder see
A father near him on his knee,
Who wishes all the while to trace
The mother in his future face;
But 'tis to her alone uprise
His wakening arms; to her those eyes
Open with joy and not surprise.
WALTER SAVAGE LANDOR.

CASTLES IN THE AIR.

The bonnie, bonnie bairn, who sits poking
   in the ase,
Glowering in the fire with his wee round
   face;
Laughing at the fuffin' lowe, what sees he
   there?
Ha! the young dreamer's bigging castles
   in the air.
His wee chubby face and his touzie curly
   pow,
Are laughing and nodding to the dancing
   lowe;
He'll brown his rosy cheeks, and singe his
   sunny hair,
Glowering at the imps wi' their castles in
   the air.

He sees muckle castles towering to the
   moon!
He sees little sogers pu'ing them a' doun!
Worlds whombling up and down, bleezing
   wi' a flare,
See how he loups! as they glimmer in the
   air.
For a' sae sage he looks, what can the laddie
   ken?
He's thinking upon naething, like mony
   mighty men,
A wee thing maks us think, a sma' thing
   maks us stare,
There are mair folk than him bigging
   castles in the air.

Sic a night in winter may weel mak him
   cauld:
His chin upon his buffy hand will soon
   mak him auld;
His brow is brent sae braid, oh, pray that
   daddy Care
Would let the wean alane wi' his castles in
   the air.
He'll glower at the fire! and he'll keek at
   the light!
But mony sparkling stars are swallow'd up
   by night;
Aulder een than his are glamour'd by a
   glare,
Hearts are broken, heads are turn'd, wi'
   castles in the air.
              JAMES BALLANTYNE.

THE LITTLE BLACK BOY.

My mother bore me in the southern wild,
   And I am black, but, oh, my soul is
   white!
White as an angel is the English child,
   But I am black, as if bereaved of light.

My mother taught me underneath a tree;
   And, sitting down before the heat of
   day,
She took me on her lap and kissèd me,
   And, pointing to the East, began to say:

"Look on the rising sun: there God does
   live,
And gives his light, and gives his heat
   away,
And flowers, and trees, and beasts, and men,
   receive
Comfort in morning, joy in the noon-
   day.

"And we are put on earth a little space,
   That we may learn to bear the beams
   of love;
And these black bodies and this sunburnt
   face
Are but a cloud, and like a shady grove.

"For, when our souls have learn'd the heat
   to bear,
The cloud will vanish, we shall hear
   His voice
Saying: 'Come from the grove, my love
   and care,
And round my golden tent like lambs
   rejoice.'"

Thus did my mother say, and kissèd me,
   And thus I say to little English boy.
When I from black, and he from white
   cloud free,
   And round the tent of God like lambs
   we joy,

I'll shade him from the heat, till he can
   bear
To lean in joy upon our Father's knee;
And then I'll stand and stroke his silver
   hair,
And be like him, and he will then love
   me.
              WILLIAM BLAKE.

BALLAD OF THE TEMPEST.

WE were crowded in the cabin,
  Not a soul would dare to sleep,—
It was midnight on the waters,
  And a storm was on the deep.

'Tis a fearful thing in Winter
  To be shattered in the blast,
And to hear the rattling trumpet
  Thunder: "Cut away the mast!"

So we shuddered there in silence,—
  For the stoutest held his breath,
While the hungry sea was roaring,
  And the breakers talked with Death.

As thus we sat in darkness,
  Each one busy in his prayers,
"We are lost!" the captain shouted
  As he staggered down the stairs.

But his little daughter whispered,
  As she took his icy hand:
"Isn't God upon the ocean
  Just the same as on the land?"

Then we kissed the little maiden,
  And we spoke in better cheer,
And we anchored safe in harbor
  When the morn was shining clear.
                    JAMES T. FIELDS.

LITTLE BELL.

He prayeth well, who loveth well
Both man and bird and beast.
                ANCIENT MARINER.

PIPED the blackbird on the beechwood
    spray:
"Pretty maid, slow wandering this way,
  What's your name?" quoth he—
"What's your name? Oh stop and straight
    unfold,
Pretty maid with showery curls of gold,"—
  "Little Bell," said she.

Little Bell sat down beneath the rocks—
Tossed aside her gleaming golden locks—
  "Bonny bird," quoth she,
"Sing me your best song before I go."
"Here's the very finest song I know,
  Little Bell," said he.

And the blackbird piped; you never heard
Half so gay a song from any bird—
  Full of quips and wiles,
Now so round and rich, now soft and slow,
All for love of that sweet face below,
  Dimpled o'er with smiles.

And the while the bonny bird did pour
His full heart out freely o'er and o'er
  'Neath the morning skies,
In the little childish heart below
All the sweetness seemed to grow and grow,
And shine forth in happy overflow
  From the blue, bright eyes.

Down the dell she tripped and through the
    glade,
Peeped the squirrel from the hazel shade,
  And from out the tree
Swung and leaped, and frolicked, void of
    fear,—
While bold blackbird piped that all might
    hear—
  "Little Bell," piped he.

Little Bell sat down amid the fern—
"Squirrel, squirrel, to your task return—
  Bring me nuts," quoth she.
Up, away the frisky squirrel hies—
Golden wood-lights glancing in his eyes—
  And adown the tree,
Great ripe nuts, kissed brown by July sun,
In the little lap dropped one by one—
Hark, how blackbird pipes to see the fun!
  "Happy Bell," pipes he.

Little Bell looked up and down the glade—
"Squirrel, squirrel, if you're not afraid,
  Come and share with me!"
Down came squirrel eager for his fare—
Down came bonny blackbird, I declare;
Little Bell gave each his honest share—
  Ah the merry three!
And the while these frolic playmates twain
Piped and frisked from bough to bough
    again,
  'Neath the morning skies,
In the little childish heart below
All the sweetness seemed to grow and grow,
And shine out in happy overflow
  From her blue, bright eyes.

By her snow-white cot at close of day
Knelt sweet Bell, with folded palms to
    pray—

Very calm and clear
Rose the praying voice to where, unseen,
In blue heaven, an angel shape serene
  Paused a while to hear—
"What good child is this," the angel said,
"That with happy heart, beside her bed
  Prays so lovingly?"
Low and soft, oh! very low and soft,
Crooned the blackbird in the orchard croft,
  "Bell, dear Bell!" crooned he.

"Whom God's creatures love," the angel fair
Murmured, "God doth bless with angels' care;
Child, thy bed shall be
Folded safe from harm—Love, deep and kind,
Shall watch around and leave good gifts behind,
  Little Bell, for thee!"
            THOMAS WESTWOOD.

THE RECONCILIATION.

As thro' the land at eve we went,
  And pluck'd the ripen'd ears,
We fell out, my wife and I,
We fell out—I know not why—
  And kiss'd again with tears.
And blessings on the falling-out
  That all the more endears,
When we fall out with those we love
  And kiss again with tears!
For when we came where lies the child
  We lost in other years,
There above the little grave,
Oh there above the little grave,
  We kiss'd again with tears.
            ALFRED TENNYSON.

GOLDEN-TRESSÈD ADELAIDE.

A SONG FOR A CHILD.

SING, I pray, a little song,
    Mother dear!
Neither sad nor very long:
It is for a little maid,
Golden-tressèd Adelaide!
Therefore let it suit a merry, merry ear,
    Mother dear!

Let it be a merry strain,
    Mother dear!
Shunning e'en the thought of pain:
For our gentle child will weep
If the theme be dark and deep;
And *we* will not draw a single, single tear,
    Mother dear!

Childhood should be all divine,
    Mother dear!
And like an endless summer shine;
Gay as Edward's shouts and cries,
Bright as Agnes' azure eyes:
Therefore bid thy song be merry:—dost thou hear,
    Mother dear?
            BRYAN WALLER PROCTER.

CASA WAPPY.

AND hast thou sought thy heavenly home,
    Our fond, dear boy—
The realms where sorrow dare not come,
    Where life is joy?
Pure at thy death, as at thy birth,
Thy spirit caught no taint from earth;
Even by its bliss we mete our dearth,
    Casa Wappy!

Despair was in our last farewell,
    As closed thine eye;
Tears of our anguish may not tell
    When thou didst die;
Words may not paint our grief for thee;
Sighs are but bubbles on the sea
Of our unfathom'd agony!
    Casa Wappy!

Thou wert a vision of delight,
    To bless us given;
Beauty embodied to our sight—
    A type of heaven!
So dear to us thou wert, thou art
Even less thine own self, than a part
Of mine, and of thy mother's heart,
    Casa Wappy!

Thy bright, brief day knew no decline—
    'Twas cloudless joy;
Sunrise and night alone were thine,
    Beloved boy!
This morn beheld thee blythe and gay;
That found thee prostrate in decay;
And ere a third shone, clay was clay,
    Casa Wappy!

Gem of our hearth, our household pride,
    Earth's undefiled,
Could love have saved, thou hadst not died,
    Our dear, sweet child!
Humbly we bow to Fate's decree;
Yet had we hoped that Time should see
Thee mourn for us, not us for thee,
    Casa Wappy!

Do what I may, go where I will,
    Thou meet'st my sight;
There dost thou glide before me still—
    A form of light!
I feel thy breath upon my cheek—
I see thee smile, I hear thee speak—
Till oh! my heart is like to break,
    Casa Wappy!

Methinks thou smil'st before me now,
    With glance of stealth;
The hair thrown back from thy full brow
    In buoyant health;
I see thine eyes' deep violet light—
Thy dimpled cheek carnation'd bright—
Thy clasping arms so round and white—
    Casa Wappy!

The nursery shows thy pictured wall,
    Thy bat—thy bow—
Thy cloak and bonnet—club and ball;
    But where art thou?
A corner holds thine empty chair;
Thy playthings, idly scatter'd there,
But speak to us of our despair,
    Casa Wappy!

Even to the last, thy every word—
    To glad—to grieve—
Was sweet, as sweetest song of bird
    On summer's eve;
In outward beauty undecay'd,
Death o'er thy spirit cast no shade,
And, like the rainbow, thou didst fade,
    Casa Wappy!

We mourn for thee, when blind, blank night
    The chamber fills;
We pine for thee, when morn's first light
    Reddens the hills;
The sun, the moon, the stars, the sea,
All—to the wall-flower and wild-pea—
Are changed; we saw the world thro' thee,
    Casa Wappy!

And though, perchance, a smile may gleam
    Of casual mirth,
It doth not own, whate'er may seem,
    An inward birth;
We miss thy small step on the stair;—
We miss thee at thine evening prayer;
All day we miss thee—everywhere—
    Casa Wappy!

Snows muffled earth when thou didst go,
    In life's spring-bloom,
Down to the appointed house below—
    The silent tomb.
But now the green leaves of the tree,
The cuckoo and "the busy bee,"
Return, but with them bring not thee,
    Casa Wappy!

'Tis so; but can it be—while flowers
    Revive again—
Man's doom, in death that we and ours
    For aye remain?
Oh can it be, that, o'er the grave,
The grass renew'd should yearly wave,
Yet God forget our child to save?
    Casa Wappy!

It cannot be; for were it so
    Thus man could die,
Life were a mockery—thought were woe—
    And truth a lie;
Heaven were a coinage of the brain—
Religion frenzy—virtue vain—
And all our hopes to meet again,
    Casa Wappy!

Then be to us, O dear lost child!
    With beam of love,
A star, death's uncongenial wild
    Smiling above!
Soon, soon thy little feet have trod
The skyward path, the seraph's road,
That led thee back from man to God,
    Casa Wappy!

Yet, 'tis sweet balm to our despair,
    Fond, fairest boy,
That heaven is God's, and thou art there,
    With him in joy;
There past are death and all its woes;
There beauty's stream for ever flows;
And pleasure's day no sunset knows,
    Casa Wappy!

RETURNING HOME.

Farewell, then—for a while, farewell—
    Pride of my heart!
It cannot be that long we dwell
    Thus torn apart.
Time's shadows like the shuttle flee;
And, dark howe'er life's night may be,
Beyond the grave I'll meet with thee,
    Casa Wappy!
DAVID MACBETH MOIR.

WILLIE WINKIE.

WEE Willie Winkie rins through the town,
Up stairs and doon stairs, in his nicht gown,
Tirlin' at the window, cryin' at the lock,
"Are the weans in their bed?—for it's now
    ten o'clock."

Hey, Willie Winkie! are ye comin' ben?
The cat's singin' gay thrums to the sleepin'
    hen,
The doug's speldered on the floor, and disna
    gie a cheep;
But here's a waukrife laddie that winna fa'
    asleep.

Onything but sleep, ye rogue!—glowerin'
    like the moon,
Rattlin' in an airn jug wi' an airn spoon,
Rumblin', tumblin' roun' about, crawin'
    like a cock,
Skirlin' like a kenna-what — wauknin'
    sleepin' folk.

Hey, Willie Winkie! the wean's in a creel!
Waumblin' aff a bodie's knee like a vera
    eel,
Ruggin' at the cat's lug, and ravellin' a' her
    thrums:
Hey, Willie Winkie!—See, there he comes!

Weary is the mither that has a storie wean,
A wee stumpie stoussie, that canna rin his
    lane,
That has a battle aye wi' sleep before he'll
    close an ee;
But a kiss frae aff his rosy lips gies strength
    anew to me.
WILLIAM MILLER.

THE BABIE.

NAE shoon to hide her tiny taes,
    Nae stockin' on her feet;
Her supple ankles white as snaw,
    Or early blossoms sweet.

Her simple dress o' sprinkled pink,
    Her double, dimplit chin,
Her puckered lips and balmy mou'
    With na ane tooth within.

Her een sae like her mither's een,
    Twa gentle, liquid things;
Her face is like an angel's face:
    We're glad she has nae wings.

She is the buddin' o' our luve,
    A giftie God gied us:
We maun na luve the gift owre weel;
    'Twad be na blessin' thus.

We still maun lo'e the Giver mair,
    An' see Him in the given;
An' sae she'll lead us up to Him,
    Our babie straight frae heaven.
J. E. RANKIN.

THE DUMB CHILD.

SHE is my only girl:
I ask'd for her as some most precious thing,
For all unfinish'd was love's jewell'd ring
    Till set with this soft pearl:
The shade that time brought forth I could
    not see;
How pure, how perfect, seem'd the gift to
    me!

Oh, many a soft old tune
I used to sing unto that deaden'd ear,
And suffer'd not the lightest footstep near,
    Lest she might wake too soon,
And hush'd her brothers' laughter while
    she lay—
Ah, needless care! I might have let them
    play!

'Twas long ere I believed
That this one daughter might not speak to
    me:
Waited and watch'd. God knows how
    patiently!
How willingly deceived!
Vain Love was long the untiring nurse of
    Faith,
And tended Hope until it starved to death.

Oh if she could but hear
For one short hour, till I her tongue might
    teach
To call me mother, in the broken speech
    That thrills the mother's ear!
Alas! those seal'd lips never may be stirr'd
To the deep music of that lovely word.

My heart it sorely tries
To see her kneel, with such a reverent air,
Beside her brothers, at their evening
    prayer;
    Or lift those earnest eyes
To watch our lips, as though our words
    she knew,—
Then move her own, as she were speaking
    too.

    I've watch'd her looking up
To the bright wonder of a sunset sky,
With such a depth of meaning in her eye,
    That I could almost hope
The struggling soul *would* burst its binding cords,
And the long pent-up thoughts flow forth in words.

    The song of bird and bee,
The chorus of the breezes, streams, and groves,
All the grand music to which Nature moves,
    Are wasted melody
To her; the world of sound a nameless void,
While even Silence hath its charms destroy'd.

    Her face is very fair:
Her blue eye beautiful: of finest mould
The soft, white brow, o'er which in waves of gold
    Ripples her shining hair.
Alas! this lovely temple closed must be;
For He who made it keeps the master-key.

    Wills He the mind within
Should from earth's Babel-clamor be kept free,
E'en that His still small voice and step might be
    Heard at its inner shrine,
Through that deep hush of soul, with clearer thrill?
Then should I grieve? O murmuring heart, be still!

    She seems to have a sense
Of quiet gladness in her noiseless play.
She hath a pleasant smile, a gentle way,
    Whose voiceless eloquence
Touches all hearts, though I had once the fear
That even her *father* would not care for her.

Thank God it is not so!
And when his sons are playing merrily,
She comes and leans her head upon his knee.
    Oh, at such times I know,
By his full eye and tones subdued and mild,
How his heart yearns over his *silent* child.

    Not of *all* gifts bereft,
Even now. How could I say she did not speak?
What real language lights her eye and cheek,
    And renders thanks to Him who left
Unto her soul yet open, avenues
For joy to enter, and for love to use!

    And God in love doth give
To her defect a beauty of its own:
And we a deeper tenderness have known,
    Through that for which we grieve.
Yet shall the seal be melted from her ear,
Yes, and *my* voice shall fill it—but not here!

    When that new sense is given,
What rapture will its first experience be,
That never woke to meaner melody
    Than the rich songs of Heaven—
To hear the full-toned anthem swelling round,
While angels teach the ecstasies of sound!

Author Unknown.

THE WONDERFU' WEAN.

Our wean's the most wonderfu' wean e'er
    I saw;
It would tak me a lang simmer day to
    tell a'
His pranks, frae the mornin' till night
    shuts his ee,
When he sleeps like a peerie, 'tween father
    and me;

For in his quite turns siccan questions he'll spier!
How the moon can stick up in the sky that's sae clear?
What gars the wind blaw? and whar frae comes the rain?
He's a perfec' divirt—he's a wonderfu' wean!

Or wha was the first bodie's father? and wha
Made the vera first snaw-shooer that ever did fa'?
And wha made the first bird that sang on a tree?
And the water that sooms a' the ships in the sea?
But after I've told him as weel as I ken,
Again he begins wi' his wha and his when;
And he looks aye sae wistfu' the whiles I explain:
He's as auld as the hills—he's an auld-farrant wean.

And folk wha hae skill o' the lumps on the head
Hint there's mae ways than toilin' o' winnin' ane's bread;
How he'll be a rich man, and hae men to work for him,
Wi' a kyte like a baillie's, shug-shuggin' afore him;
Wi' a face like the moon—sober, sonsy, and douce—
And a back, for its breadth, like the side o' a house.
'Tweel! I'm unco ta'en up wi't—they mak a' sae plain.
He's just a town's talk; he's a by-ord'nar wean!

I ne'er can forget sic a laugh as I gat,
To see him put on father's waistcoat and hat;
Then the lang-leggit boots gaed sae far owre his knees
The tap-loops wi' his fingers he grippit wi' ease;
Then he march'd through the house, he march'd but, he march'd ben,
Like owre mony mae o' our great little men,
That I leuch clean outright, for I cou'dna contain:
He was sic a conceit—sic an ancient-like wean!

But 'mid a' his daffin sic kindness he shows,
That he's dear to my heart as the dew to the rose;
And the unclouded hinny-beam aye in his ee
Maks him every day dearer and dearer to me.
Though Fortune be saucy, and dorty, and dour,
And gloom through her fingers like hills through a shooer,
When bodies hae gat a bit bit bairn o' their ain,
How he cheers up their hearts!—he's a wonderfu' wean!

WILLIAM MILLER.

JAMES MELVILLE'S CHILD.

ONE time my soul was pierced as with a sword,
   Contending still with men untaught and wild,
When He who to the prophet lent his gourd
   Gave me the solace of a pleasant child.

A summer gift my precious flower was given,
   A very summer fragrance was its life;
Its clear eyes soothed me as the blue of heaven,
   When home I turn'd, a weary man of strife.

With unform'd laughter, musically sweet,
   How soon the wakening babe would meet my kiss:
With outstretch'd arms its care-wrought father greet!
   Oh, in the desert, what a spring was this!

A few short months it blossom'd near my heart:
   A few short months, else toilsome all, and sad;
But that home-solace nerved me for my part,
   And of the babe I was exceeding glad.

Alas! my pretty bud, scarce form'd, was
    dying
  (The prophet's gourd, it wither'd in a
    night);
And He who gave me all, my heart's pulse
    trying,
  Took gently home the child of my delight.

Not rudely cull'd, not suddenly it perish'd,
  But gradual faded from our love away:
As if, still, secret dews, its life that cherish'd,
  Were drop by drop withheld, and day
    by day.

My blessed Master saved me from repining,
  So tenderly He sued me for His own;
So beautiful He made my babe's declining,
  Its dying bless'd me as its birth had done.

And daily to my board at noon and even
    Our fading flower I bade his mother
      bring,
  That we might commune of our rest in
    Heaven,
    Gazing the while on death, without its
      sting.

And of the ransom for that baby paid
  So very sweet at times our converse
    seem'd,
That the sure truth of grief a gladness
    made:
  Our little lamb by God's own Lamb redeem'd!

There were two milk-white doves my wife
    had nourish'd;
  And I too loved, erewhile, at times to
    stand
Marking how each the other fondly cherish'd,
  And fed them from my baby's dimpled
    hand!

So tame they grew that, to his cradle flying,
  Full oft they coo'd him to his noontide
    rest;
And to the murmurs of his sleep replying,
  Crept gently in and nestled in his breast.

'Twas a fair sight: the snow-pale infant
    sleeping,
  So fondly guardian'd by those creatures
    mild,
Watch o'er his closèd eyes their bright
    eyes keeping:
  Wondrous the love betwixt the birds
    and child!

Still as he sicken'd seem'd the doves too
    dwining,
  Forsook their food, and loathed their
    pretty play;
And on the day he died, with sad note
    pining,
  One gentle bird would not be fray'd
    away.

His mother found it, when she rose, sad-hearted,
  At early dawn, with sense of nearing ill;
And when, at last, the little spirit parted,
  The dove died too, as if of its heart-chill.

The other flew to meet my sad home-riding,
  As with a human sorrow in its coo;
To my dear child and its dead mate then
    guiding,
  Most pitifully plain'd—and parted too.

'Twas my first hansel and propine to
    Heaven;
  And as I laid my darling 'neath the sod,
Precious His comforts—once an infant
    given,
  And offer'd with two turtle-doves to
    God!
        MRS. A. STUART MENTEATH.

A CHILD'S THOUGHT OF GOD.

THEY say that God lives very high.
  But if you look above the pines
You cannot see our God; and why?

And if you dig down in the mines,
  You never see Him in the gold,
Though from Him all that's glory shines.

God is so good, He wears a fold
  Of heaven and earth across His face,
Like secrets kept for love untold.

But still I feel that His embrace
  Slides down by thrills through all things
    made,
Through sight and sound of every place.

As if my tender mother laid
  On my shut lids her kisses' pressure,
Half waking me at night, and said,
    "Who kissed you through the dark, dear guesser?"
          ELIZABETH BARRETT BROWNING.

THE SLEEPING BABE.

    THE baby wept;
The mother took it from the nurse's arms,
And soothed its griefs, and stilled its vain alarms,
    And baby slept.

    Again it weeps,
And God doth take it from the mother's arms,
From present pain and future unknown harms,
    And baby sleeps.
          SAMUEL HINDS.

WHICH SHALL IT BE?

"WHICH shall it be? Which shall it be?"
I look'd at John—John look'd at me
(Dear, patient John, who loves me yet
As well as though my locks were jet);
And when I found that I must speak,
My voice seem'd strangely low and weak:
"Tell me again what Robert said."
And then I, listening, bent my head.
"This is his letter: 'I will give
A house and land while you shall live,
If, in return, from out your seven,
One child to me for aye is given.'"
I look'd at John's old garments worn,
I thought of all that John had borne
Of poverty and work and care,
Which I, though willing, could not share;
I thought of seven mouths to feed,
Of seven little children's need,
And then of this. "Come, John," said I,
"We'll choose among them as they lie
Asleep;" so, walking hand in hand,
Dear John and I survey'd our band.
First to the cradle lightly stepp'd,
Where the new nameless baby slept.
"Shall it be Baby?" whispered John.
I took his hand, and hurried on
To Lily's crib. Her sleeping grasp
Held her old doll within its clasp;
Her dark curls lay like gold alight,
A glory 'gainst the pillow white.
Softly her father stoop'd to lay
His rough hand down in loving way,
When dream or whisper made her stir,
Then huskily said John, "Not her, not her!"
We stopp'd beside the trundle-bed,
And one long ray of lamplight shed
Athwart the boyish faces there,
In sleep so pitiful and fair;
I saw on Jamie's rough, red cheek
A tear undried. Ere John could speak,
"He's but a baby, too," said I,
And kiss'd him as we hurried by.
Pale, patient Robbie's angel face
Still in his sleep bore suffering's trace.
"No, for a thousand crowns, not him!"
We whisper'd, while our eyes were dim.
Poor Dick! bad Dick! our wayward son,
Turbulent, reckless, idle one—
Could he be spared? Nay; He who gave
Bids us befriend him to his grave;
Only a mother's heart can be
Patient enough for such as he;
"And so," said John, "I would not dare
To send him from her bedside prayer."
Then stole we softly up above
And knelt by Mary, child of love.
"Perhaps for her 'twould better be,"
I said to John. Quite silently
He lifted up a curl astray
Across her cheek in wilful way,
And shook his head: "Nay, love; not thee,"
The while my heart beat audibly.
Only one more, our eldest lad,
Trusty and truthful, good and glad—
So like his father. "No, John, no—
I cannot, will not, let him go."
And so we wrote, in courteous way,
We could not give one child away;
And afterward toil lighter seem'd,
Thinking of that of which we dream'd,
Happy in truth that not one face
We miss'd from its accustom'd place;
Thankful to work for all the seven,
Trusting the rest to One in heaven.
          ETHEL LYNN BEERS.

THE CHILDREN'S HOUR.

BETWEEN the dark and the daylight,
  When the night is beginning to lower,
Comes a pause in the day's occupations,
  That is known as the Children's Hour.

I hear in the chamber above me
  The patter of little feet,
The sound of a door that is opened,
  And voices soft and sweet.

From my study I see in the lamplight,
  Descending the broad hall stair,
Grave Alice, and laughing Allegra,
  And Edith with golden hair.

A whisper, and then a silence:
  Yet I know by their merry eyes
They are plotting and planning together
  To take me by surprise.

A sudden rush from the stairway,
  A sudden raid from the hall!
By three doors left unguarded
  They enter my castle wall!

They climb up into my turret
  O'er the arms and back of my chair;
If I try to escape, they surround me;
  They seem to be everywhere.

They almost devour me with kisses,
  Their arms about me entwine,
Till I think of the Bishop of Bingen
  In his Mouse-Tower on the Rhine!

Do you think, O blue-eyed banditti,
  Because you have scaled the wall,
Such an old moustache as I am
  Is not a match for you all?

I have you fast in my fortress,
  And will not let you depart,
But put you down into the dungeon
  In the round-tower of my heart.

And there will I keep you for ever,
  Yes, for ever and a day,
Till the walls shall crumble to ruin,
  And moulder in dust away!
        HENRY WADSWORTH LONGFELLOW.

THE MITHERLESS BAIRN.

WHEN a' ither bairnies are hush'd to their hame
By aunty, or cousin, or frecky grand-dame,
Wha stands last and lanely, an' naebody carin'?
'T is the puir doited loonie,—the mitherless bairn!

The mitherless bairn gangs to his lane bed;
Nane covers his cauld back or haps his bare head;
His wee hackit heelies are hard as the airn,
An' litheless the lair o' the mitherless bairn.

Aneath his cauld brow siccan dreams hover there
O' hands that wont kindly to kame his dark hair;
But mornin' brings clutches, a' reckless an' stern,
That lo'e nae the locks o' the mitherless bairn!

Yon sister that sang o'er his saftly-rock'd bed
Now rests in the mools where her mammie is laid;
The father toils sair their wee bannock to earn,
An' kens na the wrangs o' his mitherless bairn.

Her spirit, that passed in yon hour o' his birth,
Still watches his wearisome wanderings on earth;
Recording in heaven the blessings they earn
Wha couthilie deal wi' the mitherless bairn!

Oh, speak him na harshly,—he trembles the while,
He bends to your bidding, and blesses your smile;
In their dark hour o' anguish the heartless shall learn
That God deals the blow for the mitherless bairn!
        WILLIAM THOM.

THE ORPHAN BOY'S TALE.

STAY, lady, stay, for mercy's sake,
  And hear a helpless orphan's tale;
Ah, sure my looks must pity wake,—
  'Tis want that makes my cheek so pale;
Yet I was once a mother's pride,
  And my brave father's hope and joy;

But in the Nile's proud fight he died,
   And I am now an orphan boy!

Poor, foolish child! how pleased was I,
   When news of Nelson's victory came,
Along the crowded streets to fly,
   To see the lighted windows flame!
To force me home my mother sought,—
   She could not bear to hear my joy;
For with my father's life 'twas bought,—
   And made me a poor orphan boy!

The people's shouts were long and loud;
   My mother, shuddering, closed her ears;
"*Rejoice!* REJOICE!" still cried the crowd,—
   My mother answer'd with her tears!
"Oh why do tears steal down your cheek,"
   Cried I, "while others shout for joy?"
She kiss'd me; and in accents weak,
   She call'd me her poor orphan boy!

"What is an orphan boy?" I said;
   When suddenly she gasp'd for breath,
And her eyes closed! I shriek'd for aid,
   But ah! her eyes were closed in death.
My hardships since I will not tell;
   But now, no more a parent's joy,
Ah, lady, I have learn'd *too* well
   What 'tis to be an orphan boy!

Oh, were I by your bounty fed!—
   Nay, gentle lady, do not chide;
Trust me, I mean to earn my bread,—
   The sailor's orphan boy has pride.
Lady, you weep; what is't you say?
   You'll give me clothing, food, employ?
Look down, dear parents! look and see
   Your happy, happy orphan boy!
                           AMELIA OPIE.

ROMANCE OF THE SWAN'S NEST.

LITTLE Ellie sits alone
   'Mid the beeches of a meadow,
   By a stream-side on the grass,
And the trees are showering down
   Doubles of their leaves in shadow
   On her shining hair and face.

She has thrown her bonnet by,
   And her feet she has been dipping
   In the shallow water's flow.
   Now she holds them nakedly
In her hands, all sleek and dripping,
   While she rocketh to and fro.

Little Ellie sits alone,
   And the smile she softly uses
   Fills the silence like a speech,
   While she thinks what shall be done,—
And the sweetest pleasure chooses
   For her future within reach.

Little Ellie, in her smile,
Chooses, . . . "I will have a lover,
   Riding on a steed of steeds!
   He shall love me without guile,
And to *him* I will discover
   The swan's nest among the reeds.

"And the steed shall be red-roan,
   And the lover shall be noble,
   With an eye that takes the breath;
   And the lute he plays upon
Shall strike ladies into trouble,
   As his sword strikes men to death.

"And the steed it shall be shod
   All in silver, housed in azure,
   And the mane shall swim the wind,
   And the hoofs along the sod
Shall flash onward and keep measure,
   Till the shepherds look behind.

"But my lover will not prize
   All the glory that he rides in,
   When he gazes in my face.
   He will say, 'O Love, thine eyes
Build the shrine my soul abides in,
   And I kneel here for thy grace.'

"Then, ay, then—he shall kneel low,
   With the red-roan steed a-near him,
   Which shall seem to understand,—
   Till I answer, 'Rise and go!
For the world must love and fear him
   Whom I gift with heart and hand.'

"Then he will arise so pale,
I shall feel my own lips tremble
   With a *yes* I must not say,
   Nathless maiden brave, 'Farewell,'
I will utter, and dissemble—
   'Light to-morrow with to-day.'

"Then he'll ride among the hills
   To the wide world past the river,
   There to put away all wrong,
   To make straight distorted wills,
And to empty the broad quiver
   Which the wicked bear along.

"Three times shall a young foot-page
Swim the stream and climb the mountain
  And kneel down beside my feet:
'Lo, my master sends this gage,
Lady, for thy pity's counting!
  What wilt thou exchange for it?'

"And the first time I will send
A white rosebud for a guerdon,—
  And the second time, a glove;
But the third time I may bend
From my pride, and answer, 'Pardon
  If he comes to take my love.'

"Then the young foot-page will run—
Then my lover will ride faster,
  Till he kneeleth at my knee:
'I am a duke's eldest son!
Thousand serfs do call me master,—
  But, O Love, I love but *thee!*'

"He will kiss me on the mouth
Then, and lead me as a lover
  Through the crowds that praise his deeds:
And, when soul-tied by one troth,
Unto *him* I will discover
  That swan's nest among the reeds."

Little Ellie, with her smile
Not yet ended, rose up gayly,
  Tied the bonnet, donned the shoe,
And went homeward, round a mile,
Just to see, as she did daily,
  What more eggs were with the two.

Pushing through the elm-tree copse,
Winding up the stream, light-hearted,
  Where the osier pathway leads—
Past the boughs she stoops—and stops.
Lo, the wild swan had deserted—
  And a rat had gnawed the reeds.

Ellie went home sad and slow.
If she found the lover ever,
  With his red-roan steed of steeds,
Sooth I know not; but I know
She could never show him—never
  That swan's nest among the reeds!
              ELIZABETH BARRETT BROWNING.

MY CHILD.

I CANNOT make him dead:
  His fair sunshiny head
Is ever bounding round my study-chair;
Yet, when my eyes, now dim
  With tears, I turn to him,
The vision vanishes—he is not there!

I walk my parlor floor,
  And through the open door
I hear a footfall on the chamber stair;
  I'm stepping toward the hall
  To give the boy a call;
And then bethink me that—he is not there!

I thread the crowded street;
  A satchell'd lad I meet,
With the same beaming eyes and color'd hair:
  And, as he's running by,
  Follow him with my eye,
Scarcely believing that—he is not there!

I know his face is hid
  Under the coffin-lid;
Closed are his eyes; cold is his forehead fair;
  My hand that marble felt;
  O'er it in prayer I knelt;
Yet my heart whispers that—he is not there!

I cannot *make* him dead!
  When passing by the bed,
So long watch'd over with parental care,
  My spirit and my eye
  Seek it inquiringly,
Before the thought comes that—he is not there!

When, at the cool, gray break
  Of day, from sleep I wake,
With my first breathing of the morning air
  My soul goes up, with joy,
  To Him who gave my boy,
Then comes the sad thought that—he is not there!

When at the day's calm close,
  Before we seek repose,
I'm with his mother, offering up our prayer,
  Whate'er I may be *saying*,
  I am, in spirit, praying
For our boy's spirit, though—he is not there!

Not there! Where, then, is he?
  The form I used to see
Was but the *raiment* that he used to wear;

The grave, that now doth press
　Upon that cast-off dress,
Is but his wardrobe lock'd;—*he* is not
　　there!

He lives! In all the past
　He lives; nor, to the last,
Of seeing him again will I despair;
　In dreams I see him now;
　And, on his angel brow,
I see it written, "Thou shalt see me *there!*"

Yes, we all live to God!
　Father, thy chastening rod
So help us, thine afflicted ones, to bear,
　That, in the spirit-land,
　Meeting at thy right hand,
'Twill be our heaven to find that—he is
　　there!
　　　　　　　　　　　JOHN PIERPONT.

LUCY.

SHE dwelt among the untrodden ways
　Beside the springs of Dove,
A maid whom there were none to praise,
　And very few to love:

A violet by a mossy stone
　Half hidden from the eye;
Fair as a star, when only one
　Is shining in the sky.

She lived unknown, and few could know
　When Lucy ceased to be;
But she is in her grave, and, oh,
　The difference to me!
　　　　　　　　　　WILLIAM WORDSWORTH.

THREE YEARS SHE GREW.

THREE years she grew in sun and shower;
Then Nature said, "A lovelier flower
　On earth was never sown;
This child I to myself will take;
She shall be mine, and I will make
　A lady of my own.

"Myself will to my darling be
Both law and impulse, and with me
　The girl, in rock and plain,
In earth and heaven, in glade and bower,
Shall feel an overseeing power
　To kindle or restrain.

"She shall be sportive as the fawn,
That wild with glee across the lawn

Or up the mountain springs;
And hers shall be the breathing balm,
And hers the silence and the calm
　Of mute, insensate things.

"The floating clouds their state shall lend
To her; for her the willow bend:
　Nor shall she fail to see
Even in the motions of the storm
Grace that shall mould the maiden's form
　By silent sympathy.

"The stars of midnight shall be dear
To her; and she shall lean her ear
　In many a secret place,
Where rivulets dance their wayward round,
And beauty born of murmuring sound
　Shall pass into her face.

"And vital feelings of delight
Shall rear her form to stately height,
　Her virgin bosom swell;
Such thoughts to Lucy I will give
While she and I together live
　Here in this happy dell."

Thus Nature spake; the work was done—
How soon my Lucy's race was run!
　She died, and left to me
This heath, this calm and quiet scene,
The memory of what has been,
　And never more will be.
　　　　　　　　　　WILLIAM WORDSWORTH.

THE MORNING-GLORY.

WE wreathed about our darling's head
　The morning-glory bright;
Her little face looked out beneath,
　So full of life and light,
So lit as with a sunrise,
　That we could only say,
"She is the morning-glory true,
　And her poor types are they."

So always from that happy time
　We called her by their name,
And very fitting did it seem;
　For sure as morning came,
Behind her cradle-bars she smiled
　To catch the first faint ray,
As from the trellis smiles the flower
　And opens to the day.

But not so beautiful they rear
　Their airy cups of blue

As turned her sweet eyes to the light,
　Brimmed with sleep's tender dew;
And not so close their tendrils fine
　Round their supports are thrown
As those dear arms whose outstretched plea
　Clasped all hearts to her own.

We used to think how she had come,
　Even as comes the flower,
The last and perfect added gift
　To crown Love's morning hour;
And how in her was imaged forth
　The love we could not say,
As on the little dewdrops round
　Shines back the heart of day.

We never could have thought, O God,
　That she must wither up
Almost before a day was flown,
　Like the morning-glory's cup;
We never thought to see her droop
　Her fair and noble head,
Till she lay stretched before our eyes,
　Wilted, and cold, and dead!

The morning-glory's blossoming
　Will soon be coming round;
We see their rows of heart-shaped leaves
　Upspringing from the ground;
The tender things the winter killed
　Renew again their birth,
But the glory of our morning
　Has passed away from earth.

O Earth! in vain our aching eyes
　Stretch over thy green plain!
Too harsh thy dews, too gross thine air,
　Her spirit to sustain;
But up in groves of Paradise
　Full surely we shall see
Our morning-glory beautiful
　Twine round our dear Lord's knee.
MARIA WHITE LOWELL.

THE BABE.

NAKED on parent's knees, a new-born child,
Weeping thou sat'st when all around thee smiled:
So live, that, sinking to thy last long sleep,
Thou then mayst smile while all around thee weep.
SIR WILLIAM JONES.

THE THREE SONS.

I HAVE a son, a little son, a boy just five years old,
With eyes of thoughtful earnestness and mind of gentle mould.
They tell me that unusual grace in all his ways appears,
That my child is grave and wise of heart beyond his childish years.
I cannot say how this may be; I know his face is fair—
And yet his chiefest comeliness is his sweet and serious air;
I know his heart is kind and fond, I know he loveth me,
But loveth yet his mother more with grateful fervency.
But that which others most admire is the thought which fills his mind—
The food for grave, inquiring speech he everywhere doth find.
Strange questions doth he ask of me when we together walk;
He scarcely thinks as children think, or talks as children talk;
Nor cares he much for childish sports, dotes not on bat or ball,
But looks on manhood's ways and works, and aptly mimics all.
His little heart is busy still, and oftentimes perplext
With thoughts about this world of ours, and thoughts about the next.
He kneels at his dear mother's knee; she teacheth him to pray;
And strange and sweet and solemn then are the words which he will say.
Oh, should my gentle child be spared to manhood's years, like me,
A holier and a wiser man I trust that he will be;
And when I look into his eyes and stroke his thoughtful brow,
I dare not think what I should feel were I to lose him now.

I have a son, a second son, a simple child of three;
I'll not declare how bright and fair his little features be,
How silver sweet those tones of his when he prattles on my knee;

I do not think his light-blue eye is, like
   his brother's, keen,
Nor his brow so full of childish thought
   as his hath ever been;
But his little heart's a fountain pure of
   kind and tender feeling,
And his every look's a gleam of light, rich
   depths of love revealing.
When he walks with me, the country folk,
   who pass us in the street,
Will shout for joy, and bless my boy, he
   looks so mild and sweet.
A playfellow is he to all; and yet, with
   cheerful tone,
Will sing his little song of love when left
   to sport alone.
His presence is like sunshine sent to glad-
   den home and hearth,
To comfort us in all our griefs, and sweeten
   all our mirth.
Should he grow up to riper years, God
   grant his heart may prove
As sweet a home for heavenly grace as now
   for earthly love;
And if, beside his grave, the tears our
   aching eyes must dim,
God comfort us for all the love which we
   shall lose in him.

I have a son, a third sweet son, his age I
   cannot tell,
For they reckon not by years and months
   where he is gone to dwell.
To us, for fourteen anxious months, his
   infant smiles were given,
And then he bade farewell to earth, and
   went to live in heaven.
I cannot tell what form is his, what looks
   he weareth now,
Nor guess how bright a glory crowns his
   shining seraph brow.
The thoughts that fill his sinless soul, the
   bliss which he doth feel,
Are number'd with the secret things which
   God will not reveal.
But I know (for God hath told me this)
   that he is now at rest,
Where other blessed infants be—on their
   Saviour's loving breast.
I know his spirit feels no more this weary
   load of flesh,
But his sleep is bless'd with endless dreams
   of joy for ever fresh.
I know the angels fold him close beneath
   their glittering wings,
And soothe him with a song that breathes
   of heaven's divinest things.
I know that we shall meet our babe (his
   mother dear and I)
Where God for aye shall wipe away all
   tears from every eye.
Whate'er befalls his brethren twain, his
   bliss can never cease;
Their lot may here be grief and fear, but
   his is certain peace.
It may be that the tempter's wiles their
   souls from bliss may sever;
But, if our own poor faith fail not, he
   must be ours for ever.
When we think of what our darling is,
   and what we still must be—
When we muse on that world's perfect
   bliss and this world's misery—
When we groan beneath this load of sin,
   and feel this grief and pain—
Oh, we'd rather lose our other two than
   have him here again!
JOHN MOULTRIE.

WE ARE SEVEN.

—A SIMPLE child,
   That lightly draws its breath,
And feels its life in every limb,
   What should it know of death?

I met a little cottage girl;
   She was eight years old, she said;
Her hair was thick with many a curl
   That cluster'd round her head.

She had a rustic, woodland air,
   And she was wildly clad:
Her eyes were fair, and very fair—
   Her beauty made me glad.

"Sisters and brothers, little maid,
   How many may you be?"
"How many? Seven in all," she said,
   And wondering look'd at me.

"And where are they? I pray you tell
   She answer'd, "Seven are we;
And two of us at Conway dwell,
   And two are gone to sea.

"Two of us in the churchyard lie.
   My sister and my brother;

And in the churchyard cottage I
  Dwell near them with my mother."

" You say that two at Conway dwell,
  And two are gone to sea,
Yet ye are seven! I pray you tell,
  Sweet maid, how this may be?"

Then did the little maid reply:
  "Seven boys and girls are we;
Two of us in the churchyard lie,
  Beneath the churchyard tree."

" You run about, my little maid,
  Your limbs they are alive;
If two are in the churchyard laid,
  Then ye are only five."

"Their graves are green, they may be seen,"
  The little maid replied,
"Twelve steps or more from my mother's door,
  And they are side by side.

" My stockings there I often knit,
  My kerchief there I hem;
And there upon the ground I sit—
  I sit and sing to them.

" And often after sunset, sir,
  When it is light and fair,
I take my little porringer,
  And eat my supper there.

" The first that died was little Jane;
  In bed she moaning lay,
Till God released her of her pain;
  And then she went away.

" So in the churchyard she was laid;
  And when the grass was dry,
Together round her grave we play'd,
  My brother John and I.

And when the ground was white with snow,
  And I could run and slide,
My brother John was forced to go,
  And he lies by her side."

" How many are you, then," said I,
  " If they two are in Heaven?"
The little maiden did reply,
  " Oh, master, we are seven!"

" But they are dead—those two are dead,
  Their spirits are in Heaven!"
'Twas throwing words away, for still
  The little maid would have her will,
And said, " Nay, we are seven!"
                WILLIAM WORDSWORTH.

THE MOTHER'S HOPE.

Is there, where the winds are singing
  In the happy summer-time,
Where the raptured air is ringing
With Earth's music heavenward springing
  Forest chirp, and village chime;
Is there, of the sounds that float
  Minglingly, a single note
Half so sweet, and clear, and wild,
As the laughter of a child?

Listen; and be now delighted.
  Morn hath touch'd her golden strings,
Earth and sky their vows have plighted,
Life and light are reunited,
  Amid countless carollings;
Yet, delicious as they are,
There's a sound that's sweeter far—
One that makes the heart rejoice
More than all,—the human voice!

Organ, finer, deeper, clearer,
Though it be a stranger's tone;
Than the winds or waters dearer,
More enchanting to the hearer,
  For it answereth his own.
But of all its witching words,
Sweeter than the songs of birds,
Those are sweetest, bubbling wild
Through the laughter of a child.

Harmonies from time-touch'd towers,
  Haunted strains from rivulets,
Hum of bees among the flowers,
Rustling leaves, and silver showers,—
  These ere long the ear forgets;
But in mine there is a sound
Ringing on the whole year round;
Heart-deep laughter that I heard,
Ere my child could speak a word.

Ah! 'twas heard by ear far purer,
  Fondlier form'd to catch the strain—
Ear of one whose love is surer;
Hers, the mother, the endurer
  Of the deepest share of pain;

Hers the deepest bliss, to treasure
Memories of that cry of pleasure;
Hers to hoard, a lifetime after,
Echoes of that infant laughter.

Yes, a mother's large affection
  Hears with a mysterious sense;
Breathings that evade detection,
Whisper faint, and fine inflection,
  Thrill in her with power intense.
Childhood's honey'd tones untaught
Heareth she, in loving thought!
Tones that never thence depart,
For she listens—with her heart!
LAMAN BLANCHARD.

THE GAMBOLS OF CHILDREN.

DOWN the dimpled green-sward dancing,
  Bursts a flaxen-headed bevy—
Bud-lipt boys and girls advancing,
  Love's irregular little levy.

Rows of liquid eyes in laughter,
  How they glimmer, how they quiver!
Sparkling one another after,
  Like bright ripples on a river.

Tipsy band of rubious faces,
  Flush'd with Joy's ethereal spirit,
Make your mocks and sly grimaces
  At Love's self, and do not fear it.
GEORGE DARLEY.

UNDER MY WINDOW.

UNDER my window, under my window,
  All in the Midsummer weather,
Three little girls with fluttering curls
  Flit to and fro together:—
There's Bell with her bonnet of satin sheen,
And Maud with her mantle of silver green,
  And Kate with her scarlet feather.

Under my window, under my window,
  Leaning stealthily over,
Merry and clear, the voice I hear,
  Of each glad-hearted rover.
Ah! sly little Kate, she steals my roses;
And Maud and Bell twine wreaths and posies,
  As merry as bees in clover.

Under my window, under my window,
  In the blue Midsummer weather,
Stealing slow, on a hush'd tip-toe,
  I catch them all together:—
Bell with her bonnet of satin sheen,
And Maud with her mantle of silver-green,
  And Kate with the scarlet feather.

Under my window, under my window,
  And off through the orchard closes;
While Maud she flouts, and Bell she pouts,
  They scamper and drop their posies;
But dear little Kate takes naught amiss,
And leaps in my arms with a loving kiss,
  And I give her all my roses.
THOMAS WESTWOOD.

BOYHOOD.

AH! then how sweetly closed those crowded days!
The minutes parting one by one like rays,
  That fade upon a summer's eve.
  But oh! what charm, or magic numbers
  Can give me back the gentle slumbers
Those weary, happy days did leave?
When by my bed I saw my mother kneel,
And with her blessing took her nightly kiss:
Whatever Time destroys, he cannot this—
E'en now that nameless kiss I feel.
WASHINGTON ALLSTON.

THE CHILDREN IN THE WOOL.

NOW ponder well, you parents deare,
  These wordes, which I shall write;
A doleful story you shall heare,
  In time brought forth to light:
A gentleman of good account
  In Norfolke dwelt of late,
Who did in honor far surmount
  Most men of his estate.

Sore sicke he was, and like to dye,
  No helpe his life could save;
His wife by him as sicke did lye,
  And both possest one grave.
No love between these two was lost,
  Each was to other kinde;
In love they liv'd, in love they dyed,
  And left two babes behinde:

The one a fine and pretty boy,
  Not passing three yeares olde;
The other a girl more young than he,
  And fram'd in beautyes moulde.
The father left his little son,
  As plainlye doth appeare,
When he to perfect age should come,
  Three hundred poundes a yeare.

And to his little daughter Jane
  Five hundred poundes in gold,
To be paid downe on marriage-day,
  Which might not be controll'd;
But if the children chance to dye
  Ere they to age should come,
Their uncle should possesse their wealth,
  For so the wille did run.

Now, brother, said the dying man,
  Look to my children deare;
Be good unto my boy and girl,
  No friendes else have they here:
To God and you I recommend
  My children deare this daye;
But little while be sure we have
  Within this world to staye.

You must be father and mother both,
  And uncle all in one;
God knowes what will become of them
  When I am dead and gone.
With that bespake their mother deare,
  Oh brother kinde, quoth shee,
You are the man must bring our babes
  To wealth or miserie:

And if you keep them carefully,
  Then God will you reward;
But if you otherwise should deal,
  God will your deedes regard.
With lippes as cold as any stone,
  They kist their children small:
God bless you both, my children deare;
  With that the teares did fall.

These speeches then their brother spake
  To this sicke couple there:
The keeping of your little ones,
  Sweet sister, do not feare:
God never prosper me nor mine,
  Nor aught else that I have,
If I do wrong your children deare,
  When you are layd in grave.

The parents being dead and gone,
  The children home he takes,
And bringes them straite unto his house,
  Where much of them he makes.
He had not kept these pretty babes
  A twelvemonth and a daye,
But, for their wealth, he did devise
  To make them both awaye.

He bargain'd with two ruffians strong,
  Which were of furious mood,
That they should take these children young,
  And slaye them in a wood.
He told his wife an artful tale,
  He would the children send
To be brought up in faire Londòn,
  With one that was his friend.

Away then went those pretty babes,
  Rejoycing at that tide,
Rejoycing with a merry minde,
  They should on cock-horse ride.
They prate and prattle pleasantly,
  As they rode on the waye,
To those that should their butchers be,
  And work their lives decaye:

So that the pretty speeche they had,
  Made Murder's heart relent:
And they that undertooke the deed
  Full sore did now repent.
Yet one of them more hard of heart,
  Did vowe to do his charge,
Because the wretch, that hired him,
  Had paid him very large.

The other won't agree thereto,
  So here they fall to strife;
With one another they did fight,
  About the childrens life:
And he that was of mildest mood,
  Did slaye the other there,
Within an unfrequented wood;
  The babes did quake for feare!

He took the children by the hand,
  Teares standing in their eye,
And bad them straitwaye follow him,
  And look they did not crye;
And two long miles he ledd them on,
  While they for food complaine:
Staye here, quoth he, I'll bring you bread.
  When I come back againe.

These pretty babes, with hand in hand,
  Went wandering up and downe,
But never more could see the man
  Approaching from the towne:
Their prettye lippes, with black-berries,
  Were all besmear'd and dyed,
And, when they sawe the darksome night,
  They sat them downe and cry'd.

Thus wandered these poor innocents,
  Till deathe did end their grief;
In one anothers arms they dyed,
  As wanting due relief.
No burial " this " pretty " pair "
  Of any man receives,
Till Robin-red-breast piously
  Did cover them with leaves.

And now the heavy wrathe of God
  Upon their uncle fell;
Yea, fearfull fiends did haunt his house,
  His conscience felt an hell.
His barnes were fir'd, his goodes consum'd,
  His landes were barren made;
His cattle dyed within the field,
  And nothing with him stayd.

And in a voyage to Portugal
  Two of his sonnes did dye;
And to conclude, himselfe was brought
  To want and miserye:
He pawn'd and mortgaged all his land
  Ere seven years came about.
And now at length this wicked act
  Did by this meanes come out:

The fellowe, that did take in hand
  These children for to kill,
Was for a robbery judg'd to dye,
  Such was God's blessed will:
Who did confess the very truth,
  As here hath been display'd:
Their uncle having dyed in gaol,
  Where he for debt was layd.

You that executors be made,
  And overseers eke
Of children that be fatherless,
  And infants mild and meek;
Take you example by this thing,
  And yield to each his right,
Lest God, with such like miserye,
  Your wicked minds requite.

          AUTHOR UNKNOWN.

THE CHILD AND THE MOURNERS.

A LITTLE child, beneath a tree,
Sat and chanted cheerily
A little song, a pleasant song,
Which was—she sang it all day long—
" When the wind blows the blossoms fall;
But a good God reigns over all."

There pass'd a lady by the way,
Moaning in the face of day:
There were tears upon her cheek,
Grief in her heart too great to speak;
Her husband died but yester-morn,
And left her in the world forlorn.

She stopp'd and listen'd to the child
That look'd to heaven, and, singing, smiled;
And saw not, for her own despair,
Another lady, young and fair,
Who also passing, stopp'd to hear
The infant's anthem ringing clear.

For she but few sad days before
Had lost the little babe she bore;
And grief was heavy at her soul
As that sweet memory o'er her stole,
And show'd how bright had been the past,
The present drear and overcast.

And as they stood beneath the tree
Listening, soothed and placidly,
A youth came by, whose sunken eyes
Spake of a load of miseries;
And he, arrested like the twain,
Stopp'd to listen to the strain.

Death had bow'd the youthful head
Of his bride beloved, his bride unwed:
Her marriage robes were fitted on,
Her fair young face with blushes shone,
When the destroyer smote her low,
And changed the lover's bliss to woe.

And these three listen'd to the song,
Silver-toned, and sweet, and strong,
Which that child, the livelong day,
Chanted to itself in play:
" When the wind blows the blossoms fall·
But a good God reigns over all."

The widow's lips impulsive moved;
The mother's grief, though unreproved,
Soften'd, as her trembling tongue
Repeated what the infant sung;
And the sad lover, with a start,
Conn'd it over to his heart.

And though the child—if child it were,
And not a seraph sitting there—
Was seen no more, the sorrowing three
Went on their way resignedly,

The song still ringing in their ears—
Was it music of the spheres?

Who shall tell? They did not know.
But in the midst of deepest woe
The strain recurr'd, when sorrow grew,
To warn them, and console them too:
"When the wind blows the blossoms fall;
But a good God reigns over all."
CHARLES MACKAY.

LUCY GRAY; OR, SOLITUDE.

OFT I had heard of Lucy Gray;
  And, when I cross'd the wild,
I chanced to see at break of day
  The solitary child.

No mate, no comrade Lucy knew;
  She dwelt on a wide moor,—
The sweetest thing that ever grew
  Beside a human door.

You yet may spy the fawn at play,
  The hare upon the green,
But the sweet face of Lucy Gray
  Will nevermore be seen.

"To-night will be a stormy night;
  You to the town must go,
And take a lantern, child, to light
  Your mother through the snow."

"That, father, will I gladly do;
  'Tis scarcely afternoon;
The minster clock has just struck two,
  And yonder is the moon."

At this the father raised his hook,
  And snapp'd a fagot-band;
He plied his work; and Lucy took
  The lantern in her hand.

Not blither is the mountain roe:
  With many a wanton stroke
Her feet disperse the powdery snow,
  That rises up like smoke.

The storm came on before its time:
  She wander'd up and down,
And many a hill did Lucy climb,
  But never reach'd the town.

The wretched parents all that night
  Went shouting far and wide,
But there was neither sound nor sight
  To serve them for a guide.

At daybreak on a hill they stood
  That overlook'd the moor,
And thence they saw the bridge of wood,
  A furlong from their door.

They wept, and turning homeward, cried.
  "In heaven we all shall meet:"
When in the snow the mother spied
  The print of Lucy's feet.

Half breathless, from the steep hill's edge
  They track'd the foot-marks small,
And through the broken hawthorn-hedge,
  And by the long stone wall,

And then an open field they cross'd:
  The marks were still the same;
They track'd them on, nor ever lost,
  And to the bridge they came.

They follow'd from the snowy bank
  Those foot-marks one by one,
Into the middle of the plank,
  And further there were none.

Yet some maintain that to this day
  She is a living child;
That you may see sweet Lucy Gray
  Upon the lonesome wild.

O'er rough and smooth she trips along,
  And never looks behind;
And sings a solitary song
  That whistles in the wind.
WILLIAM WORDSWORTH.

THE WIDOW AND CHILD.

HOME they brought her warrior dead:
  She nor swoon'd, nor utter'd cry:
All her maidens, watching, said,
  "She must weep or she will die."

Then they praised him, soft and low,
  Called him worthy to be loved,
Truest friend and noblest foe;
  Yet she neither spoke nor moved.

Stole a maiden from her place,
  Lightly to the warrior stept,
Took the face-cloth from the face;
  Yet she neither moved nor wept.

Rose a nurse of ninety years,
  Set his child upon her knee—
Like summer tempest came her tears—
  "Sweet my child, I live for thee."
            ALFRED TENNYSON.

THE SCHOOLMISTRESS.

AH me! full sorely is my heart forlorn,
  To think how modest worth neglected lies;
While partial fame doth with her blasts adorn
  Such deeds alone as pride and pomp disguise;
  Deeds of ill sort, and mischievous emprize:
Lend me thy clarion, goddess! let me try
  To sound the praise of merit, ere it dies;
Such as I oft have chancèd to espy,
Lost in the dreary shades of dull obscurity.

In every village mark'd with little spire,
  Embower'd in trees, and hardly known to fame,
There dwells in lowly shed, and mean attire,
  A matron old, whom we schoolmistress name;
  Who boasts unruly brats with birch to tame;
They grieven sore, in piteous durance pent,
  Awed by the pow'r of this relentless dame;
And oft-times, on vagaries idly bent,
For unkempt hair, or task unconn'd, are sorely shent.

And all in sight doth rise a birchen tree,
  Which learning near her little dome did stow;
Whilom a twig of small regard to see,
  Tho' now so wide its waving branches flow;
  And work the simple vassals mickle woe;
For not a wind might curl the leaves that blew,
  But their limbs shudder'd and their pulse beat low;
And as they look'd they found their horror grew,
And shaped it into rods, and tingled at the view.

So have I seen (who has not, may conceive)
  A lifeless phantom near a garden placed;
So doth it wanton birds of peace bereave,
  Of sport, of song, of pleasure, of repast;
  They start, they stare, they wheel, they look aghast:
Sad servitude! such comfortless annoy
  May no bold Briton's riper age e'er taste!
Ne superstition clog his dance of joy,
Ne vision empty, vain, his native bliss destroy.

Near to this dome is found a patch so green,
  On which the tribe their gambols do display;
And at the door impris'ning board is seen,
  Lest weakly wights of smaller size should stray,
  Eager, perdie, to bask in sunny day!
The noises intermix'd, which thence resound,
  Do learning's little tenement betray:
Where sits the dame, disguised in look profound,
And eyes her fairy throng, and turns her wheel around.

Her cap, far whiter than the driven snow,
  Emblem right meet of decency does yield;
Her apron dyed in grain, as blue, I trow,
  As is the harebell that adorns the field:
  And in her hand, for sceptre, she does wield
Tway birchen sprays; with anxious fear entwined,
  With dark distrust, and sad repentance fill'd;
And steadfast hate, and sharp affliction join'd,
And fury uncontroll'd and chastisement unkind.

Few but have kenn'd, in semblance meet portray'd,
  The childish faces of old Eol's train;
Libs, Notus, Auster; these in frowns array'd,
  How then would fare or earth, or sky, or main,

Were the stern god to give his slaves
    the rein?
And were not she rebellious breasts to
    quell,
And were not she her statutes to main-
    tain,
The cot no more, I ween, were deem'd the
    cell,
Where comely peace of mind and decent
    order dwell.

A russet stole was o'er her shoulders
    thrown;
A russet kirtle fenced the nipping air;
'Twas simple russet, but it was her own;
    'Twas her own country bred the flock so
        fair;
    'Twas her own labor did the fleece pre-
        pare;
And, sooth to say, her pupils, ranged
    around,
    Through pious awe, did term it passing
        rare;
For they in gaping wonderment abound,
And think, no doubt, she been the greatest
    wight on ground.

Albeit ne flattery did corrupt her truth,
    Ne pompous title did debauch her ear;
Goody, good woman, gossip, n' aunt, for-
    sooth,
    Or dame, the sole additions she did
        hear;
    Yet these she challenged, these she held
        right dear:
Ne would esteem him act as mought be-
    hove,
    Who should not honor'd eld with these
        revere;
For never title yet so mean could prove,
But there was eke a mind which did that
    title love.

One ancient hen she took delight to feed,
    The plodding pattern of the busy dame,
Which ever and anon, impell'd by need,
    Into her school, begirt with chickens,
        came;
    Such favor did her past deportment
        claim;
And, if neglect had lavish'd on the
    ground
Fragment of bread, she would collect
    the same,
For well she knew, and quaintly could ex-
    pound,
What sin it were to waste the smallest
    crumb she found.

Herbs, too, she knew, and well of each
    could speak
    That in her garden sipp'd the silv'ry
        dew,
Where no vain flow'r disclosed a gaudy
    streak;
But herbs for use and physic, not a few,
    Of gray renown, within those borders
        grew:
The tufted basil, pun-provoking thyme,
    Fresh balm, and marygold of cheerful
        hue,
The lowly gill, that never dares to climb;
And more I fain would sing, disdaining
    here to rhyme.

Yet euphrasy may not be left unsung,
    That gives dim eyes to wander leagues
        around;
And pungent radish, biting infant's tongue,
    And plantain ribb'd, that heals the reap-
        er's wound,
    And marj'ram sweet, in shepherd's posie
        found,
And lavender, whose spikes of azure bloom
    Shall be erewhile in arid bundles bound,
To lurk amidst the labors of her loom,
And crown her kerchiefs clean with mickle
    rare perfume.

And here trim rosemarine, that whilom
    crown'd
    The daintiest garden of the proudest
        peer,
Ere, driven from its envied site, it found
    A sacred shelter for its branches here;
    Where, edged with gold, its glitt'ring
        skirts appear.
Oh, wassel days! oh, customs meet and
    well!
Ere this was banish'd from his lofty
    sphere:
Simplicity then sought this humble cell,
Nor ever would she more with thane and
    lordling dwell.

Here oft the dame, on Sabbath's decent
  eve,
  Hymnèd such psalms as Sternhold forth
    did mete;
If winter 'twere, she to her hearth did
  cleave,
  But in her garden found a summer-
    seat:
Sweet melody! to hear her then repeat
How Israel's sons, beneath a foreign king,
  While taunting foemen did a song en-
    treat,
All, for the nonce, untuning ev'ry string,
Uphung their useless lyres; small heart
  had they to sing.

For she was just, and friend to virtuous
    lore,
  And pass'd much time in truly virtuous
    deed,
And in those elfins' ears would oft deplore
  The times when truth by popish rage
    did bleed,
  And tortuous death was true devotion's
    meed,
And simple faith in iron chains did mourn,
  That nould on wooden image placed her
    creed,
And lawny saints in smould'ring flames did
    burn;
Ah! dearest Lord, forfend thilk days should
    e'er return!

In elbow-chair, like that of Scottish stem,
  By the sharp tooth of cank'ring eld de-
    faced,
In which, when he receives his diadem,
  Our sov'reign prince and liefest liege is
    placed,
  The matron sate; and some with rank
    she graced
(The source of children's and of cour-
    tiers' pride),
  Redress'd affronts, for vile affronts there
    pass'd,
  And warn'd them not the fretful to de-
    ride,
But love each other dear, whatever them
    betide.

Right well she knew each temper to descry:
  To thwart the proud, and the submiss to
    raise;

Some with vile copper prize exalt on high,
  And some entice with pittance small of
    praise;
  And other some with baneful sprig she
    'frays:
Ev'n absent, she the reins of power doth
    hold,
  While with quaint arts the giddy crowd
    she sways
Forewarn'd, if little bird their pranks be-
    hold,
'Twill whisper in her ear, and all the scene
    unfold.

Lo now with state she utters the command!
  Eftsoons the urchins to their tasks repair;
  Their books of stature small they take in
    hand,
  Which with pellucid horn securèd are;
  To save from fingers wet the letters fair:
The work so gay, that on their back is seen,
  St. George's high achievements does de-
    clare;
On which thilk wight that has y-gazing been,
Kens the forthcoming rod, unpleasing sight,
    I ween!

Ah, luckless he, and born beneath the
    beam
  Of evil star! it irks me whilst I write!
As erst the bard by Mulla's silver stream,
  Oft, as he told of deadly dolorous plight,
  Sigh'd as he sung, and did in tears
    indite.
For, brandishing the rod, she doth begin
  To loose the brogues, the stripling's late
    delight!
And down they drop; appears his dainty
    skin,
Fair as the furry coat of whitest ermilin.

Oh, ruthful scene! when from a nook ob-
    scure
  His little sister doth his peril see:
All playful as she sate, she grows demure;
  She finds full soon her wonted spirits flee;
  She meditates a pray'r to set him free;
Nor gentle pardon could this dame deny
  (If gentle pardon could with dames
    agree)
To her sad grief that swells in either eye,
And wrings her so that all for pity she
    could die.

No longer can she now her shrieks command;
  And hardly she forbears, through awful fear,
To rushen forth, and, with presumptuous hand,
  To stay hard justice in its mid career.
  On thee she calls, on thee her parent dear!
(Ah! too remote to ward the shameful blow!)
She sees no kind domestic visage near,
And soon a flood of tears begins to flow;
And gives a loose at last to unavailing woe.

But, ah! what pen his piteous plight may trace?
  Or what device his loud laments explain?
The form uncouth of his disguisèd face?
  The pallid hue that dyes his looks amain?
  The plenteous shower that does his cheek disdain?
When he in abject-wise implores the dame,
  Ne hopeth aught of sweet reprieve to gain;
Or when from high she levels well her aim,
And, through the thatch, his cries each falling stroke proclaim.

The other tribe aghast, with sore dismay,
  Attend, and con their tasks with mickle care:
By turns, astonied, ev'ry twig survey,
  And, from their fellow's hateful wounds, beware;
  Knowing, I wist, how each the same may share;
Till fear has taught them a performance meet,
  And to the well-known chest the dame repair;
Whence oft with sugar'd cates she doth 'em greet,
And ginger-bread y-rare; now, certes, doubly sweet!

See to their seats they hie with merry glee,
  And in beseemly order sitten there;
All but the wight of bum y-gallèd; he
  Abhorreth bench, and stool, and form, and chair
  (This hand in mouth y-fix'd, that rends his hair);
And eke with snubs profound, and heaving breast,
  Convulsions intermitting! does declare
His grievous wrongs; his dame's unjust behest,
And scorns her offer'd love, and shuns to be caress'd.

His face besprent with liquid crystal shines,
  His blooming face that seems a purple flow'r
Which low to earth its drooping head declines,
  All smear'd and sullied by a vernal show'r.
Oh, the hard bosoms of despotic pow'r!
All, all, but she, the author of his shame,
  All, all, but she, regret this mournful hour:
Yet hence the youth, and hence the flow'r shall claim,
If so I deem aright, transcending worth and fame.

Behind some door, in melancholy thought.
  Mindless of food, he, dreary caitiff, pines;
Ne for his fellows' joyaunce careth aught,
  But to the wind all merriment resigns;
  And deems it shame if he to peace inclines;
And many a sullen look askance is sent,
  Which for his dame's annoyance he designs;
And still the more to pleasure him she's bent,
The more doth he, perverse, her 'havior past resent.

Ah, me! how much I fear lest pride it be!
  But if that pride it be, which thus inspires,
Beware, ye dames, with nice discernment see
  Ye quench not too the sparks of nobler fires:

Ah, better far than all the muses' lyres,
All coward arts, is valor's gen'rous heat;
 The firm fixt breast which fit and right requires,
Like Vernon's patriot soul; more justly great
Than craft that pimps for ill, or flow'ry false deceit.

Yet, nursed with skill, what dazzling fruits appear!
 Ev'n now sagacious foresight points to show
A little bench of heedless bishops here!
And there a chancellor in embryo,
Or bard sublime, if bard may e'er be so,
As Milton, Shakespeare, names that ne'er shall die!
 Though now he crawl along the ground so low,
Nor weeting how the muse should soar on high,
Wisheth, poor starv'ling elf! his paper kite may fly.

And this perhaps, who censuring the design,
 Low lays the house which that of cards doth build,
Shall Dennis be! if rigid fates incline,
And many an epic to his rage shall yield;
And many a poet quit th' Aonian field;
And, sour'd by age, profound he shall appear,
 As he who now with 'sdainful fury thrill'd,
Surveys mine work; and levels many a sneer,
And furls his wrinkly front, and cries, "What stuff is here?"

But now Dan Phœbus gains the middle sky,
And liberty unbars her prison-door;
And like a rushing torrent out they fly,
 And now the grassy cirque han cover'd o'er
 With boist'rous revel-rout and wild uproar;
A thousand ways in wanton rings they run,
Heav'n shield their short-lived pastimes I implore
For well may freedom, erst so dearly won,
Appear to British elf more gladsome than the sun

Enjoy, poor imps! enjoy your sportive trade,
And chase gay flies, and cull the fairest flow'rs;
For when my bones in grass-green sods are laid;
For never may ye taste more careless hours
In knightly castles, or in ladies' bow'rs.
Oh, vain to seek delight in earthly thing!
But most in courts where proud ambition tow'rs;
Deluded wight, who weens fair peace can spring
Beneath the pompous dome of kesar or of king.

See in each sprite some various bent appear!
These rudely carol most incondite lay;
Those sauntering on the green, with jocund leer
Salute the stranger passing on his way;
Some builden fragile tenements of clay;
Some to the standing lake their courses bend,
With pebbles smooth at duck and drake to play;
Thilk to the huxter's sav'ry cottage tend,
In pastry kings and queens th' allotted mite to spend.

Here, as each season yields a different store,
Each season's stores in order rangèd been;
Apples with cabbage-net y-cover'd o'er,
Galling full sore th' unmoney'd wight, are seen;
And goose-b'rie clad in liv'ry red or green;
And here of lovely dye, the cath'rine pear,
Fine pear! as lovely for thy juice I ween
Oh, may no wight e'er penniless come there,
Lest smit with ardent love he pine with hopeless care!

See! cherries here, ere cherries yet abound,
With thread so white in tempting posies tied,
Scattering like blooming maid their glances round,
With pamper'd look draw little eyes aside;

And must be bought, though penury betide.
The plum all azure, and the nut all brown,
And here each season do those cakes abide,
Whose honor'd names th' inventive city own,
Rend'ring through Britain's isle Salopia's praises known.

Admired Salopia! that with venial pride
Eyes her bright form in Severn's ambient wave,
Famed for her loyal cares in perils tried,
Her daughters lovely and her striplings brave:
Ah! midst the rest, may flowers adorn his grave,
Whose art did first these dulcet cates display!
A motive fair to learning's imps he gave,
Who cheerless o'er her darkling region stray;
Till reason's morn arise, and light them on their way.

WILLIAM SHENSTONE.

THE CHILDREN.

WHEN the lessons and tasks are all ended,
And the school for the day is dismiss'd,
The little ones gather around me,
To bid me good-night and be kiss'd:
Oh, the little white arms that encircle
My neck in their tender embrace!
Oh the smiles that are halos of heaven,
Shedding sunshine of love on my face!

And when they are gone I sit dreaming
Of my childhood, too lovely to last:
Of joy that my heart will remember
While it wakes to the pulse of the past,
Ere the world and its wickedness made me
A partner of sorrow and sin;
When the glory of God was about me,
And the glory of gladness within.

All my heart grows as weak as a woman's,
And the fountains of feeling will flow,
When I think of the paths steep and stony,
Where the feet of the dear ones must go;
Of the mountains of sin hanging o'er them,
Of the tempest of Fate blowing wild;
Oh, there's nothing on earth half so holy
As the innocent heart of a child!

They are idols of hearts and of households;
They are angels of God in disguise;
His sunlight still sleeps in their tresses,
His glory still gleams in their eyes.
Those truants from home and from heaven,
They have made me more manly and mild,
And I know now how Jesus could liken
The kingdom of God to a child.

I ask not a life for the dear ones,
All radiant, as others have done,
But that life may have just enough shadow
To temper the glare of the sun:
I would pray God to guard them from evil,
But my prayer would bound back to myself;
Ah! a seraph may pray for a sinner,
But a sinner must pray for himself.

The twig is so easily bended,
I have banish'd the rule and the rod;
I have taught them the goodness of knowledge,
They have taught me the goodness of God;
My heart is the dungeon of darkness,
Where I shut them for breaking a rule;
My frown is sufficient correction;
My love is the law of the school.

I shall leave the old house in the autumn,
To traverse its threshold no more;
Ah! how I shall sigh for the dear ones
That meet me each morn at the door!
I shall miss the "good-nights" and the kisses,
And the gush of their innocent glee,
The group on the green, and the flowers
That are brought every morning for me.

I shall miss them at morn and at even,
Their song in the school and the street;
I shall miss the low hum of their voices,
And the tread of their delicate feet.

When the lessons of life are all ended,
   And Death says, "The school is dismiss'd!"
May the little ones gather around me,
   To bid me good-night, and be kiss'd!
CHARLES M. DICKINSON.

THE CRY OF THE CHILDREN.

Do ye hear the children weeping, O my brothers,
   Ere the sorrow comes with years?
They are leaning their young heads against their mothers,
   And *that* cannot stop their tears.
The young lambs are bleating in the meadows,
   The young birds are chirping in the nest,
The young fawns are playing with the shadows,
   The young flowers are blowing toward the west—
But the young, young children, O my brothers,
   They are weeping bitterly!
They are weeping in the playtime of the others,
   In the country of the free.

Do you question the young children in their sorrow
   Why their tears are falling so?
The old man may weep for his to-morrow
   Which is lost in Long Ago;
The old tree is leafless in the forest,
   The old year is ending in the frost,
The old wound, if stricken, is the sorest,
   The old hope is hardest to be lost:
But the young, young children, O my brothers,
   Do you ask them why they stand
Weeping sore before the bosoms of their mothers,
   In our happy Fatherland?

They look up with their pale and sunken faces,
   And their looks are sad to see,
For the man's hoary anguish draws and presses
   Down the cheeks of infancy;

"Your old earth," they say, "is very dreary,
   Our young feet," they say, "are very weak;
Few paces have we taken, yet are weary—
   Our grave-rest is very far to seek:
Ask the aged why they weep, and not the children,
   For the outside earth is cold,
And we young ones stand without, in our bewildering,
   And the graves are for the old.

"True," say the children, "it may happen
   That we die before our time:
Little Alice died last year, her grave is shapen
   Like a snowball, in the rime.
We looked into the pit prepared to take her:
   Was no room for any work in the close clay!
From the sleep wherein she lieth none will wake her,
   Crying, 'Get up little Alice! it is day.'
If you listen by that grave, in sun and shower,
   With your ear down, little Alice never cries;
Could we see her face, be sure we should not know her,
   For the smile has time for growing in her eyes:
And merry go her moments, lull'd and still'd in
   The shroud by the kirk-chime.
It is good when it happens," say the children,
   "That we die before our time."

Alas, alas, the children! they are seeking
   Death in life, as best to have:
They are binding up their hearts away from breaking,
   With a cerement from the grave.
Go out, children, from the mine and from the city,
   Sing out, children, as the little thrushes do;
Pluck your handfuls of the meadow-cowslips pretty,
   Laugh aloud, to feel your fingers let them through!

But they answer, "Are your cowslips of
    the meadows
  Like our weeds a-near the mine?
Leave us quiet in the dark of the coal-
    shadows,
  From your pleasures fair and fine!

"For oh," say the children, "we are weary,
  And we cannot run or leap;
If we cared for any meadows, it were
    merely
  To drop down in them and sleep.
Our knees tremble sorely in the stooping,
  We fall upon our faces, trying to go;
And, underneath our heavy eyelids droop-
    ing,
  The reddest flower would look as pale as
    snow.
For all day we drag our burden tiring
  Through the coal-dark, underground;
Or all day we drive the wheels of iron
  In the factories, round and round.

"For all day the wheels are droning, turn-
    ing;
  Their wind comes in our faces,
Till our hearts turn, our heads with pulses
    burning,
  And the walls turn in their places:
Turns the sky in the high window blank
    and reeling,
  Turns the long light that drops adown
    the wall,
Turn the black flies that crawl along the
    ceiling,
  All are turning, all the day, and we with
    all.
And all day the iron wheels are droning,
  And sometimes we could pray,
'O ye wheels' (breaking out in a mad
    moaning)
  'Stop! be silent for to-day!'"

Ay, be silent! Let them hear each other
    breathing
  For a moment, mouth to mouth!
Let them touch each other's hands, in a
    fresh wreathing
  Of their tender human youth!
Let them feel that this cold metallic mo-
    tion
  Is not all the life God fashions or re-
    veals;
Let them prove their living souls against
    the notion
  That they live in you, or under you, O
    wheels!
Still, all day, the iron wheels go onward,
  Grinding life down from its mark;
And the children's souls, which God is
    calling sunward,
  Spin on blindly in the dark.

Now tell the poor young children, O my
    brothers,
  To look up to Him and pray;
So the blessed One who blesseth all the
    others,
  Will bless them another day.
They answer, "Who is God, that He should
    hear us,
  While the rushing of the iron wheels is
    stirr'd?
When we sob aloud, the human creatures
    near us
  Pass by, hearing not, or answer not a
    word.
And *we* hear not (for the wheels in their
    resounding)
  Strangers speaking at the door:
Is it likely God, with angels singing round
    Him,
  Hears our weeping any more?

"Two words, indeed, of praying we re-
    member,
  And at midnight's hour of harm,
'Our Father,' looking upward in the cham-
    ber,
  We say softly for a charm.
We know no other words except 'Our
    Father,'
  And we think that, in some pause of
    angels' song,
God may pluck them with the silence
    sweet to gather,
  And hold both within His right hand
    which is strong.
'Our Father!' If He heard us He would
    surely
  (For they call Him good and mild)
Answer, smiling down the steep world very
    purely,
  'Come and rest with me, my child.'

"But no!" say the children, weeping faster,
"He is speechless as a stone:
And they tell us of His image is the master,
Who commands us to work on.
Go to!" say the children,—"up in heaven,
Dark, wheel-like, turning clouds are all we find.
Do not mock us; grief has made us unbelieving:
We look up for God, but tears have made us blind."
Do you hear the children weeping and disproving,
O my brothers, what ye preach?
For God's possible is taught by His world's loving,
And the children doubt of each.

And well may the children weep before you!
They are weary ere they run;
They have never seen the sunshine, nor the glory
Which is brighter than the sun.
They know the grief of man, without its wisdom;
They sink in man's despair, without its calm;
Are slaves, without the liberty in Christdom,
Are martyrs, by the pang without the palm:
Are worn as if with age, yet unretrievingly
The harvest of its memories cannot reap,—
Are orphans of the earthly love and heavenly.
Let them weep! let them weep!

They look up with their pale and sunken faces,
And their look is dread to see,
For they 'mind you of their angels in high places,
With eyes turned on Deity.
"How long," they say, "how long, O cruel nation,
Will you stand, to move the world, on a child's heart,—
Stifle down with a mailed heel its palpitation,
And tread onward to your throne amid the mart?

Our blood splashes upward, O gold-heaper,
And your purple shows your path!
But the child's sob in the silence curses deeper
Than the strong man in his wrath."
ELIZABETH BARRETT BROWNING.

TO A HIGHLAND GIRL.

(AT INVERSNEYDE, UPON LOCH LOMOND.)

SWEET Highland Girl, a very shower
Of beauty is thy earthly dower!
Twice seven consenting years have shed
Their utmost bounty on thy head:
And, these gray Rocks; this household Lawn;
These Trees, a veil just half withdrawn;
This fall of water, that doth make
A murmur near the silent Lake;
This little Bay, a quiet Road
That holds in shelter thy Abode;
In truth, together do ye seem
Like something fashion'd in a dream:
Such Forms as from their covert peep
When earthly cares are laid asleep!
Yet, dream and vision as thou art,
I bless thee with a human heart:
God shield thee to thy latest years!
I neither know thee nor thy peers;
And yet my eyes are fill'd with tears.

With earnest feeling I shall pray
For thee when I am far away:
For never saw I mien or face,
In which more plainly I could trace
Benignity and home-bred sense
Ripening in perfect innocence.
Here scatter'd like a random seed,
Remote from men, thou dost not need
The embarrass'd look of shy distress,
And maidenly shamefacedness:
Thou wear'st upon thy forehead clear
The freedom of a Mountaineer:
A face with gladness overspread!
Soft smiles by human kindness bred!
And seemliness complete, that sways
Thy courtesies, about thee plays:
With no restraint, but such as springs
From quick and eager visitings
Of thoughts that lie beyond the reach
Of thy few words of English speech:

A bondage sweetly brook'd, a strife
That gives thy gestures grace and life!
So have I, not unmoved in mind,
Seen birds of tempest-loving kind,
Thus beating up against the wind.

What hand but would a garland cull
For thee who art so beautiful?
Oh happy pleasure! here to dwell
Beside thee in some heathy dell;
Adopt your homely ways, and dress,
A Shepherd, thou a Shepherdess!
But I could frame a wish for thee
More like a grave reality:
Thou art to me but as a wave
Of the wild sea: and I would have
Some claim upon thee, if I could,
Though but of common neighborhood.
What joy to hear thee, and to see!
Thy elder Brother I would be,
Thy Father, anything to thee!

Now thanks to Heaven! that of its grace
Hath led me to this lonely place.
Joy have I had; and going hence
I bear away my recompense.
In spots like these it is we prize
Our Memory, feel that she hath eyes:
Then, why should I be loth to stir?
I feel this place was made for her;
To give new pleasure like the past,
Continued long as life shall last.
Nor am I loth, though pleased at heart,
Sweet Highland Girl! from thee to part;
For I, methinks, till I grow old,
As fair before me shall behold,
As I do now, the Cabin small,
The Lake, the Bay, the Waterfall;
And thee, the Spirit of them all!
WILLIAM WORDSWORTH.

MAIDENHOOD.

MAIDEN! with the meek, brown eyes,
In whose orbs a shadow lies
Like the dusk in evening skies!

Thou whose locks outshine the sun,
Golden tresses, wreath'd in one,
As the braided streamlets run!

Standing, with reluctant feet,
Where the brook and river meet,
Womanhood and childhood fleet!

Gazing, with a timid glance,
On the brooklet's swift advance,
On the river's broad expanse;

Deep and still, that gliding stream
Beautiful to thee must seem,
As the river of a dream.

Then why pause with indecision,
When bright angels in thy vision
Beckon thee to fields Elysian?

Seest thou shadows sailing by,
As the dove, with startled eye,
Sees the falcon's shadow fly?

Hearest thou voices on the shore,
That our ears perceive no more,
Deafen'd by the cataract's roar?

O thou child of many prayers!
Life hath quicksands,—life hath snares!
Care and age come unawares.

Like the swell of some sweet tune,
Morning rises into noon,
May glides onward into June.

Childhood is the bough, where slumber'd
Birds and blossoms many-number'd:—
Age, that bough with snows encumber'd.

Gather, then, each flower that grows,
When the young heart overflows,
To embalm that tent of snows.

Bear a lily in thy hand;
Gates of brass cannot withstand
One touch of that magic wand.

Bear through sorrow, wrong, and ruth,
In thy heart the dew of youth,
On thy lips the smile of truth.

Oh, that dew, like balm, shall steal
Into wounds that cannot heal,
Even as sleep our eyes doth seal;

And that smile, like sunshine, dart
Into many a sunless heart,
For a smile of God thou art.
HENRY WADSWORTH LONGFELLOW.

THE BLIND BOY.

Oh, say what is that thing call'd Light,
   Which I must ne'er enjoy?
What are the blessings of the sight,
   Oh, tell your poor blind boy!

You talk of wondrous things you see,
   You say the sun shines bright;
I feel him warm, but how can he
   Or make it day or night?

My day or night myself I make
   Whene'er I sleep or play;
And could I ever keep awake
   With me 'twere always day.

With heavy sighs I often hear
   You mourn my hapless woe;
But sure with patience I can bear
   A loss I ne'er can know.

Then let not what I cannot have
   My cheer of mind destroy;
Whilst thus I sing, I am a king,
   Although a poor blind boy.
              COLLEY CIBBER.

HOW'S MY BOY?

"Ho, sailor of the sea!
   How's my boy—my boy?"
"What's your boy's name, good wife,
   And in what good ship sailed he?"

"My boy John—
   He that went to sea—
What care I for the ship, sailor?
   My boy's my boy to me.

"You come back from sea,
   And not know my John?
I might as well have ask'd some landsman
   Yonder down in the town.
There's not an ass in all the parish
   But knows my John

"How's my boy—my boy?
   And unless you let me know,
I'll swear you are no sailor,
   Blue jacket or no,
Brass buttons or no, sailor,
   Anchor and crown or no!
Sure his ship was the 'Jolly Briton'"—
"Speak low, woman, speak low!"

"And why should I speak low, sailor,
   About my own boy John?
If I was loud as I am proud
   I'd sing him over the town!
Why should I speak low, sailor?"
"That good ship went down."

"How's my boy—my boy?
   What care I for the ship, sailor,
I was never aboard her?
   Be she afloat or be she aground,
Sinking or swimming, I'll be bound
   Her owners can afford her!
I say, how's my John?"
"Every man on board went down,
   Every man aboard her."

"How's my boy—my boy?
   What care I for the men, sailor?
I'm not their mother—
   How's my boy—my boy?
Tell me of him and no other!
   How's my boy—my boy?"
              SYDNEY DOBELL.

THE NIGHT BEFORE CHRISTMAS.

'Twas the night before Christmas, when all through the house
Not a creature was stirring, not even a mouse;
The stockings were hung by the chimney with care,
In hopes that St. Nicholas soon would be there;
The children were nestled all snug in their beds,
While visions of sugar-plums danced through their heads;
And mamma in her kerchief, and I in my cap,
Had just settled our brains for a long winter's nap,
When out on the lawn there arose such a clatter,
I sprang from my bed to see what was the matter.
Away to the window I flew like a flash,
Tore open the shutters and threw up the sash.
The moon, on the breast of the new-fallen snow,
Gave a lustre of mid-day to objects below;

When what to my wondering eyes should appear,
But a miniature sleigh, and eight tiny reindeer,
With a little old driver, so lively and quick,
I knew in a moment it must be St. Nick.
More rapid than eagles his coursers they came,
And he whistled, and shouted, and call'd them by name:
"Now, Dasher! now, Dancer! now, Prancer! now, Vixen!
On, Comet! on, Cupid! on, Donder and Blitzen!—
To the top of the porch, to the top of the wall!
Now, dash away, dash away, dash away all!"
As dry leaves that before the wild hurricane fly,
When they meet with an obstacle, mount to the sky,
So, up to the house-top the coursers they flew,
With the sleigh full of toys, and St. Nicholas too.
And then in a twinkling I heard on the roof
The prancing and pawing of each little hoof.
As I drew in my head, and was turning around,
Down the chimney St. Nicholas came with a bound.
He was dress'd all in fur from his head to his foot,
And his clothes were all tarnish'd with ashes and soot;
A bundle of toys he had flung on his back,
And he look'd like a peddler just opening his pack.
His eyes how they twinkled! his dimples how merry!
His cheeks were like roses, his nose like a cherry,
His droll little mouth was drawn up like a bow,
And the beard on his chin was as white as the snow.
The stump of a pipe he held tight in his teeth,
And the smoke, it encircled his head like a wreath.
He had a broad face and a little round belly
That shook, when he laugh'd, like a bowl full of jelly.
He was chubby and plump—a right jolly old elf—
And I laugh'd when I saw him, in spite of myself.
A wink of his eye, and a twist of his head,
Soon gave me to know I had nothing to dread.
He spake not a word, but went straight to his work,
And filled all the stockings; then turn'd with a jerk,
And laying his finger aside of his nose,
And giving a nod, up the chimney he rose.
He sprang to his sleigh, to his team gave a whistle,
And away they all flew like the down of a thistle;
But I heard him exclaim, ere he drove out of sight,
"Happy Christmas to all, and to all a good-night!"
                                    CLEMENT C. MOORE.

INTRODUCTION TO "SONGS OF INNOCENCE."

PIPING down the valleys wild,
  Piping songs of pleasant glee,
On a cloud I saw a child,
  And he laughing said to me:

"Pipe a song about a lamb!"
  So I piped with merry cheer.
"Piper, pipe that song again;"
  So I piped; he wept to hear.

"Drop thy pipe, thy happy pipe;
  Sing thy songs of happy cheer!"
So I sang the same again,
  While he wept with joy to hear.

"Piper, sit thee down and write
  In a book, that all may read."
So he vanish'd from my sight;
  And I pluck'd a hollow reed,

And I made a rural pen,
  And I stain'd the water clear,
And I wrote my happy songs
  Every child may joy to hear.
                                    WILLIAM BLAKE.

THE MAY QUEEN.

You must wake and call me early, call me
    early, mother dear;
To-morrow 'ill be the happiest time of all
    the glad New-year;
Of all the glad New-year, mother, the
    maddest, merriest day;
For I'm to be Queen o' the May, mother,
    I'm to be Queen o' the May.

There's many a black black eye, they say,
    but none so bright as mine;
There's Margaret and Mary, there's Kate
    and Caroline:
But none so fair as little Alice in all the
    land, they say,
So I'm to be Queen o' the May, mother,
    I'm to be Queen o' the May.

I sleep so sound all night, mother, that I
    shall never wake,
If you do not call me loud, when the day
    begins to break:
But I must gather knots of flowers, and
    buds and garlands gay,
For I'm to be Queen o' the May, mother,
    I'm to be Queen of the May.

As I came up the valley, whom think ye
    should I see,
But Robin leaning on the bridge beneath
    the hazel tree?
He thought of that sharp look, mother, I
    gave him yesterday—
But I'm to be Queen o' the May, mother,
    I'm to be Queen o' the May.

He thought I was a ghost, mother, for I
    was all in white,
And I ran by him without speaking, like
    a flash of light.
They call me cruel-hearted, but I care not
    what they say,
For I'm to be Queen o' the May, mother,
    I'm to be Queen o' the May.

They say he's dying all for love, but that
    can never be:
They say his heart is breaking, mother—
    what is that to me?
There's many a bolder lad 'ill woo me any
    summer day,
And I'm to be Queen o' the May, mother,
    I'm to be Queen o' the May.

Little Effie shall go with me to-morrow to
    the green,
And you'll be there too, mother, to see me
    made the queen;
For the shepherd lads on every side 'ill
    come from far away,
And I'm to be Queen o' the May, mother,
    I'm to be Queen o' the May.

The honeysuckle round the porch has
    wov'n its wavy bowers,
And by the meadow-trenches blow the
    faint sweet cuckoo-flowers;
And the wild marsh-marigold shines like
    fire in swamps and hollows gray,
And I'm to be Queen o' the May, mother,
    I'm to be Queen o' the May.

The night winds come and go, mother,
    upon the meadow grass,
And the happy stars above them seem to
    brighten as they pass;
There will not be a drop of rain the whole
    of the livelong day,
And I'm to be Queen o' the May, mother,
    I'm to be Queen o' the May.

All the valley, mother, 'ill be fresh and
    green and still,
And the cowslip and the crowfoot are over
    all the hill,
And the rivulet in the flowery dale 'ill
    merrily glance and play,
For I'm to be Queen o' the May, mother,
    I'm to be Queen o' the May.

So you must wake and call me early, call
    me early, mother dear,
To-morrow 'ill be the happiest time of all
    the glad New-year:
To-morrow 'ill be of all the year the maddest, merriest day,
For I'm to be Queen o' the May, mother,
    I'm to be Queen o' the May.

NEW-YEAR'S EVE.

If you're waking call me early, call me
    early, mother dear,
For I would see the sun rise upon the glad
    New-year.
It is the last New-year that I shall ever see,
Then you may lay me low i' the mould and
    think no more of me.

To night I saw the sun set: he set and left
   behind
The good old year, the dear old time, and
   all my peace of mind;
And the New-year's coming up, mother,
   but I shall never see
The blossom on the blackthorn, the leaf
   upon the tree.

Last May we made a crown of flowers: we
   had a merry day;
Beneath the hawthorn on the green they
   made me Queen of May;
And we danced about the may-pole and in
   the hazel copse,
Till Charles's Wain came out above the
   tall white chimney-tops.

There's not a flower on all the hills: the
   frost is on the pane:
I only wish to live till the snow-drops come
   again:
I wish the snow would melt and the sun
   come out on high:
I long to see a flower so before the day I
   die.

The building rook 'ill caw from the windy
   tall elm tree,
And the tufted plover pipe along the fallow
   lea,
And the swallow 'ill come back again with
   summer o'er the wave,
But I shall lie alone, mother, within the
   mouldering grave.

Upon the chancel-casement, and upon that
   grave of mine,
In the early early morning the summer
   sun 'ill shine,
Before the red cock crows from the farm
   upon the hill,
When you are warm-asleep, mother, and
   all the world is still.

When the flowers come again, mother,
   beneath the waning light
You'll never see me more in the long gray
   fields at night;
When from the dry dark wold the summer
   airs blow cool
On the oat-grass and the sword-grass, and
   the bulrush in the pool.

You'll bury me, my mother, just beneath
   the hawthorn shade,
And you'll come sometimes and see me
   where I am lowly laid.
I shall not forget you, mother; I shall hear
   you when you pass,
With your feet above my head in the long
   and pleasant grass.

I have been wild and wayward, but you'll
   forgive me now;
You'll kiss me, my own mother, and forgive
   me ere I go;
Nay, nay, you must not weep, nor let your
   grief be wild,
You should not fret for me, mother, you
   have another child.

If I can I'll come again, mother, from out
   my resting-place;
Tho' you'll not see me, mother, I shall look
   upon your face;
Tho' I cannot speak a word, I shall hearken
   what you say,
And be often, often with you when you
   think I'm far away.

Good-night, good-night, when I have said
   good-night for evermore,
And you see me carried out from the
   threshold of the door;
Don't let Effie come to see me till my grave
   be growing green:
She'll be a better child to you than ever I
   have been.

She'll find my garden-tools upon the gran-
   ary floor:
Let her take 'em: they are hers: I shall
   never garden more:
But tell her, when I'm gone, to train the
   rose-bush that I set
About the parlor-window, and the box of
   mignonette.

Good-night, sweet mother: call me before
   the day is born.
All night I lie awake, but I fall asleep at
   morn;
But I would see the sun rise upon the glad
   New-year,
So, if you're waking, call me, call me early,
   mother dear.

Conclusion.

I thought to pass away before, and yet alive I am;
And in the fields all round I hear the bleating of the lamb.
How sadly, I remember, rose the morning of the year!
To die before the snow-drop came, and now the violet's here.

Oh, sweet is the new violet, that comes beneath the skies,
And sweeter is the young lamb's voice to me that cannot rise,
And sweet is all the land about, and all the flowers that blow,
And sweeter far is death than life to me that long to go.

It seem'd so hard at first, mother, to leave the blessed sun,
And now it seems as hard to stay; and yet, His will be done!
But still I think it can't be long before I find release;
And that good man, the clergyman, has told me words of peace.

Oh, blessings on his kindly voice and on his silver hair,
And blessings on his whole life long, until he meet me there!
Oh, blessings on his kindly heart and on his silver head!
A thousand times I blest him, as he knelt beside my bed.

He taught me all the mercy, for he show'd me all the sin.
Now, tho' my lamp was lighted late, there's One will let me in;
Nor would I now be well, mother, again, if that could be,
For my desire is but to pass to Him that died for me.

I did not hear the dog howl, mother, or the death-watch beat,
There came a sweeter token when the night and morning meet;
But sit beside my bed, mother, and put your hand in mine,
And Effie on the other side, and I will tell the sign.

All in the wild March-morning I heard the angels call;
It was when the moon was setting, and the dark was over all;
The trees began to whisper, and the wind began to roll,
And in the wild March-morning I heard them call my soul.

For lying broad awake I thought of you and Effie dear;
I saw you sitting in the house, and I no longer here;
With all my strength I pray'd for both, and so I felt resign'd,
And up the valley came a swell of music on the wind.

I thought that it was fancy, and I listen'd in my bed,
And then did something speak to me—I know not what was said,
For great delight and shuddering took hold of all my mind,
And up the valley came again the music on the wind.

But you were sleeping, and I said, "It's not for them, it's mine;"
And if it comes three times, I thought, I take it for a sign.
And once again it came, and close beside the window-bars,
Then seem'd to go right up to heaven and die among the stars.

So now I think my time is near. I trust it is. I know
The blessed music went that way my soul will have to go.
And for myself, indeed, I care not if I go to-day,
But, Effie, you must comfort *her* when I am pass'd away.

And say to Robin a kind word, and tell him not to fret;
There's many a worthier than I would make him happy yet.
If I had lived—I cannot tell—I might have been his wife,
But all these things have ceased to be, with my desire of life.

Oh, look! the sun begins to rise, the heavens are in a glow;
He shines upon a hundred fields, and all of them I know.
And there I move no longer now, and there his light may shine—
Wild flowers in the valley for other hands than mine.

Oh, sweet and strange it seems to me, that ere this day is done
The voice, that now is speaking, may be beyond the sun,
For ever and for ever with those just souls and true;
And what is life that we should moan? why make we such ado?

For ever and for ever, all in a blessed home,
And there to wait a little while till you and Effie come,
To lie within the light of God, as I lie upon your breast,
And the wicked cease from troubling, and the weary are at rest.
ALFRED TENNYSON.

A FAREWELL.

My fairest child, I have no song to give you;
  No lark could pipe to skies so dull and gray;
Yet, ere we part, one lesson I can leave you
    For every day.

Be good, sweet maid, and let who will be clever;
  Do noble things, not dream them, all day long;
And so make life, death, and that vast forever
    One grand, sweet song.
CHARLES KINGSLEY.

The lillies blossom in the pond
  The bird builds in the tree,
The dark pines sing on Ramoth hill
  The slow song of the sea.

The winds so sweet with birch and fern
  A sweeter memory blow,
And there in spring the veeries sing
  The song of long ago.

John Greenleaf Whittier

Poems

OF

Memory and Retrospection.

I Remember, I Remember.

I REMEMBER, I remember,
  The house where I was born,
The little window where the sun
  Came peeping in at morn:
He never came a wink too soon,
  Nor brought too long a day;
But now, I often wish the night
  Had borne my breath away.

I remember, I remember,
  The roses, red and white;
The violets and the lily-cups,
  Those flowers made of light!
The lilacs where the robin built,
  And where my brother set
The laburnum on his birthday,—
  The tree is living yet!

I remember, I remember,
  Where I was used to swing;
And thought the air must rush as fresh
  To swallows on the wing:
My spirit flew in feathers then,
  That is so heavy now,
And summer pools could hardly cool
  The fever on my brow!

I remember, I remember,
  The fir trees dark and high;
I used to think their slender tops
  Were close against the sky:
It was a childish ignorance,
  But now 'tis little joy
To know I'm farther off from heaven
  Than when I was a boy.
              THOMAS HOOD.

The Old Arm-Chair.

I LOVE it, I love it; and who shall dare
To chide me for loving that old arm-chair?
I've treasured it long as a sainted prize;
I've bedew'd it with tears, and embalm'd
    it with sighs.
'Tis bound by a thousand bands to my
    heart;
Not a tie will break, not a link will start.
Would ye learn the spell?—a mother sat
    there;
And a sacred thing is that old arm-chair.

In childhood's hour I linger'd near
The hallow'd seat with listening ear;
And gentle words that mother would give
To fit me to die, and teach me to live.
She told me shame would never betide,
With truth for my creed and God for my
    guide;
She taught me to lisp my earliest prayer,
As I knelt beside that old arm-chair.

I sat and watch'd her many a day,
When her eye grew dim, and her locks
    were gray:
And I almost worshipp'd her when she
    smiled,
And turn'd from her Bible, to bless her
    child.
Years roll'd on: but the last one sped—
My idol was shatter'd; my earth-star fled:
I learnt how much the heart can bear,
When I saw her die in that old arm-chair.

'Tis past, 'tis past, but I gaze on it now
With quivering breath and throbbing
    brow:

'Twas there she nursed me; 'twas there
    she died:
And Memory flows with lava tide.
Say it is folly, and deem me weak,
While the scalding drops start down my
    cheek;
But I love it, I love it; and cannot tear
My soul from a mother's old arm-chair.
Eliza Cook.

ROCK ME TO SLEEP.

BACKWARD, turn backward, O Time, in
    your flight,
Make me a child again just for to-night!
Mother, come back from the echoless shore,
Take me again to your heart as of yore;
Kiss from my forehead the furrows of care,
Smooth the few silver threads out of my
    hair;
Over my slumbers your loving watch
    keep;—
Rock me to sleep, mother,—rock me to
    sleep!

Backward, flow backward, O tide of the
    years!
I am so weary of toil and of tears,—
Toil without recompense, tears all in
    vain,—
Take them, and give me my childhood
    again!
I have grown weary of dust and decay,—
Weary of flinging my soul-wealth away;
Weary of sowing for others to reap;—
Rock me to sleep, mother,—rock me to
    sleep!

Tired of the hollow, the base, the untrue,
Mother! O mother! my heart calls for you!
Many a summer the grass has grown green,
Blossom'd, and faded our faces between,
Yet with strong yearning and passionate
    pain
Long I to-night for your presence again.
Come from the silence so long and so
    deep;—
Rock me to sleep, mother,—rock me to
    sleep!

Over my heart, in the days that are flown,
No love like mother-love ever has shone;
No other worship abides and endures,—
Faithful, unselfish, and patient like yours:

None like a mother can charm away pain
From the sick soul and the world-weary
    brain.
Slumber's soft calms o'er my heavy lids
    creep;—
Rock me to sleep, mother,—rock me to
    sleep!

Come, let your brown hair, just lighted
    with gold,
Fall on your shoulders again as of old;
Let it drop over my forehead to-night,
Shading my faint eyes away from the light;
For with its sunny-edged shadows once
    more
Haply will throng the sweet visions of
    yore;
Lovingly, softly, its bright billows sweep;—
Rock me to sleep, mother,—rock me to
    sleep!

Mother, dear mother, the years have been
    long
Since I last listen'd your lullaby song:
Sing, then, and unto my soul it shall seem
Womanhood's years have been only a
    dream.
Clasp'd to your heart in a loving embrace,
With your light lashes just sweeping my
    face,
Never hereafter to wake or to weep;—
Rock me to sleep, mother,—rock me to
    sleep!
Elizabeth Akers Allen.

THE OLD OAKEN BUCKET.

How dear to this heart are the scenes of
    my childhood,
  When fond recollection presents them
    to view!
The orchard, the meadow, the deep-tangled
    wild wood,
  And every loved spot which my infancy
    knew;
The wide-spreading pond, and the mill
    which stood by it,
  The bridge and the rock where the cat-
    aract fell;
The cot of my father, the dairy-house nigh
    it,
  And e'en the rude bucket which hung
    in the well:

The old oaken bucket, the iron-bound bucket,
The moss-cover'd bucket, which hung in the well.

That moss-cover'd vessel I hail as a treasure;
  For often, at noon, when return'd from the field,
I found it the source of an exquisite pleasure,
  The purest and sweetest that Nature can yield.
How ardent I seized it, with hands that were glowing!
  And quick to the white-pebbled bottom it fell;
Then soon, with the emblem of truth overflowing,
  And dripping with coolness, it rose from the well:
The old oaken bucket, the iron-bound bucket,
The moss-cover'd bucket arose from the well.

How sweet from the green mossy brim to receive it,
  As poised on the curb it inclined to my lips!
Not a full blushing goblet could tempt me to leave it,
  Though fill'd with the nectar that Jupiter sips.
And now, far removed from the loved situation,
  The tear of regret will intrusively swell,
As fancy reverts to my father's plantation,
  And sighs for the bucket which hangs in the well:
The old oaken bucket, the iron-bound bucket,
The moss-cover'd bucket, which hangs in the well.
                SAMUEL WOODWORTH.

WOODMAN, SPARE THAT TREE!

WOODMAN, spare that tree!
  Touch not a single bough!
In youth it shelter'd me,
  And I'll protect it now.
'Twas my forefather's hand
  That placed it near his cot;
There, woodman, let it stand,
  Thy axe shall harm it not!

That old familiar tree,
  Whose glory and renown
Are spread o'er land and sea—
  And would'st thou hew it down?
Woodman, forbear thy stroke!
  Cut not its earth-bound ties;
Oh, spare that agèd oak,
  Now towering to the skies!

When but an idle boy,
  I sought its grateful shade;
In all their gushing joy
  Here, too, my sisters play'd.
My mother kiss'd me here;
  My father press'd my hand—
Forgive this foolish tear,
  But let that old oak stand!

My heart-strings round thee cling,
  Close as thy bark, old friend!
Here shall the wild bird sing,
  And still thy branches bend.
Old tree! the storm still brave!
  And, woodman, leave the spot;
While I've a hand to save,
  Thy axe shall harm it not!
                GEORGE P. MORRIS.

THE STRANGER ON THE SILL.

BETWEEN the broad fields of wheat and corn
Is the lowly home where I was born;
The peach tree leans against the wall,
And the woodbine wanders over all;
There is the shaded doorway still,
But a stranger's foot has cross'd the sill.

There is the barn, and, as of yore,
I can smell the hay from the open door,
And see the busy swallows throng,
And hear the pewee's mournful song;
But the stranger comes — oh, painful proof!—
His sheaves are piled to the heated roof.

There is the orchard—the very trees
Where my childhood knew long hours of ease,

And watch'd the shadowy moments run
Till my life imbibed more shade than sun:
The swing from the bough still sweeps the air,
But the stranger's children are swinging there.

There bubbles the shady spring below,
With its bulrush brook where the hazels grow;
'Twas there I found the calamus root,
And watched the minnows poise and shoot,
And heard the robin lave his wing:—
But the stranger's bucket is at the spring.

O ye who daily cross the sill,
Step lightly, for I love it still;
And when you crowd the old barn eaves,
Then think what countless harvest sheaves
Have pass'd within that scented door
To gladden eyes that are no more.

Deal kindly with these orchard trees;
And when your children crowd your knees,
Their sweetest fruit they shall impart,
As if old memories stirr'd their heart:
To youthful sport still leave the swing,
And in sweet reverence hold the spring.
THOMAS BUCHANAN READ.

THE OLD CLOCK ON THE STAIRS.

SOMEWHAT back from the village street
Stands the old-fashion'd country-seat.
Across its antique portico
Tall poplar trees their shadows throw:
And from its station in the hall
An ancient timepiece says to all,—
"Forever—never!
Never—forever!"

Halfway up the stairs it stands,
And points and beckons with its hands
From its case of massive oak,
Like a monk, who, under his cloak,
Crosses himself, and sighs, alas!
With sorrowful voice to all who pass,—
"Forever—never!
Never—forever!"

By day its voice is low and light;
But in the silent dead of night,
Distinct as a passing footstep's fall,
It echoes along the vacant hall,
Along the ceiling, along the floor,
And seems to say, at each chamber-door,—
"Forever—never!
Never—forever!"

Through days of sorrow and of mirth,
Through days of death and days of birth,
Through every swift vicissitude
Of changeful time, unchanged it has stood,
And as if, like God, it all things saw,
It calmly repeats those words of awe,—
"Forever—never!
Never—forever!"

In that mansion used to be
Free-hearted Hospitality;
His great fires up the chimney roar'd;
The stranger feasted at his board;
But, like the skeleton at the feast,
That warning timepiece never ceased,—
"Forever—never!
Never—forever!"

There groups of merry children play'd,
There youths and maidens dreaming stray'd;
O precious hours! O golden prime,
And affluence of love and time!
Even as a miser counts his gold,
Those hours the ancient timepiece told,—
"Forever—never!
Never—forever!"

From that chamber, clothed in white,
The bride came forth on her wedding-night;
There, in that silent room below,
The dead lay in his shroud of snow;
And in the hush that follow'd the prayer,
Was heard the old clock on the stair,—
"Forever—never!
Never—forever!"

All are scatter'd now and fled,
Some are married, some are dead;
And when I ask with throbs of pain,
"Ah! when shall they all meet again,
As in the days long since gone by?"
The ancient timepiece makes reply,—
"Forever—never!
Never—forever!"

Never here, forever there,
Where all parting, pain, and care,

And death, and time shall disappear,—
Forever there, but never here!
The horologe of Eternity
Sayeth this incessantly,—
   "Forever—never!
   Never—forever!"
HENRY WADSWORTH LONGFELLOW.

THE OLD FAMILIAR FACES.

I HAVE had playmates, I have had companions,
In my days of childhood, in my joyful school-days;
All, all are gone, the old familiar faces.

I have been laughing, I have been carousing,
Drinking late, sitting late, with my bosom cronies;
All, all are gone, the old familiar faces.

I loved a love once, fairest among women:
Closed are her doors on me; I must not see her;
All, all are gone, the old familiar faces.

I have a friend, a kinder friend has no man;
Like an ingrate, I left my friend abruptly;
Left him, to muse on the old familiar faces.

Ghost-like I paced round the haunts of my childhood;
Earth seem'd a desert I was bound to traverse,
Seeking to find the old familiar faces.

Friend of my bosom, thou more than a brother,
Why wert not thou born in my father's dwelling?
So might we talk of the old familiar faces—

How some they have died, and some they have left me,
And some are taken from me; all are departed,—
All, all are gone, the old familiar faces.
CHARLES LAMB.

OFT, IN THE STILLY NIGHT.

OFT, in the stilly night,
  Ere Slumber's chain has bound me,
Fond Memory brings the light
  Of other days around me;
    The smiles, the tears,
    Of boyhood's years,
  The words of love then spoken;
    The eyes that shone,
    Now dimm'd and gone,
  The cheerful hearts now broken!
Thus, in the stilly night,
  Ere Slumber's chain has bound me,
Sad Memory brings the light
  Of other days around me.

When I remember all
  The friends, so link'd together,
I've seen around me fall,
  Like leaves in wintry weather;
    I feel like one,
    Who treads alone
  Some banquet-hall deserted,
    Whose lights are fled,
    Whose garlands dead,
  And all but he departed!
Thus, in the stilly night,
  Ere Slumber's chain has bound me,
Sad Memory brings the light
  Of other days around me.
THOMAS MOORE.

SATURDAY AFTERNOON.

I LOVE to look on a scene like this,
  Of wild and careless play,
And persuade myself that I am not old,
  And my locks are not yet gray;
For it stirs the blood in an old man's heart,
  And makes his pulses fly,
To catch the thrill of a happy voice,
  And the light of a pleasant eye.

I have walk'd the world for fourscore years;
  And they say that I am old,
That my heart is ripe for the reaper, Death,
  And my years are wellnigh told.

It is very true; it is very true;
   I'm old, and I "bide my time;"
But my heart will leap at a scene like this,
   And I half renew my prime.

Play on, play on; I am with you there,
   In the midst of your merry ring;
I can feel the thrill of the daring jump,
   And the rush of the breathless swing.
I hide with you in the fragrant hay,
   And I whoop the smother'd call,
And my feet slip up on the seedy floor,
   And I care not for the fall.

I am willing to die when my time shall come,
   And I shall be glad to go;
For the world at best is a weary place,
   And my pulse is getting low;
But the grave is dark, and the heart will fail
   In treading its gloomy way;
And it wiles my heart from its dreariness,
   To see the young so gay.
            NATHANIEL PARKER WILLIS.

TWENTY YEARS AGO.

I'VE wander'd to the village, Tom, I've sat beneath the tree,
Upon the school-house play-ground, which shelter'd you and me;
But none were there to greet me, Tom, and few were left to know,
That play'd with us upon the grass some twenty years ago.

The grass is just as green, Tom—barefooted boys at play,
Were sporting just as we did then, with spirits just as gay;
But the "master" sleeps upon the hill, which, coated o'er with snow,
Afforded us a sliding-place, just twenty years ago.

The old school-house is alter'd some, the benches are replaced
By new ones, very like the same our penknives had defaced;
But the same old bricks are in the wall, the bell swings to and fro,
It's music, just the same, dear Tom, 'twas twenty years ago.

The boys were playing some old game, beneath the same old tree—
I do forget the name just now; you've play'd the same with me
On that same spot; 'twas play'd with knives, by throwing so and so,
The loser had a task to do, there, just twenty years ago.

The river's running just as still, the willows on its side
Are larger than they were, Tom, the stream appears less wide;
But the grapevine swing is ruin'd now where once we play'd the beau,
And swung our sweethearts—"pretty girls"
—just twenty years ago.

The spring that bubbled 'neath the hill, close by the spreading beech,
Is very low—'twas once so high that we could almost reach;
And kneeling down to get a drink, dear Tom, I even started so!
To see how much that I am changed since twenty years ago.

Near by the spring, upon an elm, you know I cut your name,
Your sweetheart's just beneath it, Tom, and you did mine the same—
Some heartless wretch had peel'd the bark, 'twas dying sure but slow,
Just as the one whose name was cut, died twenty years ago.

My lids have long been dry, Tom, but tears came in my eyes,
I thought of her I loved so well—those early broken ties—
I visited the old churchyard, and took some flowers to strew
Upon the graves of those we loved, some twenty years ago.

Some are in the churchyard laid, some sleep beneath the sea,
But few are left of our old class, excepting you and me,
And when our time is come, Tom, and we are call'd to go,
I hope they'll lay us where we play'd, just twenty years ago.
            AUTHOR UNKNOWN.

SCHOOL AND SCHOOL-FELLOWS.
"Floreat Etona."

TWELVE years ago I made a mock
  Of filthy trades and traffics:
I wonder'd what they meant by stock;
  I wrote delightful sapphics;
I knew the streets of Rome and Troy,
  I supp'd with Fates and Furies;—
Twelve years ago I was a boy,
  A happy boy at Drury's.

Twelve years ago!—how many a thought
  Of faded pains and pleasures
Those whisper'd syllables have brought
  From Memory's hoarded treasures!
The fields, the farms, the bats, the books,
  The glories and disgraces,
The voices of dear friends, the looks
  Of old familiar faces!

Kind Mater smiles again to me,
  As bright as when we parted;
I seem again the frank, the free,
  Stout-limb'd and simple-hearted!
Pursuing every idle dream,
  And shunning every warning;
With no hard work but Bovney stream,
  No chill except Long Morning:

Now stopping Harry Vernon's ball
  That rattled like a rocket;
Now hearing Wentworth's "Fourteen all!"
  And striking for the pocket;
Now feasting on a cheese and flitch,—
  Now drinking from the pewter;
Now leaping over Chalvey ditch,
  Now laughing at my tutor.

Where are my friends? I am alone;
  No playmate shares my beaker:
Some lie beneath the churchyard stone,
  And some—before the Speaker;
And some compose a tragedy,
  And some compose a rondo;
And some draw sword for Liberty,
  And some draw pleas for John Doe.

Tom Mill was used to blacken eyes
  Without the fear of sessions;
Charles Medlar loath'd false quantities,
  As much as false professions;
Now Mill keeps order in the land,
  A magistrate pedantic;

And Medlar's feet repose unscann'd
  Beneath the wide Atlantic.

Wild Nick, whose oaths made such a din,
  Does Dr. Martext's duty;
And Mullion, with that monstrous chin,
  Is married to a beauty;
And Darrel studies, week by week,
  His Mant, and not his Manton;
And Ball, who was but poor at Greek,
  Is very rich at Canton.

And I am eight-and-twenty now;—
  The world's cold chains have bound me;
And darker shades are on my brow,
  And sadder scenes around me:
In Parliament I fill my seat,
  With many other noodles;
And lay my head in Jermyn street,
  And sip my hock at Boodle's.

But often, when the cares of life,
  Have set my temples aching,
When visions haunt me of a wife,
  When duns await my waking,
When Lady Jane is in a pet,
  Or Hoby in a hurry,
When Captain Hazard wins a bet,
  Or Beaulieu spoils a curry,—

For hours and hours I think and talk
  Of each remember'd hobby;
I long to lounge in Poets' Walk,
  To shiver in the lobby;
I wish that I could run away
  From House, and Court, and Levee,
Where bearded men appear to-day
  Just Eton boys, grown heavy,—

That I could bask in childhood's sun,
  And dance o'er childhood's roses,
And find huge wealth in one pound one,
  Vast wit in broken noses,
And play Sir Giles at Datchet Lane,
  And call the milkmaids Houris,—
That I could be a boy again,—
  A happy boy,—at Drury's.
          WINTHROP MACKWORTH PRAED.

A REFLECTIVE RETROSPECT.

'TIS twenty years, and something more,
  Since, all athirst for useful knowledge,

I took some draughts of classic lore,
  Drawn very mild, at ——rd College;
Yet I remember all that one
  Could wish to hold in recollection;
The boys, the joys, the noise, the fun;
  But not a single Conic Section.

I recollect those harsh affairs,
  The morning bells, that gave us panics;
I recollect the formal prayers,
  That seemed like lessons in Mechanics;
I recollect the drowsy way
  In which the students listen'd to them,
As clearly, in my wig, to-day,
  As when a boy I slumber'd through them.

I recollect the tutors all
  As freshly now, if I may say so,
As any chapter I recall,
  In Homer or Ovidius Naso.
I recollect extremely well
  "Old Hugh," the mildest of fanatics;
I well remember Matthew Bell,
  But very faintly Mathematics.

I recollect the prizes paid
  For lessons fathom'd to the bottom;
(Alas that pencil-marks should fade!)
  I recollect the chaps who got 'em,—
The light equestrians who soar'd
  O'er every passage reckon'd stony;
And took the chalks,—but never scored
  A single honor to the pony!

Ah me! what changes Time has wrought,
  And how predictions have miscarried!
A few have reach'd the goal they sought,
  And some are dead, and some are married!
And some in city journals war;
  And some as politicians bicker;
And some are pleading at the bar—
  For jury-verdicts, or for liquor!

And some on Trade and Commerce wait;
  And some in school with dunces battle;
And some the gospel propagate;
  And some the choicest breeds of cattle;
And some are living at their ease;
  And some were wreck'd in "the revulsion;"
Some serve the State for handsome fees,
  And one, I hear, upon compulsion!

Lamont, who, in his college days,
  Thought e'en a cross a moral scandal,
Has left his Puritanic ways,
  And worships now with bell and candle;
And Mann, who mourn'd the negro's fate,
  And held the slave as most unlucky,
Now holds him, at the market rate,
  On a plantation in Kentucky!

Tom Knox—who swore in such a tone
  It fairly might be doubted whether
It was really himself alone,
  Or *Knox* and Erebus together—
Has grown a very alter'd man,
  And, changing oaths for mild entreaty,
Now recommends the Christian plan
  To savages in Otaheite!

Alas for young ambition's vow!
  How envious Fate may overthrow it!—
Poor Harvey is in Congress now,
  Who struggled long to be a poet;
Smith carves (quite well) memorial stones,
  Who tried in vain to make the law go;
Hall deals in hides; and "Pious Jones"
  Is dealing faro in Chicago!

And, sadder still, the brilliant Hays,
  Once honest, manly, and ambitious,
Has taken latterly to ways
  Extremely profligate and vicious;
By slow degrees—I can't tell how—
  He's reach'd at last the very groundsel,
And in New York he figures now,
  A member of the Common Council!
            John G. Saxe.

THE BOYS.

Has there any old fellow got mix'd with the boys?
If there has, take him out, without making a noise.
Hang the Almanac's cheat and the Catalogue's spite!
Old Time is a liar! We're twenty to-night!

We're twenty! We're twenty! Who says we are more?
He's tipsy,—young jackanapes!—show him the door!

"Gray temples at twenty?"—Yes! *white*,
   if we please;
Where the snow-flakes fall thickest there's
   nothing can freeze!

Was it snowing I spoke of? Excuse the
   mistake!
Look close,—you will see not a sign of a
   flake!
We want some new garlands for those we
   have shed,—
And these are white roses in place of the
   red.

We've a trick, we young fellows, you may
   have been told,
Of talking (in public) as if we were old:
That boy we call "Doctor," and this we
   call "Judge";—
It's a neat little fiction,—of course it's all
   fudge.

That fellow's the "Speaker,"—the one on
   the right;
"Mr. Mayor," my young one, how are you
   to-night?
That's our "Member of Congress," we say
   when we chaff;
There's the "Reverend" What's his name?
   —don't make me laugh!

That boy with the grave mathematical
   look
Made believe he had written a wonderful
   book,
And the ROYAL SOCIETY thought it was
   true!
So they chose him right in,—a good joke
   it was too!

There's a boy, we pretend, with a three-
   decker brain,
That could harness a team with a logical
   chain;
When he spoke for our manhood in syl-
   labled fire,
We call'd him "The Justice," but now
   he's "The Squire."

And there's a nice youngster of excellent
   pith,—
Fate tried to conceal him by naming him
   Smith;

But he shouted a song for the brave and
   the free,—
Just read on his medal, "My country,"
   "of thee!"

You hear that boy laughing?—You think
   he's all fun;
But the angels laugh, too, at the good he
   has done;
The children laugh loud as they troop to
   his call,
And the poor man that knows him laughs
   loudest of all!

Yes, we're boys,—always playing with
   tongue or with pen;
And I sometimes have ask'd, Shall we ever
   be men?
Shall we always be youthful, and laughing,
   and gay,
Till the last dear companion drops smil-
   ing away?

Then here's to our boyhood, its gold and
   its gray!
The stars of its winter, the dews of its
   May!
And when we have done with our life-last-
   ing toys,
Dear Father, take care of thy children,
   THE BOYS.

OLIVER WENDELL HOLMES

AULD LANG SYNE.

SHOULD auld acquaintance be forgot,
   And never brought to mind?
Should auld acquaintance be forgot,
   And auld lang syne?
      For auld lang syne, my dear,
      For auld lang syne,
      We'll tak' a cup o' kindness yet,
      For auld lang syne.

And surely ye'll be your pint stowp!
   And surely I'll be mine!
And we'll tak' a cup o' kindness yet,
   For auld lang syne.
      For auld lang syne, my dear,
      For auld lang syne,
      We'll tak' a cup o' kindness yet,
      For auld lang syne.

We twa ha'e run about the braes,
    And pou'd the gowans fine;
But we've wander'd mony a weary fitt
    Sin' auld lang syne.
        For auld lang syne, my dear,
            For auld lang syne,
        We'll tak' a cup o' kindness yet,
            For auld lang syne.

We twa ha'e paidl'd in the burn,
    Frae morning sun till dine;
But seas between us braid ha'e roar'd
    Sin' auld lang syne.
        For auld lang syne, my dear,
            For auld lang syne,
        We'll tak' a cup o' kindness yet,
            For auld lang syne.

And there's a hand, my trusty fiere!
    And gie's a hand o' thine!
And we'll tak' a right gude-willie waught,
    For auld lang syne.
        For auld lang syne, my dear,
            For auld lang syne,
        We'll tak' a cup o' kindness yet,
            For auld lang syne.
                      ROBERT BURNS.

MY PLAYMATE.

THE pines were dark on Ramoth hill,
    Their song was soft and low;
The blossoms in the sweet May wind
    Were falling like the snow.

The blossoms drifted at our feet,
    The orchard birds sang clear;
The sweetest and the saddest day
    It seem'd of all the year.

For, more to me than birds or flowers,
    My playmate left her home,
And took with her the laughing spring,
    The music and the bloom.

She kiss'd the lips of kith and kin,
    She laid her hand in mine:
What more could ask the bashful boy
    Who fed her father's kine?

She left us in the bloom of May:
    The constant years told o'er
Their seasons with as sweet May morns,
    But she came back no more.

I walk, with noiseless feet, the round
    Of uneventful years;
Still o'er and o'er I sow the spring
    And reap the autumn ears.

She lives where all the golden year
    Her summer roses blow;
The dusky children of the sun
    Before her come and go.

There haply with her jewell'd hands
    She smooths her silken gown,—
No more the homespun lap wherein
    I shook the walnuts down.

The wild grapes wait us by the brook,
    The brown nuts on the hill,
And still the May-day flowers make sweet
    The woods of Follymill.

The lilies blossom in the pond,
    The bird builds in the tree,
The dark pines sing on Ramoth hill
    The slow song of the sea.

I wonder if she thinks of them,
    And how the old time seems,—
If ever the pines of Ramoth wood
    Are sounding in her dreams.

I see her face, I hear her voice:
    Does she remember mine?
And what to her is now the boy
    Who fed her father's kine?

What cares she that the orioles build
    For other eyes than ours,—
That other hands with nuts are fill'd,
    And other laps with flowers?

O playmate in the golden time!
    Our mossy seat is green,
Its fringing violets blossom yet,
    The old trees o'er it lean.

The winds so sweet with birch and fern
    A sweeter memory blow;
And there in spring the veeries sing
    The song of long ago.

And still the pines of Ramoth wood
    Are moaning like the sea,—
The moaning of the sea of change
    Between myself and thee!
                      JOHN GREENLEAF WHITTIER.

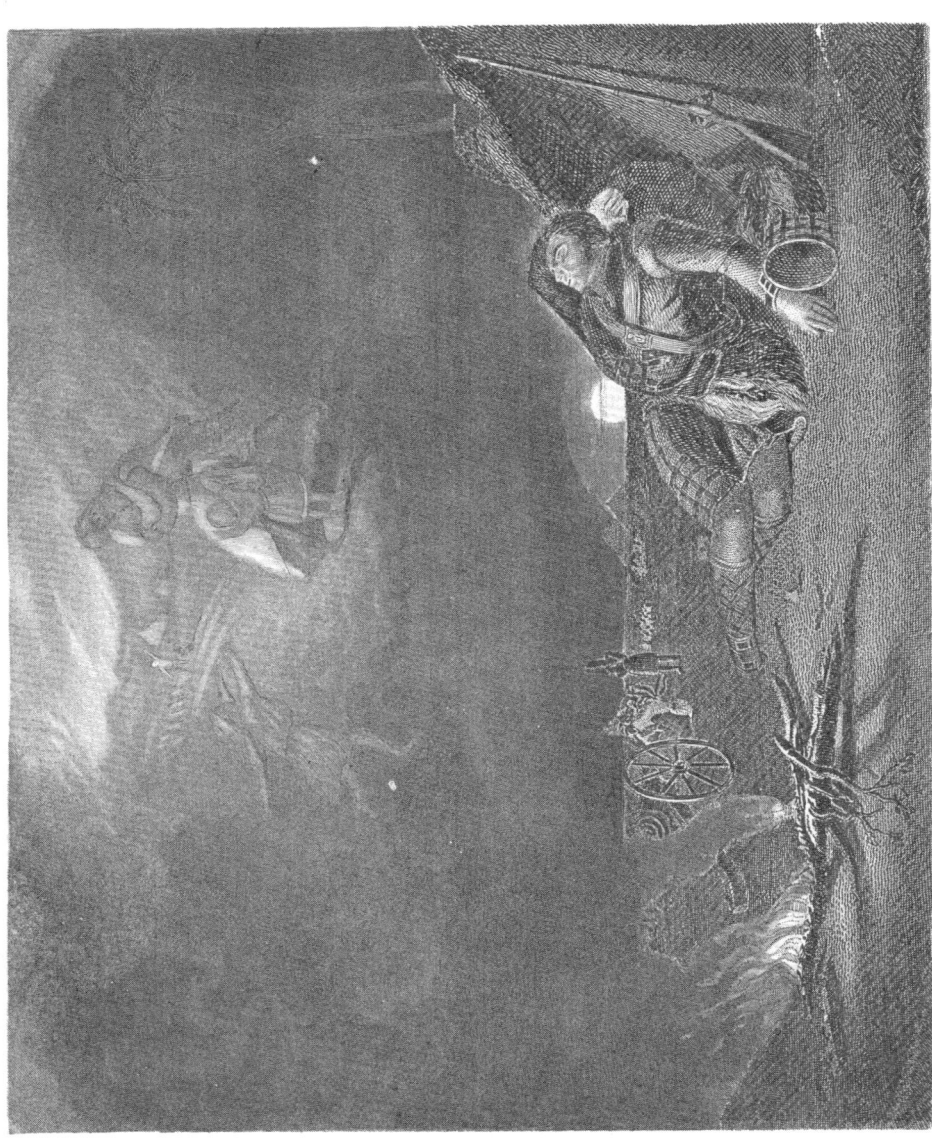

"AT THE DEAD OF THE NIGHT A SWEET VISION I SAW,
AND THRICE ERE THE MORNING I DREMT IT AGAIN"

I HAE NAEBODY NOW.

I HAE naebody now, I hae naebody now,
  To meet me upon the green,
Wi' light locks waving o'er her brow,
  An' joy in her deep blue e'en;
Wi' the raptured kiss, an' the happy smile,
  An' the dance o' the lightsome fay,
An' the wee bit tale o' news the while
  That had happen'd when I was away.

I hae naebody now, I hae naebody now,
  To clasp to my bosom at even,
O'er her calm sleep to breathe the vow,
  An' pray for a blessing from Heaven;
An' the wild embrace, an' the gleesome face,
  In the morning that met my eye,
Where are they now? where are they now?
  In the cauld, cauld grave they lie.

There's naebody kens, there's naebody kens,
  An' oh, may they never prove,
That sharpest degree o' agony
  For the child o' their earthly love.
To see a flower, in its vernal hour,
  By slow degrees decay,
Then calmly aneath the hand o' death,
  Breathe its sweet soul away!

Oh, dinna break, my poor auld heart,
  Nor at thy loss repine,
For the unseen hand that threw the dart
  Was sent frae her Father and thine.
Yet I maun mourn, an' I will mourn,
  Even till my latest day,
For though my darling can never return,
  I shall follow thee soon away.
    JAMES HOGG.

THE SOLDIER'S DREAM.

OUR bugles sang truce, for the night-cloud had lower'd,
  And the sentinel stars set their watch in the sky,
And thousands had sunk on the ground overpower'd,
  The weary to sleep, and the wounded to die.

When reposing that night on my pallet of straw,
  By the wolf-scaring fagot that guarded the slain,
At the dead of the night a sweet vision I saw,
  And thrice ere the morning I dream'd it again.

Methought from the battle-field's dreadful array,
  Far, far I had roam'd on a desolate track:
'Twas Autumn, and sunshine arose on the way
  To the home of my fathers, that welcomed me back.

I flew to the pleasant fields traversed so oft
  In life's morning march, when my bosom was young;
I heard my own mountain-goats bleating aloft,
  And knew the sweet strain that the corn-reapers sung.

Then pledged we the wine-cup, and fondly I swore
  From my home and my weeping friends never to part;
My little ones kiss'd me a thousand times o'er,
  And my wife sobb'd aloud in her fulness of heart.

"Stay, stay with us; rest,—thou art weary and worn!"
  And fain was their war-broken soldier to stay,
But sorrow return'd with the dawning of morn,
  And the voice in my dreaming ear melted away.
    THOMAS CAMPBELL.

BINGEN ON THE RHINE.

A SOLDIER of the Legion lay dying in Algiers,
There was lack of woman's nursing, there was dearth of woman's tears,
But a comrade stood beside him, while his life-blood ebb'd away,
And bent, with pitying glances, to hear what he might say.
The dying soldier falter'd as he took that comrade's hand,
And he said, "I never more shall see my own, my native land;
Take a message and a token to some distant friends of mine,
For I was born at Bingen—at Bingen on the Rhine.

"Tell my brothers and companions, when
        they meet and crowd around
To hear my mournful story in the pleasant
        vineyard ground,
That we fought the battle bravely, and
        when the day was done
Full many a corpse lay ghastly pale be-
        neath the setting sun.

And 'midst the dead and dying were some
        grown old in wars,
The death-wound on their gallant breasts,
        the last of many scars;
But some were young, and suddenly beheld
        life's morn decline,
And one had come from Bingen, fair Bin-
        gen on the Rhine.

"Tell my mother that her other sons shall
        comfort her old age,
And I was aye a truant bird, that thought
        his home a cage,
For my father was a soldier, and even as a
        child
My heart leap'd forth to hear him tell of
        struggles fierce and wild;
And when he died, and left us to divide
        his scanty hoard,
I let them take whate'er they would, but
        kept my father's sword,
And with boyish love I hung it where the
        bright light used to shine
On the cottage-wall at Bingen—calm Bin-
        gen on the Rhine.

"Tell my sister not to weep for me, and
        sob with drooping head,
When the troops are marching home again
        with glad and gallant tread,
But to look upon them proudly, with a
        calm and steadfast eye,
For her brother was a soldier too, and not
        afraid to die.
And if a comrade seek her love, I ask her
        in my name
To listen to him kindly, without regret or
        shame,
And to hang the old sword in its place
        (my father's sword and mine),
For the honor of old Bingen—dear Bin-
        gen on the Rhine.

"There's another—not a sister: in the
        happy days gone by,
You'd have known her by the merriment
        that sparkled in her eye;
Too innocent for coquetry, too fond for
        idle scorning,
O friend, I fear the lightest heart makes
        sometimes heaviest mourning;

Tell her the last night of my life (for ere
        the moon be risen
My body will be out of pain—my soul be
        out of prison),
I dream'd I stood with her, and saw the
        yellow sunlight shine
On the vineclad hills of Bingen—fair
        Bingen on the Rhine.

"I saw the blue Rhine sweep along—I
        heard, or seemed to hear,
The German songs we used to sing, in
        chorus sweet and clear,
And down the pleasant river, and up the
        slanting hill,
The echoing chorus sounded through the
        evening calm and still;
And her glad blue eyes were on me as we
        pass'd with friendly talk
Down many a path beloved of yore, and
        well-remember'd walk,
And her little hand lay lightly, confid-
        ingly in mine;
But we'll meet no more at Bingen—loved
        Bingen on the Rhine."

His voice grew faint and hoarser—his
        grasp was childish weak—
His eyes put on a dying look—he sigh'd
        and ceased to speak;
His comrade bent to lift him, but the spark
        of life had fled—
The soldier of the Legion in a foreign
        land was dead!
And the soft moon rose up slowly, and
        calmly she look'd down
On the red sand of the battle-field, with
        bloody corpses strown;
Yea, calmly on that dreadful scene her
        pale light seem'd to shine,
As it shone on distant Bingen—fair Bin-
        gen on the Rhine.

CAROLINE NORTON.

THE CHESS-BOARD.

My little love, do you remember,
  Ere we were grown so sadly wise,
Those evenings in the bleak December,
Curtain'd warm from the snowy weather,
When you and I play'd chess together,
  Checkmated by each other's eyes?
Ah, still I see your soft white hand
Hovering warm o'er Queen and Knight.
  Brave Pawns in valiant battle stand:
The double Castles guard the wings:
The Bishop, bent on distant things,
Moves sidling through the fight.
  Our fingers touch; our glances meet,
  And falter; falls your golden hair
Against my cheek; your bosom sweet
Is heaving. Down the field, your Queen
Rides slow her soldiery all between,
  And checks me unaware.
Ah me! the little battle's done,
Dispersed is all its chivalry;
Full many a move since then have we
Mid Life's perplexing checkers made,
And many a game with Fortune play'd,—
  What is it we have won?
This, this at least—if this alone;—
That never, never, never more,
As in those old still nights of yore
  (Ere we were grown so sadly wise),
  Can you and I shut out the skies,
Shut out the world, and wintry weather,
  And, eyes exchanging warmth with eyes,
Play chess, as then we play'd, together!
              ROBERT BULWER LYTTON.

WE PARTED IN SILENCE.

We parted in silence, we parted by night,
  On the banks of that lonely river;
Where the fragrant limes their boughs unite,
  We met—and we parted for ever!
The night-bird sung, and the stars above
  Told many a touching story,
Of friends long pass'd to the kingdom of love,
  Where the soul wears its mantle of glory.

We parted in silence—our cheeks were wet
  With the tears that were past controlling;
We vow'd we would never—no, never forget,
  And those vows at the time were consoling;
But those lips that echo'd the sounds of mine
  Are as cold as that lonely river;
And that eye, that beautiful spirit's shrine,
  Has shrouded its fires for ever.

And now on the midnight sky I look,
  And my heart grows full of weeping;
Each star is to me a sealèd book,
  Some tale of that loved one keeping.
We parted in silence—we parted in tears,
  On the banks of that lonely river:
But the odor and bloom of those bygone years
  Shall hang o'er its waters for ever.
              JULIA CRAWFORD.

FAREWELL! BUT WHENEVER YOU WELCOME THE HOUR.

Farewell! but whenever you welcome the hour
That awakens the night-song of mirth in your bower,
Then think of the friend who once welcomed it too.
And forgot his own griefs to be happy with you.
His griefs may return—not a hope may remain
Of the few that have brighten'd his pathway of pain—
But he ne'er will forget the short vision that threw
Its enchantment around him while lingering with you!

And still on that evening, when pleasure fills up
To the highest top-sparkle each heart and each cup,
Where'er my path lies, be it gloomy or bright,
My soul, happy friends! shall be with you that night—
Shall join in your revels, your sports, and your wiles,
And return to me beaming all o'er with your smiles;

Too blest if it tells me that, mid the gay
    cheer,
Some kind voice had murmur'd, "I wish
    he were here!"
Let Fate do her worst, there are relics of
    joy,
Bright dreams of the past, which she can-
    not destroy!
Which come in the night-time of sorrow
    and care,
And bring back the features that joy used
    to wear.
Long, long be my heart with such memo-
    ries fill'd!
Like the vase in which roses have once
    been distill'd;
You may break, you may ruin the vase if
    you will,
But the scent of the roses will hang round
    it still.
            THOMAS MOORE.

WHEN WE TWO PARTED.

WHEN we two parted
    In silence and tears,
Half broken-hearted,
    To sever for years,
Pale grew thy cheek and cold,
    Colder thy kiss;
Truly that hour foretold
    Sorrow to this.

The dew of the morning
    Sunk chill on my brow—
It felt like the warning
    Of what I feel now.
Thy vows are all broken,
    And light is thy fame;
I hear thy name spoken,
    And share in its shame.

They name thee before me,
    A knell to mine ear;
A shudder comes o'er me—
    Why wert thou *so* dear?
They know not I knew thee,
    Who knew thee too well:—
Long, long shall I rue thee,
    Too deeply to tell.

In secret we met—
    In silence I grieve,
That thy heart could forget,
    Thy spirit deceive.

If I should meet thee
    After long years,
How should I greet thee?—
    With silence and tears.
            LORD BYRON.

LAMENT OF THE IRISH EMIGRANT.

I'M sittin' on the stile, Mary,
    Where we sat side by side
On a bright May mornin' long ago,
    When first you were my bride;
The corn was springin' fresh and green,
    And the lark sang loud and high;
And the red was on your lip, Mary,
    And the love-light in your eye.

The place is little changed, Mary;
    The day is bright as then;
The lark's loud song is in my ear,
    And the corn is green again;
But I miss the soft clasp of your hand,
    And your breath, warm on my cheek;
And I still keep list'nin' for the words
    You never more will speak.

'Tis but a step down yonder lane,
    And the little church stands near—
The church where we were wed, Mary;
    I see the spire from here.
But the graveyard lies between, Mary,
    And my step might break your rest—
For I've laid you, darling, down to sleep,
    With your baby on your breast.

I'm very lonely now, Mary,
    For the poor make no new friends;
But, oh! they love the better still
    The few our Father sends!
And you were all I had, Mary—
    My blessin' and my pride:
There's nothing left to care for now,
    Since my poor Mary died.

Yours was the good, brave heart, Mary,
    That still kept hoping on,
When the trust in God had left my soul,
    And my arm's young strength was
        gone;
There was comfort ever on your lip,
    And the kind look on your brow—
I bless you, Mary, for that same,
    Though you cannot hear me now.

I thank you for the patient smile
  When your heart was fit to break—
When the hunger-pain was gnawin' there,
  And you hid it for my sake;
I bless you for the pleasant word,
  When your heart was sad and sore—
Oh! I'm thankful you are gone, Mary,
  Where grief can't reach you more!

I'm biddin' you a long farewell,
  My Mary—kind and true!
But I'll not forget you, darling,
  In the land I'm goin' to;
They say there's bread and work for all,
  And the sun shines always there—
But I'll not forget old Ireland,
  Were it fifty times as fair!

And often in those grand old woods
  I'll sit, and shut my eyes,
And my heart will travel back again
  To the place where Mary lies!
And I'll think I see the little stile
  Where we sat side by side,
And the springin' corn, and the bright May morn,
  When first you were my bride.
LADY DUFFERIN.

THE AGE OF WISDOM.

Ho, pretty page with the dimpled chin
  That never has known the barber's shear,
All your wish is woman to win,
This is the way that boys begin,—
  Wait till you come to Forty Year.

Curly gold locks cover foolish brains,
  Billing and cooing is all your cheer;
Sighing and singing of midnight strains,
Under Bonnybell's window-panes,—
  Wait till you come to Forty Year!

Forty times over let Michaelmas pass,
  Grizzling hair the brain doth clear—
Then you know a boy is an ass,
Then you know the worth of a lass,
  Once you have come to Forty Year.

Pledge me round, I bid ye declare,
  All good fellows whose beards are grey,
Did not the fairest of the fair
Common grow and wearisome ere
  Ever a month was pass'd away?

The reddest lips that ever have kiss'd,
  The brightest eyes that ever have shone,
May pray and whisper, and we not list,
Or look away, and never be miss'd,
  Ere yet ever a month is gone.

Gillian's dead, God rest her bier!
  How I loved her twenty years syne!
Marian's married, but I sit here
Alone and merry at Forty Year,
  Dipping my nose in the Gascon wine.
WILLIAM MAKEPEACE THACKERAY.

ODE TO AN INDIAN GOLD COIN.

WRITTEN IN CHÉRICAL, MALABAR.

SLAVE of the dark and dirty mine!
  What vanity has brought thee here?
How can I love to see thee shine
  So bright, whom I have bought so dear?—
The tent-ropes flapping lone I hear,
For twilight converse, arm in arm;
  The jackal's shriek bursts on mine ear
When mirth and music wont to charm.

By Chérical's dark wandering streams,
  Where cane-tufts shadow all the wild,
Sweet visions haunt my waking dreams
  Of Teviot, loved while still a child,
  Of castled rocks stupendous piled
By Esk or Eden's classic wave,
  Where loves of youth and friendships smiled,
Uncursed by thee, vile yellow slave!

Fade, day-dreams sweet, from memory fade!—
  The perish'd bliss of youth's first prime,
That once so bright on fancy play'd,
  Revives no more in after time.
  Far from my sacred natal clime,
I haste to an untimely grave;
  The daring thoughts that soar'd sublime
Are sunk in ocean's southern wave.

Slave of the mine! thy yellow light
  Gleams baleful as the tomb-fire drear.
A gentle vision comes by night
  My lonely widow'd heart to cheer;
  Her eyes are dim with many a tear,
That once were guiding stars to mine:

Her fond heart throbs with many a fear!
I cannot bear to see thee shine.

For thee, for thee, vile yellow slave,
  I left a heart that loved me true!
I cross'd the tedious ocean-wave,
  To roam in climes unkind and new.
The cold wind of the stranger blew
Chill on my wither'd heart: the grave
  Dark and untimely met my view,—
And all for thee, vile yellow slave!

Ha! com'st thou now so late to mock
  A wanderer's banish'd heart forlorn,
Now that his frame the lightning shock
  Of sun-rays tipt with death has borne?
From love, from friendship, country, torn,
To memory's fond regrets the prey;
  Vile slave, thy yellow dross I scorn!
Go mix thee with thy kindred clay!
              JOHN LEYDEN.

BREAK, BREAK, BREAK.

BREAK, break, break,
  On thy cold, gray stones, O sea!
And I would that my tongue could utter
  The thoughts that arise in me.

Oh, well for the fisherman's boy
  That he shouts with his sister at play!
Oh, well for the sailor lad
  That he sings in his boat on the bay!

And the stately ships go on
  To the haven under the hill;
But oh, for the touch of a vanish'd hand,
  And the sound of a voice that is still!

Break, break, break,
  At the foot of thy crags, O sea!
But the tender grace of a day that is dead
  Will never come back to me.
              ALFRED TENNYSON.

ON THIS DAY I COMPLETE MY THIRTY-SIXTH YEAR.

        MISSOLONGHI, Jan. 22, 1824.

'TIS time this heart should be unmoved,
  Since others it has ceased to move:
Yet, though I cannot be beloved,
    Still let me love!

My days are in the yellow leaf;
  The flowers and fruits of love are gone;
The worm, the canker, and the grief
    Are mine alone!

The fire that on my bosom preys
  Is lone as some volcanic isle;
No torch is kindled at its blaze—
    A funeral pile!

The hope, the fear, the jealous care,
  The exalted portion of the pain
And power of love, I cannot share,
    But wear the chain.

But 'tis not *thus*—and 'tis not *here*—
  Such thoughts would shake my soul, nor *now*,
Where glory decks the hero's bier,
    Or binds his brow.

The sword, the banner, and the field,
  Glory and Greece, around me see!
The Spartan, borne upon his shield,
    Was not more free.

Awake! (not Greece—she *is* awake)
  Awake, my spirit! Think through *whom*
Thy life-blood tracks its parent lake,
    And then strike home!

Tread those reviving passions down,
  Unworthy manhood!—unto thee
Indifferent should the smile or frown
    Of beauty be.

If thou regret'st thy youth, *why live?*
  The land of honorable death
Is here:—up to the field, and give
    Away thy breath!

Seek out—less often sought than found—
  A soldier's grave, for thee the best;
Then look around, and choose thy ground
    And take thy rest.
              LORD BYRON.

OLD LETTERS.

OLD LETTERS! wipe away the tear
  For vows and hopes so vainly worded?
A pilgrim finds his journal here
  Since first his youthful loins were girded

Yes, here are wails from Clapham Grove,
  How could philosophy expect us
To live with Dr. Wise, and love
  Rice-pudding and the Greek Delectus?

Explain why childhood's path is sown
  With moral and scholastic tin-tacks;

"AND THE STATELY SHIPS GO ON
TO THE HAVEN UNDER THE HILL."
Break, break, break

Ere sin original was known,
  Did Adam groan beneath the syntax?
How strange to parley with the dead!
  Keep ye your green, wan leaves? How many
From Friendship's tree untimely shed!
  And here is one as sad as any;

A ghastly bill! "I disapprove,"
  And yet She helped me to defray it—
What tokens of a mother's love!
  Oh, bitter thought! I can't repay it.

And here's the offer that I wrote
  In '33 to Lucy Diver;
And here John Wylie's begging note,—
  He never paid me back a stiver.

And here my feud with Major Spike,
  Our bet about the French Invasion;
I must confess I acted like
  A donkey upon that occasion.

Here's news from Paternoster Row!
  How mad I was when first I learn'd it:
They would not take my book, and now
  I'd give a trifle to have burnt it.

And here a pile of notes, at last,
  With "love," and "dove," and "sever," "never:"
Though hope, though passion may be past,
  Their perfume is as sweet as ever.

A human heart should beat for two,
  Despite the scoffs of single scorners;
And all the hearths I ever knew
  Had got a pair of chimney corners.

See here a double violet—
  Two locks of hair—a deal of scandal;
I'll burn what only brings regret—
  Go, Betty, fetch a lighted candle.
                    FREDERICK LOCKER.

THE BALLAD OF BOUILLABAISSE.

A STREET there is in Paris famous,
  For which no rhyme our language yields,
Rue Neuve des Petits Champs its name is—
  The New Street of the Little Fields.
And here's an inn, not rich and splendid,
  But still in comfortable case;
The which in youth I oft attended,
  To eat a bowl of Bouillabaisse.

This Bouillabaisse a noble dish is—
  A sort of soup or broth, or brew,
Or hotchpotch of all sorts of fishes,
  That Greenwich never could outdo;
Green herbs, red peppers, mussels, saffron,
  Soles, onions, garlic, roach, and dace:
All these you eat at TERRÉ's tavern,
  In that one dish of Bouillabaisse.

Indeed, a rich and savory stew 'tis;
  And true philosophers, methinks,
Who love all sorts of natural beauties,
  Should love good victuals and good drinks.
And Cordelier or Benedictine
  Might gladly, sure, his lot embrace,
Nor find a fast-day too afflicting,
  Which served him up a Bouillabaisse.

I wonder if the house still there is?
  Yes, here the lamp is, as before;
The smiling red-cheek'd écaillère is
  Still opening oysters at the door.
Is TERRÉ still alive and able?
  I recollect his droll grimace:
He'd come and smile before your table.
  And hope you liked your Bouillabaisse.

We enter—nothing's changed or older.
  "How's Monsieur TERRÉ, waiter, pray?"
The waiter stares and shrugs his shoulder—
  "Monsieur is dead this many a day."
"It is the lot of saint and sinner,
  So honest TERRÉ's run his race."
"What will Monsieur require for dinner?"
  "Say, do you still cook Bouillabaisse?"

"Oh, oui, Monsieur,"'s the waiter's answer;
  "Quel vin Monsieur desire-t-il?"
"Tell me a good one."—"That I can, sir:
  The Chambertin with yellow seal."
"So TERRÉ's gone," I say, and sink in
  My old accustom'd corner-place;
"He's done with feasting and with drinking,
  With Burgundy and Bouillabaisse."

My old accustom'd corner here is,
  The table still is in the nook;
Ah! vanish'd many a busy year is
  This well-known chair since last I took.

When first I saw ye, *cari luoghi*,
  I'd scarce a beard upon my face,
And now, a grizzled, grim old fogy,
  I sit and wait for Bouillabaisse.

Where are you, old companions trusty
  Of early days here met to dine?
Come, waiter! quick, a flagon crusty—
  I'll pledge them in the good old wine.
The kind old voices and old faces
  My memory can quick retrace;
Around the board they take their places,
  And share the wine and Bouillabaisse.

There's JACK has made a wondrous marriage;
  There's laughing TOM is laughing yet;
There's brave AUGUSTUS drives his carriage;
  There's poor old FRED in the Gazette;
On JAMES's head the grass is growing:
  Good Lord! the world has wagg'd apace
Since here we set the Claret flowing,
  And drank, and ate the Bouillabaisse.

Ah me! how quick the days are flitting!
  I mind me of a time that's gone,
When here I'd sit, as now I'm sitting,
  In this same place—but not alone.
A fair young form was nestled near me,
  A dear, dear face look'd fondly up,
And sweetly spoke and smiled to cheer me.
  —There's no one now to share my cup.

   *   *   *   *   *   *

I drink it as the Fates ordain it.
  Come, fill it, and have done with rhymes:
Fill up the lonely glass and drain it
  In memory of dear old times.
Welcome the wine, whate'er the seal is;
  And sit you down and say your grace
With thankful heart, whate'er the meal is.
  —Here comes the smoking Bouillabaisse!
              WILLIAM MAKEPEACE THACKERAY.

ON LENDING A PUNCH-BOWL.

THIS ancient silver bowl of mine,—it tells of good old times,
Of joyous days, and jolly nights, and merry Christmas chimes;
They were a free and jovial race, but honest, brave, and true,
That dipp'd their ladle in the punch when this old bowl was new.

A Spanish galleon brought the bar,—so runs the ancient tale;
'Twas hammer'd by an Antwerp smith, whose arm was like a flail;
And now and then between the strokes, for fear his strength should fail,
He wiped his brow, and quaff'd a cup of good old Flemish ale.

'Twas purchased by an English squire to please his loving dame,
Who saw the cherubs, and conceived a longing for the same;
And oft as on the ancient stock another twig was found,
'Twas fill'd with caudle spiced and hot, and handed smoking round.

But, changing hands, it reach'd at length a Puritan divine,
Who used to follow Timothy, and take a little wine,
But hated punch and prelacy; and so it was, perhaps,
He went to Leyden, where he found conventicles and schnaps.

And then,—of course you know what's next—it left the Dutchman's shore
With those that in the Mayflower came,—a hundred souls and more,
Along with all the furniture to fill their new abodes:
To judge by what is still on hand, at least a hundred loads.

'Twas on a dreary winter's eve, the night was closing dim,
When old Miles Standish took the bowl, and fill'd it to the brim;
The little Captain stood and stirr'd the posset with his sword,
And all his sturdy men-at-arms were ranged about the board.

He poured the fiery Hollands in,—the man that never fear'd,—
He took a long and solemn draught, and wiped his yellow beard;

And one by one the musketeers, the men
    that fought and pray'd,
All drank as 'twere their mother's milk,
    and not a man afraid.

That night, affrighted from his nest the
    screaming eagle flew,
He heard the Pequot's ringing whoop, the
    soldier's wild halloo;
And there the sachem learn'd the rule he
    taught to kith and kin,
"Run from the white man when you find
    he smells of Hollands gin!"

A hundred years, and fifty more, had
    spread their leaves and snows,
A thousand rubs had flatten'd down each
    little cherub's nose,
When once again the bowl was fill'd, but
    not in mirth or joy—
'Twas mingled by a mother's hand to cheer
    her parting boy.

"Drink, John," she said, "'twill do you
    good,—poor child, you'll never bear
This working in the dismal trench, out in
    the midnight air;
And if—God bless me!—you were hurt,
    'twould keep away the chill;"
So John *did* drink,—and well he wrought
    that night at Bunker's Hill!

I tell you, there was generous warmth in
    good old English cheer;
I tell you, 'twas a pleasant thought to
    bring its symbol here.
'Tis but the fool that loves excess;—hast
    thou a drunken soul?
Thy bane is in thy shallow skull, not in
    my silver bowl!

I love the memory of the past,—its press'd
    yet fragrant flowers—
The moss that clothes its broken walls,—
    the ivy on its towers;
Nay, this poor bauble it bequeath'd—my
    eyes grow moist and dim,
To think of all the vanish'd joys that
    danced around its brim.

Then fill a fair and honest cup, and bear
    it straight to me;
The goblet hallows all it holds, whate'er
    the liquid be;

And may the cherubs on its face protect
    me from the sin
That dooms one to those dreadful words,
    "My dear, where *have* you been?"
OLIVER WENDELL HOLMES.

THE DAYS THAT ARE NO MORE.

TEARS, idle tears, I know not what
    they mean,
Tears from the depth of some divine despair
Rise in the heart, and gather to the eyes,
In looking on the happy autumn fields,
And thinking of the days that are no
    more.

Fresh as the first beam glittering on a
    sail,
That brings our friends up from the under-world,
Sad as the last which reddens over one
That sinks with all we love below the
    verge;
So sad, so fresh, the days that are no
    more.

Ah, sad and strange as in dark summer
    dawns
The earliest pipe of half-awaken'd birds
To dying ears, when unto dying eyes
The casement slowly grows a glimmering
    square;
So sad, so strange, the days that are no
    more.

Dear as remember'd kisses after death,
And sweet as those by hopeless fancy
    feign'd
On lips that are for others: deep as love,
Deep as first love, and wild with all regret;
Oh, death in life! the days that are no
    more.
ALFRED TENNYSON.

THE PAST.

THOU unrelenting Past!
Strong are the barriers round thy dark
    domain,
    And fetters, sure and fast,
Hold all that enter thy unbreathing reign.

Far in thy realm withdrawn
Old empires sit in sullenness and gloom,
    And glorious ages gone
Lie deep within the shadow of thy womb.

    Childhood, with all its mirth,
Youth, Manhood, Age that draws us to
    the ground,
    And last, Man's life on earth,
Glide to thy dim dominions, and are bound.

    Thou hast my better years,
Thou hast my earlier friends—the good—
    the kind,
    Yielded to thee with tears—
The venerable form—the exalted mind.

    My spirit yearns to bring
The lost ones back—yearns with desire
    intense,
    And struggles hard to wring
Thy bolts apart, and pluck thy captives
    thence.

    In vain—thy gates deny
All passage save to those who hence depart;
    Nor to the streaming eye
Thou giv'st them back—nor to the broken
    heart.

    In thy abysses hide
Beauty and excellence unknown—to thee
    Earth's wonder and her pride
Are gather'd, as the waters to the sea;

    Labors of good to man,
Unpublish'd charity, unbroken faith,—
    Love, that 'midst grief began,
And grew with years, and falter'd not in
    death.

    Full many a mighty name
Lurks in thy depths, unutter'd, unrevered;
    With thee are silent fame,
Forgotten arts, and wisdom disappear'd.

    Thine for a space are they—
Yet shalt thou yield thy treasures up at
    last;
    Thy gates shall yet give way,
Thy bolts shall fall, inexorable Past!

    All that of good and fair
Has gone into thy womb from earliest time,
    Shall then come forth to wear
The glory and the beauty of its prime.

    They have not perish'd—no!
Kind words, remember'd voices once so
    sweet,
    Smiles, radiant long ago,
And features, the great soul's apparent seat.

    All shall come back, each tie
Of pure affection shall be knit again;
    Alone shall Evil die,
And Sorrow dwell a prisoner in thy reign.

    And then shall I behold
Him by whose kind paternal side I sprung,
    And her who, still and cold,
Fills the next grave—the beautiful and
    young.
                    WILLIAM CULLEN BRYANT.

THE RETREAT.

HAPPY those early days, when I
Shined in my angel-infancy!
Before I understood this place
Appointed for my second race,
Or taught my soul to fancy aught
But a white celestial thought;
When yet I had not walk'd above
A mile or two from my first love,
And looking back at that short space
Could see a glimpse of his bright face;
When on some gilded cloud or flower
My gazing soul would dwell an hour,
And in those weaker glories spy
Some shadows of eternity;
Before I taught my tongue to wound
My conscience with a sinful sound,
Or had the black art to dispense
A several sin to every sense,
But felt through all this fleshly dress
Bright shoots of everlastingness.

Oh how I long to travel back,
And tread again that ancient track!
That I might once more reach that plain
Where first I left my glorious train;
From whence th' enlighten'd spirit sees
That shady City of Palm trees:
But ah! my soul with too much stay
Is drunk, and staggers in the way:
Some men a forward motion love,
But I by backward steps would move
And when this dust falls to the urn,
In that state I came, return.
                    HENRY VAUGHAN.

THE NABOB.

When silent time, wi' lightly foot,
  Had trod on thirty years,
I sought again my native land
  Wi' mony hopes and fears.
Wha kens gin the dear friends I left
  May still continue mine?
Or gin I e'er again shall taste
  The joys I left langsyne?

As I drew near my ancient pile
  My heart beat a' the way;
Ilk place I pass'd seem'd yet to speak
  O' some dear former day;
Those days that follow'd me afar,
  Those happy days o' mine,
Whilk made me think the present joys
  A' naething to langsyne!

The ivied tower now met my eye
  Where minstrels used to blaw;
Nae friend stepp'd forth wi' open hand,
  Nae weel-kenn'd face I saw;
Till Donald totter'd to the door,
  Wham I left in his prime,
And grat to see the lad return
  He bore about langsyne.

I ran to ilka dear friend's room,
  As if to find them there,
I knew where ilk ane used to sit,
  And hang o'er mony a chair;
Till soft remembrance threw a veil
  Across these e'en o' mine,
I closed the door, and sobb'd aloud,
  To think on auld langsyne.

Some pensy chiels, a new-sprung race,
  Wad next their welcome pay,
Wha shudder'd at my Gothic wa's
  And wish'd my groves away.
"Cut, cut," they cried, "those aged elms;
  Lay low yon mournfu' pine."
Na! na! our fathers' names grow there,
  Memorials o' langsyne.

To wean me frae these waefu' thoughts,
  They took me to the town;
But sair on ilka weel-kenn'd face
  I miss'd the youthfu' bloom.
At balls they pointed to a nymph
  Wham a' declared divine;
But sure her mother's blushing cheeks
  Were fairer far langsyne!

In vain I sought in music's sound
  To find that magic art,
Which oft in Scotland's ancient lays
  Has thrill'd through a' my heart.
The song had mony an artfu' turn;
  My ear confess'd 'twas fine;
But miss'd the simple melody
  I listen'd to langsyne.

Ye sons to comrades o' my youth,
  Forgi'e an auld man's spleen,
Wha 'midst your gayest scenes still mourns
  The days he ance has seen.
When time has pass'd and seasons fled,
  Your hearts will feel like mine;
And aye the sang will maist delight
  That minds ye o' langsyne!

SUSANNA BLAMIRE.

ONCE UPON A TIME.

I mind me of a pleasant time,
  A season long ago;
The pleasantest I've ever known,
  Or ever now shall know.
Bees, birds, and little tinkling rills
  So merrily did chime;
The year was in its sweet spring-tide,
  And I was in my prime.

I've never heard such music since,
  From every bending spray;
I've never pluck'd such primroses,
  Set thick on bank and brae;
I've never smelt such violets
  As all that pleasant time
I found by every hawthorn root—
  When I was in my prime.

Yon moory down, so black and bare,
  Was gorgeous then and gay
With golden gorse—bright blossoming—
  As none blooms nowaday.
The blackbird sings but seldom now
  Up there in the old lime,
Where hours and hours he used to sing—
  When I was in my prime.

Such cutting winds came never then
  To pierce one through and through;
More softly fell the silent shower,
  More balmily the dew.

The morning mist and evening haze—
  Unlike this cold gray rime—
Seem'd woven warm of golden air
  When I was in my prime.

And blackberries—so mawkish now—
  Were finely flavor'd then;
And nuts—such reddening clusters ripe
  I ne'er shall pull again;
Nor strawberries blushing bright—as rich
  As fruits of sunniest clime;
How all is alter'd for the worse
  Since I was in my prime!
          CAROLINE BOWLES SOUTHEY.

FORGET ME NOT.

Go, youth beloved, in distant glades
  New friends, new hopes, new joys to find,
Yet sometimes deign, 'midst fairer maids,
  To think on her thou leav'st behind.
Thy love, thy fate, dear youth, to share,
  Must never be my happy lot,
But thou mayst grant this humble prayer,
  Forget me not, forget me not!

Yet should the thought of my distress
  Too painful to thy feelings be,
Heed not the wish I now express,
  Nor ever deign to think on me;
But, oh, if grief thy steps attend,
  If want, if sickness be thy lot,
And thou require a soothing friend;
  Forget me not, forget me not!
          AMELIA OPIE.

YOUTH AND AGE.

VERSE, a breeze 'mid blossoms straying,
  Where Hope clung feeding, like a bee—
Both were mine! Life went a-maying
  With Nature, Hope, and Poesy,
      When I was young!
When I was young?—Ah, woful When!
Ah! for the change 'twixt Now and Then!
This breathing house not built with hands,
This body that does me grievous wrong,
O'er aery cliffs and glittering sands
How lightly then it flash'd along:
Like those trim skiffs, unknown of yore,
On winding lakes and rivers wide,
That ask no aid of sail or oar,
That fear no spite of wind or tide!

Naught cared this body for wind or weather
When Youth and I lived in 't together.

Flowers are lovely; Love is flower-like;
Friendship is a sheltering tree;
Oh the joys, that came down shower-like,
Of Friendship, Love, and Liberty,
      Ere I was old!
Ere I was old?—Ah, woful Ere,
Which tells me, Youth's no longer here!
O Youth! for years so many and sweet
'Tis known that thou and I were one,
I'll think it but a fond conceit—
It cannot be, that thou art gone!
Thy vesper-bell hath not yet toll'd:—
And thou wert aye a masker bold!
What strange disguise hast now put on
To make believe that thou art gone?
I see these locks in silvery slips,
This drooping gait, this alter'd size:
But springtide blossoms on thy lips,
And tears take sunshine from thine eyes!
Life is but Thought: so think I will
That Youth and I are housemates still.

Dew-drops are the gems of morning,
But the tears of mournful eve!
Where no hope is, life's a warning
That only serves to make us grieve,
      When we are old:
—That only serves to make us grieve
With oft and tedious taking-leave,
Like some poor nigh-related guest
That may not rudely be dismist,
Yet hath outstay'd his welcome while,
And tells the jest without the smile.
          SAMUEL TAYLOR COLERIDGE.

STANZAS.

WHEN midnight o'er the moonless skies
  Her pall of transient death has spread,
When mortals sleep, when spectres rise,
  And naught is wakeful but the dead;

No bloodless shape my way pursues,
  No sheeted ghost my couch annoys;
Visions more sad my fancy views,
  Visions of long-departed joys!

The shade of youthful hope is there,
  That linger'd long, and latest died:

Ambition all dissolved to air,
  With phantom honors by his side.

What empty shadows glimmer nigh?
  They once were Friendship, Truth, and
    Love!
Oh, die to thought, to memory die,
  Since lifeless to my heart ye prove!
        WILLIAM ROBERT SPENCER.

GO WHERE GLORY WAITS THEE.

Go where glory waits thee;
But while fame elates thee,
  Oh still remember me!
When the praise thou meetest
To thine ear is sweetest,
  Oh then remember me!
Other arms may press thee,
Dearer friends caress thee,
All the joys that bless thee
  Sweeter far may be;
But when friends are nearest,
And when joys are dearest,
  Oh then remember me!

When at eve thou rovest
By the star thou lovest,
  Oh then remember me!
Think, when home returning,
Bright we've seen it burning,
  Oh thus remember me!
Oft as summer closes,
When thine eye reposes
On its lingering roses,
  Once so loved by thee,
Think of her who wove them,
Her who made thee love them—
  Oh then remember me!

When around thee dying
Autumn leaves are lying,
  Oh then remember me!
And at night when gazing
On the gay hearth blazing,
  Oh still remember me!
Then should music, stealing
All the soul of feeling,
To thy heart appealing,
  Draw one tear from thee;
Then let memory bring thee
Strains I used to sing thee—
  Oh then remember me!
        THOMAS MOORE.

THE CLOSING YEAR.

'TIS midnight's holy hour, and silence now
Is brooding like a gentle spirit o'er
The still and pulseless world. Hark! on
  the winds
The bell's deep tones are swelling,—'tis
  the knell
Of the departed year. No funeral train
Is sweeping past; yet, on the stream and
  wood,
With melancholy light, the moonbeams
  rest
Like a pale, spotless shroud; the air is
  stirr'd
As by a mourner's sigh; and on yon cloud
That floats so still and placidly through
  heaven,
The spirits of the seasons seem to stand,—
Young Spring, bright Summer, Autumn's
  solemn form,
And Winter with its aged locks,—and
  breathe,
In mournful cadences that come abroad
Like the far wind-harp's wild and touching
  wail,
A melancholy dirge o'er the dead year,
Gone from the Earth for ever.

                            'Tis a time
For memory and for tears. Within the
  deep,
Still chambers of the heart, a spectre dim,
Whose tones are like the wizard voice of
  Time
Heard from the tomb of ages, points its
  cold
And solemn finger to the beautiful
And holy visions that have pass'd away,
And left no shadow of their loveliness
On the dead waste of life. That spectre
  lifts
The coffin-lid of Hope, and Joy, and Love,
And, bending mournfully above the pale,
Sweet forms that slumber there, scatters
  dead flowers
O'er what has pass'd to nothingness.

                            The year
Has gone, and with it many a glorious
  throng
Of happy dreams. Its mark is on each
  brow,

Its shadow in each heart. In its swift course
It waved its sceptre o'er the beautiful,—
And they are not. It laid its pallid hand
Upon the strong man,—and the haughty form
Is fallen, and the flashing eye is dim.
It trod the hall of revelry, where throng'd
The bright and joyous,—and the tearful wail
Of stricken ones is heard where erst the song
And reckless shout resounded.

                              It pass'd o'er
The battle-plain, where sword, and spear, and shield,
Flash'd in the light of mid-day,—and the strength
Of serried hosts is shiver'd, and the grass,
Green from the soil of carnage, waves above
The crush'd and mouldering skeleton. It came,
And faded like a wreath of mist at eve ;
Yet, ere it melted in the viewless air,
It heralded its millions to their home
In the dim land of dreams.

                          Remorseless Time !
Fierce spirit of the glass and scythe !—what power
Can stay him in his silent course, or melt
His iron heart to pity ? *On, still on,
He presses, and for ever. The proud bird,
The condor of the Andes, that can soar
Through heaven's unfathomable depths, or brave
The fury of the northern hurricane,
And bathe his plumage in the thunder's home,
Furls his broad wings at nightfall, and sinks down
To rest upon his mountain-crag,—but Time
Knows not the weight of sleep or weariness,
And night's deep darkness has no chain to bind
His rushing pinions.

                        Revolutions sweep
O'er earth, like troubled visions o'er the breast
Of dreaming sorrow,—cities rise and sink
Like bubbles on the water,—fiery isles
Spring blazing from the ocean, and go back
To their mysterious caverns,—mountains rear
To heaven their bald and blacken'd cliffs, and bow
Their tall heads to the plain,—new empires rise,
Gathering the strength of hoary centuries,
And rush down like the Alpine avalanche,
Startling the nations,—and the very stars,
Yon bright and burning blazonry of God,
Glitter a while in their eternal depths,
And, like the Pleiad, loveliest of their train,
Shoot from their glorious spheres, and pass away
To darkle in the trackless void,—yet Time,
Time, the tomb-builder, holds his fierce career,
Dark, stern, all-pitiless, and pauses not
Amid the mighty wrecks that strew his path
To sit and muse, like other conquerors,
Upon the fearful ruin he has wrought.
                              GEORGE D. PRENTICE.

Bedouin Song.

From the Desert I come to thee,
   On a stallion shod with fire,
And the winds are left behind
   In the speed of my desire.
Under thy window I stand,
   And the midnight hears my cry:
I love thee, I love but thee,
   With a love that never shall die,

Oct. 29, 1853.   Bayard Taylor.

POEMS OF LOVE.

LOVE'S PHILOSOPHY.

The fountains mingle with the river,
   And the rivers with the ocean,
The winds of heaven mix for ever
   With a sweet emotion;
Nothing in the world is single;
   All things by a law divine
In one another's being mingle—
   Why not I with thine?

See the mountains kiss high heaven,
   And the waves clasp one another;
No sister flower would be forgiven
   If it disdain'd its brother:
And the sunlight clasps the earth,
   And the moonbeams kiss the sea;—
What are all these kissings worth,
   If thou kiss not me?
                PERCY BYSSHE SHELLEY.

LOVE WILL FIND OUT THE WAY.

Over the mountains
   And over the waves;
Under the fountains
   And under the graves;
Under floods that are deepest,
   Which Neptune obey;
Over rocks that are steepest,
   Love will find out the way.

Where there is no place
   For the glow-worm to lye;
Where there is no space
   For receipt of a fly;
Where the midge dares not venture,
   Lest herself fast she lay;
If love come he will enter,
   And soon find out his way.

You may esteem him
   A child for his might;
Or you may deem him
   A coward from his flight:
But if she whom love doth honor
   Be conceal'd from the day,
Set a thousand guards upon her,
   Love will find out the way.

Some think to lose him
   By having him confined;
And some do suppose him,
   Poor thing, to be blind;
But if ne'er so close ye wall him,
   Do the best that you may,
Blind love, if so ye call him,
   Will find out his way.

You may train the eagle
   To stoop to your fist;
Or you may inveigle
   The phœnix of the East;
The lioness, ye may move her
   To give o'er her prey;
But you'll ne'er stop a lover,
   He will find out his way.
                AUTHOR UNKNOWN.

AH, HOW SWEET IT IS TO LOVE!

Ah, how sweet it is to love!
   Ah, how gay is young desire!
And what pleasing pains we prove
   When we first approach love's fire!
      Pains of love be sweeter far
      Than all other pleasures are.

Sighs which are from lovers blown
   Do but gently heave the heart;
E'en the tears they shed alone,
   Cure, like trickling balm, their smart.
      Lovers, when they lose their breath,
      Bleed away in easy death.

Love and time with reverence use—
  Treat them like a parting friend,
Nor the golden gifts refuse
  Which in youth sincere they send;
    For each year their price is more,
    And they less simple than before.

Love, like spring-tides, full and high,
  Swells in every youthful vein;
But each tide does less supply,
  Till they quite shrink in again;
    If a flow in age appear,
    'Tis but rain, and runs not clear.
                    JOHN DRYDEN.

LOVE IS A SICKNESS.

LOVE is a sickness full of woes,
  All remedies refusing;
A plant that with most cutting grows,
  Most barren with best using:
    Why so?
  More we enjoy it, more it dies;
  If not enjoy'd, it sighing cries,
    Hey, ho!

Love is a torment of the mind.
  A tempest everlasting;
And Jove hath made it of a kind
  Not well, nor full, nor fasting:
    Why so?
  More we enjoy it, more it dies;
  If not enjoy'd, it sighing cries,
    Hey, ho!
                    SAMUEL DANIEL.

PANGLORY'S WOOING SONG.

LOVE is the blossom where there blows
Everything that lives or grows:
Love doth make the heavens to move,
And the sun doth burn in love;
Love the strong and weak doth yoke,
And makes the ivy climb the oak,
Under whose shadows lions wild,
Soften'd by love, grow tame and mild.
Love no med'cine can appease;
He burns the fishes in the seas;
Not all the skill his wounds can stanch;
Not all the sea his fire can quench.
Love did make the bloody spear
Once a leafy coat to wear,
While in his leaves there shrouded lay
Sweet birds, for love that sing and play;
And of all love's joyful flame
I the bud and blossom am.
  Only bend thy knee to me—
  Thy wooing shall thy winning be.

See! see the flowers that below
Now freshly as the morning blow,
And of all, the virgin rose,
That as bright Aurora shows—
How they all unleavèd die,
Losing their virginity;
Like unto a summer shade,
But now born, and now they fade:
Everything doth pass away;
There is danger in delay.
Come, come, gather then the rose;
Gather it, or it you lose.
All the sand of Tagus' shore
In my bosom casts its ore;
All the valleys' swimming corn
To my house is yearly borne;
Every grape of every vine
Is gladly bruised to make me wine;
While ten thousand kings, as proud
To carry up my train, have bow'd;
And a world of ladies send me,
In my chambers to attend me;
All the stars in heaven that shine,
And ten thousand more, are mine.
  Only bend thy knee to me—
  Thy wooing shall thy winning be.
                    GILES FLETCHER.

ROSALIND'S MADRIGAL.

LOVE in my bosom, like a bee,
    Doth suck his sweet;
Now with his wings he plays with me,
    Now with his feet.
Within mine eyes he makes his nest,
His bed amidst my tender breast;
My kisses are his daily feast,
And yet he robs me of my rest:
    Ah, wanton, will ye?

And if I sleep, then percheth he
    With pretty flight,
And makes his pillow of my knee
    The livelong night.

Strike I my lute, he tunes the string:
He music plays if so I sing;
He lends me every lovely thing,
Yet cruel he my heart doth sting:
    Whist, wanton, still ye:

Else I with roses every day
    Will whip you hence,
And bind you, when you long to play,
    For your offence;
I'll shut mine eyes to keep you in,
I'll make you fast it for your sin,
I'll count your power not worth a pin:
Alas! what hereby shall I win,
    If he gainsay me?

What if I beat the wanton boy
    With many a rod?
He will repay me with annoy,
    Because a god.
Then sit thou safely on my knee,
And let thy bower my bosom be;
Lurk in mine eyes,—I like of thee,
O Cupid! so thou pity me,
    Spare not, but play thee.
              THOMAS LODGE.

LOVE STILL HATH SOMETHING OF THE SEA.

LOVE still hath something of the sea,
    From whence his mother rose;
No time his slaves from love can free,
    Nor give their thoughts repose.

They are becalm'd in clearest days,
    And in rough weather toss'd;
They wither under cold delays,
    Or are in tempests lost.

One while they seem to touch the port;
    Then straight into the main
Some angry wind, in cruel sport,
    The vessel drives again.

At first disdain and pride they fear,
    Which if they chance to 'scape,
Rivals and falsehood soon appear
    In a more dreadful shape.

By such degrees to joy they come,
    And are so long withstood;
So slowly they receive the sum,
    It hardly does them good.

'Tis cruel to prolong a pain;
    And to defer a bliss,
Believe me, gentle Hermoine,
    No less inhuman is.

A hundred thousand oaths your fears
    Perhaps would not remove;
And if I gazed a thousand years,
    I could no deeper love.

'Tis fitter much for you to guess
    Than for me to explain,
But grant, oh! grant that happiness
    Which only does remain.
              SIR CHARLES SEDLEY.

LOVE'S OMNIPRESENCE.

WERE I as base as is the lowly plain,
And you, my Love, as high as heaven above,
Yet should the thoughts of me your humble swain
Ascend to heaven, in honor of my Love.
Were I as high as heaven above the plain,
And you, my Love, as humble and as low
As are the deepest bottoms of the main,
Wheresoe'er you were, with you my love should go.
Were you the earth, dear Love, and I the skies,
My love should shine on you like to the sun,
And look upon you with ten thousand eyes
Till heaven wax'd blind, and till the world were done.
Wheresoe'er I am, below, or else above you,
Wheresoe'er you are, my heart shall truly love you.
              JOSHUA SYLVESTER.

CUPID AND CAMPASPE.

CUPID and my Campaspe playd
At cardes for kisses; Cupid payd:
He stakes his quiver, bow and arrows,
His mothers doves, and teame of sparrows;
Loses them too; then down he throws
The coral of his lippe, the rose
Growing on's cheek (but none knows how),
With these, the crystal of his browe,
And then the dimple of his chinne;
All these did my Campaspe winne.
At last he set her both his eyes,
She won, and Cupid blind did rise.

O Love! has she done this to thee?
What shall, alas! become of mee?
JOHN LYLY.

LOVE.

ALL thoughts, all passions, all delights,
  Whatever stirs this mortal frame,
All are but ministers of Love,
  And feed his sacred flame.

Oft in my waking dreams do I
  Live o'er again that happy hour,
When midway on the mount I lay,
  Beside the ruin'd tower.

The moonshine, stealing o'er the scene,
  Had blended with the lights of eve;
And she was there, my hope, my joy,
  My own dear Genevieve!

She leant against the armèd man,
  The statue of the armèd knight;
She stood and listen'd to my lay,
  Amid the lingering light.

Few sorrows hath she of her own
  My hope! my joy! my Genevieve!
She loves me best, whene'er I sing
  The songs that make her grieve.

I play'd a soft and doleful air,
  I sang an old and moving story—
An old rude song, that suited well
  That ruin wild and hoary.

She listen'd with a flitting blush,
  With downcast eyes and modest grace;
For well she knew, I could not choose
  But gaze upon her face.

I told her of the Knight that wore
  Upon his shield a burning brand;
And that for ten long years he woo'd
  The Lady of the Land.

I told her how he pined; and ah!
  The deep, the low, the pleading tone
With which I sang another's love,
  Interpreted my own.

She listen'd with a flitting blush,
  With downcast eyes, and modest grace;
And she forgave me, that I gazed
  Too fondly on her face.

But when I told the cruel scorn
  That crazed that bold and lovely Knight,
And that he cross'd the mountain-woods,
  Nor rested day nor night;

That sometimes from the savage den,
  And sometimes from the darksome shade,
And sometimes starting up at once
  In green and sunny glade,

There came and look'd him in the face
  An angel beautiful and bright;
And that he knew it was a Fiend,
  This miserable Knight!

And that, unknowing what he did,
  He leap'd amid a murderous band,
And saved from outrage worse than death
  The Lady of the Land!

And how she wept, and clasp'd his knees;
  And how she tended him in vain—
And ever strove to expiate
  The scorn that crazed his brain.

And that she nursed him in a cave;
  And how his madness went away,
When on the yellow forest-leaves
  A dying man he lay.

His dying words—but when I reach'd
  That tenderest strain of all the ditty,
My faltering voice and pausing harp
  Disturb'd her soul with pity!

All impulses of soul and sense
  Had thrill'd my guileless Genevieve;
The music, and the doleful tale,
  The rich and balmy eve;

And hopes, and fears that kindle hope,
  An undistinguishable throng,
And gentle wishes long subdued,
  Subdued and cherish'd long!

She wept with pity and delight,
  She blush'd with love, and virgin-shame;
And like the murmur of a dream,
  I heard her breathe my name.

Her bosom heaved—she stepp'd aside,
  As conscious of my look she stepp'd—
Then suddenly, with timorous eye
  She fled to me and wept.

She half enclosed me with her arms,
  She press'd me with a meek embrace;
And bending back her head, look'd up,
  And gazed upon my face.

'Twas partly Love, and partly Fear,
  And partly 'twas a bashful art,
That I might rather feel than see,
  The swelling of her heart.

I calm'd her fears, and she was calm,
  And told her love with virgin pride.
And so I won my Genevieve,
  My bright and beauteous Bride.
            SAMUEL TAYLOR COLERIDGE.

NOT OURS THE VOWS.

NOT ours the vows of such as plight
  Their troth in sunny weather,
While leaves are green and skies are bright,
  To walk on flowers together.

But we have loved as those who tread
  The thorny path of sorrow,
With clouds above, and cause to dread
  Yet deeper gloom to-morrow.

That thorny path, those stormy skies,
  Have drawn our spirits nearer,
And rendered us, by sorrow's ties,
  Each to the other dearer.

Love, born in hours of joy and mirth,
  With mirth and joy may perish;
That to which darker hours gave birth
  Still more and more we cherish.

It looks beyond the clouds of time,
  And through death's shadowy portal,
Made by adversity sublime,
  By faith and hope immortal.
            BERNARD BARTON.

SONNET.

THE doubt which ye misdeem, fair love, is vain,
  That fondly fear to lose your liberty;
When, losing one, two liberties ye gain,
  And make him bound that bondage erst did fly.
Sweet be the bands, the which true love doth tye
  Without constraint, or dread of any ill:
The gentle bird feels no captivity
  Within her cage; but sings and feeds her fill;
There pride dare not approach, nor discord spill
  The league 'twixt them that loyal love hath bound;
But simple truth, and mutual good-will,
  Seeks, with sweet peace, to salve each other's wound;
There faith doth fearless dwell in brazen tower,
And spotless pleasure builds her sacred bower.
            EDMUND SPENSER.

ABSENCE.

WHAT shall I do with all the days and hours
  That must be counted ere I see thy face?
How shall I charm the interval that lowers
  Between this time and that sweet time of grace?

Still I in slumber steep each weary sense—
  Weary with longing? Shall I flee away
Into past days, and with some fond pretence
  Cheat myself to forget the present day?

Shall love for thee lay on my soul the sin
  Of casting from me God's great gift of time?
Shall I, these mists of memory locked within,
  Leave and forget life's purposes sublime?

Oh, how, or by what means, may I contrive
  To bring the hour that brings thee back more near?
How may I teach my drooping hope to live
  Until that blessed time, and thou art here?

I'll tell thee; for thy sake I will lay hold
  Of all good aims, and consecrate to thee,
In worthy deeds, each moment that is told
  While thou, beloved one! art far from me.

For thee I will arouse my thoughts to try
  All heavenward flights, all high and holy strains;
For thy dear sake I will walk patiently
  Through these long hours, nor call their minutes pains.

I will this dreary blank of absence make
  A noble task-time; and will therein strive
To follow excellence, and to o'ertake
  More good than I have won since yet I
    live.
So may this doomèd time build up in me
  A thousand graces, which shall thus be
    thine;
So may my love and longing hallowed be,
  And thy dear thought an influence
    divine.
              FRANCES ANNE KEMBLE.

HOW MANY TIMES.

How many times do I love thee, dear?
  Tell me how many thoughts there be
    In the atmosphere
    Of a new-fallen year,
Whose white and sable hours appear
  The latest flake of Eternity;
So many times do I love thee, dear.

How many times do I love thee, again?
  Tell me how many beads there are
    In a silver chain
    Of the evening rain,
Unravelled from the tumbling main,
  And threading the eye of a yellow star;
So how many times do I love, again.
              THOMAS LOVELL BEDDOES.

FAIR INES.

OH, saw ye not fair Ines?
  She's gone into the West,
To dazzle when the sun is down,
  And rob the world of rest:
She took our daylight with her,
  The smiles that we love best,
With morning blushes on her cheek,
  And pearls upon her breast.

Oh turn again, fair Ines,
  Before the fall of night,
For fear the moon should shine alone,
  And stars unrivall'd bright;
And blessed will the lover be
  That walks beneath their light,
And breathes the love against thy cheek
  I dare not even write!

Would I had been, fair Ines,
  That gallant cavalier,
Who rode so gayly by thy side,
  And whisper'd thee so near!

Were there no bonny dames at home,
  Or no true lovers here,
That he should cross the seas to win
  The dearest of the dear?

I saw thee, lovely Ines!
  Descend along the shore,
With bands of noble gentlemen,
  And banners waved before;
And gentle youth and maidens gay,
  And snowy plumes they wore;
It would have been a beauteous dream,
  If it had been no more!

Alas, alas, fair Ines!
  She went away with song,
With music waiting on her steps,
  And shoutings of the throng;
But some were sad and felt no mirth,
  But only music's wrong,
In sounds that sang, Farewell, farewell,
  To her you've loved so long!

Farewell, farewell, fair Ines!
  That vessel never bore
So fair a lady on its deck,
  Nor danced so light before;
Alas for pleasure on the sea,
  And sorrow on the shore!
The smile that blest one lover's heart
  Has broken many more!
              THOMAS HOOD.

HE CAME TOO LATE.

HE came too late! Neglect had tried
  Her constancy too long;
Her love had yielded to her pride
  And the deep sense of wrong.
She scorned the offering of a heart
  Which lingered on its way
Till it could no delight impart,
  Nor spread one cheering ray.

He came too late! At once he felt
  That all his power was o'er;
Indifference in her calm smile dwelt—
  She thought of him no more.
Anger and grief had passed away,
  Her heart and thoughts were free;
She met him, and her words were gay—
  No spell had Memory.

He came too late! The subtle chords
  Of love were all unbound,

Not by offence of spoken words,
　But by the slights that wound.
She knew that life held nothing now
　That could the past repay,
Yet she disdained his tardy vow,
　And coldly turned away.

He came too late! Her countless dreams
　Of hope had long since flown;
No charms dwelt in his chosen themes,
　Nor in his whispered tone.
And when with word and smile he tried
　Affection still to prove,
She nerved her heart with woman's pride,
　And spurned his fickle love.
　　　　　　ELIZABETH BOGART.

CUPID SWALLOWED.

T'OTHER day, as I was twining
Roses, for a crown to dine in,
What, of all things, midst the heap,
Should I light on, fast asleep,
But the little desperate elf,
The tiny traitor,—Love himself!
By the wings I pinch'd him up
Like a bee, and in a cup
Of my wine I plunged and sank him;
And what d'ye think I did?—I drank him!
Faith, I thought him dead. Not he!
There he lives with tenfold glee;
And now this moment, with his wings
I feel him tickling my heart-strings.
　　　　　　LEIGH HUNT.

WALY, WALY, BUT LOVE BE BONNY.

OH waly waly up the bank,
　And waly waly down the brae,
And waly waly yon burn side,
　Where I and my love were wont to gae.
I leant my back unto an aik,
　I thought it was a trusty tree!
But first it bow'd, and syne it brak,
　Sae my true love did lichtly me.

Oh waly waly gin love be bonny,
　A little time while it is new;
But when its auld, it waxeth cauld,
　And fades awa' like morning dew.
Oh wherefore shuld I busk my head?
　Or wherefore shuld I kame my hair?
For my true love has me forsook,
　And says he'll never lo'e me mair.

Now Arthur-seat sall be my bed,
　The sheets sall ne'er be fyl'd by me:
Saint Anton's well sall be my drink,
　Since my true love has forsaken me.
Marti'mas wind, when wilt thou blaw,
　And shake the green leaves aff the tree?
O gentle death, whan wilt thou cum?
　For of my life I am wearìe.

Tis not the frost, that freezes fell,
　Nor blawing snaws inclemencìe;
'Tis not sic cauld, that makes me cry,
　But my loves heart grown cauld to me.
When we came in by Glasgowe town,
　We were a comely sight to see,
My love was cled in black velvet,
　And I my sell in cramasìe.

But had I wist, before I kisst,
　That love had been sae ill to win;
I had lockt my heart in a case of gowd,
　And pinn'd it with a siller pin.
And, oh! if my young babe were born,
　And set upon the nurses knee,
And I my sell were dead and gane!
　For a maid again Ise never be.
　　　　　　AUTHOR UNKNOWN.

LINES TO AN INDIAN AIR.

I ARISE from dreams of thee
　In the first sweet sleep of night,
When the winds are breathing low,
　And the stars are shining bright:
I arise from dreams of thee,
　And a spirit in my feet
Has led me—who knows how?—
　To thy chamber-window, sweet!

The wandering airs they faint
　On the dark, the silent stream—
The champak odors fail
　Like sweet thoughts in a dream;
The nightingale's complaint,
　It dies upon her heart,
As I must on thine,
　Beloved as thou art!

Oh lift me from the grass!
　I die, I faint, I fail!
Let thy love in kisses rain
　On my lips and eyelids pale.

My cheek is cold and white, alas!
　My heart beats loud and fast,
Oh! press it close to thine again,
　Where it will break at last.
　　　　　　　　PERCY BYSSHE SHELLEY.

WHY SO PALE?

WHY so pale and wan, fond lover?
　Prethee, why so pale?
Will, when looking well can't move her,
　Looking ill prevail?
　Prethee why so pale?

Why so dull and mute, young sinner?
　Prethee, why so mute?
Will, when speaking well can't win her,
　Saying nothing do't?
　Prethee why so mute?

Quit, quit for shame; this will not move,
　This cannot take her;
If of herself she will not love,
　Nothing can make her,
　The devil take her!
　　　　　　　　SIR JOHN SUCKLING.

LADY GERALDINE'S COURTSHIP.

A ROMANCE OF THE AGE.

A poet writes to his friend. PLACE—*A room in Wycombe Hall.* TIME—*Late in the evening.*

DEAR my friend and fellow-student, I
　would lean my spirit o'er you!
Down the purple of this chamber tears
　should scarcely run at will.
I am humbled who was humble. Friend,
　I bow my head before you:
You should lead me to my peasants, but
　their faces are too still.

There's a lady, an earl's daughter—she is
　proud and she is noble,
And she treads the crimson carpet, and
　she breathes the perfumed air,
And a kingly blood sends glances up, her
　princely eye to trouble,
And the shadow of a monarch's crown is
　soften'd in her hair.

She has halls among the woodlands, she
　has castles by the breakers,
She has farms and she has manors, she
　can threaten and command,
And the palpitating engines snort in steam
　across her acres,
As they mark upon the blasted heaven
　the measure of the land.

There are none of England's daughters
　who can show a prouder presence;
Upon princely suitors, praying, she has
　look'd in her disdain,
She was sprung of English nobles, I was
　born of English peasants;
What was *I* that I should love her, save
　for competence to pain?

I was only a poor poet, made for singing
　at her casement,
As the finches or the thrushes, while she
　thought of other things.
Oh, she walk'd so high above me, she appear'd to my abasement,
In her lovely silken murmur, like an
　angel clad in wings!

Many vassals bow before her as her carriage sweeps their door-ways;
　She has blest their little children, as a
　priest or queen were she:
Far too tender, or too cruel far, her smile
　upon the poor was,
For I thought it was the same smile
　which she used to smile on *me*.

She has voters in the commons, she has
　lovers in the palace,
And of all the fair court-ladies, few have
　jewels half as fine;
Oft the prince has named her beauty 'twixt
　the red wine and the chalice:
Oh, and what was *I* to love her? my beloved, my Geraldine!

Yet I could not choose but love her: I was
　born to poet-uses,
To love all things set above me, all of
　good and all of fair.
Nymphs of mountain, not of valley, we
　are wont to call the Muses;
And in nympholeptic climbing, poets
　pass from mount to star.

And because I was a poet, and because the
　public praised me,
With a critical deduction for the modern
　writer's fault,

I could sit at rich men's tables—though
    the courtesies that raised me,
Still suggested clear between us the pale
    spectrum of the salt.
And they praised me in her presence ;—
    " Will your book appear this summer ?"
Then returning to each other—"Yes,
    our plans are for the moors."
Then with whisper dropp'd behind me—
    " There he is ! the latest comer.
Oh, she only likes his verses ! what is
    over, she endures.

" Quite low-born, self-educated ! somewhat
    gifted though by Nature,
And we make a point of asking him—
    of being very kind.
You may speak, he does not hear you !
    and besides he writes no satire—
All these serpents kept by charmers leave
    the natural sting behind."

I grew scornfuller, grew colder, as I stood
    up there among them,
Till as frost intense will burn you, the
    cold scorning scorch'd my brow ;
When a sudden silver speaking, gravely
    cadenced, overrung them,
And a sudden silken stirring touch'd
    my inner nature through.

I look'd upward and beheld her. With a
    calm and regnant spirit,
Slowly round she swept her eyelids, and
    said clear before them all—
" Have you such superfluous honor, sir,
    that, able to confer it,
You will come down, Mister Bertram, as
    my guest to Wycombe Hall ?"

Here she paused ; she had been paler at
    the first word of her speaking,
But because a silence follow'd it, blush'd
    somewhat, as for shame,
Then, as scorning her own feeling, resumed
    calmly—" I am seeking
More distinction than these gentlemen
    think worthy of my claim.

" Ne'ertheless, you see, I seek it—not because I am a woman "
    (Here her smile sprang like a fountain,
    and, so, overflow'd her mouth),

" But because my woods in Sussex have
    some purple shades at gloaming
Which are worthy of a king in state, or
    poet in his youth.

" I invite you, Mister Bertram, to no scene
    for worldly speeches—
Sir, I scarce should dare—but only
    where God ask'd the thrushes first :
And if *you* will sing beside them, in the
    covert of my beeches,
I will thank you for the woodlands, . . .
    for the human world, at worst."

Then she smiled around right childly, then
    she gazed around right queenly,
And I bow'd—I could not answer ; alternated light and gloom—
While as one who quells the lions, with a
    steady eye serenely,
She, with level fronting eyelids, pass'd
    out stately from the room.

Oh, the blessèd woods of Sussex, I can hear
    them still around me,
With their leafy tide of greenery still
    rippling up the wind.
Oh, the cursèd woods of Sussex ! where the
    hunter's arrow found me,
When a fair face and a tender voice had
    made me mad and blind !

In that ancient hall of Wycombe throng'd
    the numerous guests invited,
And the lovely London ladies trod the
    floors with gliding feet ;
And their voices low with fashion, not with
    feeling, softly freighted
All the air about the windows with elastic laughter sweet.

For at eve the open windows flung their
    light out on the terrace
Which the floating orbs of curtains did
    with gradual shadow sweep,
While the swans upon the river, fed at
    morning by the heiress,
Trembled downward through their snowy
    wings at music in their sleep.

And there evermore was music, both of
    instrument and singing,
Till the finches of the shrubberies grew
    restless in the dark ;

But the cedars stood up motionless, each
    in a moonlight ringing,
And the deer, half in the glimmer,
    strew'd the hollows of the park.

And though sometimes she would bind me
    with her silver-corded speeches
To commix my words and laughter with
    the converse and the jest,
Oft I sate apart, and, gazing on the river
    through the beeches,
Heard, as pure the swans swam down it,
    her pure voice o'erfloat the rest.

In the morning, horn of huntsman, hoof
    of steed, and laugh of rider,
Spread out cheery from the courtyard
    till we lost them in the hills,
While herself and other ladies, and her
    suitors left beside her,
Went a-wandering up the gardens
    through the laurels and abeles.

Thus, her foot upon the new-mown grass,
    bareheaded, with the flowing
Of the virginal white vesture gather'd
    closely to her throat,
And the golden ringlets in her neck just
    quicken'd by her going,
And appearing to breathe sun for air,
    and doubting if to float,—

With a bunch of dewy maple, which her
    right hand held above her,
And which trembled a green shadow in
    betwixt her and the skies,
As she turn'd her face in going, thus, she
    drew me on to love her,
And to worship the divineness of the
    smile hid in her eyes.

For her eyes alone smile constantly; her
    lips have serious sweetness,
And her front is calm, the dimple rarely
    ripples on the cheek;
But her deep-blue eyes smile constantly,
    as if they in discreetness
Kept the secret of a happy dream she
    did not care to speak.

Thus she drew me the first morning, out
    across into the garden,
And I walk'd among her noble friends,
    and could not keep behind.

Spake she unto all and unto me—"Behold, I am the warden
Of the song-birds in these lindens,
    which are cages to their mind.

"But within this swarded circle into which
    the lime-walk brings us,
Whence the beeches, rounded greenly,
    stand away in reverent fear,
I will let no music enter, saving what the
    fountain sings us
Which the lilies round the basin may
    seem pure enough to hear.

"The live air that waves the lilies waves
    the slender jet of water
Like a holy thought sent feebly up from
    soul of fasting saint:
Whereby lies a marble Silence, sleeping
    (Lough the sculptor wrought her),
So asleep she is forgetting to say Hush;
    —a fancy quaint.

"Mark how heavy white her eyelids! not
    a dream between them lingers;
And the left hand's index droppeth from
    the lips upon the cheek:
While the right hand—with the symbol-rose held slack within the fingers—
Has fallen backward in the basin—yet
    this Silence will not speak!

"That the essential meaning growing may
    exceed the special symbol,
Is the thought as I conceive it: it applies more high and low.
Our true noblemen will often through
    right nobleness grow humble,
And assert an inward honor by denying
    outward show."

"Nay, your Silence," said I, "truly, holds
    her symbol-rose but slackly,
Yet *she holds it*, or would scarcely be a
    Silence to our ken:
And your nobles wear their ermine on the
    outside, or walk blackly
In the presence of the social law as mere
    ignoble men.

"Let the poets dream such dreaming!
    madam, in these British islands
'Tis the substance that wanes ever, 'tis
    the symbol that exceeds.

Soon we shall have naught but symbol, and,
   for statues like this Silence,
Shall accept the rose's image—in another
   case, the weed's."

"Not so quickly," she retorted—"I con-
   fess, where'er you go, you
Find for things, names—shows for ac-
   tions, and pure gold for honor clear:
But when all is run to symbol in the Social,
   I will throw you
The world's book which now reads drily,
   and sit down with Silence here."

Half in playfulness she spoke, I thought,
   and half in indignation;
Friends who listen'd laugh'd her words
   off, while her lovers deem'd her fair:
A fair woman, flush'd with feeling, in her
   noble-lighted station
Near the statue's white reposing—and
   both bathed in sunny air!

With the trees round, not so distant but
   you heard their vernal murmur,
And beheld in light and shadow the
   leaves in and outward move,
And the little fountain leaping toward the
   sun-heart to be warmer,
Then recoiling in a tremble from the too
   much light above.

'Tis a picture for remembrance. And thus,
   morning after morning,
Did I follow as she drew me by the spirit
   to her feet.
Why, her greyhound followed also! dogs—
   we both were dogs for scorning—
To be sent back when she pleased it and
   her path lay through the wheat.

And thus, morning after morning, spite of
   vows and spite of sorrow,
Did I follow at her drawing, while the
   week-days pass'd along,
Just to feed the swans this noontide, or to
   see the fawns to-morrow,
Or to teach the hillside echo some sweet
   Tuscan in a song.

Ay, for sometimes on the hillside, while
   we sate down in the gowans,
With the forest green behind us and its
   shadow cast before,

And the river running under, and across it
   from the rowans
A brown partridge whirring near us till
   we felt the air it bore—

There, obedient to her praying, did I read
   aloud the poems
Made to Tuscan flutes, or instruments
   more various of our own;
Read the pastoral parts of Spenser, or the
   subtle interflowings
Found in Petrarch's sonnets—here's the
   book, the leaf is folded down!

Or at times a modern volume, Wordsworth's
   solemn-thoughted idyl,
Howitt's ballad-verse, or Tennyson's
   enchanted reverie—
Or from Browning some "Pomegranate,"
   which, if cut deep down the middle,
Shows a heart within blood-tinctured,
   of a vein'd humanity.

Or at times I read there, hoarsely, some
   new poem of my making:
Poets ever fail in reading their own
   verses to their worth,
For the echo in you breaks upon the words
   which you are speaking,
And the chariot wheels jar in the gate
   through which you drive them forth.

After, when we were grown tired of books,
   the silence round us flinging
A slow arm of sweet compression, felt
   with beatings at the breast,
She would break out on a sudden in a gush
   of woodland singing,
Like a child's emotion in a god—a naiad
   tired of rest.

Oh, to see or hear her singing! scarce I
   know which is divinest,
For her looks sing too—she modulates
   her gestures on the tune,
And her mouth stirs with the song, like
   song; and when the notes are finest,
'Tis the eyes that shoot out vocal light
   and seem to swell them on.

Then we talk'd—oh, how we talk'd! her
   voice, so cadenced in the talking,
Made another singing—of the soul! a
   music without bars:

While the leafy sounds of woodlands, humming round where we were walking,
Brought interposition worthy-sweet—as skies about the stars.

And she spake such good thoughts natural, as if she always thought them;
She had sympathies so rapid, open, free as bird on branch,
Just as ready to fly east as west, whichever way besought them,
In the birchen-wood a chirrup, or a cock-crow in the grange.

In her utmost lightness there is truth— and often she speaks lightly,
Has a grace in being gay which even mournful souls approve,
For the root of some grave earnest thought is understruck so rightly
As to justify the foliage and the waving flowers above.

And she talk'd on—*we* talk'd, rather!— upon all things, substance, shadow,
Of the sheep that browsed the grasses, of the reapers in the corn,
Of the little children from the schools, seen winding through the meadow,
Of the poor rich world beyond them, still kept poorer by its scorn.

So, of men, and so, of letters—books are men of higher stature,
And the only men that speak aloud for future times to hear;
So, of mankind in the abstract, which grows slowly into nature,
Yet will lift the cry of "progress," as it trod from sphere to sphere.

And her custom was to praise me when I said—"The Age culls simples,
With a broad clown's back turn'd broadly to the glory of the stars.
We are gods by our own reck'ning, and may well shut up the temples,
And wield on, amid the incense-steam, the thunder of our cars.

"For we throw out acclamations of self-thanking, self-admiring,
With, at every mile run faster,—'O the wondrous, wondrous age!'

Little thinking if we work our SOULS as nobly as our iron,
Or if angels will commend us at the goal of pilgrimage.

"Why, what *is* this patient entrance into nature's deep resources
But the child's most gradual learning to walk upright without bane?
When we drive out, from the cloud of steam, majestical white horses,
Are we greater than the first men who led black ones by the mane?

"If we trod the deeps of ocean, if we struck the stars in rising,
If we wrapp'd the globe intensely with one hot electric breath,
'Twere but power within our tether, no new spirit-power comprising,
And in life we were not greater men, nor bolder men in death."

She was patient with my talking; and I loved her, loved her, certes,
As I loved all heavenly objects, with uplifted eyes and hands;
As I loved pure inspirations, loved the graces, loved the virtues,
In a Love content with writing his own name on desert sands.

Or at least I thought so, purely; thought no idiot Hope was raising
Any crown to crown Love's silence, silent love that sate alone:
Out, alas! the stag is like me, he that tries to go on grazing
With the great deep gun-wound in his neck, then reels with sudden moan.

It was thus I reel'd. I told you that her hand had many suitors;
But she smiles them down imperially, as Venus did the waves,
And with such a gracious coldness that they cannot press their futures
On the present of her courtesy, which yieldingly enslaves.

And this morning as I sat alone within the inner chamber
With the great saloon beyond it, lost in pleasant thought serene,

For I had been reading Camöens, that
    poem, you remember,
  Which his lady's eyes are praised in as
    the sweetest ever seen.

And the book lay open, and my thought
    flew from it, taking from it
  A vibration and impulsion to an end be-
    yond its own,
As the branch of a green osier, when a
    child would overcome it,
  Springs up freely from his claspings and
    goes swinging in the sun.

As I mused I heard a murmur; it grew
    deep as it grew longer,
  Speakers using earnest language—"Lady
    Geraldine, you *would !*"
And I heard a voice that pleaded, ever on
    in accents stronger,
  As a sense of reason gave it power to
    make its rhetoric good.

Well I knew that voice; it was an earl's,
    of soul that match'd his station,
  Soul completed into lordship, might and
    right read on his brow;
Very finely courteous; far too proud to
    doubt his domination
  Of the common people, he atones for
    grandeur by a bow.

High straight forehead, nose of eagle, cold
    blue eyes of less expression
  Than resistance, coldly casting off the
    looks of other men,
As steel, arrows; unelastic lips which seem
    to taste possession,
  And be cautious lest the common air
    should injure or distrain.

For the rest, accomplish'd, upright—ay,
    and standing by his order
  With a bearing not ungraceful; fond of
    art and letters too;
Just a good man made a proud man—as
    the sandy rocks that border
  A wild coast, by circumstances, in a
    regnant ebb and flow.

Thus, I knew that voice, I heard it, and I
    could not help the hearkening:
  In the room I stood up blindly, and my
    burning heart within

Seem'd to seethe and fuse my senses till
    they ran on all sides darkening,
  And scorch'd, weigh'd like melted metal
    round my feet that stood therein.

And that voice, I heard it pleading, for
    love's sake, for wealth, position,
  For the sake of liberal uses and great
    actions to be done—
And she interrupted gently, "Nay, my
    lord, the old tradition
  Of your Normans, by some worthier hand
    than mine is, should be won."

"Ah, that white hand!" he said quickly—
    and in his he either drew it
  Or attempted—for with gravity and in-
    stance she replied,
"Nay indeed, my lord, this talk is vain,
    and we had best eschew it
  And pass on, like friends, to other points
    less easy to decide."

What he said again, I know not: it is
    likely that his trouble
  Work'd his pride up to the surface, for
    she answer'd in slow scorn,
"And your lordship judges rightly. Whom
    I marry, shall be noble,
  Ay, and wealthy. I shall never blush to
    think how he was born."

There, I madden'd! her words stung me.
    Life swept through me into fever.
  And my soul sprang up astonish'd,
    sprang full-statured in an hour.
Know you what it is when anguish, with
    apocalyptic NEVER,
  To a Pythian height dilates you, and
    despair sublimes to power?

From my brain the soul-wings budded,
    waved a flame about my body,
  Whence conventions coil'd to ashes. I
    felt self-drawn out, as man,
From amalgamate false natures, and I saw
    the skies grow ruddy
  With the deepening feet of angels, and I
    knew what spirits can.

I was mad, inspired—say either! (anguish
    worketh inspiration)
  Was a man or beast—perhaps so, for the
    tiger roars when spear'd;

And I walk'd on, step by step along the
    level of my passion—
O my soul! and pass'd the doorway to
    her face, and never fear'd.

He had left her, peradventure, when my
    footstep proved my coming,
But for *her*—she half arose, then sate,
    grew scarlet and grew pale.
Oh, she trembled! 'tis so always with a
    worldly man or woman
In the presence of true spirits; what else
    can they do but quail?

Oh, she flutter'd like a tame bird, in
    among its forest brothers
Far too strong for it; then drooping,
    bow'd her face upon her hands;
And I spake out wildly, fiercely, brutal
    truths of her and others;
I, she planted in the desert, swathed her,
    windlike, with my sands.

I pluck'd up her social fictions, bloody-
    rooted though leaf-verdant,
Trod them down with words of shaming,
    all the purple and the gold,
All the "landed stakes" and lordships,
    all that spirits pure and ardent
Are cast out of love and honor because
    chancing not to hold.

"For myself I do not argue," said I,
    "though I love you, madam,
But for better souls that nearer to the
    height of yours have trod.
And this age shows, to my thinking, still
    more infidels to Adam
Than directly, by profession, simple infi-
    dels to God.

"Yet, O God," I said, "O grave," I said,
    "O mother's heart and bosom,
With whom first and last are equal, saint
    and corpse and little child,
We are fools to your deductions in these
    figments of heart-closing,
We are traitors to your causes in these
    sympathies defiled.

"Learn more reverence, madam; not for
    rank or wealth—*that* needs no learn-
    ing;
That comes quickly, quick as sin does;
    ay, and culminates to sin;

But for Adam's seed, MAN! Trust me, 'tis
    a clay above your scorning,
With God's image stamp'd upon it, and
    God's kindling breath within.

"What right have you, madam, gazing in
    your palace mirror daily,
Getting so by heart your beauty, which
    all others must adore,
While you draw the golden ringlets down
    your fingers, to vow gaily
You will wed no man that's only good to
    God, and nothing more?

"Why, what right have you, made fair by
    that same God, the sweetest woman
Of all women he has fashion'd, with
    your lovely spirit-face,
Which would seem too near to vanish if
    its smile were not so human,
And your voice of holy sweetness, turn-
    ing common words to grace,

"What right *can* you have, God's other
    works to scorn, despise, revile them
In the gross, as mere men, broadly—not
    as *noble* men, forsooth—
As mere Pariahs of the outer world, forbid-
    den to assoil them
In the hope of living, dying, near that
    sweetness of your mouth?

"Have you any answer, madam? If my
    spirit were less earthly,
If its instrument were gifted with a
    better silver string,
I would kneel down where I stand, and
    say, 'Behold me! I am worthy
Of thy loving, for I love thee! I am
    worthy as a king.'

"As it is—your ermined pride, I swear,
    shall feel this stain upon her,
That *I*, poor, weak, tost with passion,
    scorn'd by me and you again,
Love you, madam, dare to love you, to
    my grief and your dishonor,
To my endless desolation and your im-
    potent disdain!"

More mad words like these—mere mad-
    ness! friend, I need not write them
    fuller,
For I hear my hot soul dropping on the
    lines in showers of tears.

Oh, a woman! friend, a woman! why, a
  beast had scarce been duller
Than roar bestial loud complaints
  against the shining of the spheres.

But at last there came a pause. I stood
  all vibrating with thunder
Which my soul had used. The silence
  drew her face up like a call.
Could you guess what word she utter'd?
  She look'd up, as if in wonder,
With tears beaded on her lashes, and
  said, "Bertram!"—it was all.

If she had cursed me—and she might
  have—or if even with queenly bear-
  ing
Which at need is used by women, she
  had risen up and said,
"Sir, you are my guest, and therefore I
  have given you a full hearing;
Now, beseech you, choose a name exact-
  ing somewhat less, instead!"

I had borne it: but that "Bertram"—why,
  it lies there on the paper
A mere word, without her accent; and
  you cannot judge the weight
Of the calm which crush'd my passion:
  I seem'd drowning in a vapor,
And her gentleness destroy'd me whom
  her scorn made desolate.

So, struck backward and exhausted by
  that inward flow of passion
Which had rush'd on, sparing nothing,
  into forms of abstract truth,
By a logic agonizing through unseemly
  demonstration,
And by youth's own anguish turning
  grimly gray the hairs of youth,

By the sense accursed and instant, that if
  even I spake wisely
I spake basely, using truth, if what I
  spake indeed was true,
To avenge wrong on a woman—*her*, who
  sate there weighing nicely
A poor manhood's worth, found guilty of
  such deeds as I could do!—

By such wrong and woe exhausted—what I
  suffer'd and occasion'd,—
As a wild horse through a city runs with
  lightning in his eyes,
And then dashing at a church's cold and
  passive wall, impassion'd,
Strikes the death into his burning brain,
  and blindly drops and dies—

So I fell, struck down before her—do you
  blame me, friend, for weakness?
'Twas my strength of passion slew me!
  —fell before her like a stone;
Fast the dreadful world roll'd from me
  on its roaring wheels of blackness:
When the light came, I was lying in this
  chamber and alone.

Oh, of course, she charged her lacqueys to
  bear out the sickly burden,
And to cast it from her scornful sight,
  but not *beyond* the gate;
She is too kind to be cruel, and too haughty
  not to pardon
Such a man as I; 'twere something to be
  level to her hate.

But for me—you now are conscious why,
  my friend, I write this letter,
How my life is read all backward, and
  the charm of life undone.
I shall leave her house at dawn; I would
  to-night, if I were better—
And I charge my soul to hold my body
  strengthen'd for the sun.

When the sun hath dyed the oriel, I depart
  with no last gazes,
No weak moanings (one word only, left
  in writing for her hands),
Out of reach of all derision, and some un-
  availing praises,
To make front against this anguish in
  the far and foreign lands.

Blame me not. I would not squander life
  in grief—I am abstemious.
I but nurse my spirit's falcon that its
  wing may soar again.
There's no room for tears of weakness in
  the blind eyes of a Phemius:
Into work the poet kneads them, and he
  does not die *till then*.

CONCLUSION.

Bertram finish'd the last pages, while
  along the silence ever
Still in hot and heavy splashes fell the
  tears on every leaf.

Having ended, he leans backward in his
    chair, with lips that quiver
From the deep unspoken, ay, and deep
    unwritten thoughts of grief.

Soh! how still the lady standeth! 'tis a
    dream—a dream of mercies!
'Twixt the purple lattice-curtains how
    she standeth still and pale!
'Tis a vision, sure, of mercies, sent to soften
    his self-curses,
Sent to sweep a patient quiet o'er the
    tossing of his wail.

"Eyes," he said, "now throbbing through
    me! are ye eyes that did undo me?
Shining eyes, like antique jewels set in
    Parian statue-stone!
Underneath that calm white forehead, are
    ye ever burning torrid
O'er the desolate sand-desert of my heart
    and life undone?"

With a murmurous stir uncertain, in the
    air the purple curtain
Swelleth in and swelleth out around her
    motionless pale brows,
While the gliding of the river sends a
    rippling noise for ever
Through the open casement whiten'd by
    the moonlight's slant repose.

Said he: "Vision of a lady! stand there
    silent, stand there steady!
Now I see it plainly, plainly, now I can-
    not hope or doubt—
There, the brows of mild repression—there,
    the lips of silent passion,
Curved like an archer's bow to send the
    bitter arrows out."

Ever, evermore the while in a slow silence
    she kept smiling,
And approach'd him slowly, slowly, in a
    gliding measured pace;
With her two white hands extended as if
    praying one offended,
And a look of supplication gazing earnest
    in his face.

Said he: "Wake me by no gesture—sound
    of breath, or stir of vesture!
Let the blessèd apparition melt not yet
    to its divine!
No approaching—hush, no breathing! or
    my heart must swoon to death in
The too utter life thou bringest, O thou
    dream of Geraldine!"

Ever, evermore the while in a slow silence
    she kept smiling,
But the tears ran over lightly from her
    eyes and tenderly:—
"Dost thou, Bertram, truly love me? Is
    no woman far above me
Found more worthy of thy poet-heart
    than such a one as *I?*"

Said he: "I would dream so ever, like the
    flowing of that river,
Flowing ever in a shadow greenly onward
    to the sea!
So, thou vision of all sweetness, princely
    to a full completeness,
Would my heart and life flow onward,
    deathward, through this dream of
    THEE!"

Ever, evermore the while in a slow silence
    she kept smiling,
While the silver tears ran faster down
    the blushing of her cheeks;
Then with both her hands enfolding both
    of his, she softly told him,
"Bertram, if I say I love thee, . . . 'tis
    the vision only speaks."

Soften'd, quicken'd to adore her, on his
    knee he fell before her,
And she whisper'd low in triumph, "It
    shall be as I have sworn.
Very rich he is in virtues, very noble—
    noble, certes;
And I shall not blush in knowing that
    men call him lowly-born."
ELIZABETH BARRETT BROWNING.

THE NUT-BROWN MAID.

BE it ryght, or wrong, these men among
    On women do complayne;
Affyrmynge this, how that it is
    A labour spent in vayne,
To love them wele; for never a dele
    They love a man agayne:
For late a man do what he can,
    Theyr favour to attayne,

Yet, yf a newe do them persue,
  Theyr first true lover than
Laboureth for nought: for from her thought
  He is a banysh'd man.

I say nat nay, but that all day
  It is bothe writ and sayd
That womans faith is, as who sayth,
  All utterly decayd;
But, neverthelesse ryght good wytnèsse
  In this case might be layd,
That they love true, and continùe:
  Recorde the Not-browne Mayde:
Which, when her love came, her to prove,
  To her to make his mone,
Wolde nat depart; for in her hart
  She loved but hym alone.

Than betwaine us late us dyscus
  What was all the manere
Betwayne them two: we wyll also
  Tell all the payne, and fere,
That she was in. Now I begyn
  So that ye me answère;
Wherfore, all ye that present be
  I pray you, gyve an ere:
" I am the knyght; I come by nyght,
  As secret as I can;
Sayinge, Alas! thus standeth the case,
  I am a banysh'd man."

SHE.

And I your wyll for to fulfyll
  In this wyll nat refuse;
Trustying to shewe, in wordès fewe,
  That men have an yll use
(To theyr own shame) women to blame,
  And causelesse them accuse;
Therfore to you I answere nowe,
  All women to excuse,—
Myne owne hart dere, with you what chere?
  I pray you, tell anone;
For, in my mynde, of all mankynde
  I love but you alone.

HE.

It standeth so; a dede is do
  Whereof grete harme shall growe;
My destiny is for to dy
  A shamefull deth, I trowe;
Or elles to fle: the one must be.
  None other way I knowe,

But to withdrawe as an outlawe,
  And take me to my bowe.
Wherfore, adue, my owne hart true!
  None other rede I can;
For I must to the grene wode go,
  Alone, a banysh'd man.

SHE.

O Lord, what is thys worldys blysse,
  That changeth as the mone!
My somers day in lusty may
  Is derked before the none.
I here you say farewell: Nay, nay,
  We dèpart nat so sone.
Why say ye so? wheder wyll ye go?
  Alas! what have ye done?
All my welfàre to sorrowe and care
  Sholde chaunge, yf ye were gone;
For in my mynde, of all mankynde
  I love but you alone.

HE.

I can beleve, it shall you greve,
  And somewhat you dystrayne;
But, aftyrwarde, your paynes harde
  Within a day or twayne
Shall sone aslake; and ye shall take
  Comfort to you agayne.
Why sholde ye ought? for, to make thought,
  Your labour were in vayne.
And thus I do; and pray you to
  As hartely, as I can;
For I must to the grene wode go,
  Alone, a banysh'd man.

SHE.

Now, syth that ye have shew'd to me
  The secret of your mynde,
I shall be playne to you agayne,
  Lyke as ye shall me fynde.
Syth it is so, that ye wyll go,
  I wolle not leve behynde:
Shall never be sayd, the Not-browne Mayd
  Was to her love unkynde:
Make you redy, for so am I,
  Allthough it were anone;
For, in my mynde, of all mankynde
  I love but you alone.

HE.

Yet I you rede to take good hede
  What men wyll thynke, and say:

Of yonge, and olde it shall be tolde,
  That ye be gone away,
Your wanton wyll for to fulfill,
  In grene wode you to play;
And that ye myght from your delyght
  No lenger make delay.
Rather than ye sholde thus for me
  Be called an yll womàn,
Yet wolde I to the grene wode go
  Alone, a banysh'd man.

SHE.

Though it be songe of old and yonge,
  That I sholde be to blame,
Theyrs be the charge, that speke so large
  In hurtynge of my name:
For I wyll prove, that faythfulle love
  It is devoyd of shame;
In your dystresse, and hevynesse,
  To part with you, the same:
And sure all tho, that do not so,
  True lovers are they none;
For, in my mynde, of all mankynde
  I love but you alone.

HE.

I counceyle you, remember howe,
  It is no maydens lawe,
Nothynge to dout, but to renne out
  To wode with an outlàwe:
For ye must there in your hand bere
  A bowe, redy to drawe;
And, as a thefe, thus must you lyve,
  Ever in drede and awe;
Wherby to you grete harme myght growe:
  Yet had I lever than,
That I had to the grene wode go,
  Alone, a banysh'd man.

SHE.

I thinke nat nay, but as ye say,
  It is no maidens lore:
But love may make me for your sake,
  As I have sayd before
To come on fote, to hunt, and shote
  To gete us mete in store;
For so that I your company
  May have, I aske no more:
From which to part, it maketh my hart
  As colde as ony stone;
For in my mynde, of all mankynde
  I love but you alone.

HE.

For an outlawe this is the lawe,
  That men hym take and bynde;
Without pytè, hangèd to be,
  And waver with the wynde,
If I had nede, (as God forbede!)
  What rescous coude ye fynde?
Forsoth, I trowe, ye and your bowe
  For fere wolde drawe behynde:
And no mervayle; for lytell avayle
  Were in your counceyle than:
Wherfore I wyll to the grene wode go,
  Alone, a banysh'd man.

SHE.

Right wele know ye, that woman be
  But feble for to fyght;
No womanhede it is indede
  To be bolde as a knyght:
Yet, in such fere yf that ye were
  With enemyes day or nyght,
I wolde withstande, with bowe in hande
  To greve them as I myght,
And you to save; as women have
  From deth 'men' many one:
For, in my mynde, of all mankynde
  I love but you alone.

HE.

Yet take good hede; for ever I drede
  That ye coude nat sustayne
The thornie wayes, the deep vallèies,
  The snowe, the frost, the rayne,
The colde, the hete: for dry, or wete,
  We must lodge on the playne;
And, us above, none other rofe
  But a brake bush, or twayne:
Which sone sholde greve you, I beleve;
  And ye wolde gladly than
That I had to the grene wode go,
  Alone, a banysh'd man.

SHE.

Syth I have here bene partynère
  With you of joy and blysse,
I must also part of your wo
  Endure, as reson is:
Yet am I sure of one plesùre
  And, shortely, it is this:
That, where ye be, me semeth, pardè,
  I could not fare amysse.

Without more speche, I you beseche
  That we were sone agone:
For in my mynde, of all mankynde
  I love but you alone.

HE.

If ye go thyder, ye must consyder,
  Whan ye have lust to dyne,
There shall no mete be for you gete,
  Nor drinke, bere, ale, ne wyne.
No schetès clene, to lye betwene,
  Made of threde and twyne;
None other house, but leves and bowes,
  To cover your hed and myne.
O myne harte swete, this evyll dyète
  Sholde make you pale and wan;
Wherfore I wyll to the grene wode go,
  Alone, a banysh'd man.

SHE.

Amonge the wild dere, such an archère,
  As men say that ye be,
Ne may nat fayle of good vitayle,
  Where is so grete plentè:
And water clere of the ryvère
  Shall be full swete to me;
With which in hele I shall ryght wele
  Endure, as ye shall see;
And, or we go, a bedde or two
  I can provyde anone;
For, in my mynde, of all mankynde
  I love but you alone.

HE.

Lo yet, before, ye must do more,
  Yf ye wyll go with me:
As cut your here up by your ere,
  Your kyrtel by the kne;
With bowe in hande, for to withstande
  Your enemyes yf nede be;
And this same nyght before day-light,
  To wode-warde wyll I fle.
Yf that ye wyll all this fulfill,
  Do it shortely as ye can;
Els wyll I to the grene wode go,
  Alone, a banysh'd man.

SHE.

I shall as nowe do more for you
  Than longeth to womanhede;
To shote my here, a bowe to bere,
  To shote in tyme of nede.
O my swete mother, before all other
  For you I have most drede:
But nowe, adue! I must ensue,
  Where fortune doth me lede.
All this make ye: Now let us fle:
  The day cometh fast upon;
For, in my mynde, of all mankynde
  I love but you alone.

HE.

Nay, nay, nat so; ye shall nat go,
  And I shall tell ye why,—
Your appetyght is to be lyght
  Of love, I wele espy:
For, lyke as ye have sayd to me,
  In lyke wyse hardely
Ye wolde answère whosoever it were,
  In way of company.
It is sayd of olde, Sone hote, sone colde:
  And so is a womàn.
Wherfore I to the wode wyll go,
  Alone, a banysh'd man.

SHE.

Yf ye take hede, it is no nede
  Such wordes to say by me;
For oft ye pray'd, and longe assay'd,
  Or I you loved, pardè;
And though that I of auncestry
  A barons daughter be,
Yet have you proved howe I you loved
  A squyer of lowe degrè;
And ever shall, whatso befall;
  To dy therfore anone;
For in my mynde, of all mankynde
  I love but you alone.

HE.

A barons chylde to be begylde!
  It were a cursèd dede;
To be felàwe with an outlawe!
  Almighty God forbede!
Yet beter were, the pore squyère
  Alone to forest yede,
Than ye sholde say another day,
  That, by my cursèd dede,
Ye were betray'd: Wherfore, good mayd,
  The best rede that I can,
Is, that I to the grene wode go,
  Alone, a banysh'd man.

SHE.

Whatever befall, I never shall
  Of this thyng you upbrayd:
But yf ye go, and leve me so,
  Then have ye me betrayd.
Remember you wele, howe that ye dele;
  For, yf ye, as ye sayd,
Be so unkynde, to leve behynde
  Your love the Not-browne Mayd,
Trust me truly, that I shall dy
  Sone after ye be gone;
For, in my mynde, of all mankynde
  I love but you alone.

HE.

Yf that ye went, ye sholde repent;
  For in the forest nowe
I have purvay'd me of a mayd,
  Whom I love more than you;
Another fayrère, than ever ye were,
  I dare it wele avowe;
And of ye bothe eche sholde be wrothe
  With other, as I trowe:
It were myne ese, to lyve in pese;
  So wyll I, yf I can;
Wherfore I to the wode wyll go,
  Alone, a banysh'd man.

SHE.

Though in the wode I undyrstode
  Ye had a paramour,
All this may nought remove my thought,
  But that I will be your:
And she shall fynde me soft, and kynde,
  And courteys every hour;
Glad to fulfyll all that she wyll
  Commaunde me to my power:
For had ye, lo, an hundred mo,
  'Of them I wolde be one;'
For, in my mynde, of all mankynde
  I love but you alone.

HE.

Myne owne dere love, I se the prove
  That ye be kynde, and true:
Of mayde, and wyfe, in all my lyfe,
  The best that ever I knewe.
Be mery and glad, be no more sad,
  The case is chaungèd newe;
For it were ruthe, that, for your truthe,
  Ye sholde have cause to rewe.
Be nat dismay'd; whatsoever I sayd
  To you, whan I began,
I wyll nat to the grene wode go,
  I am no banysh'd man.

SHE.

These tydings be more gladd to me,
  Than to be made a quene,
Yf I were sure they sholde endure;
  But it is often sene,
Whan men wyll breke promyse, they speke
  The wordès on the splene.
Ye shape some wyle me to begyle,
  And stele from me, I wene:
Than were the case worse than it was,
  And I more wo-begone:
For, in my mynde, of all mankynde
  I love but you alone.

HE,.

Ye shall nat nede further to drede;
  I will nat dysparàge
You (God forfend!), syth ye descend
  Of so grete a lynàge.
Nowe undyrstande; to Westmarlande,
  Which is myne herytage,
I wyll you brynge, and with a rynge
  By way of maryage
I wyll you take, and lady make,
  As shortely as I can:
Thus have you won an erlys son
  And not a banysh'd man.

AUTHOR.

Here may ye se, that women be
  In love, meke, kynde, and stable;
Late never man reprove them than,
  Or call them variable;
But, rather, pray God that we may
  To them be comfortable.
Which sometyme proveth such, as he loveth,
  Yf they be charytable.
For syth men wolde that women sholde
  Be meke to them each one,
Moche more ought they to God obey,
  And serve but Hym alone.

AUTHOR UNKNOWN.

THE FRIAR OF ORDERS GRAY.

It was a friar of orders gray
    Walkt forth to tell his beades;
And he met with a lady faire
    Clad in a pilgrime's weedes.

Now Christ thee save, thou reverend friar,
    I pray thee tell to me,
If ever at yon holy shrine
    My true love thou didst see.

And how should I know your true love
    For many another one?
O, by his cockle hat, and staff,
    And by his sandal shoone.

But chiefly by his face and mien,
    That were so fair to view;
His flaxen locks that sweetly curl'd,
    And eyne of lovely blue.

O lady, he is dead and gone!
    Lady, he's dead and gone!
And at his head a green grass turfe,
    And at his heels a stone.

Within these holy cloysters long
    He languisht and he dyed,
Lamenting of a ladyes love,
    And 'plaining of her pride.

Here bore him barefaced on his bier
    Six proper youths and tall,
And many a tear bedew'd his grave
    Within yon kirk-yard wall.

And art thou dead, thou gentle youth!
    And art thou dead and gone!
And didst thou dye for love of me!
    Break, cruel heart of stone!

O weep not, lady, weep not soe:
    Some ghostly comfort seek:
Let not vain sorrow rive thy heart,
    Ne teares bedew thy cheek.

O do not, do not, holy friar,
    My sorrows now reprove;
For I have lost the sweetest youth
    That e'er wan ladyes love.

And nowe, alas! for thy sad losse,
    I'll evermore weep and sigh:
For thee I only wisht to live,
    For thee I wish to dye.

Weep no more, lady, weep no more,
    Thy sorrowe is in vaine:
For violets pluckt the sweetest showers
    Will ne'er make grow againe.

Our joys as wingèd dreams doe flye,
    Why, then, should sorrow last?
Since grief but aggravates thy losse,
    Grieve not for what is past.

O say not soe, thou holy friar;
    I pray thee say not soe:
For since my true-love dyed for mee,
    'Tis meet my tears should flow.

And will he ne'er come again?
    Will he ne'er come again?
Ah! no, he is dead and laid in his grave,
    For ever to remain.

His cheek was redder than the rose;
    The comeliest youth was he!
But he is dead and laid in his grave:
    Alas, and woe is me!

Sigh no more, lady, sigh no more,
    Men were deceivers ever:
One foot on sea and one on land,
    To one thing constant never.

Hadst thou been fond, he had been false,
    And left thee sad and heavy;
For young men ever were fickle found,
    Since summer trees were leafy.

Now say not soe, thou holy friar,
    I pray thee say not soe;
My love he had the truest heart:
    O he was ever true!

And art thou dead, thou much-loved youth,
    And didst thou dye for mee?
Then farewell home, for ever-more
    A pilgrim I will bee.

But first upon my true-loves grave
    My weary limbs I'll lay,
And thrice I'll kiss the green-grass turf,
    That wraps his breathless clay.

Yet stay, fair lady: rest a while
    Beneath this cloyster wall:
See through the hawthorn blows the cold wind,
    And drizzly rain doth fall.

O stay me not, thou holy friar;
  O stay me not, I pray;
No drizzly rain that falls on me,
  Can wash my fault away.

Yet stay, fair lady, turn again,
  And dry those pearly tears;
For see beneath this gown of gray
  Thy owne true-love appears.

Here forced by grief and hopeless love,
  These holy weeds I sought:
And here amid these lonely walls
  To end my days I thought.

But haply, for my year of grace
  Is not yet pass'd away,
Might I still hope to win thy love,
  No longer would I stay.

Now farewell grief, and welcome joy
  Once more unto my heart;
For since I have found thee, lovely youth,
  We never more will part.
                        THOMAS PERCY.

SONNET.

TO THE MOON.

WITH how sad steps, O Moon, thou climb'st the skies!
  How silently, and with how wan a face!
  What! may it be, that e'en in heav'nly place
That busy archer his sharp arrows tries?
Sure, if that long-with-love-acquainted eyes
  Can judge of love, thou feel'st a lover's case;
  I read it in thy looks; thy languish'd grace
To me, that feel the like, thy state descries.
  Then, ev'n of fellowship, O Moon, tell me,
Is constant love deem'd there but want of wit?
  Are beauties there as proud as here they be?
Do they above love to be loved, and yet
  Those lovers scorn, whom that love doth possess?
Do they call virtue there ungratefulness?
                        SIR PHILIP SIDNEY.

JEANIE MORRISON.

I'VE wander'd east, I've wander'd west,
  Through mony a weary way;
But never, never can forget
  The luve o' life's young day!
The fire that's blawn on Beltane e'en
  May weel be black gin Yule;
But blacker fa' awaits the heart
  Where first fond luve grows cule.

Oh dear, dear Jeanie Morrison,
  The thochts o' bygane years
Still fling their shadows ower my path,
  And blind my een wi' tears:
They blind my een wi' saut, saut tears,
  And sair and sick I pine,
As memory idly summons up
  The blithe blinks o' langsyne.

'Twas then we luvit ilk ither weel,
  'Twas then we twa did part;
Sweet time—sad time! twa bairns at scule,
  Twa bairns, and but ae heart!
'Twas then we sat on ae laigh bink,
  To leir ilk ither lear;
And tones and looks and smiles were shed,
  Remember'd evermair.

I wonder, Jeanie, aften yet,
  When sitting on that bink,
Cheek touchin' cheek, loof lock'd in loof,
  What our wee heads could think.
When baith bent doun ower ae braid page,
  Wi' ae buik on our knee,
Thy lips were on thy lesson, but
  My lesson was in thee.

Oh, mind ye how we hung our heads,
  How cheeks brent red wi' shame,
Whene'er the scule-weans, laughin,' said
  We cleek'd thegither hame?
And mind ye o' the Saturdays
  (The scule then skail't at noon),
When we ran off to speel the braes,—
  The broomy braes o' June?

My head rins round and round about—
  My heart flows like a sea,
As ane by ane the thochts rush back
  O' scule-time and o' thee.
Oh mornin' life! oh mornin' luve!
  Oh lichtsome days and lang,
When hinny'd hopes around our hearts
  Like simmer blossoms sprang!

Oh, mind ye, luve, how aft we left
   The deavin' dinsome toun,
To wander by the green burnside,
   And hear its waters croon?
The simmer leaves hung ower our heads,
   The flowers burst round our feet,
And in the gloamin' o' the wood
   The throssil whusslit sweet;

The throssil whusslit in the wood,
   The burn sang to the trees—
And we, with Nature's heart in tune,
   Concerted harmonies:
And on the knowe abune the burn
   For hours thegither sat
In the silentness o' joy, till baith
   Wi' very gladness grat.

Ay, ay, dear Jeanie Morrison,
   Tears trinkled doun your cheek
Like dew-beads on a rose, yet nane
   Had ony power to speak!
That was a time, a blessed time,
   When hearts were fresh and young,
When freely gush'd all feelings forth,
   Unsyllabled—unsung!

I marvel, Jeanie Morrison,
   Gin I hae been to thee
As closely twined wi' earliest thochts
   As ye hae been to me?
Oh, tell me gin their music fills
   Thine ear as it does mine?
Oh, say gin e'er your heart grows grit
   Wi' dreamings o' langsyne?

I've wander'd east, I've wander'd west,
   I've borne a weary lot;
But in my wanderings, far or near,
   Ye never were forgot.
The fount that first burst frae this heart
   Still travels on its way;
And channels deeper, as it rins,
   The luve o' life's young day.

O dear, dear Jeanie Morrison,
   Since we were sinder'd young
I've never seen your face, nor heard
   The music o' your tongue;
But I could hug all wretchedness,
   And happy could I dee,
Did I but ken your heart still dream'd
   O' bygone days and me!
            WILLIAM MOTHERWELL.

SWEET WILLIAM'S FAREWELL TO BLACK-EYED SUSAN.

ALL in the Downs the fleet was moor'd,
   The streamers waving in the wind,
When black-eyed Susan came aboard:—
   "Oh! where shall I my true-love find?
Tell me, ye jovial sailors! tell me true
If my sweet William sails among the crew."

William, who high upon the yard
   Rock'd with the billow to and fro,
Soon as her well-known voice he heard,
   He sigh'd, and cast his eyes below:
The cord slides swiftly through his glowing hands,
And quick as lightning on the deck he stands.

So the sweet lark, high poised in air,
   Shuts close his pinions to his breast,
If chance his mate's shrill call he hear,
   And drops at once into her nest.
The noblest captain in the British fleet
Might envy William's lip those kisses sweet.

"O Susan! Susan! lovely dear,
   My vows shall ever true remain;
Let me kiss off that falling tear;
   We only part to meet again.
Change as ye list, ye winds! my heart shall be
The faithful compass that still points to thee.

"Believe not what the landmen say
   Who tempt with doubts thy constant mind:
They'll tell thee, sailors, when away,
   In every port a mistress find:
Yes, yes, believe them when they tell thee so,
For thou art present wheresoe'er I go.

"If to far India's coast we sail,
   Thy eyes are seen in diamonds bright,
Thy breath is Afric's spicy gale,
   Thy skin is ivory, so white:
Thus every beauteous object that I view
Wakes in my soul some charm of lovely Sue.

"Though battle call me from thy arms,
   Let not my pretty Susan mourn;

Though cannons roar, yet safe from harms
　William shall to his dear return.
Love turns aside the balls that round me
　　fly,
Lest precious tears should drop from
　　Susan's eye."

The boatswain gave the dreadful word;
　The sails their swelling bosom spread;
No longer must she stay aboard;
　They kiss'd; she sigh'd; he hung his head.
Her lessening boat unwilling rows to land:
"Adieu!" she cries; and waved her lily
　　hand.
　　　　　　　　　　　　JOHN GAY.

HIGHLAND MARY.

YE banks, and braes, and streams around
　The castle o' Montgomery,
Green be your woods, and fair your flowers,
　Your waters never drumlie!
There simmer first unfauld her robes,
　And there the langest tarry;
For there I took the last fareweel
　O' my sweet Highland Mary.

How sweetly bloom'd the gay green birk,
　How rich the hawthorn's blossom,
As, underneath their fragrant shade,
　I clasp'd her to my bosom!
The golden hours, on angel wings,
　Flew o'er me and my dearie;
For dear to me as light and life
　Was my sweet Highland Mary!

Wi' mony a vow, and lock'd embrace,
　Our parting was fu' tender;
And, pledging aft to meet again,
　We tore oursels asunder;
But, oh, fell death's untimely frost,
　That nipp'd my flower sae early!
Now green's the sod and cauld's the clay,
　That wraps my Highland Mary!

Oh, pale, pale now, those rosy lips
　I aft ha'e kiss'd sae fondly!
And closed for aye the sparkling glance
　That dwalt on me sae kindly!
And mouldering now in silent dust,
　That heart that lo'ed me dearly;
But still within my bosom's core
　Shall live my Highland Mary!
　　　　　　　　　　ROBERT BURNS.

SALLY IN OUR ALLEY.

OF all the girls that are so smart,
　There's none like pretty Sally;
She is the darling of my heart,
　And she lives in our alley.
There is no lady in the land
　Is half so sweet as Sally;
She is the darling of my heart,
　And she lives in our alley.

Her father he makes cabbage-nets,
　And through the streets does cry 'em;
Her mother she sells laces long
　To such as please to buy 'em:
But sure such folks could ne'er beget
　So sweet a girl as Sally!
She is the darling of my heart,
　And she lives in our alley.

When she is by, I leave my work,
　I love her so sincerely;
My master comes like any Turk,
　And bangs me most severely—
But let him bang his bellyful,
　I'll bear it all for Sally;
She is the darling of my heart,
　And she lives in our alley.

Of all the days that's in the week
　I dearly love but one day—
And that's the day that comes betwixt
　A Saturday and Monday;
For then I'm drest all in my best
　To walk abroad with Sally;
She is the darling of my heart,
　And she lives in our alley.

My master carries me to church,
　And often am I blamed
Because I leave him in the lurch
　As soon as text is named;
I leave the church in sermon-time
　And slink away to Sally;
She is the darling of my heart,
　And she lives in our alley.

When Christmas comes about again,
　Oh then I shall have money;
I'll hoard it up, and box it all,
　I'll give it to my honey:
I would it were ten thousand pound,
　I'd give it all to Sally;
She is the darling of my heart,
　And she lives in our alley.

My master and the neighbors all
  Make game of me and Sally,
And, but for her, I'd better be
  A slave and row a galley;
But when my seven long years are out,
  Oh then I'll marry Sally,—
Oh then we'll wed, and then we'll bed,
  But not in our alley.
HENRY CAREY.

A SUPPLICATION.

AWAKE, awake, my Lyre!
  And tell thy silent master's humble tale
In sounds that may prevail;
  Sounds that gentle thoughts inspire:
Though so exalted she
  And I so lowly be,
Tell her, such different notes make all thy harmony.

Hark! how the strings awake:
  And, though the moving hand approach not near,
Themselves with awful fear
  A kind of numerous trembling make.
Now all thy forces try;
  Now all thy charms apply;
Revenge upon her ear the conquests of her eye.

Weak Lyre! thy virtue sure
  Is useless here, since thou art only found
To cure, but not to wound,
  And she to wound, but not to cure.
Too weak too wilt thou prove
  My passion to remove;
Physic to other ills, thou'rt nourishment to love.

Sleep, sleep again, my Lyre!
  For thou canst never tell my humble tale
In sounds that will prevail,
  Nor gentle thoughts in her inspire;
All thy vain mirth lay by,
  Bid thy strings silent lie,
Sleep, sleep again, my Lyre, and let thy master die.
ABRAHAM COWLEY.

WISHES FOR THE SUPPOSED MISTRESS.

WHOE'ER she be,
That not impossible She
That shall command my heart and me;

Where'er she lie,
Lock'd up from mortal eye
In shady leaves of destiny:

Till that ripe birth
Of studied Fate stand forth,
And teach her fair steps to our earth;

Till that divine
Idea take a shrine
Of crystal flesh, through which to shine:

—Meet you her, my Wishes,
Bespeak her to my blisses,
And be ye call'd, my absent kisses.

I wish her beauty
That owes not all its duty
To gaudy tire, or glist'ring shoe-tie:

Something more than
Taffata or tissue can,
Or rampant feather, or rich fan.

A face that's best
By its own beauty drest,
And can alone command the rest:

A face made up
Out of no other shop
Than what Nature's white hand sets ope.

Sydneian showers
Of sweet discourse, whose powers
Can crown old Winter's head with flowers.

Whate'er delight
Can make day's forehead bright
Or give down to the wings of night.

Soft silken hours,
Open suns, shady bowers;
'Bove all, nothing within that lowers.

Days, that need borrow
No part of their good morrow
From a fore-spent night of sorrow:

Days, that in spite
Of darkness, by the light
Of a clear mind are day all night.

Life, that dares send
A challenge to his end,
And when it comes, say, "Welcome, friend."

I wish her store
Of worth may leave her poor
Of wishes; and I wish——no more.

—Now, if Time knows
That Her, whose radiant brows
Weave them a garland of my vows;

Her that dares be
What these lines wish to see:
I seek no further, it is She.

'Tis She, and here
Lo! I unclothe and clear
My wishes' cloudy character.

Such worth as this is
Shall fix my flying wishes,
And determine them to kisses.

Let her full glory,
My fancies, fly before ye;
Be ye my fictions:—but her story.
RICHARD CRASHAW.

LOVELY MARY DONNELLY.

O LOVELY Mary Donnelly, it's you I love the best!
If fifty girls were around you, I'd hardly see the rest;
Be what it may the time of day, the place be where it will,
Sweet looks of Mary Donnelly, they bloom before me still.

Her eyes like mountain water that's flowing on a rock,
How clear they are, how dark they are! and they give me many a shock;
Red rowans warm in sunshine, and wetted with a shower,
Could ne'er express the charming lip that has me in its power.

Her nose is straight and handsome, her eyebrows lifted up,
Her chin is very neat and pert, and smooth like a china cup;
Her hair's the brag of Ireland, so weighty and so fine—
It's rolling down upon her neck, and gather'd in a twine.

The dance o' last Whit Monday night exceeded all before—
No pretty girl for miles around was missing from the floor;
But Mary kept the belt of love, and oh! but she was gay;
She danced a jig, she sung a song, and took my heart away!

When she stood up for dancing, her steps were so complete,
The music nearly kill'd itself, to listen to her feet;
The fiddler mourn'd his blindness, he heard her so much praised;
But bless'd himself he wasn't deaf when once her voice she raised.

And evermore I'm whistling or lilting what you sung;
Your smile is always in my heart, your name beside my tongue.
But you've as many sweethearts as you'd count on both your hands,
And for myself there's not a thumb or little finger stands.

Oh, you're the flower of womankind, in country or in town;
The higher I exalt you, the lower I'm cast down.
If some great lord should come this way and see your beauty bright,
And you to be his lady, I'd own it was but right.

Oh, might we live together in lofty palace hall
Where joyful music rises, and where scarlet curtains fall!
Oh, might we live together in a cottage mean and small,
With sods of grass the only roof, and mud the only wall!

O lovely Mary Donnelly, your beauty's my
    distress—
It's far too beauteous to be mine, but I'll
    never wish it less;
The proudest place would fit your face, and
    I am poor and low,
But blessings be about you, dear, wherever
    you may go!
                    WILLIAM ALLINGHAM.

SHALL I TELL YOU WHOM I LOVE?

SHALL I tell you whom I love?
  Hearken then a while to me;
And if such a woman move
  As I now shall versify,
Be assured 'tis she, or none,
That I love, and love alone.

Nature did her so much right
  As she scorns the help of art.
In as many virtues dight
  As e'er yet embraced a heart.
So much good so truly tried,
Some for less were deified.

Wit she hath, without desire
  To make known how much she hath;
And her anger flames no higher
  Than may fitly sweeten wrath.
Full of pity as may be,
Though perhaps not so to me.

Reason masters every sense,
  And her virtues grace her birth;
Lovely as all excellence,
  Modest in her most of mirth.
Likelihood enough to prove
Only worth could kindle love.

Such she is; and if you know
  Such a one as I have sung;
Be she brown, or fair, or so
  That she be but somewhile young;
Be assured 'tis she, or none,
That I love, and love alone.
                      WILLIAM BROWNE.

TO VIRGINS, TO MAKE MUCH OF TIME.

GATHER ye rosebuds while ye may,
  Old Time is still a-flying,
And this same flower that smiles to-day,
  To-morrow will be dying.

The glorious lamp of heaven, the sun,
  The higher he's a-getting
The sooner will his race be run,
  And nearer he's to setting.

That age is best which is the first,
  When youth and blood are warmer,
But being spent, the worse, and worst
  Times still succeed the former.

Then be not coy, but use your time,
  And while ye may, go marry;
For having lost but once your prime,
  You may for ever tarry.
                      ROBERT HERRICK.

ROSALINE.

LIKE to the clear in highest sphere
Where all imperial glory shines,
Of selfsame color is her hair,
Whether unfolded, or in twines;
  Heigh ho, fair Rosaline!
Her eyes are sapphires set in snow,
Resembling heaven by every wink;
The gods do fear whenas they glow,
And I do tremble when I think.
  Heigh ho, would she were mine!

Her cheeks are like the blushing cloud
That beautifies Aurora's face,
Or like the silver crimson shroud
That Phœbus' smiling looks doth grace;
  Heigh ho, fair Rosaline!
Her lips are like two budded roses
Whom ranks of lilies neighbor nigh,
Within which bounds she balm encloses
Apt to entice a deity;
  Heigh ho, would she were mine!

Her neck is like a stately tower
Where Love himself imprison'd lies,
To watch for glances every hour
From her divine and sacred eyes:
  Heigh ho, fair Rosaline!
Her paps are centres of delight,
Her breasts are orbs of heavenly frame,
Where Nature moulds the dew of light
To feed perfection with the same;
  Heigh ho, would she were mine!

With orient pearl, with ruby red,
With marble white, with sapphire blue,

Her body every way is fed,
Yet soft in touch and sweet in view;
　Heigh ho, fair Rosaline!
Nature herself her shape admires;
The gods are wounded in her sight,
And Love forsakes his heavenly fires
And at her eyes his brand doth light;
　Heigh ho, would she were mine!

Then muse not, nymphs, though I bemoan
The absence of fair Rosaline,
Since for a fair there's fairer none,
Nor for her virtues so divine;
　Heigh ho, fair Rosaline;
Heigh ho, my heart! would God that she were mine!
　　　　　　　　THOMAS LODGE.

TO ALTHEA, FROM PRISON.

WHEN Love, with unconfinèd wings,
　Hovers within my gates,
And my divine Althea brings
　To whisper at my grates;
When I lye tangled in her haire;
　And fetter'd with her eye,
The birds that wanton in the aire
　Know no such libertye.

When flowing cups run swiftly round
　With no allaying Thames,
Our carelesse heads with roses crown'd,
　Our hearts with loyal flames;
When thirsty griefe in wine we steepe,
　When healths and draughts goe free,
Fishes, that tipple in the deepe,
　Know no such libertìe.

When, linnet-like, confinèd I
　With shriller note shall sing
The mercye, sweetness, majestye,
　And glories of my king;
When I shall voyce aloud how good
　He is, how great should be,
Th' enlarged windes, that curle the flood,
　Know no such libertìe.

Stone walls doe not a prison make,
　Nor iron barres a cage,
Mindes, innocent, and quiet, take
　That for an hermitage:
If I have freedom in my love,
　And in my soule am free,

Angels alone, that soare above,
　Enjoy such libertìe.
　　　　　　　RICHARD LOVELACE.

LINES ON ISABELLA MARKHAM.

WHENCE comes my love? O heart, disclose;
It was from cheeks that shamed the rose,
From lips that spoil the ruby's praise,
From eyes that mock the diamond's blaze:
Whence comes my woe? as freely own;
Ah me! 'twas from a heart like stone.

The blushing cheek speaks modest mind,
The lips befitting words most kind,
The eye does tempt to love's desire,
And seems to say 'tis Cupid's fire;
Yet all so fair but speak my moan,
Sith naught doth say the heart of stone.

Why thus, my love, so kind bespeak
Sweet eye, sweet lip, sweet blushing cheek—
Yet not a heart to save my pain?
O Venus, take thy gifts again!
Make not so fair to cause our moan,
Or make a heart that's like our own.
　　　　　　　JOHN HARRINGTON.

SONG.

FOLLOW a shadow, it still flies you;
　Seem to fly it, it will pursue:
So court a mistress, she denies you;
　Let her alone, she will court you.
Say, are not women truly, then,
Styled but the shadows of us men?

At morn and even shades are longest;
　At noon they are or short or none;
So men at weakest they are strongest,
　But grant us perfect, they're not known.
Say, are not women truly, then,
Styled but the shadows of us men?
　　　　　　　BEN JONSON.

TO LUCASTA,

ON GOING TO THE WARS.

TELL me not, sweet, I am unkinde,
　That from the nunnerie
Of thy chaste breast and quiet minde,
　To warre and armes I flee.

True, a new mistresse now I chase—
　　The first foe in the field;
And with a stronger faith imbrace
　　A sword, a horse, a shield.

Yet this inconstancy is such
　　As you, too, should adore;
I could not love thee, deare, so much,
　　Loved I not honor more.
　　　　　　　　RICHARD LOVELACE.

TO LUCASTA.

IF to be absent were to be
Away from thee:
Or that, when I am gone,
You or I were alone;
Then, my Lucasta, might I crave
Pity from blustering wind or swallowing
　　wave.

But I'll not sigh one blast or gale
To swell my sail,
Or pay a tear to 'suage
The foaming blue-god's rage;
For, whether he will let me pass
Or no, I'm still as happy as I was.

Though seas and lands be 'twixt us both,
Our faith and troth,
Like separated souls,
All time and space controls:
Above the highest sphere we meet,
Unseen, unknown; and greet as angels
　　greet.

So, then, we do anticipate
Our after-fate,
And are alive i' th' skies,
If thus our lips and eyes
Can speak like spirits unconfined
In heaven—their earthly bodies left be-
　　hind.
　　　　　　　　RICHARD LOVELACE.

THE WELCOME.

WELCOME, welcome, do I sing,
　　Far more welcome than the spring;
He that parteth from you never,
　　Shall enjoy a spring for ever.

Love that to the voice is near,
　　Breaking from your ivory pale,
Need not walk abroad to hear
　　The delightful nightingale.
　　　　Welcome, welcome, then I sing,
　　Far more welcome than the spring;
　　He that parteth from you never,
　　Shall enjoy a spring for ever.

Love, that still looks on your eyes,
　　Though the winter have begun
To benumb our arteries,
　　Shall not want the summer's sun.
　　　　Welcome, welcome, then I sing,
　　Far more welcome than the spring;
　　He that parteth from you never,
　　Shall enjoy a spring for ever.

Love, that still may see your cheeks,
　　Where all rareness still reposes,
Is a fool if e'er he seeks
　　Other lilies, other roses.
　　　　Welcome, welcome, then I sing,
　　Far more welcome than the spring;
　　He that parteth from you never,
　　Shall enjoy a spring for ever.

Love, to whom your soft lip yields,
　　And perceives your breath in kissing,
All the odors of the fields
　　Never, never shall be missing.
　　　　Welcome, welcome, then I sing,
　　Far more welcome than the spring;
　　He that parteth from you never,
　　Shall enjoy a spring for ever.

Love, that question would anew
　　What fair Eden was of old,
Let him rightly study you,
　　And a brief of that behold.
　　　　Welcome, welcome, then I sing,
　　Far more welcome than the spring;
　　He that parteth from you never,
　　Shall enjoy a spring for ever.
　　　　　　　　WILLIAM BROWNE

'TWAS WHEN THE SEAS WERE ROARING.

'TWAS when the seas were roaring
　　With hollow blasts of wind;
A damsel lay deploring,
　　All on a rock reclined,
Wide o'er the roaring billows
　　She cast a wistful look;

Her head was crown'd with willows,
　That tremble o'er the brook.

Twelve months are gone and over,
　And nine long, tedious days,
Why didst thou, vent'rous lover,
　Why didst thou trust the seas?
Cease, cease, thou cruel ocean,
　And let my lover rest:
Ah! what's thy troubled motion
　To that within my breast?

The merchant robb'd of pleasure,
　Sees tempests in despair;
But what's the loss of treasure
　To losing of my dear?
Should you some coast be laid on
　Where gold and diamonds grow,
You'd find a richer maiden,
　But none that loves you so.

How can they say that Nature
　Has nothing made in vain;
Why then beneath the water
　Should hideous rocks remain?
No eyes the rocks discover,
　That lurk beneath the deep,
To wreck the wandering lover,
　And leave the maid to weep.

All melancholy lying,
　Thus wail'd she for her dear;
Repaid each blast with sighing,
　Each billow with a tear;
When, o'er the white wave stooping,
　His floating corpse she spied;
Then like a lily drooping,
　She bow'd her head and died.
　　　　　　　　　　JOHN GAY.

JEAN.

OF a' the airts the wind can blaw
　I dearly like the West,
For there the bonnie lassie lives,
　The lassie I lo'e best;
There wild woods grow, and rivers row,
　And mony a hill between,
But day and night my fancy's flight
　Is ever wi' my Jean.

I see her in the dewy flowers,
　I see her sweet and fair,
I hear her in the tunefu' birds,
　I hear her charm the air;
There's not a bonnie flower that springs
　By fountain, shaw, or green,
There's not a bonnie bird that sings
　But 'minds me o' my Jean.

Oh blaw ye westlin winds, blaw saft
　Amang the leafy trees;
Wi' gentle gale, frae muir and dale,
　Bring hame the laden bees;
And bring the lassie back to me
　That's aye sae neat and clean;
Ae blink o' her wad banish care,
　Sae charming is my Jean.

What sighs and vows amang the knowes
　Hae pass'd atween us twa!
How fain to meet, how wae to part
　That day she gaed awa!
The Powers aboon can only ken,
　To whom the heart is seen,
That nane can be sae dear to me
　As my sweet lovely Jean!
　　　　　　　　　　ROBERT BURNS.

A SONG.

　　To thy lover,
　　Dear, discover
That sweet blush of thine, that shameth
　　(When those roses
　　It discloses)
All the flowers that Nature nameth.

　　In free air
　　Flow thy hair,
That no more summer's best dresses
　　Be beholden
　　For their golden
Locks, to Phœbus' flaming tresses.

　　Oh, deliver
　　Love his quiver.
From thy eyes he shoots his arrows,
　　Where Apollo
　　Cannot follow,
Feather'd with his mother's sparrows.

　　Oh, envy not
　　(That we die not)
Those dear lips, whose door encloses
　　All the Graces
　　In their places,
Brother pearls, and sister roses.

From these treasures
Of ripe pleasures
One bright smile to clear the weather;
Earth and heaven
Thus made even,
Both will be good friends together.

The air does woo thee,
Winds cling to thee;
Might a word once fly from out thee,
Storm and thunder
Would sit under,
And keep silence round about thee.

But if Nature's
Common creatures
So dear glories dare not borrow,
Yet thy beauty
Owes a duty
To my loving, lingering sorrow.

When, to end me,
Death shall send me
All his terrors to affright me,
Thine eyes' graces
Gild their faces,
And those terrors shall delight me.

When my dying
Life is flying,
Those sweet airs that often slew me,
Shall revive me,
Or reprieve me,
And to many deaths renew me.
RICHARD CRASHAW.

THE NIGHT PIECE.

TO JULIA.

HER eyes the glow-worme lend thee,
The shooting-starres attend thee;
And the elves also,
Whose little eyes glow
Like the sparks of fire, befriend thee.

No Will-o'-th'-wispe mislight thee,
Nor snake nor slow-worm bite thee;
But on thy way,
Not making stay,
Since ghost there's none t' affright thee!

Let not the darke thee cumber;
What though the moon does slumber?

The stars of the night
Will lend thee their light,
Like tapers cleare, without number.

Then, Julia, let me woo thee,
Thus, thus to come unto me;
And when I shall meet
Thy silvery feet,
My soule I'le pour into thee!
ROBERT HERRICK.

A DITTY.

MY true-love hath my heart, and I have
his,
By just exchange one to the other given:
I hold his dear, and mine he cannot miss,
There never was a better bargain driven:
My true-love hath my heart, and I have
his.

His heart in me keeps him and me in one,
My heart in him his thoughts and senses
guides:
He loves my heart, for once it was his own,
I cherish his because in me it bides:
My true-love hath my heart, and I have
his.
SIR PHILIP SIDNEY.

THE EVE OF ST. AGNES.

I.

ST. AGNES' EVE—Ah, bitter chill it was!
The owl, for all his feathers, was a-cold;
The hare limp'd trembling through the
frozen grass,
And silent was the flock in woolly fold:
Numb were the beadsman's fingers while
he told
His rosary, and while his frosted breath,
Like pious incense from a censer old,
Seem'd taking flight for heaven without a
death,
Past the sweet virgin's picture, while his
prayer he saith.

II.

His prayer he saith, this patient, holy man;
Then takes his lamp, and riseth from his
knees,
And back returneth, meagre, barefoot, wan,
Along the chapel aisle by slow degrees:

The sculptured dead, on each side seem
    to freeze,
Emprison'd in black, purgatorial rails:
  Knights, ladies, praying in dumb
    orat'ries,
He passeth by; and his weak spirit fails
  To think how they may ache in icy hoods
    and mails.

III.

Northward he turneth through a little door,
  And scarce three steps, ere Music's gold-
    en tongue
Flatter'd to tears this aged man and poor;
  But no—already had his death-bell rung;
  The joys of all his life were said and sung:
His was harsh penance on St. Agnes' Eve;
  Another way he went, and soon among
Rough ashes sat he for his soul's reprieve,
And all night kept awake, for sinners' sake
    to grieve.

IV.

That ancient beadsman heard the prelude
    soft;
  And so it chanced, for many a door was
    wide,
From hurry to and fro. Soon, up aloft,
  The silver, snarling trumpets 'gan to
    chide;
  The level chambers, ready with their
    pride,
Were glowing to receive a thousand
    guests;
  The carvèd angels, ever eager-eyed,
Stared, where upon their heads the cornice
    rests,
With hair blown back, and wings put cross-
    wise on their breasts.

V.

At length burst in the argent revelry,
  With plume, tiara, and all rich array,
Numerous as shadows haunting fairily
  The brain, new-stuff'd, in youth, with
    triumphs gay
  Of old romance. These let us wish away,
And turn, sole-thoughted, to one lady there
  Whose heart had brooded, all that win-
    try day,
On love, and wing'd St. Agnes' saintly care,
As she had heard old dames full many
    times declare.

VI.

They told her how, upon St. Agnes' Eve,
  Young virgins might have visions of
    delight,
And soft adorings from their loves receive
  Upon the honey'd middle of the night,
  If ceremonies due they did aright;
As, supperless to bed they must retire,
  And couch supine their beauties, lily
    white;
Nor look behind, nor sideways, but require
Of heaven with upward eyes for all that
    they desire.

VII.

Full of this whim was thoughtful Made-
    line;
  The music, yearning like a god in pain,
She scarcely heard; her maiden eyes di-
    vine,
  Fix'd on the floor, saw many a sweeping
    train
  Pass by—she heeded not at all; in vain
Came many a tiptoe, amorous cavalier,
  And back retired; not cool'd by high
    disdain,
But she saw not; her heart was other-
    where;
She sigh'd for Agnes' dreams, the sweetest
    of the year.

VIII.

She danced along with vague, regardless
    eyes,
  Anxious her lips, her breathing quick
    and short;
The hallow'd hour was near at hand; she
    sighs
  Amid the timbrels, and the throng'd re-
    sort
  Of whisperers in anger, or in sport;
'Mid looks of love, defiance, hate and scorn,
  Hoodwink'd with fairy fancy; all amort,
Save to St. Agnes and her lambs unshorn,
And all the bliss to be before to-morrow
    morn.

IX.

So, purposing each moment to retire,
  She linger'd still. Meantime, across the
    moors,
Had come young Porphyro, with heart on
    fire
  For Madeline. Beside the portal doors,

Buttress'd from moonlight, stands he,
  and implores
All saints to give him sight of Madeline,
But for one moment in the tedious hours,
That he might gaze and worship all unseen;
Perchance speak, kneel, touch, kiss—in
  sooth such things have been.

X.

He ventures in: let no buzz'd whisper
  tell:
All eyes be muffled, or a hundred swords
Will storm his heart, Love's feverous
  citadel:
For him, those chambers held barbarian
  hordes,
Hyena foemen, and hot-blooded lords,
Whose very dogs would execrations howl
  Against his lineage: not one breast
  affords
Him any mercy, in that mansion foul,
Save one old beldame, weak in body and
  in soul.

XI.

Ah, happy chance! the agèd creature came,
  Shuffling along with ivory-headed wand,
To where he stood, hid from the torch's
  flame,
  Behind a broad hall-pillar, far beyond
The sound of merriment and chorus
  bland:
He startled her; but soon she knew his
  face,
  And grasp'd his fingers in her palsied
  hand,
Saying, "Mercy, Porphyro! hie thee from
  this place;
They are all here to-night, the whole
  bloodthirsty race!

XII.

"Get hence! get hence! there's dwarfish
  Hildebrand;
He had a fever late, and in the fit
He cursed thee and thine, both house and
  land:
Then there's that old Lord Maurice, not
  a whit
More tame for his gray hairs—Alas me!
  flit!
Flit like a ghost away!"—"Ah, gossip dear,
We're safe enough; here in this armchair sit,
And tell me how"—"Good saints, not here,
  not here;
Follow me, child, or else these stones will
  be thy bier."

XIII.

He follow'd through a lowly archèd way,
  Brushing the cobwebs with his lofty
  plume;
And as she mutter'd "Well-a—well-a-day!"
  He found him in a little moonlight room,
  Pale, latticed, chill, and silent as a tomb.
"Now tell me where is Madeline," said he,
  "Oh tell me, Angela, by the holy loom
Which none but secret sisterhood may see,
When they St. Agnes' wool are weaving
  piously."

XIV.

"St. Agnes! Ah! it is St. Agnes' Eve—
  Yet men will murder upon holy days:
Thou must hold water in a witch's sieve,
  And be liege-lord of all the elves and fays,
  To venture so. It fills me with amaze
To see thee, Porphyro!—St. Agnes' Eve!
  God's help! my lady fair the conjurer
  plays
This very night: good angels her deceive!
But let me laugh a while, I've mickle time
  to grieve."

XV.

Feebly she laugheth in the languid moon,
  While Porphyro upon her face doth look,
Like puzzled urchin on an aged crone
  Who keepeth closed a wondrous riddle-book,
  As spectacled she sits in chimney-nook.
But soon his eyes grew brilliant, when she
  told
  His lady's purpose; and he scarce could
  brook
Tears, at the thought of those enchantments cold,
And Madeline asleep in lap of legends old.

XVI.

Sudden a thought came like a full-blown
  rose
  Flushing his brow, and in his painèd
  heart

Made purple riot: then doth he propose
  A stratagem, that makes the beldame start:
"A cruel man and impious thou art!
Sweet lady, let her pray, and sleep and dream
Alone with her good angels, far apart
From wicked men like thee. Go, go! I deem
Thou canst not surely be the same that thou didst seem."

XVII.

"I will not harm her, by all saints I swear!"
  Quoth Porphyro. "Oh, may I ne'er find grace
When my weak voice shall whisper its last prayer,
  If one of her soft ringlets I displace,
Or look with ruffian passion in her face:
Good Angela, believe me by these tears;
  Or I will, even in a moment's space,
Awake with horrid shout my foemen's ears,
And beard them, though they be more fang'd than wolves and bears."

XVIII.

"Ah, why wilt thou affright a feeble soul?
  A poor, weak, palsy-stricken, church-yard thing,
Whose passing-bell may ere the midnight toll;
  Whose prayers for thee, each morn and evening,
Were never miss'd." Thus plaining doth she bring
A gentler speech from burning Porphyro;
  So woeful, and of such deep sorrowing,
That Angela gives promise she will do
Whatever he shall wish, betide her weal or woe.

XIX.

Which was, to lead him, in close secrecy,
  Even to Madeline's chamber, and there hide
Him in a closet, of such privacy
  That he might see her beauty unespied,
And win perhaps that night a peerless bride,
While legion'd fairies paced the coverlet,
  And pale enchantment held her sleepy-eyed.
Never on such a night have lovers met,
Since Merlin paid his demon all the monstrous debt.

XX.

"It shall be as thou wishest," said the dame;
  "All cates and dainties shall be storèd there
Quickly on this feast-night; by the tambour-frame
  Her own lute thou wilt see: no time to spare,
For I am slow and feeble, and scarce dare
On such a catering trust my dizzy head.
  Wait here, my child, with patience kneel in prayer
The while: Ah! thou must needs the lady wed,
Or may I never leave my grave among the dead."

XXI.

So saying she hobbled off with busy fear.
  The lover's endless minutes slowly pass'd;
The dame return'd, and whisper'd in his ear
  To follow her; with agèd eyes aghast
From fright of dim espial. Safe at last,
Through many a dusky gallery, they gain
  The maiden's chamber, silken, hush'd and chaste;
Where Porphyro took covert, pleased amain.
His poor guide hurried back with agues in her brain.

XXII.

Her faltering hand upon the balustrade,
  Old Angela was feeling for the stair,
When Madeline, St. Agnes' charmèd maid,
  Rose, like a mission'd spirit, unaware:
With silver taper's light, and pious care,
She turn'd, and down the aged gossip led
  To a safe level matting. Now prepare,
Young Porphyro, for gazing on that bed;
She comes, she comes again, like ring-dove fray'd and fled.

XXIII.

Out went the taper as she hurried in;
   Its little smoke, in pallid moonshine, died:
She closed the door, she panted, all akin
   To spirits of the air, and visions wide:
No utter'd syllable, or, woe betide!
But to her heart, her heart was voluble,
   Paining with eloquence her balmy side;
As though a tongueless nightingale should swell
Her throat in vain, and die, heart-stifled, in her dell.

XXIV.

A casement high and triple-arch'd there was,
   All garlanded with carven imageries
Of fruits, and flowers, and bunches of knot-grass,
   And diamonded with panes of quaint device,
   Innumerable of stains and splendid dyes,
As are the tiger-moth's deep-damask'd wings;
   And in the midst, 'mong thousand heraldries,
And twilight saints, and dim emblazonings,
A shielded scutcheon blush'd with blood of queens and kings.

XXV.

Full on this casement shone the wintry moon,
   And threw warm gules on Madeline's fair breast,
As down she knelt for Heaven's grace and boon;
   Rose-bloom fell on her hands, together prest,
   And on her silver cross soft amethyst,
And on her hair a glory, like a saint:
   She seem'd a splendid angel, newly drest,
Save wings, for heaven. Porphyro grew faint:
She knelt, so pure a thing, so free from mortal taint.

XXVI.

Anon his heart revives: her vespers done,
   Of all its wreathèd pearls her hair she frees;
Unclasps her warmèd jewels one by one;
   Loosens her fragrant bodice; by degrees
   Her rich attire creeps rustling to her knees:
Half-hidden, like a mermaid in sea-weed,
   Pensive a while she dreams awake, and sees,
In fancy, fair St. Agnes in her bed,
But dares not look behind, or all the charm is fled.

XXVII.

Soon trembling in her soft and chilly nest,
   In sort of wakeful swoon, perplex'd she lay,
Until the poppied warmth of sleep oppress'd
   Her soothèd limbs, and soul fatigued away;
   Flown, like a thought, until the morrow-day;
Blissfully haven'd both from joy and pain;
   Clasp'd like a missal where swart Paynims pray;
Blinded alike from sunshine and from rain,
As though a rose should shut, and be a bud again.

XXVIII.

Stolen to this paradise, and so entranced,
   Porphyro gazed upon her empty dress,
And listen'd to her breathing, if it chanced
   To wake into a slumberous tenderness;
   Which when he heard, that minute did he bless,
And breathed himself: then from the closet crept,
   Noiseless as fear in a wide wilderness,
And over the hush'd carpet, silent stept,
And 'tween the curtains peep'd, where, lo!—how fast she slept.

XXIX.

Then by the bed-side, where the faded moon
   Made a dim, silver twilight, soft he set

A table, and, half anguish'd, threw thereon
  A cloth of woven crimson, gold, and jet:—
  Oh for some drowsy Morphean amulet!
The boisterous, midnight, festive clarion,
  The kettle-drum, and far-heard clarionet,
Affray his ears, though but in dying tone:—
The hall-door shuts again, and all the noise is gone.

XXX.

And still she slept an azure-lidded sleep,
  In blanchèd linen, smooth, and lavender'd;
While he from forth the closet brought a heap
  Of candied apple, quince, and plum, and gourd;
With jellies soother than the creamy curd,
  And lucent syrops, tinct with cinnamon;
Manna and dates, in argosy transferr'd
From Fez; and spicèd dainties, every one,
From silken Samarcand to cedar'd Lebanon.

XXXI.

These delicates he heap'd with glowing hand
  On golden dishes and in baskets bright
Of wreathèd silver. Sumptuous they stand
  In the retired quiet of the night,
  Filling the chilly room with perfume light.—
"And now, my love, my seraph fair, awake!
  Thou art my heaven, and I thine eremite;
Open thine eyes, for meek St. Agnes' sake,
Or I shall drowse beside thee, so my soul doth ache."

XXXII.

Thus whispering, his warm, unnervèd arm
  Sank in her pillow. Shaded was her dream
By the dusk curtains:—'twas a midnight charm
  Impossible to melt as icèd stream:
  The lustrous salvers in the moonlight gleam;
Broad golden fringe upon the carpet lies;
  It seem'd he never, never could redeem
From such a steadfast spell his lady's eyes;
So mused a while, entoil'd in woofèd phantasies.

XXXIII.

Awakening up, he took her hollow lute,—
  Tumultuous,—and, in chords that tenderest be,
He play'd an ancient ditty, long since mute,
  In Provence called "La belle dame sans mercy:"
Close to her ear touching the melody;—
  Wherewith disturb'd, she utter'd a soft moan:
He ceased—she panted quick—and suddenly
  Her blue affrayèd eyes wide open shone:
Upon his knees he sank, pale as smooth-sculptured stone.

XXXIV.

Her eyes were open, but she still beheld,
  Now wide awake, the vision of her sleep:
There was a painful change, that nigh expell'd
  The blisses of her dream so pure and deep.
At which fair Madeline began to weep,
  And moan forth witless words with many a sigh;
While still her gaze on Porphyro would keep;
  Who knelt, with joinèd hands and piteous eye,
Fearing to move or speak, she look'd so dreamingly.

XXXV.

"Ah, Porphyro!" said she, "but even now
  Thy voice was at sweet tremble in mine ear,
Made tunable with every sweetest vow;
  And those sad eyes were spiritual and clear:
How changed thou art! how pallid, chill and drear!
Give me that voice again, my Porphyro,
  Those looks immortal, those complainings dear!
Oh leave me not in this eternal woe,
For if thou diest, my love, I know not where to go."

XXXVI.

Beyond a mortal man impassion'd far
  At these voluptuous accents, he arose,

Ethereal, flush'd, and like a throbbing star
  Seen 'mid the sapphire heaven's deep repose;
Into her dream he melted, as the rose
Blendeth its odor with the violet,—
  Solution sweet: meantime the frost-wind blows
Like love's alarum pattering the sharp sleet
Against the window-panes; St. Agnes' moon hath set.

XXXVII.

'Tis dark: quick pattereth the flaw-blown sleet:
"This is no dream, my bride, my Madeline!"
'Tis dark: the icèd gusts still rave and beat:
"No dream, alas! alas! and woe is mine!
Porphyro will leave me here to fade and pine.—
Cruel! what traitor could thee hither bring?
I curse not, for my heart is lost in thine,
Though thou forsakest a deceivèd thing;—
A dove forlorn and lost, with sick, unprunèd wing."

XXXVIII.

"My Madeline! sweet dreamer! lovely bride!
Say, may I be for aye thy vassal blest?
Thy beauty's shield, heart-shaped and vermeil-dyed?
Ah, silver shrine, here will I take my rest
After so many hours of toil and quest,
A famish'd pilgrim,—saved by miracle.
Though I have found, I will not rob thy nest,
Saving of thy sweet self; if thou think'st well
To trust, fair Madeline, to no rude infidel.

XXXIX.

"Hark! 'tis an elfin storm from faery land,
  Of haggard seeming, but a boon indeed:
Arise—arise! the morning is at hand;—
  The bloated wassailers will never heed.
Let us away, my love, with happy speed;
There are no ears to hear, or eyes to see,—
  Drown'd all in Rhenish and the sleepy mead.
Awake! arise! my love, and fearless be,
For o'er the southern moors I have a home for thee."

XL.

She hurried at his words, beset with fears,
  For there were sleeping dragons all around,
At glaring watch, perhaps, with ready spears—
  Down the wide stairs a darkling way they found,
In all the house was heard no human sound.
A chain-droop'd lamp was flickering by each door;
The arras, rich with horseman, hawk, and hound,
Flutter'd in the besieging wind's uproar;
And the long carpets rose along the gusty floor.

XLI.

They glide like phantoms into the wide hall!
  Like phantoms to the iron porch they glide,
Where lay the porter, in uneasy sprawl,
  With a huge empty flagon by his side:
The wakeful bloodhound rose, and shook his hide,
But his sagacious eye an inmate owns:
By one and one the bolts full easy slide:
The chains lie silent on the footworn stones;
The key turns, and the door upon its hinges groans.

XLII.

And they are gone: ay, ages long ago
  These lovers fled away into the storm.
That night the baron dreamt of many a woe,
  And all his warrior-guests, with shade and form
Of witch, and demon, and large coffin-worm,
Were long benightmared. Angela the old
Died palsy-twitched, with meagre face deform;

The beadsman, after thousand aves told,
For aye unsought-for slept among his
    ashes cold.
                                JOHN KEATS.

JOCK OF HAZELDEAN.

"WHY weep ye by the tide, ladie?
    Why weep ye by the tide?
I'll wed ye to my youngest son,
    And ye sall be his bride;
And ye sall be his bride, ladie,
    Sae comely to be seen;"—
But aye she loot the tears down fa'
    For Jock of Hazeldean.

"Now let this wilful grief be done,
    And dry that cheek so pale;
Young Frank is chief of Errington,
    And lord of Langley-dale;
His step is first in peaceful ha',
    His sword in battle keen;"—
But aye she loot the tears down fa'
    For Jock of Hazeldean.

"A chain of gold ye shall not lack,
    Nor braid to bind your hair,
Nor mettled hound, nor managed hawk,
    Nor palfrey fresh and fair;
And you, the foremost o' them a',
    Shall ride our forest queen;"—
But aye she loot the tears down fa'
    For Jock of Hazeldean.

The kirk was deck'd at morning tide,
    The tapers glimmer'd fair,
The priest and bridegroom wait the bride,
    And dame and knight are there.
They sought her baith by bower and ha',
    The lady was not seen!—
She's o'er the Border, and awa'
    Wi' Jock of Hazeldean!
                        SIR WALTER SCOTT.

SONNETS FROM THE PORTUGUESE.

IF thou must love me, let it be for naught
    Except for love's sake only. Do not say
    "I love her for her smile, her look, her
        way
Of speaking gently,—for a trick of thought
That falls in well with mine, and certes
        brought
A sense of pleasant ease on such a
    day—"
For these things in themselves, beloved,
    may
Be changed, or change for thee,—and
    love, so wrought,
May be unwrought so. Neither love me
    for
Thine own dear pity's wiping my cheeks
    dry,—
A creature might forget to weep, who
    bore
Thy comfort long, and lose thy love
    thereby!
But love me for love's sake, that ever-
    more
Thou mayst love on, through love's
    eternity.

I NEVER gave a lock of hair away
    To a man, dearest, except this to thee,
Which now upon my fingers thought-
        fully
I ring out to the full brown length, and
        say,
"Take it." My day of youth went yester-
        day:
My hair no longer bounds to my foot's
    glee,
Nor plant I it from rose or myrtle tree,
As girls do, any more: it only may
Now shade on two pale cheeks the mark
    of tears,
Taught drooping from the head that
    hangs aside
Through sorrow's trick. I thought the
    funeral shears
Would take this first, but love is justi-
    fied,—
Take it thou,—finding pure, from all those
    years,
The kiss my mother left here when she
    died.

SAY over again, and yet once over again,
    That thou dost love me. Though the
        word repeated
Should seem "a cuckoo-song," as thou
        dost treat it.
Remember, never to the hill or plain,

Valley and wood, without her cuckoo-
    strain,
  Comes the fresh Spring in all her green
    completed.
Beloved, I, amid the darkness greeted
  By a doubtful spirit-voice, in that doubt's
    pain
Cry, "Speak once more—thou lovest!"
    Who can fear
  Too many stars, though each in heaven
    shall roll—
Too many flowers, though each shall crown
    the year?
  Say thou dost love me, love me, love
    me—toll
The silver iterance!—only minding, dear,
  To love me also in silence with thy soul.

My letters! all dead paper, . . . mute and
    white!
  And yet they seem alive and quivering
    Against my tremulous hands which
    loose the string
And let them drop down on my knee to-
    night.
This said, . . . he wish'd to have me in
    his sight
  Once, as a friend: this fix'd a day in
    spring
  To come and touch my hand . . . a
    simple thing,
Yet I wept for it! this, . . . the paper's
    light, . . .
Said, *Dear, I love thee;* and I sank and
    quail'd
  As if God's future thunder'd on my past.
This said, *I am thine,*—and so its ink has
    paled
  With lying at my heart that beat too
    fast.
And this . . . O Love, thy words have ill
    avail'd,
  If what this said, I dared repeat at last!

If I leave all for thee, wilt thou exchange
  And be all to me? Shall I never miss
  Home-talk and blessing and the com-
    mon kiss
That comes to each in turn, nor count it
    strange,
When I look up, to drop on a new range
  Of walls and floors—another home than
    this?
  Nay, wilt thou fill that place by me
    which is
Fill'd by dead eyes too tender to know
    change?
That's hardest. If to conquer love has tried,
  To conquer grief tries more, as all things
    prove;
For grief indeed is love and grief beside.
  Alas, I have grieved so, I am hard to
    love.
Yet love me—wilt thou? Open thine
    heart wide,
  And fold within the wet wings of thy dove.

First time he kiss'd me, he but only kiss'd
  The fingers of this hand wherewith I
    write;
  And ever since, it grew more clean and
    white,
Slow to world-greetings, quick with its
    "Oh, list,"
When the angels speak. A ring of ame-
    thyst
  I could not wear here, plainer to my
    sight,
  Than that first kiss. The second pass'd
    in height
The first, and sought the forehead, and
    half miss'd,
Half falling on the hair. Oh, beyond
    meed!
  That was the chrism of love, which love's
    own crown,
With sanctifying sweetness, did precede.
  The third upon my lips was folded down
In perfect, purple state; since when, in-
    deed,
  I have been proud, and said, "My love,
    my own!"

How do I love thee? Let me count the
    ways:
  I love thee to the depth and breadth
    and height
  My soul can reach, when feeling out of
    sight
For the ends of being and ideal grace.

I love thee to the level of every day's
  Most quiet need, by sun and candlelight.
I love thee freely, as men strive for right;
  I love thee purely, as they turn from praise.
I love thee with the passion put to use
  In my old griefs, and with my childhood's faith.
I love thee with a love I seem'd to lose
  With my lost saints. I love thee with the breath,
Smiles, tears, of all my life; and, if God choose,
  I shall but love thee better after death.
                ELIZABETH BARRETT BROWNING.

LOCHINVAR.

OH, young Lochinvar is come out of the West,—
Through all the wide Border his steed was the best,
And save his good broadsword he weapons had none,—
He rode all unarm'd and he rode all alone.
So faithful in love, and so dauntless in war,
There never was knight like the young Lochinvar.

He stay'd not for brake, and he stopp'd not for stone,
He swam the Eske river where ford there was none,
But ere he alighted at Netherby gate,
The bride had consented, the gallant came late;
For a laggard in love and a dastard in war
Was to wed the fair Ellen of brave Lochinvar.

So boldly he enter'd the Netherby hall,
'Mong bridesmen and kinsmen and brothers and all.
Then spoke the bride's father, his hand on his sword
(For the poor craven bridegroom said never a word),
"Oh, come ye in peace here, or come ye in war,
Or to dance at our bridal, young Lord Lochinvar?"

"I long woo'd your daughter,—my suit you denied;
Love swells like the Solway, but ebbs like its tide;
And now am I come, with this lost love of mine
To lead but one measure, drink one cup of wine.
There are maidens in Scotland more lovely, by far,
That would gladly be bride to the young Lochinvar."

The bride kiss'd the goblet, the knight took it up,
He quaff'd off the wine and he threw down the cup.
She look'd down to blush, and she look'd up to sigh,
With a smile on her lips and a tear in her eye.
He took her soft hand ere her mother could bar:
"Now tread we a measure," said young Lochinvar.

So stately his form, and so lovely her face,
That never a hall such a galliard did grace,
While her mother did fret, and her father did fume,
And the bridegroom stood dangling his bonnet and plume,
And the bridemaidens whisper'd, "'Twere better by far
To have match'd our fair cousin with young Lochinvar."

One touch to her hand, and one word in her ear,
When they reach'd the hall-door, and the charger stood near;
So light to the croupe the fair lady he swung,
So light to the saddle before her he sprung!
"She is won! we are gone, over bank, bush, and scaur;
They'll have fleet steeds that follow," quoth young Lochinvar.

There was mounting 'mong Græmes of the
  Netherby clan;
Forsters, Fenwicks, and Musgraves, they
  rode and they ran;
There was racing and chasing on Cannobie
  Lee,
But the lost bride of Netherby ne'er did
  they see.
So daring in love, and so dauntless in
  war,
Have ye e'er heard of gallant like young
  Lochinvar?
SIR WALTER SCOTT.

AULD ROBIN GRAY.

WHEN the sheep are in the fauld, when
  the kye's come hame,
When a' the weary warld to rest are
  gane,
The waes o' my heart fa' in showers frae
  my ee,
Unkenn'd by my gudeman, wha sleeps
  sound by me.

Young Jamie lo'ed me weel, and sought
  me for his bride;
But saving ae crown-piece, he had naething
  beside;
To make the crown a pound, my Jamie
  gaed to sea;
And the crown and the pound,—they
  were baith for me!

He hadna been gane a twelvemonth and
  a day,
When my father brake his arm, and the
  cow was stown away;
My mither she fell sick—my Jamie was at
  sea—
And Auld Robin Gray came a-courting
  me.

My father cou'dna wark, my mother
  cou'dna spin;
I toil'd day and night, but their bread I
  cou'dna win;
Auld Robin maintain'd them baith, and,
  wi' tears in his ee,
Said, "Jeanie, oh! for their sakes, will ye
  no marry me?"

My heart it said na, and I look'd for Jamie
  back;
But hard blew the winds, and his ship was
  a wrack:
His ship was a wrack—Why didna Jamie
  dee?
Or, why am I spared to cry, Wae is me!

My father urged me sair—my mother didna
  speak,
But she lookèd in my face till my heart
  was like to break;
They gied him my hand—my heart was in
  the sea—
And so Robin Gray he was gudeman to
  me.

I hadna been his wife a week but only
  four,
When mournfu' as I sat on the stane at
  my door,
I saw my Jamie's ghaist, for I cou'dna
  think it he,
Till he said, "I'm come hame, love, to
  marry thee!"

Oh sair, sair did we greet, and mickle say
  of a';
I gied him ae kiss, and bade him gang
  awa'—
I wish that I were dead, but I'm na like to
  dee;
For, though my heart is broken, I'm but
  young, Wae is me!

I gang like a ghaist, and I carena much to
  spin;
I darena think o' Jamie, for that wad be
  a sin;
But I'll do my best a gude wife to be,
For, oh! Robin Gray, he is kind to me.
LADY ANNE BARNARD.

TO MARY IN HEAVEN.

THOU lingering star, with lessening ray,
  That lov'st to greet the early morn,
Again thou usher'st in the day
  My Mary from my soul was torn.

O Mary! dear departed shade!
  Where is thy place of blissful rest?

Seest thou thy lover lowly laid?
  Hear'st thou the groans that rend his breast?

That sacred hour can I forget,
  Can I forget the hallow'd grove,
Where by the winding Ayr we met,
  To live one day of parting love?

Eternity will not efface
  Those records dear of transports past;
Thy image at our last embrace;
  Ah! little thought we 'twas our last!

Ayr gurgling kiss'd his pebbled shore,
  O'erhung with wild woods, thickening, green,
The fragrant birch, and hawthorn hoar,
  Twined amorous round the raptured scene.

The flowers sprang wanton to be press'd,
  The birds sang love on every spray,
Till too, too soon, the glowing west
  Proclaim'd the speed of wingèd day.

Still o'er these scenes my memory wakes,
  And fondly broods with miser care!
Time but the impression deeper makes,
  As streams their channels deeper wear.

My Mary, dear departed shade!
  Where is thy blissful place of rest?
Seest thou thy lover lowly laid?
  Hear'st thou the groans that rend his breast?
                ROBERT BURNS.

THE LADY'S YES.

"YES," I answer'd you last night;
  "No," this morning, sir, I say:
Colors seen by candle-light
  Will not look the same by day.

When the viols play'd their best,
  Lamps above and laughs below,
Love me sounded like a jest,
  Fit for *yes* or fit for *no*.

Call me false or call me free,
  Vow, whatever light may shine,—
No man on your face shall see
  Any grief for change on mine.

Yet the sin is on us both;
  Time to dance is not to woo;
Wooing light makes fickle troth,
  Scorn of *me* recoils on *you*.

Learn to win a lady's faith
  Nobly, as the thing is high,
Bravely, as for life and death,
  With a loyal gravity.

Lead her from the festive boards,
  Point her to the starry skies;
Guard her, by your truthful words
  Pure from courtship's flatteries.

By your truth she shall be true,
  Ever true, as wives of yore;
And her *yes*, once said to you,
  SHALL be Yes for evermore.
              ELIZABETH BARRETT BROWNING.

LADY CLARE.

IT was the time when lilies blow,
  And clouds are highest up in air,
Lord Ronald brought a lily-white doe
  To give his cousin, Lady Clare.

I trow they did not part in scorn:
  Lovers long betroth'd were they:
They two will wed the morrow morn:
  God's blessing on the day!

"He does not love me for my birth,
  Nor for my lands so broad and fair;
He loves me for my own true worth,
  And that is well," said Lady Clare.

In there came old Alice the nurse,
  Said, "Who was this that went from thee?"
"It was my cousin," said Lady Clare,
  "To-morrow he weds with me."

"Oh, God be thank'd!" said Alice the nurse,
  "That all comes round so just and fair:
Lord Ronald is heir of all your lands,
  And you are not the Lady Clare."

"Are ye out of your mind, my nurse, my nurse?"
  Said Lady Clare, "that ye speak so wild?"
"As God's above," said Alice the nurse,
  "I speak the truth: you are my child.

"The old earl's daughter died at my breast;
  I speak the truth, as I live by bread!
I buried her like my own sweet child,
  And put my child in her stead."

"Falsely, falsely have ye done,
  O mother," she said, "if this be true,
To keep the best man under the sun
  So many years from his due."

"Nay now, my child," said Alice the nurse,
  "But keep the secret for your life,
And all you have will be Lord Ronald's,
  When you are man and wife."

"If I'm a beggar born," she said,
  "I will speak out, for I dare not lie.
Pull off, pull off the brooch of gold,
  And fling the diamond necklace by."

"Nay now, my child," said Alice the nurse,
  "But keep the secret all ye can."
She said, "Not so: but I will know
  If there be any faith in man."

"Nay now, what faith?" said Alice the nurse,
  "The man will cleave unto his right."
"And he shall have it," the lady replied,
  "Though I should die to-night."

"Yet give one kiss to your mother, dear!
  Alas, my child, I sinn'd for thee."
"O mother, mother, mother," she said,
  "So strange it seems to me!

"Yet here's a kiss for my mother dear,
  My mother dear, if this be so,
And lay your hand upon my head,
  And bless me, mother, ere I go."

She clad herself in a russet gown,
  She was no longer Lady Clare:
She went by dale, and she went by down,
  With a single rose in her hair.

The lily-white doe Lord Ronald had brought
  Leapt up from where she lay,
Dropp'd her head in the maiden's hand,
  And follow'd her all the way.

Down stepp'd Lord Ronald from his tower:
  "O Lady Clare, you shame your worth!
Why come you dress'd like a village maid,
  That are the flower of the earth?"

"If I come dress'd like a village maid,
  I am but as my fortunes are:
I am a beggar born," she said,
  "And not the Lady Clare."

"Play me no tricks," said Lord Ronald,
  "For I am yours in word and in deed.
Play me no tricks," said Lord Ronald,
  "Your riddle is hard to read."

Oh, and proudly stood she up!
  Her heart within her did not fail:
She look'd into Lord Ronald's eyes,
  And told him all her nurse's tale.

He laugh'd a laugh of merry scorn:
  He turn'd and kiss'd her where she stood:
"If you are not the heiress born,
  And I," said he, "the next in blood—

"If you are not the heiress born,
  And I," said he, "the lawful heir,
We two will wed to-morrow morn,
  And you shall still be Lady Clare."
                                ALFRED TENNYSON.

LOVE NOT ME FOR COMELY GRACE.

LOVE not me for comely grace,
  For my pleasing eye or face,
Nor for any outward part,
No, nor for my constant heart,—
  For those may fail, or turn to ill,
  So thou and I shall sever:
Keep therefore a true woman's eye,
And love me still, but know not why—
  So hast thou the same reason still
    To doat upon me ever!
                                AUTHOR UNKNOWN.

THE LOVELINESS OF LOVE.

IT is not beauty I demand,
  A crystal brow, the moon's despair,
Nor the snow's daughter, a white hand,
  Nor mermaid's yellow pride of hair:

Tell me not of your starry eyes,
  Your lips that seem on roses fed,
Your breasts, where Cupid tumbling lies,
  Nor sleeps for kissing of his bed:—

A bloomy pair of vermeil cheeks
　Like Hebe's in her ruddiest hours,
A breath that softer music speaks
　Than summer winds a-wooing flowers,

These are but gauds : nay what are lips?
　Coral beneath the ocean stream,
Whose brink when your adventurer slips
　Full oft he perisheth on them.

And what are cheeks, but ensigns oft
　That wave hot youth to fields of blood?
Did Helen's breast, though ne'er so soft,
　Do Greece or Ilium any good?

Eyes can with baleful ardor burn ;
　Poison can breath, that erst perfumed ;
There's many a white hand holds an urn
　With lovers' hearts to dust consumed.

For crystal brows there's naught within ;
　They are but empty cells for pride ;
He who the siren's hair would win
　Is mostly strangled in the tide.

Give me, instead of Beauty's bust,
　A tender heart, a loyal mind
Which with temptation I would trust,
　Yet never link'd with error find,—

One in whose gentle bosom I
　Could pour my secret heart of woes,
Like the care-burthen'd honey-fly
　That hides his murmurs in the rose,—

My earthly Comforter ! whose love
　So indefeasible might be
That, when my spirit wonn'd above,
　Hers could not stay, for sympathy.
　　　　　　　　　AUTHOR UNKNOWN.

MILK-MAID'S SONG.
THE SHEPHERD TO HIS LOVE.

COME live with me, and be my love,
And we will all the pleasures prove
That valleys, groves, or hills, or field,
Or woods and steepy mountains yield ;

Where we will sit upon the rocks,
And see the shepherds feed our flocks
By shallow rivers, to whose falls
Melodious birds sing madrigals.

And I will make thee beds of roses,
And then a thousand fragrant posies,
A cap of flowers, and a kirtle
Embroider'd all with leaves of myrtle ;

A gown made of the finest wool
Which from our pretty lambs we pull ;
Slippers lined choicely for the cold,
With buckles of the purest gold ;

A belt of straw and ivy buds,
With coral clasps and amber studs ;
And if these pleasures may thee move,
Come live with me, and be my love.

Thy silver dishes for my meat,
As precious as the gods do eat,
Shall, on an ivory table, be
Prepared each day for thee and me.

The shepherd swains shall dance and sing
For thy delight, each May morning.
If these delights thy mind may move,
Then live with me and be my love.
　　　　　　　　　CHRISTOPHER MARLOWE.

MILK-MAID'S MOTHER'S ANSWER.
THE NYMPH'S REPLY.

IF all the world and love were young,
And truth in every shepherd's tongue,
These pretty pleasures might me move
To live with thee and be thy love.

But time drives flocks from field to fold,
When rivers rage and rocks grow cold ;
Then Philomel becometh dumb,
And age complains of care to come.

The flowers do fade, and wanton fields
To wayward winter reckoning yields.
A honey tongue, a heart of gall,
Is fancy's spring, but sorrow's fall.

Thy gowns, thy shoes, thy beds of roses,
Thy cap, thy kirtle, and thy posies,
Soon break, soon wither, soon forgotten :
In folly ripe, in reason rotten.

Thy belt of straw and ivy buds,
Thy coral clasps and amber studs,
All these in me no means can move
To come to thee, and be thy love.

What should we talk of dainties, then,
Of better meat than's fit for men?
These are but vain: that's only good
Which God hath bless'd, and sent for
  food.

But could youth last and love still breed,
Had joys no date, nor age no need,
Then those delights my mind might move
To live with thee, and be thy love.
SIR WALTER RALEIGH.

ON A DAY, ALACK THE DAY!

ON a day, alack the day!
Love, whose month is ever May,
Spied a blossom passing fair
Playing in the wanton air:
Through the velvet leaves the wind
All unseen 'gan passage find;
That the lover, sick to death,
Wish'd himself the heaven's breath.
Air, quoth he, thy cheeks may blow;
Air, would I might triumph so!
But, alack, my hand is sworn
Ne'er to pluck thee from thy thorn:
Vow, alack, for youth unmeet;
Youth so apt to pluck a sweet.
Do not call it sin in me
That I am forsworn for thee:
Thou for whom e'en Jove would swear
Juno but an Ethiope were,
And deny himself for Jove,
Turning mortal for thy love.
WILLIAM SHAKESPEARE.

WOMAN'S INCONSTANCY.

I LOVED thee once, I'll love no more,
  Thine be the grief as is the blame;
Thou art not what thou wast before,
  What reason I should be the same?
    He that can love unloved again,
    Hath better store of love than brain:
  God send me love my debts to pay,
  While unthrifts fool their love away.

Nothing could have my love o'erthrown,
  If thou hadst still continued mine;
Yea, if thou hadst remain'd thy own,
  I might perchance have yet been thine.

But thou thy freedom did recall,
  That if thou might elsewhere inthrall;
And then how could I but disdain
  A captive's captive to remain?

When new desires had conquer'd thee,
  And changed the object of thy will,
It had been lethargy in me,
  Not constancy, to love thee still.
    Yea, it had been a sin to go
    And prostitute affection so,
  Since we are taught no prayers to say
  To such as must to others pray.

Yet do thou glory in thy choice,
  Thy choice of his good fortune boast;
I'll neither grieve nor yet rejoice,
  To see him gain what I have lost;
    The height of my disdain shall be,
    To laugh at him, to blush for thee;
  To love thee still, but go no more
  A begging to a beggar's door.
SIR ROBERT AYTON.

THE MAID'S LAMENT.

I LOVED him not; and yet now he is
    gone,
  I feel I am alone.
I checkt him while he spoke; yet could
    he speak,
  Alas! I would not check.
For reasons not to love him once I
    sought,
  And wearied all my thought
To vex myself and him: I now would give
  My love, could he but live
Who lately lived for me, and when he
    found
  'Twas vain, in holy ground
He hid his face amid the shades of death!
  I waste for him my breath
Who wasted his for me; but mine returns,
  And this lone bosom burns
With stifling heat, heaving it up in sleep,
  And waking me to weep
Tears that had melted his soft heart: for
    years
  Wept he as bitter tears!
"Merciful God!" such was his latest prayer
  "These may she never share!"
Quieter is his breath, his breast more cold
  Than daisies in the mould,

Where children spell athwart the church-
yard gate
His name and life's brief date.
Pray for him, gentle souls, whoe'er ye be,
And oh, pray, too, for me!
WALTER SAVAGE LANDOR.

THE SHEPHERD'S WIFE'S SONG.

AH! what is love? It is a pretty thing,
As sweet unto a shepherd as a king,
And sweeter too;
For kings have cares that wait upon a
crown,
And cares can make the sweetest face to
frown:
Ah then, ah then,
If country loves such sweet desires gain,
What lady would not love a shepherd
swain?

His flocks are folded; he comes home at
night
As merry as a king in his delight,
And merrier too;
For kings bethink them what the state re-
quire,
Where shepherds, careless, carol by the fire:
Ah then, ah then,
If country love such sweet desires gain,
What lady would not love a shepherd
swain?

He kisseth first, then sits as blithe to eat
His cream and curd as doth the king his
meat,
And blither too;
For kings have often fears when they sup,
Where shepherds dread no poison in their
cup:
Ah then, ah then,
If country loves such sweet desires gain,
What lady would not love a shepherd
swain?

Upon his couch of straw he sleeps as sound
As doth the king upon his beds of down,
More sounder too;
For cares cause kings full oft their sleep to
spill,
Where weary shepherds lie and snort their
fill:
Ah then, ah then,
If country loves such sweet desires gain,
What lady would not love a shepherd swain?

Thus with his wife he spends the year as
blithe
As doth the king at every tide or syth,
And blither too;
For kings have wars and broils to take in
hand,
When shepherds laugh, and love upon the
land:
Ah then, ah then,
If country loves such sweet desires gain,
What lady would not love a shepherd
swain?
ROBERT GREENE.

LOVE IN THE VALLEY.

UNDER yonder beech-tree standing on the
green sward,
Couch'd with her arms behind her little
head,
Her knees folded up, and her tresses on her
bosom,
Lies my young love sleeping in the shade.
Had I the heart to slide one arm beneath
her,
Press her dreaming lips as her waist I
folded slow,
Waking on the instant she could not but
embrace me—
Ah! would she hold me, and never let me go?

Shy as the squirrel, and wayward as the
swallow;
Swift as the swallow when, athwart the
western flood,
Circleting the surface, he meets his mir-
ror'd winglets—
Is that dear one in her maiden bud.
Shy as the squirrel whose nest is in the
pine tops;
Gentle—ah! that she were jealous—as the
dove!
Full of all the wildness of the woodland
creatures,
Happy in herself is the maiden that I love!

What can have taught her distrust of all I
tell her?
Can she truly doubt me when looking on
my brows?

Nature never teaches distrust of tender love-tales—
What can have taught her distrust of all my vows?
No, she does not doubt me! on a dewy eve-tide,
Whispering together beneath the listening moon,
I pray'd till her cheek flush'd, implored till she falter'd—
Flutter'd to my bosom—ah! to fly away so soon!

When her mother tends her before the laughing mirror,
Tying up her laces, looping up her hair,
Often she thinks—Were this wild thing wedded,
I should have more love, and much less care.
When her mother tends her before the bashful mirror,
Loosening her laces, combing down her curls,
Often she thinks—Were this wild thing wedded,
I should lose but one for so many boys and girls.

Clambering roses peep into her chamber;
Jasmine and woodbine breathe sweet, sweet;
White-neck'd swallows, twittering of summer,
Fill her with balm and nested peace from head to feet.
Ah! will the rose-bough see her lying lonely,
When the petals fall and fierce bloom is on the leaves?
Will the autumn garners see her still ungather'd,
When the fickle swallows forsake the weeping eaves?

Comes a sudden question—should a strange hand pluck her!
Oh, what an anguish smites me at the thought!
Should some idle lordling bribe her mind with jewels!—
Can such beauty ever thus be bought?

Sometimes the huntsmen, prancing down the valley,
Eye the village lasses, full of sprightly mirth;
They see, as I see, mine is the fairest!
Would she were older and could read my worth!

Are there not sweet maidens, if she still deny me?
Show the bridal heavens but one bright star?
Wherefore thus then do I chase a shadow,
Clattering one note like a brown eve-jar?
So I rhyme and reason till she darts before me—
Through the milky meadows from flower to flower she flies,
Sunning her sweet palms to shade her dazzled eyelids
From the golden love that looks too eager in her eyes.

When at dawn she wakens, and her fair face gazes
Out on the weather through the window-panes,
Beauteous she looks! like a white water-lily
Bursting out of bud on the rippled river plains.
When from bed she rises, clothed from neck to ankle
In her long night-gown, sweet as boughs of May,
Beauteous she looks! like a tall garden lily,
Pure from the night and perfect for the day!

Happy, happy time, when the gray star twinkles
Over the fields all fresh with bloomy dew;
When the cold-cheek'd dawn grows ruddy up the twilight,
And the gold sun wakes and weds her in the blue.
Then when my darling tempts the early breezes,
She the only star that dies not with the dark!
Powerless to speak all the ardor of my passion,
I catch her little hand as we listen to the lark.

Shall the birds in vain then valentine their
    sweethearts?
Season after season tell a fruitless tale?
Will not the virgin listen to their voices?
Take the honey'd meaning, wear the bridal
    veil?
Fears she frosts of winter, fears she the
    bare branches?
Waits she the garlands of spring for her
    dower?
Is she a nightingale that will not be nested
Till the April woodland has built her bridal
    bower?

Then come, merry April, with all thy birds
    and beauties!
With thy crescent brows and thy flowery,
    showery glee;
With thy budding leafage and fresh green
    pastures;
And may thy lustrous crescent grow a hon-
    eymoon for me!
Come, merry month of the cuckoo and the
    violet!
Come, weeping loveliness in all thy blue
    delight!
Lo! the nest is ready, let me not languish
    longer!
Bring her to my arms on the first May night.
                      GEORGE MEREDITH.

DUNCAN GRAY.

DUNCAN GRAY cam here to woo,
    Ha, ha, the wooing o't,
On blythe Yule night when we were fou,
    Ha, ha, the wooing o't:
Maggie coost her head fu' high,
Look'd asklent and unco' skeigh,
Gart poor Duncan stand abeigh;
    Ha, ha, the wooing o't!

Duncan fleech'd, and Duncan pray'd,
    Ha, ha, the wooing o't;
Meg was deaf as Ailsa Craig;
    Ha, ha, the wooing o't.
Duncan sigh'd baith out and in,
Grat his een baith bleert an' blin',
Spak o' lowpin o'er a linn;
    Ha, ha, the wooing o't.

Time and chance are but a tide,
    Ha, ha, the wooing o't;
Slighted love is sair to bide,
    Ha, ha, the wooing o't.
Shall I, like a fool, quoth he,
For a haughty hizzie dee?
She may gae to—France for me!
    Ha, ha, the wooing o't.

How it comes let doctors tell,
    Ha, ha, the wooing o't;
Meg grew sick—as he grew heal,
    Ha, ha, the wooing o't.
Something in her bosom wrings,
For relief a sigh she brings;
And oh, her een, they spak sic things!
    Ha, ha, the wooing o't.

Duncan was a lad o' grace,
    Ha, ha, the wooing o't;
Maggie's was a piteous case,
    Ha, ha, the wooing o't.
Duncan couldna be her death,
Swelling pity smoor'd his wrath;
Now they're crouse and canty baith,
    Ha, ha, the wooing o't.
                      ROBERT BURNS.

RUTH.

SHE stood breast-high amid the corn,
Clasp'd by the golden light of morn,
Like the sweetheart of the sun,
Who many a glowing kiss had won.

On her cheek an autumn flush
Deeply ripen'd;—such a blush
In the midst of brown was born,
Like red poppies grown with corn.

Round her eyes her tresses fell,
Which were blackest none could tell,
But long lashes veil'd a light,
That had else been all too bright.

And her hat, with shady brim,
Made her tressy forehead dim;
Thus she stood amid the stooks,
Praising God with sweetest looks:—

Sure, I said, heav'n did not mean,
Where I reap thou shouldst but glean,
Lay thy sheaf adown and come,
Share my harvest and my home.
                      THOMAS HOOD.

PHILLIDA AND CORYDON.

In the merrie moneth of Maye,
In a morne by break of daye,
With a troope of damselles playing
Forthe "I yode" forsooth a-maying:

When anon by a wood side,
Where as Maye was in his pride,
I espièd all alone
Phillida and Corydon.

Much adoe there was, god wot;
He wold love, and she wold not.
She sayde, never man was trewe;
He sayes, none was false to you.

He sayde, hee had lovde her longe:
She sayes, love should have no wronge.
Corydon wold kisse her then:
She sayes, maydes must kisse no men,

Tyll they doe for good and all.
When she made the shepperde call
All the heavens to wytnes truthe,
Never loved a truer youthe.

Then with manie a prettie othe,
Yea and nay, and faith and trothe;
Suche as seelie shepperdes use
When they will not love abuse;

Love, that had bene long deluded,
Was with kisses sweete concluded;
And Phillida with garlands gaye
Was made the lady of the Maye.
NICHOLAS BRETON.

MAID OF ATHENS.

Maid of Athens, ere we part,
Give, oh, give me back my heart!
Or, since that has left my breast,
Keep it now, and take the rest!
Hear my vow before I go,
Ζώη μοῦ, σὰς ἀγαπῶ.

By those tresses unconfined,
Woo'd by each Ægean wind;
By those lids whose jetty fringe
Kiss thy soft cheeks' blooming tinge,
By those wild eyes like the roe,
Ζώη μοῦ, σὰς ἀγαπῶ.

By that lip I long to taste;
By that zone-encircled waist;
By all the token-flowers that tell
What words can never speak so well;
By love's alternate joy and woe,
Ζώη μοῦ, σὰς ἀγαπῶ.

Maid of Athens! I am gone:
Think of me, sweet! when alone.—
Though I fly to Istambol,
Athens holds my heart and soul:
Can I cease to love thee? No!
Ζώη μοῦ, σὰς ἀγαπῶ.
LORD BYRON.

ADELGITHA.

The Ordeal's fatal trumpet sounded,
  And sad, pale *Adelgitha* came,
When forth a valiant champion bounded,
  And slew the slanderer of her fame.

She wept, deliver'd from her danger;
  But when he knelt to claim her glove—
"Seek not," she cried, "O gallant stranger,
  For hapless Adelgitha's love.

"For he is in a foreign far land
  Whose arm should now have set me free;
And I must wear the willow garland
  For him that's dead, or false to me."

"Nay! say not that his faith is tainted!"—
  He raised his visor,—at the sight
She fell into his arms and fainted;
  It was indeed her own true knight.
THOMAS CAMPBELL.

BONNIE LESLEY.

Oh saw ye bonnie Lesley
  As she gaed o'er the border?
She's gane, like Alexander,
  To spread her conquests farther.

To see her is to love her,
  And love but her for ever;
For Nature made her what she is,
  And never made anither.

Thou art a queen, fair Lesley—
  Thy subjects we, before thee;
Thou art divine, fair Lesley—
  The hearts o' men adore thee.

The deil he could na scaith thee,
  Or aught that wad belang thee;
He'd look into thy bonnie face,
  And say, "I canna wrang thee."

The powers aboon will tent thee;
  Misfortune sha'na steer thee;
Thou'rt like themsel' sae lovely,
  That ill they'll ne'er let near thee.

Return again, fair Lesley!
  Return to Caledonie!
That we may brag we hae a lass
  There's nane again sae bonnie.
               ROBERT BURNS.

THE GIRL OF CADIZ.

OH never talk again to me
  Of northern climes and British ladies;
It has not been your lot to see,
  Like me, the lovely girl of Cadiz.
Although her eye be not of blue,
  Nor fair her locks, like English lasses,
How far its own expressive hue
  The languid azure eye surpasses!

Prometheus-like, from heaven she stole
  The fire that through those silken lashes
In darkest glances seems to roll,
  From eyes that cannot hide their flashes;
And as along her bosom steal
  In lengthen'd flow her raven tresses,
You'd swear each clustering lock could feel,
  And curl'd to give her neck caresses.

Our English maids are long to woo,
  And frigid even in possession;
And if their charms be fair to view,
  Their lips are slow at Love's confession:
But born beneath a brighter sun,
  For love ordain'd the Spanish maid is,
And who—when fondly, fairly won,—
  Enchants you like the Girl of Cadiz?

The Spanish maid is no coquette,
  Nor joys to see a lover tremble,
And if she love, or if she hate,
  Alike she knows not to dissemble.
Her heart can ne'er be bought or sold—
  Howe'er it beats, it beats sincerely;
And, though it will not bend to gold,
  'Twill love you long and love you dearly.

The Spanish girl that meets your love
  Ne'er taunts you with a mock denial,
For every thought is bent to prove
  Her passion in the hour of trial.
When thronging foemen menace Spain,
  She dares the deed and shares the danger;
And should her lover press the plain,
  She hurls the spear, her love's avenger.

And when, beneath the evening star,
  She mingles in the gay Bolero,
Or sings to her attuned guitar
  Of Christian knight or Moorish hero,
Or counts her beads with fairy hand
  Beneath the twinkling rays of Hesper,
Or joins devotion's choral band,
  To chaunt the sweet and hallow'd vesper,

In each her charms the heart must move
  Of all who venture to behold her;
Then let not maids less fair reprove
  Because her bosom is not colder:
Through many a clime 'tis mine to roam,
  Where many a soft and melting maid is,
But none abroad, and few at home,
  May match the dark-eyed girl of Cadiz
               LORD BYRON.

I LOVE MY LOVE.

WHAT is the meaning of the song
  That rings so clear and loud,
Thou nightingale amid the copse,
  Thou lark above the cloud?
What says thy song, thou joyous thrush,
  Up in the walnut tree?
"I love my Love, because I know
  My Love loves me."

What is the meaning of thy thought,
  O maiden fair and young?
There is such pleasure in thine eyes,
  Such music on thy tongue;
There is such glory on thy face,
  What can the meaning be?
"I love my Love, because I know
  My Love loves me."

Oh happy words! at Beauty's feet
  We sing them ere our prime,
And when the early summers pass,
  And Care comes on with Time,

THE GIRL OF CADIZ.

Still be it ours, in Care's despite,
  To join the chorus free:
"I love my Love, because I know
  My Love loves me."
CHARLES MACKAY.

COME, REST IN THIS BOSOM.

COME, rest in this bosom, my own stricken deer,
Though the herd have fled from thee, thy home is still here;
Here still is the smile that no cloud can o'ercast,
And a heart and a hand all thy own to the last.

Oh, what was love made for, if 'tis not the same
Through joy and through torment, through glory and shame?
I know not, I ask not, if guilt's in that heart,
I but know that I love thee, whatever thou art.

Thou hast call'd me thy angel in moments of bliss,
And thy angel I'll be 'mid the horrors of this,
Through the furnace, unshrinking, thy steps to pursue,
And shield thee, and save thee,—or perish there too!
THOMAS MOORE.

THE SILLER CROUN.

"AND ye sall walk in silk attire,
  And siller hae to spare,
Gin ye'll consent to be his bride,
  Nor think o' Donald mair."

Oh wha wad buy a silken goun
  Wi' a puir broken heart?
Or what's to me a siller croun
  Gin frae my love I part?

The mind, whose meanest wish is pure,
  Far dearest is to me,
And ere I'm forced to break my faith,
  I'll lay me doun an' dee.

For I hae vow'd a virgin's vow
  My lover's fate to share,
An' he has gi'en to me his heart,
  And what can man do mair?

His mind and manners won my heart:
  He gratefu' took the gift;
And did I wish to seek it back,
  It wad be waur than theft.

The langest life can ne'er repay
  The love he bears to me,
And ere I'm forced to break my faith,
  I'll lay me doun an' dee.
SUSANNA BLAMIRE.

MARY MORISON.

O MARY, at thy window be!
  It is the wish'd, the trysted hour!
Those smiles and glances let me see
  That make the miser's treasure poor:
How blithely wad I bide the stoure,
  A weary slave frae sun to sun,
Could I the rich reward secure,
  The lovely Mary Morison!

Yestreen' when to the trembling string
  The dance gaed through the lighted ha',
To thee my fancy took its wing,—
  I sat, but neither heard nor saw:
Though this was fair, and that was braw,
  And yon the toast of a' the town,
I sigh'd, and said amang them a',
  "Ye are na Mary Morison."

O Mary, canst thou wreck his peace
  Wha for thy sake wad gladly dee?
Or canst thou break that heart of his,
  Whase only faut is loving thee?
If love for love thou wilt na gie,
  At least be pity to me shown;
A thought ungentle canna be
  The thought o' Mary Morison.
ROBERT BURNS.

THE MINSTREL'S SONG.

OH, sing unto my roundelay!
  Oh, drop the briny tear with me!
Dance no more at holiday;
  Like a running river be.
    My love is dead,
    Gone to his death bed,
  All under the willow tree.

Black his hair as the winter night,
  White his neck as the summer snow,
Ruddy his face as the morning light;
  Cold he lies in the grave below.
    My love is dead,
    Gone to his death bed,
    All under the willow tree.

Sweet his tongue as the throstle's note;
  Quick in dance as thought can be;
Deft his tabor, cudgel stout;
  Oh, he lies by the willow tree!
    My love is dead,
    Gone to his death bed,
    All under the willow tree.

Hark! the raven flaps his wing
  In the brier'd dell below;
Hark! the death-owl loud doth sing
  To the nightmares as they go.
    My love is dead,
    Gone to his death bed,
    All under the willow tree.

See! the white moon shines on high;
  Whiter is my true-love's shroud,
Whiter than the morning sky,
  Whiter than the evening cloud.
    My love is dead,
    Gone to his deathbed,
    All under the willow tree.

Here, upon my true-love's grave
  Shall the baren flowers be laid,
Nor one holy saint to save
  All the coldness of a maid.
    My love is dead,
    Gone to his death bed,
    All under the willow tree.

With my hands I'll bind the briers
  Round his holy corse to gre;
Ouphante fairy, light your fires;
  Here my body still shall be.
    My love is dead,
    Gone to his death bed,
    All under the willow tree.

Come, with acorn-cup and thorn,
  Drain my heart's blood all away;
Life and all its good I scorn,
  Dance by night, or feast by day.
    My love is dead,
    Gone to his death bed,
    All under the willow tree.

Water-witches, crown'd with reytes,
  Bear me to your lethal tide.
I die! I come! my true love waits.
  Thus the damsel spake, and died.
      THOMAS CHATTERTON.

ONE WORD IS TOO OFTEN PROFANED.

ONE word is too often profaned
  For me to profane it,
One feeling too falsely disdain'd
  For thee to disdain it.
One hope is too like despair
  For prudence to smother,
And pity from thee more dear
  Than that from another.

I can give not what men call love;
  But wilt thou accept not
The worship the heart lifts above
  And the heavens reject not;
The desire of the moth for the star,
  Of the night for the morrow,
The devotion to something afar
  From the sphere of our sorrow?
      PERCY BYSSHE SHELLEY.

TO HIS FORSAKEN MISTRESS.

I DO confess thou'rt smooth and fair,
  And I might have gone near to love thee,
Had I not found the lightest prayer
  That lips could speak, had power to move thee:
But I can let thee now alone,
As worthy to be loved by none.

I do confess thou'rt sweet; yet find
  Thee such an unthrift of thy sweets,
Thy favors are but like the wind,
  That kisses everything it meets;
And since thou canst with more than one,
Thou'rt worthy to be kiss'd by none.

The morning rose that untouch'd stands
  Arm'd with her briers, how sweetly smells!
But pluck'd and strain'd through ruder hands,
  No more her sweetness with her dwells,
But scent and beauty both are gone,
And leaves fall from her, one by one.

Such fate, erelong, will thee betide,
  When thou hast handled been a while,—
Like sere flowers to be thrown aside:
  And I will sigh, while some will smile,
To see thy love for more than one
Hath brought thee to be loved by none.
                    SIR ROBERT AYTON.

LOCKSLEY HALL.

COMRADES, leave me here a little, while as yet 'tis early morn:
Leave me here, and when you want me, sound upon the bugle horn.

'Tis the place, and all around it, as of old, the curlews call,
Dreary gleams about the moorland flying over Locksley Hall;

Locksley Hall that in the distance overlooks the sandy tracts,
And the hollow ocean-ridges roaring into cataracts.

Many a night from yonder ivied casement, ere I went to rest,
Did I look on great Orion sloping slowly to the West.

Many a night I saw the Pleiads, rising thro' the mellow shade,
Glitter like a swarm of fire-flies tangled in a silver braid.

Here about the beach I wander'd, nourishing a youth sublime
With the fairy tales of science, and the long result of Time;

When the centuries behind me like a fruitful land reposed;
When I clung to all the present for the promise that it 'closed:

When I dipt into the future far as human eye could see;
Saw the Vision of the world, and all the wonder that would be.——

In the Spring a fuller crimson comes upon the robin's breast;
In the Spring the wanton lapwing gets himself another crest:

In the Spring a livelier iris changes on the burnish'd dove;
In the Spring a young man's fancy lightly turns to thoughts of love.

Then her cheek was pale and thinner than should be for one so young,
And her eyes on all my motions with a mute observance hung.

And I said, "My cousin Amy, speak, and speak the truth to me,
Trust me, cousin, all the current of my being sets to thee."

On her pallid cheek and forehead came a color and a light,
As I have seen the rosy red flushing in the northern night.

And she turn'd—her bosom shaken with a sudden storm of sighs—
All the spirit deeply dawning in the dark of hazel eyes—

Saying, "I have hid my feelings, fearing they should do me wrong:"
Saying, "Dost thou love me, cousin?" weeping, "I have loved thee long."

Love took up the glass of Time, and turn'd it in his glowing hands;
Every moment, lightly shaken, ran itself in golden sands.

Love took up the harp of Life, and smote on all the chords with might;
Smote the chord of Self, that, trembling, pass'd in music out of sight.

Many a morning on the moorland did we hear the copses ring,
And her whisper throng'd my pulses with the fullness of the Spring.

Many an evening by the waters did we watch the stately ships,
And our spirits rush'd together at the touching of the lips.

O my cousin, shallow-hearted! O my Amy, mine no more!
O the dreary, dreary moorland! O the barren, barren shore!

Falser than all fancy fathoms, falser than
    all songs have sung,
Puppet to a father's threat, and servile to
    a shrewish tongue!

Is it well to wish thee happy?—having
    known me—to decline
On a range of lower feelings and a nar-
    rower heart than mine!

Yet it shall be: thou shalt lower to his
    level day by day,
What is fine within thee growing coarse to
    sympathize with clay.

As the husband is, the wife is: thou art
    mated with a clown,
And the grossness of his nature will have
    weight to drag thee down.

He will hold thee, when his passion shall
    have spent its novel force,
Something better than his dog, a little
    dearer than his horse.

What is this? his eyes are heavy: think
    not they are glazed with wine.
Go to him: it is thy duty: kiss him: take
    his hand in thine.

It may be my lord is weary, that his brain
    is overwrought;
Soothe him with thy finer fancies, touch
    him with thy lighter thought.

He will answer to the purpose, easy things
    to understand—
Better thou wert dead before me, tho' I
    slew thee with my hand!

Better thou and I were lying, hidden from
    the heart's disgrace,
Roll'd in one another's arms, and silent in
    a last embrace.

Curséd be the social wants that sin against
    the strength of youth!
Curséd be the social lies that warp us from
    the living truth!

Curséd be the sickly forms that err from
    honest Nature's rule!
Curséd be the gold that gilds the straiten'd
    forehead of the fool!

Well—'tis well that I should bluster!—
    Hadst thou less unworthy proved—
Would to God—for I had loved thee more
    than ever wife was loved.

Am I mad, that I should cherish that
    which bears but bitter fruit?
I will pluck it from my bosom, tho' my
    heart be at the root.

Never, tho' my mortal summers to such
    length of years should come
As the many winter'd crow that leads the
    clanging rookery home.

Where is comfort? in division of the rec-
    ords of the mind?
Can I part her from herself, and love her,
    as I knew her, kind?

I remember one that perish'd: sweetly did
    she speak and move:
Such a one do I remember, whom to look
    at was to love.

Can I think of her as dead, and love her
    for the love she bore?
No—she never loved me truly: love is love
    for evermore.

Comfort? comfort scorn'd of devils! this
    is truth the poet sings,
That a sorrow's crown of sorrow is remem-
    bering happier things.

Drug thy memories, lest thou learn it, lest
    thy heart be put to proof,
In the dead unhappy night, and when the
    rain is on the roof.

Like a dog, he hunts in dreams, and thou
    art staring at the wall,
Where the dying night-lamp flickers, and
    the shadows rise and fall.

Then a hand shall pass before thee, point-
    ing to his drunken sleep,
To thy widow'd marriage-pillows, to the
    tears that thou wilt weep.

Thou shalt hear the "Never, never," whis-
    per'd by the phantom years,
And a song from out the distance in the
    ringing of thine ears;

And an eye shall vex thee, looking ancient kindness on thy pain.
Turn thee, turn thee on thy pillow: get thee to thy rest again.

Nay, but Nature brings thee solace; for a tender voice will cry.
'Tis a purer life than thine; a lip to drain thy trouble dry.

Baby lips will laugh me down: my latest rival brings thee rest.
Baby fingers, waxen touches, press me from the mother's breast.

Oh, the child too clothes the father with a dearness not his due.
Half is thine and half is his: it will be worthy of the two.

Oh, I see thee old and formal, fitted to thy petty part,
With a little hoard of maxims preaching down a daughter's heart.

"They were dangerous guides the feelings —she herself was not exempt—
Truly, she herself had suffer'd"—Perish in thy self-contempt!

Overlive it—lower yet—be happy! wherefore should I care?
I myself must mix with action, lest I wither by despair.

What is that which I should turn to, lighting upon days like these?
Every door is barr'd with gold, and opens but to golden keys.

Every gate is throng'd with suitors, all the markets overflow.
I have but an angry fancy: what is that which I should do?

I had been content to perish, falling on the foeman's ground,
When the ranks are roll'd in vapour, and the winds are laid with sound.

But the jingling of the guinea helps the hurt that Honor feels,
And the nations do but murmur, snarling at each other's heels.

Can I but re-live in sadness? I will turn that earlier page.
Hide me from my deep emotion, O thou wondrous Mother-Age!

Make me feel the wild pulsation that I felt before the strife,
When I heard my days before me, and the tumult of my life;

Yearning for the large excitement that the coming years would yield,
Eager-hearted as a boy when first he leaves his father's field,

And at night along the dusky highway near and nearer drawn,
Sees in heaven the light of London flaring like a dreary dawn;

And his spirit leaps within him to be gone before him then,
Underneath the light he looks at, in among the throngs of men:

Men, my brothers, men the workers, ever reaping something new;
That which they have done but earnest of the things that they shall do;

For I dipt into the future, far as human eye could see,
Saw the vision of the world, and all the wonder that would be;

Saw the heavens fill with commerce, argosies of magic sails,
Pilots of the purple twilight, dropping down with costly bales;

Heard the heavens fill with shouting, and there rain'd a ghastly dew
From the nations' airy navies grappling in the central blue;

Far along the world-wide whisper of the south wind rushing warm,
With the standards of the peoples plunging thro' the thunderstorm;

Till the war-drum throbb'd no longer, and the battle-flags were furl'd
In the Parliament of man, the Federation of the world.

There the common sense of most shall
    hold a fretful realm in awe,
And the kindly earth shall slumber, lapt
    in universal law.

So I triumph'd ere my passion sweeping
    thro' me left me dry,
Left me with the palsied heart, and left
    me with the jaundiced eye;

Eye, to which all order festers, all things
    here are out of joint;
Science moves, but slowly, slowly, creep-
    ing on from point to point;

Slowly comes a hungry people, as a lion
    creeping nigher,
Glares at one that nods and winks behind
    a slowly dying fire.

Yet I doubt not thro' the ages one increas-
    ing purpose runs,
And the thoughts of men are widen'd with
    the process of the suns.

What is that to him that reaps not harvest
    of his youthful joys,
Tho' the deep heart of existence beat for
    ever like a boy's?

Knowledge comes, but wisdom lingers, and
    I linger on the shore,
And the individual withers, and the world
    is more and more.

Knowledge comes but wisdom lingers, and
    he bears a laden breast,
Full of sad experience, moving toward the
    stillness of his rest.

Hark! my merry comrades call me, sound-
    ing on the bugle-horn,
They to whom my foolish passion were a
    target for their scorn;

Shall it not be scorn to me to harp on such
    a moulder'd string?
I am shamed thro' all my nature to have
    loved so slight a thing.

Weakness to be wroth with weakness!
    woman's pleasure, woman's pain,—
Nature made them blinder motions bound-
    ed in a shallower brain;

Woman is the lesser man, and all thy pas-
    sions, match'd with mine,
Are as moonlight unto sunlight, and as
    water unto wine—

Here at least, where Nature sickens, noth-
    ing. Ah, for some retreat
Deep in yonder shining Orient, where my
    life began to beat;

Where in wild Mahratta-battle fell my
    father evil-starr'd;—
I was left a trampled orphan, and a selfish
    uncle's ward.

Or to burst all links of habit—there to
    wander far away,
On from island unto island at the gateways
    of the day.

Larger constellations burning, mellow
    moons and happy skies,
Breadths of tropic shade and palms in
    cluster, knots of Paradise.

Never comes the trader, never floats an
    European flag,
Slides the bird o'er lustrous woodland,
    swings the trailer from the crag;

Droops the heavy-blossom'd bower, hangs
    the heavy-fruited tree—
Summer isles of Eden lying in dark-purple
    spheres of sea.

There methinks would be enjoyment more
    than in this march of mind,
In the steamship, in the railway, in the
    thoughts that shake mankind.

There the passions cramp'd no longer shall
    have scope and breathing-space,
I will take some savage woman, she shall
    rear my dusky race.

Iron-jointed, supple-sinew'd, they shall
    dive, and they shall run,
Catch the wild-goat by the hair, and hurl
    their lances in the sun;

Whistle back the parrot's call, and leap the
    rainbows of the brooks,
Not with blinded eyesight poring over
    miserable books—

Fool, again the dream, the fancy! but I
 know my words are wild,
But I count the gray barbarian lower than
 the Christian child.

I, to herd with narrow foreheads, vacant
 of our glorious gains,
Like a beast with lower pleasures, like a
 beast with lower pains!

Mated with a squalid savage—what to me
 were sun or clime?
I the heir of all the ages, in the foremost
 files of time—

I that rather held it better men should
 perish one by one,
Than that earth should stand at gaze like
 Joshua's moon in Ajalon!

Not in vain the distance beacons. For-
 ward, forward let us range,
Let the great world spin for ever down the
 ringing grooves of change.

Thro' the shadow of the globe we sweep
 into the younger day:
Better fifty years of Europe than a cycle
 of Cathay.

Mother-Age (for mine I knew not), help
 me as when life begun:
Rift the hills, and roll the waters, flash the
 lightnings, weigh the Sun.

Oh, I see the crescent promise of my spirit
 hath not set.
Ancient founts of inspiration well thro' all
 my fancy yet.

Howsoever these things be, a long farewell
 to Locksley Hall!
Now for me the woods may wither, now
 for me the roof-tree fall.

Comes a vapor from the margin, blacken-
 ing over heath and holt,
Cramming all the blast before it, in its
 breast a thunderbolt.

Let it fall on Locksley Hall, with rain or
 hail, or fire or snow;
For the mighty wind arises, roaring sea-
 ward, and I go.
 ALFRED TENNYSON.

THE STEADFAST SHEPHERD.

HENCE away, thou Syren; leave me.
 Pish! unclasp those wanton arms;
Sugred words shall ne'er deceive me—
 Though thou prove a thousand charms.
Fie, fie, forbear; no common snare
 Can ever my affection chain:
Your painted baits, and poor deceits,
 Are all bestow'd on me in vain.

I'm no slave to such as you be;
 Neither shall a snowy breast,
Wanton eye, or lip of ruby,
 Ever rob me of my rest.
Go, go, display your beauty's ray
 To some o'er-soon enamor'd swain:
Those common wiles, of sighs and smiles,
 Are all bestow'd on me in vain.

I have elsewhere vow'd my duty;
 Turn away your tempting eyes;
Show not me a naked beauty;
 Those impostures I despise:
My spirit loathes where gaudy clothes
 And feignèd oaths may love obtain:
I love her so whose look swears *no*,
 That all your labors will be vain.

Can he prize the tainted posies,
 Which on every breast are worn,
That may pluck the spotless roses
 From their never-touchèd thorn?
I can go rest on her sweet breast
 That is the pride of Cynthia's train;
Then hold your tongues; your mermaid
 songs
 Are all bestow'd on me in vain.

He's a fool that basely dallies
 Where each peasant mates with him
Shall I haunt the throngèd valleys,
 While there's noble hills to climb?
No, no, though clowns are scared with
 frowns,
 I know the best can but disdain:
And those I'll prove: so shall your love
 Be all bestow'd on me in vain.

Yet I would not deign embraces
 With the fairest queens that be,
If another shared those graces
 Which they had bestow'd on me.
I'll grant that one my love, where none
 Shall come to rob me of my gain:
The fickle heart makes tears and art,
 And all, bestow'd on me in vain.

I do scorn to vow a duty,
  Where each lustful lad may woo;
Give me her whose sunlike beauty
  Buzzards dare not soar unto:
She, she it is affords that bliss,
  For which I would refuse no pain;
But such as you, fond fools, adieu,
  You seek to captive me in vain.

She, that's proud in the beginning,
  And disdains each looker-on,
If a coy one in the winning,
  Proves a true one, being won.
Whate'er betide, she'll ne'er divide
  The favor she to one doth deign;
But your fond love will fickle prove,
  And all, that trust in you, are vain.

Therefore know, when I enjoy one,
  And for love employ my breath,
She I court shall be a coy one
  Though I win her with my breath.
A favor there few aim at dare;
  And if, perhaps, some lover plain,
She is not won, nor I undone
  By placing of my love in vain.

Leave me, then, thou Syren, leave me;
  Take away these charmèd arms;
Crafty wiles cannot deceive me,
  I am proof 'gainst women's charms:
You labor may to lead astray
  The heart, that constant must remain;
And I the while will sit and smile
  To see you spend your time in vain.
                    GEORGE WITHER.

FAREWELL TO NANCY.

AE fond kiss and then we sever!
Ae farewell, and then for ever!
Deep in heart-wrung tears I'll pledge thee;
Warring sighs and groans I'll wage thee.
Who shall say that Fortune grieves him,
While the star of hope she leaves him?
Me, nae cheerful twinkle lights me;
Dark despair around benights me.

I'll ne'er blame my partial fancy—
Naething could resist my Nancy:
But to see her was to love her,
Love but her and love for ever.
Had we never loved sae kindly,
Had we never loved sae blindly,
Never met—or never parted,
We had ne'er been broken-hearted.

Fare thee weel, thou first and fairest!
Fare thee weel, thou best and dearest!
Thine be ilka joy and treasure,
Peace, enjoyment, love, and pleasure!

Ae fond kiss, and then we sever!
Ae farewell, alas! for ever!
Deep in heart-wrung tears I'll pledge thee;
Warring sighs and groans I'll wage thee.
                    ROBERT BURNS.

A PRAISE OF HIS LOVE.

GIVE place, ye lovers, here before
  That spent your boasts and brags in vain;
My lady's beauty passeth more
  The best of yours, I dare well sayen,
Than doth the sun the candlelight,
Or brightest day the darkest night;

And thereto hath a troth as just
  As had Penelope the fair;
For what she saith ye may it trust,
  As it by writing sealèd were;—
And virtues hath she many mo'
Than I with pen have skill to show.

I could rehearse, if that I would,
  The whole effect of Nature's plaint,
When she had lost the perfect mould,
  The like to whom she could not paint.
With wringing hands, how did she cry!
And what she said, I know it aye.

I know she swore, with raging mind,
  Her kingdom only set apart,
There was no loss by law of kind
  That could have gone so near her heart;
And this was chiefly all her pain—
"She could not make the like again."

Sith Nature thus gave her the praise
  To be the chiefest work she wrought,
In faith, methink, some better ways
  On your behalf might well be sought,
Than to compare, as ye have done,
To match the candle with the sun.
           HENRY HOWARD (Earl of Surrey).

SWEET ARE THE CHARMS.

SWEET are the charms of her I love:
  More fragrant than the damask rose,
Soft as the down of turtle dove,
  Gentle as air when Zephyr blows,
Refreshing as descending rains
To sunburnt climes and thirsty plains.

True as the needle to the pole,
   Or as the dial to the sun ;
Constant as gliding waters roll,
   Whose swelling tides obey the moon—
From every other charmer free,
My life and love shall follow thee.

The lamb the flowery thyme devours,
   The dam the tender kid pursues ;
Sweet Philomel in shady bowers
   Of verdant spring her note renews :
All follow what they most admire,
As I pursue my soul's desire.

Nature must change her beauteous face,
   And vary as the seasons rise,
As winter to the spring gives place,
   Summer th' approach of autumn flies :
No change on love the seasons bring,—
Love only knows perpetual spring.

Devouring Time with stealing pace,
   Makes lofty oaks and cedars bow ;
And marble towers and gates of brass
   In his rude march he levels low ;
But Time, destroying far and wide,
Love from the soul can ne'er divide.

Death only, with his cruel dart,
   The gentle godhead can remove,
And drive him from the bleeding heart,
   To mingle with the blest above,
Where, known to all his kindred train,
He finds a lasting rest from pain.

Love and his sister fair, the Soul,
   Twin born, from heaven together came ;
Love will the universe control
   When dying seasons lose their name ;
Divine abodes shall own his power,
When Time and Death shall be no more.
                  BARTON BOOTH.

GENEVIEVE.

MAID of my love, sweet Genevieve ;
   In beauty's light you glide along ;
Your eye is like the star of eve,
   And sweet your voice as seraph's song.
Yet not your heavenly beauty gives
   This heart with passion soft to glow ;
Within your soul a voice there lives,
   It bids you hear the tale of woe.

When sinking low the sufferer wan
   Beholds no hand outstretch'd to save ;
Fair as the bosom of the swan
   That rises graceful o'er the wave,
I've seen your breast with pity heave,
And *therefore* love I you, sweet Genevieve.
                  SAMUEL TAYLOR COLERIDGE.

THE MILLER'S DAUGHTER.

IT is the miller's daughter,
   And she is grown so dear, so dear,
That I would be the jewel
   That trembles in her ear ;
For hid in ringlets day and night,
I'd touch her neck so warm and white.

And I would be the girdle
   About her dainty dainty waist,
And her heart would beat against me,
   In sorrow and in rest ;
And I should know if it beat right,
I'd clasp it round so close and tight.

And I would be the necklace,
   And all day long to fall and rise
Upon her balmy bosom,
   With her laughter or her sighs,
And I would lie so light, so light,
I scarce should be unclasp'd at night.
                  ALFRED TENNYSON.

THE LASS OF PATIE'S MILL.

THE lass of Patie's mill,
   Sae bonnie, blithe, and gay,
In spite of all my skill
   She stole my heart away.
When tedding of the hay,
   Bareheaded on the green,
Love 'midst her locks did play,
   And wanton'd in her een.

Her arms white, round, and smooth ;
   Breasts rising in their dawn ;
To age it would give youth
   To press them with his hand.
Through all my spirits ran
   An ecstasy of bliss,
When I such sweetness fand
   Wrapt in a balmy kiss.

Without the help of art,
   Like flow'rs which grace the wild,

She did her sweets impart,
    Whene'er she spoke or smiled;
Her looks they were so mild,
    Free from affected pride,
She me to love beguiled;—
    I wish'd her for my bride.

Oh, had I a' the wealth
    Hopetoun's high mountains fill,
Insured lang life and health,
    And pleasure at my will,
I'd promise and fulfil
    That none but bonnie she,
The lass of Patie's mill,
    Should share the same with me.
ALLAN RAMSAY.

ROSADER'S SONETTO.

Turn I my looks unto the skies,
Love with his arrows wounds mine eyes;
If so I look upon the ground,
Love then in every flower is found;
Search I the shade to flee my pain,
Love meets me in the shades again;
Want I to walk in secret grove,
E'en there I meet with sacred love;
If so I bathe me in the spring,
E'en on the brink I hear him sing;
If so I meditate alone,
He will be partner of my moan;
If so I mourn, he weeps with me,
And where I am there will he be;
When as I talk of Rosalind,
The god from coyness waxeth kind,
And seems in self-same frame to fly,
Because he loves as well as I.
Sweet Rosalind, for pity rue,
For why, than love I am more true:
He, if he speed, will quickly fly,
But in thy love I live and die.
THOMAS LODGE.

KISSES.

My love and I for kisses play'd:
    She would keep stakes—I was content;
But when I won, she would be paid;
    This made me ask her what she meant.
"Pray, since I see," quoth she, "your wrangling vein,
Take your own kisses; give me mine again."
WILLIAM STRODE.

A STOLEN KISS.

Now gentle sleep hath closèd up those eyes
    Which, waking, kept my boldest thoughts in awe;
And free access unto that sweet lip lies,
    From whence I long the rosy breath to draw.
Methinks no wrong it were, if I should steal
    From those melting rubies, one poor kiss;
None sees the theft that would the theft reveal,
    Nor rob I her of aught what she can miss:
Nay, should I twenty kisses take away,
    There would be little sign I would do so;
Why, then, should I this robbery delay?
    Oh, she may wake, and therewith angry grow!
Well, if she do, I'll back restore that one,
And twenty hundred thousand more for loan.
GEORGE WITHER.

CUPID CARRYING PROVISIONS.

There was once a gentle time
Whenne the world was in its prime;
And everie day was holydaye,
And everie monthe was lovelie Maye.—
Cupide thenne hadde but to goe
With his purple winges and bowe;
And in blossomede vale and grove
Everie shepherde knelte to Love.

Then a rosie, dimpleded cheeke,
And a blue eye fonde and meeke;
And a ringlette-wreathenne browe,
Like hyacynthes on a bed of snowe;
And a lowe voice silverre sweete
From a lippe without deceite:
Onlie those the heartes could move
Of the simple swaines to love.

But thatte time is gone and paste;
Canne the summerre alwayes laste!
And the swaines are wiser growne,
And the hearte is turnede to stone,
And the maidenne's rose may witherre!
Cupide's fled, no manne knowes whitherre!

But anotherre CUPIDE'S come,
With a browe of care and gloome;
Fixede upon the earthlie moulde,
Thinkinge of the sullenne golde:
In his hande the bowe no more,
At his backe the householde store,
That the bridalle colde muste buye;
Uselesse nowe the smile ande sighe:
But he weares the pinion stille,
Flyinge at the sighte of ille.
Oh, for the olde true-love time,
Whenne the worlde was in its prime!
GEORGE CROLY.

A RED, RED ROSE.

MY luve is like a red, red rose
   That's newly sprung in June;
My luve is like the melodie
   That's sweetly play'd in tune.
As fair art thou, my bonnie lass,
   So deep in luve am I,
And I will luve thee still, my dear,
   Till a' the seas gang dry;

Till a' the seas gang dry, my dear,
   And the rocks melt wi' the sun;
And I will luve thee still, my dear,
   While the sands o' life shall run.
And fare thee well, my only Luve!
   And fare thee well a while,
And I will come again, my Luve,
   Tho' 'twere ten thousand mile.
ROBERT BURNS.

STANZAS.

OH, talk not to me of a name great in story;
The days of our youth are the days of our glory,
And the myrtle and ivy of sweet two-and twenty
Are worth all your laurels, though ever so plenty.

What are garlands and crowns to the brow that is wrinkled?
'Tis but as a dead flower with May-dew besprinkled;
Then away with all such from the head that is hoary,—
What care I for the wreaths that can only give glory?

O Fame! if I e'er took delight in thy praises,
'Twas less for the sake of thy high-sounding phrases
Than to see the bright eyes of the dear one discover
She thought that I was not unworthy to love her.

There chiefly I sought thee, there only I found thee;
Her glance was the best of the rays that surround thee;
When it sparkled o'er aught that was bright in my story,
I knew it was love, and I felt it was glory.
LORD BYRON.

STANZAS FOR MUSIC.

THERE be none of Beauty's daughters
   With a magic like thee,
And like music on the waters
   Is thy sweet voice to me;
When, as if its sound were causing
The charmèd ocean's pausing,
The waves lie still and gleaming,
And the lull'd winds seem dreaming.

And the midnight moon is weaving
   Her bright chain o'er the deep,
Whose breast is gently heaving
   As an infant's asleep;
So the spirit bows before thee
To listen and adore thee,
With a full but soft emotion,
Like the swell of Summer's ocean.
LORD BYRON.

THOU HAST SWORN BY THY GOD, MY JEANIE.

THOU hast sworn by thy God, my Jeanie,
   By that pretty white hand o' thine,
And by a' the lowing stars in heaven,
   That thou wad ay be mine;
And I hae sworn by my God, my Jeanie,
   And by that kind heart o' thine,

By a' the stars sown thick owre heaven,
  That thou shalt ay be mine.

Then foul fa' the hands that wad loose sic
    bands,
  An' the heart that wad part sic love;
But there's nae hand can loose the band,
  Save the finger o' God above.
Though the wee wee cot maun be my
    bield,
  An' my claithing e'er sae mean,
I wad lap me up rich i' the faulds o' luve,
  Heaven's armfu' o' my Jean.

Her white arm wad be a pillow to me
  Fu' safter than the down;
An' Love wad winnow owre us his kind
    kind wings,
  An' sweetly I'd sleep, an' soun'.
Come here to me, thou lass o' my luve,
  Come here, an' kneel wi' me,
The morning is fu' o' the presence o'
    God,
  An' I canna pray but thee.

The morn-wind is sweet 'mang the beds o'
    new flowers,
  The wee birds sing kindlie an' hie,
Our gudeman leans owre his kail-yard
    dyke,
  An' a blythe auld body is he.
The Book maun be ta'en when the carl
    comes hame,
  Wi' the holie psalmodie,
An' thou maun speak o' me to thy God,
  An' I will speak o' thee.
ALLAN CUNNINGHAM.

THE WELCOME.

I.

COME in the evening, or come in the
    morning;
Come when you're looked for, or come
    without warning;
Kisses and welcome you'll find here before
    you,
And the oftener you come here the more
    I'll adore you!
  Light is my heart since the day we were
      plighted;
  Red is my cheek that they told me was
      blighted;
The green of the trees looks far greener
    than ever,
And the linnets are singing, "True
    lovers don't sever!"

II.

I'll pull you sweet flowers, to wear if you
    choose them!
Or, after you've kiss'd them, they'll lie on
    my bosom;
I'll fetch from the mountain its breeze to
    inspire you;
I'll fetch from my fancy a tale that won't
    tire you.
  Oh, your step's like the rain to the
      summer-vex'd farmer,
  Or sabre and shield to a knight without
      armor;
I'll sing you sweet songs till the stars
    rise above me,
Then, wandering, I'll wish you in silence
    to love me.

III.

We'll look through the trees at the cliff
    and the eyrie;
We'll tread round the rath on the track of
    the fairy;
We'll look on the stars, and we'll list to
    the river,
Till you ask of your darling what gift you
    can give her.
  Oh, she'll whisper you,—"Love, as un-
      changeably beaming,
  And trust, when in secret, most tunefully
      streaming;
Till the starlight of heaven above us
    shall quiver,
As our souls flow in one down eternity's
    river."

IV.

So come in the evening, or come in the
    morning;
Come when you're look'd for, or come
    without warning;
Kisses and welcome you'll find here before
    you,
And the oftener you come here the more
    I'll adore you!
  Light is my heart since the day we were
      plighted;
  Red is my cheek that they told me was
      blighted;

The green of the trees looks far greener
    than ever,
And the linnets are singing, "True
    lovers don't sever!"
                THOMAS OSBORNE DAVIS.

THE HERMIT.

"TURN, gentle hermit of the dale,
    And guide my lonely way
To where yon taper cheers the vale
    With hospitable ray.

"For here forlorn and lost I tread,
    With fainting steps and slow;
Where wilds, immeasurably spread,
    Seem lengthening as I go."

"Forbear, my son," the hermit cries,
    "To tempt the dangerous gloom;
For yonder faithless phantom flies
    To lure thee to thy doom.

"Here to the houseless child of want
    My door is open still;
And though my portion is but scant,
    I give it with good will.

"Then turn to-night, and freely share
    Whate'er my cell bestows;
My rushy couch and frugal fare,
    My blessing and repose.

"No flocks that range the valley free
    To slaughter I condemn;
Taught by that power that pities me,
    I learn to pity them;

"But from the mountain's grassy side
    A guiltless feast I bring;
A scrip with herbs and fruits supplied,
    And water from the spring.

"Then, pilgrim, turn; thy cares forego;
    All earth-born cares are wrong;
Man wants but little here below,
    Nor wants that little long."

Soft as the dew from heaven descends,
    His gentle accents fell;
The modest stranger lowly bends,
    And follows to the cell.

Far in a wilderness obscure
    The lonely mansion lay;
A refuge to the neighboring poor,
    And strangers led astray.

No stores beneath its humble thatch
    Required a master's care:
The wicket, opening with a latch,
    Received the harmless pair.

And now, when busy crowds retire
    To take their evening rest,
The hermit trimm'd his little fire,
    And cheer'd his pensive guest;

And spread his vegetable store,
    And gaily prest and smiled;
And, skill'd in legendary lore,
    The lingering hours beguiled.

Around, in sympathetic mirth,
    Its tricks the kitten tries;
The cricket chirrups on the hearth;
    The crackling fagot flies.

But nothing could a charm impart
    To soothe the stranger's woe;
For grief was heavy at his heart,
    And tears began to flow.

His rising cares the hermit spied,
    With answering care opprest:
"And whence, unhappy youth," he cried,
    "The sorrows of thy breast?

"From better habitations spurn'd,
    Reluctant dost thou rove?
Or grieve for friendship unreturn'd,
    Or unregarded love?

"Alas! the joys that fortune brings
    Are trifling, and decay;
And those who prize the paltry things,
    More trifling still than they.

"And what is friendship but a name,
    A charm that lulls to sleep;
A shade that follows wealth or fame,
    And leaves the wretch to weep?

"And love is still an emptier sound,
    The modern fair one's jest;
On earth unseen, or only found
    To warm the turtle's nest.

"For shame, fond youth! thy sorrows hush,
    And spurn the sex," he said;
But, while he spoke, a rising blush
    His lovelorn guest betray'd.

Surprised, he sees new beauties rise,
  Swift mantling to the view;
Like colors o'er the morning skies,
  As bright, as transient too.

The bashful look, the rising breast,
  Alternate spread alarms:
The lovely stranger stands confest,
  A maid in all her charms.

"And, ah! forgive a stranger rude,
  A wretch forlorn," she cried;
"Whose feet unhallow'd thus intrude
  Where heaven and you reside.

"But let a maid thy pity share,
  Whom love has taught to stray;
Who seeks for rest, but finds despair
  Companion of her way.

"My father lived beside the Tyne,
  A wealthy lord was he;
And all his wealth was mark'd as mine,
  He had but only me.

"To win me from his tender arms,
  Unnumber'd suitors came;
Who praised me for imputed charms,
  And felt, or feign'd, a flame.

"Each hour a mercenary crowd
  With richest proffers strove:
Among the rest young Edwin bow'd,
  But never talk'd of love.

"In humble, simplest habit clad,
  No wealth nor power had he;
Wisdom and worth were all he had,
  But these were all to me.

"And when beside me in the dale
  He caroll'd lays of love,
His breath lent fragrance to the gale,
  And music to the grove.

"The blossom opening to the day,
  The dews of heaven refined,
Could naught of purity display
  To emulate his mind.

"The dew, the blossom on the tree,
  With charms inconstant shine;
Their charms were his, but, woe to me!
  Their constancy was mine.

"For still I tried each fickle art,
  Importunate and vain;
And while his passion touch'd my heart,
  I triumph'd in his pain:

"Till, quite dejected with my scorn,
  He left me to my pride;
And sought a solitude forlorn,
  In secret, where he died.

"But mine the sorrow, mine the fault,
  And well my life shall pay;
I'll seek the solitude he sought,
  And stretch me where he lay.

"And there forlorn, despairing, hid,
  I'll lay me down and die;
'Twas so for me that Edwin did,
  And so for him will I."

"Forbid it, Heaven!" the hermit cried,
  And clasp'd her to his breast;
The wondering fair one turn'd to chide,—
  'Twas Edwin's self that prest.

"Turn, Angelina, ever dear,
  My charmer, turn to see
Thy own, thy long-lost Edwin here,
  Restored to love and thee.

"Thus let me hold thee to my heart,
  And every care resign;
And shall we never, never part,
  My life—my all that's mine?

"No, never from this hour to part,
  We'll live and love so true;
The sigh that rends thy constant heart
  Shall break thy Edwin's too."
OLIVER GOLDSMITH.

THE TRIUMPH OF CHARIS.

SEE the chariot at hand here of Love!
  Wherein my lady rideth!
Each that draws is a swan, or a dove—
  And well the car Love guideth.
As she goes, all hearts do duty
  Unto her beauty;
And, enamor'd, do wish, so they might
  But enjoy such a sight,
That they still were to run by her side
Through swords, through seas, whither
  she would ride.

Do but look on her eyes! they do light
   All that Love's world compriseth;
Do but look on her hair! it is bright
   As Love's star when it riseth!
Do but mark—her forehead's smoother
   Than words that soothe her!
And from her arch'd brows such a grace
Sheds itself through the face,
   As alone there triumphs to the life,
All the gain, all the good, of the elements'
   strife.

Have you seen but a bright lily grow,
   Before rude hands have touch'd it?
Have you mark'd but the fall of the snow,
   Before the soil hath smutch'd it?
Have you felt the wool of the beaver?
   Or swan's down ever?
Or have smelt o' the bud of the brier?
   Or the nard i' the fire?
Or have tasted the bag of the bee?
Oh, so white! oh, so soft! oh, so sweet is she!
                 BEN JONSON.

TELL ME HOW TO WOO THEE.

IF doughty deeds my lady please,
   Right soon I'll mount my steed;
And strong his arm, and fast his seat
   That bears frae me the meed.
I'll wear thy colors in my cap,
   Thy picture at my heart;
And he that bends not to thine eye
   Shall rue it to his smart!
     Then tell me how to woo thee, Love;
       Oh tell me how to woo thee!
     For thy dear sake, nae care I'll take,
       Tho' ne'er another trow me.

If gay attire delight thine eye
   I'll dight me in array;
I'll tend thy chamber door all night,
   And squire thee all the day.
If sweetest sounds can win thine ear,
   These sounds I'll strive to catch;
Thy voice I'll steal to woo thysell,
   That voice that nane can match.

But if fond love thy heart can gain,
   I never broke a vow;
Nae maiden lays her skaith to me,
   I never loved but you.
For you alone I ride the ring,
   For you I wear the blue;
For you alone I strive to sing,
   Oh tell me how to woo!
     Then tell me how to woo thee, Love;
       Oh tell me how to woo thee,
     For thy dear sake, nae care I'll take,
       Tho' ne'er another trow me.
               ROBERT GRAHAM OF GARTMORE.

O NANNY, WILT THOU GO WITH ME.

O NANNY, wilt thou go with me,
   Nor sigh to leave the flaunting town?
Can silent glens have charms for thee,—
   The lowly cot and russet gown?
No longer drest in silken sheen,
   No longer deck'd with jewels rare,—
Say, canst thou quit each courtly scene,
   Where thou wert fairest of the fair?

O Nanny, when thou'rt far away,
   Wilt thou not cast a wish behind?
Say, canst thou face the parching ray,
   Nor shrink before the wintry wind?
Oh, can that soft and gentle mien
   Extremes of hardship learn to bear,
Nor sad regret each courtly scene,
   Where thou wert fairest of the fair?

O Nanny, canst thou love so true,
   Through perils keen with me to go;
Or when thy swain mishap shall rue,
   To share with him the pang of woe?
Say, should disease or pain befall,
   Wilt thou assume the nurse's care,
Nor wistful those gay scenes recall,
   Where thou wert fairest of the fair?

And when at last thy love shall die,
   Wilt thou receive his parting breath,
Wilt thou repress each struggling sigh,
   And cheer with smiles the bed of death?
And wilt thou o'er his breathless clay
   Strew flowers and drop the tender tear,
Nor then regret those scenes so gay,
   Where thou wert fairest of the fair?
                 THOMAS PERCY.

WHEN MAGGY GANGS AWAY.

OH, what will a' the lads do
   When Maggy gangs away?
Oh, what will a' the lads do
   When Maggy gangs away?

There's no a heart in a' the glen
  That disna dread the day:
Oh, what will a' the lads do
  When Maggy gangs away?

Young Jock has ta'en the hill for't,
  A waefu' wight is he;
Poor Harry's ta'en the bed for't,
  An' laid him down to dee;
An' Sandy's gane unto the kirk,
  An' learnin' fast to pray:
And oh, what will the lads do
  When Maggy gangs away?

The young laird o' the Lang-Shaw
  Has drunk her health in wine;
The priest has said—in confidence—
  The lassie was divine,
And that is mair in maiden's praise
  Than ony priest should say:
But oh, what will the lads do
  When Maggy gangs away?

The wailing in our green glen
  That day will quaver high;
'Twill draw the redbreast frae the wood,
  The laverock frae the sky;
The fairies frae their beds o' dew
  Will rise an' join the lay:
An' hey! what a day 'twill be
  When Maggy gangs away!
JAMES HOGG.

BELIEVE ME, IF ALL THOSE ENDEARING YOUNG CHARMS.

BELIEVE me, if all those endearing young charms,
  Which I gaze on so fondly to-day,
Were to change by to-morrow, and fleet in my arms,
  Like fairy-gifts fading away,
Thou wouldst still be adored, as this moment thou art,
  Let thy loveliness fade as it will,
And around the dear ruin each wish of my heart
  Would entwine itself verdantly still.

It is not while beauty and youth are thine own,
  And thy cheeks unprofaned by a tear,
That the fervor and faith of a soul can be known,
  To which time will but make thee more dear;
No, the heart that has truly loved never forgets,
  But as truly loves on to the close,
As the sun-flower turns on her god, when he sets,
  The same look which she turn'd when he rose.
THOMAS MOORE.

THE YOUNG MAY MOON.

THE young May moon is beaming, love,
The glow-worm's lamp is gleaming, love,
    How sweet to rove
    Through Morna's grove
When the drowsy world is dreaming, love!
Then awake! the heavens look bright, my dear,
'Tis never too late for delight, my dear,
    And the best of all ways
    To lengthen our days
Is to steal a few hours from the night, my dear.

Now all the world is sleeping, love,
But the sage, his star-watch keeping, love,
    And I, whose star,
    More glorious far,
Is the eye from that casement peeping, love.
Then awake! till rise of sun, my dear,
The sage's glass we'll shun, my dear,
    Or, in watching the flight
    Of bodies of light,
He might happen to take thee for one, my dear.
THOMAS MOORE.

GO, PRETTY BIRDS.

YE little birds that sit and sing
  Amidst the shady valleys,
And see how Phillis sweetly walks
  Within her garden-alleys,—
Go, pretty birds, about her bower;
Sing, pretty birds, she may not lower:
Ah me! methinks I see her frown!
  Ye pretty wantons, warble.

Go tell her through your chirping bills,
  As you by me are bidden,
To her is only known my love,
  Which from the world is hidden,—
Go, pretty birds, and tell her so;
See that your notes strain not too low,
For still, methinks, I see her frown.
  Ye pretty wantons, warble.

Go, tune your voices' harmony,
  And sing I am her lover;
Strain loud and sweet, that every note
  With sweet content may move her;
And she that hath the sweetest voice,
Tell her I will not change my choice;
Yet still, methinks, I see her frown.
  Ye pretty wantons, warble.

Oh fly! make haste! see, see, she falls
  Into a pretty slumber;
Sing round about her rosy bed,
  That, waking, she may wonder;
Say to her 'tis her lover true
That sendeth love to you, to you;
And when you hear her kind reply
  Return with pleasant warblings.
                THOMAS HEYWOOD.

TOUJOURS AMOUR.

PRITHEE tell me, Dimple-Chin,
At what age does Love begin?
Your blue eyes have scarcely seen
Summers three, my fairy queen,
But a miracle of sweets,
Soft approaches, sly retreats,
Show the little archer there,
Hidden in your pretty hair;
When didst learn a heart to win?
Prithee tell me, Dimple-Chin!

' Oh!" the rosy lips reply,
" I can't tell you if I try.
'Tis so long I can't remember:
  Ask some younger lass than I!"

Tell, oh tell me, Grizzled-Face,
Do your heart and head keep pace?
When does hoary Love expire,
When do frosts put out the fire?
Can its embers burn below
All that chill December snow?
Care you still soft hands to press,
Bonny heads to smooth and bless?

When does Love give up the chase?
Tell, oh tell me, Grizzled-Face!

" Ah!" the wise old lips reply,
" Youth may pass, and strength may die;
But of Love I can't foretoken:
  Ask some older sage than I!"
                EDMUND CLARENCE STEDMAN.

SWEET-AND-TWENTY.

O, MISTRESS mine, where are you roaming?
Oh, stay and hear; your true love's coming,
  That can sing both high and low:
Trip no farther, pretty sweeting;
Journeys end in lovers' meeting,
  Every wise man's son doth know.

What is love? 'tis not hereafter;
Present mirth hath present laughter;
  What's to come is still unsure:
In delay there lies no plenty;
Then come kiss me, Sweet-and-Twenty,
  Youth's a stuff will not endure.
                WILLIAM SHAKESPEARE.

JESSIE, THE FLOWER O' DUMBLANE.

THE sun has gane down o'er the lofty Ben-lomond,
  And left the red clouds to preside o'er the scene,
While lanely I stray in the calm simmer gloamin',
  To muse on sweet Jessie, the Flow'r o' Dumblane.

How sweet is the brier, wi' its saft fauldin' blossom,
  And sweet is the birk, wi' its mantle o' green;
Yet sweeter and fairer, and dear to this bosom,
  Is lovely young Jessie, the Flow'r o' Dumblane.

She's modest as ony, and blithe as she's bonnie,—
  For guileless simplicity marks her its ain;
And far be the villain, divested of feeling,
  Wha'd blight in its bloom the sweet Flow'r o' Dumblane.

Sing on, thou sweet mavis, thy hymn to
  the e'ening!—
Thou'rt dear to the echoes of Calder-
  wood glen:
Sae dear to this bosom, sae artless and
  winning,
  Is charming young Jessie, the Flow'r o'
    Dumblane.

How lost were my days till I met wi' my
  Jessie!
The sports o' the city seem'd foolish
  and vain:
I ne'er saw a nymph I would ca' my dear
  lassie
  Till charm'd wi' sweet Jessie, the Flow'r
    o' Dumblane.

Though mine were the station o' loftiest
  grandeur,
Amidst its profusion I'd languish in
  pain,
And reckon as naething the height o' its
  splendor,
  If wanting sweet Jessie, the Flow'r o'
    Dumblane.
            ROBERT TANNAHILL.

MARY OF CASTLE CARY.

"SAW ye my wee thing, saw ye my ain
  thing,
  Saw ye my true love down on yon lea?
Cross'd she the meadow yestreen at the
  gloaming,
  Sought she the burnie where flowers
    the haw tree?
Her hair it is lint-white, her skin it is
  milk-white,
  Dark is the blue of her saft-rolling ee;
Red, red her ripe lips, and sweeter than
  roses—
  Where could my wee thing wander frae
    me?"

'I saw nae your wee thing, I saw nae your
  ain thing,
  Nor saw I your true love down by yon
    lea;
But I met my bonny thing late in the
  gloaming,
  Down by the burnie where flowers the
    haw tree:

Her hair it was lint-white, her skin it
  was milk-white,
  Dark was the blue of her saft-rolling ee;
Red were her ripe lips, and sweeter than
  roses—
  Sweet were the kisses that she gave to
    me."

"It was nae my wee thing, it was nae my
  ain thing,
  It was nae my true love ye met by the
    tree;
Proud is her leal heart, and modest her
  nature;
  She never loved ony till ance she lo'ed
    me.
Her name it is Mary; she's frae Castle
  Cary;
  Aft has she sat when a bairn on my
    knee:
Fair as your face is, were't fifty times
  fairer,
  Young bragger, she ne'er wad gie kisses
    to thee."

"It was then your Mary; she's frae Castle
  Cary;
  It was then your true love I met by the
    tree;
Proud as her heart is, and modest her
  nature,
  Sweet were the kisses that she gave to
    me."
Sair gloom'd his dark brow, blood-red his
  cheek grew,
  Wild flash'd the fire frae his red-rolling
    ee;
"Ye'se rue sair this morning your boasts
  and your scorning,
  Defend ye, fause traitor; fu' loudly ye
    lie."

"Away wi' beguiling!" cried the youth,
  smiling—
  Off went the bonnet, the lint-white
    locks flee,
The belted plaid fa'ing, her white bosom
  shawing,
  Fair stood the loved maid wi' the dark-
    rolling ee.
"Is it my wee thing, is it my ain thing,
  Is it my true love here that I see?"

"O Jamie, forgie me; your heart's constant to me;
I'll never mair wander, dear laddie, frae thee."
HECTOR MACNEILL.

RORY O'MORE.

YOUNG Rory O'More courted Kathleen bawn;
He was bold as the hawk, and she soft as the dawn;
He wish'd in his heart pretty Kathleen to please,
And he thought the best way to do that was to tease.
"Now, Rory, be aisy," sweet Kathleen would cry,
Reproof on her lip, but a smile in her eye—
"With your tricks, I don't know, in troth, what I'm about;
Faith, you've teased till I've put on my cloak inside out."
"Och! jewel," says Rory, "that same is the way
You've thrated my heart for this many a day;
And 'tis plased that I am, and why not, to be sure?
For 'tis all for good luck," says bold Rory O'More.

"Indeed, then," says Kathleen, "don't think of the like,
For I half gave a promise to soothering Mike;
The ground that I walk on *he* loves, I'll be bound."
"Faith!" says Rory, "I'd rather love *you* than the ground."
"Now, Rory, I'll cry if you don't let me go;
Sure I dhrame every night that I'm hating you so."
"Och!" says Rory, "that same I'm delighted to hear,
For dhrames always go by conthraries, my dear.
So, jewel, keep dhramin' that same till you die,
And bright mornin' will give dirty night the black lie;

And 'tis plased that I am, and why not, to be sure?
Since 'tis all for good luck," says bold Rory O'More.

"Arrah, Kathleen, my darlint, you've teased me enough;
Sure I've thrash'd, for your sake, Dinny Grimes and Jim Duff;
And I've made myself, dhrinkin' your health, quite a *baste*,
So I think, after that, *I may talk to the priest*."
Then Rory, the rogue, stole his arm round her neck,
So soft and so white, without freckle or speck;
And he look'd in her eyes, that were beaming with light,
And he kiss'd her sweet lips—don't you think he was right?
"Now, Rory, leave off, sir, you'll hug me no more,
That's eight times to-day that you've kiss'd me before."
"Then here goes another," says he, "to make sure,
For there's luck in odd numbers," says Rory O'More.
SAMUEL LOVER.

THE LOW-BACKED CAR.

WHEN first I saw sweet Peggy,
  'Twas on a market-day;
A low-back'd car she drove, and sat
  Upon a truss of hay;
But when that hay was blooming grass,
  And deck'd with flowers of spring,
No flower was there that could compare
  With the blooming girl I sing.
As she sat in the low-back'd car,
  The man at the turnpike bar
    Never ask'd for the toll,
    But just rubb'd his owld poll,
And look'd after the low-back'd car.

In battle's wild commotion,
  The proud and mighty Mars
With hostile scythes demands his tithes
  Of death—in warlike cars;
While Peggy, peaceful goddess,
  Has darts in her bright eye

That knock men down in the market-town,
    As right and left they fly;
While she sits in her low-back'd car,
Than battle more dangerous far,—
      For the doctor's art
      Cannot cure the heart
That is hit from that low-back'd car.

Sweet Peggy round her car, sir,
    Has strings of ducks and geese,
But the scores of hearts she slaughters
    By far outnumber these;
While she among her poultry sits,
    Just like a turtle-dove,
Well worth the cage, I do engage,
    Of the blooming god of love;
While she sits in her low-back'd car,
The lovers come near and far,
      And envy the chicken
      That Peggy is pickin',
As she sits in her low-back'd car.

Oh, I'd rather own that car, sir,
    With Peggy by my side,
Than a coach and four, and gold *galore*,
    And a lady for my bride;
For the lady would sit forninst me,
    On a cushion made with taste,
While Peggy would sit beside me,
    With my arm around her waist,
While we drove in the low-back'd car
To be married by Father Maher;
      Oh, my heart would beat high
      At her glance and her sigh,
Though it beat in a low-back'd car.
                SAMUEL LOVER.

JESSY.

HERE's a health to ane I lo'e dear,
Here's a health to ane I lo'e dear;
Thou art sweet as the smile when fond
    lovers meet,
And soft as their parting tear, Jessy!

    Altho' thou maun never be mine,
    Altho' even hope is denied,
'Tis sweeter for thee despairing
    Than aught in the world beside, Jessy.

I mourn thro' the gay, gaudy day,
    As, hopeless, I muse on thy charms,
But welcome the dream o' sweet slumber,
    For then I am lock'd in thine arms, Jessy.

I guess by the dear angel smile,
    I guess by thy love-rolling ee;
But why urge the tender confession
    'Gainst fortune's fell cruel decree, Jessy?

Here's a health to ane I lo'e dear,
Here's a health to ane I lo'e dear;
Thou art sweet as the smile when fond
    lovers meet,
And soft as their parting tear, Jessy.
                ROBERT BURNS.

THE DULE'S I' THIS BONNET O' MINE.

THE dule's i' this bonnet o' mine:
    My ribbins'll never be reet;
Here, Mally, aw'm like to be fine,
    For Jamie'll be comin' to-neet;
He met me i' th' lone t' other day
    (Aw wur gooin' for wayter to th' well),
An' he begg'd that aw'd wed him i' May,
    Bi th' mass, if he'll let me, aw will!

When he took my two honds into his,
    Good Lord, heaw they trembled between!
An' aw durstn't look up in his face,
    Becose on him seein' my e'en.
My cheek went as red as a rose;
    There's never a mortal con tell
Heaw happy aw felt,—for, thae knows,
    One couldn't ha' ax'd him theirsel'.

But th' tale wur at th' end o' my tung:
    To let it eawt wouldn't be reet,
For aw thought to seem forrud wur wrung,
    So aw towd him aw'd tell him to-neet.
But, Mally, thae knows very weel,
    Though it isn't a thing one should own,
Iv aw'd th' pikein' o' th' world to mysel',
    Aw'd oather ha' Jamie or noan.

Neaw, Mally, aw've towd thae my mind;
    What would to do iv it wur thee?
" Aw'd tak him just while he'se inclined,
    An' a farrantly bargain he'll be;
For Jamie's as greadly a lad
    As ever stept eawt into th' sun.
Go, jump at thy chance, an' get wed;
    An' mak th' best o' th' job when it's done!"

Eh, dear! but it's time to be gwon:
    Aw shouldn't like Jamie to wait;

Aw connut for shame be too soon,
 An' aw wouldn't for th' wuld be too late.
Aw'm o' ov a tremble to th' heel;
 Dost think 'at my bonnet 'll do?
"Be off, lass,—thae looks very weel;
 He wants noan o' th' bonnet, thae foo!"
EDWIN WAUGH.

WHEN THE KYE COMES HAME.

COME, all ye jolly shepherds,
 That whistle through the glen,
I'll tell ye of a secret
 That courtiers dinna ken;
What is the greatest bliss
 That the tongue o' man can name?
'Tis to woo a bonny lassie
 When the kye comes hame,
  When the kye comes hame,
  When the kye comes hame,
 'Tween the gloaming and the mirk,
  When the kye comes hame.

'Tis not beneath the coronet,
 Nor canopy of state,
'Tis not on couch of velvet,
 Nor arbor of the great—
'Tis beneath the spreading birk,
 In the glen without the name,
Wi' a bonny bonny lassie,
 When the kye comes hame.

There the blackbird bigs his nest,
 For the mate he lo'es to see,
And on the topmost bough
 Oh, a happy bird is he!
Where he pours his melting ditty,
 And love is a' the theme,
And he'll woo his bonny lassie,
 When the kye comes hame.

When the blewart bears a pearl,
 And the daisy turns a pea,
And the bonny lucken gowan
 Has fauldit up her ee,
Then the laverock, frae the blue lift,
 Drops down and thinks nae shame
To woo his bonny lassie
 When the kye comes hame.

See yonder pawkie shepherd,
 That lingers on the hill,
His ewes are in the fauld,
 An' his lambs are lying still,
Yet he downa gang to bed,
 For his heart is in a flame,
To meet his bonny lassie
 When the kye comes hame.

When the little wee bit heart
 Rises high in the breast,
An' the little wee bit starn
 Rises red in the east,
Oh, there's a joy sae dear
 That the heart can hardly frame,
Wi' a bonny bonny lassie,
 When the kye comes hame.

Then since all Nature joins
 In this love without alloy,
Oh, wha wad prove a traitor
 To Nature's dearest joy?
Or wha wad choose a crown,
 Wi' its perils and its fame,
And miss his bonny lassie,
 When the kye comes hame?
JAMES HOGG.

MAUD MULLER.

MAUD MULLER, on a summer's day,
Raked the meadow sweet with hay.

Beneath her torn hat glow'd the wealth
Of simple beauty and rustic health.

Singing, she wrought, and her merry glee
The mockbird echo'd from his tree.

But, when she glanced to the far-off town,
White from its hillslope looking down,

The sweet song died, and a vague unrest
And a nameless longing fill'd her breast,—

A wish, that she hardly dared to own,
For something better than she had known.

The judge rode slowly down the lane,
Smoothing his horse's chestnut mane.

He drew his bridle in the shade
Of the apple trees to greet the maid,

And ask a draught from the spring that flow'd
Through the meadow across the road.

She stoop'd where the cool spring bubbled
    up,
And fill'd for him her small tin cup,

And blush'd as she gave it, looking down
On her feet so bare, and her tatter'd gown.

"Thanks!" said the judge; "a sweeter
    draught
From a fairer hand was never quaff'd."

He spoke of the grass and flowers and trees,
Of the singing birds and the humming
    bees;

Then talk'd of the haying, and wonder'd
    whether
The cloud in the west would bring foul
    weather.

And Maud forgot her brier-torn gown,
And her graceful ankles bare and brown;

And listen'd, while a pleased surprise
Look'd from her long-lash'd hazel eyes.

At last, like one who for delay
Seeks a vain excuse, he rode away.

Maud Muller look'd and sigh'd: "Ah me!
That I the judge's bride might be!

"He would dress me up in silks so fine,
And praise and toast me at his wine.

"My father should wear a broadcloth coat,
My brother should sail a painted boat.

"I'd dress my mother so grand and gay,
And the baby should have a new toy each
    day.

"And I'd feed the hungry and clothe the
    poor,
And all should bless me who left our door."

The judge look'd back as he climb'd the
    hill,
And saw Maud Muller standing still.

"A form more fair, a face more sweet
Ne'er hath it been my lot to meet.

"And her modest answer and graceful air
Show her wise and good as she is fair.

"Would she were mine, and I to-day,
Like her a harvester of hay:

"No doubtful balance of rights and wrongs,
Nor weary lawyers with endless tongues,

"But low of cattle and song of birds,
And health and quiet and loving words."

But he thought of his sisters proud and
    cold,
And his mother vain of her rank and gold.

So, closing his heart, the judge rode on,
And Maud was left in the field alone.

But the lawyers smiled that afternoon,
When he humm'd in court an old love-
    tune;

And the young girl mused beside the well,
Till the rain on the unraked clover fell.

He wedded a wife of richest dower,
Who lived for fashion, as he for power.

Yet oft, in his marble hearth's bright glow,
He watch'd a picture come and go;

And sweet Maud Muller's hazel eyes
Look'd out in their innocent surprise.

Oft, when the wine in his glass was red,
He long'd for the wayside well instead;

And closed his eyes on his garnish'd rooms,
To dream of meadows and clover-blooms.

And the proud man sigh'd, with a secret
    pain,
"Ah, that I were free again!—

"Free as when I rode that day,
Where the barefoot maiden raked her
    hay."

She wedded a man unlearn'd and poor,
And many children play'd round her
    door.

But care and sorrow, and childbirth pain,
Left their traces on heart and brain.

And oft, when the summer sun shone hot
On the new-mown hay in the meadow lot,

And she heard the little spring brook fall
Over the roadside, through the wall,

In the shade of the apple tree again
She saw a rider draw his rein.

And, gazing down with timid grace,
She felt his pleased eyes read her face.

Sometimes her narrow kitchen walls
Stretch'd away into stately halls;

The weary wheel to a spinnet turn'd,
The tallow candle an astral burn'd,

And for him who sat by the chimney lug,
Dozing and grumbling o'er pipe and mug,

A manly form at her side she saw,
And joy was duty and love was law.

Then she took up her burden of life again,
Saying only, "It might have been."

Alas for maiden, alas for judge,
For rich repiner and household drudge!

God pity them both! and pity us all,
Who vainly the dreams of youth recall.

For of all sad words of tongue or pen,
The saddest are these: "It might have been!"

Ah, well! for us all some sweet hope lies
Deeply buried from human eyes;

And, in the hereafter, angels may
Roll the stone from its grave away!
JOHN GREENLEAF WHITTIER.

THE POWER OF LOVE.

HEAR ye, ladies that despise
  What the mighty Love has done;
Fear examples and be wise:
  Fair Calisto was a nun:
Leda, sailing on a stream,
  To deceive the hopes of man,
Love accounting but a dream,
  Doted on a silver swan;
Danaë in a brazen tower,
Where no love was, loved a shower.

Hear ye, ladies that are coy,
  What the mighty Love can do;
Fear the fierceness of the boy;
  The chaste moon he makes to woo;
Vesta, kindling holy fires,
  Circled round about with spies,
Never dreaming loose desires,
  Doting at the altar dies;

Ilion, in a short hour, higher
He can build, and once more fire.
BEAUMONT AND FLETCHER.

THE BROOKSIDE.

I WANDER'D by the brookside,
  I wander'd by the mill;
I could not hear the brook flow,
  The noisy wheel was still:
There was no burr of grasshopper,
  No chirp of any bird;
But the beating of my own heart
  Was all the sound I heard.

I sat beneath the elm tree,
  I watch'd the long, long shade,
And as it grew still longer
  I did not feel afraid;
For I listen'd for a footfall,
  I listen'd for a word:
But the beating of my own heart
  Was all the sound I heard.

He came not—no, he came not,—
  The night came on alone,—
The little stars sat one by one,
  Each on his golden throne;
The evening air pass'd by my cheek,
  The leaves above were stirr'd;
But the beating of my own heart
  Was all the sound I heard.

Fast, silent tears were flowing,
  When something stood behind;
A hand was on my shoulder,
  I knew its touch was kind;
It drew me nearer, nearer—
  We did not speak one word;
But the beating of our own hearts
  Was all the sound we heard.
RICHARD MONCKTON MILNES
(LORD HOUGHTON).

THE SHEPHERD'S RESOLUTION.

SHALL I, wasting in despair,
Die because a woman's fair?
Or make pale my cheeks with care
'Cause another's rosy are?
Be she fairer than the day
Or the flowery meads of May,
  If she be not so to me
  What care I how fair she be?

Shall my foolish heart be pined
    'Cause I see a woman kind;
Or a well-disposèd nature
Joinèd to a lovely feature?
Be she meeker, kinder than
Turtle-dove or pelican,
    If she be not so to me
    What care I how kind she be?

Shall a woman's virtues move
Me to perish for her love?
Or her merit's value known
Make me quite forget my own?
Be she with that goodness blest,
Which may gain her name of Best;
    If she be not such to me,
    What care I how good she be?

'Cause her fortunes seem too high,
Shall I play the fool and die?
Those that bear a noble mind
Where they want of riches find,
Think what with them they would do
That without them dare to woo;
    And unless that mind I see,
    What care I how great she be?

Great or good, or kind or fair,
I will ne'er the more despair;
If she love me, this believe,
I will die ere she shall grieve;
If she slight me when I woo,
I can scorn and bid her go;
    For if she be not for me,
    What care I for whom she be?
                    GEORGE WITHER.

SONNET.

SINCE there's no help, come, let us kiss
    and part,—
    Nay, I have done, you get no more of
      me,
And I am glad, yea, glad with all my
    heart,
    That thus so clearly I myself can free;
Shake hands for ever, cancel all our vows,
    And, when we meet at any time again,
Be it not seen in either of our brows,
    That we one jot of former love retain.
Now, at the last gasp of Love's latest
    breath,
    When, his pulse failing, Passion speechless lies,
When Faith is kneeling by his bed of
    death,
    And Innocence is closing up his eyes,
Now, if thou wouldst, when all have given
    him over,
From death to life thou mightst him yet
    recover.
                    MICHAEL DRAYTON.

SONG.

DAY, in melting purple dying,
Blossoms all around me sighing,
Fragrance, from the lilies straying,
Zephyr, with my ringlets playing,
    Ye but waken my distress:
    I am sick of loneliness.

Thou to whom I love to hearken,
Come, ere night around me darken;
Though thy softness but deceive me,
Say thou'rt true, and I'll believe thee;
    Veil, if ill, thy soul's intent!
    Let me think it innocent!

Save thy toiling, spare thy treasure:
All I ask is friendship's pleasure:
Let the shining ore lie darkling,
Bring no gem in lustre sparkling;
    Gifts and gold are naught to me:
    I would only look on thee!

Tell to thee the high-wrought feeling,
Ecstasy but in revealing;
Paint to thee the deep sensation,
Rapture in participation,
    Yet but torture, if comprest
    In a lone unfriended breast.

Absent still? Ah! come and bless me!
Let these eyes again caress thee;
Once, in caution, I could fly thee:
Now, I nothing could deny thee:
    In a look if death there be,
    Come and I will gaze on thee!
                    MARIA BROOKS.

THE BANKS O' DOON.

YE banks and braes o' bonnie Doon,
    How can ye bloom sae fresh and fair?
How can ye chant, ye little birds,
    And I sae weary fu' o' care!

Thou'll break my heart, thou warbling bird,
    That wantons thro' the flowering thorn:
Thou minds me o' departed joys,
    Departed never to return.

Aft hae I roved by bonnie Doon,
    To see the rose and woodbine twine;
And ilka bird sang o' its luve,
    And fondly sae did I o' mine;
Wi' lightsome heart I pu'd a rose,
    Fu' sweet upon its thorny tree!
And my fause luver staw my rose,
    But ah! he left the thorn wi' me.
ROBERT BURNS.

FLORENCE VANE.

I LOVED thee long and dearly,
    Florence Vane;
My life's bright dream and early
    Hath come again;
I renew in my fond vision
    My heart's dear pain,
My hopes and thy derision,
    Florence Vane!

The ruin, lone and hoary,
    The ruin old,
Where thou didst hark my story,
    At even told,
That spot, the hues elysian
    Of sky and plain
I treasure in my vision,
    Florence Vane!

Thou wast lovelier than the roses
    In their prime;
Thy voice excell'd the closes
    Of sweetest rhyme;
Thy heart was as a river
    Without a main,
Would I had loved thee never,
    Florence Vane.

But fairest, coldest wonder!
    Thy glorious clay
Lieth the green sod under;
    Alas the day!
And it boots not to remember
    Thy disdain,
To quicken love's pale ember,
    Florence Vane!

The lilies of the valley
    By young graves weep,
The daisies love to dally
    Where maidens sleep.
May their bloom, in beauty vying,
    Never wane
Where thine earthly part is lying,
    Florence Vane.
PHILIP PENDLETON COOKE.

I PRITHEE SEND ME BACK MY HEART.

I PRITHEE send me back my heart,
    Since I cannot have thine,
For if from yours you will not part,
    Why, then, shouldst thou have mine?

Yet now I think on't, let it lie;
    To find it were in vain;
For thou'st a thief in either eye
    Would steal it back again.

Why should two hearts in one breast lie,
    And yet not lodge together?
O Love! where is thy sympathy,
    If thus our breasts thou sever?

But love is such a mystery,
    I cannot find it out;
For when I think I'm best resolved,
    I then am in most doubt.

Then farewell care, and farewell woe,
    I will no longer pine;
For I'll believe I have her heart,
    As much as she has mine.
SIR JOHN SUCKLING.

THE NUN.

IF you become a nun, dear,
    A friar I will be;
In any cell you run, dear,
    Pray look behind for me.
The roses all turn pale, too;
The doves all take the veil, too;
    The blind will see the show:

What! you become a nun, my dear?
　I'll not believe it, no!

If you become a nun, dear,
　The bishop Love will be;
The Cupids every one, dear,
　Will chant, "We trust in thee!"
The incense will go sighing,
　The candles fall a-dying,
　　The water turn to wine:
What! you go take the vows, my dear?
　You may—but they'll be mine.
LEIGH HUNT.

SHE IS NOT FAIR TO OUTWARD VIEW.

SHE is not fair to outward view
　As many maidens be;
Her loveliness I never knew
　Until she smiled on me.
Oh then I saw her eye was bright,
A well of love, a spring of light.

But now her looks are coy and cold,
　To mine they ne'er reply,
And yet I cease not to behold
　The love-light in her eye:
Her very frowns are fairer far
Than smiles of other maidens are.
HARTLEY COLERIDGE.

SONNET.

TIME wasteth years, and months, and hours;
　Time doth consume fame, honor, wit, and strength;
Time kills the greenest herbs and sweetest flowers;
　Time wears out Youth and Beauty's looks at length;
　　Time doth convey to ground both foe and friend,
　　And each thing else but Love, which hath no end.
Time maketh every tree to die and rot;
　Time turneth oft our pleasure into pain;
Time causeth wars and wrongs to be forgot;
　Time clears the sky which first hung full of rain;
　Time makes an end of all humane desire,
　But only this which sets my heart on fire.
Time turneth into naught each princely state;
　Time brings a flood from new-resolvèd snow;
Time calms the sea where tempest was of late;
　Time eats whate'er the moon can see below:
　And yet no time prevails in my behoof,
　Nor any time can make me cease to love!
THOMAS WATSON.

THE AWAKENING OF ENDYMION.

LONE upon a mountain, the pine trees wailing round him,
　Lone upon a mountain the Grecian youth is laid;
Sleep, mystic sleep, for many a year has bound him,
　Yet his beauty, like a statue's, pale and fair, is undecay'd.
　　　When will he awaken?

When will he awaken? a loud voice hath been crying,
　Night after night, and the cry has been in vain;
Winds, woods, and waves found echoes for replying,
　But the tones of the beloved one were never heard again.
　　　When will he awaken?
　Asked the midnight's silver queen.

Never mortal eye has look'd upon his sleeping;
　Parents, kindred, comrades, have mourn'd for him as dead;
By day the gather'd clouds have had him in their keeping,
　And at night the solemn shadows round his rest are shed.
　　　When will he awaken?

Long has been the cry of faithful love's
    imploring;
Long has hope been watching with soft
    eyes fix'd above;
When will the fates, the life of life restor-
    ing,
    Own themselves vanquish'd by much-
    enduring love?
              When will he awaken?
Asks the midnight's weary queen.

Beautiful the sleep that she has watch'd
    untiring,
    Lighted up with visions from yonder ra-
    diant sky,
Full of an immortal's glorious inspiring,
    Soften'd by the woman's meek and lov-
    ing sigh.
              When will he awaken?

He has been dreaming of old heroic
    stories,
    And the poet's passionate world has
    enter'd in his soul;
He has grown conscious of life's ancestral
    glories,
    When sages and when kings first upheld
    the mind's control.
              When will he awaken?
Asks the midnight's stately queen.

Lo, the appointed midnight! the present
    hour is fated!
    It is Endymion's planet that rises on the
    air,
How long, how tenderly his goddess-love
    has waited,
    Waited with a love too mighty for
    despair!
              Soon he will awaken.

Soft amid the pines is a sound as if of sing-
    ing,
    Tones that seem the lute's from the
    breathing flowers depart;
Not a wind that wanders o'er Mount Latmos
    but is bringing
    Music that is murmur'd from nature's
    inmost heart.
              Soon he will awaken
To his and midnight's queen!

Lovely is the green earth,—she knows the
    hour is holy;
Starry are the heavens, lit with eternal
    joy;
Light like their own is dawning sweet and
    slowly
O'er the fair and sculptured forehead of
    that yet dreaming boy.
              Soon he will awaken!

Red as the red rose toward the morning
    turning,
    Warms the youth's lip to the watcher's
    near his own;
While the dark eyes open, bright, intense,
    and burning
    With a life more glorious than, ere they
    closed, was known.
              Yes, he has awaken'd
For the midnight's happy queen!

What is this old history, but a lesson
    given,
    How true love still conquers by the
    deep strength of truth—
How all the impulses, whose native home
    is heaven,
    Sanctify the visions of hope, and faith,
    and youth?
              'Tis for such they waken!

When every worldly thought is utterly for-
    saken,
    Comes the starry midnight, felt by life's
    gifted few;
Then will the spirit from its earthly sleep
    awaken
    To a being more intense, more spiritual,
    and true.
              So doth the soul awaken,
Like that youth to night's fair queen!
        LÆTITIA ELIZABETH LANDON MACLEAN.

A PASTORAL.

MY time, O ye Muses, was happily spent,
When Phœbe went with me wherever I
    went;
Ten thousand sweet pleasures I felt in my
    breast;
Sure never fond shepherd like Colin was
    blest.

But now she is gone, and has left me behind,
What a marvellous change on a sudden I find!
When things were as fine as could possibly be,
I thought 'twas the spring; but, alas! it was she.

With such a companion, to tend a few sheep,
To rise up and play, or to lie down and sleep,
I was so good-humor'd, so cheerful and gay,
My heart was as light as a feather all day.
But now I so cross and so peevish am grown,
So strangely uneasy as never was known.
My fair one is gone, and my joys are all drown'd,
And my heart—I am sure it weighs more than a pound.

The fountain that wont to run sweetly along,
And dance to soft murmurs the pebbles among;
Thou know'st, little Cupid, if Phœbe were there,
'Twas pleasure to look at, 'twas music to hear,
But now she is absent, I walk by its side,
And still as it murmurs do nothing but chide.
Must you be so cheerful while I go in pain?
Peace there with your bubbling, and hear me complain.

When my lambkins around me would oftentimes play,
And when Phœbe and I were as joyful as they,
How pleasant their sporting, how happy the time,
When spring, love, and beauty were all in their prime?
But now in their frolics when by me they pass,
I fling at their fleeces a handful of grass:
Be still, then I cry; for it makes me quite mad,
To see you so merry while I am so sad.

My dog I was ever well pleasèd to see
Come wagging his tail at my fair one and me:
And Phœbe was pleased too, and to my dog said,
"Come hither, poor fellow;" and patted his head.
But now, when he's fawning, I with a sour look
Cry, Sirrah! and give him a blow with my crook.
And I'll give him another; for why should not Tray
Be as dull as his master, when Phœbe's away?

When walking with Phœbe, what sights have I seen!
How fair was the flower, how fresh was the green!
What a lovely appearance the trees and the shade,
The corn-fields and hedges, and everything made!
But now she has left me, though all are still there,
They none of them now so delightful appear:
'Twas naught but the magic, I find, of her eyes,
Made so many beautiful prospects arise.

Sweet music went with us both all the wood through,
The lark, linnet, throstle and nightingale too;
Winds over us whisper'd, flocks by us did bleat,
And chirp! went the grasshopper under our feet.
But now she is absent, though still they sing on,
The woods are but lonely, the melody's gone:
Her voice in the concert, as now I have found,
Gave everything else its agreeable sound.

Rose, what is become of thy delicate hue?
And where is the violet's beautiful blue?
Does aught of its sweetness the blossom beguile?
That meadow, those daisies, why do they not smile?

Ah! rivals, I see what it was that you
    dress'd
And made yourselves fine for—a place in
    her breast;
You put on your colors to pleasure her
    eye,
To be pluck'd by her hand, on her bosom
    to die.

How slowly Time creeps, till my Phœbe
    return!
While amidst the soft zephyr's cool breezes
    I burn!
Methinks if I knew whereabouts he would
    tread,
I could breathe on his wings, and 'twould
    melt down the lead.
Fly swifter, ye minutes, bring hither my
    dear,
And rest so much longer for't when she is
    here.
Ah, Colin! old Time is full of delay,
Nor will budge one foot faster for all thou
    canst say.

Will no pitying power that hears me com-
    plain,
Or cure my disquiet or soften my pain?
To be cured thou must, Colin, thy passion
    remove;
But what swain is so silly to live without
    love?
No, deity, bid the dear nymph to return,
For ne'er was poor shepherd so sadly for-
    lorn.
Ah! what shall I do? I shall die with
    despair!
Take heed, all ye swains, how ye part with
    your fair.
                      JOHN BYROM.

WILLIAM AND MARGARET.

'TWAS at the silent, solemn hour,
    When night and morning meet;
In glided Margaret's grimly ghost,
    And stood at William's feet.

Her face was like an April morn,
    Clad in a wintry cloud;
And clay-cold was her lily hand,
    That held her sable shroud.

So shall the fairest face appear,
    When youth and years are flown:
Such is the robe that kings must wear,
    When death has reft their crown.

Her bloom was like the springing flower,
    That sips the silver dew;
The rose was budded in her cheek,
    Just opening to the view.

But love had, like the canker-worm,
    Consumed her early prime;
The rose grew pale, and left her cheek—
    She died before her time.

"Awake," she cried, "thy true love calls,
    Come from her midnight grave;
Now let thy pity hear the maid,
    Thy love refused to save.

"This is the dark and dreary hour,
    When injured ghosts complain;
When yawning graves give up their dead,
    To haunt the faithless swain.

"Bethink thee, William, of thy fault,
    Thy pledge and broken oath!
And give me back my maiden vow,
    And give me back my troth.

"Why did you promise love to me,
    And not that promise keep?
Why did you swear my eyes were bright,
    Yet leave those eyes to weep?

"How could you say my face was fair,
    And yet that face forsake?
How could you win my virgin heart,
    Yet leave that heart to break?

"Why did you say my lip was sweet,
    And made the scarlet pale?
And why did I, young witless maid!
    Believe the flatt'ring tale?

"That face, alas! no more is fair,
    Those lips no longer red;
Dark are my eyes now closed in death,
    And every charm is fled.

"The hungry worm my sister is;
    This winding-sheet I wear:
And cold and weary lasts our night,
    Till that last morn appear.

"But hark! the cock has warn'd me hence;
  A long and last adieu!
Come see, false man, how low she lies,
  Who died for love of you."

The lark sung loud; the morning smiled
  With beams of rosy red;
Pale William quaked in every limb,
  And raving left his bed.

He hied him to the fatal place,
  Where Margaret's body lay;
And stretch'd him on the green grass turf,
  That wrapt her breathless clay.

And thrice he call'd on Margaret's name,
  And thrice he wept full sore;
Then laid his cheek to her cold grave,
  And word spake never more.
                DAVID MALLET.

WHERE SHALL THE LOVER REST?

WHERE shall the lover rest
  Whom the Fates sever
From his true maiden's breast
  Parted for ever?
Where, through groves deep and high
  Sounds the far billow,
Where early violets die
  Under the willow.
    Eleu loro
Soft shall be his pillow.

There, through the summer day
  Cool streams are laving,
There, while the tempests sway,
  Scarce are boughs waving;
There thy rest shalt thou take,
  Parted for ever,
Never again to wake
  Never, oh never!
    Eleu loro
Never, oh never!

Where shall the traitor rest,
  He, the deceiver,
Who could win maiden's breast,
  Ruin, and leave her?
In the lost battle,
  Borne down by the flying,
Where mingles war's rattle
  With groans of the dying;
    Eleu loro
There shall he be lying.

Her wing shall the eagle flap
  O'er the false-hearted;
His warm blood the wolf shall lap
  Ere life be parted:
Shame and dishonor sit
  By his grave ever;
Blessing shall hallow it
  Never, oh never!
    Eleu loro
Never, oh never!
                SIR WALTER SCOTT.

THE OUTLAW.

OH, Brignall banks are wild and fair,
  And Greta woods are green,
And you may gather garlands there
  Would grace a summer queen.
And as I rode by Dalton Hall
  Beneath the turrets high,
A Maiden on the castle-wall
  Was singing merrily:
"Oh Brignall banks are fresh and fair,
  And Greta woods are green;
I'd rather rove with Edmund there
  Than reign our English queen."

"If, Maiden, thou wouldst wend with me,
  To leave both tower and town,
Thou first must guess what life lead we
  That dwell by dale and down.
And if thou canst that riddle read,
  As read full well you may,
Then to the greenwood shalt thou speed
  As blithe as Queen of May."
Yet sung she "Brignall banks are fair,
  And Greta woods are green;
I'd rather rove with Edmund there
  Than reign our English queen.

"I read you by your bugle-horn
  And by your palfrey good,
I read you for a Ranger sworn
  To keep the king's greenwood."
"A Ranger, lady, winds his horn,
  And 'tis at peep of light;

His blast is heard at merry morn,
  And mine at dead of night."
Yet sung she " Brignall banks are fair,
  And Greta woods are gay;
I would I were with Edmund there
  To reign his Queen of May!

" With burnish'd brand and musketoon
  So gallantly you come,
I read you for a bold Dragoon,
  That lists the tuck of drum."
" I list no more the tuck of drum,
  No more the trumpet hear;
But when the beetle sounds his hum
  My comrades take the spear.
And oh! though Brignall banks be fair
  And Greta woods be gay,
Yet mickle must the maiden dare
  Would reign my Queen of May.

"Maiden! a nameless life I lead,
  A nameless death I'll die!
The fiend whose lantern lights the mead
  Were better mate than I!
And when I'm with my comrades met
  Beneath the greenwood bough,
What once we were we all forget,
  Nor think what we are now."
Yet Brignall banks are fresh and fair,
  And Greta woods are green,
And you may gather garlands there
  Would grace a summer queen.
                    SIR WALTER SCOTT.

BEDOUIN SONG.

FROM the desert I come to thee,
  On a stallion shod with fire;
And the winds are left behind
  In the speed of my desire.
Under thy window I stand,
  And the midnight hears my cry:
I love thee, I love but thee,
  With a love that shall not die
    Till the sun grows cold,
    And the stars are old,
    And the leaves of the Judgment
      Book unfold!

Look from thy window, and see
  My passion and my pain;
I lie on the sands below,
  And I faint in thy disdain.
Let the night-winds touch thy brow
  With the heat of my burning sigh,
And melt thee to hear the vow
  Of a love that shall not die
    Till the sun grows cold,
    And the stars are old,
    And the leaves of the Judgment
      Book unfold!

My steps are nightly driven,
  By the fever in my breast,
To hear from thy lattice breathed
  The word that shall give me rest.
Open the door of thy heart,
  And open thy chamber door,
And my kisses shall teach thy lips
  The love that shall fade no more
    Till the sun grows cold,
    And the stars are old,
    And the leaves of the Judgment
      Book unfold!
                    BAYARD TAYLOR.

COME INTO THE GARDEN, MAUD.

COME into the garden, Maud,
  For the black bat, night, has flown!
Come into the garden, Maud,
  I am here at the gate alone;
And the woodbine spices are wafted abroad,
  And the musk of the rose is blown.

For a breeze of morning moves,
  And the planet of Love is on high,
Beginning to faint in the light that she loves,
  On a bed of daffodil sky,—
To faint in the light of the sun she loves,
  To faint in his light, and to die.

All night have the roses heard
  The flute, violin, bassoon;
All night has the casement jessamine stirr'd
  To the dancers dancing in tune,—
Till a silence fell with the waking bird,
  And a hush with the setting moon.

I said to the lily, " There is but one
  With whom she has heart to be gay.
When will the dancers leave her alone?
  She is weary of dance and play."
Now half to the setting moon are gone,
  And half to the rising day;

Low on the sand and loud on the stone
  The last wheel echoes away.

I said to the rose, "The brief night goes
  In babble and revel and wine.
O young lord-lover, what sighs are those
  For one that will never be thine?
But mine, but mine," so I sware to the rose,
  "For ever and ever mine!"

And the soul of the rose went into my
    blood,
  As the music clash'd in the hall;
And long by the garden lake I stood,
  For I heard your rivulet fall
From the lake to the meadow and on to
    the wood,
  Our wood, that is dearer than all;

From the meadow your walks have left so
    sweet
  That whenever a March wind sighs,
He sets the jewel-print of your feet
  In violets blue as your eyes,
To the woody hollows in which we meet,
  And the valleys of Paradise.

The slender acacia would not shake
  One long milk-bloom on the tree;
The white lake-blossom fell into the lake,
  As the pimpernel dozed on the lea;
But the rose was awake all night for your
    sake,
  Knowing your promise to me;
The lilies and roses were all awake,
  They sigh'd for the dawn and thee.

Queen rose of the rosebud garden of girls,
  Come hither, the dances are done,
In gloss of satin and glimmer of pearls,
  Queen lily and rose in one;
Shine out, little head, sunning over with
    curls,
  To the flowers, and be their sun.

There has fallen a splendid tear
  From the passion-flower at the gate.
She is coming, my dove, my dear;
  She is coming, my life, my fate!
The red rose cries, "She is near, she is
    near;"
  And the white rose weeps, "She is late;"
The larkspur listens, "I hear, I hear;"
  And the lily whispers, "I wait."

She is coming, my own, my sweet!
  Were it ever so airy a tread,
My heart would hear her and beat,
  Were it earth in an earthy bed;
My dust would hear her and beat,
  Had I lain for a century dead;
Would startle and tremble under her feet,
  And blossom in purple and red.
                    ALFRED TENNYSON.

THE CALL.

AWAKE thee, my lady-love,
  Wake thee and rise;
The sun through the bower peeps
  Into thine eyes.

Behold how the early lark
  Springs from the corn;
Hark, hark! how the flower-bird
  Winds her wee horn.

The swallow's glad shriek is heard
  All through the air,
The stock-dove is murmuring
  Loud as she dare.

Apollo's wing'd bugleman
  Cannot contain,
But peals his loud trumpet-call
  Once and again.

Then wake thee, my lady-love,
  Bird of my bower,
The sweetest and sleepiest
  Bird at this hour.
                    GEORGE DARLEY.

A HEALTH.

I FILL this cup to one made up
  Of loveliness alone,
A woman, of her gentle sex
  The seeming paragon;
To whom the better elements
  And kindly stars have given
A form so fair, that, like the air,
  'Tis less of earth than heaven.

Her every tone is music's own,
  Like those of morning birds,
And something more than melody
  Dwells ever in her words;

The coinage of her heart are they,
    And from her lips each flows,
As one may see the burden'd bee
    Forth issue from the rose.

Affections are as thoughts to her,
    The measures of her hours,
Her feelings have the fragrancy,
    The freshness of young flowers;
And lovely passions, changing oft,
    So fill her, she appears
The image of themselves by turns,—
    The idol of past years!

Of her bright face one glance will trace
    A picture on the brain,
And of her voice in echoing hearts
    A sound must long remain;
But memory, such as mine of her,
    So very much endears,
When death is nigh my latest sigh
    Will not be life's, but hers.

I fill this cup to one made up
    Of loveliness alone,
A woman, of her gentle sex
    The seeming paragon;—
Her health! and would on earth there stood
    Some more of such a frame,
That life might all be poetry,
    And weariness a name.
            EDWARD COATE PINKNEY.

CASTARA.

LIKE the violet, which alone
    Prospers in some happy shade,
My Castara lives unknown,
    To no ruder eye betray'd;
For she's to herself untrue
Who delights i' the public view.

Such is her beauty as no arts
    Have enrich'd with borrow'd grace.
Her high birth no pride imparts,
    For she blushes in her place.
Folly boasts a glorious blood,—
She is noblest being good.

Cautious, she knew never yet
    What a wanton courtship meant;
Nor speaks loud to boast her wit,
    In her silence eloquent.
Of herself survey she takes,
But 'tween men no difference makes.

She obeys with speedy will
    Her grave parents' wise commands;
And so innocent, that ill
    She nor acts, nor understands.
Women's feet run still astray
If to ill they know the way.

She sails by that rock, the court,
    Where oft virtue splits her mast;
And retiredness thinks the port,
    Where her fame may anchor cast.
Virtue safely cannot sit
Where vice is enthroned for wit.

She holds that day's pleasure best
    Where sin waits not on delight;
Without mask, or ball, or feast,
    Sweetly spends a winter's night.
O'er that darkness whence is thrust
Prayer and sleep, oft governs lust.

She her throne makes reason climb,
    While wild passions captive lie;
And each article of time,
    Her pure thoughts to heaven fly;
All her vows religious be,
And she vows her love to me.
            WILLIAM HABINGTON.

SUPERSTITION.

I CARE not though it be
By the preciser sort thought popery;
    We poets can a license show
    For everything we do:
Hear, then, my little saint, I'll pray to
    thee.

If now thy happy mind
Amid its various joys can leisure find
    To attend to anything so low
    As what I say or do,
Regard, and be what thou wast ever—kind.

Let not the bless'd above
Engross thee quite, but sometimes hither
    rove;
    Fain would I thy sweet image see,
    And sit and talk with thee;
Nor is it curiosity, but love.

Ah! what delight 'twould be
Wouldst thou sometimes by stealth con-
    verse with me!
  How should I thine sweet commune prize,
    And other joys despise!
Come, then; I ne'er was yet denied by thee.

I would not long detain
Thy soul from bliss, nor keep thee here in
    pain;
  Nor should thy fellow-saints e'er know
    Of thy escape below:
Before thou'rt miss'd thou shouldst return
    again.

Sure, heaven must needs thy love
As well as other qualities improve;
  Come, then, and recreate my sight
    With rays of thy pure light:
'Twill cheer my eyes more than the lamps
    above.

But if Fate's so severe
As to confine thee to thy blissful sphere
  (And by thy absence I shall know
    Whether thy state be so),
Live happy, but be mindful of me there.
                              JOHN NORRIS.

LIGHT.

THE night has a thousand eyes,
  And the day but one;
Yet the light of the bright world dies,
  With the dying sun.

The mind has a thousand eyes,
  And the heart but one;
Yet the light of a whole life dies,
  When love is done.
                      FRANCIS W. BOURDILLON.

DISDAIN RETURNED.

HE that loves a rosy cheek,
  Or a coral lip admires,
Or from star-like eyes doth seek
  Fuel to maintain his fires,—
As old Time makes these decay,
So his flames must waste away.

But a smooth and steadfast mind,
  Gentle thoughts and calm desires,
Hearts with equal love combined,
  Kindle never-dying fires.
Where these are not, I despise
Lovely cheeks, or lips, or eyes.

No tears, Celia, now shall win
  My resolved heart to return;
I have search'd thy soul within,
  And find naught but pride and scorn;
I have learn'd thy arts, and now
Can disdain as much as thou.
Some power, in my revenge, convey
That love to her I cast away.
                              THOMAS CAREW.

AUX ITALIENS.

AT Paris it was, at the opera there;—
  And she look'd like a queen in a book
      that night,
With the wreath of pearl in her raven
      hair,
  And the brooch on her breast so bright.

Of all the operas that Verdi wrote,
  The best, to my taste, is the Trovatore;
And Mario can soothe, with a tenor note,
  The souls in purgatory.

The moon on the tower slept soft as snow;
  And who was not thrill'd in the stran-
      gest way,
As we heard him sing, while the gas
      burn'd low,
  "Non ti scordar di me"?

The emperor there, in his box of state,
  Look'd grave, as if he had just then
      seen
The red flag wave from the city gate,
  Where his eagles in bronze had been.

The empress, too, had a tear in her eye:
  You'd have said that her fancy had gone
      back again,
For one moment, under the old blue sky,
  To the old glad life in Spain.

Well, there in our front-row box we sat
  Together, my bride betroth'd and I;
My gaze was fixed on my opera-hat,
  And hers on the stage hard by.

And both were silent, and both were sad;
  Like a queen she lean'd on her full
      white arm,
With that regal, indolent air she had,
  So confident of her charm!

I have not a doubt she was thinking then
  Of her former lord, good soul that he
    was,
Who died the richest and roundest of
    men,
  The Marquis of Carabas.

I hope that, to get to the kingdom of
    heaven,
  Through a needle's eye he had not to
    pass;
I wish him well, for the jointure given
  To my lady of Carabas.

Meanwhile, I was thinking of my first
    love,
  As I had not been thinking of aught for
    years,
Till over my eyes there began to move
  Something that felt like tears.

I thought of the dress that she wore last
    time,
  When we stood 'neath the cypress trees to-
    gether,
In that lost land, in that soft clime,
  In the crimson evening weather;

Of that muslin dress (for the eve was
    hot),
  And her warm white neck in its golden
    chain,
And her full, soft hair, just tied in a knot,
  And falling loose again;

And the jasmine flower in her fair young
    breast,
  (Oh, the faint, sweet smell of that jasmine
    flower!)
And the one bird singing alone to his nest,
  And the one star over the tower.

I thought of our little quarrels and strife,
  And the letter that brought me back my
    ring;
And it all seem'd then, in the waste of
    life,
  Such a very little thing!

For I thought of her grave below the hill,
  Which the sentinel cypress tree stands
    over,
And I thought, "Were she only living
    still,
  How I could forgive her, and love her!"

And I swear, as I thought of her thus, in
    that hour,
  And of how, after all, old things were
    best,
That I smelt the smell of that jasmine
    flower
  Which she used to wear in her breast.

It smelt so faint, and it smelt so sweet,
  It made me creep, and it made me
    cold;
Like the scent that steals from the crum-
    bling sheet
  Where a mummy is half unroll'd.

And I turn'd and look'd: she was sitting
    there,
  In a dim box over the stage, and drest
In that muslin dress, with that full, soft
    hair,
  And that jasmine in her breast.

I was here: and she was there:
  And the glittering horse-shoe curved be-
    tween,
From my bride betroth'd, with her raven
    hair,
  And her sumptuous, scornful mien,

To my early love, with her eyes downcast,
  And over her primrose face the shade.
(In short, from the future back to the
    past
  There was but a step to be made.)

To my early love from my future bride
  One moment I look'd. Then I stole to
    the door,
I traversed the passage, and down at her
    side
  I was sitting, a moment more.

My thinking of her, or the music's strain,
  Or something which never will be ex-
    prest,
Had brought her back from the grave
    again,
  With the jasmine in her breast.

She is not dead, and she is not wed,
  But she loves me now, and she loved me
    then!
And the very first word that her sweet
    lips said,
  My heart grew youthful again.

The Marchioness there, of Carabas,
  She is wealthy, and young, and handsome still,
And but for her,—well, we'll let that pass—
  She may marry whomever she will.

But I will marry my own first love,
  With her primrose face, for old things are best,
And the flower in her bosom, I prize it above
  The brooch in my lady's breast.

The world is fill'd with folly and sin,
  And love must cling where it can, I say,
For beauty is easy enough to win,
  But one isn't loved every day.

And I think, in the lives of most women and men,
  There's a moment when all would go smooth and even,
If only the dead could find out when
  To come back and be forgiven.

But oh, the smell of that jasmine flower!
  And oh, that music! and oh, the way
That voice rang out from the donjon tower:
  Non ti scordar di me,
  Non ti scordar di me!
ROBERT BULWER LYTTON.

TO SIGH, YET FEEL NO PAIN.

To sigh, yet feel no pain,
  To weep, yet scarce know why;
To sport an hour with beauty's chain,
  Then throw it idly by;
To kneel at many a shrine,
  Yet lay the heart on none;
To think all other charms divine,
  But those we just have won;
This is love, faithless love,
  Such as kindleth hearts that rove.

To keep one sacred flame,
  Through life unchill'd, unmoved,
To love in wintry age the same
  As first in youth we loved;
To feel that we adore,
  Ev'n to such fond excess,
That, though the heart would break with more,
  It could not live with less;
This is love, faithful love,
  Such as saints might feel above.
THOMAS MOORE.

A PASTORAL.

On a hill there grows a flower,
  Fair befall the dainty sweet!
By that flower there is a bower,
  Where the heavenly Muses meet.

In that bower there is a chair,
  Fringèd all about with gold,
Where doth sit the fairest fair
  That ever eye did yet behold.

It is Phillis, fair and bright,
  She that is the shepherds' joy,
She that Venus did despite,
  And did blind her little boy.

This is she, the wise, the rich,
  That the world desires to see;
This is *ipsa quae,* the which
  There is none but only she.

Who would not this face admire?
  Who would not this saint adore?
Who would not this sight desire,
  Though he thought to see no more?

O fair eyes, yet let me see
  One good look, and I am gone:
Look on me, for I am he,
  The poor silly Corydon.

Thou that art the shepherds' queen,
  Look upon thy silly swain;
By thy comfort have been seen
  Dead men brought to life again.
NICHOLAS BRETON.

THE SILENT LOVER.

Passions are likened best to floods and streams,
  The shallow murmur, but the deep are dumb;
So when affection yields discourse, it seems
  The bottom is but shallow whence they come;

They that are rich in words must needs
    discover
They are but poor in that which makes
    a lover.

Wrong not, sweet mistress of my heart,
    The merit of true passion,
With thinking that he feels no smart
    Who sues for no compassion.

Since if my plaints were not t' approve
    The conquest of thy beauty,
It comes not from defect of love,
    But fear t' exceed my duty.

For, knowing that I sue to serve
    A saint of such perfection
As all desire, but none deserve
    A place in her affection,

I rather choose to want relief
    Than venture the revealing:—
Where glory recommends the grief,
    Despair disdains the healing.

Thus those desires that boil so high
    In any mortal lover,
When reason cannot make them die,
    Discretion them must cover.

Yet when discretion doth bereave
    The plaints that I should utter,
Then your discretion may perceive
    That silence is a suitor.

Silence in love bewrays more woe
    Than words, though ne'er so witty:
A beggar that is dumb, you know,
    May challenge double pity.

Then wrong not, dearest to my heart,
    My love, for secret passion:
He smarteth most that hides his smart,
    And sues for no compassion.
            SIR WALTER RALEIGH.

THE GROOMSMAN TO THE BRIDESMAID.

EVERY wedding, says the proverb,
    Makes another, soon or late;
Never yet was any marriage
    Enter'd in the book of fate,
But the names were also written
    Of the patient pair that wait.

Blessings, then, upon the morning
    When my friend, with fondest look,
By the solemn rites' permission,
    To his heart his true love took,
And the destinies recorded
    Other two within their book.

While the priest fulfill'd his office,
    Still the ground the lovers eyed,
And the parents and the kinsmen
    Aim'd their glances at the bride;
But the groomsmen eyed the virgins
    Who were waiting at her side.

Three there were that stood beside her;
    One was dark, and one was fair;
But nor fair nor dark the other,
    Save her Arab eyes and hair;
Neither dark nor fair I call her,
    Yet she was the fairest there.

While the groomsman—shall I own it?
    Yes to thee, and only thee—
Gazed upon this dark-eyed maiden
    Who was fairest of the three,
Thus he thought: "How blest the bridal
    Where the bride were such as she!"

Then I mused upon the adage,
    Till my wisdom was perplex'd,
And I wonder'd, as the churchman
    Dwelt upon his holy text,
Which of all who heard his lesson
    Should require the service next.

Whose will be the next occasion
    For the flowers, the feast, the wine?
Thine, perchance, my dearest lady;
    Or, who knows?—it may be mine,
What if 'twere—forgive the fancy—
    What if 'twere—both mine and thine?
            THOMAS WILLIAM PARSONS.

ZARA'S EAR-RINGS.

MY ear-rings! my ear-rings! they've
    dropp'd into the well,
And what to say to Muça, I cannot, cannot
    tell—
'Twas thus, Granada's fountain by, spoke
    Albuharez' daughter:—
The well is deep—far down they lie, beneath the cold blue water;

To me did Muça give them when he spake
　　his sad farewell,
And what to say when he comes back,
　　alas! I cannot tell.

My ear-rings! my ear-rings!—they were
　　pearls in silver set,
That, when my Moor was far away, I ne'er
　　should him forget;
That I ne'er to other tongues should list,
　　nor smile on other's tale,
But remember he my lips had kiss'd, pure
　　as those ear-rings pale.
When he comes back, and hears that I
　　have dropp'd them in the well,
Oh, what will Muça think of me?—I can-
　　not, cannot tell!

My ear-rings! my ear-rings!—he'll say
　　they should have been,
Not of pearl and of silver, but of gold
　　and glittering sheen,
Of jasper and of onyx, and of diamond
　　shining clear,
Changing to the changing light, with
　　radiance insincere;
That changeful mind unchanging gems are
　　not befitting well,
Thus will he think—and what to say, alas!
　　I cannot tell.

He'll think when I to market went I
　　loiter'd by the way;
He'll think a willing ear I lent to all the
　　lads might say;
He'll think some other lover's hand, among
　　my tresses noosed,
From the ears where he had placed them
　　my rings of pearl unloosed;
He'll think when I was sporting so beside
　　this marble well
My pearls fell in—and what to say, alas!
　　I cannot tell.

He'll say I am a woman, and we are all
　　the same;
He'll say I loved when he was here to
　　whisper of his flame—
But when he went to Tunis, my virgin
　　troth had broken,
And thought no more of Muça, and cared
　　not for his token.

My ear-rings! my ear-rings! O luckless,
　　luckless well,—
For what to say to Muça—alas! I cannot
　　tell.
I'll tell the truth to Muça—and I hope he
　　will believe—
That I thought of him at morning and
　　thought of him at eve;
That, musing on my lover, when down the
　　sun was gone,
His ear-rings in my hand I held, by the
　　fountain all alone;
And that my mind was o'er the sea, when
　　from my hand they fell,
And that deep his love lies in my heart, as
　　they lie in the well.
　　　　　　　　　(From the Spanish.)
　　　　　　　　JOHN GIBSON LOCKHART.

LOOK OUT, BRIGHT EYES.

LOOK out, bright eyes, and bless the air!
Even in shadows you are fair.
Shut-up beauty is like fire,
That breaks out clearer still and higher.
Though your beauty be confined,
　　And soft Love a prisoner bound,
Yet the beauty of your mind
　　Neither check nor chain hath found.
Look out nobly, then, and dare
Even the fetters that you wear.
　　　　　　　　BEAUMONT AND FLETCHER.

TAKE, OH TAKE THOSE LIPS AWAY.

TAKE, oh take those lips away
　　That so sweetly were forsworn,
And those eyes, the break of day,
　　Lights that do mislead the morn!
But my kisses bring again,
Seals of love, though seal'd in vain.

Hide, oh hide those hills of snow
　　Which thy frozen bosom bears,
On whose tops the pinks that grow
　　Are yet of those that April wears.
But first set my poor heart free,
Bound in those icy chains by thee.
　　　　　　　　BEAUMONT AND FLETCHER.

GO, LOVELY ROSE.

"Go, lovely rose!
  Tell her that wastes her time and me,
That now she knows
    When I resemble her to thee,
    How sweet and fair she seems to be.

"Tell her that's young,
  And shuns to have her graces spied,
That hadst thou sprung
    In deserts, where no men abide,
    Thou must have uncommended died.

"Small is the worth
  Of beauty from the light retired:
Bid her come forth,
    Suffer herself to be desired,
    And not blush so to be admired.

"Then die! that she
  The common fate of all things rare
May read in thee,
    How small a part of time they share
    That are so wondrous sweet and fair."
                EDMUND WALLER.

MUSIC, WHEN SOFT VOICES DIE.

MUSIC, when soft voices die,
Vibrates in the memory—
Odors, when sweet violets sicken,
Live within the sense they quicken.

Rose-leaves, when the rose is dead,
Are heap'd for the beloved's bed;
And so thy thoughts, when thou art gone,
Love itself shall slumber on.
                PERCY BYSSHE SHELLEY.

TO HIS MISTRESS, THE QUEEN OF BOHEMIA.

YOU meaner beauties of the night,
  That poorly satisfy our eyes
More by your number than your light—
  You common people of the skies—
  What are you when the moon shall rise?

You curious chanters of the wood,
  That warble forth dame Nature's lays,
Thinking your passions understood
  By your weak accents—what's your praise
When Philomel her voice shall raise?

You violets that first appear,
  By your pure purple mantles known,
Like the proud virgins of the year,
  As if the spring were all your own—
  What are you when the rose is blown?

So when my mistress shall be seen
  In form and beauty of her mind;
By virtue first, then choice, a queen—
  Tell me, if she were not design'd
  Th' eclipse and glory of her kind?
                SIR HENRY WOTTON.

ON A GIRDLE.

THAT which her slender waist confined
Shall now my joyful temples bind;
No monarch but would give his crown,
His arms might do what this has done.

It was my heaven's extremest sphere,
The pale which held that lovely deer:
My joy, my grief, my hope, my love,
Did all within this circle move.

A narrow compass! and yet there
Dwelt all that's good, and all that's fair.
Give me but what this ribbon bound,
Take all the rest the sun goes round!
                EDMUND WALLER.

THERE IS A GARDEN IN HER FACE.

THERE is a garden in her face,
  Where roses and white lilies blow;
A heavenly paradise is that place,
  Wherein all pleasant fruits do grow;
There cherries grow that none may buy,
Till cherry-ripe themselves do cry.

Those cherries fairly do enclose
  Of orient pearl a double row,
Which when her lovely laughter shows,
  They look like rosebuds filled with snow;
Yet them no peer nor prince may buy,
Till cherry-ripe themselves do cry.

Her eyes like angels watch them still,
  Her brows like bended bows do stand,

Threatening with piercing frowns to kill
 All that approach with eye or hand
These sacred cherries to come nigh,
Till cherry-ripe themselves do cry.
RICHARD ALISON.

JENNY KISSED ME.

JENNY kiss'd me when we met,
 Jumping from the chair she sat in;
Time, you thief! who love to get
 Sweets into your list, put that in.
Say I'm weary, say I'm sad;
 Say that health and wealth have miss'd me;
Say I'm growing old, but add—
Jenny kiss'd me!
LEIGH HUNT.

ALLEN-A-DALE.

ALLEN-A-DALE has no fagot for burning,
Allen-a-Dale has no furrow for turning,
Allen-a-Dale has no fleece for the spinning,
Yet Allen-a-Dale has red gold for the winning.
Come, read me my riddle! come, hearken my tale!
And tell me the craft of bold Allen-a-Dale.

The Baron of Ravensworth prances in pride,
And he views his domains upon Arkindale side,
The mere for his net, and the land for his game,
The chase for the wild, and the park for the tame;
Yet the fish of the lake, and the deer of the vale,
Are less free to Lord Dacre than Allen-a-Dale!

Allen-a-Dale was ne'er belted a knight,
Though his spur be as sharp, and his blade be as bright;
Allen-a-Dale is no baron or lord,
Yet twenty tall yeomen will draw at his word;
And the best of our nobles his bonnet will veil,
Who at Rere-cross on Stanmore meets Allen-a-Dale.

Allen-a-Dale to his wooing is come;
The mother, she ask'd of his household and home:
"Though the castle of Richmond stand fair on the hill,
My hall," quoth bold Allen, "shows gallanter still;
'Tis the blue vault of heaven, with its crescent so pale,
And with all its bright spangles!" said Allen-a-Dale.

The father was steel, and the mother was stone;
They lifted the latch, and they bade him be gone;
But loud, on the morrow, their wail and their cry;
He had laugh'd on the lass with his bonny black eye,
And she fled to the forest to hear a lovetale,
And the youth it was told by was Allen-a-Dale!
SIR WALTER SCOTT.

THE HEATH THIS NIGHT MUST BE MY BED.

THE heath this night must be my bed,
The bracken curtain for my head,
My lullaby the warder's tread,
 Far, far from love and thee, Mary;
To-morrow eve, more stilly laid,
My couch may be my bloody plaid,
My vesper song thy wail, sweet maid!
 It will not waken me, Mary!

I may not, dare not, fancy now
The grief that clouds thy lovely brow;
I dare not think upon thy vow,
 And all it promised me, Mary.
No fond regret must Norman know;
When bursts Clan-Alpine on the foe,
His heart must be like bended bow,
 His foot like arrow free, Mary.

A time will come with feeling fraught!
For, if I fall in battle fought,
Thy hapless lover's dying thought
 Shall be a thought on thee, Mary.

And if return'd from conquer'd foes,
How blithely will the evening close,
How sweet the linnet sing repose
To my young bride and me, Mary!
SIR WALTER SCOTT.

SIGH NO MORE, LADIES.

SIGH no more, ladies, sigh no more;
  Men were deceivers ever;
One foot in sea, and one on shore,
  To one thing constant never:
    Then sigh not so,
    But let them go,
  And be you blythe and bonny;
  Converting all your sounds of woe
  Into, Hey nonny, nonny.

Sing no more ditties, sing no mo
  Of dumps so dull and heavy;
The fraud of men was ever so,
  Since summer first was leavy:
    Then sigh not so,
    But let them go,
  And be you blythe and bonny;
  Converting all your sounds of woe
  Into, Hey nonny, nonny.
WILLIAM SHAKESPEARE.

LOVE NOT.

LOVE not, love not! ye hapless sons of clay!
  Hope's gayest wreaths are made of earthly flowers—
Things that are made to fade and fall away
  Ere they have blossom'd for a few short hours.
Love not!

Love not! the thing ye love may change!
  The rosy lip may cease to smile on you,
The kindly-beaming eye grow cold and strange,
  The heart still warmly beat, yet not be true.
Love not!

Love not! the thing you love may die—
  May perish from the gay and gladsome earth;
The silent stars, the blue and smiling sky,
  Beam o'er its grave, as once upon its birth.
Love not!

Love not! oh, warning vainly said
  In present hours as in years gone by;
Love flings a halo round the dear one's head,
  Faultless, immortal, till they change or die.
Love not!
CAROLINE NORTON.

A WOMAN'S QUESTION.

BEFORE I trust my Fate to thee,
  Or place my hand in thine,
Before I let thy Future give
  Color and form to mine,
Before I peril all for thee, question thy
  soul to-night for me.

I break all slighter bonds, nor feel
  A shadow of regret:
Is there one link within the Past
  That holds thy spirit yet?
Or is thy Faith as clear and free as that
  which I can pledge to thee?

Does there within thy dimmest dreams
  A possible future shine,
Wherein thy life could henceforth breathe,
  Untouch'd, unshared by mine?
If so, at any pain or cost, oh tell me before
  all is lost.

Look deeper still. If thou canst feel
  Within thy inmost soul,
That thou hast kept a portion back,
  While I have staked the whole;
Let no false pity spare the blow, but in
  true mercy tell me so.

Is there within thy heart a need
  That mine cannot fulfil?
One chord that any other hand
  Could better wake or still?
Speak now—lest at some future day my
  whole life wither and decay.

Lives there within thy nature hid
  The demon-spirit Change,
Shedding a passing glory still
  On all things new and strange?
It may not be thy fault alone—but shield
  my heart against thy own.

Couldst thou withdraw thy hand one day
 And answer to my claim,
That Fate, and that to-day's mistake—
 Not thou—had been to blame?
Some soothe their conscience thus; but
 thou wilt surely warn and save me
 now.

Nay, answer *not*,—I dare not hear,
 The words would come too late;
Yet I would spare thee all remorse,
 So comfort thee, my Fate—
Whatever on my heart may fall—remember, I *would* risk it all!
ADELAIDE ANNE PROCTER.

A WOMAN'S ANSWER.

I WILL not let you say a woman's part
 Must be to give exclusive love alone;
Dearest, although I love you so, my heart
 Answers a thousand claims besides your
 own.

I love—what do I not love? Earth and
 air
 Find space within my heart, and myriad
 things
You would not deign to heed are cherish'd
 there,
 And vibrate on its very inmost strings.

I love the Summer, with her ebb and flow
 Of light, and warmth, and music, that
 have nursed
Her tender buds to blossoms . . . and you
 know
 It was in summer that I saw you first.

I love the Winter dearly too, . . . but then
 I owe it so much; on a winter's day,
Bleak, cold, and stormy, you return'd
 again,
 When you had been those weary months
 away.

I love the Stars like friends; so many
 nights
 I gazed at them, when you were far from
 me,
Till I grew blind with tears; . . . those far-
 off lights
 Could watch you, whom I long'd in vain
 to see.

I love the flowers; happy hours lie
 Shut up within their petals close and
 fast:
You have forgotten, dear; but they and I
 Keep every fragment of the golden past.

I love, too, to be loved; all loving praise
 Seems like a crown upon my life,—to
 make
It better worth the giving, and to raise
 Still nearer to your own the heart you
 take.

I love all good and noble souls;—I heard
 One speak of you but lately, and for
 days,
Only to think of it, my soul was stirr'd
 In tender memory of such generous
 praise.

I love all those who love you: all who owe
 Comfort to you; and I can find regret
Even for those poorer hearts who once
 could know,
 And once could love you, and can now
 forget.

Well, is my heart so narrow,—I, who spare
 Love for all these? Do I not even hold
My favorite books in special tender care,
 And prize them as a miser does his gold?—

The poets that you used to read to me
 While summer twilights faded in the
 sky;
But most of all I think Aurora Leigh,
 Because — because — do you remember
 why?

Will you be jealous? Did you guess before
 I loved so many things?—Still you the
 best:—
Dearest, remember that I love you more,
 Oh more a thousand times, than all the
 rest!
ADELAIDE ANNE PROCTER.

MAUDE CLARE.

OUT of the church she follow'd them
 With a lofty step and mien:
His bride was like a village maid,
 Maude Clare was like a queen.

"Son Thomas," his lady mother said,
  With smiles, almost with tears:
"May Nell and you but live as true
  As we have done for years;

"Your father thirty years ago
  Had just your tale to tell;
But he was not so pale as you,
  Nor I so pale as Nell."

My lord was pale with inward strife,
  And Nell was pale with pride;
My lord gazed long on pale Maude Clare
  Or ever he kiss'd the bride.

"Lo, I have brought my gift, my lord,
  Have brought my gift," she said:
"To bless the hearth, to bless the board,
  To bless the marriage-bed.

"Here's my half of the golden chain
  You wore about your neck,
That day we waded ankle-deep
  For lilies in the beck:

"Here's my half of the faded leaves
  We pluck'd from budding bough,
With feet amongst the lily-leaves,—
  The lilies are budding now."

He strove to match her scorn with scorn,
  He falter'd in his place:
"Lady," he said,—"Maude Clare," he said,—
  "Maude Clare:"—and hid his face.

She turn'd to Nell: "My Lady Nell,
  I have a gift for you;
Though were it fruit, the bloom were gone,
  Or, were it flowers, the dew.

"Take my share of a fickle heart,
  Mine of a paltry love:
Take it or leave it as you will,
  I wash my hands thereof."

"And what you leave," said Nell, "I'll take,
  And what you spurn, I'll wear;
For he's my lord for better and worse,
  And him I love, Maude Clare.

"Yea, though you're taller by the head,
  More wise, and much more fair;
I'll love him till he loves me best,
  Me best of all, Maude Clare."
          CHRISTINA GEORGINA ROSSETTI.

A SERENADE.

AH! County Guy, the hour is nigh,
  The sun has left the lea,
The orange-flower perfumes the bower,
  The breeze is on the sea.
The lark, his lay who trill'd all day,
  Sits hush'd his partner nigh;
Breeze, bird, and flower confess the hour,
  But where is County Guy?

The village maid steals through the shade,
  Her shepherd's suit to hear;
To beauty shy, by lattice high,
  Sings high-born cavalier.
The star of Love, all stars above,
  Now reigns o'er earth and sky,
And high and low the influence know,
  But where is County Guy?
          SIR WALTER SCOTT.

TO A VERY YOUNG LADY.

AH, Chloris! could I now but sit
  As unconcern'd as when
Your infant beauty could beget
  No happiness or pain!
When I the dawn used to admire,
  And praised the coming day,
I little thought the rising fire
  Would take my rest away.

Your charms in harmless childhood lay
  Like metals in a mine;
Age from no face takes more away
  Than youth conceal'd in thine.
But as your charms insensibly
  To their perfection prest,
So love as unperceived did fly,
  And centred in my breast.

My passion with your beauty grew.
  While Cupid at my heart
Still as his mother favor'd you
  Threw a new flaming dart;
Each gloried in their wanton part;
  To make a lover he
Employ'd the utmost of his art—
  To make a beauty, she.

Though now I slowly bend to love
  Uncertain of my fate,
If your fair self my chains approve,
  I shall my freedom hate.

Lovers, like dying men, may well
  At first disorder'd be,
Since none alive can truly tell
  What fortune they must see.
    SIR CHARLES SEDLEY.

SONNET.

LIKE as the culver, on the barèd bough,
  Sits mourning for the absence of her
    mate,
And in her songs sends many a wishful
    vow
  For his return that seems to linger late;
So I alone, now left disconsolate,
  Mourn to myself the absence of my
    love,
And, wand'ring here and there, all desolate,
  Seek with my plaints to match that
    mournful dove;
Ne joy of aught that under heaven doth
    hove
  Can comfort me but her own joyous
    sight,
Whose sweet aspect both God and men
    can move,
  In her unspotted pleasures to delight.
Dark is my day, whiles her fair light I
    miss,
And dead my life, that wants such lively
    bliss.
    EDMUND SPENSER.

SONNET.

SINCE I did leave the presence of my
    love,
  Many long, weary days I have outworn,
And many nights that slowly seem'd to
    move
  Their sad protract from evening until
    morn.
For, when as day the heaven doth adorn,
  I wish that night the noyous day would
    end,
And when as night hath us of light forlorn,
  I wish that day would shortly reascend.
Thus I the time with expectation spend,
  And fain my grief with changes to beguile,

That further seems his term still to extend,
  And maketh every minute seem a mile.
So sorrow still doth seem too long to last,
But joyous hours do fly away too fast.
    EDMUND SPENSER.

A RENUNCIATION.

IF women could be fair, and yet not fond,
  Or that their love were firm, not fickle
    still,
I would not marvel that they make men
    bond
  By service long to purchase their goodwill,
But when I see how frail those creatures
    are,
I muse that men forget themselves so far.

To mark the choice they make, and how
    they change,
  How oft from Phœbus they do flee to
    Pan,
Unsettled still, like haggards wild they
    range,
  These gentle birds that fly from man to
    man;
Who would not scorn and shake them
    from the fist,
And let them fly, fair fools, which way
    they list.

Yet for disport we fawn and flatter both,
  To pass the time when nothing else can
    please,
And train them to our lure with subtle
    oath,
  Till, weary of their wiles, ourselves we
    ease;
And then we say when we their fancy
    try,
To play with fools, oh, what a fool was I!
    EDWARD VERE, Earl of Oxford.

BLAME NOT MY LUTE.

BLAME not my Lute! for he must sound
  Of this or that as liketh me;
For lack of wit the Lute is bound
  To give such tunes as pleaseth me;

Though my songs be somewhat strange,
And speak such words as touch my change,
    Blame not my Lute!

My Lute, alas! doth not offend,
  Though that perforce he must agree
  To sound such tunes as I intend
  To sing to them that heareth me;
Then though my songs be somewhat plain,
And toucheth some that use to feign,
    Blame not my Lute!

My Lute and strings may not deny,
  But as I strike they must obey;
Break not them so wrongfully,
  But wreak thyself some other way;
And though the songs which I indite
Do quit thy change with rightful spite,
    Blame not my Lute!

Spite asketh spite, and changing change,
  And falsèd faith must needs be known;
The faults so great, the case so strange;
  Of right it must abroad be blown:
Then since that by thine own desert
My songs do tell how true thou art,
    Blame not my Lute!

Blame but thyself that hast misdone,
  And well deservèd to have blame;
Change thou thy way, so evil begone,
  And then my Lute shall sound that same!
But if till then my fingers play,
By thy desert their wonted way,
    Blame not my Lute!

Farewell, unknown; for though thou break
  My strings in spite with great disdain,
Yet have I found out, for thy sake,
  Strings for to string my Lute again:
And if perchance this silly rhyme
Do make thee blush at any time,
    Blame not my Lute!
        SIR THOMAS WYATT.

SONNET.

O HAPPY Thames that didst my Stella bear!
  I saw myself with many a smiling line
Upon thy cheerful face, joy's livery wear,
  While those fair planets on thy streams did shine;
The boat for joy could not to dance forbear;
  While wanton winds, with beauties so divine
Ravish'd, staid not till in her golden hair
  They did themselves, O sweetest prison! twine;
And fain those Eol's youth there would their stay
  Have made, but forced by Nature still to fly,
First did with puffing kiss those locks display.
  She so dishevell'd, blush'd:—from window I,
With sight thereof, cried out, O fair disgrace!
Let honor's self to thee grant highest place.
        SIR PHILIP SIDNEY.

THE RE-CURED LOVER EXULTETH IN HIS FREEDOM.

I AM as I am, and so will I be:
But how that I am none knoweth truly.
Be it ill, be it well, be I bond, be I free,
I am as I am, and so will I be.

I lead my life indifferently;
I mean nothing but honesty;
And though folks judge full diversely,
I am as I am, and so will I die.

I do not rejoice nor yet complain,
Both mirth and sadness I do refrain,
And use the means since folks will feign;
Yet I am as I am, be it pleasant or pain.

Divers do judge as they do trow,
Some of pleasure and some of woe,
Yet for all that, nothing they know;
But I am as I am, wheresoever I go.

But since judgers do thus decay,
Let every man his judgment say;
I will it take in sport and play,
For I am as I am, whosoever say nay.

Who judgeth well, well God them send;
Who judgeth evil, God them amend;
To judge the best therefore intend,
For I am as I am, and so will I end.

Yet some there be that take delight,
To judge folks' thought for envy and spite;
But whether they judge me wrong or right,
I am as I am, and so do I write.

Praying you all that this do read,
To trust it as you do your creed;
And not to think I change my weed,
For I am as I am, however I speed.

But how that is I leave to you;
Judge as ye list, false or true,
Ye know no more than afore ye knew,
Yet I am as I am, whatever ensue.

And from this mind I will not flee,
But to you all that misjudge me,
I do protest, as ye may see,
That I am as I am, and so will be.
Sir Thomas Wyatt.

SONNET.

Having this day my horse, my hand, my lance
  Guided so well, that I obtain'd the prize,
  Both by the judgment of the English eyes,
And of some sent from that sweet enemy France;
Horsemen my skill in horsemanship advance;
  Townfolks my strength; a daintier judge applies
  His praise to sleight which from good use doth rise;
Some lucky wits impute it but to chance;
  Others, because of both sides I do take
My blood from them who did excel in this,
  Think Nature me a man of arms did make.
How far they shot awry! the true cause is
  Stella look'd on, and from her heavenly face
Sent forth the beams which made so fair my race.
Sir Philip Sidney.

A FRAGMENT FROM SAPPHO.

Blest as the immortal gods is he,
The youth who fondly sits by thee,
And hears and sees thee all the while
Softly speak and sweetly smile.

'Twas this deprived my soul of rest,
And raised such tumults in my breast:
For while I gazed, in transport tost,
My breath was gone, my voice was lost.

My bosom glow'd; the subtle flame
Ran quick through all my vital frame:
O'er my dim eyes a darkness hung;
My ears with hollow murmurs rung.

In dewy damps my limbs were chill'd;
My blood with gentle horrors thrill'd·
My feeble pulse forgot to play—
I fainted, sunk, and died away.
Ambrose Philips.

ASK ME NO MORE.

Ask me no more: the moon may draw the sea;
  The cloud may stoop from heaven and take the shape,
  With fold to fold, of mountain or of cape;
But, oh too fond, when have I answer'd thee?
  Ask me no more.

Ask me no more: what answer should I give?
  I love not hollow cheek or faded eye;
  Yet, O my friend, I will not have thee die!
Ask me no more, lest I should bid thee live;
  Ask me no more.

Ask me no more: thy fate and mine are seal'd.
  I strove against the stream, and all in vain.
Let the great river take me to the main.
No more, dear love, for at a touch I yield;
  Ask me no more!
Alfred Tennyson.

ASK ME NO MORE WHERE JOVE BESTOWS.

Ask me no more, where Jove bestows,
When June is past, the fading rose;
For in your beauties, orient deep,
These flow'rs, as in their causes, sleep.

Ask me no more, whither do stray
The golden atoms of the day;
For, in pure love, heaven did prepare
Those powders to enrich your hair.

Ask me no more, whither doth haste
The nightingale, when May is past;
For in your sweet dividing throat
She winters, and keeps warm her note.

Ask me no more, where those stars light,
That downward fall in dead of night;
For in your eyes they sit, and there
Fixèd become, as in their sphere.

Ask me no more if east or west
The Phœnix builds her spicy nest;
For unto you at last she flies,
And in your fragrant bosom dies.
THOMAS CAREW.

MY DEAR AND ONLY LOVE.

PART FIRST.

My dear and only love, I pray,
　This noble world of thee
Be govern'd by no other sway
　But purest monarchie.
For if confusion have a part,
　Which virtuous souls abhor,
And hold a synod in thy heart,
　I'll never love thee more.

Like Alexander I will reign,
　And I will reign alone,
My thoughts shall evermore disdain
　A rival on my throne.
He either fears his fate too much,
　Or his deserts are small,
That puts it not unto the touch,
　To win or lose it all.

But I must rule and govern still,
　And always give the law,
And have each subject at my will,
　And all to stand in awe.
But 'gainst my battery if I find
　Thou shun'st the prize so sore
As that thou set'st me up a blind,
　I'll never love thee more.

If in the empire of thy heart,
　Where I should solely be,
Another do pretend a part,
　And dares to vie with me;
Or if committees thou erect,
　And go on such a score,
I'll sing and laugh at thy neglect,
　And never love thee more.

But if thou wilt be constant then,
　And faithful of thy word,
I'll make thee glorious by my pen,
　And famous by my sword.
I'll serve thee in such noble ways
　Was never heard before;
I'll crown and deck thee all with bays.
　And love thee evermore.

PART SECOND.

My dear and only love, take heed,
　Lest thou thyself expose,
And let all longing lovers feed
　Upon such looks as those.
A marble wall then build about,
　Beset without a door;
But if thou let thy heart fly out,
　I'll never love thee more.

Let not their oaths, like volleys shot,
　Make any breach at all;
Nor smoothness of their language plot
　Which way to scale the wall;
Nor balls of wild-fire love consume
　The shrine which I adore;
For if such smoke about thee fume,
　I'll never love thee more.

I think thy virtues be too strong
　To suffer by surprise;
Those victuall'd by my love so long,
　The siege at length must rise,
And leave thee rulèd in that health
　And state thou wast before;
But if thou turn a commonwealth,
　I'll never love thee more.

Or if by fraud, or by consent,
　Thy heart to ruine come,
I'll sound no trumpet as I wont,
　Nor march by tuck of drum;
But hold my arms, like ensigns, up,
　Thy falsehood to deplore,
And bitterly will sigh and weep,
　And never love thee more.

I'll do with thee as Nero did,
  When Rome was set on fire,
Not only all relief forbid,
  But to a hill retire,
And scorn to shed a tear to see
  Thy spirit grown so poor;
But smiling sing, until I die,
  I'll never love thee more.

Yet, for the love I bare thee once,
  Lest that thy name should die,
A monument of marble-stone
  The truth shall testifie:
That every pilgrim passing by
  May pity and deplore
My case, and read the reason why
  I can love thee no more.

The golden laws of love shall be
  Upon this pillar hung,—
A simple heart, a single eye,
  A true and constant tongue;
Let no man for more love pretend
  Than he has hearts in store;
True love begun shall never end;
  Love one and love no more.

Then shall thy heart be set by mine,
  But in far different case;
But mine was true, so was not thine,
  But lookt like Janus' face.
For as the waves with every wind,
  So sail'st thou every shore,
And leav'st my constant heart behind,—
  How can I love thee more?

My heart shall with the sun be fix'd
  For constancy most strange,
And thine shall with the moon be mix'd,
  Delighting aye in change.
Thy beauty shined at first more bright,
  And woe is me therefore,
That ever I found thy love so light
  I could love thee no more!

The misty mountains, smoking lakes,
  The rocks' resounding echo,
The whistling wind that murmur makes
  Shall with me sing hey ho!
The tossing seas, the tumbling boats,
  Tears dropping from each shore,
Shall tune with me their turtle notes—
  I'll never love thee more.

As doth the turtle, chaste and true.
  Her fellow's death regrete,
And daily mourns for his adieu,
  And ne'er renews her mate;
So, though thy faith was never fast,
  Which grieves me wondrous sore,
Yet I shall live in love so chast,
  That I shall love no more.

And when all gallants ride about
  These monuments to view,
Whereon is written, in and out,
  Thou traitorous and untrue;
Then in a passion they shall pause,
  And thus say, sighing sore,
"Alas! he had too just a cause,
  Never to love thee more."

And when that tracing goddess Fame
  From east to west shall flee,
She shall record it to thy shame,
  How thou hast lovèd me;
And how in odds our love was such
  As few have been before:
Thou loved too many, and I too much,
  So I can love no more.
JAMES GRAHAM, Marquis of Montrose.

OH, HAD WE SOME BRIGHT LITTLE ISLE OF OUR OWN!

OH, had we some bright little isle of our own,
In a blue summer ocean, far off and alone,
Where a leaf never dies in the still blooming bowers,
And the bee banquets on through a whole year of flowers;
  Where the sun loves to pause
    With so fond a delay,
  That the night only draws
    A thin veil o'er the day.
Where simply to feel that we breathe, that we live,
Is worth the best joy that life elsewhere can give.

There, with souls ever ardent and pure as the clime,
We should love as they loved in the first golden time;

The glow of the sunshine, the balm of the air,
Would steal to our hearts and make all
    summer there.
  With affection as free
    From decline as the bowers,
  And with hope, like the bee,
    Living always on flowers,
Our life should resemble a long day of light,
And our death come on, holy and calm as
    the night.
                            THOMAS MOORE.

TO CELIA.

DRINK to me only with thine eyes,
  And I will pledge with mine;
Or leave a kiss but in the cup,
  And I'll not look for wine.
The thirst that from the soul doth rise
  Doth ask a drink divine;
But might I of Jove's nectar sup,
  I would not change for thine.

I sent thee late a rosy wreath,
  Not so much honoring thee
As giving it a hope that there
  It could not wither'd be;
But thou thereon didst only breathe
  And sent'st it back to me;
Since when it grows, and smells, I swear,
  Not of itself, but thee!
                        (From the Greek.)
                            BEN JONSON.

AT SETTING DAY AND RISING MORN.

AT setting day and rising morn,
  With soul that still shall love thee,
I'll ask of Heaven thy safe return,
  With all that can improve thee.
I'll visit aft the birken bush,
  Where first thou kindly told me
Sweet tales of love, and hid thy blush,
  Whilst round thou didst enfold me.
To all our haunts I will repair,
  By greenwood shaw or fountain,
Or where the summer day I'd share
  With thee upon yon mountain;
There will I tell the trees and flowers,
  From thoughts unfeign'd and tender,
By vows you're mine, by love is yours
  A heart that cannot wander.
                            ALLAN RAMSAY.

SONG OF MARGARET.

AY, I saw her, we have met;—
  Married eyes, how sweet they be!
Are you happier, Margaret,
  Than you might have been with me?
Silence! make no more ado!
  Did she think I should forget?
Matters nothing, though I knew,
  Margaret, Margaret.

Once those eyes, full sweet, full shy,
  Told a certain thing to mine;
What they told me I put by,
  Oh, so careless of the sign.
Such an easy thing to take,
  And I did not want it then;
Fool! I wish my heart would break;
  Scorn is hard on hearts of men.

Scorn of self is bitter work,—
  Each of us has felt it now;
Bluest skies she counted mirk,
  Self-betray'd of eyes and brow;
As for me, I went my way,
  And a better man drew nigh,
Fain to earn, with long essay,
  What the winner's hand threw by.

Matters not in deserts old,
  What was born, and wax'd, and yearn'd,
Year to year its meaning told,
  I am come,—its deeps are learn'd;
Come, but there is naught to say,—
  Married eyes with mine have met.
Silence! Oh, I had my day,
  Margaret, Margaret.
                            JEAN INGELOW.

LOCHABER NO MORE.

FAREWELL to Lochaber, and farewell, my
    Jean,
Where heartsome with thee I hae mony
    day been!
For Lochaber no more, Lochaber no more,
We'll maybe return to Lochaber no more!
These tears that I shed, they are a' for
    my dear,
And no for the dangers attending on
    war,
Though borne on rough seas to a far bloody
    shore,
Maybe to return to Lochaber no more.

Though hurricanes rise, and rise every
  wind,
They'll ne'er make a tempest like that in
  my mind;
Though loudest of thunder on louder
  waves roar,
That's naething like leaving my love on
  the shore.
To leave thee behind me my heart is sair
  pain'd;
By ease that's inglorious no fame can be
  gain'd;
And beauty and love's the reward of the
  brave,
And I must deserve it before I can crave.

Then glory, my Jeany, maun plead my ex-
  cuse;
Since honor commands me, how can I re-
  fuse?
Without it I ne'er can have merit for
  thee,
And without thy favor I'd better not be.
I gae then, my lass, to win honor and
  fame,
And if I should luck to come gloriously
  hame,
I'll bring a heart to thee with love run-
  ning o'er,
And then I'll leave thee and Lochaber no
  more.
              ALLAN RAMSAY.

TERNISSA.

TERNISSA, you are fled!
  I say not to the dead,
But to the happy ones who rest below;
  For, surely, surely, where
  Your voice and graces are,
Nothing of death can any feel or know.
  Girls who delight to dwell
  Where grows most asphodel,
Gather to their calm breasts each word you
  speak;
  The mild Persephone
  Places you on her knee,
And your cool palm smooths down stern
  Pluto's cheek.
              WALTER SAVAGE LANDOR.

EVELYN HOPE.

BEAUTIFUL Evelyn Hope is dead!
  Sit and watch by her side an hour.
That is her book-shelf, this her bed;
  She pluck'd that piece of geranium-
    flower,
Beginning to die, too, in the glass.
  Little has yet been changed, I think;
The shutters are shut—no light may pass,
  Save two long rays thro' the hinges'
    chink.

Sixteen years old when she died!
  Perhaps she had scarcely heard my
    name—
It was not her time to love; beside,
  Her life had many a hope and aim,
Duties enough and little cares;
  And now was quiet, now astir—
Till God's hand beckon'd unawares,
  And the sweet white brow is all of her.

Is it too late, then, Evelyn Hope?
  What! your soul was pure and true;
The good stars met in your horoscope,
  Made you of spirit, fire, and dew;
And just because I was thrice as old,
  And our paths in the world diverged so
    wide,
Each was naught to each, must I be told?
  We were fellow-mortals—naught beside?

No, indeed! for God above
  Is great to grant, as mighty to make,
And creates the love to reward the love;
  I claim you still, for my own love's sake!
Delay'd, it may be, for more lives yet,
  Through worlds I shall traverse, not a
    few;
Much is to learn and much to forget
  Ere the time be come for taking you.

But the time will come—at last it will—
  When, Evelyn Hope, what meant, I shall
    say,
In the lower earth—in the years long still—
  That body and soul so gay?
Why your hair was amber I shall divine,
  And your mouth of your own geranium's
    red—
And what you would do with me, in fine,
  In the new life come in the old one's
    stead.

I have lived, I shall say, so much since then,
  Given up myself so many times,
Gain'd me the gains of various men,
  Ransack'd the ages, spoil'd the climes;
Yet one thing—one—in my soul's full scope,
  Either I miss'd or itself miss'd me—
And I want and find you, Evelyn Hope!
  What is the issue? let us see!

I loved you, Evelyn, all the while;
  My heart seem'd full as it could hold—
There was place and to spare for the frank young smile
  And the red young mouth and the hair's young gold.
So hush! I will give you this leaf to keep;
  See, I shut it inside the sweet, cold hand.
There, that is our secret! go to sleep;
  You will wake, and remember, and understand.
ROBERT BROWNING.

COME AWAY, COME AWAY, DEATH.

COME away, come away, Death,
  And in sad cypres let me be laid;
Fly away, fly away, breath;
  I am slain by a fair cruel maid.
My shroud of white, stuck all with yew,
  Oh prepare it!
My part of death no one so true
  Did share it.

Not a flower, not a flower sweet
  On my black coffin let there be strown;
Not a friend, not a friend greet
  My poor corpse, where my bones shall be thrown:
A thousand thousand sighs to save,
  Lay me, oh where
Sad true lover never find my grave,
  To weep there.
WILLIAM SHAKESPEARE.

COLIN AND LUCY.

OF Leinster, famed for maidens fair,
  Bright Lucy was the grace;
Nor e'er did Liffy's limpid stream
  Reflect so fair a face.

Till luckless love and pining care
  Impair'd her rosy hue,
Her coral lip, and damask cheek,
  And eyes of glossy blue.

Oh, have you seen a lily pale,
  When beating rains descend?
So droop'd the slow-consuming maid;
  Her life now near its end.

By Lucy warn'd, of flattering swains
  Take heed, ye easy fair;
Of vengeance due to broken vows
  Ye perjured swains beware.

Three times, all in the dead of night,
  A bell was heard to ring;
And at her window, shrieking thrice,
  The raven flapp'd his wing.

Too well the love-lorn maiden knew
  That solemn boding sound;
And thus in dying words bespoke
  The virgins weeping round:

" I hear a voice you cannot hear,
  Which says I must not stay;
I see a hand you cannot see,
  Which beckons me away.

" By a false heart and broken vows,
  In early youth I die.
Am I to blame because his bride
  Is thrice as rich as I?

"Ah, Colin! give not her thy vows,
  Vows due to me alone:
Nor thou, fond maid, receive his kiss,
  Nor think him all thy own.

" To-morrow in the church to wed,
  Impatient, both prepare,
But know, fond maid, and know, false youth,
  That Lucy will be there.

" Then bear my corse, ye comrades, bear,
  The bridegroom blithe to meet;
He in his wedding-trim so gay,
  I in my winding-sheet."

She spoke, she died;—her corse was borne
  The bridegroom blithe to meet;
He in his wedding-trim so gay,
  She in her winding-sheet.

Then what were perjured Colin's thoughts?
　How were those nuptials kept?
The bride-men flock'd round Lucy dead,
　And all the village wept.

Confusion, shame, remorse, despair,
　At once his bosom swell;
The damps of death bedew'd his brow,
　He shook, he groan'd, he fell.

From the vain bride (ah, bride no more!)
　The varying crimson fled,
When, stretch'd before her rival's corse,
　She saw her husband dead.

Then to his Lucy's new-made grave,
　Convey'd by trembling swains,
One mould with her beneath one sod,
　For ever now remains.

Oft at their grave the constant hind
　And plighted maid are seen;
With garlands gay, and true-love knots
　They deck the sacred green.

But, swain forsworn, whoe'er thou art,
　This hallow'd spot forbear,
Remember Colin's dreadful fate,
　And fear to meet him there.
　　　　　　　　THOMAS TICKELL.

LORD LOVEL.

LORD LOVEL he stood at his castle-gate
　Combing his milk-white steed;
When up came Lady Nancy Belle,
　To wish her lover good speed, speed,
　To wish her lover good speed.

"Where are you going, Lord Lovel?" she said,
　"Oh! where are you going?" said she;
"I'm going, my Lady Nancy Belle,
　Strange countries for to see, to see,
　Strange countries for to see."

"When will you be back, Lord Lovel?"
　she said;
　"Oh! when will you come back?" said
　she;
"In a year or two—or three, at the most,
　I'll return to my fair Nancy-cy,
　I'll return to my fair Nancy."

But he had not been gone a year and a day,
　Strange countries for to see,
When languishing thoughts came into his head,
　Lady Nancy Belle he would go see, see,
　Lady Nancy Belle he would go see.

So he rode and he rode on his milk-white steed,
　Till he came to London town,
And there he heard St. Pancras' bells,
　And the people all mourning, round, round,
　And the people all mourning round.

"Oh! what is the matter?" Lord Lovel he said,
　"Oh! what is the matter?" said he;
"A lord's lady is dead," a woman replied,
　"And some call her Lady Nancy-cy,
　And some call her Lady Nancy."

So he order'd the grave to be open'd wide,
　And the shroud he turnèd down,
And there he kiss'd her clay-cold lips,
　Till the tears came trickling down, down,
　Till the tears came trickling down.

Lady Nancy she died as it might be to-day,
　Lord Lovel he died as to-morrow;
Lady Nancy she died out of pure, pure grief,
　Lord Lovel he died out of sorrow, sorrow,
　Lord Lovel he died out of sorrow.

Lady Nancy was laid in St. Pancras' church,
　Lord Lovel was laid in the choir;
And out of her bosom there grew a red rose,
　And out of her lover's a brier, brier,
　And out of her lover's a brier.

They grew, and they grew, to the church-steeple top,
　And then they could grow no higher:
So there they entwined in a true-lover's knot,
　For all lovers true to admire-mire,
　For all lovers true to admire.
　　　　　　　　AUTHOR UNKNOWN.

ANNIE LAURIE.

MAXWELTON braes are bonnie
　Where early fa's the dew,
And it's there that Annie Laurie
　Gie'd me her promise true—
Gie'd me her promise true,
　Which ne'er forgot will be;
And for bonnie Annie Laurie
　I'd lay me doune and dee.

Her brow is like the snaw-drift;
　Her throat is like the swan;
Her face it is the fairest
　That e'er the sun shone on—
That e'er the sun shone on—
　And dark blue is her ee;
And for bonnie Annie Laurie
　I'd lay me doune and dee.

Like dew on the gowan lying
　Is the fa' o' her fairy feet;
And like the winds in summer sighing,
　Her voice is low and sweet—
Her voice is low and sweet—
　And she's a' the world to me;
And for bonnie Annie Laurie
　I'd lay me doune and dee.
　　　　　　　AUTHOR UNKNOWN.

WHAT AILS THIS HEART O' MINE?

WHAT ails this heart o' mine?
　What ails this watery ee?
What gars me a' turn pale as death
　When I take leave o' thee?
When thou art far awa',
　Thou'lt dearer grow to me;
But change o' place and change o' folk
　May gar thy fancy jee.

When I gae out at e'en,
　Or walk at morning air,
Ilka rustling bush will seem to say,
　I used to meet thee there.
Then I'll sit down and cry,
　And live aneath the tree,
And when a leaf fa's i' my lap,
　I'll ca' 't a word frae thee.

I'll hie me to the bower
　That thou wi' roses tied,
And where wi' mony a blushing bud
　I strove myself to hide.

I'll doat on ilka spot
　Where I hae been wi' thee;
And ca' to mind some kindly word,
　By ilka burn and tree.
　　　　　　　SUSANNA BLAMIRE.

THE PORTRAIT.

MIDNIGHT past! Not a sound of aught
　Through the silent house, but the wind
　　at his prayers.
I sat by the dying fire, and thought
　Of the dear dead woman up stairs.

A night of tears! for the gusty rain
　Had ceased, but the eaves were dripping
　　yet;
And the moon look'd forth, as though in
　　pain,
　With her face all white and wet:

Nobody with me, my watch to keep,
　But the friend of my bosom, the man I
　　love:
And grief had sent him fast to sleep
　In the chamber up above.

Nobody else, in the country place
　All round, that knew of my loss beside,
But the good young Priest with the Ra-
　　phael-face,
Who confess'd her when she died.

That good young Priest is of gentle nerve.
　And my grief had moved him beyond
　　control;
For his lip grew white, as I could observe,
　When he speeded her parting soul.

I sat by the dreary hearth alone:
　I thought of the pleasant days of yore:
I said, "The staff of my life is gone:
　The woman I loved is no more.

"On her cold dead bosom my portrait lies,
　Which next to her heart she used to
　　wear—
Haunting it o'er with her tender eyes
　When my own face was not there.

"It is set all round with rubies red,
　And pearls which a Peri might have kept.
For each ruby there my heart hath bled.
　For each pearl my eyes have wept."

And I said—"The thing is precious to me:
  They will bury her soon in the church-
    yard clay;
It lies on her heart, and lost must be
  If I do not take it away."

I lighted my lamp at the dying flame,
  And crept up the stairs that creak'd for
    fright,
Till into the chamber of death I came,
  Where she lay all in white.

The moon shone over her winding-sheet,
  There stark she lay on her carven bed:
Seven burning tapers about her feet,
  And seven about her head.

As I stretch'd my hand, I held my breath;
  I turn'd as I drew the curtains apart:
I dared not look on the face of death:
  I knew where to find her heart.

I thought at first, as my touch fell there,
  It had warm'd that heart to life, with
    love;
For the thing I touch'd was warm, I swear,
  And I could feel it move.

'Twas the hand of a man, that was moving
    slow
  O'er the heart of the dead,—from the
    other side:
And at once the sweat broke over my
    brow:
  "Who is robbing the corpse?" I cried.

Opposite me by the tapers' light,
  The friend of my bosom, the man I
    loved,
Stood over the corpse, and all as white,
  And neither of us moved.

"What do you here, my friend?" . . . The
    man
  Look'd first at me, and then at the dead.
"There is a portrait here," he began;
  "There is. It is mine," I said.

Said the friend of my bosom, "Yours, no
    doubt,
  The portrait was, till a month ago,
When this suffering angel took that out,
  And placed mine there, I know."

"This woman, she loved me well," said I.
  "A month ago," said my friend to me:
"And in your throat," I groan'd, "you
    lie!"
He answer'd, . . . "Let us see."

"Enough!" I return'd, "let the dead de-
    cide:
And whose soever the portrait prove,
  His shall it be, when the cause is tried,
    Where Death is arraign'd by Love."

We found the portrait there, in its place:
  We open'd it by the tapers' shine:
The gems were all unchanged: the face
  Was—neither his nor mine.

"One nail drives out another, at least!
  The face of the portrait there," I cried,
"Is our friend's the Raphael-faced young
    Priest,
Who confess'd her when she died."

The setting is all of rubies red,
  And pearls which a Peri might have
    kept.
For each ruby there my heart hath bled:
  For each pearl my eyes have wept.

         ROBERT BULWER LYTTON.
         (OWEN MEREDITH.)

AMYNTA.

My sheep I neglected, I broke my sheep-
    hook,
And all the gay haunts of my youth I
    forsook;
No more for Amynta fresh garlands I
    wove:
For ambition, I said, would soon cure me
    of love.

Oh, what had my youth with ambition
    to do?
Why left I Amynta? Why broke I my
    vow?
Oh, give me my sheep, and my sheep-
    hook restore,
And I'll wander from love and Amynta
    no more.

Through regions remote in vain do I
    rove,
And bid the wide ocean secure me from
    love!

O fool! to imagine that aught could subdue
A love so well founded, a passion so true!
  Oh, what had my youth with ambition
    to do?
  Why left I Amynta? Why broke I my
    vow?
  Oh, give me my sheep, and my sheep-
    hook restore,
  And I'll wander from love and Amynta
    no more.

Alas! 'tis too late at thy fate to repine;
Poor shepherd, Amynta can never be thine:
Thy tears are all fruitless, thy wishes are vain,
The moments neglected return not again.
  Oh, what had my youth with ambition
    to do?
  Why left I Amynta? Why broke I my
    vow?
  Oh, give me my sheep, and my sheep-
    hook restore,
  And I'll wander from love and Amynta
    no more.
SIR GILBERT ELLIOT.

THE LORD OF BURLEIGH.

In her ear he whispers gayly,
  "If my heart by signs can tell,
Maiden, I have watch'd thee daily,
  And I think thou lov'st me well."
She replies, in accents fainter,
  "There is none I love like thee."
He is but a landscape-painter,
  And a village maiden she.
He to lips, that fondly falter,
  Presses his without reproof:
Leads her to the village altar,
  And they leave her father's roof.
"I can make no marriage present;
  Little can I give my wife.
Love will make our cottage pleasant,
  And I love thee more than life."
They by parks and lodges going
  See the lordly castles stand;
Summer woods, about them blowing,
  Made a murmur in the land.
From deep thought himself he rouses,
  Says to her that loves him well,
"Let us see these handsome houses
  Where the wealthy nobles dwell."

So she goes, by him attended,
  Hears him lovingly converse,
Sees whatever fair and splendid
  Lay betwixt his home and hers:
Parks with oak and chestnut shady,
  Parks and order'd gardens great,
Ancient homes of lord and lady,
  Built for pleasure and for state.
All he shows her makes him dearer:
  Evermore she seems to gaze
On that cottage growing nearer,
  Where they twain will spend their days.
Oh but she will love him truly!
  He shall have a cheerful home;
She will order all things duly,
  When beneath his roof they come.
Thus her heart rejoices greatly,
  Till a gateway she discerns
With armorial bearings stately,
  And beneath the gate she turns;
Sees a mansion more majestic
  Than all those she saw before:
Many a gallant gay domestic
  Bows before him at the door.
And they speak in gentle murmur,
  When they answer to his call,
While he treads with footstep firmer,
  Leading on from hall to hall.
And, while now she wonders blindly,
  Nor the meaning can divine,
Proudly turns he round and kindly,
  "All of this is mine and thine."
Here he lives in state and bounty,
  Lord of Burleigh, fair and free,
Not a lord in all the county
  Is so great a lord as he.
All at once the color flushes
  Her sweet face from brow to chin:
As it were with shame she blushes,
  And her spirit changed within.
Then her countenance all over
  Pale again as death did prove;
But he clasp'd her like a lover,
  And he cheer'd her soul with love.
So she strove against her weakness,
  Tho' at times her spirit sank:
Shaped her heart with woman's meekness
  To all duties of her rank:
And a gentle consort made he,
  And her gentle mind was such
That she grew a noble lady,
  And the people loved her much.

But a trouble weigh'd upon her,
  And perplex'd her, night and morn,
With the burden of an honor
  Unto which she was not born.
Faint she grew, and ever fainter,
  As she murmur'd, "Oh, that he
Were once more that landscape-painter
  Which did win my heart from me!"
So she droop'd and droop'd before him,
  Fading slowly from his side:
Three fair children first she bore him,
  Then before her time she died.
Weeping, weeping late and early,
  Walking up and pacing down,
Deeply mourn'd the Lord of Burleigh,
  Burleigh-house by Stamford-town.
And he came to look upon her,
  And he look'd at her and said,
"Bring the dress and put it on her,
  That she wore when she was wed."
Then her people, softly treading,
  Bore to earth her body, drest
In the dress that she was wed in,
  That her spirit might have rest.
            ALFRED TENNYSON.

MY ONLY JO AND DEARIE, O.

THY cheek is o' the rose's hue,
  My only jo and dearie, O;
Thy neck is like the siller dew
  Upon the banks sae briery, O;
Thy teeth are o' the ivory,
Oh, sweet's the twinkle o' thine ee!
Nae joy, nae pleasure, blinks on me,
  My only jo and dearie, O.

The birdie sings upon the thorn
  Its sang o' joy, fu' cheerie, O,
Rejoicing in the summer morn,
  Nae care to make it eerie, O;
But little kens the sangster sweet
Aught o' the cares I hae to meet,
That gar my restless bosom beat,
  My only jo and dearie, O.

Whan we were bairnies on yon brae,
  And youth was blinking bonny, O,
Aft we wad daff the lee-lang day,
  Our joys fu' sweet and mony, O;
Aft I wad chase thee o'er the lee,
And round about the thorny tree,
Or pu' the wild-flowers a' for thee,
  My only jo and dearie, O.

I hae a wish I canna tine
  'Mang a' the cares that grieve me, O;
I wish thou wert for ever mine,
  And never mair to leave me, O:
Then I wad daut thee night and day,
Nor ither warldly care wad hae,
Till life's warm stream forgot to play,
  My only jo and dearie, O.
            RICHARD GALL.

LUCY'S FLITTIN'.

'TWAS when the wan leaf frae the birk
  tree was fa'in,
  And Martinmas dowie had wound up
    the year,
That Lucy rowed up her wee kist wi' her
  a' in't,
  And left her auld maister and neibours
    sae dear:
For Lucy had served i' the glen a' the
  simmer;
  She cam there afore the bloom cam on
    the pea;
An orphan was she, and they had been
  gude till her,
  Sure that was the thing brocht the tear
    to her ee.

She gaed by the stable where Jamie was
  stannin';
  Richt sair was his kind heart her flittin'
    to see.
"Fare ye weel, Lucy!" quo' Jamie, and
  ran in;
  The gatherin' tears trickled fast frae
    her ee.
As down the burnside she gaed slow wi'
  her flittin',
  "Fare ye weel, Lucy!" was ilka bird's
    sang;
She heard the craw sayin't, high on the
  tree sittin',
  And the robin was chirpin't the brown
    leaves amang.

"Oh, what is't that pits my puir heart in
  a flutter?
  And what gars the tears come sae fast
    to my ee?
If I wasna ettled to be ony better,
  Then what gars me wish ony better to
    be?

I'm just like a lammie that loses its
    mither;
  Nae mither or friend the puir lammie
    can see;
I fear I hae tint my puir heart a'thegither,
  Nae wonder the tear fa's sae fast frae
    my ee.

'Wi' the rest o' my claes I hae rowed up
    the ribbon,
  The bonnie blue ribbon that Jamie gae
    me;
Yestreen, when he gae me't, and saw I was
    sabbin',
  I'll never forget the wae blink o' his ee.
Though now he said naething but 'Fare
    ye weel, Lucy!'
  It made me I neither could speak, hear,
    nor see:
He couldna say mair but just, 'Fare ye
    weel, Lucy!'
  Yet that I will mind till the day that
    I dee."

The lamb likes the gowan wi' dew when
    it's droukit;
  The hare likes the brake and the braird
    on the lea;
But Lucy likes Jamie;—she turn'd and
    she lookit,
  She thocht the dear place she wad never
    mair see.
Ah, weel may young Jamie gang dowie
    and cheerless!
  And weel may he greet on the bank o'
    the burn!
For bonnie sweet Lucy, sae gentle and
    peerless,
  Lies cauld in her grave, and will never
    return!
                            WILLIAM LAIDLAW.

LILIAN.

AIRY, fairy Lilian,
  Flitting, fairy Lilian,
When I ask her if she love me,
Clasps her tiny hands above me,
  Laughing all she can:
She'll not tell me if she love me,
  Cruel little Lilian.

When my passion seeks
  Pleasance in love-sighs,
She, looking thro' and thro' me
Thoroughly to undo me,
  Smiling, never speaks:
So innocent-arch, so cunning-simple,
From beneath her gather'd wimple
  Glancing with black-beaded eyes,
Till the lightning laughters dimple
  The baby-roses in her cheeks;
Then away she flies.

Prythee weep, May Lilian!
  Gayety without eclipse
Wearieth me, May Lilian:
Thro' my very heart it thrilleth
  When from crimson-threaded lips
Silver-treble laughter trilleth:
Prythee weep, May Lilian.

Praying all I can,
  If prayers will not hush thee,
Airy Lilian,
Like a rose-leaf I will crush thee,
  Fairy Lilian.
                            ALFRED TENNYSON.

LOVE AND DEATH.

GLORIES, pleasures, pomps, delights, and
    ease,
  Can but please
The outward senses, when the mind
Is or untroubled, or by peace refined.
Crowns may flourish and decay,
Beauties shine, but fade away.
Youth may revel, yet it must
Lie down in a bed of dust.
Earthly honors flow and waste,
Time alone doth change and last.
Sorrows mingled with contents, prepare
  Rest for care;
Love only reigns in death; though art
Can find no comfort for a broken heart.
                            JOHN FORD.

LANGLEY LANE.

IN all the land, range up, range down,
  Is there ever a place so pleasant and
    sweet
As Langley Lane, in London town,
  Just out of the bustle of square and
    street?

Little white cottages, all in a row,
Gardens, where bachelors'-buttons grow,
Swallows' nests in roof and wall,
And up above the still blue sky,
Where the woolly-white clouds go sailing
    by,—
  I seem to be able to see it all!

For now, in summer, I take my chair,
  And sit outside in the sun, and hear
The distant murmur of street and square,
  And the swallows and sparrows chirping
    near;
And Fanny, who lives just over the way,
Comes running many a time each day,
  With her little hand's-touch so warm
    and kind;
And I smile and talk, with the sun on my
    cheek,
And the little live hand seems to stir and
    speak,—
  For Fanny is dumb and I am blind.

Fanny is sweet thirteen, and she
  Has fine black ringlets, and dark eyes
    clear,
And I am older by summers three,—
  Why should we hold one another so
    dear?
Because she cannot utter a word,
Nor hear the music of bee or bird,
  The water-cart's splash, or the milkman's
    call.
Because I have never seen the sky,
Nor the little singers that hum and fly,—
  Yet know she is gazing upon them all.

For the sun is shining, the swallows fly,
  The bees and the blue-flies murmur low,
And I hear the water-cart go by,
  With its cool splash-splash down the
    dusty row;
And the little one, close at my side, per-
    ceives
Mine eyes upraised to the cottage eaves,
  Where birds are chirping in summer
    shine,
And I hear, though I cannot look, and
    she,
Though she cannot hear, can the singers
    see,—
  And the little soft fingers flutter in
    mine.

Hath not the dear little hand a tongue,
  When it stirs on my palm for the love of
    me?
Do I not know she is pretty and young?
  Hath not my soul an eye to see?
'Tis pleasure to make one's bosom stir,
To wonder how things appear to her,
  That I only hear as they pass around;
And as long as we sit in the music and
    light,
She is happy to keep God's sight,
  And *I* am happy to keep God's sound.

Why, I know her face, though I am
    blind—
I made it of music long ago:
Strange large eyes, and dark hair twined
Round the pensive light of a brow of
    snow;
And when I sit by my little one,
And hold her hand, and talk in the sun,
  And hear the music that haunts the
    place,
I know she is raising her eyes to me,
And guessing how gentle my voice must
    be,
  And *seeing* the music upon my face.

Though, if ever Lord God should grant
  me a prayer
(I know the fancy is only vain),
I should pray: Just once, when the weather
  is fair,
To see little Fanny and Langley Lane;
Though Fanny, perhaps, would pray to
  hear
The voice of the friend that she holds so
  dear,
  The song of the birds, the hum of the
    street,—
It is better to be as we have been,—
Each keeping up something, unheard, un-
    seen,
  To make God's heaven more strange and
    sweet.

Ah! life is pleasant in Langley Lane!
  There is always something sweet to
    hear!
Chirping of birds, or patter of rain;
  And Fanny, my little one, always near;

And though I am weak, and cannot live
    long,
And Fanny, my darling, is far from strong,
And though we can never married be,—
What then?—since we hold one another so
    dear,
For the sake of the pleasure one cannot
    hear,
And the pleasure that only one can see?
                   ROBERT BUCHANAN.

A PASTORAL BALLAD.
IN FOUR PARTS.
I. ABSENCE.

YE shepherds so cheerful and gay,
    Whose flocks never carelessly roam;
Should Corydon's happen to stray,
    Oh call the poor wanderers home.
Allow me to muse and to sigh,
    Nor talk of the change that ye find;
None once was so watchful as I:
    I have left my dear Phillis behind.

Now I know what it is, to have strove
    With the torture of doubt and desire;
What it is, to admire and to love,
    And to leave her we love and admire.
Ah lead forth my flock in the morn,
    And the damps of each ev'ning repel;
Alas! I am faint and forlorn:
    I have bade my dear Phyllis farewell.

Since Phillis vouchsafed me a look,
    I never once dreamt of my vine;
May I lose both my pipe and my crook,
    If I knew of a kid that was mine.
I prized every hour that went by,
    Beyond all that had pleased me before;
But now they are past, and I sigh;
    And I grieve that I prized them no more.

But why do I languish in vain?
    Why wander thus pensively here?
Oh, why did I come from the plain,
    Where I fed on the smiles of my dear?
They tell me my favorite maid,
    The pride of that valley, is flown;
Alas! where with her I have stray'd,
    I could wander with pleasure, alone.

When forced the fair nymph to forego,
    What anguish I felt at my heart!
Yet I thought—but it might not be so—
    'Twas with pain that she saw me depart.
She gazed, as I slowly withdrew;
    My path I could hardly discern;
So sweetly she bade me adieu,
    I thought that she bade me return.

The pilgrim that journeys all day
    To visit some far-distant shrine,
If he bear but a relic away,
    Is happy, nor heard to repine.
Thus widely removed from the fair,
    Where my vows, my devotion, I owe,
Soft hope is the relic I bear,
    And my solace wherever I go.

II. HOPE.

MY banks they are furnish'd with bees,
    Whose murmur invites one to sleep;
My grottos are shaded with trees,
    And my hills are white-over with sheep.
I seldom have met with a loss,
    Such health do my fountains bestow—
My fountains all border'd with moss,
    Where the harebells and violets grow.

Not a pine in my grove is there seen,
    But with tendrils of woodbine is bound:
Not a beech's more beautiful green,
    But a sweetbrier entwines it around.
Not my fields, in the prime of the year,
    More charms than my cattle unfold:
Not a brook that is limpid and clear,
    But it glitters with fishes of gold.

One would think she might like to retire
    To the bow'r I have labor'd to rear;
Not a shrub that I heard her admire,
    But I hasted and planted it there.
Oh how sudden the jessamine strove
    With the lilac to render it gay!
Already it calls for my love,
    To prune the wild branches away.

From the plains, from the woodlands and
    groves,
    What strains of wild melody flow?
How the nightingales warble their loves
    From the thickets of roses that blow!
And when her bright form shall appear,
    Each bird shall harmoniously join
In a concert so soft and so clear,
    As—she may not be fond to resign.

I have found out a gift for my fair;
　I have found where the wood-pigeons
　　breed:
But let me that plunder forbear,
　She will say 'twas a barbarous deed.
For he ne'er could be true, she averr'd,
　Who could rob a poor bird of its young;
And I loved her the more, when I heard
　Such tenderness fall from her tongue.

I have heard her with sweetness unfold
　How that pity was due to—a dove:
That it ever attended the bold,
　And she called it the sister of Love.
But her words such a pleasure convey,
　So much I her accents adore,
Let her speak, and whatever she say,
　Methinks I should love her the more.

Can a bosom so gentle remain
　Unmoved when her Corydon sighs?
Will a nymph that is fond of the plain,
　These plains and this valley despise?
Dear regions of silence and shade!
　Soft scenes of contentment and ease!
Where I could have pleasingly stray'd,
　If aught, in her absence, could please.

But where does my Phyllida stray?
　And where are her grots and her bo'wrs?
Are the groves and the valleys as gay,
　And the shepherds as gentle as ours?
The groves may perhaps be as fair,
　And the face of the valleys as fine;
The swains may in manners compare,
　But their love is not equal to mine.

III. SOLICITUDE.

WHY will you my passion reprove?
　Why term it a folly to grieve?
Ere I show you the charms of my love,
　She is fairer than you can believe.
With her mien she enamors the brave;
　With her wit she engages the free;
With her modesty pleases the grave;
　She is ev'ry way pleasing to me.

O you that have been of her train,
　Come and join in my amorous lays;
I could lay down my life for the swain
　That will sing but a song in her praise.
When he sings, may the nymphs of the
　town
Come trooping, and listen the while
Nay, on him let not Phyllida frown;
　—But I cannot allow her to smile.

For when Paridel tries in the dance
　Any favor with Phyllis to find,
Oh how, with one trivial glance,
　Might she ruin the peace of my mind!
In ringlets he dresses his hair,
　And his crook is bestudded around;
And his pipe—oh may Phyllis beware
　Of a magic there is in the sound!

'Tis his with mock passion to glow;
　'Tis his in smooth tales to unfold,
"How her face is as bright as the snow,
　And her bosom, be sure, is as cold!
How the nightingales labor the strain,
　With the notes of his charmer to vie;
How they vary their accents in vain,
　Repine at her triumphs, and die."

To the grove or the garden he strays,
　And pillages every sweet;
Then, suiting the wreath to his lays,
　He throws it at Phyllis's feet.
"O Phyllis," he whispers, "more fair,
　More sweet than the jessamine's flow'r!
What are pinks, in a morn, to compare?
　What is eglantine, after a show'r?

"Then the lily no longer is white,
　Then the rose is deprived of its bloom,
Then the violets die with despite,
　And the woodbines give up their per-
　　fume."
Thus glide the soft numbers along,
　And he fancies no shepherd his peer,
Yet I never should envy the song,
　Were not Phyllis to lend it an ear.

Let his crook be with hyacinths bound,
　So Phyllis the trophy despise;
Let his forehead with laurels be crown'd,
　So they shine not in Phyllis's eyes.
The language that flows from the heart
　Is a stranger to Paridel's tongue,
Yet may she beware of his art,
　Or sure I must envy the song.

IV. Disappointment.

Ye shepherds, give ear to my lay,
  And take no more heed of my sheep;
They have nothing to do but to stray,—
  I have nothing to do but to weep.
Yet do not my folly reprove;
  She was fair—and my passion begun;
She smiled—and I could not but love;
  She is faithless—and I am undone.

Perhaps I was void of all thought;
  Perhaps it was plain to foresee,
That a nymph so complete would be sought
  By a swain more engaging than me.
Ah! love every hope can inspire;
  It banishes wisdom the while,
And the lip of the nymph we admire
  Seems for ever adorn'd with a smile.

She is faithless, and I am undone;
  Ye that witness the woes I endure,
Let reason instruct you to shun
  What it cannot instruct you to cure.
Beware how ye loiter in vain
  Amid nymphs of a higher degree;
It is not for me to explain
  How fair and how fickle they be.

Alas! from the day that we met,
  What hope of an end to my woes,
When I cannot endure to forget
  The glance that undid my repose?
Yet time may diminish the pain;
  The flow'r, and the shrub, and the tree,
Which I rear'd for her pleasure in vain,
  In time may have comfort for me.

The sweets of a dew-sprinkled rose,
  The sound of a murmuring stream,
The peace which from solitude flows,
  Henceforth shall be Corydon's theme.
High transports are shown to the sight,
  But we are not to find them our own;
Fate never bestow'd such delight
  As I with my Phyllis had known.

O ye woods, spread your branches apace;
  To your deepest recesses I fly;
I would hide with the beasts of the chase;
  I would vanish from every eye.
Yet my reed shall resound thro' the grove
  With the same sad complaint it begun;
How she smiled, and I could not but love;
  Was faithless, and I am undone!
WILLIAM SHENSTONE.

Her Letter.

I'm sitting alone by the fire,
  Dress'd just as I came from the dance,
In a robe even *you* would admire—
  It cost a cool thousand in France;
I'm be-diamonded out of all reason,
  My hair is done up in a cue:
In short, sir, "the belle of the season"
  Is wasting an hour on you.

A dozen engagements I've broken;
  I left in the midst of a set;
Likewise a proposal, half spoken,
  That waits—on the stairs—for me yet.
They say he'll be rich—when he grows up—
  And then he adores me indeed;
And you, sir, are turning your nose up,
  Three thousand miles off, as you read.

"And how do I like my position?"
  "And what do I think of New York?"
"And now, in my higher ambition,
  With whom do I waltz, flirt, or talk?"
"And isn't it nice to have riches,
  And diamonds and silks, and all that?"
"And aren't it a change to the ditches
  And tunnels of Poverty Flat?"

Well, yes—if you saw us out driving
  Each day in the park, four-in-hand—
If you saw poor dear mamma contriving
  To look supernaturally grand—
If you saw papa's picture, as taken
  By Brady, and tinted at that,—
You'd never suspect he sold bacon
  And flour at Poverty Flat.

And yet just this moment, when sitting
  In the glare of the grand chandelier—
In the bustle and glitter befitting
  The "finest *soireé* of the year,"

In the mists of a *gaze de Chambéry,*
  And the hum of the smallest of talk—
Somehow, Joe, I thought of the "Ferry,"
  And the dance that we had on "The
    Fork;"

Of Harrison's barn, with its muster
  Of flags festoon'd over the wall;
Of the candles that shed their soft lustre
  And tallow on head-dress and shawl;
Of the steps that we took to one fiddle;
  Of the dress of my queer *vis-à-vis,*
And how I once went down the middle
  With the man that shot Sandy McGee;

Of the moon that was quietly sleeping
  On the hill, when the time came to go;
Of the few baby peaks that were peeping
  From under their bedclothes of snow;
Of that ride—that to me was the rarest;
  Of—the something you said at the gate:
Ah, Joe, then I wasn't an heiress
  To "the best-paying lead in the State."

Well, well, it's all past; yet it's funny
  To think, as I stood in the glare
Of fashion and beauty and money,
  That I should be thinking, right there,
Of some one who breasted high water,
  And swam the North Fork, and all that,
Just to dance with old Folinsbee's daughter,
  The Lily of Poverty Flat.

But goodness! what nonsense I'm writing!
  (Mamma says my taste still is low),
Instead of my triumphs reciting,
  I'm spooning on Joseph—heigh-ho!
And I'm to be "finish'd" by travel—
  Whatever's the meaning of that—
Oh, why did papa strike pay gravel
  In drifting on Poverty Flat?

Good-night—here's the end of my paper;
  Good-night—if the longitude please—
For maybe, while wasting my taper,
  Your sun's climbing over the trees.
But know, if you haven't got riches,
  And are poor, dearest Joe, and all that,
That my heart's somewhere there in the
    ditches,
  And you've struck it—on Poverty Flat.
F. BRET HARTE.

MY LOVE.

Not as all other women are
  Is she that to my soul is dear;
Her glorious fancies come from far,
  Beneath the silver evening-star;
  And yet her breast is ever near.

Great feelings hath she of her own,
  Which lesser souls may never know;
God giveth them to her alone,
  And sweet they are as any tone
Wherewith the wind may choose to blow.

Yet in herself she dwelleth not,
  Although no home were half so fair;
No simplest duty is forgot;
  Life hath no dim and lowly spot
  That doth not in her sunshine share.

She doeth little kindnesses,
  Which most leave undone or despise;
For naught that sets one heart at ease,
  And giveth happiness or peace,
  Is low-esteemèd in her eyes.

She hath no scorn of common things;
  And, though she seem of other birth,
Round us her heart entwines and clings,
  And patiently she folds her wings
  To tread the humble paths of earth.

Blessing she is; God made her so;
  And deeds of week-day holiness
Fall from her noiseless as the snow;
  Nor hath she ever chanced to know
  That aught were easier than to bless.

She is most fair, and thereunto
  Her life doth rightly harmonize;
Feeling or thought that was not true
  Ne'er made less beautiful the blue,
  Unclouded heaven of her eyes.

She is a woman—one in whom
  The spring-time of her childish years
Hath never lost its fresh perfume,
  Though knowing well that life hath room
  For many blights and many tears.

I love her with a love as still
  As a broad river's peaceful might,
Which, by high tower and lowly mill,
  Goes wandering at its own will,
  And yet doth ever flow aright.

And, on its full, deep breast serene,
  Like quiet isles, my duties lie;
It flows around them and between,
  And makes them fresh and fair and green—
    Sweet homes wherein to live and die.
JAMES RUSSELL LOWELL.

THE BRIDAL OF ANDALLA.

"RISE up, rise up, Xarifa! lay the golden cushion down;
Rise up, come to the window, and gaze with all the town!
From gay guitar and violin the silver notes are flowing,
And the lovely lute doth speak between the trumpet's lordly blowing,
And banners bright from lattice light are waving everywhere,
And the tall, tall plume of our cousin's bridegroom floats proudly in the air.
Rise up, rise up, Xarifa! lay the golden cushion down;
Rise up, come to the window, and gaze with all the town!

"Arise, arise, Xarifa! I see Andalla's face—
He bends him to the people with a calm and princely grace;
Through all the land of Xeres and banks of Guadalquiver
Rode forth bridegroom so brave as he, so brave and lovely, never.
Yon tall plume waving o'er his brow, of purple mixed with white,
I guess 'twas wreath'd by Zara, whom he will wed to-night.
Rise up, rise up, Xarifa! lay the golden cushion down;
Rise up, come to the window, and gaze with all the town!

"What aileth thee, Xarifa—what makes thine eyes look down?
Why stay ye from the window far, nor gaze with all the town?
I've heard you say on many a day—and sure you said the truth—
Andalla rides without a peer among all Granada's youth:
Without a peer he rideth, and yon milk-white horse doth go
Beneath his stately master with a stately step and slow:—
Then rise—oh rise, Xarifa, lay the golden cushion down;
Unseen here through the lattice you may gaze with all the town!"

The Zegri lady rose not, nor laid her cushion down,
Nor came she to the window to gaze with all the town;
But though her eyes dwelt on her knee, in vain her fingers strove,
And though her needle press'd the silk, no flower Xarifa wove;
One bonny rosebud she had traced before the noise drew nigh—
That bonny bud a tear effaced, slow drooping from her eye—
"No—no!" she sighs—"bid me not rise, nor lay my cushion down,
To gaze upon Andalla with all the gazing town!"

"Why rise ye not, Xarifa, nor lay your cushion down?
Why gaze ye not, Xarifa, with all the gazing town?
Hear, hear the trumpet how it swells, and how the people cry;
He stops at Zara's palace-gate—why sit ye still—oh, why?"
—"At Zara's gate stops Zara's mate; in him shall I discover
The dark-eyed youth pledged me his truth with tears, and was my lover?
I will not rise, with weary eyes, nor lay my cushion down,
To gaze on false Andalla with all the gazing town!"
From the Spanish.
JOHN GIBSON LOCKHART.

THE CAPTIVE BEE.

As Julia once a-slumbering lay,
It chanced a bee did fly that way.
After a dew, or dew-like shower,
To tipple freely in a flower.
For some rich flower he took the lip
Of Julia, and began to sip:

But when he felt he suck'd from thence
Honey, and in the quintessence,
He drank so much he scarce could stir;
So Julia took the pilferer—
And thus surprised, as filchers use,
He thus began himself t' excuse:

"Sweet Lady-flower, I never brought
Hither the least one thieving thought;
But, taking those rare lips of yours
For some fresh, fragrant, luscious flowers,
I though I might there take a taste
Where so much syrup ran at waste.
Besides, know this,—I never sting
The flower that gives me nourishing:
But with a kiss or thanks, do pay
For honey that I bear away."

This said, he laid his little scrip
Of honey 'fore her ladyship;
And told her, as some tears did fall,
That that he took, and that was all.
At which she smiled, and bade him go
And take his bag, but thus much know:
When next he came a-pilfering so,
He should from her full lips derive
Honey enough to fill his hive.
     ROBERT HERRICK.

TO DIANEME.

SWEET, be not proud of those two eyes,
Which, star-like, sparkle in their skies;
Nor be you proud, that you can see
All hearts your captives, yours yet free;
Be you not proud of that rich haire,
Which wantons with the love-sick aire;
When as that rubie which you weare,
Sunk from the tip of your soft eare,
Will last to be a precious stone,
When all your world of beautie's gone.
     ROBERT HERRICK.

THE MAIDEN'S CHOICE.

 GENTEEL in personage,
 Conduct and equipage;
 Noble by heritage;
  Generous and free;

 Brave, not romantic;
 Learn'd, not pedantic;
 Frolic, not frantic—
  This must he be.

 Honor maintaining,
 Meanness disdaining,
 Still entertaining,
  Engaging, and new;

 Neat, but not finical;
 Sage, but not cynical;
 Never tyrannical,
  But ever true,
     HENRY CAREY.

LADY CLARA VERE DE VERE.

LADY Clara Vere de Vere,
 Of me you shall not win renown;
You thought to break a country heart
 For pastime, ere you went to town.
At me you smiled, but unbeguiled
 I saw the snare, and I retired:
The daughter of a hundred Earls,
 You are not one to be desired.

Lady Clara Vere de Vere,
 I know you proud to bear your name,
Your pride is yet no mate for mine,
 Too proud to care from whence I came
Nor would I break for your sweet sake
 A heart that doats on truer charms.
A simple maiden in her flower
 Is worth a hundred coats-of-arms.

Lady Clara Vere de Vere,
 Some meeker pupil you must find,
For were you queen of all that is,
 I could not stoop to such a mind.
You sought to prove how I could love,
 And my disdain is my reply.
The lion on your old stone gates
 Is not more cold to you than I.

Lady Clara Vere de Vere,
 You put strange memories in my head.
Not thrice your branching limes have
  blown
Since I beheld young Laurence dead.
Oh, your sweet eyes, your low replies:
 A great enchantress you may be;
But there was that across his throat
 Which you had hardly cared to see.

Lady Clara Vere de Vere,
  When thus he met his mother's view,
She had the passions of her kind,
  She spake some certain truths of you.
Indeed, I heard one bitter word
  That scarce is fit for you to hear;
Her manners had not that repose
  Which stamps the caste of Vere de Vere.

Lady Clara Vere de Vere,
  There stands a spectre in your hall:
The guilt of blood is at your door:
  You changed a wholesome heart to gall.
You held your course without remorse,
  To make him trust his modest worth,
And, last, you fixed a vacant stare,
  And slew him with your noble birth.

Trust me, Clara Vere de Vere,
  From yon blue heavens above us bent,
The grand old gardener and his wife
  Smile at the claims of long descent.
Howe'er it be, it seems to me,
  'Tis only noble to be good.
Kind hearts are more than coronets,
  And simple faith than Norman blood.

I know you, Clara Vere de Vere:
  You pine among your halls and towers:
The languid light of your proud eyes
  Is wearied of the rolling hours.
In glowing health, with boundless wealth,
  But sickening of a vague disease,
You know so ill to deal with time,
  You needs must play such pranks as these.

Clara, Clara Vere de Vere,
  If time be heavy on your hands,
Are there no beggars at your gate,
  Nor any poor about your lands?
Oh teach the orphan boy to read,
  Or teach the orphan girl to sew,
Pray heaven for a human heart,
  And let the foolish yeoman go.
          ALFRED TENNYSON.

AT THE CHURCH GATE.

ALTHOUGH I enter not,
  Yet round about the spot
    Ofttimes I hover;
And near the sacred gate,
  With longing eyes I wait,
    Expectant of her.

The minster bell tolls out
Above the city's rout,
  And noise and humming;
They've hush'd the minster bell:
The organ 'gins to swell:
  She's coming, she's coming!

My lady comes at last,
Timid, and stepping fast,
  And hastening hither,
With modest eyes downcast:
She comes—she's here—she's past—
  May Heaven go with her!

Kneel undisturb'd, fair saint!
Pour out your praise or plaint
  Meekly and duly;
I will not enter there,
To sully your pure prayer
  With thoughts unruly.

But suffer me to pace
Round the forbidden place,
  Lingering a minute,
Like outcast spirits who wait
And see through heaven's gate
  Angels within it.
          WILLIAM MAKEPEACE THACKERAY.

IN A YEAR.

NEVER any more
  While I live,
Need I hope to see his face
  As before.
Once his love grown chill,
  Mine may strive,—
Bitterly we re-embrace,
  Single still.

Was it something said,
  Something done,
Vex'd him? was it touch of **hand,**
  Turn of head?
Strange! that very way
  Love begun.
I as little understand
  Love's decay.

When I sew'd or drew,
  I recall
How he look'd as if I **sang**
  —Sweetly too.

If I spoke a word,
  First of all
Up his cheek the color sprang,
  Then he heard.

Sitting by my side,
  At my feet,
So he breathed the air I breathed,
  Satisfied!
I, too, at love's brim
  Touch'd the sweet.
I would die if death bequeath'd
  Sweet to him.

"Speak,—I love thee best!"
  He exclaim'd,—
"Let thy love my own foretell."
  I confess'd:
"Clasp my heart on thine
  Now unblamed,
Since upon thy soul as well
  Hangeth mine!"

Was it wrong to own,
  Being truth?
Why should all the giving prove
  His alone?
I had wealth and ease,
  Beauty, youth,—
Since my lover gave me love,
  I gave these.

That was all I meant,
  —To be just,
And the passion I had raised
  To content.
Since he chose to change
  Gold for dust,
If I gave him what he praised,
  Was it strange?

Would he loved me yet,
  On and on,
While I found some way undream'd,
  —Paid my debt!
Gave more life and more,
  Till, all gone,
He should smile, "She never seem'd
  Mine before.

"What—she felt the while,
  Must I think?
Love's so different with us men,"
  He should smile.

"Dying for my sake—
  White and pink!
Can't we touch these bubbles then
  But they break?"

Dear, the pang is brief.
  Do thy part,
Have thy pleasure. How perplext
  Grows belief?
Well, this cold clay clod
  Was man's heart.
Crumble it,—and what comes next?
  Is it God?
                ROBERT BROWNING.

SONG.

LAY a garland on my hearse
  Of the dismal yew:
Maidens, willow branches bear;
  Say I died true.
My love was false, but I was firm,
  From my hour of birth;
Upon my buried body, lie
  Lightly, gentle earth!
             BEAUMONT AND FLETCHER.

SONNET.

To live in hell, and heaven to behold,
  To welcome life, and die a living death,
To sweat with heat, and yet be freezing cold,
  To grasp at stars, and lie the earth beneath,
To tread a maze that never shall have end,
  To burn in sighs, and starve in daily tears,
To climb a hill, and never to descend,
  Giants to kill, and quake at childish fears,
To pine for food, and watch the Hesperian tree,
  To thirst for drink, and nectar still to draw,
To live accursed, whom men hold blest to be,
  And weep those wrongs, which never creature saw;
If this be love, if love in these be founded,
My heart is love, for these in it are grounded.
                HENRY CONSTABLE.

TO IANTHE.

IANTHE! you are call'd to cross the sea!
  A path forbidden *me!*
Remember, while the sun his blessing sheds
  Upon the mountain-heads,
How often we have watcht him laying down
  His brow, and dropt our own
Against each other's, and how faint and short
  And sliding the support!
What will succeed it now? Mine is unblest,
  Ianthe! nor will rest
But on the very thought that swells with pain.
  Oh bid me hope again!
Oh give me back what Earth, what (without you)
  Not Heaven itself can do,
One of the golden days that we have past;
  And let it be my last!
Or else the gift would be, however sweet,
  Fragile and incomplete.
WALTER SAVAGE LANDOR.

EUPHROSYNE.

I WILL not say that thou wast true,
  Yet let me say that thou wast fair!
And they that lovely face who view,
  They should not ask if truth be there.

Truth—what is truth? Two bleeding hearts
  Wounded by men, by Fortune tried,
Out-wearied with their lonely parts,
  Vow to beat henceforth side by side.

The world to them was stern and drear,
  Their lot was but to weep and moan;
Ah, let them keep their faith sincere,
  For neither could subsist alone!

But souls whom some benignant breath
  Has charm'd at birth from gloom and care,
These ask no love, these plight no faith,
  For they are happy as they are.

The world to them may homage make,
  And garlands for their forehead weave;
And what the world can give, they take—
  But they bring more than they receive.

They smile upon the world. Their ears
  To one demand alone are coy;
They will not give us love and tears—
  They bring us light, and warmth, and joy.

On one she smiled, and he was blest!
  She smiles elsewhere—we make a din!
But 'twas not love which heaved her breast,
  Fair child!—it was the bliss within.
MATTHEW ARNOLD.

JEALOUSY, THE TYRANT OF THE MIND.

WHAT state of life can be so blest
As love, that warms a lover's breast?
Two souls in one, the same desire
To grant the bliss, and to require!
But if in heaven a hell we find,
'Tis all from thee,
O Jealousy!
'Tis all from thee,
O Jealousy!
Thou tyrant, tyrant Jealousy,
Thou tyrant of the mind!

All other ills though sharp they prove,
Serve to refine and perfect love:
In absence, or unkind disdain,
Sweet hope relieves the lover's pain.
But, ah! no cure but death we find,
To set us free from Jealousy:
O Jealousy!
Thou tyrant, tyrant Jealousy,
Thou tyrant of the mind!

False in thy glass all objects are,
Some set too near, and some too far;
Thou art the fire of endless night,
The fire that burns, and gives no light.
All torments of the damn'd we find
In only thee,
O Jealousy!
Thou tyrant, tyrant Jealousy,
Thou tyrant of the mind.
JOHN DRYDEN.

SIXTEEN.

In Clementina's artless mien
    Lucilla asks me what I see,—
And are the roses of sixteen
    Enough for me?

Lucilla asks, if that be all,
    Have I not cull'd as sweet before?
Ah yes, Lucilla! and their fall
    I still deplore.

I now behold another scene,
    Where pleasure beams with heaven's
      own light,—
More pure, more constant, more serene,
    And not less bright:

Faith, on whose breast the Loves repose,
    Whose chain of flowers no force can
      sever;
And Modesty, who, when she goes,
    Is gone for ever.
              WALTER SAVAGE LANDOR.

COMIN' THROUGH THE RYE.

    Gin a body meet a body
      Comin' through the rye,
    Gin a body kiss a body,
      Need a body cry?
    Every lassie has her laddie—
      Ne'er a ane hae I;
    Yet a' the lads they smile at me
      When comin' through the rye.
Amang the train there is a swain
    I dearly lo'e mysel';
But whaur his hame, or what his name,
    I dinna care to tell.

    Gin a body meet a body
      Comin' frae the town,
    Gin a body greet a body,
      Need a body frown?
    Every lassie has her laddie—
      Ne'er a ane hae I;
    Yet a' the lads they smile at me
      When comin' through the rye.
Amang the train there is a swain
    I dearly lo'e mysel';
But whaur his hame, or what his name,
    I dinna care to tell.
              AUTHOR UNKNOWN.

CHERRY-RIPE.

Cherry-ripe, ripe, ripe, I cry,
    Full and fair ones; come and buy;
If so be you ask me where
    They do grow, I answer, there,
Where my Julia's lips do smile,
    There's the land, or cherry isle,
Whose plantations fully show
    All the year where cherries grow.
              ROBERT HERRICK.

THE WHITE ROSE.

SENT BY A YORKISH LOVER TO HIS LANCASTRIAN MISTRESS.

If this fair rose offend thy sight,
    Placed in thy bosom bare,
'Twill blush to find itself less white,
    And turn Lancastrian there.

But if thy ruby lip it spy,
    As kiss it thou mayst deign,
With envy pale 'twill lose its dye,
    And Yorkish turn again.
              AUTHOR UNKNOWN.

THE PRIMROSE.

Ask me why I send you here
    This sweet Infanta of the year?
Ask me why I send to you
    This primrose, thus bepearl'd with dew?
I will whisper to your ears,
    The sweets of love are mixt with tears.

Ask me why this flower does show
    So yellow-green, and sickly, too?
Ask me why the stalk is weak
    And bending, yet it doth not break?
I will answer: these discover
    What fainting hopes are in a lover.
              ROBERT HERRICK.

HERE'S TO THEE, MY SCOTTISH LASSIE.

Here's to thee, my Scottish lassie! here's
    a hearty health to thee!
For thine eye so bright, thy form so light,
    and thy step so firm and free;

For all thine artless elegance, and all thy
    native grace;
For the music of thy mirthful voice, and
    the sunshine of thy face;
For thy guileless look and speech sincere,
    yet sweet as speech can be,—
Here's a health, my Scottish lassie! here's
    a hearty health to thee!

Here's to thee, my Scottish lassie! Though
    my glow of youth is o'er,
And I, as once I felt and dream'd, must
    feel and dream no more;
Though the world, with all its frosts and
    storms, has chill'd my soul at last,
And genius with the foodful looks of
    youthful friendship pass'd;
Though my path is dark and lonely, now,
    o'er this world's dreary sea,
Here's a health, my Scottish lassie! here's
    a hearty health to thee!

Here's to thee, my Scottish lassie! though
    I know that not for me
Is thine eye so bright, thy form so light,
    and thy step so firm and free;
Though thou, with cold and careless looks,
    wilt often pass me by,
Unconscious of my swelling heart and of
    my wistful eye;
Though thou wilt wed some Highland love,
    nor waste one thought on me,
Here's a health, my Scottish lassie! here's
    a hearty health to thee!

Here's to thee, my Scottish lassie! when I
    meet thee in the throng
Of merry youths and maidens dancing
    lightsomely along,
I'll dream away an hour or twain, still
    gazing on thy form,
As it flashes through the baser crowd, like
    lightning through a storm;
And I, perhaps, shall touch thy hand, and
    share thy looks of glee,
And for once, my Scottish lassie, dance a
    giddy dance with thee!

Here's to thee, my Scottish lassie! I shall
    think of thee at even,
When I see its first and fairest star come
    smiling up through heaven;
I shall hear thy sweet and touching voice
    in every wind that grieves,
As it whirls from the abandon'd oak its
    wither'd autumn leaves;
In the gloom of the wild forest, in the still-
    ness of the sea,
I shall think, my Scottish lassie, I shall
    often think of thee!

Here's to thee, my Scottish lassie! In my
    sad and lonely hours,
The thought of thee comes o'er me like the
    breath of distant flowers:
Like the music that enchants mine ear, the
    sights that bless mine eye,
Like the verdure of the meadow, like the
    azure of the sky,
Like the rainbow in the evening, like the
    blossoms on the tree,
Is the thought, my Scottish lassie, is the
    lonely thought of thee.

Here's a health, my Scottish lassie!—here's
    a parting health to thee!
May thine be still a cloudless lot, though
    it be far from me!
May still thy laughing eye be bright, and
    open still thy brow,
Thy thoughts as pure, thy speech as free,
    thy heart as light as now
And, whatsoe'er my after-fate, my dearest
    toast shall be,—
Still a health, my Scottish lassie! still a
    hearty health to thee;
                      JOHN MOULTRIE.

GOOD-MORROW SONG.

PACK, clouds, away, and welcome, day,
    With night we banish sorrow;
Sweet air, blow soft, mount, larks, aloft,
    To give my Love good-morrow!
Wings from the wind to please her mind,
    Notes from the lark I'll borrow;
Bird, prune thy wing, nightingale, sing,
    To give my Love good-morrow;
        To give my Love good-morrow
    Notes from them both I'll borrow.

Wake from thy nest, Robin redbreast,
    Sing, birds, in every furrow;
And from each hill let music shrill
    Give my fair Love good-morrow!

Blackbird and thrush in every bush,
  Stare, linnet, and cock-sparrow!
You pretty elves, amongst yourselves
  Sing my fair Love good-morrow;
    To give my Love good-morrow
    Sing, birds, in every furrow!
THOMAS HEYWOOD.

THE SONG OF THE CAMP.

"GIVE us a song!" the soldiers cried,
  The outer trenches guarding,
When the heated guns of the camps allied
  Grew weary of bombarding.

The dark Redan, in silent scoff,
  Lay grim and threatening under;
And the tawny mound of the Malakoff
  No longer belch'd its thunder.

There was a pause. A guardsman said:
  "We storm the forts to-morrow;
Sing while we may, another day
  Will bring enough of sorrow."

They lay along the battery's side,
  Below the smoking cannon:
Brave hearts from Severn and from Clyde,
  And from the banks of Shannon.

They sang of love, and not of fame;
  Forgot was Britain's glory:
Each heart recall'd a different name,
  But all sang "Annie Laurie."

Voice after voice caught up the song,
  Until its tender passion
Rose like an anthem, rich and strong,—
  Their battle-eve confession.

Dear girl, her name he dared not speak,
  But as the song grew louder,
Something upon the soldier's cheek
  Wash'd off the stains of powder.

Beyond the darkening ocean burn'd
  The bloody sunset's embers,
While the Crimean valleys learn'd
  How English love remembers.

And once again a fire of hell
  Rain'd on the Russian quarters,
With scream of shot, and burst of shell,
  And bellowing of the mortars!

And Irish Nora's eyes are dim
  For a singer dumb and gory;
And English Mary mourns for him
  Who sang of "Annie Laurie."

Sleep, soldiers! still in honor'd rest
  Your truth and valor wearing:
The bravest are the tenderest,—
  The loving are the daring.
BAYARD TAYLOR.

URANIA.

SHE smiles and smiles, and will not sigh,
While we for hopeless passion die;
Yet she could love, those eyes declare,
Were but men nobler than they are.

Eagerly once her gracious ken
Was turn'd upon the sons of men;
But light the serious visage grew—
She look'd, and smiled, and saw them through.

Our petty souls, our strutting wits,
Our labor'd, puny passion-fits—
Ah, may she scorn them still, till we
Scorn them as bitterly as she!

Yet show her once, ye heavenly powers,
One of some worthier race than ours!
One for whose sake she once might prove
How deeply she who scorns can love.

His eyes be like the starry lights—
His voice like sounds of summer nights—
In all his lovely mien let pierce
The magic of the universe!

And she to him will reach her hand,
And gazing in his eyes will stand,
And know her friend, and weep for glee,
And cry, "Long, long I've look'd for thee."

Then will she weep!—with smiles, till then,
Coldly she mocks the sons of men.
Till then her lovely eyes maintain
Their pure, unwavering, deep disdain.
MATTHEW ARNOLD.

TO EVA.

O FAIR and stately maid, whose eyes
Were kindled in the upper skies
  At the same torch that lighted mine;
For so I must interpret still
Thy sweet dominion o'er my will,
  A sympathy divine.

Ah, let me blameless gaze upon
Features that seem at heart my own;
  Nor fear those watchful sentinels,
Who charm the more their glance forbids,
Chaste-glowing, underneath their lids,
  With fire that draws while it repels.
           RALPH WALDO EMERSON.

WHO IS SYLVIA?

WHO is Sylvia? what is she,
  That all the swains commend her?
Holy, fair, and wise is she;
  The heavens such grace did lend her
That she might adorèd be.

Is she kind, or is she fair?
  For beauty lives with kindness.
Love does to her eyes repair
  To help him of his blindness—
And, being help'd, inhabits there.

Then to Sylvia let us sing
  That Sylvia is excelling;
She excels each mortal thing
  Upon the dull earth dwelling;
To her let us garlands bring.
           WILLIAM SHAKESPEARE.

AUF WIEDERSEHEN.
SUMMER.

THE little gate was reach'd at last,
  Half hid in lilacs down the lane;
She push'd it wide, and, as she past,
  A wistful look she backward cast,
    And said, "*Auf Wiedersehen!*"

With hand on latch, a vision white
  Lingered reluctant, and again,
Half doubting if she did aright,
Soft as the dews that fell that night,
    She said, "*Auf Wiedersehen!*"

The lamp's clear gleam flits up the stair;
  I linger in delicious pain;
Ah, in that chamber, whose rich air
To breathe in thought I scarcely dare,
    Thinks she, "*Auf Wiedersehen!*"

'Tis thirteen years: once more I press
  The turf that silences the lane;
I hear the rustle of her dress,
I smell the lilacs, and—ah yes,
    I hear, "*Auf Wiedersehen!*"

Sweet piece of bashful maiden art!
  The English words had seem'd too fain!
But these—they drew us heart to heart,
Yet held us tenderly apart;
    She said, "*Auf Wiedersehen!*"
           JAMES RUSSELL LOWELL.

THE LOVE-KNOT.

TYING her bonnet under her chin,
She tied her raven ringlets in;
But not alone in its silken snare
Did she catch her lovely floating hair,
For, tying her bonnet under her chin,
She tied a young man's heart within.

They were strolling together up the hill,
Where the wind comes blowing merry and
    chill;
And it blew the curls a frolicsome race
All over the happy peach-color'd face,
Till, scolding and laughing, she tied them
    in,
Under her beautiful dimpled chin.

And it blew a color, bright as the bloom
Of the pinkest fuschia's tossing plume,
All over the cheeks of the prettiest girl
That ever imprison'd a romping curl,
Or, in tying her bonnet under her chin,
Tied a young man's heart within.

Steeper and steeper grew the hill—
Madder, merrier, chillier still
The western wind blew down and play'd
The wildest tricks with the little maid,
As, tying her bonnet under her chin,
She tied a young man's heart within.

O western wind, do you think it was fair
To play such tricks with her floating hair?

To gladly, gleefully do your best
To blow her against the young man's
    breast?
Where he as gladly folded her in;
He kiss'd her mouth and dimpled chin.

Oh, Ellery Vane, you little thought,
An hour ago, when you besought
This country lass to walk with you,
After the sun had dried the dew,
What perilous danger you'd be in,
As she tied her bonnet under her chin.
                            NORA PERRY.

WHEN STARS ARE IN THE QUIET SKIES.

WHEN stars are in the quiet skies,
    Then most I pine for thee;
Bend on me then thy tender eyes,
    As stars look on the sea!
For thoughts, like waves that glide by
        night,
    Are stillest when they shine;
Mine earthly love lies hush'd in light
    Beneath the heaven of thine.

There is an hour when angels keep
    Familiar watch o'er men,
When coarser souls are wrapt in sleep—
    Sweet spirit, meet me then!
There is an hour when holy dreams
    Through slumber fairest glide;
And in that mystic hour it seems
    Thou shouldst be by my side.

My thoughts of thee too sacred are
    For daylight's common beam:
I can but know thee as my star,
    My angel and my dream;
When stars are in the quiet skies,
    Then most I pine for thee;
Bend on me then thy tender eyes,
    As stars look on the sea!
                    EDWARD BULWER LYTTON.

SHE'S GANE TO DWALL IN HEAVEN.

SHE's gane to dwall in heaven, my lassie,
    She gane to dwall in heaven;
Ye're owre pure, quo' the voice o' God,
    For dwelling out o' heaven.

Oh, what'll she do in heaven, my lassie,
    Oh, what'll she do in heaven?
She'll mix her ain thoughts wi' angels'
        sangs,
    An' make them mair meet for heaven.

She was beloved by a', my lassie,
    She was beloved by a',
But an angel fell in love wi' her,
    An' took her frae us a'.

Lowly there thou lies, my lassie,
    Lowly there thou lies;
A bonnier form ne'er went to the yird,
    Nor frae it will arise.

Fu' soon I'll follow thee, my lassie,
    Fu' soon I'll follow thee;
Thou left me naught to covet ahin',
    But took gudeness sel' wi' thee.

I look'd on thy death-cold face, my lassie,
    I look'd on thy death-cold face;
Thou seem'd a lily new cut i' the bud,
    An' fading in its place.

I look'd on thy death-shut eye, my lassie,
    I look'd on thy death-shut eye;
An' a lovelier light in the brow of heaven
    Fell Time shall ne'er destroy.

Thy lips were ruddy and calm, my lassie,
    Thy lips were ruddy and calm;
But gane was the holy breath o' heaven,
    That sing the evening psalm.

There's naught but dust now mine, lassie,
    There's naught but dust now mine;
My soul's wi' thee i' the cauld grave,
    An' why should I stay behin'?
                        ALLAN CUNNINGHAM.

SONNET.

LET me not to the marriage of true minds
    Admit impediments; love is not love
Which alters when it alteration finds,
    Or bends with the remover to remove.
Oh no! it is an ever-fixèd mark,
    That looks on tempests, and is never
        shaken;
It is the star to every wandering bark,
    Whose worth's unknown, although his
        height be taken.

Love's not Time's fool, though rosy lips
    and cheeks
  Within his bending sickle's compass
    come;
Love alters not with his brief hours and
    weeks,
  But bears it out even to the edge of doom.
If this be error, and upon me proved,
  I never writ, nor no man ever loved.
                    WILLIAM SHAKESPEARE.

SONNET.

TIRED with all these, for restful death I
    cry,
As to behold desert a beggar born,
And needy nothing trimm'd in jollity,
And purest faith unhappily forsworn,
And gilded honor shamefully misplaced,
And maiden virtue rudely strumpeted,
And right perfection wrongfully disgraced,
And strength by limping sway disabled,
And art made tongue-tied by authority,
And folly, doctor-like, controlling skill,
And simple truth miscall'd simplicity,
  And captive Good attending Captain
    Ill;—
Tired with all these, from these would I
    be gone,
Save that, to die, I leave my Love alone.
                    WILLIAM SHAKESPEARE.

SONNET.

No longer mourn for me when I am dead,
  Than you shall hear the surly, sullen
    bell
  Give warning to the world that I am fled
    From this vile world, with vilest worms
      to dwell.
Nay, if you read this line, remember not
  The hand that writ it, for I love you so,
That I in your sweet thoughts would be
    forgot,
  If thinking on me then should make
    you woe.
Oh, if, I say, you look upon this verse
  When I perhaps compounded am with
    clay,
Do not so much as my poor name rehearse,
  But let your love even with my life de-
    cay,

Lest the wise world should look into your
    moan,
And mock you with me after I am gone.
                    WILLIAM SHAKESPEARE.

SONNET.

THAT time of year thou may'st in me be-
    hold,
  When yellow leaves, or none, or few do
    hang
Upon those boughs which shake against
    the cold,
  Bare ruin'd choirs, where late the sweet
    birds sang.
In me thou seest the twilight of such day
  As after sunset fadeth in the west,
Which by and by black night doth take
    away,
  Death's second self, that seals up all in
    rest;
In me thou seest the glowing of such fire
  That on the ashes of his youth doth lie,
As the deathbed whereon it must expire,
  Consumed with that which it was nour-
    ish'd by.
This thou perceiv'st, which makes thy
    love more strong,
To love that well which thou must leave
    ere long.
                    WILLIAM SHAKESPEARE.

SONNET.

WHEN in disgrace with fortune and men's
    eyes,
I all alone beweep my outcast state,
And trouble deaf Heaven with my boot-
    less cries,
  And look upon myself, and curse my
    fate,
Wishing me like to one more rich in
    hope,
  Featured like him, like him with friends
    possess'd,
Desiring this man's art, and that man's
    scope,
  With what I most enjoy contented least;
Yet in these thoughts myself almost de-
    spising,
  Haply I think on thee, and then my
    state

(Like to the lark at break of day arising
  From sullen earth) sings hymns at heaven's gate:
For thy sweet love remember'd such wealth brings,
That then I scorn to change my state with kings.
WILLIAM SHAKESPEARE.

SONNET.

WHEN in the chronicle of wasted time
  I see descriptions of the fairest wights,
And beauty making beautiful old rhyme
  In praise of ladies dead, and lovely knights;
Then in the blazon of sweet beauty's best,
  Of hand, of foot, of lip, of eye, of brow,
I see their antique pen would have exprest
  Ev'n such a beauty as you master now.
So all their praises are but prophecies
  Of this our time, all you prefiguring;
And for they look'd but with divining eyes,
  They had not skill enough your worth to sing;
For we, which now behold these present days,
Have eyes to wonder, but lack tongues to praise.
WILLIAM SHAKESPEARE.

SONNET.

SHALL I compare thee to a summer's day?
  Thou art more lovely and more temperate;
Rough winds do shake the darling buds of May,
  And summer's lease hath all too short a date.
Sometime too hot the eye of heaven shines,
  And often is his gold complexion dimm'd,
And every fair from fair sometime declines,
  By chance, or Nature's changing course, untrimm'd.
But thy eternal summer shall not fade,
  Nor lose possession of that fair thou owest,
Nor shall death brag thou wanderest in his shade,
  When in eternal lines to time thou growest.
So long as men can breathe, or eyes can see,
So long lives this, and this gives life to thee.
WILLIAM SHAKESPEARE.

EPITHALAMIUM.

I SAW two clouds at morning,
  Tinged by the rising sun,
And in the dawn they floated on,
  And mingled into one;
I thought that morning cloud was bless'd,
It moved so sweetly to the west.

I saw two summer currents
  Flow smoothly to their meeting,
And join their course, with silent force,
  In peace each other greeting;
Calm was their course through banks of green,
While dimpling eddies play'd between.

Such be your gentle motion,
  Till life's last pulse shall beat;
Like summer's beam, and summer's stream,
  Float on, in joy, to meet
A calmer sea, where storms shall cease—
A purer sky, where all is peace.
JOHN G. C. BRAINARD.

BRIDAL SONG.

To the sound of timbrels sweet
Moving slow our solemn feet,
We have borne thee on the road
To the virgin's blest abode;
With thy yellow torches gleaming,
And thy scarlet mantle streaming,
And the canopy above
Swaying as we slowly move.

Thou hast left the joyous feast,
And the mirth and wine have ceased;
And now we set thee down before
The jealously-unclosing door,
That the favor'd youth admits
Where the veilèd virgin sits
In the bliss of maiden fear,
Waiting our soft tread to hear,
And the music's brisker din
At the bridegroom's entering in—
Entering in, a welcome guest,
To the chamber of his rest.
HENRY HART MILMAN.

Green be the turf above thee,
　Friend of my better days!
None knew thee but to love thee,
　Nor named thee but to praise—

Fitz-Greene Halleck

PERSONAL POEMS.

THE GRAVE OF MACAURA.

AND this is thy grave, Macaura,
  Here by the pathway lone,
Where the thorn-blossoms are bending
  Over thy moulder'd stone.
Alas! for the sons of glory;
  O thou of the darken'd brow,
And the eagle plume, and the belted clans,
  Is it here thou art sleeping now?

Oh wild is the spot, Macaura,
  In which they have laid thee low—
The field where thy people triumph'd
  Over a slaughter'd foe;
And loud was the banshee's wailing,
  And deep was the clansmen's sorrow,
When, with bloody hands and burning tears,
  They buried thee here, Macaura!

And now thy dwelling is lonely,
  King of the rushing horde;
And now thy battles are over,
  Chief of the shining sword;
And the rolling thunder echoes
  O'er torrent and mountain free,
But alas! and alas! Macaura,
  It will not awaken thee.

Farewell to thy grave, Macaura,
  Where the slanting sunbeams shine,
And the brier and waving fern
  Over thy slumbers twine;
Thou whose gathering summons
  Could waken the sleeping glen;
Macaura, alas for thee and thine,
  'Twill never be heard again!
                MARY DOWNING.

ON A BUST OF DANTE.

SEE, from this counterfeit of him
  Whom Arno shall remember long,
How stern of lineament, how grim,
  The father was of Tuscan song!
There but the burning sense of wrong,
  Perpetual care, and scorn, abide—
Small friendship for the lordly throng,
  Distrust of all the world beside.

Faithful if this wan image be,
  No dream his life was—but a fight;
Could any Beatrice see
  A lover in that anchorite?
To that cold Ghibeline's gloomy sight
  Who could have guessed the visions came
Of beauty, veiled with heavenly light,
  In circles of eternal flame?

The lips as Cumæ's cavern close,
  The cheeks with fast and sorrow thin,
The rigid front, almost morose,
  But for the patient hope within,
Declare a life whose course hath been
  Unsullied still, though still severe,
Which, through the wavering days of sin,
  Kept itself icy-chaste and clear.

Not wholly such his haggard look
  When wandering once, forlorn, he strayed,
With no companion save his book,
  To Corvo's hushed monastic shade;
Where, as the Benedictine laid
  His palm upon the pilgrim guest,
The single boon for which he prayed
  The convent's charity was rest.

Peace dwells not here—this rugged face
  Betrays no spirit of repose;
The sullen warrior sole we trace,
  The marble man of many woes.

Such was his mien when first arose
  The thought of that strange tale divine—
When hell he peopled with his foes,
  The scourge of many a guilty line.

War to the last he waged with all
  The tyrant canker-worms of earth;
Baron and duke, in hold and hall,
  Cursed the dark hour that gave him birth.
He used Rome's harlot for his mirth;
  Plucked bare hypocrisy and crime;
But valiant souls of knightly worth
  Transmitted to the rolls of Time.

O Time! whose verdicts mock our own,
  The only righteous judge art thou;
That poor, old exile, sad and lone,
  Is Latium's other Virgil now.
Before his name the nations bow;
  His words are parcel of mankind,
Deep in whose hearts, as on his brow,
  The marks have sunk of Dante's mind.
            THOMAS WILLIAM PARSONS.

PRISONED IN WINDSOR, HE RECOUNTETH HIS PLEASURE THERE PASSED.

So cruel prison how could betide, alas!
  As proud Windsor? where I in lust and joy,
With a King's son, my childish years did pass,
  In greater feast than Priam's sons of Troy.
Where each sweet place returns a taste full sour.
The large green courts, where we were wont to hove,
  With eyes cast up into the Maiden's Tower,
And easy sighs, such as folk draw in love.
The stately seats, the ladies bright of hue,
  The dances short, long tales of great delight;
With words, and looks, that tigers could but rue,
  Where each of us did plead the other's right.
The palme-play, where despoilèd for the game,
  With dazèd eyes oft we by gleams of love
Have miss'd the ball, and got sight of our dame,
  To bait her eyes, which kept the leads above.
The gravel'd ground, with sleeves tied on the helm,
  On foaming horse, with swords and friendly hearts;
With chere, as though one should another whelm,
  Where we have fought, and chasèd oft with darts.
With silver drops the mead yet spread for ruth,
  In active games of nimbleness and strength,
Where we did strain, trainèd with swarms of youth,
  Our tender limbs, that yet shot up in length.
The secret groves, which oft we made resound
  Of pleasant plaint, and of our ladies' praise;
Recording oft what grace each one had found,
  What hope of speed, what dread of long delays:
The wild forest, the clothèd holts with green;
  With reins avail'd, and swift-ybreathèd horse,
With cry of hounds and merry blasts between,
  Where we did chase the fearful hart of force.
The void vales, eke, that harbor'd us each night;
  Wherewith, alas! reviveth in my breast
The sweet accord, such sleeps as yet delight;
  The pleasant dreams, the quiet bed of rest;
The secret thoughts, imparted with such trust;
  The wanton talk, the divers change of play;
The friendship sworn, each promise kept so just,
  Wherewith we past the winter night away.
And with this thought the blood forsakes the face,
  The tears berain my cheeks of deadly hue:

The which, as soon as sobbing sighs, alas,
  Upsuppèd have, thus I my plaint renew:
O place of bliss! renewer of my woes!
  Give me account, where is my noble fere?
Whom in thy walls thou dost each night enclose;
  To other lief; but unto me most dear:
Echo, alas! that doth my sorrow rue,
  Returns thereto a hollow sound of plaint.
Thus I alone, where all my freedom grew,
  In prison pine with bondage and restraint.
And with remembrance of the greater grief,
To banish the less, I find my chief relief.
        HENRY HOWARD, Earl of Surrey.

THE GOOD LORD CLIFFORD.

SONG AT THE FEAST OF BROUGHAM CASTLE UPON THE RESTORATION OF LORD CLIFFORD, THE SHEPHERD, TO THE ESTATES AND HONORS OF HIS ANCESTORS.

HIGH in the breathless hall the minstrel sate,
  And Emont's murmur mingled with the song.
The words of ancient time I thus translate,
  A festal strain that hath been silent long.
"From town to town, from tower to tower,
The red rose is a gladsome flower.
Her thirty years of winter past,
The red rose is revived at last;
She lifts her head for endless spring,
For everlasting blossoming:
Both roses flourish, red and white.
In love and sisterly delight
The two that were at strife are blended,
And all old troubles now are ended.
Joy! joy to both! but most to her
Who is the flower of Lancaster!
Behold her how she smiles to-day
On this great throng, this bright array!
Fair greeting doth she send to all
From every corner of the Hall;
But, chiefly, from above the board
Where sits in state our rightful lord,
A Clifford to his own restored!

"They came with banner, spear, and shield:
And it was proved in Bosworth field.
Not long the avenger was withstood—
Earth help'd him with the cry of blood
St. George was with us, and the might
Of blessed angels crown'd the right.
Loud voice the land has utter'd forth,
We loudest in the faithful north:
Our fields rejoice, our mountains ring,
Our streams proclaim a welcoming;
Our strong abodes and castles see
The glory of their loyalty.

"How glad is Skipton at this hour—
Though she is but a lonely tower!
To vacancy and silence left;
Of all her guardian sons bereft—
Knight, squire, or yeoman, page or groom;
We have them at the feast of Brougham.
How glad Pendragon—though the sleep
Of years be on her!—She shall reap
A taste of this great pleasure, viewing
As in a dream her own renewing.
Rejoiced is Brough, right glad, I deem,
Beside her little humble stream;
And she that keepeth watch and ward
Her statelier Eden's course to guard;
They both are happy at this hour,
Though each is but a lonely tower:—
But here is perfect joy and pride
For one fair House by Emont's side,
This day, distinguish'd without peer,
To see her Master, and to cheer
Him and and his Lady Mother dear!

"Oh! it was a time forlorn,
When the fatherless was born—
Give her wings that she may fly,
Or she sees her infant die!
Swords that are with slaughter wild
Hunt the mother and the child.
Who will take them from the light?
—Yonder is a man in sight—
Yonder is a house—but where?
No, they must not enter there.
To the caves, and to the brooks,
To the clouds of heaven she looks·
She is speechless, but her eyes
Pray in ghostly agonies.
Blissful Mary, mother mild,
Maid and mother undefiled,
Save a mother and her child!

"Now who is he that bounds with joy
On Carrock's side—a Shepherd Boy?
No thoughts hath he but thoughts that pass
Light as the wind along the grass.

Can this be he who hither came
In secret, like a smother'd flame?
O'er whom such thankful tears were shed
For shelter, and a poor man's bread!
God loves the child, and God hath will'd
That those dear words should be fulfill'd,
The lady's words, when forced away,
The last she to her babe did say,
'My own, my own, thy fellow-guest
I may not be; but rest thee, rest,
For lowly shepherd's life is best!'

"Alas! when evil men are strong
No life is good, no pleasure long.
The boy must part from Mosedale's groves
And leave Blencathara's rugged coves,
And quit the flowers that summer brings
To Glenderamakin's lofty springs;
Must vanish, and his careless cheer
Be turn'd to heaviness and fear.
—Give Sir Lancelot Threlkeld praise!
Hear it, good man, old in days!
Thou free of covert and of rest
For this young bird that is distrest;
Among the branches safe he lay,
And he was free to sport and play
When falcons were abroad for prey.

"A recreant harp, that sings of fear
And heaviness in Clifford's ear!
I said, when evil men are strong,
No life is good, no pleasure long,—
A weak and cowardly untruth!
Our Clifford was a happy youth,
And thankful through a weary time
That brought him up to manhood's prime.
—Again he wanders forth at will
And tends a flock from hill to hill:
His garb is humble: ne'er was seen
Such garb with such a noble mien:
Among the Shepherd-grooms no mate
Hath he, a child of strength and state!
Yet lacks not friends for solemn glee,
And a cheerful company,
That learn'd of him submissive ways,
And comforted his private days.
To his side the fallow-deer
Came, and rested without fear;
The eagle, lord of land and sea,
Stoop'd down to pay him fealty;
And both the undying fish that swim
Through Bowscale Tarn did wait on him,

The pair were servants of his eye
In their immortality;
They moved about in open sight,
To and fro, for his delight.
He knew the rocks which angels haunt
On the mountains visitant;
He hath kenn'd them taking wing:
And the caves where faëries sing
He hath enter'd;—and been told
By voices how men lived of old.
Among the heavens his eye can see
Face of thing that is to be;
And, if men report him right,
He could whisper words of might.
—Now another day is come,
Fitter hope, and nobler doom:
He hath thrown aside his crook,
And hath buried deep his book;
Armor rusting in his halls
On the blood of Clifford calls;—
'Quell the Scot,' exclaims the lance—
Bear me to the heart of France,
Is the longing of the shield—
Tell thy name, thou trembling field;
Field of death, where'er thou be,
Groan thou with our victory!
Happy day, and mighty hour,
When our Shepherd, in his power,
Mail'd and horsed, with lance and sword,
To his ancestors restored,
Like a re-appearing star,
Like a glory from afar,
First shall head the flock of war!"

Alas! the fervent harper did not know
  That for a tranquil soul the lay was
    framed,
Who, long compell'd in humble walks to go,
  Was soften'd into feeling, soothed, and
    tamed.

Love had he found in huts where poor
    men lie;
  His daily teachers had been woods and
    rills,
The silence that is in the starry sky,
  The sleep that is among the lonely hills.

In him the savage virtue of the race,
  Revenge, and all ferocious thoughts were
    dead:
Nor did he change; but kept in lofty
    place
  The wisdom which adversity had bred.

Glad were the vales, and every cottage hearth;
　The Shepherd Lord was honor'd more and more:
And ages after he was laid in earth,
　"The good Lord Clifford" was the name he bore.
　　　　　　　　WILLIAM WORDSWORTH.

INSCRIPTION FOR A STATUE OF CHAUCER AT WOODSTOCK.

SUCH was old Chaucer: such the placid mien
Of him who first with harmony inform'd
The language of our fathers. Here he dwelt
For many a cheerful day. These ancient walls
Have often heard him, while his legends blithe
He sang; of love, or knighthood, or the wiles
Of homely life; through each estate and age,
The fashions and the follies of the world
With cunning hand portraying. Though perchance
From Blenheim's towers, O stranger, thou art come
Glowing with Churchill's trophies; yet in vain
Dost thou applaud them, if thy breast be cold
To him, this other hero; who in times
Dark and untaught, began with charming verse
To tame the rudeness of his native land.
　　　　　　　　MARK AKENSIDE.

TO MISTRESS MARGARET HUSSEY.

　MERRY Margaret,
　As midsummer flower,
　Gentle as falcon,
　Or hawk of the tower;
　With solace and gladness,
　Much mirth and no madness,
　All good and no badness;
　So joyously,
　So maidenly,
　So womanly
　Her demeaning,—
　In everything
　Far, far passing
That I can indite,
Or suffice to write,
Of merry Margaret,
As midsummer flower,
Gentle as falcon
Or hawk of the tower;
As patient and as still,
And as full of good-will,
As fair Isiphil,
Coliander,
Sweet Pomander,
Good Cassander;
Steadfast of thought,
Well made, well wrought;
Far may be sought
Ere you can find
So courteous, so kind,
As merry Margaret,
This midsummer flower,
Gentle as falcon,
Or hawk of the tower.
　　　　　　　　JOHN SKELTON.

EPIGRAM ON SIR FRANCIS DRAKE.

THE stars above will make thee known,
　If man were silent here:
The sun himself cannot forget
　His fellow-traveller.
　　　　　　　　BEN JONSON.

AN ODE—TO HIMSELF.

WHERE dost thou careless lie
　Buried in ease and sloth?
Knowledge that sleeps, doth die:
And this security,
　It is the common moth,
That eats on wits and arts, and so destroys them both.

Are all the Aonian springs
　Dried up? lies Thespia waste?
Doth Clarius' harp want strings,
That not a nymph now sings?
　Or droop they as disgraced
To see their seats and bowers by chattering pies defaced?

If hence thy silence be,
　As 'tis too just a cause—
Let this thought quicken thee;
Minds that are great and free
　Should not on fortune pause?
'Tis crown enough to virtue still, her own applause.

What though the greedy fry
  Be taken with false baits
Of worded balladry,
  And think it poesy?
They die with their conceits,
And only piteous scorn upon their folly
    waits.

Then take in hand thy lyre,
  Strike in thy proper strain;
With Japhet's line aspire
Sol's chariot for new fire
  To give the world again;
Who aided him, will thee, the issue of
    Jove's brain.

And since our dainty age
  Cannot indure reproof,
Make not thyself a page
To that strumpet, the stage;
  But sing high and aloof
Safe from the wolf's black jaw, and the
    dull ass's hoof.
BEN JONSON.

SONNET.

ON HIS BEING ARRIVED TO THE AGE OF TWENTY-THREE.

How soon hath Time, the subtle thief of
    youth,
  Stolen on his wing my three-and-twenti-
    eth year!
My hasting days fly on with full career,
  But my late spring no bud or blossom
    show'th.
Perhaps my semblance might deceive the
    truth,
  That I to manhood am arrived so near;
  And inward ripeness doth much less ap-
    pear
That some more timely-happy spirits en-
    du'th.
Yet be it less or more, or soon or slow,
  It shall be still in strictest measure even
    To that same lot, however mean or high,
Toward which Time leads me, and the will
    of heaven:
  All is, if I have grace to use it so,
    As ever in my great Task-master's eye.
JOHN MILTON.

EPITAPH ON A LIVING AUTHOR.

HERE, passenger, beneath this shed,
Lies Cowley, tho' entomb'd, not dead;
Yet freed from human toil and strife,
And all th' impertinence of life.

Who in his poverty is neat,
And even in retirement great.
With Gold, the people's idol, he
Holds endless war and enmity.

Can you not say, he has resigned
His breath, to this small cell confined?
With this small mansion let him have
The rest and silence of the grave:

Strew roses here as on his hearse,
And reckon this his funeral verse:
With wreaths of fragrant herbs adorn
The yet surviving poet's urn.
ABRAHAM COWLEY.

ON MY DEAR SON, GERVASE BEAUMONT.

CAN I, who have for others oft compiled
The songs of death, forget my sweetest
    child,
Which like a flower crushed with a blast is
    dead,
And ere full time hangs down his smiling
    head,
Expecting with clear hope to live anew,
Among the angels fed with heavenly dew?
We have this sign of joy, that many days,
While on the earth his struggling spirit
    stays,
The name of Jesus in his mouth contains
His only food, his sleep, his ease from
    pains.
Oh, may that sound be rooted in my mind,
Of which in him such strong effect I find!
Dear Lord, receive my son, whose winning
    love
To me was like a friendship, far above
The course of nature or his tender age;
Whose looks could all my bitter griefs as-
    suage:
Let his pure soul—ordain'd seven years to
    be
In that frail body, which was part of me—

Remain my pledge in heaven, as sent to
  show
How to this port at every step I go.
                    Sir John Beaumont.

An Epitaph upon the Right Honourable Sir Phillip Sidney.

To praise thy life, or waile thy worthie
    death,
  And want thy wit, thy wit high, pure,
    divine,
  Is far beyond the powre of mortall line,
Nor any one hath worth that draweth
    breath.

Yet rich in zeale, though poore in learn-
    ings lore,
  And friendly care obscurde in secret brest,
  And love that envie in thy life supprest,
Thy deere life done, and death hath
    doubled more.

And I, that in thy time and living state,
  Did onely praise thy vertues in my
    thought,
  As one that feeld the rising sun hath
    sought,
With words and teares now waile thy
    timelesse fate.

Drawne was thy race aright from princely
    line,
  Nor lesse than such (by gifts that nature
    gave,
  The common mother that all creatures
    have)
Doth vertue shew, and princely linage shine.

A king gave thee thy name: a kingly minde
  That God thee gave; who found it now
    too deere
  For this base world, and hath resumde
    it neere,
To sit in skies, and sort with powres divine.

Kent thy birth daies, and Oxford held thy
    youth;
  The heavens made hast, and staid nor
    yeers, nor time:
  The fruits of age grew ripe in thy first
    prime;
Thy will, thy words; thy words the seales
    of truth.

Great gifts and wisedom rare imployd thee
    thence,
  To treat from kings with those more
    great than kings;
  Such hope men had to lay the highest
    things
On thy wise youth, to be transported hence.

Whence to sharpe wars sweet honor did
    thee call,
  Thy countries love, religion, and thy
    friends:
  Of worthy men the marks, the lives, and
    ends,
And her defence, for whom we labor all.

There didst thou vanquish shame and
    tedious age,
  Griefe, sorrow, sicknes, and base fortunes
    might:
  Thy rising day saw never wofull night,
But past with praise from off this worldly
    stage.

Back to the campe, by thee that day was
    brought,
  First thine owne death, and after thy
    long fame;
  Teares to the soldiers, the proud Castil-
    ians shame,
Vertue exprest, and honor truly taught.

What hath he lost that such great grace
    hath won?
  Yoong yeeres for endless yeeres, and
    hope unsure
  Of fortunes gifts for wealth that still
    shall dure:
Oh, happie race with so great praises run!

England doth hold thy lims that bred the
    same,
  Flaunders thy valure where it last was
    tried,
  The campe thy sorrow where thy bodie
    died,
Thy friends thy want; the world thy ver-
    tues fame:

Nations thy wit, our mindes lay up thy
    love;
  Letters thy learning, thy losse yeeres
    long to come:

In worthy harts sorrow hath made thy
    tombe;
Thy soule and spright enrich the heavens
    above.

Thy liberall hart imbalmd in gratefull
    teares,
  Yoong sighes, sweet sighes, sage sighes,
    bewaile thy fall;
  Envie her sting, and Spite hath left her
    gall,
Malice her selfe a mourning garment
    weares.

That day their Hanniball died, our Scipio
    fell!
  Scipio, Cicero, and Petrarch of our time!
  Whose vertues, wounded by my worth-
    lesse rime,
Let Angels speake, and heaven thy praises
    tell.
                    SIR WALTER RALEIGH.

TEARS WEPT AT THE GRAVE OF SIR ALBERTUS MORTON.

SILENCE, in truth, would speak my sorrow
    best,
  For deepest wounds can least their feel-
    ings tell;
Yet let me borrow from mine own unrest
  But time to bid him, whom I loved, fare-
    well.

O my unhappy lines! you that before
  Have served my youth to vent some
    wanton cries,
And now, congeal'd with grief, can scarce
    implore
  Strength to accent, "Here my Albertus
    lies!"

This is the sable stone, this is the cave
  And womb of earth, that doth his corpse
    embrace:
While others sing his praise, let me en-
    grave
  These bleeding numbers to adorn the
    place.

Here will I paint the characters of woe;
  Here will I pay my tribute to the dead;
And here my faithful tears in showers shall
    flow,
  To humanize the flints whereon I tread.

Where, though I mourn my matchless loss
    alone,
  And none between my weakness judge
    and me,
Yet even these gentle walls allow my moan,
  Whose doleful echoes to my plaints agree.

But is he gone? and live I rhyming here,
  As if some Muse would listen to my lay,
When all, distuned, sit wailing for their
    dear,
  And bathe the banks where he was wont
    to play?

Dwell thou in endless light, dischargèd
    soul,
  Freed now from Nature's and from For-
    tune's trust,
While on this fluent globe my glass shall
    roll,
  And run the rest of my remaining dust.
                    SIR HENRY WOTTON.

UPON THE DEATH OF SIR ALBERTUS MORTON'S WIFE.

HE first deceased; she for a little tried
To live without him, liked it not, and died.
                    SIR HENRY WOTTON.

TO THE MEMORY OF MY BELOVED, THE AUTHOR, MR. WILLIAM SHAKESPEARE, AND WHAT HE HATH LEFT US.

To draw no envy (Shakespeare) on thy
    name,
Am I thus ample to thy book, and fame;
While I confess thy writings to be such,
As neither man, nor muse, can praise too
    much;
'Tis true, and all men's suffrage; but these
    ways
Were not the path I meant unto thy praise:
For seeliest ignorance on these may light,
Which, when it sounds at best, but echoes
    right,
Or blind affection, which doth ne'er advance
The truth, but gropes, and urgeth all by
    chance;
Or crafty malice might pretend this praise.
And think to ruin, where it seem'd to
    raise:

These are, as some infamous bawd, or whore,
Should praise a matron: what could hurt her more?
But thou art proof against them; and, indeed,
Above th' ill fortune of them, or the need.
I therefore will begin:—Soul of the age,
The applause, delight, the wonder of our stage,
My Shakespeare, rise! I will not lodge thee by
Chaucer, or Spenser; or bid Beaumont lie
A little further, to make thee a room;
Thou art a monument without a tomb;
And art alive still, while thy book doth live,
And we have wits to read, and praise to give.
That I not mix thee so, my brain excuses;
I mean, with great but disproportion'd muses:
For, if I thought my judgment were of years,
I should commit thee surely with thy peers;
And tell how far thou didst our Lyly outshine,
Or sporting Kyd, or Marlowe's mighty line:
And though thou hadst small Latin, and less Greek,
From thence to honor thee, I would not seek
For names; but call forth thundering Æschylus,
Euripides, and Sophocles, to us,
Pacuvius, Accius, him of Cordova dead,
To live again, to hear thy buskin tread
And shake a stage; or, when thy socks were on,
Leave thee alone, for the comparison
Of all that insolent Greece, or haughty Rome,
Sent forth, or since did from their ashes come.
Triumph, my Britain! thou hast one to show,
To whom all scenes of Europe homage owe.
He was not of an age, but for all time;
And all the muses still were in their prime,
When like Apollo he came forth to warm
Our ears, or like a Mercury to charm.
Nature herself was proud of his designs,
And joy'd to wear the dressing of his lines:
Which were so richly spun, and woven so fit,
As since she will vouchsafe no other wit.
The merry Greek, tart Aristophanes,
Neat Terence, witty Plautus, now not please;
But antiquated and deserted lie,
As they were not of Nature's family.
Yet must I not give Nature all; thy art,
My gentle Shakespeare, must enjoy a part:
For though the poet's matter nature be,
His art doth give the fashion; and that he,
Who casts to write a living line, must sweat
(Such as thine are), and strike the second heat
Upon the muses' anvil; turn the same
(And himself with it) that he thinks to frame;
Or for the laurel he may gain a scorn,
For a good poet's made as well as born:
And such wert thou. Look, how the father's face
Lives in his issue; even so the race
Of Shakespeare's mind, and manners, brightly shines
In his well-turnèd and true-filed lines;
In each of which he seems to shake a lance,
As brandish'd at the eyes of ignorance.
Sweet Swan of Avon, what a sight it were,
To see thee in our water yet appear;
And make those flights upon the banks of Thames,
That so did take Eliza, and our James.
But stay; I see thee in the hemisphere
Advanced, and made a constellation there:
Shine forth, thou star of poets; and with rage,
Or influence, chide, or cheer, the drooping stage;
Which, since thy flight from hence, hath mourn'd like night,
And despairs day, but for thy volume's light.

BEN JONSON.

AN EPITAPH ON THE ADMIRABLE DRAMATIC POET, W. SHAKESPEARE.

What need my Shakespeare for his honour'd bones,
The labour of an age in pilèd stones;
Or that his hallow'd reliques should be hid
Under a star-ypointed pyramid?
Dear son of memory, great heir of fame,
What need'st thou such dull witness of thy name?
Thou, in our wonder and astonishment,
Hast built thyself a lasting monument:
For whilst, to the shame of slow-endeavouring art,
Thy easy numbers flow; and that each part
Hath, from the leaves of thy unvalued book,
Those Delphic lines with deep impression took;
Then thou, our fancy of herself bereaving,
Dost make us marble with too much conceiving;
And, so sepulchred, in such pomp dost lie,
That kings for such a tomb would wish to die.
John Milton.

LINES ON THE PORTRAIT OF SHAKESPEARE.

This figure, that thou here seest put,
It was for gentle Shakespeare cut;
Wherein the Graver had a strife
With Nature to outdo the life:
Oh, could he but have drawn his wit
As well in brass, as he hath hit
His face; the Print would then surpass
All that was ever writ in brass.
But since he cannot, Reader, look
Not at his picture, but his book.
Ben Jonson.

LINES.
Written the Night before his Execution.

E'en such is time; which takes on trust
  Our youth, our joys, our all we have,
And pays us but with earth and dust;
  Which in the dark and silent grave,
When we have wander'd all our ways,
  Shuts up the story of our days:
But from this earth, this grave, this dust,
My God shall raise me up, I trust.
Sir Walter Raleigh.

UPON THE SUDDEN RESTRAINT OF THE EARL OF SOMERSET, THEN FALLING FROM FAVOR.

Dazzled thus with height of place,
  Whilst our hopes our wits beguile,
No man marks the narrow space
  'Twixt a prison and a smile.

Then, since Fortune's favors fade,
  You that in her arms do sleep
Learn to swim, and not to wade,
  For the hearts of kings are deep.

But if greatness be so blind
  As to trust in towers of air,
Let it be with goodness lined,
  That at least the fall be fair.

Then, though darken'd, you shall say,
  When friends fail and princes frown,
Virtue is the roughest way
  But proves at night a bed of down.
Sir Henry Wotton.

TO THE LADY MARGARET, COUNTESS OF CUMBERLAND.

He that of such a height hath built his mind,
And rear'd the dwelling of his thoughts so strong,
As neither fear nor hope can shake the frame
Of his resolvèd powers; nor all the wind
Of vanity or malice pierce to wrong
His settled peace, or to disturb the same:
What a fair seat hath he, from whence he may
The boundless wastes and wilds of man survey!

And with how free an eye doth he look down
Upon these lower regions of turmoil!

Where all the storms of passions mainly
    beat
On flesh and blood: where honor, power,
    renown
Are only gay afflictions, golden toil;
Where greatness stands upon as feeble
    feet
As frailty doth; and only great doth
    seem
To little minds, who do it so esteem.

He looks upon the mightiest monarch's
    wars
But only as on stately robberies;
Where evermore the fortune that prevails
Must be the right; the ill-succeeding
    Mars
The fairest and the best-faced enterprise.
Great pirate Pompey lesser pirates quails;
Justice, he sees, (as if seducèd) still
Conspires with power, whose cause must
    not be ill.

He sees the face of right t' appear as
    manifold
As are the passions of uncertain man;
Who puts it in all colors, all attires,
To serve his ends, and make his courses
    hold.
He sees, that let deceit work what it
    can,
Plot and contrive base ways to high de-
    sires;
That the all-guiding Providence doth
    yet
All disappoint, and mocks the smoke of
    wit.

Nor is he moved with all the thunder-
    cracks
Of tyrants' threats, or with the surly brow
Of Power, that proudly sits on others'
    crimes;
Charged with more crying sins than those
    he checks.
The storms of sad confusion, that may
    grow
Up in the present for the coming times,
Appal not him that hath no side at all,
But of himself, and knows the worst can
    fall.

Although his heart (so near allied to earth)
Cannot but pity the perplexèd state
Of troublous and distress'd mortality,
That thus make way unto the ugly birth
Of their own sorrows, and do still beget
Affliction upon imbecility;
Yet seeing thus the course of things must
    run,
He looks thereon not strange, but as fore-
    done.

And whilst distraught ambition compasses,
And is encompass'd; whilst as craft de-
    ceives,
And is deceived; whilst man doth ransack
    man,
And builds on blood, and rises by distress,
And th' inheritance of desolation leaves
To great-expecting hopes; he looks there-
    on,
As from the shore of peace, with unwet
    eye,
And bears no venture in impiety.

Thus, madam, fares that man, that hath
    prepared
A rest for his desires, and sees all things
Beneath him; and hath learn'd this book
    of man,
Full of the notes of frailty; and compared
The best of glory with her sufferings;
By whom, I see, you labor all you can
To plant your heart; and set your thoughts
    as near
His glorious mansion as your powers can
    bear.

Which, madam, are so soundly fashionèd
By that clear judgment that hath carried
    you
Beyond the feeble limits of your kind,
As they can stand against the strongest
    head
Passion can make; inured to any hue
The world can cast; that cannot cast that
    mind
Out of her form of goodness, that doth see
Both what the best and worst of earth can
    be.

Which makes, that whatsoever here be-
    falls,
You in the region of yourself remain,
Where no vain breath of th' impudent mo-
    lests,
That hath secured within the brazen walls

Of a clear conscience, that (without all
    stain)
Rises in peace, in innocency rests;
Whilst all what Malice from without pro-
    cures,
Shows her own ugly heart, but hurts not
    yours.

And whereas none rejoice more in re-
    venge
Than women use to do; yet you well
    know,
That wrong is better checked by being con-
    temn'd,
Than being pursued; leaving to Him t'
    avenge
To whom it appertains. Wherein you
    show
How worthily your clearness hath con-
    demn'd
Base malediction, living in the dark,
That at the rays of goodness still doth
    bark.

Knowing the heart of man is set to be
The centre of this world, about the which
These revolutions of disturbances
Still roll; where all th' aspects of misery
Predominate; whose strong effects are such
As he must bear, being powerless to re-
    dress;
And that unless above himself he can
Erect himself, how poor a thing is man!

And how turmoil'd they are that level lie
With earth, and cannot lift themselves
    from thence;
That never are at peace with their desires,
But work beyond their years; and even
    deny
Dotage her rest, and hardly will dispense
With death: that when ability expires,
Desire lives still—so much delight they
    have
To carry toil and travel to the grave.

Whose ends you see; and what can be the
    best
They reach unto, when they have cast the
    sum
And reckonings of their glory. And you
    know,
This floating life hath but this port of
    rest,
A heart prepared, that fears no ill to
    come;
And that man's greatness rests but in his
    show,
The best of all whose days consumèd
    are,
Either in war, or peace conceiving war.

This concord, madam, of a well-tuned mind
Hath been so set by that all-working Hand
Of heaven, that though the world hath
    done his worst
To put it out by discords most unkind,
Yet doth it still in perfect union stand
With God and man; nor ever will be forced
From that most sweet accord, but still agree,
Equal in fortune's inequality.

And this note, madam, of your worthiness
Remains recorded in so many hearts,
As time nor malice cannot wrong your
    right,
In th' inheritance of fame you must pos-
    sess:
You that have built you by your great de-
    serts
(Out of small means) a far more exquisite
And glorious dwelling for your honor'd
    name
Than all the gold that leaden minds can
    frame.
SAMUEL DANIEL.

AN EPITAPH ON SALATHIEL PAVY,
A CHILD OF QUEEN ELIZABETH'S CHAPEL.

WEEP with me, all you that read
    This little story;
And know, for whom a tear you shed
    Death's self is sorry.
'Twas a child that so did thrive
    In grace and feature,
As heaven and nature seem'd to strive
    Which own'd the creature.
Years he number'd scarce thirteen
    When fates turn'd cruel,
Yet three fill'd Zodiacs had he been
    The stage's jewel;
And did act, what now we moan,
    Old men so duly,
As, sooth, the Parcæ thought him one,
    He play'd so truly.

So by error to his fate
    They all consented;
But viewing him since, alas, too late!
    They have repented;
And have sought, to give new birth,
    In baths to steep him;
But being so much too good for earth,
    Heaven vows to keep him.
                  BEN JONSON.

EPITAPH ON ELIZABETH L. H.

WOULDST thou heare what man can say
In a little?—reader, stay!
Underneath this stone doth lye
As much beauty as could dye;
Which in life did harbor give
To more vertue than doth live.
If at all she had a fault,
Leave it buried in this vault.
One name was Elizabeth—
Th' other, let it sleep with death:
Fitter, where it dyed to tell,
Than that it lived at all.   Farewell!
                    BEN JONSON.

EPITAPH ON THE COUNTESS OF PEMBROKE.

UNDERNEATH this sable hearse
Lies the subject of all verse,
Sidney's sister, Pembroke's mother;
Death! ere thou hast slain another,
Learn'd and fair and good as she,
Time shall throw a dart at thee.
                    BEN JONSON.

TO VINCENT CORBET, MY SON.

WHAT I shall leave thee, none can tell,
But all shall say I wish thee well.
I wish thee, Vin, before all wealth,
Both bodily and ghostly health;
Nor too much wealth nor wit come to thee,
So much of either may undo thee.
I wish thee learning not for show,
Enough for to instruct and know;
Not such as gentlemen require
To prate at table or at fire.
I wish thee all thy mother's graces,
Thy father's fortunes and his places.
I wish thee friends, and one at court,
Not to build on, but support;
To keep thee not in doing many
Oppressions, but from suffering any.
I wish thee peace in all thy ways,
Nor lazy nor contentious days;
And, when thy soul and body part,
As innocent as now thou art.
                    RICHARD CORBET.

ON LUCY, COUNTESS OF BEDFORD.

THIS morning, timely rapt with holy fire,
  I thought to form unto my zealous Muse,
What kind of creature I could most desire,
  To honor, serve, and love; as poets use,
I meant to make her fair, and free, and wise,
  Of greatest blood, and yet more good than great;
I meant the day-star should not brighter rise,
  Nor lend like influence from his lucent seat.
I meant she should be courteous, facile, sweet,
  Hating that solemn vice of greatness, pride;
I meant each softest virtue there should meet,
  Fit in that softer bosom to reside.
Only a learnèd and a manly soul
  I purposed her; that should, with even powers,
The rock, the spindle, and the shears control
  Of Destiny, and spin her own free hours.
Such when I meant to feign, and wish'd to see,
My Muse bade, Bedford write, and that was she.
                    BEN JONSON.

OF MYSELF.

THIS only grant me, that my means may lie
Too low for envy, for contempt too high.
  Some honor I would have,
Not from great deeds, but good alone;
The unknown are better than ill known:
  Rumor can ope the grave.

Acquaintance I would have, but when 't depends
Not on the number, but the choice, of friends.

Books should, not business, entertain the light,
And sleep, as undisturb'd as death, the night.
My house a cottage more
Than palace; and should fitting be
For all my use, no luxury.
My garden painted o'er
With Nature's hand, not Art's; and pleasures yield,
Horace might envy in his Sabine field.

Thus would I double my life's fading space;
For he that runs it well twice runs his race.
And in this true delight,
These unbought sports, this happy state,
I would not fear, nor wish, my fate;
But boldly say each night,
To-morrow let my sun his beams display,
Or in clouds hide them; I have lived to-day.

ABRAHAM COWLEY.

SONNET.

TO THE LORD GENERAL CROMWELL.

CROMWELL, our chief of men, who through a cloud
Not of war only, but detractions rude,
Guided by faith and matchless fortitude,
To peace and truth thy glorious way hast plough'd
And on the neck of crownèd fortune proud
Hast rear'd God's trophies, and his work pursued,
While Darwen stream with blood of Scots imbrued,
And Dunbar field resounds thy praises loud,
And Worcester's laureat wreath. Yet much remains
To conquer still; peace hath her victories
No less renown'd than war. New foes arise
Threatening to bind our souls with secular chains:
Help us to save free conscience from the paw
Of hireling wolves, whose gospel is their maw.

JOHN MILTON.

SONNET.

TO CYRIAC SKINNER.

CYRIAC, this three years day these eyes, tho' clear
To outward view of blemish or of spot,
Bereft of light, their seeing have forgot;
Nor to their idle orbs doth sight appear
Of sun, or moon, or star, throughout the year,
Or man, or woman. Yet I argue not
Against Heaven's hand or will, nor bate a jot
Of heart or hope; but still bear up and steer
Right onward. What supports me, dost thou ask?
The conscience, friend, t' have lost them overplied
In liberty's defence, my noble task.
Of which all Europe rings from side to side.
This thought might lead me through the world's vain mask,
Content though blind, had I no better guide.

JOHN MILTON.

SONNET

ON HIS BLINDNESS.

WHEN I consider how my light is spent,
Ere half my days in this dark world and wide,
And that one talent which is death to hide,
Lodged with me useless, though my soul more bent
To serve therewith my Maker, and present
My true account, lest He returning chide;
"Doth God exact day-labor, light denied?"
I fondly ask: but Patience, to prevent
That murmur, soon replies, "God doth not need
Either man's work or his own gifts: who best

Bear his mild yoke, they serve him best:
his state
Is kingly; thousands at his bidding speed,
And post o'er land and ocean without rest;
They also serve who only stand and
wait."
JOHN MILTON.

MILTON'S PRAYER OF PATIENCE.

I AM old and blind!
Men point at me as smitten by God's
frown;
Afflicted and deserted of my kind,
Yet am I not cast down.

I am weak, yet strong;
I murmur not that I no longer see;
Poor, old, and helpless, I the more belong,
Father Supreme! to Thee.

All-merciful One!
When men are furthest, then art Thou most
near;
When friends pass by, my weaknesses to
shun,
Thy chariot I hear.

Thy glorious face
Is leaning toward me; and its holy light
Shines in upon my lonely dwelling-place,—
And there is no more night.

On my bended knee
I recognize Thy purpose clearly shown:
My vision Thou hast dimm'd, that I may see
Thyself,—Thyself alone.

I have naught to fear;
This darkness is the shadow of Thy wing;
Beneath it I am almost sacred; here
Can come no evil thing.

Oh, I seem to stand
Trembling, where foot of mortal ne'er hath
been,
Wrapp'd in that radiance from the sinless
land,
Which eye hath never seen!

Visions come and go:
Shapes of resplendent beauty round me
throng;
From angel lips I seem to hear the flow
Of soft and holy song.

It is nothing now,
When heaven is opening on my sightless
eyes,
When airs from Paradise refresh my brow,
The earth in darkness lies.

In a purer clime
My being fills with rapture,—waves of
thought
Roll in upon my spirit,—strains sublime
Break over me unsought.

Give me now my lyre!
I feel the stirrings of a gift divine:
Within my bosom glows unearthly fire,
Lit by no skill of mine.
ELIZABETH LLOYD HOWELL.

TO THE LADY MARGARET LEY.

DAUGHTER to that good earl, once President
Of England's Council, and her Treasury,
Who lived in both, unstain'd with gold
or fee,
And left them both, more in himself content,
Till the sad breaking of that Parliament
Broke him, as that dishonest victory
At Chæronea, fatal to liberty,
Kill'd with report that old man eloquent.
Though later born than to have known the
days
Wherein your father flourish'd, yet by
you,
Madam, methinks I see him living yet;
So well your words his noble virtues praise,
That all both judge you to relate them
true,
And to possess them, honor'd Margaret.
JOHN MILTON.

LYCIDAS.

YET once more, O ye laurels, and once
more
Ye myrtles brown, with ivy never sere,
I come to pluck your berries harsh and
crude,
And with forced fingers rude
Shatter your leaves before the mellowing
year.
Bitter constraint, and sad occasion dear,

Compels me to disturb your season due;
For Lycidas is dead, dead ere his prime,
Young Lycidas, and hath not left his peer.
Who would not sing for Lycidas? he knew
Himself to sing, and build the lofty rhyme.
He must not float upon his watery bier
Unwept, and welter to the parching wind,
Without the meed of some melodious tear.
  Begin then, sisters of the sacred well,
That from beneath the seat of Jove doth spring,
Begin, and somewhat loudly sweep the string.
Hence with denial vain, and coy excuse;
So may some gentle muse
With lucky words favor my destined urn,
And as he passes turn,
And bid fair peace be to my sable shroud.
For we were nursed upon the self-same hill,
Fed the same flock by fountain, shade, and rill.
  Together both, ere the high lawns appear'd
Under the opening eyelids of the morn,
We drove a-field, and both together heard
What time the gray-fly winds her sultry horn,
Batt'ning our flocks with the fresh dews of night
Oft till the star that rose at evening bright
Toward heaven's descent had sloped his west'ring wheel.
Meanwhile the rural ditties were not mute,
Temper'd to th' oaten flute;
Rough satyrs danced and fauns with cloven heel
From the glad song would not be absent long,
And old Damætus loved to hear our song.
  But oh, the heavy change, now thou art gone—
Now thou art gone, and never must return!
Thee, shepherd, thee the woods, and desert caves,
With wild thyme and the gadding vine o'ergrown,
And all their echoes, mourn;
The willows, and the hazel copses green,
Shall now no more be seen,
Fanning their joyous leaves to thy soft lays.
As killing as the canker to the rose,
Or taint-worm to the weanling herds that graze,
Or frost to flowers, that their gay wardrobe wear,
When first the white-thorn blows;
Such, Lycidas, thy loss to shepherds' ear.
  Where were ye, nymphs, when the remorseless deep
Closed o'er the head of your loved Lycidas?
For neither were ye playing on the steep,
Where your old bards, the famous druids, lie,
Nor on the shaggy top of Mona high,
Nor yet where Deva spreads her wizard stream.
Ay me! I fondly dream!
Had ye been there, for what could that have done?
What could the muse herself that Orpheus bore,
The muse herself for her enchanting son,
Whom universal Nature did lament,
When, by the rout that made the hideous roar,
His gory vision down the stream was sent,
Down the swift Hebrus to the Lesbian shore?
  Alas! what boots it with incessant care
To tend the homely, slighted shepherd's trade,
And strictly meditate the thankless muse?
Were it not better done, as others use,
To sport with Amaryllis in the shade,
Or with the tangles of Neæra's hair?
Fame is the spur that the clear spirit doth raise
(That last infirmity of noble mind)
To scorn delights and live laborious days;
But the fair guerdon when we hope to find,
And think to burst out into sudden blaze,
Comes the blind fury with th' abhorrèd shears,
And slits the thin-spun life. But not the praise,
Phœbus replied, and touch'd my trembling ears;

Fame is no plant that grows on mortal soil,
Nor in the glistering foil
Set off to th' world, nor in broad rumor lies;
But lives and spreads aloft by those pure eyes
And perfect witness of all-judging Jove;
As he pronounces lastly on each deed,
Of so much fame in heaven expect thy meed.
  O fountain Arethuse, and thou honor'd flood,
Smooth-sliding Mincius, crown'd with vocal reeds,
That strain I heard was of a higher mood;
But now my oat proceeds,
And listens to the herald of the sea
That came in Neptune's plea;
He ask'd the waves, and ask'd the felon winds,
What hard mishap hath doom'd this gentle swain?
And question'd every gust of rugged wings
That blows from off each beakèd promontory:
They knew not of his story;
And sage Hippotades their answer brings,
That not a blast was from his dungeon stray'd;
The air was calm, and on the level brine
Sleek Panope with all her sisters play'd.
It was that fatal and perfidious bark,
Built in th' eclipse, and rigg'd with curses dark,
That sunk so low that sacred head of thine.
  Next Camus, reverend sire, went footing slow,
His mantle hairy, and his bonnet sedge,
Inwrought with figures dim, and on the edge
Like to that sanguine flower inscribed with woe.
Ah! who hath reft (quoth he) my dearest pledge?
Last came, and last did go,
The pilot of the Galilean Lake;
Two massy keys he bore of metals twain
(The golden opes, the iron shuts amain);
He shook his mitred locks, and stern bespake:

How well could I have spared for thee, young swain,
Enow of such as for their bellies' sake
Creep, and intrude, and climb into the fold?
Of other care they little reckoning make,
Than how to scramble at the shearers' feast,
And shove away the worthy bidden guest;
Blind mouths! that scarce themselves know how to hold
A sheep-hook, or have learn'd aught else the least
That to the faithful herdsman's art belongs!
What recks it them? what need they? they are sped;
And when they list, their lean and flashy songs
Grate on their scrannel pipes of wretched straw;
The hungry sheep look up, and are not fed,
But swoln with wind and the rank mist they draw,
Rot inwardly, and foul contagion spread;
Besides what the grim wolf with privy paw
Daily devours apace, and nothing said;
But that two-handed engine at the door
Stands ready to smite once, and smite no more.
  Return, Alpheus, the dread voice is past,
That shrunk thy streams: return, Sicilian muse,
And call the vales, and bid them hither cast
Their bells, and flow'rets of a thousand hues.
Ye valleys low, where the mild whispers use
Of shades, and wanton winds, and gushing brooks,
On whose fresh lap the swart-star sparely looks,
Throw hither all your quaint enamell'd eyes,
That on the green turf suck the honey'd showers,
And purple all the ground with vernal flowers.
Bring the rathe primrose that forsaken dies,
The tufted crow-toe, and pale jessamine,

The white pink, and the pansy freak'd with jet,
The glowing violet,
The musk-rose, and the well-attired woodbine,
With cowslips wan that hang the pensive head,
And every flower that sad embroidery wears;
Bid amaranthus all his beauty shed,
And daffodillies fill their cups with tears,
To strew the laureat hearse where Lycid lies.
For so to interpose a little ease,
Let our frail thoughts dally with false surmise.
Ay me! whilst thee the shores and sounding seas
Wash far away where'er thy bones are hurl'd,
Whether beyond the stormy Hebrides,
Where thou perhaps under the whelming tide
Visit'st the bottom of the monstrous world;
Or whether thou, to our moist vows denied,
Sleep'st by the fable of Bellerus old,
Where the great vision of the guarded mount
Looks toward Namancos and Bayona's hold;
Look homeward angel now, and melt with ruth!
And, O ye dolphins, waft the hapless youth!
  Weep no more, woeful shepherds, weep no more!
For Lycidas your sorrow is not dead,
Sunk though he be beneath the watery floor.
So sinks the day-star in the ocean bed,
And yet anon repairs his drooping head,
And tricks his beams, and with new-spangled ore
Flames in the forehead of the morning sky;
So Lycidas sunk low, but mounted high,
Through the dear might of Him that walk'd the waves,
Where, other groves and other streams along,
With nectar pure his oozy locks he laves,
And hears the unexpressive nuptial song,
In the blest kingdoms meek of joy and love.

There entertain him all the saints above,
In solemn troops and sweet societies,
That sing, and singing in their glory move,
And wipe the tears for ever from his eyes.
Now, Lycidas, the shepherds weep no more;
Henceforth thou art the Genius of the shore,
In thy large recompense, and shalt be good
To all that wander in that perilous flood.
  Thus sang the uncouth swain to th' oaks and rills,
While the still morn went out with sandals gray;
He touch'd the tender stops of various quills,
With eager thought warbling his Doric lay.
And now the sun had stretch'd out all the hills,
And now was dropt into the western bay;
At last he rose, and twitch'd his mantle blue:
To-morrow to fresh woods and pastures new.
                JOHN MILTON.

AN HORATIAN ODE.
UPON CROMWELL'S RETURN FROM IRELAND.

THE forward youth that would appear,
Must now forsake his Muses dear,
  Nor in the shadows sing
  His numbers languishing.

'Tis time to leave the books in dust,
And oil the unused armor's rust,
  Removing from the wall
  The corselet of the hall.

So restless Cromwell could not cease
In the inglorious arts of peace,
  But through adventurous war
  Urgèd his active star:

And like the three-fork'd lightning first,
Breaking the clouds where it was nurst,
  Did thorough his own side
  His fiery way divide;

For 'tis all one to courage high,
The emulous, or enemy;
  And with such, to enclose
  Is more than to oppose.

Then burning through the air he went,
And palaces and temples rent,
    And Cæsar's head at last
    Did through his laurels blast.

'Tis madness to resist or blame
The face of angry Heaven's flame,
    And if we would speak true,
    Much to the Man is due

Who, from his private gardens, where
He lived reservèd and austere
    (As if his highest plot
    To plant the bergamot),

Could by industrious valor climb
To ruin the great work of time,
    And cast the Kingdoms old
    Into another mould.

Though Justice against Fate complain,
And plead the ancient rights in vain—
    But those do hold or break
    As men are strong or weak.

Nature, that hateth emptiness,
Allows of penetration less,
    And therefore must make room
    Where greater spirits come.

What field of all the civil war
Where his were not the deepest scar?
    And Hampton shows what part
    He had of wiser art,

Where, twining subtle fears with hope,
He wove a net of such a scope
    That Charles himself might chase
    To Carisbrook's narrow case;

That thence the royal actor borne
The tragic scaffold might adorn,
    While round the armèd bands
    Did clap their bloody hands;

He nothing common did or mean
Upon that memorable scene,
    But with his keener eye
    The axe's edge did try;

Nor call'd the gods, with vulgar spite,
To vindicate his helpless right,
    But bow'd his comely head
    Down, as upon a bed.

This was that memorable hour
Which first assured the forcèd power,
    So when they did design
    The Capitol's first line,

A bleeding head, where they begun,
Did fright the architects to run;
    And yet in that the State
    Foresaw its happy fate!

And now the Irish are ashamed
To see themselves in one year tamed;
    So much one man can do
    That does both act and know.

They can affirm his praises best,
And have, though overcome, confest
    How good he is, how just,
    And fit for highest trust;

Nor yet grown stiffer with command,
But still in the Republic's hand—
    How fit he is to sway
    That can so well obey!

He to the Commons' feet presents
A Kingdom for his first year's rents,
    And (what he may) forbears
    His fame, to make it theirs;

And has his sword and spoils ungirt,
To lay them at the public's skirt.
    So when the falcon high
    Falls heavy from the sky,

She, having kill'd, no more does search
But on the next green bough to perch,
    Where, when he first does lure,
    The falconer has her sure.

What may not then our Isle presume
While victory his crest does plume?
    What may not others fear
    If thus he crowns each year?

As Cæsar he, ere long, to Gaul,
To Italy an Hannibal,
    And to all states not free
    Shall climacteric be.

The Pict no shelter now shall find
Within his parti-color'd mind,
    But from this valor, sad
    Shrink underneath the plaid—

Happy if in the tufted brake
The English hunter him mistake,
 Nor lay his hounds in near
 The Caledonian deer.

But thou, the War's and Fortune's son,
March indefatigably on,
 And for the last effect
 Still keep the sword erect.

Besides the force it has to fright
The spirits of the shady night,
 The same arts that did gain
 A power, must it maintain.
ANDREW MARVELL.

THE PICTURE OF T. C.
IN A PROSPECT OF FLOWERS.

SEE with what simplicity
 This nymph begins her golden days!
In the green grass she loves to lie,
 And there with her fair aspect tames
 The wilder flowers, and gives them names;
 But only with the roses plays,
 And them does tell
What color best becomes them, and what smell.

Who can foretell for what high cause
 This darling of the gods was born?
See! this is she whose chaster laws
 The wanton Love shall one day fear,
 And, under her command severe,
 See his bow broke and ensigns torn.
  Happy who can
Appease this virtuous enemy of man!

Oh, then let me in time compound
 And parley with those conquering eyes,—
Ere they have tried their force to wound,
 Ere with their glancing wheels they drive
 In triumph over hearts that strive,
 And them that yield but more despise:
  Let me be laid
Where I may see the glory from some shade.

Meanwhile, whilst every verdant thing
 Itself does at thy beauty charm,
Reform the errors of the spring:
 Make that the tulips may have share
 Of sweetness, seeing they are fair;
 And roses of their thorns disarm;
  But most procure
That violets may a longer age endure.

But, O young beauty of the woods,
 Whom Nature courts with fruit and flowers,
Gather the flowers, but spare the buds,
 Lest Flora, angry at thy crime
 To kill her infants in their prime,
 Should quickly make the example yours;
  And, ere we see,
Nip in the blossom all our hopes in thee.
ANDREW MARVELL.

LINES WRITTEN UNDER THE PICTURE OF JOHN MILTON,
BEFORE HIS "PARADISE LOST."

THREE Poets, in three distant ages born,
Greece, Italy, and England did adorn.
The first in loftiness of thought surpass'd;
The next in majesty; in both the last.
The force of Nature could no further go;
To make a third, she joined the former two.
JOHN DRYDEN.

SONNET.
TO MILTON.

MILTON! thou shouldst be living at this hour:
 England hath need of thee: she is a fen
 Of stagnant waters: altar, sword, and pen,
Fireside, the heroic wealth of hall and bower,
Have forfeited their ancient English dower
 Of inward happiness. We are selfish men:
 Oh raise us up, return to us again;
And give us manners, virtue, freedom, power!
Thy soul was like a Star, and dwelt apart;
 Thou hadst a voice whose sound was like the sea;
 Pure as the naked heavens, majestic, free,
So didst thou travel on life's common way
 In cheerful godliness; and yet thy heart
The lowliest duties on herself did lay.
WILLIAM WORDSWORTH.

LOYALTY CONFINED.

Beat on, proud billows; Boreas blow;
   Swell, curlèd waves, high as Jove's roof:
Your incivility doth show,
   That innocence is tempest proof;
Though surly Nereus frown, my thoughts are calm;
Then strike, Affliction, for thy wounds are balm.

That which the world miscalls a jail,
   A private closet is to me:
Whilst a good conscience is my bail,
   And innocence my liberty:
Locks, bars, and solitude, together met,
Make me no prisoner, but an anchoret.

I, whilst I wisht to be retired,
   Into this private room was turn'd;
As if their wisdoms had conspired
   The salamander should be burn'd:
Or like those sophists, that would drown a fish,
I am constrain'd to suffer what I wish.

The cynick loves his poverty:
   The pelican her wilderness;
And 'tis the Indian's pride to be
   Naked on frozen Caucasus:
Contentment cannot smart, Stoicks we see
Make torments easie to their apathy.

These manacles upon my arm
   I, as my mistress' favours, wear;
And for to keep my ankles warm,
   I have some iron shackles there:
These walls are but my garrison; this cell,
Which men call jail, doth prove my citadel.

I'm in the cabinet lockt up,
   Like some high-prized margarite,
Or, like the great mogul or pope,
   Am cloyster'd up from publick sight:
Retiredness is a piece of majesty,
And thus, proud sultan, I'm as great as thee.

Here sin for want of food must starve,
   Where tempting objects are not seen!
And these strong walls do only serve
   To keep vice out, and keep me in:
Malice of late's grown charitable, sure,
I'm not committed, but am kept secure.

So he that struck at Jason's life,
   Thinking t' have made his purpose sure,
By a malicious friendly knife
   Did only wound him to a cure:
Malice, I see, wants wit; for what is meant
Mischief, oft-times proves favour by th' event.

When once my prince affliction hath,
   Prosperity doth treason seem;
And to make smooth so rough a path,
   I can learn patiènce from him:
Now not to suffer shows no loyal heart,
When kings want ease subjects must bear a part.

What though I cannot see my king
   Neither in person nor in coin;
Yet contemplation is a thing
   That renders what I have not, mine:
My king from me what adamant can part,
Whom I do wear engraven on my heart!

Have you not seen the nightingale,
   A prisoner like, coopt in a cage,
How doth she chaunt her wonted tale,
   In that her narrow hermitage!
Even then her charming melody doth prove,
That all her bars are trees, her cage a grove.

I am that bird, whom they combine
   Thus to deprive of liberty;
But though they do my corps confine,
   Yet maugre hate, my soul is free;
And though immured, yet can I chirp, and sing
Disgrace to rebels, glory to my king.

My soul is free, as ambient air,
   Although my baser part's immew'd,
Whilst loyal thoughts do still repair
   T' accompany my solitude:
Although rebellion do my body binde,
My king alone can captivate my minde.
              Sir Roger L'Estrange.

EPITAPH EXTEMPORE.

Nobles and heralds, by your leave,
   Here lies what once was Matthew Prior,
The son of Adam and of Eve;
   Can Stuart or Nassau claim higher?
              Matthew Prior.

PROLOGUE TO MR. ADDISON'S TRAGEDY OF "CATO."

To wake the soul by tender strokes of art,
To raise the genius, and to mend the heart,
To make mankind, in conscious virtue bold,
Live o'er each scene, and be what they behold:
For this the tragic Muse first trod the stage,
Commanding tears to stream through every age;
Tyrants no more their savage nature kept,
And foes to virtue wonder'd how they wept.
Our author shuns by vulgar springs to move
The hero's glory, or the virgin's love;
In pitying love, we but our weakness show,
And wild ambition well deserves its woe.
Here tears shall flow from a more generous cause.
Such tears as patriots shed for dying laws:
He bids your breasts with ancient ardor rise,
And calls forth Roman drops from British eyes.
Virtue confess'd in human shape he draws,
What Plato thought, and godlike Cato was:
No common object to your sight displays,
But what with pleasure Heaven itself surveys,
A brave man struggling in the storms of fate,
And greatly falling, with a falling state.
While Cato gives his little senate laws,
What bosom beats not in his country's cause?
Who sees him act, but envies every deed?
Who hears him groan, and does not wish to bleed?
Even when proud Cæsar, 'midst triumphal cars,
The spoils of nations, and the pomp of wars,
Ignobly vain, and impotently great,
Show'd Rome her Cato's figure drawn in state;
As her dead father's reverend image pass'd
The pomp was darken'd, and the day o'ercast;
The triumph ceased, tears gush'd from every eye;
The world's great victor pass'd unheeded by;
Her last good man dejected Rome adored,
And honor'd Cæsar's less than Cato's sword.
Britons, attend: be worth like this approved,
And show you have the virtue to be moved.
With honest scorn the first famed Cato view'd
Rome learning arts from Greece, whom she subdued;
Your scene precariously subsists too long
On French translation, and Italian song.
Dare to have sense yourselves; assert the stage,
Be justly warm'd with your own native rage:
Such plays alone should win a British ear,
As Cato's self had not disdain'd to hear.
                                ALEXANDER POPE.

TO THE EARL OF WARWICK ON THE DEATH OF MR. ADDISON.

IF, dumb too long, the drooping Muse hath stay'd,
And left her debt to Addison unpaid,
Blame not her silence, Warwick, but bemoan,
And judge, oh judge my bosom by your own.
What mourner ever felt poetic fires?
Slow comes the verse that real woe inspires;
Grief unaffected suits but ill with art,
Or flowing numbers with a bleeding heart.
  Can I forget the dismal night that gave
My soul's best part for ever to the grave?
How silent did his old companions tread,
By midnight lamps, the mansions of the dead,
Through breathing statues, then unheeded things,
Through rows of warriors, and through walks of kings!
What awe did the slow, solemn knell inspire;
The pealing organ, and the pausing choir;

The duties by the lawn-robed prelate paid;
And the last words, that dust to dust convey'd?
While speechless o'er thy closing grave we bend,
Accept these tears, thou dear, departed friend.
Oh, gone for ever! take this long adieu;
And sleep in peace, next thy loved Montague.
To strew fresh laurels let the task be mine,
A frequent pilgrim, at thy sacred shrine;
Mine with true sighs thy absence to bemoan
And grave with faithful epitaphs thy stone.
If e'er from me thy loved memorial part,
May shame afflict this alienated heart;
Of thee forgetful, if I form a song,
My lyre be broken, and untuned my tongue;
My grief be doubled from thy image free,
And mirth a torment, unchastised by thee.
Oft let me range the gloomy aisles alone,
Sad luxury! to vulgar minds unknown;
Along the walls where speaking marbles show
What worthies form the hallow'd mould below;
Proud names, who once the reins of empire held;
In arms who triumph'd, or in arts excell'd;
Chiefs, graced with scars, and prodigal of blood;
Stern patriots, who for sacred freedom stood;
Just men, by whom impartial laws were given;
And saints who taught, and led, the way to heaven;
Ne'er to these chambers, where the mighty rest,
Since their foundation, came a nobler guest;
Nor e'er was to the bowers of bliss convey'd
A fairer spirit or more welcome shade.
In what new region to the just assign'd,
What new employments please th' unbodied mind?

A wingèd Virtue, through th' ethereal sky,
From world to world unwearied does he fly?
Or curious trace the long, laborious maze
Of Heaven's decrees, where wondering angels gaze?
Does he delight to hear bold seraphs tell
How Michael battled, and the dragon fell;
Or, mix'd with milder cherubim, to glow
In hymns of love, not ill essay'd below?
Or dost thou warn poor mortals left behind?—
A task well suited to thy gentle mind.
Oh! if sometimes thy spotless form descend;
To me, thy aid, thou guardian genius, lend!
When rage misguides me, or when fear alarms,
When pain distresses, or when pleasure charms,
In silent whisperings purer thoughts impart,
And turn from ill a frail and feeble heart;
Lead through the paths thy virtue trod before,
Till bliss shall join, nor death can part us more.
That awful form, which, so the heavens decree,
Must still be loved and still deplored by me,
In nightly visions seldom fails to rise,
Or, roused by fancy, meets my waking eyes.
If business calls, or crowded courts invite,
Th' unblemish'd statesman seems to strike my sight;
If in the stage I seek to soothe my care,
I meet his soul which breathes in Cato there;
If pensive to the rural shades I rove,
His shape o'ertakes me in the lonely grove;
'Twas there of just and good he reason'd strong,
Clear'd some great truth, or raised some serious song,
There patient show'd us the wise course to steer,
A candid censor, and a friend severe;
There taught us how to live; and (oh too high
The price for knowledge!) taught us how to die.

Thou Hill, whose brow the antique structures grace,
Rear'd by bold chiefs of Warwick's noble race,
Why, once so loved, whene'er thy bower appears,
O'er my dim eyeballs glance the sudden tears!
How sweet were once thy prospects fresh and fair,
Thy sloping walks, and unpolluted air!
How sweet the glooms beneath thy agèd trees,
Thy noontide shadow, and thy evening breeze!
His image thy forsaken bowers restore;
Thy walks and airy prospects charm no more;
No more the summer in thy glooms allay'd,
Thy evening breezes, and thy noonday shade.
From other hills, however Fortune frown'd,
Some refuge in the Muse's art I found;
Reluctant now I touch the trembling string,
Bereft of him, who taught me how to sing;
And these sad accents, murmur'd o'er his urn,
Betray that absence they attempt to mourn.
Oh! must I then (now fresh my bosom bleeds,
And Craggs in death to Addison succeeds)
The verse, begun to one lost friend, prolong,
And weep a second in th' unfinish'd song!
These works divine, which, on his deathbed laid
To thee, O Craggs, th' expiring sage convey'd,
Great, but ill-omen'd, monument of fame,
Nor he survived to give, nor thou to claim.
Swift after him thy social spirit flies,
And close to his, how soon! thy coffin lies.
Blest pair! whose union future bards shall tell
In future tongues; each other's boast! farewell,
Farewell! whom join'd in fame, in friendship tried,
No chance could sever, nor the grave divide.

THOMAS TICKELL.

ODE ON THE DEATH OF MR. THOMSON.

IN yonder grave a Druid lies
Where slowly winds the stealing wave!
The year's best sweets shall duteous rise,
To deck its poet's sylvan grave!

In yon deep bed of whispering reeds
His airy harp shall now be laid,
That he whose heart in sorrow bleeds,
May love through life the soothing shade.

Then maids and youths shall linger here,
And, while its sounds at distance swell,
Shall sadly seem in pity's ear
To hear the woodland pilgrim's knell.

Remembrance oft shall haunt the shore
When Thames in summer wreaths is drest,
And oft suspend the dashing oar
To bid his gentle spirit rest!

And oft as ease and health retire
To breezy lawn or forest deep,
The friend shall view yon whitening spire,
And 'mid the varied landscape weep.

But thou, who own'st that earthly bed,
Ah! what will every dirge avail?
Or tears which love and pity shed,
That mourn beneath the gliding sail?

Yet lives there one, whose heedless eye
Shall scorn thy pale shrine glimmering near?
With him, sweet bard, may fancy die,
And joy desert the blooming year.

But thou, lorn stream, whose sullen tide
No sedge-crown'd sisters now attend,
Now waft me from the green hill's side
Whose cold turf hides the buried friend!

And see, the fairy valleys fade,
Dun night has veil'd the solemn view!
Yet once again, dear parted shade,
Meek Nature's child, again adieu!

The genial meads assign'd to bless
Thy life, shall mourn thy early doom;
Their hinds and shepherd girls shall dress
With simple hands thy rural tomb.

Long, long, thy stone and pointed clay
  Shall melt the musing Briton's eyes,
O vales and wild woods, shall he say,
  In yonder grave your Druid lies!
                WILLIAM COLLINS.

ON THE DEATH OF DR. LEVETT.

CONDEMN'D to hope's delusive mine,
  As on we toil from day to day,
By sudden blasts, or slow decline,
  Our social comforts drop away.

Well tried through many a varying year,
  See Levett to the grave descend,
Officious, innocent, sincere,
  Of every friendless name the friend.

Yet still he fills affection's eye,
  Obscurely wise and coarsely kind;
Nor, letter'd arrogance, deny
  Thy praise to merit unrefined.

When fainting Nature call'd for aid,
  And hovering Death prepared the blow,
His vigorous remedy display'd
  The power of art without the show.

In misery's darkest cavern known,
  His useful care was ever nigh,
Where hopeless anguish pour'd his groan,
  And lonely want retired to die.

No summons mock'd by chill delay,
  No petty gain disdain'd by pride;
The modest wants of every day
  The toil of every day supplied.

His virtues walk'd their narrow round,
  Nor made a pause, nor left a void;
And sure the Eternal Master found
  The single talent well employ'd.

The busy day, the peaceful night,
  Unfelt, uncounted, glided by;
His frame was firm, his powers were bright,
  Though now his eightieth year was nigh.

Then with no fiery throbbing pain,
  No cold gradations of decay,
Death broke at once the vital chain,
  And freed his soul the nearest way.
                SAMUEL JOHNSON.

TO MRS. UNWIN.

MARY! I want a lyre with other strings,
  Such aid from heaven as some have feign'd they drew,
An eloquence scarce given to mortals, new
And undebased by praise of meaner things,

That ere through age or woe I shed my wings
  I may record thy worth with honor due,
In verse as musical as thou art true,
And that immortalizes whom it sings.

But thou hast little need. There is a Book
By seraphs writ with beams of heavenly light,
On which the eyes of God not rarely look,

A chronicle of actions just and bright—
There all thy deeds, my faithful Mary, shine:
And since thou own'st that praise, I spare thee mine.
                WILLIAM COWPER.

TO MARY.

THE twentieth year is well-nigh past
Since first our sky was overcast;
Ah, would that this might be the last!
  My Mary!

Thy spirits have a fainter flow,
I see thee daily weaker grow—
'Twas my distress that brought thee low,
  My Mary!

Thy needles, once a shining store,
For my sake restless heretofore,
Now rust disused, and shine no more;
  My Mary!

For though thou gladly wouldst fulfil
The same kind office for me still,
Thy sight now seconds not thy will,
  My Mary!

But well thou play'dst the housewife's part,
And all thy threads with magic art
Have wound themselves about this heart,
  My Mary!

Thy indistinct expressions seem
Like language utter'd in a dream;
Yet me they charm, whate'er the theme,
My Mary!

Thy silver locks, once auburn bright,
Are still more lovely in my sight
Than golden beams of Orient light,
My Mary!

For could I view nor them nor thee,
What sight worth seeing could I see?
The sun would rise in vain for me,
My Mary!

Partakers of thy sad decline,
Thy hands their little force resign;
Yet gently press'd, press gently mine,
My Mary!

Such feebleness of limbs thou prov'st
That now at every step thou mov'st
Upheld by two; yet still thou lov'st,
My Mary!

And still to love, though press'd with ill,
In wintry age to feel no chill,
With me is to be lovely still,
My Mary!

But ah! by constant heed I know
How oft the sadness that I show
Transforms thy smiles to looks of woe,
My Mary!

And should my future lot be cast
With much resemblance of the past,
Thy worn-out heart will break at last—
My Mary!
     WILLIAM COWPER.

COWPER'S GRAVE.

IT is a place where poets crown'd may feel the heart's decaying;
It is a place where happy saints may weep amid their praying,
Yet let the grief and humbleness as low as silence languish:
Earth surely now may give her calm to whom she gave her anguish.

O poets, from a maniac's tongue was pour'd the deathless singing!
O Christians, at your cross of hope a hopeless hand was clinging!
O men, this man in brotherhood your weary paths beguiling,
Groan'd inly while he taught you peace, and died while ye were smiling!

And now, what time ye all may read through dimming tears his story,
How discord on the music fell and darkness on the glory,
And how when, one by one, sweet sounds and wandering lights departed,
He wore no less a loving face because so broken-hearted,—

He shall be strong to sanctify the poet's high vocation,
And bow the meekest Christian down in meeker adoration;
Nor ever shall he be, in praise, by wise or good forsaken,
Named softly as the household name of one whom God hath taken.

With quiet sadness and no gloom I learn to think upon him,
With meekness that is gratefulness to God whose heaven hath won him,
Who suffer'd once the madness-cloud to His own love to blind him,
But gently led the blind along where breath and bird could find him;

And wrought within his shatter'd brain such quick poetic senses
As hills have language for, and stars, harmonious influences:
The pulse of dew upon the grass kept his within its number,
And silent shadows from the trees refresh'd him like a slumber.

Wild timid hares were drawn from woods to share his home-caresses,
Uplooking to his human eyes with sylvan tendernesses:
The very world, by God's constraint, from falsehood's ways removing,
Its women and its men became, beside him, true and loving.

And though, in blindness, he remain'd unconscious of that guiding,
And things provided came without the sweet sense of providing,

He testified this solemn truth, while frenzy
    desolated,
—Nor man nor nature satisfies whom only
    God created.

Like a sick child that knoweth not his
    mother while she blesses,
And drops upon his burning brow the cool-
    ness of her kisses,—
That turns his fever'd eyes around—"My
    mother! where's my mother?"—
As if such tender words and deeds could
    come from any other!—

The fever gone, with leaps of heart he sees
    her bending o'er him,
Her face all pale from watchful love, the
    unweary love she bore him!—
Thus woke the poet from the dream his
    life's long fever gave him,
Beneath those deep pathetic eyes which
    closed in death to save him.

Thus? oh, not *thus!* no type of earth can
    image that awaking,
Wherein he scarcely heard the chant of
    seraphs, round him breaking,
Or felt the new immortal throb of soul
    from body parted,
But felt those eyes alone, and knew,—"*My*
    Saviour! *not* deserted!"

Deserted! Who hath dreamt that when
    the cross in darkness rested,
Upon the Victim's hidden face no love was
    manifested?
What frantic hands outstretch'd have e'er
    th' atoning drops averted?
What tears have wash'd them from the
    soul, that *one* should be deserted?

Deserted! God could separate from His
    own essence rather;
And Adam's sins *have* swept between the
    righteous Son and Father:
Yea, once, Immanuel's orphan'd cry His
    universe hath shaken—
It went up single, echoless, "My God, I am
    forsaken!"

It went up from the Holy's lips amid His
    lost creation,
That, of the lost, no son should use those
    words of desolation!

That earth's worst frenzies, marring hope,
    should mar not hope's fruition,
And I, on Cowper's grave, should see his
    rapture in a vision.
        ELIZABETH BARRETT BROWNING.

ELEGY ON CAPTAIN MATTHEW HENDERSON,

A GENTLEMAN WHO HELD THE PATENT FOR HIS HONORS IMMEDIATELY FROM ALMIGHTY GOD.

"Should the poor be flattered?"—SHAKESPEARE.

O DEATH! thou tyrant fell and bloody!
    The meikle devil wi' a woodie
Haurl thee hame to his black smiddie,
        O'er hurcheon hides,
And like stock-fish come o'er his studdie
        Wi' thy auld sides!

He's gane! he's gane! he's frae us torn,
The ae best fellow e'er was born!
Thee, Matthew, Nature's sel' shall mourn
        By wood and wild,
Where, haply, Pity strays forlorn,
        Frae man exiled.

Ye hills, near neibors o' the starns,
That proudly cock your cresting cairns!
Ye cliffs, the haunts of sailing earns,
        Where echo slumbers!
Come join, ye Nature's sturdiest bairns,
        My wailing numbers!

Mourn, ilka grove the cushat kens!
Ye haz'ly shaws and briery dens!
Ye burnies, wimplin' down your glens,
        Wi' toddlin' din,
Or foaming strang, wi' hasty stens,
        Frae lin to lin!

Mourn, little harebells o'er the lea;
Ye stately foxgloves, fair to see;
Ye woodbines, hanging bonnilie,
        In scented bow'rs;
Ye roses on your thorny tree,
        The first o' flow'rs.

At dawn, when ev'ry grassy blade
Droops with a diamond at its head,
At ev'n, when beans their fragrance shed
        I' th' rustling gale,
Ye maukins whiddin thro' the glade,
        Come join my wail.

Mourn, ye wee songsters o' the wood;
Ye grouse that crap the heather bud;
Ye curlews calling thro' a clud;
  Ye whistling plover;
An' mourn, ye whirring paitrick brood!—
  He's gane for ever!

Mourn, sooty coots, and speckled teals;
Ye fisher herons, watching eels:
Ye duck and drake, wi' airy wheels
  Circling the lake;
Ye bitterns, till the quagmire reels,
  Rair for his sake.

Mourn, clam'ring craiks, at close o' day,
'Mang fields o' flow'ring clover gay;
And when ye wing your annual way
  Frae our cauld shore,
Tell thae far warlds, wha lies in clay,
  Wham we deplore.

Ye houlets, frae your ivy bow'r,
In some auld tree or eldritch tow'r,
What time the moon, wi' silent glow'r,
  Sets up her horn,
Wail thro' the dreary midnight hour
  Till waukrife morn!

O rivers, forests, hills, and plains!
Oft have ye heard my cantie strains:
But now what else for me remains
  But tales of woe?
And frae my een the drapping rains
  Maun ever flow.

Mourn, Spring, thou darling of the year!
Ilk cowslip cup shall kep a tear:
Thou Simmer, while each corny spear
  Shoots up its head,
Thy gay, green, flow'ry tresses shear
  For him that's dead.

Thou Autumn, wi' thy yellow hair,
In grief thy sallow mantle tear!
Thou, Winter, hurling thro' the air
  The roaring blast,
Wide o'er the naked world declare
  The worth we've lost!

Mourn him, thou Sun, great source of light!
Mourn, Empress of the silent night!

And you, ye twinkling starnies bright,
  My Matthew mourn!
For through your orbs he's ta'en his flight,
  Ne'er to return.

O Henderson! the man—the brother!
And art thou gone, and gone for ever?
And hast thou crost that unknown river,
  Life's dreary bound?
Like thee, where shall I find another,
  The world around?

Go to your sculptured tombs, ye great,
In a' the tinsel trash o' state!
But by thy honest turf I'll wait,
  Thou man of worth!
And weep the ae best fellow's fate
  E'er lay in earth.

The Epitaph.

Stop, passenger!—my story's brief,
  And truth I shall relate, man;
I tell nae common tale o' grief—
  For Matthew was a great man.

If thou uncommon merit hast,
  Yet spurn'd at fortune's door, man,
A look of pity hither cast—
  For Matthew was a poor man.

If thou a noble sodger art,
  That passest by this grave, man,
There moulders here a gallant heart—
  For Matthew was a brave man.

If thou on men, their works and ways,
  Canst throw uncommon light, man,
Here lies wha weel had won thy praise—
  For Matthew was a bright man.

If thou at Friendship's sacred ca'
  Wad life itself resign, man,
Thy sympathetic tear maun fa'—
  For Matthew was a kind man.

If thou art staunch without a stain,
  Like the unchanging blue, man,
This was a kinsman o' thy ain—
  For Matthew was a true man.

If thou hast wit, and fun, and fire,
  And ne'er guid wine did fear, man,
This was thy billie, dam, and sire—
  For Matthew was a queer man.

If ony whiggish whingin sot,
  To blame poor Matthew dare, man,
May dool and sorrow be his lot!
  For Matthew was a rare man.

But now his radiant course is run,
  For Matthew's was a bright one!
His soul was like the glorious sun,
  A matchless, heav'nly light, man.
ROBERT BURNS.

BURNS.

TO A ROSE BROUGHT FROM NEAR ALLOWAY KIRK, IN AYRSHIRE, IN THE AUTUMN OF 1822.

WILD rose of Alloway! my thanks:
  Thou 'mind'st me of that autumn noon
When first we met upon "the banks
  And braes o' bonny Doon."

Like thine, beneath the thorn tree's bough,
  My sunny hour was glad and brief;
We've cross'd the winter sea, and thou
  Art wither'd—flower and leaf.

And will not thy death-doom be mine—
  The doom of all things wrought of clay?
And wither'd my life's leaf like thine,
  Wild rose of Alloway?

Not so his memory for whose sake
  My bosom bore thee far and long—
His, who a humbler flower could make
  Immortal as his song,

The memory of Burns—a name
  That calls, when brimm'd her festal cup,
A nation's glory and her shame,
  In silent sadness up.

A nation's glory—be the rest
  Forgot—she's canonized his mind,
And it is joy to speak the best
  We may of humankind.

I've stood beside the cottage-bed
  Where the bard-peasant first drew breath;
A straw-thatch'd roof above his head,
  A straw-wrought couch beneath.

And I have stood beside the pile,
  His monument—that tells to Heaven
The homage of earth's proudest isle
  To that bard-peasant given.

Bid thy thoughts hover o'er that spot,
  Boy-minstrel, in thy dreaming hour;
And know, however low his lot,
  A poet's pride and power;

The pride that lifted Burns from earth,
  The power that gave a child of song
Ascendency o'er rank and birth,
  The rich, the brave, the strong;

And if despondency weigh down
  Thy spirit's fluttering pinions then,
Despair—thy name is written on
  The roll of common men.

There have been loftier themes than his,
  And longer scrolls, and louder lyres,
And lays lit up with Poesy's
  Purer and holier fires;

Yet read the names that know not death;
  Few nobler ones than Burns are there;
And few have won a greener wreath
  Than that which binds his hair.

His is that language of the heart
  In which the answering heart would speak,
Thought, word, that bids the warm tear start,
  Or the smile light the cheek;

And his that music to whose tone
  The common pulse of man keeps time,
In cot or castle's mirth or moan,
  In cold or sunny clime.

And who hath heard his song, nor knelt
  Before its spell with willing knee,
And listen'd and believed, and felt
  The poet's mastery

O'er the mind's sea, in calm and storm,
  O'er the heart's sunshine and its showers,
O'er Passion's moments, bright and warm,
  O'er Reason's dark, cold hours;

On fields where brave men "die or do,"
  In halls where rings the banquet's mirth,
Where mourners weep, where lovers woo,
  From throne to cottage hearth?

What sweet tears dim the eye unshed,
  What wild vows falter on the tongue,
When "Scots wha hae wi' Wallace bled,"
  Or "Auld Lang Syne," is sung!

Pure hopes, that lift the soul above,
  Come with his Cotter's hymn of praise,
And dreams of youth, and truth, and love
  With "Logan's" banks and braes.

And when he breathes his master-lay
  Of Alloway's witch-haunted wall,
All passions in our frames of clay
  Come thronging at his call.

Imagination's world of air,
  And our own world, its gloom and glee,
Wit, pathos, poetry, are there,
  And death's sublimity.

And Burns—though brief the race he ran,
  Though rough and dark the path he trod—
Lived, died, in form and soul a man,
  The image of his God.

Through care, and pain, and want, and woe,
  With wounds that only death could heal,
Tortures the poor alone can know,
  The proud alone can feel;

He kept his honesty and truth,
  His independent tongue and pen,
And moved, in manhood as in youth,
  Pride of his fellow-men.

Strong sense, deep feeling, passions strong,
  A hate of tyrant and of knave,
A love of right, a scorn of wrong,
  Of coward and of slave;

A kind, true heart, a spirit high,
  That could not fear, and would not bow,
Were written in his manly eye
  And on his manly brow.

Praise to the bard! his words are driven,
  Like flower-seeds by the far winds sown,
Where'er, beneath the sky of heaven,
  The birds of fame have flown.

Praise to the man! a nation stood
  Beside his coffin with wet eyes,
Her brave, her beautiful, her good,
  As when a loved one dies.

And still, as on his funeral-day,
  Men stand his cold earth-couch around,
With the mute homage that we pay
  To consecrated ground.

And consecrated ground it is,
  The last, the hallow'd home of one
Who lives upon all memories,
  Though with the buried gone.

Such graves as his are pilgrim-shrines,
  Shrines to no code or creed confined—
The Delphian vales, the Palestines,
  The Meccas, of the mind.

Sages, with Wisdom's garland wreath'd,
  Crown'd kings, and mitred priests of power,
And warriors with their bright swords sheath'd,
  The mightiest of the hour;

And lowlier names, whose humble home
  Is lit by Fortune's dimmer star,
Are there—o'er wave and mountain come,
  From countries near and far;

Pilgrims, whose wandering feet have press'd
  The Switzer's snow, the Arab's sand,
Or trod the piled leaves of the West,
  My own green forest-land.

All ask the cottage of his birth,
  Gaze on the scenes he loved and sung,
And gather feelings not of earth
  His fields and streams among.

They linger by the Doon's low trees,
  And pastoral Nith, and wooded Ayr,
And round thy sepulchres, Dumfries!
  The Poet's tomb is there.

But what to them the sculptor's art,
  His funeral columns, wreaths, and urns?
Wear they not graven on the heart
  The name of Robert Burns?
                FITZ-GREENE HALLECK.

ODE ON THE CENTENARY OF BURNS.

WE hail this morn
  A century's noblest birth;
A Poet peasant-born,
  Who more of Fame's immortal dower

Unto his country brings
Than all her kings!

As lamps high set
Upon some earthly eminence—
And to the gazer brighter thence
Than the sphere-lights they flout—
  Dwindle in distance and die out,
  While no star waneth yet;
So through the past's far-reaching night
Only the star-souls keep their light.

  A gentle boy,
With moods of sadness and of mirth,
  Quick tears and sudden joy,
Grew up beside the peasant's hearth.
  His father's toil he shares;
  But half his mother's cares
From his dark, searching eyes,
Too swift to sympathize,
  Hid in her heart she bears.

  At early morn
His father calls him to the field;
Through the stiff soil that clogs his feet,
  Chill rain, and harvest heat,
He plods all day; returns at eve outworn,
  To the rude fare a peasant's lot doth yield—
To what else was he born?

  The God-made king
  Of every living thing
(For his great heart in love could hold them all);
The dumb eyes meeting his by hearth and stall—
  Gifted to understand!—
  Knew it and sought his hand;
And the most timorous creature had not fled
Could she his heart have read,
Which fain all feeble things had bless'd and shelter èd.

  To Nature's feast,
  Who knew her noblest guest
  And entertain'd him best,
Kingly he came. Her chambers of the east
  She draped with crimson and with gold,
  And pour'd her pure joy-wines
    For him, the poet-soul'd;
    For him her anthem roll'd
  From the storm-wind among the winter pines,
Down to the slenderest note
Of a love-warble from the linnet's throat.

  But when begins
The array for battle, and the trumpet blows,
A king must leave the feast and lead the fight;
And with its mortal foes,
Grim gathering hosts of sorrows and of sins,
  Each human soul must close;
  And Fame her trumpet blew
Before him, wrapp'd him in her purple state,
And made him mark for all the shafts of Fate
That henceforth round him flew.

  Though he may yield,
Hard-press'd, and wounded fall
Forsaken on the field;
His regal vestments soil'd;
His crown of half its jewels spoil'd;
  He is a king for all.

  Had he but stood aloof!
Had he array'd himself in armor proof
Against temptation's darts!
So yearn the good—so those the world calls wise,
  With vain, presumptuous hearts,
  Triumphant moralize.

  Of martyr-woe
A sacred shadow on his memory rests—
Tears have not ceased to flow—
Indignant grief yet stirs impetuous breasts,
To think—above that noble soul brought low,
That wise and soaring spirit fool'd, enslaved—
Thus, thus he had been saved!

  It might not be!
  That heart of harmony
  Had been too rudely rent;
Its silver chords, which any hand could wound,
By no hand could be tuned,
Save by the Maker of the instrument,
  Its every string who knew,
And from profaning touch his heavenly gift withdrew.

Regretful love
His country fain would prove,
By grateful honors lavish'd on his grave;
Would fain redeem her blame
That he so little at her hands can claim,
Who unrewarded gave
To her his life-bought gift of song and fame.

The land he trod
Hath now become a place of pilgrimage;
Where dearer are the daisies of the sod
That could his song engage.
The hoary hawthorn, wreath'd
Above the bank on which his limbs he flung
While some sweet plaint he breath'd;
The streams he wander'd near;
The maidens whom he loved; the songs he sung—
All, all are dear!

The arch blue eyes—
Arch but for love's disguise—
Of Scotland's daughters, soften at his strain;
Her hardy sons, sent forth across the main
To drive the ploughshare through earth's virgin soils,
Lighten with it their toils:
And sister-lands have learn'd to love the tongue
In which such songs are sung.

For doth not song
To the whole world belong?
Is it not given wherever tears can fall,
Wherever hearts can melt, or blushes glow,
Or mirth and sadness mingle as they flow,
A heritage to all?
ISA CRAIG KNOX.

BURIAL OF SIR JOHN MOORE.

NOT a drum was heard, not a funeral note,
　As his corse to the rampart we hurried;
Not a soldier discharged his farewell shot
　O'er the grave where our hero we buried.

We buried him darkly, at dead of night,
　The sods with our bayonets turning;
By the struggling moonbeam's misty light,
　And the lantern dimly burning.

No useless coffin enclosed his breast,
　Not in sheet or in shroud we wound him;
But he lay like a warrior taking his rest,
　With his martial cloak around him.

Few and short were the prayers we said,
　And we spoke not a word of sorrow;
But we steadfastly gazed on the face that was dead,
　And we bitterly thought of the morrow.

We thought as we hollow'd his narrow bed,
　And smooth'd down his lonely pillow,
That the foe and the stranger would tread o'er his head,
　And we far away on the billow!

Lightly they'll talk of the spirit that's gone,
　And o'er his cold ashes upbraid him;
But little he'll reck, if they let him sleep on
　In the grave where a Briton has laid him.

But half of our heavy task was done
　When the clock struck the hour for retiring;
And we heard the distant and random gun
　That the foe was sullenly firing.

Slowly and sadly we laid him down,
　From the field of his fame fresh and gory;
We carved not a line, and we raised not a stone—
　But we left him alone with his glory.
CHARLES WOLFE.

OH, BREATHE NOT HIS NAME.
ROBERT EMMETT.

OH, breathe not his name! let it sleep in the shade,
Where cold and unhonor'd his relics are laid:
Sad, silent, and dark be the tears that we shed,
As the night-dew that falls on the grave o'er his head.

But the night-dew that falls, though in silence it weeps,
Shall brighten with verdure the grave where he sleeps;

And the tear that we shed, though in secret it rolls,
Shall long keep his memory green in our souls.
THOMAS MOORE.

ON THE DEATH OF JOSEPH RODMAN DRAKE.

GREEN be the turf above thee,
  Friend of my better days!
None knew thee but to love thee,
  Nor named thee but to praise.

Tears fell, when thou wert dying,
  From eyes unused to weep,
And long, where thou art lying,
  Will tears the cold turf steep.

When hearts, whose truth was proven,
  Like thine, are laid in earth,
There should a wreath be woven
  To tell the world their worth;

And I, who woke each morrow
  To clasp thy hand in mine,
Who shared thy joy and sorrow,
  Whose weal and woe were thine,—

It should be mine to braid it
  Around thy faded brow,
But I've in vain essay'd it,
  And feel I cannot now.

While memory bids me weep thee,
  Nor thoughts nor words are free,
The grief is fix'd too deeply
  That mourns a man like thee.
FITZ-GREENE HALLECK.

ADONAIS.

AN ELEGY ON THE DEATH OF JOHN KEATS.

I WEEP for Adonais—he is dead!
  Oh, weep for Adonais! though our tears
Thaw not the frost which binds so dear a head!
  And thou, sad Hour, selected from all years
  To mourn our loss, rouse thy obscure compeers,
And teach them thine own sorrow: say, "With me
Died Adonais; till the Future dares
Forget the Past, his fate and fame shall be
An echo and a light unto eternity!"

Where wert thou, mighty mother, when he lay,
  When thy son lay, pierced by the shaft which flies
In darkness? where was lorn Urania
  When Adonais died? With veilèd eyes,
  'Mid listening echoes, in her paradise
She sate, while one, with soft enamor'd breath,
Rekindled all the fading melodies,
With which, like flowers that mock the corse beneath,
He had adorn'd and hid the coming bulk of death.

Oh, weep for Adonais—he is dead!
  Wake, melancholy mother, wake and weep!
Yet wherefore? Quench within their burning bed
  Thy fiery tears, and let thy loud heart keep,
  Like his, a mute and uncomplaining sleep;
For he is gone, where all things wise and fair
Descend:—oh, dream not that the amorous Deep
Will yet restore him to the vital air;
Death feeds on his mute voice, and laughs at our despair.

Most musical of mourners, weep again!
  Lament anew, Urania!—He died,
Who was the sire of an immortal strain,
  Blind, old, and lonely, when his country's pride
  The priest, the slave, and the liberticide,
Trampled and mock'd with many a loathèd rite
Of lust and blood; he went, unterrified,
Into the gulf of death; but his clear sprite
Yet reigns o'er earth; the third among the sons of light.

Most musical of mourners, weep anew!
  Not all to that bright station dared to climb;

And happier they their happiness who
    knew,
  Whose tapers yet burn through that
    night of time
  In which suns perish'd; others more
    sublime,
Struck by the envious wrath of man or
    God,
  Have sunk, extinct in their refulgent
    prime;
And some yet live, treading the thorny
    road,
Which leads, through toil and hate, to
    Fame's serene abode.

But now, thy youngest, dearest one, has
    perish'd,
  The nursling of thy widowhood, who
    grew
Like a pale flower by some sad maiden
    cherish'd,
  And fed with true love tears instead of
    dew;
Most musical of mourners, weep anew!
Thy extreme hope, the loveliest and the
    last,
  The bloom, whose petals nipt before they
    blew
Died on the promise of the fruit, is
    waste;
The broken lily lies—the storm is over-
    past.

To that high capital, where kingly Death
  Keeps his pale court in beauty and
    decay,
He came; and bought, with price of
    purest breath,
  A grave among the eternal.—Come
    away!
  Haste, while the vault of blue Italian
    day
Is yet his fitting charnel-roof! while
    still
He lies, as if in dewy sleep he lay;
Awake him not! surely he takes his fill
Of deep and liquid rest, forgetful of all
    ill.

He will awake no more, oh, never more!
  Within the twilight chamber spreads
    apace
The shadow of white Death, and at the
    door
  Invisible Corruption waits to trace
  His extreme way to her dim dwelling-
    place;
The eternal Hunger sits, but pity and
    awe
  Soothe her pale rage, nor dares she to
    deface
So fair a prey, till darkness and the law
Of change, shall o'er his sleep the mortal
    curtain draw.

Oh, weep for Adonais!—the quick Dreams,
  The passion-wingèd ministers of Thought,
Who were his flocks, whom near the living
    streams
  Of his young spirit he fed, and whom he
    taught
The love which was its music, wander
    not—
Wander no more, from kindling brain
    to brain,
  But droop there, whence they sprung;
    and mourn their lot
Round the cold heart, where, after their
    sweet pain,
They ne'er will gather strength, nor find
    a home again.

And one with trembling hand clasps his
    cold head,
  And fans him with her moonlight wings,
    and cries,
"Our love, our hope, our sorrow, is not
    dead;
  See, on the silken fringe of his faint
    eyes,
  Like dew upon a sleeping flower, there
    lies
A tear some Dream has loosen'd from his
    brain."
  Lost angel of a ruin'd paradise!
She knew not 'twas her own; as with no
    stain
She faded, like a cloud which had outwept
    its rain.

One from a lucid urn of starry dew
  Wash'd his light limbs, as if embalm-
    ing them;
Another clipt her profuse locks, and threw
  The wreath upon him, like an anadem,

Which frozen tears instead of pearls
    begem;
Another in her wilful grief would break
    Her bow and wingèd reeds, as if to
        stem
A greater loss with one which was more
        weak;
And dull the barbèd fire against his frozen
    cheek.

Another Splendor on his mouth alit,
    That mouth whence it was wont to draw
        the breath
Which gave it strength to pierce the
        guarded wit,
    And pass into the panting heart be-
        neath
    With lightning and with music: the
        damp death
Quench'd its caress upon its icy lips;
And as a dying meteor stains a wreath
Of moonlight vapor, which the cold night
    clips,
It flush'd through his pale limbs, and
    pass'd to its eclipse.

And others came,—Desires and Adora-
    tions,
Wingèd Persuasions, and veil'd Desti-
    nies,
Splendors, and Glooms, and glimmering
    Incarnations
Of hopes and fears, and twilight Phan-
    tasies;
And Sorrow, with her family of Sighs,
And Pleasure, blind with tears, led by the
    gleam
Of her own dying smile instead of eyes,
Came in slow pomp;—the moving pomp
    might seem
Like pageantry of mist on an autumnal
    stream.

All he had loved, and moulded into
    thought
    From shape, and hue, and odor, and
        sweet sound,
Lamented Adonais. Morning sought
    Her eastern watch-tower, and her hair
        unbound,
    Wet with the tears which should adorn
        the ground,

Dimm'd the aërial eyes that kindle day;
    Afar the melancholy Thunder moan'd,
Pale Ocean in unquiet slumber lay,
And the wild Winds flew around, sobbing
    in their dismay.

Lost Echo sits amid the voiceless mountains,
    And feeds her grief with his remember'd
        lay,
And will no more reply to winds or foun-
    tains,
    Or amorous birds perch'd on the young
        green spray,
    Or herdsman's horn, or bell at closing day,
Since she can mimic not his lips, more dear
    Than those for whose disdain they pined
        away
Into a shadow of all sounds:—a drear
Murmur, between their songs, is all the
    woodmen hear.

Grief made the young Spring wild, and she
    threw down
    Her kindling buds, as if she Autumn
        were,
Or they dead leaves; since her delight is
    flown,
    For whom should she have waked the
        sullen year?
To Phœbus was not Hyacinth so dear,
Nor to himself Narcissus, as to both
Thou, Adonais: wan they stand and sere
Amid the faint companions of their
    youth,
With dew all turn'd to tears; odor, to
    sighing ruth.

Thy spirit's sister, the lorn nightingale,
    Mourns not her mate with such melo-
        dious pain;
Not so the eagle, who like thee could scale
    Heaven, and could nourish in the sun's
        domain
    Her mighty youth with morning, doth
        complain,
Soaring and screaming round her empty
    nest,
    As Albion wails for thee: the curse of
        Cain
Light on his head who pierced thy inno-
    cent breast,
And scared the angel soul that was its
    earthly guest!

Ah, woe is me! Winter is come and gone,
  But grief returns with the revolving year;
The airs and streams renew their joyous tone;
  The ants, the bees, the swallows reappear;
  Fresh leaves and flowers deck the dead Seasons' bier;
The amorous birds now pair in every brake,
  And build their mossy homes in field and brere:
And the green lizard, and the golden snake,
Like unimprison'd flames, out of their trance awake.

Through wood, and stream, and field, and hill and ocean,
  A quickening life from the Earth's heart has burst,
As it has ever done, with change and motion,
  From the great morning of the world when first
  God dawn'd on Chaos; in its stream immersed,
The lamps of Heaven flash with a softer light;
  All baser things pant with life's sacred thirst;
Diffuse themselves; and spend in love's delight,
The beauty and the joy of their renewèd might.

The leprous corpse, touch'd by this spirit tender,
  Exhales itself in flowers of gentle breath;
Like incarnations of the stars, when splendor
  Is changed to fragrance, they illumine death,
  And mock the merry worm that wakes beneath;
Naught we know dies. Shall that alone which knows
Be as a sword consumed before the sheath
By sightless lightning? th' intense atom glows
A moment, then is quench'd in a most cold repose.

Alas! that all we loved of him should be,
  But for our grief, as if it had not been,
And grief itself be mortal! Woe is me!
  Whence are we, and why are we? of what scene
  The actors or spectators? Great and mean
Meet mass'd in death, who lends what life must borrow.
As long as skies are blue, and fields are green,
Evening must usher night, night urge the morrow,
Month follow month with woe, and year wake year to sorrow.

He will awake no more, oh, never more!
  "Wake thou!" cried Misery, "childless mother, rise
Out of thy sleep, and slake, in thy heart's core,
  A wound more fierce than his tears and sighs."
  And all the Dreams that watch'd Urania's eyes,
And all the Echoes whom their sister's song
Had held in holy silence, cried "Arise!"
Swift as a Thought by the snake Memory stung,
From her ambrosial rest the fading Splendor sprung.

She rose like an autumnal Night, that springs
  Out of the East, and follows wild and drear
The golden Day, which, on eternal wings,
  Even as a ghost abandoning a bier,
  Has left the Earth a corpse. Sorrow and fear
So struck, so roused, so rapt, Urania,
So sadden'd round her like an atmosphere
Of stormy mist; so swept her on her way,
Even to the mournful place where Adonais lay.

Out of her secret paradise she sped,
  Through camps and cities rough with stone, and steel,
And human hearts, which to her aëry tread
  Yielding not, wounded the invisible

Palms of her tender feet where'er they
    fell:
And barbèd tongues, and thoughts more
    sharp than they,
Rent the soft Form they never could repel,
Whose sacred blood, like the young tears
    of May,
Paved with eternal flowers that unde-
    serving way.

In the death-chamber for a moment Death,
    Shamed by the presence of that living
    Might,
Blush'd to annihilation, and the breath
    Revisited those lips, and life's pale light
Flash'd through those limbs, so late her
    dear delight.
"Leave me not wild and drear and com-
    fortless,
    As silent lightning leaves the starless
    night!
Leave me not!" cried Urania: her distress
Roused Death: Death rose and smiled,
    and met her vain caress.

"Stay yet a while! speak to me once again;
    Kiss me, so long but as a kiss may live;
And in my heartless breast and burning
    brain
That word, that kiss, shall all thoughts
    else survive,
    With food of saddest memory kept alive,
Now thou art dead, as if it were a part
Of thee, my Adonais! I would give
All that I am to be as thou now art!
But I am chain'd to Time, and cannot
    thence depart!

"O gentle child, beautiful as thou wert,
    Why didst thou leave the trodden paths
    of men
Too soon, and with weak hands though
    mighty heart
    Dare the unpastured dragon in his den?
Defenceless as thou wert, oh! where was
    then
Wisdom the mirror'd shield, or scorn the
    spear?
Or hadst thou waited the full cycle, when
Thy spirit should have fill'd its crescent
    sphere,
The monsters of life's waste had fled from
    thee like deer.

"The herded wolves, bold only to pur-
    sue;
    The obscene ravens, clamorous o'er the
    dead;
The vultures, to the conqueror's banner
    true,
    Who feed where Desolation first has
    fed,
And whose wings rain contagion;—how
    they fled,
When, like Apollo, from his golden bow,
    The Pythian of the age one arrow sped
And smiled!—The spoilers tempt no sec-
    ond blow,
They fawn on the proud feet that spurn
    them lying low.

"The sun comes forth, and many reptiles
    spawn;
He sets, and each ephemeral insect then
Is gather'd into death without a dawn,
    And the immortal stars awake again;
    So it is in the world of living men:
A godlike mind soars forth, in its delight
    Making earth bare and veiling heaven,
    and when
It sinks, the swarms that dimm'd or shared
    its light
Leave to its kindred lamps the spirit's aw-
    ful night."

Thus ceased she: and the mountain-shep-
    herds came,
    Their garlands sere, their magic mantles
    rent;
The Pilgrim of Eternity, whose fame
    Over his living head like Heaven is
    bent,
An early but enduring monument,
Came, veiling all the lightnings of his
    song
    In sorrow; from her wilds Ierne sent
The sweetest lyrist of her saddest wrong,
And love taught grief to fall like music
    from his tongue.

'Midst others of less note came one frail
    Form,
    A phantom among men; companionless
As the last cloud of an expiring storm,
    Whose thunder is its knell: he as I
    guess,
Had gazed on Nature's naked loveliness,

Actæon-like, and now he fled astray
  With feeble steps o'er the world's wilderness,
And his own thoughts, along that rugged way,
  Pursued, like raging hounds, their father and their prey.

A pard-like Spirit beautiful and swift—
  A Love in desolation mask'd;—a power
Girt round with weakness;—it can scarce uplift
  The weight of the superincumbent hour;
  It is a dying lamp, a falling shower,
A breaking billow;—even whilst we speak
  Is it not broken? On the withering flower
The killing sun smiles brightly: on a cheek
The life can burn in blood, even while the heart may break.

His head was bound with pansies overblown,
  And faded violets, white, and pied, and blue;
And a light spear topp'd with a cypress cone,
  Round whose rude shaft dark ivy-tresses grew,
  Yet dripping with the forest's noonday dew,
Vibrated, as the ever-beating heart
  Shook the weak hand that grasp'd it; of that crew
He came the last, neglected and apart;
A herd-abandon'd deer, struck by the hunter's dart.

All stood aloof, and at his partial moan
  Smiled through their tears; well knew that gentle band
Who in another's fate now wept his own;
  As in the accents of an unknown land
He sang new sorrow; sad Urania scann'd
The Stranger's mien, and murmur'd: "Who art thou?"
He answer'd not, but with a sudden hand
Made bare his branded and ensanguined brow,
Which was like Cain's or Christ's.—Oh! that it should be so!

What softer voice is hushèd over the dead?
  Athwart what brow is that dark mantle thrown?
What form leans sadly o'er the white deathbed,
  In mockery of monumental stone,
  The heavy heart heaving without a moan?
If it be he, who, gentlest of the wise,
  Taught, soothed, loved, honor'd the departed one;
Let me not vex, with inharmonious sighs,
The silence of that heart's accepted sacrifice.

Our Adonais has drunk poison—oh!
  What deaf and viperous murderer could crown
Life's early cup with such a draught of woe?
  The nameless worm would now itself disown:
  It felt, yet could escape the magic tone
Whose prelude held all envy, hate, and wrong,
  But what was howling in one breast alone,
Silent with the expectation of the song,
Whose master's hand is cold, whose silver lyre unstrung.

Live thou, whose infamy is not thy fame!
  Live! fear no heavier chastisement from me,
Thou noteless blot on a remember'd name!
  But be thyself, and know thyself to be!
  And ever at thy season be thou free
To spill the venom when thy fangs o'erflow:
  Remorse and self-contempt shall cling to thee;
Hot shame shall burn upon thy secret brow,
And like a beaten hound tremble thou shalt—as now.

Nor let us weep that our delight is fled
  Far from these carrion-kites that scream below;
He wakes or sleeps with the enduring dead;
  Thou canst not soar where he is sitting now.

Dust to the dust! but the pure spirit shall
  flow
Back to the burning fountain whence it
  came,
A portion of the Eternal, which must glow
Through time and change, unquenchably
  the same,
Whilst thy cold embers choke the sordid
  hearth of shame.

Peace, peace! he is not dead, he doth not
  sleep—
He hath awaken'd from the dream of
  life—
'Tis we, who, lost in stormy visions, keep
With phantoms an unprofitable strife,
And in mad trance strike with our
  spirit's knife
Invulnerable nothings.— *We* decay
Like corpses in a charnel; fear and grief
Convulse us and consume us day by day,
And cold hopes swarm like worms with-
  in our living clay.

He has outsoar'd the shadow of our night;
Envy and calumny, and hate and pain,
And that unrest which men miscall delight,
  Can touch him not and torture not again;
From the contagion of the world's slow
  stain
He is secure, and now can never mourn
A heart grown cold, a head grown gray
  in vain;
Nor, when the spirit's self has ceased to
  burn,
With sparkless ashes load an unlamented
  urn.

He lives, he wakes—'tis Death is dead, not
  he;
  Mourn not for Adonais—Thou young
    Dawn,
Turn all thy dew to splendor, for from
    thee
  The spirit thou lamentest is not gone;
  Ye caverns and ye forests, cease to moan!
Cease, ye faint flowers and fountains, and
    thou Air,
  Which like a morning veil thy scarf
    hadst thrown
O'er the abandoned Earth, now leave it bare
Even to the joyous stars which smile on
    its despair!

He is made one with Nature: there is
  heard
His voice in all her music, from the
  moan
Of thunder, to the song of night's sweet
  bird;
He is a presence to be felt and known
In darkness and in light, from herb and
  stone,
Spreading itself where'er that Power may
  move
Which has withdrawn his being to its
  own;
Which wields the world with never-
  wearied love,
Sustains it from beneath, and kindles it
  above.

He is a portion of the loveliness
  Which once he made more lovely: he
    doth bear
His part, while the one Spirit's plastic
    stress
  Sweeps through the dull dense world,
    compelling there
All new successions to the forms they wear
Torturing th' unwilling dross that checks
    its flight
To its own likeness, as each mass may
    bear;
And bursting in its beauty and its might
From trees and beasts and men into the
    Heavens' light.

The splendors of the firmament of time
  May be eclipsed, but are extinguish'd
    not:
Like stars to their appointed height they
    climb,
  And death is a low mist which cannot
    blot
  The brightness it may veil. When lofty
    thought
Lifts a young heart above its mortal lair,
  And love and life contend in it, for what
Shall be its earthly doom, the dead live
    there,
  And move like winds of light on dark
    and stormy air.

The inheritors of unfulfill'd renown
  Rose from their thrones, built beyond
    mortal thought,

Far in the unapparent. Chatterton
　Rose pale, his solemn agony had not
　　Yet faded from him; Sidney, as he
　　　fought,
And as he fell, and as he lived and
　　loved,
　Sublimely mild, a Spirit without spot,
Arose; and Lucan, by his death approved:
Oblivion as they rose shrank like a thing
　reproved.

And many more, whose names on earth
　are dark,
　But whose transmitted effluence cannot
　　die
So long as fire outlives the parent spark,
　Rose, robed in dazzling immortality.
"Thou art become as one of us," they
　cry;
"It was for thee yon kingless sphere has
　long
Swung blind in unascended majesty,
Silent alone amid a heaven of song.
Assumed thy wingèd throne, thou Vesper
　of our throng!"

Who mourns for Adonais? oh come forth,
　Fond wretch! and know thyself and
　　him aright.
Clasp with thy panting soul the pendulous
　Earth;
　As from a centre, dart thy spirit's light
　Beyond all worlds, until its spacious
　　might
Satiate the void circumference; then shrink
　Even to a point within our day and
　　night;
And keep thy heart light, lest it make thee
　sink
When hope has kindled hope, and lured
　thee to the brink.

Or go to Rome, which is the sepulchre,
　Oh, not of him, but of our joy: 'tis
　　naught
That ages, empires, and religions there
　Lie buried in the ravage they have
　　wrought;
For such as he can lend,—they borrow not
Glory from those who made the world their
　prey;
And he is gather'd to the kings of thought
Who waged contention with their time's
　decay,
And of the past are all that cannot pass
　away.

Go thou to Rome—at once the paradise,
　The grave, the city, and the wilderness:
And where its wrecks like shatter'd mountains rise,
　And flowering weeds and fragrant copses
　　dress
The bones of Desolation's nakedness,
Pass, till the Spirit of the spot shall lead
Thy footsteps to a slope of green access,
Where, like an infant's smile, over the dead
A light of laughing flowers along the grass
　is spread,

And gray walls moulder round, on which
　dull Time
Feeds, like slow fire upon a hoary brand;
And one keen pyramid with wedge sublime,
　Pavilioning the dust of him who plann'd
This refuge for his memory, doth stand
Like flame transform'd to marble: and
　beneath
A field is spread, on which a newer band
Have pitch'd in Heaven's smile their camp
　of death,
Welcoming him we lose with scarce extinguish'd breath.

Here pause: these graves are all too young
　as yet
To have outgrown the sorrow which consign'd
　Its charge to each; and if the seal is set,
Here, on one fountain of a mourning
　mind,
Break it not thou! too surely shalt thou
　find
Thine own well full, if thou returnest
　home,
　Of tears and gall. From the world's
　　bitter wind
Seek shelter in the shadow of the tomb.
What Adonais is, why fear we to become?

The One remains, the many change and
　pass:
　Heaven's light for ever shines, Earth's
　　shadows fly;

Life, like a dome of many-color'd glass,
   Stains the white radiance of Eternity,
   Until death tramples it to fragments.—
      Die,
If thou wouldst be with that which thou
      dost seek!
   Follow where all is fled!—Rome's azure
      sky,
Flowers, ruins, statues, music, words are
      weak
The glory they transfuse with fitting truth
      to speak.

Why linger, why turn back, why shrink,
   my Heart?
   Thy hopes are gone before: from all
      things here
They have departed; thou shouldst now
      depart!
A light is past from the revolving year,
   And man, and woman; and what still is
      dear
Attracts to crush, repels to make thee
      wither.
   The soft sky smiles,—the low wind
      whispers near:
'Tis Adonais calls! oh, hasten thither,
No more let Life divide what Death can
      join together.

That light whose smile kindles the Uni-
   verse,
   That Beauty in which all things work
      and move,
That Benediction which the eclipsing
   Curse
   Of birth can quench not, that sustain-
      ing Love
Which through the web of being blindly
      wove
By man and beast, and earth, and air, and
   sea,
   Burns bright or dim, as each are mirrors
      of
The fire for which all thirst, now beams
      on me,
Consuming the last clouds of cold mor-
      tality.

The breath whose might I have invoked in
   song
   Descends on me; my spirit's bark is
      driven
Far from the shore, far from the trembling
   throng
   Whose sails were never to the tempest
      given,
The massy earth and spherèd skies are
      riven!
I am borne darkly, fearfully afar;
   Whilst burning through the inmost veil
      of Heaven,
The soul of Adonais, like a star,
Beacons from the abode where the eternal
      are.
            PERCY BYSSHE SHELLEY.

STANZAS WRITTEN IN DEJECTION NEAR NAPLES.

THE sun is warm, the sky is clear,
   The waves are dancing fast and bright,
Blue isles and snowy mountains wear
   The purple noon's transparent light:
   The breath of the moist air is light
Around its unexpanded buds;
   Like many a voice of one delight,
The winds, the birds, the ocean-floods,
The City's voice itself is soft like Soli-
   tude's.

I see the Deep's untrampled floor
   With green and purple sea-weeds strown;
I see the waves upon the shore
   Like light dissolved in star-showers
      thrown:
   I sit upon the sands alone,
The lightning of the noon-tide ocean
   Is flashing round me, and a tone
Arises from its measured motion,
How sweet! did any heart now share in
   my emotion.

Alas! I have nor hope nor health,
   Nor peace within nor calm around,
Nor that content surpassing wealth
   The sage in meditation found,
   And walk'd with inward glory crown'd—
Nor fame, nor power, nor love, nor leisure;
   Others I see whom these surround—
Smiling they live, and call life pleasure:
To me that cup has been dealt in another
   measure.

Yet now despair itself is mild
   Even as the winds and waters are;

I could lie down like a tired child,
  And weep away the life of care
Which I have borne, and yet must bear,
Till death like sleep might steal on me,
And I might feel in the warm air
My cheek grow cold, and hear the sea
Breathe o'er my dying brain its last monotony.

Some might lament that I were cold,
  As I, when this sweet day is gone,
Which my lost heart, too soon grown old,
  Insults with this untimely moan;
They might lament—for I am one
  Whom men love not,—and yet regret,
Unlike this day, which, when the sun
Shall on its stainless glory set,
Will linger, though enjoy'd, like joy in memory yet.
                    PERCY BYSSHE SHELLEY.

RANDOLPH OF ROANOKE.

O MOTHER EARTH! upon thy lap
  Thy weary ones receiving,
And o'er them, silent as a dream,
  Thy grassy mantle weaving,
Fold softly in thy long embrace
  That heart so worn and broken,
And cool its pulse of fire beneath
  Thy shadows old and oaken.

Shut out from him the bitter word
  And serpent hiss of scorning;
Nor let the storms of yesterday
  Disturb his quiet morning.
Breathe over him forgetfulness
  Of all save deeds of kindness,
And, save to smiles of grateful eyes,
  Press down his lids in blindness.

There, where with living ear and eye
  He heard Potomac's flowing,
And, through his tall ancestral trees,
  Saw autumn's sunset glowing,
He sleeps,—still looking to the west,
  Beneath the dark wood shadow,
As if he still would see the sun
  Sink down on wave and meadow.

Bard, Sage, and Tribune!—in himself
  All moods of mind contrasting,—
The tenderest wail of human woe,
  The scorn-like lightning blasting;
The pathos which from rival eyes
  Unwilling tears could summon,
The stinging taunt, the fiery burst
  Of hatred scarcely human!

Mirth, sparkling like a diamond shower,
  From lips of lifelong sadness;
Clear picturings of majestic thought
  Upon a ground of madness;
And over all romance and song
  A classic beauty throwing,
And laurell'd Clio at his side
  Her storied pages showing.

All parties fear'd him: each in turn
  Beheld its schemes disjointed,
As right or left his fatal glance
  And spectral finger pointed.
Sworn foe of Cant, he smote it down
  With trenchant wit unsparing,
And, mocking, rent with ruthless hand
  The robe Pretence was wearing.

Too honest or too proud to feign
  A love he never cherish'd,
Beyond Virginia's border-line
  His patriotism perish'd.
While others hail'd in distant skies
  Our eagle's dusky pinion,
He only saw the mountain bird
  Stoop o'er his Old Dominion!

Still through each change of fortune strange,
  Rack'd nerve, and brain all burning,
His loving faith in motherland
  Knew never shade of turning;
By Britain's lakes, by Neva's wave,
  Whatever sky was o'er him,
He heard her rivers' rushing sound,
  Her blue peaks rose before him.

He held his slaves, yet made withal
  No false and vain pretences,
Nor paid a lying priest to seek
  For scriptural defences.
His harshest words of proud rebuke,
  His bitterest taunt and scorning,
Fell fire-like on the Northern brow
  That bent to him in fawning.

He held his slaves: yet kept the while
  His reverence for the human:

In the dark vassals of his will
  He saw but man and woman!
No hunter of God's outraged poor
  His Roanoke valley enter'd;
No trader in the souls of men
  Across his threshold ventured.

And when the old and wearied man
  Lay down for his last sleeping,
And at his side, a slave no more,
  His brother-man stood weeping,
His latest thought, his latest breath,
  To freedom's duty giving,
With failing tongue and trembling hand
  The dying blest the living.

Oh, never bore his ancient State
  A truer son or braver!
None trampling with a calmer scorn
  On foreign hate or favor.
He knew her faults, yet never stoop'd
  His proud and manly feeling
To poor excuses of the wrong
  Or meanness of concealing.

But none beheld with clearer eye
  The plague-spot o'er her spreading,
None heard more sure the steps of Doom
  Along her future treading.
For her as for himself he spake,
  When, his gaunt frame upbracing,
He traced with dying hand "REMORSE!"
  And perish'd in the tracing.

As from the grave where Henry sleeps,
  From Vernon's weeping willow,
And from the grassy pall which hides
  The sage of Monticello,
So from the leaf-strewn burial-stone
  Of Randolph's lowly dwelling,
Virginia! o'er thy land of slaves
  A warning voice is swelling!

And hark! from thy deserted fields
  Are sadder warnings spoken,
From quench'd hearths, where thy exiled sons
  Their household gods have broken.
The curse is on thee,—wolves for men,
  And briers for corn-sheaves giving!
Oh more than all thy dead renown
  Were now one hero living!
          JOHN GREENLEAF WHITTIER.

THE LOST LEADER.

JUST for a handful of silver he left us;
  Just for a ribbon to stick in his coat—
Found the one gift of which fortune bereft us,
  Lost all the others she lets us devote.
They, with the gold to give, doled him out silver,
  So much was their's who so little allow'd.
How all our copper had gone for his service!
  Rags—were they purple, his heart had been proud!
We that had loved him so, follow'd him, honor'd him,
  Lived in his mild and magnificent eye,
Learn'd his great language, caught his clear accents,
  Made him our pattern to live and to die!
Shakespeare was of us, Milton was for us,
  Burns, Shelley, were with us—they watch from their graves!
He alone breaks from the van and the freemen;
  He alone sinks to the rear and the slaves!

We shall march prospering—not through his presence;
  Songs may inspirit us—not from his lyre;
Deeds will be done—while he boasts his quiescence,
  Still bidding crouch whom the rest bade aspire.
Blot out his name, then—record one lost soul more,
  One task more declined, one more foot-path untrod,
One more triumph for devils, and sorrow for angels,
  One wrong more to man, one more insult to God!
Life's night begins: let him never come back to us!
  There would be doubt, hesitation, and pain,
Forced praise on our part—the glimmer of twilight,
  Never glad, confident morning again!

Best fight on well, for we taught him—
    strike gallantly,
  Aim at our heart ere we pierce through
    his own;
Then let him receive the new knowledge
    and wait us,
  Pardon'd in heaven, the first by the
    throne!
ROBERT BROWNING.

CHARADE.

CAMP-BELL.

COME from my first, ay, come!
    The battle-dawn is nigh;
And the screaming trump and the thunder-
    ing drum
    Are calling thee to die!
Fight as thy father fought;
    Fall as thy father fell;
Thy task is taught; thy shroud is
    wrought;
    So forward and farewell!

Toll ye my second! toll!
    Fling high the flambeau's light,
And sing the hymn for a parted soul
    Beneath the silent night!
The helm upon his head,
    The cross upon his breast;
Let the prayer be said and the tear be
    shed;
    Now take him to his rest!

Call ye my whole,—go, call
    The lord of lute and lay;
And let him greet the sable pall
    With a noble song to-day.
Ay, call him by his name;
    No fitter hand may crave
To light the flame of a soldier's fame
    On the turf of a soldier's grave!
WINTHROP MACKWORTH PRAED.

DRYBURGH ABBEY.

And Scott—that Ocean 'mid the stream of men!
That Alp, amidst all mental greatness reared!—

'TWAS morn—but not the ray which falls
    the summer boughs among,
When Beauty walks in gladness forth, with
    all her light and song:

'Twas morn—but mist and cloud hung
    deep upon the lonely vale,
And shadows, like the wings of death,
    were out upon the gale.

For He whose spirit woke the dust of
    nations into life—
That o'er the waste and barren earth spread
    flowers and fruitage rife—
Whose genius, like the sun, illumed the
    mighty realms of mind—
Had fled for ever from the fame, love,
    friendship of mankind!

To wear a wreath in glory wrought his
    spirit swept afar,
Beyond the soaring wing of thought, the
    light of moon or star;
To drink immortal waters, free from every
    taint of earth—
To breathe before the shrine of life, the
    source whence worlds had birth!

There was wailing on the early breeze, and
    darkness in the sky,
When with sable plume, and cloak, and
    pall, a funeral train swept by;
Methought—St. Mary shield us well!—
    that other forms moved there
Than those of mortal brotherhood, the
    noble, young, and fair!

Was it a dream? how oft, in sleep, we ask,
    "Can this be true?"
Whilst warm Imagination paints her mar-
    vels to our view;—
Earth's glory seems a tarnish'd crown to
    that which we behold,
When dreams enchant our sight with
    things whose meanest garb is gold!

Was it a dream?—Methought the daunt-
    less Harold pass'd me by—
The proud Fitz-James, with martial step,
    and dark intrepid eye;
That Marmion's haughty crest was there,
    a mourner for his sake;
And she,—the bold, the beautiful!—sweet
    Lady of the Lake.

The Minstrel whose *last lay* was o'er, whose
    broken harp lay low,
And with him glorious Waverley, with
    glance and step of woe;

And Stuart's voice rose there, as when,
   'mid fate's disastrous war,
He led the wild, ambitious, proud, and
   brave Vich Ian Vohr.

Next, marvelling at his sable suit, the
   Dominie stalk'd past,
With Bertram, Julia by his side, whose
   tears were flowing fast;
Guy Mannering, too, moved there, o'er-
   power'd by that afflicting sight;
And Merrilies, as when she wept on
   Ellangowan's height.

Solemn and grave, Monkbarns appear'd,
   amidst that burial line;
And Ochiltree leant o'er his staff, and
   mourn'd for "Auld lang syne!"
Slow march'd the gallant McIntyre, whilst
   Lovel mused alone;
For *once*, Miss Wardour's image left that
   bosom's faithful throne.

With coronach, and arms reversed, forth
   came MacGregor's clan—
Red Dougal's cry peal'd shrill and wild—
   Rob Roy's bold brow look'd wan:
The fair Diana kiss'd her cross, and bless'd
   its sainted ray;
And "Wae is me!" the Baillie sigh'd,
   "that I should see this day!"

Next rode, in melancholy guise, with som-
   bre vest and scarf,
Sir Edward, Laird of Ellieslaw, the far-re-
   nown'd Black Dwarf;
Upon his left, in bonnet blue, and white
   locks flowing free—
The pious sculptor of the grave—stood
   Old Mortality!

Balfour of Burley, Claverhouse, the Lord
   of Evandale,
And stately Lady Margaret, whose woe
   might naught avail!
Fierce Bothwell on his charger black, as
   from the conflict won;
And pale Habakkuk Mucklewrath, who
   cried "God's will be done!"

And like a rose, a young white rose, that
   blooms 'mid wildest scenes,
Pass'd she,—the modest, eloquent, and
   virtuous Jeanie Deans;

And Dumbiedikes, that silent laird, with
   love too *deep* to *smile*,
And Effie, with her noble friend, the good
   Duke of Argyle.

With lofty brow, and bearing high, dark
   Ravenswood advanced,
Who on the false Lord Keeper's mien with
   eye indignant glanced:—
Whilst graceful as a lonely fawn, 'neath
   covert close and sure,
Approach'd the beauty of all hearts—the
   Bride of Lammermoor!

Then Annot Lyle, the fairy queen of light
   and song, stepp'd near,
The Knight of Ardenvohr, and *he*, the
   gifted Hieland Seer;
Dalgetty, Duncan, Lord Menteith, and Ran-
   ald met my view;
The hapless Children of the Mist, and bold
   Mhichconnel Dhu!

On swept Bois-Guilbert—Front de Bœuf
   —De Bracy's plume of woe;
And Cœur de Lion's crest shone near the
   valiant Ivanhoe;
While soft as glides a summer cloud
   Rowena closer drew,
With beautiful Rebecca, peerless daughter
   of the Jew!

I saw the courtly Euphuist, with Halbert
   of the Dell,
And, like a ray of moonlight, pass'd the
   White Maid of Avenel;
Lord Morton, Douglas, Bolton, and the
   Royal Earl march'd there,
To the slow and solemn funeral chant of
   the monks of Kennaquhair.

And she, on whose imperial brow a god
   had set his seal,
The glory of whose loveliness grief might
   not all conceal;
The loved in high and princely halls, in
   lone and lowly cots,
Stood Mary, the illustrious, yet helpless
   Queen of Scots.

The firm, devoted Catherine, the senti-
   mental Graeme,
Lochleven, whose worn brow reveal'd an
   early-blighted name,

The enthusiastic Magdalen, the pilgrim of
    that shrine,
Whose spirit triumphs o'er the tomb and
    makes its dust divine.

With Leicester, Lord of Kenilworth, in
    mournful robes, was seen
The gifted, great Elizabeth, high Eng-
    land's matchless queen.
Tressilian's wild and manly glance, and
    Varney's darker gaze,
Sought Amy Robsart's brilliant form, too
    fair for earthly praise.

Next Norna of the Fitful-head, the wild
    Reim-kennar, came,
But shiver'd lay her magic wand, and dim
    her eye of flame;
Young Minna Troil the lofty-soul'd, whom
    Cleveland's love betray'd,
The generous old Udaller, and Mordaunt's
    sweet island maid.

Slow follow'd Lord Glenvarloch, first of
    Scotia's gallant names,
With the fair, romantic Margaret, and the
    erudite King James;
The woo'd and wrong'd Hermione, whose
    lord all hearts despise,
Sarcastic Malagrowther, and the faithful
    Moniplies.

Then stout Sir Geoffrey of the Peak, and
    Peveril swept near;
Stern Bridgenorth, and the fiery Duke,
    with knight and cavalier;
The fairest of fantastic elves, Fenella,
    glided on,
And Alice, from whose beauteous lip the
    light of joy was gone.

And Quentin's haughty helm flash'd there;
    Le Balafrè's stout lance;
Orleans, Crevecœur, the brave Dunois, the
    noblest knight of France;
The wild Hayraddin, follow'd by the silent
    Jean de Troyes,
The mournful Lady Hameline, and Isa-
    belle de Croyes.

Pale sorrow mark'd young Tyrrell's mien,
    grief dimm'd sweet Clara's eye,
And Ronan's laird breathed many a prayer
    for days and friends gone by;

Oh, mourn not, pious Cargill cried; should
    his death woe impart,
Whose cenotaph's the universe, whose
    elegy's the heart!

Forth bore the noble Fairford his fascina-
    ting bride,
The lovely Lilias, with the brave Red-
    gauntlet by her side;
Black Campbell, and the bold redoubted
    Maxwell met my view,
And Wandering Willie's solemn wreath
    of dark funereal yew.

As foes who meet upon some wild, some
    far and foreign shore,
Wreck'd by the same tempestuous surge,
    recall past feuds no more,
Thus prince and peasant, peer and slave,
    thus friend and foe combine,
To pour the homage of their heart upon
    one common shrine.

There Lacey, famed Cadwallon, and the
    fierce Gwenwyn march'd on,
Whilst horn and halbert, pike and bow,
    dart, glaive, and javelin shone;
Sir Damian and the elegant young Eveline
    pass'd there,
Stout Wilkin, and the hopeless Rose, with
    wild, dishevell'd hair.

Around, in solemn grandeur, swept the
    banners of the brave,
And deep and far the clarions waked the
    wild dirge of the glave;
On came the Champion of the Cross, and
    near him, like a star,
The regal Berengaria, beauteous daughter
    of Navarre;

The high, heroic Saladin, with proud and
    haughty mien,
The rich and gorgeous Saracen, and the
    fiery Nazarene;
There Edith and her Nubian slave breathed
    many a thought divine,
Whilst rank on rank—a glorious train—
    rode the Knights of Palestine.

Straight follow'd Zerubbabel and Joliffe
    of the Tower,
Young Wildrake, Markham, Hazeldine,
    and the forest nymph Mayflower;

The democratic Cromwell, stern, resolute,
    and free,
The knight of Woodstock and the light
    and lovely Alice Lee.

And there the crafty Proudfute for once
    true sorrow felt;
Craigdallie, Chartres, and the recreant
    Conachar the Celt,
And he whose chivalry had graced a more
    exalted birth,
The noble-minded Henry, and the famed
    Fair Maid of Perth.

The intrepid Anne of Geierstein, the false
    Lorraine stepp'd near;
Proud Margaret of Anjou, and the faith-
    ful, brave De Vere;
There Arnold, and the King René, and
    Charles the Bold had met
The dauntless Donnerkugel and the grace-
    ful young Lizette.

Forth rode the glorious Godfrey, by the
    gallant Hugh the Great,
While wept the brave and beautiful their
    noble minstrel's fate;
Then Hereward the Varangian, with
    Bertha at his side,
The valorous Count of Paris and his Ama-
    zonian bride.

At last, amidst that princely train, waved
    high De Walton's plume,
Near fair Augusta's laurel-wreath, which
    Time shall ne'er consume,
And Anthony, with quiver void, his last
    fleet arrow sped,
Leant, mourning o'er his broken bow, and
    mused upon the dead.

Still onward like the gathering night ad-
    vanced that funeral train—
Like billows when the tempest sweeps
    across the shadowy main;
Where'er the eager gaze might reach, in
    noble ranks were seen
Dark plume, and glittering mail and crest,
    and woman's beauteous mien!

A sound thrill'd through that length'ning
    host! methought the vault was
    closed,
Where, in his glory and renown, fair
    Scotia's bard reposed!

A sound thrill'd through that length'ning
    host! and forth my vision fled!
But, ah! that mournful dream proved true,
    —the immortal Scott was dead!

The vision and the voice are o'er! their
    influence waned away,
Like music o'er a summer lake at the gold-
    en close of day:
The vision and the voice are o'er!—but
    when will be forgot
The buried Genius of Romance—the im-
    perishable Scott?
CHARLES SWAIN.

ICHABOD.

So fallen! so lost! the light withdrawn
    Which once he wore!
The glory from his gray hairs gone
    For evermore!

Revile him not—the tempter hath
    A snare for all;
And pitying tears, not scorn and wrath,
    Befit his fall!

Oh! dumb be passion's stormy rage,
    When he who might
Have lighted up and led his age,
    Falls back in night.

Scorn! Would the angels laugh, to mark
    A bright soul driven,
Fiend-goaded, down the endless dark,
    From hope and Heaven?

Let not the land, once proud of him,
    Insult him now;
Nor brand with deeper shame his dim,
    Dishonor'd brow.

But let its humbled sons, instead,
    From sea to lake,
A long lament, as for the dead,
    In sadness make.

Of all we loved and honor'd, naught
    Save power remains—
A fallen angel's pride of thought,
    Still strong in chains.

All else is gone; from those great eyes
　　The soul has fled:
When faith is lost, when honor dies,
　　The man is dead!

Then, pay the reverence of old days
　　To his dead fame;
Walk backward, with averted gaze,
　　And hide the shame!
　　　　　　JOHN GREENLEAF WHITTIER.

NAPOLEON.

THE mighty sun had just gone down
　　Into the chambers of the deep,
The ocean birds had upward flown,
　　Each in his cave to sleep,
And silent was the island shore,
And breathless all the broad red sea,
And motionless beside the door
　　Our solitary tree.
Our only tree, our ancient palm,
　　Whose shadow sleeps our door beside,
Partook the universal calm
　　When Buonaparte died.
An ancient man, a stately man,
　　Came forth beneath the spreading tree;
His silent thoughts I could not scan,
　　His tears I needs must see.
A trembling hand had partly cover'd
　　The old man's weeping countenance,
Yet something o'er his sorrow hover'd,
　　That spake of war and France;
Something that spake of other days,
　　When trumpets pierced the kindling air,
And the keen eye could firmly gaze
　　Through battle's crimson glare.
Said I, "Perchance this faded hand,
　　When life beat high and hope was young,
By Lodi's wave, or Syria's sand,
　　The bolt of death had flung.
Young Buonaparte's battle-cry
　　Perchance hath kindled this old cheek;
It is no shame that he should sigh—
　　His heart is like to break!
He hath been with him young and old,
　　He climb'd with him the Alpine snow,
He heard the cannon when they roll'd
　　Along the river Po.
His soul was as a sword, to leap
　　At his accustom'd leader's word;
I love to see the old man weep—
　　He knew no other lord.
As if it were but yesternight,
　　This man remembers dark Eylau;
His dreams are of the eagle's flight
　　Victorious long ago.
The memories of worser time
　　Are all as shadows unto him;
Fresh stands the picture of his prime—
　　The later trace is dim."
I enter'd, and I saw him lie
　　Within the chamber all alone;
I drew near very solemnly
　　To dead Napoleon.
He was not shrouded in a shroud,
He lay not like the vulgar dead,
Yet all of haughty, stern, and proud,
　　From his pale brow was fled.
He had put harness on to die;
　　The eagle star shone on his breast,
His sword lay bare his pillow nigh,
　　The sword he liked the best.
But calm, most calm, was all his face,
　　A solemn smile was on his lips,
His eyes were closed in pensive grace,—
　　A most serene eclipse!
Ye would have said some sainted sprite
　　Had left its passionless abode,—
Some man, whose prayer at morn and night
　　Had duly risen to God.
What thoughts had calm'd his dying breast
　　(For calm he died) cannot be known;
Nor would I wound a warrior's rest,—
　　Farewell, Napoleon!
　　　　　　JOHN GIBSON LOCKHART.

THE RETURN OF NAPOLEON FROM ST. HELENA.

Ho! city of the gay!
　　Paris! what festal rite
Doth call thy thronging million forth,
　　All eager for the sight?
Thy soldiers line the streets
　　In fix'd and stern array,
With buckled helm and bayonet,
　　As on the battle-day.

By square, and fountain side,
　　Heads in dense masses rise,

And tower and battlement and tree
  Are studded thick with eyes.
Comes there some conqueror home
  In triumph from the fight,
With spoil and captives in his train,
  The trophies of his might?

The "Arc de Triomphe" glows!
  A martial host are nigh,
France pours in long succession forth
  Her pomp of chivalry.
No clarion marks their way,
  No victor trump is blown;
Why march they on so silently,
  Told by their tread alone?

Behold! in glittering show,
  A gorgeous car of state!
The white-plumed steeds, in cloth of gold,
  Bow down beneath its weight;
And the noble war-horse, led
  Caparison'd along,
Seems fiercely for his lord to ask,
  As his red eye scans the throng.

Who rideth on yon car?
  The incense flameth high,—
Comes there some demigod of old?
  No answer!—No reply!
Who rideth on yon car?—
  No shout his minions raise,
But by a lofty chapel dome
  The muffled hero stays.

A king is standing there,
  And with uncover'd head
Receives him in the name of France:
  Receiveth whom?—*The dead!*
Was he not buried deep
  In island-cavern drear;
Girt by the sounding ocean surge?
  How came that sleeper here?

Was there no rest for him
  Beneath a peaceful pall,
That thus he brake his stony tomb,
  Ere the strong angel's call?
Hark! hark! the requiem swells,
  A deep, soul-thrilling strain!
An echo, never to be heard
  By mortal ear again.

A requiem for the chief,
  Whose fiat millions slew,

The soaring eagle of the Alps,
  The crush'd at Waterloo:—
The banish'd who return'd,
  The dead who rose again,
And rode in his shroud the billows proud
  To the sunny banks of Seine.

They laid him there in state,
  That warrior strong and bold,
The imperial crown, with jewels bright,
  Upon his ashes cold,
While round those columns proud
  The blazon'd banners wave,
That on a hundred fields he won,
  With the heart's blood of the brave;

And sternly there kept guard
  His veterans scarr'd and old,
Whose wounds of Lodi's cleaving bridge
  Or purple Leipsic told.
Yes, there, with arms reversed,
  Slow pacing, night and day,
Close watch beside the coffin kept
  Those veterans grim and gray.

A cloud is on their brow,—
  Is it sorrow for the dead?
Or memory of the fearful strife
  Where their country's legions fled?
Of Borodino's blood?
  Of Beresina's wail?
The horrors of that dire retreat,
  Which turn'd old History pale?

A cloud is on their brow,—
  Is it sorrow for the dead?
Or a shuddering at the wintry shaft
  By Russian tempests sped?
Where countless mounds of snow
  Mark'd the poor conscripts' grave,
And, pierced by frost and famine, sank
  The bravest of the brave.

A thousand trembling lamps
  The gather'd darkness mock,
And velvet drapes his hearse, who died
  On bare Helena's rock;
And from the altar near
  A never-ceasing hymn
Is lifted by the chanting priests
  Beside the taper dim.

Mysterious one, and proud!
  In the land where shadows reign,

Hast thou met the flocking ghosts of those
  Who at thy nod were slain?
Oh, when the cry of that spectral host
  Like a rushing blast shall be,
What will thine answer be to them?
  And what thy God's to thee?
            LYDIA HUNTLEY SIGOURNEY.

ODE ON THE DEATH OF THE DUKE OF WELLINGTON.

I.

BURY the Great Duke
  With an empire's lamentation,
  Let us bury the Great Duke
    To the noise of the mourning of a mighty nation,
Mourning when their leaders fall,
Warriors carry the warrior's pall,
And sorrow darkens hamlet and hall.

II.

Where shall we lay the man whom we deplore?
Here, in streaming London's central roar.
Let the sound of those he wrought for,
And the feet of those he fought for,
Echo round his bones for evermore.

III.

Lead out the pageant: sad and slow,
  As fits an universal woe,
Let the long, long procession go,
And let the sorrowing crowd about it grow,
And let the mournful martial music blow;
The last great Englishman is low.

IV.

Mourn, for to us he seems the last,
Remembering all his greatness in the past.
No more in soldier fashion will he greet
With lifted hand the gazer in the street.
O friends, our chief state-oracle is dead:
Mourn for the man of long-enduring blood,
The statesman-warrior, moderate, resolute,
Whole in himself, a common good.
Mourn for the man of amplest influence,
Yet clearest of ambitious crime,
Our greatest yet with least pretence,
Great in council and great in war,
Foremost captain of his time,
Rich in saving common-sense,
And, as the greatest only are,
In his simplicity sublime.
O good gray head which all men knew,
O voice from which their omens all men drew,
O iron nerve to true occasion true,
Oh fall'n at length that tower of strength
Which stood four-square to all the winds that blew!
Such was he whom we deplore.
The long self-sacrifice of life is o'er.
The great World-victor's victor will be seen no more.

V.

All is over and done:
Render thanks to the Giver,
England, for thy son.
Let the bell be toll'd.
Render thanks to the Giver,
And render him to the mould.
Under the cross of gold
That shines over city and river,
There he shall rest for ever
Among the wise and the bold.
Let the bell be toll'd:
And a reverent people behold
The towering car, the sable steeds:
Bright let it be with his blazon'd deeds,
Dark in its funeral fold.
Let the bell be toll'd:
And a deeper knell in the heart be knoll'd;
And the sound of the sorrowing anthem roll'd
Through the dome of the golden cross;
And the volleying cannon thunder his loss;
He knew their voices of old.
For many a time in many a clime
His captain's ear has heard them boom
Bellowing victory, bellowing doom:
When he with those deep voices wrought,
Guarding realms and kings from shame;
With those deep voices our dead captain taught
The tyrant, and asserts his claim
In that dread sound to the great name,
Which he has worn so pure of blame,

In praise and in dispraise the same,
A man of well-attemper'd frame.
O civic muse, to such a name,
To such a name for ages long,
To such a name,
Preserve a broad approach of fame,
And ever-echoing avenues of song.

VI.

Who is he that cometh, like an honor'd guest,
With banner and with music, with soldier and with priest,
With a nation weeping, and breaking on my rest?
Mighty seaman, this is he
Was great by land as thou by sea.
Thine island loves thee well, thou famous man,
The greatest sailor since our world began.
Now, to the roll of muffled drums,
To thee the greatest soldier comes;
For this is he
Was great by land as thou by sea:
His foes were thine; he kept us free;
Oh give him welcome, this is he,
Worthy of our gorgeous rites,
And worthy to be laid by thee;
For this is England's greatest son,
He that gain'd a hundred fights,
Nor ever lost an English gun;
This is he that far away
Against the myriads of Assaye
Clash'd with his fiery few and won;
And underneath another sun,
Warring on a later day,
Round affrighted Lisbon drew
The treble works, the vast designs
Of his labor'd rampart-lines,
Where he greatly stood at bay,
Whence he issued forth anew,
And ever great and greater grew,
Beating from the wasted vines
Back to France her banded swarms,
Back to France with countless blows,
Till o'er the hills her eagles flew
Past the Pyrenean pines;
Follow'd up in valley and glen
With blare of bugle, clamor of men,
Roll of cannon and clash of arms,
And England pouring on her foes.
Such a war had such a close.
Again their ravening eagle rose
In anger, wheel'd on Europe-shadowing wings,
And barking for the thrones of kings;
Till one that sought but Duty's iron crown
On that loud Sabbath shook the spoiler down;
A day of onsets of despair!
Dash'd on every rocky square
Their surging charges foam'd themselves away;
Last, the Prussian trumpet blew;
Through the long tormented air
Heaven flash'd a sudden jubilant ray,
And down we swept and charged and overthrew.
So great a soldier taught us there,
What long-enduring hearts could do
In that world-earthquake, Waterloo!
Mighty seaman, tender and true,
And pure as he from taint of craven guile,
O savior of the silver-coasted isle,
O shaker of the Baltic and the Nile,
If aught of things that here befall
Touch a spirit among things divine,
If love of country move thee there at all,
Be glad, because his bones are laid by thine!
And through the centuries let a people's voice
In full acclaim,
A people's voice,
The proof and echo of all human fame,
A people's voice, when they rejoice
At civic revel and pomp and game,
Attest their great commander's claim
With honor, honor, honor, honor to him,
Eternal honor to his name.

VII.

A people's voice! we are a people yet.
Though all men else their nobler dreams forget,
Confused by brainless mobs and lawless powers;
Thank Him who isled us here, and roughly set
His Briton in blown seas and storming showers,
We have a voice, with which to pay the debt

Of boundless love and reverence and regret
To those great men who fought, and kept it ours.
And keep it ours, O God, from brute control;
O statesmen, guard us, guard the eye, the soul
Of Europe, keep our noble England whole,
And save the one true seed of freedom sown
Betwixt a people and their ancient throne,
That sober freedom out of which there springs
Our loyal passion for our temperate kings;
For, saving that, ye help to save mankind
Till public wrong be crumbled into dust,
And drill the raw world for the march of mind,
Till crowds at length be sane and crowns be just.
But wink no more in slothful overtrust.
Remember him who led your hosts;
He bade you guard the sacred coasts.
Your cannons moulder on the seaward wall;
His voice is silent in your council-hall
For ever; and whatever tempests lower
For ever silent; even if they broke
In thunder, silent; yet remember all
He spoke among you, and the Man who spoke;
Who never sold the truth to serve the hour,
Nor palter'd with eternal God for power;
Who let the turbid streams of rumor flow
Through either babbling world of high and low;
Whose life was work, whose language rife
With rugged maxims hewn from life;
Who never spoke against a foe;
Whose eighty winters freeze with one rebuke
All great self-seekers trampling on the right:
Truth-teller was our England's Alfred named;
Truth-lover was our English Duke;
Whatever record leap to light
He never shall be shamed.

VIII.

Lo, the leader in these glorious wars
Now to glorious burial slowly borne,
Follow'd by the brave of other lands,
He, on whom from both her open hands
Lavish Honor shower'd all her stars,
And affluent Fortune emptied all her horn.
Yea, let all good things await
Him who cares not to be great,
But as he saves or serves the state.
Not once or twice in our rough island-story,
The path of duty was the way to glory:
He that walks it, only thirsting
For the right, and learns to deaden
Love of self, before his journey closes,
He shall find the stubborn thistle bursting
Into glossy purples, which outredden
All voluptuous garden-roses.
Not once or twice in our fair island-story,
The path of duty was the way to glory:
He, that ever following her commands,
On with toil of heart and knees and hands
Through the long gorge to the far light has won
His path upward, and prevail'd,
Shall find the toppling crags of Duty scaled
Are close upon the shining table-lands
To which our God Himself is moon and sun.
Such was he: his work is done.
But while the races of mankind endure,
Let his great example stand
Colossal, seen of every land,
And keep the soldier firm, the statesman pure;
Till in all lands and through all human story
The path of duty be the way to glory:
And let the land whose hearths he saved from shame
For many and many an age proclaim
At civic revel and pomp and game,
And when the long-illumined cities flame,
Their ever-loyal iron leader's fame,
With honor, honor, honor, honor to him,
Eternal honor to his name.

IX.

Peace, his triumph will be sung
By some yet unmoulded tongue
Far on in summers that we shall not see:
Peace, it is a day of pain

For one about whose patriarchal knee
Late the little children clung:
O peace, it is a day of pain
For one upon whose hand and heart and
    brain
Once the weight and fate of Europe hung.
Ours the pain, be his the gain!
More than is of man's degree
Must be with us, watching here
At this, our great solemnity.
Whom we see not we revere.
We revere, and we refrain
From talk of battles loud and vain,
And brawling memories all too free
For such a wise humility
As befits a solemn fane:
We revere, and while we hear
The tides of Music's golden sea
Setting toward eternity,
Uplifted high in heart and hope are we,
Until we doubt not that for one so true
There must be other nobler work to do
Than when he fought at Waterloo,
And Victor he must ever be.
For though the Giant Ages heave the hill
And break the shore, and evermore
Make and break, and work their will;
Though world on world in myriad myriads
    roll
Round us, each with different powers,
And other forms of life than ours,
What know we greater than the soul?
On God and godlike men we build our trust.
Hush, the Dead March wails in the peo-
    ple's ears:
The dark crowd moves, and there are sobs
    and tears:
The black earth yawns: the mortal disap-
    pears;
Ashes to ashes, dust to dust;
He is gone who seem'd so great.—
Gone; but nothing can bereave him
Of the force he made his own
Being here, and we believe him
Something far advanced in state,
And that he wears a truer crown
Than any wreath that man can weave him.
Speak no more of his renown,
Lay your earthly fancies down,
And in the vast cathedral leave him.
God accept him, Christ receive him.
                  ALFRED TENNYSON.

TO THE SISTER OF ELIA.

COMFORT thee, O thou mourner, yet a while!
Again shall Elia's smile
Refresh thy heart, where heart can ache
    no more.
What is it we deplore?

He leaves behind him, freed from griefs
    and years,
Far worthier things than tears.
The love of friends without a single foe:
Unequall'd lot below!

His gentle soul, his genius, these are thine;
For these dost thou repine?
He may have left the lowly walks of men;
Left them he has; what then?

Are not his footsteps follow'd by the eyes
Of all the good and wise?
Tho' the warm day is over, yet they seek
Upon the lofty peak

Of his pure mind the roseate light that
    glows
O'er death's perennial snows.
Behold him! from the region of the blest
He speaks: he bids thee rest.
                  WALTER SAVAGE LANDOR.

LINES WRITTEN ON THE NIGHT OF THE 30TH OF JULY, 1847.

AT THE CLOSE OF AN UNSUCCESSFUL CONTEST FOR EDINBURGH.

THE day of tumult, strife, defeat, was o'er;
    Worn out with toil, and noise, and scorn,
        and spleen,
I slumber'd, and in slumber saw once more
    A room in an old mansion, long unseen.

That room, methought, was curtain'd from
        the light;
    Yet through the curtains shone the
        moon's cold ray
Full on a cradle, where, in linen white,
    Sleeping life's first soft sleep, an infant lay

Pale flicker'd on the hearth the dying
    flame,
    And all was silent in that ancient hall,
Save when by fits on the low night-wind
    came
    The murmur of the distant waterfall.

And lo! the fairy queens who rule our
　　birth
　Drew nigh to speak the new-born baby's
　　doom:
With noiseless step, which left no trace on
　　earth,
　From gloom they came, and vanish'd
　　into gloom.

Not deigning on the boy a glance to cast,
　Swept careless by the gorgeous Queen of
　　Gain;
More scornful still, the Queen of Fashion
　　pass'd
　With mincing gait and sneer of cold dis-
　　dain.

The Queen of Power toss'd high her jew-
　　ell'd head,
　And o'er her shoulder threw a wrathful
　　frown:
The Queen of Pleasure on the pillow shed
　Scarce one stray rose-leaf from her
　　fragrant crown.

Still Fay in long procession follow'd Fay;
　And still the little couch remain'd un-
　　blest:
But, when those wayward sprites had
　　pass'd away,
　Came One, the last, the mightiest, and
　　the best.

O glorious lady, with the eyes of light,
　And laurels clustering round thy lofty
　　brow,
Who by the cradle's side didst watch that
　　night,
　Warbling a sweet, strange music, who
　　wast thou?

"Yes, darling; let them go;" so ran the
　　strain:
　"Yes; let them go, Gain, Fashion, Plea-
　　sure, Power,
And all the busy elves to whose domain
　Belongs the nether sphere, the fleeting
　　hour.

"Without one envious sigh, one anxious
　　scheme,
　The nether sphere, the fleeting hour re-
　　sign,

Mine is the world of thought, the world
　　of dream,
　Mine all the past, and all the future
　　mine.

"Fortune, that lays in sport the mighty
　　low,
　Age, that to penance turns the joys of
　　youth,
Shall leave untouch'd the gifts which I
　　bestow,
　The sense of beauty and the thirst of
　　truth.

"Of the fair brotherhood who share my
　　grace,
　I, from thy natal day, pronounce thee
　　free;
And, if for some I keep a nobler place,
　I keep for none a happier than for thee.

"There are who, while to vulgar eyes they
　　seem
　Of all my bounties largely to partake,
Of me as of some rival's handmaid deem,
　And court me but for Gain's, Power's,
　　Fashion's sake.

"To such, though deep their lore, though
　　wide their fame,
　Shall my great mysteries be all un-
　　known;
But thou, through good and evil, praise
　　and blame,
　Wilt not thou love me for myself alone?

"Yes, thou wilt love me with exceeding
　　love,
　And I will tenfold all that love repay,
Still smiling, though the tender may re-
　　prove,
　Still faithful, though the trusted may
　　betray.

"For aye mine emblem was, and aye shall
　　be,
　The ever-during plant whose bough I
　　wear,
Brightest and greenest then when every
　　tree
　That blossoms in the light of Time is
　　bare.

"In the dark hour of shame I deign'd to stand
Before the frowning peers at Bacon's side:
On a far shore I smoothed with tender hand,
Through months of pain, the sleepless bed of Hyde:
"I brought the wise and brave of ancient days
To cheer the cell where Raleigh pined alone:
I lighted Milton's darkness with the blaze
Of the bright ranks that guard the eternal throne.

"And even so, my child, it is my pleasure
That thou not then alone shouldst feel me nigh,
When in domestic bliss and studious leisure,
Thy weeks uncounted come, uncounted fly;

"Not then alone, when myriads, closely press'd
Around thy car, the shout of triumph raise,
Nor when, in gilded drawing-rooms, thy breast
Swells at the sweeter sound of woman's praise.

"No: when on restless night dawns cheerless morrow,
When weary soul and wasting body pine,
Thine am I still, in danger, sickness, sorrow,
In conflict, obloquy, want, exile, thine;

"Thine, where on mountain-waves the snow-birds scream,
Where more than Thule's winter barbs the breeze,
Where scarce, through lowering clouds, one sickly gleam
Lights the drear May-day of Antarctic seas;

"Thine, when around thy litter's track all day
White sandhills shall reflect the blinding glare;
Thine when, through forests breathing death, thy way
All night shall wind by many a tiger's lair;

"Thine most when friends turn pale, when traitors fly,
When, hard beset, thy spirit, justly proud,
For truth, peace, freedom, mercy, dares defy
A sullen priesthood and a raving crowd.

"Amidst the din of all things fell and vile,
Hate's yell, and Envy's hiss, and Folly's bray,
Remember me, and with an unforced smile
See riches, baubles, flatterers, pass away.

"Yes, they will pass away, nor deem it strange;
They come and go, as comes and goes the sea;
And let them come and go; thou, through all change,
Fix thy firm gaze on Virtue and on me."
THOMAS BABINGTON MACAULAY.

SHE IS FAR FROM THE LAND.

SHE is far from the land where her young hero sleeps,
And lovers are round her sighing;
But coldly she turns from their gaze, and weeps,
For her heart in his grave is lying.

She sings the wild song of her dear native plains,
Every note which he loved awaking;—
Ah! little they think, who delight in her strains,
How the heart of the Minstrel is breaking.

He had lived for his love, for his country he died,
They were all that to life had entwined him;
Nor soon shall the tears of his country be dried,
Nor long will his love stay behind him.

Oh make her a grave where the sunbeams
rest
When they promise a glorious morrow;
They'll shine o'er her sleep, like a smile
from the West,
From her own loved island of sorrow.
THOMAS MOORE.

KANE.
DIED FEBRUARY 16, 1857.

ALOFT upon an old basaltic crag,
Which, scalp'd by keen winds that defend the Pole,
Gazes with dead face on the seas that roll
Around the secret of the mystic zone,
A mighty nation's star-bespangled flag
Flutters alone,
And underneath, upon the lifeless front
Of that drear cliff, a simple name is
traced;
Fit type of him who, famishing and
gaunt,
But with a rocky purpose in his soul,
Breasted the gathering snows,
Clung to the drifting floes,
By want beleaguer'd, and by winter
chased,
Seeking the brother lost amid that frozen
waste.

Not many months ago we greeted him,
Crown'd with the icy honors of the
North,
Across the land his hard-won fame went
forth,
And Maine's deep woods were shaken
limb by limb;
His own mild Keystone State, sedate and
prim,
Burst from decorous quiet as he came;
Hot Southern lips with eloquence aflame
Sounded his triumph. Texas, wild and
grim,
Proffer'd its horny hand. The largelung'd West,
From out its giant breast,
Yell'd its frank welcome. And from
main to main,
Jubilant to the sky,
Thunder'd the mighty cry,
HONOR TO KANE!

In vain, in vain beneath his feet we flung
The reddening roses! All in vain we
pour'd
The golden wine, and round the shining
board
Sent the toast circling, till the rafters
rung
With the thrice-tripled honors of the
feast!
Scarce the buds wilted and the voices
ceased
Ere the pure light that sparkled in his
eyes,
Bright as auroral fires in Southern skies,
Faded and faded! And the brave young
heart
That the relentless Arctic winds had
robb'd
Of all its vital heat, in that long quest
For the lost captain, now within his
breast
More and more faintly throbb'd.
His was the victory; but as his grasp
Closed on the laurel crown with eager
clasp,
Death launch'd a whistling dart;
And ere the thunders of applause were
done
His bright eyes closed for ever on the sun!
Too late, too late the splendid prize he won
In the Olympic race of Science and of
Art!
Like to some shatter'd berg that, pale and
lone,
Drifts from the white North to a tropic
zone,
And in the burning day
Wastes peak by peak away,
Till on some rosy even
It dies with sunlight blessing it; so he
Tranquilly floated to a Southern sea,
And melted into heaven.

He needs no tears, who lived a noble life;
We will not weep for him who died so
well,
But we will gather round the hearth,
and tell
The story of his strife;
Such homage suits him well,
Better than funeral pomp or passing
bell.

What tale of peril and self-sacrifice!
Prison'd amid the fastnesses of ice,
  With hunger howling o'er the wastes of snow!
Night lengthening into months, the ravenous floe
Crunching the massive ships, as the white bear
Crunches his prey. The insufficient share
  Of loathsome food,
The lethargy of famine, the despair
  Urging to labor, nervelessly pursued,
  Toil done with skinny arms, and faces hued
Like pallid masks, while dolefully behind
Glimmer'd the fading embers of a mind!
That awful hour, when through the prostrate band
Delirium stalk'd, laying his burning hand
  Upon the ghastly foreheads of the crew.
  The whispers of rebellion, faint and few
  At first, but deepening ever till they grew
Into black thoughts of murder; such the throng
Of horrors bound the hero. High the song
Should be that hymns the noble part he play'd!
Sinking himself, yet ministering aid
  To all around him. By a mighty will
  Living defiant of the wants that kill,
Because his death would seal his comrades' fate;
  Cheering with ceaseless and inventive skill
Those Polar waters, dark and desolate.
Equal to every trial, every fate,
  He stands, until Spring, tardy with relief,
    Unlocks the icy gate,
And the pale prisoners thread the world once more,
To the steep cliffs of Greenland's pastoral shore
    Bearing their dying chief.

Time was when he should gain his spurs of gold
  From royal hands, who woo'd the knightly state;
The knell of old formalities is toll'd,
  And the world's knights are now self-consecrate.

No grander episode doth chivalry hold
  In all its annals, back to Charlemagne,
Than that lone vigil of unceasing pain,
Faithfully kept through hunger and through cold,
By the good Christian knight, ELISHA KANE!
FITZ-JAMES O'BRIEN.

IN REMEMBRANCE OF JOSEPH STURGE.

IN the fair land o'erwatch'd by Ischia's mountains,
  Across the charmèd bay
Whose blue waves keep with Capri's silver fountains
  Perpetual holiday,

A king lies dead, his wafer duly eaten,
  His gold-bought masses given;
And Rome's great altar smokes with gums to sweeten
  Her foulest gift to Heaven.

And while all Naples thrills with mute thanksgiving,
  The court of England's queen
For the dead monster, so abhorr'd while living,
  In mourning garb is seen.

With a true sorrow God rebukes that feigning;
  By lone Edgbaston's side
Stands a great city in the sky's sad raining,
  Bare-headed and wet-eyed!

Silent for once the restless hive of labor,
  Save the low funeral tread,
Or voice of craftsman whispering to his neighbor
  The good deeds of the dead.

For him no minster's chant of the immortals
  Rose from the lips of sin;
No mitred priest swung back the heavenly portals
  To let the white soul in.

But Age and Sickness framed their tearful faces
  In the low hovel's door,

And prayers went up from all the dark by-
    places
And Ghettos of the poor.

The pallid toiler and the negro chattel,
    The vagrant of the street,
The human dice wherewith in games of
    battle
    The lords of Earth compete,

Touch'd with a grief that needs no outward
    draping,
    All swell'd the long lament,
Of grateful hearts, instead of marble,
    shaping
    His viewless monument!

For never yet, with ritual pomp and splen-
    dor,
    In the long heretofore,
A heart more loyal, warm, and true, and
    tender,
    Has England's turf closed o'er.

And if there fell from out her grand old
    steeples
    No crash of brazen wail,
The murmurous woe of kindreds, tongues,
    and peoples
    Swept in on every gale.

It came from Holstein's birchen-belted
    meadows,
    And from the tropic calms
Of Indian islands in the sun-smit shadows
    Of Occidental palms;

From the lock'd roadsteads of the Both-
    nian peasants,
    And harbors of the Finn,
Where war's worn victims saw his gentle
    presence
    Come sailing, Christ-like, in,

To seek the lost, to build the old waste places,
    To link the hostile shores
Of severing seas, and sow with England's
    daisies
    The moss of Finland's moors.

Thanks for the good man's beautiful ex-
    ample,
    Who in the vilest saw
Some sacred crypt or altar of a temple
    Still vocal with God's law;

And heard with tender ear the spirit sighing
    As from its prison cell,
Praying for pity, like the mournful crying
    Of Jonah out of hell.

Not his the golden pen's or lip's persuasion,
    But a fine sense of right,
And Truth's directness, meeting each oc-
    casion
    Straight as a line of light.

His faith and works, like streams that in-
    termingle,
    In the same channel ran:
The crystal clearness of an eye kept single
    Shamed all the frauds of man.

The very gentlest of all human natures
    He join'd to courage strong,
And love outreaching unto all God's crea-
    tures
    With sturdy hate of wrong.

Tender as woman; manliness and meekness
    In him were so allied
That they who judged him by his strength
    or weakness
    Saw but a single side.

Men fail'd, betray'd him, but his zeal
    seem'd nourish'd
    By failure and by fall;
Still a large faith in human-kind he cher-
    ish'd,
    And in God's love for all.

And now he rests: his greatness and his
    sweetness
    No more shall seem at strife;
And Death has moulded into calm com-
    pleteness
    The statue of his life.

Where the dews glisten and the song-birds
    warble,
    His dust to dust is laid,
In Nature's keeping, with no pomp of
    marble
    To shame his modest shade.

The forges glow, the hammers all are ring-
    ing;
    Beneath its smoky vale,
Hard by, the city of his love is swinging
    Its clamorous iron flail.

But round his grave are quietude and beauty,
And the sweet heaven above,—
The fitting symbols of a life of duty
Transfigured into love!
JOHN GREENLEAF WHITTIER.

BROWN OF OSSAWATOMIE.

JOHN BROWN of Ossawatomie spake on his dying day:
"I will not have to shrive my soul a priest in Slavery's pay.
But let some poor slave-mother whom I have striven to free,
With her children, from the gallows-stair put up a prayer for me!"

John Brown of Ossawatomie, they led him out to die;
And lo! a poor slave-mother with her little child press'd nigh.
Then the bold blue eye grew tender, and the old harsh face grew mild,
As he stoop'd between the jeering ranks and kiss'd the negro's child!

The shadows of his stormy life that moment fell apart;
And they who blamed the bloody hand forgave the loving heart.
That kiss from all its guilty means redeem'd the good intent,
And round the grisly fighter's hair the martyr's aureole bent!

Perish with him the folly that seeks through evil good!
Long live the generous purpose unstain'd with human blood!
Not the raid of midnight terror, but the thought which underlies;
Not the borderer's pride of daring, but the Christian's sacrifice.

Nevermore may yon Blue Ridges the Northern rifle hear,
Nor see the light of blazing homes flash on the negro's spear.
But let the free-wing'd angel Truth their guarded passes scale,
To teach that right is more than might, and justice more than mail!

So vainly shall Virginia set her battle in array:
In vain her trampling squadrons knead the winter snow with clay.
She may strike the pouncing eagle, but she dares not harm the dove;
And every gate she bars to Hate shall open wide to Love!
JOHN GREENLEAF WHITTIER.

DIRGE FOR A SOLDIER.

IN MEMORY OF GEN. PHILIP KEARNEY, KILLED SEPT. 1, 1862.

CLOSE his eyes, his work is done!
  What to him is friend or foeman,
Rise of moon, or set of sun,
  Hand of man, or kiss of woman?
    Lay him low, lay him low,
    In the clover or the snow!
    What cares he? he cannot know:
    Lay him low!

As man may, he fought his fight,
  Proved his truth by his endeavor;
Let him sleep in solemn night,
  Sleep for ever and for ever.
    Lay him low, lay him low,
    In the clover or the snow!
    What cares he? he cannot know:
    Lay him low!

Fold him in his country's stars,
  Roll the drum and fire the volley!
What to him are all our wars,
  What but death bemocking folly?
    Lay him low, lay him low,
    In the clover or the snow!
    What cares he? he cannot know:
    Lay him low!

Leave him to God's watching eye,
  Trust him to the Hand that made him.
Mortal love sweeps idly by:
  God alone has power to aid him.
    Lay him low, lay him low,
    In the clover or the snow!
    What cares he? he cannot know:
    Lay him low!
GEORGE H. BOKER.

DEDICATION.

TO IDYLLS OF THE KING.

THESE to His memory—since he held them dear,
Perchance as finding there unconsciously
Some image of himself—I dedicate,
I dedicate, I consecrate with tears—
These Idylls.

   And indeed He seems to me
Scarce other than my own ideal knight,
"Who reverenced his conscience as his king;
Whose glory was redressing human wrong;
Who spake no slander, no, nor listen'd to it;
Who loved one only, and who clave to her—"
Her—over all whose realms to their last isle,
Commingled with the gloom of imminent war,
The shadow of His loss drew like eclipse,
Darkening the world. We have lost him: he is gone:
We know him now: all narrow jealousies
Are silent; and we see him as he moved,
How modest, kindly, all-accomplish'd, wise,
With what sublime repression of himself,
And in what limits, and how tenderly;
Not swaying to this faction or to that;
Not making his high place the lawless perch
Of wing'd ambitions, nor a vantage-ground
For pleasure; but thro' all this tract of years
Wearing the white flower of a blameless life,
Before a thousand peering littlenesses,
In that fierce light which beats upon a throne,
And blackens every blot: for where is he,
Who dares foreshadow for an only son
A lovelier life, a more unstain'd, than his?
Or how should England, dreaming of *his* sons,
Hope more for these than some inheritance
Of such a life, a heart, a mind as thine,
Thou noble Father of her Kings to be,
Laborious for her people and her poor—
Voice in the rich dawn of an ampler day—
Far-sighted summoner of War and Waste
To fruitful strifes and rivalries of peace—
Sweet Nature gilded by the gracious gleam
Of letters, dear to Science, dear to Art,
Dear to thy land and ours, a Prince indeed,
Beyond all titles, and a household name,
Hereafter, thro' all times, Albert the Good?

Break not, O woman's heart, but still endure;
Break not, for thou art Royal, but endure,
Remembering all the beauty of that star
Which shone so close beside Thee, that ye made
One light together, but has pass'd, and leaves
The Crown a lonely splendor.

     May all love,
His love, unseen but felt, o'ershadow Thee,
The love of all Thy sons encompass Thee
The love of all Thy daughters cherish Thee,
The love of all Thy people comfort Thee,
Till God's love set Thee at his side again.
       ALFRED TENNYSON.

ABRAHAM LINCOLN.

YOU lay a wreath on murder'd Lincoln's bier,
 You, who with mocking pencil wont to trace,
Broad for the self-complaisant British sneer,
 His length of shambling limb, his furrow'd face,

His gaunt, gnarl'd hands, his unkempt, bristling hair,
 His garb uncouth, his bearing ill at ease,
His lack of all we prize as debonair,
 Of power or will to shine, of art to please;

You, whose smart pen back'd up the pencil's laugh,
 Judging each step as though the way were plain;

Reckless, so it could point its paragraph,
  Of chief's perplexity or people's pain,—

Beside this corpse, that bears for winding-
    sheet
  The Stars and Stripes he lived to rear
    anew,
Between the mourners at his head and feet,
  Say, scurrile jester, is there room for *you?*

Yes: he had lived to shame me from my
    sneer,
  To lame my pencil and confute my pen;
To make me own this hind of princes peer,
  This rail-splitter, a true-born king of
    men.

My shallow judgment I had learn'd to rue,
  Noting how to occasion's height he rose;
How his quaint wit made home-truth seem
    more true;
  How, iron-like, his temper grew by
    blows;

How humble, yet how hopeful he could be;
  How in good fortune and in ill the same;
Nor bitter in success, nor boastful he,
  Thirsty for gold, nor feverish for fame.

He went about his work, such work as few
  Ever had laid on head and heart and
    hand,
As one who knows, where there's a task to
    do,
  Man's honest will must Heaven's good
    grace command;

Who trusts the strength will with the
    burden grow,
  That God makes instruments to work
    his will,
If but that will we can arrive to know,
  Nor tamper with the weights of good
    and ill.

So he went forth to battle, on the side
  That he felt clear was Liberty's and
    Right's,
As in his pleasant boyhood he had plied
  His warfare with rude Nature's thwart-
    ing mights—

The unclear'd forest, the unbroken soil,
  The iron bark that turns the lumberer's
    axe,

The rapid that o'erbears the boatman's
    toil,
  The prairie hiding the mazed wanderer's
    tracks,

The ambush'd Indian, and the prowling
    bear,—
  Such were the deeds that help'd his
    youth to train:
Rough culture, but such trees large fruit
    may bear,
  If but their stocks be of right girth and
    grain.

So he grew up, a destined work to do,
  And lived to do it; four long-suffering
    years'
Ill fate, ill feeling, ill report lived through,
  And then he heard the hisses change to
    cheers,

The taunts to tribute, the abuse to praise,
  And took both with the same unwaver-
    ing mood,—
Till, as he came on light, from darkling
    days,
  And seem'd to touch the goal from
    where he stood,

A felon hand, between the goal and him,
  Reach'd from behind his back, a trigger
    prest,
And those perplex'd and patient eyes
    were dim,
  Those gaunt, long-laboring limbs were
    laid to rest.

The words of mercy were upon his lips,
  Forgiveness in his heart and on his
    pen,
When this vile murderer brought swift
    eclipse
  To thoughts of peace on earth, good will
    to men.

The Old World and the New, from sea to
    sea,
  Utter one voice of sympathy and
    shame.
Sore heart, so stopp'd when it at last
    beat high!
  Sad life, cut short just as its triumph
    came!

A deed accursed! Strokes have been struck before
  By the assassin's hand, whereof men doubt
If more of horror or disgrace they bore;
  But thy foul crime, like Cain's, stands darkly out,

Vile hand, that brandest murder on a strife,
  Whate'er its grounds, stoutly and nobly striven,
And with the martyr's crown crownest a life
  With much to praise, little to be forgiven.
                                    TOM TAYLOR.

DICKENS IN CAMP.

ABOVE the pines the moon was slowly drifting,
  The river sang below;
The dim Sierras, far beyond, uplifting
  Their minarets of snow.

The roaring camp-fire, with rude humor, painted
  The ruddy tints of health
On haggard face and form that droop'd and fainted
  In the fierce race for wealth;

Till one arose, and from his pack's scant treasure
  A hoarded volume drew,
And cards were dropp'd from hands of listless leisure
  To hear the tale anew;

And then, while round them shadows gather'd faster,
  And as the firelight fell,
He read aloud the book wherein the Master
  Had writ of "Little Nell."

Perhaps 'twas boyish fancy, — for the reader
  Was youngest of them all,—
But, as he read, from clustering pine and cedar
  A silence seem'd to fall;

The fir trees, gathering closer in the shadows,
  Listen'd in every spray,
While the whole camp, with "Nell" on English meadows,
  Wander'd and lost their way.

And so in mountain solitudes—o'ertaken
  As by some spell divine—
Their cares dropp'd from them like the needles shaken
  From out the gusty pine.

Lost is that camp, and wasted all its fire:
  And he who wrought that spell?—
Ah, towering pine and stately Kentish spire,
  Ye have one tale to tell!

Lost is that camp! but let its fragrant story
  Blend with the breath that thrills
With hop-vines' incense all the pensive glory
  That fills the Kentish hills.

And on that grave where English oak and holly
  And laurel leaves entwine,
Deem it not all a too presumptuous folly,—
  This spray of Western pine!
                              FRANCIS BRET HARTE.

Then with eyes that saw not I kissed her,
And she, kissing back, could not know
That my kiss was given to her sister,
Folded close under deepening snow.

J. R. Lowell.

HISTORICAL POEMS.

THE DESTRUCTION OF SENNACHERIB.

The Assyrian came down like the wolf on the fold,
And his cohorts were gleaming in purple and gold;
And the sheen of their spears was like stars on the sea,
When the blue wave rolls nightly on deep Galilee.

Like the leaves of the forest when summer is green,
That host with their banners at sunset were seen;
Like the leaves of the forest when autumn hath blown,
That host on the morrow lay wither'd and strown.

For the Angel of Death spread his wings on the blast,
And breathed in the face of the foe as he pass'd;
And the eyes of the sleepers wax'd deadly and chill,
And their hearts but once heaved, and for ever grew still!

And there lay the steed with his nostril all wide,
But through it there roll'd not the breath of his pride;
And the foam of his gasping lay white on the turf,
And cold as the spray of the rock-beating surf.

And there lay the rider distorted and pale,
With the dew on his brow and the rust on his mail;
And the tents were all silent, the banners alone,
The lances unlifted, the trumpet unblown.

And the widows of Ashur are loud in their wail;
And the idols are broke in the temple of Baal;
And the might of the Gentile, unsmote by the sword,
Hath melted like snow in the glance of the Lord!

LORD BYRON.

HORATIUS.

Lars Porsena of Clusium,
  By the nine gods he swore
That the great house of Tarquin
  Should suffer wrong no more.
By the nine gods he swore it,
  And named a trysting-day,
And bade his messengers ride forth,
  East and west and south and north,
  To summon his array.

East and west and south and north
  The messengers ride fast,
And tower and town and cottage
  Have heard the trumpet's blast.
Shame on the false Etruscan
  Who lingers in his home,
When Porsena of Clusium
  Is on the march for Rome!

The horsemen and the footmen
  Are pouring in amain
From many a stately market-place,
  From many a fruitful plain,
From many a lonely hamlet,
  Which, hid by beech and pine,
Like an eagle's nest hangs on the crest
  Of purple Apennine;

From lordly Vollaterræ,
  Where scowls the far-famed hold
Piled by the hands of giants
  For godlike kings of old;
From sea-girt Populonia,
  Whose sentinels descry
Sardinia's snowy mountain-tops
  Fringing the southern sky;

From the proud mart of Pisæ,
  Queen of the western waves,
Where ride Massilia's triremes,
  Heavy with fair-hair'd slaves;
From where sweet Clanis wanders
  Through corn and vines and flowers;
From where Cortona lifts to heaven
  Her diadem of towers.

Tall are the oaks whose acorns
  Drop in dark Auser's rill;
Fat are the stags that champ the boughs
  Of the Ciminian hill;
Beyond all streams, Clitumnus
  Is to the herdsman dear;
Best of all pools the fowler loves
  The great Volsinian mere.

But now no stroke of woodman
  Is heard by Auser's rill;
No hunter tracks the stag's green path
  Up the Ciminian hill;
Unwatch'd along Clitumnus
  Grazes the milk-white steer;
Unharm'd the water-fowl may dip
  In the Volsinian mere.

The harvests of Arretium,
  This year, old men shall reap;
This year, young boys in Umbro
  Shall plunge the struggling sheep;
And in the vats of Luna,
  This year, the must shall foam
Round the white feet of laughing girls
  Whose sires have march'd to Rome.

There be thirty chosen prophets,
  The wisest of the land,
Who always by Lars Porsena
  Both morn and evening stand.
Evening and morn the thirty
  Have turn'd the verses o'er,
Traced from the right on linen white
  By mighty seers of yore;

And with one voice the thirty
  Have their glad answer given:
"Go forth, go forth, Lars Porsena—
  Go forth, beloved of heaven!
Go, and return in glory
  To Clusium's royal dome,
And hang round Nurscia's altars
  The golden shields of Rome!"

And now hath every city
  Sent up her tale of men;
The foot are fourscore thousand,
  The horse are thousands ten.
Before the gates of Sutrium
  Is met the great array;
A proud man was Lars Porsena
  Upon the trysting-day.

For all the Etruscan armies
  Were ranged beneath his eye,
And many a banish'd Roman,
  And many a stout ally;
And with a mighty following,
  To join the muster, came
The Tusculan Mamilius,
  Prince of the Latian name.

But by the yellow Tiber
  Was tumult and affright;
From all the spacious champaign
  To Rome men took their flight.
A mile around the city
  The throng stopp'd up the ways;
A fearful sight it was to see
  Through two long nights and days.

For aged folk on crutches,
  And women great with child,
And mothers sobbing over babes
  That hung to them and smiled,
And sick men borne in litters
  High on the necks of slaves,
And troops of sunburn'd husbandmen
  With reaping-hooks and staves,

And droves of mules and asses
  Laden with skins of wine,
And endless flocks of goats and sheep,
  And endless herds of kine,
And endless trains of wagons,
  That creak'd beneath the weight
Of corn-sacks and of household goods,
  Choked every roaring gate.

Now, from the rock Tarpeian,
  Could the wan burghers spy
The line of blazing villages
  Red in the midnight sky.
The fathers of the city,
  They sat all night and day,
For every hour some horseman came
  With tidings of dismay.

To eastward and to westward
  Have spread the Tuscan bands,
Nor house, nor fence, nor dovecote
  In Crustumerium stands.
Verbenna down to Ostia
  Hath wasted all the plain;
Astur hath storm'd Janiculum,
  And the stout guards are slain.

I wis, in all the Senate,
  There was no heart so bold
But sore it ached, and fast it beat,
  When that ill news was told.
Forthwith up rose the consul,
  Up rose the fathers all;
In haste they girded up their gowns,
  And hied them to the wall.

They held a council standing,
  Before the river-gate;
Short time was there, ye may well guess,
  For musing or debate.
Out spake the consul roundly:
  " The bridge must straight go down;
For, since Janiculum is lost,
  Naught else can save the town."

Just then a scout came flying,
  All wild with haste and fear:
" To arms! to arms! sir consul—
  Lars Porsena is here."
On the low hills to westward
  The consul fix'd his eye,
And saw the swarthy storm of dust
  Rise fast along the sky.

And nearer fast and nearer
  Doth the red whirlwind come;
And louder still, and still more loud,
From underneath that rolling cloud,
Is heard the trumpet's war-note proud,
  The trampling and the hum.
And plainly and more plainly
  Now through the gloom appears,

Far to left and far to right,
In broken gleams of dark-blue light,
The long array of helmets bright,
  The long array of spears.

And plainly and more plainly,
  Above that glimmering line,
Now might ye see the banners
  Of twelve fair cities shine;
But the banner of proud Clusium
  Was highest of them all—
The terror of the Umbrian,
  The terror of the Gaul.

And plainly and more plainly
  Now might the burghers know,
By port and vest, by horse and crest,
  Each warlike Lucumo:
There Cilnius of Arretium
  On his fleet roan was seen;
And Astur of the fourfold shield,
Girt with the brand none else may
  wield;
Tolumnius with the belt of gold,
And dark Verbenna from the hold
  By reedy Thrasymene.

Fast by the royal standard,
  O'erlooking all the war,
Lars Porsena of Clusium
  Sat in his ivory car.
By the right wheel rode Mamilius
  Prince of the Latian name;
And by the left false Sextus,
  That wrought the deed of shame.

But when the face of Sextus
  Was seen among the foes,
A yell that rent the firmament
  From all the town arose.
On the housetops was no woman
  But spat toward him and hiss'd,
No child but scream'd out curses,
  And shook its little fist.

But the consul's brow was sad,
  And the consul's speech was low,
And darkly look'd he at the wall,
  And darkly at the foe:
" Their van will be upon us
  Before the bridge goes down;
And if they once may win the bridge,
  What hope to save the town?"

Then out spake brave Horatius,
  The captain of the gate:
"To every man upon this earth
  Death cometh soon or late.
And how can man die better
  Than facing fearful odds
For the ashes of his fathers
  And the temples of his gods?

"And for the tender mother
  Who dandled him to rest,
And for the wife who nurses
  His baby at her breast,
And for the holy maidens
  Who feed the eternal flame,
To save them from false Sextus
  That wrought the deed of shame?

"Hew down the bridge, sir consul,
  With all the speed ye may;
I, with two more to help me,
  Will hold the foe in play.
In yon strait path a thousand
  May well be stopp'd by three.
Now who will stand on either hand,
  And keep the bridge with me?"

Then out spake Spurius Lartius—
  A Ramnian proud was he:
"Lo, I will stand at thy right hand,
  And keep the bridge with thee."
And out spake strong Herminius—
  Of Titian blood was he:
"I will abide on thy left side,
  And keep the bridge with thee."

"Horatius," quoth the consul,
  "As thou sayest, so let it be."
And straight against that great array
  Went forth the dauntless three.
For Romans in Rome's quarrel
  Spared neither land nor gold,
Nor son nor wife, nor limb nor life,
  In the brave days of old.

Then none was for a party—
  Then all were for the state;
Then the great man help'd the poor,
  And the poor man loved the great;
Then lands were fairly portion'd;
  Then spoils were fairly sold:
The Romans were like brothers
  In the brave days of old.

Now Roman is to Roman
  More hateful than a foe,
And the tribunes beard the high,
  And the fathers grind the low.
As we wax hot in faction,
  In battle we wax cold;
Wherefore men fight not as they fought
  In the brave days of old.

Now while the three were tightening
  Their harness on their backs,
The consul was the foremost man
  To take in hand an axe;
And fathers, mix'd with commons,
  Seized hatchet, bar, and crow,
And smote upon the planks above,
  And loosed the props below.

Meanwhile the Tuscan army,
  Right glorious to behold,
Came flashing back the noonday light,
Rank behind rank, like surges bright
  Of a broad sea of gold.
Four hundred trumpets sounded
  A peal of warlike glee,
As that great host with measured tread,
And spears advanced, and ensigns spread,
Roll'd slowly toward the bridge's head,
  Where stood the dauntless three.

The three stood calm and silent,
  And look'd upon the foes,
And a great shout of laughter
  From all the vanguard rose:
And forth three chiefs came spurring
  Before that deep array;
To earth they sprang, their swords they drew,
And lifted high their shields, and flew
  To win the narrow way.

Aunus, from green Tifernum,
  Lord of the hill of vines:
And Seius, whose eight hundred slaves
  Sicken in Ilva's mines;
And Picus, long to Clusium
  Vassal in peace and war,
Who led to fight his Umbrian powers
From that gray crag, where, girt with towers,
The fortress of Nequinum lowers
  O'er the pale waves of Nar.

Stout Lartius hurl'd down Aunus
  Into the stream beneath;
Herminius struck at Seius,
  And clove him to the teeth;
At Picus brave Horatius
  Darted one fiery thrust,
And the proud Umbrian's gilded arms
  Clash'd in the bloody dust.

Then Ocnus of Falerii
  Rush'd on the Roman three;
And Lausulus of Urgo,
  The rover of the sea;
And Aruns of Volsinium,
  Who slew the great wild boar—
The great wild boar that had his den
  Amidst the reeds of Cosa's fen,
And wasted fields, and slaughter'd men,
  Along Albinia's shore.

Herminius smote down Aruns;
  Lartius laid Ocnus low;
Right to the heart of Lausulus
  Horatius sent a blow.
"Lie there," he cried, "fell pirate!
  No more, aghast and pale,
From Ostia's walls the crowd shall mark
The track of thy destroying bark.
No more Campania's hinds shall fly
To woods and caverns when they spy
  Thy thrice-accursèd sail."

But now no sound of laughter
  Was heard among the foes.
A wild and wrathful clamor
  From all the vanguard rose.
Six spears' lengths from the entrance
  Halted that deep array,
And for a space no man came forth
  To win the narrow way.

But, hark! the cry is Astur:
  And lo! the ranks divide;
And the great lord of Luna
  Comes with his stately stride.
Upon his ample shoulders
  Clangs loud the fourfold shield,
And in his hand he shakes the brand
  Which none but he can wield.

He smiled on those bold Romans
  A smile serene and high;
He eyed the flinching Tuscans,
  And scorn was in his eye.

Quoth he, "The she-wolf's litter
  Stand savagely at bay;
But will ye dare to follow,
  If Astur clears the way?"

Then, whirling up his broadsword
  With both hands to the height,
He rush'd against Horatius,
  And smote with all his might.
With shield and blade Horatius
  Right deftly turn'd the blow.
The blow, though turn'd, came yet too nigh,
It miss'd his helm, but gash'd his thigh—
The Tuscans raised a joyful cry
  To see the red blood flow.

He reel'd, and on Herminius
  He lean'd one breathing space;
Then, like a wild-cat mad with wounds,
  Sprang right at Astur's face.
Through teeth, and skull, and helmet,
  So fierce a thrust he sped,
The good sword stood a hand-breadth out
  Behind the Tuscan's head.

And the great lord of Luna
  Fell at that deadly stroke,
As falls on Mount Alvernus
  A thunder-smitten oak.
Far o'er the crashing forest
  The giant arms lie spread;
And the pale augurs, muttering low,
  Gaze on the blasted head.

On Astur's throat Horatius
  Right firmly press'd his heel,
And thrice and four times tugg'd amain,
  Ere he wrench'd out the steel.
"And see," he cried, "the welcome,
  Fair guests, that wait you here!
What noble Lucumo comes next
  To taste our Roman cheer?"

But at his haughty challenge
  A sullen murmur ran,
Mingled with wrath, and shame, and dread,
  Along that glittering van.
There lack'd not men of prowess,
  Nor men of lordly race;
For all Etruria's noblest
  Were round the fatal place.

But all Etruria's noblest
  Felt their hearts sink to see
On the earth the bloody corpses,
  In the path the dauntless three,
And from the ghastly entrance,
  Where those bold Romans stood,
All shrank—like boys who, unaware,
  Ranging the woods to start a hare,
Come to the mouth of the dark lair
Where, growling low, a fierce old bear
  Lies amidst bones and blood.

Was none who would be foremost
  To lead such dire attack:
But those behind cried "Forward!"
  And those before cried "Back!"
And backward now, and forward,
  Wavers the deep array;
And on the tossing sea of steel
To and fro the standards reel
And the victorious trumpet-peal
  Dies fitfully away.

Yet one man for one moment
  Strode out before the crowd;
Well known was he to all the three,
  And they gave him greeting loud:
"Now welcome, welcome, Sextus!
  Now welcome to thy home!
Why dost thou stay, and turn away?
  Here lies the road to Rome."

Thrice look'd he at the city;
  Thrice look'd he at the dead;
And thrice came on in fury,
  And thrice turn'd back in dread;
And, white with fear and hatred,
  Scowl'd at the narrow way
Where, wallowing in a pool of blood,
  The bravest Tuscans lay.

But meanwhile axe and lever
  Have manfully been plied;
And now the bridge hangs tottering
  Above the boiling tide.
"Come back, come back, Horatius!"
  Loud cried the fathers all—
'Back, Lartius! back, Herminius!
  Back, ere the ruin fall!"

Back darted Spurius Lartius;
  Herminius darted back;
And, as they pass'd, beneath their feet
  They felt the timbers crack.

But when they turn'd their faces,
  And on the farther shore
Saw brave Horatius stand alone,
  They would have cross'd once more;

But with a crash like thunder
  Fell every loosen'd beam,
And, like a dam, the mighty wreck
  Lay right athwart the stream;
And a long shout of triumph
  Rose from the walls of Rome,
As to the highest turret-tops
  Was splash'd the yellow foam.

And like a horse unbroken,
  When first he feels the rein,
The furious river struggled hard,
  And toss'd his tawny mane,
And burst the curb, and bounded,
  Rejoicing to be free;
And whirling down, in fierce career,
Battlement, and plank, and pier,
  Rush'd headlong to the sea.

Alone stood brave Horatius,
  But constant still in mind—
Thrice thirty thousand foes before,
  And the broad flood behind.
"Down with him!" cried false Sextus,
  With a smile on his pale face;
"Now yield thee," cried Lars Porsena,
  "Now yield thee to our grace!"

Round turn'd he, as not deigning
  Those craven ranks to see;
Naught spake he to Lars Porsena,
  To Sextus naught spake he;
But he saw on Palatinus
  The white porch of his home;
And he spake to the noble river
  That rolls by the towers of Rome:

"O Tiber! father Tiber!
  To whom the Romans pray,
A Roman's life, a Roman's arms,
  Take thou in charge this day!"
So he spake, and, speaking, sheathed
  The good sword by his side,
And, with his harness on his back,
  Plunged headlong in the tide.

No sound of joy or sorrow
  Was heard from either bank,

But friends and foes in dumb surprise,
With parted lips and straining eyes,
  Stood gazing where he sank;
And when above the surges
  They saw his crest appear,
All Rome sent forth a rapturous cry,
And even the ranks of Tuscany
  Could scarce forbear to cheer.

But fiercely ran the current,
  Swollen high by months of rain,
And fast his blood was flowing;
  And he was sore in pain,
And heavy with his armor,
  And spent with changing blows;
And oft they thought him sinking,
  But still again he rose.

Never, I ween, did swimmer
  In such an evil case,
Struggle through such a raging flood
  Safe to the landing-place;
But his limbs were borne up bravely
  By the brave heart within,
And our good father Tiber
  Bare bravely up his chin.

"Curse on him!" quoth false Sextus,—
  "Will not the villain drown?
But for this stay, ere close of day
  We should have sack'd the town!"
"Heaven help him!" quoth Lars Porsena,
  "And bring him safe to shore;
For such a gallant feat of arms
  Was never seen before."

And now he feels the bottom;
  Now on dry earth he stands;
Now round him throng the fathers
  To press his gory hands;
And now, with shouts and clapping,
  And noise of weeping loud,
He enters through the river-gate,
  Borne by the joyous crowd.

They gave him of the corn-land,
  That was of public right,
As much as two strong oxen
  Could plough from morn till night;
And they made a molten image,
  And set it up on high—
And there it stands unto this day
  To witness if I lie.

It stands in the comitium,
  Plain for all folk to see,—
Horatius in his harness,
  Halting upon one knee;
And underneath is written,
  In letters all of gold,
How valiantly he kept the bridge
  In the brave days of old.

And still his name sounds stirring
  Unto the men of Rome,
As the trumpet-blast that cries to them
  To charge the Volscian home:
And wives still pray to Juno
  For boys with hearts as bold
As his who kept the bridge so well
  In the brave days of old.

And in the nights of winter,
  When the cold north winds blow,
And the long howling of the wolves
  Is heard amidst the snow;
When round the lonely cottage
  Roars loud the tempest's din,
And the good logs of Algidus
  Roar louder yet within;

When the oldest cask is open'd,
  And the largest lamp is lit;
When the chestnuts glow in the embers,
  And the kid turns on the spit;
When young and old in circle
  Around the firebrands close;
When the girls are weaving baskets,
  And the lads are shaping bows;

When the goodman mends his armor,
  And trims his helmet's plume;
When the goodwife's shuttle merrily
  Goes flashing through the loom;
With weeping and with laughter
  Still is the story told,
How well Horatius kept the bridge
  In the brave days of old.
THOMAS BABINGTON MACAULAY.

PERICLES AND ASPASIA.

THIS was the ruler of the land
  When Athens was the land of fame;
This was the light that led the band
  When each was like a living flame;
The centre of earth's noblest ring,
Of more than men the more than king.

Yet not by fetter, nor by spear,
  His sovereignty was held or won;
Fear'd,—but alone as freemen fear,
  Loved,—but as freemen love alone;
He waved the sceptre o'er his kind
By Nature's first great title—mind!

Resistless words were on his tongue;
  Then eloquence first flash'd below;
Full arm'd to life the portent sprung—
  Minerva from the Thunderer's brow!
And his the sole, the sacred hand
That shook her ægis o'er the land.

And throned immortal, by his side,
  A woman sits, with eye sublime,—
Aspasia, all his spirit's bride;
  But, if their solemn love were crime,
Pity the beauty and the sage,—
Their crime was in their darken'd age.

He perish'd, but his wreath was won,—
  He perish'd on his height of fame;
Then sank the cloud on Athens' sun,
  Yet still she conquer'd in his name.
Fill'd with his soul, she could not die;
Her conquest was posterity!
                    GEORGE CROLY.

ANTONY AND CLEOPATRA.

I AM dying, Egypt, dying,
  Ebbs the crimson life-tide fast,
And the dark Plutonian shadows
  Gather on the evening blast;
Let thine arms, O Queen, enfold me,
  Hush thy sobs and bow thine ear;
Listen to the great heart-secrets,
  Thou, and thou alone, must hear.

Though my scarr'd and veteran legions
  Bear their eagles high no more,
And my wreck'd and scatter'd galleys
  Strew dark Actium's fatal shore,
Though no glittering guards surround me,
  Prompt to do their master's will,
I must perish like a Roman,
  Die the great Triumvir still.

Let not Cæsar's servile minions
  Mock the lion thus laid low;
'Twas no foeman's arm that fell'd him,
  'Twas his own that struck the blow;

His who, pillow'd on thy bosom,
  Turn'd aside from glory's ray,
His who, drunk with thy caresses,
  Madly threw a world away.

Should the base plebeian rabble
  Dare assail my name at Rome,
Where my noble spouse, Octavia,
  Weeps within her widow'd home,
Seek her; say the gods bear witness—
  Altars, augurs, circling wings—
That her blood, with mine commingled,
  Yet shall mount the throne of kings.

As for thee, star-eyed Egyptian,
  Glorious sorceress of the Nile,
Light the path to Stygian horrors
  With the splendors of thy smile.
Give the Cæsar crowns and arches,
  Let his brow the laurel twine;
I can scorn the Senate's triumphs,
  Triumphing in love like thine.

I am dying, Egypt, dying;
  Hark! the insulting foeman's cry.
They are coming! quick, my falchion,
  Let me front them ere I die.
Ah! no more amid the battle
  Shall my heart exulting swell;
Isis and Osiris guard thee!
  Cleopatra, Rome, farewell!
                    WILLIAM HAINES LYTLE.

THE LAMENTATION OF DON RODERICK.

THE hosts of Don Rodrigo were scatter'd
    in dismay,
When lost was the eighth battle, nor heart
    nor hope had they;
He, when he saw that field was lost, and
    all his hope was flown,
He turn'd him from his flying host, and
    took his way alone.

His horse was bleeding, blind, and lame—
    he could no farther go;
Dismounted, without path or aim, the king
    stepp'd to and fro:
It was a sight of pity to look on Roderick,
For, sore athirst and hungry, he stagger'd
    faint and sick.

All stain'd and strew'd with dust and blood,
    like to some smouldering brand
Pluck'd from the flame, Rodrigo show'd:
    his sword was in his hand,
But it was hack'd into a saw of dark and
    purple tint;
His jewell'd mail had many a flaw, his
    helmet many a dint.

He climb'd unto a hill-top, the highest he
    could see—
Thence all about of that wide rout his
    last long look took he;
He saw his royal banners, where they lay
    drench'd and torn,
He heard the cry of victory, the Arab's
    shout of scorn.

He look'd for the brave captains that led
    the hosts of Spain,
But all were fled except the dead, and who
    could count the slain?
Where'er his eye could wander, all bloody
    was the plain,
And, while thus he said, the tears he shed
    ran down his cheeks like rain:—

" Last night I was the king of Spain—to-
    day no king am I;
Last night fair castles held my train—to-
    night where shall I lie?
Last night a hundred pages did serve me
    on the knee,—
To-night not one I call mine own:—not
    one pertains to me.

" Oh, luckless, luckless was the hour, and
    cursèd was the day,
When I was born to have the power of
    this great seniory!
Unhappy me that I should see the sun go
    down to-night!
O Death, why now so slow art thou, why
    fearest thou to smite?"

(From the Spanish.)
JOHN GIBSON LOCKHART.

HARMOSAN.

Now the third and fatal conflict for the
    Persian throne was done,
And the Moslem's fiery valor had the
    crowning victory won.

Harmosan, the last and boldest the invader
    to defy,
Captive, overborne by numbers, they were
    bringing forth to die.

Then exclaim'd that noble captive: " Lo,
    I perish in my thirst;
Give me but one drink of water, and let
    then arrive the worst!"

In his hand he took the goblet: but a while
    the draught forbore,
Seeming doubtfully the purpose of the
    foeman to explore.

Well might then have paused the bravest
    —for around him angry foes
With a hedge of naked weapons did that
    lonely man enclose.

" But what fearest thou?" cried the caliph,
    " is it, friend, a secret blow?
Fear it not! our gallant Moslems no such
    treacherous dealing know.

" Thou may'st quench thy thirst securely,
    for thou shalt not die before
Thou hast drunk that cup of water—this
    reprieve is thine—no more!"

Quick the satrap dash'd the goblet down
    to earth with ready hand,
And the liquid sank for ever, lost amid the
    burning sand.

" Thou hast said that mine my life is, till
    the water of that cup
I have drain'd; then bid thy servants that
    spill'd water gather up!"

For a moment stood the caliph as by doubt-
    ful passions stirr'd—
Then exclaim'd, " For ever sacred must
    remain a monarch's word.

" Bring another cup, and straightway to
    the noble Persian give:
Drink, I said before, and perish—now I
    bid thee drink and live!"

RICHARD CHENEVIX TRENCH.

CRESCENTIUS.

I LOOK'D upon his brow; no sign
    Of guilt or fear was there;
He stood as proud by that death-shrine
    As even o'er despair
He had a power. In his eye
    There was a quenchless energy,
A spirit that could dare
The deadliest form that death could take,
And dare it for the daring's sake.

He stood, the fetters on his hand;
    He raised them haughtily;
And had that grasp been on the brand,
    It could not wave on high
With freer pride than it waved now.
    Around he look'd with changeless brow
On many a torture nigh;
The rack, the chain, the axe, the wheel,
And, worst of all, his own red steel.

I saw him once before; he rode
    Upon a coal-black steed,
And tens of thousands throng'd the road,
    And bade their warrior speed.
His helm, his breast-plate, were of gold,
    And graved with many a dent, that told
Of many a soldier's deed;
The sun shone on his sparkling mail,
And danced his snow-plume on the gale.

But now he stood chain'd and alone,
    The headsman by his side,
The plume, the helm, the charger gone;
    The sword which had defied
The mightiest lay broken near;
    And yet no sign or sound of fear
Came from that lip of pride,
And never king's or conqueror's brow
Wore higher look than his did now.

He bent beneath the headsman's stroke
    With an uncover'd eye;
A wild shout from the numbers broke
    Who throng'd to see him die.
It was a people's loud acclaim,
    The voice of anger and of shame,
A nation's funeral cry,
Rome's wail above her only son,
Her patriot, and her latest one.
        LÆTITIA ELIZABETH LANDON MACLEAN.

THE VENGEANCE OF MUDARA.

To the chase goes Rodrigo, with hound and with hawk;
But what game he desires is reveal'd in his talk:
"Oh, in vain have I slaughter'd the Infants of Lara:
There's an heir in his hall,—there's the bastard Mudara—
There's the son of the renegade, spawn of Mahoun—
If I meet with Mudara, my spear brings him down."

While Rodrigo rides on in the heat of his wrath,
A stripling, arm'd cap-à-pie, crosses his path:
"Good morrow, young esquire." "Good morrow, old knight."
"Will you ride with our party and share our delight?"
"Speak your name, courteous stranger," the stripling replied;
"Speak your name and your lineage, ere with you I ride."

"My name is Rodrigo," thus answer'd the knight;
"Of the line of old Lara, though barr'd from my right,
For the kinsman of Salas proclaims for the heir
Of our ancestor's castles and forestries fair
A bastard, a renegade's offspring—Mudara—
Whom I'll send, if I can, to the Infants of Lara."

"I behold thee, disgrace to thy lineage!—with joy
I behold thee, thou murderer!" answer'd the boy;
"The bastard you curse, you behold him in me,
But his brothers' avenger that bastard shall be!
Draw! for I am the renegade's offspring, Mudara;
We shall see who inherits the life-blood of Lara."

"I am arm'd for the forest-chase, not for
    the fight;
Let me go for my shield and my sword,"
    cries the knight.
"Now the mercy you dealt to my brothers
    of old,
Be the hope of that mercy the comfort you
    hold;
Die, foeman to Sancha,—die, traitor to
    Lara!"
As he spake, there was blood on the spear
    of Mudara.
(From the Spanish.)
JOHN GIBSON LOCKHART.

THE BARD.

A PINDARIC ODE.

"RUIN seize thee, ruthless King!
  Confusion on thy banners wait!
Tho' fann'd by Conquest's crimson wing,
  They mock the air with idle state.
Helm, nor haüberk's twisted mail,
Nor e'en thy virtues, tyrant, shall avail
To save thy secret soul from nightly fears,
From Cambria's curse, from Cambria's
    tears!"
—Such were the sounds that o'er the
    crested pride
  Of the first Edward scatter'd wild dis-
    may,
  As down the steep of Snowdon's shaggy
    side
He wound with toilsome march his long
    array.
Stout Glo'ster stood aghast in speechless
    trance;
"To arms!" cried Mortimer, and couch'd
    his quiv'ring lance.

On a rock whose haughty brow
Frowns o'er old Conway's foaming flood,
  Robed in the sable garb of woe,
With haggard eyes the poet stood:
(Loose his beard and hoary hair
Stream'd like a meteor to the troubled air),
And with a master's hand and prophet's
    fire
Struck the deep sorrows of his lyre:
"Hark, how each giant oak and desert cave
  Sighs to the torrent's awful voice be-
    neath!

O'er thee, O King! their hundred arms they
    wave,
  Revenge on thee in hoarser murmurs
    breathe;
Vocal no more, since Cambria's fatal day,
To high-born Hoel's harp, or soft Llewel-
    lyn's lay.

"Cold is Cadwallo's tongue,
  That hush'd the stormy main:
Brave Urien sleeps upon his craggy bed:
  Mountains, ye mourn in vain
  Modred, whose magic song
Made huge Plinlimmon bow his cloud-topt
    head.
On dreary Arvon's shore they lie
Smear'd with gore and ghastly pale:
Far, far aloof the affrighted ravens sail;
  The famish'd eagle screams, and passes
    by.
Dear lost companions of my tuneful art,
  Dear as the light that visits these sad
    eyes,
  Dear as the ruddy drops that warm my
    heart,
  Ye died amidst your dying country's
    cries—
No more I weep. They do not sleep.
  On yonder cliffs, a grisly band,
I see them sit; they linger yet,
  Avengers of their native land:
With me in dreadful harmony they join,
And weave with bloody hands the tissue
    of thy line.

"Weave the warp and weave the woof,
  The winding-sheet of Edward's race:
Give ample room and verge enough
  The characters of hell to trace.
Mark the year and mark the night
When Severn shall re-echo with affright
The shrieks of death thro' Berkley's roof
    that ring,
Shrieks of an agonizing king!
  She-wolf of France, with unrelenting
    fangs,
That tear'st the bowels of thy mangled
    mate,
  From thee be born, who o'er thy country
    hangs
The scourge of Heaven! What terrors
    round him wait!

Amazement in his van, with flight com-
bined,
And Sorrow's faded form, and Solitude
behind.

"Mighty victor, mighty lord,
Low on his funeral couch he lies!
No pitying heart, no eye, afford
A tear to grace his obsequies.
Is the sable warrior fled?
Thy son is gone. He rests among the
dead.
The swarm that in thy noontide beam
were born?
—Gone to salute the rising morn.
Fair laughs the Morn, and soft the zephyr
blows,
While proudly riding o'er the azure
realm
In gallant trim the gilded vessel goes:
Youth on the prow, and Pleasure at the
helm:
Regardless of the sweeping Whirlwind's
sway,
That hush'd in grim repose expects his
evening prey.

"Fill high the sparkling bowl,
The rich repast prepare;
Reft of a crown, he yet may share the
feast:
Close by the regal chair
Fell Thirst and Famine scowl
A baleful smile upon their baffled
guest.
Heard ye the din of battle bray,
Lance to lance, and horse to horse?
Long years of havoc urge their destined
course,
And thro' the kindred squadrons mow
their way.
Ye towers of Julius, London's lasting
shame,
With many a foul and midnight murder
fed,
Revere his Consort's faith, his Father's
fame,
And spare the meek usurper's holy head.
Above, below, the rose of snow,
Twined with her blushing foe, we
spread:
The bristled boar in infant gore
Wallows beneath the thorny shade.

Now, brothers, bending o'er the accursèd
loom,
Stamp we our vengeance deep, and ratify
his doom.

"Edward, lo! to sudden fate
(Weave we the woof. The thread is
spun).
Half of thy heart we consecrate.
(The web is wove. The work is done.)
Stay, oh, stay! nor thus forlorn
Leave me unbless'd, unpitied, here to
mourn:
In yon bright track that fires the western
skies
They melt, they vanish from my eyes.
But oh, what solemn scenes on Snowdon's
height
Descending slow their glittering skirts
unroll?
Visions of glory, spare my aching sight!
Ye unborn ages, crowd not on my soul!
No more our long-lost Arthur we bewail:—
All hail, ye genuine kings! Britannia's
issue, hail!

"Girt with many a baron bold
Sublime their starry fronts they rear;
And gorgeous dames, and statesmen old
In bearded majesty, appear.
In the midst a form divine!
Her eye proclaims her of the Briton-line:
Her lion-port, her awe-commanding face
Attemper'd sweet to virgin grace.
What strings symphonious tremble in the
air,
What strains of vocal transport round
her play!
Hear from the grave, great Taliessin,
hear;
They breathe a soul to animate thy clay.
Bright Rapture calls, and soaring as she
sings,
Waves in the eye of Heaven her many-
color'd wings.

"The verse adorn again
Fierce War and faithful Love,
And Truth severe by fairy Fiction drest.
In buskin'd measures move
Pale Grief, and pleasing Pain,
With Horror, tyrant of the throbbing
breast.

A voice as of the cherub-choir
  Gales from blooming Eden bear,
  And distant warblings lessen on my ear
That lost in long futurity expire.
Fond impious man, think'st thou yon sanguine cloud
  Raised by thy breath has quench'd the orb of day?
To-morrow he repairs the golden flood
  And warms the nations with redoubled ray.
Enough for me: with joy I see
  The diff'rent doom our fates assign:
Be thine Despair and sceptred Care;
  To triumph and to die are mine."
—He spoke, and headlong from the mountain's height
Deep in the roaring tide he plunged to endless night.
                THOMAS GRAY.

BANNOCKBURN.

SCOTS, wha hae wi' Wallace bled—
Scots, wham Bruce has aften led—
Welcome to your gory bed,
    Or to victorie!

Now's the day and now's the hour;
See the front o' battle lower;
See approach proud Edward's power—
    Chains and slaverie!

Wha will be a traitor knave?
Wha can fill a coward's grave?
Wha sae base as be a slave?
    Let him turn and flee!

Wha for Scotland's king and law
Freedom's sword will strongly draw,
Freeman stand or freeman fa'—
    Let him on wi' me!

By oppression's woes and pains!
By your sons in servile chains!
We will drain our dearest veins,
    But they shall be free!

Lay the proud usurpers low!
Tyrants fall in every foe!
Liberty's in every blow!
    Let us do, or die!
                ROBERT BURNS.

A VERY MOURNFUL BALLAD.

THE Moorish king rides up and down
Through Granada's royal town;
From Elvira's gates to those
Of Bivarambla on he goes.
    Woe is me, Alhama!

Letters to the monarch tell
How Alhama's city fell:
In the fire the scroll he threw,
And the messenger he slew.
    Woe is me, Alhama!

He quits his mule, and mounts his horse,
And through the street directs his course;
Through the street of Zacatin
To the Alhambra spurring in.
    Woe is me, Alhama!

When the Alhambra walls he gain'd,
On the moment he ordain'd
That the trumpet straight should sound
With the silver clarion round.
    Woe is me, Alhama!

And when the hollow drums of war
Beat the loud alarm afar,
That the Moors of town and plain
Might answer to the martial strain,
    Woe is me, Alhama!

Then the Moors, by this aware
That bloody Mars recall'd them there,
One by one, and two by two,
To a mighty squadron grew.
    Woe is me, Alhama!

Out then spake an aged Moor
In these words the king before:
"Wherefore call on us, O king?
What may mean this gathering?"
    Woe is me, Alhama!

"Friends! ye have, alas! to know
Of a most disastrous blow,
That the Christians, stern and bold,
Have obtain'd Alhama's hold."
    Woe is me, Alhama!

Out then spake old Alfaqui,
With his beard so white to see,
"Good king, thou art justly served,
Good king, this thou hast deserved.
    Woe is me, Alhama!

"By thee were slain, in evil hour,
The Abencerrage, Granada's flower;
And strangers were received by thee
Of Cordova the chivalry.
  Woe is me, Alhama!

"And for this, O king! is sent
On thee a double chastisement,
Thee and thine, thy crown and realm,
One last wreck shall overwhelm.
  Woe is me, Alhama!

"He who holds no laws in awe,
He must perish by the law;
And Granada must be won,
And thyself with her undone."
  Woe is me, Alhama!

Fire flash'd from out the old Moor's eyes,
The monarch's wrath began to rise,
Because he answer'd, and because
He spake exceeding well of laws.
  Woe is me, Alhama!

"There is no law to say such things
As may disgust the ear of kings:"—
Thus, snorting with his choler, said
The Moorish king, and doom'd him dead.
  Woe is me, Alhama!

Moor Alfaqui! Moor Alfaqui!
Though thy beard so hoary be,
The king hath sent to have thee seized,
For Alhama's loss displeased.
  Woe is me, Alhama!

And to fix thy head upon
High Alhambra's loftiest stone;
That this for thee should be the law,
And others tremble when they saw.
  Woe is me, Alhama!

"Cavalier! and man of worth!
Let these words of mine go forth;
Let the Moorish monarch know,
That to him I nothing owe:
  Woe is me, Alhama!

"But on my soul Alhama weighs,
And on my inmost spirit preys;
And if the king his land hath lost,
Yet others may have lost the most.
  Woe is me, Alhama!

"Sires have lost their children, wives
Their lords, and valiant men their lives;
One what best his love might claim
Hath lost, another wealth or fame.
  Woe is me, Alhama!

"I lost a damsel in that hour,
Of all the land the loveliest flower;
Doubloons a hundred I would pay,
And think her ransom cheap that day."
  Woe is me, Alhama!

And as these things the old Moor said,
They sever'd from the trunk his head;
And to the Alhambra's wall with speed
'Twas carried, as the king decreed.
  Woe is me, Alhama!

And men and infants therein weep
Their loss, so heavy and so deep;
Granada's ladies, all she rears
Within her walls, burst into tears.
  Woe is me, Alhama!

And from the windows o'er the walls
The sable web of mourning falls;
The king weeps as a woman o'er
His loss, for it is much and sore.
  Woe is me, Alhama!
    (From the Spanish.)
    LORD BYRON.

THE LORD OF BUTRAGO.

"YOUR horse is faint, my King—my Lord!
  your gallant horse is sick—
His limbs are torn, his breast is gored, on
  his eye the film is thick;
Mount, mount on mine, oh, mount apace,
  I pray thee, mount and fly!
Or in my arms I'll lift Your Grace—their
  trampling hoofs are nigh!

"My King—my King! you're wounded
  sore—the blood runs from your feet;
But only lay a hand before, and I'll lift
  you to your seat:
Mount, Juan, for they gather fast!—I hear
  their coming cry—
Mount, mount, and ride for jeopardy—I'll
  save you though I die!

"Stand, noble steed! this hour of need—
    be gentle as a lamb:
I'll kiss the foam from off thy mouth—thy
    master dear I am—
Mount, Juan, mount! whate'er betide,
    away the bridle fling,
And plunge the rowels in his side.—My
    horse shall save my King!

"Nay, never speak; my sires, Lord King,
    received their land from yours,
And joyfully their blood shall spring, so
    be it thine secures:
If I should fly, and thou, my King, be
    found among the dead,
How could I stand 'mong gentlemen, such
    scorn on my gray head?

"Castile's proud dames shall never point
    the finger of disdain,
And say there's ONE that ran away when
    our good lords were slain!—
I leave Diego in your care—you'll fill his
    father's place:
Strike, strike the spur, and never spare—
    God's blessing on Your Grace!"

So spake the brave Montañez, Butrago's
    lord was he;
And turn'd him to the coming host in
    steadfastness and glee;
He flung himself among them, as they
    came down the hill—
He died, God wot! but not before his
    sword had drunk its fill.
(From the Spanish.)
JOHN GIBSON LOCKHART.

MAKE WAY FOR LIBERTY.

"MAKE way for liberty!"—he cried;
Made way for liberty, and died!

In arms the Austrian phalanx stood,
A living wall, a human wood!
A wall, where every conscious stone
Seem'd to its kindred thousands grown;
A rampart all assaults to bear,
Till time to dust their frames should wear;
A wood, like that enchanted grove
In which with fiends Rinaldo strove,
Where every silent tree possess'd
A spirit prison'd in its breast,
Which the first stroke of coming strife
Would startle into hideous life;
So dense, so still, the Austrians stood,
A living wall, a human wood!
Impregnable their front appears,
All horrent with projected spears,
Whose polish'd points before them shine,
From flank to flank, one brilliant line,
Bright as the breakers' splendors run
Along the billows, to the Sun.

Opposed to these, a hovering band
Contended for their native land:
Peasants, whose new-found strength had
    broke
From manly necks the ignoble yoke,
And forged their fetters into swords,
On equal terms to fight their lords:
And what insurgent rage had gain'd,
In many a mortal fray maintain'd;
Marshall'd once more at Freedom's call,
They came to conquer or to fall,
Where he who conquer'd, he who fell,
Was deem'd a dead or living Tell!
Such virtue had that patriot breathed,
So to the soil his soul bequeathed,
That wheresoe'er his arrows flew,
Heroes in his own likeness grew,
And warriors sprang from every sod
Which his awakening footstep trod,

And now the work of life and death
Hung on the passing of a breath;
The fire of conflict burnt within,
The battle trembled to begin:
Yet while the Austrians held their ground,
Point for attack was nowhere found.
Where'er the impatient Switzers gazed,
The unbroken line of lances blazed;
That line 'twere suicide to meet,
And perish at their tyrants' feet,—
How could they rest within their graves,
And leave their homes the homes of slaves?
Would they not feel their children tread
With clanging chains above their head?

It must not be: this day, this hour,
Annihilates the oppressor's power;
All Switzerland is in the field,
She will not fly, she cannot yield—
She must not fall; her better fate
Here gives her an immortal date.

Few were the number she could boast;
But every freeman was a host,
And felt as though himself were he
On whose sole arm hung victory.

It did depend on *one*, indeed;
Behold him—Arnold Winkelried!
There sounds not to the trump of fame
The echo of a nobler name.
Unmark'd, he stood amid the throng,
In rumination deep and long,
Till you might see, with sudden grace,
The very thought come o'er his face,
And by the motion of his form
Anticipate the bursting storm;
And by the uplifting of his brow
Tell where the bolt would strike, and how.

But 'twas no sooner thought than done,
The field was in a moment won:—

"Make way for Liberty!" he cried,
Then ran, with arms extended wide,
As if his dearest friend to clasp;
Ten spears he swept within his grasp.

"Make way for Liberty!" he cried:
Their keen points met from side to side;
He bow'd amongst them like a tree,
And thus made way for Liberty.

Swift to the breach his comrades fly;
"Make way for Liberty!" they cry,
And through the Austrian phalanx dart,
As rush'd the spears through Arnold's heart;
While, instantaneous as his fall,
Rout, ruin, panic scatter'd all:
An earthquake could not overthrow
A city with a surer blow.

Thus Switzerland again was free:
Thus death made way for liberty!
JAMES MONTGOMERY.

THE BALLAD OF AGINCOURT.

FAIR stood the wind for France
When we our sails advance,
Nor now to prove our chance
　　Longer will tarry;
But putting to the main,
At Kaux, the mouth of Seine,
With all his martial train,
　　Landed King Harry.

And taking many a fort,
Furnish'd in warlike sort,
March'd toward Agincourt
　　In happy hour—
Skirmishing day by day
With those that stopp'd his way,
Where the French gen'ral lay
　　With all his power,

Which in his height of pride,
King Henry to deride,
His ransom to provide
　　To the king sending;
Which he neglects the while,
As from a nation vile,
Yet, with an angry smile,
　　Their fall portending.

And turning to his men,
Quoth our brave Henry then:
Though they to one be ten,
　　Be not amazed;
Yet have we well begun—
Battles so bravely won
Have ever to the sun
　　By fame been raised.

And for myself, quoth he,
This my full rest shall be;
England, ne'er mourn for me,
　　Nor more esteem me.
Victor I will remain,
Or on this earth lie slain;
Never shall she sustain
　　Loss to redeem me.

Poitiers and Cressy tell,
When most their pride did swell,
Under our swords they fell;
　　No less our skill is
Than when our grandsire great,
Claiming the regal seat,
By many a warlike feat
　　Lopp'd the French lilies.

The duke of York so dread
The eager vaward led;
With the main Henry sped,
　　Amongst his henchmen.
Excester had the rear—
A braver man not there:
O Lord! how hot they were
　　On the false Frenchmen!

They now to fight are gone;
Armor on armor shone;
Drum now to drum did groan—
　　To hear was wonder;
That with the cries they make
The very earth did shake;
Trumpet to trumpet spake,
　　Thunder to thunder.

Well it thine age became,
O noble Erpingham!
Which did the signal aim
　　To our hid forces;
When, from a meadow by,
Like a storm suddenly,
The English archery
　　Struck the French horses,

With Spanish yew so strong,
Arrows a cloth-yard long,
That like to serpents stung,
　　Piercing the weather;
None from his fellow starts,
But playing manly parts,
And like true English hearts,
　　Stuck close together.

When down their bows they threw,
And forth their bilbows drew,
And on the French they flew,
　　Not one was tardy:
Arms were from shoulders sent;
Scalps to the teeth were rent;
Down the French peasants went;
　　Our men were hardy.

This while our noble king,
His broadsword brandishing,
Down the French host did ding,
　　As to o'erwhelm it;
And many a deep wound lent,
His arms with blood besprent,
And many a cruel dent
　　Bruised his helmet.

Glo'ster, that duke so good,
Next of the royal blood,
For famous England stood,
　　With his brave brother—
Clarence, in steel so bright,
Though but a maiden knight,
Yet in that furious fight
　　Scarce such another.

Warwick in blood did wade;
Oxford the foe invade,
And cruel slaughter made,
　　Still as they ran up.
Suffolk his axe did ply;
Beaumont and Willoughby
Bare them right doughtily,
　　Ferrers and Fanhope.

Upon Saint Crispin's day
Fought was this noble fray,
Which fame did not delay
　　To England to carry;
Oh, when shall Englishmen
With such acts fill a pen,
Or England breed again
　　Such a King Harry?
　　　　　　　MICHAEL DRAYTON.

THE BALLAD OF CHEVY-CHACE.

GOD prosper long our noble king,
　　Our lives and safetyes all;
A woefull hunting once there did
　　In Chevy-Chace befall;

To drive the deere with hound and horne,
　　Erle Percy took his way,
The child may rue that is unborne,
　　The hunting of that day.

The stout Erle of Northumberland
　　A vow to God did make,
His pleasure in the Scottish woods
　　Three summers days to take;

The cheefest harts in Chevy-Chace
　　To kill and beare away.
These tydings to Erle Douglas came,
　　In Scotland where he lay:

Who sent Erle Percy present word,
　　He would prevent his sport.
The English Erle, not fearing that,
　　Did to the woods resort,

With fifteen hundred bow-men bold;
　　All chosen men of might,
Who knew full well in time of neede
　　To ayme their shafts aright.

The gallant greyhounds swiftly ran,
　　To chase the fallow deere:
On Munday they began to hunt,
　　Ere daylight did appeare;

And long before high noone they had
  An hundred fat buckes slaine;
Then having dined, the drovyers went
  To rouze the deare againe.

The bow-men muster'd on the hills,
  Well able to endure;
And all their rear, with speciall care,
  That day was guarded sure.

The hounds ran swiftly through the woods,
  The nimble deere to take,
That with their cryes the hills and dales
  An eccho shrill did make.

Lord Percy to the quarry went,
  To view the slaughter'd deere;
Quoth he, Erle Douglas promisèd
  This day to meet me heere:

But if I thought he wold not come,
  Noe longer wold I stay.
With that, a brave younge gentleman
  Thus to the Erle did say:

Loe, yonder doth Erle Douglas come,
  His men in armour bright;
Full twenty hundred Scottish speres
  All marching in our sight;

All men of pleasant Tivydale,
  Fast by the river Tweede:
O cease your sports, Erle Percy said,
  And take your bowes with speede.

And now with me, my countrymen,
  Your courage forth advance;
For there was never champion yett
  In Scotland or in France,

That ever did on horsebacke come,
  But if my hap it were,
I durst encounter man for man,
  With him to break a spere.

Erle Douglas on his milke-white steede,
  Most like a baron bold,
Rode formost of his company,
  Whose armour shone like gold.

Show me, sayd hee, whose men you bee,
  That hunt soe boldly heere,
That, without my consent, doe chase
  And kill my fallow-deere.

The first man that did answer make
  Was noble Percy hee;
Who sayd, Wee list not to declare,
  Nor shew whose men we bee.

Yet wee will spend our deerest blood,
  Thy cheefest harts to slay.
Then Douglas swore a solempne oathe,
  And thus in rage did say,

Ere thus I will out-bravèd bee,
  One of us two shall dye:
I know thee well, an erle thou art;
  Lord Percy, soe am I.

But trust me, Percy, pittye it were
  And great offence to kill
Any of these our guiltlesse men,
  For they have done no ill.

Let thou and I the battell trye,
  And set our men aside.
Accurst bee he, Erle Percy sayd,
  By whom this is deny'd.

Then stept a gallant squier forth,
  Witherington was his name,
Who said, I wold not have it told
  To Henry our king for shame,

That ere my captaine fought on foote
  And I stood looking on.
You bee two erles, sayd Witherinton,
  And I a squier alone:

Ile doe the best that doe I may,
  While I have power to stand:
While I have power to weeld my sword,
  Ile fight with heart and hand.

Our English archers bent their bowes,
  Their hearts were good and trew;
Att the first flight of arrowes sent,
  Full four-score Scots they slew.

[Yet bides Earl Douglas on the bent,
  As Chieftan stout and good.
As valiant Captain, all unmoved
  The shock he firmly stood.

His host he parted had in three,
  As Leader ware and try'd,
And soon his spearmen on their foes
  Bare down on every side.

To drive the deere with hound and horne,
  Douglas bade on the bent;
Two captaines moved with mickle might
  Their speares to shivers went.

Throughout the English archery
  They dealt full many a wound:
But still our valiant Englishmen
  All firmly kept their ground:

And throwing strait their bows away,
  They grasp'd their swords so bright:
And now sharp blows, a heavy shower,
  On shields and helmets light.]

They closed full fast on everye side,
  Noe slacknes there was found;
And many a gallant gentleman
  Lay gasping on the ground.

O Christ! it was a griefe to see,
  And likewise for to heare,
The cries of men lying in their gore,
  And scatter'd here and there.

At last these two stout erles did meet,
  Like captaines of great might:
Like lyons wood, they layd on lode,
  And made a cruell fight:

They fought untill they both did sweat,
  With swords of temper'd steele;
Until the blood, like drops of rain,
  They trickling downe did feele.

Yeeld thee, Lord Percy, Douglas sayd;
  In faith I will thee bringe,
Where thou shalt high advancèd bee
  By James our Scottish king:

Thy ransome I will freely give,
  And this report of thee,
Thou art the most courageous knight
  That ever I did see.

Noe, Douglas, quoth Erle Percy then,
  Thy proffer I doe scorne;
I will not yeelde to any Scott,
  That ever yett was borne.

With that, there came an arrow keene
  Out of an English bow,
Which struck Erle Douglas to the heart,
  A deepe and deadlye blow:

Who never spake more words than these,
  Fight on, my merry men all;
For why, my life is at an end;
  Lord Percy sees my fall.

Then leaving liffe, Erle Percy tooke
  The dead man by the hand;
And said, Erle Douglas, for thy life
  Wold I had lost my land.

O Christ! my verry hert doth bleed
  With sorrow for thy sake;
For sure, a more redoubted knight
  Mischance cold never take.

A knight amongst the Scotts there was,
  Which saw Erle Douglas dye,
Who streight in wrath did vow revenge
  Upon the Lord Percye:

Sir Hugh Mountgomery was he call'd,
  Who with a speare most bright,
Well-mounted on a gallant steed,
  Ran fiercely through the fight;

And past the English archers all,
  Without all dread or feare;
And through Erle Percyes body then
  He thrust his hatefull speare;

With such a vehement force and might
  He did his body gore,
The staff ran through the other side
  A large cloth-yard, and more.

So thus did both these nobles dye,
  Whose courage none could staine·
An English archer then perceived
  The noble erle was slaine;

He had a bow bent in his hand,
  Made of a trusty tree;
An arrow of a cloth-yard long
  Up to the head drew hee:

Against Sir Hugh Mountgomerye,
  So right the shaft he sett,
The gray goose-wing that was thereon,
  In his harts blood was wett.

This fight did last from break of day
  Till setting of the sun,
For when they rung the evening bell,
  The battle scarce was done.

With stout Erle Percy, there was slaine
  Sir John of Egerton,
Sir Robert Ratcliff, and Sir John,
  Sir James that bold barrón;

And with Sir George and stout Sir James,
  Both knights of good account,
Good Sir Ralph Raby there was slaine,
  Whose prowesse did surmount.

For Witherington needs must I wayle
  As one in doleful dumpes,
For when his legs were smitten off,
  He fought upon his stumpes.

And with Erle Douglas, there was slaine
  Sir Hugh Mountgomerye,
Sir Charles Murray, that from the feeld
  One foote wold never flee.

Sir Charles Murray, of Ratcliff, too,
  His sisters sonne was hee;
Sir David Lamb, so well esteem'd,
  Yet savèd cold not bee.

And the Lord Maxwell in like case
  Did with Erle Douglas dye;
Of twenty hundred Scottish speres,
  Scarce fifty-five did flye.

Of fifteen hundred Englishmen,
  Went home but fifty-three;
The rest were slaine in Chevy-Chace,
  Under the greene woode tree.

Next day did many widowes come,
  Their husbands to bewayle;
They washt their wounds in brinish teares,
  But all wold not prevayle.

Theyr bodies, bathed in purple gore,
  They bare with them away,
They kist them dead a thousand times,
  Ere they were cladd in clay.

The newes was brought to Eddenborrow,
  Where Scotlands king did raigne,
That brave Erle Douglas suddenlye
  Was with an arrow slaine.

O heavy newes, King James did say,
  Scotland may witnesse bee,
I have not any captaine more
  Of such account as hee.

Like tydings to King Henry came,
  Within as short a space,
That Percy of Northumberland
  Was slaine in Chevy-Chace.

Now God be with him, said our king,
  Sith it will noe better bee;
I trust I have within my realme
  Five hundred as good as he;

Yett shall not Scotts nor Scotland say,
  But I will vengeance take;
Ile be revengèd on them all,
  For brave Erle Percyes sake.

This vow full well the king perform'd
  After, at Humbledowne;
In one day fifty knights were slayne,
  With lords of great renowne;

And of the rest, of small account,
  Did many thousands dye;
Thus endeth the hunting of Chevy-Chace.
  Made by the Erle Percye.

God save our king, and bless this land
  With plentye, joy, and peace;
And grant henceforth, that foule debate
  'Twixt noblemen may cease.
                    AUTHOR UNKNOWN.

EDINBURGH AFTER FLODDEN.

NEWS of battle!—news of battle!
  Hark! 'tis ringing down the street;
And the archways and the pavement
  Bear the clang of hurrying feet.
News of battle! who hath brought it?
  News of triumph? Who should bring
Tidings from our noble army,
  Greetings from our gallant King?
All last night we watch'd the beacons
  Blazing on the hills afar,
Each one bearing, as it kindled,
  Message of the open'd war,
All night long the northern streamers
  Shot across the trembling sky:
Fearful lights that never beckon
  Save when kings or heroes die.

News of battle? Who hath brought it?
  All are thronging to the gate;
"Warder—warder! open quickly!
  Man—is this a time to wait?"

And the heavy gates are open'd :
   Then a murmur long and loud,
And a cry of fear and wonder
   Bursts from out the bending crowd.
For they see in batter'd harness
   Only one hard-stricken man ;
And his weary steed is wounded,
   And his cheek is pale and wan :
Spearless hangs a bloody banner
   In his weak and drooping hand—
God! can that be Randolph Murray,
   Captain of the city band?

Round him crush the people, crying,
   "Tell us all—oh, tell us true !
Where are they who went to battle,
   Randolph Murray, sworn to you?
Where are they, our brothers—children?
   Have they met the English foe?
Why art thou alone, unfollow'd?
   Is it weal or is it woe?"
Like a corpse the grisly warrior
   Looks from out his helm of steel ;
But no word he speaks in answer—
   Only with his armèd heel
Chides his weary steed, and onward
   Up the city streets they ride ;
Fathers, sisters, mothers, children,
   Shrieking, praying by his side.
"By the God that made thee, Randolph!
   Tell us what mischance hath come."
Then he lifts his riven banner,
   And the asker's voice is dumb.

The elders of the city
   Have met within their hall—
The men whom good King James had charged
   To watch the tower and wall.
"Your hands are weak with age," he said,
   "Your hearts are stout and true ;
So bide ye in the Maiden Town,
   While others fight for you.
My trumpet from the Border-side
   Shall send a blast so clear,
That all who wait within the gate
   That stirring sound may hear.
Or, if it be the will of Heaven
   That back I never come,
And if, instead of Scottish shouts,
   Ye hear the English drum—
Then let the warning bells ring out,
   Then gird you to the fray,
Then man the walls like burghers stout,
   And fight while fight you may.
'Twere better that in fiery flame
   The roofs should thunder down,
Than that the foot of foreign foe
   Should trample in the town !"

Then in came Randolph Murray,—
   His step was slow and weak,
And, as he doff'd his dinted helm,
   The tears ran down his cheek :
They fell upon his corslet
   And on his mailèd hand,
As he gazed around him wistfully,
   Leaning sorely on his brand.
And none who then beheld him
   But straight were smote with fear,
For a bolder and a sterner man
   Had never couch'd a spear.
They knew so sad a messenger
   Some ghastly news must bring ;
And all of them were fathers,
   And their sons were with the King.

And up then rose the Provost—
   A brave old man was he,
Of ancient name, and knightly fame,
   And chivalrous degree.
He ruled our city like a lord
   Who brook'd no equal here,
And ever for the townsman's rights
   Stood up 'gainst prince and peer.
And he had seen the Scottish host
   March from the borough-muir,
With music-storm and clamorous shout,
   And all the din that thunders out
When youth's of victory sure.
But yet a dearer thought had he,—
   For, with a father's pride,
He saw his last remaining son
   Go forth by Randolph's side,
With casque on head and spur on heel,
   All keen to do and dare ;
And proudly did that gallant boy
   Dunedin's banner bear.
Oh, woeful now was the old man's look,
   And he spake right heavily—
"Now, Randolph, tell thy tidings,
   However sharp they be !
Woe is written on thy visage,
   Death is looking from thy face :
Speak! though it be of overthrow—
   It cannot be disgrace !"

Right bitter was the agony
  That wrung that soldier proud:
Thrice did he strive to answer,
  And thrice he groan'd aloud.
Then he gave the riven banner
  To the old man's shaking hand,
Saying, "That is all I bring ye
  From the bravest of the land!
Ay! ye may look upon it—
  It was guarded well and long
By your brothers and your children,
  By the valiant and the strong.
One by one they fell around it,
  As the archers laid them low,
Grimly dying, still unconquer'd,
  With their faces to the foe.
Ay, ye may well look upon it—
  There is more than honor there,
Else, be sure, I had not brought it
  From the field of dark despair.
Never yet was royal banner
  Steep'd in such a costly dye;
It hath lain upon a bosom
  Where no other shroud shall lie.
Sirs, I charge you, keep it holy;
  Keep it as a sacred thing,
For the stain ye see upon it
  Was the life-blood of your King!"

Woe, and woe, and lamentation!
  What a piteous cry was there!
Widows, maidens, mothers, children,
  Shrieking, sobbing in despair!
Through the streets the death-word rushes,
  Spreading terror, sweeping on—
"Jesu Christ! our King has fallen—
  O Great God, King James is gone!
Holy Mother Mary, shield us,
  Thou who erst didst lose thy Son!
O the blackest day for Scotland
  That she ever knew before!
O our King—the good, the noble,
  Shall we see him never more?
Woe to us, and woe to Scotland!
  O our sons, our sons and men!
Surely some have 'scaped the Southron,
  Surely some will come again!"
Till the oak that fell last winter
  Shall uprear its shatter'd stem—
Wives and mothers of Dunedin—
  Ye may look in vain for them!

But within the Council Chamber
  All was silent as the grave,
Whilst the tempest of their sorrow
  Shook the bosoms of the brave.
Well indeed might they be shaken
  With the weight of such a blow:
He was gone—their prince, their idol,
  Whom they loved and worshipp'd so!
Like a knell of death and judgment
  Rung from heaven by angel hand,
Fell the words of desolation
  On the elders of the land.
Hoary heads were bow'd and trembling,
  Wither'd hands were clasp'd and wrung;
God had left the old and feeble,
  He had ta'en away the young.

Then the Provost he uprose,
  And his lip was ashen white;
But a flush was on his brow,
  And his eye was full of light.
"Thou hast spoken, Randolph Murray,
  Like a soldier stout and true;
Thou hast done a deed of daring
  Had been perill'd but by few.
For thou hast not shamed to face us,
  Nor to speak thy ghastly tale,
Standing—thou a knight and captain—
  Here, alive within thy mail!
Now, as my God shall judge me,
  I hold it braver done,
Than hadst thou tarried in thy place,
  And died above my son!
Thou needst not tell it: he is dead.
  God help us all this day!
But speak—how fought the citizens
  Within the furious fray?
For, by the might of Mary!
  'Twere something still to tell
That no Scottish foot went backward
  When the Royal Lion fell!"

"No one fail'd him! He is keeping
  Royal state and semblance still;
Knight and noble lie around him,
  Cold on Flodden's fatal hill.
Of the brave and gallant-hearted,
  Whom ye sent with prayers away,
Not a single man departed
  From his Monarch yesterday.

Had you seen them, O my masters!
  When the night began to fall,
And the English spearmen gather'd
  Round a grim and ghastly wall!
As the wolves in winter circle
  Round the leaguer on the heath,
So the greedy foe glared upward,
  Panting still for blood and death.
But a rampart rose before them,
  Which the boldest dare not scale;
Every stone a Scottish body,
  Every step a corpse in mail!
And behind it lay our Monarch,
  Clenching still his shiver'd sword;
By his side Montrose and Athole,
  At his feet a Southron lord.
All so thick they lay together,
  When the stars lit up the sky,
That I knew not who were stricken,
  Or who yet remain'd to die.
Few there were when Surrey halted,
  And his wearied host withdrew;
None but dying men around me,
  When the English trumpet blew.
Then I stoop'd and took the banner,
  As you see it, from his breast,
And I closed our hero's eyelids,
  And I left him to his rest.
In the mountains growl'd the thunder,
  As I leap'd the woeful wall,
And the heavy clouds were settling
  Over Flodden, like a pall."

So he ended. And the others
  Cared not any answer then;
Sitting silent, dumb with sorrow,
  Sitting anguish-struck, like men
Who have seen the roaring torrent
  Sweep their happy homes away,
And yet linger by the margin,
  Staring wildly on the spray.
But, without, the maddening tumult
  Waxes ever more and more,
And the crowd of wailing women
  Gather round the council-door.
Every dusky spire is ringing
  With a dull and hollow knell,
And the Miserere's singing
  To the tolling of the bell.
Through the streets the burghers hurry,
  Spreading terror as they go;
And the rampart's throng'd with watchers
  For the coming of the foe.
From each mountain-top a pillar
  Streams into the torpid air,
Bearing token from the 'Border
  That the English host is there.
All without is flight and terror,
  All within is woe and fear—
God protect thee, Maiden City,
  For thy latest hour is near!

No! not yet, thou high Dunedin!
  Shalt thou totter to thy fall;
Though thy bravest and thy strongest
  Are not there to man the wall.
No, not yet! the ancient spirit
  Of our fathers hath not gone;
Take it to thee as a buckler
  Better far than steel or stone.
Oh, remember those who perish'd
  For thy birthright at the time
When to be a Scot was treason,
  And to side with Wallace crime!
Have they not a voice among us,
  Whilst their hallow'd dust is here?
Hear ye not a summons sounding
  From each buried warrior's bier?
Up!—they say—and keep the freedom
  Which we·won you long ago:
Up! and keep our graves unsullied
  From the insults of the foe!
Up! and if ye cannot save them,
  Come to us in blood and fire:
Midst the crash of falling turrets
  Let the last of Scots expire!

Still the bells are tolling fiercely,
  And the cry comes louder in;
Mothers wailing for their children,
  Sisters for their slaughter'd kin.
All is terror and disorder;
  Till the Provost rises up,
Calm as though he had not tasted
  Of the fell and bitter cup.
All so stately from his sorrow,
  Rose the old undaunted chief,
That you had not deem'd, to see him,
  His was more than common grief.
"Rouse ye, sirs!" he said; "we may not
  Longer mourn for what is done;
If our King be taken from us,
  We are left to guard his son.

We have sworn to keep the city
 From the foe, whate'er they be,
And the oath that we have taken
 Never shall be broke by me.
Death is nearer to us, brethren,
 Than it seem'd to those who died,
Fighting yesterday at Flodden,
 By their lord and master's side.
Let us meet it, then, in patience,
 Not in terror or in fear;
Though our hearts are bleeding yonder,
 Let our souls be steadfast here.
Up, and rouse ye! Time is fleeting,
 And we yet have much to do;
Up! and haste ye through the city,
 Stir the burghers stout and true!
Gather all our scatter'd people,
 Fling the banner out once more,—
Randolph Murray! do thou bear it,
 As it erst was borne before:
Never Scottish heart will leave it,
 When they see their Monarch's gore!

" Let them cease that dismal knelling!
 It is time enough to ring
When the fortress-strength of Scotland
 Stoops to ruin like its King.
Let the bells be kept for warning,
 Not for terror or alarm;
When they next are heard to thunder,
 Let each man and stripling arm.
Bid the women leave their wailing—
 Do they think that woeful strain,
From the bloody heaps of Flodden
 Can redeem their dearest slain?
Bid them cease,—or rather hasten
 To the churches every one;
There to pray to Mary Mother,
 And to her anointed Son,
That the thunderbolt above us
 May not fall in ruin yet;
That in fire and blood and rapine
 Scotland's glory may not set.
Let them pray,—for never women
 Stood in need of such a prayer!—
England's yeomen shall not find them
 Clinging to the altars there.
No! if we are doom'd to perish,
 Man and maiden, let us fall,
And a common gulf of ruin
 Open wide to whelm us all!
Never shall the ruthless spoiler
 Lay his hot insulting hand
On the sisters of our heroes,
 Whilst we bear a torch or brand!
Up! and rouse ye, then, my brothers,—
 But when next ye hear the bell
Sounding forth the sullen summons
 That may be our funeral knell,
Once more let us meet together,
 Once more see each other's face;
Then, like men that need not tremble,
 Go to our appointed place.
God, our Father, will not fail us
 In that last tremendous hour—
If all other bulwarks crumble,
 He will be our strength and tower:
Though the ramparts rock beneath us,
 And the walls go crashing down,
Though the roar of conflagration
 Bellow o'er the sinking town;
There is yet one place of shelter,
 Where the foeman cannot come,
Where the summons never sounded
 Of the trumpet or the drum.
There again we'll meet our children,
 Who, on Flodden's trampled sod,
For their king and for their country
 Render'd up their souls to God.
There shall we find rest and refuge,
 With our dear departed brave;
And the ashes of the city
 Be our universal grave!"
WILLIAM EDMONDSTOUNE AYTOUN.

THE FLOWERS OF THE FOREST.

I'VE heard them lilting at our ewe-milking,
 Lasses a' lilting before dawn o' day;
But now they are moaning on ilka green loaning—
 The Flowers of the Forest are a' wede away.

At bughts, in the morning, nae blythe lads are scorning,
 Lasses are lonely and dowie and wae;
Nae daffin', nae gabbin', but sighing and sabbing,
 Ilk ane lifts her leglin and hies her away.

In har'st, at the shearing, nae youths now are jeering,
 Bandsters are lyart, and runkled, and gray;

At fair or at preaching, nae wooing, nae
  fleeching,—
  The Flowers of the Forest are a' wede
    away.

At e'en, in the gloaming, nae younkers are
    roaming
  'Bout stacks wi' the lasses at bogle to
    play ;
  But ilk ane sits drearie, lamenting her
    dearie—
  The Flowers of the Forest are weded
    away.

Dool and wae for the order, sent our lads
    to the Border!
  The English, for ance, by guile wan the
    day ;
  The Flowers of the Forest, that fought aye
    the foremost,
  The prime of our land, are cauld in the
    clay.

We'll hear nae mair lilting at the ewe-
    milking,
  Women and bairns are heartless and
    wae,
  Sighing and moaning on ilka green loan-
    ing,—
  The Flowers of the Forest are a' wede
    away.
          JANE ELLIOT.

IVRY.

A SONG OF THE HUGUENOTS.

Now glory to the Lord of Hosts, from
    whom all glories are !
And glory to our Sovereign Liege, King
    Henry of Navarre !
Now let there be the merry sound of music
    and of dance,
Through thy cornfields green, and sunny
    vines, O pleasant land of France !
And thou, Rochelle, our own Rochelle,
    proud city of the waters,
Again let rapture light the eyes of all thy
    mourning daughters ;
As thou wert constant in our ills, be joyous
    in our joy,
For cold and stiff and still are they who
    wrought thy walls annoy.

Hurrah ! Hurrah ! a single field hath
    turn'd the chance of war,
Hurrah ! Hurrah ! for Ivry, and Henry of
    Navarre.

Oh, how our hearts were beating, when at
    the dawn of day
We saw the army of the League drawn
    out in long array ;
With all its priest-led citizens, and all its
    rebel peers,
And Appenzel's stout infantry, and Eg-
    mont's Flemish spears.
There rode the brood of false Lorraine, the
    curses of our land ;
And dark Mayenne was in the midst, a
    truncheon in his hand :
And, as we look'd on them, we thought of
    Seine's empurpled flood,
And good Coligni's hoary hair all dabbled
    with his blood ;
And we cried unto the living God, who
    rules the fate of war,
To fight for his own holy name, and Henry
    of Navarre.

The King is come to marshal us, in all his
    armor drest,
And he has bound a snow-white plume
    upon his gallant crest.
He look'd upon his people, and a tear was
    in his eye ;
He look'd upon the traitors, and his glance
    was stern and high.
Right graciously he smiled on us, as roll'd
    from wing to wing,
Down all our line, a deafening shout
    "God save our Lord, the King !"
"And if my standard-bearer fall, as fall
    full well he may,
For never saw I promise yet of such a
    bloody fray,
Press where ye see my white plume shine,
    amidst the ranks of war,
And be your oriflamme to-day the helmet
    of Navarre."

Hurrah ! the foes are moving. Hark to
    the mingled din,
Of fife, and steed, and trump, and drum,
    and roaring culverin.

The fiery Duke is pricking fast across Saint
  André's plain,
With all the hireling chivalry of Guelders
  and Almayne.
Now by the lips of those ye love, fair gen-
  tlemen of France,
Charge for the golden lilies! upon them
  with the lance!
A thousand spurs are striking deep, a
  thousand spears in rest,
A thousand knights are pressing close be-
  hind the snow-white crest;
And in they burst, and on they rush'd,
  while, like a guiding star,
Amidst the thickest carnage blazed the hel-
  met of Navarre.

Now, God be praised, the day is ours.
  Mayenne hath turn'd his rein.
D'Aumale hath cried for quarter. The
  Flemish count is slain.
Their ranks are breaking like thin clouds
  before a Biscay gale;
The field is heap'd with bleeding steeds,
  and flags, and cloven mail.
And then we thought on vengeance, and,
  all along our van,
"Remember St. Bartholomew!" was pass'd
  from man to man.
But out spake gentle Henry, "No French-
  man is my foe:
Down, down, with every foreigner, but let
  your brethren go."
Oh! was there ever such a knight, in
  friendship or in war,
As our Sovereign Lord, King Henry, the
  soldier of Navarre?

Right well fought all the Frenchmen who
  fought for France to-day;
And many a lordly banner God gave them
  for a prey.
But we of the religion have borne us best
  in fight;
And the good Lord of Rosny hath ta'en
  the cornet white.
Our own true Maximilian the cornet white
  hath ta'en,
The cornet white with crosses black, the
  flag of false Lorraine.
Up with it high; unfurl it wide; that all
  the host may know
How God hath humbled the proud house
  which wrought his Church such woe.
Then on the ground, while trumpets sound
  their loudest point of war,
Fling the red shreds, a footcloth meet for
  Henry of Navarre.

Ho! maidens of Vienna; ho! matrons of
  Lucerne;
Weep, weep, and rend your hair for those
  who never shall return.
Ho! Philip, send for charity thy Mexican
  pistoles,
That Antwerp monks may sing a mass for
  thy poor spearmen's souls.
Ho! gallant nobles of the League, look
  that your arms be bright;
Ho! burghers of Saint Genevieve, keep
  watch and ward to-night.
For our God hath crush'd the tyrant, our
  God hath raised the slave,
And mock'd the counsel of the wise, and
  the valor of the brave.
Then glory to His holy name, from whom
  all glories are;
And glory to our Sovereign Lord, King
  Henry of Navarre.
    THOMAS BABINGTON MACAULAY.

THE LANDING OF THE PILGRIM FATHERS IN NEW ENGLAND.

"Look now abroad;—another race has fill'd
  Those populous borders; wide the wood recedes,
And towns shoot up, and fertile realms are till'd;
  The land is full of harvests and green meads."
    BRYANT.

THE breaking waves dash'd high,
  On a stern and rock-bound coast,
And the woods against a stormy sky
  Their giant branches toss'd;

And the heavy night hung dark,
  The hills and waters o'er,
When a band of exiles moor'd their bark
  On the wild New England shore.

Not as the conqueror comes,
  They, the true-hearted, came;
Not with the roll of the stirring drums,
  And the trumpet that sings of fame;

Not as the flying come,
  In silence and in fear,—
They shook the depths of the desert gloom
  With their hymns of lofty cheer.

Amidst the storm they sang,
  And the stars heard, and the sea,
And the sounding aisles of the dim woods rang
  To the anthem of the free.

The ocean eagle soar'd
  From his nest by the white wave's foam,
And the rocking pines of the forest roar'd—
  This was their welcome home.

There were men with hoary hair
  Amidst that pilgrim band:
Why had they come to wither there,
  Away from their childhood's land?

There was woman's fearless eye,
  Lit by her deep love's truth;
There was manhood's brow serenely high,
  And the fiery heart of youth.

What sought they thus afar?
  Bright jewels of the mine?
The wealth of seas, the spoils of war?
  They sought a faith's pure shrine!

Ay, call it holy ground,
  The soil where first they trod;
They have left unstain'd what there they found—
  Freedom to worship God.
          FELICIA DOROTHEA HEMANS.

THE THREE TROOPERS.

DURING THE PROTECTORATE.

INTO the Devil tavern
  Three booted troopers strode,
From spur to feather spotted and splash'd
  With the mud of a winter road.
In each of their cups they dropp'd a crust,
  And stared at the guests with a frown;
Then drew their swords, and roar'd for a toast,
  "God send this Crum-well-down!"

A blue smoke rose from their pistol-locks,
  Their sword-blades were still wet;
There were long red smears on their jerkins of buff,
  As the table they overset.
Then into their cups they stirr'd the crusts,
  And cursed old London town;
Then waved their swords, and drank with a stamp
  "God send this Crum-well-down!"

The 'prentice dropp'd his can of beer,
  The host turn'd pale as a clout;
The ruby nose of the toping squires
  Grew white at the wild men's shout.
Then into their cups they flung the crusts,
  And show'd their teeth with a frown;
They flash'd their swords as they gave the toast,
  "God send this Crum-well-down!"

The gambler dropp'd his dog's-ear'd cards,
  The waiting-women scream'd,
As the light of the fire like stains of blood,
  On the wild men's sabres gleam'd.
Then into their cups they splash'd the crusts,
  And cursed the fool of a town,
And leap'd on the table, and roar'd a toast,
  "God send this Crum-well-down!"

Till on a sudden fire-bells rang,
  And the troopers sprang to horse;
The eldest mutter'd between his teeth,
  Hot curses—deep and coarse.
In their stirrup-cups they flung the crusts,
  And cried as they spurr'd through town,
With their keen swords drawn and their pistols cock'd,
  "God send this Crum-well-down!"

Away they dash'd through Temple Bar,
  Their red cloaks flowing free,
Their scabbards clash'd, each back-piece shone—
  None liked to touch the three.
The silver cups that held the crusts
  They flung to the startled town,
Shouting again, with a blaze of swords,
  "God send this Crum-well-down!"
          GEORGE WALTER THORNBURY.

MARCHING ALONG.
A Cavalier Song.

KENTISH Sir Byng stood for his king,
Bidding the crop-headed Parliament swing:
And, pressing a troop unable to stoop
And see the rogues flourish and honest folk droop,
March'd them along, fifty-score strong,
Great-hearted gentlemen, singing this song.

God for King Charles! Pym and such carles
To the Devil that prompts 'em their treasonous parles!
Cavaliers, up! Lips from the cup,
Hands from the pasty, nor bite take nor sup
Till you're—
Marching along, fifty-score strong,
Great-hearted gentlemen, singing this song.

Hampden to hell, and his obsequies' knell
Serve Hazelrig, Fiennes, and young Harry as well!
England, good cheer! Rupert is near!
Kentish and loyalists, keep we not here
Marching along, fifty-score strong,
Great-hearted gentlemen, singing this song?

Then, God for King Charles! Pym and his snarls
To the Devil that pricks on such pestilent carles!
Hold by the right, you double your might:
So, onward to Nottingham, fresh for the fight,
March we along, fifty-score strong,
Great-hearted gentlemen, singing this song.

ROBERT BROWNING.

JACOBITE TOAST.

GOD bless the king!—I mean the Faith's Defender;
God bless (no harm in blessing) the Pretender!
But who Pretender is, or who is king—
God bless us all!—that's quite another thing.

JOHN BYROM.

THE COVENANTERS' BATTLE-CHANT.

To battle! to battle!
 To slaughter and strife!
For a sad, broken Covenant
 We barter poor life.
The great God of Judah
 Shall smite with our hand,
And break down the idols
 That cumber the land.

Uplift every voice
 In prayer and in song;
Remember the battle
 Is not to the strong;
Lo! the Ammonites thicken,
 And onward they come,
To the vain noise of trumpet.
 Of cymbal, and drum.

They haste to the onslaught,
 With hagbut and spear;
They lust for a banquet
 That's deathful and dear.
Now horseman and footman
 Sweep down the hillside;
They come, like fierce Pharaohs,
 To die in their pride!

See, long plume and pennon
 Stream gay in the air!
They are given us for slaughter,—
 Shall God's people spare?
Nay, nay; lop them off,
 Friend, father, and son;
All earth is athirst till
 The good work be done.

Brace tight every buckler,
 And lift high the sword,
For biting must blades be
 That fight for the Lord.
Remember, remember,
 How saints' blood was shed,
As free as the rain, and
 Homes desolate made!

"A STEED! A STEED OF MATCHLESSE SPEED.
A SWORD OF METAL KEENE."
                                   The Cavalier's Song.

Among them! among them!
  Unburied bones cry,
Avenge us, or, like us,
  Faith's true martyrs die.
Hew! hew down the spoilers!
  Slay on, and spare none;
Then shout forth in gladness,
  Heaven's battle is won!
                    WILLIAM MOTHERWELL.

THE CAVALIER'S SONG.

A STEED! a steed of matchlesse speed,
  A sword of metal keene!
All else to noble heartes is drosse,
  All else on earth is meane.
The neighynge of the war-horse prowde,
  The rowlinge of the drum,
The clangor of the trumpet lowde,
  Be soundes from heaven that come;
And oh the thundering presse of knightes,
  Whenas their war-cryes swell,
May tole from heaven an angel bright,
  And rouse a fiend from hell.

Then mounte! then mounte, brave gallants all,
  And don your helmes amaine:
Deathe's couriers, fame and honour, call
  Us to the field againe.
No shrewish teares shall fill our eye
  When the sword-hilt's in our hand—
Heart whole we'll part, and no whit sighe
  For the fayrest of the land;
Let piping swaine, and craven wight,
  Thus weepe and puling crye;
Our business is like men to fight,
  And hero-like to die!
                    WILLIAM MOTHERWELL.

NASEBY.

OH, wherefore come ye forth in triumph from the north,
  With your hands, and your feet, and your raiment all red?
And wherefore doth your rout send forth a joyous shout?
  And whence be the grapes of the winepress which ye tread?

Oh, evil was the root, and bitter was the fruit,
  And crimson was the juice of the vintage that we trod;
For we trampled on the throng of the haughty and the strong,
  Who sate in the high places and slew the saints of God.

It was about the noon of a glorious day of June,
  That we saw their banners dance and their cuirasses shine,
And the Man of Blood was there, with his long essenced hair,
  And Astley, and Sir Marmaduke, and Rupert of the Rhine.

Like a servant of the Lord, with his Bible and his sword,
  The general rode along us to form us for the fight;
When a murmuring sound broke out, and swell'd into a shout
  Among the godless horsemen upon the tyrant's right.

And hark! like the roar of the billows on the shore,
  The cry of battle rises along their charging line:
For God! for the Cause! for the Church! for the Laws!
  For Charles, king of England, and Rupert of the Rhine!

The furious German comes, with his clarions and his drums,
  His bravoes of Alsatia and pages of Whitehall;
They are bursting on our flanks! Grasp your pikes! Close your ranks!
  For Rupert never comes, but to conquer, or to fall.

They are here—they rush on—we are broken—we are gone—
  Our left is borne before them like stubble on the blast.
O Lord, put forth thy might! O Lord, defend the right!
  Stand back to back, in God's name! and fight it to the last!

Stout Skippon hath a wound—the centre
　　hath given ground.
　Hark! hark! what means the trampling
　　of horsemen on our rear?
Whose banner do I see, boys? 'Tis he!
　　thank God! 'tis he, boys!
　Bear up another minute! Brave Oliver
　　is here!

Their heads all stooping low, their points
　　all in a row,
　Like a whirlwind on the trees, like a
　　deluge on the dikes,
Our cuirassiers have burst on the ranks of
　　the accurst,
　And at a shock have scatter'd the forest
　　of his pikes.

Fast, fast, the gallants ride, in some safe
　　nook to hide
　Their coward heads, predestined to rot
　　on Temple Bar;
And he—he turns! he flies! shame on
　　those cruel eyes
　That bore to look on torture, and dare
　　not look on war!

Ho, comrades! scour the plain; and ere ye
　　strip the slain,
　First give another stab to make your
　　search secure;
Then shake from sleeves and pockets their
　　broad-pieces and lockets,
　The tokens of the wanton, the plunder
　　of the poor.

Fools! your doublets shone with gold, and
　　your hearts were gay and bold,
　When you kiss'd your lily hands to your
　　lemans to-day;
And to-morrow shall the fox from her
　　chambers in the rocks
　Lead forth her tawny cubs to howl above
　　the prey.

Where be your tongues, that late mock'd
　　at heaven, and hell, and fate?
　And the fingers that once were so busy
　　with your blades?
Your perfumed satin clothes, your catches
　　and your oaths?
　Your stage-plays and your sonnets, your
　　diamonds and your spades?

Down! down! for ever down with the
　　mitre and the crown!
　With the Belial of the court, and the
　　Mammon of the Pope!
There is woe in Oxford halls, there is wail
　　in Durham's stalls;
　The Jesuit smites his bosom, the bishop
　　rends his cope.

And she of the seven hills shall mourn her
　　children's ills,
　And tremble when she thinks on the
　　edge of England's sword;
And the kings of earth in fear shall shudder
　　when they hear
　What the hand of God hath wrought for
　　the Houses and the Word!
　　　　　　　THOMAS BABINGTON MACAULAY.

ON THE FUNERAL OF CHARLES THE FIRST,

AT NIGHT IN ST. GEORGE'S CHAPEL,
WINDSOR.

THE castle clock had toll'd midnight.
　With mattock and with spade—
And silent by the torches' light—
　His corse in earth we laid.

The coffin bore his name, that those
　Of other years might know,
When earth its secrets should disclose,
　Whose bones were laid below.

"Peace to the dead!" no children sung,
　Slow pacing up the nave;
No prayers were read, no knell was rung
　As deep we dug his grave.

We only heard the winter's wind,
　In many a sullen gust,
As o'er the open grave inclined,
　We murmur'd, "Dust to dust!"

A moonbeam from the arch's height
　Stream'd, as we placed the stone;
The long aisles started into light,
　And all the windows shone.

We thought we saw the banners then
　That shook along the walls,
Whilst the sad shades of mailèd men
　Were gazing on the stalls.

'Tis gone!—Again on tombs defaced
  Sits darkness more profound;
And only by the torch we traced
  The shadows on the ground.

And now the chilling, freezing air
  Without blew long and loud;
Upon our knees we breathed one prayer,
  Where he slept in his shroud.

We laid the broken marble floor,—
  No name, no trace appears!
And when we closed the sounding door,
  We thought of him with tears.
                WILLIAM LISLE BOWLES.

WHEN THE ASSAULT WAS INTENDED TO THE CITY.

CAPTAIN, or colonel, or knight in arms,
  Whose chance on these defenceless doors may seize,
  If deed of honor did thee ever please,
Guard them, and him within protect from harms.
He can requite thee; for he knows the charms
  That call fame on such gentle acts as these,
  And he can spread thy name o'er lands and seas,
Whatever clime the sun's bright circle warms.
Lift not thy spear against the Muses' bower:
The great Emathian conqueror bid spare
The house of Pindarus, when temple and tower
Went to the ground; and the repeated air
Of sad Electra's poet had the power
  To save the Athenian walls from ruin bare.
                JOHN MILTON.

ON THE LATE MASSACRE IN PIEDMONT.

AVENGE, O Lord, thy slaughter'd saints,
  whose bones
Lie scatter'd on the Alpine mountains cold;
Even them who kept thy truth so pure of old
When all our fathers worshipt stocks and stones.

Forget not: In thy book record their groans
Who were thy sheep, and in their ancient fold
Slain by the bloody Piedmontese, that roll'd
Mother with infant down the rocks. Their moans

The vales redoubled to the hills, and they
  To Heaven. Their martyr'd blood and ashes sow
O'er all the Italian fields, where still doth sway
  The triple tyrant, that from these may grow
A hundred-fold, who, having learnt Thy way,
  Early may fly the Babylonian woe.
                JOHN MILTON.

THE EXECUTION OF MONTROSE.

COME hither, Evan Cameron!
  Come, stand behind my knee—
I hear the river roaring down
  Toward the wintry sea.
There's shouting on the mountain-side,
  There's war within the blast—
Old faces look upon me,
  Old forms go trooping past.
I hear the pibroch wailing
  Amidst the din of fight,
And my dim spirit wakes again
  Upon the verge of night.

'Twas I that led the Highland host
  Through wild Lochaber's snows,
What time the plaided clans came down
  To battle with Montrose.
I've told thee how the Southrons fell
  Beneath the broad claymore,
And how we smote the Campbell clan
  By Inverlochy's shore.
I've told thee how we swept Dundee,
  And tamed the Lindsays' pride;
But never have I told thee yet
  How the great Marquis died.

A traitor sold him to his foes;—
  O deed of deathless shame!
I charge thee, boy, if e'er thou meet
  With one of Assynt's name—
Be it upon the mountain's side,
  Or yet within the glen,
Stand he in martial gear alone,
  Or back'd by armèd men—
Face him as thou wouldst face the man
  Who wrong'd thy sire's renown;
Remember of what blood thou art,
  And strike the caitiff down!

They brought him to the Watergate,
  Hard bound with hempen span,
As though they held a lion there,
  And not a 'fenceless man.
They set him high upon a cart—
  The hangman rode below—
They drew his hands behind his back,
  And bared his noble brow.
Then, as a hound is slipp'd from leash,
  They cheer'd the common throng,
And blew the note with yell and shout,
  And bade him pass along.

It would have made a brave man's heart
  Grow sad and sick that day,
To watch the keen, malignant eyes
  Bent down on that array.
There stood the Whig west-country lords
  In balcony and bow;
There sat their gaunt and wither'd dames,
  And their daughters all a-row.
And every open window
  Was full as full might be
With black-robed Covenanting carles,
  That goodly sport to see!

But when he came, though pale and wan,
  He look'd so great and high,
So noble was his manly front,
  So calm his steadfast eye;—
The rabble rout forbore to shout,
  And each man held his breath,
For well they knew the hero's soul
  Was face to face with death.
And then a mournful shudder
  Through all the people crept,
And some that came to scoff at him
  Now turn'd aside and wept.

But onward—always onward,
  In silence and in gloom,
The dreary pageant labor'd,
  Till it reach'd the house of doom.
Then first a woman's voice was heard
  In jeer and laughter loud,
And an angry cry and a hiss arose
  From the heart of the tossing crowd:
Then, as the Græme looked upward,
  He saw the ugly smile
Of him who sold his king for gold—
  The master-fiend Argyle!

The Marquis gazed a moment,
  And nothing did he say,
But the cheek of Argyle grew ghastly pale,
  And he turn'd his eyes away.
The painted harlot by his side,
  She shook through every limb,
For a roar like thunder swept the street,
  And hands were clench'd at him;
And a Saxon soldier cried aloud,
  "Back, coward, from thy place!
For seven long years thou hast not dared
  To look him in the face."

Had I been there with sword in hand,
  And fifty Camerons by,
That day through high Dunedin's streets
  Had peal'd the slogan-cry.
Not all their troops of trampling horse,
  Nor might of mailèd men—
Not all the rebels in the south
  Had borne us backward then!
Once more his foot on Highland heath
  Had trod as free as air,
Or I, and all who bore my name,
  Been laid around him there!

It might not be. They placed him next
  Within the solemn hall,
Where once the Scottish kings were throned
  Amidst their nobles all.
But there was dust of vulgar feet
  On that polluted floor,
And perjured traitors fill'd the place
  Where good men sate before.
With savage glee came Warriston
  To read the murderous doom;
And then uprose the great Montrose
  In the middle of the room:

"Now, by my faith as belted knight
  And by the name I bear,
And by the bright St. Andrew's cross
  That waves above us there—
Yea, by a greater, mightier oath—
  And oh that such should be!—
By that dark stream of royal blood
  That lies 'twixt you and me—
I have not sought in battle-field
  A wreath of such renown,
Nor dared I hope on my dying day
  To win the martyr's crown!

"There is a chamber far away
  Where sleep the good and brave,
But a better place ye have named for me
  Than by my fathers' grave.
For truth and right, 'gainst treason's might,
  This hand hath always striven,
And ye raise it up for a witness still
  In the eye of earth and heaven.
Then nail my head on yonder tower—
  Give every town a limb—
And God who made shall gather them:
  I go from you to Him!"

The morning dawn'd full darkly,
  The rain came flashing down,
And the jagged streak of the levin-bolt
  Lit up the gloomy town;
The thunder crash'd across the heaven,
  The fatal hour was come;
Yet aye broke in, with muffled beat,
  The 'larum of the drum.
There was madness on the earth below
  And anger in the sky,
And young and old, and rich and poor,
  Came forth to see him die.

Ah, God! that ghastly gibbet!
  How dismal 'tis to see
The great tall spectral skeleton,
  The ladder and the tree!
Hark! hark! it is the clash of arms—
  The bells begin to toll—
"He is coming! he is coming!
  God's mercy on his soul!"
One last long peal of thunder—
  The clouds are clear'd away,
And the glorious sun once more looks down
  Amidst the dazzling day.

"He is coming! he is coming!"
  Like a bridegroom from his room,
Came the hero from his prison
  To the scaffold and the doom.
There was glory on his forehead,
  There was lustre in his eye,
And he never walk'd to battle
  More proudly than to die;
There was color in his visage,
  Though the cheeks of all were wan,
And they marvell'd as they saw him pass,
  That great and goodly man!

He mounted up the scaffold,
  And he turn'd him to the crowd;
But they dared not trust the people,
  So he might not speak aloud;
But he look'd upon the heavens,
  And they were clear and blue,
And in the liquid ether
  The eye of God shone through.
Yet a black and murky battlement
  Lay resting on the hill,
As though the thunder slept within—
  All else was calm and still.

The grim Geneva ministers
  With anxious scowl drew near,
As you have seen the ravens flock
  Around the dying deer.
He would not deign them word nor sign,
  But alone he bent the knee;
And veil'd his face for Christ's dear grace
  Beneath the gallows tree.
Then radiant and serene he rose,
  And cast his cloak away:
For he had ta'en his latest look
  Of earth and sun and day.

A beam of light fell o'er him,
  Like a glory round the shriven,
And he climb'd the lofty ladder
  As it were the path to heaven.
Then came a flash from out the cloud,
  And a stunning thunder-roll;
And no man dared to look aloft,
  For fear was on every soul.
There was another heavy sound,
  A hush and then a groan;
And darkness swept across the sky—
  The work of death was done!

WILLIAM EDMONDSTOUNE AYTOUN.

THE BONNETS OF BONNIE DUNDEE.

To the lords of convention 'twas Claverhouse who spoke,
"Ere the king's crown shall fall there are crowns to be broke;
So let each cavalier who loves honor and me
Come follow the bonnets of bonnie Dundee!"
  Come fill up my cup, come fill up my can;
  Come saddle your horses, and call up your men;
  Come open the Westport and let us gang free,
  And it's room for the bonnets of bonnie Dundee!

Dundee he is mounted, he rides up the street,
The bells are rung backward, the drums they are beat;
But the provost, douce man, said, "Just e'en let him be,
The gude toun is well quit of that de'il of Dundee!"
  Come fill up my cup, come fill up my can;
  Come saddle your horses, and call up your men
  Come open the Westport and let us gang free,
  And it's room for the bonnets of bonnie Dundee!

As he rode down the sanctified bends of the Bow
Ilk carline was flyting and shaking her pow;
But the young plants of grace they look'd cowthie and slee,
Thinking, Luck to thy bonnet, thou bonnie Dundee!
  Come fill up my cup, come fill up my can;
  Come saddle your horses, and call up your men;
  Come open the Westport and let us gang free,
  And it's room for the bonnets of bonnie Dundee!

With sour-featured Whigs the Grassmarket was thrang'd
As if half the west had set tryst to be hang'd;
There was spite in each look, there was fear in each ee,
As they watch'd for the bonnets of bonnie Dundee.
  Come fill up my cup, come fill up my can;
  Come saddle your horses, and call up your men;
  Come open the Westport and let us gang free,
  And it's room for the bonnets of bonnie Dundee!

These cowls of Kilmarnock had spits and had spears,
And lang-hafted gullies to kill cavaliers;
But they shrunk to close-heads, and the causeway was free
At the toss of the bonnet of bonnie Dundee.
  Come fill up my cup, come fill up my can;
  Come saddle your horses, and call up your men;
  Come open the Westport and let us gang free,
  And it's room for the bonnets of bonnie Dundee!

He spurr'd to the foot of the proud castle rock,
And with the gay Gordon he gallantly spoke:
"Let Mons Meg and her marrows speak twa words or three,
For the love of the bonnet of bonnie Dundee."
  Come fill up my cup, come fill up my can;
  Come saddle your horses, and call up your men;
  Come open the Westport and let us gang free,
  And it's room for the bonnets of bonnie Dundee!

The Gordon demands of him which way he goes—
"Where'er shall direct me the shade of Montrose!

Your Grace in short space shall hear tidings of me,
Or that low lies the bonnet of bonnie Dundee.
    Come fill up my cup, come fill up my can;
    Come saddle your horses, and call up your men;
    Come open the Westport and let us gang free,
    And it's room for the bonnets of bonnie Dundee!

"There are hills beyond Pentland and lands beyond Forth;
If there's lords in the Lowlands, there's chiefs in the north;
There are wild Duniewassals three thousand times three
Will cry 'Hoigh!' for the bonnet of bonnie Dundee.
    Come fill up my cup, come fill up my can;
    Come saddle your horses, and call up your men;
    Come open the Westport and let us gang free,
    And it's room for the bonnets of bonnie Dundee!

"There's brass on the target of barken'd bull-hide,
There's steel in the scabbard that dangles beside;
The brass shall be burnish'd, the steel shall flash free,
At a toss of the bonnet of bonnie Dundee.
    Come fill up my cup, come fill up my can;
    Come saddle your horses, and call up your men;
    Come open the Westport and let us gang free,
    And it's room for the bonnets of bonnie Dundee!

"Away to the hills, to the caves, to the rocks;
Ere I own an usurper I'll couch with the fox;
And tremble, false Whigs, in the midst of your glee,
You have not seen the last of my bonnet and me."
    Come fill up my cup, come fill up my can;
    Come saddle your horses, and call up your men;
    Come open the Westport and let us gang free,
    And it's room for the bonnets of bonnie Dundee!

He waved his proud hand, and the trumpets were blown,
The kettle-drums clash'd, and the horsemen rode on,
Till on Ravelston's cliffs and on Clermiston's lea
Died away the wild war-notes of bonnie Dundee.
    Come fill up my cup, come fill up my can;
    Come saddle the horses, and call up the men;
    Come open your doors and let me gae free,
    For it's up with the bonnets of bonnie Dundee!

                    SIR WALTER SCOTT.

THE BURIAL-MARCH OF DUNDEE.

SOUND fife, and cry the slogan—
    Let the pibroch shake the air
With its wild triumphal music,
    Worthy of the freight we bear.
Let the ancient hills of Scotland
    Hear once more the battle-song
Swell within their glens and valleys
    As the clansmen march along!
Never from the field of combat,
    Never from the deadly fray,
Was a nobler trophy carried
    Than we bring with us to-day;
Never since the valiant Douglas
    On his dauntless bosom bore
Good King Robert's heart—the priceless—
    To our dear Redeemer's shore!
Lo! we bring with us the hero—
    Lo! we bring the conquering Græme,
Crown'd as best beseems a victor
    From the altar of his fame;
Fresh and bleeding from the battle
    Whence his spirit took its flight,
Midst the crashing charge of squadrons,
    And the thunder of the fight!

Strike, I say, the notes of triumph,
　As we march o'er moor and lea!
Is there any here will venture
　To bewail our dead Dundee?
Let the widows of the traitors
　Weep until their eyes are dim!
Wail ye may full well for Scotland—
　Let none dare to mourn for him!
See! above his glorious body
　Lies the royal banner's fold—
See! his valiant blood is mingled
　With its crimson and its gold.
See how calm he looks and stately,
　Like a warrior on his shield,
Waiting till the flush of morning
　Breaks along the battle-field!
See—Oh never more, my comrades,
　Shall we see that falcon eye
Redden with its inward lightning,
　As the hour of fight drew nigh!
Never shall we hear the voice that,
　Clearer than the trumpet's call,
Bade us strike for King and Country,
　Bade us win the field, or fall!

On the heights of Killiecrankie
　Yester-morn our army lay:
Slowly rose the mist in columns
　From the river's broken way;
Hoarsely roar'd the swollen torrent,
　And the pass was wrapp'd in gloom,
When the clansmen rose together
　From their lair amidst the broom.
Then we belted on our tartans,
　And our bonnets down we drew,
And we felt our broadswords' edges,
　And we proved them to be true;
And we pray'd the prayer of soldiers,
　And we cried the gathering-cry,
And we clasp'd the hands of kinsmen,
　And we swore to do or die!
Then our leader rode before us
　On his war-horse black as night—
Well the Cameronian rebels
　Knew that charger in the fight!—
And a cry of exultation
　From the bearded warriors rose;
For we loved the house of Claver'se,
　And we thought of good Montrose.
But he raised his hand for silence—
　"Soldiers! I have sworn a vow:
Ere the evening star shall glisten
　On Schehallion's lofty brow,

Either we shall rest in triumph,
　Or another of the Græmes
Shall have died in battle-harness
　For his Country and King James!
Think upon the Royal Martyr—
　Think of what his race endure—
Think on him whom butchers murder'd
　On the field of Magus Muir:
By his sacred blood I charge ye,
　By the ruin'd hearth and shrine—
By the blighted hopes of Scotland,
　By your injuries and mine—
Strike this day as if the anvil
　Lay beneath your blows the while,
Be they Covenanting traitors,
　Or the brood of false Argyle!
Strike! and drive the trembling rebels
　Backward o'er the stormy Forth;
Let them tell their pale Convention
　How they fared within the North.
Let them tell that Highland honor
　Is not to be bought nor sold,
That we scorn their prince's anger
　As we loathe his foreign gold.
Strike! and when the fight is over,
　If you look in vain for me,
Where the dead are lying thickest
　Search for him that was Dundee!"

Loudly then the hills re-echoed
　With our answer to his call,
But a deeper echo sounded
　In the bosoms of us all.
For the lands of wide Breadalbane,
　Not a man who heard him speak
Would that day have left the battle.
　Burning eye and flushing cheek
Told the clansmen's fierce emotion,
　And they harder drew their breath;
For their souls were strong within them,
　Stronger than the grasp of death.
Soon we heard a challenge-trumpet
　Sounding in the pass below,
And the distant tramp of horses,
　And the voices of the foe;
Down we crouch'd amid the bracken,
　Till the Lowland ranks drew near,
Panting like the hounds in summer,
　When they scent the stately deer.
From the dark defile emerging,
　Next we saw the squadrons come,
Leslie's foot and Leven's troopers
　Marching to the tuck of drum;

Through the scatter'd wood of birches,
  O'er the broken ground and heath,
Wound the long battalion slowly,
  Till they gain'd the field beneath;
Then we bounded from our covert.—
  Judge how look'd the Saxons then,
When they saw the rugged mountain
  Start to life with armèd men!
Like a tempest down the ridges
  Swept the hurricane of steel,
Rose the Slogan of Macdonald—
  Flash'd the broadsword of Lochiel!
Vainly sped the withering volley
  'Mongst the foremost of our band—
On we pour'd until we met them,
  Foot to foot, and hand to hand.
Horse and man went down like drift-wood
  When the floods are black at Yule,
And their carcasses are whirling
  In the Garry's deepest pool.
Horse and man went down before us—
  Living foe there tarried none
On the field of Killiecrankie,
  When that stubborn fight was done!

And the evening star was shining
  On Schehallion's distant head,
When we wiped our bloody broadswords
  And return'd to count the dead.
There we found him gash'd and gory,
  Stretch'd upon the cumber'd plain,
As he told us where to seek him,
  In the thickest of the slain.
And a smile was on his visage,
  For within his dying ear
Peal'd the joyful note of triumph,
  And the clansmen's clamorous cheer:
So, amidst the battle's thunder,
  Shot, and steel, and scorching flame,
In the glory of his manhood
  Pass'd the spirit of the Græme!

Open wide the vaults of Athol,
  Where the bones of heroes rest—
Open wide the hallow'd portals
  To receive another guest!
Last of Scots, and last of freemen—
  Last of all that dauntless race
Who would rather die unsullied
  Than outlive the land's disgrace!

O thou lion-hearted warrior!
  Reck not of the after-time:
Honor may be deem'd dishonor,
  Loyalty be called a crime.
Sleep in peace with kindred ashes
  Of the noble and the true,
Hands that never failed their country,
  Hearts that never baseness knew.
Sleep!—and till the latest trumpet
  Wakes the dead from earth and sea,
Scotland shall not boast a braver
  Chieftain than our own Dundee!
        WILLIAM EDMONDSTOUNE AYTOUN.

HERVÉ RIEL.

On the sea and at the Hogue, sixteen hundred ninety-two,
  Did the English fight the French,—woe to France!
And the thirty-first of May, helter-skelter through the blue,
  Like a crowd of frighten'd porpoises a shoal of sharks pursue,
Came crowding ship on ship to St. Malo on the Rance,
  With the English fleet in view.

'Twas the squadron that escap'd, with the victor in full chase:
  First and foremost of the drove, in his great ship, Damfreville;
Close on him fled, great and small,
Twenty-two good ships in all;
And they signall'd to the place,
  " Help the winners of a race!
Get us guidance, give us harbor, take us quick; or, quicker still,
  Here's the English can and will!"

Then the pilots of the place put out brisk, and leap'd on board:
  " Why, what hope or chance have ships like these to pass?" laugh'd they·
" Rocks to starboard, rocks to port, all the passage scarr'd and scored.
Shall the 'Formidable' here with her twelve and eighty guns
  Think to make the river-mouth by the single narrow way,
Trust to enter where 'tis ticklish for a craft of twenty tons,

And with flow at full beside?
Now 'tis slackest ebb of tide.
Reach the mooring? Rather say,
While rock stands, or water runs,
Not a ship will leave the bay!"

Then was call'd a council straight:
Brief and bitter the debate.
"Here's the English at our heels: would you have them take in tow
All that's left us of the fleet, link'd together stern and bow,
For a prize to Plymouth Sound?
Better run the ships aground!"
(Ended Damfreville his speech.)
"Not a minute more to wait!
Let the captains all and each
Shove ashore, then blow up, burn the vessels on the beach!
France must undergo her fate."

"Give the word!" But no such word
Was ever spoke or heard:
For up stood, for out stepp'd, for in struck, amid all these,—
A captain? a lieutenant? a mate,—first, second, third?
No such man of mark and meet
With his betters to compete!
But a simple Breton sailor press'd by Tourville for the fleet,
A poor coasting-pilot he,—Hervé Riel the Croisickese.

And "What mockery or malice have we here?" cries Hervé Riel.
"Are you mad, you Malouins? Are you cowards, fools, or rogues?
Talk to me of rocks and shoals? me, who took the soundings, tell
On my fingers every bank, every shallow, every swell,
'Twixt the offing here and Grève, where the river disembogues?
Are you bought by English gold? Is it love the lying's for?
Morn and eve night and day,
Have I piloted your bay,
Enter'd free and anchor'd fast at the foot of Solidor.

Burn the fleet, and ruin France? That were worse than fifty Hogues!
Sirs, they know I speak the truth! Sirs, believe me, there's a way!
Only let me lead the line,
Have the biggest ship to steer.
Get this 'Formidable' clear,
Make the others follow mine,
And I lead them, most and least, by a passage I know well,
Right to Solidor, past Grève,
And there lay them safe and sound;
And, if one ship misbehave,—
Keel so much as grate the ground,—
Why, I've nothing but my life: here's my head!" cries Hervé Riel.

Not a minute more to wait.
"Steer us in, then, small and great!
Take the helm, lead the line, save the squadron!" cried its chief.
Captains, give the sailor place!
He is admiral, in brief.
Still the north wind, by God's grace.
See the noble fellow's face,
As the big ship, with a bound,
Clears the entry like a hound,
Keeps the passage as its inch of way were the wide sea's profound!
See, safe through shoal and rock,
How they follow in a flock!
Not a ship that misbehaves, not a keel that grates the ground,
Not a spar that comes to grief!
The peril, see, is past!
All are harbor'd to the last!
And just as Hervé Riel holloas "Anchor!" sure as fate,
Up the English come,—too late!
So the storm subsides to calm:
They see the green trees wave
On the heights o'erlooking Grève;
Hearts that bled are stanch'd with balm.
"Just our rapture to enhance,
Let the English rake the bay,
Gnash their teeth and glare askance
As they cannonade away!
'Neath rampir'd Solidor pleasant riding on the Rance!"
How hope succeeds despair on each captain's countenance!

Out burst all with one accord,
  "This is paradise for hell!
    Let France, let France's king,
    Thank the man that did the thing!"
What a shout, and all one word,
  "Hervé Riel!"
As he stepp'd in front once more;
  Not a symptom of surprise
In the frank blue Breton eyes,—
Just the same man as before.
Then said Damfreville, "My friend,
I must speak out at the end,
  Though I find the speaking hard:
Praise is deeper than the lips:
You have saved the king his ships;
  You must name your own reward.
'Faith, our sun was near eclipse!
Demand whate'er you will,
France remains your debtor still.
Ask to heart's content, and have! or my
  name's not Damfreville."

Then a beam of fun outbroke
On the bearded mouth that spoke,
  As the honest heart laugh'd through
Those frank eyes of Breton blue:—
"Since I needs must say my say;
  Since on board the duty's done,
    And from Malo Roads to Croisic Point
what is it but a run?—
Since 'tis ask and have, I may;
  Since the others go ashore,—
Come! A good whole holiday!
  Leave to go and see my wife, whom I
    call the Belle Aurore!"
That he ask'd, and that he got,—nothing more.

Name and deed alike are lost:
Not a pillar nor a post
  In his Croisic keeps alive the feat as it
    befell;
Not a head in white and black
On a single fishing-smack
  In memory of the man but for whom had
    gone to wrack
    All that France sav'd from the fight
      whence England bore the bell.
Go to Paris; rank on rank
  Search the heroes flung pell-mell
On the Louvre, face and flank:
  You shall look long enough ere you
    come to Hervé Riel.

So, for better and for worse,
Hervé Riel, accept my verse!
In my verse, Hervé Riel, do thou once
  more
Save the squadron, honor France, love thy
  wife, the Belle Aurore!
                ROBERT BROWNING.

FONTENOY.

THRICE, at the huts of Fontenoy, the English column fail'd,
And twice the lines of Saint Antoine the Dutch in vain assail'd,
For town and slope were fill'd with fort and flanking battery,
And well they swept the English ranks and Dutch auxiliary.
As vainly, through De Barri's wood, the British soldiers burst,
The French artillery drove them back, diminish'd and dispersed.
The bloody Duke of Cumberland beheld with anxious eye,
And order'd up his last reserve, his latest chance to try;
On Fontenoy, on Fontenoy, how fast his generals ride!
And mustering come his chosen troops, like clouds at eventide.

Six thousand English veterans in stately column tread,
Their cannon blaze in front and flank, Lord Hay is at their head;
Steady they step adown the slope, steady they climb the hill,
Steady they load, steady they fire, moving right onward still,
Betwixt the wood and Fontenoy, as through a furnace-blast,
Through rampart, trench, and palisade, and bullets showering fast;
And on the open plain above they rose, and kept their course,
With ready fire and grim resolve, that mock'd at hostile force:

Past Fontenoy, past Fontenoy, while thinner grow their ranks—
They break, as broke the Zuyder Zee through Holland's ocean banks.

More idly than the summer flies French tirailleurs rush round;
As stubble to the lava tide French squadrons strew the ground;
Bomb-shell, and grape, and round-shot tore, still on they march'd and fired—
Fast, from each volley, grenadier and voltigeur retired.
"Push on, my household cavalry!" King Louis madly cried:
To death they rush, but rude their shock; not unavenged they died.
On through the camp the column trod—King Louis turns his rein:
"Not yet, my liege," Saxe interposed, "the Irish troops remain;"
And Fontenoy, famed Fontenoy, had been a Waterloo,
Were not these exiles ready then, fresh, vehement, and true.

"Lord Clare," he says, "you have your wish, there are your Saxon foes!"
The Marshal almost smiles to see, so furiously he goes.
How fierce the look these exiles wear, who're wont to be so gay;
The treasured wrongs of fifty years are in their hearts to-day—
The treaty broken, ere the ink wherewith 'twas writ could dry,
Their plunder'd homes, their ruin'd shrines, their women's parting cry,
Their priesthood hunted down like wolves, their country overthrown,—
Each looks as if revenge for all were staked on him alone.
On Fontenoy, on Fontenoy, nor ever yet elsewhere,
Rush'd on to fight a nobler band than these proud exiles were.

O'Brien's voice is hoarse with joy, as, halting, he commands,
"Fix bay'nets"—"Charge;" like mountain-storm rush on these fiery bands.

Thin is the English column now, and faint their volleys grow,
Yet, must'ring all the strength they have, they make a gallant show.
They dress their ranks upon the hill to face that battle-wind,
Their bayonets the breakers' foam, like rocks the men behind;
One volley crashes from their line, when, through the surging smoke,
With empty guns clutch'd in their hands, the headlong Irish broke.
On Fontenoy, on Fontenoy, hark to that fierce huzza:
"Revenge! remember Limerick! dash down the Sacsanach!"

Like lions leaping at a fold, when mad with hunger's pang,
Right up against the English line the Irish exiles sprang;
Bright was their steel, 'tis bloody now, their guns are fill'd with gore;
Through shatter'd ranks, and sever'd files, and trampled flags they tore;
The English strove with desperate strength, paused, rallied, stagger'd, fled,—
The green hillside is matted close with dying and with dead.
Across the plain and far away pass'd on that hideous wrack,
While cavalier and fantassin dash in upon their track.
On Fontenoy, on Fontenoy, like eagles in the sun,
With bloody plumes the Irish stand—the field is fought and won!

THOMAS OSBORNE DAVIS.

BATTLE OF FONTENOY.

By our camp-fires rose a murmur
  At the dawning of the day,
And the tread of many footsteps
  Spoke the advent of the fray;
And as we took our places,
  Few and stern were our words,
While some were tightening horse-girths,
  And some were girding swords.

The trumpet-blast has sounded
  Our footmen to array—

The willing steed has bounded,
    Impatient for the fray—
The green flag is unfolded,
    While rose the cry of joy—
" Heaven speed dear Ireland's banner
    To-day at Fontenoy !"

We look'd upon that banner,
    And the memory arose
Of our homes and perish'd kindred
    Where the Lee or Shannon flows ;
We look'd upon that banner,
    And we swore to God on high,
To smite to-day the Saxon's might—
    To conquer or to die.

Loud swells the charging trumpet—
    'Tis a voice from our own land—
God of battles ! God of vengeance !
    Guide to-day the patriot's brand ;
There are stains to wash away,
    There are memories to destroy,
In the best blood of the Briton
    To-day at Fontenoy.

Plunge deep the fiery rowels
    In a thousand reeking flanks—
Down, chivalry of Ireland,
    Down on the British ranks !
Now shall their serried columns
    Beneath our sabres reel—
Through their ranks, then, with the war-horse—
    Through their bosoms with the steel.

With one shout for good King Louis,
    And the fair land of the vine,
Like the wrathful Alpine tempest,
    We swept upon their line—
Then rang along the battle-field
    Triumphant our hurrah,
And we smote them down, still cheering,
    " *Erin, slanthagal go bragh.*"

As prized as is the blessing
    From an aged father's lip—
As welcome as the haven
    To the tempest-driven ship—
As dear as to the lover
    The smile of gentle maid—
Is this day of long-sought vengeance
    To the swords of the Brigade.

See their shatter'd forces flying,
    A broken, routed line—
See, England, what brave laurels
    For your brow to-day we twine.
Oh, thrice bless'd the hour that witness'd
    The Briton turn to flee
From the chivalry of Erin
    And France's "*fleur de lis.*"

As we lay beside our camp-fires,
    When the sun had pass'd away,
And thought upon our brethren
    Who had perish'd in the fray,
We pray'd to God to grant us,
    And then we'd die with joy,
One day upon our own dear land
    Like this of Fontenoy.
                BARTHOLOMEW DOWLING.

LOCHIEL'S WARNING.
WIZARD—LOCHIEL.
WIZARD.

LOCHIEL, Lochiel ! beware of the day
When the Lowlands shall meet thee in battle-array !
For a field of the dead rushes red on my sight,
And the clans of Culloden are scatter'd in fight.
They rally, they bleed, for their kingdom and crown ;
Woe, woe to the riders that trample them down !
Proud Cumberland prances, insulting the slain,
And their hoof-beaten bosoms are trod to the plain.
But hark ! through the fast-flashing lightning of war
What steed to the desert flies frantic and far ?
'Tis thine, O Glenullin ! whose bride shall await,
Like a love-lighted watch-fire, all night at the gate.
A steed comes at morning : no rider is there ;
But its bridle is red with the sign of despair.
Weep, Albin ! to death and captivity led—
Oh weep ! but thy tears cannot number the dead ;

For a merciless sword on Culloden shall
   wave,
Culloden that reeks with the blood of the
   brave.

LOCHIEL.

Go, preach to the coward, thou death-tell-
   ing seer!
Or, if gory Culloden so dreadful appear,
Draw, dotard, around thy old wavering
   sight
This mantle, to cover the phantoms of
   fright.

WIZARD.

Ha! laugh'st thou, Lochiel, my vision to
   scorn?
Proud bird of the mountain, thy plume
   shall be torn!
Say, rush'd the bold eagle exultingly forth
From his home in the dark-rolling clouds
   of the north?
Lo! the death-shot of foemen outspeeding,
   he rode
Companionless, bearing destruction
   abroad;
But down let him stoop from his havoc on
   high!
Ah! home let him speed—for the spoiler is
   nigh.
Why flames the far summit? Why shoot
   to the blast
Those embers, like stars from the firmament
   cast?
'Tis the fire-shower of ruin, all dreadfully
   driven
From his eyrie, that beacons the darkness
   of heaven.
Oh, crested Lochiel! the peerless in might,
Whose banners arise on the battlements'
   height,
Heaven's fire is around thee, to blast and
   to burn;
Return to thy dwelling! all lonely return!
For the blackness of ashes shall mark
   where it stood,
And a wild mother scream o'er her famish-
   ing brood.

LOCHIEL.

False wizard, avaunt! I have marshall'd
   my clan;
Their swords are a thousand, their bosoms
   are one!
They are true to the last of their blood and
   their breath,
And like reapers descend to the harvest of
   death.
Then welcome be Cumberland's steed to
   the shock!
Let him dash his proud foam like a wave
   on the rock!
But woe to his kindred, and woe to his
   cause,
When Albin her claymore indignantly
   draws;
When her bonneted chieftains to victory
   crowd,
Clanronald the dauntless, and Moray the
   proud,
All plaided and plumed in their tartan
   array——

WIZARD.

——Lochiel, Lochiel! beware of the day;
For, dark and despairing, my sight I may
   seal,
But man cannot cover what God would re-
   veal;
'Tis the sunset of life gives me mystical
   lore,
And coming events casts their shadows be-
   fore.
I tell thee, Culloden's dread echoes shall
   ring
With the bloodhounds that bark for thy
   fugitive king.
Lo! anointed by heaven with the vials of
   wrath,
Behold, where he flies on his desolate path!
Now in darkness and billows he sweeps
   from my sight:
Rise, rise! ye wild tempests, and cover his
   flight!
'Tis finish'd. Their thunders are hush'd
   on the moors;
Culloden is lost, and my country de-
   plores.
But where is the iron-bound prisoner?
   where?
For the red eye of battle is shut in de-
   spair.
Say, mounts he the ocean-wave, banish'd,
   forlorn,
Like a limb from his country cast bleeding
   and torn?

Ah no! for a darker departure is near;
The war-drum is muffled and black is the bier;
His death-bell is tolling. Oh! mercy, dispel
Yon sight, that it freezes my spirit to tell!
Life flutters convulsed in his quivering limbs,
And his blood-streaming nostril in agony swims.
Accursed be the fagots that blaze at his feet,
Where his heart shall be thrown ere it ceases to beat,
With the smoke of its ashes to poison the gale——

Lochiel.

——Down, soothless insulter! I trust not the tale:
For never shall Albin a destiny meet
So black with dishonor, so foul with retreat.
Though my perishing ranks should be strew'd in their gore,
Like ocean-weeds heap'd on the surf-beaten shore,
Lochiel, untainted by flight or by chains,
While the kindling of life in his bosom remains,
Shall victor exult, or in death be laid low,
With his back to the field, and his feet to the foe!
And, leaving in battle no blot on his name,
Look proudly to heaven from the death-bed of fame.
Thomas Campbell.

YOUNG AIRLY.

Ken ye aught of brave Lochiel?
 Or ken ye aught of Airly?
They have belted on their bright broad swords,
 And off and awa' wi' Charlie.
Now bring me fire, my merry, merry men,
 And bring it red and yarely—
At mirk midnight there flash'd a light
 O'er the topmost towers of Airly.

What lowe is yon, quo' the gude Lochiel,
 Which gleams so red and rarely?
By the God of my kin, quo' young Ogilvie,
 It's my ain bonnie hame of Airly!
Put up your sword, said the brave Lochiel,
 And calm your mood, quo' Charlie;
Ere morning glow we'll raise a lowe
 Far brighter than bonnie Airly.

Oh, yon fair tower's my native tower!
 Nor will it soothe my mourning,
Were London palace, tower, and town
 As fast and brightly burning.
It's no my hame—my father's hame,
 That reddens my cheek sae sairlie—
But my wife, and twa sweet babes I left
 To smoor in the smoke of Airly.
Author Unknown.

CHARLIE IS MY DARLING.

'Twas on a Monday morning,
 Right early in the year,
That Charlie came to our town,
 The young Chevalier.
  An' Charlie is my darling,
   My darling, my darling,
  Charlie is my darling,
   The young Chevalier.

As Charlie he came up the gate,
 His face shone like the day;
I grat to see the lad come back
 That had been lang away.
  An' Charlie is my darling,
   My darling, my darling,
  Charlie is my darling,
   The young Chevalier.

Then ilka bonnie lassie sang,
 As to the door she ran,
Our king shall hae his ain again,
 An' Charlie is the man:
  For Charlie he's my darling,
   My darling, my darling,
  Charlie he's my darling,
   The young Chevalier.

Out owre yon moory mountain,
 An' down the craigy glen,
Of naething else our lasses sing
 But Charlie an' his men.

An' Charlie he's my darling,
  My darling, my darling,
Charlie he's my darling,
  The young Chevalier.

Our Highland hearts are true an' leal,
  An' glow without a stain;
Our Highland swords are metal keen,
  An' Charlie he's our ain.
    An' Charlie he's my darling,
      My darling, my darling,
    Charlie he's my darling,
      The young Chevalier.
                              JAMES HOGG.

BONNIE PRINCE CHARLIE.

CAM ye by Athol, lad wi' the philabeg,
  Down by the Tummel, or banks o' the Garry;
Saw ye our lads, wi' their bonnets and white cockades,
  Leaving their mountains to follow Prince Charlie?
Follow thee! follow thee! wha wadna follow thee?
  Lang hast thou loved and trusted us fairly:
Charlie, Charlie, wha wadna follow thee,
  King o' the Highland hearts, bonny Prince Charlie?

I hae but ae son, my gallant young Donald;
  But if I had ten, they should follow Glengary.
Health to M'Donnel, and gallant Clan-Ronald,
  For these are the men that will die for their Charlie!
Follow thee! follow thee! wha wadna follow thee?
  Lang hast thou loved and trusted us fairly:
Charlie, Charlie, wha wadna follow thee,
  King o' the Highland hearts, bonny Prince Charlie?

I'll to Lochiel and Appin, and kneel to them,
  Down by Lord Murray, and Roy of Kildarlie;
Brave M'Intosh he shall fly to the field with them;
  These are the lads I can trust wi' my Charlie!
Follow thee! follow thee! wha wadna follow thee?
  Lang hast thou loved and trusted us fairly:
Charlie, Charlie, wha wadna follow thee,
  King o' the Highland hearts, bonny Prince Charlie?

Down through the Lowlands, down wi' the Whigamore!
  Loyal true Highlanders, down wi' them rarely!
Ronald and Donald, drive on wi' the broad claymore,
  Over the necks of the foes of Prince Charlie!
Follow thee! follow thee! wha wadna follow thee?
  Lang hast thou loved and trusted us fairly:
Charlie, Charlie, wha wadna follow thee,
  King o' the Highland hearts, bonny Prince Charlie?
                              JAMES HOGG.

WAE'S ME FOR PRINCE CHARLIE!

A WEE bird came to our ha'-door;
  He warbled sweet and clearly;
And aye the o'ercome o' his sang
  Was "Wae's me for Prince Charlie!"
Oh, when I heard the bonny, bonny bird,
  The tears came drapping rarely;
I took my bonnet aff my head,
  For weel I lo'ed Prince Charlie.

Quoth I: "My bird, my bonny, bonny bird,
  Is that a tale ye borrow?
Or is't some words ye've learn'd by rote,
  Or a lilt o' dool and sorrow?"
"Oh, no, no, no!" the wee bird sang,
  "I've flown sin' morning early;
But sic a day o' wind and rain!—
  Oh, wae's me for Prince Charlie!

"On hills that are by right his ain
  He roams a lonely stranger;
On ilka hand he's press'd by want,
  On ilka side by danger.
Yestreen I met him in the glen,
  My heart near bursted fairly;
For sadly changed indeed was he—
  Oh, wae's me for Prince Charlie!

"Dark night came on; the tempest howl'd
  Out owre the hills and valleys;
And where was't that your prince lay down,
  Whase hame should be a palace?
He row'd him in a Highland plaid,
  Which cover'd him but sparely,
And slept beneath a bush o' broom—
  Oh, wae's me for Prince Charlie!"

But now the bird saw some red-coats,
  And he shook his wings wi' anger:
"Oh, this is no a land for me—
  I'll tarry here nae langer."
A while he hover'd on the wing,
  Ere he departed fairly;
But weel I mind the farewell strain,
  'Twas " Wae's me for Prince Charlie!"
                WILLIAM GLEN.

THE TEARS OF SCOTLAND.

MOURN, hapless Caledonia, mourn
Thy banish'd peace, thy laurels torn!
Thy sons, for valor long renown'd,
Lie slaughter'd on their native ground;
Thy hospitable roofs no more
Invite the stranger to the door;
In smoky ruins sunk they lie,
The monuments of cruelty.

The wretched owner sees afar
His all become the prey of war;
Bethinks him of his babes and wife,
Then smites his breast, and curses life.
Thy swains are famish'd on the rocks,
Where once they fed their wanton flocks:
Thy ravish'd virgins shriek in vain;
Thy infants perish on the plain.

What boots it, then, in every clime,
Through the wide-spreading waste of time,
Thy martial glory, crown'd with praise,
Still shone with undiminish'd blaze!

Thy tow'ring spirit now is broke,
Thy neck is bended to the yoke.
What foreign arms could never quell,
By civil rage and rancor fell.

The rural pipe and merry lay
No more shall cheer the happy day:
No social scenes of gay delight
Beguile the dreary winter night:
No strains but those of sorrow flow,
And naught be heard but sounds of woe,
While the pale phantoms of the slain
Glide nightly o'er the silent plain.

O baneful cause! O fatal morn!
Accursed to ages yet unborn!
The sons against their father stood,
The parent shed his children's blood.
Yet, when the rage of battle ceased,
The victor's soul was not appeased:
The naked and forlorn must feel
Devouring flames and murd'ring steel!

The pious mother, doom'd to death,
Forsaken wanders o'er the heath;
The bleak wind whistles round her head,
Her helpless orphans cry for bread;
Bereft of shelter, food, and friend,
She views the shades of night descend;
And, stretch'd beneath th' inclement skies
Weeps o'er her tender babes, and dies.

While the warm blood bedews my veins,
And unimpair'd remembrance reigns,
Resentment of my country's fate
Within my filial breast shall beat;
And, spite of her insulting foe,
My sympathizing verse shall flow:
" Mourn, hapless Caledonia, mourn
Thy banish'd peace, thy laurels torn."
                TOBIAS SMOLLETT.

THE POMPADOUR.

VERSAILLES!—Up the chestnut alley,
  All in flower, so white and pure,
Strut the red and yellow lacqueys
  Of this Madame Pompadour.

"Clear the way!" cry out the lacqueys,
  Elbowing the lame and poor
From the chapel's stately porches,—
  "Way for Madame Pompadour!"

Old bent soldiers, crippled veterans,
  Sigh and hobble, sad, footsore,
Jostled by the chariot-horses
  Of this woman—Pompadour.

Through the levée (poet, marquis,
  Wistful for the opening door),
With a rippling sweep of satin,
  Sail'd the queenly Pompadour.

Sighs by dozens, as she proudly
  Glides, so confident and sure,
With her fan that breaks through halberds—
  In went Madame Pompadour.

Starving abbé, wounded marshal,
  Speculator, lean and poor,
Cringe and shrink before the creatures
  Of this harlot Pompadour.

"Rose in sunshine! Summer lily!"
  Cries a poet at the door,
Squeezed and trampled by the lacqueys
  Of the witching Pompadour.

"Bathed in milk and fed on roses!"
  Sighs a pimp behind the door,
Jamm'd and bullied by the courtiers
  Of this strumpet Pompadour.

"Rose of Sharon!" chants an abbé,
  Fat and with the voice of four,
Black silk stockings soil'd by varlets
  Of this Rahab Pompadour.

"Neck so swan-like,—*Dea certe!*
  Fit for monarchs to adore!"
"Clear the way!" was still the echo,
  "For this Venus—Pompadour."

Open!—with the jar of thunder
  Fly the portals,—clocks strike four;
With a burst of drums and trumpets
  Come the king and Pompadour.
          GEORGE WALTER THORNBURY.

LOUIS XV.

THE king with all his kingly train
  Had left his Pompadour behind,
And forth he rode in Senart's wood,
  The royal beasts of chase to find.
That day by chance the monarch mused,
  And, turning suddenly away,
He struck alone into a path
  That far from crowds and courtiers lay.

He saw the pale green shadows play
  Upon the brown untrodden earth;
He saw the birds around him flit
  As if he were of peasant birth;
He saw the trees that know no king
  But him who bears a woodland axe;
He thought not, but he look'd about
  Like one who skill in thinking lacks.

Then close to him a footstep fell,
  And glad of human sound was he,
For, truth to say, he found himself
  A weight from which he fain would flee.
But that which he would ne'er have guess'd
  Before him now most plainly came;
The man upon his weary back
  A coffin bore of rudest frame.

"Why, who art thou?" exclaimed the king,
  "And what is that I see thee bear?"
"I am a laborer in the wood,
  And 'tis a coffin for Pierre.
Close by the royal hunting-lodge
  You may have often seen him toil;
But he will never work again,
  And I for him must dig the soil."

The laborer ne'er had seen the king,
  And this he thought was but a man,
Who made at first a moment's pause,
  And then anew his talk began:
"I think I do remember now,—
  He had a dark and glancing eye,
And I have seen his slender arm
  With wondrous blows the pickaxe ply.

"Pray tell me, friend, what accident
  Can thus have kill'd our good Pierre?"
"Oh, nothing more than usual, sir,
  He died of living upon air.
'Twas hunger kill'd the poor good man,
  Who long on empty hopes relied;
He could not pay gabell and tax,
  And feed his children, so he died."

The man stopp'd short, and then went on,—
  "It is, you know, a common thing;
Our children's bread is eaten up
  By courtiers, mistresses, and king."

The king look'd hard upon the man,
  And afterward the coffin eyed;
Then spurr'd to ask of Pompadour
  How came it that the peasants died.
                              JOHN STERLING.

WARREN'S ADDRESS.

STAND! the ground's your own, my braves!
Will ye give it up to slaves?
Will ye look for greener graves?
  Hope ye mercy still?
What's the mercy despots feel?
Hear it in that battle-peal!
Read it on yon bristling steel!
  Ask it,—ye who will.

Fear ye foes who kill for hire?
Will ye to your *homes* retire?
Look behind you!—they're afire!
  And, before you, see
Who have done it! From the vale
On they come!—and will ye quail?
Leaden rain and iron hail
  Let their welcome be!

In the God of battles trust!
Die we may,—and die we must:
But, oh where can dust to dust
  Be consign'd so well,
As where Heaven its dews shall shed
On the martyr'd patriot's bed,
And the rocks shall raise their head
  Of his deeds to tell?
                              JOHN PIERPONT.

PAUL REVERE'S RIDE.

LISTEN, my children, and you shall hear
Of the midnight ride of Paul Revere,
On the eighteenth of April, in Seventy-five;
Hardly a man is now alive
Who remembers that famous day and year.

He said to his friend, "If the British march
By land or sea from the town to-night,
Hang a lantern aloft in the belfry arch
Of the North Church tower as a signal light,—
One, if by land, and two, if by sea;
And I on the opposite shore will be,
Ready to ride and spread the alarm
Through every Middlesex village and farm,
For the country folk to be up and to arm."

Then he said "Good-night," and with muffled oar
Silently row'd to the Charlestown shore,
Just as the moon rose over the bay,
Where swinging wide at her moorings lay
The Somerset, British man-of-war;
A phantom ship, with each mast and spar
Across the moon like a prison bar,
And a huge black hulk, that was magnified
By its own reflection in the tide.

Meanwhile his friend, through alley and street,
Wanders and watches with eager ears,
Till in the silence around him he hears
The muster of men at the barrack-door,
The sound of arms, and the tramp of feet,
And the measured tread of the grenadiers
Marching down to their boats on the shore.

Then he climb'd the tower of the Old North Church,
By the wooden stairs, with stealthy tread,
To the belfry-chamber overhead,
And startled the pigeons from their perch
On the sombre rafters, that round him made
Masses and moving shapes of shade,—
By the trembling ladder, steep and tall,
To the highest window in the wall,
Where he paused to listen and look down
A moment on the roofs of the town,
And the moonlight flowing over all.

Beneath, in the churchyard, lay the dead,
In their night-encampment on the hill,
Wrapp'd in silence so deep and still
That he could hear, like a sentinel's tread,
The watchful night-wind, as it went
Creeping along from tent to tent,
And seeming to whisper, "All is well!"
A moment only he feels the spell
Of the place and the hour, and the secret dread
Of the lonely belfry and the dead;

For suddenly all his thoughts are bent
On a shadowy something far away,
Where the river widens to meet the bay,—
A line of black that bends and floats
On the rising tide like a bridge of boats.

Meanwhile, impatient to mount and ride,
Booted and spurr'd, with a heavy stride
On the opposite shore walk'd Paul Revere.
Now he patted his horse's side,
Now gazed at the landscape far and near,
Then, impetuous, stamp'd the earth,
And turn'd and tighten'd his saddle-girth;
But mostly he watch'd with eager search
The belfry-tower of the Old North Church,
As it rose above the graves on the hill,
Lonely and spectral and sombre and still.
And lo! as he looks on the belfry's height
A glimmer, and then a gleam of light!
He springs to the saddle, the bridle he turns,
But lingers and gazes, till full on his sight
A second lamp in the belfry burns.

A hurry of hoofs in a village street,
A shape in the moonlight, a bulk in the dark,
And beneath, from the pebbles, in passing, a spark
Struck out by a steed flying fearless and fleet:
That was all; and yet, through the gloom and the light,
The fate of a nation was riding that night;
And the spark struck out by that steed in his flight
Kindled the land into flame with its heat.

He has left the village and mounted the steep,
And beneath him, tranquil and broad and deep,
Is the Mystic, meeting the ocean tides,
And under the alders that skirt its edge,
Now soft on the sand, now loud on the ledge,
Is heard the tramp of his steed as he rides.

It was twelve by the village clock
When he cross'd the bridge into Medford town.
He heard the crowing of the cock,
And the barking of the farmer's dog,
And felt the damp of the river fog,
That rises after the sun goes down.

It was one by the village clock
When he galloped into Lexington.
He saw the gilded weathercock
Swim in the moonlight as he pass'd,
And the meeting-house windows, blank and bare,
Gaze at him with a spectral glare,
As if they already stood aghast
At the bloody work they would look upon.

It was two by the village clock
When he came to the bridge in Concord town.
He heard the bleating of the flock,
And the twitter of birds among the trees,
And felt the breath of the morning breeze
Blowing over the meadows brown.
And one was safe and asleep in his bed
Who at the bridge would be first to fall,
Who that day would be lying dead,
Pierced by a British musket-ball.

You know the rest; in the books you have read,
How the British regulars fired and fled,—
How the farmers gave them ball for ball,
From behind each fence and farmyard wall,
Chasing the red-coats down the lane,
Then crossing the fields to emerge again
Under the trees at the turn of the road,
And only pausing to fire and load.

So through the night rode Paul Revere,
And so through the night went his cry of alarm
To every Middlesex village and farm,—
A cry of defiance, and not of fear,
A voice in the darkness, a knock at the door,
And a word that shall echo for evermore!
For, borne on the night-wind of the Past,
Through all our history, to the last,
In the hour of darkness, and peril, and need,
The people will waken and listen to hear
The hurrying hoof-beats of that steed,
And the midnight message of Paul Revere.

HENRY WADSWORTH LONGFELLOW.

SONG OF MARION'S MEN.

Our band is few, but true and tried,
　Our leader frank and bold;
The British soldier trembles
　When Marion's name is told.
Our fortress is the good greenwood,
　Our tent the cypress tree;
We know the forest round us,
　As seamen know the sea;
We know its walls of thorny vines,
　Its glades of reedy grass,
Its safe and silent islands
　Within the dark morass.

Woe to the English soldiery
　That little dread us near!
On them shall light at midnight
　A strange and sudden fear;
When, waking to their tents on fire,
　They grasp their arms in vain,
And they who stand to face us
　Are beat to earth again;
And they who fly in terror deem
　A mighty host behind,
And hear the tramp of thousands
　Upon the hollow wind.

Then sweet the hour that brings release
　From danger and from toil:
We talk the battle over,
　And share the battle's spoil.
The woodland rings with laugh and shout,
　As if a hunt were up,
And woodland flowers are gather'd
　To crown the soldier's cup.
With merry songs we mock the wind
　That in the pine-top grieves,
And slumber long and sweetly
　On beds of oaken leaves.

Well knows the fair and friendly moon
　The band that Marion leads—
The glitter of their rifles,
　The scampering of their steeds.
'Tis life to guide the fiery barb
　Across the moonlight plain;
'Tis life to feel the night-wind
　That lifts his tossing mane.
A moment in the British camp—
　A moment—and away
Back to the pathless forest,
　Before the peep of day.

Grave men there are by broad Santee,
　Grave men with hoary hairs;
Their hearts are all with Marion,
　For Marion are their prayers.
And lovely ladies greet our band
　With kindliest welcoming,
With smiles like those of summer,
　And tears like those of spring.
For them we wear these trusty arms,
　And lay them down no more
Till we have driven the Briton
　For ever from our shore.
　　　　　　WILLIAM CULLEN BRYANT.

CARMEN BELLICOSUM.

In their ragged regimentals,
Stood the old Continentals,
　　Yielding not,
When the grenadiers were lunging,
And like hail fell the plunging
　　Cannon-shot;
　　　When the files
　　　Of the isles,
From the smoky night encampment,
Bore the banner of the rampant
　　Unicorn,
And grummer, grummer, grummer,
Roll'd the roll of the drummer,
　　Through the morn!

Then with eyes to the front all,
And with guns horizontal,
　　Stood our sires;
And the balls whistled deadly,
And in streams flashing redly
　　Blazed the fires;
　　　As the roar
　　　On the shore
Swept the strong battle-breakers
O'er the green-sodded acres
　　Of the plain:
And louder, louder, louder,
Crack'd the black gunpowder,
　　Crack'd amain!

Now like smiths at their forges
Work'd the red St. George's
　　Cannoneers,
And the "villainous saltpetre"
Rang a fierce discordant metre
　　Round their ears;

As the swift
　　Storm-drift
With hot sweeping anger,
Came the horseguards' clangor
　　On our flanks;
Then higher, higher, higher,
Burn'd the old-fashion'd fire
　　Through the ranks!

Then the old-fashion'd colonel
Gallop'd through the white infernal
　　Powder-cloud;
And his broad sword was swinging,
And his brazen throat was ringing
　　Trumpet loud.
　　　Then the blue
　　　Bullets flew,
And the trooper-jackets redden
At the touch of the leaden
　　Rifle-breath;
And rounder, rounder, rounder
Roar'd the iron six-pounder,
　　Hurling death!
　　　　GUY HUMPHREY MCMASTER.

LA TRICOTEUSE.

THE fourteenth of July had come,
　　And round the guillotine
The thieves and beggars, rank by rank,
　　Moved the red flags between.
A crimson heart, upon a pole,—
　　The long march had begun;
But still the little smiling child
　　Sat knitting in the sun.

The red caps of those men of France
　　Shook like a poppy-field;
Three women's heads, with gory hair,
　　The standard-bearers wield.
Cursing, with song and battle-hymn,
　　Five butchers dragg'd a gun;
Yet still the little maid sat there,
　　A-knitting in the sun.

An axe was painted on the flags,
　　A broken throne and crown,
A ragged coat, upon a lance,
　　Hung in foul black shreds down.
"More heads!" the seething rabble cry,
　　And now the drums begun;
But still the little fair-hair'd child
　　Sat knitting in the sun.

And every time a head roll'd off,
　　They roll like winter seas,
And, with a tossing up of caps,
　　Shouts shook the Tuileries.
Whizz—went the heavy chopper down,
　　And then the drums begun;
But still the little smiling child
　　Sat knitting in the sun.

The Jacobins, ten thousand strong,
　　And every man a sword;
The red caps, with the tricolors,
　　Led on the noisy horde.
"The *Sans Culottes* to-day are strong,"
　　The gossips say, and run;
But still the little maid sits there,
　　A-knitting in the sun.

Then the slow death-cart moved along;
　　And, singing patriot songs,
A pale, doom'd poet bowing comes
　　And cheers the swaying throngs.
Oh, when the axe swept shining down,
　　The mad drums all begun;
But, smiling still, the little child
　　Sat knitting in the sun.

"Le marquis," linen snowy white,
　　The powder in his hair,
Waving his scented handkerchief,
　　Looks down with careless stare.
A whirr, a chop—another head—
　　Hurrah! the work's begun;
But still the little child sat there,
　　A-knitting in the sun.

A stir, and through the parting crowd
　　The people's friends are come;
Marat and Robespierre—"Vivat!
　　Roll thunder from the drum."
The one a wild beast's hungry eye,
　　Hair tangled—hark! a gun!—
The other kindly kiss'd the child
　　A-knitting in the sun.

"And why not work all night?" the child
　　Said to the knitters there.
Oh how the furies shook their sides,
　　And toss'd their grizzled hair!
Then clapp'd a *bonnet rouge* on her,
　　And cried, "'Tis well begun!"
And laugh'd to see the little child
　　Knit, smiling in the sun.
　　　　GEORGE WALTER THORNBURY.

FRANCE: AN ODE.
FEBRUARY, 1797.

Ye Clouds! that far above me float and pause,
  Whose pathless march no mortal may control!
Ye Ocean-Waves! that, wheresoe'er ye roll,
Yield homage only to eternal laws!
  Ye Woods! that listen to the night-birds singing,
Midway the smooth and perilous slope reclined,
  Save when your own imperious branches swinging
Have made a solemn music of the wind!
  Where, like a man beloved of God,
  Through glooms, which never woodman trod,
How oft, pursuing fancies holy,
  My moonlight way o'er flowering weeds I wound,
Inspired beyond the guess of folly,
  By each rude shape and wild unconquerable sound!
O ye loud Waves! and O ye Forests high!
And O ye Clouds that far above me soar'd!
Thou rising Sun! thou blue, rejoicing Sky!
  Yea, everything that is and will be free!
Bear witness for me, wheresoe'er ye be,
With what deep worship I have still adored
The spirit of divinest Liberty.

When France in wrath her giant limbs uprear'd,
  And with that oath, which smote air, earth, and sea,
  Stamp'd her strong foot and said she would be free,
Bear witness for me, how I hoped and fear'd!
With what a joy my lofty gratulation
Unawed I sang, amid a slavish band:
  And when to whelm the disenchanted nation,
Like fiends embattled by a wizard's wand,
  The Monarchs march'd in evil day,
  And Britain join'd the dire array;
Though dear her shores and circling ocean,
Though many friendships, many youthful loves
  Had swoln the patriot emotion,
And flung a magic light o'er all her hills and groves;
  Yet still my voice, unalter'd, sang defeat
To all that braved the tyrant-quelling lance,
  And shame too long delay'd and vain retreat!
For ne'er, O Liberty! with partial aim
I dimm'd thy light or damp'd thy holy flame;
  But bless'd the pæans of deliver'd France,
And hung my head and wept at Britain's name.

"And what," I said, "though Blasphemy's loud scream
  With that sweet music of deliverance strove!
Though all the fierce and drunken passions wove
A dance more wild than e'er was maniac's dream!
  Ye Storms, that round the dawning east assembled,
The Sun was rising, though ye hid his light!"
And when to soothe my soul, that hoped and trembled,
The dissonance ceased, and all seem'd calm and bright;
  When France her front deep-scarr'd and gory
Conceal'd with clustering wreaths of glory;
When, insupportably advancing,
  Her arm made mockery of the warrior's tramp;
While timid looks of fury glancing,
  Domestic Treason, crush'd beneath her fatal stamp,
Writhed like a wounded dragon in his gore;
  Then I reproach'd my fears that would not flee;
"And soon," I said, "shall Wisdom teach her lore

In the low huts of them that toil and
    groan!
And, conquering by her happiness alone,
    Shall France compel the nations to be
        free,
    Till Love and Joy look round, and call
        the Earth their own."

Forgive me, Freedom! oh, forgive those
        dreams!
    I hear thy voice, I hear thy loud lament,
From bleak Helvetia's icy cavern sent;
I hear thy groans upon her blood-stain'd
        streams!
    Heroes, that for your peaceful country
        perish'd,
And ye that, fleeing, spot your mountain-
        snows
    With bleeding wounds; forgive me that
        I cherish'd
One thought that ever bless'd your cruel
        foes!
    To scatter rage and traitorous guilt,
    Where Peace her jealous home had built;
A patriot race to disinherit
    Of all that made their stormy wilds so
        dear;
And with inexpiable spirit
    To taint the bloodless freedom of the
        mountaineer—
O France, that mockest Heaven, adulterous,
        blind,
    And patriot only in pernicious toils,
Are these thy boasts, Champion of human
        kind?
    To mix with Kings in the low lust of
        sway,
    Yell in the hunt, and share the murderous prey;
        To insult the shrine of Liberty with
            spoils
    From freemen torn; to tempt and to
        betray?

The Sensual and the Dark rebel in vain,
    Slaves by their own compulsion! In
        mad game
    They burst their manacles and wear the
        name
Of Freedom, graven on a heavier chain!

O Liberty! with profitless endeavor
    Have I pursued thee, many a weary hour;
    But thou nor swell'st the victor's strain,
        nor ever
    Didst breathe thy soul in forms of human
        power.
    Alike from all, howe'er they praise thee
    (Nor prayer, nor boastful name delays
        thee),
Alike from Priestcraft's harpy minions,
    And factious Blasphemy's obscener
        slaves,
Thou speedest on thy subtle pinions,
    The guide of homeless winds, and playmate of the waves!
And there I felt thee!—on that sea-cliff's
        verge,
    Whose pines, scarce travell'd by the
        breeze above,
Had made one murmur with the distant
        surge!
    Yes, while I stood and gazed, my temples bare,
    And shot my being through earth, sea,
        and air,
    Possessing all things with intensest
        love,
O Liberty! my spirit felt thee there.
            SAMUEL TAYLOR COLERIDGE.

THE CHRONICLE OF THE DRUM.

PART I.

At Paris, hard by the Maine barriers,
    Whoever will choose to repair,
Midst a dozen of wooden-legg'd warriors,
    May haply fall in with old Pierre.
On the sunshiny bench of a tavern,
    He sits and he prates of old wars,
And moistens his pipe of tobacco
    With a drink that is named after Mars.

The beer makes his tongue run the quicker,
    And as long as his tap never fails,
Thus over his favorite liquor
    Old Peter will tell his old tales.
Says he, "In my life's ninety summers
    Strange changes and chances I've seen,—
So here's to all gentlemen drummers
    That ever have thump'd on a skin.

"Brought up in the art military
    For four generations we are;

My ancestors drumm'd for King Harry,
    The Huguenot lad of Navarre;
And as each man in life has his station,
    According as fortune may fix,
While Condé was waving the baton,
    My grandsire was trolling the sticks.

"Ah! those were the days for commanders!
    What glories my grandfather won,
Ere bigots, and lackeys, and panders,
    The fortunes of France had undone!
In Germany, Flanders, and Holland,—
    What foeman resisted us then?
No; my grandsire was ever victorious,
    My grandsire and Monsieur Turenne.

"He died, and our noble battalions
    The jade, fickle Fortune, forsook;
And at Blenheim, in spite of our valiance,
    The victory lay with Malbrook.
The news it was brought to King Louis;
    Corbleu! how His Majesty swore,
When he heard they had taken my grandsire,
    And twelve thousand gentlemen more!

"At Namur, Ramillies, and Malplaquet
    Were we posted, on plain or in trench;
Malbrook only need to attack it,
    And away from him scamper'd we French.
Cheer up! 'tis no use to be glum, boys,—
    'Tis written, since fighting begun,
That sometimes we fight and we conquer,
    And sometimes we fight and we run.

"To fight and to run was our fate;
    Our fortune and fame had departed;
And so perish'd Louis the Great,—
    Old, lonely, and half broken-hearted.
His coffin they pelted with mud,
    His body they tried to lay hands on;
And so having buried King Louis,
    They loyally served his great-grandson.

"God save the beloved King Louis!
    (For so he was nicknamed by some),
And now came my father to do his
    King's orders, and beat on the drum.
My grandsire was dead, but his bones
    Must have shaken, I'm certain, for joy,
To hear daddy drumming the English
    From the meadows of famed Fontenoy.

"So well did he drum in that battle,
    That the enemy show'd us their backs;
Corbleu! it was pleasant to rattle
    The sticks, and to follow old Saxe!
We next had Soubise as a leader,
    And as luck hath its changes and fits,
At Rossbach, in spite of dad's drumming,
    'Tis said we were beaten by Fritz.

"And now daddy crossed the Atlantic,
    To drum for Montcalm and his men;
Morbleu! but it makes a man frantic,
    To think we were beaten again!
My daddy he cross'd the wide ocean,
    My mother brought me on her neck,
And we came in the year fifty-seven
    To guard the good town of Quebec.

"In the year fifty-nine came the Britons,—
    Full well I remember the day,—
They knock'd at our gates for admittance,
    Their vessels were moor'd in our bay.
Says our general, 'Drive me yon red-coats
    Away to the sea, whence they come!'
So we march'd against Wolfe and his bull-dogs,
    We march'd at the sound of the drum.

"I think I can see my poor mammy
    With me in her hand as she waits,
And our regiment, slowly retreating,
    Pours back through the citadel-gates.
Dear mammy, she looks in their faces,
    And asks if her husband is come.
—He is lying all cold on the glacis,
    And will never more beat on the drum.

"Come, drink, 'tis no use to be glum, boys;
    He died like a soldier—in glory;
Here's a glass to the health of all drum-boys,
    And now I'll commence my own story.
Once more did we cross the salt ocean;
    We came in the year eighty-one;
And the wrongs of my father the drummer
    Were avenged by the drummer his son.

"In Chesapeake Bay we were landed;
    In vain strove the British to pass;
Rochambeau our armies commanded,
    Our ships they were led by De Grasse.
Morbleu! how I rattled the drumsticks,
    The day we march'd into Yorktown!
Ten thousand of beef-eating British
    Their weapons we caused to lay down.

"Then homeward returning victorious,
　In peace to our country we came,
And were thank'd for our glorious actions
　By Louis Sixteenth of the name.
What drummer on earth could be prouder
　Than I, while I drumm'd at Versailles
To the lovely court-ladies in powder,
　And lappets, and long satin tails?

"The princes that day pass'd before us,
　Our countrymen's glory and hope;
Monsieur, who was learn'd in Horace,
　D'Artois, who could dance the tight-rope.
One night we kept guard for the Queen
　At Her Majesty's opera-box,
While the King, that majestical monarch,
　Sat filing at home at his locks.

"Yes, I drumm'd for the fair Antoinette;
　And so smiling she look'd, and so tender,
That our officers, privates, and drummers
　All vow'd they would die to defend her.
But she cared not for us honest fellows,
　Who fought and who bled in her wars;
She sneer'd at our gallant Rochambeau,
　And turn'd Lafayette out of doors.

"Ventrebleu! then I swore a great oath
　No more to such tyrants to kneel;
And so, just to keep up my drumming,
　One day I drumm'd down the Bastile!
Ho, landlord! a stoup of fresh wine;
　Come, comrades, a bumper we'll try,
And drink to the year eighty-nine,
　And the glorious Fourth of July!

"Then bravely our cannon it thunder'd,
　As onward our patriots bore;
Our enemies were but a hundred,
　And we twenty thousand or more.
They carried the news to King Louis,
　He heard it as calm as you please;
And like a majestical monarch,
　Kept filing his locks and his keys.

"We show'd our republican courage,
　We storm'd and we broke the great gate in,
And we murder'd the insolent governor
　For daring to keep us a-waiting.
Lambesc and his squadrons stood by;
　They never stirr'd finger or thumb;
The saucy aristocrats trembled
　As they heard the republican drum.

"Hurrah! what a storm was a-brewing!
　The day of our vengeance was come;
Through scenes of what carnage and ruin
　Did I beat on the patriot drum!
Let's drink to the famed tenth of August:
　At midnight I beat the tattoo,
And woke up the pikemen of Paris
　To follow the bold Barbaroux.

"With pikes, and with shouts, and with torches,
　March'd onward our dusty battalions;
And we girt the tall castle of Louis,
　A million of tatterdemalions!
We storm'd the fair gardens where tower'd
　The walls of his heritage splendid;
Ah, shame on him, craven and coward,
　That had not the heart to defend it!

"With the crown of his sires on his head,
　His nobles and knights by his side,
At the foot of his ancestors' palace
　'Twere easy, methinks, to have died.
But no: when we burst through his barriers,
　'Mid heaps of the dying and dead,
In vain through the chambers we sought him,—
　He had turn'd like a craven and fled.

*　*　*　*　*　*

"You all know the Place de la Concorde?
　'Tis hard by the Tuilerie wall;
'Mid terraces, fountains, and statues,
　There rises an obelisk tall.
There rises an obelisk tall,
　All garnish'd and gilded the base is;
'Tis surely the gayest of all
　Our beautiful city's gay places.

"Around it are gardens and flowers,
　And the cities of France on their thrones,
Each crown'd with his circlet of flowers,
　Sits watching this biggest of stones!
I love to go sit in the sun there,
　The flowers and fountains to see,
And to think of the deeds that were done there,
　In the glorious year ninety-three.

"'Twas here stood the Altar of Freedom,
　And though neither marble nor gilding

Was used in those days to adorn
  Our simple republican building,
Corbleu! but the MÈRE GUILLOTINE
  Cared little for splendor or show,
So you gave her an axe and a beam,
  And a plank and a basket or so.

"Awful, and proud, and erect,
  Here sat our republican goddess;
Each morning her table we deck'd
  With dainty aristocrats' bodies.
The people each day flock'd around,
  As she sat at her meat and her wine:
'Twas always the use of our nation
  To witness the sovereign dine.

"Young virgins with fair golden tresses,
  Old silver-hair'd prelates and priests,
Dukes, marquises, barons, princesses,
  Were splendidly served at her feasts.
Ventrebleu! but we pamper'd our ogress
  With the best that our nation could bring,
And dainty she grew in her progress,
  And call'd for the head of a king!

"She call'd for the blood of our king,
  And straight from his prison we drew him;
And to her with shouting we led him,
  And took him, and bound him, and slew him.
'The monarchs of Europe against me
  Have plotted a godless alliance;
I'll fling them the head of King Louis,'
  She said, 'as my gage of defiance.'

"I see him as now, for a moment,
  Away from his jailers he broke,
And stood at the foot of the scaffold,
  And linger'd, and fain would have spoke.
'Ho, drummer! quick! silence yon Capet,'
  Says Santerre, 'with a beat of your drum;'
Lustily then did I tap it,
  And the son of St. Louis was dumb."

* * * * * *

PART II.

"THE glorious days of September
  Saw many aristocrats fall;
'Twas then that our pikes drunk the blood
  In the beautiful breast of Lamballe.
Pardi, 'twas a beautiful lady!
  I seldom have look'd on her like;
And I drumm'd for a gallant procession
  That march'd with her head on a pike.

"Let's show the pale head to the Queen,
  We said—she'll remember it well.
She look'd from the bars of her prison,
  And shriek'd as she saw it, and fell.
We set up a shout at her screaming,
  We laugh'd at the fright she had shown
At the sight of the head of her minion;
  How she'd tremble to part with her own!

"We had taken the head of King Capet,
  We call'd for the blood of his wife;
Undaunted she came to the scaffold,
  And bared her fair neck to the knife.
As she felt the foul fingers that touch'd her,
  She shrunk, but she deign'd not to speak:
She look'd with a royal disdain,
  And died with a blush on her cheek.

"'Twas thus that our country was saved:
  So told us the safety committee!
But pshaw! I've the heart of a soldier,
  All gentleness, mercy, and pity.
I loathed to assist at such deeds,
  And my drum beat its loudest of tunes
As we offered to Justice offended
  The blood of the bloody tribunes.

"Away with such foul recollections!
  No more of the axe and the block;
I saw the last fight of the sections,
  As they fell 'neath our guns at Saint Rock.
Young Bonaparte led us that day;
  When he sought the Italian frontier,
I follow'd my gallant young captain,
  I follow'd him many a long year.

"We came to an army in rags,
  Our general was but a boy,
When we first saw the Austrian flags
  Flaunt proud in the fields of Savoy.
In the glorious year ninety-six,
  We march'd to the banks of the Po;
I carried my drum and my sticks,
  And we laid the proud Austrian low.

"In triumph we enter'd Milan,
  We seized on the Mantuan keys;
The troops of the Emperor ran,
  And the Pope he fell down on his
    knees."—
Pierre's comrades here called a fresh
    bottle,
  And, clubbing together their wealth,
They drank to the Army of Italy,
  And General Bonaparte's health.

The drummer now bared his old breast,
  And show'd us a plenty of scars,
Rude presents that Fortune had made
    him
  In fifty victorious wars.
" This came when I follow'd bold Kleber—
  'Twas shot by a Mameluke gun;
And this from an Austrian sabre,
  When the field of Marengo was won.

"My forehead has many deep furrows,
  But this is the deepest of all;
A Brunswicker made it at Jena,
  Beside the fair river of Saal.
This cross, 'twas the Emperor gave it
  (God bless him!) it covers a blow;
I had it at Austerlitz fight,
  As I beat on my drum in the snow.

"'Twas thus that we conquer'd and fought;
  But wherefore continue the story?
There's never a baby in France
  But has heard of our chief and our
    glory,—
But has heard of our chief and our fame,
  His sorrows and triumphs can tell,
How bravely Napoleon conquer'd,
  How bravely and sadly he fell.

" It makes my old heart to beat higher
  To think of the deeds that I saw;
I follow'd bold Ney through the fire,
  And charged at the side of Murat."
And so did old Peter continue
  His story of twenty brave years;
His audience follow'd with comments—
  Rude comments of curses and tears.

He told how the Prussians in vain
  Had died in defence of their land;
His audience laugh'd at the story,
  And vow'd that their captain was grand!

He had fought the red English, he said,
  In many a battle of Spain;
They cursed the red English, and pray'd
  To meet them and fight them again.

He told them how Russia was lost,
  Had winter not driven them back;
And his company cursed the quick frost,
  And doubly they cursed the Cossack.
He told how the stranger arrived;
  They wept at the tale of disgrace;
And they long'd but for one battle more,
  The stain of their shame to efface!

"Our country their hordes overrun,
  We fled to the fields of Champagne,
And fought them, though twenty to one,
  And beat them again and again!
Our warrior was conquer'd at last;
  They bade him his crown to resign;
To fate and his country he yielded
  The rights of himself and his line.

" He came, and among us he stood,
  Around him we press'd in a throng,
We could not regard him for weeping,
  Who had led us and loved us so long.
'I have led you for twenty long years,'
  Napoleon said ere he went;
'Wherever was honor I found you,
  And with you, my sons, am content.

"'Though Europe against me was arm'd,
  Your chiefs and my people are true;
I still might have struggled with fortune,
  And baffled all Europe with you.

"'But France would have suffer'd the
    while;
  'Tis best that I suffer alone:
I go to my place of exile,
  To write of the deeds we have done.

"'Be true to the king that they give you;
  We may not embrace ere we part;
But, General, reach me your hand,
  And press me, I pray, to your heart.'

" He called for our old battle-standard;
  One kiss to the eagle he gave.
' Dear eagle!' he said, ' may this kiss
  Long sound in the hearts of the brave!'
'Twas thus that Napoleon left us;
  Our people were weeping and mute,

And he passed through the lines of his
  guard,
And our drums beat the notes of salute.

     *   *   *   *   *   *

" I look'd when the drumming was o'er,
  I look'd, but our hero was gone;
We were destined to see him once more,
  When we fought on the mount of St.
    John.
The Emperor rode through our files;
  'Twas June, and a fair Sunday morn;
The lines of our warriors for miles
  Stretched wide through the Waterloo
    corn.

" In thousands we stood on the plain;
  The red-coats were crowning the height;
' Go scatter yon English,' he said;
  ' We'll sup, lads, at Brussels to-night.'
We answer'd his voice with a shout;
  Our eagles were bright in the sun;
Our drums and our cannon spoke out,
  And the thundering battle begun.

" One charge to another succeeds,
  Like waves that a hurricane bears;
All day do our galloping steeds
  Dash fierce on the enemy's squares.
At noon we began the fell onset;
  We charged up the Englishman's hill;
And madly we charged it at sunset—
  His banners were floating there still.

"—Go to! I will tell you no more;
  You know how the battle was lost.
Ho! fetch me a beaker of wine,
  And, comrades, I'll give you a toast.
I'll give you a curse on all traitors,
  Who plotted our Emperor's ruin;
And a curse on those red-coated English,
  Whose bayonets help'd our undoing.

" A curse on those British assassins
  Who order'd the slaughter of Ney;
A curse on Sir Hudson, who tortured
  The life of our hero away.
A curse on all Russians—I hate them—
  On all Prussian and Austrian fry;
And, oh! but I pray we may meet them,
  And fight them again ere I die!"

'TWAS thus old Peter did conclude
  His chronicle with curses fit.
He spoke the tale in accents rude,
  In ruder verse I copied it.

Perhaps the tale a moral bears
  (All tales in time to this must come),
The story of two hundred years
  Writ on the parchment of a drum.

What Peter told with drum and stick
  Is endless theme for poet's pen:
Is found in endless quartos thick,
  Enormous books by learnèd men.

And ever since historian writ,
  And ever since a bard could sing,
Doth each exalt, with all his wit,
  The noble art of murdering.

We love to read the glorious page,
  How bold Achilles kill'd his foe,
And Turnus, fell'd by Trojans' rage,
  Went howling to the shades below.

How Godfrey led his red-cross knights,
  How mad Orlando slash'd and slew;
There's not a single bard that writes,
  But doth the glorious theme renew.

And while in fashion picturesque
  The poet rhymes of blood and blows,
The grave historian, at his desk,
  Describes the same in classic prose.

Go read the works of Reverend Cox;
  You'll duly see recorded there
The history of the selfsame knocks
  Here roughly sung by Drummer Pierre.

Of battles fierce and warriors big,
  He writes in phrases dull and slow,
And waves his cauliflower wig,
  And shouts, " St. George for Marlborow!"

Take Doctor Southey from the shelf,
  An LL.D.,—a peaceful man;
Good Lord, how doth he plume himself
  Because we beat the Corsican!

From first to last his page is fill'd
  With stirring tales how blows were
    struck.
He shows how we the Frenchmen kill'd,
  And praises God for our good luck.

Some hints, 'tis true, of politics
　The doctors give, and statesman's art;
Pierre only bangs his drum and sticks,
　And understands the bloody part.

He cares not what the cause may be,
　He is not nice for wrong and right;
But show him where's the enemy,
　He only asks to drum and fight.

They bid him fight,—perhaps he wins;
　And when he tells the story o'er,
The honest savage brags and grins,
　And only longs to fight once more.

But luck may change, and valor fail,
　Our drummer, Peter, meet reverse,
And with a moral points his tale—
　The end of all such tales—a curse.

LAST year, my love, it was my hap
　Behind a grenadier to be,
And, but he wore a hairy cap,
　No taller man, methinks, than me.

Prince Albert and the Queen, God wot!
　(Be blessings on the glorious pair!)
Before us pass'd, I saw them not,
　I only saw a cap of hair.

Your orthodox historian puts
　In foremost rank the soldier thus,
The red-coat bully in his boots,
　That hides the march of men from us.

He puts him there in foremost rank,
　You wonder at his cap of hair:
You hear his sabre's cursèd clank,
　His spurs are jingling everywhere.

Go to! I hate him and his trade:
　Who bade us so to cringe and bend,
And all God's peaceful people made
　To such as him subservient?

Tell me what find we to admire
　In epaulets and scarlet coats,
In men because they load and fire,
　And know the art of cutting throats?

　　＊　　＊　　＊　　＊　　＊　　＊

Ah, gentle, tender lady mine!
　The winter wind blows cold and shrill,
Come, fill me one more glass of wine,
　And give the silly fools their will.

And what care we for war and wrack,
　How kings and heroes rise and fall?
Look yonder; in his coffin black,
　There lies the greatest of them all!

To pluck him down, and keep him up,
　Died many million human souls;
'Tis twelve o'clock, and time to sup,
　Bid Mary heap the fire with coals.

He captured many thousand guns;
　He wrote "The Great" before his name;
And dying only left his sons
　The recollection of his shame.

Though more than half the world was his,
　He died without a rood his own;
And borrow'd from his enemies
　Six foot of ground to lie upon.

He fought a thousand glorious wars,
　And more than half the world was his,
And somewhere, now, in yonder stars,
　Can tell, mayhap, what greatness is.
　　　　WILLIAM MAKEPEACE THACKERAY.

HOHENLINDEN.

ON Linden, when the sun was low,
All bloodless lay the untrodden snow,
And dark as winter was the flow
　Of Iser, rolling rapidly.

But Linden saw another sight
When the drum beat, at dead of night,
Commanding fires of death to light
　The darkness of her scenery.

By torch and trumpet fast array'd,
Each horseman drew his battle-blade,
And furious every charger neigh'd
　To join the dreadful revelry.

Then shook the hills with thunder riven;
Then rush'd the steed to battle driven;
And, louder than the bolts of heaven,
　Far flash'd the red artillery.

But redder yet that light shall glow
On Linden's hills of stainèd snow,
And bloodier yet the torrent flow
　Of Iser, rolling rapidly.

'Tis morn; but scarce yon level sun
Can pierce the war-clouds, rolling dun,

Where furious Frank and fiery Hun
  Shout in their sulph'rous canopy.

The combat deėpens. On, ye brave,
Who rush to glory, or the grave!
Wave, Munich! all thy banners wave,
  And charge with all thy chivalry!

Few, few shall part where many meet!
The snow shall be their winding-sheet;
And every turf beneath their feet
  Shall be a soldier's sepulchre.
                    THOMAS CAMPBELL.

THE BATTLE OF THE BALTIC.

OF Nelson and the North
Sing the glorious day's renown,
When to battle fierce came forth
All the might of Denmark's crown,
And her arms along the deep proudly shone;
By each gun the lighted brand
In a bold determined hand,
And the prince of all the land
Led them on.

Like leviathans afloat
Lay their bulwarks on the brine;
While the sign of battle flew
On the lofty British line:
It was ten of April morn by the chime:
As they drifted on their path
There was silence deep as death;
And the boldest held his breath
For a time.

But the might of England flush'd
To anticipate the scene;
And her van the fleeter rush'd
O'er the deadly space between.
"Hearts of oak!" our captains cried; when each gun
From its adamantine lips
Spread a death-shade round the ships,
Like the hurricane eclipse
Of the sun.

Again! again! again!
And the havoc did not slack,
Till a feeble cheer the Dane
To our cheering sent us back;—

Their shots along the deep slowly boom—
Then ceased—and all is wail,
As they strike the shatter'd sail,
Or, in conflagration pale,
Light the gloom.

Out spoke the victor then,
As he hail'd them o'er the wave:
"Ye are brothers! ye are men!
And we conquer but to save:
So peace instead of death let us bring;
But yield, proud foe, thy fleet,
With the crews, at England's feet,
And make submission meet
To our king."

Then Denmark bless'd our chief,
That he gave her wounds repose;
And the sounds of joy and grief
From her people wildly rose,
As death withdrew his shades from the day,
While the sun look'd smiling bright
O'er a wide and woeful sight,
Where the fires of funeral light
Died away.

Now joy, Old England, raise!
For the tidings of thy might,
By the festal cities' blaze,
Whilst the wine-cup shines in light;
And yet, amidst that joy and uproar,
Let us think of them that sleep
Full many a fathom deep,
By thy wild and stormy steep,
Elsinore!

Brave hearts! to Britain's pride
Once so faithful and so true,
On the deck of fame that died,
With the gallant good Riou—
Soft sigh the winds of heaven o'er their grave!
While the billow mournful rolls,
And the mermaid's song condoles,
Singing glory to the souls
Of the brave!
                    THOMAS CAMPBELL.

INCIDENT OF THE FRENCH CAMP.

YOU know we French storm'd Ratisbon:
  A mile or so away,
On a little mound, Napoleon
  Stood on our storming-day;

With neck out-thrust, you fancy how,
  Legs wide, arms lock'd behind,
As if to balance the prone brow,
  Oppressive with its mind.

Just as perhaps he mused, "My plans
  That soar, to earth may fall,
Let once my army-leader Lannes
  Waver at yonder wall,"—
Out 'twixt the battery-smokes there flew
  A rider, bound on bound
Full galloping; nor bridle drew
  Until he reach'd the mound.

Then off there flung in smiling joy,
  And held himself erect
By just his horse's mane, a boy;
  You hardly could suspect
(So tight he kept his lips compress'd,
  Scarce any blood came through),
You look'd twice ere you saw his breast
  Was all but shot in two.

"Well," cried he, "Emperor, by God's grace
We've got you Ratisbon!
The Marshal's in the market-place,
  And you'll be there anon
To see your flag-bird flap his vans
  Where I, to heart's desire,
Perch'd him!" The chief's eye flash'd; his plans
  Soar'd up again like fire.

The chief's eye flash'd, but presently
  Soften'd itself, as sheathes
A film the mother eagle's eye
  When her bruised eaglet breathes:
"You're wounded!" "Nay," his soldier's pride
  Touch'd to the quick, he said,
"I'm kill'd, sire!" And, his chief beside,
  Smiling, the boy fell dead.
ROBERT BROWNING.

THE CONTRAST.

WRITTEN UNDER WINDSOR TERRACE, THE DAY AFTER THE FUNERAL OF GEORGE THE THIRD.

I SAW him last on this terrace proud,
  Walking in health and gladness,
Begirt with his court; and in all the crowd
  Not a single look of sadness.

Bright was the sun, and the leaves were green,
  Blithely the birds were singing;
The cymbal replied to the tambourine,
  And the bells were merrily ringing.

I have stood with the crowd beside his bier,
  When not a word was spoken;
But every eye was dim with a tear,
  And the silence by sobs was broken.

I have heard the earth on his coffin pour
  To the muffled drum's deep rolling,
While the minute-gun, with its solemn roar,
  Drown'd the death-bells' tolling.

The time since he walk'd in his glory thus,
  To the grave till I saw him carried,
Was an age of the mightiest change to us,
  But to him a night unvaried.

We have fought the fight; from his lofty throne
  The foe of our land we have tumbled;
And it gladden'd each eye, save his alone,
  For whom that foe we humbled.

A daughter beloved, a queen, a son,
  And a son's sole child, have perish'd;
And sad was each heart, save only the one
  By which they were fondest cherish'd;

For his eyes were seal'd and his mind was dark,
  And he sat in his age's lateness
Like a vision throned, as a solemn mark
  Of the frailty of human greatness;

His silver beard, o'er a bosom spread
  Unvex'd by life's commotion,
Like a yearly lengthening snow-drift shed
  On the calm of a frozen ocean.

O'er him oblivion's waters boom'd
  As the stream of time kept flowing;
And we only heard of our king when doom'd
  To know that his strength was going.

At intervals thus the waves disgorge,
  By weakness rent asunder,
A piece of the wreck of the Royal George,
  For the people's pity and wonder.
HORACE SMITH.

THE PRESENT CRISIS.

When a deed is done for Freedom, through the broad earth's aching breast
Runs a thrill of joy prophetic, trembling on from east to west,
And the slave, where'er he cowers, feels the soul within him climb
To the awful verge of manhood, as the energy sublime
Of a century bursts full-blossomed on the thorny stem of Time.

Through the walls of hut and palace shoots the instantaneous throe,
When the travail of the Ages wrings earth's systems to and fro;
At the birth of each new Era, with a recognizing start,
Nation wildly looks at nation, standing with mute lips apart,
And glad Truth's yet mightier man-child leaps beneath the Future's heart.

So the Evil's triumph sendeth, with a terror and a chill,
Under continent to continent, the sense of coming ill,
And the slave, where'er he cowers, feels his sympathies with God
In hot tear-drops ebbing earthward, to be drunk up by the sod,
Till a corpse crawls round unburied, delving in the nobler clod.

For mankind are one in spirit, and an instinct bears along,
Round the earth's electric circle, the swift flash of right or wrong;
Whether conscious or unconscious, yet Humanity's vast frame
Through its ocean-sundered fibres feels the gush of joy or shame;—
In the gain or loss of one race all the rest have equal claim.

Once to every man and nation comes the moment to decide,
In the strife of Truth with Falsehood, for the good or evil side;
Some great cause, God's new Messiah, offering each the bloom or blight,
Parts the goats upon the left hand, and the sheep upon the right,
And the choice goes by for ever 'twixt that darkness and that light.

Hast thou chosen, O my people, on whose party thou shalt stand,
Ere the Doom from its worn sandals shakes the dust against our land?
Though the cause of Evil prosper, yet 'tis Truth alone is strong,
And, albeit she wander outcast now, I see around her throng
Troops of beautiful, tall angels, to enshield her from all wrong.

Backward look across the ages, and the beacon-moments see,
That, like peaks of some sunk continent, jut through Oblivion's sea;
Not an ear in court or market for the low foreboding cry
Of those Crises, God's stern winnowers, from whose feet earth's chaff must fly;
Never shows the choice momentous till the judgment hath passed by.

Careless seems the great Avenger; history's pages but record
One death-grapple in the darkness 'twixt old systems and the Word;
Truth for ever on the scaffold, Wrong for ever on the throne,—
Yet that scaffold sways the future, and, behind the dim unknown,
Standeth God within the shadow, keeping watch above His own.

We see dimly in the Present what is small and what is great,
Slow of faith how weak an arm may turn the iron helm of fate,
But the soul is still oracular; amid the market's din,
List the ominous stern whisper from the Delphic cave within,—
"They enslave their children's children who make compromise with sin."

Slavery, the earth-born Cyclops, fellest of
 the giant brood,
Sons of brutish Force and Darkness, who
 have drenched the earth with blood,
Famished in his self-made desert, blinded
 by our purer day,
Gropes in yet unblasted regions for his miserable prey;—
Shall we guide his gory fingers where our
 helpless children play?

Then to side with Truth is noble when we
 share her wretched crust,
Ere her cause bring fame and profit, and
 'tis prosperous to be just;
Then it is the brave man chooses, while
 the coward stands aside,
Doubting in his abject spirit, till his Lord
 is crucified,
And the multitude make virtue of the faith
 they had denied.

Count me o'er earth's chosen heroes,—they
 were souls that stood alone,
While the men they agonized for hurled
 the contumelious stone,
Stood serene, and down the future saw the
 golden beam incline
To the side of perfect justice, mastered by
 their faith divine,
By one man's plain truth to manhood and
 to God's supreme design.

By the light of burning heretics Christ's
 bleeding feet I track,
Toiling up new Calvaries, ever with the
 cross that turns not back,
And these mounts of anguish number how
 each generation learned
One new word of that grand *Credo* which
 in prophet-hearts hath burned
Since the first man stood God-conquered
 with his face to heaven upturned.

For Humanity sweeps onward: where today the martyr stands,
On the morrow crouches Judas with the
 silver in his hands;
Far in front the cross stands ready and the
 crackling fagots burn,
While the hooting mob of yesterday in
 silent awe return
To glean up the scattered ashes into History's golden urn.

'Tis as easy to be heroes as to sit the idle
 slaves
Of a legendary virtue carved upon our
 fathers' graves,
Worshippers of light ancestral make the
 present light a crime;—
Was the Mayflower launched by cowards,
 steered by men behind their time?
Turn those tracks toward Past or Future,
 that make Plymouth Rock sublime?

They were men of present valor, stalwart
 old iconoclasts,
Unconvinced by axe or gibbet that all virtue was the Past's;
But we make their truth our falsehood,
 thinking that hath made us free,
Hoarding it in mouldy parchments, while
 our tender spirits flee
The rude grasp of that great Impulse which
 drove them across the sea.

They have rights who dare maintain them;
 we are traitors to our sires,
Smothering in their holy ashes Freedom's
 new-lit altar-fires;
Shall we make their creed our jailer? Shall
 we, in our haste to slay,
From the tombs of the old prophets steal
 the funeral lamps away
To light up the martyr-fagots round the
 prophets of to-day?

New occasions teach new duties; Time
 makes ancient good uncouth;
They must upward still, and onward, who
 would keep abreast of Truth;
Lo! before us gleam her camp-fires! we
 ourselves must Pilgrims be,
Launch our Mayflower, and steer boldly
 through the desperate winter sea,
Nor attempt the Future's portal with the
 Past's blood-rusted key.

JAMES RUSSELL LOWELL.

CASABIANCA.

The boy stood on the burning deck
  Whence all but he had fled;
The flame that lit the battle's wreck
  Shone round him o'er the dead.

Yet beautiful and bright he stood,
  As born to rule the storm;
A creature of heroic blood,
  A proud, though child-like form.

The flames roll'd on—he would not go
  Without his father's word;
That father, faint in death below,
  His voice no longer heard.

He call'd aloud, "Say, father, say,
  If yet my task is done?"
He knew not that the chieftain lay
  Unconscious of his son.

"Speak, father," once again he cried,
  "If I may yet be gone!"
And but the booming shots replied,
  And fast the flames roll'd on.

Upon his brow he felt their breath,
  And in his waving hair,
And look'd from that lone post of death
  In still, yet brave despair.

And shouted but once more aloud,
  "My father, must I stay?"
While o'er him fast, through sail and shroud,
  The wreathing fires made way.

They wrapt the ship in splendor wild,
  They caught the flag on high,
And stream'd above the gallant child
  Like banners in the sky.

There came a burst of thunder-sound—
  The boy!—oh, where was he?
Ask of the winds that far around
  With fragments strew'd the sea!—

With mast, and helm, and pennon fair,
  That well had borne their part,—
But the noblest thing which perish'd there
  Was that young, faithful heart!
        FELICIA DOROTHEA HEMANS.

THE ANGELS OF BUENA VISTA.

Speak and tell us, our Ximena, looking northward far away,
O'er the camp of the invaders, o'er the Mexican array,
Who is losing? who is winning? are they far or come they near?
Look abroad, and tell us, sister, whither rolls the storm we hear.

"Down the hills of Angostura still the storm of battle rolls;
Blood is flowing, men are dying; God have mercy on their souls!"
Who is losing? who is winning?—"Over hill and over plain,
I see but smoke of cannon clouding through the mountain-rain."

Holy Mother! keep our brothers! Look, Ximena, look once more.
"Still I see the fearful whirlwind rolling darkly as before,
Bearing on, in strange confusion, friend and foeman, foot and horse,
Like some wild and troubled torrent sweeping down its mountain-course."

Look forth once more, Ximena! "Ah! the smoke has roll'd away;
And I see the Northern rifles gleaming down the ranks of gray.
Hark! that sudden blast of bugles! there the troop of Minon wheels;
There the Northern horses thunder, with the cannon at their heels.

"Jesu, pity! how it thickens! now retreat and now advance!
Right against the blazing cannon shivers Puebla's charging lance!
Down they go, the brave young riders; horse and foot together fall:
Like a ploughshare in the fallow, through them ploughs the Northern ball."

Nearer came the storm and nearer, rolling fast and frightful on:
Speak, Ximena, speak and tell us, who has lost, and who has won?
"Alas! alas! I know not; friend and foe together fall,
O'er the dying rush the living; pray, my sisters, for them all!

"Lo! the wind the smoke is lifting:
 Blessed Mother, save my brain!
I can see the wounded crawling slowly out
 from heaps of slain.
Now they stagger, blind and bleeding; now
 they fall, and strive to rise;
Hasten, sisters, haste and save them, lest
 they die before our eyes!

"O my heart's love O my dear one! lay
 thy poor head on my knee:
Dost thou know the lips that kiss thee?
 Canst thou hear me? canst thou
 see?
O my husband, brave and gentle! O my
 Bernal, look once more
On the blessed cross before thee! Mercy!
 mercy! all is o'er!"

Dry thy tears, my poor Ximena; lay thy
 dear one down to rest;
Let his hands be meekly folded, lay the
 cross upon his breast;
Let his dirge be sung hereafter, and his
 funeral masses said;
To-day, thou poor bereaved one, the living
 ask thy aid.

Close beside her, faintly moaning, fair and
 young, a soldier lay,
Torn with shot and pierced with lances,
 bleeding slow his life away;
But, as tenderly before him the lorn
 Ximena knelt,
She saw the Northern eagle shining on his
 pistol-belt.

With a stifled cry of horror straight she
 turn'd away her head;
With a sad and bitter feeling look'd she
 back upon her dead;
But she heard the youth's low moaning, and
 his struggling breath of pain,
And she raised the cooling water to his
 parching lips again.

Whisper'd low the dying soldier, press'd
 her hand and faintly smiled:
Was that pitying face his mother's? did
 she watch beside her child?

All his stranger words with meaning her
 woman's heart supplied;
With her kiss upon his forehead, "Mother!" murmur'd he and died!

"A bitter curse upon them, poor boy, who
 led thee forth,
From some gentle sad-eyed mother, weeping, lonely, in the North!"
Spake the mournful Mexic woman, as she
 laid him with her dead,
And turn'd to soothe the living, and bind
 the wounds which bled.

Look forth once more, Ximena! "Like a
 cloud before the wind
Rolls the battle down the mountains, leaving blood and death behind;
Ah! they plead in vain for mercy; in the
 dust the wounded strive;
Hide your faces, holy angels! O thou
 Christ of God, forgive!"

Sink, O night, among thy mountains! let
 the cool gray shadows fall;
Dying brothers, fighting demons, drop thy
 curtain over all!
Through the thickening winter twilight,
 wide apart the battle roll'd,
In its sheath the sabre rested, and the cannon's lips grew cold.

But the noble Mexic women still their
 holy task pursued,
Through that long, dark night of sorrow,
 worn and faint and lacking food;
Over weak and suffering brothers, with a
 tender care they hung,
And the dying foeman bless'd them in a
 strange and Northern tongue.

Not wholly lost, O Father! is this evil
 world of ours;
Upward, through its blood and ashes,
 spring afresh the Eden flowers;
From its smoking hell of battle, Love and
 Pity send their prayer,
And still thy white-wing'd angels hover
 dimly in our air.
                                JOHN GREENLEAF WHITTIER.

MARCO BOZZARIS.

At midnight, in his guarded tent,
  The Turk was dreaming of the hour
When Greece, her knee in suppliance bent,
  Should tremble at his power:
In dreams, through camp and court, he bore
The trophies of a conqueror;
In dreams his song of triumph heard,
Then wore his monarch's signet-ring,
Then press'd that monarch's throne—a king;
As wild his thoughts, and gay of wing,
  As Eden's garden bird.

At midnight, in the forest shades,
  Bozzaris ranged his Suliote band,
True as the steel of their tried blades,
  Heroes in heart and hand.
There had the Persian's thousands stood,
There had the glad earth drunk their blood,
  On old Platæa's day;
And now there breathed that haunted air
The sons of sires who conquer'd there,
With arm to strike, and soul to dare,
  As quick, as far, as they.

An hour pass'd on—the Turk awoke:
  That bright dream was his last;
He woke, to hear his sentries shriek,
  "To arms! they come! the Greek! the Greek!"
He woke, to die 'midst flame, and smoke,
And shout, and groan, and sabre-stroke,
  And death-shots falling thick and fast
As lightnings from the mountain-cloud;
And heard, with voice as trumpet loud,
  Bozzaris cheer his band:
"Strike, till the last arm'd foe expires;
Strike, for your altars and your fires;
Strike, for the green graves of your sires;
  God and your native land!"

They fought, like brave men, long and well;
  They piled that ground with Moslem slain;
They conquer'd—but Bozzaris fell,
  Bleeding at every vein.
His few surviving comrades saw
His smile when rang their proud hurrah,
  And the red field was won;
Then saw in death his eyelids close
Calmly, as to a night's repose,
  Like flowers at set of sun.

Come to the bridal chamber, Death,
  Come to the mother's, when she feels,
For the first time, her first-born's breath;
  Come when the blessed seals
That close the pestilence are broke,
And crowded cities wail its stroke;
Come in consumption's ghastly form,
The earthquake-shock, the ocean-storm;
Come when the heart beats high and warm,
  With banquet-song, and dance and wine;
And thou art terrible—the tear,
The groan, the knell, the pall, the bier;
And all we know, or dream, or fear
  Of agony, are thine.

But to the hero, when his sword
  Has won the battle for the free,
Thy voice sounds like a prophet's word,
And in its hollow tones are heard
  The thanks of millions yet to be.
Come, when his task of fame is wrought,
Come, with her laurel-leaf, blood-bought,
  Come in her crowning hour, and then
Thy sunken eye's unearthly light
To him is welcome as the sight
  Of sky and stars to prison'd men;
Thy grasp is welcome as the hand
Of brother in a foreign land;
Thy summons welcome as the cry
That told the Indian isles were nigh
  To the world-seeking Genoese,
When the land-wind, from woods of palm,
And orange-groves, and fields of balm,
  Blew o'er the Haytian seas.

Bozzaris! with the storied brave
  Greece nurtured in her glory's time,
Rest thee—there is no prouder grave,
  Even in her own proud clime.
She wore no funeral weeds for thee,
  Nor bade the dark hearse wave its plume,
Like torn branch from death's leafless tree,
In sorrow's pomp and pageantry,
  The heartless luxury of the tomb.

But she remembers thee as one
Long loved, and for a season gone;
For thee her poet's lyre is wreathed,
Her marble wrought, her music breathed;
For thee she rings the birth-day bells,
Of thee her babes' first lisping tells;
For thine her evening prayer is said
At palace couch and cottage bed;
Her soldier, closing with the foe,
Gives, for thy sake, a deadlier blow;
His plighted maiden when she fears
For him, the joy of her young years,
Thinks of thy fate, and checks her tears;
And she, the mother of thy boys,
Though in her eye and faded cheek
Is read the grief she will not speak,
The memory of her buried joys,
And even she who gave thee birth,
Will, by their pilgrim-circled hearth,
Talk of thy doom without a sigh;
For thou art Freedom's now, and Fame's,
One of the few, the immortal names
That were not born to die.
    FITZ-GREENE HALLECK.

MONTEREY.

WE were not many—we who stood
Before the iron sleet that day;
Yet many a gallant spirit would
Give half his years if but he could
Have with us been at Monterey.

Now here, now there, the shot it hail'd
In deadly drifts of fiery spray,
Yet not a single soldier quail'd
When wounded comrades round them wail'd
Their dying shout at Monterey.

And on—still on our column kept
Through walls of flame its withering way;
Where fell the dead, the living stept,
Still charging on the guns which swept
The slippery streets of Monterey.

The foe himself recoil'd aghast,
When, striking where he strongest lay,
We swoop'd his flanking batteries past,
And braving full their murderous blast,
Storm'd home the towers of Monterey.

Our banners on those turrets wave,
And there our evening bugles play;
Where orange-boughs above their grave
Keep green the memory of the brave
Who fought and fell at Monterey.

We are not many—we who press'd
Beside the brave who fell that day—
But who of us has not confess'd
He'd rather share their warrior rest
Than not have been at Monterey?
    CHARLES FENNO HOFFMAN.

ON THE EXTINCTION OF THE VENETIAN REPUBLIC.

ONCE did she hold the gorgeous East in fee;
And was the safeguard of the West: the worth
Of Venice did not fall below her birth,
Venice, the eldest Child of Liberty.
She was a Maiden City, bright and free;
No guile seduced, no force could violate;
And, when She took unto herself a Mate,
She must espouse the everlasting Sea.
And what if she had seen those glories fade,
Those titles vanish, and that strength decay;
Yet shall some tribute of regret be paid
When her long life hath reach'd its final day:
Men are we, and must grieve when even the Shade
Of that which once was great is pass'd away.
    WILLIAM WORDSWORTH.

THE CHARGE OF THE LIGHT BRIGADE.

HALF a league, half a league,
 Half a league onward,
All in the valley of Death
 Rode the six hundred.
"Forward, the Light Brigade!
 Charge for the guns!" he said:
Into the valley of Death
 Rode the six hundred.

"Forward, the Light Brigade!"
Was there a man dismay'd?
Not though the soldier knew
  Some one had blunder'd:
Their's not to make reply,
Their's not to reason why,
Their's but to do and die:
Into the valley of Death
  Rode the six hundred.

Cannon to right of them,
Cannon to left of them,
Cannon in front of them
  Volley'd and thunder'd;
Storm'd at with shot and shell,
Boldly they rode and well,
Into the jaws of Death,
Into the mouth of Hell
  Rode the six hundred:

Flash'd all their sabres bare,
Flash'd as they turn'd in air,
Sabring the gunners there,
Charging an army, while
  All the world wonder'd:
Plunged in the battery-smoke,
Right through the line they broke;
  Cossack and Russian
Reel'd from the sabre-stroke
  Shatter'd and sunder'd.
Then they rode back, but not—
  Not the six hundred.

Cannon to right of them,
Cannon to left of them,
Cannon behind them
  Volley'd and thunder'd;
Storm'd at with shot and shell,
While horse and hero fell,
They that had fought so well
Came through the jaws of Death
Back from the mouth of Hell,
All that was left of them,
  Left of six hundred.

When can their glory fade?
Oh, the wild charge they made!
  All the world wonder'd.
Honor the charge they made!
Honor the Light Brigade,
  Noble six hundred!
ALFRED TENNYSON.

ALL QUIET ALONG THE POTOMAC.

"All quiet along the Potomac," they say,
  "Except, now and then, a stray picket
Is shot, as he walks on his beat to and fro,
  By a rifleman hid in the thicket."
'Tis nothing—a private or two now and then
  Will not count in the news of the battle;
Not an officer lost—only one of the men
  Moaning out, all alone, the death-rattle.

*   *   *   *   *

All quiet along the Potomac to-night,
  Where the soldiers lie peacefully dreaming;
Their tents, in the rays of the clear autumn moon
  Or the light of the watch-fire, are gleaming.
A tremulous sigh of the gentle night-wind
  Through the forest-leaves softly is creeping,
While stars up above, with their glittering eyes,
  Keep guard, for the army is sleeping.

There's only the sound of the lone sentry's tread
  As he tramps from the rock to the fountain,
And thinks of the two in the low trundle-bed
  Far away in the cot on the mountain.
His musket falls slack; his face, dark and grim,
  Grows gentle with memories tender
As he mutters a prayer for the children asleep—
  For their mother; may Heaven defend her!

The moon seems to shine just as brightly as then,
  That night when the love yet unspoken
Leaped up to his lips—when low-murmured vows
  Were pledged to be ever unbroken.

Then, drawing his sleeve roughly over his
    eyes,
He dashes off tears that are welling,
And gathers his gun closer up to its
    place,
    As if to keep down the heart-swelling.

He passes the fountain, the blasted pine
    tree,
    The footstep is lagging and weary;
Yet onward he goes through the broad belt
    of light,
    Toward the shade of the forest so
        dreary.
Hark! was it the night-wind that rustled
    the leaves?
    Was it moonlight so wondrously flash-
        ing?
It looked like a rifle—"Ha! Mary, good-
    bye!"
    The red life-blood is ebbing and plash-
        ing.

All quiet along the Potomac to-night,
    No sound save the rush of the river;
While soft falls the dew on the face of the
    dead—
    The picket's off duty for ever!
            ETHEL LYNN BEERS.

THE CUMBERLAND.

MAGNIFICENT thy fate,
    Once Mistress of the Seas!
No braver vessel ever flung
    A pennon to the breeze;
No bark e'er died a death so grand;
Such heroes never vessel manned;
Your parting broadside broke the wave
That surged above your patriot grave;
Your flag, the gamest of the game,
Sank proudly with you—not in shame,
    But in its ancient glory;
The memory of its parting gleam
Will never fade while poets dream;
The echo of your dying gun
Will last till man his race has run,
    Then live in Angel Story.
            AUTHOR UNKNOWN.

BARBARA FRIETCHIE.

UP from the meadows rich with corn,
Clear in the cool September morn,

The cluster'd spires of Frederick stand
Green-wall'd by the hills of Maryland.

Round about them orchards sweep,
Apple and peach tree fruited deep,

Fair as the garden of the Lord
To the eyes of the famish'd rebel horde,

On that pleasant morn of the early fall
When Lee march'd over the mountain-
    wall,—

Over the mountains winding down,
Horse and foot, into Frederick town.

Forty flags with their silver stars,
Forty flags with their crimson bars,

Flapp'd in the morning wind: the sun
Of noon look'd down, and saw not one.

Up rose old Barbara Frietchie then,
Bow'd with her fourscore years and ten;

Bravest of all in Frederick town,
She took up the flag the men haul'd
    down;

In her attic window the staff she set,
To show that one heart was loyal yet.

Up the street came the rebel tread,
Stonewall Jackson riding ahead.

Under his slouch'd hat left and right
He glanced: the old flag met his sight.

"Halt!"—the dust-brown ranks stood fast.
"Fire!"—out blazed the rifle-blast.

It shiver'd the window, pane and sash;
It rent the banner with seam and gash.

Quick, as it fell, from the broken staff
Dame Barbara snatch'd the silken scarf.

She lean'd far out on the window-sill,
And shook it forth with a royal will.

"Shoot, if you must, this old gray head,
But spare your country's flag," she said.

A shade of sadness, a blush of shame,
Over the face of the leader came;

The nobler nature within him stirr'd
To life at that woman's deed and word:

"Who touches a hair of yon gray head
Dies like a dog! March on!" he said.

All day long through Frederick street
Sounded the tread of marching feet:

All day long that free flag tost
Over the heads of the rebel host.

Ever its torn folds rose and fell
On the loyal winds that loved it well;

And through the hill-gaps sunset light
Shone over it with a warm good-night.

Barbara Frietchie's work is o'er,
And the rebel rides on his raids no more.

Honor to her! and let a tear
Fall, for her sake, on Stonewall's bier.

Over Barbara Frietchie's grave,
Flag of Freedom and Union, wave!

Peace and order and beauty draw
Round thy symbol of light and law;

And ever the stars above look down
On thy stars below in Frederick town!
    JOHN GREENLEAF WHITTIER.

SHERIDAN'S RIDE.

UP from the south, at break of day,
Bringing to Winchester fresh dismay,
The affrighted air with a shudder bore,
Like a herald in haste to the chieftain's
 door,
The terrible grumble, and rumble, and
 roar,
Telling the battle was on once more,
 And Sheridan twenty miles away.

And wider still those billows of war
Thunder'd along the horizon's bar;
And louder yet into Winchester roll'd
The roar of that red sea uncontroll'd,
Making the blood of the listener cold,
As he thought of the stake in that fiery fray,
 And Sheridan twenty miles away.

But there is a road from Winchester town,
A good broad highway leading down;
And there, through the flush of the morn-
 ing light,
A steed as black as the steeds of night
Was seen to pass, as with eagle flight,
As if he knew the terrible need;
He stretch'd away with his utmost speed;
Hills rose and fell; but his heart was gay,
 With Sheridan fifteen miles away.

Still sprang from those swift hoofs, thun-
 dering south,
The dust, like smoke from the cannon's
 mouth,
Or the trail of a comet, sweeping faster
 and faster,
Foreboding to traitors the doom of disaster.
The heart of the steed and the heart of the
 master
Were beating like prisoners assaulting
 their walls,
Impatient to be where the battle-field calls;
Every nerve of the charger was strain'd
 to full play,
 With Sheridan only ten miles away.

Under his spurning feet, the road
Like an arrowy Alpine river flow'd
And the landscape sped away behind
Like an ocean flying before the wind;
And the steed, like a bark fed with furnace
 ire,
Swept on, with his wild eye full of fire.
But, lo! he is nearing his heart's desire;
He is snuffing the smoke of the roaring
 fray,
 With Sheridan only five miles away.

The first that the general saw were the
 groups
Of stragglers, and then the retreating
 troops;
What was done? what to do? a glance
 told him both.
Then striking his spurs with a terrible
 oath,
He dash'd down the line, 'mid a storm of
 huzzas,
And the wave of retreat check'd its course
 there, because
The sight of the master compell'd it to
 pause.

With foam and with dust the black charger
    was gray;
By the flash of his eye, and the red nos-
    tril's play
He seem'd to the whole great army to say,
" I have brought you Sheridan all the way
From Winchester down, to save the day."

Hurrah! hurrah for Sheridan!
Hurrah! hurrah for horse and man!
And when their statues are placed on high,
Under the dome of the Union sky,
The American soldier's Temple of Fame,
There with the glorious general's name
Be it said, in letters both bold and bright:
  " Here is the steed that saved the day
By carrying Sheridan into the fight,
    From Winchester—twenty miles away!"
        THOMAS BUCHANAN READ.

HISTORY.

THOU chronicle of crimes! I read no
    more—
For I am one who willingly would love
His fellow-kind. O gentle Poesy,
Receive me from the court's polluted
    scenes,
From dungeon horrors, from the fields of
    war,
Receive me to your haunts,—that I may
    nurse
My nature's better feelings, for my soul
Sickens at man's misdeeds!
                I spake—when lo!
There stood before me, in her majesty,
Clio, the strong-eyed Muse. Upon her
    brow
Sate a calm anger. Go, young man, she
    cried,
Sigh among myrtle bowers, and let thy
    soul
Effuse itself in strains so sorrowful sweet,
That love-sick maids may weep upon thy
    page,
Soothed with delicious sorrow. Oh shame!
    shame!
Was it for this I waken'd thy young
    mind?
Was it for this I made thy swelling heart
Throb at the deeds of Greece, and thy
    boy's eye
So kindle when that glorious Spartan
    died?
Boy! boy! deceive me not! what if the
    tale
Of murder'd millions strike a chilling
    pang,
What if Tiberius in his island stews,
And Philip at his beads, alike inspire
Strong anger and contempt; hast thou
    not risen
With nobler feelings? with a deeper love
For freedom? Yes; if righteously thy
    soul
Loathes the black history of human crimes
And human misery, let that spirit fill
Thy song, and it shall teach thee, boy! to
    raise
Strains such as Cato might have deign'd
    to hear,
As Sidney in his hall of bliss may love.
                ROBERT SOUTHEY.

And when I kneel and try to pray,
  My thoughts are never free,
But cling to those who toil and fight
  And die for you and me.
And when I pray for victory,
  It seems almost a sin
To fold my hands and ask for what
  I will not help to win.

J. G. Holland

POEMS OF PATRIOTISM.

THE STAR-SPANGLED BANNER.

OH, say, can you see by the dawn's early light
  What so proudly we hail'd at the twilight's last gleaming—
Whose broad stripes and bright stars through the perilous fight,
  O'er the ramparts we watch'd, were so gallantly streaming?
And the rocket's red glare, the bombs bursting in air,
Gave proof through the night that our flag was still there;
Oh, say, does that star-spangled banner yet wave
O'er the land of the free, and the home of the brave?

On that shore, dimly seen through the mists of the deep,
  Where the foe's haughty host in dread silence reposes,
What is that which the breeze, o'er the towering steep,
  As it fitfully blows, now conceals, now discloses?
Now it catches the gleam of the morning's first beam,
In full glory reflected, now shines on the stream;
'Tis the star-spangled banner; oh, long may it wave
O'er the land of the free, and the home of the brave!

And where are the foes who so vauntingly swore
  That the havoc of war and the battle's confusion
A home and a country should leave us no more?
  Their blood has wash'd out their foul footsteps' pollution.
No refuge could save the hireling and slave
From the terror of flight, or the gloom of the grave;
And the star-spangled banner in triumph doth wave
O'er the land of the free, and the home of the brave.

Oh, thus be it ever, when freemen shall stand
  Between their loved homes and the war's desolation!
Blest with victory and peace, may the heaven-rescued land
  Praise the Power that hath made and preserved us a nation.
Then conquer we must, when our cause it is just;
And this be our motto: "In God is our trust;"
And the star-spangled banner in triumph shall wave
O'er the land of the free, and the home of the brave.
                FRANCIS SCOTT KEY.

THE AMERICAN FLAG.

WHEN Freedom from her mountain-height
  Unfurl'd her standard to the air,
She tore the azure robe of night,
  And set the stars of glory there;
She mingled with its gorgeous dyes
The milky baldric of the skies,
And striped its pure celestial white
With streakings of the morning light;

Then from his mansion in the sun
She call'd her eagle-bearer down,
And gave into his mighty hand
The symbol of her chosen land.

Majestic monarch of the cloud!
  Who rear'st aloft thy regal form,
To hear the tempest-trumpings loud,
And see the lightning lances driven,
  When strive the warriors of the storm,
And rolls the thunder-drum of heaven—
Child of the sun! to thee 'tis given
  To guard the banner of the free,
To hover in the sulphur-smoke,
To ward away the battle-stroke,
And bid its blendings shine afar,
Like rainbows on the cloud of war,
  The harbingers of victory!

Flag of the brave! thy folds shall fly,
The sign of hope and triumph high,
When speaks the signal trumpet-tone,
And the long line comes gleaming on;
Ere yet the life-blood, warm and wet,
Has dimm'd the glistening bayonet,
Each soldier eye shall brightly turn
To where thy sky-born glories burn,
And as his springing steps advance
Catch war and vengeance from the glance.
And when the cannon-mouthings loud
Heave in wild wreaths the battle-shroud,
And gory sabres rise and fall
Like shoots of flame on midnight's pall,
Then shall thy meteor glances glow,
  And cowering foes shall sink beneath
Each gallant arm that strikes below
  That lovely messenger of death.

Flag of the seas! on ocean wave
Thy stars shall glitter o'er the brave;
When death, careering on the gale,
Sweeps darkly round the bellied sail,
And frighted waves rush wildly back
Before the broadside's reeling rack,
Each dying wanderer of the sea
Shall look at once to heaven and thee,
And smile to see thy splendors fly
In triumph o'er his closing eye.

Flag of the free heart's hope and home!
  By angel hands to valor given;
Thy stars have lit the welkin dome,
  And all thy hues were born in heaven.
For ever float that standard sheet!
  Where breathes the foe but falls before us,
With freedom's soil beneath our feet,
  And freedom's banner streaming o'er us?
JOSEPH RODMAN DRAKE.

AMERICA.

My country, 'tis of thee,
Sweet land of liberty,
  Of thee I sing;
Land where my fathers died,
Land of the pilgrim's pride,
From every mountain-side
  Let freedom ring.

My native country, thee—
Land of the noble, free—
  Thy name I love;
I love thy rocks and rills,
Thy woods and templed hills;
My heart with rapture thrills
  Like that above.

Let music swell the breeze,
And ring from all the trees
  Sweet freedom's song:
Let mortal tongues awake;
Let all that breathe partake;
Let rocks their silence break,—
  The sound prolong.

Our fathers' God, to Thee,
Author of liberty,
  To Thee we sing;
Long may our land be bright
With freedom's holy light;
Protect us by Thy might,
  Great God, our King.
SAMUEL F. SMITH.

BATTLE-HYMN OF THE REPUBLIC.

Mine eyes have seen the glory of the
  coming of the Lord:
He is trampling out the vintage where the
  grapes of wrath are stored;
He hath loosed the fateful lightning of
  His terrible swift sword:
    His truth is marching on.

I have seen Him in the watch-fires of a
    hundred circling camps ;
They have builded Him an altar in the
    evening dews and damps ;
I can read His righteous sentence by the
    dim and flaring lamps :
        His day is marching on.

I have read a fiery gospel writ in burnish'd
    rows of steel :
" As ye deal with my contemners, so with
    you my grace shall deal ;
Let the Hero, born of woman, crush the
    serpent with his heel,
        Since God is marching on."

He has sounded forth the trumpet that
    shall never call retreat ;
He is sifting out the hearts of men before
    His judgment-seat :
Oh, be swift, my soul, to answer Him ! be
    jubilant, my feet !
        Our God is marching on.

In the beauty of the lilies Christ was born
    across the sea,
With a glory in His bosom that trans-
    figures you and me :
As He died to make men holy, let us die to
    make men free,
        While God is marching on.
            JULIA WARD HOWE.

RULE, BRITANNIA.

WHEN Britain first, at Heaven's com-
    mand,
  Arose from out the azure main,
This was the charter of the land,
  And guardian angels sang this strain :
        Rule, Britannia, rule the waves ;
        Britons never will be slaves.

The nations, not so blest as thee,
  Must in their turns to tyrants fall ;
While thou shalt flourish, great and free,
  The dread and envy of them all :
        Rule, Britannia, rule the waves ;
        Britons never will be slaves.

Still more majestic shalt thou rise,
  More dreadful from each foreign stroke :

As the loud blast that tears the skies
  Serves but to root thy native oak :
        Rule, Britannia, rule the waves ;
        Britons never will be slaves.

Thee haughty tyrants ne'er shall tame ;
  All their attempts to bend thee down
Will but arouse thy generous flame,
  But work their woe, and thy renown.
        Rule, Britannia, rule the waves ;
        Britons never will be slaves.

To thee belongs the rural reign ;
  Thy cities shall with commerce shine :
All thine shall be the subject main,
  And every shore it circles, thine :
        Rule, Britannia, rule the waves ;
        Britons never will be slaves.

The Muses, still with Freedom found,
  Shall to thy happy coast repair ;
Blest isle ! with matchless beauty crown'd,
  And manly hearts to guard the fair :
        Rule, Britannia, rule the waves ;
        Britons never will be slaves.
            JAMES THOMSON.

GOD SAVE THE KING.

GOD save our gracious king !
Long live our noble king !
    God save the king !
Send him victorious,
Happy and glorious,
Long to reign over us—
    God save the king !

O Lord our God, arise !
Scatter his enemies,
    And make them fall,
Confound their politics,
Frustrate their knavish tricks ;
On him our hopes we fix,
    God save us all !

Thy choicest gifts in store
On him be pleased to pour ;
    Long may he reign.
May he defend our laws,
And ever give us cause,
To sing with heart and voice—
    God save the king !
        HENRY CAREY.

MEN OF ENGLAND.

Men of England! who inherit
  Rights that cost your sires their
    blood!
Men whose undegenerate spirit
  Has been proved on field and flood!—

By the foes you've fought uncounted,
  By the glorious deeds you've done,
Trophies captured—breaches mounted—
  Navies conquer'd—kingdoms won!

Yet, remember, England gathers
  Hence but fruitless wreaths of fame,
If the freedom of your fathers
  Glow not in your hearts the same.

What are monuments of bravery
  Where no public virtues bloom?
What avail, in lands of slavery,
  Trophied temples, arch and tomb?

Pageants!—Let the world revere us
  For our people's rights and laws,
And the breasts of civic heroes
  Bared in Freedom's holy cause.

Yours are Hampden's, Russell's glory,
  Sidney's matchless shade is yours,—
Martyrs in heroic story,
  Worth a hundred Agincourts!

We're the sons of sires that baffled
  Crown'd and mitred tyranny;—
They defied the field and scaffold
  For their birthrights—so will we!
                THOMAS CAMPBELL.

YE MARINERS OF ENGLAND.

Ye Mariners of England
That guard our native seas!
Whose flag has braved, a thousand
    years,
The battle and the breeze!
Your glorious standard launch again
To match another foe:
And sweep through the deep,
While the stormy winds do blow;
While the battle rages loud and long
And the stormy winds do blow.

The spirits of your fathers
Shall start from every wave—
For the deck it was their field of fame,
And Ocean was their grave:
Where Blake and mighty Nelson fell
Your manly hearts shall glow,
As ye sweep through the deep,
While the stormy winds do blow;
While the battle rages loud and long
And the stormy winds do blow.

Britannia needs no bulwarks,
No towers along the steep;
Her march is o'er the mountain-waves,
Her home is on the deep.
With thunders from her native oak
She quells the floods below—
As they roar on the shore,
When the stormy winds do blow;
When the battle rages loud and long,
And the stormy winds do blow.

The meteor flag of England
Shall yet terrific burn;
Till danger's troubled night depart,
And the star of peace return.
Then, then, ye ocean-warriors!
Our song and feast shall flow
To the fame of your name,
When the storm has ceased to blow;
When the fiery fight is heard no more,
And the storm has ceased to blow.
                THOMAS CAMPBELL.

SONNET.

On a Distant View of England.

Yes! from mine eyes the tears unbidden
    start,
As thee, my country, and the long-lost
    sight
Of thy own cliffs, that lift their summits
    white
Above the wave, once more my beating
    heart
With eager hope and filial transport
    hails!
Scenes of my youth, reviving gales ye
    bring,
As when erewhile the tuneful morn of
    spring
Joyous awoke amidst your hawthorn vales,

And fill'd with fragrance every village
  lane:
  Fled are those hours, and all the joys
    they gave!
  Yet still I gaze, and count each rising
    wave
That bears me nearer to my home again:
If haply, 'mid those woods and vales so
  fair,
Stranger to Peace, I yet may meet her
    there.
          WILLIAM LISLE BOWLES.

THE BROADSWORDS OF SCOTLAND.

Now there's peace on the shore, now
    there's calm on the sea,
  Fill a glass to the heroes whose swords
    kept us free,
Right descendants of Wallace, Montrose,
    and Dundee.
    Oh, the broadswords of old Scotland!
    And oh, the old Scottish broadswords!

Old Sir Ralph Abercromby, the good and
    the brave—
Let him flee from our board, let him sleep
    with the slave,
Whose libation comes slow while we honor
    his grave.
    Oh, the broadswords of old Scotland!
    And oh, the old Scottish broadswords!

Though he died not, like him, amid
    victory's roar,
Though disaster and gloom wove his shroud
    on the shore,
Not the less we remember the spirit of
    Moore.
    Oh, the broadswords of old Scotland!
    And oh, the old Scottish broadswords!

Yea, a place with the fallen the living
    shall claim;
We'll entwine in one wreath every glori-
    ous name,
The Gordon, the Ramsay, the Hope, and
    the Graham,
    All the broadswords of old Scotland!
    And oh, the old Scottish broadswords!

Count the rocks of the Spey, count the
    groves of the Forth,
Count the stars in the clear, cloudless
    heaven of the north;
Then go blazon their numbers, their names,
    and their worth,
    All the broadswords of old Scotland!
    And oh, the old Scottish broadswords!

The highest in splendor, the humblest in
    place,
Stand united in glory, as kindred in race,
For the private is brother in blood to His
    Grace.
    Oh, the broadswords of old Scotland!
    And oh, the old Scottish broadswords!

Then sacred to each and to all let it be,
Fill a glass to the heroes whose swords
    kept us free,
Right descendants of Wallace, Montrose,
    and Dundee.
    Oh, the broadswords of old Scotland!
    And oh, the old Scottish broadswords!
          JOHN GIBSON LOCKHART.

IT'S HAME, AND IT'S HAME.

IT's hame, and it's hame, hame fain wad I
    be,
An' it's hame, hame, hame, to my ain
    countree!
When the flower is i' the bud and the leaf
    is on the tree,
The lark shall sing me hame in my ain
    countree;
It's hame, and it's hame, hame fain wad I
    be,
An' it's hame, hame, hame, to my ain
    countree!

The green leaf o' loyaltie's beginning for to
    fa',
The bonnie white rose it is withering
    an' a';
But I'll water 't wi' the blude of usurping
    tyrannie,
An' green it will grow in my ain countree.
It's hame, and it's hame, hame fain wad I
    be,
An' it's hame, hame, hame, to my ain
    countree!

There's naught now frae ruin my country can save
But the keys o' kind Heaven to open the grave,
That a' the noble martyrs who died for loyaltie
May rise again and fight for their ain countree.
It's hame, and it's hame, hame fain wad I be,
An' it's hame, hame, hame, to my ain countree!

The great now are gane, a' who ventured to save,
The new grass is springing on the tap o' their grave;
But the sun thro' the mirk blinks blythe in my ee:
"I'll shine on ye yet in your ain countree."
It's hame, and it's hame, hame fain wad I be,
An' it's hame, hame, hame, to my ain countree!

ALLAN CUNNINGHAM.

THE SUN RISES BRIGHT IN FRANCE.

THE sun rises bright in France,
  And fair sets he;
But he has tint the blythe blink he had
  In my ain countree.

Oh, it's nae my ain ruin
  That saddens aye my ee,
But the dear Marie I left ahin',
  Wi' sweet bairnies three.

My lanely hearth burn'd bonnie,
  An' smiled my ain Marie;
I've left a' my heart behin'
  In my ain countree.

The bud comes back to summer,
  And the blossom to the bee,
But I'll win back—oh never
  To my ain countree.

Oh, I am leal to high Heaven,
  Where soon I hope to be,
An' there I'll meet you a' soon
  Frae my ain countree!

ALLAN CUNNINGHAM.

MY HEART'S IN THE HIGHLANDS.

MY heart's in the Highlands, my heart is not here;
My heart's in the Highlands a-chasing the deer;
Chasing the wild deer, and following the roe,
My heart's in the Highlands, wherever I go.
Farewell to the Highlands, farewell to the North,
The birthplace of valor, the country of worth:
Wherever I wander, wherever I rove,
The hills of the Highlands for ever I love.

Farewell to the mountains high cover'd with snow;
Farewell to the straths and green valleys below;
Farewell to the forests and wild-hanging woods;
Farewell to the torrents and loud-pouring floods.
My heart's in the Highlands, my heart is not here,
My heart's in the Highlands a-chasing the deer.
Chasing the wild deer, and following the roe,
My heart's in the Highlands, wherever I go.

ROBERT BURNS.

BORDER BALLAD.

MARCH, march, Ettrick and Teviotdale,
  Why the de'il dinna ye march forward in order?
March, march, Eskdale and Liddesdale,
  All the blue bonnets are bound for the border.
    Many a banner spread,
    Flutters above your head,
Many a crest that is famous in story.
    Mount and make ready, then,
    Sons of the mountain-glen,
Fight for the Queen and our old Scottish glory.

Come from the hills where your hirsels are grazing,
  Come from the glen of the buck and the roe;

Come to the crag where the beacon is
    blazing,
  Come with the buckler, the lance, and
    the bow.
      Trumpets are sounding,
      War-steeds are bounding,
  Stand to your arms and march in good
    order,
      England shall many a day
      Tell of the bloody fray,
  When the blue bonnets came over the
    border.
            SIR WALTER SCOTT.

PIBROCH OF DONUIL DHU.

PIBROCH of Donuil Dhu,
    Pibroch of Donuil,
  Wake thy wild voice anew,
    Summon Clan-Conuil.
  Come away, come away,
    Hark to the summons!
  Come in your war-array,
    Gentles and commons.

Come from the deep glen, and
    From mountain so rocky,
  The war-pipe and pennon
    Are at Inverlochy.
  Come every hill-plaid, and
    True heart that wears one,
  Come every steel blade, and
    Strong hand that bears one.

Leave untended the herd,
    The flock without shelter;
  Leave the corpse uninterr'd,
    The bride at the altar;
  Leave the deer, leave the steer,
    Leave nets and barges:
  Come with your fighting gear,
    Broadswords and targes.

Come as the winds come, when
    Forests are rended;
  Come as the waves come, when
    Navies are stranded:
  Faster come, faster come,
    Faster and faster,
  Chief, vassal, page, and groom,
    Tenant and master.

Fast they come, fast they come;
    See how they gather!
  Wide waves the eagle plume,
    Blended with heather.
  Cast your plaids, draw your blades,
    Forward each man set!
  Pibroch of Donuil Dhu,
    Knell for the onset!
            SIR WALTER SCOTT.

THE EXILE OF ERIN.

THERE came to the beach a poor exile of
    Erin,
  The dew on his thin robe was heavy and
    chill;
For his country he sigh'd when at twilight
    repairing
  To wander alone by the wind-beaten hill.
But the day-star attracted his eye's sad de-
    votion,
For it rose o'er his own native isle of the
    ocean,
Where once, in the fervor of youth's warm
    emotion,
  He sung the bold anthem of Erin go
    bragh.

Sad is my fate! said the heart-broken
    stranger,
  The wild deer and wolf to a covert can
    flee;
But I have no refuge from famine and
    danger,
  A home and a country remain not to me.
Never again, in the green sunny bowers,
Where my forefathers lived, shall I spend
    the sweet hours,
Or cover my harp with the wild woven
    flowers,
  And strike to the numbers of Erin go
    bragh.

Erin, my country! though sad and for-
    saken,
  In dreams I revisit thy sea-beaten shore,
But, alas! in a far foreign land I awaken,
  And sigh for the friends who can meet
    me no more!
Oh, cruel Fate! wilt thou never replace me
In a mansion of peace, where no perils
    can chase me?
Never again shall my brothers embrace me?
  They died to defend me, or live to de-
    plore!

Where is my cabin-door, fast by the wild-
  wood?
 Sisters and sire, did ye weep for its
  fall?
Where is the mother that look'd on my
  childhood,
 And where is the bosom-friend, dearer
  than all?
Oh, my sad heart, long abandon'd by
  pleasure,
Why did it dote on a fast-fading treasure?
Tears, like the rain-drops, may fall with-
  out measure,
 But rapture and beauty they cannot re-
  call.

Yet, all its sad recollections suppressing,
 One dying wish my lone bosom can
  draw;
Erin, an exile bequeaths thee his bless-
  ing;
Land of my forefathers! Erin go bragh!
Buried and cold, when my heart stills her
  motion,
Green be thy fields, sweetest isle of the
  ocean!
And thy harp-striking bards sing aloud
  with devotion,
 Erin mavournin! Erin go bragh!
                        THOMAS CAMPBELL.

SONG OF THE GREEK POET.

THE isles of Greece, the isles of Greece!
 Where burning Sappho loved and sung,—
Where grew the arts of war and peace,—
 Where Delos rose, and Phœbus sprung!
Eternal summer gilds them yet;
But all except their sun is set.

The Scian and the Teian muse,
 The hero's harp, the lover's lute,
Have found the fame your shores refuse;
 Their place of birth alone is mute
To sounds which echo further west
Than your sires' "Islands of the Blest."

The mountains look on Marathon,
 And Marathon looks on the sea;
And musing there an hour alone,
 I dream'd that Greece might still be free;
For standing on the Persians' grave,
I could not deem myself a slave.

A king sate on the rocky brow
 Which looks o'er sea-born Salamis;
And ships by thousands lay below,
 And men in nations,—all were his!
He counted them at break of day,—
And when the sun set, where were they?

And where are they? and where art thou,
 My country? On thy voiceless shore
The heroic lay is tuneless now,—
 The heroic bosom beats no more!
And must thy lyre, so long divine,
Degenerate into hands like mine?

'Tis something, in the dearth of fame,
 Though link'd among a fetter'd race,
To feel at least a patriot's shame,
 E'en as I sing, suffuse my face;
For what is left the poet here?
For Greeks a blush,—for Greece a tear.

Must we but weep o'er days more blest?
 Must we but blush?—our fathers bled.
Earth! render back from out thy breast
 A remnant of our Spartan dead!
Of the three hundred, grant but three
To make a new Thermopylæ!

What, silent still? and silent all?
 Ah no! the voices of the dead
Sound like a distant torrent's fall,
 And answer, "Let one living head,
But one, arise,—we come, we come!"
'Tis but the living who are dumb.

In vain,—in vain; strike other chords;
 Fill high the cup with Samian wine!
Leave battles to the Turkish hordes,
 And shed the blood of Scio's vine!
Hark! rising to the ignoble call,
How answers each bold Bacchanal!

You have the Pyrrhic dance as yet,
 Where is the Pyrrhic phalanx gone?
Of two such lessons, why forget
 The nobler and the manlier one?
You have the letters Cadmus gave,—
Think ye he meant them for a slave?

Fill high the bowl with Samian wine!
 We will not think of themes like these!
It made Anacreon's song divine;
 He served—but served Polycrates,—
A tyrant; but our masters then
Were still, at least, our countrymen.

The tyrant of the Chersonese
  Was freedom's best and bravest friend;
That tyrant was Miltiades!
  Oh that the present hour would lend
Another despot of the kind!
Such chains as his were sure to bind.

Fill high the bowl with Samian wine!
  On Suli's rock and Parga's shore
Exists the remnant of a line,
  Such as the Doric mothers bore;
And there perhaps some seed is sown
The Heracleidan blood might own.

Trust not for freedom to the Franks,—
  They have a king who buys and sells.
In native swords and native ranks
  The only hope of courage dwells;
But Turkish force and Latin fraud
Would break your shield, however broad.

Fill high the bowl with Samian wine!
  Our virgins dance beneath the shade,—
I see their glorious black eyes shine;
  But, gazing on each glowing maid,
My own the burning tear-drop laves,
To think such breasts must suckle slaves.

Place me on Sunium's marbled steep,
  Where nothing, save the waves and I,
May hear our mutual murmurs sweep;
  There, swan-like, let me sing and die.
A land of slaves shall ne'er be mine,—
Dash down yon cup of Samian wine!
                      LORD BYRON.

A COURT LADY.

HER hair was tawny with gold, her eyes
  with purple were dark,
Her cheeks' pale opal burnt with a red and
  restless spark.

Never was lady of Milan nobler in name
  and in race;
Never was lady of Italy fairer to see in the
  face.

Never was lady on earth more true as
  woman and wife,
Larger in judgment and instinct, prouder
  in manners and life.

She stood in the early morning, and said
  to her maidens, "Bring
That silken robe made ready to wear at
  the court of the king.

"Bring me the clasps of diamond, lucid,
  clear of the mote,
Clasp me the large at the waist, and clasp
  me the small at the throat.

"Diamonds to fasten the hair, and diamonds to fasten the sleeves,
Laces to drop from their rays, like a powder of snow from the eaves."

Gorgeous she entered the sunlight, which
  gather'd her up in a flame,
While straight in her open carriage she
  to the hospital came.

In she went at the door, and gazing from
  end to end,
"Many and low are the pallets, but each
  is the place of a friend."

Up she pass'd through the wards, and
  stood at a young man's bed:
Bloody the band on his brow, and livid
  the droop of his head.

"Art thou a Lombard, my brother? Happy
  art thou," she cried,
And smiled like Italy on him: he dream'd
  in her face and died.

Pale with his passing soul, she went on
  still to a second:
He was a grave hard man, whose years by
  dungeons were reckon'd.

Wounds in his body were sore, wounds in
  his life were sorer.
"Art thou a Romagnole?" Her eyes
  drove the lightnings before her.

"Austrian and priest had join'd to double
  and tighten the cord
Able to bind thee, O strong one,—free by
  the stroke of a sword.

"Now be grave for the rest of us, using
  the life overcast
To ripen our wine of the present (too
  new) in glooms of the past."

Down she stepp'd to a pallet where lay a
    face like a girl's,
Young, and pathetic with dying,—a deep
    black hole in the curls.

"Art thou from Tuscany, brother? and
    seest thou, dreaming in pain,
Thy mother stand in the piazza, searching
    the list of the slain?"

Kind as a mother herself, she touch'd his
    cheeks with her hands:
"Blessed is she who has borne thee,
    although she should weep as she
    stands."

On she pass'd to a Frenchman, his arm
    carried off by a ball:
Kneeling, . . . "O more than my brother!
    how shall I thank thee for all?

"Each of the heroes around us has fought
    for his land and line,
But *thou* hast fought for a stranger, in hate
    of a wrong not thine.

"Happy are all free peoples, too strong to
    be dispossess'd:
But blessed are those among nations who
    dare to be strong for the rest!"

Ever she pass'd on her way, and came to a
    couch where pined
One with a face from Venetia, white with
    a hope out of mind.

Long she stood and gazed, and twice she
    tried at the name,
But two great crystal tears were all that
    falter'd and came.

Only a tear for Venice?—she turn'd as in
    passion and loss,
And stoop'd to his forehead and kiss'd it,
    as if she were kissing the cross.

Faint with that strain of heart, she moved
    on then to another,
Stern and strong in his death. "And
    dost thou suffer, my brother?"

Holding his hands in hers:—"Out of the
    Piedmont lion
Cometh the sweetness of freedom! sweetest
    to live or to die on."

Holding his cold rough hands,—"Well, oh,
    well have ye done
In noble, noble Piedmont, who would not
    be noble alone."

Back he fell while she spoke. She rose to
    her feet with a spring,—
"That was a Piedmontese! and this is the
    Court of the King."
ELIZABETH BARRETT BROWNING.

THE HARP THAT ONCE THROUGH TARA'S HALLS.

THE harp that once through Tara's halls
    The soul of music shed,
Now hangs as mute on Tara's walls
    As if that soul were fled.
So sleeps the pride of former days,
    So glory's thrill is o'er,
And hearts that once beat high for praise,
    Now feel that pulse no more.

No more to chiefs and ladies bright
    The harp of Tara swells;
The chord alone that breaks at night
    Its tale of ruin tells.
Thus Freedom now so seldom wakes,
    The only throb she gives
Is when some heart indignant breaks,
    To show that still she lives.
THOMAS MOORE.

THE EXILE'S SONG.

OH, why left I my hame?
    Why did I cross the deep?
Oh, why left I the land
    Where my forefathers sleep?
I sigh for Scotia's shore,
    And I gaze across the sea,
But I canna get a blink
    O' my ain countree!

The palm tree waveth high,
    And fair the myrtle springs;
And to the Indian maid
    The bulbul sweetly sings;
But I dinna see the broom
    Wi' its tassels on the lea,
Nor hear the lintie's sang
    O' my ain countree!

Oh, here no Sabbath bell
　Awakes the Sabbath morn,
Nor song of reapers heard
　Amang the yellow corn :
For the tyrant's voice is here,
　And the wail of slaverie ;
But the sun of Freedom shines
　In my ain countree !

There's a hope for every woe,
　And a balm for every pain,
But the first joys o' our heart
　Come never back again.
There's a track upon the deep,
　And a path across the sea ;
But the weary ne'er return
　To their ain countree !
　　　　　　ROBERT GILFILLAN.

HOW SLEEP THE BRAVE.

How sleep the Brave who sink to rest
By all their Country's wishes blest !
When Spring, with dewy fingers cold,
Returns to deck their hallow'd mould,
She there shall dress a sweeter sod
Than Fancy's feet have ever trod.

By fairy hands their knell is rung,
By forms unseen their dirge is sung :
There Honor comes, a pilgrim gray,
To bless the turf that wraps their clay,
And Freedom shall a while repair
To dwell a weeping hermit there !
　　　　　　WILLIAM COLLINS.

AN ODE.

IN IMITATION OF ALCÆUS.

WHAT constitutes a state ?
Not high-raised battlement or labor'd
　　mound,
　Thick wall or moated gate ;
Not cities proud with spires and turrets
　　crown'd ;
　Not bays and broad-arm'd ports,
Where, laughing at the storm, rich navies
　　ride ;
　Not starr'd and spangled courts,
Where low-brow'd baseness wafts perfume
　　to pride.

　No : men, high-minded men,
With powers as far above dull brutes en-
　　dued
　In forest, brake, or den,
As beasts excel cold rocks and brambles
　　rude,
　Men who their duties know,
But know their rights, and, knowing, dare
　　maintain,
　Prevent the long-aim'd blow,
And crush the tyrant while they rend the
　　chain :
　These constitute a state ;
And sovereign Law, that state's collected
　　will,
　O'er thrones and globes elate
Sits empress, crowning good, repressing ill.
　Smit by her sacred frown,
The fiend Dissension like a vapor sinks,
　And e'en the all-dazzling Crown
Hides his faint rays, and at her bidding
　　shrinks.

　Such was this heaven-loved isle,
Than Lesbos fairer and the Cretan shore !
　No more shall Freedom smile ?
Shall Britons languish, and be men no
　　more ?
　Since all must life resign,
Those sweet rewards which decorate the
　　brave
　'Tis folly to decline,
And steal inglorious to the silent grave.
　　　　　　SIR WILLIAM JONES.

AS BY THE SHORE AT BREAK OF DAY.

As by the shore at break of day,
A vanquish'd chief expiring lay,
Upon the sands, with broken sword,
　He traced his farewell to the free ;
And there the last unfinish'd word
　He dying wrote, was " Liberty !"

At night a sea-bird shriek'd the knell
Of him who thus for freedom fell ;
The words he wrote, ere evening came,
　Were cover'd by the sounding sea ;—
So pass away the cause and name
　Of him who dies for liberty !
　　　　　　THOMAS MOORE.

A FORCED RECRUIT AT SOLFERINO.

In the ranks of the Austrian you found him;
 He died with his face to you all:
Yet bury him here, where around him
 You honor your bravest that fall.

Venetian, fair-featured and slender,
 He lies shot to death in his youth,
With a smile on his lips over-tender
 For any mere soldier's dead mouth.

No stranger, and yet not a traitor!
 Though alien the cloth on his breast,
Underneath it how seldom a greater
 Young heart has a shot sent to rest!

By your enemy tortured and goaded
 To march with them, stand in their file,
His musket (see!) never was loaded—
 He facing your guns with that smile.

As orphans yearn on their mothers,
 He yearned to your patriot bands,—
"Let me die for one Italy, brothers,
 If not in your ranks, by your hands!

"Aim straightly, fire steadily; spare me
 A ball in the body, which may
Deliver my heart here, and tear me
 This badge of the Austrian away."

So thought he, so died he this morning.
 What then? many others have died.
Ay—but easy for men to die scorning
 The death-stroke, who fought side by side;

One tricolor floating above them;
 Struck down mid triumphant acclaims
Of an Italy rescued to love them,
 And brazen the brass with their names.

But he—without witness or honor,
 Mixed, shared in his country's regard,
With the tyrants who march in upon her—
 Died faithful and passive: 'twas hard.

'Twas sublime. In a cruel restriction
 Cut off from the guerdon of sons,
With most filial obedience, conviction,
 His soul kissed the lips of her guns.

That moves you? Nay, grudge not to show it,
 While digging a grave for him here.
The others who died, says our poet,
 Have glory: let *him* have a tear.
 ELIZABETH BARRETT BROWNING.

BOAT-SONG.

Hail to the Chief who in triumph advances!
 Honor'd and bless'd be the ever-green Pine!
Long may the tree, in his banner that glances,
 Flourish, the shelter and grace of our line!
  Heaven send it happy dew,
  Earth lend it sap anew,
Gayly to bourgeon, and broadly to grow,
  While every Highland glen
  Send our shout back again,—
"Roderigh Vich Alpine dhu, ho! ieroe!"

Ours is no sapling, chance-sown by the fountain,
 Blooming at Beltane, in winter to fade;
When the whirlwind has stripp'd every leaf on the mountain,
 The more shall Clan-Alpine exult in her shade.
  Moor'd in the rifted rock,
  Proof to the tempest's shock,
Firmer he roots him the ruder it blow;
  Menteith and Breadalbane, then,
  Echo his praise again,—
"Roderigh Vich Alpine dhu, ho! ieroe!"

Proudly our pibroch has thrill'd in Glen Fruin,
 And Bannachar's groans to our slogan replied;
Glen Luss and Ross-dhu, they are smoking in ruin,
 And the best of Loch Lomond lie dead on her side.
  Widow and Saxon maid
  Long shall lament our raid,
Think of Clan-Alpine with fear and with woe;
  Lennox and Leven-Glen
  Shake when they hear again,—
"Roderigh Vich Alpine dhu, ho! ieroe!"

Row, vassals, row, for the pride of the
    Highlands!
Stretch to your oars, for the ever-green
    pine!
Oh! that the rosebud that graces yon
    islands,
  Were wreathed in a garland around him
    to twine!
    Oh that some seedling gem,
    Worthy such noble stem,
Honor'd and bless'd in their shadow might
    grow!
    Loud should Clan-Alpine then
    Ring from his deepmost glen,—
"Roderigh Vich Alpine dhu, ho! ieroe!"
              SIR WALTER SCOTT.

IT IS GREAT FOR OUR COUNTRY TO DIE.

OH! it is great for our country to die
    where ranks are contending:
Bright is the wreath of our fame; glory
    awaits us for aye—
Glory, that never is dim, shining on with
    light never ending—
Glory that never shall fade—never, oh!
    never away.

Oh! it is sweet for our country to die!
    How softly reposes
Warrior youth on his bier, wet by the
    tears of his love,
Wet by a mother's warm tears! they crown
    him with garlands of roses,
Weep, and then joyously turn, bright
    where he triumphs above.

Not to the shades shall the youth descend
    who for country hath perished;
Hebe awaits him in heaven, welcomes
    him there with her smile;
There, at the banquet divine, the patriot
    spirit is cherished;
Gods love the young who ascend pure
    from the funeral pile.

Not to Elysian fields, by the still, oblivious
    river;
Not to the isles of the blest, over the
    blue-rolling sea;
But on Olympian heights shall dwell the
    devoted for ever;
There shall assemble the good, there the
    wise, valiant, and free.

Oh! then, how great for our country to die,
    in the front rank to perish,
Firm with our breast to the foe, victory's
    shout in our ear!
Long they our statues shall crown, in songs
    our memory cherish;
We shall look forth from our heaven,
    pleased the sweet music to hear.
              JAMES GATES PERCIVAL.

THE HEART OF THE WAR.
(1864.)

PEACE in the clover-scented air,
    And stars within the dome;
And underneath, in dim repose,
    A plain, New England home.
Within, a murmur of low tones
    And sighs from hearts oppressed,
Merging in prayer, at last, that brings
    The balm of silent rest.

I've closed a hard day's work, Marty,—
    The evening chores are done;
And you are weary with the house,
    And with the little one.
But he is sleeping sweetly now,
    With all our pretty brood;
So come and sit upon my knee,
    And it will do me good.

Oh, Marty! I must tell you all
    The trouble in my heart,
And you must do the best you can
    To take and bear your part.
You've seen the shadow on my face;
    You've felt it day and night;
For it has filled our little home,
    And banished all its light.

I did not mean it should be so,
    And yet I might have known
That hearts which live as close as ours
    Can never keep their own.
But we are fallen on evil times,
    And, do whate'er I may,
My heart grows sad about the war,
    And sadder every day.

I think about it when I work,
  And when I try to rest,
And never more than when your head
  Is pillowed on my breast;
For then I see the camp-fires blaze,
  And sleeping men around,
Who turn their faces toward their homes,
  And dream upon the ground.

I think about the dear, brave boys,
  My mates in other years,
Who pine for home and those they love,
  Till I am choked with tears.
With shouts and cheers they marched away
  On glory's shining track,
But, ah! how long, how long they stay!
  How few of them come back!

One sleeps beside the Tennessee,
  And one beside the James,
And one fought on a gallant ship
  And perished in its flames.
And some, struck down by fell disease,
  Are breathing out their life;
And others, maimed by cruel wounds,
  Have left the deadly strife.

Ah, Marty! Marty, only think
  Of all the boys have done
And suffered in this weary war!
  Brave heroes, every one!
Oh, often, often in the night
  I hear their voices call:
"*Come on and help us! Is it right
  That we should bear it all?*"

And when I kneel and try to pray,
  My thoughts are never free,
But cling to those who toil and fight
  And die for you and me.
And when I pray for victory,
  It seems almost a sin
To fold my hands and ask for what
  I will not help to win.

Oh, do not cling to me and cry,
  For it will break my heart;
I'm sure you'd rather have me die
  Than not to bear my part.
You think that some should stay at home
  To care for those away;
But still I'm helpless to decide
  If I should go or stay.

For, Marty, all the soldiers love,
  And all are loved again;
And I am loved, and love, perhaps,
  No more than other men.
I cannot tell—I do not know—
  Which way my duty lies,
Or where the Lord would have me build
  My fire of sacrifice.

I feel—I know—I am not mean;
  And, though I seem to boast,
I'm sure that I would give my life
  To those who need it most.
Perhaps the Spirit will reveal
  That which is fair and right;
So, Marty, let us humbly kneel
  And pray to Heaven for light.

Peace in the clover-scented air,
  And stars within the dome;
And underneath, in dim repose,
  A plain, New England home.
Within, a widow in her weeds,
  From whom all joy is flown,
Who kneels among her sleeping babes,
  And weeps and prays alone.
                J. G. HOLLAND.

CAVALRY SONG.

OUR good steeds snuff the evening air,
  Our pulses with their purpose tingle;
The foeman's fires are twinkling there;
  He leaps to hear our sabres jingle!
    HALT!
Each carbine sends its whizzing ball:
Now, cling! clang! forward all,
    Into the fight!

Dash on beneath the smoking dome:
  Through level lightnings gallop nearer!
One look to Heaven! No thoughts of home:
  The guidons that we bear are dearer.
    CHARGE!
Cling! clang! forward all!
Heaven help those whose horses fall!
    Cut left and right!

They flee before our fierce attack!
  They fall! they spread in broken surges!
Now, comrades, bear our wounded back,
  And leave the foeman to his dirges.
    WHEEL!
The bugles sound the swift recall:
Cling! clang! backward all!
    Home, and good-night!
                EDMUND CLARENCE STEDMAN.

For the moon never beams without bringing me dreams
    Of the beautiful Annabel Lee;
And the stars never rise but I see the bright eyes
    Of the beautiful Annabel Lee;
And so, all the night-tide, I lie down by the side
Of my darling, my darling, my life and my bride
    In her sepulchre there by the sea —
    In her tomb by the side of the sea.

                              Edgar A. Poe

LEGENDARY AND BALLAD POETRY.

SIR PATRICK SPENS.

The king sits in Dunfermline town,
    Drinking the blude-red wine:
"Oh where will I get a skeely skipper
    To sail this ship of mine?"

Oh up and spake an eldern knight,
    Sat at the king's right knee:
"Sir Patrick Spens is the best sailor
    That ever sail'd the sea."

Our king has written a braid letter,
    And seal'd it with his hand,
And sent it to Sir Patrick Spens,
    Was walking on the strand.

"To Noroway, to Noroway,
    To Noroway o'er the faem;
The king's daughter of Noroway,
    'Tis thou maun bring her hame!"

The first word that Sir Patrick read,
    Sae loud, loud laughèd he;
The neist word that Sir Patrick read,
    The tear blinded his e'e.

"Oh wha is this has done this deed,
    And tauld the king o' me,
To send us out at this time of the year,
    To sail upon the sea?

"Be't wind or weet, be't hail or sleet,
    Our ship maun sail the faem;
The king's daughter of Noroway,
    'Tis we must fetch her hame."

They hoysed their sails on Monenday morn
    Wi' a' the speed they may;
They hae landed in Noroway
    Upon a Wodensday.

They hadna been a week, a week
    In Noroway, but twae,
When that the lords o' Noroway
    Began aloud to say:

"Ye Scottishmen spend a' our king's goud
    And a' our queenis fee."
"Ye lie, ye lie, ye liars loud!
    Fu' loud I hear ye lie!

"For I hae brought as much white monie
    As gane my men and me,—
And I hae brought a half-fou o' gude red
      goud
    Out owre the sea wi' me.

"Make ready, make ready, my merry men
      a'!
    Our gude ship sails the morn."
"Now, ever alake! my master dear,
    I fear a deadly storm!

"I saw the new moon, late yestreen,
    Wi' the auld moon in her arm;
And if we gang to sea, master,
    I fear we'll come to harm."

They hadna sail'd a league, a league,
    A league, but barely three,
When the lift grew dark, and the wind
      blew loud,
    And gurly grew the sea.

The ankers brak, and the topmasts lap,
    It was sic a deadly storm;
And the waves cam o'er the broken ship
    Till a' her sides were torn.

"Oh where will I get a gude sailor
    To take my helm in hand,
Till I get up to the tall topmast
    To see if I can spy land?"

"Oh here am I, a sailor gude,
    To take the helm in hand,

Till you go up to the tall topmast,—
But I fear you'll ne'er spy land."

He hadna gane a step, a step,
A step, but barely ane,
When a boult flew out of our goodly ship,
And the salt sea it came in.

"Gae fetch a web o' the silken claith,
Another o' the twine,
And wap them into our ship's side,
And let nae the sea come in."

They fetch'd a web o' the silken claith,
Another o' the twine,
And they wapp'd them round that gude ship's side,
—But still the sea came in.

Oh laith, laith were our gude Scots lords
To weet their cork-heel'd shoon!
But lang or a' the play was play'd,
They wat their hats aboon.

And mony was the feather-bed
That float'd on the faem;
And mony was the gude lord's son
That never mair cam hame.

The ladyes wrang their fingers white,—
The maidens tore their hair;
A' for the sake of their true loves,—
For them they'll see nae mair.

Oh lang, lang may the ladyes sit,
Wi' their fans into their hand,
Before they see Sir Patrick Spens
Come sailing to the strand!

And lang, lang may the maidens sit,
Wi' their goud kaims in their hair,
A' waiting for their ain dear loves,—
For them they'll see nae mair.

Half owre, half owre to Aberdour
'Tis fifty fathoms deep,
And there lies gude Sir Patrick Spens
Wi' the Scots lords at his feet.
AUTHOR UNKNOWN.

THE HEIR OF LINNE.

PART FIRST.

LITHE and listen, gentlemen,
To sing a song I will beginne:
It is of a lord of faire Scotlànd,
Which was the unthrifty heire of Linne.

His father was a right good lord,
His mother a lady of high degree;
But they, alas! were dead, him froe,
And he lov'd keeping companie.

To spend the daye with merry cheare,
To drink and revell every night,
To card and dice from eve to morne,
It was, I ween, his hearts delighte.

To ride, to runne, to rant, to roare,
To alwaye spend and never spare,
I wott, an' it were the king himselfe,
Of gold and fee he mote be bare.

Soe fares the unthrifty Lord of Linne
Till all his gold is gone and spent;
And he maun sell his landes so broad,
His house, and landes, and all his rent.

His father had a keen stewàrde,
And John o' the Scales was callèd hee:
But John is become a gentel-man,
And John has gott both gold and fee.

Sayes, Welcome, welcome, Lord of Linne,
Let naught disturb thy merry cheere;
Iff thou wilt sell thy landes soe broad,
Good store of gold Ile give thee heere.

My gold is gone, my money is spent;
My lande nowe take it unto thee:
Give me the golde, good John o' the Scales,
And thine for aye my lande shall bee.

Then John he did him to record draw,
And John he cast him a gods-pennie;
But for every pounde that John agreed,
The lande, I wis, was well worth three.

He told him the gold upon the borde.
He was right glad his land to winne;
The gold is thine, the land is mine,
And now Ile be the Lord of Linne.

Thus he hath sold his land soe broad,
Both hill and holt, and moore and fenne,
All but a poore and lonesome lodge,
That stood far off in a lonely glenne.

For soe he to his father hight.
My sonne, when I am gonne, sayd hee,
Then thou wilt spend thy lande so broad,
And thou wilt spend thy gold so free;

But sweare me nowe upon the roode,
  That lonesome lodge thou'lt never spend;
For when all the world doth frown on thee,
  Thou there shalt find a faithful friend.

The heire of Linne is full of golde:
  And come with me, my friends, sayd hee,
Let's drinke, and rant, and merry make,
  And he that spares, ne'er mote he thee.

They ranted, drank, and merry made,
  Till all his gold it waxèd thinne;
And then his friendes they slunk away;
  They left the unthrifty heire of Linne.

He had never a penny left in his purse,
  Never a penny left but three,
And one was brass, another was lead,
  And another it was white monèy.

Nowe well-aday, sayd the heire of Linne,
  Nowe well-adaye, and woe is mee,
For when I was the Lord of Linne,
  I never wanted gold nor fee.

But many a trustye friend have I,
  And why shold I feel dole or care?
Ile borrow of them all by turnes,
  Soe need I not be never bare.

But one, I wis, was not at home;
  Another had payd his gold away;
Another call'd him thriftless loone,
  And bade him sharpely wend his way.

Now well-aday, sayd the heire of Linne,
  Now well-aday, and woe is me;
For when I had my landes so broad,
  On me they liv'd right merrilee.

To beg my bread from door to door,
  I wis, it were a brenning shame:
To rob and steal it were a sinne:
  To worke my limbs I cannot frame.

Now Ile away to lonesome lodge,
  For there my father bade me wend:
When all the world should frown on mee
  I there shold find a trusty friend.

Part Second.

Away then hyed the heire of Linne
  O'er hill and holt, and moor and fenne,
Untill he came to lonesome lodge,
  That stood so lowe in a lonely glenne.

He lookèd up, he lookèd downe,
  In hope some comfort for to winne:
But bare and lothly were the walles.
  Here's sorry cheare, quo' the heire of Linne.

The little windowe dim and darke
  Was hung with ivy, brere, and yewe;
No shimmering sunn here ever shone,
  No halesome breeze here ever blew.

No chair, ne table he mote spye,
  No cheerful hearth, ne welcome bed,
Naught save a rope with renning noose,
  That dangling hung up o'er his head.

And over it in broad lettèrs,
  These words were written so plain to see:
"Ah! gracelesse wretch, hast spent thine all
  And brought thyself to penurie?

"All this my boding mind misgave,
  I therefore left this trusty friend:
Let it now sheeld thy foule disgrace,
  And all thy shame and sorrows end."

Sorely shent wi' this rebuke,
  Sorely shent was the heire of Linne;
His heart, I wis, was near to brast
  With guilt and sorrowe, shame and sinne.

Never a word spake the heire of Linne,
  Never a word he spake but three:
"This is a trusty friend indeed,
  And is right welcome unto mee."

Then round his necke the corde he drewe,
  And sprang aloft with his bodìe:
When lo! the ceiling burst in twaine,
  And to the ground come tumbling hee.

Astonyed lay the heire of Linne,
  Ne knewe if he were live or dead:
At length he look'd, and sawe a bille,
  And in it a key of gold so redd.

He took the bill, and lookt it on,
  Strait good comfort found he there:
Itt told him of a hole in the wall,
  In which there stood three chests in-fere.

Two were full of the beaten golde,
    The third was full of white monèy;
And over them in broad letters
    These words were written so plaine to see:

"Once more, my sonne, I sette thee clere;
    Amend thy life and follies past;
For but thou amend thee of thy life,
    That rope must be thy end at last."

And let it bee, sayd the heire of Linne;
    And let it bee, but if I amend:
For here I will make mine avow,
    This reade shall guide me to the end.

Away then went with a merry cheare,
    Away then went the heire of Linne;
I wis, he neither ceas'd ne blanne,
    Till John o' the Scales house he did winne.

And when he came to John o' the Scales,
    Upp at the speere then lookèd hee;
There sate three lords upon a rowe,
    Were drinking of the wine so free.

And John himselfe sate at the bord-head,
    Because now Lord of Linne was hee.
I pray thee, he said, good John o' the Scales,
    One forty pence for to lend mee.

Away, away, thou thriftless loone;
    Away, away, this may not bee:
For Christs curse on my head, he sayd,
    If ever I trust thee one pennìe.

Then bespake the heir of Linne,
    To John o' the Scales wife then spake hee:
Madame, some almes on me bestowe,
    I pray for sweet saint Charitìe.

Away, away, thou thriftless loone,
    I sweare thou gettest no almes of mee;
For if we should hang any losel heere,
    The first we wold begin with thee.

Then bespake a good fellòwe,
    Which sat at John o' the Scales his bord;
Sayd, Turn againe, thou heire of Linne;
    Some time thou wast a well good lord:

Some time a good fellow thou hast been,
    And sparedst not thy gold and fee;
Therefore Ile lend thee forty pence,
    And other forty if need bee.

And ever I pray thee, John o' the Scales,
    To let him sit in thy companie:
For well I wot thou hadst his land,
    And a good bargain it was to thee.

Up then spake him John o' the Scales,
    All wood he answer'd him againe:
Now Christs curse on my head, he sayd,
    But I did lose by that bargàine.

And here I proffer thee, heire of Linne,
    Before these lords so faire and free,
Thou shalt have it backe again better cheape,
    By a hundred markes, than I had it of thee.

I drawe you to record, lords, he said.
    With that he cast him a gods-pennie:
Now by my fay, sayd the heire of Linne,
    And here, good John, is thy monèy.

And he pull'd forth three bagges of gold,
    And layd them down upon the bord:
All woe begone was John o' the Scales,
    Soe shent he cold say never a word.

He told him forth the good red gold,
    He told it forth mickle dinne.
The gold is thine, the land is mine,
    And now Ime againe the Lord of Linne.

Sayes, Have thou here, thou good fellòwe,
    Forty pence thou didst lend mee:
Now I am againe the Lord of Linne,
    And forty pounds I will give thee.

Ile make thee keeper of my forrest,
    Both of the wild deere and the tame;
For but I reward thy bounteous heart,
    I wis, good fellowe, I were to blame.

Now welladay! sayth Joan o' the Scales:
    Now welladay! and woe is my life!
Yesterday I was Lady of Linne,
    Now Ime but John o' the Scales his wife.

Now fare thee well, sayd the heire of Linne;
    Farewell now, John o' the Scales, said hee:
Christs curse light on me, if ever again
    I bring my lands in jeopardy.

AUTHOR UNKNOWN.

SKIPPER IRESON'S RIDE.

Of all the rides since the birth of time,
Told in story or sung in rhyme,—
On Apuleius's Golden Ass,
Or one-eyed Calender's horse of brass,
Witch astride of a human back,
Islam's prophet on Al Borák,—
The strangest ride that ever was sped
Was Ireson's, out from Marblehead!
    Old Floyd Ireson, for his hard heart,
    Tarr'd and feather'd and carried in a
      a cart
    By the women of Marblehead!

Body of turkey, head of owl,
Wings a-droop like a rain'd-on fowl,
Feather'd and ruffled in every part,
Skipper Ireson stood in the cart.
Scores of women, old and young,
Strong of muscle, and glib of tongue,
Push'd and pull'd up the rocky lane,
Shouting and singing the shrill refrain:
    "Here's Flud Oirson, fur his horrd
      horrt,
    Torr'd an' futherr'd an' corr'd in a
      corrt
    By the women o' Morble'ead!"

Wrinkled scolds with hands on hips,
Girls in bloom of cheek and lips,
Wild-eyed, free-limb'd, such as chase
Bacchus round some antique vase,
Brief of skirt, with ankles bare,
Loose of kerchief and loose of hair,
With conch-shells blowing and fish-horn's
    twang,
Over and over the Mænads sang:
    "Here's Flud Oirson, fur his horrd
      horrt,
    Torr'd an' futherr'd an' corr'd in a
      corrt
    By the women o' Morble'ead!"

Small pity for him!—He sail'd away
From a leaking ship, in Chaleur Bay,—
Sail'd away from a sinking wreck,
With his own town's-people on her deck!
"Lay by! lay by!" they call'd to him.
Back he answer'd, "Sink or swim!
Brag of your catch of fish again!"
And off he sail'd through the fog and
    rain!
    Old Floyd Ireson, for his hard heart,
    Tarr'd and feather'd and carried in a
      cart
    By the women of Marblehead!

Fathoms deep in dark Chaleur
That wreck shall lie for evermore.
Mother and sister, wife and maid,
Look'd from the rocks of Marblehead
Over the moaning and rainy sea,—
Look'd for the coming that might not be!
What did the winds and sea-birds say
Of the cruel captain who sail'd away?—
    Old Floyd Ireson, for his hard heart,
    Tarr'd and feather'd and carried in a
      cart
    By the women of Marblehead!

Through the street, on either side,
Up flew windows, doors swung wide;
Sharp-tongued spinsters, old wives gray,
Treble lent the fish-horn's bray.
Sea-worn grandsires, cripple-bound,
Hulks of old sailors run aground,
Shook head, and fist, and hat, and cane,
And crack'd with curses the hoarse refrain:
    "Here's Flud Oirson, for his horrd
      horrt,
    Torr'd an' futherr'd an' corr'd in a
      corrt
    By the women o' Morble'ead!"

Sweetly along the Salem road
Bloom of orchard and lilac show'd.
Little the wicked skipper knew
Of the fields so green and the sky so blue.
Riding there in his sorry trim,
Like an Indian idol glum and grim,
Scarcely he seem'd the sound to hear
Of voices shouting far and near:
    "Here's Flud Oirson, for his horrd
      horrt,
    Torr'd an' futherr'd an' corr'd in a
      corrt
    By the women o' Morble'ead!"

"Hear me, neighbors!" at last he cried,—
"What to me is this noisy ride?
What is the shame that clothes the skin
To the nameless horror that lives within?
Waking or sleeping, I see a wreck
And hear a cry from a reeling deck!

Hate me and curse me,—I only dread
The hand of God and the face of the
    dead!"
  Said old Floyd Ireson, for his hard
      heart,
    Tarr'd and feather'd and carried in a
        cart
    By the women of Marblehead!

Then the wife of the skipper lost at sea
Said, "God has touch'd him!—why should
    we?"
Said an old wife mourning her only son,
"Cut the rogue's tether and let him run!"
So with soft relentings and rude excuse,
Half scorn, half pity, they cut him loose,
And gave him a cloak to hide him in,
And left him alone with his shame and
    sin.
  Poor Floyd Ireson, for his hard heart,
    Tarr'd and feather'd and carried in a
        cart
    By the women of Marblehead.
            JOHN GREENLEAF WHITTIER.

HOW THEY BROUGHT THE GOOD NEWS FROM GHENT TO AIX.

I SPRANG to the stirrup, and Joris, and
    he;
I gallop'd, Dirck gallop'd, we gallop'd all
    three;
"Good speed!" cried the watch, as the
    gate-bolts undrew;
"Speed!" echo'd the wall to us galloping
    through;
Behind shut the postern, the lights sank to
    rest,
And into the midnight we gallop'd
    abreast.

Not a word to each other; we kept the
    great pace
Neck by neck, stride by stride, never
    changing our place;
I turn'd in my saddle and made its girths
    tight,
Then shorten'd each stirrup, and set the
    pique right,
Rebuckled the check-strap, chain'd slacker
    the bit,
Nor gallop'd less steadily Roland a whit.

'Twas moonset at starting; but while we
    drew near
Lokeren, the cocks crew and twilight
    dawn'd clear;
At Boom, a great yellow star came out to
    see;
At Düffeld, 'twas morning as plain as
    could be;
And from Mecheln church-steeple we heard
    the half-chime,
So Joris broke silence with, "Yet there is
    time!"

At Aerschot, up leap'd of a sudden the
    sun,
And against him the cattle stood black
    every one,
To stare through the mist at us galloping
    past,
And I saw my stout galloper Roland at
    last,
With resolute shoulders, each butting away
The haze, as some bluff river headland its
    spray.

And his low head and crest, just one sharp
    ear bent back
For my voice, and the other prick'd out on
    his track;
And one eye's black intelligence,—ever
    that glance
O'er its white edge at me, his own master,
    askance!
And the thick heavy spume flakes which
    aye and anon
His fierce lips shook upward in galloping
    on.

By Hasselt, Dirck groan'd; and cried
    Joris, "Stay spur!
Your Roos gallop'd bravely, the fault's not
    in her;
We'll remember at Aix—" for one heard
    the quick wheeze
Of her chest, saw the stretch'd neck, and
    staggering knees,
And sunk tail, and horrible heave of the
    flank,
As down on her haunches she shudder'd
    and sank.

So we were left galloping, Joris and I,
Past Looz and past Tongres, no cloud in the sky;
The broad sun above laugh'd a pitiless laugh,
'Neath our feet broke the brittle bright stubble like chaff;
Till over by Dalhem a dome-spire sprang white,
And "Gallop," gasp'd Joris, "for Aix is in sight!

"How they'll greet us!"—and all in a moment his roan
Roll'd neck and croup over, lay dead as a stone;
And there was my Roland to bear the whole weight
Of the news which alone could save Aix from her fate,
With his nostrils like pits full of blood to the brim,
And with circles of red for his eye-sockets' rim.

Then I cast loose my buff coat, each holster let fall,
Shook off both my jack-boots, let go belt and all,
Stood up in the stirrup, lean'd, patted his ear,
Call'd my Roland his pet-name, my horse without peer;
Clapp'd my hands, laugh'd and sang, any noise, bad or good,
Till at length into Aix Roland gallop'd and stood.

And all I remember is, friends flocking round
As I sate with his head 'twixt my knees on the ground,
And no voice but was praising this Roland of mine,
As I pour'd down his throat our last measure of wine,
Which (the burgesses voted by common consent)
Was no more than his due who brought good news from Ghent.

ROBERT BROWNING.

THE LAMENTATION FOR CELIN.

AT the gate of old Granada, when all its bolts are barr'd,
At twilight, at the Vega-gate, there is a trampling heard;
There is a trampling heard, as of horses treading slow,
And a weeping voice of women, and a heavy sound of woe.
What tower is fallen? what star is set? what chief come these bewailing?
"A tower is fallen! a star is set!—Alas! alas for Celin!"

Three times they knock, three times they cry,—and wide the doors they throw;
Dejectedly they enter, and mournfully they go;
In gloomy lines they mustering stand beneath the hollow porch,
Each horseman grasping in his hand a black and flaming torch;
Wet is each eye as they go by, and all around is wailing,—
For all have heard the misery,—"Alas! alas for Celin!"

Him yesterday a Moor did slay, of Bencerraje's blood,—
'Twas at the solemn jousting,—around the nobles stood;
The nobles of the land were by, and ladies bright and fair
Look'd from their latticed windows, the haughty sight to share:
But now the nobles all lament,—the ladies are bewailing,—
For he was Granada's darling knight,—"Alas! alas for Celin!"

Before him ride his vassals, in order two by two,
With ashes on their turbans spread, most pitiful to view;
Behind him his four sisters, each wrapp'd in sable veil,
Between the tambour's dismal strokes take up their doleful tale;
When stops the muffled drum, ye hear their brotherless bewailing,
And all the people, far and near, cry,—"Alas! alas for Celin!"

Oh, lovely lies he on the bier, above the
    purple pall,
The flower of all Granada's youth, the
    loveliest of them all;
His dark, dark eyes are closèd, his rosy lip
    is pale,
The crust of blood lies black and dim upon
    his burnish'd mail;
And evermore the hoarse tambour breaks
    in upon their wailing,—
Its sound is like no earthly sound,—"Alas!
    alas for Celin!"

The Moorish maid at the lattice stands,—
    the Moor stands at his door;
One maid is wringing of her hands, and
    one is weeping sore;
Down to the dust men bow their heads,
    and ashes black they strew
Upon their broider'd garments, of crimson, green, and blue;
Before each gate the bier stands still,—
    then bursts the loud bewailing,
From door and lattice, high and low,—
    "Alas! alas for Celin!"

An old, old woman cometh forth when she
    hears the people cry,—
Her hair is white as silver, like horn her
    glazèd eye;
'Twas she that nursed him at her breast,—
    that nursed him long ago:
She knows not whom they all lament, but
    soon she well shall know!
With one deep shriek, she through doth
    break, when her ears receive their
    wailing,—
"Let me kiss my Celin, ere I die!—Alas!
    alas for Celin!"
(From the Spanish.)
John Gibson Lockhart.

THE WANDERING JEW.

When as in faire Jerusalem
    Our Saviour Christ did live,
And for the sins of all the worlde
    His owne deare life did give;
The wicked Jewes with scoffes and scornes
    Did daily him molest,
That never till he left his life,
    Our Saviour could not rest.

When they had crown'd his head with
    thornes,
    And scourged him to disgrace,
In scornfull sort they led him forthe
    Unto his dying place,
Where thousand thousands in the streete
    Beheld him passe along,
Yet not one gentle heart was there,
    That pity'd this his wrong.

Both old and young revilèd him,
    As in the streete he wente,
And naught he found but churlish tauntes,
    By every ones consente:
His owne deare crosse he bore himselfe,
    A burthen far too great,
Which made him in the streete to fainte,
    With blood and water sweat.

Being weary thus, he sought for rest,
    To ease his burthen'd soule,
Upon a stone; the which a wretch
    Did churlishly controule;
And sayd, Awaye, thou King of Jewes,
    Thou shalt not rest thee here;
Pass on; thy execution-place
    Thou seest nowe draweth neare.

And thereupon he thrust him thence;
    At which our Saviour sayd,
I sure will rest, but thou shalt walke,
    And have no journey stay'd.
With that this cursèd shoemaker,
    For offering Christ this wrong,
Left wife and children, house and all,
    And went from thence along.

Where after he had seene the bloude
    Of Jesus Christ thus shed,
And to the crosse his bodye nail'd,
    Awaye with speed he fled,
Without returning backe againe
    Unto his dwelling-place,
And wandred up and downe the worlde,
    A runnagate most base.

No resting could he finde at all,
    No ease, nor hearts content;
No house, nor home, nor biding-place:
    But wandring forth he went
From towne to towne in foreigne landes,
    With grievèd conscience still,
Repenting for the heinous guilt
    Of his fore-passèd ill.

Thus after some fewe ages past
  In wandring up and downe;
He much again desired to see
  Jerusalems renowne,
But finding it all quite destroyd,
  He wandred thence with woe,
Our Saviours wordes, which he had spoke,
  To verifie and showe.

"I'll rest, sayd hee, but thou shalt walke."
  So doth this wandring Jew
From place to place, but cannot rest
  For seeing countries newe;
Declaring still the power of Him,
  Whereas he comes or goes,
And of all things done in the east,
  Since Christ his death he showes.

The world he hath still compast round
  And seene those nations strange,
That hearing of the name of Christ,
  Their idol gods doe change:
To whom he hath told wondrous thinges
  Of time forepast, and gone,
And to the princes of the worlde
  Declares his cause of moane:

Desiring still to be dissolved,
  And yeild his mortal breath;
But if the Lord hath thus decreed,
  He shall not yet see death.
For neither lookes he old nor young,
  But as he did those times,
When Christ did suffer on the crosse
  For mortall sinners crimes.

He hath past through many a foreigne place,
  Arabia, Egypt, Africa,
Grecia, Syria, and great Thrace,
  And throughout all Hungaria,
Where Paul and Peter preachèd Christ,
  Those blest apostles deare;
There he hath told our Saviours wordes,
  In countries far and neare.

And lately in Bohemia,
  With many a German towne;
And now in Flanders, as 'tis thought,
  He wandreth up and downe:
Where learnèd men with him conferre
  Of those his lingering dayes,
And wonder much to heare him tell
  His journeyes, and his wayes.

If people give this Jew an almes,
  The most that he will take
Is not above a groat a time:
  Which he, for Jesus' sake,
Will kindlye give unto the poore,
  And thereof make no spare,
Affirming still that Jesus Christ
  Of him hath dailye care.

He ne'er was seene to laugh nor smile,
  But weepe and make great moane;
Lamenting still his miseries,
  And dayes forepast and gone:
If he heare any one blaspheme,
  Or take God's name in vaine,
He telles them that they crucifie
  Their Saviour Christe againe.

If you had seene his death, saith he,
  As these mine eyes have done,
Ten thousand thousand times would yee
  His torments think upon:
And suffer for his sake all paine
  Of torments, and all woes.
These are his wordes and eke his life
  Whereas he comes or goes.
AUTHOR UNKNOWN.

THE DREAM OF EUGENE ARAM.

'TWAS in the prime of summer-time,
  An evening calm and cool,
And four-and-twenty happy boys
  Came bounding out of school:
There were some that ran and some that leapt,
  Like troutlets in a pool.

Away they sped with gamesome minds,
  And souls untouch'd by sin;
To a level mead they came, and there
  They drave the wickets in:
Pleasantly shone the setting sun
  Over the town of Lynn.

Like sportive deer they coursed about,
  And shouted as they ran,—
Turning to mirth all things of earth
  As only boyhood can;
But the Usher sat remote from all,
  A melancholy man!

His hat was off, his vest apart,
  To catch Heaven's blessed breeze;
For a burning thought was in his brow,
  And his bosom ill at ease:
So he lean'd his head on his hands, and read
  The book between his knees.

Leaf after leaf he turn'd it o'er,
  Nor ever glanced aside,
For the peace of his soul he read that book
  In the golden eventide:
Much study had made him very lean,
  And pale, and leaden-eyed.

At last he shut the ponderous tome,
  With a fast and fervent grasp
He strain'd the dusky covers close,
  And fixed the brazen hasp:
"O God! could I so close my mind,
  And clasp it with a clasp!"

Then leaping on his feet upright,
  Some moody turns he took,—
Now up the mead, then down the mead,
  And past a shady nook,—
And, lo! he saw a little boy
  That pored upon a book.

"My gentle lad, what is't you read—
  Romance or fairy fable?
Or is it some historic page,
  Of kings and crowns unstable?"
The young boy gave an upward glance,—
  "It is 'The Death of Abel.'"

The Usher took six hasty strides,
  As smit with sudden pain,—
Six hasty strides beyond the place,
  Then slowly back again,
And down he sat beside the lad,
  And talk'd with him of Cain;

And, long since then, of bloody men,
  Whose deeds tradition saves,
Of lonely folk cut off unseen,
  And hid in sudden graves,
Of horrid stabs, in groves forlorn,
  And murders done in caves;

And how the sprites of injured men
  Shriek upward from the sod,—
Ay, how the ghostly hand will point
  To show the burial clod,
And unknown facts of guilty acts
  Are seen in dreams from God!

He told how murderers walk the earth,
  Beneath the curse of Cain,
With crimson clouds before their eyes,
  And flames about their brain:
For blood has left upon their souls
  Its everlasting stain.

"And well," quoth he, "I know for truth,
  Their pangs must be extreme;
Woe, woe, unutterable woe,
  Who spill life's sacred stream!
For why? Methought, last night I wrought
  A murder in a dream.

"One that had never done me wrong,
  A feeble man and old;
I led him to a lonely field,
  The moon shone clear and cold:
Now here, said I, this man shall die,
  And I will have his gold!

"Two sudden blows with ragged stick,
  And one with a heavy stone,
One hurried gash with a hasty knife,—
  And then the deed was done:
There was nothing lying at my foot
  But lifeless flesh and bone!

"Nothing but lifeless flesh and bone,
  That could not do me ill,
And yet I fear'd him all the more,
  For lying there so still;
There was a manhood in his look
  That murder could not kill!

"And lo! the universal air
  Seem'd lit with ghastly flame;
Ten thousand thousand dreadful eyes
  Were looking down in blame:
I took the dead man by his hand,
  And call'd upon his name!

"O God! it made me quake to see
  Such sense within the slain;
But when I touch'd the lifeless clay,
  The blood gush'd out amain!
For every clot, a burning spot
  Was scorching in my brain!

"My head was like an ardent coal,
  My heart as solid ice;
My wretched, wretched soul, I knew,
  Was at the Devil's price:
A dozen times I groan'd; the dead
  Had never groan'd but twice!

" And now, from forth the frowning sky,
  From the heavens' topmost height,
I heard a voice—the awful voice
  Of the blood-avenging Sprite:—
' Thou guilty man! take up thy dead
  And hide it from my sight!'

" I took the dreary body up,
  And cast it in a stream,—
A sluggish water, black as ink,
  The depth was so extreme:—
My gentle Boy, remember this
  Is nothing but a dream!

" Down went the corse with a hollow plunge,
  And vanish'd in the pool;
Anon I cleansed my bloody hands,
  And wash'd my forehead cool,
And sat among the urchins young,
  That evening in the school.

" Oh, Heaven! to think of their white souls,
  And mine so black and grim!
I could not share in childish prayer,
  Nor join in Evening Hymn:
Like a Devil of the Pit I seem'd,
  'Mid holy Cherubim!

" And peace went with them, one and all,
  And each calm pillow spread;
But Guilt was my grim Chamberlain
  That lighted me to bed;
And drew my midnight curtains round,
  With fingers bloody red!

" All night I lay in agony,
  In anguish dark and deep;
My fever'd eyes I dared not close,
  But stared aghast at Sleep:
For Sin had render'd unto her
  The keys of Hell to keep!

" All night I lay in agony,
  From weary chime to chime,
With one besetting, horrid hint,
  That rack'd me all the time;
A mighty yearning, like the first
  Fierce impulse unto crime!

" One stern, tyrannic thought, that made
  All other thoughts its slave;
Stronger and stronger every pulse
  Did that temptation crave,—
Still urging me to go and see
  The dead man in his grave!

" Heavily I rose up, as soon
  As light was in the sky,
And sought the black accursed pool
  With a wild misgiving eye;
And I saw the Dead in the river bed,
  For the faithless stream was dry.

" Merrily rose the lark, and shook
  The dewdrop from its wing;
But I never mark'd its morning flight,
  I never heard it sing:
For I was stooping once again
  Under the horrid thing.

" With breathless speed, like a soul in chase,
  I took him up and ran;—
There was no time to dig a grave
  Before the day began:
In a lonesome wood, with heaps of leaves,
  I hid the murder'd man!

" And all that day I read in school,
  But my thought was other where;
As soon as the midday task was done,
  In secret I was there:
And a mighty wind had swept the leaves,
  And still the corse was bare!

" Then down I cast me on my face,
  And first began to weep,
For I knew my secret then was one
  That earth refused to keep:
Or land or sea, though he should be
  Ten thousand fathoms deep.

" So wills the fierce avenging Sprite,
  Till blood for blood atones!
Ay, though he's buried in a cave,
  And trodden down with stones,
And years have rotted off his flesh,—
  The world shall see his bones!

" O God! that horrid, horrid dream
  Besets me now awake!

Again—again, with dizzy brain,
  The human life I take;
And my right red hand grows raging hot,
  Like Cranmer's at the stake.

"And still no peace for the restless clay,
  Will wave or mould allow;
The horrid thing pursues my soul,—
  It stands before me now!"
The fearful boy look'd up and saw
  Huge drops upon his brow.

That very night, while gentle sleep
  The urchin eyelids kiss'd,
Two stern-faced men set out from Lynn,
  Through the cold and heavy mist;
And Eugene Aram walk'd between,
  With gyves upon his wrist.
                THOMAS HOOD.

THE INCHCAPE ROCK.

No stir in the air, no stir in the sea,
The ship was still as she could be;
Her sails from heaven received no motion,
Her keel was steady in the ocean.

Without either sign or sound of their shock
The waves flow'd over the Inchcape Rock;
So little they rose, so little they fell,
They did not move the Inchcape Bell.

The Abbot of Aberbrothok
Had placed that bell on the Inchcape Rock;
On a buoy in the storm it floated and swung,
And over the waves its warning rung.

When the rock was hid by the surges' swell,
The mariners heard the warning bell,
And then they knew the perilous rock,
And bless'd the Abbot of Aberbrothok.

The sun in heaven was shining gay,
All things were joyful on that day;
The sea-birds scream'd as they wheel'd round,
And there was joyaunce in their sound.

The buoy of the Inchcape Bell was seen
A darker speck on the ocean green;
Sir Ralph the Rover walk'd his deck,
And he fix'd his eye on the darker speck.

He felt the cheering power of spring,
It made him whistle, it made him sing,
His heart was mirthful to excess,
But the Rover's mirth was wickedness.

His eye was on the Inchcape float;
Quoth he, "My men, put out the boat,
And row me to the Inchcape Rock,
And I'll plague the Abbot of Aberbrothok."

The boat is lower'd, the boatmen row,
And to the Inchcape Rock they go;
Sir Ralph bent over from the boat,
And he cut the bell from the Inchcape float.

Down sank the bell with a gurgling sound,
The bubbles rose and burst around;
Quoth Sir Ralph, "The next who comes to the rock
Won't bless the Abbot of Aberbrothok."

Sir Ralph the Rover sail'd away,
He scour'd the seas for many a day,
And now, grown rich with plunder'd store,
He steers his course for Scotland's shore.

So thick a haze o'erspreads the sky,
They cannot see the sun on high;
The wind hath blown a gale all day,
At evening it hath died away.

On the deck the Rover takes his stand;
So dark it is they see no land.
Quoth Sir Ralph, "It will be lighter soon,
For there is the dawn of the rising moon."

"Canst hear," said one, "the breakers roar?
For methinks we should be near the shore."
"Now, where we are I cannot tell,
But I wish I could hear the Inchcape Bell."

They hear no sound, the swell is strong,
Though the wind hath fallen, they drift along,
Till the vessel strikes with a shivering shock,—
"O Death! it is the Inchcape Rock."

Sir Ralph the Rover tore his hair,
He cursed himself in his despair;
The waves rush in on every side,
The ship is sinking beneath the tide.

But, even in his dying fear,
One dreadful sound could the Rover hear,
A sound as if, with the Inchcape Bell,
The Devil below was ringing his knell.
ROBERT SOUTHEY.

CUMNOR HALL.

THE dews of summer night did fall,
 The moon, sweet regent of the sky,
Silver'd the walls of Cumnor Hall
 And many an oak that grew thereby.

Now naught was heard beneath the skies,
 The sounds of busy life were still,
Save an unhappy lady's sighs,
 That issued from that lonely pile.

"Leicester," she cried, "is this thy love
 That thou so oft has sworn to me,
To leave me in this lonely grove,
 Immured in shameful privity?

"No more thou com'st with lover's speed,
 Thy once-belovèd bride to see,
But be she alive, or be she dead,
 I fear, stern Earl, 's the same to thee.

"Not so the usage I received
 When happy in my father's hall;
No faithless husband then me grieved,
 No chilling fears did me appall.

"I rose up with the cheerful morn,
 No lark more blithe, no flower more gay,
And like the bird that haunts the thorn,
 So merrily sung the livelong day.

"If that my beauty is but small,
 Among court ladies all despised,
Why didst thou rend it from that hall,
 Where, scornful Earl, it well was prized?

"And when you first to me made suit,
 How fair I was you oft would say!
And, proud of conquest, pluck'd the fruit,
 Then left the blossom to decay.

"Yes! now neglected and despised,
 The rose is pále, the lily's dead,
But he that once their charms so prized
 Is sure the cause those charms are fled.

"For know, when sickening grief doth prey,
 And tender love's repaid with scorn,
The sweetest beauty will decay,—
 What floweret can endure the storm?

"At court, I'm told, is beauty's throne,
 Where every lady's passing rare,
That Eastern flowers, that shame the sun,
 Are not so glowing, not so fair.

"Then, Earl, why didst thou leave the beds
 Where roses and where lilies vie,
To seek a primrose, whose pale shades
 Must sicken when those gauds are by?

"'Mong rural beauties I was one,
 Among the fields wild flowers are fair;
Some country swain might me have won,
 And thought my beauty passing rare.

"But, Leicester (or I much am wrong),
 Or 'tis not beauty lures thy vows;
Rather ambition's gilded crown
 Makes thee forget thy humble spouse.

"Then, Leicester, why, again I plead
 (The injured surely may repine),
Why didst thou wed a country maid,
 When some fair princess might be thine?

"Why didst thou praise my humble charms,
 And, oh! then leave them to decay?
Why didst thou win me to thy arms,
 Then leave to mourn the livelong day?

"The village maidens of the plain
 Salute me lowly as they go;
Envious they mark my silken train,
 Nor think a countess can have woe.

"The simple nymphs! they little know
 How far more happy's their estate;
To smile for joy, than sigh for woe—
 To be content, than to be great.

"How far less blest am I than them?
 Daily to pine and waste with care!
Like the poor plant, that, from its stem
 Divided, feels the chilling air.

"Nor, cruel Earl! can I enjoy
 The humble charms of solitude;
Your minions proud my peace destroy,
 By sullen frowns or pratings rude.

"Last night, as sad I chanced to stray,
  The village death-bell smote my ear;
They wink'd aside, and seem'd to say,
  'Countess, prepare, thy end is near!'

"And now, while happy peasants sleep,
  Here I sit lonely and forlorn;
No one to soothe me as I weep,
  Save Philomel on yonder thorn.

"My spirits flag—my hopes decay—
  Still that dread death-bell smites my ear;
And many a boding seems to say,
  'Countess, prepare, thy end is near!'"

Thus sore and sad that lady grieved,
  In Cumnor Hall, so lone and drear;
And many a heartfelt sigh she heaved,
  And let fall many a bitter tear.

And ere the dawn of day appear'd,
  In Cumnor Hall, so lone and drear,
Full many a piercing scream was heard,
  And many a cry of mortal fear.

The death-bell thrice was heard to ring,
  An aërial voice was heard to call,
And thrice the raven flapp'd its wing
  Around the towers of Cumnor Hall.

The mastiff howl'd at village door,
  The oaks were shatter'd on the green;
Woe was the hour—for never more
  That hapless Countess e'er was seen.

And in that manor now no more
  Is cheerful feast and sprightly ball;
For ever since that dreary hour
  Have spirits haunted Cumnor Hall.

The village maids, with fearful glance,
  Avoid the ancient moss-grown wall;
Nor ever lead the merry dance,
  Among the groves of Cumnor Hall.

Full many a traveller oft hath sigh'd,
  And pensive wept the Countess' fall,
As wandering onward they've espied
  The haunted towers of Cumnor Hall.
                    WILLIAM JULIUS MICKLE.

EDWARD, EDWARD.

QUHY dois zour brand sae drop wi' bluid,
      Edward, Edward?
Quhy dois zour brand sae drop wi' bluid?
  And quhy sae sad gang zee, O?
O, I hae kill'd my hauke sae guid,
      Mither, mither:
O, I hae kill'd my hauke sae guid:
  And I had nae mair bot hee, O.

Zour haukis bluid was nevir sae reid,
      Edward, Edward.
Zour haukis bluid was nevir sae reid,
  My deir son I tell thee, O.
O, I hae kill'd my reid-roan steid,
      Mither, mither:
O, I hae kill'd my reid-roan steid,
  That erst was sae fair and free, O.

Zour steid was auld, and ze hae gat mair,
      Edward, Edward:
Zour steid was auld, and ze hae gat mair,
  Sum other dule ze drie, O.
O, I hae kill'd my fadir deir,
      Mither, mither:
O, I hae kill'd my fadir deir,
  Alas! and wae is mee, O!

And quhatten penance wul ze drie for that,
      Edward, Edward?
And quhatten penance will ze drie for that?
  My deir son, now tell me, O.
Ile set my feit in zonder boat,
      Mither, mither:
Ile set my feit in zonder boat,
  And Ile fare ovir the sea, O.

And quhat wul ze doe wi' zour towirs and zour ha',
      Edward, Edward?
And quhat wul ze doe wi' zour towirs and zour ha',
  That ware sae fair to see, O?
Ile let thame stand til they doun fa',
      Mither, mither:
Ile let thame stand til they doun fa',
  For here nevir mair maun I bee, O.

And quhat wul ze leive to zour bairns and
  zour wife,
            Edward, Edward?
And quhat wul ze leive to zour bairns and
  zour wife,
    Quhan ze gang ovir the sea, O?
The warldis room, let thame beg throw
  life,
            Mither, mither:
The warldis room, let thame beg throw
  life,
    For thame nevir mair wul I see, O.

And quhat wul ze leive to zour ain mither
  deir,
            Edward, Edward?
And quhat wul ze leive to zour ain mither
  deir?
    My deir son, now tell me, O.
The curse of hell frae me sall ze beir,
            Mither, mither:
The curse of hell frae me sall ze beir,
    Sic counseils ze gave to me, O.
                    AUTHOR UNKNOWN.

LORD ULLIN'S DAUGHTER.

A CHIEFTAIN, to the Highlands bound,
  Cries, "Boatman, do not tarry!
And I'll give thee a silver pound
  To row us o'er the ferry."

"Now, who be ye would cross Loch Gyle,
  This dark and stormy water?"
"Oh! I'm the chief of Ulva's isle,
  And this—Lord Ullin's daughter.

"And fast before her father's men,
  Three days we've fled together,
For should he find us in the glen,
  My blood would stain the heather.

"His horsemen hard behind us ride;
  Should they our steps discover,
Then who will cheer my bonny bride
  When they have slain her lover?"

Out spake the hardy Highland wight,
  "I'll go, my chief—I'm ready:
It is not for your silver bright,
  But for your winsome lady:

"And, by my word! the bonny bird
  In danger shall not tarry;
So, though the waves are raging white,
  I'll row you o'er the ferry."

By this, the storm grew loud apace,
  The water-wraith was shrieking;
And, in the scowl of heaven, each face
  Grew dark as they were speaking.

But still, as wilder blew the wind,
  And as the night grew drearer,
Adown the glen rode armèd men,
  Their trampling sounded nearer.

"Oh haste thee, haste!" the lady cries,
  "Though tempests round us gather,
I'll meet the raging of the skies,
  But not an angry father."

The boat has left a stormy land,
  A stormy sea before her—
When, oh, too strong for human hand,
  The tempest gather'd o'er her.

And still they row'd, amidst the roar
  Of waters fast prevailing:
Lord Ullin reach'd that fatal shore,
  His wrath was changed to wailing.

For, sore dismay'd, through storm and
  shade,
  His child he did discover;
One lovely arm she stretch'd for aid,
  And one was round her lover.

"Come back! come back!" he cried in
  grief,
"Across this stormy water:
And I'll forgive your Highland chief,
  My daughter! O my daughter!"

'Twas vain: the loud waves lash'd the
  shore,
  Return, or aid preventing:
The waters wild went o'er his child,
  And he was left lamenting.
                    THOMAS CAMPBELL.

THE DOWIE DENS OF YARROW.

LATE at e'en, drinking the wine,
  And ere they paid the lawing,
They set a combat them between,
  To fight it in the dawing.

"Oh stay at hame, my noble lord!
  Oh stay at hame, my marrow!
My cruel brother will you betray
  On the dowie houms of Yarrow."

"Oh fare ye weel, my ladye gaye!
  Oh fare ye weel, my Sarah!
For I maun gae, though I ne'er return
  Frae the dowie banks o' Yarrow."

She kiss'd his cheek, she kaim'd his hair,
  As oft she had done before, oh;
She belted him with his noble brand,
  And he's away to Yarrow.

As he gaed up the Tennies bank,
  I wot he gaed wi' sorrow,
Till, down in a den, he spied nine arm'd men,
  On the dowie houms of Yarrow.

"Oh come ye here to part your land,
  The bonnie forest thorough?
Or come ye here to wield your brand,—
  On the dowie houms of Yarrow?"—

"I come not here to part my land,
  And neither to beg nor borrow;
I come to wield my noble brand,
  On the bonnie banks of Yarrow.

"If I see all, ye're nine to ane;
  And that's an unequal marrow:
Yet will I fight, while lasts my brand,
  On the bonnie banks of Yarrow."

Four has he hurt, and five has slain,
  On the bonnie braes of Yarrow,
Till that stubborn knight came him behind,
  And ran his body thorough.

"Gae hame, gae hame, good brother John,
  And tell your sister Sarah,
To come and lift her leafu' lord;
  He's sleepin' sound on Yarrow."—

"Yestreen I dream'd a dolefu' dream:
  I fear there will be sorrow!
I dream'd I pu'd the heather green,
  Wi' my true love, on Yarrow.

"O gentle wind, that bloweth south,
  From where my love repaireth,
Convey a kiss from his dear mouth,
  And tell me how he fareth!

"But in the glen strive armèd men;
  They've wrought me dole and sorrow;
They've slain—the comeliest knight they've slain—
  He bleeding lies on Yarrow."

As she sped down yon high, high hill,
  She gaed wi' dole and sorrow,
And in the den spied ten slain men,
  On the dowie banks of Yarrow.

She kiss'd his cheeks, she kaim'd his hair,
  She search'd his wounds all thorough;
She kiss'd them, till her lips grew red,
  On the dowie houms of Yarrow.

"Now haud your tongue, my daughter dear!
  For a' this breeds but sorrow;
I'll wed ye to a better lord
  Than him ye lost on Yarrow."—

"Oh haud your tongue, my father dear!
  Ye 'mind me but of sorrow;
A fairer rose did never bloom
  Than now lies cropp'd on Yarrow."

AUTHOR UNKNOWN.

THE BRAES OF YARROW.

BUSK ye, busk ye, my bonny bonny bride,
  Busk ye, busk ye, my winsome marrow,
Busk ye, busk ye, my bonny bonny bride,
  And think nae mair on the Braes of Yarrow.

Where gat ye that bonny bonny bride?
  Where gat ye that winsome marrow?
I gat her where I dare na weil be seen,
  Pu'ing the birks on the Braes of Yarrow.

Weep not, weep not, my bonny bonny bride,
  Weep not, weep not, my winsome marrow;
Nor let thy heart lament to leive,
  Pu'ing the birks on the Braes of Yarrow.

Why does she weep, thy bonny bonny bride?
  Why does she weep, thy winsome marrow?
And why dare ye nae mair weil be seen
  Pu'ing the birks on the Braes of Yarrow?

Lang maun she weep, lang maun she,
　　maun she weep,
　Lang maun she weep with dule and sor-
　　row;
And lang maun I nae mair weil be seen
　Pu'ing the birks on the Braes of Yarrow.

For she has tint her luver, luver dear,
　Her luver dear, the cause of sorrow;
And I hae slain the comeliest swain,
　That eir pu'd birks on the Braes of Yar-
　　row.

Why rins thy stream, O Yarrow, Yarrow,
　　reid?
　Why on thy braes heard the voice of
　　sorrow?
And why yon melancholious weids
　Hung on the bonny birks of Yarrow?

What's yonder floats on the rueful rueful
　　flude?
　What's yonder floats? Oh dule and sor-
　　row!
Oh 'tis he the comely swain I slew
　Upon the duleful Braes of Yarrow.

Wash, oh wash his wounds, his wounds in
　　tears,
　His wounds in tears with dule and sor-
　　row;
And wrap his limbs in mourning weids,
　And lay him on the Braes of Yarrow.

Then build, then build, ye sisters, sisters
　　sad,
　Ye sisters sad, his tomb with sorrow;
And weep around in waeful wise
　His hapless fate on the Braes of Yar-
　　row.

Curse ye, curse ye, his useless, useless
　　shield,
　My arm that wrought the deed of sor-
　　row;
The fatal spear that pierced his breast,
　His comely breast, on the Braes of Yar-
　　row.

Did I not warn thee, not to, not to luve?
　And warn from fight? but to my sor-
　　row
Too rashly bauld a stronger arm
　Thou mett'st, and fell'st on the Braes of
　　Yarrow.

Sweet smells the birk, green grows, green
　　grows the grass,
　Yellow on Yarrow's bank the gowan,
Fair hangs the apple frae the rock,
　Sweet the wave of Yarrow flowan.

Flows Yarrow sweet? as sweet, as sweet
　　flows Tweed,
　As green its grass, its gowan as yellow,
As sweet smells on its braes the birk,
　The apple frae its rocks as mellow.

Fair was thy luve, fair fair indeed thy
　　luve,
　In flow'ry bands thou didst him fetter;
Tho' he was fair, and weil beluv'd again
　Than me he never luv'd thee better.

Busk ye, then busk, my bonny bonny
　　bride,
　Busk ye, busk ye, my winsome marrow,
Busk ye, and luve me on the banks of
　　Tweed,
　And think nae mair on the Braes of
　　Yarrow.

How can I busk a bonny bonny bride?
　How can I busk a winsome marrow?
How luve him upon the banks of Tweed,
　That slew my luve on the Braes of Yar-
　　row?

O Yarrow fields, may never never rain
　Nor dew thy tender blossoms cover,
For there was basely slain my luve,
　My luve, as he had not been a lover.

The boy put on his robes, his robes of
　　green,
　His purple vest, 'twas my awn sewing:
Ah, wretched me! I little, little kenn'd
　He was in these to meet his ruin.

The boy took out his milk-white, milk-
　　white steed,
　Unheedful of my dule and sorrow:
But ere the toofall of the night
　He lay a corps on the Braes of Yarrow.

Much I rejoyced that waeful waeful day;
　I sang, my voice the woods returning:
But lang e'er night the spear was flown,
　That slew my luve, and left me mourn-
　　ing.

What can my barbarous barbarous father do,
  But with his cruel rage pursue me?
My luver's blood is on thy spear,
  How canst thou, barbarous man, then wooe me?

My happy sisters may be, may be proud
  With cruel and ungentle scoffin',
May bid me seek on Yarrow's Braes
  My luver nailèd in his coffin.

My brother Douglas may upbraid, upbraid,
  And strive with threat'ning words to muve me:
My luver's blood is on thy spear,
  How canst thou ever bid me luve thee?

Yes, yes, prepare the bed, the bed of luve,
  With bridal sheets my body cover,
Unbar, ye bridal maids, the door,
  Let in the expected husband-lover.

But who the expected husband husband is?
  His hands, methinks, are. bathed in slaughter:
Ah me! what ghastly spectre's yon
  Comes in his pale shroud, bleeding after.

Pale as he is, here lay him, lay him down,
  Oh lay his cold head on my pillow;
Take aff, take aff these bridal weids,
  And crown my careful head with willow.

Pale tho' thou art, yet best, yet best beluv'd,
  Oh could my warmth to life restore thee!
Yet lye all night between my breists,
  No youth lay ever there before thee.

Pale, pale indeed, O luvely luvely youth!
  Forgive, forgive so foul a slaughter:
And lye all night between my breists;
  No youth shall ever lye there after.

Return, return, O mournful mournful bride,
  Return, and dry thy useless sorrow:
Thy luver heeds none of thy sighs,
  He lyes a corps in the Braes of Yarrow.

    WILLIAM HAMILTON OF BANGOUR.

THE BRAES OF YARROW.

THY braes were bonny, Yarrow stream,
  When first on them I met my lover;
Thy braes how dreary, Yarrow stream,
  When now thy waves his body cover!
For ever now, O Yarrow stream!
  Thou art to me a stream of sorrow;
For never on thy banks shall I
  Behold my love, the flower of Yarrow.

He promised me a milk-white steed
  To bear me to his father's bowers;
He promised me a little page
  To squire me to his father's towers;
He promised me a wedding-ring,—
  The wedding-day was fix'd to-morrow;—
Now he is wedded to his grave,
  Alas, his watery grave, in Yarrow!

Sweet were his words when last we met;
  My passion I as freely told him;
Clasp'd in his arms, I little thought
  That I should never more behold him!
Scarce was he gone, I saw his ghost;
  It vanish'd with a shriek of sorrow;
Thrice did the water-wraith ascend,
  And gave a doleful groan thro' Yarrow.

His mother from the window look'd
  With all the longing of a mother;
His little sister weeping walk'd
  The greenwood path to meet her brother;
They sought him east, they sought him west,
  They sought him all the forest thorough;
They only saw the cloud of night,
  They only heard the roar of Yarrow.

No longer from thy window look—
  Thou hast no son, thou tender mother!
No longer walk, thou lovely maid;
  Alas, thou hast no more a brother!
No longer seek him east or west,
  And search no more the forest thorough;
For, wandering in the night so dark,
  He fell a lifeless corpse in Yarrow.

The tear shall never leave my cheek,
  No other youth shall be my marrow—
I'll seek thy body in the stream,
  And then with thee I'll sleep in Yarrow.

—The tear did never leave her cheek,
  No other youth became her marrow;
She found his body in the stream,
  And now with him she sleeps in Yarrow.
                           JOHN LOGAN.

THE CHILD OF ELLE.

ON yonder hill a castle standes
  With walles and towres bedight,
And yonder lives the Child of Elle,
  A younge and comely knighte.

The child of Elle to his garden went,
  And stood at his garden pale,
Whan, lo! he beheld fair Emmelines page
  Come trippinge downe the dale.

The Child of Elle he hyed him thence,
  Y-wis he stoode not stille,
And soone he mette fair Emmelines page
  Come climbing up the hille.

Nowe Christe thee save, thou little foot-page,
  Now Christe thee save and see!
Oh tell me how does thy ladye gaye,
  And what may thy tydinges bee?

My lady she is all woe-begone,
  And the teares they falle from her eyne;
And aye she laments the deadlye feude
  Betweene her house and thine.

And here shee sends thee a silken scarfe
  Bedewde with many a teare,
And biddes thee sometimes thinke on her,
  Who lovèd thee so deare.

And here she sends thee a ring of golde,
  The last boone thou mayst have,
And biddes thee weare it for her sake,
  When she is layde in grave.

For, ah! her gentle heart is broke,
  And in grave soon must shee bee,
Sith her father hath chose her a new new love,
  And forbidde her to think of thee.

Her father hath brought her a carlish knight,
  Sir John of the north countràye,
And within three dayes shee must him wedde,
  Or he vowes he will her slaye.

Nowe hye thee backe, thou little foot-page,
  And greet thy ladye from mee,
And tell her that I her owne true love
  Will dye, or sette her free.

Nowe hye thee backe, thou little foot-page,
  And let thy fair ladye know
This night will I bee at her bowre-windòwe,
  Betide me weale or woe.

The boye he tripped, the boye he ranne,
  He neither stint ne stayd
Untill he came to fair Emmelines bowre,
  Whan kneeling downe he sayd,

O ladye, I've been with thy own true love,
  And he greets thee well by mee;
This night will he be at thy bowre-windòwe,
  And dye or sette thee free.

Nowe daye was gone and night was come,
  And all were fast asleepe,
All save the ladye Emmeline,
  Who sate in her bowre to weepe:

And soone she heard her true loves voice
  Lowe whispering at the walle,
Awake, awake, my dear ladyè,
  'Tis I thy true love call.

Awake, awake, my ladye deare,
  Come, mount this faire palfràye;
This ladder of ropes will lette thee downe,
  Ile carrye thee hence awaye.

Nowe nay, nowe nay, thou gentle knight,
  Nowe nay, this may not bee;
For aye shold I tint my maiden fame,
  If alone I should wend with thee.

O ladye, thou with a knighte so true
  Mayst safely wend alone,
To my ladye mother I will thee bringe,
  Where marriage shall make us one.

"My father he is a baron bolde,
  Of lynage proude and hye;
And what would he saye if his daughtèr
  Awaye with a knight should fly?

Ah! well I wot, he never would rest,
  Nor his meate should doe him no goode
Until he had slayne thee, Child of Elle,
  And seene thy deare hearts bloode."

O ladye, wert thou in thy saddle sette,
  And a little space him fro,
I would not care for thy cruel fathèr,
  Nor the worst that he could doe.

O ladye, wert thou in thy saddle sette,
  And once without this walle,
I would not care for thy cruel fathèr,
  Nor the worst that might befalle.

Faire Emmeline sighed, fair Emmeline
    wept,
  And aye her heart was woe:
At length he seized her lilly-white hand,
  And downe the ladder he drewe:

And thrice he clasp'd her to his breste,
  And kist her tenderlìe:
The teares that fell from her fair eyes
  Ranne like the fountayne free.

Hee mounted himselfe on his steede so
    talle,
  And her on a fair palfràye,
And slung his bugle about his necke,
  And roundlye they rode awaye.

All this beheard her own damsèlle,
  In her bed whereas shee ley,
Quoth shee, My lord shall knowe of this,
  Soe I shall have golde and fee.

Awake, awake, thou baron bolde!
  Awake, my noble dame!
Your daughter is fledde with the Child of
    Elle
  To doe the deede of shame.

The baron he woke, the baron he rose,
  And call'd his merrye men all:
"And come thou forth, Sir John the
    knighte,
  Thy ladye is carried to thrall."

Faire Emmeline scant had ridden a mile,
  A mile forth of the towne,
When she was aware of her fathers men
  Come galloping over the downe:

And foremost came the carlish knight,
  Sir John of the north countràye:
"Nowe stop, nowe stop, thou false traitòure,
  Nor carry that ladye awaye.

For she is come of hye linèage,
  And was of a ladye borne,
And ill it beseemes thee a false churl's
    sonne
  To carrye her hence to scorne."

Nowe loud thou lyest, Sir John the knight,
  Nowe thou doest lye of mee;
A knight mee gott, and a ladye me bore,
  Soe never did none by thee.

But light nowe downe, my ladye faire,
  Light downe, and hold my steed,
While I and this discourteous knighte
  Doe trye this arduous deede.

But light nowe downe, my deare ladyè,
  Light downe, and hold my horse;
While I and this discourteous knight
  Doe trye our valour's force.

Fair Emmeline sigh'd, fair Emmeline
    wept,
  And aye her heart was woe,
While 'twixt her love and the carlish
    knight
  Past many a baleful blowe.

The Child of Elle hee fought soe well,
  As his weapon he waved amaine,
That soone he had slaine the carlish knight,
  And layd him upon the plaine.

And nowe the baron and all his men
  Full fast approachèd nye:
Ah! what may ladye Emmeline doe?
  'Twere nowe no boote to flye.

Her lover he put his horne to his mouth,
  And blew both loud and shrill,
And soone he saw his owne merry men
  Come ryding over the hill.

"Nowe hold thy hand, thou bold baròn,
  I pray thee hold thy hand,
Nor ruthless rend two gentle hearts
  Fast knit in true love's band.

Thy daughter I have dearly loved
  Full long and many a day;
But with such love as holy kirke
  Hath freelye said wee may.

Oh give consent shee may be mine,
  And bless a faithfull paire:
My lands and livings are not small,
  My house and lineage faire:

My mother she was an earl's daughtèr,
  And a noble knyght my sire—"
The baron he frown'd and turn'd away
  With mickle dole and ire.

Faire Emmeline sigh'd, faire Emmeline wept,
  And did all tremblinge stand:
At lengthe she sprang upon her knee,
  And held his lifted hand.

Pardon, my lorde and father deare,
  This fair yong knyght and mee:
Trust me, but for the carlish knyght,
  I never had fled from thee.

Oft have you call'd your Emmeline
  Your darling and your joye;
Oh let not then your harsh resolves
  Your Emmeline destroye.

The baron he stroakt his dark-brown cheeke,
  And turn'd his heade asyde
To whipe aweye the starting teare
  He proudly strave to hyde.

In deepe revolving thought he stoode,
  And mused a little space:
Then raised faire Emmeline from the grounde
  With many a fond embrace.

Here take her, Child of Elle, he sayd,
  And gave her lillye white hand;
Here take my deare and only child,
  And with her half my land:

Thy father once mine honour wrongde
  In dayes of youthful pride;
Do thou the injurye repayre
  In fondnesse for thy bride.

And as thou love her, and hold her deare,
  Heaven prosper thee and thine:
And nowe my blessing wend wi' thee,
  My lovelye Emmeline.
         AUTHOR UNKNOWN.

HART-LEAP WELL.

THE Knight had ridden down from Wensley Moor
  With the slow motion of a summer's cloud;
He turned aside toward a Vassal's door,
  And "Bring another horse!" he cried aloud.

"Another horse!"—That shout the Vassal heard,
  And saddled his best steed, a comely gray;
Sir Walter mounted him; he was the third
  Which he had mounted on that glorious day.

Joy sparkled in the prancing Courser's eyes;
  The horse and horseman are a happy pair;
But, though Sir Walter like a falcon flies,
  There is a doleful silence in the air.

A rout this morning left Sir Walter's Hall,
  That as they gallop'd made the echoes roar;
But horse and man are vanish'd, one and all;
  Such race, I think, was never seen before.

Sir Walter, restless as a veering wind,
  Calls to the few tired dogs that yet remain:
Blanch, Swift, and Music, noblest of their kind,
  Follow, and up the weary mountain strain.

The knight halloo'd, he cheer'd and chid them on
  With suppliant gestures and upbraiding stern;
But breath and eyesight fail; and, one by one,
  The dogs are stretch'd among the mountain-fern.

Where is the throng, the tumult of the race?
  The bugles that so joyfully were blown?
This chase it looks not like an earthly chase;
  Sir Walter and the Hart are left alone.

The poor Hart toils along the mountain-
        side;
    I will not stop to tell how far he fled,
Nor will I mention by what death he
        died:
    But now the Knight beholds him lying
        dead.

Dismounting, then, he lean'd against a
        thorn,
    He had no follower, Dog, nor Man, nor
        Boy:
He neither crack'd his whip, nor blew his
        horn,
    But gazed upon the spoil with silent joy.

Close to the thorn on which Sir Walter
        lean'd,
    Stood his dumb partner in this glorious
        feat;
Weak as a lamb the hour that it is yean'd,
    And white with foam as if with cleaving
        sleet.

Upon his side the Hart was lying stretch'd:
    His nostril touch'd a spring beneath a
        hill,
And with the last deep groan his breath
        had fetch'd
    The waters of the spring were trembling
        still.

And now, too happy for repose or rest
    (Never had living man such joyful lot!),
Sir Walter walk'd all round, north, south,
        and west,
    And gazed and gazed upon that darling
        spot.

And climbing up the hill (it was at least
    Nine roods of sheer ascent), Sir Walter
        found
Three several hoof-marks which the hunted
        beast
    Had left imprinted on the grassy ground.

Sir Walter wiped his face, and cried, "Till
        now
    Such sight was never seen by living
        eyes:
Three leaps have borne him from this lofty
        brow
    Down to the very fountain where he lies.

I'll build a Pleasure-house upon this spot,
    And a small Arbor, made for rural joy;
'Twill be the Traveller's shed, the Pilgrim's
        cot,
    A place of love for Damsels that are coy.

A cunning Artist will I have to frame
    A basin for that fountain in the dell!
And they who do make mention of the
        same
    From this day forth shall call it HART-
        LEAP WELL.

And, gallant Stag! to make thy praises
        known,
    Another monument shall here be raised;
Three several Pillars, each a rough-hewn
        Stone,
    And planted where thy hoofs the turf
        have grazed.

And, in the summer-time when days are
        long,
    I will come hither with my Paramour;
And with the Dancers and the Minstrel's
        song
    We will make merry in that pleasant
        Bower.

Till the foundations of the mountains fail
    My Mansion with its Arbor shall en-
        dure;—
The joy of them who till the fields of
        Swale,
    And them who dwell among the woods
        of Ure!"

Then home he went, and left the Hart,
        stone-dead,
    With breathless nostrils stretch'd above
        the spring.
—Soon did the Knight perform what he
        had said,
    And far and wide the fame thereof did
        ring.

Ere thrice the Moon into her port had
        steer'd,
    A Cup of stone received the living
        Well;
Three Pillars of rude stone Sir Walter
        rear'd,
    And built a house of Pleasure in the
        dell.

And near the fountain, flowers of stature tall
  With trailing plants and trees were intertwined,—
Which soon composed a little sylvan Hall,
  A leafy shelter from the sun and wind.

And thither, when the summer-days were long,
  Sir Walter led his wondering Paramour;
And with the Dancers and the Minstrel's song
  Made merriment within that pleasant Bower.

The Knight, Sir Walter, died in course of time,
  And his bones lie in his paternal vale.—
But there is matter for a second rhyme,
  And I to this would add another tale.

Part Second.

The moving accident is not my trade,
  To freeze the blood I have no ready arts;
'Tis my delight, alone in summer shade,
  To pipe a simple song for thinking hearts.

As I from Hawes to Richmond did repair,
  It chanced that I saw standing in a dell
Three Aspens at three corners of a square,
  And one, not four yards distant, near a Well.

What this imported I could ill divine,
  And, pulling now the rein my horse to stop,
I saw three Pillars standing in a line,
  The last Stone Pillar on a dark hill-top.

The trees were gray, with neither arms nor head,
  Half wasted the square Mound of tawny green,
So that you just might say, as then I said,
  "Here in old time the hand of man hath been."

I look'd upon the hill both far and near;
  More doleful place did never eye survey;
It seem'd as if the spring-time came not here,
  And Nature here were willing to decay.

I stood in various thoughts and fancies lost,
  When one, who was in Shepherd's garb attired,
Came up the Hollow; him did I accost,
  And what this place might be I then inquired.

The Shepherd stopp'd, and that same story told
  Which in my former rhyme I have rehearsed.
"A jolly place," said he, "in times of old,
  But something ails it now; the spot is curst.

You see these lifeless Stumps of aspen wood,—
  Some say that they are beeches, others elms,—
These were the Bower, and here a Mansion stood,
  The finest palace of a hundred realms.

The Arbor does its own condition tell;
  You see the Stones, the Fountain, and the Stream,
But as to the great Lodge, you might as well
  Hunt half a day for a forgotten dream.

There's neither dog nor heifer, horse nor sheep,
  Will wet his lips within that Cup of stone,
And oftentimes, when all are fast asleep,
  This water doth send forth a dolorous groan.

Some say that here a murder has been done,
  And blood cries out for blood; but for my part,
I've guess'd, when I've been sitting in the sun,
  That it was all for that unhappy Hart.

What thoughts must through the Creature's brain have pass'd!
  Even from the topmost Stone upon the Steep
Are but three bounds; and look, sir, at this last;—
  Oh, Master! it has been a cruel leap!

For thirteen hours he ran a desperate
    race,
And in my simple mind we cannot tell
What cause the Hart might have to love
    this place,
And come and make his deathbed near
    the Well.

Here on the grass perhaps asleep he sank,
    Lull'd by the Fountain in the summer-
    tide;
This water was perhaps the first he drank
When he had wander'd from his moth-
    er's side.

In April here beneath the scented thorn
    He heard the birds their morning carols
    sing,
And he, perhaps, for aught we know, was
    born
Not half a furlong from that selfsame
    spring.

Now, here is neither grass nor pleasant
    shade,
The sun on drearier Hollow never shone;
So will it be, as I have often said,
Till Trees, and Stones, and Fountain, all
    are gone."

"Gray-headed Shepherd, thou hast spoken
    well;
Small difference lies between thy creed
    and mine;
This Beast not unobserved by Nature fell:
His death was mourn'd by sympathy di-
    vine.

The Being, that is in the clouds and air,
    That is in the green leaves among the
    groves,
Maintains a deep and reverential care
For the unoffending creatures whom He
    loves.

The Pleasure-house is dust,—behind, be-
    fore,
This is no common waste, no common
    gloom,
But Nature, in due course of time, once
    more
Shall here put on her beauty and her
    bloom.

She leaves these objects to a slow decay,
    That what we are, and have been, may
    be known;
But at the coming of the milder day
    These monuments shall all be overgrown.

One lesson, Shepherd, let us two divide,
    Taught both by what she shows, and
    what conceals,
Never to blend our pleasure or our pride
    With sorrow of the meanest thing that
    feels."
                      WILLIAM WORDSWORTH.

ROBIN HOOD AND ALLEN-A-DALE.

COME listen to me, you gallants so free,
    All you that love mirth for to hear,
And I will tell you of a bold outlàw,
    That lived in Nottinghamshire.

As Robin Hood in the forest stood,
    All under the greenwood tree,
There he was aware of a brave young man,
    As fine as fine might be.

The youngster was clad in scarlet red,
    In scarlet fine and gay;
And he did frisk it over the plain,
    And chaunted a roundelay.

As Robin Hood next morning stood
    Amongst the leaves so gay,
There did he espy the same young man
    Come drooping along the way.

The scarlet he wore the day before
    It was clean cast away;
And at every step he fetch'd a sigh,
    "Alas! and a-well-a-day!"

Then steppèd forth brave Little John,
    And Midge, the miller's son;
Which made the young man bend his bow,
    When as he see them come.

"Stand off! stand off!" the young man said,
    "What is your will with me?"
"You must come before our master straight,
    Under yon greenwood tree."

And when he came bold Robin before,
    Robin ask'd him courteously,
"Oh, hast thou any money to spare,
    For my merry men and me?"

"I have no money," the young man said,
  "But five shillings and a ring;
And that I have kept this seven long years,
  To have at my wedding.

"Yesterday I should have married a maid,
  But she was from me ta'en,
And chosen to be an old knight's delight,
  Whereby my poor heart is slain."

"What is thy name?" then said Robin Hood,
  "Come tell me, without any fail."
"By the faith of my body," then said the young man,
  "My name it is Allen-a-Dale."

"What wilt thou give me," said Robin Hood,
  "In ready gold or fee,
To help thee to thy true love again,
  And deliver her unto thee?"

"I have no money," then quoth the young man,
  "In ready gold nor fee,
But I will swear upon a book
  Thy true servant for to be."

"How many miles is it to thy true love?
  Come tell me without guile."
"By the faith of my body," then said the young man,
  "It is but five little mile."

Then Robin he hasted over the plain;
  He did neither stint nor lin,
Until he came unto the church
  Where Allen should keep his weddin'.

"What hast thou here?" the bishop then said;
  "I prithee now tell unto me."
"I am a bold harper," quoth Robin Hood,
  "And the best in the north country."

"Oh welcome, oh welcome," the bishop he said;
  "That music best pleaseth me."
"You shall have no music," said Robin Hood,
  "Till the bride and bridegroom I see."

With that came in a wealthy knight,
  Which was both grave and old;
And after him a finikin lass,
  Did shine like the glistering gold.

"This is not a fit match," quoth Robin Hood,
  "That you do seem to make here;
For since we are come into the church,
  The bride shall choose her own dear."

Then Robin Hood put his horn to his mouth,
  And blew blasts two or three;
When four-and-twenty yeomen bold
  Came leaping over the lea.

And when they came into the churchyard,
  Marching all in a row,
The first man was Allen-a-Dale,
  To give bold Robin his bow.

"This is thy true love," Robin he said,
  "Young Allen, as I hear say;
And you shall be married this same time,
  Before we depart away."

"That shall not be," the bishop he cried,
  "For thy word shall not stand;
They shall be three times ask'd in the church,
  As the law is of our land."

Robin Hood pull'd off the bishop's coat,
  And put it upon Little John;
"By the faith of my body," then Robin said,
  "This cloth doth make thee a man."

When Little John went into the quire,
  The people began to laugh;
He ask'd them seven times into church,
  Lest three times should not be enough.

"Who gives me this maid?" said Little John,
  Quoth Robin Hood, "That do I;
And he that takes her from Allen-a-Dale,
  Full dearly he shall her buy."

And then having ended this merry wedding,
  The bride look'd like a queen;
And so they return'd to the merry green wood,
  Amongst the leaves so green.

AUTHOR UNKNOWN.

BETH-GÊLERT; OR, THE GRAVE OF THE GREYHOUND.

The Spearmen heard the bugle sound,
   And cheerily smiled the morn,
And many a brach and many a hound
   Obey'd Llewelyn's horn.

And still he blew a louder blast,
   And gave a lustier cheer:
"Come, Gêlert, come, wert never last
   Llewelyn's horn to hear.

"Oh! where does faithful Gêlert roam,
   The flow'r of all his race?
So true, so brave; a lamb at home,
   A lion in the chase!"

'Twas only at Llewelyn's board
   The faithful Gêlert fed;
He watch'd, he serv'd, he cheer'd his lord,
   And sentinell'd his bed.

In sooth he was a peerless hound,
   The gift of royal John;
But now no Gêlert could be found,
   And all the chase rode on.

And now, as o'er the rocks and dells
   The gallant chidings rise,
All Snowdon's craggy chaos yells
   The many-mingled cries!

That day Llewelyn little loved
   The chase of Hart or Hare,
And scant and small the booty proved,
   For Gêlert was not there.

Unpleased, Llewelyn homeward hied:
   When, near the portal seat,
His truant Gêlert he espied
   Bounding his lord to greet.

But, when he gained his castle door,
   Aghast the chieftain stood:
The hound all o'er was smear'd with gore,
   His lips, his fangs, ran blood.

Llewelyn gazed with fierce surprise:
   Unused such looks to meet,
His fav'rite check'd his joyful guise,
   And crouch'd and lick'd his feet.

Onward in haste Llewelyn pass'd,
   And on went Gêlert too,
And still, where'er his eyes he cast,
   Fresh blood-gouts shock'd his view.

O'erturn'd his infant's bed he found,
   With blood-stain'd covert rent;
And all around, the walls and ground
   With recent blood besprent.

He call'd his child, no voice replied;
   He search'd with terror wild;
Blood, blood he found on ev'ry side;
   But nowhere found his child.

"Hell-hound! my child by thee's devour'd!"
   The frantic father cried;
And to the hilt his vengeful sword
   He plunged in Gêlert's side.

His suppliant looks as prone he fell,
   No pity could impart;
But still his Gêlert's dying yell
   Pass'd heavy o'er his heart.

Aroused by Gêlert's dying yell
   Some slumb'rer waken'd nigh:
What words the parent's joy could tell
   To hear his infant's cry!

Conceal'd beneath a tumbled heap
   His hurried search had miss'd,
All glowing from his rosy sleep,
   The cherub boy he kiss'd.

Nor scath had he, nor harm, nor dread;
   But the same couch beneath
Lay a gaunt wolf, all torn and dead,
   Tremendous still in death.

Ah, what was then Llewelyn's pain!
   For now the truth was clear;
His gallant hound the wolf had slain,
   To save Llewelyn's heir.

Vain, vain was all Llewelyn's woe:
   "Best of thy kind, adieu!
The frantic blow, which laid thee low,
   This heart shall ever rue."

And now a gallant tomb they raise,
   With costly sculpture deckt;
And marbles, storied with his praise,
   Poor Gêlert's bones protect.

There never could the spearman pass,
   Or forester, unmoved;

There oft the tear-besprinkled grass
　Llewelyn's sorrow proved.

And there he hung his sword and spear,
　And there as evening fell,
In Fancy's ear he oft would hear
　Poor Gêlert's dying yell.

And till great Snowdon's rocks grow old,
　And cease the storm to brave,
The consecrated spot shall hold
　The name of "Gêlert's Grave."
　　　　　　WILLIAM ROBERT SPENCER.

KATHARINE JANFARIE.

THERE was a may, and a weel-fared may,
　Lived high up in yon glen :
Her name was Katharine Janfarie,
　She was courted by mony men.

Doun cam' the Laird o' Lamington,
　Doun frae the South Countrie ;
And he is for this bonnie lass,
　Her bridegroom for to be.

He ask'd no her father and mither,
　Nor the chief o' a' her kin ;
But he whisper'd the bonny lass hersel',
　And did her favor win.

Doun cam' an English gentleman,
　Doun frae the English border ;
He is for this bonny lass,
　To keep his house in order.

He ask'd her father and mither,
　And a' the lave o' her kin ;
But he never ask'd the lassie hersel'
　Till on her wedding-e'en.

But she has wrote a long letter,
　And seal'd it with her hand ;
And sent it away to Lamington,
　To let him understand.

The first line o' the letter he read,
　He was baith fain and glad ;
But or he has read the letter o'er,
　He's turn'd baith wan and sad.

Then he has sent a messenger,
　To run through all his land ;
And four and twenty armèd men
　Were all at his command.

But he has left his merry men all,
　Left them on the lee ;
And he's awa' to the wedding-house,
　To see what he could see.

They all rose up to honor him,
　For he was of high renown ;
They all rose up to welcome him,
　And bade him to sit down.

Oh mickle was the gude red wine
　In silver cups did flow ;
But aye she drank to Lamington,
　And fain with him would go.

"Oh come ye here to fight, young lord?
　Or come ye here to play ?
Or come ye here to drink gude wine
　Upon the wedding-day ?"

"I come na here to fight," he said,
　" I come na here to play ;
I'll but lead a dance wi' the bonny bride,
　And mount and go my way."

He's caught her by the milk-white hand,
　And by the grass-green sleeve ;
He's mounted her hie behind himsel',
　At her kinsfolk spier'd na leave.

It's up, it's up the Couden bank,
　It's doun the Couden brae ;
And aye they made the trumpet sound,
　" It's a' fair play !"

Now, a' ye lords and gentlemen
　That be of England born,
Come ye na doun to Scotland thus,
　For fear ye get the scorn !

They'll feed ye up wi' flattering words,
　And play ye foul play ;
They'll dress you frogs instead of fish
　Upon your wedding-day !
　　　　　　AUTHOR UNKNOWN.

FAIR ANNIE OF LOCHROYAN.

"Oh wha will shoe my fair foot,
  And wha will glove my han'?
And wha will lace my middle jimp
  Wi' a new-made London ban'?

"Or wha will kemb my yellow hair
  Wi' a new-made silver kemb?
Or wha'll be father to my young bairn,
  Till love Gregor come hame?"

"Your father'll shoe your fair foot,
  Your mother glove your han';
Your sister lace your middle jimp
  Wi' a new-made London ban';

"Your brethren will kemb your yellow hair
  Wi' a new-made silver kemb;
And the King o' heaven will father your bairn,
  Till love Gregor come hame."

"Oh gin I had a bonny ship,
  And men to sail wi' me,
It's I would gang to my true love,
  Sin he winna come to me!"

Her father's gien her a bonny ship,
  And sent her to the stran';
She's ta'en her young son in her arms,
  And turn'd her back to the lan'.

She hadna been o' the sea sailin'
  About a month or more,
Till landed has she her bonny ship
  Near her true love's door.

The nicht was dark, and the wind blew cald,
  And her love was fast asleep,
And the bairn that was in her twa arms
  Fu' sair began to greet.

Lang stood she at her true love's door,
  And lang tirl'd at the pin;
At length up gat his fause mother,
  Says, "Wha's that wad be in?"

"Oh it is Annie of Lochroyan,
  Your love, come o'er the sea,
But and your young son in her arms;
  So open the door to me."

"Awa', awa', ye ill woman!
  You're nae come here for gude;
You're but a witch, or a vile warlock,
  Or mermaid o' the flude."

"I'm nae a witch or vile warlock,
  Or mermaiden," said she;—
"I'm but your Annie of Lochroyan;—
  Oh open the door to me!"

"Oh gin ye be Annie of Lochroyan,
  As I trust not ye be,
What taiken can ye gie that e'er
  I kept your companie?"

"Oh dinna ye mind, love Gregor," she says,
  "Whan we sat at the wine,
How we changed the napkins frae our necks?
  It's nae sae lang sinsyne.

"And yours was gude, and gude enough,
  But nae sae gude as mine;
For yours was o' the cambric clear,
  But mine o' the silk sae fine.

"And dinna ye mind, love Gregor," she says,
  "As we twa sat at dine,
How we changed the rings frae our fingers,
  And I can shew thee thine:

"And yours was gude, and gude enough,
  Yet nae sae gude as mine;
For yours was o' the gude red gold,
  But mine o' the diamonds fine.

"Sae open the door, now, love Gregor,
  And open it wi' speed;
Or your young son, that is in my arms,
  For cald will soon be dead."

"Awa', awa', ye ill woman!
  Gae frae my door for shame;
For I hae gotten anither fair love—
  Sae ye may hie you hame."

"Oh hae ye gotten anither fair love,
  For a' the oaths ye sware?
Then fare ye weel, now, fause Gregor:
  For me ye's never see mair!"

Oh hooly, hooly gaed she back,
  As the day began to peep;

She set her foot on good shipboard,
  And sair, sair did she weep.

"Tak down, tak down the mast o' goud;
  Set up the mast o' tree;
Ill sets it a forsaken lady
  To sail sae gallantlie.

"Tak down, tak down, the sails o' silk:
  Set up the sails o' skin;
Ill sets the outside to be gay,
  Whan there's sic grief within!"

Love Gregor started frae his sleep,
  And to his mother did say:
"I dreamt a dream this night, mither,
  That maks my heart richt wae;

"I dreamt that Annie of Lochroyan,
  The flower o' a' her kin,
Was standin' mournin' at my door;
  But nane wad lat her in."

"Oh there was a woman stood at the door,
  Wi' a bairn intill her arms;
But I wadna let her within the bower,
  For fear she had done you harm."

Oh quickly, quickly raise he up,
  And fast ran to the strand;
And there he saw her, fair Annie,
  Was sailing frae the land.

And "Heigh, Annie!" and "How, Annie!
  O Annie, winna ye bide?"
But aye the louder that he cried "Annie,"
  The higher rair'd the tide.

And "Heigh, Annie!" and "How, Annie!
  O Annie, speak to me!"
But aye the louder that he cried "Annie,"
  The louder rair'd the sea.

The wind grew loud, and the sea grew rough,
  And the ship was rent in twain;
And soon he saw her, fair Annie,
  Come floating o'er the main.

He saw his young son in her arms,
  Baith toss'd aboon the tide;
He wrang his hands, and fast he ran,
  And plunged in the sea sae wide.

He catch'd her by the yellow hair,
  And drew her to the strand;
But cald and stiff was every limb,
  Before he reach'd the land.

Oh first he kist her cherry cheek,
  And syne he kist her chin:
And sair he kist her ruby lips,
  But there was nae breath within.

Oh he has mourn'd o'er fair Annie,
  Till the sun was ganging down;
Syne wi' a sich his heart it brast,
  And his saul to heaven has flown.
AUTHOR UNKNOWN.

O'CONNOR'S CHILD;
OR,
"THE FLOWER OF LOVE LIES BLEEDING."

OH! once the harp of Innisfail
  Was strung full high to notes of gladness;
But yet it often told a tale
  Of more prevailing sadness.
Sad was the note, and wild its fall,
  As winds that moan at night forlorn
Along the isles of Fion-Gall,
  When for O'Connor's child to mourn,
The harper told how lone, how far
From any mansion's twinkling star,
From any path of social men,
Or voice, but from the fox's den,
The lady in the desert dwelt;
And yet no wrongs, no fear she felt.
Say, why should dwell in place so wild
O'Connor's pale and lovely child?

Sweet lady! she no more inspires
  Green Erin's hearts with beauty's power,
As in the palace of her sires
  She bloom'd a peerless flower.
Gone from her hand and bosom, gone,
  The royal brooch, the jewell'd ring,
That o'er her dazzling whiteness shone,
  Like dews on lilies of the spring.
Yet why, though fall'n her brother's kerne,
Beneath De Bourgo's battle stern,
While yet in Leinster unexplored,
Her friends survive the English sword,—
Why lingers she from Erin's host,
So far on Galway's shipwreck'd coast?
Why wanders she a huntress wild,—
O'Connor's pale and lovely child?

And, fix'd on empty space, why burn
  Her eyes with momentary wildness;
And wherefore do they then return
  To more than woman's mildness?
Dishevell'd are her raven locks;
  On Connocht Moran's name she calls;
And oft amidst the lonely rocks
  She sings sweet madrigals.
Placed midst the foxglove and the moss,
Behold a parted warrior's cross!
That is the spot where, evermore,
The lady at her shieling door,
Enjoys that, in communion sweet,
The living and the dead can meet;
For lo! to love-lorn fantasy,
The hero of her heart is nigh.

Bright as the bow that spans the storm,
  In Erin's yellow vesture clad,
A son of light, a lovely form,
  He comes and makes her glad:
Now on the grass-green turf he sits,
  His tassell'd horn beside him laid;
Now o'er the hills in chase he flits,
  The hunter and the deer a shade!
Sweet mourner! these are shadows vain,
That cross the twilight of her brain;
Yet she will tell you she is blest,
Of Connocht Moran's tomb possess'd,
More richly than in Aghrim's bower,
When bards high praised her beauty's power,
And kneeling pages offer'd up
The morat in a golden cup.

"A hero's bride! this desert bower,
  It ill befits thy gentle breeding.
And wherefore dost thou love this flower
  To call 'My love lies bleeding'?"
"This purple flower my tears have nursed,—
  A hero's blood supplied its bloom:
I love it, for it was the first
  That grew on Connocht Moran's tomb.
Oh, hearken, stranger, to my voice!
This desert mansion is my choice;
And blest, though fatal, be the star
That led me to its wilds afar.
For here these pathless mountains free
Gave shelter to my love and me;
And every rock and every stone
Bore witness that he was my own.

"O'Connor's child, I was the bud
  Of Erin's royal tree of glory;
But woe to them that wrapt in blood
  The tissue of my story!
Still, as I clasp my burning brain,
  A death-scene rushes on my sight;
It rises o'er and o'er again,—
  The bloody feud, the fatal night,
When, chafing Connocht Moran's scorn,
They call'd my hero basely born,
And bade him choose a meaner bride
Than from O'Connor's house of pride.
Their tribe, they said, their high degree,
Was sung in Tara's psaltery;
Witness their Eath's victorious brand,
And Cathal of the bloody hand.
Glory (they said) and power and honor
Were in the mansion of O'Connor;
But he, my loved one, bore in field
A humbler crest, a meaner shield.

"Ah! brothers, what did it avail,
  That fiercely and triumphantly
Ye fought the English of the Pale,
  And stemm'd De Bourgo's chivalry?
And what was it to love and me,
  That barons by your standard rode,
Or beal-fires for your jubilee
  Upon a hundred mountains glow'd?
What though the lords of tower and dome
From Shannon to the North Sea foam,—
Thought ye your iron hands of pride
Could break the knot that love had tied?
No—let the eagle change his plume,
The leaf its hue, the flower its bloom;
But ties around this heart were spun
That could not, would not, be undone!

"At bleating of the wild watch-fold,
  Thus sang my love: 'Oh, come with me!
Our bark is on the lake, behold!
  Our steeds are fasten'd to the tree.
Come far from Castle Connor's clans,
  Come with thy belted forestere;
And I, beside the lake of swans,
  Shall hunt for thee the fallow deer,
And build thy hut, and bring thee home
The wild-fowl and the honeycomb,
And berries from the wood provide,
And play my clarshech by thy side.
Then come, my love!' How could I stay?
Our nimble stag-hounds track'd the way,

And I pursued, by moonless skies,
　The light of Connocht Moran's eyes.

" And fast and far, before the star
　　Of day-spring, rush'd we through the glade,
And saw at dawn the lofty bawn
　Of Castle Connor fade.
Sweet was to us the hermitage
　Of this unplough'd, untrodden shore;
Like birds all joyous from the cage,
　For man's neglect we loved it more.
And well he knew, my huntsman dear,
To search the game with hawk and spear;
While I, his evening food to dress,
　Would sing to him in happiness.
But oh, that midnight of despair!
When I was doom'd to rend my hair,—
The night, to me, of shrieking sorrow!
The night, to him, that had no morrow!

" When all was hush'd, at even-tide
　I heard the baying of their beagle.
' Be hush'd !' my Connocht Moran cried;
　' 'Tis but the screaming of the eagle.'
Alas! 'twas not the eyrie's sound;
　Their bloody bands had track'd us out;
Up listening starts our couchant hound,—
　And hark! again, that nearer shout
Brings faster on the murderers.
Spare—spare him! Brazil—Desmond fierce!
In vain!—no voice the adder charms;
　Their weapons cross'd my sheltering arms:
Another's sword has laid him low—
　Another's, and another's;
And every hand that dealt the blow—
　Ah me! it was a brother's.
Yes, when his moanings died away,
　Their iron hands had dug the clay,
And o'er his burial-turf they trod;
　And I beheld—O God! O God!—
His life-blood oozing from the sod.

" Warm in his death-wounds sepulchred,
　Alas! my warrior's spirit brave
Nor mass nor ulla-lulla heard,
　Lamenting, soothe his grave.
Dragg'd to their hated mansion back,
　How long in thraldom's grasp I lay
I knew not, for my soul was black,
　And knew no change of night or day.
One night of horror round me grew;
Or if I saw, or felt, or knew,

'Twas but when those grim visages,
　The angry brothers of my race,
Glared on each eyeball's aching throb,
　And check'd my bosom's power to sob,
Or when my heart, with pulses drear,
　Beat like a death-watch to my ear.

" But Heaven, at last, my soul's eclipse
　Did with a vision bright inspire:
I woke, and felt upon my lips
　A prophetess's fire.
Thrice in the east a war-drum beat,—
　I heard the Saxon's trumpet sound,
And ranged, as to the judgment-seat,
　My guilty, trembling brothers round.
Clad in the helm and shield they came;
For now De Bourgo's sword and flame
　Had ravaged Ulster's boundaries,
And lighted up the midnight skies.
The standard of O'Connor's sway
　Was in the turret where I lay;
That standard, with so dire a look,
As ghastly shone the moon and pale,
　I gave, that every bosom shook
Beneath its iron mail.

" ' And go !' I cried, ' the combat seek,
　Ye hearts that unappallèd bore
The anguish of a sister's shriek,
　Go!—and return no more!
For sooner guilt the ordeal brand
　Shall grasp unhurt, than ye shall hold
The banner with victorious hand,
　Beneath a sister's curse unroll'd.'
O stranger, by my country's loss!
And by my love! and by the cross!
I swear I never could have spoke
　The curse that sever'd Nature's yoke,
But that a spirit o'er me stood,
And fired me with the wrathful mood;
And frenzy to my heart was given,
　To speak the malison of Heaven.

" They would have cross'd themselves all mute;
　They would have pray'd to burst the spell;
But at the stamping of my foot,
　Each hand down powerless fell.
' And go to Athunree!' I cried,
' High lift the banner of your pride!
But know that where its sheet unrolls,
The weight of blood is on your souls!

Go where the havoc of your kerne
Shall float as high as mountain-fern!
Men shall no more your mansion know;
The nettles on your hearth shall grow;
   Dead, as the green oblivious flood
That mantles by your walls, shall be
    The glory of O'Connor's blood!
Away! away to Athunree!
Where, downward when the sun shall fall,
The raven's wing shall be your pall:
And not a vassal shall unlace
The visor from your dying face!'

"A bolt that overhung our dome,
   Suspended till my curse was given,
Soon as it pass'd these lips of foam,
   Peal'd in the blood-red heaven.
Dire was the look that o'er their backs
   The angry parting brothers threw;
But now, behold! like cataracts,
   Come down the hills in view
O'Connor's plumèd partisans:
   Thrice ten Kilnagorvian clans
    Were marching to their doom.
A sudden storm their plumage toss'd,
A flash of lightning o'er them cross'd
    And all again was gloom.

"Stranger, I fled the home of grief,
   At Connocht Moran's tomb to fall.
I found the helmet of my chief,
   His bow still hanging on our wall,
And took it down, and vow'd to rove
   This desert place a huntress bold;
Nor would I change my buried love
   For any heart of living mould.
No! for I am a hero's child;
I'll hunt my quarry in the wild;
   And still my home this mansion make,
   Of all unheeded and unheeding;
   And cherish, for my warrior's sake,
'The flower of love lies bleeding.'"
THOMAS CAMPBELL.

THE PRISONER OF CHILLON.

ETERNAL Spirit of the chainless Mind!
   Brightest in dungeons, Liberty, thou art,
   For there thy habitation is the heart—
The heart which love of thee alone can bind;

And when thy sons to fetters are consign'd—
   To fetters, and the damp vault's dayless gloom—
   Their country conquers with their martyrdom,
And freedom's fame finds wings on every wind.
Chillon! thy prison is a holy place,
   And thy sad floor an altar—for 'twas trod
Until his very steps have left a trace,
   Worn as if thy cold pavement were a sod,
By Bonnivard!—May none those marks efface!
   For they appeal from tyranny to God.

I.

My hair is gray, but not with years,
    Nor grew it white
    In a single night,
As men's have grown from sudden fears;
My limbs are bow'd, though not with toil,
   But rusted with a vile repose;
For they have been a dungeon's spoil,
   And mine has been the fate of those
To whom the goodly earth and air
Are bann'd and barr'd—forbidden fare.
But this was for my father's faith
I suffer'd chains and courted death.
That father perish'd at the stake
For tenets he would not forsake;
And for the same his lineal race
In darkness found a dwelling-place.
We were seven, who now are one—
   Six in youth, and one in age,
Finish'd as they had begun,
   Proud of Persecution's rage;
One in fire, and two in field,
Their belief with blood have seal'd:
Dying, as their father died,
For the God their foes denied.
Three were in a dungeon cast,
Of whom this wreck is left the last.

II.

There are seven pillars, of Gothic mould,
In Chillon's dungeons deep and old;
There are seven columns, massy and gray,
Dim with a dull imprison'd ray,
A sunbeam which hath lost its way,

And through the crevice and the cleft
Of the thick wall is fallen and left;
Creeping o'er the floor so damp,
Like a marsh's meteor lamp:
And in each pillar there is a ring,
   And in each ring there is a chain;
That iron is a cankering thing,
   For in these limbs its teeth remain,
With marks that will not wear away
Till I have done with this new day,
Which now is painful to these eyes,
Which have not seen the sun so rise
For years—I cannot count them o'er;
I lost their long and heavy score
When my last brother droop'd and died,
And I lay living by his side.

III.

They chain'd us each to a column stone
And we were three—yet each alone.
We could not move a single pace;
We could not see each other's face,
But with that pale and livid light
That made us strangers in our sight;
And thus together, yet apart—
Fetter'd in hand, but join'd in heart;
'Twas still some solace, in the dearth
Of the pure elements of earth,
To hearken to each other's speech,
And each turn comforter to each
With some new hope, or legend old,
Or song heroically bold;
But even these at length grew cold.
Our voices took a dreary tone,
An echo of the dungeon-stone,
   A grating sound—not full and free,
   As they of yore were wont to be;
   It might be fancy—but to me
They never sounded like our own.

IV.

I was the eldest of the three;
   And to uphold and cheer the rest
I ought to do, and did, my best—
And each did well in his degree.
   The youngest, whom my father loved,
Because our mother's brow was given
To him—with eyes as blue as heaven—
   For him my soul was sorely moved;
And truly might it be distress'd
To see such bird in such a nest;
For he was beautiful as day
(When day was beautiful to me
As to young eagles, being free),
A polar day, which will not see
A sunset till its summer's gone,
   Its sleepless summer of long light,
The snow-clad offspring of the sun:
   And thus he was as pure and bright,
And in his natural spirit gay,
With tears for naught but other's ills;
And then they flow'd like mountain-rills,
Unless he could assuage the woe
Which he abhorr'd to view below.

V.

The other was as pure of mind,
But form'd to combat with his kind;
Strong in his frame, and of a mood
Which 'gainst the world in war had stood,
And perish'd in the foremost rank
   With joy; but not in chains to pine.
His spirit wither'd with their clank;
   I saw it silently decline—
   And so, perchance, in sooth, did mine:
But yet I forced it on to cheer
Those relics of a home so dear.
He was a hunter of the hills,
   Had follow'd there the deer and wolf;
   To whom this dungeon was a gulf,
And fetter'd feet the worst of ills.

VI.

   Lake Leman lies by Chillon's walls.
A thousand feet in depth below,
Its massy waters meet and flow;
Thus much the fathom-line was sent
From Chillon's snow-white battlement,
   Which round about the wave enthralls;
A double dungeon wall and wave
Have made—and like a living grave,
Below the surface of the lake
The dark vault lies wherein we lay;
We heard it ripple night and day;
   Sounding o'er our heads it knock'd;
And I have felt the winter's spray
Wash through the bars when winds were high,
And wanton in the happy sky;
   And then the very rock hath rocked,
   And I have felt it shake, unshock'd,
Because I could have smiled to see
The death that would have set me free.

VII.

I said my nearer brother pined;
I said his mighty heart declined.
He loathed and put away his food;
It was not that 'twas coarse and rude,
For we were used to hunter's fare,
And for the like had little care.
The milk drawn from the mountain-goat
Was changed for water from the moat;
Our bread was such as captives' tears
Have moisten'd many a thousand years,
Since man first pent his fellow-men,
Like brutes, within an iron den.
But what were these to us or him?
These wasted not his heart or limb;
My brother's soul was of that mould
Which in a palace had grown cold,
Had his free breathing been denied
The range of the steep mountain's side.
But why delay the truth?—he died.
I saw, and could not hold his head,
Nor reach his dying hand—nor dead,
Though hard I strove, but strove in vain,
To rend and gnash my bonds in twain.
He died—and they unlock'd his chain,
And scoop'd for him a shallow grave
Even from the cold earth of our cave.
I begg'd them, as a boon, to lay
His corse in dust whereon the day
Might shine—it was a foolish thought;
But then within my brain it wrought,
That even in death his freeborn breast
In such a dungeon could not rest.
I might have spared my idle prayer—
They coldly laugh'd, and laid him there,
The flat and turfless earth above
The being we so much did love;
His empty chain above it leant—
Such murder's fitting monument!

VIII.

But he, the favorite and the flower,
Most cherish'd since his natal hour,
His mother's image in fair face,
The infant love of all his race,
His martyr'd father's dearest thought,
My latest care—for whom I sought
To hoard my life, that his might be
Less wretched now, and one day free—
He, too, who yet had held untired
A spirit natural or inspired—
He, too, was struck, and day by day
Was wither'd on the stalk away.
O God! it is a fearful thing
To see the human soul take wing
In any shape, in any mood:
I've seen it rushing forth in blood;
I've seen it on the breaking ocean
Strive with a swoln, convulsive motion;
I've seen the sick and ghastly bed
Of sin, delirious with its dread;
But these were horrors—this was woe
Unmix'd with such—but sure and slow.
He faded, and so calm and meek,
So softly worn, so sweetly weak,
So tearless, yet so tender—kind,
And grieved for those he left behind;
With all the while a cheek whose bloom
Was as a mockery of the tomb,
Whose tints as gently sunk away
As a departing rainbow's ray—
An eye of most transparent light,
That almost made the dungeon bright,
And not a word of murmur, not
A groan o'er his untimely lot—
A little talk of better days,
A little hope my own to raise;
For I was sunk in silence—lost
In this last loss, of all the most;
And then the sighs he would suppress
Of fainting Nature's feebleness,
More slowly drawn, grew less and less.
I listen'd, but I could not hear—
I call'd, for I was wild with fear;
I knew 'twas hopeless, but my dread
Would not be thus admonishèd;
I call'd, and thought I heard a sound—
I burst my chain with one strong bound,
And rush'd to him: I found him not,
I only stirr'd in this black spot,
I only lived—I only drew
The accursèd breath of dungeon-dew;
The last, the sole, the dearest link
Between me and the eternal brink,
Which bound me to my failing race,
Was broken in this fatal place.
One on the earth and one beneath—
My brothers—both had ceased to breathe.
I took that hand which lay so still—
Alas! my own was full as chill;
I had not strength to stir or strive,
But felt that I was still alive—

A frantic feeling, when we know
That what we love shall ne'er be so.
  I know not why
  I could not die,
I had no earthly hope—but faith,
And that forbade a selfish death.

IX.

What next befell me then and there
  I know not well—I never knew.
First came the loss of light and air,
  And then of darkness too.
I had no thought, no feeling—none:
Among the stones I stood a stone;
And was, scarce conscious what I wist,
As shrubless crags within the mist;
For all was blank, and bleak, and gray;
It was not night—it was not day;
It was not even the dungeon-light,
So hateful to my heavy sight;
But vacancy absorbing space,
And fixedness, without a place;
There were no stars, no earth, no time,
No check, no change, no good, no crime;
But silence, and a stirless breath,
Which neither was of life nor death;
A sea of stagnant idleness,
Blind, boundless, mute, and motionless!

X.

A light broke in upon my brain—
  It was the carol of a bird;
It ceased, and then it came again—
  The sweetest song ear ever heard;
And mine was thankful till my eyes
Ran over with the glad surprise,
And they that moment could not see
I was the mate of misery;
But then by dull degrees came back
My senses to their wonted track:
I saw the dungeon walls and floor
Close slowly round me as before;
I saw the glimmer of the sun
Creeping as it before had done;
But through the crevice where it came
That bird was perch'd as fond and tame,
  And tamer than upon the tree—
A lovely bird with azure wings,
And song that said a thousand things,
  And seem'd to say them all for me!
I never saw its like before—
I ne'er shall see its likeness more.

It seem'd, like me, to want a mate,
But was not half so desolate;
And it was come to love me when
None lived to love me so again,
And, cheering from my dungeon's brink,
Had brought me back to feel and think.
I know not if it late were free,
  Or broke its cage to perch on mine;
But knowing well captivity,
  Sweet bird! I could not wish for thine—
Or if it were, in wingèd guise,
A visitant from Paradise;
For—Heaven forgive that thought! the while
Which made me both to weep and smile;
I sometimes deem'd that it might be
My brother's soul come down to me;
But then at last away it flew,
And then 'twas mortal well I knew;
For he would never thus have flown,
And left me twice so doubly lone—
Lone as the corse within its shroud,
Lone as a solitary cloud,
  A single cloud on a sunny day,
While all the rest of heaven is clear,
A frown upon the atmosphere,
That hath no business to appear
  When skies are blue, and earth is gay.

XI.

A kind of change came in my fate—
My keepers grew compassionate.
I know not what had made them so—
They were inured to sights of woe;
But so it was—my broken chain
With links unfasten'd did remain;
And it was liberty to stride
Along my cell from side to side,
And up and down, and then athwart,
And tread it over every part;
And round the pillars one by one,
Returning where my walk begun—
Avoiding only, as I trod,
My brothers' graves without a sod;
For if I thought with heedless tread
My step profaned their lowly bed,
My breath came gaspingly and thick,
And my crush'd heart fell blind and sick.

XII.

I made a footing in the wall:
  It was not therefrom to escape,

For I had buried one and all
  Who loved me in a human shape;
And the whole earth would henceforth be
  A wider prison unto me;
No child, no sire, no kin had I,
  No partner in my misery.
I thought of this, and I was glad,
For thought of them had made me mad;
But I was curious to ascend
To my barr'd windows, and to bend
Once more upon the mountains high
The quiet of a loving eye.

XIII.

I saw them—and they were the same;
They were not changed, like me, in frame;
I saw their thousand years of snow
On high—their wide, long lake below,
And the blue Rhone in fullest flow;
I heard the torrents leap and gush
O'er channell'd rock and broken bush;
I saw the white-wall'd distant town.
And whiter sails go skimming down;
And then there was a little isle,
Which in my very face did smile—
  The only one in view;
A small, green isle, it seem'd no more,
Scarce broader than my dungeon-floor;
But in it there were three tall trees,
And o'er it blew the mountain-breeze,
And by it there were waters flowing,
And on it there were young flow'rs growing
  Of gentle breath and hue.
The fish swam by the castle-wall,
And they seem'd joyous, each and all;
The eagle rode the rising blast—
Methought he never flew so fast
As then to me he seem'd to fly;
And then new tears came in my eye,
And I felt troubled, and would fain
I had not left my recent chain;
And when I did descend again
The darkness of my dim abode
Fell on me as a heavy load;
It was as is a new-dug grave,
Closing o'er one we sought to save;
And yet my glance, too much oppress'd,
Had almost need of such a rest.

XIV.

It might be months, or years, or days—
  I kept no count, I took no note—
I had no hope my eyes to raise,
  And clear them of their dreary mote;
At last men came to set me free,
  I ask'd not why, and reck'd not where;
It was at length the same to me,
Fetter'd or fetterless to be;
  I learn'd to love despair.
And thus, when they appear'd at last,
And all my bonds aside were cast,
These heavy walls to me had grown
A hermitage—and all my own!
And half I felt as they were come
To tear me from a second home.
With spiders I had friendship made,
And watch'd them in their sullen trade;
Had seen the mice by moonlight play;
And why should I feel less than they?
We were all inmates of one place,
And I, the monarch of each race,
Had power to kill; yet, strange to tell!
In quiet we had learn'd to dwell.
My very chains and I grew friends,
So much a long communion tends
To make us what we are:—even I
Regain'd my freedom with a sigh.
                LORD BYRON.

FAIR HELEN.

I WISH I were where Helen lies;
Night and day on me she cries;
Oh that I were where Helen lies,
  On fair Kirconnell lea!

Curst be the heart that thought the thought,
And curst the hand that fired the shot,
When in my arms burd Helen dropt,
  And died to succor me!

Oh think na but my heart was sair,
When my love dropt down and spak nae mair!
I laid her down wi' meikle care,
  On fair Kirconnell lea.

As I went down the water-side,
None but my foe to be my guide—
None but my foe to be my guide,
  On fair Kirconnell lea—

I lighted down my sword to draw;
I hackèd him in pieces sma'—
I hackèd him in pieces sma',
  For her sake that died for me.

O Helen fair, beyond compare,
I'll make a garland of thy hair
Shall bind my heart for evermair,
    Until the day I die!

Oh that I were where Helen lies!
Night and day on me she cries;
Out of my bed she bids me rise—
    Says, "Haste and come to me!"

O Helen fair! O Helen chaste!
If I were with thee I were blest,
Where thou lies low, and takes thy rest,
    On fair Kirconnell lea.

I wish my grave were growing green,
A winding-sheet drawn ower my een,
And I in Helen's arms lying,
    On fair Kirconnell lea.

I wish I were where Helen lies!
Night and day on me she cries;
And I am weary of the skies,
    Since my love died for me.
                  AUTHOR UNKNOWN.

HELEN OF KIRKCONNELL.

I WISH I were where Helen lies,
For night and day on me she cries;
And, like an angel, to the skies
    Still seems to beckon me!
For me she lived, for me she sigh'd,
For me she wish'd to be a bride;
For me in life's sweet morn she died
    On fair Kirkconnell-Lee!

Where Kirtle waters gently wind,
As Helen on my arm reclined,
A rival with a ruthless mind
    Took deadly aim at me:
My love, to disappoint the foe,
Rush'd in between me and the blow;
And now her corse is lying low
    On fair Kirkconnell-Lee!

Though Heaven forbids my wrath to swell,
I curse the hand by which she fell—
The fiend who made my heaven a hell,
    And tore my love from me!
For if, where all the graces shine—
Oh, if on earth there's aught divine,
My Helen! all these charms were thine—
    They centred all in thee!

Ah, what avails it that, amain,
I clove the assassin's head in twain?
No peace of mind, my Helen slain,
    No resting-place for me:
I see her spirit in the air—
I hear the shriek of wild despair,
When Murder laid her bosom bare
    On fair Kirkconnell-Lee!

Oh! when I'm sleeping in my grave,
And o'er my head the rank weeds wave,
May He who life and spirit gave
    Unite my love and me!
Then from this world of doubts and sighs,
My soul on wings of peace shall rise;
And, joining Helen in the skies,
    Forget Kirkconnell-Lee!
                    JOHN MAYNE.

ROSABELLE.

OH listen, listen, ladies gay!
    No haughty feat of arms I tell;
Soft is the note, and sad the lay
    That mourns the lovely Rosabelle.

"Moor, moor the barge, ye gallant crew,
    And, gentle lady, deign to stay!
Rest thee in Castle Ravensheuch,
    Nor tempt the stormy firth to-day.

"The blackening wave is edged with white;
    To inch and rock the sea-mews fly;
The fishers have heard the Water-Sprite,
    Whose screams forbode that wreck is nigh.

"Last night the gifted seer did view
    A wet shroud swathed round lady gay;
Then stay thee, Fair, in Ravensheuch;
    Why cross the gloomy firth to-day?"

"'Tis not because Lord Lindesay's heir
    To-night at Roslin leads the ball,
But that my lady-mother there
    Sits lonely in her castle-hall.

"'Tis not because the ring they ride,
    And Lindesay at the ring rides well,
But that my sire the wine will chide
    If 'tis not fill'd by Rosabelle."

—O'er Roslin all that dreary night
    A wondrous blaze was seen to gleam;

'Twas broader than the watch-fire's light,
   And redder than the bright moonbeam.

It glared on Roslin's castled rock,
   It ruddied all the copse-wood glen;
'Twas seen from Dryden's groves of oak,
   And seen from cavern'd Hawthornden.

Seem'd all on fire that chapel proud
   Where Roslin's chiefs uncoffin'd lie,
Each baron, for a sable shroud,
   Sheath'd in his iron panoply.

Seem'd all on fire within, around,
   Deep sacristy and altar's pale;
Shone every pillar foliage-bound,
   And glimmer'd all the dead men's mail.

Blazed battlement and pinnet high,
   Blazed every rose-carved buttress fair—
So still they blaze, when fate is nigh
   The lordly line of high Saint Clair.

There are twenty of Roslin's barons bold
   Lie buried within that proud chapelle;
Each one the holy vault doth hold,
   But the sea holds lovely Rosabelle!

And each Saint Clair was buried there
   With candle, with book, and with knell;
But the sea-caves rung, and the wild winds
     sung
   The dirge of lovely Rosabelle.
SIR WALTER SCOTT.

CARÇAMON.

HIS steed was old, his armor worn,
   And he was old and worn and gray;
The light that lit his patient eyes,
   It shone from very far away.

Through gay Provence he journeyed on,
   To one high quest his life was true;
And so they called him Carçamon—
   The knight who seeketh the world through.

A pansy blossomed on his shield;
   "A token 'tis,' the people say,
'That still across the world's wide field
   He seeks *la dame de ses pensées.*"

For somewhere on a painted wall,
   Or in the city's shifting crowd,
Or looking from a casement tall,
   Or shaped of dream or evening cloud—

Forgotten when, forgotten where—
   Her face had filled his careless eye
A moment ere he turned and passed,
   Nor knew it was his destiny.

But ever in his dreams it came,
   Divine and passionless and strong,
A smile upon the imperial lips
   No lover's kiss had dared to wrong.

He took his armor from the wall—
   Ah! gone since then was many a day—
He led his steed from out the stall
   And sought *la dame de ses pensées.*

The ladies of the Troubadours
   Came riding through the chestnut grove:
"Sir Minstrel, string that lute of yours,
   And sing us a gay song of love."

"O ladies of the Troubadours,
   My lute has but a single string;
Sirventes fit for paramours
   My heart is not in tune to sing.

"The flower that blooms upon my shield,
   It has another soil and spring
Than that wherein the gaudy rose
   Of light Provence is blossoming.

"The lady of my dreams doth hold
   Such royal state within my mind,
No thought that comes unclad in gold
   To that high court may entrance find."

So through the chestnut groves he passed,
   And through the land and far away;
Nor know I whether in the world
   He found *la dame de ses pensées.*

Only I know that in the South
   Long to the harp his tale was told;
Sweet as new wine within the mouth
   The small, choice words and music old.

To scorn the promise of the Real;
   To seek and seek and not to find;
Yet cherish still the fair Ideal,—
   It is thy fate, O restless Mind!
HENRY AUGUSTIN BEERS.

CURFEW MUST NOT RING TO-NIGHT.

SLOWLY England's sun was setting o'er the
   hilltops far away,
Filling all the land with beauty at the close
   of one sad day;

And the last rays kissed the forehead of a
    man and maiden fair,
He with footsteps slow and weary, she with
    sunny, floating hair;
He with bowed head, sad and thoughtful,
    she with lips all cold and white,
Struggling to keep back the murmur, "Cur-
    few must not ring to-night!"

"Sexton," Bessie's white lips faltered,
    pointing to the prison old,
With its turrets tall and gloomy, with its
    walls dark, damp, and cold—
"I've a lover in that prison, doomed this
    very night to die
At the ringing of the Curfew, and no
    earthly help is nigh.
Cromwell will not come till sunset;" and
    her face grew strangely white
As she breathed the husky whisper, "Cur-
    few must not ring to-night!"

"Bessie," calmly spoke the sexton—and his
    accents pierced her heart
Like the piercing of an arrow, like a dead-
    ly poisoned dart—
"Long, long years I've rung the Curfew
    from that gloomy shadowed tower;
Every evening, just at sunset, it has told
    the twilight hour;
I have done my duty ever, tried to do it
    just and right,
Now I'm old, I still must do it: Curfew,
    girl, must ring to-night!"

Wild her eyes and pale her features, stern
    and white her thoughtful brow,
And within her secret bosom Bessie made
    a solemn vow.
She had listened while the judges read,
    without a tear or sigh,
"At the ringing of the Curfew, Basil Un-
    derwood must die."
And her breath came fast and faster, and
    her eyes grew large and bright,
As in undertone she murmured, "Curfew
    must not ring to-night!"

With quick step she bounded forward,
    sprang within the old church-door,
Left the old man threading slowly paths
    he'd trod so oft before;

Not one moment paused the maiden, but
    with eye and cheek aglow
Mounted up the gloomy tower, where the
    bell swung to and fro:
As she climbed the dusty ladder, on which
    fell no ray of light,
Up and up, her white lips saying, "Curfew
    shall not ring to-night!"

She has reached the topmost ladder, o'er
    her hangs the great dark bell,
Awful is the gloom beneath her like the
    pathway down to hell;
Lo, the ponderous tongue is swinging, 'tis
    the hour of Curfew now,
And the sight has chilled her bosom, stopped
    her breath and paled her brow.
Shall she let it ring? No, never! Flash her
    eyes with sudden light,
And she springs and grasps it firmly: "Cur-
    few shall not ring to-night!"

Out she swung, far out; the city seemed a
    speck of light below;
She 'twixt heaven and earth suspended
    as the bell swung to and fro;
And the sexton at the bell-rope, old and
    deaf, heard not the bell,
But he thought it still was ringing fair
    young Basil's funeral knell.
Still the maiden clung more firmly, and,
    with trembling lips and white,
Said, to hush her heart's wild beating,
    "Curfew shall not ring to-night!"

It was o'er: the bell ceased swaying, and
    the maiden stepped once more
Firmly on the dark old ladder, where for
    hundred years before
Human foot had not been planted; but
    the brave deed she had done
Should be told long ages after:—often as
    the setting sun
Should illume the sky with beauty, agèd
    sires, with heads of white,
Long should tell the little children, "Cur-
    few did not ring that night."

O'er the distant hills came Cromwell; Bes-
    sie sees him, and her brow,
Full of hope and full of gladness, has no
    anxious traces now.

At his feet she tells her story, shows her
    hands all bruised and torn;
And her face so sweet and pleading, yet
    with sorrow pale and worn,
Touched his heart with sudden pity—lit
    his eye with misty light;
"Go, your lover lives!" said Cromwell;
    "Curfew shall not ring to-night!"
ROSA HARTWICK THORPE.

GLENLOGIE.

THREESCORE o' nobles rade up the king's
    ha',
But bonnie Glenlogie's the flower o' them
    a',
Wi' his milk-white steed and his bonnie
    black e'e,
"Glenlogie, dear mither, Glenlogie for me!"

"Oh, haud your tongue, daughter, ye'll get
    better than he."
"Oh, say nae sae, mither, for that canna be;
Though Doumlie is richer and greater than
    he,
Yet if I maun tak him, I'll certainly dee.

"Where will I get a bonnie boy, to win
    hose and shoon,
Will gae to Glenlogie, and come again
    soon?"
"Oh, here am I, a bonnie boy, to win hose
    and shoon,
Will gae to Glenlogie, and come again
    soon."

When he gaed to Glenlogie, 'twas "Wash
    and go dine;"
'Twas "Wash ye, my pretty boy, wash and
    go dine."
"Oh, 'twas ne'er my father's fashion, and it
    ne'er shall be mine
To gar a lady's errand wait till I dine.

"But there is, Glenlogie, a letter for thee."
The first line that he read, a low laugh
    gave he;
The next line that he read, the tear blindit
    his e'e;
But the last line that he read, he gart the
    table flee.

"Gar saddle the black horse, gar saddle
    the brown;
Gar saddle the swiftest steed e'er rade frae
    a town:"
But lang ere the horse was drawn and
    brought to the green,
Oh, bonnie Glenlogie was twa mile his lane.

When he came to Glenfeldy's door, little
    mirth was there;
Bonnie Jean's mother was tearing her hair.
"Ye're welcome, Glenlogie, ye're wel-
    come," said she,—
"Ye're welcome, Glenlogie, your Jeanie to
    see."

Pale and wan was she when Glenlogie
    gaed ben,
But red and rosy grew she whene'er he
    sat down;
She turn'd awa' her head, but the smile
    was in her e'e,
"Oh, binna fear'd, mither, I'll maybe no
    dee."
AUTHOR UNKNOWN.

GINEVRA.

IF thou shouldst ever come by choice or
    chance
To Modena, where still religiously
Among her ancient trophies is preserved
Bologna's bucket (in its chain it hangs
Within that reverend tower, the Guir-
    landine)
Stop at a Palace near the Reggio gate,
Dwelt in of old by one of the Orsini.
Its noble gardens, terrace above terrace,
And rich in fountains, statues, cypresses,
Will long detain thee; thro' their archèd
    walks,
Dim at noonday, discovering many a
    glimpse
Of knights and dames, such as in old
    romance,
And lovers, such as in heroic song,
Perhaps the two, for groves were their
    delight,
That in the spring-time, as alone they sat,
Venturing together on a tale of love,
Read only part that day.—A summer sun
Sets ere one half is seen; but ere thou go,

Enter the house—prythee, forget it not—
And look a while upon a picture there.
  'Tis of a Lady in her earliest youth,
The very last of that illustrious race,
Done by Zampieri—but I care not whom.
He who observes it, ere he passes on
Gazes his fill, and comes and comes again,
That he may call it up when far away.
  She sits, inclining forward as to speak,
Her lips half open, and her finger up,
As tho' she said, "Beware!" her vest of gold
Broider'd with flowers, and clasp'd from head to foot,
An emerald stone in every golden clasp;
And on her brow, fairer than alabaster,
A coronet of pearls. But then her face,
So lovely, yet so arch, so full of mirth,
The overflowings of an innocent heart—
It haunts me still, tho' many a year has fled,
Like some wild melody!
              Alone it hangs
Over a mouldering heirloom, its companion,
An oaken chest, half eaten by the worm,
But richly carved by Antony of Trent
With Scripture stories from the Life of Christ;
A chest that came from Venice, and had held
The ducal robes of some old Ancestor.
That by the way—it may be true or false—
But don't forget the picture; and thou wilt not
When thou hast heard the tale they told me there.
  She was an only child; from infancy
The joy, the pride of an indulgent Sire.
Her Mother dying of the gift she gave,
That precious gift, what else remained to him?
The young Ginevra was his all in life,
Still as she grew, for ever in his sight;
And in her fifteenth year became a bride,
Marrying an only son, Francesco Doria,
Her playmate from her birth, and her first love.
  Just as she looks there in her bridal dress,
She was all gentleness, all gaiety,
Her pranks the favorite theme of every tongue.
But now the day was come, the day, the hour;
Now, frowning, smiling, for the hundredth time,
The nurse, that ancient lady, preach'd decorum;
And, in the lustre of her youth, she gave
Her hand, with her heart in it, to Francesco.
  Great was the joy; but at the Bridal-feast,
When all sat down, the Bride was wanting there.
Nor was she to be found! Her Father cried,
"'Tis but to make a trial of our love!"
And filled his glass to all; but his hand shook,
And soon from guest to guest the panic spread.
'Twas but that instant she had left Francesco,
Laughing and looking back and flying still,
Her ivory tooth imprinted on his finger.
But now, alas, she was not to be found;
Nor from that hour could anything be guess'd,
But that she was not!
              Weary of his life,
Francesco flew to Venice, and forthwith
Flung it away in battle with the Turk.
Orsini lived; and long might'st thou have seen
An old man wandering as in quest of something,
Something he could not find—he knew not what.
When he was gone, the house remain'd a while
Silent and tenantless—then went to strangers.
  Full fifty years were past, and all forgot,
When on an idle day, a day of search
'Mid the old lumber in the Gallery,
That mouldering chest was noticed: and 'twas said
By one as young, as thoughtless as Ginevra,
"Why not remove it from its lurking-place?"
'Twas done as soon as said; but on the way

It burst, it fell; and lo, a skeleton,
With here and there a pearl, an emerald stone,
A golden clasp, clasping a shred of gold.
All else had perish'd—save a nuptial ring,
And a small seal, her mother's legacy,
Engraven with a name, the name of both,
"GINEVRA."
    There then had she found a grave!
Within that chest had she conceal'd herself,
Fluttering with joy, the happiest of the happy;
When a spring-lock, that lay in ambush there,
Fasten'd her down for ever!
SAMUEL ROGERS.

THE BULL-FIGHT OF GAZUL.

KING ALMANZOR of Granada, he hath bid the trumpet sound,
He hath summon'd all the Moorish lords from the hills and plains around;
From Vega and Sierra, from Betis and Xenil,
They have come with helm and cuirass of gold and twisted steel.

'Tis the holy Baptist's feast they hold in royalty and state,
And they have closed the spacious lists, beside the Alhambra's gate;
In gowns of black with silver laced, within the tented ring,
Eight Moors to fight the bull are placed in presence of the king.

Eight Moorish lords, of valor tried, with stalwart arm and true,
The onset of the beasts abide, as they come rushing through:
The deeds they've done, the spoils they've won, fill all with hope and trust;
Yet, ere high in heaven appears the sun, they all have bit the dust.

Then sounds the trumpet clearly, then clangs the loud tambour:
Make room, make room for Gazul!—throw wide, throw wide the door!—

Blow, blow the trumpet clearer still! more loudly strike the drum!—
The alcaydè of Algava to fight the bull doth come.

And first before the king he pass'd, with reverence stooping low;
And next he bow'd him to the queen, and the Infantas all a-row;
Then to his lady's grace he turn'd, and she to him did throw
A scarf from out her balcony was whiter than the snow.

With the life-blood of the slaughter'd lords all slippery is the sand,
Yet proudly in the centre hath Gazul ta'en his stand;
And ladies look with heaving breast, and lords with anxious eye:
But firmly he extends his arm—his look is calm and high.

Three bulls against the knight are loosed, and two come roaring on:
He rises high in stirrup, forth stretching his *rejón;*
Each furious beast upon the breast he deals him such a blow,
He blindly totters and gives back across the sand to go.

"Turn, Gazul—turn!" the people cry: the third comes up behind;
Low to the sand his head holds he, his nostrils snuff the wind;—
The mountaineers that lead the steers without stand whispering low,
"Now thinks this proud alcaydè to stun Harpado so?"

From Gaudiana comes he not, he comes not from Xenil,
From Guadalarif of the plain, or Barves of the hill;
But where from out the forest burst Xarama's waters clear,
Beneath the oak trees was he nursed,—this proud and stately steer.

Dark is his hide on either side, but the blood within doth boil,
And the dun hide glows, as if on fire, as he paws to the turmoil:

His eyes are jet, and they are set in crys-
    tal rings of snow;
But now they stare with one red glare of
    brass upon the foe.

Upon the forehead of the bull the horns
    stand close and near,—
From out the broad and wrinkled skull
    like daggers they appear;
His neck is massy, like the trunk of some
    old, knotted tree,
Whereon the monster's shagged mane, like
    billows curl'd ye see.

His legs are short, his hams are thick, his
    hoofs are black as night;
Like a strong flail he holds his tail in
    fierceness of his might;
Like some thing molten out of iron, or
    hewn from forth the rock,
Harpado of Xarama stands, to bide the
    alcaydè's shock.

Now stops the drum: close, close they come;
    thrice meet, and thrice give back;
The white foam of Harpado lies on the
    charger's breast of black,—
The white foam of the charger on Har-
    pado's front of dun;—
Once more advance upon his lance,—once
    more, thou fearless one!

Once more, once more!—in dust and gore
    to ruin must thou reel!—
In vain, in vain thou tearest the sand with
    furious heel!—
In vain, in vain, thou noble beast!—I see,
    I see thee stagger!
Now keen and cold thy neck must hold
    the stern alcaydè's dagger!

They have slipp'd a noose around his feet,
    six horses are brought in,
And away they drag Harpado with a loud
    and joyful din.
Now stoop thee, lady, from thy stand, and
    the ring of price bestow
Upon Gazul of Algava, that hath laid
    Harpado low.

(From the Spanish.)
JOHN GIBSON LOCKHART.

GOD'S JUDGMENT ON A WICKED BISHOP.

THE summer and autumn had been so wet,
That in winter the corn was growing yet.
'Twas a piteous sight to see all around
The grain lie rotting on the ground.

Every day the starving poor
Crowded around Bishop Hatto's door,
For he had a plentiful last year's store,
And all the neighborhood could tell
His granaries were furnish'd well.

At last Bishop Hatto appointed a day
To quiet the poor without delay;
He bade them to his great barn repair,
And they should have food for the winter
    there.

Rejoiced the tidings good to hear,
The poor folk flock'd from far and near;
The great barn was full as it could hold
Of women and children, and young and
    old.

Then, when he saw it could hold no more,
Bishop Hatto he made fast the door,
And while for mercy on Christ they call,
He set fire to the barn, and burnt them
    all.

"I' faith, 'tis an excellent bonfire!" quoth
    he,
"And the country is greatly obliged to
    me
For ridding it, in these times forlorn,
Of rats that only consume the corn."

So then to his palace returnèd he,
And he sat down to supper merrily,
And he slept that night like an innocent
    man;
But Bishop Hatto never slept again.

In the morning, as he enter'd the hall
Where his picture hung against the wall,
A sweat like death all over him came,
For the rats had eaten it out of the frame.

As he look'd, there came a man from his
    farm,
He had a countenance white with alarm:

"My Lord, I open'd your granaries this morn,
And the rats had eaten all your corn."

Another came running presently,
And he was pale as pale could be.
"Fly, my lord bishop, fly!" quoth he,
"Ten thousand rats are coming this way,
The Lord forgive you for yesterday!"

"I'll go to my tower on the Rhine," replied he;
"'Tis the safest place in Germany;
The walls are high, and the shores are steep,
And the stream is strong, and the water deep."

Bishop Hatto fearfully hasten'd away,
And he cross'd the Rhine without delay,
And reach'd his tower, and barr'd with care
All the windows, doors, and loopholes there.

He laid him down and closed his eyes,
But soon a scream made him arise;
He started, and saw two eyes of flame
On his pillow, from whence the screaming came.

He listen'd and look'd,—it was only the cat,
But the bishop he grew more fearful for that,
For she sat screaming, mad with fear,
At the army of rats that were drawing near.

For they have swum over the river so deep,
And they have climb'd the shores so steep,
And up the tower their way is bent,
To do the work for which they were sent.

They are not to be told by the dozen or score;
By thousands they come, and by myriads and more;
Such numbers had never been heard of before,
Such a judgment had never been witness'd of yore.

Down on his knees the bishop fell,
And faster and faster his beads did he tell,
As louder and louder, drawing near,
The gnawing of their teeth he could hear.

And in at the windows, and in at the door,
And through the walls helter-skelter they pour;
And down from the ceiling and up through the floor,
From the right and the left, from behind and before,
From within and without, from above and below,—
And all at once to the bishop they go.

They have whetted their teeth against the stones,
And now they pick the bishop's bones;
They gnaw'd the flesh from every limb,
For they were sent to do judgment on him!
ROBERT SOUTHEY.

ANNABEL LEE.

It was many and many a year ago,
  In a kingdom by the sea,
That a maiden there lived, whom you may know
  By the name of Annabel Lee;
And this maiden she lived with no other thought
  Than to love, and be loved by me.

I was a child and she was a child,
  In this kingdom by the sea;
But we loved with a love that was more than love,
  I and my Annabel Lee—
With a love that the wingèd seraphs of heaven
  Coveted her and me.

And this was the reason that, long ago,
  In this kingdom by the sea,
A wind blew out of a cloud, chilling
  My beautiful Annabel Lee;

So that her high-born kinsman came
   And bore her away from me,
To shut her up in a sepulchre
   In this kingdom by the sea.

The angels, not half so happy in heaven,
   Went envying her and me,
Yes! that was the reason (as all men know,
   In this kingdom by the sea)
That the wind came out of the cloud by night,
   Chilling and killing my Annabel Lee.

But our love it was stronger by far than the love
   Of those who were older than we,
   Of many far wiser than we;
And neither the angels in heaven above,
   Nor the demons down under the sea,
Can ever dissever my soul from the soul
   Of the beautiful Annabel Lee.

For the moon never beams without bringing me dreams
   Of the beautiful Annabel Lee,
And the stars never rise, but I feel the bright eyes
   Of the beautiful Annabel Lee;
And so, all the night-tide, I lie down by the side
   Of my darling—my darling—my life and my bride,
     In the sepulchre there by the sea,
     In her tomb by the sounding sea.
EDGAR ALLAN POE.

THE GLOVE AND THE LIONS.

KING FRANCIS was a hearty king, and loved a royal sport,
And one day, as his lions fought, sat looking on the court.
The nobles fill'd the benches, with the ladies in their pride,
And 'mongst them sat the Count de Lorge, with one for whom he sigh'd:
And truly 'twas a gallant thing to see that crowning show,
Valor and love, and a king above, and the royal beasts below.

Ramp'd and roar'd the lions, with horrid laughing jaws;
They bit, they glared, gave blows like beams, a wind went with their paws,
With wallowing might and stifled roar they roll'd on one another,
Till all the pit with sand and mane was in a thunderous smother;
The bloody foam above the bars came whisking through the air;
Said Francis then, "Faith, gentlemen, we're better here than there."

De Lorge's love o'erheard the king, a beauteous, lively dame,
With smiling lips and sharp bright eyes, which always seem'd the same;
She thought, The Count my lover is brave as brave can be;
He surely would do wondrous things to show his love of me;
King, ladies, lovers, all look on; the occasion is divine;
I'll drop my glove, to prove his love; great glory will be mine.

She dropp'd her glove, to prove his love, then look'd at him and smiled;
He bow'd, and in a moment leap'd among the lions wild:
The leap was quick, return was quick, he has regain'd his place,
Then threw the glove, but not with love, right in the lady's face.
"By heaven," said Francis, "rightly done!" and he rose from where he sat;
"No love," quoth he, "but vanity, sets love a task like that."
LEIGH HUNT.

THE THREE RAVENS.

THERE were three ravens sat on a tree,
They were as black as they might be.

The one of them said to his mate,
"Where shall we our breakfast take?"

"Down in yonder green field,
There lies a knight slain under his shield;

"His hounds they lie down at his feet,
  So well do they their master keep;

"His hawks they fly so eagerly,
  There's no fowl dare come him nigh."

Down there comes a fallow doe,
  As great with young as she might go.

She lifted up his bloody head,
  And kiss'd his wounds that were so red.

She got him up upon her back,
  And carried him to earthen lake.

She buried him before the prime,
  She was dead herself before even-song time.

God send every gentleman
  Such hawks, such hounds, and such a leman.
                        AUTHOR UNKNOWN.

THE TWA CORBIES.

As I gaed doun by yon house-en'
Twa corbies there were sittan their lane:
The tane unto the tother sae,
"Oh where shall we gae dine to-day?"

"Oh down beside yon new-faun birk
There lies a new-slain knicht;
Nae livin kens that he lies there,
But his horse, his hounds, and his lady fair.

"His horse is to the huntin gane,
His hounds to bring the wild deer hame;
His lady's ta'en another mate;
Sae we may make our dinner swate.

"Oh we'll sit on his bonnie briest-bane,
And we'll pyke out his bonnie gray een;
Wi' ae lock o' his gowden hair
We'll theek our nest when it blaws bare.

"Mony a ane for him maks mane,
But nane sall ken where he is gane;
Ower his banes, when they are bare,
The wind sall blaw for evermair!"
                        AUTHOR UNKNOWN.

BURD HELEN.

LORD JOHN stood in his stable door,
  Said he was boun' to ride:
Burd Helen stood in her bouir door,
  Said she'd run by his side.

"The corn is turning ripe, Lord John;
  The nuts are growing fu':
An' ye are boun' for your ain countrie;
  Fain wad I go with you."

"Wi' me, Helen! wi' me, Helen!
  What wad ye do wi' me?
I've mair need o' a little foot-page,
  Than of the like o' thee."

"O, I will be your little foot-boy,
  To wait upon your steed;
And I will be your little foot-page,
  Your leish of hounds to lead."

"But my hounds will eat the breid o' wheat,
  And ye the dust and bran;
Then will ye sit and sigh, Helen,
  That e'er ye lo'ed a man."

"O, your dogs may eat the gude wheat-breid,
  And I the dust and bran;
Yet will I sing and say, weel's me,
  That e'er I lo'ed a man!"

"O, better ye'd stay at hame, Helen,
  And sew your silver seam;
For my house is in the far Hielands,
  And ye'll ha'e puir welcome hame."

"I winna stay, Lord John," she said,
  "To sew my silver seam;
Though your house is in the far Hielands,
  And I'll ha'e puir welcome hame."

"Then if you'll be my foot-page, Helen,
  As you tell unto me,
Then you must cut your gown of green
  An inch abune your knee.

"So you must cut your yellow locks
  An inch abune your e'e;
You must tell no man what is my name:
  My foot-page then you'll be."

Then he has luppen on his white steed,
  And straight awa' did ride;
Burd Helen, dressed in men's array,
  She ran fast by his side.

And he was ne'er sae lack a knicht,
  As ance wad bid her ride;
And she was ne'er sae mean a May,
  As ance wad bid him bide.

Lord John he rade, Burd Helen ran,
  A live-long summer day;
Until they cam to Clyde-water,
  Was filled frae bank to brae.

"Seest thou yon water, Helen," said he,
  "That flows from bank to brim?"
"I trust to God, Lord John," she said,
  "You ne'er will see me swim!"

But he was ne'er sae lack a knicht,
  As ance wad bid her ride;
Nor did he sae much as reach his hand,
  To help her ower the tide.

The firsten step that she wade in,
  She wadit to the knee;
"Ochone, alas," quo' that ladye fair,
  "This water's no for me!"

The second step that she wade in,
  She steppit to the middle:
Then, sighing, said that fair ladye,
  "I've wet my gowden girdle."

The thirden step that she wade in,
  She steppit to the neck;
When that the bairn that she was wi',
  For cauld began to quake.

"Lie still, my babe; lie still, my babe;
  Lie still as lang's ye may:
Your father, that rides on horseback high,
  Cares little for us twae."

And when she cam to the other side,
  She sat down on a stane;
Says, "Them that made me, help me now;
  For I am far frae hame!

"O, tell me this, now, good Lord John;
  In pity tell to me;
How far is it to your lodging,
  Where we this nicht maun be?"

"O, dinna ye see yon castle, Helen,
  Stands on yon sunny lea?
There ye'se get ane o' my mother's men:
  Ye'se get nae mair o' me."

"O, weel see I your bonnie castell
  Stands on yon sunny lea;
But I'se hae nane o' your mother's men,
  Though I never get mair o' thee."

"But there is in yon castle, Helen,
  That stands on yonder lea,
There is a lady in yon castle,
  Will sinder you and me."

"I wish nae ill to that ladye,
  She comes na in my thocht:
But I wish the maid maist o' your love,
  That dearest has you bocht."

When he cam to the porter's yett,
  He tirled at the pin;
And wha sae ready as the bauld porter,
  To open and let him in?

Many a lord and lady bright
  Met Lord John in the closs;
But the bonniest lady among them a'
  Was hauding Lord John's horse.

Four and twenty gay ladyes
  Led him through bouir and ha';
But the fairest lady that was there
  Led his horse to the sta'.

Then up bespak Lord John's sister;
  These were the words spak she:
"You have the prettiest foot-page, brother,
  My eyes did ever see—

"But that his middle is sae thick,
  His girdle sae wond'rous hie:
Let him, I pray thee, good Lord John,
  To chamber go with me."

"It is not fit for a little foot-page,
  That has run through moss and mire,
To go into chamber with any ladye
  That wears so rich attire.

"It were more meet for a little foot-page,
  That has run through moss and mire,
To take his supper upon his knee,
  And sit doun by the kitchen fire."

When bells were rung, and mass was sung,
  And a' men boun' to meat,
Burd Helen was, at the bye-table,
  Amang the pages set.

"O, eat and drink, my bonnie boy,
  The white breid and the beer."
"The never a bit can I eat or drink;
  My heart's sae fu' o' fear."

"O, eat and drink, my bonnie boy,
  The white breid and the wine."
"O, the never a bit can I eat or drink;
  My heart's sae fu' o' pyne."

But out and spak Lord John his mother,
  And a skeely woman was she:
"Where met ye, my son, wi' that bonnie boy,
  That looks sae sad on thee?

"Sometimes his cheek is rosy red,
  And sometimes deidly wan:
He's liker a woman grit wi' child,
  Than a young lord's serving-man."

"O, it maks me laugh, my mother dear,
  Sic words to hear frae thee;
He is a squire's ae dearest son,
  That for love has followed me.

"Rise up, rise up, my bonnie boy;
  Gi'e my horse corn and hay."
"O that I will, my master deir,
  As quickly as I may."

She took the hay aneath her arm,
  The corn intill her hand;
But atween the stable door and the sta'
  Burd Helen made a stand.

"O room ye round, my bonnie broun steids;
  O room ye near the wa';
For the pain that strikes through my twa
      sides,
  I fear, will gar me fa'."

She leaned her back again' the wa';
  Strong travail came her on;
And, e'en among the great horse' feet,
  She has brought forth her son.

When bells were rung, and mass was sung,
  And a' men boun' for bed,
Lord John's mother and sister gay
  In ae bouir they were laid.

Lord John hadna weel got aff his claes,
  Nor was he weel laid doun,
Till his mother heard a bairn greet,
  And a woman's heavy moan.

"Win up, win up, Lord John," she said;
  "Seek neither stockings nor shoen:
For I ha'e heard a bairn loud greet,
  And a woman's heavy moan!"

Richt hastilie he rase him up,
  Socht neither hose nor shoen;
And he's doen him to the stable door,
  By the lee licht o' the mune.

"O, open the door, Burd Helen," he said,
  "O, open and let me in;
I want to see if my steed be fed,
  Or my greyhounds fit to rin."

"O lullaby, my own deir child!
  Lullaby, deir child, deir!
I wold thy father were a king,
  Thy mother laid on a bier!"

"O, open the door, Burd Helen," he says,
  "O, open the door to me;
Or, as my sword hangs by my gair,
  I'll gar it gang in three!"

"That never was my mother's custome,
  And I hope it's ne'er be mine;
A knicht into her companie,
  When she dries a' her pyne."

He hit the door then wi' his foot,
  Sae did he wi' his knee;
Till door o' deal, and locks o' steel,
  In splinders he gart flee.

"An askin', an askin', Lord John," she says,
  "An askin' ye'll grant me;
The meanest maid about your house,
  To bring a drink to me.

"An askin', an askin', my dear Lord John,
  An askin' ye'll grant me;
The warsten bouir in a' your touirs,
  For thy young son and me!"

"I grant, I grant your askins, Helen,
  An' that and mair frae me;
The very best bouir in a' my touirs,
  For my young son and thee.

"O, have thou comfort, fair Helen,
  Be of good cheer, I pray;
And your bridal and your kirking baith
  Shall stand upon ae day."

And he has ta'en her Burd Helen,
  And rowed her in the silk;
And he has ta'en his ain young son,
  And washed him in the milk.

And there was ne'er a gayer bridegroom,
   Nor yet a blyther bride,
As they, Lord John and Lady Helen,
   Neist day to kirk did ride.
AUTHOR UNKNOWN.

THE HIGH TIDE ON THE COAST OF LINCOLNSHIRE. (1571.)

THE old mayor climb'd the belfry tower,
   The ringers rang by two, by three;
" Pull, if ye never pull'd before;
   Good ringers, pull your best," quoth he,
" Play uppe, play uppe, O Boston bells!
Ply all your changes, all your swells,
   Play up, 'The Brides of Enderby.' "

Men say it was a stolen tyde—
   The Lord that sent it, He knows all;
But in myne ears doth still abide
   The message that the bells let fall:
And there was naught of strange, beside
The flights of mews and peewits pied
   By millions crouch'd on the old sea wall.

I sat and spun within the doore,
   My thread brake off, I raised myne eyes;
The level sun, like ruddy ore,
   Lay sinking in the barren skies;
And dark against day's golden death
She moved where Lindis wandereth,
   My sonne's faire wife, Elizabeth.

"Cusha! Cusha! Cusha!" calling,
   Ere the early dews were falling,
   Farre away I heard her song.
"Cusha! Cusha!" all along;
Where the reedy Lindis floweth,
   Floweth, floweth,
From the meads where melick groweth
   Faintly came her milking-song—

"Cusha! Cusha! Cusha!" calling,
" For the dews will soon be falling;
   Leave your meadow-grasses mellow,
      Mellow, mellow;
   Quit your cowslips, cowslips yellow;
   Come uppe, Whitefoot, come uppe, Lightfoot;
   Quit the stalks of parsley hollow,
      Hollow, hollow;
   Come uppe, Jetty, rise and follow,
      From the clovers lift your head;
   Come up, Whitefoot, come up, Lightfoot,
   Come uppe, Jetty, rise and follow,
      Jetty, to the milking-shed."

If it be long, ay, long ago,
   When I beginne to think howe long,
Againe I hear the Lindis flow,
   Swift as an arrowe sharp and strong;
And all the aire, it seemeth mee,
Bin full of floating bells (sayth shee),
   That ring the tune of Enderby.

Alle fresh the level pasture lay,
   And not a shadowe mote be seene,
Save where full fyve good miles away
   The steeple tower'd from out the greene;
And lo! the great bell farre and wide
Was heard in all the country side
   That Saturday at eventide.

The swanherds where their sedges are
   Moved on in sunset's golden breath,
The shepherd-lads I heard afarre,
   And my sonne's wife, Elizabeth;
Till floating o'er the grassy sea
Came downe that kindly message free,
   The "Brides of Mavis Enderby."

Then some look'd uppe into the sky,
   And all along where Lindis flows
To where the goodly vessels lie,
   And where the lordly steeple shows.
They sayde, "And why should this thing be?
What danger lowers by land or sea?
   They ring the tune of Enderby!

" For evil news from Mablethorpe,
   Of pyrate galleys warping down;
For shippes ashore beyond the scorpe,
   They have not spared to wake the towne:
But while the west bin red to see,
And storms be none, and pyrates flee,
   Why ring 'The Brides of Enderby'?"

I look'd without, and lo! my sonne
   Came riding down with might and main;
He raised a shout as he drew on,
   Till all the welkin rang again,
"Elizabeth! Elizabeth!"
(A sweeter woman ne'er drew breath
   Than my sonne's wife, Elizabeth.)

"The old sea wall," he cried, "is downe,
   The rising tide comes on apace,
And boats adrift in yonder towne
   Go sailing uppe the market-place."
He shook as one that looks on death:
"God, save you, mother!" straight he saith;
"Where is my wife, Elizabeth?"

"Good sonne, where Lindis winds her way,
   With her two bairns I mark'd her long,
And ere yon bells beganne to play
   Afar I heard her milking song."
He look'd across the grassy lea,
To right, to left, "Ho, Enderby!"
They rang "The Brides of Enderby!"

With that he cried and beat his breast;
   For, lo! along the river's bed
A mighty eygre rear'd his crest,
   And uppe the Lindis raging sped.
It swept with thunderous noises loud,
Shaped like a curling snow-white cloud
Or like a demon in a shroud.

And rearing Lindis backward press'd
   Shook all her trembling bankes amaine,
Then madly at the eygre's breast
   Flung uppe her weltering walls again.
Then bankes came down with ruin and rout,
Then beaten foam flew round about,
Then all the mighty floods were out.

So farre, so fast the eygre drave,
   The heart had hardly time to beat,
Before a shallow seething wave
   Sobb'd in the grasses at oure feet;
The feet had hardly time to flee
Before it brake against the knee,
And all the world was in the sea.

Upon the roof we sate that night,
   The noise of bells went sweeping by;
I mark'd the lofty beacon light
   Stream from the church tower, red and high;
A lurid mark and dread to see;
And awesome bells they were to mee,
That in the dark rang "Enderby."

They rang the sailor lads to guide
   From roofe to roofe who fearless row'd;
And I—my sonne was at my side,
   And yet the ruddy beacon glow'd;
And yet he moan'd beneath his breath,
"Oh come in life, or come in death,
O lost! my love, Elizabeth."

And didst thou visit him no more?
   Thou didst, thou didst, my daughter deare;
The waters laid thee at his doore,
   Ere yet the early dawn was clear.
Thy pretty bairns in fast embrace,
The lifted sun shone on thy face,
Downe drifted to thy dwelling-place.

That flow strew'd wrecks about the grass,
   That ebbe swept out the flocks to sea;
A fatal ebbe and flow, alas!
   To manye more than myne and mee;
But each will mourn his own (she saith),
And sweeter woman ne'er drew breath
Than my sonne's wife, Elizabeth.

I shall never hear her more
   By the reedy Lindis shore,
"Cusha! Cusha! Cusha!" calling,
   Ere the early dews be falling;
I shall never hear her song,
   "Cusha! Cusha!" all along
Where the sunny Lindis floweth,
     Goeth, floweth;
From the meads where melick groweth,
When the water winding down,
Onward floweth to the town.

I shall never see her more
Where the reeds and rushes quiver,
   Shiver, quiver;
Stand beside the sobbing river,
Sobbing, throbbing, in its falling
To the sandy, lonesome shore;
I shall never hear her calling,
"Leave your meadow grasses mellow,
   Mellow, mellow;
Quit your cowslips, cowslips yellow;
Come uppe Whitefoot, come uppe Lightfoot,
Quit your pipes of parsley hollow,
   Hollow, hollow;
Come uppe Lightfoot, rise and follow,
   Lightfoot, Whitefoot,
From your clovers lift the head;
Come uppe, Jetty, follow, follow,
Jetty, to the milking-shed."
JEAN INGELOW.

THE SANDS OF DEE.

"OH, Mary, go and call the cattle home,
  And call the cattle home,
  And call the cattle home,
    Across the sands of Dee."
The western wind was wild and dank with
    foam,
  And all alone went she.

The western tide crept up along the sand,
  And o'er and o'er the sand,
  And round and round the sand,
    As far as eye could see.
The rolling mist came down and hid the
    land:
  And never home came she.

"Oh! is it weed, or fish, or floating hair—
  A tress of golden hair,
  A drownèd maiden's hair,
    Above the nets at sea?"
Was never salmon yet that shone so fair
  Among the stakes on Dee.

They row'd her in across the rolling
    foam,
  The cruel crawling foam,
  The cruel hungry foam,
    To her grave beside the sea.
But still the boatmen hear her call the
    cattle home
  Across the sands of Dee.
            CHARLES KINGSLEY.

BARBARA ALLEN'S CRUELTY.

ALL in the merry month of May,
  When green buds they were swelling,
Young Jemmy Grove on his death-bed lay
  For love o' Barbara Allen.

He sent his man unto her then,
  To the town where she was dwelling:
"Oh haste and come to my master dear,
  If your name be Barbara Allen."

Slowly, slowly rase she up,
  And she cam' where he was lying;
And when she drew the curtain by,
  Says, "Young man, I think you're
    dying."

"Oh, it's I am sick, and very, very sick,
  And it's a' for Barbara Allen."

"Oh the better for me ye'se never be,
  Tho' your heart's blude were a-spilling!

"O, dinna ye min', young man," she says,
  "When the red wine ye were filling,
That ye made the healths gae round and
    round,
  And ye slighted Barbara Allen?"

He turn'd his face unto the wa',
  And death was wi' him dealing:
"Adieu, adieu, my dear friends a';
  Be kind to Barbara Allen."

As she was walking o'er the fields,
  She heard the dead-bell knelling;
And every jow the dead-bell gave,
  It cried, "Woe to Barbara Allen!"

"O mother, mother, mak' my bed,
  To lay me down in sorrow.
My love has died for me to-day,
  I'll die for him to-morrow."
            AUTHOR UNKNOWN.

LAMENT OF THE BORDER WIDOW.

MY love he built me a bonny bower,
And clad it a' wi' lily flower;
A brawer bower ye ne'er did see,
Than my true-love he built for me.

There came a man by middle day,
He spied his sport, and went away;
And brought the king that very night,
Who brake my bower and slew my knight.

He slew my knight, to me sae dear;
He slew my knight, and poin'd his gear:
My servants all for life did flee,
And left me in extremitie.

I sew'd his sheet, making my mane;
I watch'd the corpse mysell alane;
I watch'd his body night and day;
No living creature came that way.

I took his body on my back,
And whiles I gaed, and whiles I sat;
I digg'd a grave, and laid him in,
And happ'd him with the sod sae green.

But think nae ye my heart was sair,
When I laid the moul' on his yellow hair?

Oh, think nae ye my heart was wae,
When I turn'd about, away to gae?

Nae living man I'll love again,
Since that my lovely knight is slain;
Wi' ae lock o' his yellow hair
I'll chain my heart for evermair.
AUTHOR UNKNOWN.

THE CRUEL SISTER.

THERE were two sisters sat in a bour,
    Binnorie, O Binnorie;
There came a knight to be their wooer;
    By the bonny milldams of Binnorie.

He courted the eldest with glove and ring,
    Binnorie, O Binnorie;
But he lo'ed the youngest abune a' thing;
    By the bonny milldams of Binnorie.

He courted the eldest with broach and knife,
    Binnorie, O Binnorie;
But he lo'ed the youngest abune his life;
    By the bonny milldams of Binnorie.

The eldest she was vexèd sair,
    Binnorie, O Binnorie;
And sore envied her sister fair;
    By the bonny milldams of Binnorie.

The eldest said to the youngest ane,
    Binnorie, O Binnorie;
"Will ye go and see our father's ships come in?"
    By the bonny milldams of Binnorie.

She's ta'en her by the lily hand,
    Binnorie, O Binnorie;
And led her down to the river strand;
    By the bonny milldams of Binnorie.

The youngest stude upon a stane,
    Binnorie, O Binnorie;
The eldest came and push'd her in;
    By the bonny milldams of Binnorie.

She took her by the middle sma',
    Binnorie, O Binnorie;
And dash'd her bonny back to the jaw;
    By the bonny milldams of Binnorie.

"O sister, sister, reach your hand,
    Binnorie, O Binnorie;
And ye shall be heir of half my land."—
    By the bonny milldams of Binnorie.

"O sister, I'll not reach my hand,
    Binnorie, O Binnorie;
And I'll be heir of all your land;
    By the bonny milldams of Binnorie.

"Shame fa' the hand that I should take,
    Binnorie, O Binnorie:
It's twined me and my world's make."—
    By the bonny milldams of Binnorie.

"O sister, reach me but your glove,
    Binnorie, O Binnorie;
And sweet William shall be your love."—
    By the bonny milldams of Binnorie.

"Sink on, nor hope for hand or glove!
    Binnorie, O Binnorie;
And sweet William shall better be my love,
    By the bonny milldams of Binnorie.

"Your cherry cheeks and your yellow hair,
    Binnorie, O Binnorie;
Garr'd me gang maiden evermair."
    By the bonny milldams of Binnorie.

Sometimes she sunk, and sometimes she swam,
    Binnorie, O Binnorie;
Until she cam to the miller's dam;
    By the bonny milldams of Binnorie.

"O father, father, draw your dam!
    Binnorie, O Binnorie;
There's either a mermaid, or a milk-white swan."
    By the bonny milldams of Binnorie.

The miller hasted and drew his dam!
    Binnorie, O Binnorie;
And there he found a drown'd woman;
    By the bonny milldams of Binnorie.

You could not see her yellow hair,
    Binnorie, O Binnorie;
For gowd and pearls that were so rare;
    By the bonny milldams of Binnorie.

You could not see her middle sma',
    Binnorie, O Binnorie;
Her gowden girdle was sae' bra';
    By the bonny milldams of Binnorie.

A famous harper passing by,
    Binnorie, O Binnorie;
The sweet pale face he chanced to spy;
    By the bonny milldams of Binnorie.

And when he look'd that lady on,
    Binnorie, O Binnorie;
He sigh'd and made a heavy moan;
    By the bonny milldams of Binnorie.

He made a harp of her breast-bone,
    Binnorie, O Binnorie;
Whose sounds would melt a heart of stone;
    By the bonny milldams of Binnorie.

The strings he framed of her yellow hair,
    Binnorie, O Binnorie;
Whose notes made sad the listening ear;
    By the bonny milldams of Binnorie.

He brought it to her father's hall,
    Binnorie, O Binnorie;
And there was the court assembled all;
    By the bonny milldams of Binnorie.

He laid his harp upon a stone,
    Binnorie, O Binnorie;
And straight it began to play alone;
    By the bonny milldams of Binnorie.

" Oh yonder sits my father, the king,
    Binnorie, O Binnorie;
And yonder sits my mother, the queen;
    By the bonny milldams of Binnorie.

" And yonder stands my brother Hugh,
    Binnorie, O Binnorie;
And by him my William, sweet and true."
    By the bonny milldams of Binnorie.

But the last tune that the harp play'd then,
    Binnorie, O Binnorie;
Was—" Woe to my sister, false Helen!"
    By the bonny milldams of Binnorie.
                  AUTHOR UNKNOWN.

BONNIE GEORGE CAMPBELL.

HIE upon Hielands,
    And low upon Tay,
Bonnie George Campbell
    Rade out on a day.

Saddled and bridled
    And gallant rade he;
Hame cam his gude horse,
    But never cam he.

Out cam his old mither
    Greeting fu' sair,
And out cam his bonnie bride
    Rivin' her hair.
Saddled and bridled
    And booted rade he;
Toom hame cam the saddle,
    But never cam he.

" My meadow lies green,
    And my corn is unshorn;
My barn is to build,
    And my baby's unborn."
Saddled and bridled
    And booted rade he;
Toom hame cam the saddle,
    But never cam he!
                  AUTHOR UNKNOWN.

THE LAST BUCCANEER.

OH, England is a pleasant place for them that's rich and high;
But England is a cruel place for such poor folks as I;
And such a port for mariners I ne'er shall see again
As the pleasant Isle of Avès, beside the Spanish main.

There were forty craft in Avès that were both swift and stout,
All furnish'd well with small-arms and cannons round about;
And a thousand men in Avès made laws so fair and free
To choose their valiant captains and obey them loyally.

Thence we sail'd against the Spaniard with his hoards of plate and gold,
Which he wrung with cruel tortures from the Indian folk of old;
Likewise the merchant captains, with hearts as hard as stone,
Who flog men and keel-haul them and starve them to the bone.

Oh the palms grew high in Avès and fruits
    that shone like gold,
And the colibris and parrots they were
    gorgeous to behold;
And the negro maids to Avès from bondage
    fast did flee,
To welcome gallant sailors a-sweeping in
    from sea.

Oh sweet it was in Avès to hear the land-
    ward breeze
A-swing with good tobacco in a net be-
    tween the trees,
With a negro lass to fan you while you lis-
    ten'd to the roar
Of the breakers on the reef outside that
    never touch'd the shore.

But Scripture saith, an ending to all fine
    things must be,
So the King's ships sail'd on Avès, and
    quite put down were we.
All day we fought like bulldogs, but they
    burst the booms at night;
And I fled in a piragua sore wounded from
    the fight.

Nine days I floated starving, and a negro
    lass beside,
Till for all I tried to cheer her, the poor
    young thing she died;
But as I lay a-gasping a Bristol sail came
    by,
And brought me home to England here to
    beg until I die.

And now I'm old and going—I'm sure I
    can't tell where;
One comfort is, this world's so hard I can't
    be worse off there:
If I might but be a sea-dove I'd fly across
    the main,
To the pleasant Isle of Avès, to look at it
    once again.   CHARLES KINGSLEY.

THE KING OF DENMARK'S RIDE.

WORD was brought to the Danish king
    (Hurry!)
That the love of his heart lay suffering
And pined for the comfort his voice would
    bring;
    (Oh ride as though you were flying!)
Better he loves each golden curl
On the brow of that Scandinavian girl
Than his rich crown jewels of ruby and
    pearl;
And his Rose of the Isles is dying!

Thirty nobles saddled with speed;
    (Hurry!)
Each one mounting a gallant steed
Which he kept for battle and days of
    need;
    (Oh ride as though you were flying!)
Spurs were struck in the foaming flank;
Worn-out chargers stagger'd and sank;
Bridles were slacken'd, and girths were
    burst;
But ride as they would, the king rode
    first,
For his Rose of the Isles lay dying!

His nobles are beaten one by one;
    (Hurry!)
They have fainted, and falter'd, and home-
    ward gone;
His little fair page now follows alone,
    For strength and for courage trying.
The king look'd back at that faithful child;
Wan was the face that answering smiled;
They pass'd the drawbridge with clattering
    din,
Then he dropp'd; and only the king rode
    in
Where his Rose of the Isles lay dying!

The king blew a blast on his bugle horn;
    (Silence!)
No answer came; but faint and forlorn
An echo return'd on the cold gray morn,
    Like the breath of a spirit sighing.
The castle portal stood grimly wide;
None welcomed the king from that weary
    ride;
For dead, in the light of the dawning
    day,
The pale sweet form of the welcomer lay,
    Who had yearn'd for his voice while
    dying!

The panting steed, with a drooping crest,
    Stood weary.
The king return'd from her chamber of
    rest,
The thick sobs choking in his breast;
    And, that dumb companion eying,

The tears gush'd forth which he strove to
    check;
He bow'd his head on his charger's neck:
"O steed—that every nerve didst strain,
Dear steed, our ride hath been in vain
    To the halls where my love lay dying!"
                  CAROLINE NORTON.

A SONG OF THE NORTH.

"AWAY! away!" cried the stout Sir John,
"While the blossoms are on the trees;
For the summer is short and the time speeds on,
    As we sail for the northern seas.
Ho! gallant Crozier and brave Fitz James!
    We will startle the world, I trow,
When we find a way through the Northern seas
    That never was found till now!
A good stout ship is the Erebus
    As ever unfurl'd a sail,
And the Terror will match with as brave a one
    As ever outrode a gale."

So they bade farewell to their pleasant homes,
    To the hills and the valleys green,
With three hearty cheers for their native isle,
    And three for the English queen.
They sped them away beyond cape and bay,
    Where the day and the night are one—
Where the hissing light in the heavens grew bright
    And flamed like a midnight sun.
There was naught below save the fields of snow,
    That stretch'd to the icy Pole;
And the Esquimaux, in his strange canoe,
    Was the only living soul!

Along the coast like a giant host
    The glittering icebergs frown'd,
Or they met on the main like a battle-plain,
    And crash'd with a fearful sound!
The seal and the bear, with a curious stare,
    Look'd down from the frozen heights,
And the stars in the skies with their great wild eyes,
    Peer'd out from the Northern Lights.
The gallant Crozier and brave Fitz James,
    And even the stout Sir John,
Felt a doubt like a chill through their warm hearts thrill
    As they urged the good ships on.

They sped them away, beyond cape and bay,
    Where even the tear-drops freeze;
But no way was found by a strait or sound,
    To sail through the Northern seas;
They sped them away, beyond cape and bay,
    And they sought, but they sought in vain,
For no way was found, through the ice around,
    To return to their homes again.
Then the wild waves rose, and the waters froze
    Till they closed like a prison-wall;
And the icebergs stood, in the sullen flood,
    Like their jailers grim and tall.
O God! O God!—it was hard to die
    In that prison-house of ice!
For what was fame, or a mighty name,
    When life was the fearful price?

The gallant Crozier and brave Fitz James,
    And even the stout Sir John,
Had a secret dread and their hopes all fled,
    As the weeks and the months pass'd on.
Then the Ice King came, with his eyes of flame,
    And look'd on that fated crew;
His chilling breath was as cold as death,
    And it pierced their warm hearts through.
A heavy sleep, that was dark and deep,
    Came over their weary eyes,
And they dream'd strange dreams of the hills and streams,
    And the blue of their native skies.

The Christmas chimes of the good old times
    Were heard in each dying ear,

And the dancing feet and the voices sweet
  Of their wives and their children dear!
But it faded away—away—away!
  Like a sound on a distant shore;
And deeper and deeper grew the sleep,
  Till they slept to wake no more!

Oh, the sailor's wife and the sailor's child!
  They will weep and watch and pray;
And the Lady Jane, she will hope in vain
  As the long years pass away!
The gallant Crozier and brave Fitz James,
  And the good Sir John have found
An open way to a quiet bay,
  And a port where we all are bound.
Let the waters roar on the ice-bound shore
  That circles the frozen Pole,
But there is no sleep and no grave so deep
  That can hold a human *soul*.
ELIZABETH DOTEN.

THE LAKE OF THE DISMAL SWAMP.

"THEY made her a grave too cold and damp
  For a soul so warm and true;
And she's gone to the Lake of the Dismal Swamp,
  Where all night long, by a firefly lamp,
    She paddles her white canoe.
"And her firefly lamp I soon shall see,
  And her paddle I soon shall hear;
Long and loving our life shall be,
And I'll hide the maid in a cypress tree,
  When the footstep of death is near."

Away to the Dismal Swamp he speeds,—
  His path was rugged and sore,
Through tangled juniper, beds of reeds,
Through many a fen where the serpent feeds,
  And man never trod before.

And when on the earth he sank to sleep,
  If slumber his eyelids knew,
He lay where the deadly vine doth weep
Its venomous tear, and nightly steep
  The flesh with blistering dew!

And near him the she-wolf stirr'd the brake,
  And the copper-snake breathed in his ear,
Till he starting cried, from his dream awake,
"Oh when shall I see the dusky Lake,
  And the white canoe of my dear?"

He saw the Lake, and a meteor bright
  Quick over its surface play'd,—
"Welcome," he said, "my dear one's light!"
And the dim shore echo'd for many a night
  The name of the death-cold maid.

Till he hollow'd a boat of the birchen bark,
  Which carried him off from shore;
Far, far he follow'd the meteor spark,
The wind was high and the clouds were dark,
  And the boat return'd no more.

But oft, from the Indian hunter's camp,
  This lover and maid so true
Are seen at the hour of midnight damp
To cross the Lake by a firefly lamp,
  And paddle their white canoe!
THOMAS MOORE.

Build thee more stately mansions, O my Soul,
   As the swift seasons roll!
   Leave thy low-vaulted past!
Let each new temple, nobler than the last,
Shut thee from heaven with a dome more vast,
   Till thou at length art free,
Leaving thine outgrown shell by life's unresting sea!

Oliver Wendell Holmes.

POEMS OF NATURE.

A HYMN.

THE SEASONS.

THESE, as they change, Almighty Father, these
Are but the varied God. The rolling year
Is full of Thee. Forth in the pleasing spring
Thy Beauty walks, thy Tenderness and Love.
Wide flush the fields; the softening air is balm;
Echo the mountains round; the forest smiles;
And every sense, and every heart, is joy.
Then comes thy Glory in the summer months,
With light and heat refulgent. Then thy Sun
Shoots full perfection through the swelling year;
And oft thy Voice in dreadful thunder speaks,
And oft at dawn, deep noon, or falling eve,
By brooks and groves, in hollow-whispering gales.
Thy Bounty shines in autumn unconfined,
And spreads a common feast for all that lives.
In winter awful Thou! with clouds and storms
Around Thee thrown, tempest o'er tempest roll'd,
Majestic darkness! On the whirlwind's wing,
Riding sublime, Thou bid'st the World adore,
And humblest Nature with thy northern blast.

Mysterious round! what skill, what force divine,
Deep felt, in these appear! a simple train,
Yet so delightful mix'd, with such kind art,
Such beauty and beneficence combined;
Shade, unperceived, so softening into shade;
And all so forming an harmonious whole,
That, as they still succeed, they ravish still.
But wandering oft, with brute unconscious gaze,
Man marks not Thee, marks not the mighty Hand,
That, ever busy, wheels the silent spheres;
Works in the secret deep; shoots, steaming, thence
The fair profusion that o'erspreads the spring;
Flings from the sun direct the flaming day;
Feeds every creature; hurls the tempest forth;
And, as on earth this grateful change revolves,
With transport touches all the springs of life.
Nature, attend! join, every living soul
Beneath the spacious temple of the sky,
In adoration join; and, ardent, raise
One general song! To Him, ye vocal gales,
Breathe soft, whose Spirit in your freshness breathes:
Oh, talk of Him in solitary glooms;
Where, o'er the rock, the scarcely waving pine
Fills the brown shade with a religious awe.
And ye, whose bolder note is heard afar,

Who shake the astonish'd world, lift high
    to heaven
The impetuous song, and say from whom
    you rage.
His praise, ye brooks, attune, ye trembling
    rills;
And let me catch it as I muse along.
Ye headlong torrents, rapid and profound;
Ye softer floods, that lead the humid
    maze
Along the vale; and thou, majestic main,
A secret world of wonders in thyself,
Sound His stupendous praise, whose greater
    voice
Or bids you roar, or bids your roarings
    fall.
Soft roll your incense, herbs, and fruits,
    and flowers,
In mingled clouds to Him, whose sun
    exalts,
Whose breath perfumes you, and whose
    pencil paints.
Ye forests, bend, ye harvests, wave, to Him;
Breathe your still song into the reaper's
    heart,
As home he goes beneath the joyous
    moon.
Ye that keep watch in heaven, as earth
    asleep
Unconscious lies, effuse your mildest
    beams,
Ye constellations, while your angels strike,
Amid the spangled sky, the silver lyre.
Great source of day! best image here below
Of thy Creator, ever pouring wide,
From world to world, the vital ocean
    round,
On Nature write with every beam His
    praise.
The thunder rolls: be hush'd the prostrate
    world,
While cloud to cloud returns the solemn
    hymn.
Bleat out afresh, ye hills; ye mossy rocks,
Retain the sound; the broad responsive
    low,
Ye valleys, raise; for the Great Shepherd
    reigns,
And His unsuffering kingdom yet will
    come.

Ye woodlands all, awake: a boundless
    song
Burst from the groves; and when the restless day,
Expiring, lays the warbling world asleep,
Sweetest of birds! sweet Philomela, charm
The listening shades, and teach the night
    His praise.
Ye chief, for whom the whole creation
    smiles,
At once the head, the heart, and tongue
    of all,
Crown the great hymn! in swarming cities
    vast,
Assembled men to the deep organ join
The long-resounding voice, oft breaking
    clear,
At solemn pauses, through the swelling
    bass;
And, as each mingling flame increases
    each,
In one united ardor rise to heaven.
Or if you rather choose the rural shade,
And find a fane in every sacred grove,
There let the shepherd's flute, the virgin's
    lay,
The prompting seraph, and the poet's
    lyre,
Still sing the God of Seasons, as they
    roll.
For me, when I forget the darling theme,
Whether the blossom blows, the summer
    ray
Russets the plain, inspiring autumn gleams,
Or winter rises in the blackening east,
Be my tongue mute, my fancy paint no
    more,
And, dead to joy, forget my heart to beat!
Should fate command me to the farthest
    verge
Of the green earth, to distant barbarous
    climes,
Rivers unknown to song,—where first the
    sun
Gilds Indian mountains, or his setting
    beam
Flames on the Atlantic isles,—'tis naught
    to me:
Since God is ever present, ever felt,
In the void waste, as in the city full,
And where He vital breathes, there must
    be joy.

When even at last the solemn hour shall
    come,
And wing my mystic flight to future
    worlds,
I cheerful will obey; there, with new
    powers,
Will rising wonders sing: I cannot go
Where Universal Love not smiles around,
Sustaining all yon orbs, and all their
    suns;
From seeming evil still educing good,
And better thence again, and better still,
In infinite progression. But I lose
Myself in Him, in Light ineffable!
Come, then, expressive Silence, muse His
    praise.
                              JAMES THOMSON.

TO PAN.

ALL ye woods, and trees, and bowers,
All ye virtues and ye powers
That inhabit in the lakes,
In the pleasant springs or brakes,
        Move your feet
        To our sound,
        Whilst we greet
        All this ground
With his honor and his name
That defends our flocks from blame.

He is great, and he is just,
He is ever good, and must
Thus be honor'd. Daffodillies,
Roses, pinks, and lovèd lilies,
        Let us fling,
        Whilst we sing,
        Ever hòly,
        Ever holy,
Ever honor'd, ever young!
Thus great Pan is ever sung.
                    BEAUMONT AND FLETCHER.

DESCRIPTION OF SPRING.

THE soote season, that bud and bloom forth
    brings,
  With green hath clad the hill, and eke
    the vale;
The nightingale with feathers new she
    sings;
  The turtle to her make hath told her
    tale.
Summer is come, for every spray now
    springs;
  The hart hath hung his old head on the
    pale,
The buck in brake his winter coat he
    slings;
  The fishes flete with new repairèd
    scale;
The adder all her slough away she flings;
  The swift swallow pursueth the flies
    smale;
The busy bee her honey now she mings;
  Winter is worn that was the flowres'
    bale.
And thus I see among these pleasant
    things
  Each care decays, and yet my sorrow
    springs.
                              HENRY HOWARD
                              (Earl of Surrey).

TO SPRING.

SWEET Spring, thou turn'st with all thy
    goodly train,
  Thy head with flames, thy mantle bright
    with flowers;
  The zephyrs curl the green locks of the
    plain,
The clouds for joy in pearls weep down
    their showers.
Thou turn'st, sweet youth—but, ah! my
    pleasant hours
  And happy days, with thee come not
    again;
  The sad memorials only of my pain
Do with thee turn, which turn my sweets
    in sours.
Thou art the same which still thou wast
    before,
  Delicious, wanton, amiable, fair;
But she whose breath embalm'd thy whole-
    some air
  Is gone; nor gold nor gems her can re-
    store.
Neglected Virtue, seasons go and come,
When thine forgot lie closèd in a tomb.

    What doth it serve to see sun's burning
        face?
And skies enamell'd with both Indies'
    gold?

Or moon at night in jetty chariot roll'd,
 And all the glory of that starry place?
What doth it serve earth's beauty to behold,
 The mountain's pride, the meadow's flowery grace;
The stately comeliness of forests old,
 The sport of floods which would themselves embrace?
What doth it serve to hear the sylvans' songs,
 The wanton merle, the nightingale's sad strains,
Which in dark shades seem to deplore my wrongs?
For what doth serve all that this world contains,
Sith she, for whom those once to me were dear,
No part of them can have now with me here?
WILLIAM DRUMMOND.

CHORUS.

FROM "ATALANTA IN CALYDON."

WHEN the hounds of spring are on winter's traces,
 The mother of months in meadow or plain
Fills the shadows and windy places
 With lisp of leaves and ripple of rain;
And the brown bright nightingale amorous
Is half assuaged for Itylus,
For the Thracian ships and the foreign faces;
The tongueless vigil, and all the pain.

Come with bows bent and with emptying of quivers,
 Maiden most perfect, lady of light,
With a noise of winds and many rivers,
 With a clamor of waters, and with might;
Bind on thy sandals, O thou most fleet,
Over the splendor and speed of thy feet!
For the faint east quickens, the wan west shivers,
 Round the feet of the day and the feet of the night.

Where shall we find her, how shall we sing to her,
 Fold our hands round her knees and cling?
Oh that man's heart were as fire, and could spring to her,
 Fire, or the strength of the streams that spring!
For the stars and the winds are unto her
As raiment, as songs of the harp-player;
For the risen stars and the fallen cling to her,
 And the south-west wind and the west wind sing.

For winter's rains and ruins are over,
 And all the season of snows and sins;
The days dividing lover and lover,
 The light that loses, the night that wins;
And time remember'd is grief forgotten,
And frosts are slain and flowers begotten,
And in green underwood and cover
 Blossom by blossom the spring begins.

The full streams feed on flower of rushes,
 Ripe grasses trammel a travelling foot,
The faint fresh flame of the young year flushes
 From leaf to flower and flower to fruit;
And fruit and leaf are as gold and fire,
And the oat is heard above the lyre,
And the hoof'd heel of a satyr crushes
 The chestnut-husk at the chestnut-root.

And Pan by noon and Bacchus by night,
 Fleeter of foot than the fleet-foot kid,
Follow with dancing and fill with delight
 The Mænad and the Bassarid;
And soft as lips that laugh and hide,
The laughing leaves of the trees divide,
And screen from seeing and leave in sight
 The god pursuing, the maiden hid.

The ivy falls with the Bacchanal's hair
 Over her eyebrows, shading her eyes;
The wild vine slipping down leaves bare
 Her bright breast shortening into sighs;
The wild vine slips with the weight of its leaves,
But the berried ivy catches and cleaves
To the limbs that glitter, the feet that scare
 The wolf that follows, the fawn that flies.
ALGERNON CHARLES SWINBURNE.

ODE.

ON THE SPRING.

Lo! where the rosy-bosom'd Hours,
    Fair Venus' train, appear,
Disclose the long-expecting flowers
    And wake the purple year!
The Attic warbler pours her throat
Responsive to the cuckoo's note,
    The untaught harmony of spring:
While, whispering pleasure as they fly,
Cool Zephyrs through the clear blue sky
    Their gather'd fragrance fling.

Where'er the oak's thick branches stretch
    A broader, browner shade,
Where'er the rude and moss-grown beech
    O'er-canopies the glade,
Beside some water's rushy brink
With me the Muse shall sit, and think
    (At ease reclined in rustic state)
How vain the ardor of the crowd,
How low, how little are the proud,
    How indigent the great!

Still is the toiling hand of Care;
    The panting herds repose:
Yet hark, how thro' the peopled air
    The busy murmur glows!
The insect youth are on the wing,
Eager to taste the honey'd spring
    And float amid the liquid noon:
Some lightly o'er the current skim,
Some show their gayly-gilded trim
    Quick-glancing to the sun.

To Contemplation's sober eye
    Such is the race of man;
And they that creep, and they that fly
    Shall end where they began.
Alike the busy and the gay
But flutter thro' life's little day,
    In Fortune's varying colors drest:
Brush'd by the hand of rough Mischance
Or chill'd by Age, their airy dance
    They leave, in dust to rest.

Methinks I hear in accents low
    The sportive kind reply:
Poor moralist! and what art thou?
    A solitary fly!
Thy joys no glittering female meets,
No hive hast thou of hoarded sweets,
No painted plumage to display:
On hasty wings thy youth is flown;
Thy sun is set, thy spring is gone—
    We frolic while 'tis May.
        THOMAS GRAY.

SPRING.

SPRING, the sweet spring, is the year's
    pleasant king;
Then blooms each thing, then maids dance
    in a ring.
Cold doth not sting, the pretty birds do
    sing,
    Cuckoo, jug-jug, pu-we, to-witta-woo!

The palm and may make country houses
    gay,
Lambs frisk and play, the shepherds pipe
    all day,
And we hear aye birds tune this merry
    lay,
    Cuckoo, jug-jug, pu-we, to-witta-woo!

The fields breathe sweet, the daisies kiss
    our feet,
Young lovers meet, old wives a-sunning
    sit,
In every street these tunes our ears do
    greet,
    Cuckoo, jug-jug, pu-we, to-witta-woo!
      Spring! the sweet spring!
        THOMAS NASH.

SONG. ON MAY MORNING.

Now the bright morning star, day's har-
    binger,
Comes dancing from the east, and leads
    with her
The flowery May, who from her green lap
    throws
The yellow cowslip and the pale prim-
    rose.
Hail, bounteous May, that doth inspire
Mirth, and youth, and warm desire!
Woods and groves are of thy dressing,
Hill and dale doth boast thy blessing.
Thus we salute thee with our early song,
And welcome thee, and wish thee long.
        JOHN MILTON.

SONG TO MAY.

May! queen of blossoms
    And fulfilling flowers,
With what pretty music
    Shall we charm the hours?
Wilt thou have pipe and reed,
Blown in the open mead?
Or to the lute give heed
    In the green bowers?

Thou hast no need of us,
    Or pipe or wire,
That hast the golden bee
    Ripen'd with fire;
And many thousand more
Songsters, that thee adore,
Filling earth's grassy floor
    With new desire.

Thou hast thy mighty herds,
    Tame, and free livers;
Doubt not, thy music too
    In the deep rivers;
And the whole plumy flight,
Warbling the day and night—
Up at the gates of light,
    See, the lark quivers!

When with the jacinth
    Coy fountains are tress'd:
And for the mournful bird
    Green woods are dress'd,
That did for Tereus pine;
Then shall our songs be thine,
To whom our hearts incline:
    May, be thou bless'd!
Lord Thurlow.

SONNET.

MAY.

When May is in his prime, and youthful Spring
    Doth clothe the tree with leaves and ground with flowers,
And time of year reviveth everything,
    And lovely Nature smiles, and nothing lowers;
Then Philomela most doth strain her breast
With night-complaints, and sits in little rest.
This bird's estate I may compare with mine,
    To whom fond Love doth work such wrongs by day,
That in the night my heart must needs repine,
    And storm with sighs to ease me as I may;
Whilst others are becalm'd or lie them still,
Or sail secure with tide and wind at will.
And as all those which hear this bird complain,
    Conceive in all her tunes a sweet delight,
Without remorse or pitying her pain;
    So she, for whom I wail both day and night,
Doth sport herself in hearing my complaint;
A just reward for serving such a saint!
Thomas Watson.

CORINNA'S GOING A-MAYING.

Get up, get up, for shame! the blooming morn
Upon her wings presents the god unshorn.
    See how Aurora throws her fair
    Fresh-quilted colors through the air!
    Get up, sweet slug-a-bed, and see
    The dew bespangling herb and tree.
Each flower has wept and bow'd toward the east,
Above an hour since, yet you not drest—
    Nay, not so much as out of bed,
    When all the birds have matins said,
    And sung their thankful hymns: 'tis sin,
    Nay, profanation, to keep in,
Whenas a thousand virgins on this day
Spring sooner than the lark to fetch in May.

Rise, and put on your foliage, and be seen
To come forth, like the spring-time, fresh and green,
    And sweet as Flora. Take no care
    For jewels for your gown or hair:
    Fear not, the leaves will strew
    Gems in abundance upon you;

Besides, the childhood of the day has kept,
Against you come, some orient pearls unwept.
　Come, and receive them while the light
　Hangs on the dew-locks of the night;
　And Titan on the eastern hill
　Retires himself, or else stands still
Till you come forth. Wash, dress, be brief in praying:
Few beads are best, when once we go a-Maying.

Come, my Corinna, come! and, coming, mark
How each field turns a street, each street a park
　Made green and trimm'd with trees; see how
　Devotion gives each house a bough
　Or branch; each porch, each door, ere this
　An ark, a tabernacle is,
Made up of white thorn neatly interwove,
As if here were those cooler shades of love.
　Can such delights be in the street
　And open fields, and we not see 't?
　Come! we'll abroad, and let's obey
　The proclamation made for May;
And sin no more, as we have done, by staying,
But, my Corinna, come! let's go a-Maying.

There's not a budding boy or girl, this day,
But is got up, and gone to bring in May.
　A deal of youth, ere this, is come
　Back, and with white thorn laden home.
　Some have despatch'd their cakes and cream
　Before that we have left to dream;
And some have wept and woo'd and plighted troth,
And chose their priest, ere we can cast off sloth.
　Many a green gown has been given;
　Many a kiss, both odd and even;
　Many a glance, too, has been sent
　From out the eye, love's firmament;

Many a jest told of the key's betraying
This night, and locks pick'd: yet w' are not a-Maying.

Come! let us go while we are in our prime,
And take the harmless folly of the time;
　We shall grow old apace, and die
　Before we know our liberty.
　Our life is short, and our days run
　As fast away as does the sun;
And as a vapor, or a drop of rain
Once lost, can ne'er be found again,
　So when or you or I are made
　A fable, song, or fleeting shade,
　All love, all liking, all delight
　Lies drown'd with us in endless night.
Then, while time serves, and we are but decaying,
Come, my Corinna, come! let's go a-Maying.
　　　　　　　　　　　ROBERT HERRICK.

SUMMER LONGINGS.

*Las mañanas floridas
De Abril y Mayo.*
　　　　CALDERON.

AH! my heart is weary waiting—
　Waiting for the May—
Waiting for the pleasant rambles,
Where the fragrant hawthorn brambles,
　With the woodbine alternating,
　Scent the dewy way.
Ah! my heart is weary waiting—
　Waiting for the May.

Ah! my heart is sick with longing,
　Longing for the May—
Longing to escape from study,
To the young face fair and ruddy,
　And the thousand charms belonging
　To the summer's day.
Ah! my heart is sick with longing,
　Longing for the May.

Ah! my heart is sore with sighing,
　Sighing for the May—
Sighing for their sure returning,
When the summer beams are burning,
　Hopes and flowers that, dead or dying,
　All the winter lay.
Ah! my heart is sore with sighing,
　Sighing for the May.

Ah! my heart is pain'd with throbbing,
    Throbbing for the May—
Throbbing for the seaside billows,
Or the water-wooing willows;
    Where, in laughing and in sobbing,
    Glide the streams away.
Ah! my heart, my heart is throbbing,
    Throbbing for the May.

Waiting sad, dejected, weary,
    Waiting for the May:
Spring goes by with wasted warnings—
Moonlit evenings, sunbright mornings—
    Summer comes, yet dark and dreary
    Life still ebbs away;
Man is ever weary, weary,
    Waiting for the May!
              DENIS FLORENCE MCCARTHY.

THEY COME! THE MERRY SUMMER MONTHS.

THEY come! the merry summer months
    of beauty, song, and flowers;
They come! the gladsome months that
    bring thick leafiness to bowers.
Up, up, my heart! and walk abroad; fling
    cark and care aside;
Seek silent hills, or rest thyself where
    peaceful waters glide;
Or, underneath the shadow vast of patri-
    archal tree,
Scan through its leaves the cloudless sky
    in rapt tranquillity.

The grass is soft, its velvet touch is grate-
    ful to the hand;
And, like the kiss of maiden love, the
    breeze is sweet and bland;
The daisy and the buttercup are nodding
    courteously;
It stirs their blood with kindest love, to
    bless and welcome thee;
And mark how with thine own thin locks
    —they now are silvery gray—
That blissful breeze is wantoning, and
    whispering, "Be gay!"

There is no cloud that sails along the
    ocean of yon sky
But hath its own wing'd mariners to give
    it melody;
Thou seest their glittering fans outspread,
    all gleaming like red gold;
And hark! with shrill pipe musical, their
    merry course they hold.
God bless them all, those little ones, who,
    far above this earth,
Can make a scoff of its mean joys, and
    vent a nobler mirth!

But soft! mine ear upcaught a sound,—
    from yonder wood it came!
The spirit of the dim green glade did
    breathe his own glad name;—
Yes, it is he! the hermit bird, that, apart
    from all his kind,
Slow spells his beads monotonous to the
    soft western wind;
Cuckoo! cuckoo! he sings again,—his
    notes are void of art;
But simplest strains do soonest sound the
    deep founts of the heart.

Good Lord! it is a gracious boon for
    thought-crazed wight like me
To smell again these summer flowers be-
    neath this summer tree!
To suck once more in every breath their
    little souls away,
And feed my fancy with fond dreams of
    youth's bright summer day,
When, rushing forth like untamed colt, the
    reckless, truant boy
Wander'd through greenwoods all day
    long, a mighty heart of joy!

I'm sadder now,—I have had cause; but
    oh, I'm proud to think
That each pure joy-fount, loved of yore, I
    yet delight to drink;—
Leaf, blossom, blade, hill, valley, stream,
    the calm, unclouded sky,
Still mingle music with my dreams, as in
    the days gone by.
When summer's loveliness and light fall
    round me dark and cold,
I'll bear indeed life's heaviest curse,—a
    heart that hath wax'd old!
              WILLIAM MOTHERWELL.

SPRING.

Spring, with that nameless pathos in the air
Which dwells with all things fair,
Spring, with her golden suns and silver rain,
Is with us once again.

Out in the lonely woods the jasmine burns
Its fragrant lamps, and turns
Into a royal court, with green festoons
The banks of dark lagoons.

In the deep heart of every forest tree
The blood is all aglee,
And there's a look about the leafless bowers
As if they dreamed of flowers.

Yet still on every side we trace the hand
Of Winter in the land,
Save where the maple reddens on the lawn,
Flushed by the season's dawn;

Or where, like those strange semblances we find
That age to childhood bind,
The elm puts on, as if in Nature's scorn,
The brown of autumn corn.

As yet the turf is dark, although you know
That, not a span below,
A thousand germs are groping through the gloom,
And soon will burst their tomb.

In gardens you may note amid the dearth,
The crocus breaking earth;
And near the snowdrop's tender white and green,
The violet in its screen.

But many gleams and shadows need must pass
Along the budding grass,
And weeks go by, before the enamored South
Shall kiss the rose's mouth.

Still, there's a sense of blossoms yet unborn
In the sweet airs of morn;
One almost looks to see the very street
Grow purple at his feet.

At times a fragrant breeze comes floating by,
And brings, you know not why,
A feeling as when eager crowds await
Before a palace-gate

Some wondrous pageant; and you scarce would start,
If from a beech's heart
A blue-eyed Dryad, stepping forth, should say,
"Behold me! I am May!"
Henry Timrod.

THE AIRS OF SPRING.

Sweetly breathing, vernal air,
That with kind warmth doth repair
Winter's ruins; from whose breast
All the gums and spice of th' East
Borrow their perfumes; whose eye
Gilds the morn, and clears the sky;
Whose dishevelled tresses shed
Pearls upon the violet bed;
On whose brow, with calm smiles drest,
The halcyon sits and builds her nest;
Beauty, youth, and endless spring,
Dwell upon thy rosy wing!

Thou, if stormy Boreas throws
Down whole forests when he blows,
With a pregnant, flowery birth,
Canst refresh the teeming earth.
If he nip the early bud;
If he blast what's fair or good;
If he scatter our choice flowers;
If he shake our halls or bowers;
If his rude breath threaten us,—
Thou canst stroke great Æolus,
And from him the grace obtain,
To bind him in an iron chain.
Thomas Carew.

SONG TO MAY.

Born in yon blaze of orient sky,
  Sweet May! thy radiant form unfold,
Unclose thy blue voluptuous eye,
  And wave thy shadowy locks of gold.

For thee the fragrant zephyrs blow,
  For thee descends the sunny shower;
The rills in softer murmurs flow,
  And brighter blossoms gem the bower.

Light graces decked in flowery wreaths,
  And tiptoe joys their hands combine;
And Love his sweet contagion breathes,
  And, laughing, dances round thy shrine.

Warm with new life, the glittering throng
  On quivering fin and rustling wing,
Delighted join their votive song,
  And hail thee Goddess of the Spring!
                ERASMUS DARWIN.

THE REIGN OF MAY.

I FEEL a newer life in every gale;
  The winds that fan the flowers,
And with their welcome breathings fill the sail,
  Tell of serener hours,—
    Of hours that glide unfelt away
    Beneath the sky of May.

The spirit of the gentle south wind calls
  From his blue throne of air,
And where his whispering voice in music falls,
  Beauty is budding there;
    The bright ones of the valley break
    Their slumbers, and awake.

The waving verdure rolls along the plain,
  And the wide forest weaves,
To welcome back its playful mates again,
  A canopy of leaves;
    And from its darkening shadow floats
    A gush of trembling notes.

Fairer and brighter spreads the reign of May;
  The tresses of the woods
With the light dallying of the west wind play;
  And the full-brimming floods,
    As gladly to their goal they run,
    Hail the returning sun.
                JAMES GATES PERCIVAL.

JULY.

LOUD is the Summer's busy song,
The smallest breeze can find a tongue,
While insects of each tiny size
Grow teasing with their melodies,
Till noon burns with its blistering breath
Around, and day lies still as death.

The busy noise of man and brute
Is on a sudden lost and mute;
Even the brook that leaps along,
Seems weary of its bubbling song,
And, so soft its waters creep,
Tired silence sinks in sounder sleep;

The cricket on its bank is dumb;
The very flies forget to hum;
And, save the wagon rocking round,
The landscape sleeps without a sound.
The breeze is stopped, the lazy bough
Hath not a leaf that danceth now;

The taller grass upon the hill,
And spider's threads, are standing still;
The feathers, dropped from moorhen's wing
Which to the water's surface cling,
Are steadfast, and as heavy seem
As stones beneath them in the stream;

Hawkweed and groundsel's fanny downs
Unruffled keep their seedy crowns;
And in the overheated air
Not one light thing is floating there,
Save that to the earnest eye
The restless heat seems twittering by.

Noon swoons beneath the heat it made,
And flowers e'en within the shade;
Until the sun slopes in the west,
Like weary traveller, glad to rest
On pillowed clouds of many hues.
Then Nature's voice its joy renews,

And checkered field and grassy plain
Hum with their summer songs again,
A requiem to the day's decline,
Whose setting sunbeams coolly shine
As welcome to day's feeble powers
As falling dews to thirsty flowers.
                JOHN CLARE.

SONNET.
SUMMER.

THE Summer, the divinest Summer burns,
  The skies are bright with azure and with gold,
The mavis and the nightingale by turns
  Amid the woods a soft enchantment hold:
The flowering woods, with glory and delight,
  Their tender leaves unto the air have spread;
.The wanton air, amid their alleys bright,
  Doth softly fly, and a light fragrance shed:
The nymphs within the silver fountains play,
  The angels on the golden banks recline,
Wherein great Flora, in her bright array,
  Hath sprinkled her ambrosial sweets divine:
Or, else, I gaze upon that beauteous face,
O Amoret! and think these sweets have place.
                LORD THURLOW.

SONG OF THE SUMMER WINDS.

UP the dale and down the bourne,
  O'er the meadow swift we fly;
Now we sing, and now we mourn,
  Now we whistle, now we sigh.

By the grassy-fringèd river,
  Through the murmuring reeds we sweep;
'Mid the lily-leaves we quiver,
  To their very hearts we creep.

Now the maiden rose is blushing
  At the frolic things we say,
While aside her cheek we're rushing,
  Like some truant bees at play.

Through the blooming groves we rustle,
  Kissing every bud we pass,—
As we did it in the bustle,
  Scarcely knowing how it was.

Down the glen, across the mountain,
  O'er the yellow heath we roam,
Whirling round about the fountain,
  Till its little breakers foam.

Bending down the weeping willows,
  While our vesper hymn we sigh;
Then unto our rosy pillows
  On our weary wings we hie.

There of idlenesses dreaming,
  Scarce from waking we refrain,
Moments long as ages deeming
  Till we're at our play again.
                GEORGE DARLEY.

REVE DU MIDI.

WHEN o'er the mountain-steeps
The hazy noontide creeps,
And the shrill cricket sleeps
  Under the grass;
When soft the shadows lie,
And clouds sail o'er the sky,
And the idle winds go by
With the heavy scent of blossoms as they pass—

Then, when the silent stream
Lapses as in a dream,
And the water-lilies gleam
  Up to the sun;
When the hot and burden'd day
Rests on its downward way,
When the moth forgets to play
And the plodding ant may dream her work is done—

Then, from the noise of war
And the din of earth afar,
Like some forgotten star
  Dropt from the sky—
The sounds of love and fear,
All voices sad and clear,
Banish'd to silence drear—
The willing thrall of trances sweet I lie.

Some melancholy gale
Breathes its mysterious tale,
Till the rose's lips grow pale
  With her sighs;
And o'er my thoughts are cast
Tints of the vanish'd past,
Glories that faded fast,
Renew'd to splendor in my dreaming eyes.

As poised on vibrant wings,
Where its sweet treasure swings,
The honey-lover clings
  To the red flowers;
So, lost in vivid light,
So, rapt from day and night,
I linger in delight,
  Enraptured o'er the vision-freighted hours.
            ROSE TERRY COOKE.

A NOCTURNAL REVERIE.

IN such a night, when every louder wind
Is to its distant cavern safe confined,
And only gentle Zephyr fans his wings,
And lonely Philomel still waking sings;
Or from some tree, famed for the owl's delight,
She, holloaing clear, directs the wanderer right:
In such a night, when passing clouds give place,
Or thinly veil the heavens' mysterious face;
When in some river overhung with green
The waving moon and trembling leaves are seen;
When freshen'd grass now bears itself upright,
And makes cool banks to pleasing rest invite,
Whence springs the woodbine, and the bramble rose,
And where the sleepy cowslip shelter'd grows;
Whilst now a paler hue the foxglove takes,
Yet checkers still with red the dusky brakes;
When scatter'd glow-worms, but in twilight fine,
Show trivial beauties, watch their hour to shine;
Whilst Salisbury stands the test of every light,
In perfect charms and perfect virtue bright;
When odors which declined repelling day
Through temperate air uninterrupted stray;
When darken'd groves their softest shadows wear,
And falling waters we distinctly hear;
When through the gloom more venerable shows
Some ancient fabric, awful in repose;
While sunburnt hills their swarthy looks conceal,
And swelling haycocks thicken up the vale;
When the loosed horse now, as his pasture leads,
Comes slowly grazing through the adjoining meads,
Whose stealing pace and lengthen'd shade we fear,
Till torn-up forage in his teeth we hear;
When nibbling sheep at large pursue their food,
And unmolested kine rechew the cud;
When curlews cry beneath the village walls,
And to her straggling brood the partridge calls;
Their short-lived jubilee the creatures keep,
Which but endures whilst tyrant man does sleep;
When a sedate content the spirit feels,
And no fierce light disturbs, whilst it reveals;
But silent musings urge the mind to seek
Something too high for syllables to speak;
Till the free soul to a composedness charm'd,
Finding the elements of rage disarm'd,
O'er all below a solemn quiet grown,
Joys in the inferior world, and thinks it like her own:
In such a night let me abroad remain,
Till morning breaks, and all's confused again;
Our cares, our toils, our clamors are renew'd,
Our pleasures, seldom reach'd, again pursued.
            ANNE, COUNTESS OF WINCHELSEA.

SEPTEMBER.

SWEET is the voice that calls
  From babbling waterfalls,
In meadows where the downy seeds are flying;
  And soft the breezes blow,
  And eddying come and go,
In faded gardens where the rose is dying.

Among the stubbled corn
The blithe quail pipes at morn;
The merry partridge drums in hidden places,
And glittering insects gleam
Above the reedy stream,
Where busy spiders spin their filmy laces.

At eve, cool shadows fall
Across the garden-wall,
And on the cluster'd grapes to purple turning,
And pearly vapors lie
Along the eastern sky,
Where the broad harvest-moon is redly burning.

Ah, soon on field and hill
The winds shall whistle chill,
And patriarch swallows call their flocks together
To fly from frost and snow,
And seek for lands where blow
The fairer blossoms of a balmier weather.

The pollen-dusted bees
Search for the honey-lees
That linger in the last flowers of September,
While plaintive mourning doves
Coo sadly to their loves
Of the dead summer they so well remember.

The cricket chirps all day,
"O fairest Summer, stay!"
The squirrel eyes askance the chestnuts browning;
The wild-fowl fly afar
Above the foamy bar,
And hasten southward ere the skies are frowning.

Now comes a fragrant breeze
Through the dark cedar trees,
And round about my temples fondly lingers,
In gentle playfulness,
Like to the soft caress
Bestow'd in happier days by loving fingers.

Yet, though a sense of grief
Comes with the falling leaf,
And memory makes the summer doubly pleasant,
In all my autumn dreams
A future summer gleams,
Passing the fairest glories of the present!
GEORGE ARNOLD.

TO AUTUMN.

SEASON of mists and mellow fruitfulness!
Close bosom-friend of the maturing sun!
Conspiring with him how to load and bless
With fruit the vines that round the thatch-eaves run—
To bend with apples the moss'd cottage trees,
And fill all fruit with ripeness to the core—
To swell the gourd, and plump the hazel-shells
With a sweet kernel—to set budding more,
And still more, later flowers for the bees,
Until they think warm days will never cease,
For Summer has o'er-brimm'd their clammy cells.

Who hath not seen thee oft amid thy store?
Sometimes whoever seeks abroad may find
Thee sitting careless on a granary-floor,
Thy hair soft-lifted by the winnowing wind;
Or on a half-reap'd furrow sound asleep,
Drowsed with the fume of poppies, while thy hook
Spares the next swath and all its twinèd flowers;
And sometime like a gleaner thou dost keep
Steady thy laden head across a brook;
Or by a cider-press, with patient look,
Thou watchest the last oozings, hours by hours.

Where are the songs of Spring? Ay,
    where are they?
Think not of them—thou hast thy music
    too,
While barrèd clouds bloom the soft-dying
    day,
And touch the stubble-plains with rosy
    hue;
Then in a wailful choir the small gnats
    mourn
Among the river-sallows, borne aloft
    Or sinking, as the light wind lives or
    dies;
And full-grown lambs loud bleat from
    hilly bourn;
    Hedge-crickets sing; and now with
    treble soft
The red-breast whistles from a garden-
    croft,
    And gathering swallows twitter in the
    skies.
                  JOHN KEATS.

AUTUMN.
A DIRGE.

THE warm sun is failing, the bleak wind is
    wailing,
The bare boughs are sighing, the pale
    flowers are dying,
        And the year
On the earth her deathbed, in a shroud of
    leaves dead,
        Is lying.
    Come, months, come away,
    From November to May,
    In your saddest array;
    Follow the bier
    Of the dead cold year.
And like dim shadows watch by her
    sepulchre.

The chill rain is falling, the nipt worm is
    crawling,
The rivers are swelling, the thunder is
    knelling
        For the year;
The blithe swallows are flown, and the
    lizards each gone
        To his dwelling;
    Come, months, come away,
    Put on white, black, and gray,
    Let your light sisters play—

    Ye follow the bier
    Of the dead cold year,
And make her grave green with tear on
    tear.
                  PERCY BYSSHE SHELLEY.

ODE TO THE WEST WIND.
I.

O WILD West Wind, thou breath of au-
    tumn's being,
Thou from whose unseen presence the
    leaves dead
Are driven, like ghosts from an enchanter
    fleeing,

Yellow, and black, and pale, and hectic
    red,
Pestilence-stricken multitudes: O thou
Who chariotest to their dark wintry bed

The wingèd seeds, where they lie cold and
    low,
Each like a corpse within its grave, until
Thine azure sister of the spring shall
    blow

Her clarion o'er the dreaming earth, and
    fill
(Driving sweet buds like flocks to feed in
    air)
With living hues and odors plain and hill:

Wild spirit, which art moving everywhere;
Destroyer and preserver; hear, oh hear!

II.

Thou on whose stream, 'mid the steep sky's
    commotion,
Loose clouds like earth's decaying leaves
    are shed,
Shook from the tangled boughs of heaven
    and ocean,

Angels of rain and lightning; there are
    spread
On the blue surface of thine airy surge,
Like the bright hair uplifted from the head

Of some fierce Mænad, even from the dim
    verge
Of the horizon to the zenith's height,
The locks of the approaching storm. Thou
    dirge

Of the dying year, to which this closing
    night
Will be the dome of a vast sepulchre,
Vaulted with all thy congregated might

Of vapors, from whose solid atmosphere
Black rain and fire and hail will burst: oh
    hear!

III.

Thou who didst waken from his summer
    dreams
The blue Mediterranean, where he lay
Lull'd by the coil of his crystalline streams

Beside a pumice isle in Baiæ's bay,
And saw in sleep old palaces and towers
Quivering within the wave's intenser day,

All overgrown with azure moss and flowers
So sweet, the sense faints picturing them!
    Thou
For whose path the Atlantic's level powers

Cleave themselves into chasms, while far
    below
The sea-blooms and the oozy woods which
    wear
The sapless foliage of the ocean know

Thy voice, and suddenly grow gray with
    fear,
And tremble, and despoil themselves: oh
    hear!

IV.

If I were a dead leaf thou mightest bear;
If I were a swift cloud to fly with thee;
A wave to pant beneath thy power, and
    share

The impulse of thy strength, only less free
Than thou, O uncontrollable! if even
I were as in my boyhood, and could be

The comrade of thy wanderings over
    heaven,
As then, when to outstrip the skyey speed
Scarce seem'd a vision, I would ne'er have
    striven

As thus with thee in prayer in my sore
    need.
Oh, lift me as a wave, a leaf, a cloud!
I fall upon the thorns of life! I bleed!

A heavy weight of hours has chain'd and
    bow'd
One too like thee: tameless and swift and
    proud.

V.

Make me thy lyre, even as the forest is:
What if my leaves are falling like its own!
The tumult of thy mighty harmonies

Will take from both a deep autumnal tone,
Sweet though in sadness. Be thou, spirit
    fierce,
My spirit! be thou me, impetuous one!

Drive my dead thoughts over the universe
Like wither'd leaves to quicken a new
    birth;
And, by the incantation of this verse,

Scatter, as from an unextinguish'd hearth
Ashes and sparks, my words among man-
    kind!
Be through my lips to unawaken'd earth

The trumpet of a prophecy! O wind,
If winter comes, can spring be far behind?
        PERCY BYSSHE SHELLEY.

THE FIRST SNOW-FALL.

THE snow had begun in the gloaming,
    And busily all the night
Had been heaping field and highway
    With a silence deep and white.

Every pine and fir and hemlock
    Wore ermine too dear for an earl,
And the poorest twig on the elm tree
    Was ridged inch-deep with pearl.

From sheds new-roof'd with Carrara
    Came Chanticleer's muffled crow,
The stiff rails were soften'd to swan's-down,
    And still flutter'd down the snow.

I stood and watch'd by the window
    The noiseless work of the sky,
And the sudden flurries of snow-birds,
    Like brown leaves whirling by.

I thought of a mound in sweet Auburn
    Where a little headstone stood;
How the flakes were folding it gently,
    As did robins the babes in the wood.

Up spoke our own little Mabel,
  Saying, "Father, who makes it snow?"
And I told of the good All-father
  Who cares for us here below.

Again I look'd at the snow-fall,
  And thought of the leaden sky
That arch'd o'er our first great sorrow,
  When that mound was heap'd so high.

I remember'd the gradual patience
  That fell from that cloud like snow,
Flake by flake, healing and hiding
  The scar of our deep-plunged woe.

And again to the child I whisper'd,
  "The snow that husheth all,
Darling, the merciful Father
  Alone can make it fall!"

Then, with eyes that saw not, I kiss'd her;
  And she, kissing back, could not know
That *my* kiss was given to her sister,
  Folded close under deepening snow.
              JAMES RUSSELL LOWELL.

WHEN ICICLES HANG BY THE WALL.

WHEN icicles hang by the wall
  And Dick the shepherd blows his nail,
And Tom bears logs into the hall,
  And milk comes frozen home in pail,
When blood is nipp'd, and ways be foul,
Then nightly sings the staring owl,
          To-who;
Tu-whit, to-who, a merry note,
While greasy Joan doth keel the pot.

When all aloud the wind doth blow,
  And coughing drowns the parson's saw,
And birds sit brooding in the snow,
  And Marian's nose looks red and raw,
When roasted crabs hiss in the bowl,
Then nightly sings the staring owl,
          To-who;
Tu-whit, to-who, a merry note,
While greasy Joan doth keel the pot.
              WILLIAM SHAKESPEARE.

BLOW, BLOW, THOU WINTER WIND.

BLOW, blow, thou winter wind,
  Thou art not so unkind
    As man's ingratitude;
  Thy tooth is not so keen,
  Because thou art not seen,
    Although thy breath be rude.
Heigh-ho! sing heigh-ho! unto the green holly:
Most friendship is feigning, most loving mere folly:
  Then, heigh-ho! the holly!
  This life is most jolly!

  Freeze, freeze, thou bitter sky,
  Thou dost not bite so nigh
    As benefits forgot:
  Though thou the waters warp,
  Thy sting is not so sharp
    As friend remember'd not.
Heigh-ho! sing heigh-ho! unto the green holly:
Most friendship is feigning, most loving mere folly:
  Then, heigh-ho! the holly!
  This life is most jolly!
              WILLIAM SHAKESPEARE.

THE DEATH OF THE OLD YEAR.

FULL knee-deep lies the winter snow,
  And the winter winds are wearily sighing:
Toll ye the church-bell sad and slow,
And tread softly and speak low,
  For the Old year lies a-dying
    Old year, you must not die;
    You came to us so readily,
    You lived with us so steadily,
  Old year, you shall not die.

He lieth still: he doth not move:
  He will not see the dawn of day.
He hath no other life above.
He gave me a friend, and a true true-love,
  And the New year will take 'em away.
    Old year, you must not go;
    So long as you have been with us,
    Such joy as you have seen with us,
  Old year, you shall not go.

He froth'd his bumpers to the brim;
  A jollier year we shall not see.
But though his eyes are waxing dim,
And though his foes speak ill of him,
  He was a friend to me.
    Old year, you shall not die;
    We did so laugh and cry with you,
    I've half a mind to die with you,
    Old year, if you must die.

He was full of joke and jest,
  But all his merry quips are o'er.
To see him die, across the waste
His son and heir doth ride post-haste,
  But he'll be dead before.
    Every one for his own.
      The night is starry and cold, my
        friend,
      And the New year blithe and bold,
        my friend,
    Comes up to take his own.

How hard he breathes! Over the snow
  I heard just now the crowing cock.
The shadows flicker to and fro:
The cricket chirps: the light burns low:
  'Tis nearly twelve o'clock.
    Shake hands before you die.
      Old year, we'll dearly rue for you:
      What is it we can do for you?
    Speak out before you die.

His face is growing sharp and thin.
  Alack! our friend is gone.
Close up his eyes: tie up his chin:
Step from the corpse and let him in
  That standeth there alone,
    And waiteth at the door.
      There's a new foot on the floor, my
        friend,
      And a new face at the door, my
        friend,
    A new face at the door.
              ALFRED TENNYSON.

MORNING.

HARK—hark! the lark at heaven's gate
    sings,
  And Phœbus 'gins arise,
His steeds to water at those springs
  On chaliced flowers that lies:
And winking Mary-buds begin
  To ope their golden eyes;
With everything that pretty bin,
  My lady sweet, arise;
    Arise, arise!
              WILLIAM SHAKESPEARE.

SONNET.

FULL many a glorious morning have I
    seen
  Flatter the mountain-tops with sov-
    ereign eye,
Kissing with golden face the meadows
    green,
  Gilding pale streams with heavenly al-
    chemy;
Anon permit the basest clouds to ride
  With ugly rack on his celestial face,
And from the forlorn world his visage hide,
  Stealing unseen to west with this dis-
    grace.
Even so my sun one early morn did shine,
  With all triumphant splendor on my
    brow;
But out, alack! he was but one hour
    mine,
  The region cloud hath mask'd him from
    me now.
Yet him for this my love no whit dis-
    daineth;
Suns of the world may stain, when heaven's
    sun staineth.
              WILLIAM SHAKESPEARE.

THE SABBATH MORNING.

WITH silent awe I hail the sacred morn,
  That slowly wakes while all the fields
    are still!
A soothing calm on every breeze is borne;
  A graver murmur gurgles from the rill;
And Echo answers softer from the hill;
And softer sings the linnet from the thorn;
  The skylark warbles in a tone less shrill.
Hail, light serene! hail, sacred Sabbath
    morn!
  The rooks float silent by in airy drove;
The sun a placid yellow lustre throws;
  The gales that lately sigh'd along the
    grove,

Have hush'd their downy wings in dead
    repose;
  The hovering rack of clouds forgets to
    move—
So smiled the day when the first morn
    arose!
                    JOHN LEYDEN.

ODE TO EVENING.

IF aught of oaten stop, or pastoral song,
May hope, O pensive Eve, to soothe thine
    ear,
    Like thy own brawling springs,
    Thy springs, and dying gales;

O nymph reserved, while now the bright-
    hair'd sun
Sits in yon western tent whose cloudy
    skirts,
    With brede ethereal wove,
    O'erhang his wavy bed:

Now air is hush'd, save where the weak-
    eyed bat,
With short shrill shriek flits by on leathern
    wing,
    Or where the beetle winds
    His small but sullen horn,

As oft he rises midst the twilight path,
Against the pilgrim borne in needless
    hum:
    Now teach me, maid composed,
    To breathe some soften'd strain,

Whose numbers stealing through thy dark-
    ening vale
May not unseemly with its stillness suit;
    As musing slow I hail
    Thy genial loved return!

For when thy folding star arising shows
His paly circlet, at his warning lamp
    The fragrant Hours and Elves
    Who slept in buds the day,

And many a nymph who wreathes her
    brows with sedge,
And sheds the freshening dew, and, love-
    lier still,
    The pensive Pleasures sweet,
    Prepare thy shadowy car.

Then let me rove some wild and heathy
    scene,
Or find some ruin midst its dreary dells,
    Whose walls more awful nod
    By thy religious gleams.

Or if chill blustering winds, or driving
    rain,
Prevent my willing feet, be mine the hut
    That from the mountain's side
    Views wilds and swelling floods,

And hamlets brown, and dim-discover'd
    spires,
And hears their simple bell, and marks
    o'er all
    Thy dewy fingers draw
    The gradual dusky veil.

While Spring shall pour his showers, as
    oft he wont,
And bathe thy breathing tresses, meekest
    Eve!
    While Summer loves to sport
    Beneath thy lingering light;

While sallow Autumn fills thy lap with
    leaves;
Or Winter, yelling through the troublous
    air,
    Affrights thy shrinking train,
    And rudely rends thy robes;

So long, regardful of thy quiet rule,
Shall Fancy, Friendship, Science, smiling
    Peace
    Thy gentlest influence own,
    And love thy favorite name.
                    WILLIAM COLLINS.

THE MIDGES DANCE ABOON THE BURN.

THE midges dance aboon the burn;
    The dews begin to fa';
The pairtricks down the rushy holm
    Set up their e'ening ca'.
Now loud and clear the blackbird's sang
    Rings through the briery shaw,
While, flitting gay, the swallows play
    Around the castle-wa'.

Beneath the golden gloamin' sky
    The mavis mends her lay;

The redbreast pours his sweetest strains
  To charm the lingering day;
While weary yeldrins seem to wail
  Their little nestlings torn,
The merry wren, frae den to den,
  Gaes jinking through the thorn.

The roses fauld their silken leaves,
  The foxglove shuts its bell;
The honeysuckle and the birk
  Spread fragrance through the dell.
Let others crowd the giddy court
  Of mirth and revelry,
The simple joys that Nature yields
  Are dearer far to me.
            ROBERT TANNAHILL.

SONNET.

IT is a beauteous Evening, calm and free;
  The holy time is quiet as a Nun
Breathless with adoration; the broad sun
  Is sinking down in its tranquillity;
The gentleness of heaven is on the Sea:
  Listen! the mighty Being is awake,
And doth with his eternal motion make
  A sound like thunder—everlastingly.
Dear Child! dear Girl! that walkest with me here,
  If thou appear'st untouch'd by solemn thought,
Thy nature is not therefore less divine:
Thou liest in Abraham's bosom all the year;
  And worshipp'st at the Temple's inner shrine,
God being with thee when we know it not.
            WILLIAM WORDSWORTH.

SABBATH EVENING.

How calmly sinks the parting sun!
  Yet twilight lingers still;
And beautiful as dream of heaven
  It slumbers on the hill;
Earth sleeps, with all her glorious things,
  Beneath the Holy Spirit's wings,
And, rendering back the hues above,
Seems resting in a trance of love.

Round yonder rocks the forest trees
  In shadowy groups recline,
Like saints at evening bow'd in prayer
  Around their holy shrine;
And through their leaves the night-winds blow,
So calm and still, their music low
Seems the mysterious voice of prayer,
Soft echo'd on the evening air.

And yonder western throng of clouds,
  Retiring from the sky,
So calmly move, so softly glow,
  They seem to Fancy's eye
Bright creatures of a better sphere,
Come down at noon to worship here,
And, from their sacrifice of love,
Returning to their home above.

The blue isles of the golden sea,
  The night-arch floating high,
The flowers that gaze upon the heavens,
  The bright streams leaping by,
Are living with religion—deep
On earth and sea its glories sleep,
And mingle with the starlight rays,
Like the soft light of parted days.

The spirit of the holy eve
  Comes through the silent air
To Feeling's hidden spring, and wakes
  A gush of music there!
And the far depths of ether beam
So passing fair, we almost dream
That we can rise and wander through
Their open paths of trackless blue.

Each soul is fill'd with glorious dreams,
  Each pulse is beating wild;
And thought is soaring to the shrine
  Of glory undefiled!
And holy aspirations start,
Like blessed angels, from the heart,
And bind—for earth's dark ties are riven—
Our spirits to the gates of heaven.
            GEORGE DENISON PRENTICE.

TO NIGHT.

MYSTERIOUS Night! when our first parent knew
  Thee from report divine, and heard thy name,
  Did he not tremble for this lovely frame,
This glorious canopy of light and blue?

Yet 'neath the curtain of translucent dew,
  Bathed in the rays of the great setting flame,
Hesperus with the host of heaven came,
And lo! creation widen'd in man's view.
Who could have thought such darkness lay conceal'd
  Within thy beams, O Sun! or who could find,
While fly, and leaf, and insect lay reveal'd,
  That to such countless orbs thou mad'st us blind!
Why do we, then, shun Death with anxious strife?—
If Light can thus deceive, wherefore not Life?
                    JOSEPH BLANCO WHITE.

TO NIGHT.

SWIFTLY walk over the western wave,
        Spirit of Night!
Out of the misty eastern cave,
Where all the long and lone daylight
Thou wovest dreams of joy and fear
Which make thee terrible and dear,—
        Swift be thy flight!

Wrap thy form in a mantle gray
        Star-inwrought!
Blind with thine hair the eyes of day,
Kiss her until she be wearied out,
Then wander o'er city, and sea, and land,
Touching all with thine opiate wand—
        Come, long-sought!

When I arose and saw the dawn,
        I sigh'd for thee;
When light rode high, and the dew was gone,
And noon lay heavy on flower and tree,
And the weary Day turn'd to his rest,
Lingering like an unloved guest,
        I sigh'd for thee.

Thy brother Death came, and cried,
        Wouldst thou me?
Thy sweet child Sleep, the filmy-eyed,
Murmur'd like a noontide bee,
Shall I nestle near thy side?
Wouldst thou me?—And I replied,
        No, not thee!

Death will come when thou art dead,
        Soon, too soon—
Sleep will come when thou art fled;
Of neither would I ask the boon
I ask of thee, belovèd Night—
Swift be thine approaching flight,
        Come soon, soon!
                    PERCY BYSSHE SHELLEY.

THE EVENING CLOUD.

A CLOUD lay cradled near the setting sun,
  A gleam of crimson tinged its braided snow;
Long had I watch'd the glory moving on
  O'er the still radiance of the lake below.
Tranquil its spirit seem'd, and floated slow!
  Even in its very motion there was rest;
While every breath of eve that chanced to blow
  Wafted the traveller to the beauteous west.
Emblem, methought, of the departed soul!
  To whose white robe the gleam of bliss is given
And by the breath of mercy made to roll
  Right onward to the golden gates of heaven,
Where to the eye of faith it peaceful lies,
And tells to man his glorious destinies.
                    JOHN WILSON.

THE EVENING WIND.

SPIRIT that breathest through my lattice; thou
  That cool'st the twilight of the sultry day!
Gratefully flows thy freshness round my brow;
  Thou hast been out upon the deep at play,
Riding all day the wild blue waves till now,
  Roughening their crests, and scattering high their spray,
And swelling the white sail. I welcome thee
To the scorch'd land, thou wanderer of the sea!

Nor I alone,—a thousand bosoms round
  Inhale thee in the fulness of delight;
And languid forms rise up, and pulses
    bound
  Livelier, at coming of the wind of night;
And languishing to hear thy welcome
    sound,
  Lies the vast inland, stretch'd beyond
    the sight.
Go forth into the gathering shade; go
    forth,—
God's blessing breathed upon the fainting
    earth!

Go, rock the little wood-bird in his nest;
  Curl the still waters, bright with stars;
    and rouse
The wide old wood from his majestic rest,
  Summoning, from the innumerable
    boughs,
The strange deep harmonies that haunt his
    breast.
  Pleasant shall be thy way where meekly
    bows
The shutting flower, and darkling waters
    pass,
And where the o'ershadowing branches
    sweep the grass.

Stoop o'er the place of graves, and softly
    sway
  The sighing herbage by the gleaming
    stone,
That they who near the churchyard wil-
    lows stray,
  And listen in the deepening gloom,
    alone,
May think of gentle souls that pass'd
    away,
  Like thy pure breath, into the vast un-
    known,
Sent forth from heaven among the sons of
    men,
And gone into the boundless heaven again.

The faint old man shall lean his silver
    head
  To feel thee; thou shalt kiss the child
    asleep,
And dry the moisten'd curls that over-
    spread
  His temples, while his breathing grows
    more deep;

And they who stand about the sick man's
    bed
  Shall joy to listen to thy distant
    sweep,
And softly part his curtains to allow
Thy visit, grateful to his burning brow.

Go,—but the circle of eternal change,
  Which is the life of Nature, shall re-
    store,
With sounds and scents from all thy
    mighty range,
  Thee to thy birthplace of the deep
    once more.
Sweet odors in the sea-air, sweet and
    strange,
  Shall tell the homesick mariner of the
    shore;
And, listening to thy murmur, he shall
    deem
He hears the rustling leaf and running
    stream.
            WILLIAM CULLEN BRYANT.

THE RAINBOW.

STILL young and fine, but what is still in
    view
We slight as old and soil'd, though fresh
    and new.
How bright wert thou, when Shem's ad-
    miring eye
Thy burnish'd, flaming arch did first des-
    cry!
When Terah, Nahor, Haran, Abram,
    Lot,
The youthful world's gray fathers, in one
    knot
Did with intentive looks watch every
    hour
For thy new light, and trembled at each
    shower!
When thou dost shine, darkness looks
    white and fair,
Forms turn to music, clouds to smiles and
    air:
Rain gently spends his honey-drops, and
    pours
Balm on the cleft earth, milk on grass
    and flowers.

Bright pledge of peace and sunshine! the sure tie
Of thy Lord's hand, the object of His eye!
When I behold thee though my light be dim,
Distinct, and low, I can in thine see Him,
Who looks upon thee from His glorious throne,
And minds the covenant betwixt all and One.
HENRY VAUGHAN.

TO THE RAINBOW.

TRIUMPHAL arch that fill'st the sky
  When storms prepare to part,
I ask not proud Philosophy
  To teach me what thou art—

Still seem, as to my childhood's sight,
  A mid-way station given
For happy spirits to alight
  Betwixt the earth and heaven.

Can all that Optics teach, unfold
  Thy form to please me so,
As when I dream'd of gems and gold
  Hid in thy radiant bow?

When Science from Creation's face
  Enchantment's veil withdraws,
What lovely visions yield their place
  To cold material laws!

And yet, fair bow, no fabling dreams
  But words of the Most High,
Have told why first thy robe of beams
  Was woven in the sky.

When o'er the green undeluged earth
  Heaven's covenant thou did'st shine,
How came the world's gray fathers forth
  To watch thy sacred sign!

And when its yellow lustre smiled
  O'er mountains yet untrod,
Each mother held aloft her child
  To bless the bow of God.

Methinks, thy jubilee to keep,
  The first-made anthem rang
On earth, deliver'd from the deep,
  And the first poet sang.

Nor ever shall the Muse's eye
  Unraptured greet thy beam;
Theme of primeval prophecy,
  Be still the prophet's theme!

The earth to thee her incense yields,
  The lark thy welcome sings,
When, glittering in the freshen'd fields,
  The snowy mushroom springs.

How glorious is thy girdle cast
  O'er mountain, tower, and town,
Or mirror'd in the ocean vast,
  A thousand fathoms down!

As fresh in yon horizon dark,
  As young thy beauties seem,
As when the eagle from the ark
  First sported in thy beam.

For, faithful to its sacred page,
  Heaven still rebuilds thy span,
Nor lets the type grow pale with age
  That first spoke peace to man.
THOMAS CAMPBELL.

THE RAINBOW.

MY heart leaps up when I behold
  A Rainbow in the sky:
So was it when my life began;
So is it now I am a Man;
So be it when I shall grow old,
  Or let me die!
The Child is Father of the Man;
And I could wish my days to be
Bound each to each by natural piety.
WILLIAM WORDSWORTH.

THE CLOUD.

I BRING fresh showers for the thirsting flowers,
  From the seas and the streams;
I bear light shade for the leaves when laid
  In their noonday dreams.
From my wings are shaken the dews that waken
  The sweet birds every one,
When rock'd to rest on their mother's breast,
  As she dances about the sun.

I wield the flail of the lashing hail,
  And whiten the green plains under;
And then again I dissolve it in rain;
  And laugh as I pass in thunder.

I sift the snow on the mountains below,
  And their great pines groan aghast;
And all the night 'tis my pillow white,
  While I sleep in the arms of the blast.
Sublime on the towers of my skyey bowers
  Lightning, my pilot, sits;
In a cavern under is fetter'd the thunder;
  It struggles and howls at fits.
Over earth and ocean, with gentle motion,
  This pilot is guiding me,
Lured by the love of the genii that move
  In the depths of the purple sea;
Over the rills, and the crags, and the hills,
  Over the lakes and the plains,
Wherever he dream, under mountain or stream,
  The Spirit he loves remains;
And I all the while bask in heaven's blue smile,
  Whilst he is dissolving in rains.

The sanguine sunrise, with his meteor eyes,
  And his burning plumes outspread,
Leaps on the back of my sailing rack,
  When the morning star shines dead.
As, on the jag of a mountain-crag
  Which an earthquake rocks and swings,
An eagle, alit, one moment may sit
  In the light of its golden wings;
And when sunset may breathe, from the lit sea beneath,
  Its ardors of rest and of love,
And the crimson pall of eve may fall
  From the depth of heaven above,
With wings folded I rest on mine airy nest,
  As still as a brooding dove.

That orbèd maiden with white fire laden,
  Whom mortals call the moon,
Glides glimmering o'er my fleece-like floor
  By the midnight breezes strewn;
And wherever the beat of her unseen feet,
  Which only the angels hear,
May have broken the woof of my tent's thin roof,
  The stars peep behind her and peer;
And I laugh to see them whirl and flee,
  Like a swarm of golden bees,
When I widen the rent in my wind-built tent,
  Till the calm rivers, lakes, and seas,
Like strips of the sky fallen through me on high,
  Are each paved with the moon and these.

I bind the sun's throne with a burning zone,
  And the moon's with a girdle of pearl;
The volcanoes are dim, and the stars reel and swim,
  When the whirlwinds my banner unfurl.
From cape to cape, with a bridge-like shape,
  Over a torrent sea,
Sunbeam-proof, I hang like a roof,
  The mountains its columns be.
The triumphal arch, through which I march
  With hurricane, fire, and snow,
When the powers of the air are chain'd to my chair,
  Is the million-color'd bow;
The sphere-fire above its soft colors wove,
  While the moist earth was laughing below.

I am the daughter of earth and water,
  And the nursling of the sky;
I pass through the pores of the ocean and shores;
  I change, but I cannot die.
For after the rain, when, with never a stain,
  The pavilion of heaven is bare,
And the winds and sunbeams, with their convex gleams,
  Build up the blue dome of air—
I silently laugh at my own cenotaph,
  And out of the caverns of rain,
Like a child from the womb, like a ghost from the tomb,
  I arise and unbuild it again.

PERCY BYSSHE SHELLEY.

FANCY IN NUBIBUS;
OR, THE POET IN THE CLOUDS.

OH, it is pleasant, with a heart at ease,
  Just after sunset, or by moonlight skies,
To make the shifting clouds be what you
    please,
  Or let the easily-persuaded eyes
Own each quaint likeness issuing from the
    mould
  Of a friend's fancy; or with head bent
    low
And cheek aslant see rivers flow of gold
  'Twixt crimson banks; and then, a trav-
    veller, go
From mount to mount through Cloudland,
    gorgeous land!
Or list'ning to the tide, with closèd sight,
Be that blind bard, who on the Chian strand
  By those deep sounds possess'd with in-
    ward light,
Beheld the Iliad and the Odyssee
Rise to the swelling of the voiceful sea.
SAMUEL TAYLOR COLERIDGE.

DRINKING.

THE thirsty earth soaks up the rain,
And drinks, and gapes for drink again;
The plants suck in the earth, and are,
With constant drinking, fresh and fair;
The sea itself (which one would think
Should have but little need of drink)
Drinks ten thousand rivers up,
So filled that they o'erflow the cup.
The busie sun (and one would guess
By 's drunken fiery face no less)
Drinks up the sea, and when he 'as done,
The moon and stars drink up the sun:
They drink and dance by their own light;
They drink and revel all the night.
Nothing in Nature's sober found,
But an eternal "health" goes round.
Fill up the bowl then, fill it high—
Fill all the glasses there; for why
Should every creature drink but I;
Why, man of morals, tell me why?
ANACREON (Greek).
Translation of ABRAHAM COWLEY.

TO CYNTHIA.

QUEEN and huntress, chaste and fair,
  Now the sun is laid to sleep,
Seated in thy silver chair
  State in wonted manner keep:
Hesperus entreats thy light,
Goddess excellently bright!

Earth, let not thy envious shade
  Dare itself to interpose;
Cynthia's shining orb was made
  Heaven to clear when day did close;
Bless us, then, with wishèd sight,
Goddess excellently bright!

Lay thy bow of pearl apart,
  And thy crystal-shining quiver;
Give unto thy flying hart
  Space to breathe, how short soever;
Thou that mak'st a day of night,
Goddess excellently bright!
BEN JONSON.

TO THE MOON.

ART thou pale for weariness
Of climbing heaven, and gazing on the earth,
  Wandering companionless
Among the stars that have a different
    birth,—
And ever changing, like a joyless eye
That finds no object worth its constancy?
PERCY BYSSHE SHELLEY.

SONNET.
TO THE MOON.

O MOON, that shinest on this heathy
    wild,
  And light'st the hill of Hastings with
    thy ray,
How am I with thy sad delight beguiled!
  How hold with fond imagination play!
By thy broad taper I call up the time
  When Harold on the bleeding verdure
    lay;
Though great in glory, overstain'd with
    crime,
  And fallen by his fate from kingly sway!
On bleeding knights, and on war-broken
    arms,
  Torn banners, and the dying steeds you
    shone,
When this fair England, and her peerless
    charms,
  And all, but honor, to the foe were gone!

Here died the king, whom his brave sub-
    jects chose,
But, dying, lay amid his Norman foes!
                            LORD THURLOW.

TO THE EVENING STAR.

How sweet thy modest light to view,
    Fair star, to love and lovers dear,
While trembling on the falling dew,
    Like beauty shining through a tear!

Or hanging o'er that mirror-stream,
    To mark that image trembling there,
Thou seem'st to smile with softer gleam,
    To see thy lovely face so fair.

Though, blazing o'er the arch of night,
    The moon thy timid beams outshine
As far as thine each starry light,—
    Her rays can never vie with thine.

Thine are the soft enchanting hours
    When twilight lingers on the plain,
And whispers to the closing flowers
    That soon the sun will rise again.

Thine is the breeze that, murmuring bland
    As music, wafts the lover's sigh,
And bids the yielding heart expand
    In love's delicious ecstasy.

Fair star! though I be doom'd to prove
    That rapture's tears are mix'd with pain,
Ah! still I feel 'tis sweet to love,—
    But sweeter to be loved again.
                            JOHN LEYDEN.

SONG.

TO THE EVENING STAR.

STAR that bringest home the bee,
And sett'st the weary laborer free!
    If any star shed peace, 'tis thou
    That send'st it from above,
Appearing when Heaven's breath and brow
    Are sweet as hers we love.

Come to the luxuriant skies
Whilst the landscape's odors rise,
Whilst far-off lowing herds are heard,
    And songs, when toil is done,
From cottages whose smoke unstirr'd
    Curls yellow in the sun.

Star of love's soft interviews!
Parted lovers on thee muse;
    Their remembrancer in Heaven
        Of thrilling vows thou art,
    Too delicious to be riven
        By absence from the heart.
                        THOMAS CAMPBELL.

ON A SPRIG OF HEATH.

FLOWER of the waste! the heathfowl shuns
    For thee the brake and tangled wood—
To thy protecting shade she runs,
    Thy tender buds supply her food;
Her young forsake her downy plumes
To rest upon thy opening blooms.

Flower of the desert though thou art!
    The deer that range the mountain free,
The graceful doe, the stately hart,
    Their food and shelter seek from thee;
The bee thy earliest blossom greets,
And draws from thee her choicest sweets.

Gem of the heath! whose modest bloom
    Sheds beauty o'er the lonely moor,
Though thou dispense no rich perfume,
    Nor yet with splendid tints allure,
Both valor's crest and beauty's bower
Oft hast thou deck'd, a favorite flower.

Flower of the wild! whose purple glow
    Adorns the dusky mountain's side,
Not the gay hues of Iris' bow,
    Nor garden's artful varied pride,
With all its wealth of sweets, could cheer,
Like thee, the hardy mountaineer.

Flower of his heart! thy fragrance mild
    Of peace and freedom seems to breathe;
To pluck thy blossoms in the wild,
    And deck his bonnet with the wreath,
Where dwelt of old his rustic sires,
Is all his simple wish requires.

Flower of his dear-loved native land!
    Alas, when distant, far more dear!
When he from some cold foreign strand
    Looks homeward through the blinding
        tear,
How must his aching heart deplore,
That home and thee he sees no more!
                            ANNE GRANT.

FLOWERS.

Spake full well, in language quaint and
    olden,
One who dwelleth by the castled Rhine,
When he call'd the flowers, so blue and
    golden,
  Stars, that in earth's firmament do shine.

Stars they are, wherein we read our his-
    tory,
  As astrologers and seers of eld;
Yet not wrapp'd about with awful mystery,
  Like the burning stars which they beheld.

Wondrous truths, and manifold as won-
    drous,
  God hath written in those stars above;
But not less in the bright flowerets under
    us
  Stands the revelation of his love.

Bright and glorious is that revelation,
  Written all over this great world of
      ours—
Making evident our own creation,
  In these stars of earth, these golden
      flowers.

And the poet, faithful and far-seeing,
  Sees, alike in stars and flowers, a part
Of the self-same, universal being
  Which is throbbing in his brain and
      heart.

Gorgeous flowerets in the sunlight shin-
    ing,
  Blossoms flaunting in the eye of day,
Tremulous leaves, with soft and silver lin-
    ing,
  Buds that open only to decay;

Brilliant hopes, all woven in gorgeous
    tissues,
  Flaunting gayly in the golden light;
Large desires, with most uncertain issues,
  Tender wishes, blossoming at night;

These in flowers and men are more than
    seeming;
  Workings are they of the self-same
      powers
Which the poet, in no idle dreaming,
  Seeth in himself and in the flowers.

Everywhere about us are they glowing—
  Some, like stars, to tell us Spring is born;
Others, their blue eyes with tears o'erflow-
    ing,
  Stand, like Ruth, amid the golden corn.

Not alone in Spring's armorial bearing,
  And in Summer's green-emblazon'd
      field,
But in arms of brave old Autumn's wear-
    ing,
  In the centre of his brazen shield;

Not alone in meadows and green alleys,
  On the mountain-top, and by the brink
Of sequester'd pools in woodland valleys,
  Where the slaves of Nature stoop to
      drink;

Not alone in her vast dome of glory,
  Not on graves of bird and beast alone,
But in old cathedrals, high and hoary,
  On the tombs of heroes, carved in stone;

In the cottage of the rudest peasant;
  In ancestral homes, whose crumbling
      towers,
Speaking of the Past unto the Present,
  Tell us of the ancient Games of Flowers.

In all places, then, and in all seasons,
  Flowers expand their light and soul-like
      wings,
Teaching us, by most persuasive reasons,
  How akin they are to human things.

And with childlike, credulous affection,
  We behold their tender buds expand—
Emblems of our own great resurrection,
  Emblems of the bright and better land.
        Henry Wadsworth Longfellow.

FLOWERS.

Sweet nurslings of the vernal skies,
  Bathed in soft airs, and fed with dew,
What more than magic in you lies
  To fill the heart's fond view!
In childhood's sports companions gay;
In sorrow, on life's downward way,
How soothing! in our last decay,
  Memorials prompt and true.

Relics ye are of Eden's bowers,
  As pure, as fragrant, and as fair,

As when ye crown'd the sunshine hours
  Of happy wanderers there.
Fall'n all beside,—the world of life
How is it stain'd with fear and strife!
In reason's world what storms are rife,
  What passions rage and glare!

But cheerful, and unchanged the while,
  Your first and perfect form ye show,
The same that won Eve's matron smile
  In the world's opening glow.
The stars of heaven a course are taught,
Too high above our human thought;—
Ye may be found if ye are sought,
  And as we gaze, we know.

Ye dwell beside our paths, and homes,
  Our paths of sin, our homes of sorrow,
And guilty man, where'er he roams,
  Your innocent mirth may borrow.
The birds of air before us fleet,
They cannot brook our shame to meet,—
But we may taste your solace sweet,
  And come again to-morrow.

Ye fearless in your nests abide;
  Nor may we scorn, too proudly wise,
Your silent lessons, undescried
  By all but lowly eyes;
For ye could draw th' admiring gaze
Of Him who worlds and hearts surveys;
Your order wild, your fragrant maze,
  He taught us how to prize.

Ye felt your Maker's smile that hour,
  As when He paused, and own'd you good,
His blessing on earth's primal bower,
  Ye felt it all renew'd.
What care ye now, if winter's storm
Sweep restless o'er each silken form?
Christ's blessing at your heart is warm,
  Ye fear no vexing mood.

Alas! of thousand bosoms kind,
  That daily court you, and caress,
How few the happy secret find
  Of your calm loveliness!
"Live for to-day!" to-morrow's light
To-morrow's cares shall bring to sight.
Go, sleep like closing flowers at night,
  And Heaven thy morn will bless.

JOHN KEBLE.

CHORUS OF THE FLOWERS.

WE are the sweet Flowers,
  Born of sunny showers,
Think, whene'er you see us, what our beauty saith;
  Utterance mute and bright
  Of some unknown delight,
We fill the air with pleasure, by our simple breath:
  All who see us love us;
  We befit all places;
Unto sorrow we give smiles; and unto graces, graces.

Mark our ways, how noiseless
  All, and sweetly voiceless,
Though the March-winds pipe to make our passage clear;
  Not a whisper tells
  Where our small seed dwells,
Nor is known the moment green when our tips appear.
  We thread the earth in silence,
  In silence build our bowers;
And leaf by leaf in silence show, till we laugh atop, sweet Flowers.

The dear lumpish baby,
  Humming with the May bee,
Hails us with his bright stare, stumbling through the grass;
  The honey-dropping moon,
  On a night in June,
Kisses our pale pathway leaves, that felt the bridegroom pass.
  Age, the wither'd clinger,
  On us mutely gazes,
And wraps the thought of his last bed in his childhood's daisies.

See, and scorn all duller
  Taste, how Heaven loves color;
How great Nature, clearly, joys in red and green;
  What sweet thoughts she thinks
  Of violets and pinks,
And a thousand flashing hues made solely to be seen;
  See her whitest lilies
  Chill the silver showers,
And what a red mouth has her rose, the woman of the Flowers.

Uselessness divinest,
Of a use the finest,
Painteth us, the teachers of the end of
  use;
Travellers, weary-eyed,
Bless us, far and wide;
Unto sick and prison'd thoughts we give
  sudden truce;
Not a poor town-window
Loves its sickliest planting,
But its wall speaks loftier truth than
  Babylon's whole vaunting.

Sage are yet the uses
Mix'd with our sweet juices,
Whether man or May-fly profits of the
  balm;
As fair fingers heal'd
Knights from the olden field,
We hold cups of mightiest force to give
  the wildest calm.
E'en the terror, poison,
Hath its plea for blooming;
Life it gives to reverent lips, though death
  to the presuming.

And oh! our sweet soul-taker,
That thief, the honey-maker,
What a house hath he, by the thymy glen!
In his talking rooms
How the feasting fumes,
Till his gold cups overflow to the mouths
  of men!
The butterflies come aping
Those fine thieves of ours,
And flutter round our rifled tops, like
  tickled flowers with flowers.

See those tops, how beauteous!
What fair service duteous
Round some idol waits, as on their lord the
  Nine?
Elfin court twould seem,
And taught, perchance, that dream
Which the old Greek mountain dreamt
  upon nights divine.
To expound such wonder
Human speech avails not,
Yet there dies no poorest weed, that such
  a glory exhales not.

Think of all these treasures,
Matchless works and pleasures,
Every one a marvel, more than thought
  can say;
Then think in what bright showers
We thicken fields and bowers,
And with what heaps of sweetness half
  stifle wanton May;
Think of the mossy forests
By the bee-birds haunted,
And all those Amazonian plains, lone
  lying as enchanted.

Trees themselves are ours;
Fruits are born of flowers;
Peach and roughest nut were blossoms in
  the Spring;
The lusty bee knows well
The news, and comes pell-mell,
And dances in the bloomy thicks with
  darksome antheming.
Beneath the very burthen
Of planet-pressing ocean
We wash our smiling cheeks in peace, a
  thought for meek devotion.

Tears of Phœbus—missings
Of Cytherea's kissings,
Have in us been found, and wise men find
  them still;
Drooping grace unfurls
Still Hyacinthus' curls,
And Narcissus loves himself in the selfish
  rill;
Thy red lip, Adonis,
Still is wet with morning;
And the step that bled for thee the rosy
  brier adorning.

Oh! true things are fables,
Fit for sagest tables,
And the flowers are true things, yet no fa-
  bles they;
Fables were not more
Bright, nor loved of yore—
Yet they grew not, like the flowers, by
  every old pathway;
Grossest hand can test us;
Fools may prize us never;
Yet we rise, and rise, and rise, marvels
  sweet for ever.

Who shall say that flowers
Dress not heaven's own bowers?

Who its love, without them, can fancy—or
    sweet floor?
  Who shall even dare
    To say we sprang not there,
And came not down, that Love might bring
    one piece of heaven the more?
  Oh! pray believe that angels
    From those blue dominions
Brought us in their white laps down, 'twixt
    their golden pinions.
              LEIGH HUNT.

HYMN TO THE FLOWERS.

DAY-STARS! that ope your frownless eyes
    to twinkle
  From rainbow galaxies of earth's creation,
And dewdrops on her lonely altars sprinkle
    As a libation!

Ye matin worshippers! who bending
    lowly
  Before the uprisen sun—God's lidless
    eye—
Throw from your chalices a sweet and
    holy
    Incense on high!

Ye bright mosaics! that with storied
    beauty
  The floor of Nature's temple tessellate,
What numerous emblems of instructive
    duty
    Your forms create!

'Neath cloister'd boughs, each floral bell
    that swingeth
  And tolls its perfume on the passing air,
Makes Sabbath in the fields, and ever
    ringeth
    A call to prayer.

Not to the domes where crumbling arch
    and column
  Attest the feebleness of mortal hand,
But to that fane, most catholic and solemn,
    Which God hath plann'd;

To that cathedral, boundless as our wonder,
  Whose quenchless lamps the sun and
    moon supply—

Its choir the winds and waves, its organ
    thunder,
    Its dome the sky.

There—as in solitude and shade I wander
  Through the green aisles, or, stretch'd
    upon the sod,
Awed by the silence, reverently ponder
    The ways of God—

Your voiceless lips, O Flowers, are living
    preachers,
  Each cup a pulpit, every leaf a book,
Supplying to my fancy numerous teachers
    From loneliest nook.

Floral apostles! that in dewy splendor
  "Weep without woe, and blush without
    a crime,"
Oh, may I deeply learn, and ne'er surrender,
    Your lore sublime!

"Thou wert not, Solomon! in all thy
    glory,
  Array'd," the lilies cry, "in robes like
    ours;
How vain your grandeur! Ah, how transitory
    Are human flowers!"

In the sweet-scented pictures, Heavenly
    Artist!
  With which thou paintest Nature's widespread hall,
What a delightful lesson thou impartest
    Of love to all!

Not useless are ye, Flowers! though made
    for pleasure;
  Blooming o'er field and wave, by day
    and night,
From every source your sanction bids me
    treasure
    Harmless delight.

Ephemeral sages! what instructors hoary
  For such a world of thought could furnish scope?
Each fading calyx a *memento mori*,
    Yet fount of hope.

Posthumous glories! angel-like collection!
  Upraised from seed or bulb interr'd in
    earth,

Ye are to me a type of resurrection,
    And second birth.

Were I in churchless solitudes remaining,
    Far from all voice of teachers and divines,
My soul would find, in flowers of God's ordaining,
        Priests, sermons, shrines!
            HORACE SMITH.

TO AN EARLY PRIMROSE.

MILD offspring of a dark and sullen sire!
Whose modest form, so delicately fine,
    Was nursed in whirling storms,
    And cradled in the winds,

Thee, when young Spring first question'd
    Winter's sway,
And dared the sturdy blusterer to the fight,
    Thee on this bank he threw
    To mark his victory.

In this low vale, the promise of the year,
Serene, thou openest to the nipping gale,
    Unnoticed and alone,
    Thy tender elegance.

So Virtue blooms, brought forth amid the storms
Of chill adversity; in some lone walk
    Of life she rears her head,
    Obscure and unobserved;

While every bleaching breeze that on her blows
Chastens her spotless purity of breast,
    And hardens her to bear
    Serene the ills of life.
            HENRY KIRKE WHITE.

TO PRIMROSES,

FILLED WITH MORNING DEW.

WHY do ye weep, sweet babes? Can tears
    Speak grief in you,
        Who were but born
        Just as the modest morn
    Teem'd her refreshing dew?
    Alas! you have not known that shower
        That mars a flower;

    Nor felt th' unkind
        Breath of a blasting wind;
Nor are ye worn with years;
    Or warp'd, as we,
        Who think it strange to see
Such pretty flowers, like to orphans young,
Speaking by tears before ye have a tongue.

Speak, whimpering younglings, and make known
    The reason why
        Ye droop and weep.
    Is it for want of sleep,
    Or childish lullaby?
Or, that ye have not seen as yet
    The violet?
        Or brought a kiss
        From that sweetheart to this?
No, no; this sorrow, shown
    By your tears shed,
    Would have this lecture read:—
" That things of greatest, so of meanest worth,
Conceived with grief are, and with tears brought forth."
            ROBERT HERRICK.

DAFFODILS.

I WANDER'D lonely as a Cloud
    That floats on high o'er Vales and Hills,
When all at once I saw a crowd,
    A host, of golden Daffodils,
Beside the Lake, beneath the trees,
Fluttering and dancing in the breeze.

Continuous as the stars that shine
    And twinkle on the Milky Way,
They stretch'd in never-ending line
    Along the margin of a bay:
Ten thousand saw I at a glance,
Tossing their heads in sprightly dance.

The waves beside them danced, but they
    Outdid the sparkling waves in glee:—
A poet could not but be gay
    In such a jocund company:
I gazed—and gazed—but little thought
What wealth the show to me had brought:

For oft, when on my couch I lie
    In vacant or in pensive mood,

They flash upon that inward eye,
  Which is the bliss of solitude,
And then my heart with pleasure fills,
And dances with the Daffodils.
WILLIAM WORDSWORTH.

TO DAFFODILS.

FAIR Daffodils, we weep to see
  You haste away so soon:
As yet the early-rising Sun
  Has not attain'd his noon.
    Stay, stay,
  Until the hasting day
    Has run
  But to the even-song;
And, having pray'd together, we
  Will go with you along.

We have short time to stay, as you,
  We have as short a Spring;
As quick a growth to meet decay
  As you, or any thing.
    We die,
  As your hours do, and dry
    Away
  Like to the Summer's rain;
Or as the pearls of morning's dew,
  Ne'er to be found again.
ROBERT HERRICK.

THE VIOLET.

O FAINT, delicious, spring-time violet!
  Thine odor, like a key,
Turns noiselessly in memory's wards to let
  A thought of sorrow free.

The breath of distant fields upon my brow
  Blows through that open door
The sound of wind-borne bells, more sweet and low,
  And sadder than of yore.

It comes afar, from that belovéd place
  And that belovéd hour,
When life hung ripening in love's golden grace,
  Like grapes above a bower.

A spring goes singing through its reedy grass;
  The lark sings o'er my head,
Drown'd in the sky—oh pass, ye visions, pass!
  I would that I were dead!—

Why hast thou open'd that forbidden door
  From which I ever flee?
O vanish'd Joy! O Love, that art no more,
  Let my vex'd spirit be!

O violet! thy odor through my brain
  Hath search'd, and stung to grief
This sunny day, as if a curse did stain
  Thy velvet leaf.
WILLIAM WETMORE STORY.

TO THE DAISY.

WITH little here to do or see
Of things that in the great world be,
Sweet Daisy, oft I talk to thee,
    For thou art worthy,
Thou unassuming Commonplace
Of Nature, with that homely face,
And yet with something of a grace,
    Which Love makes for thee!

Oft on the dappled turf at ease
I sit, and play with similes,
Loose types of things through all degrees,
    Thoughts of thy raising:
And many a fond and idle name
I give to thee, for praise or blame,
As is the humor of the game,
    While I am gazing.

A Nun demure, of lowly port;
Or sprightly Maiden of Love's Court,
In thy simplicity the sport
    Of all temptations;
A Queen in crown of rubies drest;
A Starveling in a scanty vest;
Are all, as seems to suit thee best,
    Thy appellations.

A little Cyclops, with one eye
Staring to threaten and defy,
That thought comes next—and instantly
    The freak is over,
The shape will vanish, and behold
A silver Shield with boss of gold,
That spreads itself, some Faery bold
    In fight to cover!

I see thee glittering from afar;—
And then thou art a pretty Star;
Not quite so fair as many are
    In heaven above thee!
Yet like a star, with glittering crest,
Self-poised in air thou seem'st to rest;—
May peace come never to his nest,
    Who shall reprove thee!

Sweet Flower! for by that name at last,
When all my reveries are past,
I call thee, and to that cleave fast,
    Sweet silent Creature!
That breath'st with me in sun and air,
Do thou, as thou art wont, repair
My heart with gladness, and a share
    Of thy meek nature!
              WILLIAM WORDSWORTH.

TO THE DAISY.

BRIGHT flower, whose home is everywhere!
A Pilgrim bold in Nature's care,
And oft, the long year through, the heir
    Of joy or sorrow,
Methinks that there abides in thee
Some concord with humanity,
Given to no other Flower I see
    The forest through!

And wherefore? Man is soon deprest;
A thoughtless Thing! who, once unblest,
Does little on his memory rest,
    Or on his reason;
But Thou wouldst teach him how to find
A shelter under every wind,
A hope for times that are unkind
    And every season.

Thou wander'st this wide world about,
Uncheck'd by pride or scrupulous doubt,
With friends to greet thee, or without,
    Yet pleased and willing;
Meek, yielding to the occasion's call,
And all things suffering from all,
Thy function apostolical
    In peace fulfilling.
              WILLIAM WORDSWORTH.

TO A MOUNTAIN DAISY.

ON TURNING ONE DOWN WITH THE PLOUGH, IN APRIL, 1786.

WEE, modest, crimson-tippèd flower,
Thou's met me in an evil hour,
For I maun crush amang the stoure
    Thy slender stem;
To spare thee now is past my power,
    Thou bonny gem.

Alas! it's no thy neibor sweet,
The bonny lark, companion meet,
Bending thee 'mang the dewy weet,
    Wi' speckled breast,
When upward springing, blithe, to greet
    The purpling east.

Cauld blew the bitter biting north
Upon thy early, humble birth;
Yet cheerfully thou glinted forth
    Amid the storm,
Scarce rear'd above the parent earth
    Thy tender form.

The flaunting flowers our gardens yield,
High sheltering woods and wa's maun
    shield:
But thou beneath the random bield
    O' clod or stane,
Adorns the histie stibble-field,
    Unseen, alane.

There, in thy scanty mantle clad,
Thy snawie bosom sunward spread,
Thou lifts thy unassuming head
    In humble guise;
But now the share uptears thy bed,
    And low thou lies!

Such is the fate of artless maid,
Sweet flow'ret of the rural shade!
By love's simplicity betray'd,
    And guileless trust,
Till she, like thee, all soil'd is laid
    Low i' the dust.

Such is the fate of simple bard,
On life's rough ocean luckless starr'd!
Unskilful he to note the card
    Of prudent lore,
Till billows rage, and gales blow hard,
    And whelm him o'er!

Such fate to suffering worth is given,
Who long with wants and woes has striven,
By human pride or cunning driven
    To misery's brink,
Till, wrench'd of every stay but Heaven,
    He, ruin'd, sink!

Even thou who mourn'st the Daisy's fate,
That fate is thine,—no distant date:
Stern Ruin's ploughshare drives, elate,
    Full on thy bloom,
Till crush'd beneath the furrow's weight
    Shall be thy doom!
                ROBERT BURNS.

THE RHODORA.

ON BEING ASKED, WHENCE IS THE FLOWER?

IN May, when sea-winds pierced our solitudes,
I found the fresh Rhodora in the woods
Spreading its leafless blooms in a damp nook,
To please the desert and the sluggish brook:
  The purple petals fallen in the pool
    Made the black water with their beauty gay,—
  Here might the red-bird come his plumes to cool,
    And court the flower that cheapens his array.
Rhodora! if the sages ask thee why
  This charm is wasted on the earth and sky,
Tell them, dear, that if eyes were made for seeing,
Then beauty is its own excuse for being.
  Why thou wert there, O rival of the rose!
I never thought to ask, I never knew;
  But in my simple ignorance suppose
The self-same Power that brought me there brought you.
                RALPH WALDO EMERSON.

TO THE FRINGED GENTIAN.

THOU blossom, bright with autumn dew,
And color'd with the heaven's own blue,
That openest when the quiet light
Succeeds the keen and frosty night;

Thou comest not when violets lean
O'er wandering brooks and springs unseen,
Or columbines, in purple dress'd,
Nod o'er the ground-bird's hidden nest.

Thou waitest late, and com'st alone,
When woods are bare and birds are flown,
And frosts and shortening days portend
The aged Year is near his end.

Then doth thy sweet and quiet eye
Look through its fringes to the sky,
Blue—blue—as if that sky let fall
A flower from its cerulean wall.

I would that thus, when I shall see
The hour of death draw near to me,
Hope, blossoming within my heart,
May look to heaven as I depart.
                WILLIAM CULLEN BRYANT.

THE USE OF FLOWERS.

GOD might have bade the earth bring forth
  Enough for great and small,
The oak tree and the cedar tree,
  Without a flower at all.
We might have had enough, enough,
  For every want of ours,
For luxury, medicine, and toil,
  And yet have had no flowers.

Then wherefore, wherefore were they made,
  All dyed with rainbow-light,
All fashion'd with supremest grace,
  Upspringing day and night:—
Springing in valleys green and low,
  And on the mountains high,
And in the silent wilderness
  Where no man passes by?

Our outward life requires them not,—
  Then wherefore had they birth?—
To minister delight to man,
  To beautify the earth;
To comfort man,—to whisper hope,
  Whene'er his faith is dim,
For Who so careth for the flowers
  Will care much more for him!
                MARY HOWITT.

A THOUGHT AMONG THE ROSES.

The roses grew so thickly,
  I never saw the thorn,
Nor deem'd the stem was prickly
  Until my hand was torn.

Thus worldly joys invite us
  With rosy-color'd hue;
But, ere they long delight us,
  We find they prick us too.
              PETER SPENCER.

'TIS THE LAST ROSE OF SUMMER.

'Tis the last rose of summer,
  Left blooming alone;
All her lovely companions
  Are faded and gone;
No flower of her kindred,
  No rosebud, is nigh
To reflect back her blushes,
  Or give sigh for sigh.

I'll not leave thee, thou lone one!
  To pine on the stem;
Since the lovely are sleeping,
  Go sleep thou with them.
Thus kindly I scatter
  Thy leaves o'er the bed
Where thy mates of the garden
  Lie scentless and dead.

So soon may *I* follow,
  When friendships decay,
And from love's shining circle
  The gems drop away.
When true hearts lie wither'd,
  And fond ones are flown,
Oh, who would inhabit
  This bleak world alone?
              THOMAS MOORE.

THE IVY GREEN.

Oh! a dainty plant is the Ivy green,
  That creepeth o'er ruins old!
Of right choice food are his meals, I ween,
  In his cell so lone and cold.
The walls must be crumbled, the stones decay'd,
  To pleasure his dainty whim;
And the mouldering dust that years have made
  Is a merry meal for him.
    Creeping where no life is seen,
    A rare old plant is the Ivy green.

Fast he stealeth on, though he wears no wings,
  And a staunch old heart has he!
How closely he twineth, how tight he clings
  To his friend, the huge oak tree!
And slyly he traileth along the ground,
  And his leaves he gently waves,
And he joyously twines and hugs around
  The rich mould of dead men's graves.
    Creeping where no life is seen,
    A rare old plant is the Ivy green.

Whole ages have fled, and their works decay'd,
  And nations scatter'd been;
But the stout old Ivy shall never fade
  From its hale and hearty green.
The brave old plant in its lonely days
  Shall fatten upon the past;
For the stateliest building man can raise
  Is the Ivy's food at last.
    Creeping where no life is seen,
    A rare old plant is the Ivy green.
              CHARLES DICKENS.

THE DEATH OF THE FLOWERS.

The melancholy days are come, the saddest of the year,
Of wailing winds, and naked woods, and meadows brown and sere.
Heap'd in the hollows of the grove, the autumn leaves lie dead;
They rustle to the eddying gust, and to the rabbit's tread.
The robin and the wren are flown, and from the shrubs the jay,
And from the wood-top calls the crow through all the gloomy day.

Where are the flowers, the fair young flowers, that lately sprang and stood
In brighter light and softer airs, a beauteous sisterhood?

Alas! they all are in their graves; the
    gentle race of flowers
Are lying in their lowly beds with the fair
    and good of ours.
The rain is falling where they lie; but the
    cold November rain
Calls not from out the gloomy earth the
    lovely ones again.

The wind-flower and the violet, they perish'd long ago,
And the brier-rose and the orchis died
    amid the summer glow;
But on the hill the golden-rod, and the
    aster in the wood,
And the yellow sunflower by the brook, in
    autumn beauty stood,
Till fell the frost from the clear cold
    heaven, as falls the plague on men,
And the brightness of their smile was gone
    from upland, glade, and glen.

And now, when comes the calm mild day,
    as still such days will come,
To call the squirrel and the bee from out
    their winter home;
When the sound of dropping nuts is heard,
    though all the trees are still,
And twinkle in the smoky light the waters
    of the rill,
The south wind searches for the flowers
    whose fragrance late he bore,
And sighs to find them in the wood and by
    the stream no more.

And then I think of one who in her youthful beauty died,
The fair meek blossom that grew up and
    faded by my side.
In the cold moist earth we laid her when
    the forest cast the leaf,
And we wept that one so lovely should
    have a life so brief;
Yet not unmeet it was that one, like that
    young friend of ours,
So gentle and so beautiful, should perish
    with the flowers.
        WILLIAM CULLEN BRYANT.

TO BLOSSOMS.

FAIR pledges of a fruitful tree,
    Why do ye fall so fast?
    Your date is not so past

But you may stay yet here a while
    To blush and gently smile,
    And go at last.

What! were ye born to be
    An hour or half's delight,
    And so to bid good-night?
'Tis pity Nature brought ye forth,
    Merely to show your worth,
    And lose you quite.

But you are lovely leaves, where we
    May read how soon things have
    Their end, though ne'er so brave;
And, after they have shown their pride
    Like you a while, they glide
    Into the grave.
        ROBERT HERRICK.

ALMOND-BLOSSOM.

BLOSSOM of the almond trees,
April's gift to April's bees,
Birthday ornament of spring,
Flora's fairest daughterling;—
Coming when no flowerets dare
Trust the cruel outer air,
When the royal king-cup bold
Dares not don his coat of gold,
And the sturdy blackthorn spray
Keeps his silver for the May;—
Coming when no flowerets would,
Save thy lowly sisterhood,
Early violets, blue and white,
Dying for their love of light,—
Almond-blossom, sent to teach us
That the spring days soon will reach us,
Lest, with longing over-tried,
We die as the violets died,—
Blossom, clouding all the tree
With thy crimson 'broidery,
Long before a leaf of green
On the bravest bough is seen,—
Ah! when winter winds are swinging
All thy red bells into ringing,
With a bee in every bell,
Almond-bloom, we greet thee well.
        EDWIN ARNOLD.

SONG.

UNDER the greenwood tree
Who loves to lie with me

And tune his merry note
    Unto the sweet bird's throat,
Come hither, come hither, come hither;
    Here shall he see
    No enemy
But Winter and rough weather.

Who doth ambition shun
    And loves to live i' the sun,
Seeking the food he eats,
    And pleased with what he gets,
Come hither, come hither, come hither;
    Here shall he see
    No enemy
But Winter and rough weather.
WILLIAM SHAKESPEARE.

THE HOLLY TREE.

O READER! hast thou ever stood to see
    The holly tree?
The eye that contemplates it well, perceives
    Its glossy leaves,
Ordered by an intelligence so wise
As might confound the atheist's sophistries.

Below, a circling fence, its leaves are seen
    Wrinkled and keen;
No grazing cattle, through their prickly round,
    Can reach to wound;
But as they grow where nothing is to fear,
Smooth and unarm'd the pointless leaves appear.

I love to view these things with curious eyes,
    And moralize;
And in this wisdom of the holly tree
    Can emblems see
Wherewith, perchance, to make a pleasant rhyme,
One which may profit in the after-time.

Thus, though abroad, perchance I might appear
    Harsh and austere
To those who on my leisure would intrude,
    Reserved and rude;
Gentle at home amid my friends I'd be,
Like the high leaves upon the holly tree.

And should my youth, as youth is apt, I know,
    Some harshness show,
All vain asperities I, day by day,
    Would wear away,
Till the smooth temper of my age should be
Like the high leaves upon the holly tree.

And as, when all the summer trees are seen
    So bright and green,
The holly-leaves their fadeless hues display
    Less bright than they;
But when the bare and wintry woods we see,
What then so cheerful as the holly tree?

So, serious should my youth appear among
    The thoughtless throng;
So would I seem, amid the young and gay,
    More grave than they;
That in my age as cheerful I might be
As the green winter of the holly tree.
ROBERT SOUTHEY.

THE AGED OAK AT OAKLEY, SOMERSET.

I WAS a young fair tree:
Each spring with quivering green
My boughs were clad; and far
Down the deep vale a light
Shone from me on the eyes
Of those who pass'd,—a light
That told of sunny days,
And blossoms, and blue sky;
For I was ever first
Of all the grove to hear
The soft voice under ground
Of the warm-working spring;
And ere my brethren stirr'd
Their sheathèd buds, the kine,
And the kine's keeper, came
Slow up the valley-path,
And laid them underneath
My cool and rustling leaves;
And I could feel them there
As in the quiet shade
They stood, with tender thoughts
That pass'd along their life

Like wings on a still lake,
Blessing me; and to God,
The blessèd God, who cares
For all my little leaves,
Went up the silent praise;
And I was glad with joy
Which life of laboring things
Ill knows,—the joy that sinks
Into a life of rest.

 Ages have fled since then:
But deem not my pierced trunk
And scanty leafage serves
No high behest; my name
Is sounded far and wide;
And in the Providence
That guides the steps of men,
Hundreds have come to view
My grandeur in decay;
And there hath pass'd from me
A quiet influence
Into the minds of men:
The silver head of age,
The majesty of laws,
The very name of God,
And holiest things that are
Have won upon the heart
Of humankind the more,
For that I stand to meet
With vast and bleaching trunk
The rudeness of the sky.
HENRY ALFORD.

THE QUESTION.

I DREAM'D that as I wander'd by the way
 Bare Winter suddenly was changed to Spring,
And gentle odors led my steps astray,
 Mix'd with a sound of waters murmuring
Along a shelving bank of turf, which lay
 Under a copse, and hardly dared to fling
Its green arms round the bosom of the stream,
But kiss'd it and then fled, as thou mightest in dream.

There grew pied wind-flowers and violets,
 Daisies, those pearl'd Arcturi of the earth,
The constellated flower that never sets;
 Faint ox-lips; tender blue-bells, at whose birth
The sod scarce heaved; and that tall flower that wets
 Its mother's face with heaven-collected tears,
When the low wind, its playmate's voice, it hears.

And in the warm hedge grew lush eglantine,
 Green cow-bind and the moonlight-color'd may,
And cherry-blossoms, and white cups, whose wine
 Was the bright dew yet drain'd not by the day;
And wild roses, and ivy serpentine,
 With its dark buds and leaves, wandering astray;
And flowers azure, black, and streak'd with gold,
Fairer than any waken'd eyes behold.

And nearer to the river's trembling edge
 There grew broad flag-flowers, purple prankt with white,
And starry river-buds among the sedge,
 And floating water-lilies, broad and bright,
Which lit the oak that overhung the hedge
 With moonlight beams of their own watery light;
And bulrushes, and reeds of such deep green
As soothed the dazzled eye with sober sheen.

Methought that of these visionary flowers
 I made a nosegay, bound in such a way
That the same hues, which in their natural bowers
 Were mingled or opposed, the like array
Kept these imprison'd children of the Hours
 Within my hand,—and then, elate and gay,
I hasten'd to the spot whence I had come
That I might there present it—oh! to whom?
PERCY BYSSHE SHELLEY.

ORIGIN OF THE OPAL.

A DEWDROP came, with a spark of flame
 He had caught from the sun's last ray,

To a violet's breast, where he lay at rest
  Till the hours brought back the day.

The rose look'd down, with a blush and
    frown;
  But she smiled all at once to view
Her own bright form, with its coloring
    warm,
  Reflected back by the dew.

Then the stranger took a stolen look
  At the sky so soft and blue;
And a leaflet green, with its silver sheen,
  Was seen by the idler too.

A cold north wind, as he thus reclined,
  Of a sudden raged around;
And a maiden fair, who was walking there,
  Next morning, an *opal* found.
                AUTHOR UNKNOWN.

SONG OF THE BROOK.

I COME from haunts of coot and hern:
  I make a sudden sally
And sparkle out among the fern,
  To bicker down a valley.

By thirty hills I hurry down,
  Or slip between the ridges;
By twenty thorps, a little town,
  And half a hundred bridges.

Till last by Philip's farm I flow
  To join the brimming river;
For men may come and men may go,
  But I go on for ever.

I chatter over stony ways,
  In little sharps and trebles;
I bubble into eddying bays,
  I babble on the pebbles.

With many a curve my banks I fret
  By many a field and fallow,
And many a fairy foreland set
  With willow-weed and mallow.

I chatter, chatter, as I flow
  To join the brimming river;
For men may come and men may go,
  But I go on for ever.

I wind about, and in and out,
  With here a blossom sailing,
And here and there a lusty trout,
  And here and there a grayling.

And here and there a foamy flake
  Upon me, as I travel,
With many a silvery waterbreak
  Above the golden gravel;

And draw them all along, and flow
  To join the brimming river;
For men may come and men may go,
  But I go on for ever.

I steal by lawns and grassy plots;
  I slide by hazel covers;
I move the sweet forget-me-nots
  That grow for happy lovers.

I slip, I slide, I gloom, I glance,
  Among my skimming swallows,
I make the netted sunbeam dance
  Against my sandy shallows.

I murmur under moon and stars
  In brambly wildernesses;
I linger by my shingly bars;
  I loiter round my cresses;

And out again I curve and flow
  To join the brimming river;
For men may come and men may go,
  But I go on for ever.
                ALFRED TENNYSON.

ARETHUSA.

ARETHUSA arose
  From her couch of snows
In the Acroceraunian mountains,—
  From cloud and from crag
  With many a jag,
Shepherding her bright fountains.
  She leapt down the rocks
  With her rainbow locks
Streaming among the streams;—
  Her steps paved with green
  The downward ravine
Which slopes to the western gleams:
  And, gliding and springing,
  She went, ever singing
In murmurs as soft as sleep;
  The Earth seem'd to love her,
  And Heaven smiled above her,
As she linger'd toward the deep.

Then Alpheus bold,
  On his glacier cold,
With his trident the mountains strook;
  And open'd a chasm
  In the rocks;—with the spasm
All Erymanthus shook.
  And the black south wind
  It conceal'd behind
The urns of the silent snow,
  And earthquake and thunder
  Did rend in sunder
The bars of the springs below:
  The beard and the hair
  Of the river-god were
Seen through the torrent's sweep,
  As he follow'd the light
  Of the fleet nymph's flight
To the brink of the Dorian deep.

  "Oh, save me! Oh, guide me!
  And bid the deep hide me,
For he grasps me now by the hair!"
  The loud Ocean heard,
  To its blue depth stirr'd,
And divided at her prayer;
  And under the water
  The Earth's white daughter
Fled like a sunny beam;
  Behind her descended,
  Her billows unblended
With the brackish Dorian stream.
  Like a gloomy stain
  On the emerald main,
Alpheus rush'd behind,—
  As an eagle pursuing
  A dove to its ruin
Down the streams of the cloudy wind.

  Under the bowers
  Where the Ocean Powers
Sit on their pearlèd thrones;
  Through the coral woods
  Of the weltering floods,
Over heaps of unvalued stones;
  Through the dim beams
  Which amid the streams
Weave a network of color'd light;
  And under the caves,
  Where the shadowy waves
Are as green as the forest's night—
  Outspeeding the shark,
  And the sword-fish dark,
Under the ocean foam;
  And up through the rifts
  Of the mountain-clifts
They pass'd to their Dorian home.

  And now from their fountains
  In Enna's mountains,
Down one vale where the morning basks,
  Like friends once parted,
  Grown single-hearted,
They ply their watery tasks.
  At sunrise they leap
  From their cradles steep
In the cave of the shelving hill;
  At noontide they flow
  Through the woods below,
And the meadows of asphodel;
  And at night they sleep
  In the rocking deep
Beneath the Ortygian shore;—
  Like spirits that lie
  In the azure sky,
When they love, but live no more.
          PERCY BYSSHE SHELLEY.

SONG OF THE RIVER.

CLEAR and cool, clear and cool,
By laughing shallow and dreaming pool;
Cool and clear, cool and clear,
By shining shingle and foaming weir;
Under the crag where the ouzel sings,
And the ivied wall where the church-bell rings,
Undefiled for the undefiled;
Play by me, bathe in me, mother and child.

Dank and foul, dank and foul,
By the smoky town in its murky cowl;
Foul and dank, foul and dank,
By wharf, and sewer, and slimy bank;
Darker and darker the further I go,
Baser and baser the richer I grow;
Who dare sport with the sin-defiled?
Shrink from me, turn from me, mother and child.

Strong and free, strong and free,
The flood-gates are open, away to the sea:
Free and strong, free and strong,
Cleansing my streams as I hurry along

To the golden sands and the leaping bar,
And the taintless tide that awaits me afar,
As I lose myself in the infinite main,
Like a soul that has sinn'd and is pardon'd again,
Undefiled for the undefiled;
Play by me, bathe in me, mother and child.
CHARLES KINGSLEY.

THE SEA.

THE sea! the sea! the open sea!
The blue, the fresh, the ever free!
Without a mark, without a bound,
It runneth the earth's wide regions' round,
It plays with the clouds; it mocks the skies;
Or like a cradled creature lies.

I'm on the sea! I'm on the sea!
I am where I would ever be;
With the blue above, and the blue below,
And silence wheresoe'er I go;
If a storm should come and awake the deep,
What matter? *I* shall ride and sleep.

I love (oh *how* I love!) to ride
On the fierce foaming, bursting tide,
When every mad wave drowns the moon,
Or whistles aloft his tempest-tune,
And tells how goeth the world below,
And why the south-west blasts do blow.

I never was on the dull tame shore
But I loved the great sea more and more,
And backward flew to her billowy breast,
Like a bird that seeketh its mother's nest;
And a mother she *was*, and *is* to me;
For I was born on the open sea!

The waves were white, and red the morn,
In the noisy hour when I was born;
And the whale it whistled, the porpoise roll'd,
And the dolphins bared their backs of gold;
And never was heard such an outcry wild
As welcomed to life the ocean child!

I've lived since then, in calm and strife,
Full fifty summers a sailor's life,
With wealth to spend and a power to range,
But never have sought, nor sigh'd for change;
And Death, whenever he come to me,
Shall come on the wild unbounded sea!
BRYAN WALLER PROCTER
(BARRY CORNWALL).

THE SEA-LIMITS.

CONSIDER the sea's listless chime:
  Time's self it is, made audible,—
  The murmur of the earth's own shell.
Secret continuance sublime
  Is the sea's end: our sight may pass
  No furlong further. Since time was,
This sound hath told the lapse of time.

No quiet, which is death's,—it hath
  The mournfulness of ancient life,
  Enduring always at dull strife.
As the world's heart of rest and wrath,
  Its painful pulse is in the sands.
  Last utterly, the whole sky stands,
Gray and not known, along its path.

Listen alone beside the sea,
  Listen alone among the woods;
  Those voices of twin solitudes
Shall have one sound alike to thee:
  Hark where the murmurs of throng'd men
  Surge and sink back and surge again,—
Still the one voice of wave and tree.

Gather a shell from the strown beach
  And listen at its lips: they sigh
  The same desire and mystery,
The echo of the whole sea's speech.
  And all mankind is thus at heart
  Not anything but what thou art:
And Earth, Sea, Man, are all in each.
DANTE GABRIEL ROSSETTI.

THE TEMPEST.

THE tempest has darken'd the face of the skies,
  The winds whistle wildly across the waste plain,
The fiends of the whirlwind terrific arise,
  And mingle the clouds with the white foaming main.

All dark is the night and all gloomy the
   shore,
Save when the red lightnings the ether
   divide;
Then follows the thunder with loud-sound-
   ing roar,
And echoes in concert the billowy tide.

But though now all is murky and shaded
   with gloom,
Hope, the soother, soft whispers the tem-
   pest shall cease;
Then Nature again in her beauty shall
   bloom,
And enamor'd embrace the fair, sweet-
   smiling Peace.

For the bright blushing Morning, all rosy
   with light,
Shall convey on her wings the creator of
   day;
He shall drive all the tempests and terrors
   of night,
And Nature, enliven'd, again shall be
   gay.

Then the warblers of Spring shall attune
   the soft lay,
And again the bright floweret shall
   blush in the vale;
On the breast of the ocean the zephyr shall
   play,
And the sunbeam shall sleep on the hill
   and the dale.

If the tempests of Nature so soon sink to
   rest,
If her once-faded beauties so soon glow
   again,
Shall man be for ever by tempests op-
   press'd,—
By the tempests of passion, of sorrow,
   and pain?

Ah, no! for his passions and sorrows shall
   cease
When the troublesome fever of life shall
   be o'er:
In the night of the grave he shall slumber
   in peace,
And passion and sorrow shall vex him
   no more.

And shall not this night, and its long dis-
   mal gloom,
Like the night of the tempest again
   pass away?
Yes! the dust of the earth in bright
   beauty shall bloom,
And rise to the morning of heavenly
   day.
                  Sir Humphry Davy.

GULF-WEED.

A WEARY weed, toss'd to and fro,
   Drearily drench'd in the ocean brine,
Soaring high and sinking low,
   Lash'd along without will of mine;
Sport of the spoom of the surging sea:
   Flung on the foam, afar and anear,
Mark my manifold mystery,—
   Growth and grace in their place appear.

I bear round berries, gray and red,
   Rootless and rover though I be;
My spangled leaves, when nicely spread,
   Arboresce as a trunkless tree;
Corals curious coat me o'er,
   White and hard in apt array;
'Mid the wild waves' rude uproar
   Gracefully grow I, night and day.

Hearts there are on the sounding shore,
   Something whispers soft to me,
Restless and roaming for evermore,
   Like this weary weed of the sea;
Bear they yet on each beating breast
   The eternal type of the wondrous whole,
Growth unfolding amidst unrest,
   Grace informing with silent soul.
             Cornelius George Fenner.

THE TREASURES OF THE DEEP.

WHAT hid'st thou in thy treasure-caves
   and cells,
   Thou hollow-sounding and mysterious
   main?—
Pale glistening pearls and rainbow-color'd
   shells,
   Bright things which gleam unreck'd-of
   and in vain!—
Keep, keep thy riches, melancholy sea!
We ask not such from thee.

Yet more, the depths have more!—what
  wealth untold,
 Far down, and shining through their
  stillness lies!
Thou hast the starry gems, the burning
  gold,
 Won from ten thousand royal argosies!—
Sweep o'er thy spoils, thou wild and
  wrathful main!
Earth claims not *these* again.

Yet more, the depths have more! thy
  waves have roll'd
 Above the cities of a world gone by;
Sand hath fill'd up the palaces of old,
 Sea-weed o'ergrown the halls of rev-
  elry.—
Dash o'er them, Ocean, in thy scornful
  play!
Man yields them to decay.

Yet more, the billows and the depths have
  more!
 High hearts and brave are gather'd to
  thy breast!
They hear not now the booming waters
  roar,
 The battle-thunders will not break their
  rest.—
Keep thy red gold and gems, thou stormy
  grave!
Give back the true and brave!

Give back the lost and lovely! those for
  whom
 The place was kept at board and hearth
  so long!
The prayer went up through midnight's
  breathless gloom,
 And the vain yearning woke midst fes-
  tal song!
Hold fast thy buried isles, thy towers o'er-
  thrown,—
But all is not thine own.

To thee the love of woman hath gone
  down,
 Dark flow thy tides o'er manhood's noble
  head,
O'er youth's bright locks, and beauty's
  flowery crown;
 Yet must thou hear a voice,—Restore
  the dead!

Earth shall reclaim her precious things
  from thee!—
Restore the dead, thou sea!
                FELICIA DOROTHEA HEMANS.

THE CORAL GROVE.

DEEP in the wave is a coral grove,
Where the purple mullet and gold-fish rove;
Where the sea-flower spreads its leaves of
  blue
That never are wet with falling dew,
But in bright and changeful beauty shine
Far down in the green and glassy brine.
The floor is of sand, like the mountain-
  drift,
And the pearl-shells spangle the flinty snow;
From coral rocks the sea-plants lift
Their boughs, where the tides and billows
  flow;
The water is calm and still below,
For the winds and waves are absent there,
And the sands are bright as the stars that
  glow
In the motionless fields of upper air.
There, with its waving blade of green,
The sea-flag streams through the silent
  water,
And the crimson leaf of the dulse is seen
To blush, like a banner bathed in slaughter.
There with a light and easy motion
The fan-coral sweeps through the clear,
  deep sea;
And the yellow and scarlet tufts of ocean
Are bending like corn on the upland lea;
And life, in rare and beautiful forms,
Is sporting amid those bowers of stone,
And is safe when the wrathful spirit of
  storms
Has made the top of the wave his own.
And when the ship from his fury flies,
Where the myriad voices of ocean roar,
When the wind-god frowns in the murky
  skies,
And demons are waiting the wreck on
  shore;
Then, far below, in the peaceful sea,
The purple mullet and gold-fish rove
Where the waters murmur tranquilly,
Through the bending twigs of the coral
  grove.
                JAMES GATES PERCIVAL.

DRIFTING.

My soul to-day
Is far away,
Sailing the Vesuvian Bay;
My wingèd boat,
A bird afloat,
Swims round the purple peaks remote:—

Round purple peaks
It sails, and seeks
Blue inlets, and their crystal creeks,
Where high rocks throw,
Through deeps below,
A duplicated golden glow.

Far, vague, and dim,
The mountains swim;
While on Vesuvius' misty brim,
With outstretch'd hands,
The gray smoke stands
O'erlooking the volcanic lands.

In lofty lines,
'Mid palms and pines,
And olives, aloes, elms, and vines,
Sorrento swings
On sunset wings,
Where Tasso's spirit soars and sings.

Here Ischia smiles
O'er liquid miles;
And yonder, bluest of the isles,
Calm Capri waits,
Her sapphire gates
Beguiling to her bright estates.

I heed not, if
My rippling skiff
Float swift or slow from cliff to cliff;—
With dreamful eyes
My spirit lies
Under the walls of Paradise.

Under the walls
Where swells and falls
The Bay's deep breast at intervals,
At peace I lie,
Blown softly by,
A cloud upon this liquid sky.

The day, so mild,
Is Heaven's own child,
With Earth and Ocean reconciled;
The airs I feel
Around me steal
Are murmuring to the murmuring keel.

Over the rail
My hand I trail
Within the shadow of the sail,
A joy intense,
The cooling sense,
Glides down my drowsy indolence.

With dreamful eyes
My spirit lies
Where Summer sings and never dies,—
O'erveil'd with vines,
She glows and shines
Among her future oil and wines.

Her children, hid
The cliffs amid,
Are gambolling with the gambolling kid;
Or down the walls,
With tipsy calls,
Laugh on the rocks like waterfalls.

The fisher's child,
With tresses wild,
Unto the smooth, bright sand beguiled,
With glowing lips
Sings as she skips,
Or gazes at the far-off ships.

Yon deep bark goes
Where Traffic blows,
From lands of sun to lands of snows;—
This happier one,
Its course is run
From lands of snow to lands of sun.

O happy ship,
To rise and dip,
With the blue crystal at your lip!
O happy crew,
My heart with you
Sails, and sails, and sings anew!

No more, no more
The worldly shore
Upbraids me with its loud uproar!
With dreamful eyes
My spirit lies
Under the walls of Paradise!

THOMAS BUCHANAN READ.

AT SEA.

The night was made for cooling shade,
For silence, and for sleep;
And when I was a child, I laid
My hands upon my breast, and pray'd,
And sank to slumbers deep.

Childlike, as then, I lie to-night,
And watch my lonely cabin-light.

Each movement of the swaying lamp
  Shows how the vessel reels,
And o'er her deck the billows tramp,
And all her timbers strain and cramp
  With every shock she feels;
It starts and shudders, while it burns,
And in its hingèd socket turns.

Now swinging slow, and slanting low,
  It almost level lies:
And yet I know, while to and fro
I watch the seeming pendulum go
  With restless fall and rise,
The steady shaft is still upright,
Poising its little globe of light.

O hand of God! O lamp of peace!
  O promise of my soul!
Though weak and toss'd, and ill at ease
Amid the roar of smiting seas,—
  The ship's convulsive roll,—
I own, with love and tender awe,
Yon perfect type of faith and law.

A heavenly trust my spirit calms,—
  My soul is fill'd with light;
The ocean sings his solemn psalms;
The wild winds chant; I cross my palms;
  Happy, as if to-night,
Under the cottage-roof again,
I heard the soothing summer rain.
                JOHN T. TROWBRIDGE.

WHERE LIES THE LAND?

WHERE lies the land to which the ship
  would go?
Far, far ahead, is all her seamen know;
And where the land she travels from?
  Away,
Far, far behind, is all that they can say.

On sunny noons upon the deck's smooth
  face,
Link'd arm in arm, how pleasant here to
  pace;
Or, o'er the stern reclining, watch below
The foaming wake far widening as we go.

On stormy nights when wild north-westers
  rave,
How proud a thing to fight with wind and
  wave!

The dripping sailor on the reeling mast
Exults to bear, and scorns to wish it past.

Where lies the land to which the ship
  would go?
Far, far ahead, is all her seamen know;
And where the land she travels from?
  Away,
Far, far behind, is all that they can say.
                ARTHUR HUGH CLOUGH.

BY THE AUTUMN SEA.

FAIR as the dawn of the fairest day,
Sad as the evening's tender gray,
By the latest lustre of sunset kissed,
That wavers and wanes through an amber
  mist,
There cometh a dream of the past to me,
On the desert sands by the autumn sea.

All heaven is wrapped in a mystic veil,
And the face of the ocean is dim and pale,
And there rises a wind from the chill
  north-west
That seemeth the wail of a soul's unrest,
As the twilight falls, and the vapors flee
Far over the wastes of the autumn sea.

A single ship through the gloaming glides,
Upborne on the swell of the seaward tides;
And above the gleam of her topmast spar
Are the virgin eyes of the vesper-star
That shine with an angel's ruth on me,
A hopeless waif, by the autumn sea.

The wings of the ghostly beach-birds gleam
Through the shimmering surf, and the curlew's scream
Falls faintly shrill from the darkening
  height;
The first weird sigh on the lips of Night
Breathes low through the sedge and the
  blasted tree,
With a murmur of doom, by the autumn
  sea.

O sky-enshadowed and yearning main!
Your gloom but deepens this human pain;
Those waves seem big with a nameless care,
That sky is a type of the heart's despair,
As I linger and muse by the sombre lea,
And the night-shades close on the autumn
  sea.
                PAUL HAMILTON HAYNE.

Izaak Walton, fishing.

INVITATION TO IZAAK WALTON.

WHILST in this cold and blustering clime,
  Where bleak winds howl and tempests roar,
We pass away the roughest time
  Has been of many years before;

Whilst from the most tempestuous nooks
  The chillest blasts our peace invade,
And by great rains our smallest brooks
  Are almost navigable made;

Whilst all the ills are so improved
  Of this dead quarter of the year,
That even you, so much beloved,
  We would not now wish with us here,—

In this estate, I say, it is
  Some comfort to us to suppose
That in a better clime than this
  You, our dear friend, have more repose;

And some delight to me the while,
  Though Nature now does weep in rain,
To think that I have seen her smile,
  And haply may I do again.

If the all-ruling Power please
  We live to see another May,
We'll recompense an age of these
  Foul days in one fine fishing-day.

We then shall have a day or two,
  Perhaps a week, wherein to try
What the best master's hand can do
  With the most deadly killing fly—

A day with not too bright a beam;
A warm, but not a scorching sun;
A southern gale to curl the stream;
  And, master, half our work is done.

Then, whilst behind some bush we wait
  The scaly people to betray,
We'll prove it just, with treacherous bait,
  To make the preying trout our prey;

And think ourselves, in such an hour,
  Happier than those, though not so high,
Who, like leviathans, devour
  Of meaner men the smaller fry.

This, my best friend, at my poor home,
  Shall be our pastime and our theme;
But then, should you not deign to come,
  You make all this a flattering dream.
                      CHARLES COTTON.

THE ANGLER'S WISH.

I IN these flowery meads would be,
These crystal streams should solace me;
To whose harmonious bubbling noise
I, with my angle, would rejoice,
  Sit here, and see the turtle-dove
  Court his chaste mate to acts of love;

Or, on that bank, feel the west wind
Breathe health and plenty; please my mind,
To see sweet dewdrops kiss these flowers,
And then wash'd off by April showers;
  Here, hear my kenna sing a song:
  There, see a blackbird feed her young,

Or a laverock build her nest;
Here, give my weary spirits rest,
And raise my low-pitch'd thoughts above
Earth, or what poor mortals love.
  Thus, free from lawsuits, and the noise
  Of princes' courts, I would rejoice;

Or, with my Bryan and a book,
Loiter long days near Shawford brook;
There sit by him, and eat my meat;
There see the sun both rise and set;
There bid good-morning to next day;
There meditate my time away;
  And angle on; and beg to have
  A quiet passage to a welcome grave.
                      IZAAK WALTON.

VERSES IN PRAISE OF ANGLING.

QUIVERING fears, heart-tearing cares,
Anxious sighs, untimely tears,
  Fly, fly to courts,
  Fly to fond worldlings' sports,
Where strain'd sardonic smiles are glosing still,
And Grief is forced to laugh against her will,
  Where mirth's but mummery,
  And sorrows only real be.

Fly from our country pastimes, fly,
Sad troops of human misery,
  Come, serene looks,
  Clear as the crystal brooks,

Or the pure azured heaven that smiles to see
The rich attendance on our poverty;
    Peace and a secure mind,
    Which all men seek, we only find.

Abusèd mortals! did you know
Where joy, heart's ease, and comforts grow,
    You'd scorn proud towers,
    And seek them in these bowers,
Where winds, sometimes, our woods perhaps may shake,
But blustering care could never tempest make;
    Nor murmurs e'er come nigh us,
    Saving of fountains that glide by us.

Here's no fantastic mask nor dance,
But of our kids that frisk and prance;
    Nor wars are seen,
    Unless upon the green
Two harmless lambs are butting one the other,
Which done, both bleating run, each to his mother;
    And wounds are never found,
    Save what the ploughshare gives the ground.

Here are no entrapping baits
To hasten too, too hasty fates;
    Unless it be
    The fond credulity
Of silly fish, which (worldling-like) still look
Upon the bait, but never on the hook;
    Nor envy, 'less among
    The birds, for price of their sweet song.

Go, let the diving negro seek
For gems, hid in some forlorn creek;
    We all pearls scorn
    Save what the dewy morn
Congeals upon each little spire of grass,
Which careless shepherds beat down as they pass;
    And gold ne'er here appears,
    Save what the yellow Ceres bears.

Blest silent groves, oh may you be,
For ever, mirth's best nursery!
    May pure contents
    For ever pitch their tents
Upon these downs, these meads, these rocks, these mountains;
And peace still slumber by these purling fountains,
    Which we may every year
    Meet, when we come a-fishing here.
          Sir Henry Wotton.

THE ANGLER.

Oh the gallant fisher's life!
    It is the best of any:
'Tis full of pleasure, void of strife,
    And 'tis beloved by many;
        Other joys
        Are but toys;
        Only this
        Lawful is;
        For our skill
        Breeds no ill,
But content and pleasure.

In a morning up we rise,
    Ere Aurora's peeping;
Drink a cup to wash our eyes,
    Leave the sluggard sleeping;
        Then we go,
        To and fro,
        With our knacks
        At our backs,
        To such streams
        As the Thames,
If we have the leisure.

When we please to walk abroad
    For our recreation,
In the fields is our abode,
    Full of delectation,
        Where, in a brook,
        With a hook—
        Or a lake,—
        Fish we take;
        There we sit
        For a bit,
Till we fish entangle.

We have gentles in a horn,
    We have paste and worms too;
We can watch both night and morn,
    Suffer rain and storms too;
        None do here
        Use to swear:

    Oaths do fray
    Fish away;
    We sit still,
    Watch our quill:
Fishers must not wrangle.

If the sun's excessive heat
  Make our bodies swelter,
To an osier hedge we get,
  For a friendly shelter;
    Where—in a dyke,
    Perch or pike,
    Roach or dace,
    We do chase,
    Bleak or gudgeon,
    Without grudging;
We are still contented.

Or, we sometimes pass an hour
  Under a green willow
That defends us from a shower,
  Making earth our pillow;
    Where we may
    Think and pray,
    Before death
    Stops our breath;
    Other joys
    Are but toys,
And to be lamented.
            JOHN CHALKHILL.

THE ANGLER'S TRYSTING-TREE.

SING, sweet thrushes, forth and sing!
  Meet the morn upon the lea;
Are the emeralds of the spring
  On the angler's trysting-tree?
Tell, sweet thrushes, tell to me!
Are there buds on our willow tree?
Buds and birds on our trysting-tree?

Sing, sweet thrushes, forth and sing!
  Have you met the honey-bee,
Circling upon rapid wing,
  'Round the angler's trysting-tree?
Up, sweet thrushes, up and see!
Are there bees at our willow tree?
Birds and bees at the trysting-tree?

Sing, sweet thrushes, forth and sing!
  Are the fountains gushing free?
Is the south wind wandering
  Through the angler's trysting-tree?
Up, sweet thrushes, tell to me!
Is there wind up our willow tree?
Wind or calm at our trysting-tree?

Sing, sweet thrushes, forth and sing!
  Wile us with a merry glee;
To the flowery haunts of spring—
  To the angler's trysting-tree.
Tell, sweet thrushes, tell to me!
Are there flow'rs 'neath our willow tree?
Spring and flowers at the trysting-tree?
            THOMAS TOD STODDART.

ADDRESS TO CERTAIN GOLD-FISHES.

RESTLESS forms of living light
  Quivering on your lucid wings,
Cheating still the curious sight
  With a thousand shadowings;
Various as the tints of even,
Gorgeous as the hues of heaven,
Reflected on your native streams
In flitting, flashing, billowy gleams!
Harmless warriors, clad in mail
Of silver breastplate, golden scale—
Mail of Nature's own bestowing,
With peaceful radiance mildly glowing—
Fleet are ye as fleetest galley
Or pirate rover sent from Sallee;
Keener than the Tartar's arrow,
Sport ye in your sea so narrow.

Was the sun himself your sire?
Were ye born of vital fire?
Or of the shade of golden flowers
Such as we fetch from Eastern bowers,
To mock this murky clime of ours?
Upward, downward, now ye glance,
Weaving many a mazy dance;
Seeming still to grow in size
When ye would elude our eyes—
Pretty creatures! we might deem
Ye were happy as ye seem—
As gay, as gamesome, and as blithe,
As light, as loving, and as lithe,
As gladly earnest in your play,
As when ye gleam'd in far Cathay:

And yet since on this hapless earth
There's small sincerity in mirth,
And laughter oft is but an art
To drown the outcry of the heart;

It may be, that your ceaseless gambols,
Your wheelings, dartings, divings, rambles,
Your restless roving round and round
The circuit of your crystal bound—
Is but the task of weary pain,
An endless labor, dull and vain;
And while your forms are gayly shining,
Your little lives are inly pining!
Nay—but still I fain would dream,
That ye are happy as ye seem.
     HARTLEY COLERIDGE.

THE CHAMBERED NAUTILUS.

THIS is the ship of pearl, which, poets feign,
 Sails the unshadow'd main,—
  The venturous bark that flings
On the sweet summer wind its purpled wings
 In gulfs enchanted, where the Siren sings,
  And coral reefs lie bare,
Where the cold sea-maids rise to sun their streaming hair.

Its webs of living gauze no more unfurl;
 Wreck'd is the ship of pearl!
  And every chamber'd cell,
Where its dim dreaming life was wont to dwell,
As the frail tenant shaped his growing shell,
  Before thee lies reveal'd,—
Its iris'd ceiling rent, its sunless crypt unseal'd!

Year after year beheld the silent toil
 That spread his lustrous coil;
  Still, as the spiral grew,
He left the past year's dwelling for the new,
Stole with soft step its shining archway through,
  Built up its idle door,
Stretch'd in his last-found home, and knew the old no more.

Thanks for the heavenly message brought by thee,
 Child of the wandering sea,
  Cast from her lap, forlorn!
From thy dead lips a clearer note is born
Than ever Triton blew from wreathèd horn!
  While on mine ear it rings,
Through the deep caves of thought I hear a voice that sings:—

Build thee more stately mansions, O my soul,
 As the swift seasons roll!
  Leave thy low-vaulted past!
Let each new temple, nobler than the last,
Shut thee from heaven with a dome more vast,
  Till thou at length art free,
Leaving thine outgrown shell by life's unresting sea!
     OLIVER WENDELL HOLMES.

THE STORMY PETREL.

A THOUSAND miles from land are we,
Tossing about on the stormy sea—
From billow to bounding billow cast,
Like fleecy snow on the stormy blast.
The sails are scatter'd abroad like weeds;
The strong masts shake like quivering reeds;
The mighty cables and iron chains,
The hull, which all earthly strength disdains,—
They strain and they crack; and hearts like stone
Their natural, hard, proud strength disown.

Up and down!—up and down!
From the base of the wave to the billow's crown,
And amidst the flashing and feathery foam
The stormy petrel finds a home,—
A home, if such a place may be
For her who lives on the wide, wide sea,
On the craggy ice, in the frozen air,
And only seeketh her rocky lair
To warm her young, and to teach them to spring
At once o'er the waves on their stormy wing!

O'er the deep!—o'er the deep!
Where the whale and the shark and the swordfish sleep,—
Outflying the blast and the driving rain,
The petrel telleth her tale—in vain;
For the mariner curseth the warning bird
Which bringeth him news of the storm unheard!

Ah! thus does the prophet of good or ill
Meet hate from the creatures he serveth
    still;
Yet he ne'er falters,—so, petrel, spring
Once more o'er the waves on thy stormy
    wing!
BRYAN WALLER PROCTER
(BARRY CORNWALL).

THE LITTLE BEACH-BIRD.

THOU little bird, thou dweller by the
    sea,
  Why takest thou its melancholy voice,
    And with that boding cry
    O'er the waves dost thou fly?
Oh! rather, bird, with me
  Through the fair land rejoice!

Thy flitting form comes ghostly dim and
    pale,
  As driven by a beating storm at sea;
    Thy cry is weak and scared,
    As if thy mates had shared
The doom of us. Thy wail—
  What does it bring to me?

Thou call'st along the sand, and haunt'st
    the surge,
  Restless and sad; as if, in strange accord
    With the motion and the roar
    Of waves that drive to shore,
One spirit did ye urge—
  The Mystery—the Word.

Of thousands thou both sepulchre and
    pall,
  Old Ocean, art! A requiem o'er the
    dead
    From out thy gloomy cells
    A tale of mourning tells—
Tells of man's woe and fall,
  His sinless glory fled.

Then turn thee, little bird, and take thy
    flight
  Where the complaining sea shall sadness
    bring
    Thy spirit never more.
    Come, quit with me, the shore
For gladness, and the light
  Where birds of summer sing.
RICHARD HENRY DANA.

TO A WATERFOWL.

WHITHER, 'midst falling dew,
While glow the heavens with the last
    steps of day,
Far, through their rosy depths, dost thou
    pursue
  Thy solitary way?

  Vainly the fowler's eye
Might mark thy distant flight to do thee
    wrong,
As, darkly seen against the crimson sky,
  Thy figure floats along.

  Seek'st thou the plashy brink
Of weedy lake, or marge of river wide,
Or where the rocking billows rise and
    sink
  On the chafed ocean side?

  There is a Power whose care
Teaches thy way along that pathless
    coast,
The desert and illimitable air,
  Lone wandering, but not lost.

  All day thy wings have fann'd,
At that far height, the cold, thin atmo-
    sphere,
Yet stoop not, weary, to the welcome
    land,
  Though the dark night is near.

  And soon that toil shall end;
Soon shalt thou find a summer home and
    rest,
And scream among thy fellows; reeds
    shall bend
  Soon o'er thy shelter'd nest.

  Thou'rt gone, the abyss of heaven
Hath swallow'd up thy form; yet, on my
    heart,
Deeply hath sunk the lesson thou hast
    given,
  And shall not soon depart.

  He who, from zone to zone,
Guides through the boundless sky thy cer-
    tain flight,
In the long way that I must tread alone,
  Will lead my steps aright.
WILLIAM CULLEN BRYANT.

TO A BIRD

THAT HAUNTED THE WATERS OF LAAKEN IN THE WINTER.

O MELANCHOLY bird! a winter's day
　　Thou standest by the margin of the pool,
　　And, taught by God, dost thy whole being school
To patience, which all evil can allay.
God has appointed thee the fish thy prey,
　　And given thyself a lesson to the fool
　　Unthrifty, to submit to moral rule,
And his unthinking course by thee to weigh.
　　There need not schools nor the professor's chair,
Though these be good, true wisdom to impart;
　　He who has not enough for these to spare
Of time or gold, may yet amend his heart,
　　And teach his soul by brooks and rivers fair,—
Nature is always wise in every part.
　　　　　　　　　　LORD THURLOW.

SONG.

THE lark now leaves his watery nest,
　　And, climbing, shakes his dewy wings;
He takes this window for the east;
　　And to implore your light, he sings,—
Awake, awake, the morn will never rise,
Till she can dress her beauty at your eyes.

The merchant bows unto the seaman's star,
　　The ploughman from the sun his season takes,
But still the lover wonders what they are
　　Who look for day before his mistress wakes.
Awake, awake, break through your veils of lawn,
Then draw your curtains, and begin the dawn.
　　　　　　　　SIR WILLIAM DAVENANT.

PHILOMELA.

HARK! ah, the nightingale!
The tawny-throated!
Hark! from that moonlit cedar what a burst!
What triumph! hark—what pain!
O wanderer from a Grecian shore,
Still—after many years, in distant lands—
Still nourishing in thy bewilder'd brain
That wild, unquench'd, deep-sunken, old-world pain—
　　Say, will it never heal?
And can this fragrant lawn,
With its cool trees, and night,
And the sweet, tranquil Thames,
And moonshine, and the dew,
To thy racked heart and brain
　　Afford no balm?

　　Dost thou to-night behold,
Here, through the moonlight on this English grass,
The unfriendly palace in the Thracian wild?
　　Dost thou again peruse,
With hot cheeks and sear'd eyes,
The too clear web, and thy dumb sister's shame?
　　Dost thou once more assay
Thy flight; and feel come over thee,
Poor fugitive, the feathery change
Once more; and once more seem to make resound
With love and hate, triumph and agony,
Lone Daulis, and the high Cephissian vale?

Listen, Eugenia—
How thick the bursts come crowding through the leaves!
Again—thou hearest?
Eternal passion!
Eternal pain!
　　　　　　　　MATTHEW ARNOLD.

SONG.

'TIS sweet to hear the merry lark,
　　That bids a blithe good-morrow;

But sweeter to hark, in the twinkling dark,
  To the soothing song of sorrow.
O nightingale!   What doth she ail?
  And is she sad or jolly?
For ne'er on earth was sound of mirth
  So like to melancholy.

The merry lark, he soars on high,
  No worldly thought o'ertakes him;
He sings aloud to the clear blue sky,
  And the daylight that awakes him.
As sweet a lay, as loud, as gay,
  The nightingale is trilling;
With feeling bliss, no less than his,
  Her little heart is thrilling.

Yet ever and anon, a sigh
  Peers through her lavish mirth;
For the lark's bold song is of the sky,
  And her's is of the earth.
By night and day, she tunes her lay,
  To drive away all sorrow;
For bliss, alas! to-night must pass,
  And woe may come to-morrow.
            HARTLEY COLERIDGE.

TO A SKYLARK.

UP with me! up with me into the clouds!
  For thy song, Lark, is strong;
Up with me, up with me into the clouds!
  Singing, singing,
With clouds and sky about thee ringing,
Lift me, guide me till I find
That spot which seems so to thy mind!

I have walk'd through wildernesses dreary,
  And to-day my heart is weary;
Had I now the wings of a Faery,
  Up to thee would I fly.
There's madness about thee, and joy divine
  In that song of thine;
Lift me, guide me high and high
To thy banqueting-place in the sky.

Joyous as morning,
Thou art laughing and scorning;
Thou hast a nest for thy love and thy rest,
And, though little troubled with sloth,
Drunken Lark! thou wouldst be loth
To be such a Traveller as I.

Happy, happy Liver,
With a soul as strong as a mountain River
Pouring out praise to the Almighty Giver,
Joy and jollity be with us both!
            WILLIAM WORDSWORTH.

TO A SKYLARK.

ETHEREAL Minstrel! Pilgrim of the sky!
  Dost thou despise the earth where cares
    abound?
Or, while the wings aspire, are heart and
    eye
  Both with thy nest upon the dewy
    ground?—
Thy nest which thou canst drop into at
    will,
Those quivering wings composed, that
    music still!
To the last point of vision, and beyond,
  Mount, daring Warbler! that love-
    prompted strain
('Twixt thee and thine a never-failing
    bond)
  Thrills not the less the bosom of the
    plain:
Yet might'st thou seem, proud privilege!
    to sing
All independent of the leafy spring.

Leave to the Nightingale her shady wood;
  A privacy of glorious light is thine;
Whence thou dost pour upon the world a
    flood
  Of harmony, with instinct more divine;
Type of the wise who soar, but never
    roam;
True to the kindred points of Heaven and
    Home!
            WILLIAM WORDSWORTH.

THE SKYLARK.

BIRD of the wilderness,
Blithesome and cumberless,
Sweet be thy matin o'er moorland and
    lea!
  Emblem of happiness,
  Blest is thy dwelling-place—
Oh to abide in the desert with thee!
  Wild is thy lay, and loud,
  Far in the downy cloud;

Love gives it energy—love gave it birth.
    Where, on thy dewy wing—
    Where art thou journeying?
Thy lay is in heaven—thy love is on earth.

    O'er fell and fountain sheen,
    O'er moor and mountain green,
O'er the red streamer that heralds the day;
    Over the cloudlet dim,
    Over the rainbow's rim,
Musical cherub, soar, singing, away!
    Then, when the gloaming comes,
    Low in the heather blooms,
Sweet will thy welcome and bed of love be!
    Emblem of happiness,
    Blest is thy dwelling-place—
Oh to abide in the desert with thee!
                    JAMES HOGG.

TO A SKYLARK.

HAIL to thee, blithe spirit—
    Bird thou never wert—
    That from heaven, or near it,
    Pourest thy full heart
In profuse strains of unpremeditated art.

    Higher still and higher
    From the earth thou springest,
    Like a cloud of fire;
    The blue deep thou wingest,
And singing still dost soar, and soaring ever singest.

    In the golden lightning
    Of the setting sun,
    O'er which clouds are bright'ning,
    Thou dost float and run;
Like an embodied joy whose race is just begun.

    The pale purple even
    Melts around thy flight;
    Like a star of heaven,
    In the broad daylight
Thou art unseen, but yet I hear thy shrill delight—

    Keen as are the arrows
    Of that silver sphere,
    Whose intense lamp narrows
    In the white dawn clear,
Until we hardly see, we feel, that it is there.

    All the earth and air
    With thy voice is loud,
    As, when night is bare,
    From one lonely cloud
The moon rains out her beams, and heaven is overflow'd.

    What thou art we know not;
    What is most like thee?
    From rainbow clouds there flow not
    Drops so bright to see,
As from thy presence showers a rain of melody.

    Like a poet hidden
    In the light of thought,
    Singing hymns unbidden,
    Till the world is wrought
To sympathy with hopes and fears it heeded not;

    Like a high-born maiden
    In a palace tower,
    Soothing her love-laden
    Soul in secret hour
With music sweet as love, which overflows her bower;

    Like a glow-worm golden,
    In a dell of dew,
    Scattering unbeholden
    Its aërial hue
Among the flowers and grass which screen it from the view;

    Like a rose embower'd
    In its own green leaves,
    By warm winds deflower'd,
    Till the scent it gives
Makes faint with too much sweet these heavy-wingèd thieves.

    Sound of vernal showers
    On the twinkling grass,
    Rain-awaken'd flowers,
    All that ever was
Joyous and fresh and clear, thy music doth surpass.

    Teach us, sprite or bird,
    What sweet thoughts are thine;
    I have never heard
    Praise of love or wine
That panted forth a flood of rapture so divine.

Chorus hymeneal,
  Or triumphant chaunt,
Match'd with thine, would be all
  But an empty vaunt,—
A thing wherein we feel there is some
  hidden want.

What objects are the fountains
  Of thy happy strain?
What fields, or waves, or mountains?
  What shapes of sky or plain?
What love of thine own kind? What
  ignorance of pain?

With thy clear, keen joyance
  Languor cannot be;
Shadow of annoyance
  Never came near thee;
Thou lovest, but ne'er knew love's sad
  satiety.

Waking, or asleep,
  Thou of death must deem
Things more true and deep
  Than we mortals dream,
Or how could thy notes flow in such a
  crystal stream?

We look before and after,
  And pine for what is not;
Our sincerest laughter
  With some pain is fraught;
Our sweetest songs are those that tell of
  saddest thought.

Yet if we could scorn
  Hate and pride and fear,
If we were things born
  Not to shed a tear,
I know not how thy joy we ever should
  come near.

Better than all measures
  Of delightful sound,
Better than all treasures
  That in books are found,
Thy skill to poet were, thou scorner of the
  ground!

Teach me half the gladness
  That thy brain must know,
Such harmonious madness
  From my lips would flow,
The world should listen then, as I am lis-
  tening now.
            PERCY BYSSHE SHELLEY.

THE EARLY BLUE-BIRD.

BLUE-BIRD! on yon leafless tree,
  Dost thou carol thus to me,
"Spring is coming! Spring is here!"
  Say'st thou so, my birdie dear?
What is that, in misty shroud,
  Stealing from the darken'd cloud?
Lo! the snow-flakes' gathering mound
  Settles o'er the whiten'd ground,
Yet thou singest, blithe and clear,
  "Spring is coming! Spring is here!"

Strik'st thou not too bold a strain?
  Winds are piping o'er the plain;
Clouds are sweeping o'er the sky
  With a black and threatening eye;
Urchins, by the frozen rill,
  Wrap their mantles closer still;
Yon poor man, with doublet old,
  Doth he shiver at the cold?
Hath he not a nose of blue?
  Tell me, birdling, tell me true.

Spring's a maid of mirth and glee,
  Rosy wreaths and revelry:
Hast thou woo'd some wingèd love
  To a nest in verdant grove?
Sung to her of greenwood bower,
  Sunny skies that never lower?
Lured her with thy promise fair
  Of a lot that knows no care?
Pr'ythee, bird, in coat of blue,
  Though a lover, tell her true.

Ask her if, when storms are long,
  She can sing a cheerful song?
When the rude winds rock the tree,
  If she'll closer cling to thee?
Then the blasts that sweep the sky,
  Unappall'd shall pass thee by;
Though thy curtain'd chamber show
  Siftings of untimely snow,
Warm and glad thy heart shall be,
  Love shall make it Spring for thee.
            LYDIA HUNTLEY SIGOURNEY.

THE BLUE-BIRD.

WHEN winter's cold tempests and snows
  are no more,
Green meadows and brown-furrowed
  fields reappearing,

The fishermen hauling their shad to the shore,
  And cloud-cleaving geese to the Lakes are a-steering;
When first the lone butterfly flits on the wing;
  When red glow the maples, so fresh and so pleasing,
Oh then comes the blue-bird, the HERALD OF SPRING!
  And hails with his warblings the charms of the season.

Then loud-piping frogs make the marshes to ring;
  Then warm glows the sunshine, and fine is the weather;
The blue woodland flowers just beginning to spring,
  And spicewood and sassafras budding together:
Oh then to your gardens, ye housewives, repair!
  Your walks border up; sow and plant at your leisure;
The blue-bird will chant from his box such an air,
  That all your hard toils will seem truly a pleasure.

He flits through the orchard, he visits each tree,
  The red-flowering peach and the apple's sweet blossoms;
He snaps up *destroyers* wherever they be,
  And seizes the caitiffs that lurk in their bosoms;
He drags the vile *grub* from the corn he devours,
  The worms from their webs where they riot and welter;
His song and his services freely are ours,
  And all that he asks is in summer a shelter.

The ploughman is pleased when he gleans in his train,
  Now searching the furrows, now mounting to cheer him;
The gardener delights in his sweet simple strain,
  And leans on his spade to survey and to hear him;
The slow-lingering schoolboys forget they'll be chid,
  While gazing intent as he warbles before 'em
In mantle of sky-blue, and bosom so red,
  That each little loiterer seems to adore him.

When all the gay scenes of the summer are o'er,
  And autumn slow enters so silent and sallow,
And millions of warblers, that charmed us before,
  Have fled in the train of the sun-seeking swallow,
The blue-bird, forsaken, yet true to his home,
  Still lingers, and looks for a milder to-morrow,
Till, forced by the horrors of winter to roam,
  He sings his adieu in a lone note of sorrow.

While spring's lovely season, serene, dewy, warm,
  The green face of earth, and the pure blue of heaven,
Or love's native music have influence to charm,
  Or sympathy's glow to our feelings is given,
Still dear to each bosom the blue-bird shall be;
  His voice, like the thrillings of hope, is a treasure;
For, through bleakest storms if a calm he but see,
  He comes to remind us of sunshine and pleasure!

ALEXANDER WILSON.

THE THRUSH'S NEST.

WITHIN a thick and spreading hawthorn bush,
  That overhung a molehill large and round,

I heard from morn to morn a merry thrush
  Sing hymns of rapture, while I drank
    the sound
With joy, and oft, an unintruding guest,
  I watch'd her secret toils from day to
    day;
How true she warp'd the moss to form her
    nest,
  And modell'd it within with wood and
    clay.
And by and by, like heath-bells gilt with
    dew,
  There lay her shining eggs as bright as
    flowers,
Ink-spotted over, shells of green and blue:
  And there I witness'd in the summer
    hours
A brood of Nature's minstrels chirp and
    fly,
  Glad as the sunshine and the laughing
    sky.
JOHN CLARE.

SONNET

TO THE REDBREAST.

WHEN that the fields put on their gay
    attire,
  Thou silent sitt'st near brake or river's
    brim,
  Whilst the gay thrush sings loud from
    covert dim;
But when pale Winter lights the social
    fire,
And meads with slime are sprent and
    ways with mire,
Thou charm'st us with thy soft and solemn
    hymn,
From battlement or barn, or haystack trim;
And now not seldom tun'st, as if for hire,
  Thy thrilling pipe to me, waiting to
    catch
The pittance due to thy well-warbled song:
  Sweet bird, sing on! for oft near lonely
    hatch,
Like thee, myself have pleased the rustic
    throng,
  And oft for entrance, 'neath the peaceful
    thatch,
Full many a tale have told and ditty
    long.
JOHN BAMPFYLDE.

ROBIN REDBREAST.

GOOD-BYE, good-bye to Summer!
  For Summer's nearly done;
The garden smiling faintly,
  Cool breezes in the sun;
Our thrushes now are silent,
  Our swallows flown away,—
But Robin's here in coat of brown,
  And scarlet breast-knot gay.
Robin, Robin Redbreast,
  O Robin dear!
Robin sings so sweetly
  In the falling of the year.

Bright yellow, red, and orange,
  The leaves come down in hosts;
The trees are Indian princes,
  But soon they'll turn to ghosts;
The leathery pears and apples
  Hang russet on the bough;
It's autumn, autumn, autumn late,
  'Twill soon be winter now.
Robin, Robin Redbreast,
  O Robin dear!
And what will this poor Robin do?
  For pinching days are near.

The fireside for the cricket,
  The wheat-stack for the mouse,
When trembling night-winds whistle
  And moan all round the house.
The frosty ways like iron,
  The branches plumed with snow,—
Alas! in winter dead and dark,
  Where can poor Robin go?
Robin, Robin Redbreast,
  O Robin dear!
And a crumb of bread for Robin,
  His little heart to cheer.
WILLIAM ALLINGHAM.

TO A NIGHTINGALE.

SWEET bird! that sing'st away the early
    hours
Of winters past or coming, void of
    care;
Well pleasèd with delights which present are,
Fair seasons, budding sprays, sweet-smelling flowers—

To rocks, to springs, to rills, from leafy
    bowers
  Thou thy Creator's goodness dost de-
    clare,
  And what dear gifts on thee He did not
    spare,
A stain to human sense in sin that lowers.
  What soul can be so sick which by thy
    songs
  (Attired in sweetness) sweetly is not
    driven
  Quite to forget earth's turmoils, spites,
    and wrongs,
And lift a reverend eye and thought to
    Heaven!
  Sweet, artless songster! thou my mind
    dost raise
  To airs of spheres—yes, and to angels'
    lays.
                    WILLIAM DRUMMOND.

TO THE NIGHTINGALE.

DEAR chorister, who from those shadows
    sends—
  Ere that the blushing morn dare show
    her light—
Such sad lamenting strains, that night at-
    tends,
  Become all ear, stars stay to hear thy
    plight:
If one whose grief e'en reach of thought
    transcends,
  Who ne'er (not in a dream) did taste
    delight,
May thee importune who like case pre-
    tends,
  And seems to joy in woe, in woe's de-
    spite;
Tell me (so may thou fortune milder try,
  And long, long, sing!) for what thou thus
    complains
Since winter's gone, and sun in dappled
    sky
Enamor'd smiles on woods and flowery
    plains?
  The bird, as if my questions did her
    move,
With trembling wings sigh'd forth, "I
    love, I love."
                    WILLIAM DRUMMOND.

TO THE NIGHTINGALE.

O NIGHTINGALE, that on yon bloomy
    spray,
  Warblest at eve, when all the woods are
    still,
  Thou with fresh hope the lover's heart
    dost fill,
While the jolly hours lead on propitious
    May.
Thy liquid notes, that close the eye of
    day,
  First heard before the shallow cuckoo's
    bill,
  Portend success in love. Oh, if Jove's
    will
Have link'd that amorous power to thy
    soft lay,
  Now timely sing, ere the rude bird of
    hate
Foretell my hopeless doom in some grove
    nigh;
  As thou from year to year hast sung too
    late
For my relief, yet hadst no reason why.
  Whether the Muse, or Love call thee his
    mate,
Both them I serve, and of their train am I.
                    JOHN MILTON.

ODE TO A NIGHTINGALE.

MY heart aches, and a drowsy numbness
    pains
  My sense, as though of hemlock I had
    drunk,
Or emptied some dull opiate to the drains
  One minute past, and Lethe-ward had
    sunk.
'Tis not through envy of thy happy lot,
  But being too happy in thy happiness,
That thou, light-wingèd Dryad of the trees,
    In some melodious plot
  Of beechen green, and shadows number-
    less,
Singest of summer in full-throated ease.

Oh, for a draught of vintage, that hath been
  Cool'd a long age in the deep delvèd
    earth,
Tasting of Flora and the country green,
  Dance, and Provençal song, and sun-
    burn'd mirth!

Oh, for a beaker full of the warm South,
    Full of the true, the blushful Hippocrene,
With beaded bubbles winking at the brim,
    And purple-stainèd mouth,—
That I might drink, and leave the world unseen,
And with thee fade away into the forest dim!

Fade far away, dissolve, and quite forget
    What thou among the leaves hast never known,
The weariness, the fever, and the fret
    Here, where men sit and hear each other groan,
Where palsy shakes a few sad, last gray hairs,
    Where youth grows pale, and spectre-thin, and dies,
Where but to think is to be full of sorrow
    And leaden-eyed despairs,
    Where beauty cannot keep her lustrous eyes,
Or new love pine at them beyond to-morrow.

Away! away! for I will fly to thee,
    Not charioted by Bacchus and his pards,
But on the viewless wings of Poesy,
    Though the dull brain perplexes and retards:
Already with thee! tender is the night,
    And haply the Queen-Moon is on her throne,
    Cluster'd around by all her starry fays;
    But here there is no light,
Save what from heaven is with the breezes blown
Through verdurous glooms and winding mossy ways.

I cannot see what flowers are at my feet,
    Nor what soft incense hangs upon the boughs;
But, in embalmèd darkness, guess each sweet
    Wherewith the seasonable month endows
The grass, the thicket, and the fruit tree wild,—
    White hawthorn and the pastoral eglantine;
Fast-fading violets, cover'd up in leaves,
    And mid-May's eldest child,
    The coming musk-rose, full of dewy wine,
The murmurous haunt of flies on summer eves.

Darkling I listen, and for many a time
    I have been half in love with easeful Death,
Call'd him soft names in many a musèd rhyme,
    To take into the air my quiet breath;
Now, more than ever, seems it rich to die,
    To cease upon the midnight, with no pain,
While thou art pouring forth thy soul abroad
    In such an ecstasy!
    Still wouldst thou sing, and I have ears in vain,—
To thy high requiem become a sod.

Thou wast not born for death, immortal bird!
    No hungry generations tread thee down;
The voice I hear this passing night was heard
    In ancient days by emperor and clown;
Perhaps the selfsame song that found a path
    Through the sad heart of Ruth, when, sick for home,
She stood in tears amid the alien corn;
    The same that ofttimes hath
Charm'd magic casements opening on the foam
Of perilous seas, in fairy lands forlorn.

Forlorn! the very word is like a bell
    To toll me back from thee to my sole self?
Adieu! the Fancy cannot cheat so well
    As she is famed to do, deceiving elf.
Adieu! adieu! thy plaintive anthem fades
Past the near meadows, over the still stream,
Up the hillside, and now 'tis buried deep
    In the next valley-glades;
    Was it a vision or a waking dream?
Fled is that music,—do I wake or sleep?
                        JOHN KEATS.

THE NIGHTINGALE.

As it fell upon a day
In the merry month of May,
Sitting in a pleasant shade
Which a grove of myrtles made,
Beasts did leap and birds did sing,
Trees did grow and plants did spring,
Everything did banish moan
Save the nightingale alone.
She, poor bird, as all forlorn,
Lean'd her breast against a thorn,
And there sung the dolefullest ditty
That to hear it was great pity.
Fie, fie, fie, now would she cry;
Tereu, tereu, by and by:
That to hear her so complain
Scarce I could from tears refrain;
For her griefs so lively shown
Made me think upon mine own.
—Ah, thought I, thou mourn'st in vain,
None takes pity on thy pain:
Senseless trees, they cannot hear thee,
Ruthless beasts, they will not cheer thee;
King Pandion, he is dead,
All thy friends are lapp'd in lead:
All thy fellow-birds do sing
Careless of thy sorrowing:
Even so, poor bird, like thee
None alive will pity me.
RICHARD BARNEFIELD.

THE SONGS OF BIRDS.

WHAT bird so sings, yet so does wail?
Oh 'tis the ravish'd nightingale—
Jug, jug, jug, jug,—teru—she cries,
And still her woes at midnight rise.
Brave prick-song! who is't now we hear?
None but the lark so shrill and clear;
Now at heaven's gate she claps her wings,
The morn not waking till she sings.
Hark, hark! with what a pretty throat
Poor Robin Redbreast tunes his note;
Hark, how the jolly cuckoos sing
"Cuckoo!" to welcome in the spring.
JOHN LYLY.

ON THE DEPARTURE OF THE NIGHTINGALE.

Sweet poet of the woods—a long adieu!
  Farewell, soft minstrel of the early year!
Ah! 'twill be long ere thou shalt sing anew,
  And pour thy music on "the night's dull ear."
Whether on Spring thy wandering flights await,
  Or whether silent in our groves you dwell,
The pensive Muse shall own thee for her mate,
  And still protect the song she loves so well.
With cautious step the love-lorn youth shall glide
  Through the long brake that shades thy mossy nest;
And shepherd girls from eyes profane shall hide
  The gentle bird who sings of pity best:
For still thy voice shall soft affections move,
And still be dear to sorrow, and to love!
CHARLOTTE SMITH.

TO THE CUCKOO.

O BLITHE new-comer! I have heard,
  I hear thee and rejoice.
O Cuckoo! shall I call thee Bird,
  Or but a wandering Voice?

While I am lying on the grass
  Thy twofold shout I hear,
That seems to fill the whole air's space,
  As loud far off as near.

Though babbling only to the Vale,
  Of sunshine and of flowers,
Thou bringest unto me a tale
  Of visionary hours.

Thrice welcome, darling of the Spring!
  Even yet thou art to me
No Bird: but an invisible Thing,
  A voice, a mystery;

The same whom in my Schoolboy days
  I listen'd to; that Cry
Which made me look a thousand ways
  In bush, and tree, and sky.

To seek thee did I often rove
  Through woods and on the green;

And thou wert still a hope, a love;
    Still long'd for, never seen.

And I can listen to thee yet;
    Can lie upon the plain
And listen, till I do beget
    That golden time again.

O blessed Bird! the earth we pace
    Again appears to be
An unsubstantial, faery place;
    That is fit home for Thee!
              WILLIAM WORDSWORTH.

TO THE CUCKOO.

HAIL, beauteous stranger of the grove!
    Thou messenger of Spring!
Now Heaven repairs thy rural seat,
    And woods thy welcome sing.

Soon as the daisy decks the green,
    Thy certain voice we hear.
Hast thou a star to guide thy path,
    Or mark the rolling year?

Delightful visitant! with thee
    I hail the time with flowers,
And hear the sound of music sweet
    From birds among the bowers.

The schoolboy, wandering through the wood
    To pull the primrose gay,
Starts, thy most curious voice to hear,
    And imitates thy lay.

What time the pea puts on the bloom,
    Thou fliest thy vocal vale,
An annual guest in other lands,
    Another Spring to hail.

Sweet bird! thy bower is ever green,
    Thy sky is ever clear;
Thou hast no sorrow in thy song,
    No Winter in thy year!

Oh, could I fly, I'd fly with thee!
    We'd make, with joyful wing,
Our annual visit o'er the globe,
    Attendants on the Spring.
              JOHN LOGAN.

THE BLACK COCK.

GOOD-MORROW to thy sable beak,
And glossy plumage dark and sleek,
Thy crimson moon and azure eye,
Cock of the heath, so wildly shy!
I see thee, slyly cowering, through
That wiry web of silvery dew,
That twinkles in the morning air,
Like casement of my lady fair.

A maid there is in yonder tower,
Who, peeping from her early bower,
Half shows, like thee, with simple wile,
Her braided hair and morning smile.
The rarest things, with wayward will,
Beneath the covert hide them still;
The rarest things to light of day
Look shortly forth, and shrink away.

One fleeting moment of delight
I sunn'd me in her cheering sight;
And short, I ween, the term will be
That I shall parley hold with thee.
Through Snowdon's mist red beams the day,
The climbing herd-boy chants his lay,
The gnat-flies dance their sunny ring,—
Thou art already on the wing.
              JOANNA BAILLIE.

SONG.

OH welcome, bat and owlet gray,
Thus winging low your airy way!
And welcome, moth and drowsy fly,
That to mine ear come humming by!
And welcome, shadows dim and deep,
And stars that through the pale sky peep!
Oh welcome all! to me ye say,
My woodland love is on her way.

Upon the soft wind floats her hair;
Her breath is in the dewy air;
Her steps are in the whisper'd sound
That steals along the stilly ground.
O dawn of day, in rosy bower,
What art thou to this witching hour?
O noon of day, in sunshine bright,
What art thou to the fall of night?
              JOANNA BAILLIE.

TO THE BUTTERFLY.

CHILD of the sun! pursue thy rapturous flight,
Mingling with her thou lov'st in fields of light;
And, where the flowers of Paradise unfold,
Quaff fragrant nectar from their cups of gold.
There shall thy wings, rich as an evening sky,
Expand and shut with silent ecstasy!
—Yet wert thou once a worm, a thing that crept
On the bare earth, then wrought a tomb and slept.
And such is man; soon from his cell of clay
To burst a seraph in the blaze of day!
SAMUEL ROGERS.

ON THE GRASSHOPPER AND CRICKET.

THE poetry of earth is never dead:
When all the birds are faint with the hot sun
And hide in cooling trees, a voice will run
From hedge to hedge about the new-mown mead.
That is the Grasshopper's—he takes the lead
In summer luxury,—he has never done
With his delights; for, when tired out with fun,
He rests at ease beneath some pleasant weed.
The poetry of earth is ceasing never:
On a lone winter evening, when the frost
Has wrought a silence, from the stove there shrills
The Cricket's song, in warmth increasing ever,
And seems, to one in drowsiness half lost,
The Grasshopper's among some grassy hills.
JOHN KEATS.

TO THE GRASSHOPPER AND CRICKET.

GREEN little vaulter in the sunny grass,
  Catching your heart up at the feel of June—
Sole voice that's heard amidst the lazy noon
When even the bees lag at the summoning brass;
And you, warm little housekeeper, who class
  With those who think the candles come too soon,
  Loving the fire, and with your tricksome tune
Nick the glad silent moments as they pass;

O sweet and tiny cousins, that belong,
  One to the fields, the other to the hearth,
Both have your sunshine: both, though small, are strong
  At your clear hearts; and both seem given to earth
To ring in thoughtful ears this natural song—
  In doors and out, summer and winter, Mirth.
LEIGH HUNT.

THE HUMBLE-BEE.

BURLY, dozing humble-bee,
Where thou art is clime for me.
Let them sail for Porto Rique,
Far-off heats through seas to seek;—
I will follow thee alone,
Thou animated torrid zone!
Zigzag steerer, desert cheerer,
  Let me chase thy waving lines:
Keep me nearer, me thy hearer,
  Singing over shrubs and vines.

Insect lover of the sun,
Joy of thy dominion!
Sailor of the atmosphere,
Swimmer through the waves of air,
Voyager of light and noon,
Epicurean of June,
Wait, I prithee, till I come
Within earshot of thy hum,—
All without is martyrdom,

When the south wind, in May days,
With a net of shining haze
Silvers the horizon wall;
And, with softness touching all,

Tints the human countenance
With the color of romance;
And infusing subtle heats
Turns the sod to violets,—
Thou in sunny solitudes,
Rover of the underwoods,
The green silence dost displace
With thy mellow breezy bass.

Hot Midsummer's petted crone,
Sweet to me thy drowsy tone
Tells of countless sunny hours,
Long days, and solid banks of flowers;
Of gulfs of sweetness without bound
In Indian wildernesses found;
Of Syrian peace, immortal leisure,
Firmest cheer, and bird-like pleasure.

Aught unsavory or unclean
Hath my insect never seen;
But violets, and bilberry bells,
Maple sap, and daffodils,
Grass with green flag half-mast high,
Succory to match the sky,
Columbine with horn of honey,
Scented fern, and agrimony,
Clover, catch-fly, adder's-tongue,
And brier-roses, dwelt among:
All beside was unknown waste,
All was picture as he pass'd.
Wiser far than human seer,
Yellow-breech'd philosopher!
Seeing only what is fair,
 Sipping only what is sweet,
Thou dost mock at fate and care,
 Leave the chaff and take the wheat.
When the fierce north-western blast
Cools sea and land so far and fast,
Thou already slumberest deep;
Woe and want thou canst outsleep;
Want and woe, which torture us,
Thy sleep makes ridiculous.
RALPH WALDO EMERSON.

SONG,

MADE EXTEMPORE BY A GENTLEMAN, OCCASIONED BY A FLY DRINKING OUT OF HIS CUP OF ALE.

 BUSY, curious, thirsty fly,
 Drink with me, and drink as I;
 Freely welcome to my cup,
 Could'st thou sip and sip it up.

Make the most of life you may;
Life is short and wears away.

Both alike are mine and thine,
Hastening quick to their decline;
Thine's a summer, mine no more,
Though repeated to threescore;
Threescore summers, when they're gone,
Wilt appear as short as one.
WILLIAM OLDYS.

SONNET TO THE GLOW-WORM.

TASTEFUL illumination of the night,
 Bright scatter'd, twinkling star of spangled earth!
Hail to the nameless color'd dark and light,
 The witching nurse of thy illumined birth.
In thy still hour how dearly I delight
 To rest my weary bones, from labor free;
In lone spots out of hearing, out of sight,
 To sigh day's smother'd pains; and pause on thee,
Bedecking dangling brier and ivied tree,
 Or diamonds tipping on the grassy spear;
Thy pale-faced glimmering light I love to see,
 Gilding and glistering in the dew-drop near:
O still-hour's mate! my easing heart sobs free,
 While tiny bents low bend with many an added tear.
JOHN CLARE.

TO A MOUSE,

ON TURNING HER UP IN HER NEST WITH THE PLOUGH, NOVEMBER, 1785.

WEE, sleekit, cow'rin', tim'rous beastie,
Oh, what a panic 's in thy breastie!
Thou need na start awa' sae hasty,
 Wi' bickering brattle!
I wad be laith to rin an' chase thee,
 Wi' murd'ring pattle!

I'm truly sorry man's dominion
Has broken Nature's social union,
An' justifies that ill opinion
 Which makes thee startle
At me, thy poor earth-born companion,
 An' fellow-mortal!

I doubt na, whyles, but thou may thieve;
What then? poor beastie, thou maun live!
A daimen icker in a thrave
　　'S a sma' request:
I'll get a blessin' wi' the lave,
　　And never miss 't.

Thy wee bit housie, too, in ruin!
Its silly wa's the win's are strewin'!
An' naething now to big a new ane
　　O' foggage green!
An' bleak December's winds ensuin',
　　Baith snell and keen!

Thou saw the fields laid bare an' waste,
An' weary winter comin' fast,
An' cozie here, beneath the blast,
　　Thou thought to dwell,
'Till, crash! the cruel coulter past
　　Out through thy cell.

That wee bit heap o' leaves an' stibble
Has cost thee mony a weary nibble!
Now thou's turn'd out, for a' thy trouble,
　　But house or hald,
To thole the winter's sleety dribble,
　　An' cranreuch cauld!

But, Mousie, thou art no thy lane,
In proving foresight may be vain:
The best-laid schemes o' mice an' men
　　Gang aft agley,
An' lea'e us naught but grief and pain,
　　For promised joy.

Still thou art blest, compared wi' me!
The present only toucheth thee:
But, och! I backward cast my e'e
　　On prospects drear!
An' forward, though I canna see,
　　I guess an' fear.
　　　　　　　ROBERT BURNS.

THE KITTEN.

WANTON droll, whose harmless play
Beguiles the rustic's closing day,
When, drawn the evening fire about,
Sit aged crone and thoughtless lout,
And child upon his three-foot stool,
Waiting until his supper cool;
And maid, whose cheek outblooms the rose,
As bright the blazing fagot glows,
Who, bending to the friendly light,
Plies her task with busy sleight;
Come, show thy tricks and sportive graces,
Thus circled round with merry faces.

Backward coil'd, and crouching low,
With glaring eyeballs watch thy foe,
The housewife's spindle whirling round,
Or thread, or straw, that on the ground
Its shadow throws, by urchin sly
Held out to lure thy roving eye;
Then onward stealing, fiercely spring
Upon the tempting, faithless thing.
Now, wheeling round with bootless skill,
Thy bo-peep tail provokes thee still,
As still beyond thy curving side
Its jetty tip is seen to glide;
Till, from thy centre starting far,
Thou sidelong veer'st, with rump in air,
Erected stiff, and gait awry,
Like madam in her tantrums high,
Though ne'er a madam of them all,
Whose silken kirtle sweeps the hall,
More varied trick and whim displays
To catch the admiring stranger's gaze.

Doth power in measured verses dwell,
All thy vagaries wild to tell?
Ah, no! the start, the jet, the bound,
The giddy scamper round and round,
With leap and toss and high curvet,
And many a whirling somerset
(Permitted by the modern Muse
Expression technical to use),
These mock the deftest rhymester's skill,
But poor in art, though rich in will.

The feacest tumbler, stage-bedight,
To thee is but a clumsy wight,
Who every limb and sinew strains
To do what costs thee little pains;
For which, I trow, the gaping crowd
Requite him oft with plaudits loud.

But, stopp'd the while thy wanton play,
Applauses, too, *thy* feats repay;
For then beneath some urchin's hand
With modest pride thou tak'st thy stand,
While many a stroke of kindness glides
Along thy back and tabby sides.
Dilated swells thy glossy fur,
And loudly croons thy busy purr,
As, timing well the equal sound,
Thy clutching feet bepat the ground,

And all their harmless claws disclose,
Like prickles of an early rose;
While softly from thy whisker'd cheek
Thy half-closed eyes peer mild and meek.

But not alone by cottage fire
Do rustics rude thy feats admire;
The learnèd sage, whose thoughts explore
The widest range of human lore,
Or, with unfetter'd fancy, fly
Through airy heights of poesy,
Pausing, smiles with alter'd air
To see thee climb his elbow-chair,
Or, struggling on the mat below,
Hold warfare with his slipper'd toe.
The widow'd dame, or lonely maid,
Who in the still but cheerless shade
Of home unsocial spends her age,
And rarely turns a letter'd page,
Upon her hearth for thee lets fall
The rounded cork or paper ball,
Nor chides thee on thy wicked watch
The ends of ravell'd skein to catch,
But lets thee have thy wayward will,
Perplexing oft her better skill.

E'en he, whose mind of gloomy bent,
In lonely tower or prison pent,
Reviews the coil of former days,
And loathes the world and all its ways,
What time the lamp's unsteady gleam
Doth rouse him from his moody dream,
Feels, as thou gambol'st round his seat,
His heart of pride less fiercely beat,
And smiles, a link in thee to find
That joins it still to living kind.

Whence hast thou, then, thou witless Puss,
The magic power to charm us thus?
Is it that in thy glaring eye
And rapid movements we descry—
Whilst we at ease, secure from ill,
The chimney-corner snugly fill—
A lion darting on his prey,
A tiger at his ruthless play?
Or is it that in thee we trace,
With all thy varied wanton grace,
An emblem, view'd with kindred eye,
Of tricky, restless infancy?
Ah, many a lightly sportive child,
Who hath like thee our wits beguiled,
To dull and sober manhood grown,
With strange recoil our hearts disown.

And so, poor Kit, must thou endure
When thou becom'st a cat demure,
Full many a cuff and angry word,
Chased roughly from the tempting board.
But yet, for that thou hast, I ween,
So oft our favor'd playmate been;
Soft be the change which thou shalt prove!
When time hath spoil'd thee of our love,
Still be thou deem'd by housewife fat
A comely, careful, mousing cat,
Whose dish is, for the public good,
Replenish'd oft with savory food.
Nor, when thy span of life is past,
Be thou to pond or dunghill cast,
But, gently borne on good man's spade,
Beneath the decent sod be laid,
And children show, with glistening eyes,
The place where poor old Pussy lies.
JOANNA BAILLIE.

THE KITTEN AND THE FALLING LEAVES.

THAT way look, my Infant, lo!
What a pretty baby-show!
See the Kitten on the Wall,
Sporting with the leaves that fall,
Wither'd leaves—one—two—and three—
From the lofty Elder tree!
Through the calm and frosty air,
Of this morning bright and fair,
Eddying round and round they sink
Softly, slowly: one might think,
From the motions that are made,
Every little leaf convey'd
Sylph or Faery hither tending,—
To this lower world descending,
Each invisible and mute,
In his wavering parachute.
——But the Kitten, how she starts,
Crouches, stretches, paws, and darts!
First at one, and then its fellow
Just as light and just as yellow;
There are many now—now one—
Now they stop, and there are none;
What intenseness of desire
In her upward eye of fire!
With a tiger-leap half way
Now she meets the coming prey,
Lets it go as fast, and then
Has it in her power again:

Now she works with three or four,
Like an Indian Conjuror;
Quick as he in feats of art,
Far beyond in joy of heart.
Were her antics play'd in the eye
Of a thousand standers-by,
Clapping hands with shout and stare,
What would little Tabby care
For the plaudits of the crowd?
Over-happy to be proud,
Over-wealthy in the treasure
Of her own exceeding pleasure!

'Tis a pretty Baby-treat;
Nor, I deem, for me unmeet;
Here, for neither Babe nor me,
Other playmate can I see.
Of the countless living things,
That with stir of feet and wings
(In the sun or under shade,
Upon bough or grassy blade)
And with busy revellings,
Chirp and song, and murmurings,
Made this Orchard's narrow space,
And this Vale so blithe a place;
Multitudes are swept away,
Never more to breathe the day:
Some are sleeping; some in Bands
Travell'd into distant Lands;
Others slunk to moor and wood,
Far from human neighborhood;
And, among the Kinds that keep
With us closer fellowship,
With us openly abide,
All have laid their mirth aside.
—Where is he, that giddy Sprite,
Blue cap, with his colors bright,
Who was blest as bird could be,
Feeding in the apple tree;
Made such wanton spoil and rout,
Turning blossoms inside out;
Hung with head toward the ground,
Flutter'd, perch'd, into a round
Bound himself, and then unbound;
Lithest, gaudiest Harlequin!
Prettiest Tumbler ever seen!
Light of heart and light of limb;
What is now become of him?
Lambs, that through the mountains went
Frisking, bleating merriment,
When the year was in its prime,
They are sober'd by this time.

If you look to vale or hill,
If you listen, all is still,
Save a little neighboring Rill,
That from out the rocky ground
Strikes a solitary sound.
Vainly glitter hill and plain,
And the air is calm in vain;
Vainly Morning spreads the lure
Of a sky serene and pure;
Creature none can she decoy
Into open sign of joy:
Is it that they have a fear
Of the dreary season near?
Or that other pleasures be
Sweeter even than gayety?

Yet, whate'er enjoyments dwell
In the impenetrable cell
Of the silent heart which Nature
Furnishes to every Creature;
Whatsoe'er we feel and know
Too sedate for outward show,
Such a light of gladness breaks,
Pretty Kitten! from thy freaks,—
Spreads with such a living grace
O'er my little Laura's face;
Yes, the sight so stirs and charms
Thee, Baby, laughing in my arms,
That almost I could repine
That your transports are not mine,
That I do not wholly fare
Even as ye do, thoughtless Pair!
And I will have my careless season
Spite of melancholy reason,
Will walk through life in such a way
That, when time brings on decay,
Now and then I may possess
Hours of perfect gladsomeness.
—Pleased by any random toy;
By a Kitten's busy joy,
Or an Infant's laughing eye
Sharing in the ecstasy;
I would fare like that or this,
Find my wisdom in my bliss;
Keep the sprightly soul awake,
And have faculties to take,
Even from things by sorrow wrought,
Matter for a jocund thought,
Spite of care, and spite of grief,
To gambol with Life's falling Leaf.

WILLIAM WORDSWORTH.

THE PET LAMB.

A PASTORAL.

The dew was falling fast, the stars began
   to blink;
I heard a voice; it said, "Drink, pretty
   Creature, drink!"
And, looking o'er the hedge, before me I
   espied
A snow-white mountain Lamb with a
   Maiden at its side.

No other sheep were near, the Lamb was
   all alone,
And by a slender cord was tether'd to a
   stone;
With one knee on the grass did the little
   Maiden kneel,
While to that Mountain Lamb she gave its
   evening meal.

The Lamb, while from her hand he thus
   his supper took,
Seem'd to feast with head and ears; and
   his tail with pleasure shook.
"Drink, pretty Creature, drink." she said
   in such a tone
That I almost received her heart into my
   own.

'Twas little Barbara Lewthwaite, a Child
   of beauty rare!
I watch'd them with delight, they were a
   lovely pair.
Now with her empty Can the Maiden
   turn'd away:
But ere ten yards were gone her footsteps
   did she stay.

Right toward the Lamb she look'd; and
   from a shady place
I unobserved could see the workings of
   her face:
If Nature to her tongue could measured
   numbers bring,
Thus, thought I, to her Lamb that little
   Maid might sing:

"What ails thee, Young One? what?
   Why pull so at thy cord?
Is it not well with thee? well both for bed
   and board?

Thy plot of grass is soft, and green as
   grass can be;
Rest, little Young One, rest; what is't that
   aileth thee?

"What is it thou would'st seek? What
   is wanting to thy heart?
Thy limbs are they not strong? And beau-
   tiful thou art:
This grass is tender grass; these flowers
   they have no peers;
And that green corn all day is rustling in
   thy ears!

"If the Sun be shining hot, do but stretch
   thy woollen chain,
This beech is standing by, its covert thou
   canst gain;
For rain and mountain-storms, the like
   thou needest not fear—
The rain and storm are things that scarcely
   can come here.

"Rest, little Young One, rest; thou hast
   forgot the day
When my Father found thee first in places
   far away;
Many flocks were on the hills, but thou
   wert own'd by none,
And thy mother from thy side for ever-
   more was gone.

"He took thee in his arms, and in pity
   brought thee home:
A blessed day for thee! then whither
   wouldst thou roam?
A faithful Nurse thou hast; the dam that
   did thee yean
Upon the mountain-tops no kinder could
   have been.

"Thou knowest that twice a day I brought
   thee in this Can
Fresh water from the brook, as clear as
   ever ran;
And twice in the day, when the ground is
   wet with dew,
I bring thee draughts of milk, warm milk
   it is and new.

"Thy limbs will shortly be twice as stout
   as they are now,
Then I'll yoke thee to my cart like a pony
   in the plough;

My Playmate thou shalt be; and when the
    wind is cold
Our hearth shall be thy bed, our house
    shall be thy fold.

" It will not, will not rest!—Poor Creature,
    can it be
That 'tis thy mother's heart which is work-
    ing so in thee?
Things that I know not of belike to thee
    are dear,
And dreams of things which thou canst
    neither see nor hear.

" Alas, the mountain-tops that look so
    green and fair!
I've heard of fearful winds and darkness
    that come there;
The little brooks that seem all pastime and
    all play,
When they are angry, roar like Lions for
    their prey.

" Here thou needest not dread the raven in
    the sky;
Night and day thou art safe,—our cottage
    is hard by.
Why bleat so after me? Why pull so at
    thy chain?
Sleep—and at break of day I will come to
    thee again!'

—As homeward through the lane I went
    with lazy feet,
This song to myself did I oftentimes re-
    peat;
And it seem'd, as I retraced the ballad
    line by line,
That but half of it was hers, and one half
    of it was *mine*.

Again, and once again, did I repeat the
    song;
"Nay," said I, "more than half to the
    Damsel must belong,
For she look'd with such a look, and she
    spake with such a tone,
That I almost received her heart into my
    own."
                  WILLIAM WORDSWORTH.

THE BLOOD HORSE.

GAMARRA is a dainty steed,
Strong, black, and of a noble breed,
Full of fire, and full of bone,
With all his line of fathers known;
Fine his nose, his nostrils thin,
But blown abroad by the pride within!
His mane is like a river flowing,
And his eyes like embers glowing
In the darkness of the night,
And his pace as swift as light.

Look,—how round his straining throat
Grace and shifting beauty float;
Sinewy strength is in his reins,
And the red blood gallops through his
    veins,—
Richer, redder, never ran
Through the boasting heart of man.
He can trace his lineage higher
Than the Bourbon dare aspire,—
Douglas, Guzman, or the Guelph,
Or O'Brien's blood itself!

He, who hath no peer, was born
Here, upon a red March morn;
But his famous fathers dead
Were Arabs all, and Arab-bred,
And the last of that great line
Trod like one of a race divine!
And yet, he was but friend to one,
Who fed him at the set of sun
By some lone fountain fringed with green;
With him, a roving Bedouin,
He lived (none else would he obey
Through all the hot Arabian day),
And died untamed upon the sands
Where Balkh amidst the desert stands!
                  BRYAN WALLER PROCTER
                  (BARRY CORNWALL).

THE HIGH-METTLED RACER.

SEE the course throng'd with gazers, the
    sports are begun;
The confusion but hear: "I'll bet you,
    sir." "Done, done!"
Ten thousand strange murmurs resound
    far and near,
Lords, hawkers, and jockeys assail the
    tired ear,

While with neck like a rainbow, erecting his crest,
Pamper'd, prancing, and pleased, his head touching his breast,
Scarcely snuffing the air, he's so proud and elate,
The high-mettled racer first starts for the plate.

Now Reynard's turn'd out, and o'er hedge and ditch rush
Hounds, horses, and huntsmen, all hard at his brush;
They run him at length, and they have him at bay,
And by scent and by view cheat a long, tedious way,
While, alike born for sports of the field and the course,
Always sure to come thorough a stanch and fleet horse,
When fairly run down the fox yields up his breath,
The high-mettled racer is in at the death.

Grown aged, used up, and turn'd out of the stud,
Lame, spavin'd, and windgall'd, but yet with some blood;
While knowing postilions his pedigree trace,
Tell his dam won that sweepstakes, his sire gain'd that race,
And what matches he won to the ostlers count o'er,
As they loiter their time at some hedge ale-house door,
While the harness sore galls, and the spurs his sides goad,
The high-mettled racer's a hack on the road.

Till at last, having labor'd, drudged early and late,
Bow'd down by degrees, he bends on to his fate!
Blind, old, lean and feeble, he tugs round a mill,
Or draws sand till the sand of his hourglass stands still;

And now, cold and lifeless, exposed to the view
In the very same cart which he yesterday drew,
While a pitying crowd his sad relics surrounds,
The high-mettled racer is sold for the hounds!

CHARLES DIBDIN.

THE HORSEBACK RIDE.

WHEN troubled in spirit, when weary of life,
When I faint 'neath its burdens, and shrink from its strife,
When its fruits, turn'd to ashes, are mocking my taste,
And its fairest scene seems but a desolate waste,
Then come ye not near me, my sad heart to cheer
With friendship's soft accents or sympathy's tear.
No pity I ask, and no counsel I need,
But bring me, oh, bring me my gallant young steed,
With his high archèd neck, and his nostril spread wide,
His eye full of fire, and his step full of pride!
As I spring to his back, as I seize the strong rein,
The strength to my spirit returneth again!
The bonds are all broken that fetter'd my mind,
And my cares borne away on the wings of the wind;
My pride lifts its head, for a season bow'd down,
And the queen in my nature now puts on her crown!

Now we're off—like the winds to the plains whence they came;
And the rapture of motion is thrilling my frame!
On, on speeds my courser, scarce printing the sod,
Scarce crushing a daisy to mark where he trod!

On, on like a deer, when the hound's early
    bay
Awakes the wild echoes, away, and away!
Still faster, still farther, he leaps at my
    cheer,
Till the rush of the startled air whirs in
    my ear!
Now 'long a clear rivulet lieth his track,—
See his glancing hoofs tossing the white
    pebbles back!
Now a glen dark as midnight—what
    matter?—we'll down
Though shadows are round us, and rocks
    o'er us frown;
The thick branches shake as we're hurry-
    ing through,
And deck us with spangles of silvery dew!

What a wild thought of triumph, that this
    girlish hand
Such a steed in the might of his strength
    may command!
What a glorious creature! Ah! glance at
    him now,
As I check him a while on this green hil-
    lock's brow;
How he tosses his mane, with a shrill joy-
    ous neigh,
And paws the firm earth in his proud,
    stately play!
Hurrah! off again, dashing on as in ire,
Till the long, flinty pathway is flashing
    with fire!
Ho! a ditch!—Shall we pause? No; the
    bold leap we dare,
Like a swift-winged arrow we rush through
    the air!
Oh, not all the pleasures that poets may
    praise,
Not the 'wildering waltz in the ball-room's
    blaze,
Nor the chivalrous joust, nor the daring
    race,
Nor the swift regatta, nor merry chase,
Nor the sail, high heaving waters o'er,
Nor the rural dance on the moonlight
    shore,
Can the wild and thrilling joy exceed
Of a fearless leap on a fiery steed!

SARA JANE LIPPINCOTT
(GRACE GREENWOOD).

AFAR IN THE DESERT.

AFAR in the desert I love to ride,
With the silent Bush-boy alone by my
    side,
When the sorrows of life the soul o'ercast,
And, sick of the present, I cling to the
    past;
When the eye is suffused with regretful
    tears,
From the fond recollections of former
    years;
And shadows of things that have long
    since fled
Flit over the brain, like the ghosts of the
    dead:
Bright visions of glory that vanish'd too
    soon;
Day-dreams, that departed ere manhood's
    noon;
Attachments by fate or falsehood reft;
Companions of early days lost or left—
And my native land—whose magical name
Thrills to the heart like electric flame;
The home of my childhood; the haunts
    of my prime;
All the passions and scenes of that rap-
    turous time
When the feelings were young and the
    world was new,
Like the fresh bowers of Eden unfolding
    to view;
All—all now forsaken—forgotten—fore-
    gone!
And I—a lone exile remember'd of none—
My high aims abandon'd,—my good acts
    undone—
Aweary of all that is under the sun—
With that sadness of heart which no
    stranger may scan,
I fly to the desert afar from man.

Afar in the desert I love to ride,
With the silent Bush-boy alone by my
    side,
When the wild turmoil of this wearisome
    life,
With its scenes of oppression, corruption,
    and strife—
The proud man's frown and the base man's
    fear—
The scorner's laugh, and the sufferer's
    tear—

And malice, and meanness, and falsehood,
    and folly,
Dispose me to musing and dark melan-
    choly;
When my bosom is full and my thoughts
    are high,
And my soul is sick with the bondman's
    sigh—
Oh! then there is freedom, and joy, and
    pride,
Afar in the desert alone to ride!
There is rapture to vault on the champing
    steed,
And to bound away with the eagle's speed,
With the death-fraught firelock in my
    hand—
The only law of the Desert Land!

Afar in the desert I love to ride,
With the silent Bush-boy alone by my side.
Away—away from the dwellings of men,
By the wild deer's haunt, by the buffalo's
    glen;
By valleys remote where the oribi plays,
Where the gnu, the gazelle, and the hartè-
    beest graze,
And the kudu and eland unhunted recline
By the skirts of gray forest o'erhung with
    wild vine;
Where the elephant browses at peace in
    his wood,
And the river-horse gambols unscared in
    the flood,
And the mighty rhinoceros wallows at will
In the fen where the wild ass is drinking
    his fill.

Afar in the desert I love to ride,
With the silent Bush-boy alone by my side.
O'er the brown karroo, where the bleating
    cry
Of the springbok's fawn sounds plain-
    tively;
And the timorous quagga's shrill whistling
    neigh
Is heard by the fountain at twilight gray;
Where the zebra wantonly tosses his
    mane,
With wild hoof scouring the desolate
    plain;
And the fleet-footed ostrich over the waste
Speeds like a horseman who travels in
    haste,
Hieing away to the home of her rest,
Where she and her mate have scoop'd
    their nest,
Far hid from the pitiless plunderer's
    view
In the pathless depths of the parch'd
    karroo.

Afar in the desert I love to ride,
With the silent Bush-boy alone by my
    side.
Away—away—in the wilderness vast
Where the white man's foot hath never
    pass'd,
And the quiver'd Coranna or Bechuan
Hath rarely cross'd with his roving clan:
A region of emptiness howling and drear,
Which man hath abandon'd from famine
    and fear;
Which the snake and the lizard inhabit
    alone,
With the twilight bat from the yawning
    stone;
Where grass, nor herb, nor shrub takes
    root,
Save poisonous thorns that pierce the
    foot;
And the bitter melon for food and drink,
Is the pilgrim's fare by the salt lake's
    brink;
A region of drought, where no river glides,
Nor rippling brook with osier'd sides;
Where sedgy pool, nor bubbling fount,
Nor tree, nor cloud, nor misty mount,
Appears to refresh the aching eye;
But the barren earth and the burning
    sky,
And the blank horizon, round and round,
Spread—void of living sight or sound.
And here, while the night-winds round me
    sigh,
And the stars burn bright in the midnight
    sky,
As I sit apart by the desert stone,
Like Elijah at Horeb's cave, alone,
" A still small voice " comes through the
    wild
(Like a father consoling his fretful child),
Which banishes bitterness, wrath, and
    fear,
Saying—Man is distant, but God is near!
                          THOMAS PRINGLE.

THE ARAB'S FAREWELL TO HIS HORSE.

My beautiful! my beautiful! that standest
   meekly by,
With thy proudly arch'd and glossy neck,
   and dark and fiery eye,
Fret not to roam the desert now, with all
   thy wingèd speed;
I may not mount on thee again,—thou'rt
   sold, my Arab steed!
Fret not with that impatient hoof,—snuff
   not the breezy wind,—
The farther that thou fliest now, so far am
   I behind:
The stranger hath thy bridle-rein,—thy
   master hath *his* gold,—
Fleet-limb'd and beautiful, farewell;
   thou'rt sold, my steed, thou'rt sold.

Farewell! those free, untired limbs full
   many a mile must roam,
To reach the chill and wintry sky which
   clouds the stranger's home;
Some other hand, less fond, must now thy
   corn and bread prepare,
The silky mane, I braided once, must be
   another's care!
The morning sun shall dawn again, but
   never more with thee
Shall I gallop through the desert paths,
   where we were wont to be;
Evening shall darken on the earth, and o'er
   the sandy plain
Some other steed, with slower step, shall
   bear me home again.

Yes, thou must go! the wild, free breeze,
   the brilliant sun and sky,
Thy master's home,—from all of these my
   exiled one must fly;
Thy proud dark eye will grow less proud,
   thy step become less fleet,
And vainly shalt thou arch thy neck, thy
   master's hand to meet.
Only in sleep shall I behold that dark eye,
   glancing bright;—
Only in sleep shall hear again that step so
   firm and light;
And when I raise my dreaming arm to
   check or cheer thy speed,
Then must I, starting, wake to feel—
   thou'rt *sold*, my Arab steed!

Ah! rudely, then, unseen by me, some
   cruel hand may chide,
Till foam-wreaths lie, like crested waves,
   along thy panting side:
And the rich blood that's in thee swells, in
   thy indignant pain,
Till careless eyes, which rest on thee, may
   count each started vein.
Will they ill use thee? If I thought—but
   no, it cannot be,—
Thou art so swift, yet easy curb'd; so gen-
   tle, yet so free;
And yet, if haply, when thou'rt gone, my
   lonely heart should yearn,—
Can the hand which casts thee from it now
   command thee to return?

Return! alas! my Arab steed! what shall
   thy master do,
When thou, who wast his all of joy, hast
   vanish'd from his view?
When the dim distance cheats mine eye,
   and through the gathering tears,
Thy bright form, for a moment, like the
   false mirage appears;
Slow and unmounted shall I roam, with
   weary step alone,
Where, with fleet step and joyous bound,
   thou oft hast borne me on;
And sitting down by that green well, I'll
   pause and sadly think,
"It was here he bow'd his glossy neck
   when last I saw him drink!"

When last I saw thee drink!—Away! the
   fever'd dream is o'er,—
I could not live a day, and *know* that we
   should meet no more!
They tempted me, my beautiful!—for
   hunger's power is strong,—
They tempted me, my beautiful! but I
   have loved too long.
Who said that I had given thee up? who
   said that thou wast sold?
'Tis false,—'tis false! my Arab steed! I
   fling them back their gold!
Thus, *thus*, I leap upon thy back, and scour
   the distant plains;
Away! who overtakes us now shall claim
   thee for his pains!

                CAROLINE NORTON.

THE TROOPER TO HIS MARE.

OLD girl that has borne me far and fast
  On pawing hoofs that were never loath,
Our gallop to-day may be the last
  For thee, or for me, or perhaps for both!
As I tighten your girth do you nothing
    daunt?
Do you catch the hint of our forming line?
And now the artillery move to the front,
  Have you never a qualm, Bay Bess of
    mine?

It is dainty to see you sidle and start
  As you move to the battle's cloudy
    marge,
And to feel the swells of your wakening
    heart
  When our sonorous bugles sound a
    charge;
At the scream of the shell and the roar of
    the drum
  You feign to be frighten'd with roguish
    glance;
But up the green slopes where the bullets
    hum,
  Coquettishly, darling, I've known you
    dance.

Your skin is satin, your nostrils red,
  Your eyes are a bird's, or a loving
    girl's;
And from delicate fetlock to stately head
  A throbbing vein-cordage around you
    curls;
O joy of my heart! if you they slay,
  For triumph or rout I little care,
For there isn't in all the wide valley to-day
  Such a dear little bridle-wise, thorough-
    bred mare!   CHARLES G. HALPINE.

A-HUNTING WE WILL GO.

THE dusky night rides down the sky,
  And ushers in the morn:
The hounds all join in glorious cry,
  The huntsman winds his horn.
    And a-hunting we will go.

The wife around her husband throws
  Her arms, and begs his stay:
'My dear, it rains, and hails, and snows,
  You will not hunt to-day."
    But a-hunting we will go.

Away they fly to 'scape the rout,
  Their steeds they soundly switch;
Some are thrown in and some thrown out,
  And some thrown in the ditch.
    Yet a-hunting we will go.

Sly Reynard now like lightning flies,
  And sweeps across the vale;
And when the hounds too near he spies,
  He drops his bushy tail.
    Then a-hunting we will go.

Fond Echo seems to like the sport,
  And join the jovial cry;
The woods, the hills, the sound retort,
  And music fills the sky
    When a-hunting we do go.

At last his strength to faintness worn,
  Poor Reynard ceases flight;
Then hungry, homeward we return,
  To feast away the night.
    And a-drinking we do go.

Ye jovial hunters, in the morn
  Prepare them for the chase;
Rise at the sounding of the horn,
  And health with sport embrace
    When a-hunting we do go.
              AUTHOR UNKNOWN.

TO MY HORSE.

WITH a glancing eye and curving mane
He neighs and champs on the bridle-rein;
One spring, and his saddled back I press,
And ours is a common happiness!
'Tis the rapture of motion! a hurrying
    cloud
When the loosen'd winds are breathing
    loud:—
A shaft from the painted Indian's bow,
A bird—in the pride of speed we go.

Dark thoughts that haunt me, where are
    ye now?
While the cleft air gratefully cools my
    brow,
And the dizzy earth seems reeling by,
And naught is at rest but the arching sky;
And the tramp of my steed, so swift and
    strong,
Is dearer than fame and sweeter than song!

There is life in the breeze as we hasten
    on;
With each bound some care of earth has
    gone,
And the languid pulse begins to play,
And the night of my soul is turn'd to day;
A richer verdure the earth o'erspreads,
Sparkles the streamlet more bright in the
    meads;
And its voice to the flowers that bend
    above
Is soft as the whisper of early love;
With fragrance spring flowers have bur-
    den'd the air
And the blue-bird and robin are twittering
    clear.

Lovely tokens of gladness, I mark'd ye
    not'
When last I roam'd o'er this self-same
    spot.
Ah! then the deep shadows of sorrow's
    mien
Fell, like a blight, on the happy scene;
And Nature, with all her love and grace,
In the depths of the spirit could find no
    place.

So the vex'd breast of the mountain-lake,
When wind and rain mad revelry make,
Turbid and gloomy, and wildly tost,
Retain no trace of the beauty lost.
But when through the moist air, bright
    and warm,
The sun looks down with his golden
    charm,
And clouds have fled, and the wind is
    lull,
Oh! then the changed lake, how beautiful!

The glistening trees, in their shady ranks,
And the ewe with its lamb along the
    banks,
And the kingfisher perch'd on the with-
    er'd bough,
And the pure blue heaven all pictured
    below!
Bound proudly, my steed, nor bound proud-
    ly in vain,
Since thy master is now himself again.
And thine be the praise when the leech's
    power
Is idle, to conquer the darken'd hour,

By the might of the sounding hoof to win
Beauty without and joy within;
Beauty else to my eyes unseen,
And joy, that then had a stranger been.
                    AUTHOR UNKNOWN.

THE TIGER.

TIGER! tiger! burning bright,
In the forest of the night,
What immortal hand or eye
Could frame thy fearful symmetry?

In what distant deeps or skies
Burn'd the ardor of thine eyes?
On what wings dare he aspire?
What the hand dare seize the fire?

And what shoulder, and what art,
Could twist the sinews of thy heart?
And when thy heart began to beat,
What dread hand forged thy dread feet?

What the hammer, what the chain?
In what furnace was thy brain?
What the anvil; what dread grasp
Dare its deadly terrors clasp?

When the stars threw down their spears,
And water'd heaven with their tears,
Did He smile His work to see?
Did He who made the lamb make thee?

Tiger! tiger! burning bright,
In the forest of the night,
What immortal hand or eye
Dare frame thy fearful symmetry?
                    WILLIAM BLAKE.

THE HUNTER OF THE PRAIRIES.

AY, this is freedom!—these pure skies
    Were never stain'd with village smoke;
The fragrant wind, that through them
        flies,
    Is breathed from wastes by plough un-
        broke.
Here, with my rifle and my steed,
    And her who left the world for me,
I plant me, where the red-deer feed
    In the green desert—and am free.

For here the fair savannas know
   No barriers in the bloomy grass;
Wherever breeze of heaven may blow,
   Or beam of heaven may glance, I pass.
In pastures, measureless as air,
   The bison is my noble game;
The bounding elk, whose antlers tear
   The branches, falls before my aim.

Mine are the river-fowl that scream
   From the long stripe of waving sedge;
The bear that marks my weapon's gleam
   Hides vainly in the forest's edge;
In vain the she-wolf stands at bay;
   The brinded catamount, that lies
High in the boughs to watch his prey,
   Even in the act of springing dies.

With what free growth the elm and plane
   Fling their huge arms across my way,
Gray, old, and cumber'd with a train
   Of vines, as huge, and old, and gray!
Free stray the lucid streams, and find
   No taint in these fresh lawns and shades;
Free spring the flowers that scent the wind
   Where never scythe has swept the glades.

Alone the Fire, when frost-winds sere
   The heavy herbage of the ground,
Gathers his annual harvest here,
   With roaring like the battle's sound,
And hurrying flames that sweep the plain,
   And smoke-streams gushing up the sky.
I meet the flames with flames again,
   And at my door they cower and die.

Here, from dim woods, the aged Past
   Speaks solemnly; and I behold
The boundless Future in the vast
   And lonely river, seaward roll'd.
Who feeds its founts with rain and dew?
   Who moves, I ask, its gliding mass,
And trains the bordering vines whose blue
   Bright clusters tempt me as I pass?

Broad are these streams—my steed obeys,
   Plunges, and bears me through the tide:
Wide are these woods—I thread the maze
   Of giant stems, nor ask a guide.

I hunt till day's last glimmer dies
   O'er woody vale and grassy height;
And kind the voice and glad the eyes
   That welcome my return at night.
              WILLIAM CULLEN BRYANT.

FOLDING THE FLOCKS.

SHEPHERDS all, and maidens fair,
Fold your flocks up; for the air
'Gins to thicken, and the sun
Already his great course hath run.
See the dewdrops, how they kiss
Every little flower that is;
Hanging on their velvet heads,
Like a string of crystal beads.
See the heavy clouds low falling
And bright Hesperus down calling
The dead night from under ground;
At whose rising, mists unsound,
Damps and vapors, fly apace,
And hover o'er the smiling face
Of these pastures; where they come,
Striking dead both bud and bloom.
Therefore from such danger lock
Every one his lovèd flock;
And let your dogs lie loose without,
Lest the wolf come as a scout
From the mountain and, ere day,
Bear a lamb or kid away;
Or the crafty, thievish fox
Break upon your simple flocks.
To secure yourself from these,
Be not too secure in ease;
So shall you good shepherds prove,
And deserve your master's love.
Now, good-night! may sweetest slumbers
And soft silence fall in numbers
On your eyelids. So farewell:
Thus I end my evening knell.
              BEAUMONT AND FLETCHER.

THE RETIREMENT.

FAREWELL, thou busy world, and may
   We never meet again;
Here I can eat, and sleep, and pray,
   And do more good in one short day
Than he who his whole age out-wears
   Upon the most conspicuous theatres,
Where naught but vanity and vice appears.

Good God! how sweet are all things here!
How beautiful the fields appear!
    How cleanly do we feed and lie!
Lord! what good hours do we keep!
How quietly we sleep!
    What peace, what unanimity!
How innocent from the lewd fashion
Is all our business, all our recreation!

  Oh, how happy here's our leisure!
  Oh, how innocent our pleasure!
  O ye valleys! O ye mountains!
  O ye groves, and crystal fountains!
    How I love at liberty
  By turns to come and visit ye!

  Dear solitude, the soul's best friend,
That man acquainted with himself dost make,
  And all his Maker's wonders to intend,
    With thee I here converse at will
    And would be glad to do so still,
For it is thou alone that keep'st the soul awake.

How calm and quiet a delight
  Is it, alone
To read, and meditate, and write,
  By none offended, and offending none;
To walk, ride, sit, or sleep at one's own ease;
And, pleasing a man's self, none other to displease.

  O my belovèd nymph, fair Dove,
  Princess of rivers, how I love
    Upon thy flowery banks to lie,
    And view thy silver stream,
  When gilded by a Summer's beam!
    And in it all thy wanton fry
      Playing at liberty,
    And with my angle upon them
      The all of treachery
  I ever learn'd industriously to try!

Such streams Rome's yellow Tiber cannot show,
  The Iberian Tagus, or Ligurian Po;
  The Maese, the Danube, and the Rhine,
Are puddle-water, all, compared with thine;
And Loire's pure streams yet too polluted are
With thine, much purer, to compare;

The rapid Garonne and the winding Seine
  Are both too mean,
  Belovèd Dove, with thee
    To vie priority;
Nay, Tame and Isis, when conjoined, submit,
And lay their trophies at thy silver feet.

O my belovèd rocks that rise
To awe the earth and brave the skies,
  From some aspiring mountain's crown
How dearly do I love,
  Giddy with pleasure, to look down,
And, from the vales, to view the noble heights above!
O my belovèd caves! from dog-star's heat,
And all anxieties, my safe retreat;
What safety, privacy, what true delight,
In the artificial night
  Your gloomy entrails make,
  Have I taken, do I take!
How oft, when grief has made me fly,
To hide me from society
E'en of my dearest friends, have I,
  In your recesses' friendly shade,
  All my sorrows open laid,
And my most secret woes entrusted to your privacy!

Lord! would men let me alone,
What an over-happy one
  Should I think myself to be,
Might I in this desert place
(Which most men in discourse disgrace)
  Live but undisturb'd and free!
Here, in this despised recess,
  Would I, maugre Winter's cold,
And the Summer's worst excess,
  Try to live out to sixty full years old;
And, all the while,
  Without an envious eye
On any thriving under Fortune's smile,
  Contented live, and then contented die.
CHARLES COTTON.

THE PRAISE OF A COUNTRYMAN'S LIFE.

  OH, the sweet contentment
  The countryman doth find,

High trolollie, lollie, lol; high trolollie, lee;
  That quiet contemplation
  Possesseth all my mind:
Then care away, and wend along with me.

  For courts are full of flattery,
  As hath too oft been tried,
High trolollie, lollie, lol; high trolollie, lee;
  The city full of wantonness,
  And both are full of pride;
Then care away, and wend along with me.

  But, oh! the honest countryman
  Speaks truly from his heart,
High trolollie, lollie, lol; high trolollie, lee;
  His pride is in his tillage,
  His horses and his cart:
Then care away, and wend along with me.

  Our clothing is good sheep-skins,
  Gray russet for our wives,
High trolollie, lollie, lol; high trolollie, lee;
  'Tis warmth and not gay clothing
  That doth prolong our lives:
Then care away, and wend along with me.

  The ploughman, though he labor hard,
  Yet on the holy day,
High trolollie, lollie, lol; high trolollie, lee;
  No emperor so merrily
  Does pass his time away:
Then care away, and wend along with me.

  To recompense our tillage
  The heavens afford us showers,
High trolollie, lollie, lol; high trolollie, lee;
  And for our sweet refreshments
  The earth affords us bowers;
Then care away, and wend along with me.

  The cuckoo and the nightingale
  Full merrily do sing,
High trolollie, lollie, lol; high trolollie, lee;
  And with their pleasant roundelays
  Bid welcome to the spring:
Then care away, and wend along with me.

  This is not half the happiness
  The countryman enjoys,
High trolollie, lollie, lol; high trolollie, lee;
  Though others think they have as much,
  Yet he that says so lies:
Then care away, and wend along with me.
                  JOHN CHALKHILL.

THOUGHTS IN A GARDEN.

How vainly men themselves amaze
To win the palm, the oak, or bays,
And their incessant labors see
Crown'd from some single herb or tree,
Whose short and narrow vergèd shade
Does prudently their toils upbraid;
While all the flowers and trees do close
To weave the garlands of Repose.

Fair Quiet, have I found thee here,
And Innocence thy sister dear?
Mistaken long, I sought you then
In busy companies of men:
Your sacred plants, if here below,
Only among the plants will grow:
Society is all but rude
To this delicious solitude.

No white nor red was ever seen
So amorous as this lovely green.
Fond lovers, cruel as their flame,
Cut in these trees their mistress' name:
Little, alas, they know or heed
How far these beauties her exceed!
Fair trees! where'er your barks I wound,
No name shall but your own be found.

When we have run our passion's heat
Love hither makes his best retreat:
The gods, who mortal beauty chase,
Still in a tree did end their race:
Apollo hunted Daphne so
Only that she might laurel grow;
And Pan did after Syrinx speed
Not as a nymph, but for a reed.

What wondrous life is this I lead!
Ripe apples drop about my head;
The luscious clusters of the vine
Upon my mouth do crush their wine;

The nectarine and curious peach
Into my hands themselves do reach;
Stumbling on melons, as I pass,
Ensnared with flowers, I fall on grass.

Meanwhile the mind from pleasure less
Withdraws into its happiness—
The mind, that ocean where each kind
Does straight its own resemblance find;
Yet it creates, transcending these,
Far other worlds, and other seas;
Annihilating all that's made
To a green thought in a green shade.

Here at the fountain's sliding foot
Or at some fruit tree's mossy root,
Casting the body's vest aside
My soul into the boughs does glide;
There, like a bird, it sits and sings,
Then whets and claps its silver wings,
And, till prepared for longer flight,
Waves in its plumes the various light.

Such was that happy Garden state
While man there walk'd without a mate:
After a place so pure and sweet,
What other help could yet be meet?
But 'twas beyond a mortal's share
To wander solitary there:
Two paradises are in one,
To live in Paradise alone.

How well the skilful gardener drew
Of flowers and herbs this dial new!
Where, from above, the milder sun
Does through a fragrant zodiac run:
And, as it works, th' industrious bee
Computes its time as well as we.
How could such sweet and wholesome hours
Be reckon'd, but with herbs and flowers!
ANDREW MARVELL.

THE BRAES O' BALQUHITHER.

LET us go, lassie, go,
 To the Braes o' Balquhither,
Where the blae-berries grow
 'Mang the bonnie Highland heather;
Where the deer and the rae,
 Lightly bounding together,
Sport the lang summer day
 On the braes o' Balquhither.

I will twine thee a bower
 By the clear siller fountain,
And I'll cover it o'er
 Wi' the flowers o' the mountain;
I will range through the wilds,
 And the deep glens sae drearie,
And return wi' their spoils
 To the bower o' my dearie.

When the rude wintry win'
 Idly raves round our dwelling,
And the roar of the linn
 On the night-breeze is swelling,
So merrily we'll sing,
 As the storm rattles o'er us,
Till the dear shieling ring
 Wi' the light lilting chorus.

Now the simmer's in prime
 Wi' the flowers richly blooming,
And the wild mountain-thyme
 A' the moorlands perfuming;
To our dear native scenes
 Let us journey together,
Where glad innocence reigns
 'Mang the braes o' Balquhither.
ROBERT TANNAHILL.

AN ITALIAN SONG.

DEAR is my little native vale,
 The ring-dove builds and murmurs there;
Close by my cot she tells her tale
 To every passing villager.
The squirrel leaps from tree to tree,
And shells his nuts at liberty.

In orange-groves and myrtle bowers,
 That breathe a gale of fragrance round,
I charm the fairy-footed hours
 With my loved lute's romantic sound;
Or crowns of living laurel weave
For those that win the race at eve.

The shepherd's horn at break of day,
 The ballet danced in twilight glade,
The canzonet and roundelay
 Sung in the silent greenwood shade,—
These simple joys that never fail
Shall bind me to my native vale.
SAMUEL ROGERS.

SONNET.

To one who has been long in city pent,
   'Tis very sweet to look into the fair
   And open face of heaven,—to breathe a prayer
Full in the smile of the blue firmament.
Who is more happy, when, with heart content,
   Fatigued he sinks into some pleasant lair
   Of wavy grass, and reads a debonair
And gentle tale of love and languishment?
Returning home at evening, with an ear
Catching the notes of Philomel,—an eye
   Watching the sailing cloudlet's bright career,
He mourns that day so soon has glided by:
   E'en like the passage of an angel's tear
That falls through the clear ether silently.
JOHN KEATS.

MORNING SONG.

Up! quit thy bower; late wears the hour;
Long have the rooks caw'd round thy tower;
On flower and tree loud hums the bee;
The wilding kid sports merrily:
A day so bright, so fresh, so clear,
Showeth when good fortune's near.

Up! lady fair, and braid thy hair,
And rouse thee in the breezy air;
The lulling stream that soothed thy dream
Is dancing in the sunny beam;
And hours so sweet, so bright, so gay,
Will waft good fortune on its way.

Up! time will tell: the friar's bell
Its service sound hath chimèd well;
The aged crone keeps house alone,
And reapers to the fields are gone;
The active day, so boon and bright,
May bring good fortune ere the night.
JOANNA BAILLIE.

THE INVITATION.

Best and brightest, come away!
Fairer far than this fair Day,
Which, like thee, to those in sorrow
Comes to bid a sweet good-morrow
To the rough Year just awake
In its cradle on the brake.
The brightest hour of unborn Spring
Through the winter wandering,
Found, it seems, the halcyon Morn
To hoar February born;
Bending from heaven, in azure mirth,
It kiss'd the forehead of the Earth,
And smiled upon the silent sea,
And bade the frozen streams be free,
And waked to music all their fountains,
And breathed upon the frozen mountains,
And like a prophetess of May
Strew'd flowers upon the barren way,
Making the wintry world appear
Like one on whom thou smilest, dear.

Away, away, from men and towns
To the wild wood and the downs—
To the silent wilderness
Where the soul need not repress
Its music, lest it should not find
An echo in another's mind,
While the touch of Nature's art
Harmonizes heart to heart.
I leave this notice on my door
For each accustom'd visitor:—
" I am gone into the fields
To take what this sweet hour yields.
Reflection, you may come to-morrow;
Sit by the fireside with Sorrow.
You with the unpaid bill, Despair,—
You tiresome verse-reciter, Care,—
I will pay you in the grave,—
Death will listen to *your* stave.
Expectation too, be off!
To-day is for itself enough.
Hope, in pity, mock not Woe
With smiles, nor follow where I go;
Long having lived on your sweet food,
At length I find one moment's good
After long pain: with all your love,
This you never told me of."

Radiant Sister of the Day,
Awake! arise! and come away!
To the wild woods and the plains,
And the pools where winter rains
Image all their roof of leaves,
Where the pine its garland weaves

Of sapless green, and ivy dun,
Round stems that never kiss the sun,
Where the lawns and pastures be
And the sand-hills of the sea,
Where the melting hoar-frost wets
The daisy-star that never sets,
And wind-flowers and violets
Which yet join not scent to hue
Crown the pale year weak and new;
When the night is left behind
In the deep east, dun and blind,
And the blue noon is over us,
And the multitudinous
Billows murmur at our feet,
Where the earth and ocean meet,
And all things seem only one
In the universal Sun.
PERCY BYSSHE SHELLEY.

FANCY.

EVER let the Fancy roam,
Pleasure never is at home:
At a touch sweet Pleasure melteth,
Like to bubbles when rain pelteth;
Then let wingèd Fancy wander
Through the thought still spread beyond her:
Open wide the mind's cage-door,
She'll dart forth, and cloudward soar.

O sweet Fancy! let her loose;
Summer's joys are spoilt by use,
And the enjoying of the Spring
Fades as does its blossoming:
Autumn's red-lipp'd fruitage too,
Blushing through the mist and dew,
Cloys with tasting. What do then?
Sit thee by the ingle, when
The sere fagot blazes bright,
Spirit of a winter's night;
When the soundless earth is muffled,
And the cakèd snow is shuffled
From the ploughboy's heavy shoon;
When the Night doth meet the Noon
In a dark conspiracy
To banish Even from her sky.
—Sit thee there, and send abroad
With a mind self-overawed
Fancy, high-commission'd:—send her!
She has vassals to attend her;

She will bring, in spite of frost,
Beauties that the earth hath lost;
She will bring thee, all together,
All delights of summer weather;
All the buds and bells of May
From dewy sward or thorny spray;
All the heapèd Autumn's wealth,
With a still, mysterious stealth;
She will mix these pleasures up
Like three fit wines in a cup,
And thou shalt quaff it;—thou shalt hear
Distant harvest-carols clear;
Rustle of the reapèd corn;
Sweet birds antheming the morn;
And in the same moment—hark!
'Tis the early April lark,
Or the rooks, with busy caw,
Foraging for sticks and straw.
Thou shalt, at one glance, behold
The daisy and the marigold;
White-plumed lilies, and the first
Hedge-grown primrose that hath burst;
Shaded hyacinth, alway
Sapphire queen of the mid-May;
And every leaf, and every flower
Pearlèd with the selfsame shower.
Thou shalt see the field-mouse peep
Meagre from its cellèd sleep;
And the snake all winter-thin
Cast on sunny bank its skin;
Freckled nest-eggs thou shalt see
Hatching in the hawthorn tree,
When the hen-bird's wing doth rest
Quiet on her mossy nest;
Then the hurry and alarm
When the bee-hive casts its swarm;
Acorns ripe down-pattering
While the autumn breezes sing.

O sweet Fancy! let her loose;
Everything is spoilt by use:
Where's the cheek that doth not fade,
Too much gazed at? Where's the maid
Whose lip mature is ever new?
Where's the eye, however blue,
Doth not weary? Where's the face
One would meet in every place?
Where's the voice, however soft,
One would hear so very oft?
At a touch sweet Pleasure melteth
Like to bubbles when rain pelteth.

Let then wingèd Fancy find
Thee a mistress to thy mind:
Dulcet-eyed as Ceres' daughter,
Ere the god of torment taught her
How to frown and how to chide;
With a waist and with a side
White as Hebe's, when her zone
Slipt its golden clasp, and down
Fell her kirtle to her feet
While she held the goblet sweet,
And Jove grew languid.—Break the mesh
Of the Fancy's silken leash;
Quickly break her prison-string,
And such joys as these she'll bring:
—Let the wingèd Fancy roam,
Pleasure never is at home.
JOHN KEATS.

THE NYMPH COMPLAINING OF THE DEATH OF HER FAWN.

THE wanton troopers, riding by,
Have shot my fawn, and it will die.
Ungentle men! they cannot thrive
Who kill'd thee. Thou ne'er didst, alive,
Them any harm; alas! nor could
Thy death yet do them any good.
I'm sure I never wish'd them ill,
Nor do I for all this, nor will;
But, if my simple prayers may yet
Prevail with Heaven to forget
Thy murder, I will join my tears,
Rather than fail. But, oh my fears!
It cannot die so. Heaven's king
Keeps register of everything;
And nothing may we use in vain;
Even beasts must be with justice slain,
Else men are made their deodands.
Though they should wash their guilty
 hands
In this warm life-blood, which doth part
From thine and wound me to the heart,
Yet could they not be clean—their stain
Is dyed in such a purple grain;
There is not such another in
The world to offer for their sin.
 Inconstant Sylvio, when yet
I had not found him counterfeit,
One morning (I remember well)
Tied in this silver chain and bell,
Gave it to me; nay, and I know
What he said then—I'm sure I do;

Said he, "Look how your huntsman here
Hath taught a fawn to hunt his deer!"
But Sylvio soon had me beguiled—
This waxèd tame, while he grew wild,
And, quite regardless of my smart,
Left me his fawn, but took his heart.
 Thenceforth, I set myself to play
My solitary time away,
With this, and, very well content,
Could so mine idle life have spent.
For it was full of sport, and light
Of foot and heart, and did invite
Me to its game. It seem'd to bless
Itself in me. How could I less
Than love it? Oh, I cannot be
Unkind to a beast that loveth me.
 Had it lived long, I do not know
Whether it, too, might have done so
As Sylvio did—his gifts might be
Perhaps as false, or more, than he.
For I am sure, for aught that I
Could in so short a time espy,
Thy love was far more better than
The love of false and cruel man.
 With sweetest milk and sugar first
I it at mine own fingers nursed;
And as it grew, so every day
It wax'd more white and sweet than they.
It had so sweet a breath! and oft
I blush'd to see its foot more soft
And white—shall I say than my hand?
Nay, any lady's of the land.
 It is a wondrous thing how fleet
'Twas on those little silver feet!
With what a pretty, skipping grace
It oft would challenge me the race!
And when 't had left me far away,
'Twould stay, and run again, and stay;
For it was nimbler, much, than hinds,
And trod as if on the four winds.
 I have a garden of my own—
But so with roses overgrown,
And lilies, that you would it guess
To be a little wilderness;
And all the spring-time of the year
It lovèd only to be there.
Among the beds of lilies I
Have sought it oft, where it should lie;
Yet could not, till itself would rise,
Find it, although before mine eyes;
For in the flaxen lilies' shade
It like a bank of lilies laid.

Upon the roses it would feed,
Until its lips ev'n seem'd to bleed;
And then to me 'twould boldly trip,
And print those roses on my lip.
But all its chief delight was still
On roses thus itself to fill;
And its pure virgin limbs to fold
In whitest sheets of lilies cold.
Had it lived long, it would have been
Lilies without, roses within.

 Oh help! oh help! I see it faint,
And die as calmly as a saint,
See how it weeps! the tears do come,
Sadly, slowly, dropping like a gum.
So weeps the wounded balsam; so
The holy frankincense doth flow;
The brotherless Heliades
Melt in such amber tears as these.

 I in a golden vial will
Keep these two crystal tears; and fill
It, till it do o'erflow, with mine;
Then place it in Diana's shrine.
Now my sweet fawn is vanish'd to
Whither the swans and turtles go;
In fair Elysium to endure,
With milk-white lambs, and ermines pure.
Oh do not run too fast! for I
Will but bespeak thy grave, and die.

 First my unhappy statue shall
Be cut in marble; and withal,
Let it be weeping too! But there
Th' engraver sure his art may spare,
For I so truly thee bemoan
That I shall weep though I be stone;
Until my tears, still drooping, wear
My breast, themselves engraving there.
There at my feet shalt thou be laid,
Of purest alabaster made;
For I would have thine image be
White as I can, though not as thee.
     ANDREW MARVELL.

ECHO AND SILENCE.

IN eddying course when leaves began to fly,
 And Autumn in her lap the store to strew,
 As 'mid wild scenes I chanced the muse to woo,
Through glens untrod, and woods that frown'd on high,
Two sleeping nymphs with wonder mute I spy!
 And, lo, she's gone!—In robe of dark-green hue
 'Twas Echo from her sister Silence flew,
For quick the hunter's horn resounded to the sky!
In shade affrighted Silence melts away.
 Not so her sister.—Hark! for onward still,
 With far-heard step, she takes her listening way,
Bounding from rock to rock, and hill to hill.
Ah, mark the merry maid in mockful play,
 With thousand mimic tones the laughing forest fill!
     SIR EGERTON BRYDGES.

BUGLE SONG.

THE splendor falls on castle-walls
 And snowy summits old in story:
The long light shakes across the lakes,
 And the wild cataract leaps in glory.
Blow, bugle, blow, set the wild echoes flying,
Blow, bugle; answer, echoes, dying, dying, dying.

Oh hark! oh hear! how thin and clear,
 And thinner, clearer, farther going!
Oh sweet and far, from cliff and scar,
 The horns of Elfland faintly blowing!
Blow, let us hear the purple glens replying:
Blow, bugle; answer, echoes, dying, dying, dying.

O love, they die in yon rich sky,
 They faint on hill or field or river:
Our echoes roll from soul to soul,
 And grow for ever and for ever.
Blow, bugle, blow, set the wild echoes flying,
And answer, echoes, answer, dying, dying, dying.
     ALFRED TENNYSON.

"What an image of peace and rest,
  Is this little church among its graves!
All is so quiet; the troubled breast,
The wounded spirit, the heart oppressed,
  Here may find the repose it craves.
            Henry W. Longfellow.

POEMS OF PLACES.

THE CHIMES OF ENGLAND.

THE chimes, the chimes of Motherland,
   Of England green and old,
That out from fane and ivied tower
   A thousand years have toll'd—
How glorious must their music be
   As breaks the hallow'd day,
And calleth with a seraph's voice
   A nation up to pray!

Those chimes that tell a thousand tales—
   Sweet tales of olden time!—
And ring a thousand memories
   At vesper, and at prime:
At bridal and at burial,
   For cottager and king—
Those chimes—those glorious Christian chimes,
   How blessedly they ring!

Those chimes, those chimes of Motherland,
   Upon a Christmas morn,
Outbreaking, as the angels did,
   For a Redeemer born,—
How merrily they call afar,
   To cot and baron's hall,
With holly deck'd and misletoe,
   To keep the festival!

The chimes of England, how they peal
   From tower and Gothic pile,
Where hymn and swelling anthem fill
   The dim cathedral aisle;
Where windows bathe the holy light
   On priestly heads that falls,
And stain the florid tracery
   And banner-dighted walls!

And then, those Easter bells, in Spring,
   Those glorious Easter chimes,—
How loyally they hail thee round,
   Old queen of holy times!

From hill to hill, like sentinels,
   Responsively they cry,
And sing the rising of the Lord,
   From vale to mountain high.

I love ye, chimes of Motherland,
   With all this soul of mine,
And bless the Lord that I am sprung
   Of good old English line!
And, like a son, I sing the lay
   That England's glory tells;
For she is lovely to the Lord,
   For you, ye Christian bells!

And heir of her ancestral fame,
   And happy in my birth,
Thee, too, I love, my forest-land,
   The joy of all the earth;
For thine thy mother's voice shall be,
   And here, where God is King,
With English chimes, from Christian spires,
   The wilderness shall ring.
ARTHUR CLEVELAND COXE.

SONNET.

COMPOSED UPON WESTMINSTER BRIDGE.

EARTH has not anything to show more fair;
   Dull would he be of soul who could pass by
   A sight so touching in its majesty:
This city now doth like a garment wear
The beauty of the morning; silent, bare,
   Ships, towers, domes, theatres, and temples lie
   Open unto the fields, and to the sky;
All bright and glittering in the smokeless air.

Never did sun more beautifully steep
  In his first splendor valley, rock, or hill;
Ne'er saw I, never felt, a calm so deep!
  The river glideth at his own sweet will;
Dear God! the very houses seem asleep,
  And all that mighty heart is lying still.
              WILLIAM WORDSWORTH.

ON THE TOMBS IN WESTMINSTER ABBEY.

MORTALITY, behold and fear
What a change of flesh is here!
Think how many royal bones
Sleep within these heaps of stones!
Here they lie, had realms and lands,
Who now want strength to stir their hands,
Where from their pulpits seal'd with dust
They preach, "In greatness is no trust."
Here's an acre sown indeed
With the richest, royallest seed
That the earth did e'er suck in
Since the first man died for sin;
Here the bones of birth have cried,
"Though gods they were, as men they died!"
Here are sands, ignoble things,
Dropt from the ruin'd sides of kings;
Here's a world of pomp and state
Buried in dust, once dead by fate.
              FRANCIS BEAUMONT.

LINES ON THE MERMAID TAVERN.

  SOULS of poets dead and gone,
  What Elysium have ye known—
  Happy field or mossy cavern—
  Choicer than the Mermaid Tavern?
  Have ye tippled drink more fine
  Than mine host's Canary wine?
  Or are fruits of Paradise
  Sweeter than those dainty pies
  Of venison? O generous food!
  Drest as though bold Robin Hood
  Would, with his maid Marian,
  Sup and bowse from horn and can.

I have heard that on a day
Mine host's signboard flew away,
Nobody knew whither, till
An astrologer's old quill
To a sheepskin gave the story:
Said he saw you in your glory
Underneath a new old-sign,
Sipping beverage divine,
And pledging with contented smack
The mermaid in the Zodiac!
Souls of poets dead and gone,
What Elysium have ye known—
Happy field or mossy cavern—
Choicer than the Mermaid Tavern?
              JOHN KEATS.

SONNET.

WRITTEN AFTER SEEING WINDSOR CASTLE.

FROM beauteous Windsor's high and storied halls
Where Edward's chiefs start from the glowing walls,
To my low cot from ivory beds of state,
Pleased I return unenvious of the great.
So the bee ranges o'er the varied scenes
Of corn, of heaths, of fallows, and of greens,
Pervades the thicket, soars above the hill,
Or murmurs to the meadow's murmuring rill:
Now haunts old hollow'd oaks, deserted cells,
Now seeks the low vale lily's silver bells;
Sips the warm fragrance of the greenhouse bowers,
And tastes the myrtle and the citron's flowers;
At length returning to the wonted comb,
Prefers to all his little straw-built home.
              THOMAS WARTON.

ON A DISTANT PROSPECT OF ETON COLLEGE.

YE distant spires, ye antique towers,
  That crown the wat'ry glade,
Where grateful Science still adores
  Her Henry's holy shade;
And ye that from the stately brow
Of Windsor's heights th' expanse below
  Of grove, of lawn, of mead survey,
Whose turf, whose shade, whose flowers among
Wanders the hoary Thames along
  His silver winding way:

Ah, happy hills! ah, pleasing shade!
  Ah, fields beloved in vain!—
Where once my careless childhood stray'd,
  A stranger yet to pain!
I feel the gales that from ye blow
A momentary bliss bestow,
  As, waving fresh their gladsome wing,
My weary soul they seem to soothe,
And, redolent of joy and youth,
  To breathe a second spring.

Say, Father Thames—for thou hast seen
  Full many a sprightly race,
Disporting on thy margent green,
  The paths of pleasure trace—
Who foremost now delight to cleave,
With pliant arm, thy glassy wave?
  The captive linnet which enthrall?
What idle progeny succeed
To chase the rolling circle's speed,
  Or urge the flying ball?

While some, on urgent business bent,
  Their murmuring labors ply
'Gainst graver hours that bring constraint
  To sweeten liberty;
Some bold adventurers disdain
The limits of their little reign,
  And unknown regions dare descry;
Still as they run they look behind,
They hear a voice in every wind,
  And snatch a fearful joy.

Gay hope is theirs by Fancy fed,
  Less pleasing when possest;
The tear forgot as soon as shed,
  The sunshine of the breast:
Theirs buxom health, of rosy hue,
Wild wit, invention ever new,
  And lively cheer, of vigor born;
The thoughtless day, the easy night,
The spirits pure, the slumbers light,
  That fly th' approach of morn.

Alas! regardless of their doom,
  The little victims play;
No sense have they of ills to come,
  Nor care beyond to-day;
Yet see, how all around them wait
The ministers of human fate,
  And black Misfortune's baleful train!
Ah, show them where in ambush stand,
To seize their prey, the murderous band!
  Ah, tell them, they are men!

These shall the fury Passions tear,
  The vultures of the mind,
Disdainful Anger, pallid Fear,
  And Shame that skulks behind;
Or pining Love shall waste their youth,
Or Jealousy, with rankling tooth,
  That inly gnaws the secret heart:
And Envy wan, and faded Care,
Grim-visaged, comfortless Despair,
  And Sorrow's piercing dart.

Ambition this shall tempt to rise,
  Then whirl the wretch from high,
To bitter Scorn a sacrifice,
  And grinning Infamy.
The stings of Falsehood those shall try,
And hard Unkindness' alter'd eye,
  That mocks the tears it forced to flow
And keen Remorse, with blood defiled,
And moody Madness, laughing wild
  Amid severest woe.

Lo! in the vale of years beneath
  A grisly troop are seen,
The painful family of Death,
  More hideous than their queen;
This racks the joints, this fires the veins,
That every laboring sinew strains,
  Those in the deeper vitals rage:
Lo! Poverty, to fill the band,
That numbs the soul with icy hand,
  And slow-consuming Age.

To each his suff'rings: all are men,
  Condemn'd alike to groan;
The tender for another's pain,
  Th' unfeeling for his own.
Yet, ah! why should they know their fate,
Since sorrow never comes too late,
  And happiness too swiftly flies?
Thought would destroy their paradise.
No more:—where ignorance is bliss,
  'Tis folly to be wise!
                    THOMAS GRAY.

ELEGIAC STANZAS.

SUGGESTED BY A PICTURE OF PEELE CASTLE IN A STORM, PAINTED BY SIR GEORGE BEAUMONT.

I WAS thy Neighbor once, thou rugged Pile!
  Four summer weeks I dwelt in sight of thee:

I saw thee every day; and all the while
  Thy Form was sleeping on a glassy sea.

So pure the sky, so quiet was the air!
  So like, so very like, was day to day!
Whene'er I look'd, thy Image still was
    there;
  It trembled, but it never pass'd away.

How perfect was the calm! it seem'd no
    sleep;
  No mood, which season takes away or
    brings:
I could have fancied that the mighty
    Deep
  Was even the gentlest of all gentle
    Things.

Ah! THEN, if mine had been the Painter's
    hand,
  To express what then I saw; and add
    the gleam,
The light that never was on sea or land,
  The consecration, and the Poet's dream;

I would have planted thee, thou Hoary
    Pile!
  Amid a world how different from this!
Beside a sea that could not cease to smile;
  On tranquil land, beneath a sky of bliss.

A Picture had it been of lasting ease,
  Elysian quiet, without toil or strife;
No motion but the moving tide, a breeze,
  Or merely silent Nature's breathing life.

Such, in the fond illusion of my heart,
  Such Picture would I at that time have
    made,
And seen the soul of truth in every part;
  A faith, a trust, that could not be be-
    tray'd.

So once it would have been,—'tis so no more;
  I have submitted to a new control:
A power is gone, which nothing can re-
    store;
  A deep distress hath humanized my
    Soul.

Not for a moment could I now behold
  A smiling sea, and be what I have been:
The feeling of my loss will ne'er be old;
  This, which I know, I speak with mind
    serene.

Then, Beaumont, Friend! who would have
    been the Friend,
  If he had liv'd, of him whom I deplore,
This Work of thine I blame not, but com-
    mend;
  This sea in anger, and that dismal shore.

Oh 'tis a passionate Work!—yet wise and
    well;
  Well chosen is the spirit that is here;
That Hulk which labors in the deadly
    swell,
  This rueful sky, this pageantry of fear!

And this huge Castle, standing here sub-
    lime,
  I love to see the look with which it
    braves,
Cased in the unfeeling armor of old time,
  The lightning, the fierce wind, and
    trampling waves.

Farewell, farewell the heart that lives
    alone,
  Housed in a dream, at distance from
    the Kind!
Such happiness, wherever it be known,
  Is to be pitied; for 'tis surely blind.

But welcome, fortitude and patient cheer,
  And frequent sights of what is to be
    borne!
Such sights, or worse, as are before me
    here,—
  Not without hope we suffer and we
    mourn.
                  WILLIAM WORDSWORTH.

GRONGAR HILL.

SILENT nymph, with curious eye!
Who, the purple eve, dost lie
On the mountain's lonely van,
Beyond the noise of busy man,
Painting fair the form of things,
While the yellow linnet sings,
Or the tuneful nightingale
Charms the forest with her tale,—
Come, with all thy various hues,
Come and aid thy sister Muse.
Now, while Phœbus, riding high,
Gives lustre to the land and sky,
Grongar Hill invites my song,—
Draw the landscape bright and strong;

Grongar, in whose mossy cells
Sweetly musing Quiet dwells;
Grongar, in whose silent shade,
For the modest Muses made,
So oft I have, the evening still,
At the fountain of a rill,
Sat upon a flowery bed,
With my hand beneath my head,
While stray'd my eyes o'er Towy's flood,
Over mead and over wood,
From house to house, from hill to hill,
Till Contemplation had her fill.

About his checker'd sides I wind,
And leave his brooks and meads behind,
And groves and grottos where I lay,
And vistas shooting beams of day.
Wide and wider spreads the vale,
As circles on a smooth canal.
The mountains round, unhappy fate!
Sooner or later, of all height,
Withdraw their summits from the skies,
And lessen as the others rise.
Still the prospect wider spreads,
Adds a thousand woods and meads;
Still it widens, widens still,
And sinks the newly-risen hill.

Now I gain the mountain's brow;
What a landscape lies below!
No clouds, no vapors intervene;
But the gay, the open scene
Does the face of Nature show,
In all the hues of heaven's bow;
And, swelling to embrace the light,
Spreads around beneath the sight.

Old castles on the cliffs arise,
Proudly towering in the skies;
Rushing from the woods, the spires
Seem from hence ascending fires;
Half his beams Apollo sheds
On the yellow mountain-heads,
Gilds the fleeces of the flocks,
And glitters on the broken rocks.

Below me trees unnumber'd rise,
Beautiful in various dyes:
The gloomy pine, the poplar blue,
The yellow beech, the sable yew,
The slender fir that taper grows,
The sturdy oak with broad-spread boughs;
And, beyond the purple grove,
Haunt of Phyllis, queen of love!
Gaudy as the opening dawn,
Lies a long and level lawn,
On which a dark hill, steep and high,
Holds and charms the wandering eye.
Deep are his feet in Towy's flood:
His sides are clothed with waving wood,
And ancient towers crown his brow,
That cast an awful look below;
Whose ragged wall the ivy creeps,
And with her arms from falling keeps;
So both a safety from the wind
In mutual dependence find.
'Tis now the raven's bleak abode;
'Tis now the apartment of the toad;
And there the fox securely feeds;
And there the poisonous adder breeds,
Conceal'd in ruins, moss, and weeds;
While, ever and anon, there fall
Huge heaps of hoary moulder'd wall.
Yet Time has seen,—that lifts the low
And level lays the lofty brow,—
Has seen this broken pile complete,
Big with the vanity of state.
But transient is the smile of Fate!
A little rule, a little sway,
A sunbeam in a winter's day,
Is all the proud and mighty have
Between the cradle and the grave.

And see the rivers, how they run
Through woods and meads, in shade and sun,
Sometimes swift, sometimes slow,—
Wave succeeding wave, they go
A various journey to the deep,
Like human life to endless sleep!
Thus is Nature's vesture wrought,
To instruct our wandering thought:
Thus she dresses green and gay,
To disperse our cares away.

Ever charming, ever new,
When will the landscape tire the view?
The fountain's fall, the river's flow;
The woody valleys, warm and low;
The windy summit, wild and high,
Roughly rushing on the sky;
The pleasant seat, the ruin'd tower,
The naked rock, the shady bower;
The town and village, dome and farm—
Each gives each a double charm,
As pearls upon an Ethiop's arm.
See on the mountain's southern side
Where the prospect opens wide,
Where the evening gilds the tide;

How close and small the hedges lie!
What streaks of meadow cross the eye!
A step, methinks, may pass the stream,
So little distant dangers seem;
So we mistake the Future's face,
Eyed through Hope's deluding glass;
As yon summits, soft and fair,
Clad in colors of the air,
Which, to those who journey near,
Barren, brown, and rough appear;
Still we tread the same coarse way,
The present's still a cloudy day.

Oh, may I with myself agree,
And never covet what I see;
Content me with an humble shade,
My passions tamed, my wishes laid;
For while our wishes wildly roll,
We banish quiet from the soul:
'Tis thus the busy beat the air,
And misers gather wealth and care.

Now, even now, my joys run high,
As on the mountain-turf I lie;
While the wanton Zephyr sings,
And in the vale perfumes his wings;
While the waters murmur deep;
While the shepherd charms his sheep,
While the birds unbounded fly,
And with music fill the sky,
Now, even now, my joys run high.

Be full, ye courts: be great who will;
Search for Peace with all your skill:
Open wide the lofty door,
Seek her on the marble floor.
In vain you search; she is not there!
In vain you search the domes of Care!
Grass and flowers Quiet treads,
On the meads and mountain-heads,
Along with Pleasure, close allied,
Ever by each other's side;
And often, by the murmuring rill,
Hears the thrush, while all is still
Within the groves of Grongar Hill.
JOHN DYER.

ON REVISITING THE RIVER LODDON.

AH! what a weary race my feet have run
  Since first I trod thy banks with alders crown'd,
  And thought my way was all through fairy ground,
Beneath the azure sky and golden sun—
When first my Muse to lisp her notes begun.
  While pensive memory traces back the round
Which fills the varied interval between;
Much pleasure, more of sorrow, marks the scene.
Sweet native stream! those skies and suns so pure,
  No more return to cheer my evening road:
Yet still one joy remains, that not obscure
  Nor useless, all my vacant days have flow'd
From youth's gay dawn to manhood's prime mature,
  Nor with the Muse's laurel unbestow'd.
THOMAS WARTON.

THE CATARACT OF LODORE.

"How does the water
  Come down at Lodore?"
My little boy ask'd me
  Thus, once on a time;
And moreover he task'd me
  To tell him in rhyme.
    Anon at the word,
There first came one daughter,
  And then came another,
  To second and third
The request of their brother,
And to hear how the water
  Comes down at Lodore,
  With its rush and its roar,
    As many a time
They had seen it before.
So I told them in rhyme,
For of rhymes I had store;
  And 'twas in my vocation
    For their recreation
    That so I should sing;
  Because I was Laureate
  To them and the King.

From its sources which well
  In the tarn on the fell;
  From its fountains
  In the mountains,
Its rills and its gills;

Through moss and through brake
It runs and it creeps
For a while, till it sleeps
In its own little lake.
And thence at departing,
Awakening and starting,
It runs through the reeds,
And away it proceeds,
Through meadow and glade,
In sun and in shade,
And through the wood-shelter,
Among crags in its flurry,
Helter-skelter,
Hurry-skurry.
Here it comes sparkling,
And there it lies darkling,
Now smoking and frothing
Its tumult and wrath in,
Till in this rapid race
On which it is bent,
It reaches the place
Of its steep descent.

The cataract strong
Then plunges along,
Striking and raging
As if a war waging
Its caverns and rocks among;
Rising and leaping,
Sinking and creeping,
Swelling and sweeping,
Showering and springing,
Flying and flinging,
Writhing and ringing,
Eddying and whisking,
Spouting and frisking,
Turning and twisting,
Around and around
With endless rebound;
Smiting and fighting,
A sight to delight in;
Confounding, astounding,
Dizzying and deafening the ear with its sound.

Collecting, projecting,
Receding and speeding,
And shocking and rocking,
And darting and parting,
And threading and spreading,
And whizzing and hissing,
And dripping and skipping,
And hitting and splitting,
And shining and twining,
And rattling and battling,
And shaking and quaking,
And pouring and roaring,
And waving and raving,
And tossing and crossing,
And flowing and going,
And running and stunning,
And foaming and roaming,
And dinning and spinning,
And dropping and hopping,
And working and jerking,
And guggling and struggling,
And heaving and cleaving,
And moaning and groaning;

And glittering and frittering,
And gathering and feathering,
And whitening and brightening,
And quivering and shivering,
And hurrying and skurrying,
And thundering and floundering;

Dividing and gliding and sliding,
And falling and brawling and sprawling,
And driving and riving and striving,
And sprinkling and twinkling and wrinkling,
And sounding and bounding and rounding,
And bubbling and troubling and doubling,
And grumbling and rumbling and tumbling,
And clattering and battering and shattering;

Retreating and beating and meeting and sheeting,
Delaying and straying and playing and spraying,
Advancing and prancing and glancing and dancing,
Recoiling, turmoiling and toiling and boiling,
And gleaming and streaming and steaming and beaming,
And rushing and flushing and brushing and gushing,
And flapping and rapping and clapping and slapping,
And curling and whirling and purling and twirling,

And thumping and plumping and bumping
    and jumping,
And dashing and flashing and splashing
    and clashing;
And so never ending, but always descending,
Sounds and motions for ever and ever are
    blending,
All at once and all o'er, with a mighty
    uproar,
And this way the water comes down at
    Lodore.
ROBERT SOUTHEY.

YARROW UNVISITED.

FROM Stirling Castle we had seen
    The mazy Forth unravell'd;
Had trod the banks of Clyde and Tay,
    And with the Tweed had travell'd;
And when we came to Clovenford,
    Then said my "*winsome Marrow*,"
"Whate'er betide, we'll turn aside,
    And see the Braes of Yarrow."

"Let Yarrow Folk, frae Selkirk Town,
    Who have been buying, selling,
Go back to Yarrow, 'tis their own;
    Each Maiden to her Dwelling!
On Yarrow's banks let herons feed,
    Hares couch, and rabbits burrow!
But we will downward with the Tweed,
    Nor turn aside to Yarrow.

"There's Galla Water, Leader Haughs,
    Both lying right before us;
And Dryborough, where with the chiming
    Tweed
The Lintwhites sing in chorus;
There's pleasant Tiviotdale, a land
    Made blithe with plough and harrow:
Why throw away a needful day
    To go in search of Yarrow?

"What's Yarrow but a River bare,
    That glides the dark hills under?
There are a thousand such elsewhere
    As worthy of your wonder."
—Strange words they seem'd of slight and
    scorn:
My true-love sigh'd for sorrow;
And look'd me in the face, to think
    I thus could speak of Yarrow!

"Oh! green," said I, "are Yarrow's
    Holms
And sweet is Yarrow flowing!
Fair hangs the apple frae the rock,
    But we will leave it growing.
O'er hilly path, and open Strath,
    We'll wander Scotland thorough;
But, though so near, we will not turn
    Into the Dale of Yarrow.

"Let beeves and home-bred kine partake
    The sweets of Burn-mill meadow;
The swan on still St. Mary's Lake
    Float double, swan and shadow!
We will not see them; will not go,
    To-day, nor yet to-morrow;
Enough if in our hearts we know
    There's such a place as Yarrow.

"Be Yarrow Stream unseen, unknown!
    It must, or we shall rue it:
We have a vision of our own;
    Ah, why should we undo it?
The treasured dreams of times long past,
    We'll keep them, winsome Marrow!
For when we're there, although 'tis fair,
    'Twill be another Yarrow!

"If Care with freezing years should come.
    And wandering seem but folly,—
Should we be loath to stir from home,
    And yet be melancholy;
Should life be dull, and spirits low,
    'Twill soothe us in our sorrow,
That earth has something yet to show,
    The bonny Holms of Yarrow!"
WILLIAM WORDSWORTH.

YARROW VISITED.

AND is this—Yarrow?—*This* the Stream
    Of which my fancy cherish'd,
So faithfully, a waking dream?
    An image that hath perish'd!
Oh that some Minstrel's harp were near
    To utter notes of gladness,
And chase this silence from the air,
    That fills my heart with sadness!

Yet why?—a silvery current flows
    With uncontroll'd meanderings;
Nor have these eyes by greener hills
    Been soothed, in all my wanderings.

And, through her depths, Saint Mary's
    Lake
Is visibly delighted;
For not a feature of those hills
    Is in the mirror slighted.

A blue sky bends o'er Yarrow Vale,
    Save where that pearly whiteness
Is round the rising sun diffused,
    A tender hazy brightness;
Mild dawn of promise! that excludes
    All profitless dejection;
Though not unwilling here to admit
    A pensive recollection.

Where was it that the famous Flower
    Of Yarrow Vale lay bleeding?
His bed perchance was yon smooth mound
    On which the herd is feeding:
And haply from this crystal pool,
    Now peaceful as the morning,
The Water-wraith ascended thrice,—
    And gave his doleful warning.

Delicious is the Lay that sings
    The haunts of happy Lovers,
The path that leads them to the grove,
    The leafy grove that covers:
And Pity sanctifies the verse
    That paints, by strength of sorrow,
The unconquerable strength of love;
    Bear witness, rueful Yarrow!

But thou, that didst appear so fair
    To fond Imagination,
Dost rival in the light of day
    Her delicate creation:
Meek loveliness is round thee spread
    A softness still and holy;
The grace of forest charms decay'd,
    And pastoral melancholy.

That region left, the Vale unfolds
    Rich groves of lofty stature,
With Yarrow winding through the pomp
    Of cultivated Nature;
And, rising from those lofty groves,
    Behold a ruin hoary!
The shatter'd front of Newark's Towers,
    Renown'd in Border story.

Fair scenes for childhood's opening bloom,
    For sportive youth to stray in;
For manhood to enjoy his strength;
    And age to wear away in!
Yon Cottage seems a bower of bliss,
    A covert for protection
Of tender thoughts that nestle there,
    The brood of chaste affection.

How sweet, on this autumnal day,
    The wild-wood fruits to gather,
And on my True-love's forehead plant
    A crest of blooming heather!
And what if I enwreathed my own?
    'Twere no offence to reason;
The sober Hills thus deck their brows
    To meet the wintry season.

I see—but not by sight alone,
    Loved Yarrow, have I won thee;
A ray of Fancy still survives—
    Her sunshine plays upon thee!
Thy ever-youthful waters keep
    A course of lively pleasure;
And gladsome notes my lips can breathe,
    Accordant to the measure.

The vapors linger round the Heights,
    They melt—and soon must vanish;
One hour is theirs, nor more is mine—
    Sad thought, which I would banish,
But that I know, where'er I go,
    Thy genuine image, Yarrow!
Will dwell with me—to heighten joy,
    And cheer my mind in sorrow.
WILLIAM WORDSWORTH.

YARROW REVISITED.

THE gallant Youth who may have gain'd,
    Or seeks, a "Winsome Marrow,"
Was but an Infant in the lap
    When first I look'd on Yarrow;
Once more, by Newark's Castle-gate
    Long left without a Warder,
I stood, look'd, listen'd, and with Thee,
    Great Minstrel of the Border!

Grave thoughts ruled wide on that sweet day,
    Their dignity installing
In gentle bosoms, while sere leaves
    Were on the bough, or falling;
But breezes play'd, and sunshine gleam'd—
    The forest to embolden;
Redden'd the fiery hues, and shot
    Transparence through the golden.

For busy thoughts the Stream flow'd on
  In foamy agitation;
And slept in many a crystal pool
  For quiet contemplation:
No public and no private care
  The freeborn mind enthralling,
We made a day of happy hours,
  Our happy days recalling.

Brisk Youth appear'd, the Morn of youth,
  With freaks of graceful folly,—
Life's temperate Noon, her sober Eve,
  Her Night not melancholy,
Past, present, future, all appear'd
  In harmony united,
Like guests that meet, and some from far,
  By cordial love invited.

And if, as Yarrow, through the woods
  And down the meadow ranging,
Did meet us with unalter'd face,
  Though we were changed and changing;
If, *then*, some natural shadows spread
  Our inward prospect over,
The soul's deep valley was not slow
  Its brightness to recover.

Eternal blessings on the Muse,
  And her divine employment!
The blameless Muse, who trains her Sons
  For hope and calm enjoyment;
Albeit sickness lingering yet
  Has o'er their pillow brooded,
And Care waylay their steps—a sprite
  Not easily eluded.

For thee, O Scott! compell'd to change
  Green Eildon-hill and Cheviot
For warm Vesuvio's vine-clad slopes;
  And leave thy Tweed and Teviot
For mild Sorrento's breezy waves;
  May classic Fancy, linking
With native Fancy her fresh aid,
  Preserve thy heart from sinking!

Oh! while they minister to thee,
  Each vying with the other,
May Health return to mellow Age,
  With Strength, her venturous brother;
And Tiber, and each brook and rill
  Renown'd in song and story,
With unimagined beauty shine,
  Nor lose one ray of glory!

For Thou, upon a hundred streams,
  By tales of love and sorrow,
Of faithful love, undaunted truth,
  Hast shed the power of Yarrow;
And streams unknown, hills yet unseen,
  Where'er thy path invite thee,
At parent Nature's grateful call,
  With gladness must requite Thee.

A gracious welcome shall be thine,
  Such looks of love and honor
As thy own Yarrow gave to me
  When first I gazed upon her;
Beheld what I had fear'd to see,
  Unwilling to surrender
Dreams treasured up from early days,
  The holy and the tender.

And what, for this frail world, were all
  That mortals do or suffer
Did no responsive harp, no pen,
  Memorial tribute offer?
Yea, what were mighty Nature's self,
  Her features, could they win us,
Unhelp'd by the poetic voice
  That hourly speaks within us?

Nor deem that localized Romance
  Plays false with our affections;
Unsanctifies our tears—made sport
  For fanciful dejections:
Ah, no! the visions of the past
  Sustain the heart in feeling
Life as she is—our changeful Life,
  With friends and kindred dealing.

Bear witness, Ye, whose thoughts that day
  In Yarrow's groves were centred;
Who through the silent portal arch
  Of mouldering Newark enter'd,
And clomb the winding stair that once
  Too timidly was mounted
By the "Last Minstrel" (not the last),
  Ere he his Tale recounted.

Flow on for ever, Yarrow Stream!
  Fulfil thy pensive duty,
Well pleased that future Bards should chant
  For simple hearts thy beauty,
To dreamlight dear while yet unseen,
  Dear to the common sunshine,
And dearer still, as now I feel,
  To memory's shadowy moonshine!

WILLIAM WORDSWORTH.

ALNWICK CASTLE.

Home of the Percy's high-born race,
  Home of their beautiful and brave,
Alike their birth- and burial-place,
  Their cradle and their grave!
Still sternly o'er the castle-gate
Their house's Lion stands in state,
  As in his proud departed hours,
And warriors frown in stone on high,
And feudal banners "flout the sky"
  Above his princely towers.

A gentle hill its side inclines,
  Lovely in England's fadeless green,
To meet the quiet stream which winds
  Through this romantic scene
As silently and sweetly still,
As when, at evening, on that hill,
  While summer's wind blew soft and low,
Seated by gallant Hotspur's side,
His Katherine was a happy bride,
  A thousand years ago.

Gaze on the Abbey's ruin'd pile:
  Does not the succoring ivy, keeping
Her watch around it, seem to smile,
  As o'er a loved one sleeping?
One solitary turret gray
  Still tells, in melancholy glory,
The legend of the Cheviot day,
  The Percy's proudest border-story.

That day its roof was triumph's arch;
  Then rang, from aisle to pictured dome,
The light step of the soldier's march,
  The music of the trump and drum;
And babe and sire, the old, the young,
And the monk's hymn, and minstrel's song,
  And woman's pure kiss, sweet and long,
  Welcomed her warrior home.

Wild roses by the Abbey towers
  Are gay in their young bud and bloom;
They were born of a race of funeral flowers
  That garlanded, in long-gone hours,
  A templar's knightly tomb.
He died, his sword in his mailèd hand,
On the holiest spot of the Blessed Land,
  Where the Cross was damp'd with his
    dying breath,
When blood ran free as festal wine,

And the sainted air of Palestine
  Was thick with the darts of death.

Wise with the lore of centuries,
What tales, if there be "tongues in trees,"
  Those giant oaks could tell
Of beings born and buried here;
Tales of the peasant and the peer,
Tales of the bridal and the bier,
  The welcome and farewell,
Since on their boughs the startled bird
First, in her twilight slumbers, heard
  The Norman's curfew-bell!

I wander'd through the lofty halls
  Trod by the Percys of old fame,
And traced upon the chapel walls
  Each high, heroic name,
From him who once his standard set
Where now, o'er mosque and minaret,
  Glitter the Sultan's crescent moons,
To him who, when a younger son,
Fought for King George at Lexington,
  A major of dragoons.

That last half stanza—it has dash'd
  From my warm lip the sparkling cup;
The light that o'er my eyebeam flash'd,
  The power that bore my spirit up
Above this bank-note world—is gone;
And Alnwick's but a market-town,
  And this, alas! its market-day,
And beasts and borderers throng the way
Oxen and bleating lambs in lots,
Northumbrian boors and plaided Scots,
  Men in the coal and cattle line;
From Teviot's bard and hero land,
From royal Berwick's beach of sand,
From Wooller, Morpeth, Hexham, and
  Newcastle-upon-Tyne.

These are not the romantic times
So beautiful in Spenser's rhymes,
  So dazzling to the dreaming boy:
Ours are the days of fact, not fable,
Of knights, but not of the Round Table,
  Of Bailie Jarvie, not Rob Roy:
'Tis what "our President," Monroe,
  Has called "the era of good feeling:"
The Highlander, the bitterest foe
To modern laws, has felt their blow,
  Consented to be tax'd, and vote,
  And put on pantaloons and coat,
    And leave off cattle-stealing:

Lord Stafford mines for coal and salt,
The Duke of Norfolk deals in malt,
　The Douglass in red herrings;
And noble name and cultured land,
Palace, and park, and vassal-band,
　Are powerless to the notes of hand
　　Of Rothschild or the Barings.

The age of bargaining, said Burke,
Has come: to-day the turban'd Turk
(Sleep, Richard of the lion heart!
Sleep on, nor from your cerements start)
　Is England's friend and fast ally;
The Moslem tramples on the Greek,
　And on the Cross and altar-stone,
　And Christendom looks tamely on,
And hears the Christian maiden shriek,
　And sees the Christian father die;
And not a sabre-blow is given
For Greece and fame, for faith and heaven,
　By Europe's craven chivalry.

You'll ask if yet the Percy lives
　In the arm'd pomp of feudal state?
The present representatives
　Of Hotspur and his "gentle Kate"
Are some half dozen serving-men
　In the drab coat of William Penn;
　A chambermaid, whose lip and eye,
And cheek, and brown hair, bright and curling
　　Spoke Nature's aristocracy;
And one, half groom, half seneschal,
Who bowed me through court, bower, and hall,
　From donjon-keep to turret wall,
　　For ten-and-sixpence sterling.
　　　　　　　FITZ-GREENE HALLECK.

HELLVELLYN.

I CLIMB'D the dark brow of the mighty Hellvellyn.
　Lakes and mountains beneath me gleam'd misty and wide;
All was still, save by fits, when the eagle was yelling,
　And starting around me the echoes replied.
On the right, Striden-edge round the Red-tarn was bending,
And Catchedicam its left verge was defending,
One huge nameless rock in the front was ascending,
　When I mark'd the sad spot where the wanderer had died.

Dark green was that spot 'mid the brown mountain-heather,
　Where the Pilgrim of Nature lay stretch'd in decay,
Like the corpse of an outcast abandon'd to weather,
　Till the mountain-winds wasted the tenantless clay.
Nor yet quite deserted, though lonely extended,
For, faithful in death, his mute favorite attended,
The much-loved remains of her master defended,
　And chased the hill-fox and the raven away.

How long didst thou think that his silence was slumber?
　When the wind waved his garment, how oft didst thou start?
How many long days and long weeks didst thou number,
　Ere he faded before thee, the friend of thy heart?
And, oh, was it meet, that—no requiem read o'er him,
No mother to weep, and no friend to deplore him,
And thou, little guardian, alone stretch'd before him,—
　Unhonor'd the Pilgrim from life should depart?

When a Prince to the fate of the Peasant has yielded,
　The tapestry waves dark round the dim-lighted hall;
With scutcheons of silver the coffin is shielded,
　And pages stand mute by the canopied pall:

Through the courts at deep midnight the
   torches are gleaming;
In the proudly-arch'd chapel the banners
   are beaming;
Far adown the long aisle sacred music is
   streaming,
   Lamenting a Chief of the People should
      fall.

But meeter for thee, gentle lover of Nature,
   To lay down thy head like the meek
      mountain-lamb,
When, 'wilder'd, he drops from some cliff
      huge in stature,
And draws his last sob by the side of his
      dam.
And more stately thy couch by this desert
   lake lying,
Thy obsequies sung by the gray plover
   flying,
With one faithful friend but to witness thy
   dying,
   In the arms of Hellvellyn and Catche
      dicam.
                  SIR WALTER SCOTT.

ODE TO LEVEN WATER.

ON Leven's banks, while free to rove,
And tune the rural pipe to love,
I envied not the happiest swain
That ever trod the Arcadian plain.
   Pure stream, in whose transparent wave
My youthful limbs I wont to lave;
No torrents stain thy limpid source,
No rocks impede thy dimpling course,
That sweetly warbles o'er its bed,
With white round polish'd pebbles spread;
While, lightly poised, the scaly brood
In myriads cleave thy crystal flood;
The springing trout in speckled pride,
The salmon, monarch of the tide;
The ruthless pike, intent on war,
The silver eel, and mottled par.
Devolving from thy parent lake,
A charming maze thy waters make,
By bowers of birch and groves of pine,
And hedges flower'd with eglantine.
   Still on thy banks, so gayly green,
May numerous flocks and herds be seen:
And lasses chanting o'er the pail,
And shepherds piping in the dale;

And ancient faith that knows no guile,
And industry embrown'd with toil;
And hearts resolved and hands prepared
The blessings they enjoy to guard!
                  TOBIAS SMOLLETT.

FLOW GENTLY, SWEET AFTON.

FLOW gently, sweet Afton, among thy
   green braes,
Flow gently, I'll sing thee a song in thy
   praise;
My Mary's asleep by thy murmuring
   stream,
Flow gently, sweet Afton, disturb not her
   dream.

Thou stock-dove whose echo resounds
   through the glen,
Ye wild whistling blackbirds in yon thorny
   den,
Thou green-crested lapwing, thy scream-
   ing forbear,
I charge you disturb not my slumbering
   fair.

How lofty, sweet Afton, thy neighboring
   hills,
Far mark'd with the courses of clear
   winding rills;
There daily I wander as noon rises high,
My flocks and my Mary's sweet cot in my
   eye.

How pleasant thy banks and green valleys
   below,
Where wild in the woodlands the prim-
   roses blow;
There oft, as mild Evening weeps over the
   lea,
The sweet-scented birk shades my Mary
   and me.

Thy crystal stream, Afton, how lovely it
   glides,
And winds by the cot where my Mary re-
   sides;
How wanton thy waters her snowy feet lave,
As, gathering sweet flow'rets, she stems
   thy clear wave!

Flow gently, sweet Afton, among thy green
   braes,
Flow gently, sweet river, the theme of my
   lays;

My Mary's asleep by thy murmuring
    stream,
Flow gently, sweet Afton, disturb not her
    dream.
ROBERT BURNS.

THE BELLS OF SHANDON.

> *Sabbata pango;*
> *Funera plango;*
> *Solemnia clango.*
> INSCRIPTION ON AN OLD BELL.

WITH deep affection
And recollection
I often think of
    Those Shandon bells,
Whose sounds so wild would,
In the days of childhood,
Fling round my cradle
    Their magic spells.

On this I ponder
Where'er I wander,
And thus grow fonder,
    Sweet Cork, of thee—
With thy bells of Shandon,
That sound so grand on
The pleasant waters
    Of the river Lee.

I've heard bells chiming
Full many a clime in,
Tolling sublime in
    Cathedral shrine,
While at a glibe rate
Brass tongues would vibrate;
But all their music
    Spoke naught like thine.

For memory, dwelling
On each proud swelling
Of the belfry knelling
    Its bold notes free,
Made the bells of Shandon
Sound far more grand on
The pleasant waters
    Of the river Lee.

I've heard bells tolling
Old Adrian's Mole in,
Their thunder rolling
    From the Vatican—
And cymbals glorious
Swinging uproarious
In the gorgeous turrets
    Of Notre Dame;

But thy sounds were sweeter
Than the dome of Peter
Flings o'er the Tiber,
    Pealing solemnly.
Oh! the bells of Shandon
Sound far more grand on
The pleasant waters
    Of the river Lee.

There's a bell in Moscow;
While on tower and kiosk, oh,
In Saint Sophia
    The Turkman gets,
And loud in air
Calls men to prayer
From the tapering summit
    Of tall minarets.

Such empty phantom
I freely grant them;
But there's an anthem
    More dear to me—
'Tis the Bells of Shandon,
That sound so grand on
The pleasant waters
    Of the river Lee.
FRANCIS MAHONY ("Father Prout").

THE GROVES OF BLARNEY.

THE groves of Blarney they look so charming,
    Down by the purlings of sweet silent brooks—
All deck'd by posies, that spontaneous grow there,
    Planted in order in the rocky nooks.
'Tis there the daisy, and the sweet carnation,
    The blooming pink, and the rose so fair;
Likewise the lily, and the daffodilly—
    All flowers that scent the sweet, open air.

'Tis Lady Jeffers owns this plantation;
    Like Alexander, or like Helen fair,
There's no commander in all the nation
    For regulation can with her compare.

Such walls surround her, that no nine-pounder
  Could ever plunder her place of strength;
But Oliver Cromwell, he did her pommel,
  And made a breach in her battlement.

There's gravel-walks there for speculation,
  And conversation in sweet solitude;
'Tis there the lover may hear the dove, or
  The gentle plover, in the afternoon.
And if a young lady should be so engaging
  As to walk alone in those shady bowers,
'Tis there her courtier he may transport her
  In some dark fort, or under the ground.

For 'tis there's the cave where no daylight enters,
  But bats and badgers are for ever bred;
Being moss'd by Natur', that makes it sweeter
  Than a coach and six, or a feather bed.
'Tis there's the lake that is stored with perches,
  And comely eels in the verdant mud;
Besides the leeches, and the groves of beeches,
  All standing in order for to guard the flood.

'Tis there's the kitchen hangs many a flitch in,
  With the maids a-stitching upon the stair;
The bread and biske', the beer and whiskey,
  Would make you frisky if you were there.
'Tis there you'd see Peg Murphy's daughter
  A-washing praties forenent the door,
With Roger Cleary, and Father Healy,
  All blood relations to my Lord Donoughmore.

There's statues gracing this noble place in,
  All heathen goddesses so fair—
Bold Neptune, Plutarch, and Nicodemus,
  All standing naked in the open air.
So now to finish this brave narration,
  Which my poor geni' could not entwine;
But were I Homer, or Nebuchadnezzar,
  'Tis in every feature I would make it shine.

         RICHARD ALFRED MILLIKIN.

SWEET INNISFALLEN.

SWEET Innisfallen, fare thee well,
  May calm and sunshine long be thine!
How fair thou art let others tell—
  To *feel* how fair shall long be mine.

Sweet Innisfallen, long shall dwell
  In memory's dream that sunny smile,
Which o'er thee on that evening fell
  When first I saw thy fairy isle.

'Twas light, indeed, too blest for one,
  Who had to turn to paths of care—
Through crowded haunts again to run,
  And leave thee bright and silent there;

No more unto thy shores to come,
  But, on the world's rude ocean tost,
Dream of thee sometimes as a home
  Of sunshine he had seen and lost.

Far better in thy weeping hours
  To part from thee, as I do now,
When mist is o'er thy blooming bowers,
  Like sorrow's veil on beauty's brow.

For, though unrivall'd still thy grace,
  Thou dost not look, as then, too blest,
But thus in shadow, seem'st a place
  Where erring man might hope to rest—

Might hope to rest, and find in thee
  A gloom like Eden's, on the day
He left its shade, when every tree,
  Like thine, hung weeping o'er his way.

Weeping or smiling, lovely isle!
  And all the lovelier for thy tears—
For tho' but rare thy sunny smile,
  'Tis heaven's own glance when it appears.

Like feeling hearts, whose joys are few,
  But, when indeed they come, divine—
The brightest life the sun e'er threw
  Is lifeless to one gleam of thine!

         THOMAS MOORE.

THE MEETING OF THE WATERS.

THERE is not in the wide world a valley so sweet
As that vale, in whose bosom the bright waters meet;

Oh, the last rays of feeling and life must depart
Ere the bloom of that valley shall fade from my heart!

Yet it was not that Nature had shed o'er the scene
Her purest of crystal and brightest of green;
'Twas not the soft magic of streamlet or hill,—
Oh, no! it was something more exquisite still.

'Twas that friends, the beloved of my bosom, were near,
Who made every dear scene of enchantment more dear,
And who felt how the best charms of Nature improve
When we see them reflected from looks that we love.

Sweet Vale of Avoca! how calm could I rest
In thy bosom of shade, with the friends I love best:
Where the storms that we feel in this cold world should cease,
And our hearts, like thy waters, be mingled in peace.
          THOMAS MOORE.

AT DIEPPE.

THE shivering column of the moonlight lies
  Upon the crumbling sea;
Down the lone shore the flying curlew cries
  Half humanly

With hoarse, dull wash the backward dragging surge
  Its rancid pebbles rakes,
Or swelling dark runs down with toppling verge,
  And flashing breaks.

The lighthouse flares and darkens from the cliff,
  And stares with lurid eye
Fiercely along the sea and shore, as if
  Some foe to spy.

What knowing thought, O ever-moaning sea,
  Haunts thy perturbèd breast,
What dark crime weighs upon thy memory
  And spoils thy rest?

Thy soft swell lifts and swings the new-launch'd yacht
  With polish'd spars and deck,
But crawls and grovels where the bare ribs rot
  Of the old wreck.

O treacherous courtier! thy deceitful lie
  To youth is gayly told,
But in remorse I see thee cringingly
  Crouch to the old.
          WILLIAM WETMORE STORY.

THE RHINE.

'TWAS morn, and beauteous on the mountain's brow
  (Hung with the clusters of the bending vine)
Shone in the early light, when on the Rhine
We bounded, and the white waves round the prow
In murmurs parted:—varying as we go,
  Lo! the woods open, and the rocks retire,
  As some gray convent-wall or glistening spire
Mid the bright landscape's track unfolding slow!
Here dark, with furrowed aspect, like Despair,
  Frowns the bleak cliff! There on the woodland's side
The shadowy sunshine pours its streaming tide;
Whilst Hope, enchanted with the scene so fair,
Counts not the hours of a long summer's day,
Nor heeds how fast the prospect winds away.
          WILLIAM LISLE BOWLES.

HYMN.

BEFORE SUNRISE IN THE VALE OF CHAMOUNI.

HAST thou a charm to stay the morning-star
In his steep course? So long he seems to pause

On thy bald awful head, O sovran Blanc!
The Arve and Arveiron at thy base
Rave ceaselessly; but thou, most awful
    Form,
Risest from forth thy silent sea of pines,
How silently! Around thee and above,
Deep is the air and dark; substantial,
    black,
An ebon mass: methinks thou piercest it,
As with a wedge! But, when I look
    again,
It is thine own calm home, thy crystal
    shrine,
Thy habitation from eternity!
O dread and silent Mount! I gazed upon
    thee,
Till thou, still present to the bodily sense,
Didst vanish from my thought: entranced
    in prayer,
I worshipp'd the Invisible alone.

Yet, like some sweet beguiling melody,
So sweet, we know not we are listening to
    it,
Thou, the meanwhile, wast blending with
    my thought,
Yea, with my life, and life's own secret
    joy:
Till the dilating Soul, enwrapt, trans-
    fused,
Into the mighty vision passing—there,
As in her natural form, swell'd vast to
    Heaven!

Awake, my soul! Not only passive praise
Thou owest! not alone these swelling
    tears,
Mute thanks, and secret ecstasy! Awake,
Voice of sweet song! Awake, my Heart,
    awake,
Green vales and icy cliffs, all join my
    Hymn.

Thou, first and chief, sole sovran of the
    Vale!
Oh struggling with the darkness all the
    night,
And visited all night by troops of stars,
Or when they climb the sky, or when they
    sink:
Companion of the morning-star at dawn,
Thyself Earth's rosy star, and of the
    dawn

Co-herald: wake! oh wake! and utter
    praise!
Who sank thy sunless pillars deep in
    Earth?
Who fill'd thy countenance with rosy
    light?
Who made thee parent of perpetual
    streams?

And you, ye five wild torrents fiercely glad!
Who call'd you forth from night and utter
    death,
From dark and icy caverns call'd you
    forth,
Down those precipitous, black, jagged
    Rocks,
For ever shatter'd, and the same for ever?
Who gave you your invulnerable life,
Your strength, your speed, your fury, and
    your joy,
Unceasing thunder, and eternal foam?
And who commanded (and the silence
    came),
Here let the billows stiffen, and have rest?

Ye ice-falls! ye that from the mountain's
    brow
Adown enormous ravines slope amain—
Torrents, methinks, that heard a mighty
    voice,
And stopp'd at once amid their maddest
    plunge!
Motionless torrents! silent cataracts!
Who made you glorious as the gates of
    Heaven
Beneath the keen full moon? Who bade
    the sun
Clothe you with rainbows? Who with
    living flowers
Of loveliest blue spread garlands at your
    feet?
God! let the torrents, like a shout of
    nations,
Answer: and let the ice-plains echo, God!
God! sing, ye meadow-streams, with glad-
    some voice!
Ye pine groves, with your soft and soul-
    like sounds!
And they, too, have a voice, yon piles of
    snow,
And in their perilous fall shall thunder,
    God!

Ye living flowers that skirt the eternal
    frost!
Ye wild goats sporting round the eagle's
    nest!
Ye eagles, playmates of the mountain-
    storm!
Ye lightnings, the dread arrows of the
    clouds!
Ye signs and wonders of the element!
Utter forth God! and fill the hills with
    praise!

Thou, too, hoar Mount! with thy sky-
    pointing peaks,
Oft from whose feet the avalanche, un-
    heard,
Shoots downward, glittering through the
    pure serene
Into the depth of clouds, that veil thy
    breast—
Thou, too, again, stupendous Mountain!
    thou
That as I raise my head, a while bow'd
    low
In adoration, upward from thy base
Slow travelling with dim eyes suffused with
    tears,
Solemnly seemest, like a vapory cloud,
To rise before me—Rise, oh ever rise,
Rise like a cloud of incense, from the
    Earth!
Thou kingly Spirit throned among the
    hills,
Thou dread ambassador from Earth to
    Heaven,
Great hierarch! tell thou the silent sky,
And tell the stars, and tell yon rising sun,
Earth with her thousand voices praises
    God.
            SAMUEL TAYLOR COLERIDGE.

INDIAN NAMES.

E say they all have pass'd away,
    That noble race and brave,
That their light canoes have vanish'd
    From off the crested wave;
That, 'mid the forests where they roam'd,
    There rings no hunter's shout;
But their name is on your waters,
    Ye may not wash it out.

'Tis where Ontario's billow
    Like ocean's surge is curl'd;
Where strong Niagara's thunders wake
    The echo of the world;
Where red Missouri bringeth
    Rich tribute from the West,
And Rappahannock sweetly sleeps
    On green Virginia's breast.

Ye say their conelike cabins,
    That cluster'd o'er the vale,
Have fled away like wither'd leaves
    Before the autumn's gale:
But their memory liveth on your hills,
    Their baptism on your shore;
Your everlasting rivers speak
    Their dialect of yore.

Old Massachusetts wears it
    Within her lordly crown,
And broad Ohio bears it
    'Mid all her young renown;
Connecticut hath wreathed it
    Where her quiet foliage waves,
And bold Kentucky breathes it hoarse
    Through all her ancient caves.

Wachuset hides its lingering voice
    Within his rocky heart,
And Alleghany graves its tone
    Throughout his lofty chart;
Monadnock on his forehead hoar
    Doth seal the sacred trust:
Your mountains build their monument,
    Though ye destroy their dust.
            LYDIA HUNTLEY SIGOURNEY.

NIAGARA.

THE thoughts are strange that crowd into
    my brain
While I look upward to thee! It would
    seem
As if God pour'd thee from his hollow hand,
And hung his bow upon thine awful front,
And spoke in that loud voice which seem'd
    to him
Who dwelt in Patmos for his Saviour's sake
"The sound of many waters," and had bade
Thy flood to chronicle the ages back,
And notch His centuries in the eternal
    rocks.

"YE SAY THEY ALL HAVE PASS'D AWAY,
THAT NOBLE RACE AND BRAVE." Indian Names.

Deep calleth unto deep—and what are we
That hear the question of that voice sublime?
Oh, what are all the notes that ever rung
From war's vain trumpet by thy thundering side?
Yea, what is all the riot man can make,
In his short life, to thine unceasing roar?
And yet, bold babbler, what art thou to Him
Who drown'd the world and heap'd the waters far
Above its loftiest mountains?—A light wave,
That breaks and whispers of his Maker's might!
JOHN G. C. BRAINARD.

TO SENECA LAKE.

On thy fair bosom, silver lake,
   The wild swan spreads his snowy sail,
And round his breast the ripples break,
   As down he bears before the gale.

On thy fair bosom, waveless stream,
   The dipping paddle echoes far,
And flashes in the moonlight gleam,
   And bright reflects the polar star.

The waves along thy pebbly shore,
   As blows the north wind, heave their foam
And curl around the dashing oar,
   As late the boatman hies him home.

How sweet, at set of sun, to view
   Thy golden mirror spreading wide,
And see the mist of mantling blue
   Float round the distant mountain's side.

At midnight hour, as shines the moon,
   A sheet of silver spreads below,
And swift she cuts, at highest noon,
   Light clouds, like wreaths of purest snow.

On thy fair bosom, silver lake,
   Oh I could ever sweep the oar,—
When early birds at morning wake,
   And evening tells us toil is o'er.
JAMES GATES PERCIVAL.

THE ARSENAL AT SPRINGFIELD.

THIS is the Arsenal. From floor to ceiling,
   Like a huge organ, rise the burnish'd arms,
But from their silent pipes no anthem pealing
   Startles the villages with strange alarms.

Ah! what a sound will rise—how wild and dreary—
   When the death-angel touches those swift keys!
What loud lament and dismal Miserere
   Will mingle with their awful symphonies!

I hear even now the infinite fierce chorus,
   The cries of agony, the endless groan,
Which, through the ages that have gone before us,
   In long reverberations reach our own.

On helm and harness rings the Saxon hammer,
   Through Cimbric forest roars the Norseman's song,
And loud, amid the universal clamor,
   O'er distant deserts sounds the Tartar gong.

I hear the Florentine, who from his palace
   Wheels out his battle-bell with dreadful din,
And Aztec priests upon their teocallis
   Beat the wild war-drums made of serpent's skin;

The tumult of each sack'd and burning village,
   The shout that every prayer for mercy drowns,
The soldiers' revels in the midst of pillage,
   The wail of famine in beleaguer'd towns;

The bursting shell, the gateway wrench'd asunder,
   The rattling musketry, the clashing blade,
And ever and anon, in tone of thunder,
   The diapason of the cannonade.

Is it, O man, with such discordant noises,
   With such accursèd instruments as these,

Thou drownest Nature's sweet and kindly
    voices,
And jarrest the celestial harmonies?

Were half the power that fills the world
    with terror,
  Were half the wealth bestow'd on camps
    and courts,
Given to redeem the human mind from
    error,
  There were no need of arsenals or
    forts:

The warrior's name would be a name abhorrèd,
  And every nation that should lift again
Its hand against a brother, on its forehead
  Would wear for evermore the curse of
    Cain!

Down the dark future, through long generations,
  The echoing sounds grow fainter and
    then cease;
And like a bell, with solemn, sweet vibrations,
  I hear once more the voice of Christ
    say, "Peace!"

Peace!—and no longer from its brazen
    portals
  The blast of War's great organ shakes
    the skies,
But, beautiful as songs of the immortals,
  The holy melodies of love arise.
HENRY WADSWORTH LONGFELLOW.

OLD ST. DAVID'S AT RADNOR.

WHAT an image of peace and rest
  Is this little church among its graves!
All is so quiet; the troubled breast,
  The wounded spirit, the heart oppressed,
  Here may find the repose it craves.

See, how the ivy climbs and expands
  Over this humble hermitage,
And seems to caress with its little hands
The rough, gray stones, as a child that
    stands
  Caressing the wrinkled cheeks of age!

You cross the threshold; and dim and
    small
  Is the space that serves for the Shepherd's Fold;
The narrow aisle, the bare, white wall,
The pews, and the pulpit quaint and tall,
  Whisper and say: "Alas! we are old."

Herbert's chapel at Bemerton
  Hardly more spacious is than this;
But Poet and Pastor, blent in one,
Clothed with a splendor, as of the sun,
  That lowly and holy edifice.

It is not the wall of stone without
  That makes the building small or great,
But the soul's light shining round about,
And the faith that overcometh doubt,
  And the love that stronger is than hate.

Were I a pilgrim in search of peace,
  Were I a pastor of Holy Church,
More than a bishop's diocese
Should I prize this place of rest, and release
  From farther longing and farther search.

Here would I stay, and let the world
  With its distant thunder roar and roll;
Storms do not rend the sail that is furled;
Nor like a dead leaf, tossed and whirled
  In an eddy of wind, is the anchored soul.
HENRY WADSWORTH LONGFELLOW.

Give us grace, O Saviour,
To put off in might,
Deeds & dreams of darkness
For the robes of light.

A. Cleveland Coxe
Bp. of Westn. N. York.
June, 6. 1881.

"Psalms and Hymns and Spiritual Songs."
Eph. v. 19.

Watchman, Tell us of the Night.

Watchman, tell us of the night—
 What its signs of promise are!
Traveller, o'er yon mountain's height
 See that glory-beaming star!
Watchman, does its beauteous ray
 Aught of hope or joy foretell?
Traveller, yes; it brings the day—
 Promised day of Israel.

Watchman, tell us of the night—
 Higher yet that star ascends!
Traveller, blessedness and light,
 Peace and truth, its course portends.
Watchman, will its beams alone
 Gild the spot that gave them birth?
Traveller, ages are its own—
 See, it bursts o'er all the earth!

Watchman, tell us of the night,
 For the morning seems to dawn.
Traveller, darkness takes its flight—
 Doubt and terror are withdrawn.
Watchman, let thy wandering cease;
 Hie thee to thy quiet home.
Traveller, lo! the Prince of Peace—
 Lo! the Son of God, is come.
                    Sir John Bowring.

On the Morning of Christ's Nativity.

I.

This is the month, and this the happy morn,
Wherein the Son of heav'n's eternal King,
Of wedded Maid, and Virgin Mother born,
Our great redemption from above did bring;
For so the holy sages once did sing,
That He our deadly forfeit should release,
And with His Father work us a perpetual peace.

II.

That glorious form, that light unsufferable,
And that far-beaming blaze of majesty,
Wherewith He wont at heav'n's high council-table
To sit the midst of Trinal Unity,
He laid aside; and here with us to be,
Forsook the courts of everlasting day,
And chose with us a darksome house of mortal clay.

III.

Say, heav'nly Muse, shall not thy sacred vein
Afford a present to the Infant God?
Hast thou no verse, no hymn, or solemn strain,
To welcome Him to this His new abode,
Now while the heav'n, by the sun's team untrod,
Hath took no print of the approaching light,
And all the spangled host keep watch in squadrons bright?

IV.

See how from far upon the eastern road
The star-led wizards haste with odors sweet:
Oh run, prevent them with thy humble ode,
And lay it lowly at His blessed feet;
Have thou the honor first thy Lord to greet,
And join thy voice unto the Angel quire,
From out His secret altar touch'd with hallow'd fire.

THE HYMN.

I.

It was the winter wild,
While the heav'n-born Child
   All meanly wrapt in the rude manger lies;
Nature in awe to Him
Had dofft her gaudy trim,
   With her great Master so to sympathize:
It was no season then for her
To wanton with the sun, her lusty paramour.

II.

Only with speeches fair
She woos the gentle air
   To hide her guilty front with innocent snow,
And on her naked shame,
Pollute with sinful blame,
   The saintly veil of maiden white to throw;
Confounded that her Maker's eyes
Should look so near upon her foul deformities.

III.

But He her fears to cease,
Sent down the meek-eyed Peace;
   She, crown'd with olive green, came softly sliding
Down through the turning sphere
His ready harbinger,
   With turtle wing the amorous clouds dividing;
And waving wide her myrtle wand,
She strikes a universal peace through sea and land.

IV.

No war or battle's sound
Was heard the world around:
   The idle spear and shield were high up hung,
The hookèd chariot stood
Unstain'd with hostile blood,
   The trumpet spake not to the armèd throng,
And kings sat still with awful eye,
As if they surely knew their sov'reign Lord was by.

V.

But peaceful was the night,
Wherein the Prince of Light
   His reign of peace upon the earth began:
The winds with wonder whist
Smoothly the waters kist,
   Whisp'ring new joys to the mild ocean,
Who now hath quite forgot to rave,
While birds of calm sit brooding on the charmèd wave.

VI.

The stars with deep amaze
Stand fix'd in steadfast gaze,
   Bending one way their precious influence,
And will not take their flight,
For all the morning light,
   Or Lucifer that often warn'd them thence;
But in their glimmering orbs did glow,
Until their Lord Himself bespake, and bid them go.

VII.

And though the shady gloom
Had given day her room,
   The sun himself withheld his wonted speed,
And hid his head for shame,
As his inferior flame
   The new enlighten'd world no more should need;
He saw a greater Sun appear
Than his bright throne, or burning axle-tree could bear.

VIII.

The shepherds on the lawn,
Or e'er the point of dawn,
   Sat simply chatting in a rustic row;
Full little thought they then
That the mighty Pan
   Was kindly come to live with them below;
Perhaps their loves, or else their sheep,
Was all that did their silly thoughts so busy keep.

IX.

When such music sweet
Their hearts and ears did greet,
  As never was by mortal finger strook,
Divinely-warbled voice
Answering the stringèd noise,
  As all their souls in blissful rapture took;
The air such pleasure loath to lose,
With thousand echoes still prolongs each heavenly close.

X.

Nature that heard such sound,
Beneath the hollow round
  Of Cynthia's seat, the airy region thrilling,
Now was almost won
To think her part was done,
  And that her reign had here its last fulfilling;
She knew such harmony alone
Could hold all heav'n and earth in happier union.

XI.

At last surrounds their sight
A globe of circular light,
  That with long beams the shamefaced night array'd;
The helmèd Cherubim,
And sworded Seraphim,
  Are seen in glittering ranks with wings display'd,
Harping in loud and solemn quire,
With unexpressive notes to Heaven's new-born Heir.

XII.

Such music (as 'tis said)
Before was never made,
  But when of old the sons of morning sung,
While the Creator great
His constellations set,
  And the well-balanced world on hinges hung;
And cast the dark foundations deep,
And bid the welt'ring waves their oozy channel keep.

XIII.

Ring out, ye crystal spheres,
Once bless our human ears,
  If ye have pow'r to touch our senses so;
And let your silver chime
Move in melodious time,
  And let the base of heav'n's deep organ blow;
And with your ninefold harmony
Make up full consort to th' angelic symphony.

XIV.

For if such holy song
Inwrap our fancy long,
  Time will run back, and fetch the age of gold;
And speckled Vanity
Will sicken soon and die,
  And leprous Sin will melt from earthly mould;
And Hell itself will pass away,
And leave her dolorous mansions to the peering day.

XV.

Yea Truth and Justice then
Will down return to men,
  Orb'd in a rainbow; and, like glories wearing,
Mercy will sit between,
Throned in celestial sheen,
  With radiant feet the tissued clouds down steering:
And heav'n, as at some festival,
Will open wide the gates of her high palace hall.

XVI.

But wisest Fate says, no,
This must not yet be so,
  The Babe lies yet in smiling infancy,
That on the bitter cross
Must redeem our loss;
  So both Himself and us to glorify;
Yet first to those ychain'd in sleep,
The wakeful trump of doom must thunder through the deep,

XVII.

With such a horrid clang
As on Mount Sinai rang,
   While the red fire, and smouldering clouds out brake:
The agèd earth aghast,
With terror of that blast,
   Shall from the surface to the centre shake;
When at the world's last session,
The dreadful Judge in middle air shall spread His throne.

XVIII.

And then at last our bliss
Full and perfect is,
   But now begins; for from this happy day
The old Dragon under ground
In straiter limits bound,
   Not half so far casts his usurped sway,
And wroth to see his kingdom fail,
Swinges the scaly horror of his folded tail.

XIX.

The oracles are dumb,
No voice or hideous hum
   Runs thro' the archèd roof in words deceiving.
Apollo from his shrine
Can no more divine,
   With hollow shriek the steep of Delphos leaving.
No nightly trance, or breathèd spell
Inspires the pale-eyed priest from the prophetic cell.

XX.

The lonely mountains o'er,
And the resounding shore,
   A voice of weeping heard and loud lament;
From haunted spring, and dale
Edged with poplar pale,
   The parting genius is with sighing sent;
With flow'r-inwoven tresses torn
The Nymphs in twilight shade of tangled thickets mourn.

XXI.

In consecrated earth,
And on the holy hearth,
   The Lars, and Lemures moan with midnight plaint;
In urns, and altars round,
A drear and dying sound
   Affrights the Flamens at their service quaint:
And the chill marble seems to sweat,
While each peculiar Pow'r foregoes his wonted seat.

XXII.

Peor and Baälim
Forsake their temples dim,
   With that twice-batter'd god of Palestine;
And moonèd Ashtaroth,
Heav'n's queen and mother both,
   Now sits not girt with tapers' holy shine;
The Lybic Hammon shrinks his horn,
In vain the Tyrian maids their wounded Thammuz mourn.

XXIII.

And sullen Moloch fled,
Hath left in shadows dread
   His burning idol all of blackest hue;
In vain with cymbals' ring
They call the grisly king,
   In dismal dance about the furnace blue:
The brutish gods of Nile as fast,
Isis and Orus, and the dog Anubis haste.

XXIV.

Nor is Osiris seen
In Memphian grove or green,
   Trampling the unshow'r'd grass with lowings loud:
Nor can he be at rest
Within his sacred chest;
   Naught but profoundest hell can be his shroud:
In vain with timbrell'd anthems dark
The sable-stolèd sorcerers bear his worshipp'd ark.

XXV.

He feels from Juda's land
The dreaded Infant's hand,
   The rays of Bethlehem blind his dusky eyn:
Nor all the gods beside,
Longer dare abide,
   Not Typhon huge ending in snaky twine:
Our Babe, to show His Godhead true,
Can in His swaddling bands control the damnèd crew.

XXVI.

So when the sun in bed,
Curtain'd with cloudy red,
   Pillows his chin upon an orient wave,
The flocking shadows pale
Troop to th' infernal jail,
   Each fetter'd ghost slips to his several grave;
And the yellow-skirted Fayes
Fly after the night-steeds, leaving their moon-loved maze.

XXVII.

But see the Virgin blest
Hath laid her Babe to rest,
   Time is our tedious song should here have ending;
Heav'n's youngest teemèd star
Hath fix'd her polish'd car,
   Her sleeping Lord with handmaid lamp attending;
And all about the courtly stable
Bright-harness'd Angels sit in order serviceable.

JOHN MILTON.

MESSIAH.

A SACRED ECLOGUE.

YE nymphs of Solyma! begin the song:
To heavenly themes sublimer strains belong.
The mossy fountains and the sylvan shades,
The dreams of Pindus and th' Aonian maids,
Delight no more—O Thou my voice inspire
Who touch'd Isaiah's hallow'd lips with fire!
Rapt into future times the bard begun:
A Virgin shall conceive—a Virgin bear a Son!
From Jesse's root behold a Branch arise
Whose sacred flower with fragrance fills the skies:
Th' Ethereal Spirit o'er its leaves shall move,
And on its top descends the mystic Dove.
Ye heavens! from high the dewy nectar pour,
And in soft silence shed the kindly shower!
The sick and weak the healing plant shall aid—
From storms a shelter, and from heat a shade.
All crimes shall cease, and ancient fraud shall fail;
Returning Justice lift aloft her scale,
Peace o'er the world her olive wand extend,
And white-robed Innocence from heaven descend.
Swift fly the years, and rise th' expected morn!
Oh spring to light, auspicious Babe, be born!
See, Nature hastes her earliest wreaths to bring,
With all the incense of the breathing spring:
See lofty Lebanon his head advance;
See nodding forests on the mountains dance;
See spicy clouds from lowly Sharon rise,
And Carmel's flowery top perfumes the skies!
Hark! a glad voice the lonely desert cheers:
Prepare the way! a God, a God appears!
A God, a God! the vocal hills reply—
The rocks proclaim the approaching Deity.
Lo, earth receives Him from the bending skies!
Sink down, ye mountains; and ye valleys, rise!
With heads declined, ye cedars, homage pay!
Be smooth, ye rocks; ye rapid floods, give way!

The Saviour comes! by ancient bards fore-
    told—
Hear Him, ye deaf; and all ye blind, be-
    hold!
He from thick films shall purge the visual
    ray,
And on the sightless eyeball pour the
    day:
'Tis He th' obstructed paths of sound shall
    clear,
And bid new music charm th' unfolding
    ear;
The dumb shall sing; the lame his crutch
    forego,
And leap exulting like the bounding roe.
No sigh, no murmur, the wide world shall
    hear—
From every face He wipes off every tear.
In adamantine claims shall Death be
    bound,
And Hell's grim tyrant feel the eternal
    wound.
As the good shepherd tends his fleecy
    care,
Seeks freshest pasture, and the purest air,
Explores the lost, the wandering sheep di-
    rects,
By day o'ersees them, and by night pro-
    tects;
The tender lambs he raises in his arms—
Feeds from his hand, and in his bosom
    warms:
Thus shall mankind His guardian care en-
    gage—
The promised Father of the future age.
No more shall nation against nation rise,
Nor ardent warriors meet with hateful
    eyes;
Nor fields with gleaming steel be cover'd
    o'er,
The brazen trumpets kindle rage no
    more;
But useless lances into scythes shall bend,
And the broad falchion in a ploughshare
    end.
Then palaces shall rise; the joyful son
Shall finish what his short-lived sire be-
    gun;
Their vines a shadow to their race shall
    yield,
And the same hand that sow'd shall reap
    the field.

The swain in barren deserts with surprise
Sees lilies spring and sudden verdure rise;
And starts, amidst the thirsty wilds, to
    hear
New falls of water murmuring in his ear.
On rifted rocks, the dragon's late abodes,
The green reed trembles, and the bulrush
    nods;
Waste sandy valleys, once perplex'd with
    thorn,
The spiry fir and shapely box adorn;
To leafless shrubs the flow'ring palms suc-
    ceed,
And od'rous myrtle to the noisome weed;
The lambs with wolves shall graze the ver-
    dant mead,
And boys in flowery bands the tiger lead;
The steer and lion at one crib shall meet,
And harmless serpents lick the pilgrim's
    feet.
The smiling infant in his hand shall take
The crested basilisk and speckled snake—
Pleased, the green lustre of the scales
    survey,
And with their forky tongue shall inno-
    cently play.
Rise, crown'd with light, imperial Salem,
    rise!
Exalt thy tow'ry head, and lift thy eyes!
See a long race thy spacious courts adorn;
See future sons and daughters, yet un-
    born,
In crowding ranks on every side arise,
Demanding life, impatient for the skies!
See barb'rous nations at thy gates attend,
Walk in thy light, and in thy temple
    bend;
See thy bright altars throng'd with pros-
    trate kings,
And heap'd with products of Sabæan
    springs!
For thee Idume's spicy forests blow,
And seeds of gold in Ophir's mountains
    glow.
See Heaven its sparkling portals wide dis-
    play,
And break upon thee in a flood of day!
No more the rising Sun shall gild the
    morn,
Nor ev'ning Cynthia fill her silver horn;
But lost, dissolved in thy superior rays,
One tide of glory, one unclouded blaze,

O'erflow thy courts; the Light Himself
    shall shine
Reveal'd, and God's eternal day be thine!
The seas shall waste, the skies in smoke
    decay,
Rocks fall to dust, and mountains melt
    away;
But fix'd His word, His saving power re-
    mains;
Thy realm for ever lasts, thy own Messiah
    reigns!
ALEXANDER POPE.

A CHRISTMAS HYMN.

IT was the calm and silent night!
    Seven hundred years and fifty-three
Had Rome been growing up to might,
    And now was queen of land and sea.
No sound was heard of clashing wars—
    Peace brooded o'er the hush'd domain:
Apollo, Pallas, Jove, and Mars
    Held undisturb'd their ancient reign,
        In the solemn midnight,
        Centuries ago.

'Twas in the calm and silent night!
    The senator of haughty Rome,
Impatient, urged his chariot's flight,
    From lordly revel rolling home;
Triumphal arches, gleaming, swell
    His breast with thoughts of boundless
        sway;
What reck'd the Roman what befell
    A paltry province far away,
        In the solemn midnight,
        Centuries ago?

Within that province far away
    Went plodding home a weary boor;
A streak of light before him lay,
    Fallen through a half-shut stable-door
Across his path. He pass'd—for naught
    Told what was going on within;
How keen the stars, his only thought—
    The air how calm, and cold, and thin,
        In the solemn midnight,
        Centuries ago!

O strange indifference! low and high
    Drowsed over common joys and cares;
The earth was still—but knew not why
    The world was listening, unawares.

How calm a moment may precede
    One that shall thrill the world for ever!
To that still moment, none would heed,
    Man's doom was link'd no more to
        sever—
        In the solemn midnight,
        Centuries ago!

It is the calm and solemn night!
    A thousand bells ring out, and throw
Their joyous peals abroad, and smite
    The darkness—charm'd and holy now!
The night that erst no name had worn,
    To it a happy name is given;
For in that stable lay, new-born,
    The peaceful Prince of earth and heaven,
        In the solemn midnight,
        Centuries ago!
ALFRED DOMETT.

CHRISTMAS.

WHILE shepherds watch'd their flocks by
    night,
    All seated on the ground,
The angel of the Lord came down,
    And glory shone around.

"Fear not," said he (for mighty dread
    Had seized their troubled mind);
"Glad tidings of great joy I bring
    To you and all mankind.

"To you, in David's town, this day
    Is born of David's line
The Saviour who is Christ the Lord;
    And this shall be the sign:

"The heavenly Babe you there shall find
    To human view display'd,
All meanly wrapt in swathing bands,
    And in a manger laid."

Thus spake the Seraph; and forthwith
    Appear'd a shining throng
Of angels, praising God, and thus
    Address'd their joyful song:

"All glory be to God on high,
    And to the earth be peace;
Good-will henceforth from heaven to men
    Begin, and never cease!"
NAHUM TATE.

CHRISTMAS CAROL.

Carol, carol, Christians,
  Carol joyfully;
Carol for the coming
  Of Christ's Nativity;
And pray a gladsome Christmas
  For all good Christian men.
Carol, carol, Christians,
  For Christmas come again.
    Carol, carol.

Go ye to the forest,
  Where the myrtles grow;
Where the pine and laurel
  Bend beneath the snow.
Gather them for Jesus;
  Wreath them for His shrine;
Make His temple glorious
  With the box and pine.
    Carol, carol.

Wreath your Christmas garland
  Where to Christ we pray;
It shall smell like Carmel
  On our festal day;
Libanus and Sharon
  Shall not greener be
Than our holy chancel
  On Christ's Nativity.
    Carol, carol.

Carol, carol, Christians!
  Like the Magi, now
Ye must lade your caskets
  With a grateful vow:
Ye must have sweet incense,
  Myrrh, and finest gold,
At our Christmas altar
  Humbly to unfold.
    Carol, carol.

Blow, blow up the trumpet
  For our solemn feast;
Gird thine armor, Christian,
  Wear thy surplice, priest!
Go ye to the altar,
  Pray—with fervor pray—
For Jesus' second coming,
  And the Latter Day.
    Carol, carol.

Give us grace, O Saviour,
  To put off in might
Deeds and dreams of darkness,
  For the robes of light!
And to live as lowly
  As Thyself with men;
So to rise in glory
  When Thou com'st again.
    Carol, carol.
        ARTHUR CLEVELAND COXE.

COME, YE LOFTY.

Come, ye lofty, come, ye lowly,
  Let your songs of gladness ring;
In a stable lies the Holy,
  In a manger rests the King.
See, in Mary's arms reposing,
  Christ by highest heaven adored;
Come, your circle round Him closing,
  Pious hearts that love the Lord.

Come, ye poor; no pomp of station
  Robes the Child your hearts adore,
He, the Lord of all salvation,
  Shares your want, is weak and poor;
Oxen, round about behold them;
  Rafters naked, cold and bare;
See the shepherds; God has told them
  That the Prince of Life lies there.

Come, ye children, blithe and merry,
  This one Child your model make;
Christmas-holly, leaf and berry,
  All be prized for His dear sake:
Come, ye gentle hearts and tender,
  Come, ye spirits keen and bold;
All in all your homage render,
  Weak and mighty, young and old.

High above a star is shining,
  And the wise men haste from far;
Come, glad hearts, and spirits pining—
  For you all has risen the star.
Let us bring our poor oblations,
  Thanks and love, and faith and praise;
Come, ye people, come, ye nations;
  All in all draw nigh to gaze.

Hark, the Heaven of Heavens is ringing
  Christ the Lord to man is born!
Are not all our hearts, too, singing,
  Welcome, welcome, Christmas morn?
Still the Child all power possessing
  Smiles as through the ages past,
And the song of Christmas blessing
  Sweetly sinks to rest at last.
        ARCHER GURNEY.

CHRISTMAS CAROL.

CHRISTIANS, awake, salute the happy morn
Whereon the Saviour of the world was born;
Rise to adore the mystery of love
Which hosts of angels chanted from above!
With them the joyful tidings first begun
Of God incarnate and the Virgin's Son.
Then to the watchful shepherds it was told,
Who heard the angelic herald's voice:
"Behold,
I bring good tidings of a Saviour's birth
To you and all the nations upon earth:
This day hath God fulfill'd his promised word,
This day is born a Saviour, Christ the Lord.
In David's city, shepherds, ye shall find
The long-foretold Redeemer of mankind.
Wrapt up in swaddling-clothes, the babe divine
Lies in a manger: this shall be your sign."
He spake; and straightway the celestial choir
In hymns of joy, unknown before, conspire:
The praises of redeeming love they sung,
And heaven's whole orb with alleluias rung:
God's highest glory was their anthem still,
Peace upon earth, and mutual good-will.
To Bethlehem straight the enlightened shepherds ran,
To see the wonder God had wrought for man:
And found, with Joseph and the blessed maid,
Her Son, the Saviour, in a manger laid;
Amazed the wondrous story they proclaim,
The first apostles of his infant fame.
While Mary keeps and ponders in her heart
The heavenly vision which the swains impart,
They to their flocks, still praising God, return,
And their glad hearts within their bosoms burn.
Let us, like these good shepherds, then employ
Our grateful voices to proclaim the joy;
Like Mary, let us ponder in our mind
God's wondrous love in saving lost mankind;
Artless and watchful, as these favored swains,
While virgin meekness in the heart remains.
Trace we the Babe, who has retrieved our loss,
From His poor manger to His bitter cross;
Treading His steps, assisted by His grace,
Till man's first heavenly state again takes place.
Then may we hope, the angelic thrones among,
To sing, redeem'd, a glad triumphal song;
He that was born upon this joyful day
Around us all His glory shall display;
Saved by His love, incessant we shall sing
Of angels and of angel-men the King.
JOHN BYROM.

CHRISTMAS CAROL.

GOD rest you, merry gentlemen,
  Let nothing you dismay,
For Jesus Christ our Saviour
  Was born upon this day,
To save us all from Satan's power,
  When we were gone astray.
    Oh tidings of comfort and joy,
    For Jesus Christ, our Saviour, was
    born on Christmas Day!

In Bethlehem, in Jewry,
  This blessed babe was born,
And laid within a manger,
  Upon this blessed morn;
The which his mother Mary
  Nothing did take in scorn.
    Oh tidings of comfort and joy,
    For Jesus Christ, our Saviour, was
    born on Christmas Day!

From God, our Heavenly Father,
  A blessed angel came,
And unto certain shepherds
  Brought tidings of the same,
How that in Bethlehem was born
  The Son of God by name.
    Oh tidings of comfort and joy,
    For Jesus Christ, our Saviour, was
    born on Christmas Day!

Fear not, then said the angel,
  Let nothing you affright,
This day is born a Saviour,
  Of virtue, power, and might,
So frequently to vanquish all
  The friends of Satan quite.
    Oh tidings of comfort and joy,
    For Jesus Christ, our Saviour, was
    born on Christmas Day!

The shepherds at those tidings
  Rejoicèd much in mind,

And left their flocks a-feeding
  In tempest, storm, and wind,
And went to Bethlehem straightway
  This blessed babe to find.
    Oh tidings of comfort and joy,
      For Jesus Christ, our Saviour, was
        born on Christmas Day!

But when to Bethlehem they came,
  Whereat this infant lay,
They found him in a manger
  Where oxen feed on hay;
His mother Mary, kneeling,
  Unto the Lord did pray.
    Oh tidings of comfort and joy,
      For Jesus Christ, our Saviour, was
        born on Christmas Day!

Now to the Lord sing praises,
  All you within this place,
And with true love and brotherhood
  Each other now embrace;
This holy tide of Christmas
  All others doth deface.
    Oh tidings of comfort and joy,
      For Jesus Christ, our Saviour, was
        born on Christmas Day!
            AUTHOR UNKNOWN.

IT CAME UPON THE MIDNIGHT CLEAR.

IT came upon the midnight clear,
  That glorious song of old,
From angels bending near the earth
  To touch their harps of gold:
"Peace on the earth, good-will to men
  From Heaven's all-gracious King:"
The world in solemn stillness lay
  To hear the angels sing.

Still through the cloven skies they come
  With peaceful wings unfurl'd;
And still their heavenly music floats
  O'er all the weary world:
Above its sad and lowly plains
  They bend on hovering wing,
And ever o'er its Babel sounds
  The blessed angels sing.

But with the woes of sin and strife
  The world has suffer'd long;
Beneath the angel-strain have roll'd
  Two thousand years of wrong;
And man, at war with man, hears not
  The love-song which they bring:
Oh! hush the noise, ye men of strife,
  And hear the angels sing!

And ye, beneath life's crushing load
  Whose forms are bending low,
Who toil along the climbing way
  With painful steps and slow,
Look now! for glad and golden hours
  Come swiftly on the wing:
Oh! rest beside the weary road,
  And hear the angels sing!

For lo! the days are hastening on,
  By prophet-bards foretold,
When with the ever-circling years
  Comes round the age of gold;
When peace shall over all the earth
  Its ancient splendors fling,
And the whole world send back the song
  Which now the angels sing!
            EDMUND H. SEARS.

HARK! HOW ALL THE WELKIN RINGS!

HARK! how all the welkin rings!
  Glory to the King of kings!
Peace on earth, and mercy mild,
  God and sinners reconciled!
Joyful, all ye nations, rise,
  Join the triumph of the skies;
Universal Nature say,
  Christ the Lord is born to-day!

Christ, by highest Heaven adored;
  Christ, the Everlasting Lord;
Late in time behold Him come,
  Offspring of a Virgin's womb:
Veil'd in flesh the Godhead see;
  Hail the Incarnate Deity,
Pleased as man with men to appear,
  Jesus, our Immanuel here!

Hail! the heavenly Prince of Peace!
  Hail! the Sun of Righteousness!
Light and life to all He brings,
  Risen with healing in His wings.
Mild He lays His glory by,
  Born that man no more may die,
Born to raise the sons of earth,
  Born to give them second birth.

Come, Desire of nations, come,
Fix in us Thy humble home!
Rise, the woman's conquering Seed,
Bruise in us the Serpent's head!
Now display Thy saving power,
Ruin'd nature now restore,
Now in mystic union join
Thine to ours, and ours to Thine!

Adam's likeness, Lord, efface;
Stamp Thy image in its place;
Second Adam from above,
Reinstate us in Thy love!
Let us Thee, though lost, regain,
Thee, the Life, the Inner Man:
Oh, to all Thyself impart,
Form'd in each believing heart!
CHARLES WESLEY.

SHOUT THE GLAD TIDINGS.

SHOUT the glad tidings, exultingly sing;
Jerusalem triumphs, Messiah is King!

Sion, the marvellous story be telling,
  The Son of the Highest, how lowly His birth!
The brightest archangel in glory excelling,
  He stoops to redeem thee, He reigns upon earth:
    Shout the glad tidings, exultingly sing;
    Jerusalem triumphs, Messiah is King!

Tell how He cometh; from nation to nation,
  The heart-cheering news let the earth echo round:
How free to the faithful He offers salvation,
  How His people with joy everlasting are crown'd:
    Shout the glad tidings, exultingly sing;
    Jerusalem triumphs, Messiah is King!

Mortals, your homage be gratefully bringing,
  And sweet let the gladsome Hosanna arise;
Ye angels, the full Hallelujah be singing;
  One chorus resound through the earth and the skies:
    Shout the glad tidings, exultingly sing;
    Jerusalem triumphs, Messiah is King!
WILLIAM AUGUSTUS MUHLENBERG.

A CHRISTMAS CAROL.

GOD rest ye, merry gentlemen; let nothing you dismay,
For Jesus Christ, our Saviour, was born on Christmas-day.
The dawn rose red o'er Bethlehem, the stars shone through the gray,
When Jesus Christ, our Saviour, was born on Christmas-day.

God rest ye, little children; let nothing you affright,
For Jesus Christ, your Saviour, was born this happy night;
Along the hills of Galilee the white flocks sleeping lay,
When Christ, the Child of Nazareth, was born on Christmas-day.

God rest ye, all good Christians; upon this blessed morn
The Lord of all good Christians was of a woman born:
Now all your sorrows He doth heal, your sins He takes away;
For Jesus Christ, our Saviour, was born on Christmas-day.
DINAH MARIA MULOCH CRAIK.

HARK, THE GLAD SOUND.

HARK, the glad sound! the Saviour comes,
  The Saviour promised long;
Let every heart prepare a throne,
  And every voice a song!

On him the Spirit, largely pour'd,
  Exerts his sacred fire;
Wisdom and might, and zeal and love,
  His holy breast inspire.

He comes, the prisoners to release
  In Satan's bondage held;
The gates of brass before Him burst,
  The iron fetters yield.

He comes, from thickest films of vice
  To clear the mental ray,
And on the eyeballs of the blind
  To pour celestial day.

He comes, the broken heart to bind,
  The bleeding soul to cure,
And with the treasures of His grace
  To enrich the humble poor.

His silver trumpets publish loud
  The jubilee of the Lord;
Our debts are all remitted now,
  Our heritage restored.

Our glad Hosannas, Prince of Peace,
  Thy welcome shall proclaim,
And heaven's eternal arches ring
  With thy belovèd name.
PHILIP DODDRIDGE.

EPIPHANY.

BRIGHTEST and best of the sons of the morning,
  Dawn on our darkness, and lend us Thine aid!
Star of the East, the horizon adorning,
  Guide where our infant Redeemer is laid!

Cold on His cradle the dewdrops are shining;
  Low lies His head with the beasts of the stall;
Angels adore Him in slumber reclining—
  Maker, and Monarch, and Saviour of all.

Say, shall we yield Him, in costly devotion,
  Odors of Edom, and offerings divine—
Gems of the mountain, and pearls of the ocean?
  Myrrh from the forest, or gold from the mine?

Vainly we offer each ample oblation,
  Vainly with gifts would His favor secure;
Richer by far is the heart's adoration,
  Dearer to God are the prayers of the poor.

Brightest and best of the sons of the morning,
  Dawn on our darkness, and lend us Thine aid!
Star of the East, the horizon adorning,
  Guide where our infant Redeemer is laid!
REGINALD HEBER.

GETHSEMANE.

Go to dark Gethsemane,
  Ye that feel the tempter's power;
Your Redeemer's conflict see,
  Watch with Him one bitter hour;
Turn not from His griefs away,
Learn of Jesus Christ to pray!

Follow to the judgment-hall—
  View the Lord of life arraign'd;
Oh, the wormwood and the gall,
  Oh, the pangs his soul sustain'd!
Shun not suffering, shame, or loss—.
Learn of Him to bear the cross!

Calvary's mournful mountain climb;
  There, adoring at His feet,
Mark that miracle of time—
  God's own sacrifice complete!
"It is finish'd!"—hear the cry;
Learn of Jesus Christ to die.

Early hasten to the tomb
  Where they laid his breathless clay;
All is solitude and gloom;
  Who hath taken Him away?
Christ is risen! He meets our eyes!
Saviour, teach us so to rise!
JAMES MONTGOMERY.

CHRIST CRUCIFIED.

"And was crucified for us under Pontius Pilate;
He suffered, and was buried."

RIDE on, ride on in majesty!
Hark! all the tribes Hosanna cry!
Thine humble beast pursues his road,
With palms and scatter'd garments strow'd.

Ride on! ride on in majesty!
In lowly pomp ride on to die!
O Christ! Thy triumphs now begin
O'er captive Death and conquer'd Sin.

Ride on! ride on in majesty!
The wingèd squadrons of the sky
Look down with sad and wondering eyes
To see the approaching Sacrifice.

Ride on! ride on in majesty!
Thy last and fiercest strife is nigh;
The Father on His sapphire throne
Expects His own anointed Son.

Ride on! ride on in majesty!
In lowly pomp ride on to die!
Bow Thy meek head to mortal pain;
Then take, O God, Thy power, and reign!
HENRY HART MILMAN.

BOUND UPON TH' ACCURSÈD TREE.

BOUND upon th' accursèd tree,
Faint and bleeding, who is He?
By the eyes so pale and dim,
Streaming blood, and writhing limb,
By the flesh, with scourges torn,
By the crown of twisted thorn,
By the side, so deeply pierced,
By the baffled burning thirst,
By the drooping death-dew'd brow,
Son of Man! 'tis Thou, 'tis Thou!

Bound upon th' accursèd tree,
Dread and awful, who is He?
By the sun at noonday pale,
Shivering rocks, and rending veil,
By earth, that trembles at His doom,
By yonder saints, who burst their tomb,
By Eden, promised ere He died
To the felon at His side,
Lord, our suppliant knees we bow;
Son of God! 'tis Thou! 'tis Thou!

Bound upon th' accursèd tree,
Sad and dying, who is He?
By the last and bitter cry,
The ghost given up in agony,
By the lifeless body laid
In the chamber of the dead,
By the mourners, come to weep
Where the bones of Jesus sleep;
Crucified! we know Thee now;
Son of Man! 'tis Thou! 'tis Thou!

Bound upon th' accursèd tree,
Dread and awful, who is He?
By the prayer for them that slew,
"Lord, they know not what they do!"
By the spoil'd and empty grave,
By the souls He died to save,
By the conquest He hath won,
By the saints before His throne,
By the rainbow round His brow,
Son of God! 'tis Thou! 'tis Thou!
HENRY HART MILMAN.

WE SING THE PRAISE OF HIM WHO DIED.

WE sing the praise of Him who died,
Of Him who died upon the cross;
The sinner's hope let men deride,
For this we count the world but loss.

Inscribed upon the cross we see,
In shining letters, God is Love;
He bears our sins upon the tree,
He brings us mercy from above.

The Cross! it takes our guilt away;
It holds the fainting spirit up;
It cheers with hope the gloomy day,
And sweetens every bitter cup;

It makes the coward spirit brave,
And nerves the feeble arm for fight;
It takes its terror from the grave,
And gilds the bed of death with light;

The balm of life, the cure of woe,
The measure and the pledge of love,
The sinner's refuge here below,
The angels' theme in heaven above.
THOMAS KELLY.

JESUS WEPT.

DID Christ o'er sinners weep?
And shall our cheeks be dry?
Let floods of penitential grief
Burst forth from every eye.

The Son of God in tears,
The wondering angels see!
Be thou astonish'd, O my soul!
He shed those tears for thee.

He wept, that we might weep;
Each sin demands a tear;
In heaven alone no sin is found;
There is no weeping there.
BENJAMIN BEDDOME.

THE LORD IS RISEN.

"CHRIST the Lord is risen to-day,"
Sons of men and angels say:
Raise your joys and triumphs high,
Sing, ye heavens, and earth reply.

Love's redeeming work is done,
Fought the fight, the battle won:
Lo! our Sun's eclipse is o'er;
Lo! He sets in blood no more.

Vain the stone, the watch, the seal;
Christ has burst the gates of hell!
Death in vain forbids His rise;
Christ has open'd Paradise!

Lives again our glorious King:
Where, O Death, is now thy sting?
Dying once, He all doth save;
Where thy victory, O Grave?

Soar we now where Christ has led,
Following our exalted Head;
Made like Him, like Him we rise;
Ours the cross, the grave, the skies.

What though once we perish'd all,
Partners in our parents' fall?
Second life we all receive,
In our Heavenly Adam live.

Risen with Him, we upward move;
Still we seek the things above;
Still pursue, and kiss the Son
Seated on His Father's Throne.

Scarce on earth a thought bestow,
Dead to all we leave below;
Heaven our aim, and loved abode,
Hid our life with Christ in God:

Hid, till Christ our Life appear
Glorious in His members here;
Join'd to Him, we then shall shine,
All immortal, all divine.

Hail the Lord of Earth and Heaven!
Praise to Thee by both be given!
Thee we greet triumphant now!
Hail, the Resurrection Thou!

King of glory, Soul of bliss!
Everlasting life is this,
Thee to know, Thy power to prove,
Thus to sing, and thus to love!
Charles Wesley.

CHRIST RISEN.

"And the third day He rose again, according to the Scriptures."

Again the Lord of Life and Light
 Awakes the kindling ray,
Unseals the eyelids of the morn,
 And pours increasing day.

Oh what a night was that which wrapt
 The heathen world in gloom!
Oh what a sun, which broke this day
 Triumphant from the tomb!

This day be grateful homage paid,
 And loud hosannas sung;
Let gladness dwell in every heart,
 And praise on every tongue.

Ten thousand differing lips shall join
 To hail this welcome morn,
Which scatters blessings from its wings
 To nations yet unborn.

Jesus, the friend of human kind,
 With strong compassion moved,
Descended like a pitying God
 To save the souls he loved.

The powers of darkness leagued in vain
 To bind His soul in death;
He shook their kingdom, when He fell,
 With His expiring breath.

Not long the toils of hell could keep
 The hope of Judah's line;
Corruption never could take hold
 Of aught so much divine.

And now His conquering chariot-wheels
 Ascend the lofty skies;
While broke beneath His powerful cross
 Death's iron sceptre lies.

Exalted high at God's right hand,
 The Lord of all below,
Through Him is pardoning love dispensed,
 And boundless blessings flow.

And still for erring, guilty man
 A Brother's pity flows;
And still His bleeding heart is touch'd
 With memory of our woes.

To Thee, my Saviour and my King,
 Glad homage let me give;
And stand prepared like Thee to die,
 With Thee that I may live!
Anna Lætitia Barbauld.

CORONATION.

"All hail the power of Jesus' name!
 Let angels prostrate fall;
Bring forth the royal diadem,
 To crown Him Lord of all!

"Let high-born seraphs tune the lyre,
  And, as they tune it, fall
Before His face who tunes their choir,
  And crown Him Lord of all!

"Crown Him, ye morning stars of light
  Who fix'd this floating ball;
Now hail the Strength of Israel's might,
  And crown Him Lord of all!

"Crown Him, ye martyrs of your God,
  Who from His altar call;
Extol the stem of Jesse's rod,
  And crown Him Lord of all!

"Ye seed of Israel's chosen race,
  Ye ransom'd of the fall,
Hail Him who saves you by His grace,
  And crown Him Lord of all!

"Hail Him, ye heirs of David's line,
  Whom David Lord did call,
The God incarnate, man divine;
  And crown Him Lord of all!

"Sinners, whose love can ne'er forget
  The wormwood and the gall,
Go spread your trophies at His feet,
  And crown Him Lord of all!

"Let every tribe and every tongue
  That bound creation's call,
Now shout, in universal song,
  THE CROWNÈD LORD OF ALL!"
                    EDWARD PERRONET.

PSALM LXXII.

HAIL to the Lord's Anointed,
  Great David's greater Son!
Hail, in the time appointed,
  His reign on earth begun!
He comes to break oppression,
  To let the captive free,
To take away transgression,
  And rule in equity.

He comes with succor speedy
  To those who suffer wrong;
To help the poor and needy,
  And bid the weak be strong:
To give them songs for sighing,
  Their darkness turn to light,
Whose souls, condemn'd and dying,
  Were precious in His sight.

He shall come down like showers
  Upon the fruitful earth,
And love, joy, hope, like flowers,
  Spring in His path to birth;
Before Him, on the mountains,
  Shall Peace, the herald, go,
And righteousness, in fountains,
  From hill to valley flow.

Arabia's desert-ranger
  To Him shall bow the knee;
The Ethiopian stranger
  His glory come to see:
With offerings of devotion
  Ships from the isles shall meet,
To pour the wealth of ocean
  In tribute at His feet.

Kings shall fall down before Him,
  And golden incense bring;
All nations shall adore Him,
  His praise all people sing;
For He shall have dominion
  O'er river, sea, and shore;
Far as the eagle's pinion,
  Or dove's light wing, can soar.

For Him shall prayer unceasing,
  And daily vows ascend,
His kingdom still increasing,
  A kingdom without end:
The mountain-dews shall nourish
  A seed, in weakness sown,
Whose fruit shall spread and flourish,
  And shake like Lebanon.

O'er every foe victorious
  He on His throne shall rest
From age to age more glorious,
  All blessing and all-blest:
The tide of time shall never
  His covenant remove;
His Name shall stand for ever,
  That Name to us is Love.
                    JAMES MONTGOMERY.

PER PACEM AD LUCEM.

I DO not ask, O Lord, that life may be
  A pleasant road;
I do not ask that Thou wouldst take from me
  Aught of its load;

I do not ask that flowers should always spring
    Beneath my feet;
I know too well the poison and the sting
    Of things too sweet.
For one thing only, Lord, dear Lord, I plead,
    Lead me aright—
Though strength should falter, and though heart should bleed—
    Through Peace to Light.

I do not ask, O Lord, that Thou shouldst shed
    Full radiance here;
Give but a ray of peace, that I may tread
    Without a fear.

I do not ask my cross to understand,
    My way to see;
Better in darkness just to feel Thy hand
    And follow Thee.

Joy is like restless day; but peace divine
    Like quiet night:
Lead me, O Lord,—till perfect Day shall shine,
    Through Peace to Light.
        ADELAIDE ANNE PROCTER.

HAIL, THOU ONCE-DESPISÈD JESUS!

HAIL, Thou once-despisèd Jesus!
    Hail, thou Galilean King!
Thou didst suffer to release us,
    Thou didst free salvation bring:
Hail, thou agonizing Saviour,
    Bearer of our sin and shame;
By Thy merits we find favor;
    Life is given through Thy Name!

Paschal Lamb, by God appointed,
    All our sins were on Thee laid;
By Almighty Love anointed,
    Thou hast full atonement made:
All Thy people are forgiven
    Through the virtue of Thy Blood;
Open'd is the gate of heaven;
    Peace is made 'twixt man and God.

Jesus, hail! enthroned in glory,
    There for ever to abide;
All the heavenly hosts adore Thee,
    Seated at Thy Father's side.
There for sinners Thou art pleading;
    There Thou dost our place prepare;
Ever for us interceding
    Till in glory we appear.

Worship, honor, power, and blessing,
    Thou art worthy to receive;
Loudest praises, without ceasing,
    Meet it is for us to give!
Help, ye bright angelic spirits,
    Bring your sweetest, noblest lays;
Help to sing our Saviour's merits,
    Help to chant Immanuel's praise!

Soon we shall, with those in glory,
    His transcendent grace relate;
Gladly sing the amazing story
    Of His dying love so great:
In that blessed contemplation
    We for evermore shall dwell,
Crown'd with bliss and consolation,
    Such as none below can tell.
        JOHN BAKEWELL.

MY FAITH LOOKS UP TO THEE.

MY faith looks up to Thee,
Thou Lamb of Calvary,
    Saviour divine!
Now hear me while I pray:
Take all my guilt away;
Oh let me from this day
    Be wholly Thine!

May Thy rich grace impart
Strength to my fainting heart,
    My zeal inspire!
As Thou hast died for me,
Oh may my love to Thee
Pure, warm, and changeless be,
    A living fire!

While life's dark maze I tread,
And griefs around me spread,
    Be Thou my Guide!
Bid darkness turn to day,
Wipe sorrow's tears away,
Nor let me ever stray
    From Thee aside.

When ends life's transient dream,
When death's cold sullen stream
    Shall o'er me roll,
Blest Saviour! then in love
Fear and distrust remove;
Oh bear me safe above,
    A ransom'd soul!
        RAY PALMER.

LITANY.

Saviour, when in dust to Thee
Low we bend th' adoring knee;
When repentant to the skies
Scarce we lift our streaming eyes;
Oh! by all Thy pains and woe
Suffer'd once for man below,
Bending from Thy throne on high,
Hear our solemn Litany!

By Thy helpless infant years,
By Thy life of want and tears,
By Thy days of sore distress
In the savage wilderness;
By the dread mysterious hour
Of the insulting tempter's power;
Turn, oh! turn a favoring eye,
Hear our solemn Litany!

By the sacred griefs that wept
O'er the grave where Lazarus slept;
By the boding tears that flow'd
Over Salem's loved abode;
By the anguish'd sigh that told
Treachery lurk'd within Thy fold:
From Thy seat above the sky,
Hear our solemn Litany!

By Thine hour of dire despair;
By Thine agony of prayer;
By the cross, the nail, the thorn,
Piercing spear, and torturing scorn;
By the gloom that veil'd the skies
O'er the dreadful sacrifice;
Listen to our humble cry,
Hear our solemn Litany!

By Thy deep expiring groan;
By the sad sepulchral stone;
By the vault, whose dark abode
Held in vain the rising God;
Oh! from earth to heaven restored,
Mighty reascended Lord,
Listen, listen to the cry
Of our solemn Litany!
Sir Robert Grant.

O THOU, THE CONTRITE SINNERS' FRIEND.

O Thou, the contrite sinners' friend,
Who, loving, lov'st them to the end,
On this alone my hopes depend,
  That Thou wilt plead for me!

When, weary in the Christian race,
Far off appears my resting-place,
And fainting I mistrust Thy grace,
  Then, Saviour, plead for me!

When I have err'd and gone astray
Afar from Thine and Wisdom's way,
And see no glimmering guiding ray,
  Still, Saviour, plead for me!

When Satan, by my sins made bold,
Strives from Thy cross to loose my hold,
Then with Thy pitying arms enfold,
  And plead, oh plead for me!

And when my dying hour draws near,
Darken'd with anguish, guilt, and fear,
Then to my fainting sight appear,
  Pleading in Heaven for me!

When the full light of heavenly day
Reveals my sins in dread array,
Say Thou hast wash'd them all away;
  Oh say Thou plead'st for me!
Charlotte Elliott.

JESUS, I MY CROSS HAVE TAKEN.

Jesus, I my cross have taken,
  All to leave, and follow Thee;
Destitute, despised, forsaken,
  Thou, from hence, my all shalt be:
Perish every fond ambition,
  All I've sought, or hoped, or known;
Yet how rich is my condition!
  God and Heaven are still my own!

Let the world despise and leave me,
  They have left my Saviour too;
Human hearts and looks deceive me;
  Thou art not, like them, untrue:
And, while Thou shalt smile upon me,
  God of wisdom, love, and might,
Foes may hate, and friends may shun me;
  Show Thy face, and all is bright!

Go, then, earthly fame and treasure!
  Come, disaster, scorn, and pain!
In Thy service, pain is pleasure,
  With Thy favor, loss is gain!

I have call'd Thee, Abba, Father!
　I have stay'd my heart on Thee!
Storms may howl, and clouds may gather,
　All must work for good to me.

Man may trouble and distress me,
　'Twill but drive me to Thy breast;
Life with trials hard may press me,
　Heaven will bring me sweeter rest!
Oh, 'tis not in grief to harm me,
　While Thy love is left to me!
Oh, 'twere not in joy to charm me,
　Were that joy unmix'd with Thee!

Take, my soul, thy full salvation;
　Rise o'er sin, and fear, and care;
Joy to find, in every station,
　Something still to do or bear:
Think what Spirit dwells within thee!
　What a Father's smile is thine!
What a Saviour died to win thee!
　Child of Heaven, shouldst thou repine?

Haste, then, on from grace to glory,
　Arm'd by faith, and wing'd by prayer;
Heaven's eternal day's before thee,
　God's own hand shall guide thee there!
Soon shall close thy earthly mission,
　Swift shall pass thy pilgrim days;
Hope soon change to glad fruition,
　Faith to sight, and prayer to praise!
　　　　　HENRY FRANCIS LYTE.

SAVIOUR, WHO THY FLOCK ART FEEDING.

SAVIOUR, who Thy flock art feeding
　With the Shepherd's kindest care,
All the feeble gently leading,
　While the lambs Thy bosom share;

Now, these little ones receiving,
　Fold them in Thy gracious arm;
There, we know, Thy word believing,
　Only there, secure from harm!

Never, from Thy pasture roving,
　Let them be the lion's prey;
Let Thy tenderness so loving
　Keep them all life's dangerous way:

Then, within Thy fold eternal,
　Let them find a resting-place,
Feed in pastures ever vernal,
　Drink the rivers of Thy grace!
　　　　　WILLIAM AUGUSTUS MUHLENBERG.

ROCK OF AGES.

ROCK of Ages, cleft for me,
Let me hide myself in Thee!
Let the water and the blood,
From Thy riven side which flow'd,
Be of sin the double cure,
Cleanse me from its guilt and power.

Not the labors of my hands
Can fulfil Thy law's demands;
Could my zeal no respite know,
Could my tears for ever flow,
All for sin could not atone;
Thou must save, and Thou alone.

Nothing in my hand I bring;
Simply to Thy Cross I cling;
Naked, come to Thee for dress;
Helpless, look to Thee for grace;
Foul, I to the Fountain fly;
Wash me, Saviour, or I die!

While I draw this fleeting breath,
When my eyestrings break in death,
When I soar through tracts unknown,
See Thee on Thy judgment-throne;
Rock of Ages, cleft for me,
Let me hide myself in Thee!
　　　　　AUGUSTUS MONTAGUE TOPLADY.

JESU, LOVER OF MY SOUL.

JESU, lover of my soul,
　Let me to Thy bosom fly,
While the nearer waters roll,
　While the tempest still is high!
Hide me, O my Saviour, hide,
　Till the storm of life is past,
Safe into the haven guide;
　Oh receive my soul at last!

Other refuge have I none;
　Hangs my helpless soul on Thee;
Leave, ah! leave me not alone,
　Still support and comfort me!
All my trust on Thee is stay'd,
　All my help from Thee I bring:
Cover my defenceless head
　With the shadow of Thy wing!

Wilt Thou not regard my call?
　　Wilt Thou not accept my prayer?
Lo! I sink, I faint, I fall!
　　Lo! on Thee I cast my care!
Reach me out Thy gracious hand!
　　While I of Thy strength receive,
Hoping against hope I stand,
　　Dying, and behold I live!

Thou, O Christ, art all I want;
　　More than all in Thee I find:
Raise the fallen, cheer the faint,
　　Heal the sick, and lead the blind!
Just and holy is Thy Name;
　　I am all unrighteousness;
False and full of sin I am,
　　Thou art full of truth and grace.

Plenteous grace with Thee is found—
　　Grace to cover all my sin;
Let the healing streams abound;
　　Make and keep me pure within!
Thou of Life the Fountain art,
　　Freely let me take of Thee;
Spring Thou up within my heart!
　　Rise to all eternity!
　　　　　　　　　CHARLES WESLEY.

HOW SWEET THE NAME OF JESUS SOUNDS.

How sweet the Name of Jesus sounds
　　In a believer's ear!
It soothes his sorrows, heals his wounds,
　　And drives away his fear!

It makes the wounded spirit whole,
　　And calms the troubled breast;
'Tis manna to the hungry soul,
　　And to the weary rest.

Dear Name! the rock on which I build,
　　My shield and hiding-place,
My never-failing treasury, fill'd
　　With boundless stores of grace,

By Thee my prayers acceptance gain,
　　Although with sin defiled;
Satan accuses me in vain,
　　And I am own'd a child.

Jesus, my Shepherd, Husband, Friend,
　　My Prophet, Priest, and King,
My Lord, my Life, my Way, my End,
　　Accept the praise I bring.

Weak is the effort of my heart,
　　And cold my warmest thought;
But when I see Thee as Thou art,
　　I'll praise Thee as I ought.

Till then, I would Thy love proclaim
　　With every fleeting breath;
And may the music of Thy Name
　　Refresh my soul in death!
　　　　　　　　　JOHN NEWTON.

LOVEST THOU ME?

John xxi. 16.

HARK, my soul! it is the Lord,
　　'Tis thy Saviour, hear His word;
Jesus speaks, and speaks to thee:
　　"Say, poor sinner, lov'st thou Me?

"I deliver'd thee when bound,
　　And, when bleeding, heal'd thy wound;
Sought thee wandering, set thee right,
　　Turn'd thy darkness into light.

"Can a woman's tender care
　　Cease toward the child she bare?
Yes, she may forgetful be;
　　Yet will I remember thee!

"Mine is an unchanging love,
　　Higher than the heights above,
Deeper than the depths beneath,
　　Free and faithful, strong as death.

"Thou shalt see my glory soon,
　　When the work of grace is done;
Partner of my throne shalt be;
　　Say, poor sinner, lov'st thou Me?"

Lord! it is my chief complaint,
　　That my love is weak and faint;
Yet I love Thee and adore!
　　Oh! for grace to love Thee more!
　　　　　　　　　WILLIAM COWPER.

THE STRANGER AND HIS FRIEND.

A POOR wayfaring man of grief
　　Hath often cross'd me on my way,
Who sued so humbly for relief,
　　That I could never answer, Nay.
I had not power to ask his name,
Whither he went, or whence he came.
Yet there was something in his eye
That won my love, I knew not why.

Once, when my scanty meal was spread,
   He enter'd; not a word he spake;
Just perishing for want of bread;
   I gave him all; he bless'd it, brake,
And ate; but gave me part again;
Mine was an angel's portion then;
For, while I fed with eager haste,
That crust was manna to my taste.

I spied him, where a fountain burst
   Clear from the rock; his strength was gone;
The heedless water mock'd his thirst,
   He heard it, saw it hurrying on:
I ran to raise the sufferer up;
Thrice from the stream he drain'd my cup,
Dipt, and return'd it running o'er;
I drank, and never thirsted more.

'Twas night; the floods were out; it blew
   A winter hurricane aloof;
I heard his voice abroad, and flew
   To bid him welcome to my roof;
I warm'd, I clothed, I cheer'd my guest,
Laid him on my own couch to rest;
Then made the hearth my bed, and seem'd
In Eden's garden while I dream'd.

Stript, wounded, beaten, nigh to death,
   I found him by the highway-side:
I roused his pulse, brought back his breath,
   Revived his spirit, and supplied
Wine, oil, refreshment; he was heal'd:
I had myself a wound conceal'd;
But from that hour forgot the smart,
And peace bound up my broken heart.

In prison I saw him next condemn'd
   To meet a traitor's death at morn:
The tide of lying tongues I stemm'd,
   And honor'd him 'midst shame and scorn;
My friendship's utmost zeal to try,
He ask'd if I for him would die;
The flesh was weak, my blood ran chill;
But the free spirit cried, "I will."

Then in a moment to my view
   The Stranger darted from disguise;
The tokens in His hands I knew,
   My Saviour stood before mine eyes!

He spake; and my poor name He named:
"Of Me thou hast not been ashamed;
These deeds shall thy memorial be;
Fear not; thou didst them unto Me."
JAMES MONTGOMERY.

COME, HOLY SPIRIT, HEAVENLY DOVE.

COME, Holy Spirit, heavenly Dove,
   With all Thy quickening powers,
Kindle a flame of sacred love
   In these cold hearts of ours.

Look how we grovel here below,
   Fond of these trifling toys;
Our souls can neither fly nor go
   To reach eternal joys!

In vain we tune our formal songs,
   In vain we strive to rise;
Hosannas languish on our tongues,
   And our devotion dies.

Dear Lord, and shall we ever lie
   At this poor dying rate?
Our love so faint, so cold to Thee,
   And Thine to us so great!

Come, Holy Spirit, heavenly Dove,
   With all Thy quickening powers;
Come, shed abroad a Saviour's love,
   And that shall kindle ours.
ISAAC WATTS.

VENI CREATOR SPIRITUS.

COME, Holy Ghost, our souls inspire,
And lighten with celestial fire;
Thou the Anointing Spirit art,
Who dost Thy sevenfold gifts impart.
Thy blessed unction from above
Is comfort, life, and fire of love;
Enable with perpetual light
The dulness of our blinded sight;
Anoint and cheer our soilèd face
With the abundance of Thy grace;
Keep far our foes, give peace at home;
Where Thou art guide, no ill can come;
Teach us to know the Father, Son,
And Thee of Both, to be but One,
That, through the ages all along,
This may be our endless song,

"Praise to thy eternal merit,
Father, Son, and Holy Spirit!"
Amen!
AUTHOR UNKNOWN.

VENI CREATOR.

CREATOR SPIRIT, by whose aid
The world's foundations first were laid,
Come, visit every pious mind;
Come, pour Thy joys on human kind;
From sin and sorrow set us free,
And make Thy temples worthy Thee!

O source of uncreated light,
The Father's promised Paraclete!
Thrice holy fount, thrice holy fire,
Our hearts with heavenly love inspire,
Come, and Thy sacred unction bring,
To sanctify us while we sing!

Plenteous of grace, descend from high,
Rich in Thy sevenfold energy!
Thou strength of His almighty hand
Whose power does heaven and earth command!
Proceeding Spirit, our defence,
Who dost the gifts of tongues dispense,
And crown'st Thy gifts with eloquence!

Refine and purge our earthly parts;
But, oh, inflame and fire our hearts!
Our frailties help, our vice control—
Submit the senses to the soul;
And when rebellious they are grown,
Then lay Thy hand, and hold them down.

Chase from our minds th' infernal foe,
And peace, the fruit of love, bestow;
And, lest our feet should step astray,
Protect and guide us in the way.

Make us eternal truths receive,
And practise all that we believe;
Give us Thyself, that we may see
The Father, and the Son, by Thee.

Immortal honor, endless fame,
Attend the almighty Father's name!
The Saviour Son be glorified,
Who for lost man's redemption died!
And equal adoration be,
Eternal Paraclete, to Thee!
JOHN DRYDEN.

IN SORROW.

GENTLY, Lord, oh, gently lead us,
Pilgrims in this vale of tears,
Through the trials yet decreed us,
Till our last great change appears.
When temptation's darts assail us,
When in devious paths we stray,
Let Thy goodness never fail us,
Lead us in Thy perfect way.

In the hour of pain and anguish,
In the hour when death draws near,
Suffer not our hearts to languish,
Suffer not our souls to fear;
And, when mortal life is ended,
Bid us in Thine arms to rest,
Till, by angel bands attended,
We awake among the blest.
THOMAS HASTINGS.

LIGHT SHINING OUT OF DARKNESS.

GOD moves in a mysterious way
His wonders to perform;
He plants His footsteps in the sea,
And rides upon the storm.

Deep in unfathomable mines
Of never-failing skill,
He treasures up His bright designs,
And works His sovereign will.

Ye fearful saints, fresh courage take;
The clouds ye so much dread
Are big with mercy, and shall break
In blessings on your head.

Judge not the Lord by feeble sense,
But trust Him for His grace;
Behind a frowning Providence
He hides a smiling face.

His purposes will ripen fast,
Unfolding every hour;
The bud may have a bitter taste,
But sweet will be the flower.

Blind unbelief is sure to err,
And scan His work in vain;
God is His own interpreter,
And He will make it plain.
WILLIAM COWPER.

GOD IS LOVE.

God is love! His mercy brightens
  All the path in which we rove;
Bliss He wakes, and woe He lightens:
  God is wisdom! God is love!

Chance and change are busy ever;
  Man decays and ages move;
But His mercy waneth never:
  God is wisdom! God is love!

E'en the hour that darkest seemeth
  Will His changeless goodness prove;
From the gloom His brightness streameth:
  God is wisdom! God is love!

He with earthly cares entwineth
  Hope and comfort from above;
Everywhere His glory shineth:
  God is wisdom! God is love!

God is love! His mercy brightens
  All the path in which we rove;
Bliss He wakes, and woe He lightens:
  God is wisdom! God is love!
SIR JOHN BOWRING.

FATHER, THY WILL BE DONE.

He sendeth sun, He sendeth shower,—
Alike they're needful for the flower;
And joys and tears alike are sent
To give the soul fit nourishment.
  As comes to me or cloud or sun,
  Father! Thy will, not mine, be done.

Can loving children e'er reprove
With murmurs whom they trust and love?
Creator, I would ever be
A trusting, loving child to Thee;
  As comes to me or cloud or sun,
  Father! Thy will, not mine, be done.

Oh, ne'er will I at life repine;
Enough that Thou hast made it mine.
When falls the shadow cold of death,
I yet will sing with parting breath,
  As comes to me or shade or sun,
  Father! Thy will, not mine, be done.
SARAH FLOWER ADAMS.

THE ELIXER.

Teach me, my God and King,
  In all things thee to see,
And what I do in anything,
  To do it as for thee.

Not rudely, as a beast,
  To runne into an action;
But still to make thee prepossest,
  And give it his perfection.

A man that looks on glasse,
  On it may stay his eye;
Or, if he pleaseth, through it passe,
  And then the heaven espie.

All may of thee partake:
  Nothing can be so mean,
Which with his tincture (for thy sake)
  Will not grow bright and clean.

A servant with this clause
  Makes drudgerie divine:
Who sweeps a room, as for thy laws,
  Makes that and th' action fine.

This is the famous stone
  That turneth all to gold;
For that which God doth touch and own
  Cannot for lesse be told.
GEORGE HERBERT.

A HYMN.

Drop, drop, slow tears,
  And bathe those beauteous feet
Which brought from heaven
  The news and Prince of Peace!
Cease not, wet eyes,
  His mercies to entreat;
To cry for vengeance
  Sin doth never cease;
In your deep floods
  Drown all my faults and fears;
Nor let His eye
  See sin, but through my tears.
PHINEAS FLETCHER.

WITH ONE CONSENT LET ALL THE EARTH
TO GOD THEIR CHEERFUL VOICES RAISE:

Psalm C.

AN ODE.

The spacious firmament on high,
With all the blue ethereal sky,
And spangled heavens, a shining frame,
Their great Original proclaim.
The unwearied sun from day to day
Does his Creator's power display,
And publishes to every land
The work of an almighty Hand.

Soon as the evening shades prevail,
The moon takes up the wondrous tale,
And nightly, to the listening earth,
Repeats the story of her birth;
Whilst all the stars that round her burn,
And all the planets in their turn,
Confirm the tidings as they roll,
And spread the truth from pole to pole.

What though in solemn silence all
Move round the dark terrestrial ball?
What though nor real voice nor sound
Amid their radiant orbs be found?
In reason's ear they all rejoice,
And utter forth a glorious voice,
For ever singing as they shine,
The Hand that made us is divine!"
Joseph Addison.

THE UNIVERSAL PRAYER.

Deo Opt. Max.

Father of all! in every age,
  In every clime adored—
By saint, by savage, and by sage—
  Jehovah, Jove, or Lord!

Thou Great First Cause, least understood,
  Who all my sense confined
To know but this: that Thou art good,
  And that myself am blind;

Yet gave me, in this dark estate,
  To see the good from ill;
And, binding Nature fast in fate,
  Left free the human will.

What conscience dictates to be done,
  Or warns me not to do,
This teach me more than hell to shun,
  That more than heaven pursue.

What blessings Thy free bounty gives
  Let me not cast away—
For God is paid when man receives:
  To enjoy is to obey.

Yet not to earth's contracted span
  Thy goodness let me bound,
Or think Thee Lord alone of man,
  When thousand worlds are round.

Let not this weak, unknowing hand
  Presume Thy bolts to throw,
And deal damnation round the land
  On each I judge Thy foe.

If I am right, Thy grace impart
  Still in the right to stay;
If I am wrong, oh teach my heart
  To find that better way.

Save me alike from foolish pride
  Or impious discontent,
At aught Thy wisdom has denied,
  Or aught Thy goodness lent.

Teach me to feel another's woe,
  To hide the fault I see;
That mercy I to others show,
  That mercy show to me.

Mean though I am, not wholly so,
  Since quicken'd by Thy breath;
Oh lead me, wheresoe'er I go,
  Through this day's life or death.

This day be bread and peace my lot:
  All else beneath the sun
Thou know'st if best bestow'd or not,
  And let Thy will be done.

To Thee, whose temple is all space,
  Whose altar, earth, sea, skies—
One chorus let all being raise!
  All Nature's incense rise!
Alexander Pope.

PSALM C.

With one consent let all the earth
  To God their cheerful voices raise;
Glad homage pay with awful mirth,
  And sing before Him songs of praise.

Convinced that He is God alone,
  From whom both we and all proceed;

We, whom He chooses for His own,
    The flock that He vouchsafes to feed.

Oh enter, then, His temple gate,
    Thence to His courts devoutly press;
And still your grateful hymns repeat,
    And still His name with praises bless.

For He's the Lord, supremely good,
    His mercy is for ever sure:
His truth, which always firmly stood,
    To endless ages shall endure.
TATE AND BRADY.

PSALM C.

BEFORE Jehovah's awful throne,
Ye nations, bow with sacred joy;
Know that the Lord is God alone,
He can create and He destroy.

His sovereign power without our aid,
    Made us of clay, and form'd us men;
And when like wandering sheep we stray'd,
    He brought us to His fold again.

We'll crowd Thy gates with thankful songs,
    High as the heavens our voices raise;
And earth, with her ten thousand tongues,
    Shall fill Thy courts with sounding praise.

Wide as the world is Thy command,
Vast as eternity Thy love;
Firm as a rock Thy truth must stand,
When rolling years shall cease to move.
ISAAC WATTS.
(Varied by CHARLES WESLEY.)

I GIVE IMMORTAL PRAISE.

I GIVE immortal praise
    To God the Father's love,
For all my comforts here
    And better hopes above;
He sent His own eternal Son
To die for sins that man had done.

To God the Son belongs
    Immortal glory too,
Who bought us with His blood
    From everlasting woe;
And now He lives, and now He reigns,
And sees the fruit of all His pains.

To God the Spirit's name
    Immortal worship give,
Whose new-creating power
    Makes the dead sinner live;
His work completes the great design,
And fills the soul with joy divine.

Almighty God, to Thee
    Be endless honors done;
The undivided Three,
    And the mysterious One!
Where reason fails with all her powers,
There faith prevails, and love adores.
ISAAC WATTS.

THE HOLY TRINITY.

HOLY, holy, holy, Lord God Almighty!
    Early in the morning our song shall rise to Thee;
Holy, holy, holy! Merciful and Mighty!
    God in Three Persons, blessed Trinity!

Holy, holy, holy! all the saints adore Thee,
    Casting down their golden crowns around the glassy sea,
Cherubim and Seraphim falling down before Thee,
    Which wert, and art, and evermore shalt be.

Holy, holy, holy! though the darkness hide Thee,
    Though the eye of sinful man Thy glory may not see,
Only Thou art holy, there is none beside Thee,
    Perfect in power, in love, and purity.

Holy, holy, holy, Lord God Almighty!
    All Thy works shall praise Thy Name in earth and sky and sea;
Holy, holy, holy! Merciful and Mighty!
    God in Three Persons, blessed Trinity!
REGINALD HEBER.

ST. AGNES' EVE.

DEEP on the convent-roof the snows
    Are sparkling to the moon:
My breath to heaven like vapor goes:
    May my soul follow soon!

The shadows of the convent-towers
  Slant down the snowy sward,
Still creeping with the creeping hours
  That lead me to my Lord:
Make Thou my spirit pure and clear
  As are the frosty skies,
Or this first snowdrop of the year
  That in my bosom lies.

As these white robes are soil'd and dark,
  To yonder shining ground;
As this pale taper's earthly spark,
  To yonder argent round;
So shows my soul before the Lamb,
  My spirit before Thee;
So in mine earthly house I am,
  To that I hope to be.
Break up the heavens, O Lord! and far,
  Thro' all yon starlight keen,
Draw me, thy bride, a glittering star,
  In raiment white and clean.

He lifts me to the golden doors;
  The flashes come and go;
All heaven bursts her starry floors,
  And strews her lights below,
And deepens on and up! the gates
  Roll back, and far within
For me the Heavenly Bridegroom waits,
  To make me pure of sin.
The sabbaths of Eternity,
  One sabbath deep and wide—
A light upon the shining sea—
  The Bridegroom with his bride!
               ALFRED TENNYSON.

GLORYING IN THE CROSS.

WHEN I survey the wondrous cross
  On which the Prince of glory died,
My richest gain I count but loss,
  And pour contempt on all my pride.

Forbid it, Lord, that I should boast
  Save in the death of Christ, my God;
All the vain things that charm me most
  I sacrifice them to His blood.

See from His head, His hands, His feet,
  Sorrow and love flow mingled down!
Did e'er such love and sorrow meet,
  Or thorns compose so rich a crown?

His dying crimson, like a robe,
  Spreads o'er his body on the tree;
Then am I dead to all the globe,
  And all the globe is dead to me.

Were the whole realm of Nature mine,
  That were a present far too small;
Love so amazing, so divine,
  Demands my soul, my life, my all.
               ISAAC WATTS.

WHEN ALL THY MERCIES, O MY GOD.

WHEN all Thy mercies, O my God,
  My rising soul surveys,
Transported with the view, I'm lost
  In wonder, love, and praise.

Oh, how shall words with equal warmth
  The gratitude declare
That glows within my ravish'd heart?
  But Thou canst read it there.

Thy providence my life sustain'd,
  And all my wants redress'd,
When in the silent womb I lay,
  And hung upon the breast.

To all my weak complaints and cries
  Thy mercy lent an ear,
Ere yet my feeble thoughts had learnt
  To form themselves in prayer.

Unnumber'd comforts to my soul
  Thy tender care bestow'd,
Before my infant heart conceived
  From whence these comforts flow'd.

When in the slippery paths of youth
  With heedless steps I ran,
Thine arm, unseen, convey'd me safe,
  And led me up to man.

Through hidden dangers, toils, and death,
  It gently clear'd my way,
And through the pleasing snares of vice,
  More to be fear'd than they.

When worn with sickness, oft hast Thou
  With health renew'd my face,
And, when in sins and sorrows sunk,
  Revived my soul with grace.

Thy bounteous hand with worldly bliss
  Has made my cup run o'er,
And in a kind and faithful friend
  Has doubled all my store.

Ten thousand thousand precious gifts
  My daily thanks employ,
Nor is the least a cheerful heart
  That tastes those gifts with joy.

Through every period of my life
  Thy goodness I'll pursue,
And after death, in distant worlds,
  The glorious theme renew.

When Nature fails, and day and night
  Divide thy works no more,
My ever-grateful heart, O Lord,
  Thy mercy shall adore.

Through all eternity to Thee
  A joyful song I'll raise,
But oh, eternity's too short
  To utter all Thy praise!
JOSEPH ADDISON.

BLEST BE THY LOVE, DEAR LORD.

BLEST be Thy love, dear Lord,
  That taught us this sweet way,
Only to love Thee for Thyself,
  And for that love obey.

O Thou, our souls' chief hope!
  We to Thy mercy fly;
Where'er we are, Thou canst protect,
  Whate'er we need, supply.

Whether we sleep or wake,
  To Thee we both resign;
By night we see, as well as day,
  If Thy light on us shine.

Whether we live or die,
  Both we submit to Thee;
In death we live, as well as life,
  If Thine in death we be.
JOHN AUSTIN.

PRAISE TO GOD.

PRAISE to God, immortal praise,
For the love that crowns our days!
Bounteous source of every joy,
Let Thy praise our tongues employ.

For the blessings of the field,
For the stores the gardens yield;
For the vine's exalted juice,
For the generous olive's use:

Flocks that whiten all the plain;
Yellow sheaves of ripen'd grain;
Clouds that drop their fattening dews;
Suns that temperate warmth diffuse.

All that Spring with bounteous hand
Scatters o'er the smiling land;
All that liberal Autumn pours
From her rich o'erflowing stores:

These to Thee, my God, we owe,
Source whence all our blessings flow
And for these my soul shall raise
Grateful vows and solemn praise.

Yet, should rising whirlwinds tear
From its stem the ripening ear;
Should the fig tree's blasted shoot
Drop her green, untimely fruit;

Should the vine put forth no more,
Nor the olive yield her store;
Though the sickening flocks should fall,
And the herds desert the stall;

Should Thine alter'd hand restrain
The early and the latter rain;
Blast each opening bud of joy,
And the rising year destroy;

Yet to Thee my soul should raise
Grateful vows and solemn praise;
And, when every blessing's flown,
Love Thee for Thyself alone!
ANNA LÆTITIA BARBAULD.

HYMN.

LORD, with glowing heart I'd praise Thee
  For the bliss Thy love bestows,
For the pardoning grace that saves me,
  And the peace that from it flows.
Help, O God! my weak endeavor,
  This dull soul to rapture raise;
Thou must light the flame, or never
  Can my love be warm'd to praise.

Praise, my soul, the God that sought thee,
  Wretched wanderer, far astray;

Found thee lost, and kindly brought thee
  From the paths of death away.
Praise, with love's devoutest feeling,
  Him who saw thy guilt-born fear,
And, the light of hope revealing,
  Bade the blood-stain'd cross appear.

Lord! this bosom's ardent feeling
  Vainly would my lips express;
Low before Thy footstool kneeling,
  Deign Thy suppliant's prayer to bless.
Let Thy grace, my soul's chief treasure,
  Love's pure flame within me raise;
And, since words can never measure,
  Let my life show forth Thy praise.
FRANCIS SCOTT KEY.

PSALM XC.

OUR God, our help in ages past,
  Our hope for years to come,
Our shelter from the stormy blast,
  And our eternal home:

Under the shadow of Thy throne
  Thy saints have dwelt secure;
Sufficient is Thine arm alone,
  And our defence is sure.

Before the hills in order stood,
  Or earth received her frame,
From everlasting Thou art God,
  To endless years the same.

A thousand ages in Thy sight
  Are like an evening gone;
Short as the watch that ends the night
  Before the rising sun.

The busy tribes of flesh and blood,
  With all their lives and cares,
Are carried downward by Thy flood,
  And lost in following years.

Time, like an ever-rolling stream,
  Bears all its sons away;
They fly forgotten, as a dream
  Dies at the opening day.

Our God, our help in ages past;
  Our hope for years to come;
Be Thou our guard while troubles last,
  And our eternal home!
ISAAC WATTS.

PSALM XCVIII.

JOY to the world! the Lord is come:
  Let earth receive her King:
Let every heart prepare Him room,
  And heaven and nature sing.

Joy to the earth! the Saviour reigns:
  Let men their songs employ;
While fields and floods, rocks, hills, and plains,
  Repeat the sounding joy.

No more let sins and sorrows grow,
  Nor thorns infest the ground:
He comes to make His blessings flow
  Far as the curse is found.

He rules the world with truth and grace,
  And makes the nations prove
The glories of His righteousness,
  And wonders of His love.
ISAAC WATTS.

THE EMIGRANTS IN THE BERMUDAS.

WHERE the remote Bermudas ride
In th' ocean's bosom, unespied—
From a small boat, that row'd along,
The list'ning winds received this song:

  What should we do but sing His praise
That led us through the watery maze
Unto an isle so long unknown,
And yet far kinder than our own?
Where He the huge sea-monsters wracks
That lift the deep upon their backs,
He lands us on a grassy stage,
Safe from the storms, and prelate's rage.
He gave us this eternal spring
Which here enamels every thing,
And sends the fowls to us in care,
On daily visits through the air.
He hangs in shades the orange bright,
Like golden lamps in a green night,
And does in the pomegranates close
Jewels more rich than Ormus shows.
He makes the figs our mouths to meet,
And throws the melons at our feet.
But apples—plants of such a price
No tree could ever bear them twice.
With cedars, chosen by His hand
From Lebanon, He stores the land;

And makes the hollow seas, that roar,
　Proclaim the ambergris on shore.
He cast (of which we rather boast)
　The gospel's pearl upon our coast;
And in these rocks for us did frame
　A temple, where to sound His name.
Oh! let our voice His praise exalt
　Till it arrive at heaven's vault;
Which, then, perhaps rebounding, may
　Echo beyond the Mexique bay.

Thus sang they, in the English boat,
　A holy and a cheerful note;
And all the way, to guide their chime,
　With falling oars they kept the time.
　　　　　　　ANDREW MARVELL.

REBECCA'S HYMN.

WHEN Israel, of the Lord beloved,
　Out from the land of bondage came,
Her fathers' God before her moved,
　An awful guide in smoke and flame.
By day, along the astonish'd lands
　The cloudy pillar glided slow;
By night, Arabia's crimson'd sands
　Return'd the fiery column's glow.

There rose the choral hymn of praise,
　And trump and timbrel answer'd keen;
And Zion's daughters pour'd their lays,
　With priest's and warrior's voice between.
No portents now our foes amaze—
　Forsaken Israel wanders lone;
Our fathers would not know Thy ways,
　And Thou hast left them to their own.

But, present still, though now unseen,
　When brightly shines the prosperous day,
Be thoughts of Thee a cloudy screen,
　To temper the deceitful ray.
And oh, when stoops on Judah's path
　In shade and storm the frequent night,
Be Thou, long-suffering, slow to wrath,
　A burning and a shining light!

Our harps we left by Babel's streams—
　The tyrant's jest, the Gentile's scorn;
No censer round our altar beams,
　And mute are timbrel, trump, and horn.

But Thou hast said, The blood of goat,
　The flesh of rams, I will not prize—
A contrite heart, a humble thought,
　Are mine accepted sacrifice.
　　　　　　　SIR WALTER SCOTT.

SOUND THE LOUD TIMBREL.

MIRIAM'S SONG.

SOUND the loud timbrel o'er Egypt's dark sea!
Jehovah has triumph'd,—his people are free!
Sing,—for the pride of the tyrant is broken,
　His chariots, his horsemen, all splendid and brave,—
How vain was their boast, for the Lord hath but spoken,
　And chariots and horsemen are sunk in the wave.
Sound the loud timbrel o'er Egypt's dark sea!
Jehovah has triumph'd,—his people are free!

Praise to the Conqueror, praise to the Lord!
His word was our arrow, his breath was our sword.
Who shall return to tell Egypt the story
　Of those she sent forth in the hour of her pride?
For the Lord hath look'd out from his pillar of glory,
　And all her brave thousands are dash'd in the tide.
Sound the loud timbrel o'er Egypt's dark sea!
Jehovah has triumph'd,—his people are free!
　　　　　　　THOMAS MOORE.

BEHOLD, I STAND AT THE DOOR AND KNOCK.

O JESU, Thou art standing
　Outside the fast-closed door,
In lowly patience waiting
　To pass the threshold o'er:
We bear the name of Christians,
　His name and sign we bear;
Oh, shame, thrice shame upon us,
　To keep Him standing there!

O Jesu, thou art knocking,
    And lo! that hand is scarr'd,
And thorns Thy brow encircle,
    And tears Thy face have marr'd:
Oh, love that passeth knowledge,
    So patiently to wait!
Oh, sin that hath no equal,
    So fast to bar the gate!

O Jesu, Thou art pleading
    In accents meek and low,
"I died for you, my children,
    And will ye treat Me so?"
O Lord, with shame and sorrow
    We open now the door:
Dear Saviour, enter, enter,
    And leave us nevermore!
WILLIAM WALSHAM HOW.

THOU ART, O GOD!

THOU art, O God! the life and light
    Of all this wondrous world we see;
Its glow by day, its smile by night,
    Are but reflections caught from Thee.
Where'er we turn, Thy glories shine,
And all things fair and bright are Thine.

When day, with farewell beam, delays
    Among the opening clouds of even,
And we can almost think we gaze
    Through golden vistas into heaven,—
Those hues that make the sun's decline
So soft, so radiant, Lord! are Thine.

When night, with wings of starry gloom,
    O'ershadows all the earth and skies,
Like some dark, beauteous bird, whose plume
Is sparkling with unnumber'd eyes,—
That sacred gloom, those fires divine,
So grand, so countless, Lord! are Thine.

When youthful Spring around us breathes,
    Thy spirit warms her fragrant sigh;
And every flower the Summer wreathes
    Is born beneath that kindling eye.
Where'er we turn, Thy glories shine,
And all things fair and bright are Thine.
THOMAS MOORE.

PSALM CXLVIII.

COME, oh come! in pious lays
    Sound we God Almighty's praise;
Hither bring, in one consent,
    Heart and voice and instrument:
Music add of every kind,
Sound the trump, the cornet wind,
Strike the viol, touch the lute,
Let no tongue nor string be mute;
Nor a creature dumb be found
That hath either voice or sound.

Let those things which do not live
    In still music praises give;
Lowly pipe, ye worms that creep
    On the earth or in the deep:
Loud aloft your voices strain,
Beasts and monsters of the main;
Birds, your warbling treble sing;
Clouds, your peals of thunders ring;
Sun and moon, exalted higher,
And bright stars, augment this choir

Come, ye sons of human race,
    In this chorus take your place,
And amid the mortal throng
    Be you masters of the song:
Angels and supernal powers,
Be the noblest tenor yours:
Let, in praise of God, the sound
Run a never-ending round,
That our song of praise may be
Everlasting, as is He.

From earth's vast and hollow womb
    Music's deepest base may come;
Seas and floods, from shore to shore,
    Shall their counter-tenors roar:
To this concert, when we sing,
Whistling winds, your descants bring;
That our song may over-climb
All the bounds of place and time,
And ascend, from sphere to sphere,
To the great Almighty's ear.

So from heaven on earth He shall
Let His gracious blessings fall:
And this huge wide orb we see
Shall one choir, one temple be;
Where in such a praiseful tone
We will sing what He hath done,
That the cursed fiends below
Shall thereat impatient grow.
Then, oh come, in pious lays
Sound we God Almighty's praise!
GEORGE WITHER.

PSALM CXVII.

From all that dwell below the skies
Let the Creator's praise arise;
Let the Redeemer's Name be sung
Through every land by every tongue!

Eternal are Thy mercies, Lord!
Eternal truth attends Thy word;
Thy praise shall sound from shore to shore,
Till suns shall rise and set no more.

Isaac Watts.

EVENING HYMN OF THE ALPINE SHEPHERDS.

Brothers, the day declines;
  Above, the glacier brightens;
Through hills of waving pines
  The "vesper halo" lightens!
Now wake the welcome chorus
  To Him our sires adored;
To Him who watcheth o'er us,—
  Ye shepherds, praise the Lord!

From each tower's embattled crest
  The vesper-bell has toll'd;
'Tis the hour that bringeth rest
  To the shepherd and his fold:
From hamlet, rock, and chalet
  Let our evening song be pour'd;
Till mountain, rock, and valley
  Re-echo,—Praise the Lord!

Praise the Lord, who made and gave us
  Our glorious mountain-land!
Who deign'd to shield and save us
  From the despot's iron hand:
With the bread of life He feeds us;
  Enlighten'd by His word,
Through pastures green He leads us,—
  Ye shepherds, praise the Lord!

And hark, below, aloft,
  From clifts that pierce the cloud,
From blue lakes, calm and soft
  As a virgin in her shroud,
New strength our anthem gathers;
  From Alp to Alp 'tis pour'd;
So sang our sainted fathers,—
  Ye shepherds, praise the Lord!

Praise the Lord! from flood and fell
  Let the voice of old and young—
All the strength of Appenzel,
  True of heart and sweet of tongue—
The grateful theme prolong
  With souls in soft accord,
Till yon stars take up our song,—
  Hallelujah to the Lord!

William Beattie.

EVENING CONTEMPLATION.

Softly now the light of day
Fades upon my sight away;
Free from care, from labor free,
Lord, I would commune with Thee.

Thou, whose all-pervading eye
  Naught escapes, without, within!
Pardon each infirmity,
  Open fault, and secret sin.

Soon for me the light of day
Shall for ever pass away;
Then, from sin and sorrow free,
Take me, Lord, to dwell with Thee.

Thou who, sinless, yet hast known
  All of man's infirmity!
Then, from Thine eternal throne,
  Jesus, look with pitying eye.

George Washington Doane.

THE PRIEST.

I would I were an excellent divine
  That had the Bible at my fingers' ends;
That men might hear out of this mouth of mine,
  How God doth make His enemies His friends;
Rather than with a thundering and long prayer
Be led into presumption, or despair.

This would I be, and would none other be—
  But a religious servant of my God;
And know there is none other God but He,
  And willingly to suffer mercy's rod—
Joy in His grace, and live but in His love,
And seek my bliss but in the world above.

And I would frame a kind of faithful prayer
For all estates within the state of grace,
That careful love might never know despair,
Nor servile fear might faithful love deface:
And this would I both day and night devise
To make my humble spirit's exercise.

And I would read the rules of sacred life;
Persuade the troubled soul to patience;
The husband care, and comfort to the wife,
To child and servant due obedience;
Faith to the friend, and to the neighbor peace,
That love might live, and quarrels all might cease.

Prayer for the health of all that are diseased,
Confession unto all that are convicted,
And patience unto all that are displeased,
And comfort unto all that are afflicted,
And mercy unto all that have offended,
And grace to all: that all may be amended.
NICHOLAS BRETON.

MORNING HYMN.

OH, timely happy, timely wise,
Hearts that with rising morn arise!
Eyes that the beam celestial view,
Which evermore makes all things new!

New every morning is the love
Our wakening and uprising prove,
Through sleep and darkness safely brought,
Restored to life, and power, and thought.

New mercies, each returning day,
Hover around us while we pray;
New perils past, new sins forgiven,
New thoughts of God, new hopes of heaven.

If, on our daily course, our mind
Be set to hallow all we find,
New treasures still, of countless price,
God will provide for sacrifice.

Old friends, old scenes, will lovelier be,
As more of heaven in each we see;
Some softening gleam of love and prayer
Shall dawn on every cross and care.

As for some dear familiar strain
Untired we ask, and ask again,
Ever, in its melodious store,
Finding a spell unheard before;

Such is the bliss of souls serene,
When they have sworn, and steadfast mean,
Counting the cost, in all t' espy
Their God, in all themselves deny.

Oh, could we learn that sacrifice,
What lights would all around us rise!
How would our hearts with wisdom talk
Along life's dullest, dreariest walk!

We need not bid, for cloister'd cell,
Our neighbor and our work farewell,
Nor strive to wind ourselves too high
For sinful man beneath the sky;

The trivial round, the common task,
Will furnish all we ought to ask;
Room to deny ourselves,—a road
To bring us, daily, nearer God.

Seek we no more: content with these,
Let present rapture, comfort, ease,
As heaven shall bid them, come and go;
The secret this of rest below.

Only, O Lord, in Thy dear love
Fit us for perfect rest above,
And help us, this and every day,
To live more nearly as we pray!
JOHN KEBLE.

MORNING HYMN.

AWAKE, my soul, and with the sun
Thy daily stage of duty run;
Shake off dull sloth, and joyful rise
To pay thy morning sacrifice.

Thy precious time misspent redeem;
Each present day thy last esteem;

Improve thy talent with due care;
For the great day thyself prepare.

In conversation be sincere;
Keep conscience as the noontide clear;
Think how All-seeing God thy ways
And all thy secret thoughts surveys.

By influence of the light divine
Let thy own light to others shine;
Reflect all Heaven's propitious rays,
In ardent love and cheerful praise.

Wake and lift up thyself, my heart,
And with the angels bear thy part,
Who, all night long, unwearied sing
High praise to the Eternal King.

Awake! awake! Ye heavenly choir,
May your devotion me inspire,
That I, like you, my age may spend,
Like you may on my God attend!

May I, like you, in God delight,
Have all day long my God in sight,
Perform like you my Maker's will!
Oh may I never more do ill!

Had I your wings to Heaven I'd fly;
But God shall that defect supply;
And my soul, wing'd with warm desire,
Shall all day long to Heaven aspire.

All praise to Thee, who safe hast kept,
And hast refresh'd me whilst I slept!
Grant, Lord, when I from death shall wake,
I may of endless light partake!

I would not wake, nor rise again,
Ev'n Heaven itself I would disdain,
Wert thou not there to be enjoy'd,
And I in hymns to be employ'd!

Heaven is, dear Lord, where'er Thou art;
Oh never then from me depart!
For, to my soul, 'tis hell to be
But for one moment void of Thee.

Lord, I my vows to thee renew;
Disperse my sins as morning dew;
Guard my first springs of thought and will,
And with Thyself my spirit fill.

Direct, control, suggest, this day,
All I design, or do, or say;
That all my powers, with all their might,
In Thy sole glory may unite.

Praise God, from whom all blessings flow;
Praise Him, all creatures here below!
Praise Him above, ye heavenly host;
Praise Father, Son, and Holy Ghost!
THOMAS KEN.

MORNING HYMN.

SINCE Thou hast added now, O God!
　Unto my life another day,
And giv'st me leave to walk abroad,
　And labor in my lawful way;
My walks and works with me begin,
Conduct me forth, and bring me in.

In every power my soul enjoys
　Internal virtues to improve;
In every sense that she employs
　In her external works to move;
Bless her, O God! and keep me sound
From outward harm and inward wound.

Let sin nor Satan's fraud prevail
　To make mine eye of reason blind,
Or faith, or hope, or love to fail,
　Or any virtues of the mind;
But more and more let them increase,
And bring me to mine end in peace.

Lewd courses let my feet forbear;
　Keep Thou my hands from doing wrong;
Let not ill counsels pierce mine ear,
　Nor wicked words defile my tongue;
And keep the windows of each eye
That no strange lust climb in thereby.

But guard Thou safe my heart in chief;
　That neither hate, revenge, nor fear,
Nor vain desire, vain joy, or grief,
　Obtain command or dwelling there:
And, Lord! with every saving grace,
Still true to Thee maintain that place!

From open wrongs, from secret hates,
　Preserve me, likewise, Lord! this day;
From slanderous tongues, from wicked mates
　From every danger in my way;
My goods to me secure Thou too,
And prosper all the works I do.

So till the evening of this morn
　My time shall then so well be spent,
That when the twilight shall return
　I may enjoy it with content,
And to Thy praise and honor say,
That this hath proved a happy day.
GEORGE WITHER.

EVENING HYMN.

Sun of my soul, Thou Saviour dear,
It is not night if Thou be near;
Oh! may no earth-born cloud arise
To hide Thee from Thy servant's eyes!

When round Thy wondrous works below
My searching rapturous glance I throw,
Tracing out wisdom, power, and love,
In earth or sky, in stream or grove;

Or, by the light Thy words disclose,
Watch time's full river as it flows,
Scanning Thy gracious Providence,
Where not too deep for mortal sense;

When with dear friends sweet talk I hold,
And all the flowers of life unfold;
Let not my heart within me burn,
Except in all I Thee discern!

When the soft dews of kindly sleep
My wearied eyelids gently steep,
Be my last thought, How sweet to rest
For ever on my Saviour's breast!

Abide with me from morn till eve,
For without Thee I cannot live!
Abide with me when night is nigh,
For without Thee I dare not die!

Thou Framer of the light and dark,
Steer through the tempest Thine own ark!
Amid the howling wintry sea
We are in port if we have Thee.

The rulers of this Christian land,
'Twixt Thee and us ordain'd to stand,
Guide Thou their course, O Lord, aright!
Let all do all as in Thy sight!

Oh! by Thine own sad burthen, borne
So meekly up the hill of scorn,
Teach Thou Thy priests their daily cross
To bear as Thine, nor count it loss!

If some poor wandering child of Thine
Have spurn'd, to-day, the voice divine;
Now, Lord, the gracious work begin;
Let him no more lie down in sin!

Watch by the sick, enrich the poor
With blessings from Thy boundless store!
Be every mourner's sleep to-night
Like infant's slumbers, pure and light!

Come near and bless us when we wake,
Ere through the world our way we take:
Till, in the ocean of Thy love,
We lose ourselves in Heaven above!
JOHN KEBLE.

EVENING HYMN.

All praise to Thee, my God, this night,
For all the blessings of the light;
Keep me, oh keep me, King of kings,
Beneath Thine own Almighty wings!

Forgive me, Lord, for Thy dear Son,
The ill that I this day have done;
That with the world, myself, and Thee,
I, ere I sleep, at peace may be.

Teach me to live, that I may dread
The grave as little as my bed!
To die, that this vile body may
Rise glorious at the awful day!

Oh may my soul on Thee repose;
And may sweet sleep mine eyelids close;
Sleep, that may me more vigorous make
To serve my God when I awake!

When in the night I sleepless lie,
My soul with heavenly thoughts supply!
Let no ill dreams disturb my rest,
No powers of darkness me molest!

Dull sleep, of sense me to deprive!
I am but half my time alive:
Thy faithful lovers, Lord, are grieved
To lie so long of Thee bereaved.

But though sleep o'er my frailty reigns,
Let it not hold me long in chains!
And now and then let loose my heart,
Till it an hallelujah dart!

The faster sleep the senses binds,
The more unfetter'd are our minds;
Oh may my soul, from matter free,
Thy loveliness unclouded see!

Oh when shall I, in endless day,
For ever chase dark sleep away,
And hymns with the supernal choir
Incessant sing, and never tire?

Oh may my Guardian, while I sleep,
Close to my bed His vigils keep;

His love angelical instill;
Stop all the avenues of ill:

May He celestial joy rehearse,
And thought to thought with me converse;
Or in my stead, all the night long,
Sing to my God a grateful song!

Praise God, from whom all blessings flow,
Praise Him, all creatures here below!
Praise Him above, ye heavenly host!
Praise Father, Son, and Holy Ghost!
THOMAS KEN.

EVENING HYMN.

BEHOLD the sun, that seem'd but now
  Enthronèd overhead,
Beginneth to decline below
  The globe whereon we tread;
And he, whom yet we look upon
  With comfort and delight,
Will quite depart from hence anon,
  And leave us to the night.

Thus time, unheeded, steals away
  The life which Nature gave;
Thus are our bodies every day
  Declining to the grave:
Thus from us all those pleasures fly
  Whereon we set our heart;
And when the night of death draws nigh,
  Thus will they all depart.

Lord! though the sun forsake our sight,
  And mortal hopes are vain;
Let still Thine everlasting light
  Within our souls remain!
And in the nights of our distress
  Vouchsafe those rays divine,
Which from the Sun of Righteousness
  For ever brightly shine!
GEORGE WITHER.

EVENING HYMN.

THE night is come; like to the day,
Depart not thou, great God, away,
Let not my sins, black as the night,
Eclipse the lustre of Thy light.
Keep in my horizon; for to me
The sun makes not the day, but Thee.
Thou whose nature cannot sleep,
On my temples sentry keep:
Guard me 'gainst those watchful foes,
Whose eyes are open while mine close.
Let no dreams my head infest
But such as Jacob's temples blest.
Whilst I do rest, my soul advance;
Make my sleep a holy trance:
That I may, my rest being wrought,
Awake into some holy thought,
And with as active vigor run
My course, as doth the nimble sun.
Sleep is a death; oh, make me try,
By sleeping, what it is to die:
And as gently lay my head
On my grave as now my bed.
Howe'er I rest, great God, let me
Awake again at last with Thee.
And thus assured, behold I lie
Securely, or to wake or die.
These are my drowsy days; in vain
I do now wake to sleep again:
Oh, come that hour when I shall never
Sleep thus again, but wake for ever.
SIR THOMAS BROWNE.

EVENING HYMN.

SWEET SAVIOUR! bless us ere we go;
  Thy word into our minds instill,
And make our lukewarm hearts to glow
  With lowly love and fervent will;
Through life's long day and death's dark night,
O gentle Jesus, be our light.

The day is done, its hours have run,
  And Thou hast taken count of all,—
The scanty triumphs grace hath won,
  The broken vow, the frequent fall;
Through life's long day and death's dark night,
O gentle Jesus, be our light.

Grant us, dear Lord, from evil ways
  True absolution and release,
And bless us more than in past days,
  With purity and inward peace;
Through life's long day and death's dark night,
O gentle Jesus, be our light.

Do more than pardon,—give us joy,
  Sweet fear, and sober liberty,
And loving hearts without alloy,
  That only long to be like Thee;
Through life's long day and death's dark night,
O gentle Jesus, be our light.

Labor is sweet, for Thou hast toil'd,
  And care is light, for Thou hast cared:
Let not our works with self be soil'd,
  Nor in unsimple ways ensnared;
Through life's long day and death's dark night,
O gentle Jesus, be our light.

For all we love—the poor, the sad,
  The sinful—unto Thee we call;
Oh! let Thy mercy make us glad!
  Thou art our Jesus and our all;
Through life's long day and death's dark night,
O gentle Jesus, be our light.

Sweet Saviour! bless us; night is come;
  Through all its watches near us be;
Good angels watch about our home,
  And we are one day nearer Thee.
Through life's long day and death's dark night,
O gentle Jesus, be our light.
FREDERICK WILLIAM FABER.

ABIDE WITH ME.

ABIDE with me! fast falls the even-tide;
The darkness deepens; Lord, with me abide!
When other helpers fail, and comforts flee,
Help of the helpless, oh abide with me!

Swift to its close ebbs out life's little day;
Earth's joys grow dim; its glories pass away;
Change and decay in all around I see:
O Thou, who changest not, abide with me!

Not a brief glance I beg, a passing word:
But, as Thou dwell'st with Thy disciples, Lord,
Familiar, condescending, patient, free,
Come, not to sojourn, but abide, with me!

Come not in terrors, as the King of kings;
But kind and good, with healing in Thy wings;
Tears for all woes, a heart for every plea;
Come, Friend of sinners, and thus 'bide with me!

Thou on my head in early youth didst smile;
And, though rebellious and perverse meanwhile,
Thou hast not left me, oft as I left Thee.
On to the close, O Lord, abide with me!

I need Thy Presence every passing hour;
What but Thy grace can foil the Tempter's power?
Who like Thyself my guide and stay can be?
Through cloud and sunshine, oh abide with me!

I fear no foe, with Thee at hand to bless:
Ills have no weight, and tears no bitterness:
Where is Death's sting? where, Grave, thy victory?
I triumph still, if Thou abide with me!

Hold then Thy cross before my closing eyes!
Shine through the gloom, and point me to the skies!
Heaven's morning breaks, and earth's vain shadows flee;
In life and death, O Lord, abide with me!
HENRY FRANCIS LYTE.

MIDNIGHT HYMN.

My God, now I from sleep awake,
The sole possession of me take:
From midnight terrors me secure,
And guard my heart from thoughts impure!

Bless'd angels! while we silent lie,
You hallelujahs sing on high;
You joyful hymn the Ever-blest,
Before the Throne, and never rest.

I with your choir celestial join
In offering up a hymn divine;
With you in Heaven I hope to dwell,
And bid the night and world farewell.

My soul, when I shake off this dust,
Lord, in Thy arms I will entrust:
Oh make me Thy peculiar care;
Some mansion for my soul prepare!

Give me a place at Thy saints' feet,
Or some fall'n angel's vacant seat!
I'll strive to sing as loud as they,
Who sit above in brighter day.

Oh may I always ready stand
With my lamp burning in my hand:
May I in sight of Heaven rejoice,
Whene'er I hear the Bridegroom's voice!

All praise to Thee in light array'd,
Who light Thy dwelling-place hast made;
A boundless ocean of bright beams
From Thy all-glorious Godhead streams.

The Sun in its meridian height
Is very darkness in Thy sight!
My soul oh lighten and inflame,
With thought and love of Thy great Name!

Bless'd Jesu, Thou, on Heaven intent,
Whole nights hast in devotion spent;
But I, frail creature, soon am tired,
And all my zeal is soon expired.

My soul, how canst thou weary grow
Of antedating bliss below,
In sacred hymns, and heavenly love,
Which will eternal be above?

Shine on me, Lord, new life impart!
Fresh ardors kindle in my heart!
One ray of Thy all-quickening light
Dispels the sloth and clouds of night.

Lord, lest the tempter me surprise,
Watch over Thine own sacrifice!
All loose, all idle thoughts cast out,
And make my very dreams devout!

Praise God, from whom all blessings flow,
Praise Him, all creatures here below!
Praise Him above, ye heavenly host;
Praise Father, Son, and Holy Ghost!
THOMAS KEN.

HYMN.

How are Thy servants blest, O Lord!
  How sure is their defence!
Eternal wisdom is their guide,
  Their help omnipotence.

In foreign realms, and lands remote,
  Supported by Thy care,
Through burning climes I pass'd unhurt,
  And breathed in tainted air.

Thy mercy sweeten'd every soil,
  Made every region please;
The hoary Alpine hills it warm'd,
  And smooth'd the Tyrrhene seas.

Think, O my soul, devoutly think,
  How with affrighted eyes
Thou saw'st the wide-extended deep
  In all its horrors rise!

Confusion dwelt in every face,
  And fear in every heart,
When waves on waves, and gulfs in gulfs,
  O'ercame the pilot's art.

Yet then from all my griefs, O Lord,
  Thy mercy set me free;
Whilst in the confidence of prayer
  My soul took hold on Thee.

For though in dreadful whirls we hung,
  High on the broken wave;
I knew Thou wert not slow to hear,
  Nor impotent to save.

The storm was laid, the winds retired,
  Obedient to Thy will;
The sea, that roar'd at Thy command,
  At Thy command was still.

In midst of dangers, fears, and deaths,
  Thy goodness I'll adore—
And praise Thee for Thy mercies past,
  And humbly hope for more.

My life, if Thou preserv'st my life,
  Thy sacrifice shall be;
And death, if death must be my doom,
  Shall join my soul to Thee.
JOSEPH ADDISON.

THANKSGIVING HYMN.

Come, ye thankful people, come,
Raise the song of Harvest-Home!
All is safely gather'd in,
Ere the winter-storms begin;

God, our Maker, doth provide
For our wants to be supplied;
Come to God's own temple, come,
Raise the song of Harvest-Home!

We ourselves are God's own field,
Fruit unto His praise to yield;
Wheat and tares together sown,
Unto joy or sorrow grown:
First the blade, and then the ear,
Then the full corn shall appear:
Grant, O harvest Lord, that we
Wholesome grain and pure may be!

For the Lord our God shall come,
And shall take His harvest home;
From His field shall purge away
All that doth offend, that day;
Give His Angels charge at last
In the fire the tares to cast,
But the fruitful ears to store
In His garner evermore.

Then, thou Church triumphant, come,
Raise the song of Harvest-Home!
All are safely gather'd in,
Free from sorrow, free from sin;
There for ever purified,
In God's garner to abide:
Come, ten thousand Angels, come,
Raise the glorious Harvest-Home!
HENRY ALFORD.

A THANKSGIVING TO GOD FOR HIS HOUSE.

LORD, Thou hast given me a cell,
 Wherein to dwell;
A little house, whose humble roof
 Is weather-proof;
Under the sparres of which I lie
 Both soft and drie;
Where Thou, my chamber for to ward,
 Hath set a guard
Of harmlesse thoughts, to watch and keep
 Me while I sleep.
Low is my porch, as is my fate;
 Both void of state;
And yet the threshold of my doore
 Is worn by th' poore,
Who thither come and freely get
 Good words or meat.
Like as my parlour, so my hall
 And kitchin's small;
A littie butterie, and therein
 A little byn,
Which keeps my little loafe of bread
 Unchipt, unflead;
Some brittle sticks of thorne or brier
 Make me a fire,
Close by whose living coale I sit,
 And glow like it.
Lord, I confesse too, when I dine,
 The pulse is Thine,
And all those other bits that bee
 There placed by Thee;
The worts, the purslain, and the messe
 Of water-cresse,
Which of Thy kindnesse Thou hast sent;
 And my content
Makes those, and my beloved beet,
 To be more sweet.
'Tis Thou that crown'st my glittering hearth
 With guiltlesse mirth,
And giv'st me wassaile bowles to drink,
 Spiced to the brink.
Lord, 'tis Thy plenty-dropping hand,
 That soiles my land,
And giv'st me, for my bushell sowne,
 Twice ten for one;
Thou mak'st my teeming hen to lay
 Her egg each day;
Besides my healthful ewes to bear
 Me twins each yeare;
The while the conduits of my kine
 Run creame, for wine:
All these, and better Thou dost send
 Me, to this end,
That I should render, for my part,
 A thankfull heart;
Which, fired with incense, I resigne,
 As wholly Thine;
But the acceptance, that must be,
 My Christ, by Thee.
ROBERT HERRICK.

FOR NEW-YEAR'S DAY.

ETERNAL source of every joy,
Well may Thy praise our lips employ,
While in Thy temple we appear,
Whose goodness crowns the circling year.

The flowery spring at Thy command
Embalms the air and paints the land;

The summer rays with vigor shine,
To raise the corn, and cheer the vine.

Thy hand in autumn richly pours
Through all our coasts redundant stores,
And winters, soften'd by Thy care,
No more a face of horror wear.

Seasons and months and weeks and days
Demand successive songs of praise;
Still be the cheerful homage paid
With opening light and evening shade!

Oh! may our more harmonious tongues
In worlds unknown pursue the songs;
And in those brighter courts adore,
Where days and years revolve no more!
PHILIP DODDRIDGE.

SUNDAY.

O DAY most calm, most bright!
The fruit of this, the next world's bud;
The indorsement of supreme delight,
Writ by a Friend, and with His blood;
The couch of time, care's balm and bay,
The week were dark but for thy light;
  Thy torch doth show the way.

The other days and thou
Make up one man, whose face thou art,
Knocking at heaven with thy brow:
The working days are the back part,
The burden of the week lies there,
Making the whole to stoop and bow,
  Till thy release appear.

Man had straightforward gone
To endless death; but thou dost pull
And turn us round to look on One,
Whom, if we were not very dull,
We could not choose but look on still,
Since there is no place so alone,
  The which He doth not fill!

Sundays the pillars are
On which heaven's palace archèd lies:
The other days fill up the spare
And hollow room with vanities;
They are the fruitful beds and borders
Of God's rich garden; that is bare,
  Which parts their ranks and orders.

The Sundays of man's life,
Threaded together on time's string,
Make bracelets to adorn the wife
Of the eternal glorious King;
On Sunday heaven's gate stands ope;
Blessings are plentiful and rife,
  More plentiful than hope.

This day my Saviour rose,
And did enclose this light for His,
That, as each beast his manger knows,
Man might not of his fodder miss;
Christ hath took in this piece of ground,
And made a garden there for those
  Who want herbs for their wound.

The rest of our creation
Our great Redeemer did remove
With the same shake, which at His passion
Did th' earth, and all things with it, move;
As Samson bore the doors away,
Christ's hands, though nail'd, wrought our salvation,
  And did unhinge that day.

The brightness of that day
We sullied by our foul offence;
Wherefore that robe we cast away,
Having a new at His expense,
Whose drops of blood paid the full price
That was required to make us gay
  And fit for Paradise.
GEORGE HERBERT.

SON-DAYES.

BRIGHT shadows of true rest! some shoots of blisse;
  Heaven once a week;
The next world's gladnesse prepossest in this;
  A day to seek:
Eternity in time; the steps by which
  We climb above all ages; lamps that light
Man through his heap of dark days; and the rich
  And full redemption of the whole week's flight!

The pulleys unto headlong man; time's bower;
  The narrow way;
Transplanted paradise; God's walking houre;
  The cool o' th' day!

The creature's jubile; God's parle with
    dust;
Heaven here; man on those hills of myrrh
    and flowres;
Angels descending; the returns of trust;
A gleam of glory after six-days showres!

The Churche's love-feasts; time's prerog-
    ative
        And interest
Deducted from the whole; the combs and
    hive,
        And home of rest.
The milky-way chalkt out with suns; a
    clue,
    That guides through erring hours; and
        in full story
A taste of heav'n on earth; the pledge
    and cue
    Of a full feast! and the out-courts of
        glory.
                HENRY VAUGHAN.

SABBATH CHIMES.

THERE'S music in the morning air,
    A holy voice and sweet,
Far calling to the house of prayer
    The humblest peasant's feet.
From hill, and vale, and distant moor,
    Long as the chime is heard,
Each cottage sends its tenants poor
    For God's enriching word.

Where'er the British power hath trod,
    The cross of faith ascends,
And, like a radiant arch of God,
    The light of Scripture bends!
Deep in the forest wilderness
    The wood-built church is known;
A sheltering wing, in man's distress,
    Spread like the Saviour's own!

The warrior from his armèd tent,
    The seaman from his tide,
Far as the Sabbath chimes are sent
    In Christian nations wide,—
Thousands and tens of thousands bring
    Their sorrows to His shrine,
And taste the never-failing spring
    Of Jesus' love divine!

If, at an earthly chime, the tread
    Of million, million feet

Approach whene'er the Gospel's read
    In God's own temple seat,
How blest the sight, from death's dark
    sleep
To see God's saints arise;
And countless hosts of angels keep
    The Sabbath of the skies!
                CHARLES SWAIN.

TO THY TEMPLE I REPAIR.

To Thy temple I repair;
Lord, I love to worship there;
When within the veil I meet
Christ before the mercy-seat.

Thou, through Him, art reconciled;
I, through Him, became Thy child;
Abba, Father! give me grace
In Thy courts to seek Thy face!

While Thy glorious praise is sung,
Touch my lips, unloose my tongue,
That my joyful soul may bless
Thee, the Lord my Righteousness!

While the prayers of saints ascend,
God of love! to mine attend!
Hear me, for Thy Spirit pleads;
Hear, for Jesus intercedes!

While I hearken to Thy law,
Fill my soul with humble awe;
Till Thy Gospel bring to me
Life and immortality:

While Thy ministers proclaim
Peace and pardon in Thy Name,
Through their voice, by faith, may I
Hear Thee speaking from the sky!

From Thy house when I return,
May my heart within me burn;
And at evening let me say,
I have walk'd with God to-day!
                JAMES MONTGOMERY.

PARAPHRASE OF PSALM XXIII.

THE Lord my pasture shall prepare,
    And feed me with a Shepherd's care;
His presence shall my wants supply,
    And guard me with a watchful eye;
My noonday walks He shall attend,
    And all my midnight hours defend.

When in the sultry glebe I faint,
Or on the thirsty mountain pant,
To fertile vales and dewy meads
My weary, wandering steps He leads,
Where peaceful rivers, soft and slow,
Amid the verdant landscape flow.

Though in the paths of death I tread,
With gloomy horrors overspread,
My steadfast heart shall fear no ill,
For Thou, O Lord, art with me still;
Thy friendly crook shall give me aid,
And guide me through the dreadful shade.

Though in a bare and rugged way,
Through devious lonely wilds I stray,
Thy bounty shall my wants beguile;
The barren wilderness shall smile,
With sudden greens and herbage crown'd,
And streams shall murmur all around.
JOSEPH ADDISON.

PARAPHRASE OF PSALM XXIII.

HAPPY me! O happy sheep
Whom my God vouchsafes to keep;
Even my God, even He it is
That points me to these ways of bliss;
On whose pastures cheerful Spring
All the year doth sit and sing,
And, rejoicing, smiles to see
Their green backs wear His livery.
When my wayward breath is flying
He calls home my soul from dying,
Strokes and tames my rabid grief,
And does woo me into life:
When my simple weakness strays,
Tangled in forbidden ways,
He, my Shepherd, is my guide,
He's before me, on my side,
And behind me, He beguiles
Craft in all her knotty wiles:
He expounds the giddy wonder
Of my weary steps, and under
Spreads a path clear as the day,
Where no churlish rub says nay
To my joy-conduced feet,
Whilst they gladly go to meet
Grace and Peace, to meet new lays
Tuned to my great Shepherd's praise.
Come now, all ye terrors, sally,
Muster forth into the valley,
Where triumphant darkness hovers
With a sable wing, that covers
Brooding horror. Come then, Death,
Let the damps of thy dull breath
Overshadow even the shade,
And make Darkness' self afraid;
There my feet, even there, shall find
Way for a resolvèd mind.
Still my Shepherd, still my God,
Thou art with me; still thy rod,
And thy staff, whose influence
Gives direction, gives defence.
At the whisper of Thy word
Crown'd abundance spreads my board:
How my head in ointment swims!
How my cup o'erlooks her brims!
So, even so still may I move
By the line of Thy dear love;
Still may Thy sweet mercy spread
A shady arm above my head,
About my paths; so shall I find
The fair centre of my mind,
Thy temple, and those lovely walls
Bright ever with a beam that falls
Fresh from the pure glance of Thine eye,
Lighting to Eternity.
There I'll dwell for ever, there
Will I find a purer air
To feed my life with, there I'll sup,
Balm and nectar in my cup,
And thence my ripe soul will I breathe
Warm into the arms of Death.
RICHARD CRASHAW.

THY GOODNESS, LORD, OUR SOULS CONFESS.

THY goodness, Lord, our souls confess,
  Thy goodness we adore;
A spring, whose blessings never fail,
  A sea without a shore.

Sun, moon, and stars Thy love attest
  In every cheerful ray;
Love draws the curtains of the night,
  And love restores the day.

Thy bounty every season crowns
  With all the bliss it yields,
With joyful clusters bend the vines,
  With harvests wave the fields.

But chiefly Thy compassions, Lord,
  Are in the Gospel seen;

There, like the sun, Thy mercy shines
　Without a cloud between.
　　　　　　　　THOMAS GIBBONS.

BAPTISMAL HYMN.

IN token that thou shalt not fear
　Christ crucified to own,
We print the cross upon thee here,
　And stamp thee His alone.

In token that thou shalt not blush
　To glory in His name,
We blazon here upon thy front
　His glory and His shame.

In token that thou shalt not flinch
　Christ's quarrel to maintain,
But 'neath His banner manfully
　Firm at thy post remain;

In token that thou too shalt tread
　The path He travell'd by,
Endure the cross, despise the shame,
　And sit thee down on high;

Thus, outwardly and visibly,
　We seal thee for His own,
And may the brow that wears His cross
　Hereafter share His crown!
　　　　　　　　HENRY ALFORD.

FOUNTAIN OF MERCY! GOD OF LOVE!

FOUNTAIN of mercy! God of love!
　How rich Thy bounties are!
The rolling seasons, as they move,
　Proclaim Thy constant care.

When in the bosom of the earth
　The sower hid the grain,
Thy goodness mark'd its secret birth,
　And sent the early rain.

The spring's sweet influence was Thine,
　The plants in beauty grew;
Thou gavest refulgent suns to shine,
　And mild, refreshing dew.

These various mercies from above
　Matured the swelling grain,
A yellow harvest crowns Thy love,
　And plenty fills the plain.

Seed-time and harvest, Lord, alone
　Thou dost on man bestow;
Let him not then forget to own
　From Whom his blessings flow!

Fountain of love! our praise is Thine;
　To Thee our songs we'll raise,
And all created Nature join
　In sweet harmonious praise!
　　　　　　　　ANNE FLOWERDEW.

WHAT IS PRAYER?

PRAYER is the soul's sincere desire,
　Utter'd or unexpress'd;
The motion of a hidden fire
　That trembles in the breast.

Prayer is the burthen of a sigh,
　The falling of a tear,
The upward glancing of the eye,
　When none but God is near.

Prayer is the simplest form of speech
　That infant lips can try;
Prayer the sublimest strains that reach
　The Majesty on high.

Prayer is the contrite sinner's voice
　Returning from his ways,
While angels in their songs rejoice,
　And cry, Behold, he prays!

Prayer is the Christian's vital breath,
　The Christian's native air;
His watchword at the gates of death;
　He enters heaven with prayer.

The saints in prayer appear as one
　In word, and deed, and mind;
While with the Father and the Son
　Sweet fellowship they find.

Nor prayer is made by man alone:
　The Holy Spirit pleads;
And Jesus, on the eternal Throne,
　For mourners intercedes.

O Thou, by whom we come to God!
　The Life, the Truth, the Way!
The path of prayer Thyself hast trod:
　Lord! teach us how to pray!
　　　　　　　　JAMES MONTGOMERY.

THE HOUR OF PRAYER.

CHILD, amidst the flowers at play,
　While the red light fades away:
Mother, with thine earnest eye
　Ever following silently:
Father, by the breeze of eve
Call'd thy harvest-work to leave,—
Pray! ere yet the dark hours be,
Lift the heart, and bend the knee.

Traveller in the stranger's land,
Far from thine own household band:
Mourner, haunted by the tone
Of a voice from this world gone:
Captive, in whose narrow cell
Sunshine hath not leave to dwell:
Sailor, on the darkening sea,
Lift the heart, and bend the knee.

Warrior, that from battle won
Breathest now at set of sun;
Woman, o'er the lowly slain,
Weeping on his burial-plain:
Ye that triumph, ye that sigh,
Kindred by one holy tie,
Heaven's first star alike ye see,
Lift the heart and bend the knee.
　　　　　FELICIA DOROTHEA HEMANS.

HEAR MY PRAYER, O HEAVENLY FATHER.

HEAR my prayer, O Heavenly Father,
　Ere I lay me down to sleep:
Bid Thy angels, pure and holy,
　Round my bed their vigil keep.

Great my sins are, but Thy mercy
　Far outweighs them every one:
Down before Thy cross I cast them
　Trusting in Thy help alone.

Keep me, through this night of peril,
　Underneath its boundless shade;
Take me to Thy rest, I pray Thee,
　When my pilgrimage is made!

None shall measure out Thy patience
　By the span of human thought;
None shall bound the tender mercies
　Which Thy Holy Son hath wrought.

Pardon all my past transgressions;
　Give me strength for days to come;
Guide and guard me with Thy blessing,
　Till Thine angels bid me home!
　　　　　HARRIET T. PARR.

NEARER, MY GOD, TO THEE.

NEARER, my God, to Thee,
　Nearer to Thee!
E'en though it be a cross
　That raiseth me;
Still all my song shall be,
Nearer, my God, to Thee,
　Nearer to Thee!

Though like the wanderer,
　The sun gone down,
Darkness be over me,
　My rest a stone;
Yet in my dreams I'd be
Nearer, my God, to Thee,
　Nearer to Thee!

There let the way appear
　Steps unto Heaven;
All that Thou send'st to me
　In mercy given;
Angels to beckon me
Nearer, my God, to Thee,
　Nearer to Thee!

Then, with my waking thoughts
　Bright with Thy praise,
Out of my stony griefs
　Bethel I'll raise;
So by my woes to be
Nearer, my God, to Thee,
　Nearer to Thee!

Or if on joyful wing
　Cleaving the sky,
Sun, moon, and stars forgot,
　Upward I fly,
Still all my song shall be,
Nearer, my God, to Thee,
　Nearer to Thee!
　　　　　SARAH FLOWER ADAMS.

WALKING WITH GOD.
Gen. v. 24.

OH for a closer walk with God,
　A calm and heavenly frame!

A light to shine upon the road
  That leads me to the Lamb!

Where is the blessedness I knew
  When first I saw the Lord?
Where is the soul-refreshing view
  Of Jesus and His word?

What peaceful hours I once enjoy'd!
  How sweet their memory still!
But they have left an aching void
  The world can never fill.

Return, O holy Dove! return,
  Sweet messenger of rest!
I hate the sins that made Thee mourn,
  And drove Thee from my breast.

The dearest idol I have known,
  Whate'er that idol be,
Help me to tear it from Thy throne,
  And worship only Thee!

So shall my walk be close with God,
  Calm and serene my frame;
So purer light shall mark the road
  That leads me to the Lamb!
WILLIAM COWPER.

GOD.

THOU hast made me, and shall Thy work decay?
  Repair me now, for now mine end doth haste;
  I run to death, and death meets me as fast,
And all my pleasures are like yesterday.
I dare not move my dim eyes any way,
  Despair behind, and death before doth cast
  Such terror; and my feeble flesh doth waste
By sin in it, which it towards hell doth weigh.
Only Thou art above, and when towards Thee
  By Thy leave I can look, I rise again;
But our old subtle foe so tempteth me,
  That not one hour myself I can sustain:
Thy grace may wing me to prevent His art,
And Thou like adamant draw mine iron heart.
JOHN DONNE.

THE INNER CALM.

CALM me, my God, and keep me calm,
  While these hot breezes blow;
Be like the night-dew's cooling balm
  Upon earth's fever'd brow!

Calm me, my God, and keep me calm,
  Soft resting on Thy breast;
Soothe me with holy hymn and psalm,
  And bid my spirit rest.

Calm me, my God, and keep me calm;
  Let Thine outstretchèd wing
Be like the shade of Elim's palm
  Beside her desert spring.

Yes; keep me calm, though loud and rude
  The sounds my ear that greet;
Calm in the closet's solitude,
  Calm in the bustling street;

Calm in the hour of buoyant health,
  Calm in my hour of pain;
Calm in my poverty or wealth,
  Calm in my loss or gain;

Calm in the sufferance of wrong,
  Like Him who bore my shame;
Calm 'mid the threatening, taunting throng
  Who hate Thy holy Name;

Calm when the great world's news with power
  My listening spirit stir:
Let not the tidings of the hour
  E'er find too fond an ear;

Calm as the ray of sun or star,
  Which storms assail in vain,
Moving unruffled through earth's war
  Th' eternal calm to gain!
HORATIUS BONAR.

RESIGNATION.

O GOD! whose thunder shakes the sky,
  Whose eye this atom-globe surveys,
To Thee, my only rock, I fly,—
  Thy mercy in Thy justice praise.

The mystic mazes of Thy will,
  The shadows of celestial night,
Are past the power of human skill;
  But what the Eternal acts is right.

Oh teach me, in the trying hour—
   When anguish swells the dewy tear—
To still my sorrows, own Thy power,
   Thy goodness love, Thy justice fear.

If in this bosom aught but Thee,
   Encroaching, sought a boundless sway,
Omniscience could the danger see,
   And mercy look the cause away.

Then why, my soul, dost thou complain—
   Why drooping seek the dark recess?
Shake off the melancholy chain;
   For God created all to bless.

But ah! my breast is human still;
   The rising sigh, the falling tear,
My languid vitals' feeble rill,
   The sickness of my soul declare.

But yet, with fortitude resign'd,
   I'll thank the inflictor of the blow—
Forbid the sigh, compose my mind,
   Nor let the gush of misery flow.

The gloomy mantle of the night,
   Which on my sinking spirit steals,
Will vanish at the morning light,
   Which God, my east, my sun, reveals.
              THOMAS CHATTERTON.

RESIGNATION.

LORD, it belongs not to my care
   Whether I die or live:
To love and serve Thee is my share,
   And this Thy grace must give.

If life be long, I will be glad,
   That I may long obey;
If short, yet why should I be sad
   To soar to endless day?

Christ leads me through no darker rooms
   Than He went through before;
He that into God's kingdom comes
   Must enter by His door.
Come, Lord, when grace has made me meet
   Thy blessed face to see;
For if Thy work on earth be sweet,
   What will Thy glory be?

Then shall I end my sad complaints,
   And weary, sinful days;
And join with the triumphant saints,
   That sing Jehovah's praise.
My knowledge of that life is small,
   The eye of faith is dim;
But 'tis enough that Christ knows all,
   And I shall be with Him.
              RICHARD BAXTER.

THY WILL BE DONE.

MY God and Father, while I stray
Far from my home, on life's rough way,
Oh teach me from my heart to say,
   Thy will be done!

Though dark my path and sad my lot,
Let me be still and murmur not,
Or breathe the prayer divinely taught,
   Thy will be done!

What though in lonely grief I sigh
For friends beloved, no longer nigh,
Submissive still would I reply,
   Thy will be done!

Though Thou hast call'd me to resign
What most I prized, it ne'er was mine;
I have but yielded what was Thine;
   Thy will be done!

Should grief or sickness waste away
My life in premature decay,
My Father! still I strive to say,
   Thy will be done!

Let but my fainting heart be blest
With Thy sweet Spirit for its guest,
My God, to Thee I leave the rest;
   Thy will be done!

Renew my will from day to day;
Blend it with Thine; and take away
All that now makes it hard to say,
   Thy will be done!

Then, when on earth I breathe no more
The prayer, oft mix'd with tears before,
I'll sing upon a happier shore,
   Thy will be done!
              CHARLOTTE ELLIOTT.

THE WILL OF GOD.

I WORSHIP thee, sweet Will of God!
   And all Thy ways adore,

And every day I live I seem
  To love Thee more and more.

Thou wert the end, the blessed rule
  Of our Saviour's toils and tears;
Thou wert the passion of His heart
  Those three-and-thirty years.

And He hath breathed into my soul
  A special love of Thee,
A love to lose my will in His,
  And by that loss be free.

I love to see Thee bring to naught
  The plans of wily men;
When simple hearts outwit the wise,
  Oh, Thou art loveliest then!

The headstrong world, it presses hard
  Upon the Church full oft,
And then how easily Thou turn'st
  The hard ways into soft!

I love to kiss each print where Thou
  Hast set Thine unseen feet:
I cannot fear Thee, blessed Will!
  Thine empire is so sweet.

When obstacles and trials seem
  Like prison-walls to be,
I do the little I can do,
  And leave the rest to Thee.

I know not what it is to doubt;
  My heart is ever gay;
I run no risk, for come what will
  Thou always hast Thy way.

I have no cares, O blessed Will!
  For all my cares are Thine;
I live in triumph, Lord; for Thou
  Hast made Thy triumphs mine.

And when it seems no chance or change
  From grief can set me free,
Hope finds its strength in helplessness,
  And gayly waits on Thee.

Man's weakness waiting upon God
  Its end can never miss,
For men on earth no work can do
  More angel-like than this.

Ride on, ride on, triumphantly,
  Thou glorious Will! ride on;
Faith's pilgrim sons behind Thee take
  The road that Thou hast gone.

He always wins who sides with God,
  To him no chance is lost;
God's Will is sweetest to him when
  It triumphs at his cost.

Ill that He blesses is our good,
  And unblest good is ill;
And all is right that seems most wrong,
  If it be His sweet Will!
FREDERICK WILLIAM FABER.

THY WILL BE DONE.

FATHER, I know that all my life
  Is portion'd out for me,
And the changes that are sure to come
  I do not fear to see;
But I ask Thee for a present mind,
  Intent on pleasing Thee.

I ask Thee for a thoughtful love,
  Through constant watching wise,
To meet the glad with joyful smiles,
  And wipe the weeping eyes;
And a heart at leisure from itself,
  To soothe and sympathize.

I would not have the restless will
  That hurries to and fro;
Seeking for some great thing to do,
  Or secret thing to know:
I would be treated as a child,
  And guided where I go.

Wherever in the world I am,
  In whatsoe'er estate,
I have a fellowship with hearts
  To keep and cultivate,
And a work of lowly love to do,
  For the Lord on whom I wait.

So I ask Thee for the daily strength
  To none that ask denied,
And a mind to blend with outward life,
  While keeping at Thy side;
Content to fill a little space,
  If Thou be glorified.

And if some things I do not ask
  In my cup of blessing be,
I would have my spirit fill'd the more
  With grateful love to Thee;
More careful, not to serve Thee much,
  But to please Thee perfectly.

There are briers besetting every path,
  That call for patient care;

There is a cross in every lot,
  And an earnest need for prayer;
But a lowly heart, that leans on Thee,
  Is happy anywhere.

In a service which Thy will appoints
  There are no bonds for me;
For my inmost heart is taught the Truth
  That makes Thy children free;
And a life of self-renouncing love
  Is a life of liberty.
          ANNA LÆTITIA WARING.

THY WILL BE DONE.

WE see not, know not; all our way
Is night,—with Thee alone is day:
From out the torrent's troubled drift,
Above the storm our prayers we lift,
  Thy will be done!

The flesh may fail, the heart may faint,
But who are we to make complaint,
Or dare to plead, in times like these,
The weakness of our love of ease?
  Thy will be done!

We take with solemn thankfulness
Our burden up, nor ask it less,
And count it joy that even we
May suffer, serve, or wait for Thee,
  Whose will be done!

Though dim as yet in tint and line,
We trace Thy picture's wise design,
And thank Thee that our age supplies
Its dark relief of sacrifice.
  Thy will be done!

And if, in our unworthiness,
Thy sacrificial wine we press;
If from Thy ordeal's heated bars
Our feet are seam'd with crimson scars,
  Thy will be done!

If, for the age to come, this hour
Of trial hath vicarious power,
And, blest by Thee, our present pain
Be Liberty's eternal gain,
  Thy will be done!

Strike, Thou the Master, we Thy keys,
The anthem of the destinies!
The minor of Thy loftier strain,
Our hearts shall breathe the old refrain,
  Thy will be done!
          JOHN GREENLEAF WHITTIER.

JUST AS I AM.

JUST as I am, without one plea
But that Thy Blood was shed for me,
And that Thou bidd'st me come to Thee,
  O Lamb of God, I come!

Just as I am, and waiting not
To rid my soul of one dark blot,
To Thee, whose Blood can cleanse each spot,
  O Lamb of God, I come!

Just as I am, though toss'd about
With many a conflict, many a doubt,
Fightings and fears within, without,
  O Lamb of God, I come!

Just as I am, poor, wretched, blind,
Sight, riches, healing of the mind,
Yea, all I need, in Thee to find,
  O Lamb of God, I come!

Just as I am, Thou wilt receive,
Wilt welcome, pardon, cleanse, relieve!
Because Thy promise I believe,
  O Lamb of God, I come!

Just as I am (Thy Love unknown
Has broken every barrier down),
Now, to be Thine, yea, Thine alone,
  O Lamb of God, I come!

Just as I am, of that free love
The breadth, length, depth, and height to prove,
Here for a season, then above,
  O Lamb of God, I come!
          CHARLOTTE ELLIOTT.

HYMN FOR FAMILY WORSHIP.

O LORD, another day is flown;
  And we, a lonely band,
Are met once more before Thy throne
  To bless Thy fostering hand.

And wilt Thou lend a listening ear
  To praises low as ours?

Thou wilt! for Thou dost love to hear
The song which meekness pours.

And, Jesus, Thou Thy smiles wilt deign
  As we before Thee pray;
For Thou didst bless the infant train,
  And we are less than they.

Oh let Thy grace perform its part,
  And let contention cease;
And shed abroad in every heart
  Thine everlasting peace!

Thus chasten'd, cleansed, entirely Thine,
  A flock by Jesus led,
The Sun of holiness shall shine
  In glory on our head.

And Thou wilt turn our wandering feet,
  And Thou wilt bless our way,
Till worlds shall fade, and faith shall greet
  The dawn of lasting day!
HENRY KIRKE WHITE.

LEAD, KINDLY LIGHT.

LEAD, kindly Light, amid th' encircling gloom,
  Lead Thou me on;
The night is dark, and I am far from home;
  Lead Thou me on;
Keep Thou my feet; I do not ask to see
The distant scene; one step enough for me.

I was not ever thus, nor pray'd that Thou
  Shouldst lead me on;
I loved to choose and see my path; but now
  Lead Thou me on!
I loved the garish day, and, spite of fears,
Pride ruled my will. Remember not past years!

So long Thy power has blest me, sure it still
  Will lead me on
O'er moor and fen, o'er crag and torrent, till
  The night is gone,
And with the morn those angel faces smile
Which I have loved long since, and lost a while!
JOHN HENRY NEWMAN.

WHEN GATHERING CLOUDS AROUND I VIEW.

WHEN gathering clouds around I view,
And days are dark and friends are few,
On Him I lean, who not in vain
Experienced every human pain.
He sees my wants, allays my fears,
And counts and treasures up my tears.

If aught should tempt my soul to stray
From heavenly wisdom's narrow way;
To fly the good I would pursue,
Or do the sin I would not do;
Still He, who felt temptation's power,
Shall guard me in that dangerous hour.

If wounded love my bosom swell,
Deceived by those I prized too well,
He shall his pitying aid bestow,
Who felt on earth severer woe;
At once betray'd, denied, or fled,
By those who shared His daily bread.

If vexing thoughts within me rise,
And, sore dismay'd, my spirit dies;
Still He, who once vouchsafed to bear
The sickening anguish of despair,
Shall sweetly soothe, shall gently dry,
The throbbing heart, the streaming eye.

When sorrowing o'er some stone I bend,
Which covers what was once a friend,
And from his voice, his hand, his smile,
Divides me for a little while;
Thou, Saviour, mark'st the tears I shed,
For Thou didst weep o'er Lazarus dead!

And oh, when I have safely past
Through every conflict but the last,
Still, still unchanging, watch beside
My bed of death, for Thou hast died!
Then point to realms of cloudless day,
And wipe the latest tear away!
SIR ROBERT GRANT.

LONG DID I TOIL.

LONG did I toil, and knew no earthly rest;
  Far did I rove, and found no certain home;
At last I sought them in His sheltering breast,
  Who opes His arms, and bids the weary come:

With Him I found a home, a rest divine;
And I since then am His, and He is mine.

Yes! He is mine! and naught of earthly things,
  Not all the charms of pleasure, wealth, or power,
The fame of heroes, or the pomp of kings,
  Could tempt me to forego His love an hour.
Go, worthless world, I cry, with all that's thine!
Go! I my Saviour's am, and He is mine.

The good I have is from His stores supplied;
  The ill is only what He deems the best;
He for my Friend, I'm rich with naught beside;
  And poor without Him, though of all possest:
Changes may come; I take, or I resign;
Content, while I am His, while He is mine.

Whate'er may change, in Him no change is seen;
  A glorious Sun, that wanes not nor declines;
Above the clouds and storms He walks serene,
  And sweetly on His people's darkness shines:
All may depart; I fret not, nor repine,
While I my Saviour's am, while He is mine.

He stays me falling, lifts me up when down,
  Reclaims me wandering, guards from every foe;
Plants on my worthless brow the victor's crown;
  Which, in return, before His feet I throw,
Grieved that I cannot better grace His shrine,
Who deigns to own me His, as He is mine.

While here, alas! I know but half His love,
  But half discern Him, and but half adore;
But when I meet Him in the realms above,
  I hope to love Him better, praise Him more,
And feel, and tell, amid the choir divine,
How fully I am His, and He is mine.
              HENRY FRANCIS LYTE.

RISE, MY SOUL, AND STRETCH THY WINGS.

RISE, my soul, and stretch thy wings,
  Thy better portion trace;
Rise from transitory things
  Toward heaven, thy native place.
Sun and moon and stars decay;
  Time shall soon this earth remove;
Rise, my soul, and haste away
  To seats prepared above.

Rivers to the ocean run,
  Nor stay in all their course;
Fire ascending seeks the sun;
  Both speed them to their source:
So my soul, derived from God,
  Pants to view His glorious face,
Forward tends to His abode,
  To rest in His embrace.

Fly me riches, fly me cares,
  Whilst I that coast explore;
Flattering world, with all thy snares
  Solicit me no more!
Pilgrims fix not here their home;
  Strangers tarry but a night;
When the last dear morn is come,
  They'll rise to joyful light.

Cease, ye pilgrims, cease to mourn;
  Press onward to the prize;
Soon our Saviour will return
  Triumphant in the skies.
Yet a season, and you know
  Happy entrance will be given,
All our sorrows left below,
  And earth exchanged for heaven.
              ROBERT SEAGRAVE.

HOW KINDLY HAST THOU LED ME!

OH how kindly hast Thou led me,
  Heavenly Father, day by day!
Found my dwelling, clothed and fed me,
  Furnish'd friends to cheer my way!
Didst Thou bless me, didst Thou chasten,
  With Thy smile, or with Thy rod,

'Twas that still my step might hasten
  Homeward, heavenward, to my God!
Oh how slowly have I often
  Follow'd where Thy hand would draw!
How Thy kindness fail'd to soften!
  How Thy chastening fail'd to awe!
Make me for Thy rest more ready
  As Thy path is longer trod:
Keep me in Thy friendship steady,
  Till Thou call me home, my God!
THOMAS GRINFIELD.

WRESTLING JACOB.

COME, O thou Traveller unknown,
  Whom still I hold, but cannot see,
My company before is gone,
  And I am left alone with Thee;
With Thee all night I mean to stay,
And wrestle till the break of day.

I need not tell Thee who I am,
  My misery or sin declare;
Thyself hast call'd me by my name;
  Look on Thy hands, and read it there!
But Who, I ask Thee, Who art thou?
Tell me Thy Name, and tell me now.

In vain Thou strugglest to get free,
  I never will unloose my hold;
Art thou the Man that died for me?
  The secret of Thy love unfold.
Wrestling, I will not let Thee go,
Till I Thy Name, Thy Nature know.

Wilt Thou not yet to me reveal
  Thy new, unutterable Name?
Tell me, I still beseech Thee, tell;
  To know it now, resolved I am:
Wrestling, I will not let Thee go,
Till I Thy Name, Thy Nature know.

'Tis all in vain to hold Thy tongue,
  Or touch the hollow of my thigh;
Though every sinew be unstrung,
  Out of my arms Thou shalt not fly:
Wrestling, I will not let Thee go,
Till I Thy Name, Thy Nature know.

What though my shrinking flesh complain,
  And murmur to contend so long?
I rise superior to my pain;
  When I am weak, then I am strong:
And when my all of strength shall fail
I shall with the God-Man prevail.

My strength is gone; my nature dies;
  I sink beneath Thy weighty hand,
Faint to revive, and fall to rise;
  I fall, and yet by faith I stand:
I stand, and will not let Thee go,
Till I Thy Name, Thy Nature know.

Yield to me now, for I am weak,
  But confident in self-despair;
Speak to my heart, in blessings speak,
  Be conquer'd by my instant prayer!
Speak, or Thou never hence shalt move,
And tell me, if Thy Name is Love.

'Tis Love! 'tis Love! Thou diedst for me!
  I hear Thy whisper in my heart!
The morning breaks, the shadows flee;
  Pure universal Love Thou art!
To me, to all, Thy bowels move!
Thy Nature, and Thy Name, is Love!

My prayer hath power with God; the grace
  Unspeakable I now receive;
Through faith I see Thee face to face,
  I see Thee face to face and live:
In vain I have not wept and strove;
Thy Nature, and Thy Name, is Love.

I know Thee, Saviour, who Thou art;
  Jesus, the feeble sinner's Friend!
Nor wilt Thou with the night depart,
  But stay, and love me to the end!
Thy mercies never shall remove,
Thy Nature, and Thy Name, is Love!

The Sun of Righteousness on me
  Hath rose, with healing in His wings;
Wither'd my nature's strength, from Thee
  My soul its life and succor brings;
My help is all laid up above;
Thy Nature, and Thy Name, is Love.

Contented now upon my thigh
  I halt, till life's short journey end;
All helplessness, all weakness, I
  On Thee alone for strength depend;
Nor have I power from Thee to move;
Thy Nature, and Thy Name, is Love.

Lame as I am, I take the prey,
  Hell, earth, and sin with ease o'ercome;
I leap for joy, pursue my way,
  And as a bounding hart fly home!

Through all eternity to prove,
　Thy Nature, and Thy Name, is Love!
　　　　　　　　CHARLES WESLEY.

WHILST THEE I SEEK.

WHILST Thee I seek, protecting Power,
　Be my vain wishes still'd!
And may this consecrated hour
　With better hopes be fill'd.

Thy love the power of thought bestow'd:
　To Thee my thoughts would soar:
Thy mercy o'er my life has flow'd,
　That mercy I adore.

In each event of life, how clear
　Thy ruling hand I see!
Each blessing to my soul more dear,
　Because conferr'd by Thee.

In every joy that crowns my days,
　In every pain I bear,
My heart shall find delight in praise,
　Or seek relief in prayer.

When gladness wings my favor'd hour,
　Thy love my thoughts shall fill;
Resign'd, when storms of sorrow lower,
　My soul shall meet Thy will.

My lifted eye, without a tear,
　The gathering storms shall see;
My steadfast heart shall know no fear;
　That heart shall rest on Thee.
　　　　　　　　HELEN MARIA WILLIAMS.

THE RIGHT MUST WIN.

OH, it is hard to work for God,
　To rise and take His part
Upon this battle-field of earth,
　And not sometimes lose heart!

He hides Himself so wondrously,
　As though there were no God;
He is least seen when all the powers
　Of ill are most abroad.

Or He deserts us at the hour
　The fight is all but lost;
And seems to leave us to ourselves
　Just when we need Him most.

Yes, there is less to try our faith
　In our mysterious creed,
Than in the godless look of earth
　In these our hours of need.

Ill masters good, good seems to change
　To ill with greatest ease;
And, worst of all, the good with good
　Is at cross-purposes.

It is not so, but so it looks;
　And we lose courage then;
And doubts will come if God hath kept
　His promises to men.

Ah! God is other than we think;
　His ways are far above,
Far beyond reason's height, and reach'd
　Only by childlike love.

The look, the fashion of God's ways
　Love's lifelong study are;
She can be bold, and guess and act,
　When Reason would not dare.

She has a prudence of her own;
　Her step is firm and free;
Yet there is cautious science too
　In her simplicity.

Workman of God! oh lose not heart,
　But learn what God is like;
And in the darkest battle-field
　Thou shalt know where to strike.

Thrice blessed is he to whom is given
　The instinct that can tell
That God is on the field when He
　Is most invisible.

Blest too is he who can divine
　Where real right doth lie,
And dares to take the side that seems
　Wrong to man's blindfold eye.

Then learn to scorn the praise of men,
　And learn to lose with God;
For Jesus won the world through shame,
　And beckons thee His road.

God's glory is a wondrous thing,
　Most strange in all its ways,
And, of all things on earth, least like
　What men agree to praise.

As He can endless glory weave
  From what men reckon shame,
In His own world He is content
  To play a losing game.

Muse on His justice, downcast soul!
  Muse and take better heart;
Back with thine angel to the field,
  And bravely do thy part!

God's justice is a bed where we
  Our anxious hearts may lay,
And, weary with ourselves, may sleep
  Our discontent away.

For right is right, since God is God;
  And right the day must win;
To doubt would be disloyalty,
  To falter would be sin!
            FREDERICK WILLIAM FABER.

JOY AND PEACE IN BELIEVING.

SOMETIMES a light surprises
  The Christian while he sings;
It is the Lord, who rises
  With healing in His wings:
When comforts are declining,
  He grants the soul again
A season of clear shining
  To cheer it after rain.

In holy contemplation
  We sweetly then pursue
The theme of God's salvation,
  And find it ever new:
Set free from present sorrow,
  We cheerfully can say,
E'en let the unknown to-morrow
  Bring with it what it may.

It can bring with it nothing,
  But He will bear us through;
Who gives the lilies clothing
  Will clothe His people too;
Beneath the spreading heavens
  No creature but is fed;
And He, who feeds the ravens,
  Will give His children bread.

Though vine nor fig tree neither
  Their wonted fruit shall bear;
Though all the field should wither,
  Nor flocks nor herds be there;

Yet, God the same abiding,
  His praise shall tune my voice;
For, while in Him confiding,
  I cannot but rejoice.
            WILLIAM COWPER.

GUIDE ME, O THOU GREAT JEHOVAH!

GUIDE me, O Thou great Jehovah!
  Pilgrim through this barren land;
I am weak, but Thou art mighty,
  Hold me with Thy powerful hand.
    Bread of Heaven! Bread of Heaven!
Feed me now and evermore!

Open now the crystal fountain,
  Whence the healing streams do flow;
Let the fiery cloudy pillar
  Lead me all my journey through;
    Strong Deliverer! strong Deliverer!
Be thou still my Strength and Shield!

When I tread the verge of Jordan,
  Bid my anxious fears subside;
Death of deaths, and hell's destruction,
  Land me safe on Canaan's side;
    Songs of praises, songs of praises,
I will ever give to Thee!

Musing on my habitation,
  Musing on my heavenly home,
Fills my soul with holy longing;
  Come, my Jesus, quickly come.
    Vanity is all I see;
    Lord, I long to be with thee!
            WILLIAM WILLIAMS.

THE CHILD LEANS ON ITS PARENT'S BREAST.

THE child leans on its parent's breast,
Leaves there its cares, and is at rest;
The bird sits singing by his nest,
        And tells aloud
His trust in God, and so is blest
        'Neath every cloud.

He has no store, he sows no seed,
Yet sings aloud, and doth not heed;
By flowing stream or grassy mead
        He sings to shame
Men, who forget, in fear of need,
        A Father's name.

The heart that trusts for ever sings,
And feels as light as it had wings;
A well of peace within it springs;
   Come good or ill,
Whate'er to-day, to-morrow brings,
  It is His will.
    ISAAC WILLIAMS.

I LOVE THY KINGDOM, LORD.

I LOVE Thy kingdom, Lord,
 The house of Thine abode,
The Church our blest Redeemer saved
 With His own precious blood.

I love Thy Church, O God!
 Her walls before Thee stand,
Dear as the apple of Thine eye,
 And graven on Thy hand.

If e'er to bless Thy sons,
 My voice, or hands, deny,
These hands let useful skill forsake,
 This voice in silence die.

If e'er my heart forget
 Her welfare or her woe,
Let every joy this heart forsake,
 And every grief o'erflow.

For her my tears shall fall;
 For her my prayers ascend;
To her my cares and toils be given,
 Till toils and cares shall end.

Beyond my highest joy
 I prize her heavenly ways,
Her sweet communion, solemn vows,
 Her hymns of love and praise.

Jesus, Thou Friend divine,
 Our Saviour and our King,
Thy hand from every snare and foe
 Shall great deliverance bring.

Sure as Thy truth shall last,
 To Zion shall be given
The brightest glories earth can yield,
 And brighter bliss of Heaven.
    TIMOTHY DWIGHT.
 (From the Latin of ST. AMBROSE.)

"DUM VIVIMUS VIVAMUS."

"LIVE while you live!" the epicure would say,
"And seize the pleasures of the present day!"
"Live while you live!" the sacred Preacher cries,
"And give to God each moment as it flies!"
Lord, in my view let both united be:
I live in pleasure while I live to Thee.
    PHILIP DODDRIDGE.

CHILDREN OF THE HEAVENLY KING.

CHILDREN of the Heavenly King,
As ye journey, sweetly sing;
Sing your Saviour's worthy praise,
Glorious in His works and ways!

We are travelling home to God,
In the way the Fathers trod;
They are happy now; and we
Soon their happiness shall see.

O ye banish'd seed, be glad!
Christ our Advocate is made;
Us to save, our flesh assumes;
Brother to our souls becomes.

Shout, ye little flock, and blest!
You on Jesus' Throne shall rest;
There your seat is now prepared,
There your kingdom and reward.

Lift your eyes, ye sons of Light!
Zion's city is in sight:
There our endless home shall be,
There our Lord we soon shall see.

Fear not, brethren; joyful stand
On the borders of your land;
Jesus Christ, your Father's Son,
Bids you undismay'd go on.

Lord! obediently we go,
Gladly leaving all below:
Only Thou our leader be,
And we still will follow Thee!

Seal our love, our labors end;
Let us to Thy bliss ascend;

Let us to Thy kingdom come;
Lord! we long to be at home.
JOHN CENNICK.

EARLY PIETY.

BY cool Siloam's shady rill
　How sweet the lily grows!
How sweet the breath beneath the hill
　Of Sharon's dewy rose!
Lo! such the child whose early feet
　The paths of peace have trod,
Whose secret heart with influence sweet
　Is upward drawn to God.

By cool Siloam's shady rill
　The lily must decay;
The rose that blooms beneath the hill
　Must shortly fade away;
And soon, too soon, the wintry hour
　Of man's maturer age
Will shake the soul with sorrow's power,
　And stormy passion's rage.

O Thou whose infant feet were found
　Within Thy Father's shrine,
Whose years with changeless virtue crown'd
　Were all alike divine:
Dependent on Thy bounteous breath,
　We seek Thy grace alone
In childhood, manhood, age, and death,
　To keep us still Thine own.
REGINALD HEBER.

O HAPPY SOUL, THAT LIVES ON HIGH!

O HAPPY soul, that lives on high,
　While men lie grovelling here!
His hopes are fix'd above the sky,
　And faith forbids his fear.

His conscience knows no secret stings,
　While peace and joy combine
To form a life whose holy springs
　Are hidden and divine.

He waits in secret on his God,
　His God in secret sees;
Let earth be all in arms abroad,
　He dwells in heavenly peace.

His pleasures rise from things unseen,
　Beyond this world and time,
Where neither eyes nor ears have been,
　Nor thoughts of sinners climb.

He wants no pomp, nor royal throne,
　To raise his figure here;
Content and pleased to live unknown,
　Till Christ, his Life, appear.

He looks to heaven's eternal hill,
　To meet that glorious day,
And patient waits his Saviour's will,
　To fetch his soul away.
ISAAC WATTS.

HEAVENLY WISDOM.

OH, happy is the man who hears
　Instruction's warning voice,
And who celestial Wisdom makes
　His early, only choice.

For she has treasures greater far
　Than east or west unfold,
And her reward is more secure
　Than is the gain of gold.

In her right hand she holds to view
　A length of happy years,
And in her left, the prize of fame
　And honor bright appears.

She guides the young, with innocence,
　In pleasure's path to tread;
A crown of glory she bestows
　Upon the hoary head.

According as her labors rise,
　So her rewards increase;
Her ways are ways of pleasantness,
　And all her paths are peace.
JOHN LOGAN.

THE HEART'S SONG.

IN the silent midnight watches,
　List—thy bosom door!
How it knocketh, knocketh, knocketh,
　Knocketh evermore!
Say not 'tis thy pulses beating;
　'Tis thy heart of sin:
'Tis thy Saviour knocks, and crieth,
　Rise and let Me in!

Death comes down with reckless footstep
　To the hall and hut;

Think you Death will stand a-knocking
  Where the door is shut?
Jesus waiteth—waiteth—waiteth;
  But thy door is fast!
Grieved, away thy Saviour goeth:
  Death breaks in at last.

Then 'tis thine to stand entreating
  Christ to let thee in:
At the gate of heaven beating,
  Wailing for thy sin.
Nay, alas! thou foolish virgin,
  Hast thou then forgot,
Jesus waited long to know thee,
  But He knows thee not!

ARTHUR CLEVELAND COXE.

DELIGHT IN GOD ONLY.

I LOVE, and have some cause to love, the earth—
  She is my Maker's creature, therefore good.
She is my mother, for she gave me birth;
  She is my tender nurse, she gives me food:
But what's a creature, Lord, compared with Thee?
Or what's my mother or my nurse to me?

I love the air—her dainty sweets refresh
  My drooping soul, and to new sweets invite me;
Her shrill-mouth'd choir sustain me with their flesh,
  And with their polyphonian notes delight me:
But what's the air, or all the sweets that she
Can bless my soul withal, compared to Thee?

I love the sea—she is my fellow-creature,
  My careful purveyor; she provides me store;
She walls me round; she makes my diet greater;
  She wafts my treasure from a foreign shore:
But, Lord of oceans, when compared with Thee,
What is the ocean or her wealth to me?

To Heaven's high city I direct my journey,
  Whose spangled suburbs entertain mine eye—
Mine eye, by contemplation's great attorney,
  Transcends the crystal pavement of the sky:
But what is Heaven, great God, compared to Thee?
Without thy presence, Heaven's no Heaven to me.

Without Thy presence, earth gives no refection;
  Without Thy presence, sea affords no treasure;
Without Thy presence, air's a rank infection;
  Without Thy presence, Heaven itself's no pleasure:
If not possess'd, if not enjoy'd in Thee,
What's earth, or sea, or air, or Heaven to me?

The highest honors that the world can boast
  Are subjects far too low for my desire;
The brightest beams of glory are, at most,
  But dying sparkles of Thy living fire;
The proudest flames that earth can kindle be
But nightly glow-worms if compared to Thee.

Without Thy presence, wealth is bags of cares;
  Wisdom but folly; joy, disquiet sadness;
Friendship is treason, and delights are snares;
  Pleasure's but pain, and mirth but pleasing madness—
Without Thee, Lord, things be not what they be,
Nor have their being, when compared with Thee.

In having all things, and not Thee, what have I?
  Not having Thee, what have my labors got?

Let me enjoy but Thee, what further crave
    I?
  And having Thee alone, what have I
    not?
I wish nor sea, nor land, nor would I be
Possess'd of Heaven, Heaven unpossess'd
    of Thee!
                    FRANCIS QUARLES.

THE STAR OF BETHLEHEM.

WHEN marshall'd on the nightly plain,
  The glittering host bestud the sky;
One star alone, of all the train,
  Can fix the sinner's wandering eye.

Hark! hark! to God the chorus breaks,
  From every host, from every gem;
But one alone the Saviour speaks,
  It is the Star of Bethlehem.

Once on the raging seas I rode,
  The storm was loud—the night was dark,
The ocean yawn'd—and rudely blow'd
  The wind that toss'd my foundering
    bark.

Deep horror then my vitals froze,
  Death-struck, I ceased the tide to stem;
When suddenly a star arose,
  It was the Star of Bethlehem.

It was my guide, my light, my all,
  It bade my dark forebodings cease;
And through the storm and dangers' thrall
  It led me to the port of peace.

Now safely moor'd—my perils o'er,
  I'll sing, first in night's diadem,
For ever and for evermore,
  The Star—the Star of Bethlehem!
                    HENRY KIRKE WHITE.

LIFE.

IF life's pleasures cheer thee,
  Give them not thy heart,
    Lest the gifts ensnare thee
      From thy God to part:
  His praises speak, His favor seek,
    Fix there thy hopes' foundation;
  Love him, and He shall ever be
    The Rock of thy salvation.

If sorrow e'er befall thee,
  Painful though it be,
    Let not fear appall thee:
      To thy Saviour flee:
  He, ever near, thy prayer will hear,
    And calm thy perturbation;
  The waves of woe shall ne'er o'erflow
    The Rock of thy salvation.

Death shall never harm thee,
  Shrink not from his blow,
    For thy God shall arm thee,
      And victory bestow:
  For death shall bring to thee no sting,
    The grave no desolation;
  'Tis gain to die, with Jesus nigh,
    The Rock of thy salvation.
                    FRANCIS SCOTT KEY.

ART THOU WEARY?

ART thou weary, art thou languid,
    Art thou sore distress'd?
"Come to Me," saith One, "and coming,
    Be at rest."

Hath He marks to lead me to Him,
    If He be my Guide?
"In His feet and hands are wound-prints,
    And His side."

Is there diadem, as Monarch,
    That His brow adorns?
"Yea, a crown, in very surety,
    But of thorns."

If I find Him, if I follow,
    What His guerdon here?
"Many a sorrow, many a labor,
    Many a tear."

If I still hold closely to Him,
    What hath He at last?
"Sorrow vanquish'd, labor ended,
    Jordan pass'd."

If I ask Him to receive me,
    Will He say me nay?
"Not till earth, and not till heaven
    Pass away."

Finding, following, keeping, struggling,
  Is He sure to bless?
"Saints, apostles, prophets, martyrs,
    Answer, Yes."
                    JOHN MASON NEALE.
  (Translation from ST. STEPHEN THE SABAITE.)

UP-HILL.

DOES the road wind up-hill all the way?
  Yes, to the very end.
Will the day's journey take the whole long
    day.
  From morn to night, my friend.

But is there for the night a resting-place?
  *A roof for when the slow dark hours
    begin.*
May not the darkness hide it from my
    face?
  You cannot miss that inn.

Shall I meet other wayfarers at night?
  Those who have gone before.
Then must I knock, or call when just in
    sight?
  *They will not keep you standing at that
    door.*

Shall I find comfort, travel-sore and weak?
  Of labor you shall find the sum.
Will there be beds for me and all who
    seek?
  Yes, beds for all who come.
                CHRISTINA GEORGINA ROSSETTI.

NOTHING BUT LEAVES.

"He found nothing thereon but leaves."—Matt. chap.
                  xxi. v. 19.

NOTHING but leaves; the spirit grieves
  Over a wasted life;
Sin committed while conscience slept,
Promises made but never kept,
  Hatred, battle, and strife;
    Nothing but leaves!

Nothing but leaves; no garner'd sheaves
  Of life's fair, ripen'd grain;
Words, idle words, for earnest deeds;
We sow our seeds—lo! tares and weeds;
  We reap with toil and pain
    Nothing but leaves!

Nothing but leaves; memory weaves
  No veil to screen the past:
As we retrace our weary way,
Counting each lost and misspent day—
  We find, sadly, at last,
    Nothing but leaves!

And shall we meet the Master so,
  Bearing our wither'd leaves?
The Saviour looks for perfect fruit,—
We stand before him, humbled, mute;
  Waiting the words he breathes,—
    "*Nothing but leaves!*"
                LUCY EVELINA AKERMAN.

THE PILGRIMAGE.

GIVE me my scallop-shell of quiet,
  My staff of faith to walk upon;
My scrip of joy, immortal diet;
  My bottle of salvation;
My gown of glory, hope's true gauge,
And thus I'll take my pilgrimage!
Blood must be my body's balmer,
  No other balm will there be given;
Whilst my soul, like quiet palmer,
  Travelleth toward the land of Heaven:
Over the silver mountains
Where spring the nectar fountains:
There will I kiss the bowl of bliss,
And drink mine everlasting fill
Upon every milken hill.
My soul will be a-dry before,
But after, it will thirst no more.
Then by that happy, blissful day,
  More peaceful pilgrims I shall see,
That have cast off their rags of clay,
  And walk apparell'd fresh like me.
I'll take them first to quench their thirst,
  And taste of nectar's suckets
At those clear wells where sweetness
    dwells
  Drawn up by saints in crystal buckets.
And when our bottles and all we
Are fill'd with immortality,
Then the blest paths we'll travel,
Strew'd with rubies thick as gravel,—
Ceilings of diamonds, sapphire floors,
High walls of coral, and pearly bowers.
From thence to heaven's bribeless hall,
Where no corrupted voices brawl;

No conscience molten into gold,
No forged accuser, bought or sold,
No cause deferr'd, no vain-spent journey,
For there Christ is the King's Attorney;
Who pleads for all without degrees,
And He hath angels, but no fees;
And when the grand twelve million jury
Of our sins, with direful fury,
'Gainst our souls black verdicts give,
Christ pleads His death, and then we live.
Be thou my speaker, taintless pleader,
Unblotted lawyer, true proceeder!
Thou giv'st salvation even for alms,—
Not with a bribèd lawyer's palms.
And this is mine eternal plea
To Him that made heaven, earth and sea,
That since my flesh must die so soon,
And want a head to dine next noon,
Just at the stroke when my veins start and
  spread,
Set on my soul an everlasting head:
Then am I, like a palmer, fit
To tread those blest paths which before I
  writ.
Of death and judgment, heaven and hell,
Who oft doth think, must needs die well.
Sir Walter Raleigh.

THE FLOWER.

How fresh, O Lord, how sweet and
  clean
Are thy returns! e'en as the flowers in
  spring—
To which, besides their own demean,
The late-past frosts tributes of pleasure
  bring.
    Grief melts away
    Like snow in May,
As if there were no such cold thing.

Who would have thought my shrivell'd
  heart
Could have recovered greenness? It was
  gone
Quite underground; as flowers depart
To see their mother-root when they have
  blown,
    Where they together,
    All the hard weather,
Dead to the world, keep house unknown.

These are Thy wonders, Lord of power:
Killing and quick'ning, bringing down to
  hell
And up to heaven in an hour,
Making a chiming of a passing-bell.
    We say amiss,
    This or that is—
Thy word is all, if we could spell.

Oh, that I once past changing were—
Fast in Thy paradise, where no flower can
  wither!
Many a spring I shoot up fair,
Offering at heaven, growing and groaning
  thither;
    Nor doth my flower
    Want a spring-shower,
My sins and I joining together.

But, while I grow in a straight line,
Still upward bent, as if heaven were mine
  own,
Thy anger comes, and I decline;
What frost to that? what pole is not the
  zone
    Where all things burn,
    When Thou dost turn,
And the least frown of Thine is shown?

And now in age I bud again—
After so many deaths I live and write;
I once more smell the dew and rain,
And relish versing; O my only light,
    It cannot be
    That I am he
On whom Thy tempests fell all night!

These are Thy wonders, Lord of love—
To make us see we are but flowers that
  glide;
Which when we once can find and
  prove,
Thou hast a garden for us where to bide.
    Who would be more,
    Swelling through store,
Forfeit their paradise by their pride.
George Herbert.

JESU, MY STRENGTH, MY HOPE.

Jesu, my strength, my hope,
  On Thee I cast my care,
With humble confidence look up,
  And know Thou hear'st my prayer.

Give me on thee to wait
  Till I can all things do,
On Thee, Almighty to create,
  Almighty to renew!

I rest upon Thy word;
  The promise is for me;
My succor and salvation, Lord,
  Shall surely come from Thee.
But let me still abide,
  Nor from my hope remove,
Till Thou my patient spirit guide
  Into thy perfect love!

I want a sober mind,
  A self-renouncing will,
That tramples down and casts behind
  The baits of pleasing ill:
A soul inured to pain,
  To hardship, grief, and loss;
Bold to take up, firm to sustain,
  The consecrated cross.

I want a godly fear,
  A quick discerning eye,
That looks to Thee when sin is near,
  And sees the tempter fly;
A spirit still prepared,
  And arm'd with jealous care,
For ever standing on its guard,
  And watching unto prayer.

I want a heart to pray,
  To pray and never cease,
Never to murmur at Thy stay,
  Or wish my sufferings less;
This blessing, above all,
  Always to pray, I want,
Out of the deep on Thee to call,
  And never, never faint.

I want a true regard,
  A single, steady aim,
Unmoved by threat'ning or reward,
  To Thee and Thy great name;
A jealous, just concern
  For Thine immortal praise;
A pure desire that all may learn
  And glorify Thy grace.

I want with all my heart,
  Thy pleasure to fulfil,
To know myself, and what Thou art,
  And what Thy perfect will.
I want I know not what;
  I want my wants to see;
I want—alas, what want I not,
  When Thou art not in me?
                CHARLES WESLEY.

MISSIONARY HYMN.

FROM Greenland's icy mountains,
  From India's coral strand,
Where Afric's sunny fountains
  Roll down their golden sand;
From many an ancient river,
  From many a palmy plain,
They call us to deliver
  Their land from error's chain.

What though the spicy breezes
  Blow soft o'er Ceylon's isle;
Though every prospect pleases,
  And only man is vile;
In vain with lavish kindness
  The gifts of God are strown;
The heathen in his blindness
  Bows down to wood and stone.

Can we, whose souls are lighted
  With wisdom from on high,
Can we to men benighted
  The lamp of life deny?
Salvation! O salvation!
  The joyful sound proclaim,
Till each remotest nation
  Has learnt Messiah's Name.

Waft, waft, ye winds, His story,
  And you, ye waters, roll,
Till like a sea of glory
  It spreads from pole to pole;
Till o'er our ransom'd nature
  The Lamb for sinners slain,
Redeemer, King, Creator,
  In bliss returns to reign.
                REGINALD HEBER.

THE BURIAL OF MOSES.

"And he buried him in a valley in the land of Moab, over against Beth-peor; but no man knoweth of his sepulchre unto this day."

BY Nebo's lonely mountain,
  On this side Jordan's wave,
In a vale in the land of Moab
  There lies a lonely grave.
And no man knows that sepulchre,
  And no man saw it e'er,
For the angels of God upturn'd the sod
  And laid the dead man there.

That was the grandest funeral
  That ever pass'd on earth;
But no man heard the trampling,
  Or saw the train go forth—
Noiselessly as the daylight
  Comes back when night is done,
And the crimson streak on ocean's cheek
  Grows into the great sun.

Noiselessly as the spring-time
  Her crown of verdure weaves,
And all the trees on all the hills
  Open their thousand leaves;
So without sound of music,
  Or voice of them that wept,
Silently down from the mountain's crown
  The great procession swept.

Perchance the bald old eagle
  On gray Beth-peor's height,
Out of his lonely eyrie
  Look'd on the wondrous sight;
Perchance the lion stalking,
  Still shuns that hallow'd spot,
For beast and bird have seen and heard
  That which man knoweth not.

But when the warrior dieth,
  His comrades in the war,
With arms reversed and muffled drum,
  Follow his funeral car;
They show the banners taken,
  They tell his battles won,
And after him lead his masterless steed,
  While peals the minute gun.

Amid the noblest of the land
  We lay the sage to rest,
And give the bard an honor'd place,
  With costly marble drest,
In the great minster transept
  Where lights like glories fall,
And the organ rings, and the sweet choir sings
  Along the emblazon'd wall.

This was the truest warrior
  That ever buckled sword,
This the most gifted poet
  That ever breathed a word;
And never earth's philosopher
  Traced, with his golden pen,
On the deathless page, truths half so sage
  As he wrote down for men.

And had he not high honor,—
  The hillside for a pall,
To lie in state while angels wait
  With stars for tapers tall,
And the dark rock-pines like tossing plumes,
  Over his bier to wave,
And God's own hand, in that lonely land,
  To lay him in the grave?

In that strange grave without a name,
  Whence his uncoffin'd clay
Shall break again, O wondrous thought!
  Before the judgment day,
And stand with glory wrapt around
  On the hills he never trod,
And speak of the strife that won our life
  With the Incarnate Son of God.

O lonely grave in Moab's land!
  O dark Beth-peor's hill!
Speak to these curious hearts of ours,
  And teach them to be still.
God hath His mysteries of grace,
  Ways that we cannot tell;
He hides them deep, like the hidden sleep
  Of him He loved so well.
                CECIL FRANCES ALEXANDER.

THE NINETY AND NINE.

THERE were ninety and nine that safely lay
  In the shelter of the fold,
But one was out on the hills away,
  Far off from the gates of gold—
Away on the mountains wild and bare,
Away from the tender Shepherd's care.

"Lord, Thou hast here Thy ninety and nine;
  Are they not enough for Thee?"
But the Shepherd made answer: "'Tis of mine
  Has wander'd away from me;
And although the road be rough and steep,
I go to the desert to find my sheep."

But none of the ransom'd ever knew
  How deep were the waters cross'd;
Nor how dark was the night that the Lord pass'd through
  Ere He found His sheep that was lost.
Out in the desert He heard its cry—
Sick and helpless, and ready to die.

"Lord, whence are those blood-drops all
    the way
That mark out the mountain's track?"
"They were shed for one who had gone
    astray
Ere the Shepherd could bring him
    back."
"Lord, whence are Thy hands so rent and
    torn?"
"They are pierced to-night by many a
    thorn."

But all thro' the mountains, thunder-riven,
    And up from the rocky steep,
There rose a cry to the gate of heaven,
    "Rejoice! I have found My sheep!"
And the angels echo'd around the throne,
    "Rejoice, for the Lord brings back His
    own!"
ELIZABETH C. CLEPHANE.

RETIREMENT.

FAR from the world, O Lord, I flee,
    From strife and tumult far;
From scenes where Satan wages still
    His most successful war.

The calm retreat, the silent shade,
    With prayer and praise agree,
And seem by Thy sweet bounty made
    For those who follow Thee.

There, if Thy Spirit touch the soul,
    And grace her mean abode,
Oh, with what peace, and joy, and love,
    She communes with her God!

There, like the nightingale, she pours
    Her solitary lays,
Nor asks a witness of her song,
    Nor thirsts for human praise.

Author and Guardian of my life,
    Sweet Source of light divine,
And, all harmonious names in one,
    My Saviour! Thou art mine!

What thanks I owe Thee, and what love,
    A boundless, endless store,
Shall echo through the realms above
    When time shall be no more!
WILLIAM COWPER.

LORD, SHALL THY CHILDREN COME TO THEE?

LORD, shall thy children come to Thee?
    A boon of love divine we seek;
Brought to Thine arms in infancy,
    Ere heart could feel, or tongue could
    speak,
Thy children pray for grace, that they
May come themselves to Thee to-day.

Lord, shall we come? and come again,
    Oft as we see Thy table spread,
And, tokens of Thy dying pain,
    The wine pour'd out, the broken bread?
Bless, bless, O Lord, Thy children's prayer,
That they may come and find Thee there.

Lord, shall we come? not thus alone
    At holy time or solemn rite,
But every hour till life be flown,
    Through weal or woe, in gloom or light,
Come to Thy throne of grace, that we
In faith, hope, love, confirm'd may be.

Lord, shall we come, come yet again?
    Thy children ask one blessing more:
To come, not now alone, but then,
    When life, and death, and time are o'er;
Then, then to come, O Lord, and be
Confirm'd in heaven, confirm'd by Thee.
SAMUEL HINDS.

WHEN OUR HEADS ARE BOWED WITH WOE.

WHEN our heads are bow'd with woe,
When our bitter tears o'erflow,
When we mourn the lost, the dear,
Gracious Son of Mary, hear.

Thou our throbbing flesh hast worn,
Thou our mortals griefs hast borne,
Thou hast shed the human tear;
Gracious Son of Mary, hear.

When the sullen death-bell tolls
For our own departed souls,
When our final doom is near,
Gracious Son of Mary, hear.

Thou hast bow'd the dying head,
Thou the blood of life hast shed,
Thou hast fill'd a mortal bier;
Gracious Son of Mary, hear.

When the heart is sad within
With the thought of all its sin,
When the spirit shrinks with fear,
Gracious Son of Mary, hear.

Thou the shame, the grief, hast known,
Though the sins were not Thine own;
Thou hast deign'd their load to bear;
Gracious Son of Mary, hear.
HENRY HART MILMAN.

PSALM CXXI.

Up to the hills I lift mine eyes,
The eternal hills beyond the skies;
Thence all her help my soul derives,
There my Almighty Refuge lives.

He lives, the everlasting God,
That built the world, that spread the flood;
The heavens with all their hosts he made,
And the dark regions of the dead.

He guides our feet, He guards our way;
His morning smiles bless all the day;
He spreads the evening veil, and keeps
The silent hours while Israel sleeps.

Israel, a name divinely blest,
May rise secure, securely rest;
Thy holy Guardian's wakeful eyes
Admit no slumber nor surprise.

No sun shall smite thy head by day,
Nor the pale moon with sickly ray
Shall blast thy couch; no baleful star
Dart his malignant fire so far.

Should earth and hell with malice burn,
Still thou shalt go, and still return,
Safe in the Lord; His heavenly care
Defends thy life from every snare.

On thee foul spirits have no power;
And, in thy last departing hour,
Angels, that trace the airy road,
Shall bear thee homeward to thy God.
ISAAC WATTS.

A LANCASHIRE DOXOLOGY.

"Praise God from whom all blessings flow."
Praise Him who sendeth joy and woe.

The Lord who takes,—the Lord who gives,—
Oh, praise Him, all that dies and lives.

He opens and He shuts His hand,
But why, we cannot understand:
Pours and dries up His mercies' flood,
And yet is still All-perfect Good.

We fathom not the mighty plan,
The mystery of God and man;
We women, when afflictions come,
We only suffer and are dumb.

And when, the tempest passing by,
He gleams out, sunlike, through the sky,
We look up, and, through black clouds riven,
We recognize the smile of Heaven.

Ours is no wisdom of the wise,
We have no deep philosophies:
Childlike, we take both kiss and rod,
For he who loveth knoweth God.
DINAH MARIA MULOCH CRAIK.

THE GOD OF ABRAHAM PRAISE.

The God of Abraham praise,
  Who reigns enthroned above,
Ancient of everlasting days,
  And God of Love!
Jehovah! Great I Am!
  By earth and heaven confest;
I bow and bless the sacred Name,
  For ever blest!

The God of Abraham praise!
  At whose supreme command
From earth I rise, and seek the joys
  At His right hand:
I all on earth forsake,
  Its wisdom, fame, and power,
And Him my only portion make,
  My Shield and Tower.

The God of Abraham praise!
  Whose all-sufficient grace
Shall guide me all my happy days
  In all my ways:
He calls a worm His friend!
  He calls Himself my God!
And He shall save me to the end
  Through Jesus' Blood.

He by Himself hath sworn,
  I on His oath depend;
I shall, on eagle's wings upborne,
  To heaven ascend;
I shall behold His face,
  I shall His power adore,
And sing the wonders of His grace
  For evermore!

Though Nature's strength decay,
  And earth and hell withstand,
To Canaan's bounds I urge my way
  At His command:
The watery deep I pass
  With Jesus in my view,
And through the howling wilderness
  My way pursue.

The goodly land I see,
  With peace and plenty blest,
A land of sacred liberty,
  And endless rest:
There milk and honey flow,
  And oil and wine abound,
And trees of life for ever grow,
  With Mercy crown'd.

There dwells the Lord our King,
  The Lord our Righteousness,
Triumphant o'er the world and sin,
  The Prince of Peace!
On Sion's sacred height
  His kingdom still maintains,
And, glorious with His saints in light,
  For ever reigns!

He keeps His own secure;
  He guards them by His side;
Arrays in garments white and pure
  His spotless Bride;
With streams of sacred bliss,
  With groves of living joys,
With all the fruits of Paradise,
  He still supplies.

Before the great Three-One
  They all exulting stand,
And tell the wonders He hath done
  Through all their land;
The listening spheres attend
  And swell the growing fame,
And sing, in songs which never end,
  The wondrous Name!

The God who reigns on high,
  The great Archangels sing,
And, "Holy, holy, holy," cry,
  "Almighty King!
Who Was, and Is, the same,
  And evermore shall be!
Jehovah! Father! Great I Am!
  We worship Thee!"

Before the Saviour's face
  The ransom'd nations bow,
O'erwhelm'd at His Almighty grace,
  For ever new:
He shows His prints of love;
  They kindle to a flame,
And sound, through all the worlds above,
  The slaughter'd Lamb!

The whole triumphant host
  Give thanks to God on high;
"Hail! Father, Son, and Holy Ghost!"
  They ever cry:
Hail! Abraham's God, and mine!
  I join the heavenly lays;
All might and majesty are Thine,
  And endless praise!

              THOMAS OLIVERS.

O THOU, FROM WHOM ALL GOODNESS FLOWS.

O THOU, from whom all goodness flows,
  I lift my heart to Thee;
In all my sorrows, conflicts, woes,
  Dear Lord, remember me!

When groaning on my burden'd heart
  My sins lie heavily,
My pardon speak, new peace impart,
  In love remember me!

Temptations sore obstruct my way;
  And ills I cannot flee:
Oh, give me strength, Lord, as my day;
  For good remember me!

Distrest with pain, disease, and grief,
  This feeble body see!
Grant patience, rest, and kind relief;
  Hear, and remember me!

If on my face, for Thy dear Name,
  Shame and reproaches be;

All hail reproach, and welcome shame,
  If Thou remember me!

The hour is near; consign'd to death
  I own the just decree:
    Saviour!" with my last parting breath,
  I'll cry, "Remember me!"
THOMAS HAWEIS.

COME, THOU FOUNT OF EVERY BLESSING.

COME, Thou Fount of every blessing,
  Tune mine heart to sing Thy grace;
Streams of mercy, never ceasing,
  Call for songs of loudest praise.
Teach me some melodious sonnet,
  Sung by flaming tongues above;
Praise the mount—I'm fix'd upon it—
  Mount of God's unchanging love!

Here I raise my Ebenezer!
  Hither by Thine help I'm come;
And I hope, by Thy good pleasure,
  Safely to arrive at home.
Jesus sought me when a stranger,
  Wandering from the fold of God;
He, to rescue me from danger,
  Interposed with precious blood.

Oh, to grace how great a debtor
  Daily I'm constrain'd to be!
Let that grace now, like a fetter,
  Bind my wandering heart to Thee;
Prone to wander, Lord, I feel it,
  Prone to leave the God I love;
Here's mine heart, oh take and seal it;
  Seal it from Thy courts above.
ROBERT ROBINSON.

THE OMNIPOTENT DECREE.

STAND the omnipotent decree!
  Jehovah's will be done!
Nature's end we wait to see,
  And hear her final groan.
Let this earth dissolve, and blend
  In death the wicked and the just;
Let those ponderous orbs descend,
  And grind us into dust:—

Rests secure the righteous man;
  At his Redeemer's beck.
Sure to emerge and rise again,
  And mount above the wreck.
Lo! the heavenly spirit towers,
  Like flames, o'er Nature's funeral pyre,
Triumphs in immortal powers,
  And claps his wings of fire!

Nothing hath the just to lose,
  By worlds on worlds destroy'd;
Far beneath his feet he views,
  With smiles, the flaming void;
Sees this universe renew'd,
  The grand millennial reign begun;
Shouts, with all the sons of God,
  Around the eternal throne.

Resting in this glorious hope
  To be at last restored,
Yield we now our bodies up
  To earthquake, plague, or sword.
Listening for the call divine,
  The latest trumpet of the seven;
Soon our soul and dust shall join,
  And both fly up to heaven.
CHARLES WESLEY.

COMPLAINING.

Do not beguile my heart,
  Because Thou art
My power and wisdom. Put me not to shame,
  Because I am
Thy clay that weeps, Thy dust that calls.

Thou art the Lord of glory—
  The deed and story
Are both Thy due; but I, a silly fly,
  That live or die
According as the weather falls.

Art Thou all justice, Lord?
  Shows not Thy word
More attributes? Am I all throat or eye,
  To weep or cry?
Have I no parts but those of grief?

Let not Thy wrathful power
  Afflict my hour,
My inch of life; or let Thy gracious power
  Contract my hour,
That I may climb and find relief.
GEORGE HERBERT.

ON A PRAYER-BOOK
SENT TO MRS. M. R.

Lo! here a little volume, but great book,
(Fear it not, sweet,
It is no hypocrite!)
Much larger in itself than in its look!
It is—in one rich handful—heaven and all
Heaven's royal hosts encamp'd — thus small
To prove, that true schools use to tell,
A thousand angels in one point can dwell.
It is love's great artillery,
Which here contracts itself, and comes to lie
Close couch'd in your white bosom, and from thence,
As from a snowy fortress of defence,
Against the ghostly foe to take your part,
And fortify the hold of your chaste heart.

It is the armory of light—
Let constant use but keep it bright,
  You'll find it yields
To holy hands and humble hearts
  More swords and shields
Than sin hath snares, or hell hath darts.
  Only be sure
  The hands be pure
That hold these weapons, and the eyes
Those of turtles—chaste and true,
  Wakeful and wise.
Here is a friend shall fight for you;
Hold but this book before your heart,
Let prayer alone to play his part.

But oh! the heart
That studies this high art
Must be a sure housekeeper,
And yet no sleeper.

Dear soul, be strong,
Mercy will come ere long,
And bring her bosom full of blessings—
Flowers of never-fading graces,
To make immortal dressings
For worthy souls, whose wise embraces
Store up themselves for Him who is alone
The Spouse of virgins and the Virgin's Son.

But if the noble Bridegroom, when He comes,
Shall find the wandering heart from home,
  Leaving her chaste abode
  To gad abroad—
Amongst the gay mates of the god of flies
  To take her pleasures, and to play,
  And keep the devil's holiday—
To dance in the sunshine of some smiling,
  But beguiling

Spear of sweet and sugar'd lies—
  Some slippery pair
  Of false, perhaps as fair,
Flattering but forswearing eyes—
Doubtless some other heart
  Will get the start,
  And, stepping in before,
Will take possession of the sacred store
  Of hidden sweets and holy joys—
  Words which are not heard with ears
(These tumultuous shops of noise),
  Effectual whispers, whose still voice
The soul itself more feels than hears—

Amorous languishments, luminous trances,
  Sights which are not seen with eyes—
Spiritual and soul-piercing glances,
  Whose pure and subtle lightning flies
Home to the heart, and sets the house on fire,
And melts it down in sweet desire;
  Yet doth not stay
To ask the windows leave to pass that way—
Delicious deaths, soft exhalations
Of soul, dear and divine annihilations—
  A thousand unknown rites
  Of joys, and rarefied delights—
An hundred thousand loves and graces,
  And many a mystic thing
  Which the divine embraces
Of the dear Spouse of spirits with them will bring,
  For which it is no shame
That dull mortality must not know a name.
  Of all this hidden store
Of blessings, and ten thousand more,
  If, when He come,
He find the heart from home,

Doubtless He will unload
Himself some otherwhere,
   And pour abroad
   His precious sweets
On the fair soul whom first He meets.
Oh fair! oh fortunate! oh rich! oh dear!
   Oh, happy and thrice happy she—
   Dear silver-breasted dove,
   Whoe'er she be,
   Whose early love
   With wingèd vows
Makes haste to meet her morning Spouse,
And close with His immortal kisses—
   Happy soul! who never misses
   To improve that precious hour,
   And every day
   Seize her sweet prey,
   All fresh and fragrant as He rises,
   Dropping with a balmy shower,
   A delicious dew of spices!

Oh! let that happy soul hold fast
Her heavenly armful; she shall taste
At once ten thousand paradises;
   She shall have power
   To rifle and deflower
The rich and roseal spring of those rare sweets
Which, with a swelling bosom, there she meets;
Boundless and infinite, bottomless treasures
      Of pure inebriating pleasures;
Happy soul! she shall discover
   What joy, what bliss,
'How many heavens at once, it is,
To have a God become her lover.
             RICHARD CRASHAW.

TO KEEP A TRUE LENT.

   Is this a fast—to keep
      The larder lean,
      And clean
   From fat of veals and sheep?

   Is it to quit the dish
      Of flesh, yet still
      To fill
   The platter high with fish?

   Is it to fast an hour—
      Or ragged to go—
      Or show
   A downcast look, and sour?

   No! 'tis a fast to dole
      Thy sheaf of wheat,
      And meat,
   Unto the hungry soul.

   It is to fast from strife,
      From old debate
      And hate—
   To circumcise thy life.

   To show a heart grief-rent;
      To starve thy sin,
      Not bin;
   And that's to keep thy Lent.
             ROBERT HERRICK.

O GOD OF BETHEL, BY WHOSE HAND.

O GOD of Bethel, by whose hand
   Thy people still are fed,
Who through this weary pilgrimage
   Hast all our fathers led;

Our vows, our prayers, we now present
   Before Thy throne of grace;
God of our fathers! be the God
   Of their succeeding race.

Through each perplexing path of life
   Our wandering footsteps guide;
Give us each day our daily bread,
   And raiment fit provide.

Oh spread Thy covering wings around
   Till all our wanderings cease,
And at our Father's loved abode
   Our souls arrive in peace!

Such blessings from Thy gracious hand
   Our humble prayers implore;
And Thou shalt be our chosen God,
   And portion evermore.
           Variation by JOHN LOGAN.
           (From PHILIP DODDRIDGE.)

NEARER HOME.

ONE sweetly solemn thought
   Comes to me o'er and o'er;
I'm nearer my home to-day
   Than I ever have been before;

Nearer my Father's house,
  Where the many mansions be;
Nearer the great white throne;
  Nearer the crystal sea;

Nearer the bound of life,
  Where we lay our burdens down;
Nearer leaving the cross;
  Nearer gaining the crown.

But lying darkly between,
  Winding down through the night,
Is the silent, unknown stream
  That leads at last to the light.

Closer and closer my steps
  Come to the dread abysm:
Closer Death to my lips
  Presses the awful chrism.

Oh, if my mortal feet
  Have almost gain'd the brink;
If it be I am nearer home
  Even to-day than I think;

Father, perfect my trust;
  Let my spirit feel in death
That her feet are firmly set
  On the rock of a living faith!
PHŒBE CARY.

YE GOLDEN LAMPS OF HEAVEN, FAREWELL.

YE golden lamps of heaven, farewell,
  With all your feeble light:
Farewell, thou ever-changing moon,
  Pale empress of the night.

And thou, refulgent orb of day,
  In brighter flames array'd;
My soul, that springs beyond thy sphere,
  No more demands thine aid.

Ye stars are but the shining dust
  Of my divine abode,
The pavement of those heavenly courts
  Where I shall reign with God.

The Father of eternal light
  Shall there His beams display,
Nor shall one moment's darkness mix
  With that unvaried day.

No more the drops of piercing grief
  Shall swell into mine eyes;
Nor the meridian sun decline
  Amid those brighter skies.

There all the millions of His saints
  Shall in one song unite,
And each the bliss of all shall view
  With infinite delight.
PHILIP DODDRIDGE.

SONGS OF PRAISE THE ANGELS SANG.

SONGS of praise the angels sang,
Heaven with hallelujahs rang,
When Jehovah's work begun,
When He spake and it was done.

Songs of praise awoke the morn,
When the Prince of Peace was born;
Songs of praise arose when He
Captive led captivity.

Heaven and earth must pass away,
Songs of praise shall crown that day;
God will make new heavens, new earth,
Songs of praise shall hail their birth.

And can man alone be dumb,
Till that glorious kingdom come?
No: the Church delights to raise
Psalms, and hymns, and songs of praise.

Saints below, with heart and voice,
Still in songs of praise rejoice,
Learning here, by faith and love,
Songs of praise to sing above.

Borne upon their latest breath,
Songs of praise shall conquer death;
Then, amidst eternal joy,
Songs of praise their powers employ.
JAMES MONTGOMERY.

ON ANOTHER'S SORROW.

Can I see another's woe,
And not be in sorrow too?
Can I see another's grief,
And not seek for kind relief?

Can I see a falling tear,
And not feel my sorrow's share?
Can a father see his child
Weep, nor be with sorrow fill'd?

Can a mother sit and hear
An infant groan, an infant fear?
No! no! never can it be—
Never, never can it be!

And can He who smiles on all,
Hear the wren with sorrows small,
Hear the small bird's grief and care,
Hear the woes that infants bear,—

And not sit beside the nest,
Pouring pity in their breast?
And not sit the cradle near,
Weeping tear on infant's tear?

And not sit both night and day,
Wiping all our tears away?
Oh, no! never can it be—
Never, never can it be!

He doth give His joy to all;
He becomes an infant small,
He becomes a man of woe,
He doth feel the sorrow too.

Think not thou canst sigh a sigh,
And thy Maker is not nigh;
Think not thou canst weep a tear,
And thy Maker is not near.

Oh! He gives to us His joy,
That our griefs He may destroy.
Till our grief is fled and gone
He doth sit by us and moan.
WILLIAM BLAKE.

PASSING UNDER THE ROD.

I saw the young bride in her beauty and pride,
  Bedeck'd in her snowy array;
And the bright flush of joy mantled high on her cheek,
  And the future look'd blooming and gay:
And with woman's devotion she laid her fond heart
  At the shrine of idolatrous love,
And she anchor'd her hopes to this perishing earth,
  By the chain which her tenderness wove.
But I saw, when those heartstrings were bleeding and torn,
  And the chain had been sever'd in two,
She had changed her white robes for the sables of grief,
  And her bloom for the paleness of woe!
But the Healer was there, pouring balm on her heart,
  And wiping the tears from her eyes,
And He strengthen'd the chain He had broken in twain,
  And fasten'd it firm to the skies!
There had whisper'd a voice—'twas the voice of her God:
  "I love thee—I love thee—*pass under the rod!*"

I saw the young mother in tenderness bend
  O'er the couch of her slumbering boy,
And she kiss'd the soft lips as they murmur'd her name,
  While the dreamer lay smiling in joy.
Oh, sweet as a rosebud encircled with dew,
  When its fragrance is flung on the air,
So fresh and so bright to that mother he seem'd,
  As he lay in his innocence there.
But I saw when she gazed on the same lovely form,
  Pale as marble, and silent, and cold,
But paler and colder her beautiful boy,
  And the tale of her sorrow was told!
But the Healer was there who had stricken her heart,
  And taken her treasure away;
To allure her to heaven, He has placed it on high,
  And the mourner will sweetly obey.
There had whisper'd a voice—'twas the voice of her God:
  "I love thee—I love thee—*pass under the rod!*"

I saw the fond brother, with glances of love,
  Gazing down on a gentle young girl,
And she hung on his arm, and breathed soft in his ear,
  As he play'd with each graceful curl.
Oh, he loved the sweet tones of her silvery voice,
  Let her use it in sadness or glee;
And he twinèd his arms round her delicate form,
  As she sat in the eve on his knee.
But I saw when he gazed on her death-stricken face,
  And she breathed not a word in his ear,
And he claspèd his arms round an icy-cold form,
  And he moisten'd her cheek with a tear.
But the Healer was there, and He said to him thus,
  "Grieve not for thy sister's short life,"
And He gave to his arms still another fair girl,
  And he made her his own cherish'd wife!
There had whisper'd a voice—'twas the voice of his God:
  "I love thee—I love thee—*pass under the rod!*"

I saw, too, a father and mother who lean'd
  On the arms of a dear gifted son,
And the star in the future grew bright to their gaze,
  As they saw the proud place he had won;
And the fast-coming evening of life promised fair,
  And its pathway grew smooth to their feet,
And the starlight of love glimmer'd bright at the end,
  And the whispers of fancy were sweet.
And I saw them again, bending low o'er the grave,
  Where their hearts' dearest hope had been laid,
And the star had gone down in the darkness of night,
  And the joy from their bosoms had fled.
But the Healer was there, and His arms were around,
  And He led them with tenderest care;
And He show'd them a star in the bright upper world;
  'Twas *their star* shining brilliantly there!
They had each heard a voice—'twas the voice of their God:
"I love thee—I love thee—*pass under the rod!*"

MARY S. B. DANA.

THE CHANGED CROSS.

IT was a time of sadness, and my heart,
Although it knew and loved the better part,
Felt wearied with the conflict and the strife,
And all the needful discipline of life.

And while I thought on these as given to me,
My trial-tests of faith and love to be,
It seem'd as if I never could be sure
That faithful to the end I should endure.

And thus, no longer trusting to His might
Who says, "We walk by faith and not by sight,"
Doubting, and almost yielding to despair,
The thought arose, "My cross I cannot bear.

"Far heavier its weight must surely be
Than those of others which I daily see;
Oh! if I might another burden choose,
Methinks I should not fear my crown to lose."

A solemn silence reign'd on all around,
E'en Nature's voices utter'd not a sound;
The evening shadows seem'd of peace to tell,
And sleep upon my weary spirit fell.

A moment's pause,—and then a heavenly light
Beam'd full upon my wondering, raptured sight;
Angels on silvery wings seem'd everywhere,
And angels' music thrill'd the balmy air.

Then One, more fair than all the rest to see,
One to whom all the others bow'd the knee,
Came gently to me, as I trembling lay,
And, "Follow me," He said; "I am the Way."

Then, speaking thus, He led me far above,
And there, beneath a canopy of love,
Crosses of divers shape and size were seen,
Larger and smaller than my own had been.

And one there was most beauteous to behold,—
A little one, with jewels set in gold.
Ah! this, methought, I can with comfort wear,
For it will be an easy one to bear.

And so the little cross I quickly took,
But all at once my frame beneath it shook;
The sparkling jewels, fair were they to *see*,
But far too heavy was their *weight* for me.

"This may not be," I cried, and look'd again,
To see if there was any here could ease my pain;
But, one by one, I pass'd them slowly by,
Till on a lovely one I cast my eye.

Fair flowers around its sculptured form entwined,
And grace and beauty seem'd in it combined.
Wondering I gazed,—and still I wonder'd more,
To think so many should have pass'd it o'er.

But oh that form so beautiful to see
Soon made its hidden sorrows known to me;
Thorns lay beneath those flowers and colors fair;
Sorrowing I said, "This cross I may not bear."

And so it was with each and all around,
Not one to suit my *need* could there be found;
Weeping I laid each heavy burden down,
As my Guide gently said, "No cross,—no crown."

At length to Him I raised my sadden'd heart;
He knew its sorrows, bade its doubts depart;
"Be not afraid," He said, "but trust in Me;
My perfect love shall now be shown to thee."

And then, with lighten'd eyes and willing feet,
Again I turn'd, my earthly cross to meet;
With forward footsteps, turning not aside,
For fear some hidden evil might betide;

And there,—in the prepared, appointed way,
Listening to hear, and ready to obey,—
A cross I quickly found of plainest form,
With only words of love inscribed thereon.

With thankfulness I raised it from the rest,
And joyfully acknowledged it the best,—
The only one, of all the many there,
That I could feel was good for me to bear.

And while I thus my chosen one confess'd,
I saw a heavenly brightness on it rest;
And as I bent, my burden to sustain,
I recognized *my own old cross* again.

But, oh! how different did it seem to be,
Now I had learn'd its preciousness to see!
No longer could I unbelieving say,
"Perhaps another is a better way."

Ah, no! henceforth my one desire shall be,
That He, who knows me best should choose for me;
And so, whate'er His love sees good to send,
I'll trust it's best,—because He knows the end.

MRS. CHARLES HOBART.

WEARY.

I WOULD have gone; God bade me stay:
   I would have work'd; God bade me rest.
He broke my will from day to day;
   He read my yearnings unexpress'd,
      And said them nay.

Now I would stay; God bids me go:
Now I would rest; God bids me work.
He breaks my heart toss'd to and fro;
My soul is wrung with doubts that lurk
    And vex it so!

I go, Lord, where Thou sendest me;
  Day after day I plod and moil;
But, Christ my God, when will it be
  That I may let alone my toil,
    And rest with Thee?
        CHRISTINA GEORGINA ROSSETTI.

THE VALEDICTION.

VAIN world, what is in thee?
What do poor mortals see
Which should esteemèd be
  Worthy their pleasure?
Is it the mother's womb,
Or sorrows which soon come,
Or a dark grave and tomb;
  Which is their treasure?
How dost thou man deceive
  By thy vain glory?
Why do they still believe
  Thy false history?

Is it children's book and rod,
The laborer's heavy load,
Poverty undertrod,
  The world desireth?
Is it distracting cares,
Or heart-tormenting fears,
Or pining grief and tears,
  Which man requireth?
Or is it youthful rage,
  Or childish toying?
Or is decrepit age
  Worth man's enjoying?

Is it deceitful wealth,
Got by care, fraud, or stealth,
Or short, uncertain health,
  Which thus befool men?
Or do the serpent's lies,
By the world's flatteries
And tempting vanities,
  Still overrule them?
Or do they in a dream
  Sleep out their season?
Or borne down by lust's stream,
  Which conquers reason?

The silly lambs to-day
Pleasantly skip and play,
Whom butchers mean to slay,
  Perhaps to-morrow;
In a more brutish sort
Do careless sinners sport,
Or in dead sleep still snort,
  As near to sorrow;
Till life, not well begun,
  Be sadly ended,
And the web they have spun
  Can ne'er be mended.

What is the time that's gone,
And what is that to come?
Is it not now as none?
  The present stays not.
Time posteth, oh how fast!
Unwelcome death makes haste;
None can call back what's past—
  Judgment delays not;
Though God bring in the light,
  Sinners awake not—
Because hell's out of sight,
  They sin forsake not.

Man walks in a vain show;
They know, yet will not know;
Sit still when they should go—
  But run for shadows,
While they might taste and know
The living streams that flow,
And crop the flowers that grow,
  In Christ's sweet meadows.
Life's better slept away
  Than as they use it;
In sin and drunken play
  Vain men abuse it.

Malignant world, adieu!
Where no foul vice is new—
Only to Satan true,
  God still offended;
Though taught and warn'd by God,
And His chastising rod,
Keeps still the way that's broad,
  Never amended.
Baptismal vows some make,
  But ne'er perform them;
If angels from heaven spake,
  'Twould not reform them.

They dig for hell beneath,
They labor hard for death,
Run themselves out of breath
   To overtake it.
Hell is not had for naught,
Damnation's dearly bought,
And with great labor sought—
   They'll not forsake it.
Their souls are Satan's fee—
   He'll not abate it.
Grace is refused that's free—
   Mad sinners hate it.

Vile man is so perverse,
It's too rough work for verse
His badness to rehearse,
   And show his folly;
He'll die at any rates—
He God and conscience hates,
Yet sin he consecrates,
   And calls it holy.
The grace he'll not endure
   Which would renew him—
Constant to all, and sure,
   Which will undo him.

His head comes first at birth,
And takes root in the earth—
As nature shooteth forth,
   His feet grow highest,
To kick at all above,
And spurn at saving love;
His God is in his grove,
   Because it's nighest;
He loves this world of strife,
   Hates that would mend it;
Loves death that's callèd life,
   Fears what would end it.

All that is good he'd crush,
Blindly on sin doth rush—
A pricking thorny bush,
   Such Christ was crown'd with;
Their worship's like to this—
The reed, the Judas kiss:
Such the religion is
   That these abound with;
They mock Christ with the knee
   Whene'er they bow it—
As if God did not see
   The heart, and know it.

Of good they choose the least,
Despise that which is best—
The joyful, heavenly feast
   Which Christ would give them;
Heaven hath scarce one cold wish;
They live unto the flesh;
Like swine they feed on wash—
   Satan doth drive them.
Like weeds, they grow in mire
   Which vices nourish—
Where, warm'd by Satan's fire,
   All sins do flourish.

Is this the world men choose,
For which they heaven refuse,
And Christ and grace abuse,
   And not receive it?
Shall I not guilty be
Of this in some degree,
If hence God would me free,
   And I'd not leave it?
My soul, from Sodom fly,
   Lest wrath there find thee;
Thy refuge-rest is nigh—
   Look not behind thee!

There's none of this ado,
None of the hellish crew;
God's promise is most true—
   Boldly believe it.
My friends are gone before,
And I am near the shore;
My soul stands at the door—
   O Lord, receive it!
It trusts Christ and His merits—
   The dead He raises;
Join it with blessed spirits
   Who sing Thy praises.
              RICHARD BAXTER.

I WOULD NOT LIVE ALWAY.

I WOULD not live alway—live alway
   below!
Oh no, I'll not linger, when bidden to go.
The days of our pilgrimage granted us
   here
Are enough for life's woes, full enough for
   its cheer.
Would I shrink from the path which the
   prophets of God,
Apostles, and Martyrs so joyfully trod?

While brethren and friends are all hastening home,
Like a spirit unblest, o'er the earth would I roam?

I would not live alway: I ask not to stay
Where storm after storm rises dark o'er the way;
Where, seeking for rest, I but hover around
Like the patriarch's bird, and no resting is found;
Where Hope, when she paints her gay bow in the air,
Leaves her brilliance to fade in the night of despair,
And Joy's fleeting angel ne'er sheds a glad ray,
Save the gleam of the plumage that bears him away.

I would not live alway, thus fetter'd by sin,
Temptation without, and corruption within;
In a moment of strength, if I sever the chain,
Scarce the victory is mine ere I'm captive again.
E'en the rapture of pardon is mingled with fears,
And the cup of thanksgiving with penitent tears.
The festival trump calls for jubilant songs,
But my spirit her own *miserere* prolongs.

I would not live alway: no, welcome the tomb;
Immortality's lamp burns there bright 'mid the gloom.
There, too, is the pillow where Christ bow'd his head;
Oh, soft be my slumbers on that holy bed!
And then the glad morn soon to follow that night,
When the sunrise of glory shall burst on my sight,
And the full matin-song as the sleepers arise
To shout in the morning, shall peal through the skies.

Who, who would live alway, away from his God,
Away from yon Heaven, that blissful abode,
Where the rivers of pleasure flow o'er the bright plains,
And the noontide of glory eternally reigns;
Where the saints of all ages in harmony meet,
Their Saviour and brethren transported to greet,
While the anthems of rapture unceasingly roll,
And the smile of the Lord is the feast of the soul?

That heavenly music! what is it I hear?
The notes of the harpers ring sweet on my ear!
And see soft unfolding those portals of gold,
The King all array'd in His beauty behold!
Oh give me, oh give me, the wings of a dove!
Let me hasten my flight to those mansions above:
Ay! 'tis now that my soul on swift pinions would soar,
And in ecstasy bid earth adieu evermore.
           WILLIAM AUGUSTUS MUHLENBERG.

STANZAS ON THE DEATH OF A FRIEND.

THOU art gone to the grave: but we will not deplore thee,
  Though sorrows and darkness encompass the tomb:
Thy Saviour has pass'd through its portal before thee,
  And the lamp of His love is thy guide through the gloom!

Thou art gone to the grave: we no longer behold thee,
  Nor tread the rough paths of the world by thy side;
But the wide arms of Mercy are spread to enfold thee,
  And sinners may die, for the Sinless has died!

Thou art gone to the grave: and, its mansion forsaking,
  Perhaps thy weak spirit in fear linger'd long;
But the mild rays of Paradise beam'd on thy waking,
  And the sound which thou heard'st was the Seraphim's song!

Thou art gone to the grave: but we will not deplore thee;
  Whose God was thy ransom, thy Guardian, and Guide!
He gave thee, He took thee, and He will restore thee;
  And death has no sting, for the Saviour has died!
REGINALD HEBER.

BURIAL HYMN.

BROTHER, thou art gone before us; and thy saintly soul is flown
Where tears are wiped from every eye, and sorrow is unknown;
From the burden of the flesh, and from care and fear released,
Where the wicked cease from troubling, and the weary are at rest.

The toilsome way thou'st travelled o'er, and borne the heavy load;
But Christ hath taught thy languid feet to reach His blest abode:
Thou'rt sleeping now, like Lazarus upon his Father's breast,
Where the wicked cease from troubling, and the weary are at rest.

Sin can never taint thee now, nor doubt thy faith assail,
Nor thy meek trust in Jesus Christ and the Holy Spirit fail:
And there thou'rt sure to meet the good, whom on earth thou lovedst best,
Where the wicked cease from troubling, and the weary are at rest.

Earth to earth, and dust to dust, the solemn priest hath said;
So we lay the turf above thee now, and we seal thy narrow bed;

But thy spirit, brother, soars away among the faithful blest,
Where the wicked cease from troubling, and the weary are at rest.

And when the Lord shall summon us, whom thou hast left behind,
May we, untainted by the world, as sure a welcome find!
May each, like thee, depart in peace, to be a glorious guest,
Where the wicked cease from troubling, and the weary are at rest!
HENRY HART MILMAN.

A LITTLE WHILE.

BEYOND the smiling and the weeping
  I shall be soon;
Beyond the waking and the sleeping,
Beyond the sowing and the reaping,
  I shall be soon.
    Love, rest, and home!
    Sweet hope!
    Lord, tarry not, but come.

Beyond the blooming and the fading
  I shall be soon;
Beyond the shining and the shading,
Beyond the hoping and the dreading,
  I shall be soon.
    Love, rest, and home!
    Sweet hope!
    Lord, tarry not, but come.

Beyond the rising and the setting
  I shall be soon;
Beyond the calming and the fretting,
Beyond remembering and forgetting,
  I shall be soon.
    Love, rest, and home!
    Sweet hope!
    Lord, tarry not, but come.

Beyond the gathering and the strowing
  I shall be soon;
Beyond the ebbing and the flowing,
Beyond the coming and the going,
  I shall be soon.
    Love, rest, and home!
    Sweet hope!
    Lord, tarry not, but come.

Beyond the parting and the meeting
  I shall be soon;
Beyond the farewell and the greeting,
Beyond this pulse's fever beating,
  I shall be soon.
    Love, rest, and home!
    Sweet hope!
    Lord, tarry not, but come.

Beyond the frost-chain and the fever
  I shall be soon;
Beyond the rock-waste and the river,
Beyond the ever and the never,
  I shall be soon.
    Love, rest, and home!
    Sweet hope!
    Lord, tarry not, but come.
HORATIUS BONAR.

ADDRESS TO THE SOUL.

DEATHLESS principle, arise!
Soar, thou native of the skies;
Pearl of price, by Jesus bought,
To His glorious likeness wrought!

Go, to shine before His throne;
Deck His mediatorial crown;
Go, His triumphs to adorn;
Made for God, to God return!

Lo, He beckons from on high!
Fearless to His presence fly!
Thine the merit of His Blood;
Thine the Righteousness of God.

Angels, joyful to attend,
Hovering round thy pillow, bend;
Wait to catch the signal given,
And escort thee quick to Heaven.

Is thy earthly house distrest,
Willing to retain her guest?
'Tis not thou, but she, must die;
Fly, celestial tenant, fly!

Burst thy shackles, drop thy clay,
Sweetly breathe thyself away;
Singing, to thy crown remove
Swift of wing, and fired with love.

Shudder not to pass the stream;
Venture all thy care on Him;
Him, whose dying love and power
Still'd its tossing, hush'd its roar.

Safe is the expanded wave,
Gentle as a summer's eve;
Not one object of His care
Ever suffer'd shipwreck there.

See the haven full in view;
Love Divine shall bear thee through;
Trust to that propitious gale;
Weigh thy anchor, spread thy sail.

Saints, in glory perfect made,
Wait thy passage through the shade:
Ardent for thy coming o'er,
See, they throng the blissful shore!

Mount, their transports to improve;
Join the longing choir above;
Swiftly to their wish be given;
Kindle higher joy in Heaven!

Such the prospects that arise
To the dying Christian's eyes;
Such the glorious vista faith
Opens through the shades of death.
AUGUSTUS MONTAGUE TOPLADY.

THE DYING CHRISTIAN TO HIS SOUL.

VITAL spark of heavenly flame,
Quit, oh, quit this mortal frame!
Trembling, hoping, lingering, flying,
Oh, the pain, the bliss, of dying!
Cease, fond Nature, cease thy strife,
And let me languish into life!

Hark! they whisper; angels say,
Sister Spirit, come away.
What is this absorbs me quite—
Steals my senses, shuts my sight,
Drowns my spirit, draws my breath?
Tell me, my soul! can this be death?

The world recedes—it disappears!
Heaven opens on my eyes! my ears
  With sounds seraphic ring.
Lend, lend your wings! I mount, I fly
O Grave! where is thy victory?
  O Death! where is thy sting?
ALEXANDER POPE.

THEY ARE ALL GONE.

They are all gone into the world of light,
  And I alone sit lingering here!
Their very memory is fair and bright,
  And my sad thoughts doth clear.

It glows and glitters in my cloudy breast,
  Like stars upon some gloomy grove,
Or those faint beams in which this hill is drest
  After the sun's remove.

I see them walking in an air of glory,
  Whose light doth trample on my days;
My days, which are at best but dull and hoary,
  Mere glimmering and decays.

O holy hope! and high humility,—
  High as the heavens above!
These are your walks, and you have show'd them me
  To kindle my cold love.

Dear, beauteous death,—the jewel of the just,—
  Shining nowhere but in the dark!
What mysteries do lie beyond thy dust,
  Could man outlook that mark!

He that hath found some fledged bird's nest may know,
  At first sight, if the bird be flown;
But what fair dell or grove he sings in now,
  That is to him unknown.

And yet, as angels in some brighter dreams
  Call to the soul when man doth sleep,
So some strange thoughts transcend our wonted themes,
  And into glory peep.

If a star were confined into a tomb,
  Her captive flames must needs burn there;
But when the hand that lockt her up gives room,
  She'll shine through all the sphere.

O Father of eternal life, and all
  Created glories under Thee!
Resume Thy Spirit from this world of thrall
  Into true liberty!

Either disperse these mists, which blot and fill
  My perspective still as they pass;
Or else remove me hence unto that hill
  Where I shall need no glass.
         HENRY VAUGHAN.

FOR EVER WITH THE LORD.

For ever with the Lord!
  Amen! so let it be!
Life from the dead is in that word,
  'Tis immortality!

Here in the body pent,
  Absent from Him I roam,
Yet nightly pitch my moving tent
  A day's march nearer home.

My Father's house on high,
  Home of my soul! how near,
At times, to faith's far-seeing eye
  Thy golden gates appear!

Ah! then my spirit faints
  To reach the land I love,
The bright inheritance of saints,
  Jerusalem above!

Yet clouds will intervene,
  And all my prospect flies;
Like Noah's dove, I flit between
  Rough seas and stormy skies.

Anon the clouds depart,
  The winds and waters cease;
While sweetly o'er my gladden'd heart
  Expands the bow of peace!

Beneath its glowing arch,
  Along the hallow'd ground,
I see cherubic armies march,
  A camp of fire around.

I hear at morn and even,
  At noon and midnight hour,
The choral harmonies of heaven
  Earth's Babel tongues o'erpower.

Then, then I feel, that He,
  Remember'd or forgot,
The Lord is never far from me,
  Though I perceive Him not.
         JAMES MONTGOMERY.

WHAT ARE THESE IN BRIGHT ARRAY.

What are these in bright array,
  This innumerable throng,
Round the altar, night and day,
  Hymning one triumphant song?
"Worthy is the Lamb, once slain,
  Blessing, honor, glory, power,
Wisdom, riches, to obtain,
  New dominion every hour."

These through fiery trials trod;
  These from great affliction came;
Now, before the Throne of God,
  Seal'd with His Almighty Name,
Clad in raiment pure and white,
  Victor-palms in every hand,
Through their dear Redeemer's might,
  More than conquerors they stand.

Hunger, thirst, disease unknown,
  On immortal fruits they feed;
Them the Lamb amidst the Throne
  Shall to living fountains lead:
Joy and gladness banish sighs;
  Perfect love dispels all fear;
And for ever from their eyes
  God shall wipe away the tear.
            JAMES MONTGOMERY.

THE BETTER LAND.

"I hear thee speak of the better land;
Thou call'st its children a happy band;
Mother! oh where is that radiant shore—
Shall we not seek it and weep no more?
Is it where the flower of the orange blows,
  And the fire-flies glance through the myrtle boughs?"
    "Not there, not there, my child!"

"Is it where the feathery palmtrees rise,
  And the date grows ripe under sunny skies,
Or 'midst the green islands of glittering seas
Where fragrant forests perfume the breeze,
And strange, bright birds on their starry wings
Bear the rich hues of all glorious things?"
    "Not there, not there, my child!"

"Is it far away in some region old
Where the rivers wander o'er sands of gold,—
Where the burning rays of the ruby shine,
And the diamond lights up the secret mine,
And the pearl gleams forth from the coral strand,—
Is it there, sweet mother, that better land?"
    "Not there, not there, my child!

"Eye hath not seen it, my gentle boy!
Ear hath not heard its deep songs of joy,
Dreams cannot picture a world so fair,—
Sorrow and death may not enter there;
Time doth not breathe on its fadeless bloom,
For, beyond the clouds, and beyond the tomb,
    It is there, it is there, my child!"
           FELICIA DOROTHEA HEMANS.

PSALM LXXXVII.

Glorious things of thee are spoken,
  Zion, city of our God;
He, whose word cannot be broken,
  Form'd thee for His own abode:
On the Rock of Ages founded,
  What can shake thy sure repose?
With salvation's walls surrounded,
  Thou mayst smile at all thy foes.

See, the streams of living waters,
  Springing from eternal love,
Well supply thy sons and daughters,
  And all fear of want remove:
Who can faint, while such a river
  Ever flows their thirst t' assuage;
Grace, which, like the Lord the giver,
  Never fails from age to age?

Round each habitation hovering,
  See the cloud and fire appear,
For a glory and a covering:
  Showing that the Lord is near.
Thus deriving from their banner
  Light by night, and shade by day,
Safe they feed upon the manna,
  Which He gives them when they pray.

Blest inhabitants of Zion,
  Wash'd in the Redeemer's blood!
Jesus, whom their souls rely on,
  Makes them kings and priests to God:
'Tis his love his people raises
  Over self to reign as kings,
And as priests, his solemn praises
  Each for a thank-off'ring brings.

Saviour, if of Zion's city
  I, through grace, a member am,
Let the world deride or pity,
  I will glory in Thy Name;
Fading is the worldling's pleasure,
  All his boasted pomp and show;
Solid joys and lasting treasure
  None but Zion's children know.
            JOHN NEWTON.

THERE IS A HAPPY LAND.

THERE is a happy land,
  Far, far away,
Where saints in glory stand,
  Bright, bright as day.
Oh, how they sweetly sing,
Worthy is our Saviour King;
Loud let his praises ring—
  Praise, praise for aye!

Come to this happy land—
  Come, come away;
Why will ye doubting stand,
  Why still delay?
Oh, we shall happy be,
When, from sin and sorrow free,
Lord, we shall live with Thee—
  Blest, blest for aye.

Bright in that happy land
  Beams every eye:
Kept by a Father's hand,
  Love cannot die.
On, then, to glory run;
Be a crown and kingdom won;
And, bright above the sun,
  Reign, reign for aye.
            ANDREW YOUNG.

THERE IS A LAND OF PURE DELIGHT.

THERE is a land of pure delight,
  Where saints immortal reign,
Infinite day excludes the night,
  And pleasures banish pain.

There everlasting spring abides,
  And never-withering flowers;
Death, like a narrow sea, divides
  This heavenly land from ours.

Sweet fields beyond the swelling flood
  Stand dress'd in living green:
So to the Jews old Canaan stood,
  While Jordan roll'd between.

But timorous mortals start and shrink
  To cross this narrow sea,
And linger shivering on the brink,
  And fear to launch away.

Oh could we make our doubts remove,
  These gloomy doubts that rise,
And see the Canaan that we love
  With unbeclouded eyes,—

Could we but climb where Moses stood,
  And view the landscape o'er,—
Not Jordan's stream, nor death's cold flood,
  Should fright us from the shore.
            ISAAC WATTS.

THERE IS A DWELLING-PLACE ABOVE.

THERE is a dwelling-place above;
Thither, to meet the God of love,
  The poor in spirit go;
There is a paradise of rest;
For contrite hearts and souls distrest
  Its streams of comfort flow.

There is a goodly heritage,
Where earthly passions cease to rage;
  The meek that haven gain:
There is a board, where they who pine,
Hungry, athirst, for grace divine,
  May feast, nor crave again.

There is a voice to mercy true;
To them who mercy's path pursue
  That voice shall bliss impart;
There is a sight from man conceal'd;
That sight, the face of God reveal'd,
  Shall bless the pure in heart.

There is a name, in heaven bestow'd;
That name, which hails them sons of God,
　　The friends of peace shall know:
There is a kingdom in the sky,
Where they shall reign with God on high,
　　Who serve Him best below.

Lord! be it mine like them to choose
The better part, like them to use
　　The means Thy love hath given!
Be holiness my aim on earth,
That death be welcomed as a birth
　　To life and bliss in Heaven!
　　　　　　　　RICHARD MANT.

PSALM LXXXIV.

PLEASANT are Thy courts above,
In the land of light and love;
Pleasant are Thy courts below,
In this land of sin and woe.
Oh, my spirit longs and faints
For the converse of Thy saints,
For the brightness of Thy face,
For Thy fulness, God of grace!

Happy birds that sing and fly
Round Thy altars, O Most High!
Happier souls that find a rest
In a Heavenly Father's breast!
Like the wandering dove, that found
No repose on earth around,
They can to their ark repair,
And enjoy it ever there.

Happy souls! their praises flow
Even in this vale of woe;
Waters in the desert rise,
Manna feeds them from the skies:
On they go from strength to strength,
Till they reach Thy throne at length,
At Thy feet adoring fall,
Who has led them safe through all.

Lord! be mine this prize to win!
Guide me through a world of sin!
Keep me by Thy saving grace;
Give me at Thy side a place:
Sun and Shield alike Thou art;
Guide and guard my erring heart!
Grace and glory flow from Thee;
Shower, oh shower them, Lord, on me!
　　　　　　　HENRY FRANCIS LYTE.

THE PILGRIMS OF THE NIGHT.

HARK! hark! my soul! angelic songs are swelling
　O'er earth's green fields and ocean's wave-beat shore;
How sweet the truth those blessed strains are telling
　Of that new life, when sin shall be no more!
　　　Angels of Jesus,
　　　　Angels of light,
　　　Singing to welcome
　　　　The pilgrims of the night!

Darker than night life's shadows fall around us,
　And like benighted men we miss our mark:
God hides Himself, and grace hath scarcely found us,
　Ere death finds out his victims in the dark.
　　　Angels of Jesus,
　　　　Angels of light,
　　　Singing to welcome
　　　　The pilgrims of the night!

Onward we go, for still we hear them singing,
　"Come, weary souls, for Jesus bids you come;"
And through the dark, its echoes sweetly ringing,
　The music of the Gospel leads us home.
　　　Angels of Jesus,
　　　　Angels of light,
　　　Singing to welcome
　　　　The pilgrims of the night!

Far, far away, like bells at evening pealing,
　The voice of Jesus sounds o'er land and sea,
And laden souls by thousands meekly stealing,
　Kind Shepherd, turn their weary steps to Thee.
　　　Angels of Jesus,
　　　　Angels of light,
　　　Singing to welcome
　　　　The pilgrims of the night!

Rest comes at last, though life be long and
    dreary,
The day must dawn, and darksome night
    be past,
All journeys end in welcomes to the weary,
    And heaven, the heart's true home, will
    come at last.
        Angels of Jesus,
        Angels of light,
        Singing to welcome
        The pilgrims of the night!

Cheer up, my soul! faith's moonbeams
    softly glisten
Upon the breast of life's most troubled
    sea;
And it will cheer thy drooping heart to
    listen
To those brave songs which angels mean
    for thee.
        Angels of Jesus,
        Angels of light,
        Singing to welcome
        The pilgrims of the night!

Angels! sing on, your faithful watches
    keeping,
Sing us sweet fragments of the songs
    above;
While we toil on, and soothe ourselves with
    weeping,
Till life's long night shall break in endless love.
        Angels of Jesus,
        Angels of light,
        Singing to welcome
        The pilgrims of the night!
            FREDERICK WILLIAM FABER.

PARADISE.

O PARADISE! O Paradise!
    Who doth not crave for rest?
Who would not seek the happy land,
    Where they that loved are blest?
        Where loyal hearts, and true,
        Stand ever in the light,
        All rapture through and through,
        In God's most holy sight.

O Paradise! O Paradise!
    The world is growing old;
Who would not be at rest and free
    Where love is never cold,
        Where loyal hearts, and true,
        Stand ever in the light,
        All rapture through and through,
        In God's most holy sight?

O Paradise! O Paradise!
    Wherefore doth death delay,
Bright death, that is the welcome dawn
    Of our eternal day,
        Where loyal hearts, and true,
        Stand ever in the light,
        All rapture through and through,
        In God's most holy sight?

O Paradise! O Paradise!
    'Tis weary waiting here:
I long to be where Jesus is,
    To feel, to see Him near;
        Where loyal hearts, and true,
        Stand ever in the light,
        All rapture through and through,
        In God's most holy sight.

O Paradise! O Paradise!
    I want to sin no more;
I want to be as pure on earth
    As on thy spotless shore;
        Where loyal hearts, and true,
        Stand ever in the light,
        All rapture through and through,
        In God's most holy sight.

O Paradise! O Paradise!
    I greatly long to see
The special place my dearest Lord
    Is destining for me;
        Where loyal hearts, and true,
        Stand ever in the light,
        All rapture through and through,
        In God's most holy sight.
            FREDERICK WILLIAM FABER.

PRAISE.

WORSHIP, honor, glory, blessing,
    Be to Him who reigns above!
Young and old Thy Name confessing,
    Saviour! let us share Thy love!

As the saints in heaven adore Thee,
  We would bow before Thy throne;
As Thine angels bow before Thee,
  So on earth Thy will be done!
                EDWARD OSLER.

THE NEW JERUSALEM;
OR, THE SOUL'S BREATHING AFTER THE HEAVENLY COUNTRY.

"Since Christ's fair truth needs no man's art,
Take this rude song in better part."

O MOTHER dear, Jerusalem,
  When shall I come to thee?
When shall my sorrows have an end—
  Thy joys when shall I see?
O happy harbor of God's saints!
  O sweet and pleasant soil!
In thee no sorrows can be found—
  No grief, no care, no toil.

In thee no sickness is at all,
  No hurt, nor any sore;
There is no death nor ugly night,
  But life for evermore.
No dimming cloud o'ershadows thee,
  No cloud nor darksome night,
But every soul shines as the sun—
  For God himself gives light.

There lust and lucre cannot dwell,
  There envy bears no sway;
There is no hunger, thirst, nor heat,
  But pleasures every way.
Jerusalem! Jerusalem!
  Would God I were in thee!
Oh! that my sorrows had an end,
  Thy joys that I might see!

No pains, no pangs, no grieving grief,
  No woeful night is there;
No sigh, no sob, no cry is heard—
  No well-away, no fear.
Jerusalem the city is
  Of God our King alone;
The Lamb of God, the light thereof,
  Sits there upon His throne.

O God! that I Jerusalem
  With speed may go behold!
For why? the pleasures there abound
  Which here cannot be told.
Thy turrets and thy pinnacles
  With carbuncles do shine—
With jasper, pearl, and chrysolite,
  Surpassing pure and fine.

Thy houses are of ivory,
  Thy windows crystal clear,
Thy streets are laid with beaten gold—
  There angels do appear.
Thy walls are made of precious stone,
  Thy bulwarks diamond square,
Thy gates are made of orient pearl—
  O God! if I were there!

Within thy gates nothing can come
  That is not passing clean;
No spider's web, no dirt, nor dust,
  No filth may there be seen.
Jehovah, Lord, now come away,
  And end my griefs and plaints—
Take me to Thy Jerusalem,
  And place me with Thy saints!

Who there are crown'd with glory great,
  And see God face to face,
They triumph still, and aye rejoice—
  Most happy is their case.
But we that are in banishment
  Continually do moan;
We sigh, we mourn, we sob, we weep—
  Perpetually we groan.

Our sweetness mixèd is with gall,
  Our pleasures are but pain,
Our joys not worth the looking on—
  Our sorrows aye remain.
But there they live in such delight,
  Such pleasure and such play,
That unto them a thousand years
  Seems but as yesterday.

O my sweet home, Jerusalem!
  Thy joys when shall I see—
The King sitting upon His throne,
  And thy felicity?
Thy vineyards, and thy orchards,
  So wonderfully rare,
Are furnish'd with all kinds of fruit,
  Most beautifully fair.

Thy gardens and thy goodly walks
  Continually are green;
There grow such sweet and pleasant flowers
  As nowhere else are seen.
There cinnamon and sugar grow,
  There nard and balm abound;

No tongue can tell, no heart can think,
  The pleasures there are found.

There nectar and ambrosia spring—
  There music's ever sweet;
There many a fair and dainty thing
  Is trod down under feet.
Quite through the streets, with pleasant sound,
  The flood of life doth flow;
Upon the banks, on every side,
  The trees of life do grow.

These trees each month yield ripen'd fruit—
  For evermore they spring;
And all the nations of the world
  To thee their honors bring.
Jerusalem, God's dwelling-place,
  Full sore I long to see;
Oh! that my sorrows had an end,
  That I might dwell in thee!

There David stands, with harp in hand,
  As master of the choir;
A thousand times that man were blest
  That might his music hear.
There Mary sings "Magnificat,"
  With tunes surpassing sweet;
And all the virgins bear their part,
  Singing about her feet.

"Te Deum" doth St. Ambrose sing,
  St. Austin doth the like;
Old Simeon and Zacharie
  Have not their songs to seek.
There Magdalene hath left her moan,
  And cheerfully doth sing,
With all blest saints whose harmony
  Through every street doth ring.

Jerusalem! Jerusalem!
  Thy joys fain would I see;
Come quickly, Lord, and end my grief,
  And take me home to Thee;
Oh! paint Thy name on my forehead,
  And take me hence away,
That I may dwell with Thee in bliss,
  And sing Thy praises aye.

Jerusalem, the happy home—
  Jehovah's throne on high!
O sacred city, queen, and wife
  Of Christ eternally!
O comely queen with glory clad,
  With honor and degree,
All fair thou art, exceeding bright—
  No spot there is in thee!

I long to see Jerusalem,
  The comfort of us all;
For thou art fair and beautiful—
  None ill can thee befall.
In thee, Jerusalem, I say,
  No darkness dare appear—
No night, no shade, no winter foul—
  No time doth alter there.

No candle needs, no moon to shine,
  No glittering star to light;
For Christ, the King of righteousness,
  For ever shineth bright.
A Lamb unspotted, white and pure
  To Thee doth stand in lieu
Of light—so great the glory is
  Thine heavenly King to view.

He is the King of kings, beset
  In midst His servants' sight;
And they, His happy household all,
  Do serve Him day and night.
There, there the choir of angels sing—
  There the supernal sort
Of citizens, which hence are rid
  From dangers deep, do sport.

There be the prudent prophets all,
  The apostles six and six,
The glorious martyrs in a row,
  And confessors betwixt.
There doth the crew of righteous men
  And matrons all consist—
Young men and maids that here on earth
  Their pleasures did resist.

The sheep and lambs, that hardly 'scaped
  The snare of death and hell,
Triumph in joy eternally,
  Whereof no tongue can tell;
And though the glory of each one
  Doth differ in degree,
Yet is the joy of all alike
  And common, as we see

There love and charity do reign,
 And Christ is all in all,
Whom they most perfectly behold
 In joy celestial.
They love, they praise—they praise, they love;
 They "Holy, holy," cry;
They neither toil, nor faint, nor end,
 But laud continually.

Oh! happy thousand times were I,
 If, after wretched days,
I might with listening ears conceive
 Those heavenly songs of praise,
Which to the eternal King are sung
 By happy wights above,
By savèd souls and angels sweet,
 Who love the God of love.

Oh! passing happy were my state,
 Might I be worthy found
To wait upon my God and King,
 His praises there to sound;
And to enjoy my Christ above,
 His favor and His grace,
According to His promise made,
 Which here I interlace:

"O Father dear," quoth he, "let them
 Which Thou hast put of old
To me, be there where lo! I am—
 Thy glory to behold;
Which I with Thee before the world
 Was made in perfect wise,
Have had—from whence the fountain great
 Of glory doth arise."

Again: "If any man will serve
 Thee, let him follow Me;
For where I am, he there, right sure,
 Then shall My servant be."
And still: "If any man loves Me,
 Him loves My Father dear,
Whom I do love—to him Myself
 In glory will appear."

Lord, take away my misery,
 That then I may be bold
With Thee, in Thy Jerusalem,
 Thy glory to behold;
And so in Zion see my King,
 My love, my Lord, my all—

Where now as in a glass I see,
 There face to face I shall.

Oh! blessed are the pure in heart—
 Their Sovereign they shall see;
O ye most happy, heavenly wights,
 Which of God's household be!
O Lord, with speed dissolve my bands,
 These gins and fetters strong;
For I have dwelt within the tents
 Of Kedar over long.

Yet search me, Lord, and find me out!
 Fetch me Thy fold unto,
That all Thy angels may rejoice,
 While all Thy will I do.
O mother dear! Jerusalem!
 When shall I come to thee?
When shall my sorrows have an end,
 Thy joys when shall I see?

Yet once again I pray Thee, Lord,
 To quit me from all strife,
That to Thy hill I may attain,
 And dwell there all my life—
With cherubims and seraphims
 And holy souls of men,
To sing Thy praise, O God of hosts!
 For ever and amen!
AUTHOR UNKNOWN.

THE CELESTIAL COUNTRY.

THE world is very evil;
 The times are waxing late:
Be sober and keep vigil;
 The Judge is at the gate:
The Judge that comes in mercy,
 The Judge that comes with might
To terminate the evil,
 To diadem the right.
When the just and gentle Monarch
 Shall summon from the tomb,
Let man, the guilty, tremble,
 For Man, the God, shall doom.
Arise, arise, good Christian!
 Let right to wrong succeed;
Let penitential sorrow
 To heavenly gladness lead;
To the light that hath no evening,
 That knows nor moon nor sun,
The light so new and golden,
 The light that is but one.

And when the Sole-Begotten
  Shall render up once more
The kingdom to the Father
  Whose own it was before,—
Then glory yet unheard of
  Shall shed abroad its ray,
Resolving all enigmas,
  An endless Sabbath-day.
Then, then from his oppressors
  The Hebrew shall go free,
And celebrate in triumph
  The year of Jubilee;
And the sunlit land that recks not
  Of tempest nor of fight,
Shall fold within its bosom
  Each happy Israelite:
The home of fadeless splendor,
  Of flowers that fear no thorn,
Where they shall dwell as children,
  Who here as exiles mourn.
Midst power that knows no limit,
  And wisdom free from bound,
The Beatific vision
  Shall glad the saints around·
The peace of all the faithful,
  The calm of all the blest,
Inviolate, unvaried,
  Divinest, sweetest, best.
Yes, peace! for war is needless,—
  Yes, calm! for storm is past,—
And goal from finish'd labor,
  And anchorage at last.
That peace—but who may claim it?
  The guileless in their way,
Who keep the ranks of battle,
  Who mean the thing they say:
The peace that is for heaven,
  And shall be for the earth:
The palace that re-echoes
  With festal song and mirth;
The garden, breathing spices,
  The paradise on high;
Grace beautified to glory,
  Unceasing minstrelsy.
There nothing can be feeble,
  There none can ever mourn,
There nothing is divided,
  There nothing can be torn:
'Tis fury, ill, and scandal,
  'Tis peaceless peace below;
Peace, endless, strifeless, ageless,
  The halls of Sion know:

O happy, holy portion,
  Refection for the blest;
True vision of true beauty,
  Sweet cure of all distrest!
Strive, man, to win that glory;
  Toil, man, to gain that light;
Send hope before to grasp it,
  Till hope be lost in sight:
Till Jesus gives the portion
  Those blessed souls to fill,
The insatiate, yet satisfied,
  The full, yet craving still.
That fulness and that craving
  Alike are free from pain,
Where thou, midst heavenly citizens,
  A home like theirs shalt gain.
Here is the warlike trumpet;
  There, life set free from sin;
When to the last Great Supper
  The faithful shall come in:
When the heavenly net is laden
  With fishes many and great;
So glorious in its fulness,
  Yet so inviolate:
And the perfect from the shatter'd,
  And the fall'n from them that stand,
And the sheep-flock from the goat-herd
  Shall part on either hand!
And these shall pass to torment,
  And those shall triumph, then;
The new peculiar nation,
  Blest number of blest men.
Jerusalem demands them:
  They paid the price on earth,
And now shall reap the harvest
  In blissfulness and mirth:
The glorious holy people,
  Who evermore relied
Upon their Chief and Father,
  The King, the Crucified:
The sacred ransom'd number
  Now bright with endless sheen,
Who made the Cross their watchword
  Of Jesus Nazarene:
Who, fed with heavenly nectar,
  Where soul-like odors play,
Draw out the endless leisure
  Of that long vernal day:
And through the sacred lilies,
  And flowers on every side,
The happy dear-bought people
  Go wandering far and wide.

Their breasts are filled with gladness,
  Their mouths are tuned to praise,
What time, now safe for ever,
  On former sins they gaze:
The fouler was the error,
  The sadder was the fall,
The ampler are the praises
  Of Him who pardon'd all.
Their one and only anthem,
  The fulness of His love,
Who gives instead of torment
  Eternal joys above;
Instead of torment, glory;
  Instead of death, that life
Wherewith your happy country,
  True Israelites, is rife.

Brief life is here our portion,
  Brief sorrow, short-lived care,
The life that knows no ending,
  The tearless life, is there.
O happy retribution!
  Short toil, eternal rest,
For mortals and for sinners
  A mansion with the blest!
That we should look, poor wand'rers,
  To have our home on high!
That worms should seek for dwellings
  Beyond the starry sky!
To all one happy guerdon
  Of one celestial grace;
For all, for all, who mourn their fall,
  Is one eternal place;
And martyrdom hath roses
  Upon that heavenly ground,
And white and virgin lilies
  For virgin-souls abound.
There grief is turn'd to pleasure,
  Such pleasure as below
No human voice can utter,
  No human heart can know;
And after fleshly scandal,
  And after this world's night,
And after storm and whirlwind,
  Is calm, and joy, and light.
And now we fight the battle,
  But then shall wear the crown
Of full and everlasting
  And passionless renown;
And now we watch and struggle,
  And now we live in hope,

And Sion, in her anguish,
  With Babylon must cope;
But He whom now we trust in
  Shall then be seen and known,
And they that know and see Him
  Shall have Him for their own.
The miserable pleasures
  Of the body shall decay;
The bland and flattering struggles
  Of the flesh shall pass away,
And none shall there be jealous,
  And none shall there contend;
Fraud, clamor, guile—what say I?
  All ill, all ill shall end!
And there is David's Fountain,
  And life in fullest glow,
And there the light is golden,
  And milk and honey flow;
The light that hath no evening,
  The health that hath no sore,
The life that hath no ending,
  But lasteth evermore.

There Jesus shall embrace us,
  There Jesus be embraced,—
That spirit's food and sunshine
  Whence earthly love is chased.
Amidst the happy chorus.
  A place, however low,
Shall show Him us, and showing,
  Shall satiate evermo.
By hope we struggle onward,
  While here we must be fed
By milk, as tender infants,
  But there by Living Bread.
The night was full of terror,
  The morn is bright with gladness:
The Cross becomes our harbor,
  And we triumph after sadness,
And Jesus to His true ones
  Brings trophies fair to see,
And Jesus shall be loved, and
  Beheld in Galilee;
Beheld, when morn shall waken,
  And shadows shall decay,
And each true-hearted servant
  Shall shine as doth the day;
And every ear shall hear it,—
  Behold thy King's array,
Behold thy God in beauty,
  The Law hath past away!

Yes! God my King and Portion,
  In fulness of His grace,
We then shall see for ever,
  And worship face to face.
Then Jacob into Israel,
  From earthlier self estranged,
And Leah into Rachel,
  For ever shall be changed:
Then all the halls of Sion
  For aye shall be complete,
And, in the Land of Beauty,
  All things of beauty meet.

For thee, oh dear dear Country!
  Mine eyes their vigils keep;
For very love, beholding
  Thy happy name, they weep:
The mention of thy glory
  Is unction to the breast,
And medicine in sickness,
  And love, and life, and rest.
O one, O onely Mansion!
  O Paradise of Joy!
Where tears are ever banish'd,
  And smiles have no alloy;
Beside thy living waters
  All plants are, great and small,
The cedar of the forest,
  The hyssop of the wall:
With jaspers glow thy bulwarks;
  Thy streets with emeralds blaze;
The sardius and the topaz
  Unite in thee their rays:
Thine ageless walls ere bonded
  With amethyst unpriced:
Thy Saints build up its fabric,
  And the corner-stone is Christ.
The Cross is all thy splendor,
  The Crucified thy praise:
His laud and benediction
  Thy ransom'd people raise:
Jesus, the Gem of Beauty,
  True God and Man, they sing:
The never-failing Garden,
  The ever-golden Ring:
The Door, the Pledge, the Husband,
  The Guardian of his Court:
The Day-star of Salvation,
  The Porter and the Port.
Thou hast no shore, fair ocean!
  Thou hast no time, bright day!

Dear fountain of refreshment
  To pilgrims far away!
Upon the Rock of Ages
  They raise thy holy tower:
Thine is the victor's laurel,
  And thine the golden dower:
Thou feel'st in mystic rapture,
  O Bride that know'st no guile,
The Prince's sweetest kisses,
  The Prince's loveliest smile;
Unfading lilies, bracelets
  Of living pearl thine own;
The Lamb is ever near thee,
  The Bridegroom thine alone;
The Crown is He to guerdon,
  The Buckler to protect,
And He Himself the Mansion,
  And He the Architect.
The only art thou needest,
  Thanksgiving for thy lot:
The only joy thou seekest,
  The Life where Death is not:
And all thine endless leisure
  In sweetest accents sings,
The ill that was thy merit,—
  The wealth that is thy King's!

Jerusalem the golden,
  With milk and honey blest,
Beneath thy contemplation
  Sink heart and voice oppress'd:
I know not, oh I know not,
  What social joys are there;
What radiancy of glory,
  What light beyond compare!
And when I fain would sing them,
  My spirit fails and faints;
And vainly would it image
  The assembly of the Saints.
They stand, those halls of Sion,
  Conjubilant with song,
And bright with many an angel,
  And all the martyr throng:
The Prince is ever in them;
  The daylight is serene;
The pastures of the Blessed
  Are deck'd in glorious sheen.
There is the Throne of David,—
  And there, from care released,
The song of them that triumph,
  The shout of them that feast;

And they who, with their Leader,
   Have conquer'd in the fight,
For ever and for ever
   Are clad in robes of white!

O holy, placid harp-notes
   Of that eternal hymn!
O sacred, sweet refection,
   And peace of Seraphim!
O thirst for ever ardent,
   Yet evermore content!
O true peculiar vision
   Of God cunctipotent!
Ye know the many mansions
   For many a glorious name,
And divers retributions
   That divers merits claim:
For midst the constellations
   That deck our earthly sky,
This star than that is brighter,—
   And so it is on high.

Jerusalem the glorious!
   The glory of the Elect!
O dear and future vision
   That eager hearts expect:
Even now by faith I see thee:
   Even here thy walls discern:
To thee my thoughts are kindled,
   And strive and pant and yearn:
Jerusalem the onely,
   That look'st from heaven below,
In thee is all my glory;
   In me is all my woe:
And though my body may not,
   My spirit seeks thee fain,
Till flesh and earth return me
   To earth and flesh again.
Oh none can tell thy bulwarks,
   How gloriously they rise:
Oh none can tell thy capitals
   Of beautiful device:
Thy loveliness oppresses
   All human thought and heart:
And none, O Peace, O Sion,
   Can sing thee as thou art.
New mansion of new people,
   Whom God's own love and light
Promote, increase, make holy,
   Identify, unite.
Thou City of the Angels!
   Thou City of the Lord!

Whose everlasting music
   Is the glorious decachord!
And there the band of Prophets
   United praise ascribes,
And there the twelvefold chorus
   Of Israel's ransom'd tribes:
The lily-beds of virgins,
   The roses' martyr-glow,
The cohort of the Fathers
   Who kept the faith below.
And there the Sole-Begotten
   Is Lord in regal state;
He, Judah's mystic Lion,
   He, Lamb Immaculate.
O fields that know no sorrow!
   O state that fears no strife!
O princely bow'rs! O land of flow'rs!
   O realm and home of life!

Jerusalem, exulting
   On that securest shore,
I hope thee, wish thee, sing thee,
   And love thee evermore!
I ask not for my merit:
   I seek not to deny
My merit is destruction,
   A child of wrath am I:
But yet with Faith I venture
   And Hope upon my way;
For those perennial guerdons
   I labor night and day.
The best and dearest Father
   Who made me, and who saved,
Bore with me in defilement,
   And from defilement laved;
When in His strength I struggle,
   For very joy I leap,
When in my sin I totter,
   I weep, or try to weep;
And grace, sweet grace celestial,
   Shall all its love display,
And David's royal Fountain
   Purge every sin away.

O mine, my golden Sion!
   O lovelier far than gold!
With laurel-girt battalions,
   And safe victorious fold;
O sweet and blessed country,
   Shall I ever see thy face?
O sweet and blessed country,
   Shall I ever win thy grace?

I have the hope within me
  To comfort and to bless!
Shall I ever win the prize itself?
  Oh, tell me, tell me, Yes!

Exult, O dust and ashes!
  The Lord shall be thy part;
His only, His for ever,
  Thou shalt be, and thou art!
Exult, O dust and ashes!
  The Lord shall be thy part;
His only, His for ever,
  Thou shalt be, and thou art!
BERNARD OF CLUNY.
(Translation of JOHN MASON NEALE.)

CHRIST WILL GATHER IN HIS OWN.

CHRIST will gather in His own
To the place where He is gone,
Where their heart and treasure lie,
Where our life is hid on high.

Day by day the voice saith, "Come,
Enter this eternal home;"
Asking not if we can spare
This dear soul its summons there.

Had He ask'd us, well we know
We should cry, "Oh spare this blow!"
Yes, with streaming tears should pray,
"Lord, we love him; let him stay."

But the Lord doth naught amiss,
And, since He hath ordered this,
We have naught to do but still
Rest in silence on His will.

Many a heart no longer here,
Ah! was all too inly dear:
Yet, O Love, 'tis Thou dost call,
Thou wilt be our all in all.
AUTHOR UNKNOWN.

DIES IRÆ.

Dies Iræ, Dies Illa, dies tribulationis et angustiæ, dies calamitatis et miseriæ, dies tenebrarum et caliginis, dies nebulæ et turbinis, dies tubæ et clangoris super civitatis munitas, et super angulos excelsos!—*Sophonia*, i. 15, 16.

  DIES Iræ, Dies Illa!
  Solvet sæclum in favillâ,
  Teste David cum Sybillâ.

Quantus tremor est futurus,
Quando Judex est venturus,
Cuncta stricte discussurus.

Tuba mirum spargens sonum
Per sepulcra regionum,
Coget omnes ante thronum.

Mors stupebit, et natura,
Quum resurget creatura,
Judicanti responsura.

Liber scriptus proferetur,
In quo totum continetur,
Unde mundus judicetur.

Judex ergo cum sedebit,
Quidquid latet, apparebit:
Nil inultum remanebit.

Quid sum, miser! tunc dicturus,
Quem patronum rogaturus,
Quum vix justus sit securus?

Rex tremendæ majestatis,
Qui salvandos salvas gratis,
Salva me, fons pietatis!

Recordare, Jesu pie,
Quod sum causa tuæ viæ;
Ne me perdas illâ die!

Quærens me, sedisti lassus,
Redemisti, crucem passus:
Tantus labor non sit cassus.

Juste Judex ultionis,
Donum fac remissionis
Ante diem rationis.

Ingemisco tanquam reus,
Culpâ rubet vultus meus,
Supplicanti parce, Deus!

Qui Mariam absolvisti,
Et latronem exaudisti,
Mihi quoque spem dedisti.

Preces meæ non sunt dignæ,
Sed Tu bonus fac benigne
Ne perenni cremer igne!

Inter oves locum præsta,
Et ab hædis me sequestra,
Statuens in parte dextrâ.

Confutatis maledictis,
Flammis acribus addictis,
Voca me cum benedictis!

Oro supplex et acclinis,
Cor contritum quasi cinis,
Gere curam mei finis.

Lacrymosa dies illâ!
Qua resurget ex favillâ.
Judicandus homo reus;
Huic ergo parce, Deus!
THOMAS DE CELANO.

DIES IRÆ.

TRANSLATION OF WILLIAM J. IRONS.

DAY of wrath! O day of mourning!
See! once more the Cross returning,
Heaven and earth in ashes burning!

Oh what fear man's bosom rendeth
When from Heaven the Judge descendeth,
On whose sentence all dependeth!

Wondrous sound the Trumpet flingeth,
Through earth's sepulchres it ringeth,
All before the throne it bringeth!

Death is struck, and Nature quaking,
All creation is awaking,
To its Judge an answer making!

Lo, the Book, exactly worded!
Wherein all hath been recorded;
Thence shall judgment be awarded.

When the Judge His seat attaineth,
And each hidden deed arraigneth,
Nothing unavenged remaineth.

What shall I, frail man, be pleading,
Who for me be interceding,
When the just are mercy needing?

King of Majesty tremendous,
Who dost free salvation send us,
Fount of pity! then befriend us!

Think! kind Jesu, my salvation
Caused Thy wondrous incarnation;
Leave me not to reprobation!

Faint and weary Thou hast sought me,
On the Cross of suffering bought me,
Shall such grace be vainly brought me?

Righteous Judge of retribution,
Grant Thy gift of absolution,
Ere that reck'ning day's conclusion!

Guilty, now I pour my moaning,
All my shame with anguish owning;
Spare, O God, Thy suppliant groaning!

Thou the sinful woman savedst,
Thou the dying thief forgavest;
And to me a hope vouchsafest!

Worthless are my prayers and sighing,
Yet, good Lord, in grace complying,
Rescue me from fires undying!

With Thy favor'd sheep, oh place me!
Nor among the goats abase me;
But to Thy right hand upraise me.

While the wicked are confounded,
Doom'd to flames of woe unbounded,
Call me! with Thy saints surrounded.

Low I kneel with heart submission;
See, like ashes, my contrition;
Help me, in my last condition!

Ah! that Day of tears and mourning!
From the dust of earth returning,
Man for judgment must prepare him;
Spare, O God, in mercy spare him!

Lord, who didst our souls redeem,
Grant a blessed Requiem! Amen.

DIES IRÆ.

PARAPHRASE OF SIR WALTER SCOTT.

THAT day of wrath, that dreadful day,
When heaven and earth shall pass away,
What power shall be the sinner's stay?
How shall he meet that dreadful day?

When, shrivelling like a parchèd scroll,
The flaming heavens together roll;
When louder yet, and yet more dread,
Swells the high trump that wakes the dead;

Oh, on that day, that wrathful day,
When man to judgment wakes from clay,
Be Thou the trembling sinner's stay,
Though heaven and earth shall pass away!

DIES IRÆ.

Translation of John A. Dix.

Day of vengeance, without morrow!
Earth shall end in flame and sorrow,
As from saint and seer we borrow.

Ah! what terror is impending,
When the Judge is seen descending,
And each secret veil is rending!

To the throne, the trumpet sounding,
Through the sepulchres resounding,
Summons all, with voice astounding.

Death and Nature, 'mazed, are quaking,
When, the grave's long slumber breaking,
Man to judgment is awaking.

On the written volume's pages
Life is shown in all its stages,—
Judgment-record of past ages!

Sits the Judge, the raised arraigning,
Darkest mysteries explaining,
Nothing unavenged remaining.

What shall I then say, unfriended,
By no advocate attended,
When the just are scarce defended?

King of majesty tremendous,
By Thy saving grace defend us,
Fount of pity, safety send us!

Holy Jesus, meek, forbearing,
For my sins the death-crown wearing,
Save me, in that day, despairing.

Worn and weary, Thou hast sought me,
By Thy cross and passion bought me,—
Spare the hope Thy labors brought me.

Righteous Judge of retribution,
Give, oh, give me absolution
Ere the day of dissolution.

As a guilty culprit groaning,
Flush'd my face, my errors owning,
Hear, O God, my spirit's moaning!

Thou to Mary gav'st remission,
Heard'st the dying thief's petition,
Bad'st me hope in my contrition.

In my prayers no grace discerning,
Yet on me Thy favor turning,
Save my soul from endless burning.

Give me, when thy sheep confiding
Thou art from the goats dividing,
On Thy right a place abiding!

When the wicked are confounded,
And by bitter flames surrounded,
Be my joyful pardon sounded.

Prostrate, all my guilt discerning,
Heart as though to ashes turning,
Save, oh, save me from the burning!

Day of weeping, when from ashes
Man shall rise 'mid lightning-flashes,
Guilty, trembling with contrition,
Save him, Father, from perdition!

LO! HE COMES, WITH CLOUDS DESCENDING!

Lo! He comes, with clouds descending!
  Hark! the trump of God is blown,
And th' Archangel's voice attending
  Makes the high procession known:
    Sons of Adam!
  Rise, and stand before your God!

Crowns and sceptres fall before Him,
  Kings and conquerors own His sway;
Haughtiest monarchs now adore Him,
  While they see His lightnings play:
    How triumphant
  Is the world's Redeemer now!

Hear His voice, as mighty thunder
  Sounding in eternal roar,
While its echo rends in sunder
  Rocks and mountains, sea and shore:
    Hark! His accents
  Through th' unfathom'd deep resound!

"Come, Lord Jesus! Oh come quickly!"
  Oft has pray'd the mourning Bride:
"Lo!" He answers, "I come quickly!"
  Who Thy coming may abide?
    All who loved Him,
  All who long'd to see His day.

"Come," he saith, 'ye heirs of glory;
  Come, ye purchase of my blood;
Claim the Kingdom now before you,
  Rise, and fill the mount of God,
    Fix'd for ever
  Where the Lamb on Sion stands."

See! ten thousand burning seraphs
  From their thrones as lightnings fly;
"Take," they cry, "your seats above us,
  Nearest Him that rules the sky!"
    Patient sufferers,
  How rewarded are ye now!

Now their trials all are ended:
  Now the dubious warfare's o'er;
Joy no more with sorrow blended,
  They shall sigh and weep no more;
    God for ever
  Wipes the tear from every eye.

Through His passion all victorious
  Now they drink immortal wine;
In Emmanuel's likeness glorious
  As the firmament they shine;
    Shine for ever,
  With the bright and morning Star.

Shout aloud, ye ethereal choirs!
  Triumph in Jehovah's praise!
Kindle all your heavenly fires,
  All your palms of victory raise!
    Shout His conquests,
  Shout salvation to the Lamb!

In full triumph see them marching
  Through the gates of massy light,
While the City walls are sparkling
  With meridian glory bright;
    Oh how lovely
  Are the dwellings of the Lamb!

Hosts angelic all adore Him
  Circling round His orient seat;
Elders cast their crowns before Him,
  Fall and worship at His feet;
    O how holy
  And how reverend is Thy Name!

Hail, Thou Alpha and Omega!
  First and Last, of all alone!
He that is, and was, and shall be,
  And beside whom there is none!
    Take the Glory,
  Great Eternal Three in One!
          THOMAS OLIVERS.

LORD, DISMISS US WITH THY BLESSING.

LORD, dismiss us with Thy blessing,
  Fill our hearts with joy and peace;
Let us each, Thy love possessing,
  Triumph in redeeming grace;
    Oh refresh us,
  Travelling through this wilderness.

Thanks we give, and adoration,
  For Thy gospel's joyful sound;
May the fruit of Thy salvation
  In our hearts and lives abound:
    May Thy presence
  With us evermore be found.

So, whene'er the signal's given
  Us from earth to call away,
Borne on angels' wings to heaven,
  Glad the summons to obey,
    May we ever
  Reign with Christ in endless day.
          WALTER SHIRLEY.

Bride, who dost wear the widow's veil
Before the wedding flowers are pale,—
Ye deem the human heart endures
No deeper, bitterer grief than yours.

        Wm Cullen Bryant

Moral and Didactic Poetry.

LIFE.

THE World's a bubble, and the Life of Man
    Less than a span:
In his conception wretched, from the womb,
    So to the tomb;
Curst from his cradle, and brought up to years
    With cares and fears.
Who then to frail mortality shall trust,
But limns on water, or but writes in dust.

Yet whilst with sorrow here we live opprest,
    What life is best?
Courts are but only superficial schools
    To dandle fools:
The rural parts are turn'd into a den
    Of savage men:
And where's a city from foul vice so free,
But may be term'd the worst of all the three?

Domestic cares afflict the husband's bed,
    Or pains his head:
Those that live single, take it for a curse,
    Or do things worse:
Some would have children: those that have them, moan
    Or wish them gone:
What is it, then, to have, or have no wife,
But single thraldom, or a double strife?

Our own affection still at home to please
    Is a disease:
To cross the seas to any foreign soil,
    Peril and toil:
Wars with their noise affright us; when they cease,
    We are worse in peace;—
What then remains, but that we still should cry
For being born, or, being born, to die?
LORD BACON.

LIFE.

LIFE! I know not what thou art,
But know that thou and I must part;
And when, or how, or where we met
I own to me's a secret yet.

Life! we've been long together,
Through pleasant and through cloudy weather;
'Tis hard to part when friends are dear—
Perhaps 'twill cost a sigh, a tear;
—Then steal away, give little warning,
Choose thine own time;
Say not Good-Night,—but in some brighter clime
Bid me Good-Morning.
ANNA LÆTITIA BARBAULD.

MY PSALM.

I MOURN no more my vanish'd years:
    Beneath a tender rain,
An April rain of smiles and tears,
    My heart is young again.

The west winds blow, and, singing low,
    I hear the glad streams run;
The windows of my soul I throw
    Wide open to the sun.

No longer forward nor behind
    I look in hope or fear;
But, grateful, take the good I find,
    The best of now and here.

I plough no more a desert land,
    To harvest weed and tare;
The manna dropping from God's hand
    Rebukes my painful care.

I break my pilgrim staff,—I lay
    Aside the toiling oar;

The angel sought so far away
  I welcome at my door.

The airs of spring may never play
  Among the ripening corn,
Nor freshness of the flowers of May
  Blow through the autumn morn;

Yet shall the blue-eyed gentian look
  Through fringèd lids to heaven,
And the pale aster in the brook
  Shall see its image given;—

The woods shall wear their robes of praise,
  The south wind softly sigh,
And sweet, calm days, in golden haze
  Melt down the amber sky.

Not less shall manly deed and word
  Rebuke an age of wrong;
The graven flowers that wreathe the sword
  Make not the blade less strong.

But smiting hands shall learn to heal,—
  To build as to destroy;
Nor less my heart for others feel
  That I the more enjoy.

All as God wills, who wisely heeds
  To give or to withhold,
And knoweth more of all my needs
  Than all my prayers have told!

Enough that blessings undeserved
  Have mark'd my erring track;—
That wheresoe'er my feet have swerved,
  His chastening turn'd me back;—

That more and more a Providence
  Of love is understood,
Making the springs of time and sense
  Sweet with eternal good;—

That death seems but a cover'd way
  Which opens into light,
Wherein no blinded child can stray
  Beyond the Father's sight;—

That care and trial seem at last,
  Through Memory's sunset air,
Like mountain-ranges overpast,
  In purple distance fair;—

That all the jarring notes of life
  Seem blending in a psalm,
And all the angles of its strife
  Slow rounding into calm.

And so the shadows fall apart,
  And so the west winds play;
And all the windows of my heart
  I open to the day.
              JOHN GREENLEAF WHITTIER.

SONNET.

SAD is our youth, for it is ever going,
  Crumbling away beneath our very feet;
Sad is our life, for onward it is flowing
  In current unperceived, because so fleet;
Sad are our hopes, for they were sweet in sowing—
  But tares, self-sown, have overtopp'd the wheat;
Sad are our joys, for they were sweet in blowing—
  And still, oh still, their dying breath is sweet;
And sweet is youth, although it hath bereft us
  Of that which made our childhood sweeter still;
And sweet is middle life, for it hath left us
  A nearer good to cure an older ill;
And sweet are all things, when we learn to prize them
Not for their sake, but His who grants them or denies them!
              AUBREY DE VERE.

THE STREAM OF LIFE.

O STREAM descending to the sea,
  Thy mossy banks between,
The flow'rets blow, the grasses grow,
  The leafy trees are green.

In garden-plots the children play,
  The fields the laborers till,
And houses stand on either hand,
  And thou descendest still.

O life descending into death,
  Our waking eyes behold
Parent and friend thy lapse attend,
  Companions young and old.

Strong purposes our minds possess,
  Our hearts affections fill;
We toil and earn, we seek and learn,
  And thou descendest still.

O end to which our currents tend,
  Inevitable sea
To which we flow, what do we know,
  What shall we guess of thee?

A roar we hear upon thy shore,
  As we our course fulfil;
Scarce we divine a sun will shine
  And be above us still.
ARTHUR HUGH CLOUGH.

A PSALM OF LIFE.

WHAT THE HEART OF THE YOUNG MAN SAID TO THE PSALMIST.

TELL me not in mournful numbers,
  "Life is but an empty dream!"
For the soul is dead that slumbers,
  And things are not what they seem.

Life is real! Life is earnest!
  And the grave is not its goal;
"Dust thou art, to dust returnest,"
  Was not spoken of the soul.

Not enjoyment, and not sorrow,
  Is our destined end or way;
But to act, that each to-morrow
  Finds us farther than to-day.

Art is long, and time is fleeting,
  And our hearts, though stout and brave,
Still, like muffled drums, are beating
  Funeral marches to the grave.

In the world's broad field of battle,
  In the bivouac of life,
Be not like dumb, driven cattle,
  Be a hero in the strife!

Trust no future, howe'er pleasant!
  Let the dead past bury its dead!
Act—act in the living present!
  Heart within, and God o'erhead!

Lives of great men all remind us
  We can make our lives sublime,
And, departing, leave behind us
  Footprints on the sands of time—

Footprints that perhaps another,
  Sailing o'er life's solemn main
A forlorn and shipwreck'd brother,
  Seeing, shall take heart again.

Let us, then, be up and doing,
  With a heart for any fate;
Still achieving, still pursuing,
  Learn to labor and to wait.
HENRY WADSWORTH LONGFELLOW.

LIFE.

WE are born; we laugh; we weep;
  We love; we droop; we die!
Ah! wherefore do we laugh or weep?
  Why do we live or die?
Who knows that secret deep?
  Alas, not I!

Why doth the violet spring
  Unseen by human eye?
Why do the radiant seasons bring
  Sweet thoughts that quickly fly?
Why do our fond hearts cling
  To things that die?

We toil—through pain and wrong;
  We fight—and fly;
We love; we lose; and then, ere long,
  Stone-dead we lie.
O life! is all thy song
  "Endure and—die?"
BRYAN WALLER PROCTER.
(BARRY CORNWALL.)

THE SHORTNESS OF LIFE.

"He cometh forth like a flower, and is cut down."—
Job xiv. 2.

  BEHOLD,
  How short a span
  Was long enough of old
  To measure out the life of man;
In those well-temper'd days! his time
  was then
Survey'd, cast up, and found but three-
  score years and ten.

  Alas!
  And what is that?
  They come, and slide, and pass,
  Before my pen can tell thee what.

The posts of time are swift, which hav-
    ing run
Their seven short stages o'er, their short-
    lived task is done.

Our days
    Begun we lend
    To sleep, to antic plays
And toys, until the first stage end:
Twelve waning moons, twice five times
    told, we give
To unrecover'd loss: we rather breathe
    than live.

We spend
    A ten years' breath
    Before we apprehend
What 'tis to live, or fear a death:
Our childish dreams are fill'd with
    painted joys,
Which please our sense a while, and wak-
    ing, prove but toys.

How vain,
    How wretched, is
    Poor man, that doth remain
A slave to such a state as this!
His days are short, at longest; few at
    most:
They are but bad, at best; yet lavish'd out,
    or lost.

They be
    The secret springs
    That make our minutes flee
On wheels more swift than eagles'
    wings:
Our life's a clock, and every gasp of
    breath
Breathes forth a warning grief, till Time
    shall strike a death.

How soon
    Our new-born light
    Attains to full-aged noon!
And this, how soon to gray-hair'd
    night!
We spring, we bud, we blossom, and we
    blast,
Ere we can count our days, our days they
    flee so fast.

They end
    When scarce begun;
    And ere we apprehend
That we begin to live, our life is
    done:
Man, count thy days; and, if they fly
    too fast
For thy dull thoughts to count, count
    every day the last.
                    FRANCIS QUARLES.

STANZAS.

MY life is like the summer rose
    That opens to the morning sky,
But, ere the shades of evening close,
    Is scatter'd on the ground—to die!
Yet on the rose's humble bed
The sweetest dews of night are shed,
As if she wept the waste to see—
But none shall weep a tear for me!

My life is like the autumn leaf
    That trembles in the moon's pale ray;
Its hold is frail—its date is brief,
    Restless—and soon to pass away!
Yet, ere that leaf shall fall and fade,
The parent tree will mourn its shade,
The winds bewail the leafless tree—
But none shall breathe a sigh for me!

My life is like the prints which feet
    Have left on Tampa's desert strand;
Soon as the rising tide shall beat,
    All trace will vanish from the sand;
Yet, as if grieving to efface
All vestige of the human race,
On that lone shore loud moans the sea—
But none, alas! shall mourn for me!
                    RICHARD HENRY WILDE.

THE MEANS TO ATTAIN HAPPY LIFE.

MARTIAL, the things that do attain
    The happy life be these, I find—
The riches left, not got with pain;
    The fruitful ground, the quiet mind;

The equal friend; no grudge, no strife;
    No charge of rule, nor governance;
Without disease, the healthful life;
    The household of continuance;

The mean diet, no delicate fare;
　True wisdom joined with simpleness;
The night dischargèd of all care,
　Where wine the wit may not oppress;

The faithful wife, without debate;
　Such sleeps as may beguile the night.
Contented with thine own estate,
　Ne wish for Death, ne fear his might.
　　　　HENRY HOWARD, Earl of Surrey.

THE WEB OF LIFE.

MY life, which was so straight and plain,
Has now become a tangled skein,
　Yet God still holds the thread;
Weave as I may, His hand doth guide
The shuttle's course, however wide
　The chain in woof be wed.

One weary night, when months went by,
I plied my loom with tear and sigh,
　In grief unnamed, untold;
But when at last the morning's light
Broke on my vision, fair and bright
　There gleamed a cloth of gold.

And now I never lose my trust,
Weave as I may—and weave I must—
　That God doth hold the thread;
He guides my shuttle on its way,
He makes complete my task each day;
　What more, then, can be said?
　　　　CLARA J. MOORE.

THERE BE THOSE.

THERE be those who sow beside
The waters that in silence glide,
Trusting no echo will declare
Whose footsteps ever wandered there.

The noiseless footsteps pass away,
The stream flows on as yesterday;
Nor can it for a time be seen
A benefactor there had been.

Yet think not that the seed is dead
Which in the lonely place is spread;
It lives, it lives—the spring is nigh,
And soon its life shall testify.

That silent stream, that desert ground,
No more unlovely shall be found;
But scattered flowers of simplest grace
Shall spread their beauty round the place.

And soon or late a time will come
When witnesses, that now are dumb,
With grateful eloquence shall tell
From whom the seed, there scattered, fell.
　　　　BERNARD BARTON.

ENDURANCE.

How much the heart may bear, and yet **not**
　break!
How much the flesh may suffer, and **not**
　die!
I question much if any pain or ache
　Of soul or body brings our end more nigh:
Death chooses his own time: till that is
　sworn,
　　All evils may be borne.

We shrink and shudder at the surgeon's
　knife,
　Each nerve recoiling from the cruel steel
Whose edge seems searching for the quiver-
　ing life,
　Yet to our sense the bitter pangs reveal,
That still, although the trembling flesh be
　torn,
　　This also can be borne.

We see a sorrow rising in our way,
　And try to flee from the approaching ill;
We seek some small escape; we weep and
　pray;
　But when the blow falls, then our hearts
　　are still;
Not that the pain is of its sharpness shorn,
　　But that it can be borne.

We wind our life about another life;
　We hold it closer, dearer than our own:
Anon it faints and fails in deathly strife,
　Leaving us stunned, and stricken, and
　　alone;
But ah! we do not die with those we
　mourn,—
　　This also can be borne.

Behold, we live through all things—famine,
　thirst,
　Bereavement, pain; all grief and misery,
All woe and sorrow; life inflicts its worst
　On soul and body—but we cannot die.
Though we be sick, and tired, and faint,
　and worn,
　　Lo, all things can be borne.
　　　　ELIZABETH AKERS ALLEN.

GOOD-NIGHT.

GOOD-NIGHT to all the world! there's none
Beneath the "over-going" sun
To whom I feel or hate or spite,
And so to all a fair good-night.

Would I could say good-night to pain,
Good-night to conscience and her train,
To cheerless poverty, and shame
That I am yet unknown to fame!

Would I could say good-night to dreams
That haunt me with delusive gleams,
That through the sable future's veil
Like meteors glimmer, but to fail!

Would I could say a long good-night
To halting between wrong and right,
And, like a giant with new force,
Awake prepared to run my course!

But time o'er good and ill sweeps on,
And when few years have come and gone,
The past will be to me as naught,
Whether remember'd or forgot.

Yet let me hope one faithful friend
O'er my last couch shall tearful bend;
And, though no day for me was bright,
Shall bid me then a long good-night.
      ROBERT C. SANDS.

HIS LAST VERSES.

I AM! yet what I am who cares, or knows?
 My friends forsake me like a memory lost.
I am the self-consumer of my woes,
 They rise and vanish, an oblivious host,
Shadows of life, whose very soul is lost.
And yet I am—I live—though I am toss'd

Into the nothingness of scorn and noise,
 Into the living sea of waking dream,
Where there is neither sense of life nor joys,
 But the huge shipwreck of my own esteem,
And all that's dear. Even those I loved the best
Are strange—nay, they are stranger than the rest.

I long for scenes where man has never trod,
 For scenes where woman never smiled or wept;
There to abide with my Creator, God,
 And sleep as I in childhood sweetly slept,
Full of high thoughts, unborn. So let me lie,
 The grass below; above, the vaulted sky.
      JOHN CLARE.

THE DEATH OF THE VIRTUOUS.

SWEET is the scene when virtue dies!
 When sinks a righteous soul to rest,
How mildly beam the closing eyes,
 How gently heaves th' expiring breast!

So fades a summer cloud away,
 So sinks the gale when storms are o'er,
So gently shuts the eye of day,
 So dies a wave along the shore.

Triumphant smiles the victor brow,
 Fanned by some angel's purple wing:—
Where is, O grave! thy victory now?
 And where, insidious death! thy sting?

Farewell, conflicting joys and fears,
 Where light and shade alternate dwell!
How bright th' unchanging morn appears!—
 Farewell, inconstant world, farewell!

Its duty done,—as sinks the day,
 Light from its load the spirit flies;
While heaven and earth combine to say
 "Sweet is the scene when virtue dies!"
      ANNA LÆTITIA BARBAULD.

THE COMMON LOT.

ONCE, in the flight of ages past,
 There liv'd a man; and who was he?
Mortal! howe'er thy lot be cast,
 That man resembled thee.

Unknown the region of his birth,
 The land in which he died unknown;
His name has perish'd from the earth,
 This truth survives alone:

That joy, and grief, and hope, and fear,
　Alternate triumph'd in his breast;
His bliss and woe,—a smile, a tear!
　Oblivion hides the rest

He suffer'd,—but his pangs are o'er;
　Enjoy'd,—but his delights are fled;
Had friends,—his friends are now no more;
And foes,—his foes are dead.

He saw whatever thou hast seen;
　Encounter'd all that troubles thee:
He was—whatever thou hast been;
　He is what thou shalt be.

The rolling seasons, day and night,
　Sun, moon, and stars, the earth and main,
Erewhile his portion, life, and light,
　To him exist in vain.

The clouds and sunbeams, o'er his eye
　That once their shades and glory threw,
Have left in yonder silent sky
　No vestige where they flew.

The annals of the human race,
　Their ruins, since the world began,
Of him afford no other trace
　Than this,—there lived a man!
　　　　　　　　JAMES MONTGOMERY.

THE THREE WARNINGS.

THE tree of deepest root is found
Least willing still to quit the ground:
'Twas therefore said by ancient sages,
　That love of life increased with years
So much, that in our later stages,
When pains grow sharp, and sickness rages,
　The greatest love of life appears.
This great affection to believe,
Which all confess, but few perceive,
If old assertions can't prevail,—
Be pleased to hear a modern tale.
　When sports went round, and all were gay,
On neighbor Dodson's wedding-day,
Death call'd aside the jocund groom
With him into another room,
And looking grave—"You must," says he,
"Quit your sweet bride, and come with me."

"With you! and quit my Susan's side!
With you!" the hapless husband cried;
"Young as I am, 'tis monstrous hard!
Besides, in truth, I'm not prepared:
My thoughts on other matters go:
This is my wedding-day, you know."
　What more he urged, I have not heard;
　　His reasons could not well be stronger;
　So Death the poor delinquent spared,
　　And left to live a little longer.
Yet calling up a serious look—
His hour-glass trembled while he spoke—
"Neighbor," he said, "farewell! No more
Shall Death disturb your mirthful hour;
And farther, to avoid all blame
Of cruelty upon my name,
To give you time for preparation,
And fit you for your future station,
Three several warnings you shall have,
Before you're summon'd to the grave.
Willing for once I'll quit my prey,
　And grant a kind reprieve,
In hopes you'll have no more to say,
But, when I call again this way,
　Well pleased the world will leave."
To these conditions both consented,
And parted perfectly contented.
　What next the hero of our tale befell,
How long he lived, how wise, how well,
How roundly he pursued his course,
And smoked his pipe, and stroked his horse,
　The willing Muse shall tell.
He chaffer'd then, he bought, he sold,
Nor once perceived his growing old,
　Nor thought of Death as near;
His friends not false, his wife no shrew,
Many his gains, his children few,
　He pass'd his hours in peace.
But while he view'd his wealth increase,
While thus along Life's dusty road
The beaten track content he trod,
Old Time, whose haste no mortal spares,
Uncall'd, unheeded, unawares,
　Brought on his eightieth year.
And now, one night, in musing mood
　As all alone he sate,
Th' unwelcome messenger of Fate
　Once more before him stood.
Half kill'd with anger and surprise,
"So soon return'd!" old Dodson cries.
"So soon, d'ye call it?" Death replies:

"Surely, my friend, you're but in jest!
  Since I was here before
'Tis six-and-thirty years at least,
  And you are now fourscore."
"So much the worse," the clown rejoin'd;
"To spare the aged would be kind:
However, see your search be legal;
And your authority—is't regal?
Else you are come on a fool's errand,
With but a secretary's warrant.
Besides, you promised me Three Warnings,
Which I have look'd for nights and mornings;
But for that loss of time and ease,
I can recover damages."
"I know," cries Death, "that at the best
I seldom am a welcome guest;
But don't be captious, friend, at least:
I little thought you'd still be able
To stump about your farm and stable;
Your years have run to a great length;
I wish you joy, though, of your strength!"
"Hold," says the farmer, "not so fast!
I have been lame these four years past."
"And no great wonder," Death replies:
"However, you still keep your eyes;
And sure, to see one's loves and friends,
For legs and arms would make amends."
"Perhaps," says Dodson, "so it might,
But latterly I've lost my sight."
"This is a shocking tale, 'tis true,
But still there's comfort left for you:
Each strives your sadness to amuse;
I warrant you hear all the news."
"There's none," cries he; "and if there were,
I'm grown so deaf I could not hear."
"Nay, then," the spectre stern rejoin'd,
"These are unwarrantable yearnings;
If you are lame, and deaf, and blind,
  You've had your three sufficient warnings;
So, come along, no more we'll part;"
He said, and touch'd him with his dart.
And now old Dodson, turning pale,
Yields to his fate—so ends my tale.
              HESTER THRALE PIOZZI.

NOW AND AFTERWARDS.

"Two hands upon the breast, and labor is past."
              RUSSIAN PROVERB.

"Two hands upon the breast,
  And labor's done;
Two pale feet cross'd in rest,—
  The race is won;
Two eyes with coin-weights shut,
  And all tears cease;
Two lips where grief is mute,
  Anger at peace:"
So pray we oftentimes, mourning our lot;
God in His kindness answereth not.

"Two hands to work addrest
  Aye for His praise;
Two feet that never rest
  Walking His ways;
Two eyes that look above
  Through all their tears;
Two lips still breathing love,
  Not wrath, nor fears:"
So pray we afterwards, low on our knees;
Pardon those erring prayers! Father, hear these!
              DINAH MARIA MULOCK CRAIK.

TOMMY'S DEAD.

You may give over plough, boys,
  You may take the gear to the stead,
All the sweat o' your brow, boys,
  Will never get beer and bread.
The seed's waste, I know, boys,
  There's not a blade will grow, boys,
'Tis cropp'd out, I trow, boys,
  And Tommy's dead.

Send the colt to fair, boys,
  He's going blind, as I said,
My old eyes can't bear, boys,
  To see him in the shed;
The cow's dry and spare, boys,
She's neither here nor there, boys,
  I doubt she's badly bred;
Stop the mill to-morn, boys,
There'll be no more corn, boys,
  Neither white nor red;
There's no sign of grass, boys,
You may sell the goat and the ass, boys,
The land's not what it was, boys,
  And the beasts must be fed;

You may turn Peg away, boys,
  You may pay off old Ned,
We've had a dull day, boys,
  And Tommy's dead.

Move my chair on the floor, boys,
  Let me turn my head;
She's standing there in the door, boys,
  Your sister Winifred!
Take her away from me, boys,
  Your sister Winifred!
Move me round in my place, boys,
  Let me turn my head,
Take her away from me, boys,
  As she lay on her death-bed,
The bones of her thin face, boys,
  As she lay on her death-bed!
I don't know how it be, boys,
  When all's done and said,
But I see her looking at me, boys,
  Wherever I turn my head;
Out of the big oak tree, boys,
  Out of the garden bed,
And the lily as pale as she, boys,
  And the rose that used to be red.

There's something not right, boys,
  But I think it's not in my head,
I've kept my precious sight, boys,—
  The Lord be hallowèd!
Outside and in
  The ground is cold to my tread,
The hills are wizen and thin,
  The sky is shrivell'd and shred,
The hedges down by the loan
  I can count them bone by bone,
The leaves are open and spread,
But I see the teeth of the land,
  And hands like a dead man's hand,
  And the eyes of a dead man's head.
There's nothing but cinders and sand,
  The rat and the mouse have fed,
And the summer's empty and cold;
Over valley and wold
  Wherever I turn my head
There's a mildew and a mould,
  The sun's going out overhead,
And I'm very old,
  And Tommy's dead.

What am I staying for, boys?
  You're all born and bred,
'Tis fifty years and more, boys,
  Since wife and I were wed,
And she's gone before, boys,
  And Tommy's dead.

She was always sweet, boys,
  Upon his curly head,
She knew she'd never see't, boys,
  And she stole off to bed;
I've been sitting up alone, boys,
  For he'd come home, he said,
But it's time I was gone, boys,
  For Tommy's dead.

Put the shutters up, boys,
  Bring out the beer and bread,
Make haste and sup, boys,
  For my eyes are heavy as lead;
There's something wrong i' the cup, boys,
  There's something ill wi' the bread,
I don't care to sup, boys,
  And Tommy's dead.

I'm not right, I doubt, boys,
  I've such a sleepy head,
I shall nevermore be stout, boys,
  You may carry me to bed.
What are you about, boys?
  The prayers are all said,
The fire's raked out, boys,
  And Tommy's dead.

The stairs are too steep, boys,
  You may carry me to the head,
The night's dark and deep, boys,
  Your mother's long in bed,
'Tis time to go to sleep, boys,
  And Tommy's dead.

I'm not used to kiss, boys,
  You may shake my hand instead.
All things go amiss, boys,
  You may lay me where she is, boys,
  And I'll rest my old head:
'Tis a poor world, this, boys,
  And Tommy's dead.
SIDNEY DOBELL.

THE BARON'S LAST BANQUET.

O'ER a low couch the setting sun
  Had thrown its latest ray,
Where in his last strong agony
  A dying warrior lay,

The stern, old Baron Rudiger,
  Whose frame had ne'er been bent
By wasting pain, till time and toil
  Its iron strength had spent.

"They come around me here, and say
  My days of life are o'er,
That I shall mount my noble steed
  And lead my band no more;
They come, and to my beard they dare
  To tell me now, that I,
Their own liege lord and master born,—
  That I—ha! ha!—must die.

"And what is Death? I've dared him oft
  Before the Paynim spear,—
Think ye he's enter'd at my gate,
  Has come to seek me here?
I've met him, faced him, scorn'd him,
  When the fight was raging hot,—
I'll try his might—I'll brave his power;
  Defy, and fear him not.

"Ho! sound the tocsin from my tower,—
  And fire the culverin,—
Bid each retainer arm with speed,—
  Call every vassal in;
Up with my banner on the wall,—
  The banquet-board prepare,—
Throw wide the portal of my hall,
  And bring my armor there!"

A hundred hands were busy then,—
  The banquet forth was spread,—
And rung the heavy oaken floor
  With many a martial tread,
While from the rich, dark tracery
  Along the vaulted wall,
Lights gleam'd on harness, plume, and spear,
  O'er the proud old Gothic hall.

Fast hurrying through the outer gate,
  The mail'd retainers pour'd,
On through the portal's frowning arch,
  And throng'd around the board.
While at its head, within his dark,
  Carved oaken chair of state,
Armed cap-a-pie, stern Rudiger,
  With girded falchion, sate.

"Fill every beaker up, my men,
  Pour forth the cheering wine;
There's life and strength in every drop,—
  Thanksgiving to the vine!
Are ye all there, my vassals true?—
  Mine eyes are waxing dim;—
Fill round, my tried and fearless ones,
  Each goblet to the brim.

"Ye're there, but yet I see ye not.
  Draw forth each trusty sword,—
And let me hear your faithful steel
  Clash once around my board:
I hear it faintly:—Louder yet!—
  What clogs my heavy breath?
Up all,—and shout for Rudiger,
  'Defiance unto Death!'"

Bowl rang to bowl,—steel clang'd to steel
  —And rose a deafening cry
That made the torches flare around,
  And shook the flags on high:—
"Ho! cravens, do ye fear him?—
  Slaves, traitors! have ye flown?
Ho! cowards, have ye left me
  To meet him here alone?

"But *I* defy him:—let him come!"
  Down rang the massy cup,
While from its sheath the ready blade
  Came flashing half-way up;
And, with the black and heavy plumes
  Scarce trembling on his head,
There, in his dark, carved, oaken chair,
  Old Rudiger sat, *dead.*
                ALBERT G. GREENE.

THE SLEEP.

"He giveth His beloved sleep."—Psalm cxxvii. 2.

OF all the thoughts of God that are
Borne inward unto souls afar
  Along the Psalmist's music deep,
Now tell me if that any is
For gift or grace surpassing this,—
  "He giveth His beloved sleep"?

What would we give to our beloved?
The hero's heart to be unmoved,
  The poet's star-tuned harp to sweep,
The patriot's voice to teach and rouse,

The monarch's crown to light the brows?
  "He giveth *His* beloved sleep."

What do we give to our beloved?
A little faith all undisproved,
  A little dust to overweep,
And bitter memories to make
The whole earth blasted for our sake.
  "He giveth *His* beloved sleep."

"Sleep soft, beloved!" we sometimes say,
But have no tune to charm away
  Sad dreams that through the eyelids creep.
But never doleful dream again
Shall break the happy slumber when
  "He giveth *His* beloved sleep."

O earth, so full of dreary noises!
O men, with wailing in your voices!
  O delvèd gold, the wailers heap!
O strife, O curse, that o'er it fall!
God strikes a silence through you all,
  And "giveth His beloved sleep."

His dews drop mutely on the hill,
His cloud above it saileth still,
  Though on its slope men sow and reap.
More softly than the dew is shed,
Or cloud is floated overhead,
  "He giveth His beloved sleep."

Ay, men may wonder while they scan
A living, thinking, feeling man,
  Confirm'd in such a rest to keep;
But angels say—and through the word
I think their happy smile is *heard*—
  "He giveth His beloved sleep."

For me, my heart, that erst did go
Most like a tired child at a show,
  That sees through tears the mummers leap,
Would now its weary vision close,
Would childlike on *His* love repose
  Who "giveth His beloved sleep!"

And, friends, dear friends, when it shall be
That this low breath is gone from me,
  And round my bier ye come to weep,
Let one, most loving of you all,
Say, "Not a tear must o'er her fall,—
  He giveth His beloved sleep."
  ELIZABETH BARRETT BROWNING.

DEATH'S FINAL CONQUEST.

THE glories of our blood and state
  Are shadows, not substantial things;
There is no armor against fate;
  Death lays his icy hand on kings;
    Sceptre and crown
    Must tumble down,
And in the dust be equal made
With the poor crooked scythe and spade.

Some men with swords may reap the field,
  And plant fresh laurels where they kill,
But their strong nerves at last must yield;
  They tame but one another still;
    Early or late
    They stoop to fate,
And must give up their murmuring breath
When they, pale captives, creep to death.

The garlands wither on your brow;
  Then boast no more your mighty deeds;
Upon Death's purple altar now
  See where the victor-victim bleeds;
    Your heads must come
    To the cold tomb;
Only the actions of the just
Smell sweet, and blossom in their dust.
  JAMES SHIRLEY.

THE LAST CONQUEROR.

VICTORIOUS men of earth, no more
  Proclaim how wide your empires are;
Though you bind in every shore
  And your triumphs reach as far
    As night or day,
Yet you, proud monarchs, must obey,
And mingle with forgotten ashes, when
Death calls ye to the crowd of common men.

Devouring Famine, Plague, and War,
  Each able to undo mankind,
Death's servile emissaries are;
  Nor to these alone confined,
    He hath at will
    More quaint and subtle ways to kill;
A smile or kiss, as he will use the art,
Shall have the cunning skill to break a heart.
  JAMES SHIRLEY.

THANATOPSIS.

To him who in the love of Nature holds
Communion with her visible forms, she
    speaks
A various language; for his gayer hours
She has a voice of gladness, and a smile
And eloquence of beauty, and she glides
Into his darker musings, with a mild
And healing sympathy, that steals away
Their sharpness ere he is aware. When
    thoughts
Of the last bitter hour come like a blight
Over thy spirit, and sad images
Of the stern agony, and shroud, and pall,
And breathless darkness, and the narrow
    house,
Make thee to shudder, and grow sick at
    heart;—
Go forth, under the open sky, and list
To Nature's teachings, while from all
    around—
Earth and her waters, and the depths of
    air,—
Comes a still voice—Yet a few days, and
    thee
The all-beholding sun shall see no more
In all his course; nor yet in the cold
    ground,
Where thy pale form was laid, with many
    tears,
Nor in the embrace of ocean, shall exist
Thy image. Earth, that nourish'd thee,
    shall claim
Thy growth, to be resolved to earth again,
And, lost each human trace, surrendering up
Thine individual being, shalt thou go
To mix for ever with the elements,
To be a brother to the insensible rock,
And to the sluggish clod, which the rude
    swain
Turns with his share, and treads upon.
    The oak
Shall send his roots abroad, and pierce
    thy mould.

 Yet not to thine eternal resting-place
Shalt thou retire alone,—nor couldst thou
    wish
Couch more magnificent. Thou shalt lie
    down
With patriarchs of the infant world—with
    kings,
The powerful of the earth—the wise, the
    good,
Fair forms, and hoary seers of ages past,
All in one mighty sepulchre. The hills
Rock-ribb'd and ancient as the sun; the
    vales
Stretching in pensive quietness between;
The venerable woods; rivers that move
In majesty, and the complaining brooks
That make the meadows green; and, pour'd
    round all,
Old Ocean's gray and melancholy waste,—
Are but the solemn decorations all
Of the great tomb of man. The golden sun,
The planets, all the infinite host of
    heaven,
Are shining on the sad abodes of death,
Through the still lapse of ages. All that
    tread
The globe are but a handful to the tribes
That slumber in its bosom.—Take the
    wings
Of morning, pierce the Barcan wilderness,
Or lose thyself in the continuous woods
Where rolls the Oregon, and hears no
    sound
Save his own dashings—yet the dead are
    there:
And millions in those solitudes, since first
The flight of years began, have laid them
    down
In their last sleep—the dead reign there
    alone.
So shalt thou rest, and what if thou with-
    draw
In silence from the living, and no friend
Take note of thy departure? All that
    breathe
Will share thy destiny. The gay will
    laugh
When thou art gone, the solemn brood of
    care
Plod on, and each one as before will chase
His favorite phantom; yet all these shall
    leave
Their mirth and their employments, and
    shall come,
And make their bed with thee. As the
    long train
Of ages glide away, the sons of men,
The youth in life's green spring, and he
    who goes

In the full strength of years, matron and
    maid,
The speechless babe, and the gray-headed
    man,—
Shall one by one be gather'd to thy side,
By those who in their turn shall follow
    them.

  So live, that when thy summons comes
    to join
The innumerable caravan, which moves
To that mysterious realm, where each shall
    take
His chamber in the silent halls of death,
Thou go not, like the quarry-slave at
    night,
Scourged to his dungeon, but, sustain'd and
    soothed
By an unfaltering trust, approach thy
    grave
Like one who wraps the drapery of his
    couch
About him, and lies down to pleasant
    dreams.
              WILLIAM CULLEN BRYANT.

WHEN COLDNESS WRAPS THIS SUFFERING CLAY.

WHEN coldness wraps this suffering clay,
  Ah, whither strays the immortal mind?
It cannot die, it cannot stay,
  But leaves its darken'd dust behind.
Then, unembodied, doth it trace
  By steps each planet's heavenly way?
Or fill at once the realms of space,
  A thing of eyes, that all survey?

Eternal, boundless, undecay'd,
  A thought unseen, but seeing all,
All, all in earth or skies display'd,
  Shall it survey, shall it recall:
Each fainter trace that memory holds
  So darkly of departed years,
In one broad glance the soul beholds,
  And all that was at once appears.

Before creation peopled earth,
  Its eye shall roll through chaos back;
And where the farthest heaven had birth,
  The spirit trace its rising track.
And where the future mars or makes,
  Its glance dilate o'er all to be,

While sun is quench'd or system breaks,
  Fix'd in its own eternity.

Above or love, hope, hate, or fear,
  It lives all passionless and pure:
An age shall fleet like earthly year;
  Its years as moments shall endure.
Away, away, without a wing,
  O'er all, through all, its thoughts shall
    fly,—
A nameless and eternal thing,
  Forgetting what it was to die.
               LORD BYRON.

A DEATH-BED.

HER suffering ended with the day;
  Yet lived she at its close,
And breathed the long, long night away,
  In statue-like repose.

But when the sun, in all his state,
  Illumed the eastern skies,
She pass'd through glory's morning-gate,
  And walk'd in Paradise!
               JAMES ALDRICH.

THE DEATH-BED.

WE watch'd her breathing through the
    night,
  Her breathing soft and low,
As in her breast the wave of life
  Kept heaving to and fro.

So silently we seem'd to speak,
  So slowly moved about,
As we had lent her half our powers
  To eke her living out.

Our very hopes belied our fears,
  Our fears our hopes belied—
We thought her dying when she slept,
  And sleeping when she died.

For when the morn came dim and sad
  And chill with early showers,
Her quiet eyelids closed—she had
  Another morn than ours.
               THOMAS HOOD.

CORONACH.

HE is gone on the mountain,
  He is lost to the forest,
Like a summer-dried fountain,
  When our need was the sorest.

The font, reappearing,
　From the raindrops shall borrow,
But to us comes no cheering,
　To Duncan no morrow!

The hand of the reaper
　Takes the ears that are hoary,
But the voice of the weeper
　Wails manhood in glory.
The autumn winds, rushing,
　Waft the leaves that are serest;
But our flower was in flushing
　When blighting was nearest.

Fleet foot on the correi,
　Sage counsel in cumber,
Red hand in the foray,
　How sound is thy slumber!
Like the dew on the mountain,
Like the foam on the river,
Like the bubble on the fountain,
　Thou art gone, and for ever!
　　　　　　　SIR WALTER SCOTT.

THE KNIGHT'S TOMB.

WHERE is the grave of Sir Arthur O'Kellyn?
Where may the grave of that good man be?—
By the side of a spring, on the breast of Helvellyn,
Under the twigs of a young birch tree!
The oak that in summer was sweet to hear,
And rustled its leaves in the fall of the year,
And whistled and roar'd in the winter alone,
Is gone,—and the birch in its stead is grown.—
The knight's bones are dust,
And his good sword rust;—
His soul is with the saints, I trust.
　　　　　　　SAMUEL TAYLOR COLERIDGE.

THE VOICELESS.

WE count the broken lyres that rest
　Where the sweet wailing singers slumber,
But o'er their silent sister's breast
　The wild-flowers who will stoop to number?

A few can touch the magic string,
　And noisy Fame is proud to win them:—
Alas for those that never sing,
　But die with all their music in them!

Nay, grieve not for the dead alone
　Whose song has told their hearts' sad story,—
Weep for the voiceless, who have known
　The cross without the crown of glory!
Not where Leucadian breezes sweep
　O'er Sappho's memory-haunted billow,
But where the glistening night-dews weep
　On nameless sorrow's churchyard pillow.

O hearts that break and give no sign
　Save whitening lip and fading tresses,
Till Death pours out his cordial wine
　Slow-dropp'd from Misery's crushing presses,—
If singing breath or echoing chord
　To every hidden pang were given,
What endless melodies were pour'd,
　As sad as earth, as sweet as heaven!
　　　　　　　OLIVER WENDELL HOLMES.

MAN'S MORTALITY.

LIKE as the damask rose you see,
Or like the blossom on the tree,
Or like the dainty flower in May,
Or like the morning of the day,
Or like the sun, or like the shade,
Or like the gourd which Jonas had,—
E'en such is man;—whose thread is spun,
Drawn out, and cut, and so is done.—
The rose withers, the blossom blasteth,
The flower fades, the morning hasteth,
The sun sets, the shadow flies,
The gourd consumes,—and man he dies!

Like to the grass that's newly sprung,
Or like a tale that's new begun,
Or like the bird that's here to-day,
Or like the pearlèd dew of May,
Or like an hour, or like a span,
Or like the singing of a swan,—
E'en such is man;—who lives by breath,
Is here, now there, in life and death.—

The grass withers, the tale is ended,
The bird is flown, the dew's ascended.
The hour is short, the span is long,
The swan's near death,—man's life is done!
SIMON WASTELL.

OH WHY SHOULD THE SPIRIT OF MORTAL BE PROUD?

OH, why should the spirit of mortal be proud?
Like a fast-flitting meteor, a fast-flying cloud,
A flash of the lightning, a break of the wave,
He passeth from life to his rest in the grave.

The leaves of the oak and the willow shall fade,
Be scatter'd around and together be laid;
And the young and the old, and the low and the high,
Shall moulder to dust and together shall lie.

The child that a mother attended and loved,
The mother that infant's affection who proved,
The husband that mother and infant who bless'd,—
Each, all, are away to their dwellings of rest.

The maid on whose cheek, on whose brow, in whose eye,
Shone beauty and pleasure,—her triumphs are by;
And the memory of those who have loved her and praised,
Are alike from the minds of the living erased.

The hand of the king that the sceptre hath borne,
The brow of the priest that the mitre hath worn,
The eye of the sage, and the heart of the brave,
Are hidden and lost in the depths of the grave.

The peasant whose lot was to sow and to reap,
The herdsman who climb'd with his goats to the steep,
The beggar who wander'd in search of his bread,
Have faded away like the grass that we tread.

The saint who enjoy'd the communion of heaven,
The sinner who dared to remain unforgiven,
The wise and the foolish, the guilty and just,
Have quietly mingled their bones in the dust.

So the multitude goes, like the flower and the weed,
That wither away to let others succeed;
So the multitude comes, even those we behold,
To repeat every tale that hath often been told.

For we are the same things our fathers have been;
We see the same sights that our fathers have seen,—
We drink the same stream, and we feel the same sun,
And run the same course that our fathers have run.

The thoughts we are thinking our fathers would think;
From the death we are shrinking from, they too would shrink;
To the life we are clinging to, they too would cling;
But it speeds from the earth like a bird on the wing.

They loved, but their story we cannot unfold;
They scorn'd, but the heart of the haughty is cold;
They grieved, but no wail from their slumbers will come;
They joy'd, but the voice of their gladness is dumb.

They died,—ay! they died; and we things
  that are now,
Who walk on the turf that lies over their
  brow,
Who make in their dwellings a transient
  abode,
Meet the changes they met on their pil-
  grimage road.

Yea, hope and despondence, and pleasure
  and pain,
Are mingled together in sunshine and
  rain;
And the smile and the tear, the song and
  the dirge,
Still follow each other, like surge upon
  surge.

'Tis the twink of an eye, 'tis the draught
  of a breath,
From the blossom of health to the paleness
  of death,
From the gilded saloon to the bier and the
  shroud,—
Oh why should the spirit of mortal be
  proud?
                              WILLIAM KNOX.

PASSING AWAY.

WAS it the chime of a tiny bell
  That came so sweet to my dreaming ear,
Like the silvery tones of a fairy's shell
  That he winds, on the beach, so mellow
    and clear,
When the winds and the waves lie to-
  gether asleep,
And the Moon and the Fairy are watching
  the deep,
She dispensing her silvery light,
And he his notes as silvery quite,
While the boatman listens and ships his
  oar,
To catch the music that comes from the
  shore?
Hark! the notes on my ear that play
Are set to words; as they float, they say,
  "Passing away! passing away!"

But no; it was not a fairy's shell,
  Blown on the beach, so mellow and
    clear;
Nor was it the tongue of a silver bell,
  Striking the hour, that fill'd my ear

As I lay in my dream; yet was it a chime
  That told of the flow of the stream of
    time.
For a beautiful clock from the ceiling
  hung,
And a plump little girl, for a pendulum,
  swung
(As you've sometimes seen, in a little ring
That hangs in his cage, a canary-bird
  swing);
And she held to her bosom a budding
  bouquet,
And, as she enjoy'd it, she seem'd to say,
  "Passing away! passing away!"

Oh how bright were the wheels, that told
  Of the lapse of time, as they moved
    round slow;
And the hands, as they swept o'er the dial
  of gold,
Seem'd to point to the girl below.
And lo! she had changed: in a few short
  hours
Her bouquet had become a garland of
  flowers,
That she held in her outstretch'd hands,
  and flung
This way and that, as she, dancing, swung
In the fulness of grace and of womanly
  pride,
That told me she soon was to be a bride;
Yet then, when expecting her happiest
  day,
In the same sweet voice I heard her say,
  "Passing away! passing away!"

While I gazed at that fair one's cheek, a
  shade
Of thought or care stole softly over,
Like that by a cloud in a summer's day
  made,
  Looking down on a field of blossoming
    clover.
The rose yet lay on her cheek, but its
  flush
Had something lost of its brilliant blush;
And the light in her eye, and the light on
  the wheels,
That march'd so calmly round above her,
Was a little dimm'd,—as when Evening
  steals
  Upon Noon's hot face. Yet one couldn't
    but love her,

For she look'd like a mother whose first
    babe lay
Rock'd on her breast, as she swung all day;
And she seem'd, in the same silver tone,
    to say,
    " Passing away! passing away!"

While yet I look'd, what a change there
    came!
Her eye was quench'd, and her cheek
    was wan;
Stooping and staff'd was her wither'd
    frame,
Yet just as busily swung she on;
The garland beneath her had fallen to
    dust;
The wheels above her were eaten with
    rust;
The hands, that over the dial swept,
Grew crooked and tarnish'd, but on they
    kept,
And still there came that silver tone
From the shrivell'd lips of the toothless
    crone
(Let me never forget till my dying day
The tone or the burden of her lay),
    "Passing away! passing away!"
                  JOHN PIERPONT.

HER LAST VERSES.

EARTH, with its dark and dreadful ills,
    Recedes and fades away;
Lift up your heads, ye heavenly hills,
    Ye gates of death, give way!

My soul is full of whisper'd song,
    My blindness is my sight;
The shadows that I fear'd so long
    Are all alive with light.

The while my pulses faintly beat,
    My faith doth so abound,
I feel grow firm beneath my feet
    The green immortal ground.

That faith to me a courage gives,
    Low as the grave to go;
I know that my Redeemer lives:
    That I shall live I know.

The palace-walls I almost see,
    Where dwells my Lord and King;
O grave, where is thy victory?
    O death, where is thy sting?
                  ALICE CARY.

OVER THE RIVER.

OVER the river they beckon to me,—
    Loved ones who've cross'd to the farther
        side;
The gleam of their snowy robes I see,
    But their voices are drown'd in the
        rushing tide.
There's one with ringlets of sunny gold,
    And eyes, the reflection of heaven's own
        blue;
He cross'd in the twilight, gray and cold,
    And the pale mist hid him from mortal
        view.
We saw not the angels who met him there;
    The gates of the city we could not see;
Over the river, over the river,
    My brother stands waiting to welcome me!

Over the river, the boatman pale
    Carried another,—the household pet:
Her brown curls waved in the gentle
    gale—
    Darling Minnie! I see her yet.
She cross'd on her bosom her dimpled
    hands,
    And fearlessly enter'd the phantom
        bark;
We watch'd it glide from the silver sands,
    And all our sunshine grew strangely
        dark.
We know she is safe on the farther side,
    Where all the ransom'd and angels be;
Over the river, the mystic river,
    My childhood's idol is waiting for me.

For none return from those quiet shores,
    Who cross with the boatman cold and
        pale;
We hear the dip of the golden oars,
    And catch a gleam of the snowy sail,—
And lo! they have pass'd from our yearn-
    ing heart;
    They cross the stream, and are gone for
        aye;
We may not sunder the veil apart,
    That hides from our vision the gates of
        day.
We only know that their barks no more
    May sail with us o'er life's stormy sea;
Yet somewhere, I know, on the unseen
    shore,
    They watch, and beckon, and wait for me.

And I sit and think, when the sunset's gold
  Is flushing river, and hill, and shore,
I shall one day stand by the water cold,
  And list for the sound of the boatman's oar;
I shall watch for a gleam of the flapping sail;
  I shall hear the boat as it gains the strand;
I shall pass from sight, with the boatman pale,
  To the better shore of the spirit land;
I shall know the loved who have gone before,—
  And joyfully sweet will the meeting be,
When over the river, the peaceful river,
  The Angel of Death shall carry me.
NANCY A. W. WAKEFIELD.

THE HOUR OF DEATH.

LEAVES have their time to fall,
And flowers to wither at the north wind's breath,
  And stars to set,—but all,
Thou hast all seasons for thine own, O Death!

Day is for mortal care,
Eve for glad meetings round the joyous hearth,
  Night for the dreams of sleep, the voice of prayer,—
But all for thee, thou mightiest of the earth!

The banquet hath its hour,
Its feverish hour of mirth, and song, and wine;
  There comes a day for grief's o'erwhelming power,—
A time for softer tears,—but all are thine.

Youth and the opening rose
May look like things too glorious for decay,
  And smile at thee,—but thou art not of those
That wait the ripen'd bloom to seize their prey.

Leaves have their time to fall,
And flowers to wither at the north wind's breath,
  And stars to set,—but all,
Thou hast all seasons for thine own, O Death!

We know when moons shall wane,
When summer birds from far shall cross the sea,
  When autumn's hues shall tinge the golden grain,—
But who shall teach us when to look for thee?

Is it when Spring's first gale
Comes forth to whisper where the violets lie?
  Is it when roses in our paths grow pale?—
They have *one* season,—*all* are ours to die!

Thou art where billows foam,
Thou art where music melts upon the air;
  Thou art around us in our peaceful home;
And the world calls us forth,—and thou art there.

Thou art where friend meets friend,
Beneath the shadow of the elm to rest,—
  Thou art where foe meets foe, and trumpets rend
The skies, and swords beat down the princely crest.

Leaves have their time to fall,
And flowers to wither at the north wind's breath,
  And stars to set,—but all,
Thou hast all seasons for thine own, O Death!
FELICIA DOROTHEA HEMANS.

ELEGY.

WRITTEN IN A COUNTRY CHURCHYARD.

THE curfew tolls the knell of parting day,
  The lowing herd winds slowly o'er the lea,
The ploughman homeward plods his weary way,
  And leaves the world to darkness and to me.

Now fades the glimmering landscape on
    the sight,
And all the air a solemn stillness holds,
Save where the beetle wheels his droning
    flight,
And drowsy tinklings lull the distant
    folds:

Save that from yonder ivy-mantled tower
    The moping owl does to the moon complain
Of such as, wandering near her secret
    bower,
Molest her ancient solitary reign.

Beneath those rugged elms, that yew tree's
    shade,
    Where heaves the turf in many a mouldering heap,
Each in his narrow cell for ever laid,
    The rude forefathers of the hamlet sleep.

The breezy call of incense-breathing morn,
    The swallow twittering from the straw-built shed,
The cock's shrill clarion, or the echoing
    horn,
    No more shall rouse them from their lowly bed.

For them no more the blazing hearth shall
    burn
    Or busy housewife ply her evening care:
No children run to lisp their sire's return,
    Or climb his knees the envied kiss to
    share.

Oft did the harvest to their sickle yield,
    Their furrow oft the stubborn glebe has
    broke;
How jocund did they drive their team
    afield!
    How bow'd the woods beneath their
    sturdy stroke!

Let not Ambition mock their useful toil,
    Their homely joys, and destiny obscure;
Nor Grandeur hear with a disdainful
    smile
    The short and simple annals of the
    poor.

The boast of heraldry, the pomp of power,
    And all that beauty, all that wealth e'er
    gave,

Await alike th' inevitable hour:—
    The paths of glory lead but to the grave.

Nor you, ye proud, impute to these the
    fault
    If Memory o'er their tomb no trophies
    raise,
Where through the long-drawn aisle and
    fretted vault
    The pealing anthem swells the note of
    praise.

Can storied urn or animated bust
    Back to its mansion call the fleeting
    breath?
Can Honor's voice provoke the silent dust,
    Or Flattery soothe the dull cold ear of
    Death?

Perhaps in this neglected spot is laid
    Some heart once pregnant with celestial
    fire;
Hands, that the rod of empire might have
    sway'd,
    Or waked to ecstasy the living lyre:

But Knowledge to their eyes her ample
    page
    Rich with the spoils of time did ne'er
    unroll;
Chill Penury repress'd their noble rage,
    And froze the genial current of the soul.

Full many a gem of purest ray serene
    The dark unfathom'd caves of ocean
    bear:
Full many a flower is born to blush unseen,
    And waste its sweetness on the desert
    air.

Some village Hampden, that with dauntless breast
    The little tyrant of his fields withstood,
Some mute inglorious Milton here may
    rest,
    Some Cromwell, guiltless of his country's
    blood.

Th' applause of list'ning senates to command,
    The threats of pain and ruin to despise,
To scatter plenty o'er a smiling land,
    And read their history in a nation's
    eyes,

Their lot forbade: nor circumscribed alone
  Their growing virtues, but their crimes
    confined;
Forbade to wade through slaughter to a
    throne,
And shut the gates of mercy on man-
    kind;

The struggling pangs of conscious truth to
    hide,
  To quench the blushes of ingenuous
    shame,
Or heap the shrine of Luxury and Pride
  With incense kindled at the Muse's
    flame.

Far from the madding crowd's ignoble
    strife
  Their sober wishes never learn'd to stray;
Along the cool sequester'd vale of life
  They kept the noiseless tenor of their
    way.

Yet e'en these bones from insult to pro-
    tect
  Some frail memorial still erected nigh,
With uncouth rhymes and shapeless sculp-
    ture deck'd,
  Implores the passing tribute of a sigh.

Their name, their years, spelt by th' unlet-
    ter'd Muse,
  The place of fame and elegy supply:
And many a holy text around she strews
  That teach the rustic moralist to die.

For who, to dumb forgetfulness a prey,
  This pleasing anxious being e'er re-
    sign'd,
Left the warm precincts of the cheerful
    day,
  Nor cast one longing lingering look be-
    hind?

On some fond breast the parting soul relies,
  Some pious drops the closing eye re-
    quires;
E'en from the tomb the voice of Nature
    cries,
  E'en in our ashes live their wonted fires.

For thee, who, mindful of th' unhonor'd
    dead,
  Dost in these lines their artless tale re-
    late,

If chance, by lonely Contemplation led,
  Some kindred spirit shall inquire thy
    fate,—

Haply some hoary-headed swain may say,
  "Oft have we seen him at the peep of
    dawn
Brushing with hasty steps the dews away,
  To meet the sun upon the upland lawn;

"There at the foot of yonder nodding beech
  That wreathes its old fantastic roots so
    high,
His listless length at noontide would he
    stretch,
  And pore upon the brook that babbles by.

"Hard by yon wood, now smiling as in
    scorn,
  Muttering his wayward fancies he would
    rove;
Now drooping, woeful-wan, like one for-
    lorn,
  Or crazed with care, or cross'd in hope-
    less love.

"One morn I miss'd him on the 'custom'd
    hill,
  Along the heath, and near his favorite
    tree;
Another came, nor yet beside the rill,
  Nor up the lawn, nor at the wood was
    he;

"The next with dirges due in sad array
  Slow through the churchway path we
    saw him borne;
Approach and read (for thou canst read)
    the lay
  Graved on the stone beneath yon aged
    thorn."

THE EPITAPH.

Here rests his head upon the lap of Earth
  A youth, to fortune and to fame un-
    known;
Fair Science frown'd not on his humble
    birth,
  And Melancholy mark'd him for her
    own.

Large was his bounty, and his soul sin-
    cere;
  Heaven did a recompense as largely
    send:

He gave to Misery all he had,—a tear,
  He gain'd from Heaven—'twas all he wish'd—a friend.

No farther seek his merits to disclose,
  Or draw his frailties from their dread abode
(There they alike in trembling hope repose),
  The bosom of his Father and his God.
                    THOMAS GRAY.

LINES WRITTEN IN RICHMOND CHURCHYARD, YORKSHIRE.

METHINKS it is good to be here;
If thou wilt, let us build,—but for whom?
  Nor Elias nor Moses appear,
But the shadows of eve that encompass the gloom,
  The abode of the dead and the place of the tomb.

Shall we build to Ambition? Oh, no!
Affrighted, he shrinketh away;
  For, see! they would pin him below,
In a small, narrow cave, and, begirt with cold clay,
  To the meanest of reptiles a peer and a prey.

To Beauty? ah, no! She forgets
The charms which she wielded before,
  Nor knows the foul worm that he frets
The skin which but yesterday fools could adore,
  For the smoothness it held, or the tint which it wore.

Shall we build to the purple of Pride,
The trappings which 'dizen the proud?
  Alas! they are all laid aside,
And here's neither dress nor adornment allow'd,
  But the long winding-sheet and the fringe of the shroud.

To Riches? alas! 'tis in vain;
Who hid, in their turn have been hid;
  The treasures are squander'd again,
And here in the grave are all metals forbid,
  But the tinsel that shines on the dark coffin-lid.

To the pleasures which Mirth can afford,—
The revel, the laugh, and the jeer?
  Ah! here is a plentiful board!
But the guests are all mute as their pitiful cheer,
  And none but the worm is a reveller here.

Shall we build to Affection and Love?
Ah, no! they have wither'd and died,
  Or fled with the spirit above:
Friends, brothers, and sisters are laid side by side,
  Yet none have saluted, and none have replied.

Unto Sorrow?—The dead cannot grieve;
Not a sob, not a sigh meets mine ear,
  Which compassion itself could relieve.
Ah! sweetly they slumber, nor hope, love, nor fear,—
  Peace, peace is the watchword, the only one here!

Unto Death, to whom monarchs must bow?
Ah, no! for his empire is known,
  And here there are trophies enow!
Beneath, the cold dead, and around, the dark stone,
  Are the signs of a sceptre that none may disown!

The first tabernacle to Hope we will build,
And look for the sleepers around us to rise;
  The second to Faith, which ensures it fulfill'd;
And the third to the Lamb of the great sacrifice,
  Who bequeathed us them both when he rose to the skies.
                    HERBERT KNOWLES.

HALLOWED GROUND.

WHAT's hallow'd ground? Has earth a clod
Its Maker meant not should be trod
By man, the image of his God,
    Erect and free,
Unscourged by superstition's rod
    To bow the knee?

That's hallow'd ground where, mourn'd and
    miss'd,
The lips repose our love has kiss'd:—
But where's their memory's mansion? Is't
    Yon churchyard's bowers?
No! in ourselves their souls exist,
    A part of ours.

A kiss can consecrate the ground
Where mated hearts are mutual bound;
The spot where love's first links were
    wound,
    That ne'er are riven,
Is hallow'd, down to earth's profound,
    And up to heaven!

For time makes all but true love old;
The burning thoughts that then were
    told
Run molten still in memory's mould;
    And will not cool
Until the heart itself be cold
    In Lethe's pool.

What hallows ground where heroes sleep?
'Tis not the sculptured piles you heap!—
In dews that heavens far distant weep
    Their turf may bloom,
Or genii twine beneath the deep
    Their coral tomb.

But strew his ashes to the wind
Whose sword or voice has served mankind—
And is he dead whose glorious mind
    Lifts thine on high?—
To live in hearts we leave behind
    Is not to die.

Is't death to fall for Freedom's right?
He's dead alone that lacks her light!
And murder sullies in Heaven's sight
    The sword he draws:—
What can alone ennoble fight?
    A noble cause!

Give that! and welcome War to brace
Her drums, and rend Heaven's reeking
    space!
The colors planted face to face,
    The charging cheer,
Though Death's pale horse lead on the
    chase,
    Shall still be dear.

And place our trophies where men kneel
To Heaven!—But Heaven rebukes my
    zeal.
The cause of truth and human weal,
    O God above!
Transfer it from the sword's appeal
    To Peace and Love.

Peace! Love!—the cherubim that join
Their spread wings o'er Devotion's shrine!
Prayers sound in vain, and temples shine,
    Where they are not;
The heart alone can make divine
    Religion's spot.

To incantations dost thou trust,
And pompous rites in domes august?
See mouldering stones and metal's rust
    Belie the vaunt,
That men can bless one pile of dust
    With chime or chaunt.

The ticking wood-worm mocks thee, man!
Thy temples—creeds themselves grow wan!
But there's a dome of nobler span,
    A temple given
Thy faith, that bigots dare not ban—
    Its space is Heaven!

Its roof star-pictured Nature's ceiling,
Where, trancing the rapt spirit's feeling,
And God Himself to man revealing,
    The harmonious spheres
Make music, though unheard their pealing
    By mortal ears.

Fair stars! are not your beings pure?
Can sin, can death, your worlds obscure?
Else why so swell the thoughts at your
    Aspect above?
Ye must be heavens that make us sure
    Of heavenly love!

And in your harmony sublime
I read the doom of distant time:
That man's regenerate soul from crime
    Shall yet be drawn,
And reason, on his mortal clime,
    Immortal dawn.

What's hallow'd ground? 'Tis what gives
    birth
To sacred thoughts in souls of worth!—

Peace! Independence! Truth! go forth,
   Earth's compass round;
And your high priesthood shall make earth
   All hallow'd ground!
THOMAS CAMPBELL.

EPITAPH UPON HUSBAND AND WIFE

WHO DIED AND WERE BURIED TOGETHER.

To these, whom death again did wed,
This grave's the second marriage-bed,
For though the hand of fate could force
'Twixt soul and body a divorce,
It could not sever man and wife,
Because they both lived but one life.
Peace, good reader, do not weep
Peace, the lovers are asleep!
They (sweet turtles) folded lie,
In the last knot love could tie.
Let them sleep, let them sleep on,
Till this stormy night be gone,
And the eternal morrow dawn;
Then the curtains will be drawn,
And they wake into a light
Whose day shall never end in night.
RICHARD CRASHAW.

ELEGY TO THE MEMORY OF AN UNFORTUNATE LADY.

WHAT beck'ning ghost, along the moonlight shade,
Invites my steps, and points to yonder glade?
'Tis she!—but why that bleeding bosom gored?
Why dimly gleams the visionary sword?
O ever beauteous! ever friendly! tell,
Is it in Heav'n a crime to love too well?
To bear too tender or too firm a heart,
To act a lover's or a Roman's part?
Is there no bright reversion in the sky
For those who greatly think or bravely die?
  Why bade ye else, ye pow'rs! her soul aspire
Above the vulgar flight of low desire?
Ambition first sprung from your blest abodes,
The glorious fault of angels and of gods:
Thence to their images on earth it flows,
And in the breasts of kings and heroes glows.
Most souls, 'tis true, but peep out once an age,
Dull sullen pris'ners in the body's cage:
Dim lights of life, that burn a length of years,
Useless, unseen, as lamps in sepulchres;
Like Eastern kings, a lazy state they keep,
And, close confined to their own palace, sleep.
  From these perhaps (ere Nature bade her die)
Fate snatch'd her early to the pitying sky.
As into air the purer spirits flow,
And sep'rate from their kindred dregs below;
So flew the soul to its congenial place,
Nor left one virtue to redeem her race.
  But thou, false guardian of a charge too good,
Thou mean deserter of thy brother's blood!
See on these ruby lips the trembling breath,
These cheeks now fading at the blast of death!
Cold is that breast which warm'd the world before,
And those love-darting eyes must roll no more.
Thus, if eternal justice rules the ball,
Thus shall your wives, and thus your children fall:
On all the line a sudden vengeance waits,
And frequent hearses shall besiege your gates:
There passengers shall stand, and pointing say
(While the long fun'rals blacken all the way),
"Lo! these were they, whose souls the Furies steel'd,
And cursed with hearts unknowing how to yield."
Thus unlamented pass the proud away,
The gaze of fools, and pageant of a day!
So perish all, whose breast ne'er learn'd to glow
For others' good, or melt at others' woe.
  What can atone (O ever-injured shade!)
Thy fate unpitied and thy rites unpaid?

No friend's complaint, no kind domestic
    tear
Pleased thy pale ghost, or graced thy
    mournful bier;
By foreign hands thy dying eyes were
    closed,
By foreign hands thy decent limbs com-
    posed,
By foreign hands thy humble grave
    adorn'd,
By strangers honor'd and by strangers
    mourn'd.
What though no friends in sable weeds
    appear,
Grieve for an hour, perhaps, then mourn a
    year,
And bear about the mockery of woe
To midnight dances and the public
    show?
What though no weeping Loves thy ashes
    grace,
Nor polish'd marble emulate thy face?
What though no sacred earth allow thee
    room,
Nor hallow'd dirge be mutter'd o'er thy
    tomb?
Yet shall thy grave with rising flowers be
    dress'd,
And the green turf lie lightly on thy
    breast:
There shall the morn her earliest tears
    bestow,
There the first roses of the year shall
    blow:
While angels with their silver wings o'er-
    shade
The ground now sacred by thy relics
    made.
    So peaceful rests, without a stone, a
        name,
What once had beauty, titles, wealth, and
    fame.
How loved, how honor'd once, avails thee
    not,
To whom related, or by whom begot;
A heap of dust alone remains of thee,
'Tis all thou art, and all the proud shall
    be!
    Poets themselves must fall like those
        they sung,
Deaf the praised ear, and mute the tune-
    ful tongue.

Ev'n he, whose soul now melts in mourn-
    ful lays,
Shall shortly want the gen'rous tear he
    pays;
Then from his closing eyes thy form shall
    part,
And the last pang shall tear thee from his
    heart;
Life's idle business at one gasp be o'er,
The Muse forgot, and thou beloved no
    more!
                ALEXANDER POPE.

THE LAND O' THE LEAL.

I'm wearin' awa', Jean,
Like snaw-wreaths in thaw, Jean,
I'm wearin' awa'
    To the land o' the leal.
There's nae sorrow there, Jean,
There's neither cauld nor care, Jean,
The day is aye fair
    In the land o' the leal.

Our bonnie bairn's there, Jean,
She was baith gude and fair, Jean,
And oh! we grudged her sair
    To the land o' the leal.
But sorrow's sel' wears past, Jean,
And joy's a-comin' fast, Jean,
The joy that's aye to last
    In the land o' the leal.

Sae dear that joy was bought, Jean,
Sae free the battle fought, Jean,
That sinfu' man e'er brought
    To the land o' the leal.
Oh! dry your glistening e'e, Jean,
My soul langs to be free, Jean,
And angels beckon me
    To the land o' the leal.

Oh! haud ye leal and true, Jean,
Your day it's wearin' thro', Jean,
And I'll welcome you
    To the land o' the leal.
Now fare ye weel, my ain Jean,
This warld's cares are vain, Jean,
We'll meet, and we'll be fain,
    In the land o' the leal.
                LADY CAROLINA NAIRNE.

STANZAS.

Farewell, life! my senses swim,
And the world is growing dim;
Thronging shadows cloud the light,
Like the advent of the night,—
Colder, colder, colder still,
Upward steals a vapor chill;
Strong the earthy odor grows,—
I smell the mould above the rose!

Welcome, life! the spirit strives!
Strength returns and hope revives:
Cloudy fears and shapes forlorn
Fly like shadows at the morn,—
O'er the earth there comes a bloom;
Sunny light for sullen gloom,
Warm perfume for vapor cold,—
I smell the rose above the mould!
Thomas Hood.

THE DYING MAN IN HIS GARDEN.

Why, Damon, with the forward day
Dost thou thy little spot survey,
From tree to tree, with doubtful cheer,
Pursue the progress of the year,
What winds arise, what rains descend,
When thou before that year shalt end?

What do thy noontide walks avail,
To clear the leaf, and pick the snail,
Then wantonly to death decree
An insect usefuller than thee?
Thou and the worm are brother-kind,
As low, as earthy, and as blind.

Vain wretch! canst thou expect to see
The downy peach make court to thee?
Or that thy sense shall ever meet
The bean-flower's deep-embosom'd sweet
Exhaling with an evening blast?
Thy evenings then will all be past!

Thy narrow pride, thy fancied green
(For vanity's in little seen),
All must be left when Death appears,
In spite of wishes, groans, and tears;
Nor one of all thy plants that grow
But Rosemary will with thee go.
George Sewell.

DIRGE.

From "Cymbeline."

Fear no more the heat o' the sun,
  Nor the furious winter's rages;
Thou thy worldly task hast done,
  Home art gone, and ta'en thy wages:
Golden lads and lasses must,
As chimney-sweepers, come to dust.

Fear no more the frown o' the great,
  Thou art past the tyrant's stroke;
Care no more to clothe, and eat;
  To thee the reed is as the oak:
The sceptre, learning, physic, must
All follow this, and come to dust.

Fear no more the lightning flash
  Nor the all-dreaded thunder-stone;
Fear not slander, censure rash;
  Thou hast finish'd joy and moan:
All lovers young, all lovers must,
Consign to thee, and come to dust.
William Shakespeare.

DIRGE IN CYMBELINE.

Sung by Guiderus and Arviragus over Fidele, supposed to be Dead.

To fair Fidele's grassy tomb
  Soft maids and village hinds shall bring
Each opening sweet of earliest bloom,
  And rifle all the breathing spring.

No wailing ghost shall dare appear,
  To vex with shrieks this quiet grove;
But shepherd lads assemble here,
  And melting virgins own their love.

No wither'd witch shall here be seen—
  No goblins lead their nightly crew;
The female fays shall haunt the green,
  And dress thy grave with pearly dew.

The redbreast oft, at evening hours,
  Shall kindly lend his little aid,
With hoary moss, and gather'd flowers,
  To deck the ground where thou art laid.

When howling winds and beating rain
  In tempests shake the sylvan cell,
Or 'midst the chase, on every plain,
  The tender thought on thee shall dwell,

Each lonely scene shall thee restore,
  For thee the tear be duly shed;
Beloved till life can charm no more,
  And mourn'd till Pity's self be dead.
WILLIAM COLLINS.

DIRGE.

FROM "THE WHITE DEVIL."

CALL for the robin-redbreast and the wren,
  Since o'er shady groves they hover,
  And with leaves and flowers do cover
The friendless bodies of unburied men.
Call unto his funeral dole
The ant, the field-mouse, and the mole,
To raise him hillocks that shall keep him warm,
And, when gay tombs are robb'd, sustain no harm;
But keep the wolf far thence, that's foe to men,
For with his nails he'll dig them up again.
JOHN WEBSTER.

DIRGE.

SOFTLY!
  She is lying
    With her lips apart;
Softly!
  She is dying of a broken heart.

Whisper!
  She is going
    To her final rest;
Whisper!
  Life is growing
    Dim within her breast.

Gently!
  She is sleeping;
    She has breathed her last!
Gently!
  While you're weeping,
    She to heaven has pass'd.
CHARLES GAMAGE EASTMAN.

FRIEND AFTER FRIEND DEPARTS.

FRIEND after friend departs:
  Who hath not lost a friend?
There is no union here of hearts
  That finds not here an end;
Were this frail world our only rest,
Living or dying, none were blest.

Beyond the flight of time,
  Beyond this vale of death,
There surely is some blessed clime
  Where life is not a breath,
Nor life's affections transient fire,
Whose sparks fly upward to expire.

There is a world above,
  Where parting is unknown;
A whole eternity of love,
  Form'd for the good alone;
And faith beholds the dying here
Translated to that happier sphere.

Thus star by star declines,
  Till all are pass'd away,
As morning high and higher shines,
  To pure and perfect day;
Nor sink those stars in empty night;
They hide themselves in heaven's own light.
JAMES MONTGOMERY

GANE WERE BUT THE WINTER CAULD.

GANE were but the winter cauld,
  And gane were but the snaw,
I could sleep in the wild woods,
  Where primroses blaw.

Cauld's the snaw at my head,
  And cauld at my feet,
And the finger o' Death's at my e'en,
  Closing them to sleep.

Let nane tell my father
  Or my mither sae dear;
I'll meet them baith in heaven
  At the spring o' the year.
ALLAN CUNNINGHAM.

THE ALPINE SHEEP.

WHEN on my ear your loss was knell'd,
  And tender sympathy upburst,
A little spring from memory well'd,
  Which once had quench'd my bitter thirst.

And I was fain to bear to you
  A portion of its mild relief,
That it might be as healing dew,
  To steal some fever from your grief.

After our child's untroubled breath
  Up to the Father took its way,
And on our home the shade of Death
  Like a long twilight haunting lay,

And friends came round, with us to weep
  Her little spirit's swift remove,
The story of the Alpine sheep
  Was told to us by one we love.

They, in the valley's sheltering care,
  Soon crop the meadow's tender prime,
And when the sod grows brown and bare,
  The shepherd strives to make them climb

To airy shelves of pasture green,
  That hang along the mountain's side,
Where grass and flowers together lean,
  And down through mist the sunbeams
    slide.

But naught can tempt the timid things
  The steep and rugged paths to try,
Though sweet the shepherd calls and sings,
  And sear'd below the pastures lie,

Till in his arms their lambs he takes,
  Along the dizzy verge to go;
Then, heedless of the rifts and breaks,
  They follow on, o'er rock and snow.

And in those pastures, lifted fair,
  More dewy-soft than lowland mead,
The shepherd drops his tender care,
  And sheep and lambs together feed.

This parable, by Nature breathed,
  Blew on me as the south wind free
O'er frozen brooks, that flow unsheathed
  From icy thraldrom to the sea.

A blissful vision, through the night,
  Would all my happy senses sway,
Of the good Shepherd on the height,
  Or climbing up the starry way,

Holding our little lamb asleep,—
  While, like the murmur of the sea,
Sounded that voice along the deep,
  Saying, "Arise and follow me!"
                    MARIA WHITE LOWELL.

TOM BOWLING.

HERE, a sheer hulk, lies poor Tom Bowling,
  The darling of our crew;
No more he'll hear the tempest howling—
  For Death has broach'd him to.
His form was of the manliest beauty;
  His heart was kind and soft;
Faithful below he did his duty;
  But now he's gone aloft.

Tom never from his word departed—
  His virtues were so rare;
His friends were many and true-hearted;
  His Poll was kind and fair.
And then he'd sing so blithe and jolly—
  Ah, many's the time and oft!
But mirth is turn'd to melancholy,
  For Tom is gone aloft.

Yet shall poor Tom find pleasant weather,
  When He, who all commands,
Shall give, to call life's crew together,
  The word to pipe all hands.
Thus Death, who kings and tars despatches,
  In vain Tom's life has doff'd;
For, though his body's under hatches,
  His soul is gone aloft.
                    CHARLES DIBDIN.

ONLY WAITING.

ONLY waiting till the shadows
  Are a little longer grown,
Only waiting till the glimmer
  Of the day's last beam is flown;
Till the night of earth is faded
  From the heart once full of day;
Till the stars of Heaven are breaking
  Through the twilight soft and gray.

Only waiting till the reapers
  Have the last sheaf gather'd home.
For the summer-time is faded,
  And the autumn winds have come.
Quickly, reapers! gather quickly
  The last ripe hours of my heart,
For the bloom of life is wither'd,
  And I hasten to depart.

Only waiting till the angels
  Open wide the mystic gate,
At whose feet I long have linger'd,
  Weary, poor, and desolate.

Even now I hear the footsteps,
  And their voices far away;
If they call me I am waiting,
  Only waiting to obey.

Only waiting till the shadows
  Are a little longer grown,
Only waiting till the glimmer
  Of the day's last beam is flown.
Then from out the gather'd darkness,
  Holy, deathless stars shall rise,
By whose light my soul shall gladly
  Tread its pathway to the skies.
FRANCES LAUGHTON MACE.

THE CLOSING SCENE.

WITHIN his sober realm of leafless trees
  The russet year inhaled the dreamy air;
Like some tann'd reaper in his hour of ease,
  When all the fields are lying brown and bare.

The gray barns looking from their hazy hills
  O'er the dim waters widening in the vales,
Sent down the air a greeting to the mills,
  On the dull thunder of alternate flails.

All sights were mellow'd and all sounds subdued,
  The hills seem'd farther and the streams sang low;
As in a dream the distant woodman hew'd
  His winter log with many a muffled blow.

The embattled forests, erewhile arm'd in gold,
  Their banners bright with every martial hue,
Now stood, like some sad beaten host of old,
  Withdrawn afar in Time's remotest blue.

On slumb'rous wings the vulture held his flight;
  The dove scarce heard its sighing mate's complaint;
And like a star slow drowning in the light,
  The village church-vane seem'd to pale and faint.

The sentinel-cock upon the hillside crew,
  Crew thrice, and all was stiller than before,—
Silent till some replying warder blew
  His alien horn, and then was heard no more.

Where erst the jay, within the elm's tall crest,
  Made garrulous trouble round her unfledged young,
And where the oriole hung her swaying nest,
  By every light wind like a censer swung;—

Where sang the noisy masons of the eaves,
  The busy swallows circling ever near,
Foreboding, as the rustic mind believes,
  An early harvest and a plenteous year;—

Where every bird which charm'd the vernal feast,
  Shook the sweet slumber from its wings at morn,
To warn the reaper of the rosy east,—
  All now was songless, empty, and forlorn.

Alone from out the stubble piped the quail,
  And croak'd the crow through all the dreamy gloom;
Alone the pheasant, drumming in the vale,
  Made echo to the distant cottage loom.

There was no bud, no bloom, upon the bowers;
  The spiders wove their thin shrouds night by night;
The thistle-down, the only ghost of flowers,
  Sail'd slowly by, pass'd noiseless out of sight.

Amid all this, in this most cheerless air,
  And where the woodbine shed upon the porch
Its crimson leaves, as if the Year stood there
  Firing the floor with his inverted torch;

Amid all this, the centre of the scene,
  The white-hair'd matron with monotonous tread,

Plied the swift wheel, and with her joyless
  mien,
 Sat, like a Fate, and watch'd the flying
  thread.

She had known Sorrow,—he had walk'd
  with her,
 Oft supp'd and broke the bitter ashen
  crust;
And in the dead leaves still she heard the
  stir
 Of his black mantle trailing in the
  dust.

While yet her cheek was bright with sum-
  mer bloom,
 Her country summon'd and she gave her
  all;
And twice War bow'd to her his sable
  plume,—
 Regave the swords to rust upon her
  wall.

Regave the swords,—but not the hand that
  drew
 And struck for Liberty its dying blow,
Nor him who, to his sire and country true,
 Fell 'mid the ranks of the invading foe.

Long, but not loud, the droning wheel
  went on,
 Like the low murmur of a hive at noon;
Long, but not loud, the memory of the
  gone
 Breathed through her lips a sad and
  tremulous tune.

At last the thread was snapp'd: her head
  was bow'd:
 Life dropt the distaff through his hands
  serene;
And loving neighbors smoothed her care-
  ful shroud,
 While Death and Winter closed the
  autumn scene.
             THOMAS BUCHANAN READ.

THE GRAVE.

THERE is a calm for those who weep,
 A rest for weary pilgrims found;
They softly lie and sweetly sleep
      Low in the ground.

The storm that wrecks the winter sky
 No more disturbs their deep repose
Than summer evening's latest sigh
      That shuts the rose.

I long to lay this painful head
 And aching heart beneath the soil,
To slumber in that dreamless bed
      From all my toil.

For Misery stole me at my birth,
 And cast me helpless on the wild:
I perish;—O my mother Earth,
      Take home thy child.

On thy dear lap these limbs reclined,
 Shall gently moulder into thee;
Nor leave one wretched trace behind
      Resembling me.

Hark!—a strange sound affrights mine ear,
 My pulse,—my brain runs wild,—I rave:
—Ah! who art thou whose voice I hear?
      "I am the Grave!

"The Grave, that never spake before,
 Hath found at length a tongue to chide:
Oh listen!—I will speak no more:—
      Be silent, Pride!

"Art thou a Wretch of hope forlorn,
 The victim of consuming care?
Is thy distracted conscience torn
      By fell despair?

"Do foul misdeeds of former times
 Wring with remorse thy guilty breast?
And ghosts of unforgiven crimes
      Murder thy rest?

"Lash'd by the furies of the mind,
 From Wrath and Vengeance wouldst
  thou flee?
Ah! think not, hope not, fool, to find
      A friend in me.

"By all the terrors of the tomb,
 Beyond the power of tongue to tell;
By the dread secrets of my womb;
      By Death and Hell;

"I charge thee live!—repent and pray,
 In dust thine infamy deplore;
There yet is mercy—go thy way,
      And sin no more.

"Art thou a Mourner?—Hast thou known
  The joy of innocent delights,
Endearing days for ever flown,
  And tranquil nights?

"Oh live!—and deeply cherish still
  The sweet remembrance of the past:
Rely on Heaven's unchanging will
  For peace at last.

"Art thou a Wanderer?—Hast thou seen
  O'erwhelming tempests drown thy bark?
A shipwreck'd sufferer hast thou been,
  Misfortune's mark?

"Though long of winds and waves the sport,
  Condemn'd in wretchedness to roam,
Live!—thou shalt reach a sheltering port,
  A quiet home.

"To Friendship didst thou trust thy fame,
  And was thy friend a deadly foe,
Who stole into thy breast to aim
  A surer blow?

"Live!—and repine not o'er his loss,
  A loss unworthy to be told,
Thou hast mistaken sordid dross
  For friendship's gold.

"Seek the true treasure seldom found,
  Of power the fiercest griefs to calm,
And soothe the bosom's deepest wound
  With heavenly balm.

"Did Woman's charm thy youth beguile,
  And did the Fair One faithless prove?
Hath she betray'd thee with a smile,
  And sold thy love?

"Live! 'Twas a false bewildering fire:
  Too often Love's insidious dart
Thrills the fond soul with wild desire,
  But kills the heart.

"Thou yet shalt know how sweet, how dear,
  To gaze on listening Beauty's eye;
To ask,—and pause in hope and fear
  Till she reply.

"A nobler flame shall warm thy breast,
  A brighter maiden faithful prove;
Thy youth, thine age, shall yet be blest
  In woman's love.

"—Whate'er thy lot,—whoe'er thou be—
  Confess thy folly, kiss the rod,
And in thy chastening sorrows see
  The hand of God.

"A bruisèd reed He will not break;
  Afflictions all his children feel;
He wounds them for His mercy's sake,
  He wounds to heal.

"Humbled beneath His mighty hand,
  Prostrate His Providence adore:
'Tis done!—Arise! He bids thee stand,
  To fall no more.

"Now, Traveller in the vale of tears
  To realms of everlasting light,
Through Time's dark wilderness of years,
  Pursue thy flight.

"There is a calm for those who weep,
  A rest for weary Pilgrims found;
And while the mouldering ashes sleep
  Low in the ground,

"The Soul, of origin divine,
  God's glorious image, freed from clay,
In heaven's eternal sphere shall shine
  A star of day.

"The Sun is but a spark of fire,
  A transient meteor in the sky;
The Soul, immortal as its Sire,
  SHALL NEVER DIE."
      JAMES MONTGOMERY.

TO A SKELETON.

BEHOLD this ruin! 'Twas a skull
Once of ethereal spirit full.
This narrow cell was Life's retreat,
This space was Thought's mysterious seat.
What beauteous visions fill'd this spot!
What dreams of pleasure long forgot!
Nor hope, nor joy, nor love, nor fear,
Have left one trace of record here.

Beneath this mouldering canopy
Once shone the bright and busy eye,
But start not at the dismal void,—
If social love that eye employ'd,
If with no lawless fire it gleam'd,
But through the dews of kindness beam'd,
That eye shall be for ever bright
When stars and sun are sunk in night.

Within this hollow cavern hung
The ready, swift, and tuneful tongue;
If Falsehood's honey it disdain'd,
And when it could not praise was chain'd;
If bold in Virtue's cause it spoke,
Yet gentle concord never broke,—
This silent tongue shall plead for thee
When Time unveils Eternity!

Say, did these fingers delve the mine?
Or with the envied rubies shine?
To hew the rock or wear a gem
Can little now avail to them.
But if the page of Truth they sought,
Or comfort to the mourner brought,
These hands a richer meed shall claim
Than all that wait on Wealth and Fame.

Avails it whether bare or shod
These feet the paths of duty trod?
If from the bowers of Ease they fled,
To seek Affliction's humble shed;
If Grandeur's guilty bribe they spurn'd,
And home to Virtue's cot return'd,—
These feet with angel wings shall vie,
And tread the palace of the sky!
AUTHOR UNKNOWN.

THE LAST MAN.

ALL worldly shapes shall melt in gloom,
　The Sun himself must die,
Before this mortal shall assume
　Its immortality!
I saw a vision in my sleep,
That gave my spirit strength to sweep
　Adown the gulf of Time!
I saw the last of human mould
That shall Creation's death behold,
　As Adam saw her prime!

The Sun's eye had a sickly glare,
　The Earth with age was wan;
The skeletons of nations were
　Around that lonely man!
Some had expired in fight,—the brands
Still rusted in their bony hands,
　In plague and famine some!
Earth's cities had no sound nor tread;
And ships were drifting with the dead
　To shores where all was dumb!

Yet, prophet-like, that lone one stood,
　With dauntless words and high,
That shook the sere leaves from the wood,
　As if a storm pass'd by,
Saying, We are twins in death, proud Sun!
Thy face is cold, thy race is run,
　'Tis Mercy bids thee go;
For thou ten thousand thousand years
Hast seen the tide of human tears,
　That shall no longer flow.

What though beneath thee man put forth
　His pomp, his pride, his skill;
And arts that made fire, flood, and earth
　The vassals of his will?
Yet mourn I not thy parted sway,
Thou dim, discrownèd king of day;
　For all those trophied arts
And triumphs that beneath thee sprang,
Heal'd not a passion or a pang
　Entail'd on human hearts.

Go, let oblivion's curtain fall
　Upon the stage of men,
Nor with thy rising beams recall
　Life's tragedy again:
Its piteous pageants bring not back,
Nor waken flesh, upon the rack
　Of pain anew to writhe;
Stretch'd in disease's shapes abhorr'd,
Or mown in battle by the sword,
　Like grass beneath the scythe.

Even I am weary in yon skies
　To watch thy fading fire;
Test of all sumless agonies,
　Behold not me expire.
My lips that speak thy dirge of death,
Their rounded gasp and gurgling breath
　To see thou shalt not boast.
The eclipse of Nature spreads my pall,
The majesty of Darkness shall
　Receive my parting ghost!

This spirit shall return to Him
　Who gave its heavenly spark;
Yet think not, Sun, it shall be dim
　When thou thyself art dark!
No! it shall live again, and shine
In bliss unknown to beams of thine,
　By Him recall'd to breath,
Who captive led captivity,
Who robb'd the grave of Victory,
　And took the sting from Death!

Go, Sun, while Mercy holds me up
  On Nature's awful waste
To drink this last and bitter cup
  Of grief that man shall taste,—
Go, tell the night that hides thy face,
Thou saw'st the last of Adam's race,
  On Earth's sepulchral clod,
The darkening universe defy
  To quench his immortality,
  Or shake his trust in God!
THOMAS CAMPBELL.

ODE.

INTIMATIONS OF IMMORTALITY FROM RECOLLECTIONS OF EARLY CHILDHOOD.

I.

THERE was a time when meadow, grove, and stream,
  The earth, and every common sight,
    To me did seem
  Apparell'd in celestial light,
The glory and the freshness of a dream.
  It is not now as it hath been of yore;—
    Turn wheresoe'er I may,
    By night or day,
  The things which I have seen I now can see no more.

II.

  The Rainbow comes and goes,
  And lovely is the Rose,
  The Moon doth with delight
Look round her when the heavens are bare,
  Waters on a starry night
  Are beautiful and fair;
  The sunshine is a glorious birth;
  But yet I know, where'er I go,
That there hath pass'd away a glory from the earth.

III.

Now, while the birds thus sing a joyous song,
  And while the young lambs bound
  As to the tabor's sound,
To me alone there came a thought of grief:
A timely utterance gave that thought relief,
  And I again am strong:
The cataracts blow their trumpets from the steep;
  No more shall grief of mine the season wrong;
I hear the Echoes through the mountains throng,
The Winds come to me from the fields of sleep,
  And all the earth is gay;
    Land and sea
  Give themselves up to jollity,
  And with the heart of May
Doth every Beast keep holiday;—
  Thou Child of Joy,
Shout round me, let me hear thy shouts, thou happy
  Shepherd boy!

IV.

Ye blessed Creatures, I have heard the call
  Ye to each other make; I see
The heavens laugh with you in your jubilee;
  My heart is at your festival,
  My head hath its coronal,
The fulness of your bliss, I feel—I feel it all.
  O evil day! if I were sullen
  While Earth herself is adorning,
  This sweet May morning,
  And the Children are culling
    On every side,
  In a thousand valleys far and wide,
Fresh flowers; while the sun shines warm,
And the Babe leaps up on his Mother's arm:—
  I hear, I hear, with joy I hear!
—But there's a Tree, of many, one,
A single Field which I have look'd upon,
Both of them speak of something that is gone:
  The Pansy at my feet
  Doth the same tale repeat:
Whither is fled the visionary gleam?
Where is it now, the glory and the dream?

V.

Our birth is but a sleep and a forgetting:
  The Soul that rises with us, our life's Star,
    Hath had elsewhere its setting,
    And cometh from afar:
  Not in entire forgetfulness,
  And not in utter nakedness,

But trailing clouds of glory do we come
  From God, who is our home:
Heaven lies about us in our infancy!
Shades of the prison-house begin to close
  Upon the growing Boy,
But he beholds the light, and whence it flows,
  He sees it in his joy;
The Youth, who daily farther from the east
  Must travel, still is Nature's Priest,
  And by the vision splendid
  Is on his way attended;
At length the Man perceives it die away,
And fade into the light of common day.

VI.

Earth fills her lap with pleasures of her own;
  Yearnings she hath in her own natural kind,
  And, even with something of a Mother's mind,
  And no unworthy aim,
  The homely Nurse doth all she can
To make her Foster-child, her Inmate Man,
  Forget the glories he hath known,
And that imperial palace whence he came.

VII.

Behold the child among his new-born blisses,
  A six years' Darling of a pigmy size!
See, where 'mid work of his own hand he lies,
Fretted by sallies of his mother's kisses,
  With light upon him from his father's eyes!
See, at his feet, some little plan or chart,
  Some fragment from his dream of human life,
  Shaped by himself with newly-learnèd art;
    A wedding or a festival,
    A mourning or a funeral;
      And this hath now his heart,
      And unto this he frames his song:
        Then will he fit his tongue
To dialogues of business, love, or strife;
    But it will not be long
    Ere this be thrown aside,
    And with new joy and pride
The little Actor cons another part;
Filling from time to time his "humorous stage"
With all the Persons, down to palsied Age,
That Life brings with her in her equipage;
  As if his whole vocation
  Were endless imitation.

VIII.

Thou, whose exterior semblance doth belie
  The Soul's immensity;
Thou best Philosopher, who yet dost keep
  Thy heritage, thou Eye among the blind,
That, deaf and silent, read'st the eternal deep,
Haunted for ever by the eternal mind,—
  Mighty Prophet! Seer blest!
  On whom those truths do rest,
Which we are toiling all our lives to find,
In darkness lost, the darkness of the grave;
Thou, over whom thy Immortality
Broods like the Day, a Master o'er a Slave,
A Presence which is not to be put by;
Thou little Child, yet glorious in the might
Of heaven-born freedom on thy being's height,
Why with such earnest pains dost thou provoke
The years to bring the inevitable yoke,
  Thus blindly with thy blessedness at strife?
Full soon thy Soul shall have her earthly freight,
And custom lie upon thee with a weight,
Heavy as frost, and deep almost as life!

IX.

  Oh joy! that in our embers
  Is something that doth live,
  That Nature yet remembers
    What was so fugitive!
The thought of our past years in me doth breed
Perpetual benediction: not indeed
For that which is most worthy to be blest
Delight and liberty, the simple creed
Of Childhood, whether busy or at rest,
With new-fledged hope still fluttering in his breast:—
  Not for these I raise
  The song of thanks and praise:

But for those obstinate questionings
Of sense and outward things
Fallings from us, vanishings;
Blank misgivings of a Creature
Moving about in worlds not realized,
High instincts before which our mortal
Nature
Did tremble like a guilty thing surprised:
But for those first affections
Those shadowy recollections,
Which, be they what they may,
Are yet the fountain-light of all our day,
Are yet a master light of all our seeing;
Uphold us, cherish, and have power to
make
Our noisy years seem moments in the
being
Of the eternal Silence: truths that wake,
To perish never;
Which neither listlessness, nor mad endeavor,
Nor Man nor Boy,
Nor all that is at enmity with joy,
Can utterly abolish or destroy!
Hence in a season of calm weather
Though inland far we be,
Our souls have sight of that immortal sea
Which brought us hither,
Can in a moment travel thither,
And see the Children sport upon the
shore,
And hear the mighty waters rolling evermore.

X.

Then sing, ye Birds, sing, sing a joyous
song!
And let the young Lambs bound
As to the tabor's sound;
We in thought will join your throng,
Ye that pipe and ye that play,
Ye that through your hearts to-day
Feel the gladness of the May!
What though the radiance which was once
so bright
Be now for ever taken from my sight,
Though nothing can bring back the hour
Of splendor in the grass, of glory in the
flower;
We will grieve not, rather find
Strength in what remains behind;
In the primal sympathy
Which having been must ever be;
In the soothing thoughts that spring
Out of human suffering;
In the faith that looks through death.
In years that bring the philosophic mind.

XI.

And O ye Fountains, Meadows, Hills, and
Groves,
Forebode not any severing of our loves?
Yet in my heart of hearts I feel your might;
I only have relinquish'd one delight
To live beneath your more habitual sway.
I love the Brooks which down their channels fret,
Even more than when I tripp'd lightly as
they;
The innocent brightness of a new-born
Day
Is lovely yet;
The Clouds that gather round the setting
sun
Do take a sober coloring from an eye
That hath kept watch o'er man's mortality;
Another race hath been, and other palms
are won.
Thanks to the human heart by which we
live,
Thanks to its tenderness, its joys, and
fears,
To me the meanest flower that blows can
give
Thoughts that do often lie too deep for
tears.
WILLIAM WORDSWORTH.

RESIGNATION.

THERE is no flock, however watch'd and
tended,
But one dead lamb is there!
There is no fireside, howsoe'er defended,
But has one vacant chair!

The air is full of farewells to the dying,
And mournings for the dead;
The heart of Rachel, for her children crying,
Will not be comforted!

Let us be patient! These severe afflictions
Not from the ground arise,
But oftentimes celestial benedictions
Assume this dark disguise.

We see but dimly through the mists and
    vapors;
  Amid these earthly damps
What seem to us but sad, funereal tapers
  May be heaven's distant lamps.

There is no Death! What seems so is tran-
    sition:
  This life of mortal breath
Is but a suburb of the life elysian,
  Whose portal we call Death.

She is not dead,—the child of our affec-
    tion,—
  But gone unto that school
Where she no longer needs our poor pro-
    tection,
  And Christ Himself doth rule.

In that great cloister's stillness and seclu-
    sion,
  By guardian angels led,
Safe from temptation, safe from sin's pollu-
    tion,
  She lives whom we call dead.

Day after day we think what she is doing
  In those bright realms of air;
Year after year, her tender steps pursuing,
  Behold her grown more fair.

Thus do we walk with her, and keep un-
    broken
  The bond which Nature gives,
Thinking that our remembrance, though
    unspoken,
  May reach her where she lives.

Not as a child shall we again behold her;
  For when with raptures wild
In our embraces we again enfold her,
  She will not be a child:

But a fair maiden, in her Father's mansion,
  Clothed with celestial grace;
And beautiful with all the soul's expan-
    sion
  Shall we behold her face.

And though, at times, impetuous with
    emotion
  And anguish long suppress'd,
The swelling heart heaves moaning like
    the ocean,
  That cannot be at rest,—

We will be patient, and assuage the feel-
    ing
  We may not wholly stay;
By silence sanctifying, not concealing,
  The grief that must have way.
                HENRY WADSWORTH LONGFELLOW.

THE CROWDED STREET.

LET me move slowly through the street,
  Fill'd with an ever-shifting train,
Amid the sound of steps that beat
  The murmuring walks like autumn rain.

How fast the flitting figures come!
  The mild, the fierce, the stony face—
Some bright with thoughtless smiles, and
    some
  Where secret tears have left their trace.

They pass to toil, to strife, to rest—
  To halls in which the feast is spread—
To chambers where the funeral guest
  In silence sits beside the dead.

And some to happy homes repair,
  Where children, pressing cheek to cheek,
With mute caresses shall declare
  The tenderness they cannot speak.

And some, who walk in calmness here,
  Shall shudder as they reach the door
Where one who made their dwelling dear,
  Its flower, its light, is seen no more.

Youth, with pale cheek and slender frame,
  And dreams of greatness in thine eye!
Go'st thou to build an early name,
  Or early in the task to die?

Keen son of trade with eager brow!
  Who is now fluttering in thy snare?
Thy golden fortunes, tower they now,
  Or melt the glittering spires in air?

Who of this crowd to-night shall tread
  The dance till daylight gleam again?
Who sorrow o'er the untimely dead?
  Who writhe in throes of mortal pain?

Some, famine-struck, shall think how long
  The cold, dark hours, how slow the
    light;
And some, who flaunt amid the throng,
  Shall hide in dens of shame to-night.

Each where his tasks or pleasures call,
  They pass, and heed each other not.
There is Who heeds, Who holds them all
  In His large love and boundless thought.

These struggling tides of life, that seem
  In wayward, aimless course to tend,
Are eddies of the mighty stream
  That rolls to its appointed end.
                    WILLIAM CULLEN BRYANT.

THE HERMIT.

AT the close of the day, when the hamlet is still,
  And mortals the sweets of forgetfulness prove,
When naught but the torrent is heard on the hill,
  And naught but the nightingale's song in the grove,
'Twas thus, by the cave of the mountain afar,
  While his harp rung symphonious, a hermit began;
No more with himself or with Nature at war,
  He thought as a sage, though he felt as a man:

"Ah! why, all abandon'd to darkness and woe,
  Why, lone Philomela, that languishing fall?
For spring shall return, and a lover bestow,
  And sorrow no longer thy bosom inthrall.
But, if pity inspire thee, renew the sad lay,—
  Mourn, sweetest complainer, man calls thee to mourn;
Oh, soothe him whose pleasures like thine pass away!
  Full quickly they pass,—but they never return.

"Now, gliding remote on the verge of the sky,
  The moon, half extinguish'd, her crescent displays;
But lately I mark'd when majestic on high
  She shone, and the planets were lost in her blaze.
Roll on, thou fair orb, and with gladness pursue
  The path that conducts thee to splendor again!
But man's faded glory what change shall renew?
  Ah, fool! to exult in a glory so vain!

"'Tis night, and the landscape is lovely no more.
  I mourn, but, ye woodlands, I mourn not for you;
For morn is approaching your charms to restore,
  Perfumed with fresh fragrance, and glittering with dew.
Nor yet for the ravage of winter I mourn,—
  Kind Nature the embryo blossom will save;
But when shall spring visit the mouldering urn?
  Oh, when shall day dawn on the night of the grave?

"'Twas thus, by the glare of false science betray'd,
  That leads to bewilder, and dazzles to blind,
My thoughts wont to roam from shade onward to shade,
  Destruction before me, and sorrow behind.
'Oh pity, great Father of light,' then I cried,
  'Thy creature, who fain would not wander from Thee!
Lo, humbled in dust, I relinquish my pride;
  From doubt and from darkness Thou only canst free!'

"And darkness and doubt are now flying away;
  No longer I roam in conjecture forlorn.
So breaks on the traveller, faint and astray,
  The bright and the balmy effulgence of morn.

See truth, love, and mercy in triumph
    descending,
And Nature all glowing in Eden's first
    bloom!
On the cold cheek of death smiles and
    roses are blending,
And beauty immortal awakes from the
    tomb."
JAMES BEATTIE.

THE VANITY OF HUMAN WISHES.

IN IMITATION OF THE TENTH SATIRE OF JUVENAL.

LET Observation, with extensive view,
Survey mankind from China to Peru;
Remark each anxious toil, each eager
    strife,
And watch the busy scenes of crowded
    life;
Then say how hope and fear, desire and
    hate,
O'erspread with snares the clouded maze
    of fate,
Where wavering man, betray'd by ventur-
    ous pride
To chase the dreary paths without a
    guide,
As treacherous phantoms in the midst
    delude,
Shuns fancied ills, or chases airy good;
How rarely reason guides the stubborn
    choice,
Rules the bold hand, or prompts the sup-
    pliant voice;
How nations sink, by darling schemes op-
    press'd,
When Vengeance listens to the fool's re-
    quest.
Fate wings with every wish th' afflictive
    dart,
Each gift of Nature and each grace of
    art;
With fatal heat impetuous courage glows,
With fatal sweetness elocution flows,
Impeachment stops the speaker's powerful
    breath,
And restless fire precipitates on death.

But, scarce observed, the knowing and
    the bold
Fall in the general massacre of gold;
Wide wasting pest! that rages unconfined
And crowds with crimes the records of
    mankind;
For gold his sword the hireling ruffian
    draws,
For gold the hireling judge distorts the
    laws;
Wealth heap'd on wealth, nor truth nor
    safety buys,
The dangers gather as the treasures rise.

Let History tell where rival kings com-
    mand,
And dubious title shakes the madded land,
When statutes glean the refuse of the
    sword,
How much more safe the vassal than the
    lord!
Low skulks the hind below the rage of
    power,
And leaves the wealthy traitor in the
    Tower;
Untouch'd his cottage, and his slumbers
    sound,
Though Confiscation's vultures hover
    round.

The needy traveller, serene and gay,
Walks the wild heath, and sings his toil
    away.
Does envy seize thee? crush th' upbraid-
    ing joy,
Increase his riches, and his peace de-
    stroy:
Now fears in dire vicissitude invade,
The rustling brake alarms, and quivering
    shade,
Nor light nor darkness bring his pain
    relief,
One shows the plunder and one hides the
    thief.

Yet still one general cry the skies assails,
And gain and grandeur load the tainted
    gales;
Few know the toiling statesman's fear or
    care,
The insidious rival and the gaping heir.
Once more, Democritus, arise on earth,
With cheerful wisdom and instructive
    mirth;
See motley life in modern trappings dress'd,
And feed with varied fools th' eternal jest:

Thou who couldst laugh, where want enchain'd caprice,
Toil crush'd conceit, and man was of a piece;
Where wealth unloved without a mourner died,
And scarce a sycophant was fed by pride;
Where ne'er was known the form of mock debate,
Or seen a new-made mayor's unwieldy state;
Where change of favorites made no change of laws,
And senates heard before they judged a cause;
How wouldst thou shake at Britain's modish tribe,
Dart the quick taunt and edge the piercing gibe?
Attentive truth and nature to descry,
And pierce each scene with philosophic eye,
To thee were solemn toys, or empty show,
The robes of pleasure, and the veils of woe:
All aid the farce, and all thy mirth maintain,
Whose joys are causeless, or whose griefs are vain.

Such was the scorn that fill'd the sage's mind,
Renew'd at every glance on human kind;
How just that scorn ere yet thy voice declare,
Search every state, and canvass every prayer.

Unnumber'd suppliants crowd Preferment's gate,
Athirst for wealth, and burning to be great;
Delusive Fortune hears th' incessant call,
They mount, they shine, evaporate and fall.
On every stage the foes of peace attend,
Hate dogs their flight, and insult mocks their end.
Love ends with hope, the sinking statesman's door
Pours in the morning worshipper no more;
For growing names the weekly scribbler lies,
To growing wealth the dedicator flies;
From every room descends the painted face
That hung the bright palladium of the place,
And, smoked in kitchens, or in auctions sold,
To better features yields the frame of gold;
For now no more we trace in every line
Heroic worth, benevolence divine;
The form distorted justifies the fall,
And detestation rids th' indignant wall.

But will not Britain hear the last appeal,
Sign her foes' doom, or guard the favorite's zeal?
Through Freedom's sons no more remonstrance rings,
Degrading nobles and controlling kings;
Our supple tribes repress their patriot throats,
And ask no questions but the price of votes;
With weekly libels and septennial ale,
Their wish is full to riot and to rail.

In full-flown dignity see Wolsey stand,
Law in his voice, and fortune in his hand;
To him the church, the realm, their powers consign,
Through him the rays of regal bounty shine,
Turn'd by his nod the stream of honor flows,
His smile alone security bestows;
Still to new heights his restless wishes tower,
Claim leads to claim, and power advances power;
Till conquest unresisted ceased to please,
And rights submitted left him none to seize;
At length his sovereign frowns—the train of state
Mark the keen glance, and watch the sign to hate.
Where'er he turns, he meets a stranger's eye,
His suppliants scorn him, and his followers fly;

Now drops at once the pride of awful state,
The golden canopy, the glittering plate,
The regal palace, the luxurious board,
The liveried army, and the menial lord;
With age, with cares, with maladies oppress'd,
He seeks the refuge of monastic rest.
Grief aids disease, remember'd folly stings,
And his last sighs reproach the faith of kings.

Speak, thou whose thoughts at humble peace repine,
Shall Wolsey's wealth with Wolsey's end be thine?
Or liv'st thou now, with safer pride content,
The wisest justice on the banks of Trent?
For why did Wolsey, near the steeps of fate,
On weak foundations raise th' enormous weight?
Why but to sink beneath misfortune's blow,
With louder ruin to the gulfs below?

What gave great Villiers to the assassin's knife,
And fixed disease on Harley's closing life?
What murder'd Wentworth, and what exiled Hyde,
By kings protected and to kings allied?
What but their wish indulged in courts to shine
And power too great to keep or to resign?

When first the college rolls receive his name,
The young enthusiast quits his ease for fame;
Resistless burns the fever of renown,
Caught from the strong contagion of the gown;
O'er Bodley's dome his future labors spread,
And Bacon's mansion trembles o'er his head.
Are these thy views? Proceed, illustrious youth,
And Virtue guard thee to the throne of Truth!
Yet should thy soul indulge the generous heat
Till captive Science yields her last retreat;

Should Reason guide thee with her brightest ray,
And pour on misty Doubt resistless day;
Should no false kindness lure to loose delight,
Nor praise relax, nor difficulty fright;
Should tempting Novelty thy cell refrain,
And Sloth diffuse her opiate fumes in vain;
Should Beauty blunt on fops her fatal dart,
Nor claim the triumph of a letter'd heart;
Should no disease thy torpid veins invade,
Nor Melancholy's phantoms haunt thy shade;
Yet hope not life from grief or danger free,
Nor think the doom of man reversed for thee.
Deign on the passing world to turn thine eyes,
And pause a while from letters to be wise;
There mark what ills the scholar's life assail,
Toil, envy, want, the patron, and the jail.
See nations, slowly wise and meanly just,
To buried merit raise the tardy bust.
If dreams yet flatter, yet again attend,
Hear Lydiat's life and Galileo's end.

Nor deem, when Learning her last prize bestows,
The glittering eminence exempt from foes;
See, when the vulgar 'scapes, despised or awed,
Rebellion's vengeful talons seize on Laud.
From meaner minds, though smaller fines content
The plunder'd palace, or sequester'd rent,
Mark'd out by dangerous parts, he meets the shock,
And fatal Learning leads him to the block;
Around his tomb let Art and Genius weep,
But hear his death, ye blockheads, hear and sleep.

The festal blazes, the triumphal show,
The ravish'd standard, and the captive foe,
The senate's thanks, the Gazette's pompous tale,
With force resistless o'er the brave prevail.
Such bribes the rapid Greek o'er Asia whirl'd,
For such the steady Romans shook the world;

For such in distant lands the Britons shine,
And stain with blood the Danube or the Rhine;
This power has praise, that virtue scarce can warm
Till Fame supplies the universal charm.
Yet Reason frowns on War's unequal game,
Where wasted nations raise a single name;
And mortgaged states their grandsire's wreaths regret,
From age to age in everlasting debt;
Wreaths which at last the dear-bought right convey
To rust on medals, or on stones decay.

On what foundation stands the warrior's pride,
How just his hopes, let Swedish Charles decide:
A frame of adamant, a soul of fire,
No dangers fright him, and no labors tire;
O'er love, o'er fear, extends his wide domain,
Unconquer'd lord of pleasure and of pain;
No joys to him pacific sceptres yield,
War sounds the trump, he rushes to the field;
Behold surrounding kings their powers combine,
And one capitulate, and one resign;
Peace courts his hand, but spreads her charms in vain;
"Think nothing gain'd," he cries, "till naught remain,
On Moscow's walls till Gothic standards fly,
And all be mine beneath the polar sky!"
The march begins in military state,
And nations on his eye suspended wait;
Stern Famine guards the solitary coast,
And Winter barricades the realms of Frost;
He comes, nor want nor cold his course delay;—
Hide, blushing Glory, hide Pultowa's day:
The vanquish'd hero leaves his broken bands,
And shows his miseries in distant lands;
Condemn'd a needy supplicant to wait,
While ladies interpose, and slaves debate.
But did not Chance at length her error mend?
Did no subverted empire mark his end?
Did rival monarchs give the fatal wound?
Or hostile millions press him to the ground?
His fall was destined to a barren strand,
A petty fortress, and a dubious hand;
He left the name, at which the world grew pale,
To point a moral, or adorn a tale.

All times their scenes of pompous woes afford,
From Persia's tyrant to Bavaria's lord.
In gay hostility and barbarous pride,
With half mankind embattled at his side,
Great Xerxes comes to seize the certain prey,
And starves exhausted regions in his way;
Attendant Flattery counts his myriads o'er,
Till counted myriads soothe his pride no more;
Fresh praise is tried till madness fires his mind,
The waves he lashes, and enchains the wind,
New powers are claim'd, new powers are still bestow'd,
Till rude resistance lops the spreading god.
The daring Greeks deride the martial show,
And heap their valleys with the gaudy foe;
Th' insulted sea with humbler thought he gains,
A single skiff to speed his flight remains;
Th' encumber'd oar scarce leaves the dreaded coast
Through purple billows and a floating host.

The bold Bavarian, in a luckless hour,
Tries the dread summits of Cæsarean power,
With unexpected legions bursts away,
And sees defenceless realms receive his sway;
Short sway! fair Austria spreads her mournful charms,
The queen, the beauty, sets the world in arms;

From hill to hill the beacon's rousing blaze
Spreads wide the hope of plunder and of praise;
The fierce Croatian and the wild Hussar,
With all the sons of ravage crowd the war;
The baffled prince, in honor's flattering bloom
Of hasty greatness, finds the fatal doom,
His foes' derision, and his subjects' blame,
And steals to death from anguish and from shame.

"Enlarge my life with multitude of days!"
In health, in sickness, thus the suppliant prays;
Hides from himself his state, and shuns to know
That life protracted is protracted woe.
Time hovers o'er, impatient to destroy,
And shuts up all the passages of joy.
In vain their gifts the bounteous seasons pour,
The fruit autumnal and the vernal flower;
With listless eyes the dotard views the store,
He views, and wonders that they please no more;
Now pall the tasteless meats, and joyless wines,
And Luxury with sighs her slave resigns.
Approach, ye minstrels, try the soothing strain,
Diffuse the tuneful lenitives of pain:
No sounds, alas! would touch th' impervious ear,
Though dancing mountains witness'd Orpheus near:
Nor lute nor lyre his feeble powers attend,
Nor sweeter music of a virtuous friend;
But everlasting dictates crowd his tongue,
Perversely grave, or positively wrong.
The still returning tale, and lingering jest
Perplex the fawning niece and pamper'd guest,
While growing hopes scarce awe the gathering sneer,
And scarce a legacy can bribe to hear;
The watchful guests still hint the last offence;
The daughter's petulance, the son's expense;
Improve his heady rage with treacherous skill,
And mould his passions till they make his will.

Unnumber'd maladies his joints invade,
Lay siege to life, and press the dire blockade;
But unextinguish'd Avarice still remains,
And dreaded losses aggravate his pains;
He turns, with anxious heart and crippled hands,
His bonds of debt, and mortgages of lands;
Or views his coffers with suspicious eyes,
Unlocks his gold, and counts it till he dies.

But grant, the virtues of a temperate prime
Bless with an age exempt from scorn or crime;
An age that melts with unperceived decay,
And glides in modest innocence away;
Whose peaceful day Benevolence endears,
Whose night congratulating Conscience cheers;
The general favorite as the general friend;
Such age there is, and who shall wish its end?

Yet even on this her load Misfortune flings,
To press the weary minutes' flagging wings;
New sorrow rises as the day returns,
A sister sickens, or a daughter mourns;
Now kindred Merit fills the sable bier,
Now lacerated Friendship claims a tear;
Year chases year, decay pursues decay,
Still drops some joy from withering life away;
New forms arise, and different views engage,
Superfluous lags the veteran on the stage,
Till pitying Nature signs the last release,
And bids afflicted worth retire to peace.

But few there are whom hours like these await,
Who set unclouded in the gulfs of Fate.

From Lydia's monarch should the search
   descend,
By Solon caution'd to regard his end,
In life's last scene what prodigies surprise,
Fears of the brave, and follies of the wise:
From Marlborough's eyes the streams of
   dotage flow,
And Swift expires a driveller and a show!

   The teeming mother, anxious for her
     race,
Begs for each birth the fortune of a face;
Yet Vane could tell what ills from beauty
   spring;
And Sedley cursed the form that pleased a
   king.
Ye nymphs of rosy lips and radiant eyes,
Whom Pleasure keeps too busy to be wise;
Whom joys with soft varieties invite,
By day the frolic, and the dance by night;
Who frown with vanity, who smile with
   art,
And ask the latest fashion of the heart;
What care, what rules, your heedless
   charms shall save,
Each nymph your rival, and each youth
   your slave?
Against your fame with fondness hate
   combines,
The rival batters, and the lover mines:
With distant voice neglected Virtue calls,
Less heard and less, the faint remonstrance
   falls;
Tired with contempt, she quits the slippery
   reign,
And Pride and Prudence take her seat in
   vain.
In crowd at once, where none the pass defend,
The harmless freedom, and the private
   friend;
The guardians yield, by force superior
   plied:
To Interest, Prudence; and to Flattery,
   Pride.
Here Beauty falls betray'd, despised, distress'd,
And hissing Infamy proclaims the rest

   Where then shall Hope and Fear their
     objects find?
Must dull suspense corrupt the stagnant
   mind?
Must helpless man, in ignorance sedate,
Roll darkling down the torrent of his fate?
Must no dislike alarm, no wishes rise,
No cries invoke the mercies of the skies?
Inquirer, cease; petitions yet remain
Which Heaven may hear, nor deem Religion vain.
Still raise for good the supplicating voice,
But leave to Heaven the measure and the
   choice.
Safe in His power whose eyes discern
   afar
The secret ambush of a specious prayer,
Implore His aid, in His decisions rest,
Secure, whate'er He gives, He gives the
   best.
Yet, when the sense of sacred presence
   fires,
And strong devotion to the skies aspires,
Pour forth thy fervors for a healthful
   mind,
Obedient passions, and a will resign'd;
For love, which scarce collective man can
   fill;
For patience, sovereign o'er transmuted
   ill;
For faith, that, panting for a happier
   seat,
Counts death kind Nature's signal of retreat.
These goods for man the laws of Heaven
   ordain;
These goods He grants who grants the
   power to gain;
With these celestial Wisdom calms the
   mind,
And makes the happiness she does not
   find.
                SAMUEL JOHNSON.

THE VANITY OF THE WORLD.

FALSE world, thou ly'st; thou canst not lend
   The least delight:
Thy favors cannot gain a friend,
   They are so slight:
Thy morning pleasures make an end
   To please at night:
Poor are the wants that thou supply'st,
And yet thou vaunt'st, and yet thou vy'st
With heaven; fond earth, thou boast'st:
   false world, thou ly'st.

Thy babbling tongue tells golden tales
    Of endless treasure;
Thy bounty offers easy sales
    Of lasting pleasure;
Thou ask'st the conscience what she ails,
    And swear'st to ease her;
There's none can want where thou sup­ply'st:
There's none can give where thou deny'st.
Alas! fond world, thou boast'st; false world, thou ly'st.

What well-advisèd ear regards
    What earth can say?
Thy words are gold, but thy rewards
    Are painted clay:
Thy cunning can but pack the cards,
    Thou canst not play:
Thy game at weakest, still thou vy'st;
If seen, and then revy'd, deny'st:
Thou art not what thou seem'st; false world, thou ly'st.

Thy tinsel bosom seems a mint
    Of new-coin'd treasure:
A paradise, that has no stint,
    No change, no measure;
A painted cask, but nothing in't,
    Nor wealth, nor pleasure:
Vain earth! that falsely thus comply'st
With man; vain man, that thou rely'st
On earth; vain man, thou doat'st; vain earth, thou ly'st.

What mean dull souls, in this high measure,
    To haberdash
In earth's base wares, whose greatest treasure
    Is dross and trash;
The height of whose enchanting pleasure
    Is but a flash?
Are these the goods that thou supply'st
Us mortals with? Are these the high'st?
Can these bring cordial peace? False world, thou ly'st.
                FRANCIS QUARLES.

THE LIE.

Go, soul, the body's guest,
    Upon a thankless arrant;
Fear not to touch the best,
    The truth shall be thy warrant:
Go, since I needs must die,
And give the world the lie.

Go, tell the court it glows
    And shines like rotten wood;
Go, tell the Church it shows
    What's good, and doth no good.
If Church and court reply,
Then give them both the lie.

Tell potentates they live
    Acting by others' action,
Not loved unless they give,
    Not strong but by a faction.
If potentates reply,
Give potentates the lie.

Tell men of high condition
    That rule affairs of state,
Their purpose is ambition,
    Their practice only hate.
And if they once reply,
Then give them all the lie.

Tell them that brave it most,
    They beg for more by spending,
Who, in their greatest cost,
    Seek nothing but commending.
And if they make reply,
Then give them all the lie.

Tell zeal it lacks devotion,
    Tell love it is but lust,
Tell time it is but motion,
    Tell flesh it is but dust;
And wish them not reply,
For thou must give the lie.

Tell age it daily wasteth,
    Tell honor how it alters,
Tell beauty how she blasteth,
    Tell favor how it falters.
And as they shall reply,
Give every one the lie.

Tell wit how much it wrangles
    In tickle points of niceness;
Tell wisdom she entangles
    Herself in over-wiseness.
And when they do reply,
Straight give them both the lie.

Tell physic of her boldness,
    Tell skill it is pretension,
Tell charity of coldness,
    Tell law it is contention.

    And as they do reply,
      So give them still the lie.

Tell fortune of her blindness,
    Tell Nature of decay,
Tell friendship of unkindness,
    Tell justice of delay.
      And if they will reply,
      Then give them all the lie.

Tell arts they have no soundness,
    But vary by esteeming;
Tell schools they want profoundness,
    And stand too much on seeming.
      If arts and schools reply,
      Give arts and schools the lie.

Tell faith it's fled the city;
    Tell how the country erreth;
Tell, manhood shakes off pity;
    Tell, virtue least preferreth.
      And if they do reply,
      Spare not to give the lie.

So when thou hast, as I
    Commanded thee, done blabbing,
Although to give the lie
    Deserves no less than stabbing,
      Yet, stab at thee who will,
      No stab the soul can kill.
          SIR WALTER RALEIGH.

ARMSTRONG'S GOOD-NIGHT.

THIS night is my departing night,
    For here nae langer must I stay;
There's neither friend nor foe o' mine
    But wishes me away.

What I have done thro' lack o' wit
    I never, never can recall.
I hope ye're a' my friends as yet:
    Good-night! and joy be wi' you all!
          AUTHOR UNKNOWN.

MELANCHOLIA.

HENCE, all you vain delights,
    As short as are the nights
      Wherein you spend your folly:
There's naught in this life sweet
    If man were wise to see't,
      But only Melancholy,
      O sweetest Melancholy!

Welcome, folded arms and fixèd eyes,
A sigh that piercing mortifies,
A look that's fasten'd to the ground,
A tongue chain'd up without a sound!
Fountain-heads and pathless groves,
Places which pale passion loves!
Moonlight walks, when all the fowls
Are warmly housed save bats and owls!
A midnight bell, a parting groan!
    These are the sounds we feed upon;
Then stretch our bones in a still gloomy valley;
Nothing's so dainty sweet as lovely Melancholy.
          JOHN FLETCHER.

SONNET.

A GOOD that never satisfies the mind,
    A beauty fading like the April showers,
A sweet with floods of gall that runs combined,
    A pleasure passing ere in thought made ours,
A honor that more fickle is than wind,
    A glory at opinion's frown that lowers,
A treasury which bankrupt time devours,
    A knowledge than grave ignorance more blind,
A vain delight our equals to command,
    A style of greatness in effect a dream,
A swelling thought of holding sea and land,
    A servile lot deck'd with a pompous name:
Are the strange ends we toil for here below
    Till wisest death make us our errors know.
          WILLIAM DRUMMOND.

THERE'S NOT A JOY THE WORLD CAN GIVE.

THERE'S not a joy the world can give like that it takes away
When the glow of early thought declines in feeling's dull decay;
'Tis not on youth's smooth cheek the blush alone which fades so fast,
But the tender bloom of heart is gone, ere youth itself be past.

Then the few whose spirits float above the
    wreck of happiness
Are driven o'er the shoals of guilt or ocean
    of excess:
The magnet of their course is gone, or only
    points in vain
The shore to which their shiver'd sail shall
    never stretch again.

Then the mortal coldness of the soul like
    death itself comes down;
It cannot feel for others' woes, it dare not
    dream its own;
That heavy chill has frozen o'er the foun-
    tain of our tears,
And though the eye may sparkle still, 'tis
    where the ice appears.

Though wit may flash from fluent lips, and
    mirth distract the breast,
Through midnight hours that yield no more
    their former hope of rest;
'Tis but as ivy-leaves around the ruin'd
    turret wreathe,
All green and wildly fresh without, but
    worn and gray beneath.

Oh could I feel as I have felt, or be what I
    have been,
Or weep as I could once have wept o'er
    many a vanish'd scene,—
As springs in deserts found seem sweet, all
    brackish though they be,
So, midst the wither'd waste of life, those
    tears would flow to me!
                                LORD BYRON.

GOOD-BYE.

GOOD-BYE, proud world! I'm going home;
  Thou art not my friend, and I'm not thine.
Long through thy weary crowds I roam;
  A river-ark on the ocean brine,
Long I've been toss'd like the driven foam,
But now, proud world, I'm going home.

Good-bye to flattery's fawning face,
To grandeur, with his wise grimace,
To upstart wealth's averted eye,
To supple office, low and high,
To crowded halls, to court and street,
To frozen hearts and hasting feet,
To those who go and those who come,—
Good-bye, proud world! I'm going home.

I am going to my own hearthstone,
Bosom'd in yon green hills alone—
A secret nook in a pleasant land,
Whose groves the frolic fairies plann'd,
Where arches green, the livelong day,
Echo the blackbird's roundelay,
And vulgar feet have never trod,—
A spot that is sacred to thought and God.

Oh, when I am safe in my sylvan home,
I tread on the pride of Greece and Rome,
And when I am stretch'd beneath the
    pines,
Where the evening star so holy shines,
I laugh at the lore and pride of man,
At the sophist schools, and the learnèd
    clan;
For what are they all, in their high conceit,
When man in the bush with God may
    meet?
                        RALPH WALDO EMERSON.

NO AGE CONTENT WITH HIS OWN ESTATE.

LAID in my quiet bed,
  In study as I were,
I saw within my troubled head
  A heap of thoughts appear.

And every thought did show
  So lively in mine eyes,
That now I sigh'd, and then I smiled,
  As cause of thought did rise.

I saw the little boy
  In thought, how oft that he
Did wish of God to 'scape the rod,
  A tall young man to be.

The young man eke that feels
  His bones with pains oppress'd,
How he would be a rich old man,
  To live and lie at rest.

The rich old man that sees
  His end draw on so sore,
How he would be a boy again,
  To live so much the more.

Whereat full oft I smiled,
  To see how all these three,
From boy to man, from man to boy,
  Would chop and change degree.

And musing thus, I think,
   The case is very strange,
That man from wealth, to live in woe,
   Doth ever seek to change.

Thus thoughtful as I lay,
   I saw my wither'd skin,
How it doth show my dented chews,
   The flesh was worn so thin;

And eke my toothless chaps,
   The gates of my right way,
That opes and shuts as I do speak,
   Do thus unto me say:

"Thy white and hoarish hairs,
   The messengers of age,
That show, like lines of true belief,
   That this life doth assuage;

"Bid thee lay hard, and feel
   Them hanging on thy chin.
The which do write two ages past,
   The third now coming in.

"Hang up, therefore, the bit
   Of thy young wanton time,
And thou that therein beaten art,
   The happiest life define."

Whereat I sigh'd, and said,
   "Farewell my wonted joy!
Truss up thy pack, and trudge from me,
   To every little boy,

"And tell them thus from me,
   Their time most happy is,
If to their time they reason had,
   To know the truth of this."
                        HENRY HOWARD
                        (Earl of Surrey).

DIFFERENT MINDS.

SOME murmur when their sky is clear
   And wholly bright to view,
If one small speck of dark appear
   In their great heaven of blue;
And some with thankful love are fill'd
   If but one streak of light,
One ray of God's good mercy, gild
   The darkness of their night.

In palaces are hearts that ask,
   In discontent and pride,
Why life is such a dreary task,
   And all good things denied;
And hearts in poorest huts admire
   How Love has in their aid
(Love that not ever seems to tire)
   Such rich provision made.
                        RICHARD CHENEVIX TRENCH.

THE PRAISE OF A SOLITARY LIFE.

THRICE happy he, who by some shady grove,
   Far from the clamorous world, doth live his own;
Though solitary, who is not alone,
But doth converse with that eternal Love.
Oh how more sweet is bird's harmonious moan,
Or the hoarse sobbings of the widow'd dove,
   Than those smooth whisperings near a prince's throne,
Which good make doubtful, do the evil approve!
Oh! how more sweet is Zephyr's wholesome breath,
And sighs embalm'd, which new-born flowers unfold,
   Than that applause vain honor doth bequeath!
How sweet are streams to poison drank in gold!
   The world is full of horrors, troubles, slights:
Woods' harmless shades have only true delights.
                        WILLIAM DRUMMOND.

ON A CONTENTED MIND.

WHEN all is done and said,
   In the end this shall you find:
He most of all doth bathe in bliss
   That hath a quiet mind;
And, clear from worldly cares,
   To deem can be content
The sweetest time in all his life
   In thinking to be spent.

The body subject is
   To fickle Fortune's power,
And to a million of mishaps
   Is casual every hour;

And Death in time doth change
  It to a clod of clay,
When as the mind, which is divine,
  Runs never to decay.

Companion none is like
  Unto the mind alone,
For many have been harm'd by speech,
  Through thinking, few or none.
Fear oftentimes restraineth words,
  But makes not thoughts to cease,
And he speaks best that hath the skill
  When for to hold his peace.

Our wealth leaves us at death,
  Our kinsmen at the grave,
But virtues of the mind unto
  The heavens with us we have;
Wherefore, for virtue's sake,
  I can be well content
The sweetest time of all my life
  To deem in thinking spent.
              THOMAS, LORD VAUX.

A HYMN TO CONTENTMENT.

LOVELY, lasting peace of mind!
Sweet delight of human kind!
Heavenly born, and bred on high,
To crown the favorites of the sky
With more of happiness below,
Than victors in a triumph know!
Whither, oh whither art thou fled,
To lay thy meek, contented head?
What happy region dost thou please
To make the seat of calms and ease?

  Ambition searches all its sphere
Of pomp and state, to meet thee there.
Increasing Avarice would find
Thy presence in its gold enshrined.
The bold adventurer ploughs his way,
Through rocks amidst the foaming sea,
To gain thy love; and then perceives
Thou wert not in the rocks and waves.
The silent heart, which grief assails,
Treads soft and lonesome o'er the vales,
See daisies open, rivers run,
And seeks (as I have vainly done)
Amusing thought; but learns to know
That Solitude's the nurse of woe.

No real happiness is found
In trailing purple o'er the ground:
Or in a soul exalted high,
To range the circuit of the sky,
Converse with stars above, and know
All Nature in its forms below;
The rest it seeks, in seeking dies,
And doubts at last for knowledge rise.

  Lovely, lasting peace, appear!
This world itself, if thou art here,
Is once again with Eden blest,
And man contains it in his breast.

  'Twas thus, as under shade I stood,
I sung my wishes to the wood,
And, lost in thought, no more perceived
The branches whisper as they waved:
It seem'd as all the quiet place
Confess'd the presence of the Grace.
When thus she spoke—Go rule thy will,
Bid thy wild passions all be still,
Know God—and bring thy heart to know
The joys which from religion flow:
Then every Grace shall prove its guest,
And I'll be there to crown the rest.

  Oh! by yonder mossy seat,
In my hours of sweet retreat,
Might I thus my soul employ
With sense of gratitude and joy:
Raised as ancient prophets were,
In heavenly vision, praise and prayer;
Pleasing all men, hurting none,
Pleased and bless'd with God alone:
Then while the gardens take my sight,
With all the colors of delight;
While silver waters glide along,
To please my ear, and court my song;
I'll lift my voice, and tune my string,
And Thee, great Source of Nature, sing.

  The sun that walks his airy way,
To light the world, and give the day;
The moon that shines with borrow'd light;
The stars that gild the gloomy night;
The seas that roll unnumber'd waves;
The wood that spreads its shady leaves;
The field whose ears conceal the grain,
The yellow treasure of the plain;
All of these, and all I see,
Should be sung, and sung by me:
They speak their Maker as they can,
But want and ask the tongue of man.

Go search among your idle dreams,
Your busy or your vain extremes;
And find a life of equal bliss,
Or own the next begun in this.
THOMAS PARNELL.

A CONTENTED MIND.

I WEIGH not fortune's frown or smile;
I joy not much in earthly joys;
I seek not state, I reck not style;
I am not fond of fancy's toys:
I rest so pleased with what I have
I wish no more, no more I crave.

I quake not at the thunder's crack;
I tremble not at noise of war;
I swound not at the news of wrack;
I shrink not at a blazing star;
I fear not loss, I hope not gain,
I envy none, I none disdain.

I see ambition never pleased;
I see some Tantals starved in store;
I see gold's dropsy seldom eased;
I see even Midas gape for more:
I neither want, nor yet abound—
Enough's a feast, content is crown'd.

I feign not friendship where I hate;
I fawn not on the great (in show);
I prize, I praise a mean estate—
Neither too lofty nor too low:
This, this is all my choice, my cheer—
A mind content, a conscience clear.
JOSHUA SYLVESTER.

SWEET CONTENT.

ART thou poor, yet hast thou golden slumbers?
    O sweet content!
Art thou rich, yet is thy mind perplexèd?
    O punishment!
Dost thou laugh to see how fools are vexèd
To add to golden numbers, golden numbers?
O sweet content! O sweet, O sweet content!
  Work apace, apace, apace, apace;
  Honest labor bears a lovely face;
Then hey nonny nonny, hey nonny nonny!

Canst drink the waters of the crispèd spring?
    O sweet content!
Swimm'st thou in wealth, yet sink'st in thine own tears?
    O punishment!
Then he that patiently want's burden bears
No burden bears, but is a king, a king!
O sweet content! O sweet, O sweet content!
  Work apace, apace, apace, apace;
  Honest labor bears a lovely face;
Then hey nonny nonny, hey nonny nonny!
THOMAS DEKKER.

CONTENT.

SWEET are the thoughts that savor of content—
  The quiet mind is richer than a crown;
Sweet are the nights in careless slumber spent—
  The poor estate scorns fortune's angry frown:
Such sweet content, such minds, such sleep, such bliss,
Beggars enjoy, when princes oft do miss.

The homely house that harbors quiet rest,
  The cottage that affords no pride or care,
The mean that 'grees with country music best,
  The sweet consort of mirth and music's fare,
Obscurèd life sets down a type of bliss:
A mind content both crown and kingdom is.
ROBERT GREENE.

CARELESS CONTENT.

I AM content, I do not care,
  Wag as it will the world for me;
When fuss and fret was all my fare,
  It got no ground as I could see:
So when away my caring went,
I counted cost, and was content.

With more of thanks and less of thought,
  I strive to make my matters meet;

To seek what ancient sages sought,
  Physic and food in sour and sweet:
To take what passes in good part,
And keep the hiccups from the heart.

With good and gentle-humor'd hearts
  I choose to chat where'er I come,
Whate'er the subject be that starts;
  But if I get among the glum,
I hold my tongue to tell the truth,
And keep my breath to cool my broth.

For chance or change of peace or pain,
  For Fortune's favor or her frown,
For lack or glut, for loss or gain,
  I never dodge nor up nor down;
But swing what way the ship shall swim,
Or tack about with equal trim.

I suit not where I shall not speed,
  Nor trace the turn of every tide;
If simple sense will not succeed,
  I make no bustling, but abide;
For shining wealth or scaring woe,
I force no friend, I fear no foe.

Of ups and downs, of ins and outs,
  Of they're i' the wrong, and we're i' the right,
I shun the rancors and the routs;
  And wishing well to every wight,
Whatever turn the matter takes,
I deem it all but ducks and drakes.

With whom I feast I do not fawn,
  Nor if the folks should flout me, faint;
If wonted welcome be withdrawn,
  I cook no kind of a complaint:
With none disposed to disagree,
But like them best who best like me.

Not that I rate myself the rule
  How all my betters should behave;
But fame shall find me no man's fool,
  Nor to a set of men a slave:
I love a friendship free and frank,
And hate to hang upon a hank.

Fond of a true and trusty tie,
  I never loose where'er I link;
Though if a business budges by,
  I talk thereon just as I think;
My word, my work, my heart, my hand,
Still on a side together stand.

If names or notions make a noise,
  Whatever hap the question hath,
The point impartially I poise,
  And read or write, but without wrath;
For should I burn, or break my brains,
Pray, who will pay me for my pains?

I love my neighbor as myself,
  Myself like him too, by his leave;
Nor to his pleasure, power, or pelf
  Came I to crouch, as I conceive:
Dame Nature doubtless has design'd
A man the monarch of his mind.

Now taste and try this temper, sirs;
  Mood it and brood it in your breast;
Or if ye ween, for worldly stirs,
  That man does right to mar his rest,
Let me be deft, and debonair,
I am content, I do not care.
JOHN BYROM.

CHARACTER OF A HAPPY LIFE.

How happy is he born and taught
  That serveth not another's will;
Whose armor is his honest thought
  And simple truth his utmost skill!

Whose passions not his masters are,
  Whose soul is still prepared for death,
Untied unto the world by care
  Of public fame or private breath;

Who envies none that chance doth raise
  Nor vice; hath ever understood
How deepest wounds are given by praise;
  Nor rules of state, but rules of good:

Who hath his life from rumors freed,
  Whose conscience is his strong retreat;
Whose state can neither flatterers feed,
  Nor ruin make oppressors great;

Who God doth late and early pray
  More of His grace than gifts to lend;
And entertains the harmless day
  With a religious book or friend;

—This man is freed from servile bands
  Of hope to rise, or fear to fall;
Lord of himself, though not of lands;
  And having nothing, yet hath all.
SIR HENRY WOTTON.

THE PULLEY.

WHEN God at first made Man,
Having a glass of blessings standing by;
Let us (said He) pour on him all we can:
Let the world's riches, which dispersèd lie,
  Contract into a span.

So strength first made a way;
Then beauty flow'd, then wisdom, honor, pleasure:
When almost all was out, God made a stay,
Perceiving that alone of all His treasure,
  Rest in the bottom lay.

For if I should (said He)
Bestow this jewel also on My creature,
He would adore My gifts instead of Me,
And rest in Nature, not the God of Nature:
  So both should losers be.

Yet let him keep the rest,
But keep them with repining restlessness:
Let him be rich and weary, that at least,
If goodness lead him not, yet weariness
  May toss him to My breast.
          GEORGE HERBERT.

THE KINGDOM OF GOD.

I SAY to thee, do thou repeat
To the first man thou mayest meet,
In lane, highway, or open street,—

That he, and we, and all men move
Under a canopy of Love,
As broad as the blue sky above:

That doubt and trouble, fear and pain,
And anguish, all are shadows vain;
That death itself shall not remain:

That weary deserts we may tread,
A dreary labyrinth may thread,
Through dark ways underground be led;

Yet, if we will one Guide obey,
The dreariest path, the darkest way,
Shall issue out in heavenly day;

And we, on divers shores now cast,
Shall meet, our perilous voyage past,
All in our Father's home at last.

And ere thou leave him, say thou this:
Yet one word more: They only miss
The winning of that perfect bliss

Who will not count it true that Love,
Blessing, not cursing, rules above,
And that in it we live and move.

And one thing further make him know:
That to believe these things are so,
This firm faith never to forego,—

Despite of all which seems at strife
With blessing, and with curses rife,—
That this *is* blessing, this *is* life.
          RICHARD CHENEVIX TRENCH.

VIRTUE.

SWEET day, so cool, so calm, so bright,
  The bridal of the earth and sky;
The dew shall weep thy fall to-night;
  For thou must die.

Sweet rose, whose hue, angry and brave,
  Bids the rash gazer wipe his eye,
Thy root is ever in its grave—
  And thou must die.

Sweet spring, full of sweet days and roses,
  A box where sweets compacted lie,
My music shows ye have your closes,
  And all must die.

Only a sweet and virtuous soul,
  Like season'd timber, never gives;
But, though the whole world turn to coal,
  Then chiefly lives.
          GEORGE HERBERT.

THE GOOD, GREAT MAN.

How seldom, friend, a good great man inherits
  Honor and wealth, with all his worth and pains!
It seems a story from the world of spirits
When any man obtains that which he merits,
  Or any merits that which he obtains.

For shame, my friend! renounce this idle
    strain!
What wouldst thou have a good great man
    obtain?
Wealth, title, dignity, a golden chain,
Or heap of corses which his sword hath
    slain?
Goodness and greatness are not means, but
    ends.

Hath he not always treasures, always
    friends,
The great good man? Three treasures,—
    love, and light,
  And calm thoughts, equable as infant's
    breath;
And three fast friends, more sure than day
    or night,—
  Himself, his Maker, and the angel
    Death.
            SAMUEL TAYLOR COLERIDGE.

SONNET TO HOPE.

OH, ever skill'd to wear the form we love!
  To bid the shapes of fear and grief de-
    part,
Come, gentle Hope! with one gay smile
    remove
  The lasting sadness of an aching heart.
Thy voice, benign enchantress, let me
    hear;
  Say that for me some pleasures yet shall
    bloom,
That Fancy's radiance, Friendship's pre-
    cious tear,
  Shall soften, or shall chase, misfortune's
    gloom.
But come not glowing in the dazzling
    ray
  Which once with dear illusions charm'd
    my eye,
Oh, strew no more, sweet flatterer, on my
    way
  The flowers I fondly thought too bright
    to die;
Visions less fair will soothe my pensive
    breast,
  That asks not happiness, but longs for
    rest!
            HELEN MARIA WILLIAMS.

THE PROBLEM.

I LIKE a church, I like a cowl,
I love a prophet of the soul,
And on my heart monastic aisles
Fall like sweet strains or pensive smiles,
Yet not for all his faith can see
Would I that cowlèd churchman be.

Why should the vest on him allure,
Which I could not on me endure?

Not from a vain or shallow thought
His awful Jove young Phidias brought;
Never from lips of cunning fell
The thrilling Delphic oracle;
Out from the heart of Nature roll'd
The burdens of the Bible old;
The litanies of nations came,
Like the volcano's tongue of flame,
Up from the burning core below,—
The canticles of love and woe.
The hand that rounded Peter's dome,
And groin'd the aisles of Christian Rome,
Wrought in a sad sincerity.
Himself from God he could not free;
He builded better than he knew;
The conscious stone to beauty grew.

Know'st thou what wove yon wood-bird's
    nest
Of leaves, and feathers from her breast?
Or how the fish outbuilt her shell,
Painting with morn each annual cell?
Or how the sacred pine tree adds
To her old leaves new myriads?
Such and so grew these holy piles,
Whilst love and terror laid the tiles.
Earth proudly wears the Parthenon
As the best gem upon her zone;
And Morning opes with haste her lids
To gaze upon the Pyramids;
O'er England's abbeys bends the sky
As on its friends with kindred eye;
For, out of Thought's interior sphere
These wonders rose to upper air,
And Nature gladly gave them place,
Adopted them into her race,
And granted them an equal date
With Andes and with Ararat.

These temples grew as grows the grass;
Art might obey, but not surpass.

The passive Master lent his hand
To the vast Soul that o'er him plann'd,
And the same power that rear'd the shrine,
Bestrode the tribes that knelt within.
Ever the fiery Pentecost
Girds with one flame the countless host,
Trances the heart through chanting choirs,
And through the priest the mind inspires.

The word unto the prophet spoken
Was writ on tables yet unbroken;
The word by seers or sibyls told,
In groves of oak or fanes of gold,
Still floats upon the morning wind,
Still whispers to the willing mind.
One accent of the Holy Ghost
The heedless world hath never lost.
I know what say the Fathers wise,—
The Book itself before me lies,—
Old Chrysostom, best Augustine,
And he who blent both in his line,
The younger *Golden Lips* or mines,
Taylor, the Shakespeare of divines.
His words are music in my ear,
I see his cowlèd portrait dear,
And yet, for all his faith could see,
I would not the good bishop be.
RALPH WALDO EMERSON.

ABOU BEN ADHEM.

ABOU BEN ADHEM (may his tribe increase!)
Awoke one night from a deep dream of peace,
And saw within the moonlight in his room,
Making it rich, and like a lily in bloom,
An angel, writing in a book of gold;
Exceeding peace had made Ben Adhem bold,
And to the presence in the room he said,
"What writest thou?" the vision raised its head,
And with a look made of all sweet accord,
Answer'd, "The names of those who love the Lord."
"And is mine one?" said Abou. "Nay, not so,"
Replied the angel. Abou spoke more low,
But cheerly still; and said, "I pray thee, then,
Write me as one that loves his fellow-men."

The angel wrote and vanish'd. The next night
It came again, with a great wakening light,
And show'd the names whom love of God had bless'd,
And, lo! Ben Adhem's name led all the rest.
LEIGH HUNT.

ODE TO DUTY.

STERN Daughter of the Voice of God!
  O Duty! if that name thou love
Who art a Light to guide, a Rod
  To check the erring, and reprove;
Thou, who art victory and law
When empty terrors overawe;
From vain temptations dost set free;
And calm'st the weary strife of frail humanity!

There are who ask not if thine eye
  Be on them; who, in love and truth,
Where no misgiving is, rely
  Upon the genial sense of youth:
Glad hearts! without reproach or blot;
Who do thy work, and know it not:
Long may the kindly impulse last!
But thou, if they should totter, teach them to stand fast!

Serene will be our days and bright,
  And happy will our nature be,
When love is an unerring light,
  And joy its own security.
And they a blissful course may hold
Even now, who, not unwisely bold,
Live in the spirit of this creed;
Yet find that other strength, according to their need.

I, loving freedom, and untried,
  No sport of every random gust,
Yet being to myself a guide,
  Too blindly have reposed my trust:
And oft, when in my heart was heard
Thy timely mandate, I deferr'd
The task, in smoother walks to stray;
But thee I now would serve more strictly, if I may.

Through no disturbance of my soul,
  Or strong compunction in me wrought,
I supplicate for thy control;
  But in the quietness of thought:

Me this uncharter'd freedom tires;
I feel the weight of chance desires:
My hopes no more must change their name,
I long for a repose that ever is the same.

Stern Lawgiver! yet thou dost wear
  The Godhead's most benignant grace;
  Nor know we anything so fair
As is the smile upon thy face:
Flowers laugh before thee on their beds;
And Fragrance in thy footing treads;
Thou dost preserve the Stars from wrong;
And the most ancient Heavens, through
    thee, are fresh and strong.

To humbler functions, awful Power!
  I call thee: I myself commend
Unto thy guidance from this hour;
  Oh, let my weakness have an end!
Give unto me, made lowly wise,
The spirit of self-sacrifice;
The confidence of reason give;
And in the light of truth thy Bondman
    let me live!
            WILLIAM WORDSWORTH.

THE TOUCHSTONE.

A MAN there came, whence none could
    tell,
  Bearing a touchstone in his hand;
  And tested all things in the land
By its unerring spell.

Quick birth of transmutation smote
  The fair to foul, the foul to fair;
  Purple nor ermine did he spare,
Nor scorn the dusty coat.

Of heirloom jewels, prized so much,
  Were many changed to chips and
    clods,
  And even statues of the gods
Crumbled beneath its touch.

Then angrily the people cried,
  "The loss outweighs the profit far;
  Our goods suffice us as they are;
We will not have them tried."

And since they could not so avail
  To check his unrelenting quest,
  They seized him, saying, "Let him test,
How real is our jail!"

But, though they slew him with the
    sword,
  And in a fire his touchstone burn'd,
  Its doings could not be o'erturn'd,
Its undoings restored.

And when, to stop all future harm,
  They strew'd its ashes on the breeze;
  They little guess'd each grain of these
Convey'd the perfect charm.
            WILLIAM ALLINGHAM.

THE PHILOSOPHER'S SCALES.

A MONK, when his rites sacerdotal were
    o'er,
In the depths of his cell with his stone-
    cover'd floor,
Resigning to thought his chimerical brain,
Once form'd the contrivance we now shall
    explain;
But whether by magic's or alchemy's
    powers
We know not; indeed, 'tis no business of
    ours.

Perhaps it was only by patience and care,
At last, that he brought his invention to
    bear.
In youth 'twas projected, but years stole
    away,
And ere 'twas complete he was wrinkled
    and gray;
But success is secure, unless energy fails;
And at length he produced THE PHILOSO-
    PHER'S SCALES.

"What were they?" you ask. You shall
    presently see;
These scales were not made to weigh sugar
    and tea.
Oh no; for such properties wondrous had
    they,
That qualities, feelings, and thoughts they
    could weigh,
Together with articles small or immense,
From mountains or planets to atoms of
    sense.

Naught was there so bulky but there it
    would lay,
And naught so ethereal but there it would
    stay,

And naught so reluctant but in it must go:
All which some examples more clearly
    will show.

The first thing he weigh'd was the head
    of Voltaire,
Which retain'd all the wit that had ever
    been there.
As a weight, he threw in a torn scrap of a
    leaf,
Containing the prayer of the penitent
    thief;
When the skull rose aloft with so sudden
    a spell
That it bounced like a ball on the roof of
    the cell.

One time he put in Alexander the Great,
With the garment that Dorcas had made
    for a weight;
And though clad in armor from sandals to
    crown,
The hero rose up, and the garment went
    down.

A long row of almshouses, amply endow'd
By a well-esteem'd Pharisee, busy and
    proud,
Next loaded one scale; while the other
    was press'd
By those mites the poor widow dropp'd
    into the chest:
Up flew the endowment, not weighing an
    ounce,
And down, down the farthing-worth came
    with a bounce.

By further experiments (no matter how)
He found that ten chariots weigh'd less
    than one plough;
A sword with gilt trapping rose up in the
    scale,
Though balanced by only a ten-penny
    nail;
A shield and a helmet, a buckler and
    spear,
Weigh'd less than a widow's uncrystal-
    lized tear.

A lord and a lady went up at full sail,
When a bee chanced to light on the oppo-
    site scale;

Ten doctors, ten lawyers, two courtiers, one
    earl,
Ten counsellors' wigs full of powder and
    curl,
All heap'd in one balance and swinging
    from thence,
Weigh'd less than a few grains of candor
    and sense;
A first-water diamond, with brilliants
    begirt,
Than one good potato just wash'd from
    the dirt;
Yet not mountains of silver and gold could
    suffice
One pearl to outweigh,—'twas the pearl of
    great price.

Last of all, the whole world was bowl'd
    in at the grate,
With the soul of a beggar to serve for a
    weight,
When the former sprang up with so strong
    a rebuff
That it made a vast rent and escaped at
    the roof!
When balanced in air, it ascended on high,
And sailed up aloft, a balloon in the sky;
While the scale with the soul in't so
    mightily fell
That it jerk'd the philosopher out of his
    cell.
                                    JANE TAYLOR.

THE HERMIT.

FAR in a wild, unknown to public view,
From youth to age a reverend hermit
    grew;
The moss his bed, the cave his humble
    cell,
His food the fruits, his drink the crystal
    well:
Remote from man, with God he pass'd the
    days,
Prayer all his business, all his pleasure
    praise.

A life so sacred, such serene repose,
Seem'd heaven itself, till one suggestion
    rose;
That vice should triumph, virtue vice obey,
This sprung some doubt of Providence's
    sway:

His hopes no more a certain prospect boast,
And all the tenor of his soul is lost.
So when a smooth expanse receives imprest
Calm Nature's image on its watery breast,
Down bend the banks, the trees depending grow,
And skies beneath with answering colors glow;
But if a stone the gentle scene divide,
Swift ruffling circles curl on every side,
And glimmering fragments of a broken sun,
Banks, trees, and skies, in thick disorder run.

To clear this doubt, to know the world by sight,
To find if books, or swains, report it right
(For yet by swains alone the world he knew,
Whose feet came wandering o'er the nightly dew),
He quits his cell; the pilgrim-staff he bore,
And fix'd the scallop in his hat before;
Then with the sun a rising journey went,
Sedate to think, and watching each event.

The morn was wasted in the pathless grass,
And long and lonesome was the wild to pass;
But when the southern sun had warm'd the day,
A youth came posting o'er a crossing way;
His raiment decent, his complexion fair,
And soft in graceful ringlets waved his hair.
Then near approaching, "Father, hail!" he cried,
"And hail, my son," the reverend sire replied;
Words follow'd words, from question answer flow'd,
And talk of various kind deceived the road;
Till each with other pleased, and loath to part,
While in their age they differ, join in heart:

Thus stands an aged elm in ivy bound,
Thus youthful ivy clasps an elm around.

Now sunk the sun; the closing hour of day
Came onward, mantled o'er with sober gray;
Nature in silence bade the world repose:
When near the road a stately palace rose:
There by the moon through ranks of trees they pass,
Whose verdure crown'd their sloping sides of grass.
It chanced the noble master of the dome
Still made his house the wandering stranger's home:
Yet still the kindness, from a thirst of praise,
Proved the vain flourish of expensive ease.
The pair arrive: the liveried servants wait;
Their lord receives them at the pompous gate.
The table groans with costly piles of food,
And all is more than hospitably good.
Then led to rest, the day's long toil they drown,
Deep sunk in sleep, and silk, and heaps of down.

At length 'tis morn, and at the dawn of day,
Along the wide canals the zephyrs play;
Fresh o'er the gay parterres the breezes creep,
And shake the neighboring wood to banish sleep.
Up rise the guests, obedient to the call:
An early banquet deck'd the splendid hall;
Rich luscious wine a golden goblet graced,
Which the kind master forced the guests to taste.
Then, pleased and thankful, from the porch they go,
And, but the landlord, none had cause of woe;
His cup was vanish'd; for in secret guise
The younger guest purloin'd the glittering prize.

As one who spies a serpent in his way,
Glistening and basking in the summer
   ray,
Disorder'd stops to shun the danger near,
Then walks with faintness on, and looks
   with fear:
So seem'd the sire; when, far upon the
   road,
The shining spoil his wily partner show'd.
He stopp'd with silence, walk'd with trem-
   bling heart,
And much he wish'd, but durst not ask to
   part:
Murmuring he lifts his eyes, and thinks it
   hard,
That generous actions meet a base reward.

While thus they pass, the sun his glory
   shrouds,
The changing skies hang out their sable
   clouds;
A sound in air presaged approaching rain,
And beasts to covert scud across the plain.
Warn'd by the signs, the wandering pair
   retreat,
To seek for shelter at a neighboring seat.
'Twas built with turrets, on a rising ground,
And strong, and large, and unimproved
   around;
Its owner's temper, timorous and severe,
Unkind and griping, caused a desert there.

As near the miser's heavy doors they drew,
Fierce rising gusts with sudden fury blew;
The nimble lightning mix'd with showers
   began,
And o'er their heads loud-rolling thunder
   ran.
Here long they knock, but knock or call in
   vain,
Driven by the wind, and batter'd by the
   rain.
At length some pity warm'd the master's
   breast
('Twas then, his threshold first received a
   guest),
Slow creaking turns the door with jealous
   care,
And half he welcomes in the shivering
   pair;
One frugal fagot lights the naked walls,
And Nature's fervor through their limbs
   recalls:

Bread of the coarsest sort, with eager
   wine
(Each hardly granted), served them both
   to dine;
And when the tempest first appear'd to
   cease,
A ready warning bid them part in peace.

With still remark the pondering hermit
   view'd
In one so rich, a life so poor and rude;
And why should such (within himself he
   cried)
Lock the lost wealth a thousand want be-
   side?
But what new marks of wonder soon took
   place
In every settling feature of his face,
When from his vest the young companion
   bore
That cup the generous landlord own'd be-
   fore,
And paid profusely with the precious bowl
The stinted kindness of this churlish soul!

But now the clouds in airy tumult fly,
The sun emerging opes an azure sky;
A fresher green the smelling leaves display,
And, glittering as they tremble, cheer the
   day:
The weather courts them from the poor
   retreat,
And the glad master bolts the wary gate.

While hence they walk, the pilgrim's
   bosom wrought
With all the travail of uncertain thought;
His partner's acts without their cause
   appear,
'Twas there a vice, and seem'd a madness
   here:
Detesting that, and pitying this, he goes,
Lost and confounded with the various
   shows.

Now night's dim shades again involve the
   sky;
Again the wanderers want a place to lie,
Again they search, and find a lodging
   nigh:
The soil improved around, the mansion
   neat,
And neither poorly low nor idly great:

It seem'd to speak its master's turn of
    mind,
Content, and not for praise, but virtue
    kind.

Hither the walkers turn with weary feet,
Then bless the mansion, and the master
    greet:
Their greeting fair bestow'd with modest
    guise,
The courteous master hears, and thus re-
    plies:

"Without a vain, without a grudging
    heart,
To Him who gives us all, I yield a part;
From Him you come, for Him accept it
    here,
A frank and sober, more than costly
    cheer."
He spoke, and bid the welcome table
    spread,
Then talk'd of virtue till the time of
    bed,
When the grave household round his hall
    repair,
Warn'd by a bell, and close the hours with
    prayer.

At length the world, renew'd by calm re-
    pose,
Was strong for toil, the dappled morn
    arose:
Before the pilgrims part, the younger
    crept
Near the closed cradle where an infant
    slept,
And writhed his neck: the landlord's
    little pride,
Oh strange return! grew black, and gasp'd,
    and died.
Horror of horrors! what! his only son!
How look'd our hermit when the fact was
    done?
Not hell, though hell's black jaws in
    sunder part,
And breathe blue fire, could more assault
    his heart.

Confused, and struck with silence at the
    deed,
He flies, but trembling fails to fly with
    speed.

His steps the youth pursues; the country
    lay
Perplex'd with roads, a servant show'd
    the way:
A river cross'd the path; the passage o'er
Was nice to find; the servant trod be-
    fore:
Long arms of oaks an open bridge sup-
    plied,
And deep the waves beneath the bending
    glide.
The youth, who seem'd to watch a time
    to sin,
Approach'd the careless guide, and thrust
    him in;
Plunging he falls, and rising lifts his head,
Then flashing turns, and sinks among the
    dead.

Wild, sparkling rage inflames the father's
    eyes.
He bursts the bands of fear, and madly
    cries,
"Detested wretch!"—but scarce his speech
    began,
When the strange partner seem'd no
    longer man:
His youthful face grew more serenely
    sweet;
His robe turn'd white, and flow'd upon
    his feet;
Fair rounds of radiant points invest his
    hair;
Celestial odors breathe through purpled
    air;
And wings, whose colors glitter'd on the
    day,
Wide at his back their gradual plumes dis-
    play,
The form ethereal bursts upon his sight,
And moves in all the majesty of light.

Though loud at first the pilgrim's passion
    grew,
Sudden he gazed, and wist not what to
    do:
Surprise in secret chains his words sus-
    pends,
And in a calm his settling temper ends.
But silence here the beauteous angel
    broke
(The voice of music ravish'd as he
    spoke):

"Thy prayer, thy praise, thy life to vice unknown,
In sweet memorial rise before the throne:
These charms success in our bright region find,
And force an angel down, to calm thy mind;
For this commission'd, I forsook the sky,
Nay, cease to kneel—thy fellow-servant I.

"Then know the truth of government divine,
And let these scruples be no longer thine.

"The Maker justly claims that world He made,
In this the right of Providence is laid;
Its sacred majesty through all depends
On using second means to work His ends:
'Tis thus, withdrawn in state from human eye,
The Power exerts His attributes on high,
Your actions uses, nor controls your will,
And bids the doubting sons of men be still.

"What strange events can strike with more surprise
Than those which lately struck thy wondering eyes·
Yet taught by these, confess th' Almighty just,
And where you can't unriddle, learn to trust!

"The great, vain man, who fared on costly food,
Whose life was too luxurious to be good;
Who made his ivory stands with goblets shine,
And forced his guests to morning draughts of wine,
Has, with the cup, the graceless custom lost,
And still he welcomes, but with less of cost.

"The mean, suspicious wretch, whose bolted door
Ne'er moved in duty to the wandering poor;
With him I left the cup, to teach his mind
That Heaven can bless, if mortals will be kind.

Conscious of wanting worth, he views the bowl,
And feels compassion touch his grateful soul.
Thus artists melt the sullen ore of lead,
With heaping coals of fire upon its head;
In the kind warmth the metal learns to glow,
And, loose from dross, the silver runs below.

"Long had our pious friend in virtue trod,
But now the child half wean'd his heart from God;
Child of his age, for him he lived in pain,
And measured back his steps to earth again.
To what excesses had this dotage run!
But God, to save the father, took the son.
To all but thee, in fits he seem'd to go
(And 'twas my ministry to deal the blow).
The poor fond parent, humbled in the dust,
Now owns in tears the punishment was just.

"But how had all his fortune felt a wrack
Had that false servant sped in safety back!
This night his treasured heaps he meant to steal,
And what a fund of charity would fail!

"Thus Heaven instructs thy mind: this trial o'er,
Depart in peace, resign, and sin no more."

On sounding pinions here the youth withdrew,
The sage stood wondering as the seraph flew.
Thus look'd Elisha, when, to mount on high,
His master took the chariot of the sky;
The fiery pomp ascending left the view;
The prophet gazed, and wish'd to follow too.

The bending hermit here a prayer begun:
"Lord! as in heaven, on earth Thy will be done!"
Then gladly turning, sought his ancient place,
And pass'd a life of piety and peace.
THOMAS PARNELL.

THE SQUIRE'S PEW.

A SLANTING ray of evening light
  Shoots through the yellow pane;
It makes the faded crimson bright,
  And gilds the fringe again;
The window's Gothic framework falls
In oblique shadows on the walls.

And since those trappings first were new,
  How many a cloudless day,
To rob the velvet of its hue,
  Has come and pass'd away!
How many a setting sun hath made
That curious lattice-work of shade!

Crumbled beneath the hillock green
  The cunning hand must be
That carved this fretted door, I ween,
  Acorn, and fleur-de-lis;
And now the worm hath done her part
In mimicking the chisel's art.

In days of yore (as now we call),
  When the first James was king,
The courtly knight from yonder hall
  His train did hither bring,
All seated round, in order due,
With 'broider'd suit and buckled shoe.

On damask cushions deck'd with fringe
  All reverently they knelt;
Prayer-books with brazen hasp and hinge,
  In ancient English spelt,
Each holding in a lily hand,
Responsive to the priest's command.

Now, streaming down the vaulted aisle,
  The sunbeam long and lone,
Illumes the characters a while
  Of their inscription-stone;
And there in marble, hard and cold,
The knight with all his train behold.

Outstretch'd together are express'd
  He and my lady fair,
With hands uplifted on the breast,
  In attitude of prayer;
Long-visaged, clad in armor, he—
With ruffled arm and bodice she.

Set forth in order as they died,
  Their numerous offspring bend,
Devoutly kneeling side by side,
  As if they did intend
For past omissions to atone
By saying endless prayers in stone.

Those mellow days are past and dim,
  But generations new,
In regular descent from him,
  Have fill'd the stately pew,
And in the same succession go
To occupy the vaults below.

And now the polish'd modern squire
  And his gay train appear,
Who duly to the hall retire
  A season every year,
And fill the seats with belle and beau,
As 'twas so many years ago.

Perchance, all thoughtless as they tread
  The hollow-sounding floor
Of that dark house of kindred dread,
  Which shall, as heretofore,
In turn receive to silent rest
Another and another guest:

The feather'd hearse and sable train,
  In all their wonted state,
Shall wind along the village lane,
  And stand before the gate;
Brought many a distant country through,
To join the final rendezvous.

And when the race is swept away,
  All to their dusty beds,
Still shall the mellow evening ray
  Shine gayly o'er their heads,
While other faces, fresh and new,
Shall fill the squire's deserted pew.
JANE TAYLOR.

THE OLD AND YOUNG COURTIER.

An old song made by an aged old pate,
Of an old worshipful gentleman, who had a great estate,
That kept a brave old house at a bountiful rate,
And an old porter to relieve the poor at his gate:
   Like an old courtier of the queen's,
   And the queen's old courtier.

With an old lady, whose anger one word assuages,
That every quarter paid their old servants their wages,
And never knew what belong'd to coachmen, footmen, nor pages,
But kept twenty old fellows with blue coats and badges;
   Like an old courtier of the queen's,
   And the queen's old courtier.

With an old study fill'd full of learnèd old books,
With an old reverend chaplain, you might know him by his looks;
With an old buttery hatch, worn quite off the hooks,
And an old kitchen that maintain'd half a dozen old cooks;
   Like an old courtier of the queen's,
   And the queen's old courtier.

With an old hall hung about with pikes, guns, and bows,
With old swords, and bucklers that had borne many shrewd blows,
And an old frieze coat to cover his worship's trunk hose;
And a cup of old sherry to comfort his copper nose;
   Like an old courtier of the queen's,
   And the queen's old courtier.

With a good old fashion, when Christmas was come,
To call in all his old neighbors with bagpipe and drum,
With good cheer enough to furnish every old room,
And old liquor able to make a cat speak and a man dumb;
   Like an old courtier of the queen's,
   And the queen's old courtier.

With an old falconer, huntsman, and a kennel of hounds,
That never hawk'd nor hunted but in his own grounds,
Who, like a wise man, kept himself within his own bounds,
And when he died gave every child a thousand good pounds;
   Like an old courtier of the queen's,
   And the queen's old courtier.

But to his eldest son his house and lands he assign'd,
Charging him in his will to keep the old bountiful mind,
To be good to his old tenants, and to his neighbors be kind;
But in the ensuing ditty you shall hear how he was inclined;
   Like a young courtier of the king's,
   And the king's young courtier.

Like a flourishing young gallant, newly come to his land,
Who keeps a brace of painted madams at his command,
And takes up a thousand pounds upon his father's land,
And gets drunk in a tavern till he can neither go nor stand;
   Like a young courtier of the king's,
   And the king's young courtier.

With a new-fangled lady, that is dainty, nice, and spare,
Who never knew what belong'd to good housekeeping, or care;
Who buys gaudy-color'd fans to play with wanton air,
And seven or eight different dressings of other women's hair;
   Like a young courtier of the king's,
   And the king's young courtier.

With a new-fashion'd hall, built where the old one stood,
Hung round with new pictures that do the poor no good;
With a fine marble chimney, wherein burns neither coal nor wood,
And a new smooth shovel-board, whereon no victuals ne'er stood;
   Like a young courtier of the king's,
   And the king's young courtier.

With a new study stuff'd full of pamphlets
   and plays,
And a new chaplain that swears faster than
   he prays,
With a new buttery hatch that opens once
   in four or five days,
And a new French cook to devise fine kick-
   shaws and toys;
   Like a young courtier of the king's,
   And the king's young courtier.

With a new fashion, when Christmas is
   drawing on,
And a new journey to London straight we
   all must be gone,
And leave none to keep house but our new
   porter John,
Who relieves the poor with a thump on the
   back with a stone;
   Like a young courtier of the king's,
   And the king's young courtier.

With a new gentleman usher, whose car-
   riage is complete;
With a new coachman, footman, and pages
   to carry up the meat;
With a waiting gentlewoman, whose dress-
   ing is very neat,
Who, when her lady has dined, lets the
   servants *not* eat;
   Like a young courtier of the king's,
   And the king's young courtier.

With new titles of honor, bought with his
   father's old gold,
For which sundry of his ancestors' old
   manors are sold;
And this is the course most of our new
   gallants hold,
Which makes that good housekeeping is
   now grown so cold
   Among our young courtiers of the
     king,
   Or the king's young courtiers.
                 AUTHOR UNKNOWN.

THE END OF THE PLAY.

THE play is done, the curtain drops,
   Slow falling to the prompter's bell;
A moment yet the actor stops,
   And looks around to say farewell.
It is an irksome word and task,
   And when he's laugh'd and said his say,
He shows, as he removes the mask,
   A face that's anything but gay.

One word, ere yet the evening ends,—
   Let's close it with a parting rhyme,
And pledge a hand to all young friends,
   As fits the merry Christmas-time;
On life's wide scene you, too, have parts,
   That Fate ere long shall bid you play;
Good-night! with honest gentle hearts
   A kindly greeting go alway.

Good-night!—I'd say the griefs, the joys,
   Just hinted in this mimic page,
The triumphs and defeats of boys,
   Are but repeated in our age;
I'd say your woes are not less keen,
   Your hopes more vain, than those of
     men,—
Your pangs or pleasures of fifteen
   At forty-five play'd o'er again.

I'd say we suffer and we strive
   Not less nor more as men than boys,
With grizzled beards at forty-five,
   As erst at twelve in corduroys;
And if, in time of sacred youth,
   We learn'd at home to love and pray,
Pray Heaven that early love and truth
   May never wholly pass away.

And in the world, as in the school,
   I'd say how fate may change and shift,
The prize be sometimes with the fool,
   The race not always to the swift;
The strong may yield, the good may fall,
   The great man be a vulgar clown,
The knave be lifted over all,
   The kind cast pitilessly down.

Who knows the inscrutable design?
   Blessed be He who took and gave!
Why should your mother, Charles, not
     mine,
   Be weeping at her darling's grave?
We bow to Heaven that will'd it so,
   That darkly rules the fate of all,
That sends the respite or the blow,
   That's free to give or to recall.

This crowns his feast with wine and wit:
   Who brought him to that mirth and state?

His betters, see, below him sit,
    Or hunger hopeless at the gate.
Who bade the mud from Dives' wheel
    To spurn the rags of Lazarus?
Come, brother, in that dust we'll kneel,
    Confessing Heaven that ruled it thus.

So each shall mourn, in life's advance,
    Dear hopes, dear friends, untimely kill'd,
Shall grieve for many a forfeit chance,
    And longing passion unfulfill'd.
Amen! whatever fate be sent,
    Pray God the heart may kindly glow,
Although the head with cares be bent,
    And whiten'd with the winter snow.

Come wealth or want, come good or ill,
    Let young and old accept their part,
And bow before the awful Will,
    And bear it with an honest heart,
Who misses, or who wins the prize.
    Go; lose or conquer as you can,
But if you fail, or if you rise,
    Be each, pray God, a gentleman.

A gentleman, or old or young!
    (Bear kindly with my humble lays);
The sacred chorus first was sung
    Upon the first of Christmas days;
The shepherds heard it overhead,
    The joyful angels raised it then:
Glory to Heaven on high, it said,
    And peace on earth to gentle men!

My song, save this, is little worth;
    I lay the weary pen aside,
And wish you health, and love, and mirth,
    As fits the solemn Christmas-tide.
As fits the holy Christmas birth,
    Be this, good friends, our carol still,—
Be peace on earth, be peace on earth,
    To men of gentle will.
        WILLIAM MAKEPEACE THACKERAY.

THE OLD MAN'S COMFORTS,

AND HOW HE GAINED THEM.

YOU are old, Father William, the young
    man cried,
The few locks which are left you are gray;
You are hale, Father William, a hearty
    old man,
Now tell me the reason, I pray.

In the days of my youth, Father William
    replied,
I remember'd that youth would fly fast,
And abused not my health and my vigor
    at first,
That I never might need them at last.

You are old, Father William, the young
    man cried,
And pleasures with youth pass away,
And yet you lament not the days that are
    gone,
Now tell me the reason, I pray.

In the days of my youth, Father William
    replied,
I remember'd that youth could not last;
I thought of the future, whatever I did,
That I never might grieve for the past.

You are old, Father William, the young
    man cried,
And life must be hastening away;
You are cheerful, and love to converse
    upon death,
Now tell me the reason, I pray.

I am cheerful, young man, Father William
    replied;
Let the cause thy attention engage;
In the days of my youth I remember'd my
    God!
And He hath not forgotten my age.
        ROBERT SOUTHEY.

IN THE DOWN-HILL OF LIFE.

IN the down-hill of life, when I find I'm
    declining,
May my lot no less fortunate be
Than a snug elbow-chair can afford for re-
    clining,
And a cot that o'erlooks the wide sea;
With an ambling pad-pony to pace o'er
    the lawn,
While I carol away idle sorrow,
And blithe as the lark that each day hails
    the dawn,
Look forward with hope for to-morrow.

With a porch at my door, both for shelter
    and shade too,
As the sunshine or rain may prevail;

And a small spot of ground for the use of
    the spade too,
  With a barn for the use of the flail:
A cow for my dairy, a dog for my game,
    And a purse when a friend wants to
      borrow;
I'll envy no nabob his riches or fame,
    Nor what honors await him to-morrow.

From the bleak northern blast may my cot
    be completely
  Secured by a neighboring hill;
And at night may repose steal upon me
    more sweetly
  By the sound of a murmuring rill:
And while peace and plenty I find at my
    board,
  With a heart free from sickness and
    sorrow,
With my friends may I share what to-day
    may afford,
  And let them spread the table to-morrow.

And when I at last must throw off this
    frail covering
  Which I've worn for threescore years
    and ten,
On the brink of the grave I'll not seek to
    keep hovering,
  Nor my thread wish to spin o'er again:
But my face in the glass I'll serenely
    survey,
  And with smiles count each wrinkle and
    furrow;
As this old worn-out stuff, which is thread-
    bare to-day,
  May become everlasting to-morrow.
            JOHN COLLINS.

A Hundred Years to Come.

WHO'LL press for gold this crowded street,
    A hundred years to come?
Who'll tread yon church with willing feet,
    A hundred years to come?
Pale, trembling age and fiery youth,
And childhood with his brow of truth,
The rich and poor, on land, on sea,
Where will the mighty millions be,
    A hundred years to come?

We all within our graves shall sleep,
    A hundred years to come;

No living soul for us will weep,
    A hundred years to come.
But other men our land will till,
And others then our streets will fill,
And other words will sing as gay,
And bright the sunshine as to-day,
    A hundred years to come.
            WILLIAM GOLDSMITH BROWN.

The Eve of Election.

  FROM gold to gray
  Our mild sweet day
Of Indian Summer fades too soon;
  But tenderly
  Above the sea
Hangs, white and calm, the hunter's
    moon.

  In its pale fire,
  The village spire
Shows like the Zodiac's spectral lance;
  The painted walls
  Whereon it falls
Transfigured stand in marble trance!

  O'er fallen leaves
  The west wind grieves,
Yet comes a seed-time round again;
  And morn shall see
  The State sown free
With baleful tares or healthful grain.

  Along the street
  The shadows meet
Of Destiny, whose hands conceal
  The moulds of fate
  That shape the State,
And make or mar the common weal.

  Around I see
  The powers that be;
I stand by Empire's primal springs;
  And princes meet
  In every street,
And hear the tread of uncrown'd kings!

  Hark! through the crowd
  The laugh runs loud,
Beneath the sad, rebuking moon.
  God save the land,
  A careless hand
May shake or swerve ere morrow's noon!

No jest is this;
  One cast amiss
May blast the hope of Freedom's year.
  Oh, take me where
  Are hearts of prayer,
And foreheads bow'd in reverent fear!

  Not lightly fall
  Beyond recall
The written scrolls a breath can float;
  The crowning fact,
  The kingliest act
Of Freedom, is the freeman's vote!

  For pearls that gem
  A diadem
The diver in the deep sea dies;
  The regal right
  We boast to-night
Is ours through costlier sacrifice:

  The blood of Vane,
  His prison pain
Who traced the path the Pilgrim trod,
  And hers whose faith
  Drew strength from death,
And prayed her Russell up to God!

  Our hearts grow cold,
  We lightly hold
A right which brave men died to gain;
  The stake, the cord,
  The axe, the sword,
Grim nurses at its birth of pain.

  The shadow rend,
  And o'er us bend,
O martyrs, with your crowns and palms,—
  Breathe through these throngs
  Your battle-songs,
Your scaffold prayers, and dungeon psalms!

  Look from the sky,
  Like God's great eye,
Thou solemn moon, with searching beam;
  Till in the sight
  Of thy pure light
Our mean self-seekings meaner seem.

  Shame from our hearts
  Unworthy arts,
The fraud design'd, the purpose dark;
  And smite away
  The hands we lay
Profanely on the sacred ark.

  To party claims,
  And private aims,
Reveal that august face of Truth,
  Whereto are given
  The age of heaven,
The beauty of immortal youth.

  So shall our voice
  Of sovereign choice
Swell the deep bass of duty done,
  And strike the key
  Of time to be,
When God and man shall speak as one!
JOHN GREENLEAF WHITTIER.

THE BATTLE-FIELD.

ONCE this soft turf, this rivulet's sands,
  Were trampled by a hurrying crowd,
And fiery hearts and armèd hands
  Encounter'd in the battle-cloud.

Ah, never shall the land forget
  How gush'd the life-blood of her brave,—
Gush'd, warm with hope and courage yet,
  Upon the soil they fought to save.

Now all is calm, and fresh, and still;
  Alone the chirp of flitting bird,
And talk of children on the hill,
  And bell of wandering kine, are heard.

No solemn host goes trailing by
  The black-mouth'd gun and staggering wain;
Men start not at the battle-cry,—
  Oh, be it never heard again!

Soon rested those who fought; but thou
  Who minglest in the harder strife
For truths which men receive not now,
  Thy warfare only ends with life.

A friendless warfare! lingering long
  Through weary day and weary year;
A wild and many-weapon'd throng
  Hang on thy front and flank and rear.

Yet nerve thy spirit to the proof,
  And blench not at thy chosen lot;
The timid good may stand aloof,
  The sage may frown,—yet faint thou not.

Nor heed the shaft too surely cast,
  The foul and hissing bolt of scorn;

For with thy side shall dwell, at last,
    The victory of endurance born.

Truth, crush'd to earth, shall rise again,—
    The eternal years of God are hers;
But Error, wounded, writhes in pain,
    And dies among his worshippers.

Yea, though thou lie upon the dust,
    When they who help'd thee flee in fear,
Die full of hope and manly trust,
    Like those who fell in battle here.

Another hand thy sword shall wield,
    Another hand the standard wave,
Till from the trumpet's mouth is peal'd
    The blast of triumph o'er thy grave.
                    WILLIAM CULLEN BRYANT.

THE BATTLE OF BLENHEIM.

IT was a summer evening,—
    Old Kaspar's work was done,
And he before his cottage-door
    Was sitting in the sun;
And by him sported on the green
His little grandchild Wilhelmine.

She saw her brother Peterkin
    Roll something large and round,
Which he beside the rivulet,
    In playing there, had found;
He came to ask what he had found
That was so large and smooth and round.

Old Kaspar took it from the boy,
    Who stood expectant by;
And then the old man shook his head,
    And, with a natural sigh,—
"'Tis some poor fellow's skull," said he,
"Who fell in the great victory.

"I find them in the garden,
    For there's many hereabout;
And often, when I go to plough,
    The ploughshare turns them out;
For many thousand men," said he,
"Were slain in that great victory."

"Now tell us what 'twas all about,"
    Young Peterkin he cries;
And little Wilhelmine looks up
    With wonder-waiting eyes,—
"Now tell us all about the war,
And what they fought each other for."

"It was the English," Kaspar cried,
    "Who put the French to rout;
But what they fought each other for
    I could not well make out;
But everybody said," quoth he,
"That 'twas a famous victory.

"My father lived at Blenheim then,
    Yon little stream hard by;
They burnt his dwelling to the ground,
    And he was forced to fly;
So with his wife and child he fled,
Nor had he where to rest his head.

"With fire and sword the country round
    Was wasted far and wide;
And many a childing mother then,
    And new-born baby died;
But things like that, you know, must be
At every famous victory.

"They say it was a shocking sight
    After the field was won,—
For many thousand bodies here
    Lay rotting in the sun;
But things like that, you know, must be
After a famous victory.

"Great praise the Duke of Marlbro' won,
    And our good prince Eugene."
"Why, 'twas a very wicked thing!"
    Said little Wilhelmine.
"Nay, nay, my little girl!" quoth he,
"It was a famous victory.

"And everybody praised the duke
    Who this great fight did win."
"But what good came of it at last?"
    Quoth little Peterkin.
"Why, that I cannot tell," said he;
"But 'twas a famous victory."
                    ROBERT SOUTHEY.

NOT ON THE BATTLE-FIELD.

"To fall on the battle-field fighting for my dear country,—that would not be hard."—*The Neighbors.*

OH no, no,—let me lie
Not on a field of battle when I die!
    Let not the iron tread
Of the mad war-horse crush my helmèd
    head;

Nor let the reeking knife,
That I have drawn against a brother's life,
Be in my hand when Death
Thunders along, and tramples me beneath
His heavy squadron's heels,
Or gory felloes of his cannon's wheels.

From such a dying bed,
Though o'er it float the stripes of white and red,
And the bald eagle brings
The cluster'd stars upon his wide-spread wings
To sparkle in my sight,
Oh, never let my spirit take her flight!

I know that Beauty's eye
Is all the brighter where gay pennants fly,
And brazen helmets dance,
And sunshine flashes on the lifted lance;
I know that bards have sung,
And people shouted till the welkin rung,
In honor of the brave
Who on the battle-field have found a grave;
I know that o'er their bones
Have grateful hands piled monumental stones.
Some of these piles I've seen:
The one at Lexington upon the green
Where the first blood was shed
That to my country's independence led;
And others on our shore,
The "Battle Monument" at Baltimore,
And that on Bunker's Hill.
Ay, and abroad, a few more famous still;
Thy "tomb," Themistocles,
That looks out yet upon the Grecian seas,
And which the waters kiss
That issue from the Gulf of Salamis.
And thine, too, have I seen,
Thy mound of earth, Patroclus, robed in green,
That, like a natural knoll,
Sheep climb and nibble over as they stroll,
Watch'd by some turban'd boy,
Upon the margin of the plain of Troy.

Such honors grace the bed,
I know, whereon the warrior lays his head,
And hears, as life ebbs out,
The conquer'd flying, and the conqueror's shout;
But as his eye grows dim,
What is a column or a mound to him?
What to the parting soul,
The mellow note of bugles? What the roll
Of drums? No, let me die
Where the blue heaven bends o'er me lovingly,
And the soft summer air,
As it goes by me, stirs my thin white hair,
And from my forehead dries
The death-damp as it gathers, and the skies
Seem waiting to receive
My soul to their clear depth! Or let me leave
The world when round my bed
Wife, children, weeping friends are gather'd,
And the calm voice of prayer
And holy hymning shall my soul prepare
To go and be at rest
With kindred spirits,—spirits who have bless'd
The human brotherhood
By labors, cares, and counsels for their good.

And in my dying hour,
When riches, fame, and honor have no power
To bear the spirit up,
Or from my lips to turn aside the cup
That all must drink at last,
Oh, let me draw refreshment from the past!
Then let my soul run back,
With peace and joy, along my earthly track,
And see that all the seeds
That I have scatter'd there, in virtuous deeds
Have sprung up, and have given,
Already, fruits of which to taste is Heaven!
And though no grassy mound
Or granite pile say 'tis heroic ground
Where my remains repose,
Still will I hope—vain hope, perhaps!—that those

Whom I have striven to bless,
The wanderer reclaim'd, the fatherless,
   May stand around my grave,
With the poor prisoner, and the poorer slave,
   And breathe an humble prayer
That they may die like him whose bones are mouldering there.
JOHN PIERPONT.

VERSES
SUPPOSED TO BE WRITTEN BY ALEXANDER SELKIRK DURING HIS SOLITARY ABODE IN THE ISLAND OF JUAN FERNANDEZ.

I AM monarch of all I survey;
   My right there is none to dispute;
From the centre all round to the sea
   I am lord of the fowl and the brute.
O Solitude! where are the charms
   That sages have seen in thy face?
Better dwell in the midst of alarms
   Than reign in this horrible place.

I am out of humanity's reach;
   I must finish my journey alone;
Never hear the sweet music of speech—
   I start at the sound of my own.
The beasts that roam over the plain,
   My form with indifference see;
They are so unacquainted with man,
   Their tameness is shocking to me.

Society, Friendship, and Love,
   Divinely bestow'd upon man,
Oh had I the wings of a dove,
   How soon would I taste you again!
My sorrows I then might assuage
   In the ways of religion and truth,
Might learn from the wisdom of age,
   And be cheer'd by the sallies of youth.

Religion! what treasure untold
   Resides in that heavenly word!
More precious than silver and gold,
   Or all that this earth can afford.
But the sound of the church-going bell
   These valleys and rocks never heard;
Never sigh'd at the sound of a knell,
   Or smiled when a Sabbath appear'd.

Ye winds that have made me your sport,
   Convey to this desolate shore
Some cordial endearing report
   Of a land I shall visit no more:

My friends, do they now and then send
   A wish or a thought after me?
Oh tell me I yet have a friend,
   Though a friend I am never to see.
How fleet is the glance of the mind!
   Compared with the speed of its flight,
The tempest itself lags behind,
   And the swift-wingèd arrows of light.
When I think of my own native land,
   In a moment I seem to be there;
But, alas! recollection at hand
   Soon hurries me back to despair.

But the sea-fowl is gone to her nest,
   The beast is laid down in his lair;
Even here is a season of rest,
   And I to my cabin repair.
There's mercy in every place,
   And mercy—encouraging thought!—
Gives even affliction a grace,
   And reconciles man to his lot.
WILLIAM COWPER.

FAITH.

BETTER trust all and be deceived,
   And weep that trust and that deceiving,
Than doubt one heart that if believed
   Had bless'd one's life with true believing.

Oh, in this mocking world too fast
   The doubting fiend o'ertakes our youth;
Better be cheated to the last
   Than lose the blessed hope of truth.
FRANCES ANNE KEMBLE.

THE LADDER OF ST. AUGUSTINE.

SAINT AUGUSTINE! well hast thou said,
   That of our vices we can frame
A ladder, if we will but tread
   Beneath our feet each deed of shame!

All common things, each day's events,
   That with the hour begin and end,
Our pleasures and our discontents,
   Are rounds by which we may ascend.

The low desire, the base design,
   That makes another's virtues less;
The revel of the ruddy wine,
   And all occasions of excess;

The longing for ignoble things;
    The strife for triumph more than truth;
The hardening of the heart, that brings
    Irreverence for the dreams of youth;

All thoughts of ill, all evil deeds,
    That have their root in thoughts of ill;
Whatever hinders or impedes
    The action of the nobler will;—

All these must first be trampled down
    Beneath our feet, if we would gain
In the bright fields of fair renown
    The right of eminent domain.

We have not wings, we cannot soar;
    But we have feet to scale and climb,
By slow degrees, by more and more,
    The cloudy summits of our time.

The mighty pyramids of stone
    That wedge-like cleave the desert airs,
When nearer seen, and better known,
    Are but gigantic flights of stairs.

The distant mountains, that uprear
    Their solid bastions to the skies,
Are cross'd by pathways, that appear
    As we to higher levels rise.

The heights by great men reach'd and kept
    Were not attain'd by sudden flight,
But they, while their companions slept
    Were toiling upward in the night.

Standing on what too long we bore
    With shoulders bent and downcast eyes,
We may discern—unseen before—
    A path to higher destinies.

Nor deem the irrevocable Past
    As wholly wasted, wholly vain,
If, rising on its wrecks, at last
    To something nobler we attain.
        HENRY WADSWORTH LONGFELLOW.

THE RED RIVER VOYAGEUR.

OUT and in the river is winding
    The links of its long, red chain,
Through belts of dusky pine-land
    And gusty leagues of plain.

Only, at times, a smoke-wreath
    With the drifting cloud-rack joins,—
The smoke of the hunting-lodges
    Of the wild Assiniboins!

Drearily blows the north wind
    From the land of ice and snow;
The eyes that look are weary,
    And heavy the hands that row.

And with one foot on the water,
    And one upon the shore,
The Angel of Shadow gives warning
    That day shall be no more.

Is it the clang of wild-geese,
    Is it the Indian's yell,
That lends to the voice of the north wind
    The tones of a far-off bell?

The voyageur smiles as he listens
    To the sound that grows apace;
Well he knows the vesper ringing
    Of the bells of St. Boniface,—

The bells of the Roman Mission,
    That call from their turrets twain
To the boatman on the river,
    To the hunter on the plain!

Even so in our mortal journey
    The bitter north winds blow,
And thus upon life's Red River
    Our hearts, as oarsmen, row.

And when the Angel of Shadow
    Rests his feet on wave and shore,
And our eyes grow dim with watching
    And our hearts faint at the oar,

Happy is he who heareth
    The signal of his release
In the bells of the Holy City,
    The chimes of eternal peace!
        JOHN GREENLEAF WHITTIER.

THE PLACE TO DIE.

How little recks it where men die,
    When once the moment's past
In which the dim and glazing eye
    Has looked on earth its last—
Whether beneath the sculptured urn
    The coffin'd form shall rest,

Or, in its nakedness, return
  Back to its mother's breast!

Death is a common friend or foe,
  As different men may hold,
And at its summons each must go,
  The timid and the bold;
But when the spirit, free and warm,
  Deserts it, as it must,
What matter where the lifeless form
  Dissolves again to dust?

The soldier falls 'mid corses piled
  Upon the battle plain,
Where reinless war-steeds gallop wild
  Above the gory slain;
But though his corse be grim to see,
  Hoof-trampled on the sod,
What recks it when the spirit free
  Has soar'd aloft to God!

The coward's dying eye may close
  Upon his downy bed,
And softest hands his limbs compose,
  Or garments o'er him spread;
But, ye who shun the bloody fray
  Where fall the mangled brave,
Go strip his coffin-lid away,
  And see him in his grave!

'Twere sweet indeed to close our eyes
  With those we cherish near,
And, wafted upward by their sighs,
  Soar to some calmer sphere;
But whether on the scaffold high,
  Or in the battle's van,
The fittest place where man can die
  Is where he dies for man.
        MICHAEL JOSEPH BARRY.

AFTER DEATH IN ARABIA.

HE who died at Azan sends
This to comfort all his friends.

Faithful friends! It lies, I know,
Pale and white and cold as snow;
And ye say, "Abdullah's dead!"
Weeping at the feet and head.
I can see your falling tears,
I can hear your sighs and prayers;
Yet I smile, and whisper this:
"I am not the thing you kiss;
Cease your tears, and let it lie;
It *was* mine, it is not I."

Sweet friends! what the women lave
For its last bed of the grave
Is a hut which I am quitting,
Is a garment no more fitting,
Is a cage, from which at last,
Like a hawk, my soul hath pass'd.
Love the inmate, not the room—
The wearer, not the garb—the plume
Of the falcon, not the bars,
Which kept him from the splendid stars.

Loving friends! Be wise, and dry
Straightway every weeping eye;
What ye lift upon the bier
Is not worth a wistful tear;
'Tis an empty sea-shell—one
Out of which the pearl has gone;
The shell is broken—it lies there;
The pearl, the all, the soul, is here.
'Tis an earthen jar, whose lid
Allah seal'd the while it hid
That treasure of his treasury,
A mind that loved him; let it lie!
Let the shard be earth's once more,
Since the gold shines in his store!

Allah glorious! Allah good!
Now thy world is understood;
Now the long, long wonder ends!
Yet ye weep, my erring friends,
While the man whom ye call dead,
In unspoken bliss, instead,
Lives and loves you; lost, 'tis true,
By such light as shines for you;
But in the light ye cannot see
Of unfulfill'd felicity—
In enlarging paradise—
Lives a life that never dies.

Farewell, friends! Yet not farewell;
Where I am, ye too shall dwell.
I am gone before your face
A moment's time, a little space;
When ye come where I have stepped,
Ye will wonder why ye wept;
Ye will know, by wise love taught,
That here is all, and there is naught.
Weep a while, if ye are fain—
Sunshine still must follow rain;
Only not at death—for death,
Now I know, is that first breath
Which our souls draw when we enter
Life which is of all life centre.

Be ye certain all seems love,
View'd from Allah's throne above;
Be ye stout of heart, and come
Bravely onward to your home!
La Allah illa Allah! yea!
Thou Love divine! Thou Love alway!

   He that died as Azan gave
   This to those who made his grave.
                              EDWIN ARNOLD.

TWENTY-ONE.

GROWN to man's stature! O my little child!
   My bird that sought the skies so long ago!
My fair, sweet blossom, pure and undefiled,
   How have the years flown since we laid thee low!

What have they been to thee? If thou wert here,
   Standing beside thy brothers, tall and fair,
With bearded lip, and dark eyes shining clear,
   And glints of summer sunshine in thy hair,

I should look up into thy face and say,
   Wavering, perhaps, between a tear and smile,
"O my sweet son, thou art a man to-day!"
   And thou wouldst stoop to kiss my lips the while.

But—up in heaven—how is it with thee, dear?
   Art thou a man—to man's full stature grown?
Dost thou count time, as we do, year by year?
   And what of all earth's changes hast thou known?

Thou hadst not learn'd to love me. Didst thou take
   Any small germ of love to heaven with thee,
That thou hast watch'd and nurtured for my sake,
   Waiting till I its perfect flower may see?

What is it to have lived in heaven always?
   To have no memory of pain or sin?
Ne'er to have known in all the calm, bright days
   The jar and fret of earth's discordant din?

Thy brothers—they are mortal—they must tread
   Ofttimes in rough, hard ways, with bleeding feet;
Must fight with dragons, must bewail their dead,
   And fierce Apollyon face to face must meet.

I, who would give my very life for theirs—
   I cannot save them from earth's pain or loss;
I cannot shield them from its griefs or cares;
   Each human heart must bear alone its cross!

Was God, then, kinder unto thee than them,
   O thou whose little life was but a span?
Ah, think it not! In all his diadem
   No star shines brighter than the kingly man,

Who nobly earns whatever crown he wears,
   Who grandly conquers or as grandly dies,
And the white banner of his manhood bears
   Through all the years uplifted to the skies!

What lofty pæans shall the victor greet!
   What crown resplendent for his brow be fit!
O child, if earthly life be bitter-sweet,
   Hast thou not something missed in missing it?
                              JULIA CAROLINE DORR.

THE LIVING LOST.

MATRON! the children of whose love,
   Each to his grave, in youth have passed;
And now the mould is heaped above
   The dearest and the last!
Bride! who dost wear the widow's veil
Before the wedding flowers are pale!
Ye deem the human heart endures
No deeper, bitterer grief than yours.

Yet there are pangs of keener woe,
  Of which the sufferers never speak;
Nor to the world's cold pity show
  The tears that scald the cheek,
Wrung from their eyelids by the shame
And guilt of those they shrink to name,
  Whom once they loved with cheerful will,
  And love, though fallen and branded, still.

Weep, ye who sorrow for the dead,
  Thus breaking hearts their pain relieve;
And reverenced are the tears ye shed,
  And honored ye who grieve.
The praise of those who sleep in earth,
The pleasant memory of their worth,
  The hope to meet when life is past
  Shall heal the tortured mind at last.

But ye, who for the living lost
  That agony in secret bear,
Who shall with soothing words accost
  The strength of your despair?
Grief for your sake is scorn for them
Whom ye lament and all condemn;
  And o'er the world of spirits lies
  A gloom from which ye turn your eyes.
    WILLIAM CULLEN BRYANT.

ONE BY ONE.

ONE by one the sands are flowing,
  One by one the moments fall;
Some are coming, some are going;
  Do not strive to grasp them all.

One by one thy duties wait thee,
  Let thy whole strength go to each;
Let no future dreams elate thee,
  Learn thou first what these can teach.

One by one (bright gifts from Heaven)
  Joys are sent thee here below;
Take them readily when given,
  Ready too to let them go.

One by one thy griefs shall meet thee,
  Do not fear an armèd band;
One will fade as others greet thee;
  Shadows passing through the land.

Do not look at life's long sorrow;
  See how small each moment's pain;
God will help thee for to-morrow,
  So each day begin again.

Every hour that fleets so slowly
  Has its task to do or bear;
Luminous the crown, and holy,
  When each gem is set with care.

Do not linger with regretting,
  Or for passing hours despond;
Nor, the daily toil forgetting,
  Look too eagerly beyond.

Hours are golden links, God's token
  Reaching heaven; but one by one
Take them, lest the chain be broken
  Ere the pilgrimage be done.
    ADELAIDE ANNE PROCTER.

BETWEEN THE LIGHTS.

A LITTLE pause in life—while daylight lingers
  Between the sunset and the pale moonrise,
When daily labor slips from weary fingers,
  And calm, gray shadows veil the aching eyes.

Old perfumes wander back from fields of clover,
  Seen in the light of stars that long have set;
Beloved ones, whose earthly toil is over,
  Draw near as if they lived among us yet.

Old voices call me—through the dusk returning
  I hear the echo of departed feet;
And then I ask with vain and troubled yearning,
  "What is the charm which makes old things so sweet?"

"Must the old joys be evermore withholden?
  Even their memory keeps me pure and true;
And yet from our Jerusalem the golden
  God speaketh, saying, "I make all things new."

"Father," I cry, "the old must still be nearer;
  Stifle my love or give me back the past;
Give me the fair old fields, whose paths are dearer
  Than all Thy shining streets and mansions vast."

Peace! peace! the Lord of earth and heaven knoweth
The human soul in all its heat and strife;
Out of His throne no stream of Lethe floweth,
But the pure river of eternal life.

He giveth life, ay, life in all its sweetness;
Old loves, old sunny scenes will He restore;
Only the curse of sin and incompleteness
Shall vex thy soul and taint thine earth no more.

Serve Him in daily toil and holy living,
And Faith shall lift thee to His sunlit heights;
Then shall a psalm of gladness and thanksgiving
Fill the calm hour that comes between the lights.
AUTHOR UNKNOWN.

A DOUBTING HEART.

WHERE are the swallows fled?
Frozen and dead,
Perchance upon some bleak and stormy shore.
O doubting heart!
Far over purple seas,
They wait, in sunny ease,
The balmy southern breeze,
To bring them to their northern homes once more.

Why must the flowers die?
Prison'd they lie
In the cold tomb, heedless of tears or rain.
O doubting heart!
They only sleep below
The soft white ermine snow,
While winter winds shall blow,
To breathe and smile upon you soon again.

The sun has hid its rays
These many days:
Will dreary hours never leave the earth?
O doubting heart!
The stormy clouds on high
Veil the same sunny sky,
That soon (for spring is nigh)
Shall wake the summer into golden mirth.

Fair hope is dead, and light
Is quench'd in night.
What sound can break the silence of despair?
O doubting heart!
Thy sky is overcast,
Yet stars shall rise at last,
Brighter for darkness past,
And angels' silver voices stir the air.
ADELAIDE ANNE PROCTER.

THE NEGLECTED CALL.

WHEN the fields were white with harvest, and the laborers were few,
Heard I thus a voice within me, "Here is work for thee to do;
Come thou up and help the reapers, I will show thee now the way,
Come and help them bear the burden, and the toiling of the day."
"For a more convenient season," thus I answered, "will I wait,"
And the voice reproving murmur'd, "Hasten, ere it be too late."

Yet I heeded not the utterance, listening to lo! here—lo! there—
I lost sight of all the reapers in whose work I would not share;
Follow'd after strange devices—bow'd my heart to gods of stone,
Till like Ephraim join'd to idols, God wellnigh left me alone;
But the angel of His patience follow'd on my erring track,
Setting here and there a landmark, wherewithal to guide me back.

Onward yet I went, and onward, till there met me on the way
A poor prodigal *returning*, who, like me, had gone astray,
And his faith was strong and earnest that a father's house would be
Safest shelter from temptation for such sinful ones as he.

"Read the lesson," said the angel, "take
    the warning and repent;"
But the wily Tempter queried, "Ere thy
    substance be unspent?

"Hast thou need to toil and labor? art
    thou fitted for the work?
Many a hidden stone to bruise thee in the
    harvest-field doth lurk;
There are others call'd beside thee, and
    perchance the voice may be
But thy own delusive fancy, which thou
    hearest calling thee—
There is time enough before thee, all thy
    footsteps to retrace."
Then I yielded to the Tempter, and the
    angel veil'd her face.

Pleasure beckon'd in the distance, and her
    siren song was sweet,
"Through a thornless path of flowers
    gently I will guide thy feet.
Youth is as a rapid river, gliding noiseless-
    ly away,
Earth is but a pleasant garden; cull its
    roses whilst thou may;
Press the juice from purple clusters, fill
    life's chalice with the wine,
Taste the fairest fruits which tempt thee,
    all its richest fruits are thine."

Ah! the path was smooth and easy, but
    a snare was set therein,
And the feet were oft entangled in the
    fearful mesh of sin,
And the canker-worm was hidden in the
    rose-leaf folded up,
And the sparkling wine of pleasure was a
    fatal Circean cup;
All its fruits were Dead Sea apples, tempt-
    ing only to the sight,
Fair yet fill'd with dust and ashes—beau-
    tiful, but touch'd with blight.

"O my Father," cried I inly, "Thou hast
    striven—I have will'd;
Now the mission of the angel of Thy
    patience is fulfill'd;
I have tasted earthly pleasures, yet my
    soul is craving food;
Let the summons Thou hast given to Thy
    harvest be renew'd;

I am ready now to labor—wilt thou call me
    once again?
I will join thy willing reapers as they
    garner up the grain."

But the still small voice within me, earnest
    in its truth and deep,
Answer'd my awaken'd conscience, "As
    thou sowest thou shalt reap;
God is just, and retribution follows each
    neglected call;
Thou hadst thy appointed duty taught thee
    by the Lord of all;
Thou wert chosen, but another fill'd the
    place assignèd thee,
Henceforth in my field of labor thou
    mayst but a gleaner be.

"But a work is still before thee—see thou
    linger not again;
Separate the chaff thou gleanest, beat it
    from among the grain;
Follow after these my reapers, let thine
    eyes be on the field,
Gather up the precious handfuls their
    abundant wheat-sheaves yield;
Go not hence to glean, but tarry from the
    morning until night;
Be thou faithful, thou mayst yet find favor
    in thy Master's sight."

HANNAH LLOYD NEALE.

THE LOT OF THOUSANDS.

WHEN hope lies dead within the heart,
    By secret sorrow close conceal'd,
We shrink lest looks or words impart
    What must not be reveal'd.

'Tis hard to smile when one would weep;
    To speak when one would silent be;
To wake when one should wish to sleep,
    And wake to agony.

Yet such the lot by thousands cast
    Who wander in this world of care,
And bend beneath the bitter blast,
    To save them from despair.

But Nature waits her guests to greet,
    Where disappointment cannot come;
And Time guides with unerring feet
    The weary wanderers home.

ANNE HUNTER.

INFLUENCE OF TIME ON GRIEF.

O TIME, who know'st a lenient hand to lay
Softest on sorrow's wound, and slowly thence
(Lulling to sad repose the weary sense)
The faint pang stealest unperceived away;
On thee I rest my only hope at last,
And think when thou hast dried the bitter tear
That flows in vain o'er all my soul held dear,
I may look back on every sorrow past,
And meet life's peaceful evening with a smile,
As some lone bird, at day's departing hour,
Sings in the sunbeam, of the transient shower
Forgetful, though its wings are wet the while.
Yet ah! how much must that poor heart endure,
Which hopes from thee, and thee alone, a cure!
WILLIAM LISLE BOWLES.

THE CHAMELEON.

OFT has it been my lot to mark
A proud, conceited, talking spark,
With eyes that hardly served at most
To guard their master 'gainst a post,
Yet round the world the blade has been
To see whatever could be seen.
Returning from his finish'd tour
Grown ten times perter than before;
Whatever word you chance to drop,
The travell'd fool your mouth will stop;
"Sir, if my judgment you'll allow,
I've seen—and sure I ought to know,"
So begs you'd pay a due submission,
And acquiesce in his decision.

Two travellers of such a cast,
As o'er Arabia's wilds they pass'd,
And on their way, in friendly chat,
Now talk'd of this, and then of that,
Discoursed a while, 'mongst other matter,
Of the chameleon's form and nature.
"A stranger animal," cries one,
"Sure never lived beneath the sun.
A lizard's body, lean and long,
A fish's head, a serpent's tongue,
Its foot with triple claw disjoin'd,
And what a length of tail behind!
How slow its pace, and then its hue,—
Who ever saw so fine a blue?"

"Hold, there!" the other quick replies;
"'Tis green,—I saw it with these eyes,
As late with open mouth it lay,
And warm'd it in the sunny ray;
Stretch'd at its ease the beast I view'd,
And saw it eat the air for food."
"I've seen it, sir, as well as you,
And must again affirm it blue;
At leisure I the beast survey'd,
Extended in the cooling shade."
"'Tis green, 'tis green, sir, I assure ye."
"Green!" cries the other in a fury,—
"Why, sir, d'ye think I've lost my eyes?"
"'Twere no great loss," the friend replies,
"For if they always serve you thus,
You'll find them of but little use."

So high at last the contest rose,
From words they almost came to blows,
When luckily came by a third,—
To him the question they referr'd,
And begg'd he'd tell 'em, if he knew,
Whether the thing was green or blue.
"Sirs," cries the umpire, "cease your pother!
The creature's neither one nor t'other.
I caught the animal last night,
And view'd it o'er by candlelight;
I mark'd it well—'twas black as jet;
You stare,—but, sirs, I've got it yet,
And can produce it." "Pray, sir, do:
I'll lay my life the thing is blue."
"And I'll be sworn, that when you've seen
The reptile, you'll pronounce him green."

"Well then, at once to ease the doubt,"
Replies the man, "I'll turn him out,
And when before your eyes I've set him,
If you don't find him black, I'll eat him."
He said, then full before their sight
Produced the beast, and lo!—'twas white.

Both stared; the man look'd wondrous wise—
"My children," the chameleon cries

(Then first the creature found a tongue),
"You all are right, and all are wrong;
When next you talk of what you view,
Think others see as well as you;
Nor wonder, if you find that none
Prefers your eyesight to his own."
JAMES MERRICK.

I LAY IN SORROW, DEEP DISTRESSED.

I LAY in sorrow, deep distress'd;
  My grief a proud man heard;
His looks were cold, he gave me gold,
  But not a kindly word.
My sorrow pass'd,—I paid him back
  The gold he gave to me;
Then stood erect and spoke my thanks,
  And bless'd his Charity.

I lay in want, in grief and pain:
  A poor man pass'd my way;
He bound my head, he gave me bread,
  He watch'd me night and day.
How shall I pay him back again
  For all he did to me?
Oh, gold is great, but greater far
  Is heavenly Sympathy!
CHARLES MACKAY.

STANZAS.

WHEN lovely woman stoops to folly,
  And finds too late that men betray,
What charm can soothe her melancholy,
  What art can wash her guilt away?

The only art her guilt to cover,
  To hide her shame from every eye,
To give repentance to her lover
  And wring his bosom, is—to die.
OLIVER GOLDSMITH.

NIGHT.

NIGHT is the time for rest;
  How sweet, when labors close,
To gather round an aching breast
  The curtain of repose,
Stretch the tired limbs and lay the head
Down on our own delightful bed!

Night is the time for dreams:
  The gay romance of life,
When truth that is, and truth that seems,
  Mix in fantastic strife;
Ah! visions less beguiling far
Than waking dreams by daylight are!

Night is the time for toil:
  To plough the classic field,
Intent to find the buried spoil
  Its wealthy furrows yield;
Till all is ours that sages taught,
That poets sang, and heroes wrought.

Night is the time to weep:
  To wet with unseen tears
Those graves of Memory, where sleep
  The joys of other years;
Hopes that were angels at their birth,
But died when young, like things of earth.

Night is the time to watch:
  O'er ocean's dark expanse,
To hail the Pleiades, or catch
  The full moon's earliest glance,
That brings into the homesick mind
All we have loved and left behind.

Night is the time for care:
  Brooding on hours misspent,
To see the spectre of Despair
  Come to our lonely tent;
Like Brutus, 'midst his slumbering host,
Summon'd to die by Cæsar's ghost.

Night is the time to think:
  When, from the eye, the soul
Takes flight; and on the utmost brink
  Of yonder starry pole
Discerns beyond the abyss of night
The dawn of uncreated light.

Night is the time to pray:
  Our Saviour oft withdrew
To desert mountains far away;
  So will His followers do,
Steal from the throng to haunts untrod,
And commune there alone with God.

Night is the time for Death:
  When all around is peace,
Calmly to yield the weary breath,
  From sin and suffering cease,
Think of heaven's bliss, and give the sign
To parting friends;—such death be mine.
JAMES MONTGOMERY.

GOOD-NIGHT.

Downward sinks the setting sun,
  Soft the evening shadows fall;
    Light is flying,
    Day is dying,
  Darkness stealeth over all.
          Good-night!

Autumn garners in her stores—
  Foison of the fading year;
    Leaves are dying,
    Winds are sighing—
  Whispering of the Winter near.
          Good-night!

Youth is vanished, manhood wanes;
  Age its forward shadows throws;
    Day is dying,
    Years are flying,
  Life runs onward to its close.
          Good-night!
            AUTHOR UNKNOWN.

GOOD COUNSEIL OF CHAUCER.

Flee fro the pres, and duelle with sothfastnesse;
  Suffice the thy good though hit be smale;
For horde hath hate, and clymbyng tikelnesse,
  Pres hath envye, and wele is blent over alle.
Savoure no more then the behove shalle;
Rede wel thy self that other folke canst rede,
And trouthe the shal delyver, hit ys no
      drede.

Peyne the not eche croked to redresse
  In trust of hire that turneth as a balle,
Grete rest stant in lytil besynesse;
  Bewar also to spurne ayeine an nalle,
Stryve not as doth a croke with a walle;
Daunt thy selfe that dauntest otheres dede,
And trouthe the shal delyver, hit is no
      drede.

That the ys sent receyve in buxomnesse,
  The wrasteling of this world asketh a falle;
Her is no home, her is but wyldyrnesse.
  Forth pilgrime! forth best out of thy
      stalle!
Loke up on hye, and thonke God of alle;
Weyve thy lust, and let thy goste the lede,
And trouthe shal thee delyver, hit is no
      drede.
            GEOFFREY CHAUCER.

SIC VITA.

Like to the falling of a star,
Or as the flights of eagles are,
Or like the fresh spring's gaudy hue,
Or silver drops of morning dew,
Or like a wind that chafes the flood,
Or bubbles which on water stood—
E'en such is man, whose borrow'd light
Is straight called in, and paid to-night.
The wind blows out, the bubble dies,
The spring entomb'd in autumn lies,
The dew dries up, the star is shot,
The flight is past—and man forgot!
            HENRY KING.

LINES.

WRITTEN BY ONE IN THE TOWER, BEING
  YOUNG AND CONDEMNED TO DIE.

My prime of youth is but a frost of cares,
My feast of joy is but a dish of pain,
My crop of corn is but a field of tares,
  And all my goodes is but vain hope of
      gain.
The day is fled, and yet I saw no sun;
And now I live, and now my life is done!

My spring is past, and yet it hath not
      sprung,
  The fruit is dead, and yet the leaves are
      green;
My youth is past, and yet I am but young,
  I saw the world, and yet I was not seen.
My thread is cut, and yet it is not spun;
And now I live, and now my life is done!

I sought for death, and found it in the
      wombe,
  I lookt for life, and yet it was a shade,
I trade the ground, and knew it was my
      tombe,
  And now I die, and now I am but made.
The glass is full, and yet my glass is run;
And now I live, and now my life is done!
            CHIDIOCK TYCHBORN.

ON HIS DIVINE POEMS.

When we for age could neither read nor
      write,
  The subject made us able to indite:
The soul, with nobler resolutions deck'd,
  The body stooping, does herself erect:
No mortal parts are requisite to raise
Her that unbodied can her Maker praise.

The seas are quiet when the winds give o'er;
So calm are we when passions are no more.
For then we know how vain it was to boast
Of fleeting things, so certain to be lost.

Clouds of affection from our younger eyes
Conceal that emptiness which age descries.
The soul's dark cottage, batter'd and decay'd,
Lets in new light through chinks that time has made.

Stronger by weakness, wiser men become
As they draw near to their eternal home.
Leaving the old, both worlds at once they view,
That stand upon the threshold of the new.
EDMUND WALLER.

FROM "IN MEMORIAM."

I.

I HELD it truth, with him who sings
  To one clear harp in divers tones,
  That men may rise on stepping-stones
Of their dead selves to higher things.

But who shall so forecast the years
  And find in loss a gain to match?
  Or reach a hand thro' time to catch
The far-off interest of tears?

Let Love clasp Grief lest both be drown'd,
  Let darkness keep her raven gloss:
  Ah, sweeter to be drunk with loss,
To dance with death, to beat the ground,

Than that the victor Hours should scorn
  The long result of love, and boast,
  "Behold the man that loved and lost,
But all he was is overworn."

XXVII.

I envy not, in any moods,
  The captive void of noble rage,
  The linnet born within the cage,
That never knew the summer woods.

I envy not the beast that takes
  His license in the field of time,
  Unfetter'd by the sense of crime,
To whom a conscience never wakes;

Nor, what may count itself as blest,
  The heart that never plighted troth,
  But stagnates in the weeds of sloth;
Nor any want-begotten rest.

I hold it true, whate'er befall—
  I feel it, when I sorrow most—
  'Tis better to have loved and lost
Than never to have loved at all.

LIV.

Oh yet we trust that somehow good
  Will be the final goal of ill,
  To pangs of nature, sins of will,
Defects of doubt, and taints of blood;

That nothing walks with aimless feet;
  That not one life shall be destroyed,
  Or cast as rubbish to the void,
When God hath made the pile complete;

That not a worm is cloven in vain;
  That not a moth with vain desire
  Is shrivell'd in a fruitless fire,
Or but subserves another's gain.

Behold, we know not anything;
  I can but trust that good shall fall
  At last—far off—at last, to all,
And every winter change to spring.

So runs my dream: but what am I?
  An infant crying in the night:
  An infant crying for the light:
And with no language but a cry.

LXXVIII.

Again at Christmas did we weave
  The holly round the Christmas hearth;
  The silent snow possessed the earth,
And calmly fell our Christmas-eve:

The yule-clog sparkled keen with frost,
  No wing of wind the region swept,
  But over all things brooding slept
The quiet sense of something lost.

As in the winters left behind
  Again our ancient games had place,
  The mimic picture's breathing grace,
And dance and song and hoodman-blind.

Who show'd a token of distress?
  No single tear, no mark of pain:
  O sorrow, then can sorrow wane?
O grief, can grief be changed to less?

O last regret, regret can die!
  No—mixt with all this mystic frame,
  Her deep relations are the same,
But with long use her tears are dry.

CVI.

Ring out, wild bells, to the wild sky,
  The flying cloud, the frosty light:
  The year is dying in the night;
Ring out, wild bells, and let him die.

Ring out the old, ring in the new,
  Ring, happy bells, across the snow:
  The year is going, let him go;
Ring out the false, ring in the true.

Ring out the grief that saps the mind,
  For those that here we see no more;
  Ring out the feud of rich and poor,
Ring in redress to all mankind.

Ring out a slowly dying cause,
  And ancient forms of party strife;
  Ring in the nobler modes of life,
With sweeter manners, purer laws.

Ring out the want, the care, the sin,
  The faithless coldness of the times;
  Ring out, ring out my mournful rhymes,
But ring the fuller minstrel in.

Ring out false pride in place and blood,
  The civic slander and the spite;
  Ring in the love of truth and right,
Ring in the common love of good.

Ring out old shapes of foul disease;
  Ring out the narrowing lust of gold;
  Ring out the thousand wars of old,
Ring in the thousand years of peace.

Ring in the valiant man and free,
  The larger heart, the kindlier hand;
  Ring out the darkness of the land,
Ring in the Christ that is to be.

CXIV.

Who loves not Knowledge? Who shall rail
  Against her beauty? May she mix
  With men and prosper! Who shall fix
Her pillars? Let her work prevail.

But on her forehead sits a fire:
  She sets her forward countenance
  And leaps into the future chance,
Submitting all things to desire.

Half-grown as yet, a child, and vain—
  She cannot fight the fear of death.
  What is she, cut from love and faith,
But some wild Pallas from the brain

Of Demons? fiery hot to burst
  All barriers in her onward race
  For power. Let her know her place;
She is the second, not the first.

A higher hand must make her mild,
  If all be not in vain; and guide
  Her footsteps, moving side by side
With Wisdom, like the younger child:

For she is earthly of the mind,
  But Wisdom heavenly of the soul.
  Oh, friend, who camest to thy goal
So early, leaving me behind,

I would the great world grew like thee,
  Who grewest not alone in power
  And knowledge, but by year and hour
In reverence and in charity.

CXVIII.

Contemplate all this work of Time,
  The giant laboring in his youth;
  Nor dream of human love and truth,
As dying Nature's earth and lime;

But trust that those we call the dead
  Are breathers of an ampler day
  For ever nobler ends. They say,
The solid earth whereon we tread

In tracts of fluent heat began,
  And grew to seeming-random forms,
  The seeming prey of cyclic storms,
Till at the last arose the man;

Who throve and branch'd from clime to clime,
  The herald of a higher race,
  And of himself in higher place,
If so he type this work of time

Within himself, from more to more;
  Or, crown'd with attributes of woe
  Like glories, move his course, and show
That life is not as idle ore,

But iron dug from central gloom,
  And heated hot with burning fears,
  And dipt in baths of hissing tears,
And battered with the shocks of doom

To shape and use. Arise and fly
  The reeling Faun, the sensual feast;
  Move upward, working out the beast,
And let the ape and tiger die.

ALFRED TENNYSON.

Poems of Labor and Social Questions.

LABORARE EST ORARE.

Pause not to dream of the future before us;
Pause not to weep the wild cares that come o'er us;
Hark how Creation's deep, musical chorus,
Unintermitting, goes up into Heaven!
Never the ocean-wave falters in flowing;
Never the little seed stops in its growing;
More and more richly the rose-heart keeps glowing,
 Till from its nourishing stem it is riven.

"Labor is worship!" the robin is singing;
"Labor is worship!" the wild bee is ringing;
Listen! that eloquent whisper, upspringing,
 Speaks to thy soul from out Nature's great heart.
From the dark cloud flows the life-giving shower;
From the rough sod blows the soft-breathing flower;
From the small insect, the rich coral bower;
 Only man, in the plan, shrinks from his part.

Labor is life!—'Tis the still water faileth;
Idleness ever despaireth, bewaileth;
Keep the watch wound, for the dark rust assaileth:
 Flowers droop and die in the stillness of noon.
Labor is glory!—the flying cloud lightens;
Only the waving wing changes and brightens;
Idle hearts only the dark future frightens:
 Play the sweet keys, wouldst thou keep them in tune!

Labor is rest from the sorrows that greet us,
Rest from all petty vexations that meet us,
Rest from sin-promptings that ever entreat us,
 Rest from world-sirens that lure us to ill.
Work,—and pure slumbers shall wait on thy pillow;
Work,—thou shalt ride over Care's coming billow;
Lie not down wearied 'neath Woe's weeping willow!
 Work with a stout heart and resolute will!

Labor is health!—Lo! the husbandman reaping,
How through his veins goes the life-current leaping!
How his strong arm, in its stalwart pride sweeping,
 True as a sunbeam the swift sickle guides!
Labor is wealth,—in the sea the pearl groweth;
Rich the queen's robe from the frail cocoon floweth;
From the fine acorn the strong forest bloweth;
 Temple and statue the marble block hides.

Droop not, though shame, sin, and anguish are round thee;
Bravely fling off the cold chain that hath bound thee!
Look to yon pure Heaven smiling beyond thee:

Rest not content in thy darkness,—a clod!
Work for some good, be it ever so slowly;
Cherish some flower, be it ever so lowly:
Labor!—all labor is noble and holy;
   Let thy great deeds be thy prayer to thy God.
Frances Sargent Osgood.

THE USEFUL PLOUGH.

A country life is sweet!
In moderate cold and heat,
   To walk in the air, how pleasant and fair!
In every field of wheat,
   The fairest of flowers, adorning the bowers,
And every meadow's brow;
   So that I say, no courtier may
Compare with them who clothe in gray,
And follow the useful plough.

They rise with the morning lark,
And labor till almost dark;
   Then folding their sheep, they hasten to sleep;
While every pleasant park
   Next morning is ringing with birds that are singing
On each green, tender bough.
   With what content and merriment
Their days are spent, whose minds are bent
To follow the useful plough!
Author Unknown.

THE PLOUGHMAN.

Clear the brown path to meet his coulter's gleam!
Lo! on he comes, behind his smoking team,
With toil's bright dewdrops on his sunburnt brow,
The lord of earth, the hero of the plough!

First in the field before the reddening sun,
Last in the shadows when the day is done,
Line after line, along the bursting sod,
Marks the broad acres where his feet have trod;
Still where he treads the stubborn clods divide,
The smooth, fresh furrow opens deep and wide;
Matted and dense the tangled turf upheaves,
Mellow and dark the ridgy cornfield cleaves;
Up the steep hillside, where the laboring train
Slants the long track that scores the level plain,
Through the moist valley, clogg'd with oozing clay,
The patient convoy breaks its destined way;
At every turn the loosening chains resound,
The swinging ploughshare circles glistening round,
Till the wide field one billowy waste appears,
And wearied hands unbind the panting steers.

These are the hands whose sturdy labor brings
The peasant's food, the golden pomp of kings;
This is the page whose letters shall be seen
Changed by the sun to words of living green;
This is the scholar whose immortal pen
Spells the first lesson hunger taught to men;
These are the lines that heaven-commanded Toil
Shows on his deed,—the charter of the soil!

O gracious Mother, whose benignant breast
Wakes us to life, and lulls us all to rest,
How thy sweet features, kind to every clime,
Mock with their smile the wrinkled front of Time!
We stain thy flowers,—they blossom o'er the dead;
We rend thy bosom, and it gives us bread;
O'er the red field that trampling strife has torn
Waves the green plumage of thy tassell'd corn;
Our maddening conflicts scar thy fairest plain,
Still thy soft answer is the growing grain.

Yet, O our Mother, while uncounted charms
Steal round our hearts in thine embracing arms,
Let not our virtues in thy love decay,
And thy fond sweetness waste our strength away.
No! by these hills whose banners now display'd
In blazing cohorts Autumn has array'd;
By yon twin summits, on whose splintery crests
The tossing hemlocks hold the eagles' nests;
By these fair plains the mountain circle screens,
And feeds with streamlets from its dark ravines,—
True to their home, these faithful arms shall toil
To crown with peace their own untainted soil;
And, true to God, to freedom, to mankind,
If her chain'd ban-dogs Faction shall unbind,
These stately forms, that, bending even now,
Bow'd their strong manhood to the humble plough,
Shall rise erect, the guardians of the land,
The same stern iron in the same right hand,
Till o'er their hills the shouts of triumph run;
The sword has rescued what the ploughshare won!
                    OLIVER WENDELL HOLMES.

THE VILLAGE BLACKSMITH.

UNDER a spreading chestnut tree
  The village smithy stands;
The smith, a mighty man is he,
  With large and sinewy hands;
And the muscles of his brawny arms
  Are strong as iron bands.

His hair is crisp, and black, and long;
  His face is like the tan;
His brow is wet with honest sweat;
  He earns whate'er he can,
And looks the whole world in the face,
  For he owes not any man.

Week in, week out, from morn till night,
  You can hear his bellows blow;
You can hear him swing his heavy sledge,
  With measured beat and slow,
Like a sexton ringing the village bell
  When the evening sun is low.

And children coming home from school
  Look in at the open door;
They love to see the flaming forge,
  And hear the bellows roar,
And catch the burning sparks that fly
  Like chaff from a threshing-floor.

He goes on Sunday to the church,
  And sits among his boys;
He hears the parson pray and preach,
  He hears his daughter's voice
Singing in the village choir,
  And it makes his heart rejoice.

It sounds to him like her mother's voice
  Singing in Paradise!
He needs must think of her once more,
  How in the grave she lies;
And with his hard, rough hand he wipes
  A tear out of his eyes.

Toiling—rejoicing—sorrowing—
  Onward through life he goes:
Each morning sees some task begin,
  Each evening sees it close;
Something attempted—something done,
  Has earn'd a night's repose.

Thanks, thanks to thee, my worthy friend,
  For the lesson thou hast taught!
Thus at the flaming forge of Life
  Our fortunes must be wrought,
Thus on its sounding anvil shaped
  Each burning deed and thought.
                HENRY WADSWORTH LONGFELLOW.

THE FORGING OF THE ANCHOR.

COME, see the Dolphin's anchor forged!
  'tis at a white heat now—
The bellows ceased, the flames decreased,
  though, on the forge's brow,
The little flames still fitfully play through
  the sable mound,
And fitfully you still may see the grim
  smiths ranking round,

All clad in leathern panoply, their broad
    hands only bare,
Some rest upon their sledges here, some
    work the windlass there.

The windlass strains the tackle-chains,—
    the black mould heaves below,
And red and deep, a hundred veins burst
    out at every throe.
It rises, roars, rends all outright,—O Vulcan, what a glow!
'Tis blinding white, 'tis blasting bright,—
    the high sun shines not so!
The high sun sees not, on the earth, such
    fiery fearful show.
The roof-ribs swarth, the candent hearth,
    the ruddy lurid row
Of smiths, that stand, an ardent band,
    like men before the foe,
As, quivering through his fleece of flame,
    the sailing monster slow
Sinks on the anvil; all about, the faces
    fiery grow:
"Hurrah!" they shout, "leap out, leap
    out!" bang, bang! the sledges go;
Hurrah! the jetted lightnings are hissing
    high and low,
A hailing fount of fire is struck at every
    squashing blow;
The leathern mail rebounds the hail, the
    rattling cinders strow
The ground around; at every bound the
    sweltering fountains flow;
And, thick and loud, the swinking crowd
    at every stroke pant "Ho!"

Leap out, leap out, my masters! leap out,
    and lay on load;
Let's forge a goodly anchor—a bower thick
    and broad,
For a heart of oak is hanging on every
    blow, I bode,
And I see the good ship riding, all in a
    perilous road,
The low reef roaring on her lee, the roll
    of ocean pour'd
From stem to stern, sea after sea; the
    mainmast by the board;
The bulwarks down, the rudder gone, the
    boats stove at the chains;
But courage still, brave mariners, the
    bower yet remains!

And not an inch to flinch he deigns, save
    when ye pitch sky-high;
Then moves his head, as though he said,
    "Fear nothing, here am I!"

Swing in your strokes in order; let foot
    and hand keep time;
Your blows make music sweeter far than
    any steeple's chime.
But while ye swing your sledges, sing, and
    let the burthen be,
The anchor is the anvil king, and royal
    craftsmen we!
Strike in, strike in!—the sparks begin to
    dull their rustling red;
Our hammers ring with sharper din—our
    work will soon be sped;
Our anchor soon must change his bed of
    fiery rich array
For a hammock at the roaring bows, or an
    oozy couch of clay;
Our anchor soon must change the lay of
    merry craftsmen here
For the yeo-heave-o and the heave away,
    and the sighing seamen's cheer—
When, weighing slow, at eve they go, far,
    far from love and home;
And sobbing sweethearts, in a row, wail
    o'er the ocean foam.

In livid and obdurate gloom, he darkens
    down at last;
A shapely one he is, and strong, as e'er
    from cat was cast.
O trusted and trustworthy guard! if thou
    hadst life like me,
What pleasures would thy toils reward beneath the deep green sea!
O deep sea-diver, who might then behold
    such sights as thou?—
The hoary monster's palaces!—Methinks
    what joy 'twere now
To go plumb-plunging down, amid the assembly of the whales,
And feel the churn'd sea round me boil
    beneath their scourging tails!
Then deep in tangle-woods to fight the
    fierce sea-unicorn,
And send him foil'd and bellowing back,
    for all his ivory horn;

To leave the subtle sworder-fish of bony
    blade forlorn ;
And for the ghastly-grinning shark, to
    laugh his jaws to scorn ;
To leap down on the kraken's back, where
    'mid Norwegian isles
He lies, a lubber anchorage for sudden
    shallow'd miles—
Till, snorting like an under-sea volcano,
    off he rolls ;
Meanwhile to swing, a-buffeting the far
    astonish'd shoals
Of his back-browsing ocean-calves ; or,
    haply, in a cove
Shell-strown, and consecrate of old to
    some Undine's love,
To find the long-hair'd mermaidens ; or,
    hard by icy lands,
To wrestle with the sea-serpent, upon cerulean sands.

O broad-arm'd fisher of the deep ! whose
    sports can equal thine ?
The dolphin weighs a thousand tons that
    tugs thy cable line ;
And night by night 'tis thy delight, thy
    glory day by day,
Through sable sea and breaker white the
    giant game to play.
But, shamer of our little sports ! forgive
    the name I gave :
A fisher's joy is to destroy—thine office is
    to save.
O lodger in the sea-king's halls ! couldst
    thou but understand
Whose be the white bones by thy side—
    or who that dripping band,
Slow swaying in the heaving wave, that
    round about thee bend,
With sounds like breakers in a dream
    blessing their ancient friend—
Oh, couldst thou know what heroes glide
    with larger steps round thee,
Thine iron side would swell with pride—
    thou'dst leap within the sea !

Give honor to their memories who left the
    pleasant strand
To shed their blood so freely for the love
    of fatherland—
Who left their chance of quiet age and
    grassy churchyard grave
So freely, for a restless bed amid the tossing wave !
Oh, though our anchor may not be all I
    have fondly sung,
Honor him for their memory whose bones
    he goes among !
                  SAMUEL FERGUSON.

A LIFE ON THE OCEAN WAVE.

A LIFE on the ocean wave,
    A home on the rolling deep ;
Where the scatter'd waters rave,
    And the winds their revels keep !
Like an eagle caged I pine
    On this dull, unchanging shore :
Oh give me the flashing brine,
    The spray and the tempest's roar !

Once more on the deck I stand,
    Of my own swift-gliding craft :
Set sail ! farewell to the land ;
    The gale follows fair abaft.
We shoot through the sparkling foam,
    Like an ocean-bird set free,—
Like the ocean-bird, our home
    We'll find far out on the sea.

The land is no longer in view,
    The clouds have begun to frown ;
But with a stout vessel and crew,
    We'll say, Let the storm come down !
And the song of our hearts shall be,
    While the winds and the waters rave,
A home on the rolling sea !
    A life on the ocean wave !
                  EPES SARGENT.

A WET SHEET AND A FLOWING SEA.

A WET sheet and a flowing sea—
    A wind that follows fast,
And fills the white and rustling sail,
    And bends the gallant mast—
And bends the gallant mast, my boys,
    While, like the eagle free,
Away the good ship flies, and leaves
    Old England on the lee.

Oh for a soft and gentle wind!
  I heard a fair one cry;
But give to me the snoring breeze,
  And white waves heaving high—
And white waves heaving high, my boys,
  The good ship tight and free;
The world of waters is our home,
  And merry men are we.

There's tempest in yon hornèd moon,
  And lightning in yon cloud;
And hark the music, mariners!
  The wind is piping loud—
The wind is piping loud, my boys,
  The lightning flashing free;
While the hollow oak our palace is,
  Our heritage the sea.
        ALLAN CUNNINGHAM.

THE FISHERMAN'S SONG.

AWAY—away o'er the feathery crest
  Of the beautiful blue are we:
For our toil-lot lies on its boiling breast,
  And our wealth's in the glorious sea!
And we've hymn'd in the grasp of the
    fiercest night,
  To the God of the sons of toil,
As we cleft the wave by its own white
    light,
  And away with its scaly spoil.
    Then oh, for the long and the strong
      oar-sweep
    We have given, and will again!
    For when children's weal lies in the
      deep,
    Oh, their fathers *must* be men!

And we'll think, as the blast grows loud
    and long,
  That we hear our offspring's cries;
And we'll think, as the surge grows tall
    and strong,
  Of the tears in their mothers' eyes:
And we'll reel through the clutch of the
    shiv'ring green,
  For the warm, warm clasp at home—
For the welcoming shriek of each heart's
    own queen,
  When her cheek's like the flying foam.
    Then oh, for the long and the strong
      oar-sweep
    We have given, and *must* again!
    But when white waves leap, and our
      pale wives weep,
    O Heaven,—thy mercy then!

Do we yearn for the land when toss'd on
    this?
  Let it ring to the proud one's tread!
Far worse than the waters and winds may
    hiss
  Where the poor man gleans his bread.
If the adder-tongue of the upstart knave
  Can bleed what it may not bend,
'Twere better to battle the wildest wave
  That the spirit of storms could send,
    Than be singing farewell to the bold
      oar-sweep
    We have given, and will again;
    Though our souls *should* bow to the
      savage deep,
    Oh, they'll never to savage men!

And if Death, at times, through a foamy
    cloud,
  On the brown-brow'd boatman glares,
He can pay him his glance with a soul as
    proud
  As the form of a mortal bears;
And oh 'twere glorious, sure, to die,
  In our toils for *some* on shore,
With a hopeful eye fix'd calm on the sky,
  And a hand on the broken oar.
    Then oh, for the long and the strong
      oar-sweep!
    Hold to it!—hurrah!—dash on!
    If our babes must fast till we rob
      the deep,
    It is time we had begun!
        FRANCIS DAVIS.

THE MARINER'S DREAM.

IN slumbers of midnight the sailor boy
    lay;
  His hammock swung loose at the sport
    of the wind;
But watch-worn and weary, his care flew
    away,
  And visions of happiness danced o'er
    his mind.

He dream'd of his home, of his dear native
    bowers,
And pleasures that waited on life's merry
    morn;
While Memory stood sideways half cover'd
    with flowers,
And restored every rose, but secreted its
    thorn.

Then Fancy her magical pinions spread
    wide,
And bade the young dreamer in ecstasy
    rise;
Now far, far behind him the green waters
    glide,
And the cot of his forefathers blesses his
    eyes.

The jessamine clambers in flower o'er the
    thatch,
And the swallow sings sweet from her
    nest in the wall;
All trembling with transport, he raises the
    latch,
And the voices of loved ones reply to
    his call.

A father bends o'er him with looks of de-
    light;
His cheek is impearl'd with a mother's
    warm tear;
And the lips of the boy in a love-kiss
    unite
With the lips of the maid whom his
    bosom holds dear.

The heart of the sleeper beats high in his
    breast;
Joy quickens his pulses—his hardships
    seem o'er;
And a murmur of happiness steals through
    his rest—
Kind Fate, thou hast blest me—I ask for
    no more.

Ah! what is that flame which now bursts
    on his eye?
Ah! what is that sound which now
    'larums his ear?
'Tis the lightning's red glare, painting hell
    on the sky!
'Tis the crashing of thunders, the groan
    of the sphere!

He springs from his hammock—he flies to
    the deck;
Amazement confronts him with images
    dire;
Wild winds and mad waves drive the ves-
    sel a wreck;
The masts fly in splinters; the shrouds
    are on fire!

Like mountains the billows tremendously
    swell;
In vain the lost wretch calls on Mercy
    to save;
Unseen hands of spirits are ringing his
    knell;
And the death-angel flaps his broad wing
    o'er the wave!

O sailor boy! woe to thy dream of de-
    light!
In darkness dissolves the gay frost-work
    of bliss.
Where now is the picture that Fancy
    touch'd bright—
Thy parents' fond pressure and love's
    honey'd kiss?

O sailor boy! sailor boy! never again
Shall home, love, or kindred thy wishes
    repay;
Unbless'd and unhonor'd, down deep in
    the main,
Full many a fathom, thy frame shall de-
    cay.

No tomb shall e'er plead to remembrance
    for thee,
Or redeem form or frame from the mer-
    ciless surge;
But the white foam of waves shall thy
    winding-sheet be,
And winds, in the midnight of winter,
    thy dirge!

On beds of green sea-flowers thy limbs
    shall be laid;
Around thy white bones the red coral
    shall grow;
Of thy fair yellow locks threads of amber
    be made;
And every part suit to thy mansion be-
    low.

Days, months, years, and ages shall circle away,
And still the vast waters above thee shall roll;—
Earth loses thy pattern for ever and aye:—
O sailor boy! sailor boy! peace to thy soul!
WILLIAM DIMOND.

POOR JACK.

Go patter to lubbers and swabs, do ye see,
'Bout danger, and fear, and the like;
A tight water-boat and good sea-room give me,
And it ent to a little I'll strike:
Though the tempest top-gallant masts smack smooth should smite,
And shiver each splinter of wood,
Clear the wreck, stow the yards, and bouse everything tight,
And under reef'd foresail we'll scud:
Avast! nor don't think me a milksop so soft
To be taken for trifles aback;
For they say there's a Providence sits up aloft,
To keep watch for the life of poor Jack.

I heard our good chaplain palaver one day
About souls, heaven, mercy, and such;
And, my timbers! what lingo he'd coil and belay,
Why, 'twas just all as one as High Dutch:
For he said how a sparrow can't founder, d'ye see,
Without orders that come down below;
And a many fine things that proved clearly to me
That Providence takes us in tow:
For, says he, do you mind me, let storms e'er so oft
Take the topsails of sailors aback,
There's a sweet little cherub that sits up aloft,
To keep watch for the life of poor Jack.

I said to our Poll—for, d'ye see, she would cry,
When last we weigh'd anchor for sea—
What argufies sniv'lling and piping your eye?
Why, what a damn'd fool you must be!
Can't you see the world's wide, and there's room for us all,
Both for seamen and lubbers ashore?
And if to old Davy I should go, friend Poll,
You never will hear of me more:
What then? all's a hazard: come, don't be so soft,
Perhaps I may laughing come back,
For, d'ye see, there's a cherub sits smiling aloft,
To keep watch for the life of poor Jack.

D'ye mind me, a sailor should be every inch
All as one as a piece of the ship,
And with her brave the world without offering to flinch,
From the moment the anchor's a-trip.
As for me, in all weathers, all times, sides, and ends,
Naught's a trouble from duty that springs,
For my heart is my Poll's, and my rhino's my friend's,
And as for my life, 'tis the king's:
Even when my time comes, ne'er believe me so soft
As for grief to be taken aback,
For the same little cherub that sits up aloft
Will look out a good berth for poor Jack.
CHARLES DIBDIN.

HANNAH BINDING SHOES.

Poor lone Hannah,
Sitting at the window, binding shoes!
Faded, wrinkled,
Sitting, stitching, in a mournful muse!
Bright-eyed beauty once was she,
When the bloom was on the tree:
Spring and winter
Hannah's at the window, binding shoes.

Not a neighbor
Passing nod or answer will refuse
To her whisper,
"Is there from the fishers any news?"
Oh, her heart's adrift with one
On an endless voyage gone!
Night and morning
Hannah's at the window, binding shoes.

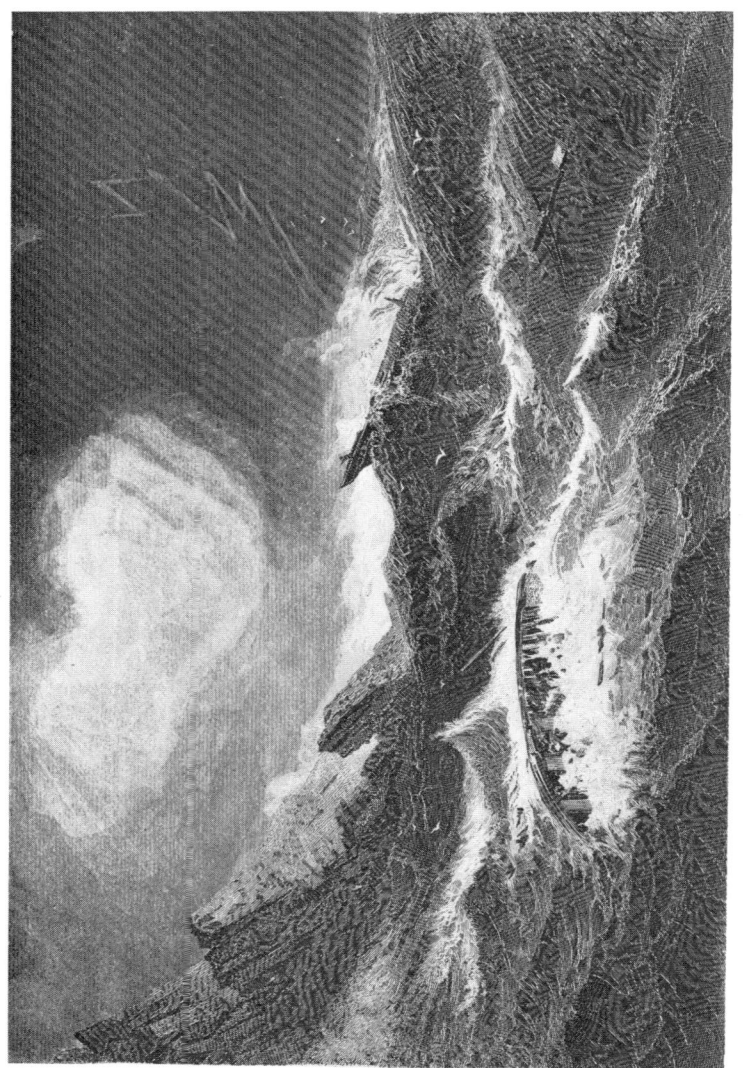

"FOR MEN MUST WORK AND WOMEN MUST WEEP
THOUGH STORMS BE SUDDEN AND WATERS DEEP"
The Three Fishers.

Fair young Hannah,
Ben, the sunburnt fisher, gayly woos;
Hale and clever,
For a willing heart and hand he sues.
  May-day skies are all aglow,
  And the waves are laughing so!
    For her wedding
Hannah leaves her window and her shoes.

    May is passing:
Mid the apple-boughs a pigeon coos.
    Hannah shudders,
For the mild south-wester mischief brews.
  Round the rocks of Marblehead,
  Outward bound, a schooner sped:
    Silent, lonesome,
Hannah's at the window, binding shoes.

    'Tis November.
Now no tears her wasted cheek bedews.
    From Newfoundland
Not a sail returning will she lose,
  Whispering hoarsely, "Fisherman,
  Have you, have you heard of Ben?"
    Old with watching,
Hannah's at the window, binding shoes.

    Twenty winters
Bleach and tear the ragged shore she views.
    Twenty seasons;—
Never one has brought her any news.
  Still her dim eyes silently
  Chase the white sail o'er the sea:
    Hopeless, faithful,
Hannah's at the window, binding shoes.
                                LUCY LARCOM.

THE THREE FISHERS.

THREE fishers went sailing away to the west—
  Away to the west as the sun went down;
Each thought on the woman who loved him the best,
  And the children stood watching them out of the town;
For men must work, and women must weep;
And there's little to earn, and many to keep,
  Though the harbor bar be moaning.

Three wives sat up in the lighthouse tower,
  And they trimm'd the lamps as the sun went down;
They look'd at the squall, and they look'd at the shower,
  And the night-rack came rolling up, ragged and brown;
But men must work, and women must weep,
Though storms be sudden, and waters deep,
  And the harbor bar be moaning.

Three corpses lay out on the shining sands
  In the morning gleam as the tide went down,
And the women are weeping and wringing their hands
  For those who will never come home to the town;
For men must work, and women must weep—
And the sooner it's over, the sooner to sleep—
  And good-bye to the bar and its moaning.
                            CHARLES KINGSLEY.

"THEY'RE DEAR FISH TO ME."

THE farmer's wife sat at the door,
  A pleasant sight to see;
And blithesome were the wee, wee bairns
  That play'd around her knee.

When, bending 'neath her heavy creel,
  A poor fish-wife came by,
And, turning from the toilsome road,
  Unto the door drew nigh.

She laid her burden on the green,
  And spread its scaly store,
With trembling hands and pleading words
  She told them o'er and o'er.

But lightly laugh'd the young guidwife,
  "We're no sae scarce o' cheer;
Tak up your creel, and gang your ways,—
  I'll buy nae fish sae dear."

Bending beneath her load again,
  A weary sight to see;
Right sorely sigh'd the poor fish-wife,
  "They're dear fish to me!

"Our boat was oot ae fearfu' night,
  And when the storm blew o'er,
My husband, and my three brave sons,
  Lay corpses on the shore.

"I've been a wife for thirty years,
  A childless widow three;
I maun buy them now to sell again,—
  They're dear fish to me!"

The farmer's wife turn'd to the door,—
  What was't upon her cheek?
What was there rising in her breast,
  That then she scarce could speak?

She thought upon her ain guid man,
  Her lightsome laddies three;
The woman's words had pierced her heart,—
  "They're dear fish to me!"

"Come back," she cried, with quivering voice
  And pity's gathering tear;
"Come in, come in, my poor woman,
  Ye're kindly welcome here.

"I kentna o' your aching heart,
  Your weary lot to dree;
I'll ne'er forget your sad, sad words:
  'They're dear fish to me!'"

Ay, let the happy-hearted learn
  To pause ere they deny
The meed of honest toil, and think
  How much their gold may buy,—

How much of manhood's wasted strength,
  What woman's misery,—
What breaking hearts might swell the cry:
  "They're dear fish to me!"
              AUTHOR UNKNOWN.

THE PEARL-WEARER.

WITHIN the midnight of her hair,
  Half hidden in its deepest deeps,
A single peerless, priceless pearl,
  All filmy-eyed, for ever sleeps.
Without the diamond's sparkling eyes,
The ruby's blushes,—there it lies!
Modest as the tender Dawn
When her purple veil's withdrawn,—
The flower of gems,—a lily, cold and pale!
Yet, what doth all avail?
All its beauty, all its grace,
All the honors of its place?
He who pluck'd it from its bed
  In the far blue Indian Ocean,
  Lieth, without life or motion,
In his earthly dwelling,—dead!
And his children, one by one,
  When they look upon the sun,
Curse the toil by which he drew
The treasure from its bed of blue.

Gentle bride, no longer wear
In thy night-black, odorous hair
Such a spoil! It is not fit
That a tender soul should sit
Under such accursed gem.
What needst thou a diadem?—
Thou, within whose Eastern eyes
Thought, a starry genius, lies?—
Thou, whom Beauty has array'd,—
Thou, whom Love and Truth have made
Beautiful?—in whom we trace
Woman's softness, angel's grace,—
All we hope for, all that streams
Upon us in our haunted dreams!

O sweet Lady! cast aside,
With a gentle, noble pride,
All to sin or pain allied.
Let the wild-eyed conqueror wear
The bloody laurel in his hair;
Let the black and snaky vine
Round the drinker's temples twine;
Let the slave-begotten gold
Weigh on bosoms hard and cold;
But be thou for ever known
By thy natural light alone!
              BRYAN WALLER PROCTER.
              (BARRY CORNWALL.)

SOLDIER, REST.

SOLDIER, rest! thy warfare o'er,
  Sleep the sleep that knows not breaking!
Dream of battled fields no more,
  Days of danger, nights of waking.
In our isle's enchanted hall
  Hands unseen thy couch are strewing,
Fairy streams of music fall,
  Every sense in slumber dewing.
Soldier, rest! thy warfare o'er,
  Dream of fighting fields no more;
Sleep the sleep that knows not breaking,
  Morn of toil, nor night of waking.

No rude sound shall reach thine ear,
　　Armor's clang or war-steed champing,
Trump nor pibroch summon here
　　Mustering clan or squadron tramping.
Yet the lark's shrill fife may come,
　　At the daybreak from the fallow,
And the bittern sound his drum,
　　Booming from the sedgy shallow.
Ruder sounds shall none be near,
Guards nor warders challenge here,
Here's no war-steed's neigh and champing,
Shouting clans or squadrons stamping.

Huntsman, rest! thy chase is done,
　　While our slumb'rous spells assail ye,
Dream not with the rising sun,
　　Bugles here shall sound reveillé.
Sleep! the deer is in his den;
　　Sleep! thy hounds are by thee lying;
Sleep! nor dream in yonder glen
　　How thy gallant steed lay dying.
Huntsman, rest! thy chase is done,
Think not of the rising sun,
For at dawning to assail ye,
Here no bugles sound reveillé.
　　　　　　　　　Sir Walter Scott.

THE BOATIE ROWS.

Oh, weel may the boatie row,
　　And better may she speed!
And weel may the boatie row,
　　That wins the bairns's bread!
The boatie rows, the boatie rows,
　　The boatie rows indeed;
And happy be the lot of a'
　　That wishes her to speed!

I cuist my line in Largo Bay,
　　And fishes I caught nine;
There's three to boil, and three to fry,
　　And three to bait the line,
The boatie rows, the boatie rows,
　　The boatie rows indeed;
And happy be the lot of a'
　　That wishes her to speed!

Oh, weel may the boatie row,
　　That fills a heavy creel,
And cleads us a' frae head to feet,
　　And buys our parritch meal.
The boatie rows, the boatie rows,
　　The boatie rows indeed;
And happy be the lot of a'
　　That wish' the boatie speed!

When Jamie vowed he would be mine,
　　And wan frae me my heart,
Oh, muckle lighter grew my creel!
　　He swore we'd never part!
The boatie rows, the boatie rows,
　　The boatie rows fu' weel;
And muckle lighter is the lade
　　When love bears up the creel.

My kurtch I put upon my head,
　　And dressed mysel' fu' braw:
I trow my heart was dowf and wae
　　When Jamie gaed awa:
But weel may the boatie row,
　　And lucky be her part;
And lightsome be the lassie's care
　　That yields an honest heart!

When Sawnie, Jock, and Janetie
　　Are up, and gotten lear,
They'll help to gar the boatie row,
　　And lighten a' our care.
The boatie rows, the boatie rows,
　　The boatie rows fu' weel;
And lightsome be her heart that bears
　　The murlain and the creel!

And when wi' age we are worn down,
　　And hirpling round the door,
They'll row to keep us hale and warm,
　　As we did them before:
Then, weel may the boatie row,
　　That wins the bairns's bread;
And happy be the lot of a'
　　That wish the boat to speed!
　　　　　　　　　John Ewen.

YE GENTLEMEN OF ENGLAND.

Ye gentlemen of England
　　That live at home at ease,
Ah! little do you think upon
　　The dangers of the seas.
Give ear unto the mariners,
　　And they will plainly show

All the cares and the fears
  When the stormy winds do blow.

If enemies oppose us
  When England is at war
With any foreign nation,
  We fear not wound or scar;
Our roaring guns shall teach 'em
  Our valor for to know,
Whilst they reel on the keel,
  And the stormy winds do blow.

Then courage, all brave mariners,
  And never be dismay'd;
While we have bold adventurers,
  We ne'er shall want a trade:
Our merchants will employ us
  To fetch them wealth, we know;
Then be bold—work for gold,
  When the stormy winds do blow.
MARTYN PARKER.

THE LABORER.

TOILING in the naked fields,
Where no bush a shelter yields,
Needy Labor dithering stands,
Beats and blows his numbing hands,
And upon the crumping snows
Stamps in vain to warm his toes.

Though all's in vain to keep him warm,
Poverty must brave the storm,
Friendship none its aid to lend,—
Constant health his only friend,
Granting leave to live in pain,
Giving strength to toil in vain.
JOHN CLARE.

CORONATION.

AT the king's gate the subtle noon
  Wove filmy yellow nets of sun;
Into the drowsy snare too soon
  The guards fell one by one.

Through the king's gate, unquestioned then,
  A beggar went, and laughed, "This brings
Me chance, at last, to see if men
  Fare better, being kings."

The king sat bowed beneath his crown,
  Propping his face with listless hand;
Watching the hour-glass sifting down
  Too slow its shining sand.

"Poor man, what wouldst thou have of me?"
  The beggar turned, and, pitying,
Replied, like one in a dream, "Of thee,
  Nothing. I want the king."

Uprose the king, and from his head
  Shook off the crown and threw it by.
"O man, thou must have known," he said,
  "A greater king than I!"

Through all the gates, unquestioned then,
  Went king and beggar hand in hand.
Whispered the king, "Shall I know when
  Before *his* throne I stand?"

The beggar laughed. Free winds in haste
  Were wiping from the king's hot brow
The crimson lines the crown had traced.
  "This is his presence now."

At the king's gate, the crafty noon
  Unwove its yellow nets of sun;
Out of their sleep in terror soon
  The guards waked one by one.

"Ho here! ho here! Has no man seen
  The king?" The cry ran to and fro;
Beggar and king, they laughed, I ween,
  The laugh that freemen know.

On the king's gate the moss grew gray:
  The king came not. They called him dead;
And made his eldest son one day
  Slave in his father's stead.
HELEN HUNT.

TOM DUNSTAN; OR, THE POLITICIAN.

Now poor Tom Dunstan's cold,
  Our shop is duller;
Scarce a story is told,
And our chat has lost the old
  Red republican color!

Though he was sickly and thin,
  'Twas a sight to see his face,—
While, sick of the country's sin,
  With bang of the fist, and chin
Thrust out, he argued the case!
He prophesied men should be free,
  And the money-bags be bled;—
"She's coming, she's coming," said he;
"Courage, boys! wait and see!
  Freedom's ahead!"

All day we sat in the heat,
  Like spiders spinning,
Stitching full fine and fleet,
While old Moses on his seat
  Sat greasily grinning;
And here Tom said his say,
  And prophesied Tyranny's death;
And the tallow burnt all day,
And we stitch'd and stitch'd away
  In the thick smoke of our breath.
Weary, weary were we,
  Our hearts as heavy as lead,—
But "Patience! she's coming!" said he;
"Courage, boys! wait and see!
  Freedom's ahead!"

And at night, when we took here
  The rest allow'd to us,
The paper came with the beer,
And Tom read, sharp and clear,
  The news out loud to us,
And then, in his witty way,
  He threw the jests about,—
The cutting things he'd say
Of the wealthy and the gay!
  How he turn'd them inside out!
And it made our breath more free
  To hearken to what he said:
"She's coming, she's coming!" said he;
"Courage, boys! wait and see!
  Freedom's ahead!"

But grim Jack Hart, with a sneer,
  Would mutter, "Master,
If Freedom means to appear,
I think she might step here
  A little faster!"
Then 'twas fine to see Tom flame,
  And argue and prove and preach,
Till Jack was silent for shame,
Or a fit of coughing came
  O' sudden to spoil Tom's speech.

Ah! Tom had the eyes to see
  When Tyranny should be sped;—
"She's coming, she's coming!" said he;
"Courage, boys! wait and see!
  Freedom's ahead!"

But Tom was little and weak;
  The hard hours shook him;
Hollower grew his cheek,
And when he began to speak
  The coughing took him.
Erelong the cheery sound
  Of his chat among us ceased,
And we made a purse all round,
That he might not starve, at least.
His pain was sorry to see,
  Yet there, on his poor, sick bed,
"She's coming, in spite of me!
Courage and wait!" cried he,
  "Freedom's ahead!"

A little before he died,
  To see his passion!
"Bring me a paper!" he cried,
And then to study it tried
  In his old sharp fashion;
And, with eyeballs glittering,
  His look on me he bent,
And said that savage thing
Of the lords o' the Parliament.
Then, dying, smiling on me,
  "What matter if one be dead?
She's coming, at last!" said he;
"Courage, boys! wait and see!
  Freedom's ahead!"

Ay, now Tom Dunstan's cold,
  The shop feels duller;
Scarce a tale is told,
And our talk has lost the old
  Red republican color.
But we see a figure gray,
  And we hear a voice of death,
And the tallow burns all day,
And we stitch and stitch away
  In the thick smoke of our breath;
Ay, while in the dark sit we,
  Tom seems to call from the dead—
"She's coming, she's coming!" says he;
"Courage, boys! wait and see!
  Freedom's ahead!"

How long, O Lord, how long
  Must Thy handmaid linger?
She who shall right the wrong,
  Make the poor sufferer strong?
Sweet morrow, bring her!
  Hasten her over the sea,
O Lord, ere hope be fled,—
  Bring her to men and to me!
O slave, pray still on thy knee,
  "Freedom's ahead!"
                ROBERT BUCHANAN.

THE DEAD POLITICIAN.

FIFTH WARD.

"'Who's dead?' Ye want to know
Whose is this funeral show—
      This A 1 corteg'?
Well, it was Jim Adair,
And the remains's hair
      Sported a short edge!

"When a man dies like Jim,
There's no expense of him
      We boys are sparing.
In life he hated fuss,
But—as he's left to us—
      Them plumes he's wearing.

"All the boys here, you see,
  Chock full each carriage!
Only one woman. She,
  Cousin by marriage.

"Who was this Jim Adair?
Who? Well, you've got me there!
Reckon one of them 'air
      Fogy 'old res'dents.'
Who? Why, that corpse you see
Ridin' so peacefully,
Head o' this jamboree—
      'Lected three Pres'dents!

"Who was he? Ask the boys
Who made the biggest noise,
      Rynders or Jimmy?
Who, when his hat he'd fling,
Knew how the 'Ayes' would ring,
      Oh no! not Jimmy!

"Who was he? Ask the Ward
Who hed the rules aboard,
      All parliament'ry?

Who ran the delegate
That ran the Empire State,
And—just as sure as fate—
      Ran the whole 'kentry?

"Who was he? S'pose you try
That chap as wipes his eye
      In that hack's corner;
Ask him, the only man
That agin Jimmy ran,—
      Now his chief mourner!

"Well, that's the last o' Jim.
Yes, we *was* proud o' him."
                F. BRET HARTE.

A MAN'S A MAN FOR A' THAT.

Is there for honest poverty
  That hangs his head, an' a' that?
The coward slave, we pass him by;
  We dare be poor for a' that!
For a' that, an' a' that,
  Our toils obscure, an' a' that;
The rank is but the guinea's stamp—
  The man's the gowd for a' that!

What tho' on hamely fare we dine,
  Wear hoddin gray, an' a' that;
Gie fools their silks, and knaves their wine—
  A man's a man for a' that!
For a' that, an' a' that,
  Their tinsel show, an' a' that;
The honest man, though e'er sae poor,
  Is king o' men for a' that!

You see yon birkie ca'd a lord,
  Wha struts, an' stares, an' a' that—
Tho' hundreds worship at his word,
  He's but a coof for a' that;
For a' that, an' a' that,
  His riband, star, an' a' that;
The man o' independent mind,
  He looks an' laughs at a' that.

A prince can mak a belted knight,
  A marquis, duke, an' a' that;
But an honest man's aboon his might—
  Gude faith, he mauna fa' that!
For a' that, an' a' that,
  Their dignities, an' a' that,
The pith o' sense, an' pride o' worth,
  Are higher rank than a' that.

Then let us pray that come it may,
  As come it will for a' that,
That sense an' worth, o'er a' the earth,
  Shall bear the gree, an' a' that.
For a' that, an' a' that,
  It's comin' yet, for a' that—
The man to man, the warld o'er,
  Shall brothers be for a' that.
ROBERT BURNS.

THE HERITAGE.

THE rich man's son inherits lands,
  And piles of brick, and stone, and gold;
And he inherits soft white hands,
  And tender flesh, that fears the cold,
  Nor dares to wear a garment old;
A heritage, it seems to me,
One scarce would wish to hold in fee.

The rich man's son inherits cares:
  The bank may break, the factory burn,
A breath may burst his bubble shares,
  And soft white hands could hardly earn
  A living that would serve his turn;
A heritage, it seems to me,
One scarce would wish to hold in fee.

The rich man's son inherits wants,
  His stomach craves for dainty fare;
With sated heart he hears the pants
  Of toiling hinds with brown arms bare,
  And wearies in his easy-chair;
A heritage, it seems to me,
One scarce would wish to hold in fee.

What doth the poor man's son inherit?
  Stout muscles and a sinewy heart,
A hardy frame, a hardier spirit;
  King of two hands, he does his part
  In every useful toil and art;
A heritage, it seems to me,
A king might wish to hold in fee.

What doth the poor man's son inherit?
  Wishes o'erjoy'd with humble things,
A rank adjudged with toil-won merit,
  Content that from employment springs,
  A heart that in his labor sings;
A heritage, it seems to me,
A king might wish to hold in fee.

What doth the poor man's son inherit?
  A patience learn'd of being poor,
Courage, if sorrow come, to bear it,
  A fellow-feeling that is sure
  To make the outcast bless his door;
A heritage, it seems to me,
A king might wish to hold in fee.

O rich man's son! there is a toil
  That with all others level stands:
Large charity doth never soil,
  But only whiten, soft white hands,—
  This is the best crop from thy lands;
A heritage, it seems to me,
Worth being rich to hold in fee.

O poor man's son! scorn not thy state;
  There is worse weariness than thine—
In merely being rich and great:
  Toil only gives the soul to shine,
  And makes rest fragrant and benign,—
A heritage, it seems to me,
Worth being poor to hold in fee.

Both, heirs to some six feet of sod,
  Are equal in the earth at last:
Both, children of the same dear God,
  Prove title to your heirship vast
  By record of a well-fill'd past;
A heritage, it seems to me,
Well worth a life to hold in fee.
JAMES RUSSELL LOWELL.

DIFFERENCES.

I.

THE king can drink the best of wine—
  So can I;
And has enough when he would dine—
  So have I;
And cannot order rain or shine—
  Nor can I.
Then where's the difference—let me see—
Betwixt my lord the king and me?

II.

Do trusty friends surround his throne
  Night and day?
Or make his interest their own?
  No, not they.
Mine love me for myself alone—
  Bless'd be they!
And that's the difference which I see
Betwixt my lord the king and me.

III.

Do knaves around me lie in wait
    To deceive?
Or fawn and flatter when they hate,
    And would grieve?
Or cruel pomps oppress my state
    By my leave?
No, Heaven be thank'd! And here you see
More difference 'twixt the king and me.

IV.

He has his fools, with jests and quips,
    When he'd play;
He has his armies and his ships—
    Great are they;
But not a child to kiss his lips;
    Well-a-day!
And that's a difference sad to see
Betwixt my lord the king and me.

V.

I wear the cap and he the crown—
    What of that?
I sleep on straw and he on down—
    What of that?
And he's the king and I'm the clown—
    What of that?
If happy I, and wretched he,
Perhaps the king would change with me.
    CHARLES MACKAY.

WE ARE BRETHREN A'.

A HAPPY bit hame this auld world would be
If men, when they're here, could make shift to agree,
An' ilk said to his neighbor, in cottage an' ha',
"Come, gi'e me your hand,—we are brethren a'."

I ken na why ane wi' anither should fight,
When to 'gree would make a' body cosie an' right,
When man meets wi' man, 'tis the best way ava,
To say, "Gi'e me your hand,—we are brethren a'."

My coat is a coarse ane, an' yours may be fine,
And I maun drink water, while you may drink wine;
But we baith ha'e a leal heart, unspotted to shaw:
Sae gi'e me your hand,—we are brethren a'.

The knave ye would scorn, the unfaithfu' deride;
Ye would stand like a rock, wi' the truth on your side;
Sae would I, an' naught else would I value a straw:
Then gi'e me your hand,—we are brethren a'.

Ye would scorn to do fausely by woman or man;
I haud by the right aye, as weel as I can;
We are ane in our joys, our affections, an' a':
Come, gi'e me your hand,—we are brethren a'.

Your mither has lo'ed you as mithers can lo'e;
An' mine has done for me what mithers can do;
We are ane high an' laigh, an' we shouldna be twa:
Sae gi'e me your hand,—we are brethren a'.

We love the same simmer day, sunny and fair;
Hame! oh, how we love it, an' a' that are there!
Frae the puir air o' heaven the same life we draw:
Come, gi'e me your hand,—we are brethren a'.

Frail shakin' auld age will soon come o'er us baith,
An' creepin' alang at his back will be death;
Syne into the same mither-yird we will fa':
Come, gi'e me your hand,—we are brethren a'.
    ROBERT NICOLL.

WITHOUT AND WITHIN.

My coachman, in the moonlight there,
  Looks through the side-light of the door;
I hear him with his brethren swear,
  As I could do,—but only more.

Flattening his nose against the pane,
  He envies me my brilliant lot,
Breathes on his aching fists in vain,
  And dooms me to a place more hot.

He sees me in to supper go,
  A silken wonder by my side,
Bare arms, bare shoulders, and a row
  Of flounces, for the door too wide.

He thinks how happy is my arm
  'Neath its white-gloved and jewell'd load;
And wishes me some dreadful harm,
  Hearing the merry corks explode.

Meanwhile I inly curse the bore
  Of hunting still the same old coon,
And envy him, outside the door,
  In golden quiets of the moon.

The winter wind is not so cold
  As the bright smile he sees me win,
Nor the host's oldest wine so old
  As our poor gabble sour and thin.

I envy him the ungyved prance
  By which his freezing feet he warms,
And drag my lady's chains and dance
  The galley-slave of dreary forms.

Oh, could he have my share of din,
  And I his quiet!—past a doubt
'Twould still be one man bored within,
  And just another bored without.
           JAMES RUSSELL LOWELL.

EACH AND ALL.

LITTLE thinks, in the field, yon red-cloak'd clown
Of thee from the hill-top looking down;
The heifer that lows in the upland farm,
Far heard, lows not thine ear to charm;
The sexton tolling his bell at noon,
Deems not that great Napoleon
Stops his horse, and lists with delight,
Whilst his files sweep round yon Alpine height;
Nor knowest thou what argument
Thy life to thy neighbor's creed has lent.
All are needed by each one;
Nothing is fair or good alone.
I thought the sparrow's note from heaven,
  Singing at dawn on the alder bough;
I brought him home, in his nest, at even;
  He sings the song, but it cheers not now,
For I did not bring home the river and sky;—
He sang to my ear,—they sang to my eye.
  The delicate shells lay on the shore;
The bubbles of the latest wave
Fresh pearls to their enamel gave;
And the bellowing of the savage sea
Greeted their safe escape to me.
I wiped away the weeds and foam,
I fetched my sea-born treasures home;
But the poor, unsightly, noisome things
  Had left their beauty on the shore,
  With the sun and the sand and the wild uproar.
The lover watch'd his graceful maid,
As 'mid the virgin train she stray'd,
Nor knew her beauty's best attire
Was woven still by the snow-white choir.
At last she came to his hermitage,
Like the bird from the woodlands to the cage;—
The gay enchantment was undone,
A gentle wife, but fairy none.
Then I said, "I covet truth;
  Beauty is unripe childhood's cheat;
I leave it behind with the games of youth."
As I spoke, beneath my feet
The ground-pine curl'd its pretty wreath,
  Running over the club-moss burrs;
I inhaled the violet's breath;
  Around me stood the oaks and firs;
Pine-cones and acorns lay on the ground;
Over me soar'd the eternal sky,
Full of light and of deity;
Again I saw, again I heard,
The rolling river, the morning bird;—
Beauty through my senses stole;
I yielded myself to the perfect whole.
           RALPH WALDO EMERSON.

NOTHING TO WEAR.

An Episode of City Life.

Miss Flora M'Flimsey, of Madison Square,
  Has made three separate journeys to Paris,
And her father assures me, each time she was there,
  That she and her friend Mrs. Harris
(Not the lady whose name is so famous in history,
But plain Mrs. H., without romance or mystery)
Spent six consecutive weeks without stopping,
In one continuous round of shopping;
Shopping alone, and shopping together,
At all hours of the day, and in all sorts of weather;
For all manner of things that a woman can put
On the crown of her head or the sole of her foot,
Or wrap round her shoulders, or fit round her waist,
Or that can be sew'd on, or pinn'd on, or laced,
Or tied on with a string, or stitch'd on with a bow,
In front or behind, above or below:
For bonnets, mantillas, capes, collars, and shawls;
Dresses for breakfasts, and dinners, and balls;
Dresses to sit in, and stand in, and walk in;
Dresses to dance in, and flirt in, and talk in;
Dresses in which to do nothing at all;
Dresses for winter, spring, summer, and fall;
All of them different in color and pattern,
Silk, muslin, and lace, crape, velvet, and satin,
Brocade, and broadcloth, and other material,
Quite as expensive and much more ethereal;
In short, for all things that could ever be thought of,
Or milliner, *modiste*, or tradesman be bought of,
From ten-thousand-francs robes to twenty-sous frills;
In all quarters of Paris, and to every store,
While M'Flimsey in vain storm'd, scolded, and swore,
  They footed the streets, and he footed the bills.

The last trip, their goods shipp'd by the steamer Arago
Form'd, M'Flimsey declares, the bulk of her cargo,
Not to mention a quantity kept from the rest,
Sufficient to fill the largest-sized chest,
Which did not appear on the ship's manifest,
But for which the ladies themselves manifested
Such particular interest that they invested
Their own proper persons in layers and rows
Of muslins, embroideries, work'd underclothes,
Gloves, handkerchiefs, scarfs, and such trifles as those;
Then, wrapp'd in great shawls, like Circassian beauties,
Gave *good-bye* to the ship, and *go-by* to the duties.
Her relations at home all marvell'd, no doubt,
Miss Flora had grown so enormously stout
  For an actual belle and a possible bride;
But the miracle ceased when she turn'd inside out,
  And the truth came to light, and the dry-goods beside,
Which, in spite of collector and custom-house sentry,
Had entered the port without any entry.

And yet, though scarce three months have pass'd since the day
This merchandise went, on twelve carts, up Broadway,
This same Miss M'Flimsey, of Madison Square,
The last time we met, was in utter despair,
Because she had nothing whatever to wear!

NOTHING TO WEAR! Now, as this is a true ditty,
I do not assert—this, you know, is between us—
That she's in a state of absolute nudity,
Like Powers' Greek Slave or the Medici Venus;
But I do mean to say, I have heard her declare,
When, at the same moment, she had on a dress
Which cost five hundred dollars, and not a cent less,
And jewelry worth ten times more, I should guess,
That she had not a thing in the wide world to wear!

I should mention just here, that out of Miss Flora's
Two hundred and fifty or sixty adorers,
I had just been selected as he who should throw all
The rest in the shade, by the gracious bestowal
On myself, after twenty or thirty rejections,
Of those fossil remains which she call'd her "affections,"
And that rather decay'd, but well-known work of art,
Which Miss Flora persisted in styling "her heart."
So we were engaged. Our troth had been plighted,
Not by moonbeam or starbeam, by fountain or grove,
But in a front parlor, most brilliantly lighted,
Beneath the gas-fixtures we whisper'd our love.
Without any romance, or raptures, or sighs,
Without any tears in Miss Flora's blue eyes,
Or blushes, or transports, or such silly actions,
It was one of the quietest business transactions,
With a very small sprinkling of sentiment, if any,
And a very large diamond imported by Tiffany.

On her virginal lips while I printed a kiss,
She exclaim'd, as a sort of parenthesis,
And by way of putting me quite at my ease,
"You know, I'm to polka as much as I please,
And flirt when I like—now stop, don't you speak—
And you must not come here more than twice in the week,
Or talk to me either at party or ball,
But always be ready to come when I call;
So don't prose to me about duty and stuff,
If we don't break this off, there will be time enough
For that sort of thing; but the bargain must be
That, as long as I choose, I am perfectly free,
For this is a sort of engagement, you see,
Which is binding on you, but not binding on me."

Well, having thus woo'd Miss M'Flimsey, and gain'd her,
With the silks, crinolines, and hoops that contain'd her,
I had, as I thought, a contingent remainder
At least in the property, and the best right
To appear as its escort by day and by night;
And it being the week of the Stuckups' grand ball—
Their cards had been out a fortnight or so,
And set all the Avenue on the tip-toe—
I considered it only my duty to call,
And see if Miss Flora intended to go.
I found her—as ladies are apt to be found,
When the time intervening between the first sound
Of the bell and the visitor's entry is shorter
Than usual—I found—I won't say, I caught—her
Intent on the pier-glass, undoubtedly meaning
To see if perhaps it didn't need cleaning.
She turn'd as I enter'd—"Why, Harry, you sinner,
I thought that you went to the Flashers' to dinner!"

"So I did," I replied, "but the dinner is
    swallow'd,
  And digested, I trust, for 'tis now nine
    and more,
So being relieved from that duty, I fol-
    low'd
  Inclination, which led me, you see, to
    your door.
And now will your ladyship so condescend
As just to inform me if you intend
Your beauty, and graces, and presence to
    lend,
  (All which, when I own, I hope no one
    will borrow)
To the Stuckups', whose party, you know,
    is to-morrow?"

The fair Flora look'd up with a pitiful air,
And answer'd quite promptly, "Why
    Harry, *mon cher*,
I should like above all things to go with
    you there;
But really and truly—I've nothing to
    wear."

"Nothing to wear! Go just as you are;
Wear the dress you have on, and you'll be
    by far,
I engage, the most bright and particular
    star
  On the Stuckup horizon"—I stopp'd,
    for her eye,
Notwithstanding this delicate onset of
    flattery,
  Open'd on me at once a most terrible
    battery
Of scorn and amazement. She made no
    reply,
But gave a slight turn to the end of her
    nose
  (That pure Grecian feature), as much as
    to say,
"How absurd that any sane man should
    suppose
That a lady would go to a ball in the
    clothes,
  No matter how fine, that she wears
    every day!"

So I ventured again—"Wear your crimson
    brocade"
(Second turn up of nose)—"That's too
    dark by a shade."

"Your blue silk"—"That's too heavy."
  "Your pink"—"That's too light."
"Wear tulle over satin"—"I can't endure
    white."
"Your rose-color'd, then, the best of the
    batch"—
"I haven't a thread of point lace to
    match."
"Your brown *moire antique*"—"Yes, and
    look like a Quaker."
"The pearl-color'd"—"I would, but that
    plaguey dressmaker
Has had it a week."—"Then that exquisite
    lilac,
In which you would melt the heart of a
    Shylock."
(Here the nose took again the same eleva-
    tion)
"I wouldn't wear that for the whole of
    creation."
  "Why not? It's my fancy, there's
    nothing could strike it
As more *comme il faut*—" "Yes, but, dear
    me, that lean
Sophronia Stuckup has got one just like
    it,
And I won't appear dress'd like a chit of
    sixteen."
"Then that splendid purple, that sweet
    mazarine;
That superb *point d'aguille*, that imperial
    green,
That zephyr-like tarletan, that rich *gren-
    adine*"—
"Not one of all which is fit to be seen,"
Said the lady, becoming excited and flush'd.
"Then wear," I exclaim'd, in a tone which
    quite crush'd
  Opposition, "that gorgeous *toilette* which
    you sported
In Paris last spring, at the grand pre-
    sentation,
When you quite turn'd the head of the
    head of the nation;
  And by all the grand court were so very
    much courted."
The end of the nose was portentously
    tipp'd up,
  And both the bright eyes shot forth in-
    dignation,
As she burst upon me with the fierce
    exclamation,

"I have worn it three times at the least calculation,
And that and the most of my dresses are ripp'd up!"
Here *I ripp'd out* something, perhaps rather rash,
  Quite innocent, though; but, to use an expression
More striking than classic, it "settled my hash,"
  And proved very soon the last act of our session.
"Fiddlesticks, is it, sir? I wonder the ceiling
Doesn't fall down and crush you—oh, you men have no feeling,
You selfish, unnatural, illiberal creatures,
Who set yourselves up as patterns and preachers.
Your silly pretence—why, what a mere guess it is!
Pray, what do you know of a woman's necessities?
I have told you and shown you I've nothing to wear,
And it's perfectly plain you not only don't care,
But you do not believe me" (here the nose went still higher):
"I suppose if you dared you would call me a liar.
Our engagement is ended, sir—yes, on the spot;
You're a brute, and a monster, and—I don't know what."
I mildly suggested the words—Hottentot, Pickpocket, and cannibal, Tartar, and thief,
As gentle expletives which might give relief;
But this only proved as spark to the powder,
And the storm I had raised came faster and louder,
It blew, and it rain'd, thunder'd, lighten'd, and hail'd
Interjections, verbs, pronouns, till language quite fail'd
To express the abusive, and then its arrears
Were brought up all at once by a torrent of tears,
And my last faint, despairing attempt at an obs-
Ervation was lost in a tempest of sobs.

Well, I felt for the lady, and felt for my hat, too,
Improvised on the crown of the latter a tattoo,
In lieu of expressing the feelings which lay
Quite too deep for words, as Wordsworth would say;
Then, without going through the form of a bow,
Found myself in the entry—I hardly knew how—
On doorstep and sidewalk, past lamp-post and square,
At home and up stairs, in my own easy-chair;
  Poked my feet into slippers, my fire into blaze,
And said to myself, as I lit my cigar,
Supposing a man had the wealth of the czar
  Of the Russias to boot, for the rest of his days,
On the whole, do you think he would have much to spare
If he married a woman with nothing to wear?
Since that night, taking pains that it should not be bruited
Abroad in society, I've instituted
A course of inquiry, extensive and thorough,
On this vital subject, and find, to my horror,
That the fair Flora's case is by no means surprising,
  But that there exists the greatest distress
In our female community, solely arising
  From this unsupplied destitution of dress,
Whose unfortunate victims are filling the air
With the pitiful wail of "Nothing to wear."
Researches in some of the "Upper Ten" districts
Reveal the most painful and startling statistics,

Of which let me mention only a few:
In one single house, on the Fifth Avenue,
Three young ladies were found, all below twenty-two,
Who have been three whole weeks without anything new
In the way of flounced silks, and thus left in the lurch
Are unable to go to ball, concert, or church.
In another large mansion near the same place
Was found a deplorable, heart-rending case
Of entire destitution of Brussels point lace.
In a neighboring block there was found, in three calls,
Total want, long continued, of camel's-hair shawls;
And a suffering family, whose case exhibits
The most pressing need of real ermine tippets;
One deserving young lady almost unable
To survive for the want of a new Russian sable;
Another confined to the house, when it's windier
Than usual, because her shawl isn't India.
Still another, whose tortures have been most terrific
Ever since the sad loss of the steamer Pacific,
In which were engulf'd, not friend or relation
(For whose fate she perhaps might have found consolation,
Or borne it, at least, with serene resignation),
But the choicest assortment of French sleeves and collars
Ever sent out from Paris, worth thousands of dollars,
And all as to style most *recherché* and rare,
The want of which leaves her with nothing to wear,
And renders her life so drear and dyspeptic
That she's quite a recluse, and almost a skeptic,
For she touchingly says that this sort of grief
Cannot find in Religion the slightest relief,
And Philosophy has not a maxim to spare
For the victims of such overwhelming despair.
But the saddest by far of all these sad features
Is the cruelty practised upon the poor creatures
By husbands and fathers, real Bluebeards and Timons,
Who resist the most touching appeals made for diamonds
By their wives and their daughters, and leave them for days
Unsupplied with new jewelry, fans, or bouquets,
Even laugh at their miseries whenever they have a chance,
And deride their demands as useless extravagance;
One case of a bride was brought to my view,
Too sad for belief, but, alas! 'twas too true,
Whose husband refused, as savage as Charon,
To permit her to take more than ten trunks to Sharon
The consequence was, that when she got there,
At the end of three weeks she had nothing to wear;
And when she proposed to finish the season
At Newport, the monster refused out and out,
For his infamous conduct alleging no reason,
Except that the waters were good for his gout;
Such treatment as this was too shocking, of course,
And proceedings are now going on for divorce.

But why harrow the feelings by lifting the curtain
From these scenes of woe? Enough, it is certain,

Has been here disclosed to stir up the pity
Of every benevolent heart in the city,
And spur up Humanity into a canter
To rush and relieve these sad cases instanter.
Won't somebody, moved by this touching description,
Come forward to-morrow and head a subscription?
Won't some kind philanthropist, seeing that aid is
So needed at once by these indigent ladies,
Take charge of the matter? or won't Peter Cooper
The corner-stone lay of some splendid super-
Structure, like that which to-day links his name
In the Union unending of honor and fame;
And found a new charity just for the care
Of these unhappy women with nothing to wear,
Which, in view of the cash which would daily be claim'd,
The *Laying-out* Hospital well might be named?
Won't Stewart, or some of our dry-goods importers,
Take a contract for clothing our wives and our daughters?
Or, to furnish the cash to supply these distresses,
And life's pathway strew with shawls, collars, and dresses,
Ere the want of them makes it much rougher and thornier.
Won't some one discover a new California?

O ladies, dear ladies, the next sunny day
Please trundle your hoops just out of Broadway,
From its whirl and its bustle, its fashion and pride,
And the temples of Trade which tower on each side,
To the alleys and lanes, where Misfortune and Guilt
Their children have gather'd, their city have built;
Where Hunger and Vice, like twin beasts of prey,
Have hunted their victims to gloom and despair;
Raise the rich, dainty dress, and the fine broider'd skirt,
Pick your delicate way through tne dampness and dirt,
Grope through the dark dens, climb the rickety stair
To the garret, where wretches, the young and the old,
Half starved and half naked, lie crouch'd from the cold.
See those skeleton limbs, those frost-bitten feet,
All bleeding and bruised by the stones of the street;
Hear the sharp cry of childhood, the deep groans that swell
From the poor dying creature who writhes on the floor,
Hear the curses that sound like the echoes of Hell,
As you sicken and shudder and fly from the door;
Then home to your wardrobes, and say, if you dare—
Spoil'd children of Fashion—you've nothing to wear!

And oh, if perchance there should be a sphere,
Where all is made right which so puzzles us here,
Where the glare, and the glitter, and tinsel of Time
Fade and die in the light of that region sublime,
Where the soul, disenchanted of flesh and of sense,
Unscreen'd by its trappings, and shows, and pretence,
Must be clothed for the life and the service above,
With purity, truth, faith, meekness, and love;
O daughters of Earth! foolish virgins, beware!
Lest in that upper realm you have nothing to wear!

WILLIAM ALLEN BUTLER.

THE COMPLAINTS OF THE POOR.

"And wherefore do the poor complain?"
　The rich man ask'd of me:
"Come, walk abroad with me," I said,
　"And I will answer thee."

'Twas evening, and the frozen streets
　Were cheerless to behold;
And we were wrapp'd and coated well,
　And yet we were a-cold.

We met an old, bareheaded man,
　His locks were thin and white;
I ask'd him what he did abroad
　In that cold winter's night.

The cold was keen, indeed, he said—
　But at home no fire had he;
And therefore he had come abroad
　To ask for charity.

We met a young barefooted child,
　And she begg'd loud and bold;
I asked her what she did abroad
　When the wind it blew so cold.

She said her father was at home,
　And he lay sick abed;
And therefore was it she was sent
　Abroad to beg for bread.

We saw a woman sitting down
　Upon a stone to rest;
She had a baby at her back,
　And another at her breast.

I ask'd her why she loiter'd there,
　When the night-wind was so chill;
She turn'd her head, and bade the child
　That scream'd behind, be still—

Then told us that her husband served,
　A soldier, far away;
And therefore to her parish she
　Was begging back her way.

We met a girl, her dress was loose
　And sunken was her eye,
Who with a wanton's hollow voice
　Address'd the passers-by;

I ask'd her what there was in guilt
　That could her heart allure
To shame, disease, and late remorse;
　She answer'd she was poor.

I turn'd me to the rich man then,
　For silently stood he;
"You ask'd me why the poor complain;
　And these have answer'd thee!"
　　　　　　　ROBERT SOUTHEY.

THE LADY'S DREAM.

THE lady lay in her bed,
　Her couch so warm and soft,
But her sleep was restless and broken still;
For, turning often and oft
From side to side, she mutter'd and moan'd,
　And toss'd her arms aloft.

At last she started up,
　And gazed on the vacant air
With a look of awe, as if she saw
　Some dreadful phantom there—
And then in the pillow she buried her face
　From visions ill to bear.

The very curtain shook,
　Her terror was so extreme,
And the light that fell on the broider'd quilt
　Kept a tremulous gleam;
And her voice was hollow, and shook as she cried,
　"Oh me! that awful dream!

"That weary, weary walk
　In the churchyard's dismal ground!
And those horrible things, with shady wings,
　That came and flitted round,—
Death, death, and nothing but death,
　In every sight and sound!

"And oh! those maidens young
　Who wrought in that dreary room,
With figures drooping and spectres thin,
　And cheeks without a bloom;—
And the voice that cried, 'For the pomp of pride
　We haste to an early tomb'!

"'For the pomp and pleasures of pride
　We toil like the African slaves,
And only to earn a home at last
　Where yonder cypress waves;'—
And then it pointed—I never saw
　A ground so full of graves!

"And still the coffins came,
  With their sorrowful trains and slow;
Coffin after coffin still,
  A sad and sickening show;
From grief exempt, I never had dreamt
  Of such a world of Woe!

"Of the hearts that daily break,
  Of the tears that hourly fall,
Of the many, many troubles of life,
  That grieve this earthly ball—
Disease and Hunger, Pain and Want,
  But now I dream of them all!

"For the blind and the cripple were there,
  And the babe that pined for bread,
And the houseless man, and the widow poor,
  Who begg'd—to bury the dead!
The naked, alas! that I might have clad,
  The famish'd I might have fed!

"The sorrow I might have soothed,
  And the unregarded tears;
For many a thronging shape was there,
  From long-forgotten years,
Ay, even the poor rejected Moor,
  Who raised my childish fears!

"Each pleading look, that long ago
  I scann'd with a heedless eye;
Each face was gazing as plainly there,
  As when I pass'd it by;
Woe, woe for me if the past should be
  Thus present when I die!

"No need of sulphurous lake,
  No need of fiery coal,
But only that crowd of humankind
  Who wanted pity and dole—
In everlasting retrospect—
  Will wring my sinful soul!

"Alas! I have walk'd through life
  Too heedless where I trod;
Nay, helping to trample my fellow-worm,
  And fill the burial sod—
Forgetting that even the sparrow falls
  Not unmark'd of God!

"I drank the richest draughts,
  And ate whatever is good—
Fish, and flesh, and fowl, and fruit,
  Supplied my hungry mood;
But I never remember'd the wretched ones
  That starve for want of food!

"I dress'd as the noble dress,
  In cloth of silver and gold,
With silk, and satin, and costly furs,
  In many an ample fold;
But I never remember'd the naked limbs,
  That froze with winter's cold.

"The wounds I might have heal'd!
  The human sorrow and smart!
And yet it never was in my soul
  To play so ill a part:
But evil is wrought by want of Thought,
  As well as want of Heart!"

She clasp'd her fervent hands,
  And the tears began to stream;
Large, and bitter, and fast they fell,
  Remorse was so extreme;
And yet, oh yet, that many a Dame
  Would dream the Lady's Dream!
                THOMAS HOOD.

GAFFER GRAY.

Ho! why dost thou shiver and shake,
  Gaffer Gray?
And why does thy nose look so blue?
  "'Tis the weather that's cold,
  'Tis I'm grown very old,
And my doublet is not very new,
  Well-a-day!"

Then line thy worn doublet with ale,
  Gaffer Gray;
And warm thy old heart with a glass.
  "Nay, but credit I've none,
  And my money's all gone;
Then say how may that come to pass?
  Well-a-day!"

Hie away to the house on the brow,
  Gaffer Gray,
And knock at the jolly priest's door.
  "The priest often preaches
  Against worldly riches,
But ne'er gives a mite to the poor,
  Well-a-day!"

The lawyer lives under the hill,
  Gaffer Gray;
Warmly fenced both in back and in front.
  "He will fasten his locks,
  And will threaten the stocks
Should he evermore find me in want,
  Well-a-day!"

The squire has fat beeves and brown ale,
    Gaffer Gray;
And the season will welcome you there.
  "His fat beeves and his beer,
    And his merry new year,
  Are all for the flush and the fair,
    Well-a-day!"

My keg is but low, I confess,
    Gaffer Gray;
What then? While it lasts, man, we'll
    live.
  "The poor man alone,
    When he hears the poor moan,
  Of his morsel a morsel will give,
    Well-a-day!"
                THOMAS HOLCROFT.

THE SONG OF THE SHIRT.

WITH fingers weary and worn,
  With eyelids heavy and red,
A woman sat, in unwomanly rags,
  Plying her needle and thread—
Stitch! stitch! stitch!
  In poverty, hunger, and dirt,
And still with a voice of dolorous pitch
  She sang the "Song of the Shirt!"

"Work! work! work!
  While the cock is crowing aloof!
And work—work—work,
  Till the stars shine through the roof!
It's oh! to be a slave
  Along with the barbarous Turk,
Where woman has never a soul to save,
  If this is Christian work!

"Work—work—work!
  Till the brain begins to swim;
Work—work—work!
  Till the eyes are heavy and dim!
Seam, and gusset, and band,
  Band, and gusset, and seam,
Till over the buttons I fall asleep,
  And sew them on in a dream!

"O men, with sisters dear!
  O men, with mothers and wives!
It is not linen you're wearing out,
  But human creatures' lives!
Stitch—stitch—stitch,
  In poverty, hunger, and dirt,
Sewing at once with a double thread,
  A shroud as well as a shirt!

"But why do I talk of Death,
  That Phantom of grisly bone?
I hardly fear his terrible shape,
  It seems so like my own—
It seems so like my own,
  Because of the fast I keep:
O God! that bread should be so dear,
  And flesh and blood so cheap!

"Work—work—work!
  My labor never flags;
And what are its wages? A bed of straw,
  A crust of bread, and rags.
A shatter'd roof—and this naked floor—
  A table—a broken chair—
And a wall so blank, my shadow I thank
  For sometimes falling there!

"Work—work—work!
  From weary chime to chime,
Work—work—work—
  As prisoners work for crime!
Band, and gusset, and seam,
  Seam, and gusset, and band,
Till the heart is sick, and the brain benumb'd,
  As well as the weary hand.

"Work—work—work
  In the dull December light,
And work—work—work
  When the weather is warm and bright—
While underneath the eaves,
  The brooding swallows cling,
As if to show me their sunny backs
  And twit me with the spring.

"Oh but to breathe the breath
  Of the cowslip and primrose sweet—
With the sky above my head,
  And the grass beneath my feet;
For only one short hour
  To feel as I used to feel,
Before I knew the woes of want,
  And the walk that costs a meal!

"Oh! but for one short hour!
  A respite however brief!
No blessed leisure for love or hope,
  But only time for grief!

A little weeping would ease my heart,
  But in their briny bed
My tears must stop, for every drop
  Hinders needle and thread!"

With fingers weary and worn,
  With eyelids heavy and red,
A woman sat in unwomanly rags,
  Plying her needle and thread—
Stitch! stitch! stitch!
  In poverty, hunger, and dirt,
And still with a voice of dolorous pitch,—
Would that its tone could reach the rich!—
  She sang this "Song of the Shirt."
THOMAS HOOD.

THE BEGGAR'S PETITION.

PITY the sorrows of a poor old man,
  Whose trembling limbs have borne him to your door,
Whose days are dwindled to the shortest span;
  Oh! give relief, and Heaven will bless your store.

These tatter'd clothes my poverty bespeak,
  These hoary locks proclaim my lengthen'd years,
And many a furrow in my grief-worn cheek
  Has been the channel to a flood of tears.

Yon house, erected on the rising ground,
  With tempting aspect, drew me from my road;
For plenty there a residence has found,
  And grandeur a magnificent abode.

Hard is the fate of the infirm and poor!
  Here, as I craved a morsel of their bread,
A pamper'd menial drove me from the door,
  To seek a shelter in an humbler shed.

Oh! take me to your hospitable dome;
  Keen blows the wind, and piercing is the cold!
Short is my passage to the friendly tomb,
  For I am poor, and miserably old.

Should I reveal the sources of my grief,
  If soft humanity e'er touch'd your breast,
Your hands would not withhold the kind relief,
  And tears of pity would not be repress'd.

Heaven sends misfortunes; why should we repine?
  'Tis Heaven has brought me to the state you see;
And your condition may be soon like mine,
  The child of sorrow and of misery.

A little farm was my paternal lot;
  Then, like the lark, I sprightly hail'd the morn;
But, ah! oppression forced me from my cot,
  My cattle died, and blighted was my corn.

My daughter, once the comfort of my age,
  Lured by a villain from her native home,
Is cast abandon'd on the world's wide stage,
  And doom'd in scanty poverty to roam.

My tender wife, sweet soother of my care,
  Struck with sad anguish at the stern decree,
Fell, lingering fell, a victim to despair,
  And left the world to wretchedness and me.

Pity the sorrows of a poor old man,
  Whose trembling limbs have borne him to your door,
Whose days are dwindled to the shortest span;
  Oh! give relief, and Heaven will bless your store.
THOMAS MOSS.

THE VAGABONDS.

WE are two travellers, Roger and I.
  Roger's my dog. — Come here, you scamp!
Jump for the gentleman,—mind your eye!
  Over the table, — look out for the lamp!—

The rogue is growing a little old;
  Five years we've tramp'd through wind
    and weather,
And slept out doors when nights were
    cold,
  And ate and drank—and starved—to-
    gether.

We've learn'd what comfort is, I tell
    you!
  A bed on the floor, a bit of rosin,
A fire to thaw our thumbs (poor fellow!
    The paw he holds up there has been
    frozen),
Plenty of catgut for my fiddle
  (This out-door business is bad for
    strings),
Then a few nice buckwheats hot from the
    griddle,
  And Roger and I set up for kings!

No, thank you, sir,—I never drink;
  Roger and I are exceedingly moral,—
Aren't we, Roger?—see him wink!—
  Well, something hot, then, we won't
    quarrel.
He's thirsty, too—see him nod his head?
  What a pity, sir, that dogs can't talk!—
He understands every word that's said,—
  And he knows good milk from water and
    chalk.

The truth is, sir, now I reflect,
  I've been so sadly given to grog,
I wonder I've not lost the respect
  (Here's to you, sir!) even of my dog.
But he sticks by, through thick and thin;
  And this old coat, with its empty pock-
    ets,
And rags that smell of tobacco and gin,
  He'll follow while he has eyes in his
    sockets.

There isn't another creature living
  Would do it, and prove, through every
    disaster,
So fond, so faithful, and so forgiving
  To such a miserable thankless master!
No, sir!—see him wag his tail and grin!
  By George! it makes my old eyes
    water!
That is, there's something in this gin
  That chokes a fellow. But no matter!

We'll have some music, if you are will-
    ing,
  And Roger (hem! what a plague a cough
    is, sir!)
Shall march a little.—Start, you villain!
  Stand straight! 'Bout face! Salute your
    officer!
Put up that paw! Dress! Take your
    rifle!
(Some dogs have arms, you see!) Now
    hold your
Cap while the gentlemen give a trifle
  To aid a poor old patriot soldier.

March! Halt! Now show how the rebel
    shakes
  When he stands up to hear his sen-
    tence.
Now tell how many drams it takes
  To honor a jolly new acquaintance.
Five yelps, that's five! he's mighty know-
    ing!
  The night's before us, fill the glasses!
Quick, sir! I'm ill,—my brain is going;
  Some brandy,—thank you; there,—it
    passes!

Why not reform? That's easily said;
  But I've gone through such wretched
    treatment,
Sometimes forgetting the taste of bread,
  And scarce remembering what meat
    meant,
That my poor stomach's past reform;
  And there are times when, mad with
    thinking,
I'd sell out Heaven for something warm
  To prop a horrible inward sinking.

Is there a way to forget to think?
  At your age, sir, home, fortune, friends,
A dear girl's love,—but I took to
    drink;—
  The same old story; you know how it
    ends.
If you could have seen these classic fea-
    tures,—
  You needn't laugh, sir; they were not
    then
Such a burning libel on God's creatures;
  I was one of your handsome men!

If you had seen her, so fair and young,
  Whose head was happy on this breast!
If you could have heard the songs I sung
  When the wine went round, you wouldn't
    have guess'd
That ever I, sir, should be straying
    From door to door with fiddle and
      dog,
Ragged and penniless, and playing
  To you to-night for a glass of grog.

She's married since, a parson's wife;
  'Twas better for her that we should part;
Better the soberest, prosiest life
  Than a blasted home and a broken
    heart.
I have seen her? Once: I was weak and
    spent
On the dusty road; a carriage stopp'd;
But little she dream'd, as on she went,
  Who kiss'd the coin that her fingers
    dropp'd!

You've set me talking, sir; I'm sorry;
  It makes me wild to think of the
    change!
What do you care for a beggar's story?
Is it amusing? you find it strange?
I had a mother so proud of me!
  'Twas well she died before. Do you
    know
If the happy spirits in Heaven can see
  The ruin and wretchedness here below?

Another glass, and strong, to deaden
  This pain; then Roger and I will start.
I wonder, has he such a lumpish, leaden,
  Aching thing, in place of a heart?
He is sad sometimes, and would weep if
    he could,
  No doubt, remembering things that
    were—
A virtuous kennel, with plenty of food,
  And himself a sober, respectable cur.

I'm better now; that glass was warming,—
  You rascal! limber your lazy feet!
We must be fiddling and performing
  For supper and bed, or starve in the
    street.—
Not a very gay life to lead, you think?
  But soon we shall go where lodgings are
    free,
And the sleepers need neither victuals nor
    drink;—
  The sooner the better for Roger and me.
                    J. T. TROWBRIDGE.

THE BRIDGE OF SIGHS.

"Drowned! drowned!"—*Hamlet.*

ONE more Unfortunate,
  Weary of breath,
Rashly importunate,
  Gone to her death!

Take her up tenderly,
  Lift her with care,—
Fashion'd so slenderly,
  Young, and so fair!

Look at her garments
Clinging like cerements;
  Whilst the wave constantly
Drips from her clothing;
  Take her up instantly,
Loving, not loathing.—

Touch her not scornfully;
Think of her mournfully,
  Gently and humanly;
Not of the stains of her,
All that remains of her
  Now is pure womanly.

Make no deep scrutiny
Into her mutiny
  Rash and undutiful:
Past all dishonor,
Death has left on her
  Only the beautiful.

Still, for all slips of hers,
One of Eve's family—
Wipe those poor lips of hers,
  Oozing so clammily.

Loop up her tresses
  Escaped from the comb,
Her fair auburn tresses;
  Whilst wonderment guesses
    Where was her home?

Who was her father?
  Who was her mother?
Had she a sister?
  Had she a brother?

Or was there a dearer one
Still, and a nearer one
   Yet, than all other?

Alas! for the rarity
Of Christian charity
   Under the sun!
Oh! it was pitiful!
Near a whole city full,
   Home she had none.

Sisterly, brotherly,
Fatherly, motherly,
   Feelings had changed:
Love, by harsh evidence,
Thrown from its eminence;
Even God's providence
   Seeming estranged.

Where the lamps quiver
So far in the river,
   With many a light
From window and casement,
From garret to basement,
She stood with amazement,
   Houseless by night.

The bleak wind of March
   Made her tremble and shiver;
But not the dark arch,
   Or the black flowing river;
Mad from life's history,
Glad to death's mystery
   Swift to be hurl'd—
Anywhere, anywhere
   Out of the world!

In she plunged boldly,
No matter how coldly
   The rough river ran,—
Over the brink of it,
Picture it—think of it,
   Dissolute man!
Lave in it, drink of it,
   Then, if you can!

Take her up tenderly,
   Lift her with care;
Fashion'd so slenderly,
   Young, and so fair!

Ere her limbs frigidly
Stiffen too rigidly,

Decently,—kindly,—
   Smooth and compose them;
And her eyes, close them,
   Staring so blindly!

Dreadfully staring
   Through muddy impurity,
As when with the daring
Last look of despairing
   Fix'd on futurity.

Perishing gloomily,
Spurr'd by contumely,
Cold inhumanity,
Burning insanity,
   Into her rest.—
Cross her hands humbly,
As if praying dumbly,
   Over her breast!

Owning her weakness,
   Her evil behavior,
And leaving, with meekness
   Her sins to her Saviour!
                              THOMAS HOOD.

BEAUTIFUL SNOW.

OH! the snow, the beautiful snow,
Filling the sky and the earth below;
Over the house-tops, over the street,
Over the heads of the people you meet:
      Dancing,
         Flirting,
            Skimming along,
Beautiful snow! it can do nothing wrong.
Flying to kiss a fair lady's cheek;
Clinging to lips in a frolicsome freak.
Beautiful snow, from the heavens above,
Pure as an angel and fickle as love!

Oh! the snow, the beautiful snow!
How the flakes gather and laugh as they
      go!
Whirling about in its maddening fun,
It plays in its glee with every one.
      Chasing,
         Laughing,
            Hurrying by,
It lights up the face and it sparkles the
      eye;
And even the dogs, with a bark and a
      bound,
Snap at the crystals that eddy around.

The town is alive, and its heart in a glow
To welcome the coming of beautiful snow.

How the wild crowd goes swaying along,
Hailing each other with humor and song!
How the gay sledges like meteors flash by—
Bright for a moment, then lost to the eye
    Ringing,
      Swinging,
        Dashing they go
Over the crest of the beautiful snow:
Snow so pure when it falls from the sky,
To be trampled in mud by the crowd rushing by:
To be trampled and track'd by the thousands of feet,
Till it blends with the filth in the horrible street.

Once I was pure as the snow—but I fell:
Fell, like the snow-flakes, from heaven—to hell:
Fell, to be tramp'd as the filth of the street:
Fell, to be scoff'd, to be spit on, and beat,
    Pleading,
      Cursing,
        Dreading to die,
Selling my soul to whoever would buy,
Dealing in shame for a morsel of bread,
Hating the living and fearing the dead.
Merciful God! have I fallen so low?
And yet I was once like this beautiful snow!

Once I was fair as the beautiful snow,
With an eye like its crystals, a heart like its glow;
Once I was loved for my innocent grace—
Flatter'd and sought for the charm of my face.
    Father,
      Mother,
        Sisters all,
God, and myself, I have lost by my fall.
The veriest wretch that goes shivering by
Will take a wide sweep, lest I wander too nigh;
For all that is on or about me, I know
There is nothing that's pure but the beautiful snow.

How strange it should be that this beautiful snow
Should fall on a sinner with nowhere to go!
How strange it would be, when the night comes again,
If the snow and the ice struck my desperate brain!
    Fainting,
      Freezing,
        Dying alone!
Too wicked for prayer, too weak for my moan
To be heard in the crash of the crazy town,
Gone mad in their joy at the snow's coming down;
To lie and to die in my terrible woe,
With a bed and a shroud of the beautiful snow!

              JOHN W. WATSON.

THE PAUPER'S DEATH-BED.

TREAD softly,—bow the head,—
  In reverent silence bow,—
No passing bell doth toll,
  Yet an immortal soul
    Is passing now.

Stranger! however great,
  With lowly reverence bow;
There's one in that poor shed—
One by that paltry bed—
    Greater than thou.

Beneath that beggar's roof,
  Lo! Death doth keep his state.
Enter, no crowds attend;
Enter, no guards defend
    This palace-gate.

That pavement, damp and cold,
  No smiling courtiers tread;
One silent woman stands,
Lifting with meagre hands
    A dying head.

No mingling voices sound,—
  An infant wail alone;
A sob suppress'd,—again
That short deep gasp, and then—
    The parting groan.

O change! O wondrous change!
  Burst are the prison-bars,—
This moment *there* so low,
So agonized, and now
  Beyond the stars.

O change! stupendous change!
  There lies the soulless clod;
The sun eternal breaks,
The new immortal wakes,—
  Wakes with his God.
CAROLINE BOWLES SOUTHEY.

THE PAUPER'S DRIVE.

THERE'S a grim one-horse hearse in a jolly round trot,—
To the churchyard a pauper is going, I wot;
The road it is rough, and the hearse has no springs;
And hark to the dirge which the mad driver sings:
  Rattle his bones over the stones!
  He's only a pauper whom nobody owns!

Oh, where are the mourners? Alas! there are none;
He has left not a gap in the world, now he's gone,—
Not a tear in the eye of child, woman, or man;
To the grave with his carcass as fast as you can:
  Rattle his bones over the stones!
  He's only a pauper whom nobody owns!

What a jolting, and creaking, and splashing, and din!
The whip, how it cracks! and the wheels, how they spin!
How the dirt, right and left, o'er the hedges is hurl'd!—
The pauper at length makes a noise in the world!
  Rattle his bones over the stones!
  He's only a pauper whom nobody owns!

Poor pauper defunct! he has made some approach
To gentility, now that he's stretch'd in a coach!
He's taking a drive in his carriage at last;
But it will not be long, if he goes on so fast:
  Rattle his bones over the stones!
  He's only a pauper whom nobody owns!

You bumpkins! who stare at your brother convey'd,
Behold what respect to a cloddy is paid!
And be joyful to think, when by death you're laid low,
You've a chance to the grave like a gemman to go!
  Rattle his bones over the stones!
  He's only a pauper whom nobody owns!

But a truce to this strain; for my soul it is sad,
To think that a heart in humanity clad
Should make, like the brutes, such a desolate end,
And depart from the light without leaving a friend!
  Bear soft his bones over the stones!
  Though a pauper, he's one whom his Maker yet owns!
THOMAS NOEL.

I see the inundation sweet,
I hear the spending of the stream
Through years, through men, through Nature
                              fleet.
Through passion, thought,—through power and dream.

                                              R. Waldo Emerson

Concord, Massachusetts —
December 10, 1878.

"WESTWARD THE COURSE OF EMPIRE TAKES ITS WAY."

POEMS OF SENTIMENT.

ON THE PROSPECT OF PLANTING ARTS AND LEARNING IN AMERICA.

The Muse, disgusted at an age and clime
  Barren of every glorious theme,
In distant lands now waits a better time,
  Producing subjects worthy fame.

In happy climes, where from the genial sun
  And virgin earth such scenes ensue,
The force of Art by Nature seems outdone,
  And fancied beauties by the true;

In happy climes, the seat of innocence,
  Where Nature guides and Virtue rules,
Where men shall not impose for truth and sense
  The pedantry of courts and schools;

There shall be sung another golden age,
  The rise of empire and of arts,
The good and great inspiring epic rage,
  The wisest heads and noblest hearts.

Not such as Europe breeds in her decay;
  Such as she bred when fresh and young,
When heavenly flame did animate her clay,
  By future poets shall be sung.

Westward the course of empire takes its way;
  The four first acts already past,
A fifth shall close the drama with the day;
  Time's noblest offspring is the last.
George Berkeley.

A MUSICAL INSTRUMENT.

What was he doing, the great god Pan,
  Down in the reeds by the river?
Spreading ruin and scattering ban,
Splashing and paddling with hoofs of a goat,
And breaking the golden lilies afloat
  With the dragon-fly on the river?

He tore out a reed, the great god Pan,
  From the deep, cool bed of the river.
The limpid water turbidly ran,
And the broken lilies a-dying lay,
And the dragon-fly had fled away,
  Ere he brought it out of the river.

High on the shore sate the great god Pan,
  While turbidly flow'd the river,
And hack'd and hew'd as a great god can
With his hard, bleak steel at the patient reed,
Till there was not a sign of a leaf indeed
  To prove it fresh from the river.

He cut it short, did the great god Pan
  (How tall it stood in the river!)
Then drew the pith like the heart of a man,
Steadily from the outside ring,
Then notch'd the poor dry empty thing
  In holes as he sate by the river.

"This is the way," laugh'd the great god Pan
  (Laugh'd while he sate by the river),
"The only way since gods began
To make sweet music, they could succeed."
Then dropping his mouth to a hole in the reed,
  He blew in power by the river.

Sweet, sweet, sweet, O Pan,
  Piercing sweet by the river!
Blinding sweet, O great god Pan!
The sun on the hill forgot to die,
And the lilies revived, and the dragon-fly
  Came back to dream on the river.

Yet half a beast is the great god Pan,
 To laugh, as he sits by the river,
Making a poet out of a man.
The true gods sigh for the cost and the pain,—
For the reed that grows nevermore again
 As a reed with the reeds of the river.
ELIZABETH BARRETT BROWNING.

ALEXANDER'S FEAST; OR, THE POWER OF MUSIC.

AN ODE IN HONOR OF ST. CECILIA'S DAY.

I.

'TWAS at the royal feast for Persia won
 By Philip's warlike son:
 Aloft, in awful state,
 The godlike hero sate
 On his imperial throne:
His valiant peers were placed around,
Their brows with roses and with myrtles bound
 (So should desert in arms be crown'd):
 The lovely Thais, by his side,
 Sate like a blooming Eastern bride,
 In flower of youth and beauty's pride.
  Happy, happy, happy pair!
   None but the brave,
   None but the brave,
   None but the brave deserves the fair.

CHORUS.

  Happy, happy, happy pair!
   None but the brave,
   None but the brave,
   None but the brave deserves the fair.

II.

Timotheus, placed on high
 Amid the tuneful quire,
 With flying fingers touch'd the lyre;
The trembling notes ascend the sky,
 And heavenly joys inspire.
The song began from Jove,
Who left his blissful seats above
(Such is the power of mighty Love).
A dragon's fiery form belied the god;
Sublime on radiant spires he rode,
 When he to fair Olympia press'd,
 And while he sought her snowy breast:

Then, round her slender waist he curl'd,
And stamp'd an image of himself, a sovereign of the world.
The listening crowd admire the lofty sound—
A present deity! they shout around;
A present deity! the vaulted roofs rebound.
  With ravish'd ears
  The monarch hears,
  Assumes the god,
  Affects to nod,
And seems to shake the spheres.

CHORUS.

  With ravish'd ears
  The monarch hears,
  Assumes the god,
  Affects to nod,
And seems to shake the spheres.

III.

The praise of Bacchus, then, the sweet musician sung—
 Of Bacchus ever fair and ever young;
 The jolly god in triumph comes:
 Sound the trumpets; beat the drums!
  Flush'd with a purple grace,
  He shows his honest face;
Now give the hautboys breath—he comes, he comes!
Bacchus, ever fair and young,
 Drinking joys did first ordain;
Bacchus' blessings are a treasure;
Drinking is the soldier's pleasure;
  Rich the treasure,
  Sweet the pleasure;
Sweet is pleasure after pain.

CHORUS.

Bacchus' blessings are a treasure;
Drinking is the soldier's pleasure;
  Rich the treasure,
  Sweet the pleasure;
Sweet is pleasure after pain.

IV.

Soothed with the sound, the king grew vain;
Fought all his battles o'er again;
And thrice he routed all his foes, and thrice he slew the slain.

The master saw the madness rise—
His glowing cheeks, his ardent eyes;
And, while he Heaven and earth defied,
Changed his hand and check'd his pride.
    He chose a mournful muse,
    Soft pity to infuse:
He sung Darius great and good,
    By too severe a fate
Fallen, fallen, fallen, fallen—
Fallen from his high estate,
    And welt'ring in his blood;
Deserted, at his utmost need,
By those his former bounty fed;
On the bare earth exposed he lies,
With not a friend to close his eyes.
With downcast looks the joyless victor sate
    Revolving in his alter'd soul
    The various turns of chance below;
    And, now and then, a sigh he stole;
    And tears began to flow.

CHORUS.

    Revolving in his alter'd soul
    The various turns of chance below;
    And, now and then, a sigh he stole;
    And tears began to flow.

V.

The mighty master smiled to see
That love was in the next degree:
'Twas but a kindred sound to move,
For pity melts the mind to love.
    Softly sweet, in Lydian measures,
    Soon he soothed his soul to pleasures.
War, he sung, is toil and trouble;
Honor but an empty bubble—
    Never ending, still beginning—
Fighting still, and still destroying;
If the world be worth thy winning,
Think, oh think it worth enjoying!
    Lovely Thais sits beside thee—
    Take the good the gods provide thee.
The many rend the sky with loud applause;
So Love was crown'd, but Music won the cause.
The prince, unable to conceal his pain,
    Gazed on the fair
    Who caused his care,
And sigh'd and look'd, sigh'd and look'd,
Sigh'd and look'd, and sigh'd again.
At length, with love and wine at once oppress'd,
The vanquish'd victor sunk upon her breast.

CHORUS.

The prince, unable to conceal his pain,
    Gazed on the fair
    Who caused his care,
And sigh'd and look'd, sigh'd and look'd,
Sigh'd and look'd, and sigh'd again.
At length, with love and wine at once oppress'd,
The vanquish'd victor sunk upon her breast.

VI.

Now strike the golden lyre again—
A louder yet, and yet a louder strain!
    Break his bands of sleep asunder,
And rouse him, like a rattling peal of thunder.
    Hark, hark! the horrid sound
    Has raised up his head!
    As awaked from the dead,
    And amazed, he stares around.
Revenge! revenge! Timotheus cries;
    See the Furies arise!
    See the snakes that they rear,
    How they hiss in their hair,
And the sparkles that flash from their eyes!
    Behold a ghastly band,
    Each a torch in his hand!
Those are Grecian ghosts, that in battle were slain,
    And unburied remain,
    Inglorious, on the plain!
    Give the vengeance due
    To the gallant crew.
Behold how they toss their torches on high,
    How they point to the Persian abodes,
And glittering temples of their hostile gods!
The princes applaud with a furious joy,
And the king seized a flambeau with zeal to destroy;
    Thais led the way
    To light him to his prey,
And, like another Helen, fired another Troy.

CHORUS.

And the king seized a flambeau with zeal to destroy;
   Thais led the way
   To light him to his prey,
And, like another Helen, fired another Troy.

VII.

   Thus, long ago—
Ere heaving bellows learn'd to blow,
   While organs yet were mute—
Timotheus, to his breathing flute
   And sounding lyre,
Could swell the soul to rage, or kindle soft desire.
   At last divine Cecilia came,
   Inventress of the vocal frame;
The sweet enthusiast, from her sacred store,
   Enlarged the former narrow bounds,
   And added length to solemn sounds,
With Nature's mother-wit, and arts unknown before.
   Let old Timotheus yield the prize,
   Or both divide the crown;
   He raised a mortal to the skies—
   She drew an angel down.

GRAND CHORUS.

   At last divine Cecilia came,
   Inventress of the vocal frame;
The sweet enthusiast, from her sacred store,
   Enlarged the former narrow bounds,
   And added length to solemn sounds,
With Nature's mother-wit, and arts unknown before.
   Let old Timotheus yield the prize,
   Or both divide the crown;
   He raised a mortal to the skies—
   She drew an angel down.
                JOHN DRYDEN.

A SONG FOR ST. CECILIA'S DAY.

I.

FROM harmony, from heavenly harmony,
   This universal frame began.
   When Nature underneath a heap
     Of jarring atoms lay,
   And could not heave her head,
   The tuneful voice was heard from high,
Arise, ye more than dead!
   Then cold, and hot, and moist, and dry
In order to their stations leap,
   And Music's power obey.
From harmony, from heavenly harmony,
   This universal frame began:
From harmony to harmony
   Through all the compass of the notes it ran,
   The diapason closing full in Man.

II.

What passion cannot Music raise and quell?
When Jubal struck the chorded shell
   His listening brethren stood around,
And, wondering, on their faces fell
   To worship that celestial sound.
Less than a god they thought there could not dwell
   Within the hollow of that shell
   That spoke so sweetly and so well.
What passion cannot Music raise and quell?

III.

   The trumpet's loud clangor
     Excites us to arms,
   With shrill notes of anger
     And mortal alarms.
The double double double beat
   Of the thundering drum
   Cries, "Hark! the foes come;
Charge, charge, 'tis too late to retreat!"

IV.

   The soft complaining flute
     In dying notes discovers
   The woes of hopeless lovers,
Whose dirge is whisper'd by the warbling lute.

V.

   Sharp violins proclaim
Their jealous pangs and desperation,
Fury, frantic indignation,
Depth of pains, and height of passion
   For the fair, disdainful dame.

VI.

But oh! what art can teach,
What human voice can reach,
The sacred organ's praise?
　Notes inspiring holy love,
Notes that wing their heavenly ways
　To mend the choirs above.

VII.

Orpheus could lead the savage race,
And trees uprooted left their place
Sequacious of the lyre:
But bright Cecilia raised the wonder
　　higher:
When to her organ vocal breath was given
An angel heard, and straight appear'd—
Mistaking Earth for Heaven!

GRAND CHORUS.

As from the power of sacred lays
　The spheres began to move,
And sung the great Creator's praise
　To all the blest above;
So when the last and dreadful hour
This crumbling pageant shall devour,
The trumpet shall be heard on high,
The dead shall live, the living die,
And Music shall untune the sky.
　　　　　　　　JOHN DRYDEN.

ODE ON ST. CECILIA'S DAY.

I.

DESCEND, ye Nine! descend and sing;
　The breathing instruments inspire;
Wake into voice each silent string,
　And sweep the sounding lyre!
In a sadly-pleasing strain
Let the warbling lute complain:
　Let the loud trumpet sound,
　Till the roofs all around
　The shrill echoes rebound:
While in more lengthen'd notes and slow
The deep, majestic, solemn organs blow.
　Hark! the numbers soft and clear
　Gently steal upon the ear;
　Now louder, and yet louder rise,
　And fill with spreading sounds the skies;
Exulting in triumph now swell the bold
　　notes,
In broken air, trembling, the wild music
　　floats:

Till by degrees, remote and small,
　The strains decay,
　And melt away
In a dying, dying fall.

II.

By Music, minds an equal temper know,
Nor swell too high, nor sink too low.
If in the breast tumultuous joys arise,
Music her soft, assuasive voice applies;
　Or, when the soul is press'd with cares,
　Exalts her in enliv'ning airs:
Warriors she fires with animated sounds;
Pours balm into the bleeding lover's
　　wounds:
　Melancholy lifts her head,
　Morpheus rouses from his bed,
　Sloth unfolds her arms and wakes,
　List'ning Envy drops her snakes,
Intestine war no more our Passions wage,
And giddy Factions hear away their rage.

III.

But when our country's cause provokes to
　　arms,
How martial music ev'ry bosom warms!
So when the first bold vessel dared the
　　seas,
High on the stern the Thracian raised his
　　strain,
　While Argo saw her kindred trees
　Descend from Pelion to the main.
Transported demigods stood round,
And men grew heroes at the sound,
　Inflamed with glory's charms:
Each chief his sevenfold shield display'd,
And half unsheathed the shining blade:
And seas, and rocks, and skies rebound,
　To arms! to arms! to arms!

IV.

But when through all th' infernal bounds,
Which flaming Phlegethon surrounds,
　Love, strong as Death, the poet led
　To the pale nations of the dead,
What sounds were heard,
What scenes appear'd
　O'er all the dreary coasts!
　　Dreadful gleams,
　　Dismal screams,
　　Fires that glow,
　　Shrieks of woe,

Sullen moans,
　Hollow groans
　And cries of tortured ghosts!
But hark! he strikes the golden lyre;
And see! the tortured ghosts respire,
　See, shady forms advance!
Thy stone, O Sisyphus, stands still,
Ixion rests upon his wheel,
　And the pale spectres dance!
The Furies sink upon their iron beds,
And snakes uncurl'd hang list'ning round
　　their heads.

V.

By the streams that ever flow,
By the fragrant winds that blow
　O'er th' Elysian flow'rs;
By those happy souls who dwell
In yellow meads of asphodel,
　Or amaranthine bow'rs;
By the heroes' armèd shades,
Glitt'ring through the gloomy glades,
By the youths that died for love,
Wand'ring in the myrtle grove;
Restore, restore Eurydice to life:
Oh take the husband, or return the wife!
He sung, and Hell consented
　To hear the poet's prayer:
Stern Proserpine relented,
　And gave him back the fair.
Thus song could prevail
O'er Death and o'er Hell,
A conquest how hard, and how glorious!
　Though Fate had fast bound her
　With Styx nine times round her,
Yet Music and Love were victorious.

VI.

But soon, too soon, the lover turns his
　　eyes:
Again she falls—again she dies—she dies!
How wilt thou now the fatal sisters move?
No crime was thine, if 'tis no crime to love.
　Now under hanging mountains,
　Beside the falls of fountains,
　Or where Hebrus wanders,
　Rolling in meanders,
　　All alone,
　　Unheard, unknown,
　　He makes his moan;
　　And calls her ghost,
　　For ever, ever, ever lost!

Now with Furies surrounded,
Despairing, confounded,
He trembles, he glows,
　Amidst Rhodope's snows:
See, wild as the winds, o'er the desert he
　　flies;
Hark! Hæmus resounds with the Bacchanals' cries—Ah see, he dies!
Yet ev'n in death Eurydice he sung,
Eurydice still trembled on his tongue,
　Eurydice the woods,
　Eurydice the floods,
Eurydice the rocks and hollow mountains
　　rung.

VII.

Music the fiercest grief can charm,
And fate's severest rage disarm;
Music can soften pain to ease,
And make despair and madness please;
Our joys below it can improve,
And antedate the bliss above.
This the divine Cecilia found,
And to her Maker's praise confined the
　　sound.
When the full organ joins the tuneful
　　quire,
Th' immortal pow'rs incline their ear;
Borne on the swelling notes our souls aspire,
While solemn airs improve the sacred
　　fire;
And angels lean from Heav'n to hear.
Of Orpheus now no more let poets tell,
To bright Cecilia greater pow'r is giv'n;
His numbers raised a shade from Hell,
Hers lift the soul to Heav'n.
　　　　　　　　ALEXANDER POPE.

THE PROGRESS OF POESY.

A PINDARIC ODE.

AWAKE, Æolian lyre, awake,
And give to rapture all thy trembling
　　strings.
From Helicon's harmonious springs
　A thousand rills their mazy progress
　　take;
The laughing flowers that round them
　　blow
Drink life and fragrance as they flow.
Now the rich stream of Music winds along,
Deep, majestic, smooth, and strong,

Through verdant vales, and Ceres' golden
   reign;
Now rolling down the steep amain
Headlong, impetuous, see it pour:
The rocks and nodding groves re-bellow
   to the roar.

O Sovereign of the willing soul,
Parent of sweet and solemn-breathing
   airs,
Enchanting shell! the sullen Cares
   And frantic Passions hear thy soft control.
On Thracia's hills the Lord of War
Has curb'd the fury of his car
And dropp'd his thirsty lance at thy command.
Perching on the sceptred hand
Of Jove, thy magic lulls the feather'd
   king
With ruffled plumes and flagging wing;
Quench'd in dark clouds of slumber lie
The terror of his beak, and lightnings of
   his eye.

   Thee the voice, the dance, obey
   Temper'd to thy warbled lay.
O'er Idalia's velvet-green
The rosy-crownèd Loves are seen
   On Cytherea's day,
With antic Sport, and blue-eyed Pleasures,
Frisking light in frolic measures;
Now pursuing, now retreating,
   Now in circling troops they meet,
To brisk notes in cadence beating
   Glance their many-twinkling feet.
Slow melting strains their Queen's approach declare:
   Where'er she turns the Graces homage
      pay.
With arms sublime that float upon the air
In gliding state she wins her easy way:
O'er her warm cheek and rising bosom
   move
The bloom of young Desire and purple
   light of Love.

   Man's feeble race what ills await!
Labor, and Penury, the racks of Pain,
Disease, and Sorrow's weeping train,
   And Death, sad refuge from the storms
      of Fate!

The fond complaint, my song, disprove,
And justify the laws of Jove.
Say, has he given in vain the heavenly
   Muse?
Night, and all her sickly dews,
Her spectres wan, and birds of boding
   cry
He gives to range the dreary sky,
Till down the eastern cliffs afar
Hyperion's march they spy, and glittering
   shafts of war.

   In climes beyond the solar road
Where shaggy forms o'er ice-built mountains roam,
The Muse has broke the twilight gloom
   To cheer the shivering native's dull
      abode.
And oft, beneath the od'rous shade
Of Chili's boundless forests laid,
She deigns to hear the savage youth repeat
In loose numbers wildly sweet
Their feather-cinctured chiefs and dusky
   loves.
Her track, where'er the goddess roves,
Glory pursue, and gen'rous Shame,
Th' unconquerable Mind, and Freedom's
   holy flame.

   Woods, that wave o'er Delphi's steep,
   Isles, that crown th' Ægean deep,
Fields, that cool Ilissus laves,
Or where Mæander's amber waves
   In lingering lab'rinths creep,
How do your tuneful echoes languish,
Mute, but to the voice of anguish!
Where each old poetic mountain
   Inspiration breathed around;
Every shade and hallow'd fountain
   Murmur'd deep a solemn sound;
Till the sad Nine, in Greece's evil hour,
   Left their Parnassus for the Latian
      plains.
Alike they scorn the pomp of tyrant
   Power,
   And coward Vice, that revels in her
      chains.
When Latium had her lofty spirit lost,
They sought, O Albion! next, thy sea-encircled coast.

Far from the sun and summer gale,
In thy green lap was Nature's darling laid,
What time, where lucid Avon stray'd,
To him the mighty mother did unveil
Her awful face: the dauntless child
Stretch'd forth his little arms, and smiled.
This pencil take (she said), whose colors clear
Richly paint the vernal year;
Thine, too, these golden keys, immortal boy!
This can unlock the gates of Joy;
Of Horror that, and thrilling Fears,
Or ope the sacred source of sympathetic Tears.

Nor second he, that rode sublime
Upon the seraph-wings of Ecstasy,
The secrets of th' abyss to spy.
 He pass'd the flaming bounds of Place and Time,
The living Throne, the sapphire-blaze
Where angels tremble while they gaze;
He saw, but, blasted with excess of light,
Closed his eyes in endless night.
Behold where Dryden's less presumptuous car
Wide o'er the fields of glory bear
Two coursers of ethereal race,
With necks in thunder clothed, and long-resounding pace.

 Hark! his hands the lyre explore!
 Bright-eyed Fancy, hovering o'er,
Scatters from her pictured urn
Thoughts that breathe, and words that burn.
But ah! 'tis heard no more—
O Lyre divine! what daring Spirit
Wakes thee now? Tho' he inherit
Nor the pride, nor ample pinion,
That the Theban eagle bear,
Sailing with supreme dominion
 Thro' the azure deep of air;
Yet oft before his infant eyes would run
Such forms as glitter in the Muse's ray
With orient hues, unborrow'd of the sun;
 Yet shall he mount, and keep his distant way
Beyond the limits of a vulgar fate,
Beneath the Good how far, but far above the Great.

       THOMAS GRAY.

THE PASSIONS.
AN ODE FOR MUSIC.

WHEN Music, heavenly maid, was young,
While yet in early Greece she sung,
The Passions oft, to hear her shell,
Throng'd around her magic cell,
Exulting, trembling, raging, fainting,
Possest beyond the Muse's painting;
By turns they felt the glowing mind
Disturb'd, delighted, raised, refined;
Till once, 'tis said, when all were fired,
Fill'd with fury, rapt, inspired,
From the supporting myrtles round
They snatch'd her instruments of sound,
And, as they oft had heard apart
Sweet lessons of her forceful art,
Each, for Madness ruled the hour,
Would prove his own expressive power.

First Fear his hand, its skill to try,
 Amid the chords bewilder'd laid,
And back recoil'd, he knew not why,
 E'en at the sound himself had made.

Next Anger rush'd; his eyes on fire,
 In lightnings own'd his secret stings:
In one rude clash he struck the lyre
 And swept with hurried hand the strings.

With woeful measures wan Despair—
 Low, sullen sounds his grief beguiled;
A solemn, strange, and mingled air;
 'Twas sad by fits, by starts 'twas wild.

But thou, O Hope, with eyes so fair,
 What was thy delighted measure?
Still it whisper'd promised pleasure,
 And bade the lovely scenes at distance hail!
Still would her touch the strain prolong;
 And from the rocks, the woods, the vale
She call'd on Echo still through all the song;
 And, where her sweetest theme she chose,
A soft responsive voice was heard at every close;
And Hope enchanted smiled, and waved her golden hair.

And longer had she sung:—but with a frown
  Revenge impatient rose:
He threw his blood-stain'd sword in thunder down;
  And with a withering look
  The war-denouncing trumpet took,
And blew a blast so loud and dread,
Were ne'er prophetic sounds so full of woe!
And ever and anon he beat
The doubling drum with furious heat;
And, though sometimes, each dreary pause between,
  Dejected Pity at his side
  Her soul-subduing voice applied,
Yet still he kept his wild unalter'd mien,
  While each strain'd ball of sight seem'd bursting from his head.

Thy numbers, Jealousy, to naught were fix'd:
  Sad proof of thy distressful state!
Of differing themes the veering song was mix'd;
  And now it courted Love, now raving call'd on Hate.

With eyes upraised, as one inspired,
Pale Melancholy sat retired;
And from her wild sequester'd seat,
In notes by distance made more sweet,
Pour'd through the mellow horn her pensive soul:
  And dashing soft from rocks around
  Bubbling runnels join'd the sound;
Through glades and glooms the mingled measure stole,
Or, o'er some haunted stream, with fond delay,
  Round an holy calm diffusing,
  Love of peace, and lonely musing,
In hollow murmurs died away.

But oh! how alter'd was its sprightlier tone
  When Cheerfulness, a nymph of healthiest hue,
  Her bow across her shoulder flung,
  Her buskins gemm'd with morning dew,
Blew an inspiring air, that dale and thicket rung,
The hunter's call to Faun and Dryad known.
  The oak-crown'd Sisters and their chaste-eyed Queen,
  Satyrs and Sylvan Boys were seen
  Peeping from forth their alleys green:
Brown Exercise rejoiced to hear;
And Sport leap'd up, and seized his beechen spear.

Last came Joy's ecstatic trial:
  He, with viny crown advancing,
  First to the lively pipe his hand addrest;
But soon he saw the brisk awakening viol
  Whose sweet entrancing voice he loved the best:
They would have thought who heard the strain
  They saw, in Tempe's vale, her native maids
  Amidst the festal-sounding shades
  To some unwearied minstrel dancing;
While, as his flying fingers kiss'd the strings,
  Love framed with Mirth a gay, fantastic round:
  Loose were her tresses seen, her zone unbound;
  And he, amidst his frolic play,
  As if he would the charming air repay,
Shook thousand odors from his dewy wings.

O Music! sphere-descended maid,
Friend of Pleasure, Wisdom's aid!
Why, goddess, why, to us denied,
Lay'st thou thy ancient lyre aside?
As in that loved Athenian bower
You learn'd an all-commanding power,
Thy mimic soul, O nymph endear'd!
Can well recall what then it heard.
Where is thy native simple heart,
Devote to Virtue, Fancy, Art?
Arise, as in that elder time,
Warm, energic, chaste, sublime!
Thy wonders, in that god-like age,
Fill thy recording Sister's page;—
'Tis said, and I believe the tale,
Thy humblest reed could more prevail,

Had more of strength, diviner rage,
Than all which charms this laggard age,
E'en all at once together found
Cecilia's mingled world of sound:—
Oh bid our vain endeavors cease:
Revive the just designs of Greece:
Return in all thy simple state!
Confirm the tales her sons relate!
WILLIAM COLLINS.

INFLUENCE OF MUSIC.

ORPHEUS with his lute made trees,
And the mountain-tops that freeze,
  Bow themselves, when he did sing:
To his music, plants and flowers
Ever sprung, as sun and showers
  There had made a lasting spring.

Everything that heard him play,
Even the billows of the sea,
  Hung their heads, and then lay by—
In sweet music is such art:
Killing care, and grief of heart,
  Fall asleep, or, hearing, die.
WILLIAM SHAKESPEARE.

WITH A GUITAR, TO JANE.

Ariel to Miranda.—Take
This slave of Music, for the sake
Of him who is the slave of thee;
And teach it all the harmony
In which thou canst, and only thou,
Make the delighted spirit glow,
Till joy denies itself again,
And, too intense, is turn'd to pain.
For by permission and command
Of thine own prince Ferdinand,
Poor Ariel sends this silent token
Of more than ever can be spoken;
Your guardian spirit, Ariel, who
From life to life must still pursue
Your happiness, for thus alone
Can Ariel ever find his own.
From Prospero's enchanted cell,
As the mighty verses tell,
To the throne of Naples he
Lit you o'er the trackless sea,
Flitting on, your prow before,
Like a living meteor.
When you die, the silent Moon
In her interlunar swoon
Is not sadder in her cell
Than deserted Ariel;
When you live again on earth,
Like an unseen star of birth
Ariel guides you o'er the sea
Of life from your nativity.
Many changes have been run
Since Ferdinand and you begun
Your course of love, and Ariel still
Has track'd your steps and served your
  will.
Now in humbler, happier lot,
This is all remember'd not;
And now, alas! the poor sprite is
Imprison'd for some fault of his
In a body like a grave—
From you he only dares to crave
For his service and his sorrow
A smile to-day, a song to-morrow.

The artist who this idol wrought
To echo all harmonious thought,
Fell'd a tree, while on the steep
The woods were in their winter sleep,
Rock'd in that repose divine
On the wind-swept Apennine;
And dreaming, some of autumn past,
And some of spring approaching fast,
And some of April buds and showers,
And some of songs in July bowers,
And all of love; and so this tree—
Oh, that such our death may be!—
Died in sleep, and felt no pain,
To live in happier form again;
From which, beneath Heaven's fairest
  star,
The artist wrought this loved guitar;
And taught it justly to reply,
To all who question skilfully,
In language gentle as thine own;
Whispering in enamor'd tone
Sweet oracles of woods and dells,
And summer winds in sylvan cells.
For it had learn'd all harmonies
Of the plains and of the skies,
Of the forests and the mountains,
And the many-voicèd fountains;
The clearest echoes of the hills,
The softest notes of falling rills,
The melodies of birds and bees,
The murmuring of summer seas,
And pattering rain, and breathing dew,
And airs of evening; and it knew
That seldom-heard mysterious sound
Which, driven on its diurnal round,

As it floats through boundless day
Our world enkindles on its way.
All this it knows, but will not tell
To those who cannot question well
The spirit that inhabits it.
It talks according to the wit
Of its companions; and no more
Is heard than has been felt before
By those who tempt it to betray
These secrets of an elder day.
But, sweetly as its answers will
Flatter hands of perfect skill,
It keeps its highest, holiest tone
For our beloved Jane alone.
PERCY BYSSHE SHELLEY.

L'ALLEGRO.

HENCE, loathèd Melancholy,
  Of Cerberus and blackest Midnight born!
  In Stygian cave forlorn,
'Mongst horrid shapes, and shrieks, and
    sights unholy,
  Find out some uncouth cell,
Where brooding Darkness spreads his
    jealous wings,
And the night raven sings;
There under ebon shades, and low-brow'd
    rocks,
  As ragged as thy locks,
  In dark Cimmerian desert ever dwell.
But come thou Goddess fair and free,
In heav'n y-clep'd Euphrosyne,
And by men, heart-easing Mirth,
Whom lovely Venus at a birth
With two sister Graces more,
To ivy-crownèd Bacchus bore;
Or whether (as some sager sing)
The frolic wind that breathes the spring,
Zephyr with Aurora playing,
As he met her once a-maying;
There on beds of violets blue,
And fresh-blown roses wash'd in dew,
Fill'd her with thee a daughter fair,
So buxom, blithe, and debonair.
  Haste thee, Nymph, and bring with thee
Jest, and youthful Jollity,
Quips, and Cranks, and wanton Wiles,
Nods, and Becks, and wreathèd Smiles,
Such as hang on Hebe's cheek,
And love to live in dimple sleek;

Sport that wrinkled Care derides,
And Laughter holding both his sides.
Come, and trip it as you go,
On the light fantastic toe;
And in thy right hand lead with thee
The mountain-nymph, sweet Liberty;
And, if I give thee honor due,
Mirth, admit me of the crew,
To live with her, and live with thee,
In unreprovèd pleasures free;
To hear the lark begin his flight,
And singing startle the dull night,
From his watch-tow'r in the skies,
Till the dappled dawn doth rise;
Then to come in spite of sorrow,
And at my window bid good-morrow,
Through the sweet-brier, or the vine,
Or the twisted eglantine:
While the cock with lively din
Scatters the rear of darkness thin,
And to the stack, or the barn-door,
Stoutly struts his dames before:
Oft list'ning how the hounds and horn
Cheerly rouse the slumb'ring morn,
From the side of some hoar hill,
Through the high wood echoing shrill:
Some time walking, not unseen,
By hedge-row elms, on hillocks green,
Right against the eastern gate,
Where the great sun begins his state,
Robed in flames, and amber light,
The clouds in thousand liveries dight;
While the ploughman near at hand
Whistles o'er the furrow'd land,
And the milkmaid singeth blithe,
And the mower whets his scythe,
And every shepherd tells his tale
Under the hawthorn in the dale.
Straight mine eye hath caught new pleasures
Whilst the landscape round it measures;
Russet lawns, and fallows gray,
Where the nibbling flocks do stray,
Mountains, on whose barren breast
The lab'ring clouds do often rest;
Meadows trim with daisies pied,
Shallow brooks, and rivers wide.
Towers and battlements it sees
Bosom'd high in tufted trees,
Where perhaps some beauty lies,
The cynosure of neighb'ring eyes.

Hard by, a cottage chimney smokes,
From betwixt two aged oaks,
Where Corydon and Thyrsis met
Are at their savory dinner set
Of herbs, and other country messes,
Which the neat-handed Phillis dresses;
And then in haste her bow'r she leaves,
With Thestylis to bind the sheaves;
Or, if the earlier season lead,
To the tann'd haycock in the mead,
Sometimes with secure delight
The upland hamlets will invite,
When the merry bells ring round,
And the jocund rebecks sound
To many a youth, and many a maid,
Dancing in the chequer'd shade;
And young and old come forth to play
On a sunshine holiday,
Till the live-long daylight fail;
Then to the spicy nut-brown ale,
With stories told of many a feat,
How fairy Mab the junkets eat;
She was pinch'd, and pull'd she said,
And he by friars' lanthorn led
Tells how the drudging Goblin sweat,
To earn his cream-bowl duly set,
When in one night, ere glimpse of morn,
His shadowy flail hath thresh'd the corn,
That ten day-lab'rers could not end;
Then lies him down the lubber fiend,
And stretch'd out all the chimney's length,
Basks at the fire his hairy strength,
And crop-full out of doors he flings,
Ere the first cock his matin rings.
Thus done the tales, to bed they creep,
By whispering winds soon lull'd asleep.
Tower'd cities please us then,
And the busy hum of men,
Where throngs of knights and barons bold
In weeds of peace high triumphs hold,
With store of ladies, whose bright eyes
Rain influence, and judge the prize
Of wit, or arms, while both contend
To win her grace, whom all commend.
There let Hymen oft appear
In saffron robe, with taper clear,
And pomp, and feast, and revelry,
With mask, and antique pageantry,
Such sights as youthful poets dream
On summer eves by haunted stream.

Then to the well-trod stage anon,
If Jonson's learnèd sock be on,
Or sweetest Shakespeare, Fancy's child,
Warble his native wood-notes wild.
  And ever against eating cares,
Lap me in soft Lydian airs,
Married to immortal verse;
Such as the meeting soul may pierce,
In notes, with many a winding bout
Of linkèd sweetness long drawn out,
With wanton heed and giddy cunning,
The melting voice through mazes running,
Untwisting all the chains that tie
The hidden soul of harmony;
That Orpheus' self may heave his head
From golden slumber on a bed
Of heap'd Elysian flowers, and hear
Such strains as would have won the ear
Of Pluto, to have quite set free
His half-regain'd Eurydice.
  These delights if thou canst give,
Mirth, with thee I mean to live.
JOHN MILTON.

SONNET TO HIS LUTE.

MY lute, be as thou wert when thou didst grow
  With thy green mother in some shady grove,
  When immelodious winds but made thee move,
And birds their ramage did on thee bestow.
Since that dear voice which did thy sounds approve,
  Which wont in such harmonious strains to flow,
  Is reft from earth to tune the spheres above,
What art thou but a harbinger of woe?
Thy pleasing notes be pleasing notes no more,
  But orphan wailings to the fainting ear;
  Each stroke a sigh, each sound draws forth a tear;
For which be silent as in woods before:
Or if that any hand to touch thee deign,
Like widow'd turtle still her loss complain.
WILLIAM DRUMMOND.

A CANADIAN BOAT-SONG.

Et remigem cantus hortatur.
QUINTILIAN.

FAINTLY as tolls the evening chime,
Our voices keep tune, and our oars keep time.
Soon as the woods on shore look dim,
We'll sing at St. Ann's our parting hymn.
Row, brothers, row! the stream runs fast,
The rapids are near, and the daylight's past!

Why should we yet our sail unfurl?—
There is not a breath the blue wave to curl.
But when the wind blows off the shore
Oh! sweetly we'll rest our weary oar.
Blow, breezes, blow! the stream runs fast,
The rapids are near, and the daylight's past!

Utawa's tide! this trembling moon
Shall see us float over thy surges soon.
Saint of this green isle, hear our prayers—
Oh! grant us cool heavens and favoring airs!
Blow, breezes, blow! the stream runs fast,
The rapids are near, and the daylight's past!

THOMAS MOORE.

IL PENSEROSO.

HENCE, vain deluding joys,
  The brood of folly without father bred,
How little you bestead,
Or fill the fixèd mind with all your toys!
Dwell in some idle brain,
And fancies fond with gaudy shapes possess,
As thick and numberless
As the gay motes that people the sunbeams,
Or likest hovering dreams,
  The fickle pensioners of Morpheus' train.
But hail, thou goddess sage and holy,
Hail, divinest Melancholy,
Whose saintly visage is too bright
To hit the sense of human sight,
And therefore to our weaker view
O'erlaid with black, staid Wisdom's hue;
Black, but such as in esteem
Prince Memnon's sister might beseem,
Or that starr'd Ethiop queen that strove
To set her beauty's praise above
The Sea-Nymphs, and their pow'rs offended:
Yet thou art higher far descended;
Thee bright-hair'd Vesta, long of yore,
To solitary Saturn bore;
His daughter she (in Saturn's reign
Such mixture was not held a stain).
Oft in glimmering bow'rs and glades
He met her, and in secret shades
Of woody Ida's inmost grove,
While yet there was no fear of Jove.
Come, pensive nun, devout and pure,
Sober, steadfast, and demure,
All in a robe of darkest grain,
Flowing with majestic train,
And sable stole of cyprus lawn
Over thy decent shoulders drawn.
Come, but keep thy wonted state,
With even step, and musing gait,
And looks commercing with the skies,
Thy rapt soul sitting in thine eyes:
There held in holy passion still,
Forget thyself to marble, till
With a sad leaden downward cast
Thou fix them on the earth as fast:
And join with thee calm Peace and Quiet,
Spare Fast, that oft with gods doth diet,
And hears the muses in a ring
Aye round about Jove's altar sing:
And add to these retired Leisure,
That in trim gardens takes his pleasure;
But first, and chiefest, with thee bring,
Him that yon soars on golden wing,
Guiding the fiery-wheelèd throne,
The cherub Contemplation;
And the mute Silence hist along,
'Less Philomel will deign a song,
In her sweetest, saddest plight,
Smoothing the rugged brow of night,
While Cynthia checks her dragon-yoke,
Gently o'er th' accustom'd oak;
Sweet bird, that shunn'st the noise of folly,
Most musical, most melancholy!
Thee, chauntress, oft the woods among
I woo, to hear thy even-song;
And missing thee, I walk unseen
On the dry smooth-shaven green,
To behold the wandering moon,
Riding near her highest noon,

Like one that had been led astray
Through the heav'n's wide pathless way;
And oft, as if her head she bow'd,
Stooping through a fleecy cloud.
Oft on a plat of rising ground,
I hear the far-off curfew sound,
Over some wide-water'd shore,
Swinging slow with sullen roar;
Or if the air will not permit,
Some still removèd place will fit,
Where glowing embers through the room
Teach light to counterfeit a gloom;
Far from all resort of mirth,
Save the cricket on the hearth,
Or the bellman's drowsy charm,
To bless the doors from nightly harm
Or let my lamp at midnight hour
Be seen in some high lonely tow'r,
Where I may oft outwatch the Bear,
With thrice-great Hermes, or unsphere
The spirit of Plato, to unfold
What worlds, or what vast regions, hold
The immortal mind, that hath forsook
Her mansion in this fleshly nook:
And of those demons that are found
In fire, air, flood, or under ground,
Whose power hath a true consent
With planet, or with element.
Sometime let gorgeous Tragedy
In sceptred pall come sweeping by,
Presenting Thebes or Pelops' line,
Or the tale of Troy divine,
Or what (though rare) of later age
Ennobled hath the buskin'd stage.
But, O sad virgin, that thy power
Might raise Musæus from his bower,
Or bid the soul of Orpheus sing
Such notes as, warbled to the string,
Drew iron tears down Pluto's cheek,
And made Hell grant what love did seek.
Or call up him that left half told
The story of Cambuscan bold,
Of Camball, and of Algarsife,
And who had Canace to wife,
That own'd the virtuous ring and glass,
And of the wondrous horse of brass,
On which the Tartar king did ride;
And if aught else great bards beside
In sage and solemn tunes have sung,
Of turneys and of trophies hung,
Of forests, and enchantments drear,
Where more is meant than meets the ear.

Thus Night oft see me in thy pale career,
Till civil-suited Morn appear,
Nor trick'd and frounced as she was wont
With the Attic boy to hunt,
But kerchief'd in a comely cloud,
While rocking winds are piping loud,
Or usher'd with a shower still
When the gust hath blown his fill,
Ending on the rustling leaves,
With minute drops from off the eaves.
And when the sun begins to fling
His flaring beams, me, goddess, bring
To archèd walks of twilight groves,
And shadows brown that Sylvan loves
Of pine, or monumental oak,
Where the rude axe with heavèd stroke
Was never heard the nymphs to daunt,
Or fright them from their hallow'd haunt.
There in close covert by some brook,
Where no profaner eye may look,
Hide me from day's garish eye,
While the bee with honey'd thigh,
That at her flow'ry work doth sing,
And the waters murmuring
With such consort as they keep,
Entice the dewy-feather'd sleep;
And let some strange, mysterious dream
Wave at his wings in aëry stream
Of lively portraiture display'd,
Softly on my eyelids laid.
And as I wake sweet music breathe
Above, about, or underneath,
Sent by some spirit to mortals good,
Or th' unseen genius of the wood.
But let my due feet never fail
To walk the studious cloisters pale,,
And love the high-embowèd roof,
With antique pillars massy proof,
And storied windows richly dight,
Casting a dim religious right:
There let the pealing organ blow,
To the full-voiced quire below,
In service high, and anthems clear,
As may with sweetness, through mine ear
Dissolve me into ecstasies,
And bring all heaven before mine eyes.
And may at last my weary age
Find out the peaceful hermitage,
The hairy gown and mossy cell,
Where I may sit and rightly spell
Of every star that heav'n doth show,
And every herb that sips the dew;

Till old experience do attain
To something like prophetic strain.
These pleasures, Melancholy, give,
And I with thee will choose to live.
JOHN MILTON.

MY MINDE TO ME A KINGDOM IS.

My minde to me a kingdom is;
  Such perfect joy therein I finde
As farre exceeds all earthly blisse
  That God or Nature hath assignde;
Though much I want, that most would have,
Yet still my minde forbids to crave.

Content I live; this is my stay—
  I seek no more than may suffice.
I presse to beare no haughtie sway;
  Look, what I lack my minde supplies.
Loe, thus I triumph like a king,
Content with that my minde doth bring.

I see how plentie surfets oft,
  And hastie clymbers soonest fall;
I see that such as sit aloft
  Mishap doth threaten most of all.
These get with toile, and keepe with feare:
Such cares my minde could never beare.

No princely pompe nor welthie store,
  No force to win the victorie,
No wylie wit to salve a sore,
  No shape to winne a lover's eye—
To none of these I yeeld as thrall;
For why, my minde despiseth all.

Some have too much, yet still they crave;
  I little have, yet seek no more.
They are but poore, though much they have,
  And I am rich with little store.
They poor, I rich; they beg, I give;
They lacke, I lend; they pine, I live.

I laugh not at another's losse,
  I grudge not at another's gaine;
No worldly wave my minde can tosse;
  I brooke that is another's bane.
I feare no foe, nor fawne on friend;
I lothe not life, nor dread mine end.

I joy not in no earthly blisse;
  I weigh not Cresus' wealth a straw;
For care, I care not what it is;
  I feare not fortune's fatal law:
My minde is such as may not move
For beautie bright, or force of love.

I wish but what I have at will;
  I wander not to seeke for more;
I like the plaine, I clime no hill;
  In greatest stormes I sitte on shore,
And laugh at them that toile in vaine
To get what must be lost againe.

I kisse not where I wish to kill;
  I feigne not love where most I hate;
I breake no sleepe to winne my will;
  I wayte not at the mightie's gate.
I scorne no poore, I feare no rich;
I feele no want, nor have too much.

The court ne cart I like ne loath—
  Extreames are counted worst of all;
The golden meane betwixt them both
  Dost surest sit, and feares no fall;
This is my choyce; for why, I finde
No wealth is like a quiet minde.

My wealth is health and perfect ease;
  My conscience clere my chiefe defence;
I never seeke by bribes to please,
  Nor by desert to give offence.
Thus do I live, thus will I die;
Would all did so as well as I!
WILLIAM BYRD.

MY DAYS AMONG THE DEAD ARE PASSED.

My days among the dead are pass'd;
  Around me I behold,
Where'er these casual eyes are cast,
  The mighty minds of old;
My never-failing friends are they,
With whom I converse day by day.

With them I take delight in weal,
  And seek relief in woe;
And while I understand and feel
  How much to them I owe,
My cheeks have often been bedew'd
With tears of thoughtful gratitude.

My thoughts are with the dead; with them
  I live in long-past years;

Their virtues love, their faults condemn,
  Partake their hopes and fears,
And from their lessons seek and find
  Instruction with an humble mind.

My hopes are with the dead; anon
  My place with them will be,
And I with them shall travel on
  Through all futurity,
Yet leaving here a name, I trust,
  That will not perish in the dust.
               ROBERT SOUTHEY.

THOUGHTS IN A LIBRARY.

SPEAK low! tread softly through these
    halls;
Here Genius lives enshrined;
Here reign, in silent majesty,
  The monarchs of the mind.

A mighty spirit-host they come
  From every age and clime;
Above the buried wrecks of years
  They breast the tide of Time.

And in their presence-chamber here
  They hold their regal state,
And round them throng a noble train,
  The gifted and the great.

O child of Earth! when round thy path
  The storms of life arise,
And when thy brothers pass thee by
  With stern, unloving eyes,

Here shall the poets chant for thee
  Their sweetest, loftiest lays,
And prophets wait to guide thy steps
  In Wisdom's pleasant ways.

Come, with these God-anointed kings
  Be thou companion here;
And in the mighty realm of mind
  Thou shalt go forth a peer!
               ANNE C. LYNCH BOTTA.

THE LAWYER'S FAREWELL TO HIS MUSE.

As, by some tyrant's stern command,
A wretch forsakes his native land,
In foreign climes condemn'd to roam
An endless exile from his home;
Pensive he treads the destined way,
And dreads to go, nor dares to stay;
Till on some neighboring mountain's
    brow
He stops, and turns his eyes below;
There, melting at the well-known view,
Drops a last tear, and bids adieu;
So I, thus doom'd from thee to part,
Gay Queen of Fancy and of Art,
Reluctant move, with doubtful mind,
Oft stop, and often look behind.
  Companion of my tender age,
Serenely gay, and sweetly sage,
How blithesome we were wont to rove
By verdant hill or shady grove,
Where fervent bees, with humming
    voice,
Around the honey'd oak rejoice,
And aged elms with awful bend
In long cathedral walks extend!
Lull'd by the lapse of gliding floods,
Cheer'd by the warbling of the woods,
How bless'd my days, my thoughts how
    free
In sweet society with thee!
Then all was joyous, all was young,
And years unheeded roll'd along:
But now the pleasing dream is o'er,
These scenes must charm me now no
    more;
Lost to the fields, and torn from you,—
Farewell!—a long, a last adieu.
  Me wrangling courts, and stubborn
    law,
To smoke, and crowds, and cities draw:
There selfish Faction rules the day,
And Pride and Avarice throng the way;
Diseases taint the murky air,
And midnight conflagrations glare;
Loose Revelry and Riot bold
In frighted streets their orgies hold;
Or, where in silence all is drown'd,
Fell Murder walks his lonely round;
No room for Peace, no room for you,
Adieu, celestial nymph, adieu!
  Shakespeare no more thy sylvan son,
Nor all the art of Addison,
Pope's heaven-strung lyre, nor Waller's
    ease,
Nor Milton's mighty self, must please:
Instead of these, a formal band
In furs and coifs around me stand;

With sounds uncouth, and accents dry,
That grate the soul of harmony;
Each pedant sage unlocks his store
Of mystic, dark, discordant lore;
And points with tottering hand the ways
That lead me to the thorny maze.

There, in a winding close retreat,
Is Justice doom'd to fix her seat;
There, fenced by bulwarks of the law,
She keeps the wondering world in awe;
And there, from vulgar sight retired,
Like Eastern queen, is more admired.

Oh let me pierce the secret shade
Where dwells the venerable maid!
There humbly mark, with reverend awe,
The guardian of Britannia's law;
Unfold with joy her sacred page,
Th' united boast of many an age;
Where mix'd, yet uniform, appears
The wisdom of a thousand years.
In that pure spring the bottom view,
Clear, deep, and regularly true;
And other doctrines thence imbibe
Than lurk within the sordid scribe;
Observe how parts with parts unite
In one harmonious rule of right;
See countless wheels distinctly tend
By various laws to one great end:
While mighty Alfred's piercing soul
Pervades and regulates the whole.

Then welcome business, welcome strife,
Welcome the cares, the thorns of life,
The visage wan, the purblind sight,
The toil by day, the lamp at night,
The tedious forms, the solemn prate,
The pert dispute, the dull debate,
The drowsy bench, the babbling hall,—
For thee, fair Justice, welcome all!
Thus though my noon of life be past,
Yet let my setting sun, at last,
Find out the still, the rural cell,
Where sage Retirement loves to dwell!
There let me taste the homefelt bliss
Of innocence and inward peace;
Untainted by the guilty bribe,
Uncursed amid the harpy tribe;
No orphan's cry to wound my ear;
My honor and my conscience clear;
Thus may I calmly meet my end,
Thus to the grave in peace descend.
Sir William Blackstone.

ON FIRST LOOKING INTO CHAPMAN'S HOMER.

Much have I travell'd in the realms of gold,
And many goodly states and kingdoms seen;
Round many western islands have I been
Which bards in fealty to Apollo hold.
Oft of one wide expanse had I been told
That deep-brow'd Homer ruled as his demesne;
Yet did I never breathe its pure serene
Till I heard Chapman speak out loud and bold:
Then felt I like some watcher of the skies
When a new planet swims into his ken;
Or like stout Cortez when with eagle eyes
He stared at the Pacific—and all his men
Look'd at each other with a wild surmise—
Silent, upon a peak in Darien.
John Keats.

A VISION UPON THIS CONCEIT OF THE FAERIE QUEENE.

Methought I saw the grave where Laura lay,
Within that temple, where the vestal flame
Was wont to burn; and passing by that way,
To see that buried dust of living fame,
Whose tomb fair Love, and fairer Virtue kept,
All suddenly I saw the Faerie Queene;
At whose approach the soul of Petrarch wept,
And, from thenceforth, those Graces were not seen;
For they this Queen attended; in whose stead
Oblivion laid him down on Laura's hearse:
Hereat the hardest stones were seen to bleed,
And groans of buried ghosts the heavens did pierce,
Where Homer's spright did tremble all for grief,
And cursed the access of that celestial thief!
Sir Walter Raleigh.

ODE.

Bards of passion and of mirth,
Ye have left your souls on earth!
Have ye souls in Heaven too,
Double-lived in regions new?
Yes, and those of Heaven commune
With the spheres of sun and moon;
With the noise of fountains wondrous,
And the parle of voices thund'rous;
With the whisper of Heaven's trees
And one another, in soft ease
Seated on Elysian lawns
Browsed by none but Dian's fawns;
Underneath large blue-bells tented,
Where the daisies are rose-scented,
And the rose herself has got
Perfume which on earth is not;
Where the nightingale doth sing
Not a senseless, trancèd thing,
But divine, melodious truth—
Philosophic numbers smooth—
Tales and golden histories
Of Heaven and its mysteries.

Thus ye live on high, and then
On the earth ye live again;
And the souls ye left behind you
Teach us here the way to find you,
Where your other souls are joying,
Never slumber'd, never cloying.
Here your earth-born souls still speak
To mortals, of their little week;
Of their sorrows and delights;
Of their passions and their spites;
Of their glory and their shame;
What doth strengthen and what maim.
Thus ye teach us, every day,
Wisdom, though fled far away.

Bards of passion and of mirth,
Ye have left your souls on earth!
Ye have souls in Heaven too,
Double-lived in regions new!
JOHN KEATS.

SONG.

Still to be neat, still to be drest,
As you were going to a feast;
Still to be powder'd, still perfumed,
Lady, it is to be presumed,
Though art's hid causes are not found,
All is not sweet, all is not sound.

Give me a look, give me a face,
That makes simplicity a grace;
Robes loosely flowing, hair as free—
Such sweet neglect more taketh me
Than all the adulteries of art;
They strike mine eyes, but not my heart.
BEN JONSON.

DELIGHT IN DISORDER.

A sweet disorder in the dress
Kindles in clothes a wantonness:
A lawn about the shoulders thrown
Into a fine distractión—
An erring lace, which here and there
Enthralls the crimson stomacher—
A cuff neglectful, and thereby
Ribbons to flow confusedly—
A winning wave, deserving note,
In the tempestuous petticoat—
A careless shoe-string, in whose tie
I see a wild civility,—
Do more bewitch me than when art
Is too precise in every part.
ROBERT HERRICK.

THE LACHRYMATORY.

From out the grave of one whose budding years
  Were cropp'd by death when Rome was in her prime,
I brought the vial of his kinsman's tears,
  There placed, as was the wont of ancient time;
Round me, that night, in meads of asphodel,
  The souls of th' early dead did come and go,
Drawn by that flask of grief, as by a spell,
  That long-imprison'd shower of human woe;
As round Ulysses, for the draught of blood,
  The heroes throng'd, those spirits flock'd to me,
Where, lonely, with that charm of tears I stood;
  Two, most of all, my dreaming eyes did see;
The young Marcellus, young, but great and good,
  And Tully's daughter mourn'd so tenderly.
CHARLES TURNER.

AGE AND SONG.

In vain men tell us time can alter
Old loves or make old memories falter,
  That with the old year the old year's life
    closes.
The old dew still falls on the old sweet
    flowers,
The old sun revives the new-fledged hours,
The old summer rears the new-born roses.

Much more a Muse that bears upon her
Raiment and wreath and flower of honor,
  Gather'd long since and long since woven,
Fades not or falls as falls the vernal
Blossoms that bear no fruit eternal,
  By summer or winter charr'd or cloven.

No time casts down, no time upraises
Such loves, such memories and such praises,
  As need no grace of sun or shower,
No saving screen from frost or thunder,
To tend and house around and under
  The imperishable and peerless flower.

Old thanks, old thoughts, old aspirations,
Outlive men's lives and lives of nations,
  Dead, but for one thing which survives—
The inalienable and unpriced treasure,
The old joy of power, the old pride of
    pleasure,
  That lives in light above men's lives.
        ALGERNON CHARLES SWINBURNE.

BEAUTY FADES.

Trust not, sweet soul, those curlèd waves
    of gold
  With gentle tides that on your temples
    flow,
  Nor temples spread with flakes of virgin
    snow,
  Nor snow of cheeks with Tyrian grain en-
    roll'd.
Trust not those shining lights which
    wrought my woe
  When first I did their azure rays be-
    hold,
  Nor voice, whose sounds more strange ef-
    fects do show
  Than of the Thracian harper have been
    told.

Look to this dying lily, fading rose,
  Dark hyacinth, of late whose blushing
    beams
Made all the neighboring herbs and grass
    rejoice,
  And think how little is 'twixt life's ex-
    tremes:
The cruel tyrant that did kill those flowers
Shall once, ah me! not spare that spring
    of yours.
        WILLIAM DRUMMOND.

SHE WALKS IN BEAUTY.

She walks in beauty like the night
  Of cloudless climes and starry skies;
And all that's best of dark and bright
  Meets in her aspect and her eyes:
Thus mellow'd to that tender light
  Which heaven to gaudy day denies.

One shade the more, one ray the less,
  Had half impair'd the nameless grace
Which waves in every raven tress,
  Or softly lightens o'er her face—
Where thoughts serenely sweet express
  How pure, how dear their dwelling-
    place.

And on that cheek, and o'er that brow,
  So soft, so calm, yet eloquent,
The smiles that win, the tints that glow,
  But tell of days in goodness spent,
A mind at peace with all below,
  A heart whose love is innocent.
        LORD BYRON.

HESTER.

When maidens such as Hester die,
Their place ye may not well supply,
Though ye among a thousand try,
  With vain endeavor.

A month or more hath she been dead,
Yet cannot I by force be led
To think upon the wormy bed
  And her, together.

A springy motion in her gait,
A rising step did indicate
Of pride and joy no common rate,
  That flush'd her spirit;

I know not by what name beside
I shall it call: if 'twas not pride,
It was a joy to that allied,
    She did inherit.

Her parents held the Quaker rule,
Which doth the human feeling cool;
But she was train'd in Nature's school—
    Nature had bless'd her.

A waking eye, a prying mind,
A heart that stirs, is hard to bind;
A hawk's keen sight ye cannot blind—
    Ye could not Hester.

My sprightly neighbor, gone before
To that unknown and silent shore!
Shall we not meet, as heretofore,
    Some summer morning,

When from thy cheerful eyes a ray
Hath struck a bliss upon the day—
A bliss that would not go away—
    A sweet forewarning?
                  CHARLES LAMB.

HAS SORROW THY YOUNG DAYS SHADED.

HAS sorrow thy young days shaded,
    As clouds o'er the morning fleet?
Too fast have those young days faded,
    That, even in sorrow, were sweet?
Does Time with his cold wing wither
    Each feeling that once was dear?—
Then, child of misfortune, come hither,
    I'll weep with thee, tear for tear.

Has love to that soul, so tender,
    Been like our Lagenian mine,
Where sparkles of golden splendor
    All over the surface shine?
But, if in pursuit we go deeper,
    Allured by the gleam that shone,
Ah! false as the dream of the sleeper,
    Like Love, the bright ore is gone.

Has Hope, like the bird in the story,
    That flitted from tree to tree
With the talisman's glittering glory—
    Has Hope been that bird to thee?
On branch after branch alighting,
    The gem did she still display,
And, when nearest and most inviting,
    Then waft the fair gem away?

If thus the young hours have fleeted,
    When sorrow itself look'd bright;
If thus the fair hope hath cheated,
    That led thee along so light;
If thus the cold world now wither
    Each feeling that once was dear:—
Come, child of misfortune, come hither,
    I'll weep with thee, tear for tear.
                  THOMAS MOORE.

STANZAS.

AND thou art dead, as young and fair
    As aught of mortal birth;
And form so soft, and charms so rare,
    Too soon return'd to earth!
Though Earth received them in her bed,
And o'er the spot the crowd may tread
    In carelessness or mirth,
There is an eye which could not brook
A moment on that grave to look.

I will not ask where thou liest low,
    Nor gaze upon the spot;
There flowers or weeds at will may grow,
    So I behold them not:
It is enough for me to prove
That what I loved, and long must love,
    Like common earth can rot;
To me there needs no stone to tell,
'Tis nothing that I loved so well.

Yet did I love thee to the last
    As fervently as thou,
Who didst not change through all the past,
    And canst not alter now.
The love where death has set his seal,
Nor age can chill, nor rival steal,
    Nor falsehood disavow:
And what were worse, thou canst not see
Or wrong, or change, or fault in me.

The better days of life were ours;
    The worst can be but mine;
The sun that cheers, the storm that lowers,
    Shall never more be thine.
The silence of that dreamless sleep
I envy now too much to weep;
    Nor need I to repine
That all those charms have pass'd away,
I might have watch'd through long decay.

The flower in ripen'd bloom unmatch'd
  Must fall the earliest prey;
Though by no hand untimely snatch'd,
  The leaves must drop away:
And yet it were a greater grief
To watch it withering, leaf by leaf,
  Than see it pluck'd to-day;
Since earthly eye but ill can bear
To trace the change to foul from fair.

I know not if I could have borne
  To see thy beauties fade;
The night that follow'd such a morn
  Had worn a deeper shade:
Thy day without a cloud hath past,
And thou wert lovely to the last;
  Extinguish'd, not decay'd;
As stars that shoot along the sky
Shine brightest as they fall from high.

As once I wept, if I could weep,
  My tears might well be shed,
To think I was not near to keep
  One vigil o'er thy bed;
To gaze, how fondly! on thy face,
To fold thee in a faint embrace,
  Uphold thy drooping head;
And show that love, however vain,
Nor thou nor I can feel again.

Yet how much less it were to gain,
  Though thou hast left me free,
The loveliest things that still remain,
  Than thus remember thee!
The all of thine that cannot die
Through dark and dread eternity
  Returns again to me,
And more thy buried love endears
Than aught, except its living years.
LORD BYRON.

OH! SNATCHED AWAY IN BEAUTY'S BLOOM.

OH! snatch'd away in beauty's bloom
On thee shall press no ponderous tomb;
  But on thy turf shall roses rear
  Their leaves, the earliest of the year;
And the wild cypress wave in tender gloom:

And oft by yon blue gushing stream
  Shall Sorrow lean her drooping head,
And feed deep thought with many a dream,
  And lingering pause and lightly tread:
Fond wretch! as if her step disturb'd
  the dead!

Away! we know that tears are vain,
  That death nor heeds nor hears distress.
Will this unteach us to complain?
  Or make one mourner weep the less?
And thou—who tell'st me to forget,
Thy looks are wan, thine eyes are wet.
LORD BYRON.

THY VOICE IS HEARD THRO' ROLLING DRUMS.

THY voice is heard thro' rolling drums,
  That beat to battle where he stands;
Thy face across his fancy comes,
  And gives the battle to his hands:
A moment, while the trumpets blow,
He sees his brood about thy knee;
The next, like fire he meets the foe,
And strikes him dead for thine and thee.
ALFRED TENNYSON.

AN ANGEL IN THE HOUSE.

How sweet it were, if without feeble fright,
Or dying of the dreadful beauteous sight,
An angel came to us, and we could bear
To see him issue from the silent air
At evening in our room, and bend on ours
His divine eyes, and bring us from his bowers
News of dear friends, and children who have never
Been dead indeed—as we shall know for ever.
Alas! we think not what we daily see
About our hearths—angels that are to be,
Or may be if they will, and we prepare
Their souls and ours to meet in happy air;
A child, a friend, a wife whose soft heart sings
In unison with ours, breeding its future wings.
LEIGH HUNT.

CHORUS.

FROM "ATALANTA IN CALYDON."

BEFORE the beginning of years
  There came to the making of man
Time, with a gift of tears;
  Grief, with a glass that ran;
Pleasure, with pain for leaven;
  Summer, with flowers that fell;
Remembrance, fallen from heaven;
  And madness risen from hell;
Strength, without hands to smite;
  Love, that endures for a breath;
Night, the shadow of light,
  And life, the shadow of death.

And the high gods took in hand
  Fire, and the falling of tears,
And a measure of sliding sand
  From under the feet of the years;
And froth and drift of the sea;
  And dust of the laboring earth;
And bodies of things to be
  In the houses of death and of birth;
And wrought with weeping and laughter,
  And fashion'd with loathing and love,
With life before and after,
  And death beneath and above,
For a day and a night and a morrow,
  That his strength might endure for a span
With travail and heavy sorrow,
  The holy spirit of man.

From the winds of the north and the south
  They gather'd as unto strife;
They breathed upon his mouth,
  They fill'd his body with life;
Eyesight and speech they wrought
  For the veils of the soul therein,
A time for labor and thought,
  A time to serve and to sin;
They gave him light in his ways,
  And love, and a space for delight,
And beauty and length of days,
  And night, and sleep in the night.
His speech is a burning fire;
  With his lips he travaileth;
In his heart is a blind desire,
  In his eyes foreknowledge of death;
He weaves, and is clothed with derision;
  Sows, and he shall not reap;
His life is a watch or a vision
  Between a sleep and a sleep.
      ALGERNON CHARLES SWINBURNE.

QUA CURSUM VENTUS.

As ships becalm'd at eve, that lay
  With canvas drooping, side by side,
Two towers of sail at dawn of day,
  Are scarce, long leagues apart, descried;

When fell the night, upsprung the breeze,
  And all the darkling hours they plied,
Nor dreamt but each the selfsame seas
  By each was cleaving, side by side:

E'en so,—but why the tale reveal
  Of those whom, year by year unchanged,
Brief absence join'd anew to feel,
  Astounded, soul from soul estranged?

At dead of night their sails were fill'd,
  And onward each rejoicing steer'd:
Ah, neither blame, for neither will'd,
  Or wist, what first with dawn appear'd!

To veer, how vain! On, onward strain,
  Brave barks! In light, in darkness too,
Through winds and tides one compass guides,—
  To that, and your own selves, be true.

But, O blithe breeze, and O great seas,
  Though ne'er, that earliest parting past,
On your wide plain they join again,
  Together lead them home at last!

One port, methought, alike they sought,
  One purpose hold where'er they fare,—
O bounding breeze, O rushing seas,
  At last, at last, unite them there.
      ARTHUR HUGH CLOUGH.

ADDRESS TO THE MUMMY IN BELZONI'S EXHIBITION.

AND thou hast walk'd about (how strange a story!)
  In Thebes' streets three thousand years ago,
When the Memnonium was in all its glory,
  And time had not begun to overthrow
Those temples, palaces, and piles stupendous,
  Of which the very ruins are tremendous?

Speak! for thou long enough hast acted dummy;
  Thou hast a tongue—come—let us hear its tune;

Thou'rt standing on thy legs, above ground, mummy!
Revisiting the glimpses of the moon—
Not like thin ghosts or disembodied creatures,
But with thy bones, and flesh, and limbs, and features.

Tell us—for doubtless thou canst recollect—
To whom should we assign the Sphinx's fame?
Was Cheops or Cephrenes architect
Of either pyramid that bears his name?
Is Pompey's Pillar really a misnomer?
Had Thebes a hundred gates, as sung by Homer?

Perhaps thou wert a Mason, and forbidden
By oath to tell the secrets of thy trade—
Then say what secret melody was hidden
In Memnon's statue, which at sunrise play'd?
Perhaps thou wert a priest—if so, my struggles
Are vain, for priestcraft never owns its juggles.

Perhaps that very hand, now pinion'd flat,
Has hob-a-nobb'd with Pharaoh, glass to glass;
Or dropp'd a half-penny in Homer's hat;
Or doff'd thine own to let Queen Dido pass;
Or held, by Solomon's own invitation,
A torch at the great temple's dedication.

I need not ask thee if that hand, when arm'd,
Has any Roman soldier maul'd and knuckled;
For thou wert dead, and buried, and embalm'd
Ere Romulus and Remus had been suckled:
Antiquity appears to have begun
Long after thy primeval race was run.

Thou could'st develop—if that wither'd tongue
Might tell us what those sightless orbs have seen—
How the world look'd when it was fresh and young,
And the great deluge still had left it green;
Or was it then so old that history's pages
Contain'd no record of its early ages?

Still silent! incommunicative elf!
Art sworn to secrecy? then keep thy vows;
But prythee tell us something of thyself—
Reveal the secrets of thy prison-house;
Since in the world of spirits thou hast slumber'd—
What hast thou seen—what strange adventures number'd?

Since first thy form was in this box extended
We have, above ground, seen some strange mutations;
The Roman empire has begun and ended—
New worlds have risen—we have lost old nations;
And countless kings have into dust been humbled,
While not a fragment of thy flesh has crumbled.

Didst thou not hear the pother o'er thy head
When the great Persian conqueror, Cambyses,
March'd armies o'er thy tomb with thundering tread—
O'erthrew Osiris, Orus, Apis, Isis;
And shook the pyramids with fear and wonder,
When the gigantic Memnon fell asunder?

If the tomb's secrets may not be confess'd,
The nature of thy private life unfold:
A heart has throbb'd beneath that leathern breast,
And tears adown that dusty cheek have roll'd;
Have children climb'd those knees and kiss'd that face?
What was thy name and station, age and race?

Statue of flesh—Immortal of the dead!
Imperishable type of evanescence!

Posthumous man—who quitt'st thy narrow bed,
  And standest undecay'd within our presence!
Thou wilt hear nothing till the judgment morning,
  When the great trump shall thrill thee with its warning.

Why should this worthless tegument endure,
  If its undying guest be lost for ever?
Oh! let us keep the soul embalm'd and pure
  In living virtue—that when both must sever,
Although corruption may our frame consume,
  The immortal spirit in the skies may bloom!

HORACE SMITH.

ODE ON A GRECIAN URN.

THOU still unravish'd bride of quietness!
  Thou foster-child of Silence and slow Time!
Sylvan historian, who canst thus express
  A flowery tale more sweetly than our rhyme!
What leaf-fringed legend haunts about thy shape
  Of deities or mortals, or of both,
    In Tempe or the dales of Arcady?
  What men or gods are these? what maidens loath?
  What mad pursuit? What struggle to escape?
    What pipes and timbrels? What wild ecstasy?

Heard melodies are sweet, but those unheard
  Are sweeter; therefore, ye soft pipes, play on—
Not to the sensual ear, but more endear'd,
  Pipe to the spirit ditties of no tone:
Fair youth beneath the trees, thou canst not leave
  Thy song, nor ever can those trees be bare;
    Bold lover, never, never, canst thou kiss,
  Though winning near the goal; yet do not grieve—
  She cannot fade, though thou hast not thy bliss;
    For ever wilt thou love, and she be fair!

Ah, happy, happy boughs! that cannot shed
  Your leaves, nor ever bid the Spring adieu:
And, happy melodist, unwearièd,
  For ever piping songs for ever new;
More happy love! more happy, happy love!
  For ever warm and still to be enjoy'd,
    For ever panting and for ever young;
All breathing human passion far above,
  That leaves a heart high sorrowful and cloy'd,
    A burning forehead and a parching tongue.

Who are these coming to the sacrifice?
  To what green altar, O mysterious priest,
Lead'st thou that heifer lowing at the skies,
  And all her silken flanks with garlands drest?
What little town by river or sea-shore,
  Or mountain-built with peaceful citadel,
    Is emptied of its folk this pious morn?
And, little town, thy streets for evermore
  Will silent be; and not a soul, to tell
    Why thou art desolate, can e'er return.

O Attic shape! Fair attitude! with brede
  Of marble men and maidens overwrought,
With forest branches and the trodden weed;
Thou, silent form! dost tease us out of thought,
  As doth eternity. Cold pastoral!
When old age shall this generation waste,
  Thou shalt remain, in midst of other woe
    Than ours, a friend to man, to whom thou say'st,

"Beauty is truth, truth beauty,"—that is all
  Ye know on earth, and all ye need to know.
JOHN KEATS.

THE MEN OF OLD.

I KNOW not that the men of old
  Were better than men now,
Of heart more kind, of hand more bold,
  Of more ingenuous brow;
I heed not those who pine for force
  A ghost of time to raise,
As if they thus could check the course
  Of these appointed days.

Still it is true, and over-true,
  That I delight to close
This book of life self-wise and new,
  And let my thoughts repose
On all that humble happiness
  The world has since foregone,—
The daylight of contentedness
  That on those faces shone!

With rights, though not too closely scann'd,
  Enjoy'd as far as known,
With will, by no reverse unmann'd,
  With pulse of even tone,
They from to-day, and from to-night,
  Expected nothing more
Than yesterday and yesternight
  Had proffer'd them before.

To them was life a simple art
  Of duties to be done,
A game where each man took his part,
  A race where all must run;
A battle whose great scheme and scope
  They little cared to know,
Content, as men-at-arms, to cope
  Each with his fronting foe.

Man now his virtue's diadem
  Puts on, and proudly wears,—
Great thoughts, great feelings, came to them
  Like instincts unawares;
Blending their souls' sublimest needs
  With tasks of every day,
They went about their gravest deeds
  As noble boys at play.

And what if Nature's fearful wound
  They did not probe and bare,
For that their spirits never swoon'd
  To watch the misery there,—
For that their love but flow'd more fast,
  Their charities more free,
Not conscious what mere drops they cast
  Into the evil sea.

A man's best things are nearest him,
  Lie close about his feet;
It is the distant and the dim
  That we are sick to greet;
For flowers that grow our hands beneath
  We struggle and aspire,—
Our hearts must die, except they breathe
  The air of fresh desire.

Yet, brothers, who up reason's hill
  Advance with hopeful cheer,—
Oh, loiter not, those heights are chill,
  As chill as they are clear;
And still restrain your haughty gaze
  The loftier that ye go,
Remembering distance leaves a haze
  On all that lies below.
RICHARD MONCKTON MILNES
(LORD HOUGHTON).

OH! THE PLEASANT DAYS OF OLD!

OH! the pleasant days of old, which so often people praise!
True, they wanted all the luxuries that grace our modern days:
Bare floors were strew'd with rushes—the walls let in the cold;
Oh! how they must have shiver'd in those pleasant days of old!

Oh! those ancient lords of old, how magnificent they were!
They threw down and imprison'd kings—to thwart them who might dare?
They ruled their serfs right sternly; they took from Jews their gold—
Above both law and equity were those great lords of old!

Oh! the gallant knights of old, for their valor so renown'd!
With sword and lance, and armor strong, they scour'd the country round;

And whenever aught to tempt them they
   met by wood or wold,
By right of sword they seized the prize—
   those gallant knights of old!

Oh! the gentle dames of old! who, quite
   free from fear or pain,
Could gaze on joust and tournament, and
   see their champions slain;
They lived on good beefsteaks and ale,
   which made them strong and bold—
Oh! more like men than women were
   those gentle dames of old!

Oh! those mighty towers of old! with
   their turrets, moat, and keep,
Their battlements and bastions, their dun-
   geons dark and deep.
Full many a baron held his court within
   the castle hold;
And many a captive languish'd there, in
   those strong towers of old.

Oh! the troubadours of old! with their
   gentle minstrelsie
Of hope and joy, or deep despair, which-
   e'er their lot might be—
For years they served their lady-love ere
   they their passions told—
Oh! wondrous patience must have had
   those troubadours of old!

Oh! those blessed times of old! with their
   chivalry and state;
I love to read their chronicles, which such
   brave deeds relate;
I love to sing their ancient rhymes, to hear
   their legends told—
But, Heaven be thank'd! I live not in
   those blessed times of old!
                FRANCES BROWN.

IS IT COME?

Is it come? they said, on the banks of the
   Nile,
   Who look'd for the world's long-promised
      day,
And saw but the strife of Egypt's toil,
   With the desert's sand and the granite
      gray.
From the pyramid, temple, and treasured
   dead,
   We vainly ask for her wisdom's plan;
They tell us of the tyrant's dread—
   Yet there was hope when that day be-
      gan.

The Chaldee came, with his starry lore,
   And built up Babylon's crown and creed;
And brick were stamp'd on the Tigris
   shore
   With signs which our sages scarce can
      read.
From Ninus' temple, and Nimrod's tower,
   The rule of the old East's empire spread
Unreasoning faith and unquestion'd pow-
   er—
   But still, Is it come? the watcher said.

The light of the Persian's worshipp'd
   flame,
   The ancient bondage its splendor threw;
And once, on the West a sunrise came,
   When Greece to her freedom's trust was
      true;
With dreams to the utmost ages dear,
   With human gods, and with god-like
      men,
No marvel the far-off day seem'd near
   To eyes that look'd through her laurels
      then.

The Romans conquer'd, and revell'd too,
   Till honor, and faith, and power, were
      gone;
And deeper old Europe's darkness grew,
   As, wave after wave, the Goth came on.
The gown was learning, the sword was
   law;
   The people served in the oxen's stead;
But ever some gleam the watcher saw,
   And evermore, Is it come? they said.

Poet and Seer that question caught,
   Above the din of life's fears and frets;
It march'd with letters, it toil'd with
   thought,
   Through schools and creeds which the
      earth forgets.
And statesmen trifle, and priests deceive,
   And traders barter our world away—
Yet hearts to that golden promise cleave,
   And still, at times, Is it come? they say.

The days of the nations bear no trace
 Of all the sunshine so far foretold;
The cannon speaks in the teacher's place—
 The age is weary with work and gold;
And high hopes wither, and memories wane;
On hearths and altars the fires are dead;
But that brave faith hath not lived in vain—
 And this is all that our watcher said.
FRANCES BROWN.

THE LONG-AGO.

EYES, which can but ill define
 Shapes that rise about and near,
Through the far horizon's line
 Stretch a vision free and clear;
Memories, feeble to retrace
 Yesterday's immediate flow,
Find a dear familiar face
 In each hour of Long-ago.

Follow yon majestic train
 Down the slopes of old renown;
Knightly forms without disdain,
 Sainted heads without a frown:
Emperors of thought and hand
 Congregate, a glorious show,
Met from every age and land
 In the plains of Long-ago.

As the heart of childhood brings
 Something of eternal joy
From its own unsounded springs,
 Such as life can scarce destroy;
So, remindful of the prime,
 Spirits wandering to and fro
Rest upon the resting-time
 In the peace of Long-ago.

Youthful Hope's religious fire,
 When it burns no longer, leaves
Ashes of impure desire
 On the altars it bereaves;
But the light that fills the Past
 Sheds a still diviner glow,
Ever farther it is cast
 O'er the scenes of Long-ago.

Many a growth of pain and care,
 Cumbering all the present hour,
Yields, when once transplanted there,
 Healthy fruit or pleasant flower.

Thoughts that hardly flourish here,
 Feelings long have ceased to blow,
Breathe a native atmosphere
 In the world of Long-ago.

On that deep-retiring shore
 Frequent pearls of beauty lie,
Where the passion-waves of yore
 Fiercely beat and mounted high;
Sorrows—that are sorrows still—
 Lose the bitter taste of woe;
Nothing's altogether ill
 In the griefs of Long-ago.

Tombs where lonely love repines,
 Ghastly tenements of tears,
Wear the look of happy shrines
 Through the golden mist of years;
Death, to those who trust in good,
 Vindicates his hardest blow;
Oh! we would not, if we could,
 Wake the sleep of Long-ago!

Though the doom of swift decay
 Shocks the soul where life is strong;
Though for frailer hearts the day
 Lingers sad and overlong;—
Still the weight will find a leaven,
 Still the spoiler's hand is slow,
While the future has its Heaven,
 And the past its Long-ago.
RICHARD MONCKTON MILNES
(LORD HOUGHTON).

GIVE ME THE OLD—

OLD WINE TO DRINK, OLD WOOD TO BURN,
OLD BOOKS TO READ, AND OLD FRIENDS
 TO CONVERSE WITH.

OLD wine to drink!—
Ay, give the slippery juice
That drippeth from the grape thrown loose
 Within the tun;
Pluck'd from beneath the cliff
Of sunny-sided Teneriffe,
 And ripen'd 'neath the blink
 Of India's sun!
 Peat whiskey hot,
Temper'd with well-boil'd water!
These make the long night shorter,--
 Forgetting not
Good stout old English porter.

Old wood to burn —
Ay, bring the hill-side beech
From where the owlets meet and screech,
    And ravens croak;
The crackling pine, and cedar sweet;
Bring too a clump of fragrant peat,
    Dug 'neath the fern;
      The knotted oak,
    A fagot too, perhap,
Whose bright flame, dancing, winking,
Shall light us at our drinking;
    While the oozing sap
Shall make sweet music to our thinking.

Old books to read!—
Ay, bring those nodes of wit,
The brazen-clasp'd the vellum writ,
    Time-honor'd tomes!
The same my sire scann'd before,
The same my grandsire thumbéd o'er,
The same his sire from college bore,
    The well-earn'd meed
      Of Oxford's domes:
    Old Homer blind,
Old Horace, rake Anacreon, by
Old Tully, Plautus, Terence lie;
Mort Arthur's olden minstrelsie,
Quaint Burton, quainter Spenser, ay!
And Gervase Markham's venerie—
    Nor leave behind
The Holye Book by which we live and die.

Old friends to talk!—
Ay, bring those chosen few,
The wise, the courtly, and the true,
    So rarely found;
Him for my wine, him for my stud,
Him for my easel, distich, bud
    In mountain-walk!
      Bring Walter good:
With soulful Fred; and learnèd Will,
And thee, my *alter ego* (dearer still
    For every mood).
These add a bouquet to my wine!
These add a sparkle to my pine!
    If these I tine,
      Can books, or fire, or wine be good?
          ROBERT HINCKLEY MESSINGER.

THE GOOD TIME COMING.

THERE'S a good time coming, boys,
    A good time coming:
We may not live to see the day,
But earth shall glisten in the ray
    Of the good time coming.
Cannon-balls may aid the truth,
    But thought's a weapon stronger;
We'll win our battle by its aid;—
    Wait a little longer.

There's a good time coming, boys,
    A good time coming:
The pen shall supersede the sword,
And Right, not Might, shall be the lord,
    In the good time coming.
Worth, not Birth, shall rule mankind,
    And be acknowledged stronger;
The proper impulse has been given;—
    Wait a little longer.

There's a good time coming, boys,
    A good time coming:
War in all men's eyes shall be
A monster of iniquity
    In the good time coming.
Nations shall not quarrel then,
    To prove which is the stronger;
Nor slaughter men for glory's sake;—
    Wait a little longer.

There's a good time coming, boys,
    A good time coming:
Hateful rivalries of creed
Shall not make their martyrs bleed
    In the good time coming.
Religion shall be shorn of pride,
    And flourish all the stronger;
And Charity shall trim her lamp;—
    Wait a little longer.

There's a good time coming, boys,
    A good time coming:
The people shall be temperate,
And shall love instead of hate,
    In the good time coming.
They shall use, and not abuse,
    And make all virtue stronger;—
The reformation has begun;—
    Wait a little longer.

There's a good time coming, boys,
    A good time coming:
Let us aid it all we can,
Every woman, every man,
    The good time coming.
Smallest helps, if rightly given,
    Make the impulse stronger;—
'Twill be strong enough one day;—
    Wait a little longer.
          CHARLES MACKAY.

A PETITION TO TIME.

Touch us gently, Time!
  Let us glide adown thy stream
Gently,—as we sometimes glide
  Through a quiet dream!
Humble voyagers are we,
Husband, wife, and children three,—
(One is lost,—an angel, fled
To the azure overhead).

Touch us gently, Time!
  We've not proud nor soaring wings;
Our ambition, our content,
  Lies in simple things.
Humble voyagers are we
O'er life's dim, unsounded sea,
Seeking only some calm clime;—
Touch us gently, gentle Time!
BRYAN WALLER PROCTER
(BARRY CORNWALL).

THE AGED MAN-AT-ARMS.

His golden locks time hath to silver turn'd;
  O time too swift, O swiftness never ceasing!
His youth 'gainst time and age hath ever spurn'd,
  But spurn'd in vain; youth waneth by increasing:
Beauty, strength, youth, are flowers but fading seen,
Duty, faith, love, are roots, and ever green.

His helmet now shall make a hive for bees,
  And, lovers' sonnets turn'd to holy psalms,
A man-at-arms must now serve on his knees,
  And feed on prayers, which are old age's alms;
But though from court to cottage he depart,
His saint is sure of his unspotted heart.

And when he saddest sits in homely cell,
  He'll teach his swains this carol for a song:
"Bless'd be the hearts that wish my sovereign well,
  Cursed be the souls that think her any wrong!"
Goddess, allow this agèd man his right,
To be your beadsman now that was your knight.
GEORGE PEELE.

THE ONE GRAY HAIR.

The wisest of the wise
Listen to pretty lies,
  And love to hear 'em told;
Doubt not that Solomon
Listen'd to many a one,—
Some in his youth, and more when he grew old.

I never sat among
The choir of Wisdom's song,
  But pretty lies loved I
As much as any king—
When youth was on the wing,
And (must it then be told?) when youth had quite gone by.

Alas! and I have not
The pleasant hour forgot,
  When one pert lady said,
"O Walter! I am quite
Bewilder'd with affright!
I see (sit quiet now!) a white hair on your head!"

Another, more benign,
Snipt it away from mine,
  And in her own dark hair
Pretended it was found. . . .
She lept, and twirl'd it round.
Fair as she was, she never was so fair.
WALTER SAVAGE LANDOR.

I'M GROWING OLD.

My days pass pleasantly away,
  My nights are bless'd with sweetest sleep;
I feel no symptoms of decay,
  I have no cause to mourn nor weep;
My foes are impotent and shy,
  My friends are neither false nor cold,
And yet, of late, I often sigh,—
  I'm growing old!

My growing talk of olden times,
  My growing thirst for early news

My growing apathy for rhymes,
  My growing love for easy shoes,
My growing hate of crowds and noise,
  My growing fear of taking cold,
All whisper, in the plainest voice,
  I'm growing old!

I'm growing fonder of my staff,
  I'm growing dimmer in the eyes,
I'm growing fainter in my laugh,
  I'm growing deeper in my sighs,
I'm growing careless of my dress,
  I'm growing frugal of my gold,
I'm growing wise, I'm growing—yes—
  I'm growing old!

I see it in my changing taste,
  I see it in my changing hair,
I see it in my growing waist,
  I see it in my growing heir;
A thousand signs proclaim the truth,
  As plain as truth was ever told,
That even in my vaunted youth
  I'm growing old!

Ah me! my very laurels breathe
  The tale in my reluctant ears;
And every boon the Hours bequeath
  But makes me debtor to the Years;
E'en Flattery's honey'd words declare
  The secret she would fain withhold,
And tells me in "How young you are!"
  I'm growing old!

Thanks for the years whose rapid flight
  My sombre muse too sadly sings;
Thanks for the gleams of golden light
  That tint the darkness of their wings,—
The light that beams from out the sky,
  Those heavenly mansions to unfold,
Where all are blest, and none may sigh,
  " I'm growing old!"
                  JOHN G. SAXE.

SONNET.

To me, fair friend, you never can be old,
  For as you were, when first your eye I eyed,
Such seems your beauty still. Three winters cold
  Have from the forests shook three summers' pride;
Three beauteous springs to yellow autumn turn'd,
  In process of the seasons have I seen;
Three April perfumes in three hot Junes burn'd,
  Since first I saw you fresh, which yet are green.
Ah! yet doth beauty, like a dial-hand,
  Steal from his figure, and no pace perceived;
So your sweet hue, which methinks still doth stand,
  Hath motion, and mine eye may be deceived:
For fear of which, hear this, thou age unbred,—
Ere you were born was beauty's summer dead.
                  WILLIAM SHAKESPEARE.

SONNET.

When I do count the clock that tells the time,
  And see the brave day sunk in hideous night;
When I behold the violet past prime,
  And sable curls all silver'd o'er with white;
When lofty trees I see barren of leaves,
  Which erst from heat did canopy the herd,
And Summer's green all girded up in sheaves,
  Borne on the bier with white and bristly beard;
Then, of thy beauty do I question make,
  That thou among the wastes of time must go,
Since sweets and beauties do themselves forsake,
  And die as fast as they see others grow;
And nothing 'gainst Time's scythe can make defence,
Save breed, to brave him, when he takes thee hence.
                  WILLIAM SHAKESPEARE.

SONNET.

Not marble, nor the gilded monuments
  Of princes, shall outlive this powerful rhyme;

But you shall shine more bright in these
contents
Than unswept stone, besmear'd with
sluttish time.
When wasteful war shall statues overturn,
And broils root out the work of ma-
sonry,
Nor Mars his sword, nor war's quick fire
shall burn
The living record of your memory.
'Gainst death and all-oblivious enmity
Shall you pace forth: your praise shall
still find room
Even in the eyes of all posterity,
That wear this world out to the ending
doom.
So, till the judgment that yourself arise,
You live in this, and dwell in lovers' eyes.
WILLIAM SHAKESPEARE.

SONNET.

OH, how much more doth beauty beau-
teous seem,
By that sweet ornament which truth
doth give!
The rose looks fair, but fairer we it deem
For that sweet odor which doth in it live.
The canker blooms have full as deep a dye,
As the perfumed tincture of the roses;
Hang on such thorns, and play as wantonly
When summer's breath their maskèd
buds discloses;
But, for their virtue only is their show,
They live unwoo'd, and unrespected fade;
Die to themselves. Sweet roses do not so;
Of their sweet deaths are sweetest odors
made:
And so of you, beauteous and lovely youth,
When that shall fade, my verse distils
your truth.
WILLIAM SHAKESPEARE.

SONNET.

WHEN to the sessions of sweet silent
thought
I summon up remembrance of things
past,
I sigh the lack of many a thing I sought,
And with old woes new wail my dear
time's waste.

Then, can I drown an eye, unused to flow,
For precious friends hid in death's date-
less night,
And weep afresh love's long-since cancell'd
woe,
And moan th' expense of many a van-
ish'd sight.
Then can I grieve at grievances foregone,
And heavily from woe to woe tell o'er
The sad account of fore-bemoanèd moan,
Which I new pay, as if not paid be-
fore;
But if the while I think on thee, dear
friend,
All losses are restored, and sorrows end.
WILLIAM SHAKESPEARE.

SONNET.

LIKE as the waves make toward the peb-
bled shore
So do our minutes hasten to their end;
Each changing place with that which
goes before,
In sequent toil all forward do contend.
Nativity once in the main of light
Crawls to maturity, wherewith being
crown'd,
Crooked eclipses 'gainst his glory fight,
And Time that gave, doth now his gift
confound.
Time doth transfix the flourish set on
youth,
And delves the parallels in beauty's
brow;
Feeds on the rarities of Nature's truth,
And nothing stands but for his scythe to
mow.
And yet, to times in hope, my verse shall
stand
Praising thy worth, despite his cruel hand.
WILLIAM SHAKESPEARE.

SONNET.

POOR Soul, the centre of my sinful earth,
Fool'd by those rebel powers that thee
array,
Why dost thou pine within, and suffer
dearth,
Painting thy outward walls so costly
gay?

Why so large cost, having so short a lease,
  Dost thou upon thy fading mansion spend?
Shall worms, inheritors of this excess,
  Eat up thy charge? is this thy body's end?
Then, Soul, live thou upon thy servant's loss,
  And let that pine to aggravate thy store;
Buy terms divine in selling hours of dross;
  Within be fed, without be rich no more:—
So shalt thou feed on death, that feeds on men,
And death once dead, there's no more dying then.
WILLIAM SHAKESPEARE.

SONNET.

THEY that have power to hurt, and will do none,
  That do not do the thing they most do show,
Who, moving others, are themselves as stone,
  Unmovèd, cold, and to temptation slow,—
They rightly do inherit Heaven's graces,
  And husband Nature's riches from expense;
They are the lords and owners of their faces,
  Others, but stewards of their excellence.
The summer's flower is to the summer sweet,
  Though to itself it only live and die;
But if that flower with base infection meet,
  The basest weed outbraves his dignity:
For sweetest things turn sourest by their deeds;
Lilies that fester smell far worse than weeds.
WILLIAM SHAKESPEARE.

THE OLD MAN'S WISH.

IF I live to grow old, as I find I go down,
Let this be my fate: in a country town
May I have a warm house, with a stone at my gate,
And a cleanly young girl to rub my bald pate.
  May I govern my passions with an absolute sway,
  Grow wiser and better as my strength wears away,
  Without gout or stone, by a gentle decay.

In a country town, by a murmuring brook,
With the ocean at distance, on which I may look,
With a spacious plain, without hedge or stile,
And an easy pad nag to ride out a mile.
  May I govern my passions with an absolute sway,
  Grow wiser and better as my strength wears away,
  Without gout or stone, by a gentle decay.

With Horace and Plutarch, and one or two more
Of the best wits that lived in the ages before;
With a dish of roast mutton, not ven'son nor teal,
And clean, though coarse linen at every meal.
  May I govern my passions with an absolute sway,
  Grow wiser and better as my strength wears away,
  Without gout or stone, by a gentle decay.

With a pudding on Sunday, and stout, humming liquor,
And remnants of Latin to puzzle the vicar;
With a hidden reserve of Burgundy wine
To drink the king's health as oft as I dine.
  May I govern my passions with an absolute sway,
  Grow wiser and better as my strength wears away,
  Without gout or stone, by a gentle decay.

With a courage undaunted may I face my last day,
And when I am dead may the better sort say,

In the morning when sober, in the even-
    ing when mellow,
"He's gone, and hain't left behind him
    his fellow;
  For he govern'd his passions with an
    absolute sway,
  And grew wiser and better as his
    strength wore away,
  Without gout or stone, by a gentle
    decay."
                              WALTER POPE.

THE LAST LEAF.

I SAW him once before,
As he pass'd by the door;
    And again
The pavement-stones resound
As he totters o'er the ground
    With his cane.

They say that in his prime,
Ere the pruning-knife of Time
    Cut him down,
Not a better man was found
By the crier on his round
    Through the town.

But now he walks the streets,
And he looks at all he meets
    Sad and wan;
And he shakes his feeble head,
That it seems as if he said,
    "They are gone."

The mossy marbles rest
On the lips that he has press'd
    In their bloom;
And the names he loved to hear
Have been carved for many a year
    On the tomb.

My grandmamma has said—
Poor old lady! she is dead
    Long ago—
That he had a Roman nose,
And his cheek was like a rose
    In the snow.

But now his nose is thin,
And it rests upon his chin
    Like a staff;
And a crook is in his back,
And a melancholy crack
    In his laugh.

I know it is a sin
For me to sit and grin
    At him here,
But the old three-corner'd hat,
And the breeches,—and all that,
    Are so queer!

And if I should live to be
The last leaf upon the tree
    In the spring,
Let them smile, as I do now,
At the old forsaken bough
    Where I cling.
                    OLIVER WENDELL HOLMES.

ODE ON SOLITUDE.

HAPPY the man, whose wish and care
  A few paternal acres bound,
Content to breathe his native air
    In his own ground.

Whose herds with milk, whose fields with
    bread,
  Whose flocks supply him with attire;
Whose trees in summer yield him shade,
    In winter, fire.

Blest, who can unconcern'dly find
  Hours, days, and years, slide soft away
In health of body, peace of mind,
    Quiet by day,

Sound sleep by night; study and ease
  Together mix'd; sweet recreation,
And innocence, which most does please
    With meditation.

Thus let me live, unseen, unknown;
  Thus unlamented let me die;
Steal from the world, and not a stone
    Tell where I lie.
                              ALEXANDER POPE.

TO MY PICTURE.

WHEN age hath made me what I am not
    now,
And every wrinkle tells me where the
    plough
Of Time hath furrow'd; when an ice shall
    flow
Through every vein, and all my head be
    snow;

When Death displays his coldness in my
    cheek,
And I myself in my own picture seek,
Not finding what I am, but what I was,
In doubt which to believe—this or my
    glass;
Yet though I alter, this remains the same
As it was drawn, retains the primitive
    frame
And first complexion; here will still be seen
Blood on the cheek and down upon the chin;
Here the smooth brow will stay, the lively
    eye,
The ruddy lip, and hair of youthful dye.
Behold what frailty we in man may see,
Whose shadow is less given to change than
    he!
                  THOMAS RANDOLPH.

CRABBÈD AGE AND YOUTH.

CRABBÈD age and youth
    Cannot live together;
Youth is full of pleasance,
    Age is full of care;
Youth like summer morn,
    Age like winter weather;
Youth like summer brave,
    Age like winter bare.
Youth is full of sport,
Age's breath is short;
    Youth is nimble, age is lame;
Youth is hot and bold,
Age is weak and cold;
    Youth is wild, and age is tame.
Age, I do abhor thee,
Youth, I do adore thee;
    Oh, my love, my love is young!
Age, I do defy thee;
O sweet shepherd! hie thee,
    For methinks thou stay'st too long.
                  WILLIAM SHAKESPEARE.

LIFE.

MADE a posy, while the day ran by:
Here will I smell my remnant out, and tie
    My life within this band.
But time did beckon to the flowers, and
    they
By noon most cunningly did steal away,
    And wither'd in my hand.

My hand was next to them, and then my
    heart;
I took, without more thinking, in good
    part,
    Time's gentle admonition;
Who did so sweetly death's sad taste con-
    vey,
Making my mind to smell my fatal day,
    Yet sugaring the suspicion.

Farewell, dear flowers, sweetly your time
    ye spent,
Fit, while ye lived, for smell or ornament,
    And after death for cures.
I follow straight without complaints or
    grief,
Since, if my scent be good, I care not if
    It be as short as yours.
                  GEORGE HERBERT.

THE DESERTED VILLAGE.

SWEET Auburn! loveliest village of the
    plain,
Where health and plenty cheer'd the
    laboring swain,
Where smiling spring its earliest visit
    paid,
And parting summer's lingering blooms
    delay'd—
Dear lovely bowers of innocence and
    ease,
Seats of my youth, when every sport could
    please—
How often have I loiter'd o'er thy green,
Where humble happiness endear'd each
    scene;
How often have I paused on every
    charm—
The shelter'd cot, the cultivated farm,
The never-failing brook, the busy mill,
The decent church that topt the neighbor-
    ing hill,
The hawthorn bush, with seats beneath
    the shade
For talking age and whispering lovers
    made;
How often have I blest the coming day,
When toil, remitting, lent its turn to play,
And all the village train, from labor free,
Led up their sports beneath the spreading
    tree;

While many a pastime circled in the shade,
The young contending as the old survey'd;
And many a gambol frolick'd o'er the ground,
And sleights of art and feats of strength went round;
And still, as each repeated pleasure tired,
Succeeding sports the mirthful band inspired:
The dancing pair, that simply sought renown
By holding out, to tire each other down;
The swain mistrustless of his smutted face,
While secret laughter titter'd round the place;
The bashful virgin's sidelong looks of love,
The matron's glance that would those looks reprove:
These were thy charms, sweet village! sports like these,
With sweet succession, taught even toil to please;
These round thy bowers their cheerful influence shed;
These were thy charms—but all these charms are fled.

Sweet-smiling village, loveliest of the lawn!
Thy sports are fled, and all thy charms withdrawn;
Amidst thy bowers the tyrant's hand is seen,
And desolation saddens all thy green;
One only master grasps the whole domain,
And half a tillage stints thy smiling plain;
No more thy glassy brook reflects the day,
But, choked with sedges, works its weedy way;
Along thy glades, a solitary guest,
The hollow-sounding bittern guards its nest;
Amidst thy desert walks the lapwing flies,
And tires their echoes with unvaried cries;
Sunk are thy bowers in shapeless ruin all,
And the long grass o'ertops the mouldering wall;
And, trembling, shrinking from the spoiler's hand,
Far, far away thy children leave the land.

Ill fares the land, to hastening ills a prey,
Where wealth accumulates, and men decay;
Princes and lords may flourish, or may fade—
A breath can make them, as a breath has made;
But a bold peasantry, their country's pride,
When once destroy'd, can never be supplied.

A time there was, ere England's griefs began,
When every rood of ground maintain'd its man:
For him light Labor spread her wholesome store—
Just gave what life required, but gave no more;
His best companions. innocence and health;
And his best riches, ignorance of wealth.

But times are alter'd: trade's unfeeling train
Usurp the land, and dispossess the swain;
Along the lawn, where scatter'd hamlets rose,
Unwieldy wealth and cumbrous pomp repose;
And every want to opulence allied,
And every pang that folly pays to pride.
Those gentle hours that plenty bade to bloom,
Those calm desires that ask'd but little room,
Those healthful sports that graced the peaceful scene,
Lived in each look, and brighten'd all the green,—
These, far departing, seek a kinder shore,
And rural mirth and manners are no more.

Sweet Auburn! parent of the blissful hour,
Thy glades forlorn confess the tyrant's power.

Here, as I take my solitary rounds
Amidst thy tangling walks and ruin'd grounds,
And, many a year elapsed, return to view
Where once the cottage stood, the hawthorn grew,
Remembrance wakes with all her busy train,
Swells at my breast, and turns the past to pain.

In all my wanderings round this world of care,
In all my griefs—and God has given my share—
I still had hopes my latest hours to crown,
Amidst these humble bowers to lay me down;
To husband out life's taper at the close,
And keep the flame from wasting by repose;
I still had hopes—for pride attends us still—
Amidst the swains to show my book-learn'd skill,
Around my fire an evening group to draw,
And tell of all I felt, and all I saw;
And, as a hare, whom hounds and horns pursue,
Pants to the place from whence at first she flew,
I still had hopes, my long vexations past,
Here to return—and die at home at last.

O blest retirement! friend to life's decline!
Retreats from care, that never must be mine!
How happy he who crowns, in shades like these,
A youth of labor with an age of ease;
Who quits a world where strong temptations try,
And, since 'tis hard to combat, learns to fly.
For him no wretches, born to work and weep,
Explore the mine, or tempt the dangerous deep;
No surly porter stands, in guilty state,
To spurn imploring famine from the gate;
But on he moves to meet his latter end,
Angels around befriending Virtue's friend;
Bends to the grave with unperceived decay,
While Resignation gently slopes the way;
And, all his prospects brightening to the last,
His heaven commences ere the world be past.

Sweet was the sound, when oft at evening's close
Up yonder hill the village murmur rose;
There, as I pass'd with careless steps and slow,
The mingling notes came soften'd from below:
The swain responsive as the milkmaid sung,
The sober herd that low'd to meet their young,
The noisy geese that gabbled o'er the pool,
The playful children just let loose from school,
The watch-dog's voice that bay'd the whispering wind,
And the loud laugh that spoke the vacant mind,—
These all in sweet confusion sought the shade,
And fill'd each pause the nightingale had made.
But now the sounds of population fail;
No cheerful murmurs fluctuate in the gale;
No busy steps the grass-grown footway tread,
For all the bloomy flush of life is fled—
All but yon widow'd, solitary thing,
That feebly bends beside the plashy spring;
She, wretched matron, forced in age, for bread,
To strip the brook with mantling cresses spread,
To pick her wintry fagot from the thorn,
To seek her nightly shed, and weep till morn,—
She only left of all the harmless train,
The sad historian of the pensive plain.

Near yonder copse, where once the garden smiled,
And still where many a garden-flower grows wild,

There, where a few torn shrubs the place disclose,
The village preacher's modest mansion rose.
A man he was to all the country dear,
And passing rich with forty pounds a year;
Remote from towns he ran his godly race,
Nor e'er had changed, nor wish'd to change, his place;
Unpractised he to fawn, or seek for power
By doctrines fashion'd to the varying hour;
Far other aims his heart had learn'd to prize—
More skilled to raise the wretched than to rise.
His house was known to all the vagrant train;
He chid their wanderings, but relieved their pain.
The long-remember'd beggar was his guest,
Whose beard, descending, swept his aged breast;
The ruin'd spendthrift, now no longer proud,
Claim'd kindred there, and had his claims allow'd;
The broken soldier, kindly bade to stay,
Sate by his fire, and talk'd the night away—
Wept o'er his wounds, or, tales of sorrow done,
Shoulder'd his crutch, and show'd how fields were won.
Pleased with his guests, the good man learn'd to glow,
And quite forgot their vices in their woe;
Careless their merits or their faults to scan,
His pity gave ere charity began.

Thus to relieve the wretched was his pride;
And e'en his failings lean'd to Virtue's side;
But in his duty prompt at every call,
He watch'd and wept, he pray'd and felt for all;
And, as a bird each fond endearment tries
To tempt its new-fledged offspring to the skies,
He tried each art, reproved each dull delay,
Allured to brighter worlds, and led the way.

Beside the bed where parting life was laid,
And sorrow, guilt, and pain by turns dismay'd,
The reverend champion stood. At his control
Despair and anguish fled the struggling soul;
Comfort came down the trembling wretch to raise,
And his last faltering accents whisper'd praise.

At church, with meek and unaffected grace,
His looks adorn'd the venerable place;
Truth from his lips prevail'd with double sway,
And fools, who came to scoff, remain'd to pray.
The service past, around the pious man,
With ready zeal, each honest rustic ran;
E'en children follow'd with endearing wile,
And pluck'd his gown, to share the good man's smile.
His ready smile a parent's warmth exprest;
Their welfare pleased him, and their cares distress'd;
To them his heart, his love, his griefs were given—
But all his serious thoughts had rest in heaven.
As some tall cliff that lifts its awful form,
Swells from the vale, and midway leaves the storm,
Though round its breast the rolling clouds are spread,
Eternal sunshine settles on its head.

Beside yon straggling fence that skirts the way,
With blossom'd furze unprofitably gay,
There, in his noisy mansion, skill'd to rule,
The village master taught his little school.
A man severe he was, and stern to view—
I knew him well, and every truant knew;

Well had the boding tremblers learn'd to trace
The day's disasters in his morning face;
Full well they laugh'd, with counterfeited glee,
At all his jokes, for many a joke had he;
Full well the busy whisper, circling round,
Convey'd the dismal tidings when he frown'd;
Yet he was kind—or, if severe in aught,
The love he bore to learning was in fault.
The village all declared how much he knew;
'Twas certain he could write, and cipher too;
Lands he could measure, terms and tides presage,
And e'en the story ran that he could gauge.
In arguing, too, the parson own'd his skill,
For, e'en though vanquish'd, he could argue still;
While words of learnèd length and thundering sound
Amazed the gazing rustics ranged around;
And still they gazed, and still the wonder grew,
That one small head could carry all he knew.
But past is all his fame; the very spot,
Where many a time he triumph'd, is forgot.

Near yonder thorn, that lifts its head on high,
Where once the sign-post caught the passing eye,
Low lies that house where nut-brown draughts inspired,
Where gray-beard mirth and smiling toil retired,
Where village statesmen talk'd with looks profound,
And news much older than their ale went round.
Imagination fondly stoops to trace
The parlor splendors of that festive place:
The whitewash'd wall, the nicely-sanded floor,
The varnish'd clock that click'd behind the door,
The chest contrived a double debt to pay—
A bed by night, a chest of drawers by day,
The pictures placed for ornament and use,
The twelve good rules, the royal game of goose;
The hearth, except when winter chill'd the day,
With aspen boughs, and flowers and fennel gay;
While broken tea-cups, wisely kept for show,
Ranged o'er the chimney, glisten'd in a row.

Vain, transitory splendors! could not all
Reprieve the tottering mansion from its fall?
Obscure it sinks, nor shall it more impart
An hour's importance to the poor man's heart;
Thither no more the peasant shall repair
To sweet oblivion of his daily care;
No more the farmer's news, the barber's tale,
No more the woodman's ballad shall prevail;
No more the smith his dusky brow shall clear,
Relax his ponderous strength, and lean to hear;
The host himself no longer shall be found
Careful to see the mantling bliss go round;
Nor the coy maid, half willing to be prest,
Shall kiss the cup to pass it to the rest.

Yes! let the rich deride, the proud disdain,
These simple blessings of the lowly train;
To me more dear, congenial to my heart,
One native charm than all the gloss of art.
Spontaneous joys, where Nature has its play,
The soul adopts, and owns their first-born sway;
Lightly they frolic o'er the vacant mind,
Unenvied, unmolested, unconfined;
But the long pomp, the midnight masquerade,
With all the freaks of wanton wealth array'd—
In these, ere triflers half their wish obtain,
The toiling pleasure sickens into pain;

And, e'en while fashion's brightest arts decoy,
The heart, distrusting, asks if this be joy.

   Ye friends to truth, ye statesmen, who survey
The rich man's joys increase, the poor's decay!
'Tis yours to judge how wide the limits stand
Between a splendid and a happy land.
Proud swells the tide with loads of freighted ore,
And shouting Folly hails them from her shore;
Hoards, e'en beyond the miser's wish, abound,
And rich men flock from all the world around.
Yet count our gains: this wealth is but a name,
That leaves our useful products still the same.
Not so the loss: the man of wealth and pride
Takes up a space that many poor supplied—
Space for his lake, his park's extended bounds—
Space for his horses, equipage, and hounds;
The robe that wraps his limbs in silken cloth
Has robb'd the neighboring fields of half their growth;
His seat, where solitary sports are seen,
Indignant spurns the cottage from the green;
Around the world each needful product flies,
For all the luxuries the world supplies;
While thus the land, adorn'd for pleasure all,
In barren splendor, feebly waits the fall.

   As some fair female, unadorn'd and plain,
Secure to please while youth confirms her reign,
Slights every borrow'd charm that dress supplies,
Nor shares with art the triumph of her eyes;
But when those charms are past—for charms are frail—
When time advances, and when lovers fail,
She then shines forth, solicitous to bless,
In all the glaring impotence of dress:
Thus fares the land, by luxury betray'd:
In Nature's simplest charms at first array'd;
But, verging to decline, its splendors rise,
Its vistas strike, its palaces surprise;
While, scourged by famine, from the smiling land
The mournful peasant leads his humble band;
And while he sinks, without one arm to save,
The country blooms—a garden and a grave.

   Where, then, ah! where shall poverty reside
To 'scape the pressure of contiguous pride?
If to some common's fenceless limits stray'd,
He drives his flock to pick the scanty blade,
Those fenceless fields the sons of wealth divide,
And even the bare-worn common is denied.
If to the city sped, what waits him there?
To see profusion that he must not share;
To see ten thousand baneful arts combined
To pamper luxury, and thin mankind;
To see those joys the sons of pleasure know
Extorted from his fellow-creatures' woe.
Here while the courtier glitters in brocade,
There the pale artist plies the sickly trade;
Here while the proud their long-drawn pomps display,
There the black gibbet glooms beside the way.
The dome where Pleasure holds her midnight reign,
Here, richly deck'd, admits the gorgeous train;
Tumultuous grandeur crowds the blazing square—
The rattling chariots clash, the torches glare.

Sure scenes like these no troubles e'er annoy!
Sure these denote one universal joy!
Are these thy serious thoughts? Ah! turn thine eyes
Where the poor, houseless, shivering female lies;
She once, perhaps, in village plenty blest,
Has wept at tales of innocence distress'd;
Her modest looks the cottage might adorn,
Sweet as the primrose peeps beneath the thorn:
Now lost to all—her friends, her virtue fled—
Near her betrayer's door she lays her head,
And, pinch'd with cold, and shrinking from the shower,
With heavy heart deplores that luckless hour
When, idly first, ambitious of the town,
She left her wheel, and robes of country brown.

Do thine, sweet Auburn—thine the loveliest train—
Do thy fair tribes participate her pain?
E'en now, perhaps, by cold and hunger led,
At proud men's doors they ask a little bread.

Ah, no! To distant climes, a dreary scene,
Where half the convex world intrudes between,
Through torrid tracts with fainting steps they go,
Where wild Altama murmurs to their woe.
Far different there, from all that charm'd before,
The various terrors of that horrid shore:
Those blazing suns that dart a downward ray,
And fiercely shed intolerable day;
Those matted woods where birds forget to sing,
But silent bats in drowsy clusters cling;
Those pois'nous fields, with rank luxuriance crown'd,
Where the dark scorpion gathers death around;
Where at each step the stranger fears to wake
The rattling terrors of the vengeful snake;
Where crouching tigers wait their hapless prey,
And savage men more murderous still than they;
While oft in whirls the mad tornado flies,
Mingling the ravaged landscape with the skies.
Far different these from every former scene—
The cooling brook, the grassy-vested green,
The breezy covert of the warbling grove,
That only shelter'd thefts of harmless love.

Good Heaven! what sorrows gloom'd that parting day
That call'd them from their native walks away;
When the poor exiles, every pleasure past,
Hung round their bowers, and fondly look'd their last,
And took a long farewell, and wish'd in vain
For seats like these beyond the western main,
And, shuddering still to face the distant deep,
Return'd and wept, and still return'd to weep!
The good old sire the first prepared to go
To new-found worlds, and wept for others' woe;
But for himself, in conscious virtue brave,
He only wish'd for worlds beyond the grave.
His lovely daughter, lovelier in her tears,
The fond companion of his helpless years,
Silent went next, neglectful of her charms,
And left a lover's for a father's arms.
With louder plaints the mother spoke her woes,
And bless'd the cot where every pleasure rose;
And kiss'd her thoughtless babes with many a tear,
And clasp'd them close, in sorrow doubly dear;
Whilst her fond husband strove to lend relief
In all the silent manliness of grief.

O Luxury! thou curst by Heaven's decree,
How ill exchanged are things like these
　for thee!
How do thy potions, with insidious joy,
Diffuse their pleasures only to destroy!
Kingdoms by thee to sickly greatness
　grown
Boast of a florid vigor not their own.
At every draught more large and large
　they grow,
A bloated mass of rank, unwieldy woe;
Till, sapp'd their strength and every part
　unsound,
Down, down they sink, and spread a ruin
　round.

Even now the devastation is begun,
And half the business of destruction done;
Even now, methinks, as pondering here I
　stand,
I see the rural virtues leave the land.
Down where yon anchoring vessel spreads
　the sail
That, idly waiting, flaps with every gale—
Downward they move, a melancholy band,
Pass from the shore, and darken all the
　strand.
Contented toil, and hospitable care,
And kind connubial tenderness are there;
And piety with wishes placed above,
And steady loyalty and faithful love.
And thou, sweet Poetry, thou loveliest
　maid,
Still first to fly where sensual joys invade—
Unfit, in these degenerate times of shame,
To catch the heart, or strike for honest
　fame;
Dear, charming nymph, neglected and de-
　cried,
My shame in crowds, my solitary pride!
Thou source of all my bliss and all my woe—
That found'st me poor at first, and keep'st
　me so;
Thou guide, by which the nobler arts
　excel,
Thou nurse of every virtue—fare thee well!
Farewell!—and oh! where'er thy voice be
　tried,
On Torno's cliffs, or Pambamarca's side—
Whether where equinoctial fervors glow,
Or winter wraps the polar world in
　snow—

Still let thy voice, prevailing over time,
Redress the rigors of th' inclement clime;
Aid slighted truth with thy persuasive
　strain,
Teach erring man to spurn the rage of gain;
Teach him that states, of native strength
　possest,
Though very poor, may still be very blest;
That trade's proud empire hastes to swift
　decay,
As ocean sweeps the labor'd mole away;
While self-dependent power can time defy,
As rocks resist the billows and the sky.
　　　　　　　　　OLIVER GOLDSMITH.

*I KNEW BY THE SMOKE THAT SO
GRACEFULLY CURLED.*

I KNEW by the smoke that so gracefully
　curl'd
　Above the green elms, that a cottage
　　was near,
And I said, "If there's peace to be found
　in the world,
　A heart that is humble might hope for
　　it here!"

It was noon, and on flowers that languish'd
　around
　In silence reposed the voluptuous bee;
Every leaf was at rest, and I heard not a
　sound
　But the woodpecker tapping the hollow
　　beech tree.

And "Here in this lone little wood," I
　exclaim'd,
　"With a maid who was lovely to soul
　　and to eye,
Who would blush when I praised her, and
　weep if I blamed,
　How blest could I live, and how calm
　　could I die!

"By the shade of yon sumac, whose red
　berry dips
　In the gush of the fountain, how sweet
　　to recline,
And to know that I sigh'd upon innocent
　lips,
　Which had never been sigh'd on by any
　　but mine!"
　　　　　　　　　THOMAS MOORE.

NEVER AGAIN.

There are gains for all our losses,
  There are balms for all our pain:
But when youth, the dream, departs,
It takes something from our hearts,
  And it never comes again.

We are stronger, and are better,
  Under manhood's sterner reign:
Still we feel that something sweet
Follow'd youth, with flying feet,
  And will never come again.

Something beautiful is vanish'd,
  And we sigh for it in vain:
We behold it everywhere,
On the earth and in the air,
  But it never comes again!
      RICHARD HENRY STODDARD.

TWO RIVERS.

Thy summer voice, Musketaquit,
  Repeats the music of the rain;
But sweeter rivers pulsing flit
  Through thee, as thou through Concord Plain.

Thou in thy narrow banks art pent:
  The stream I love unbounded goes
Through flood and sea and firmament;
  Through light, through life, it forward flows.

I see the inundation sweet,
  I hear the spending of the stream
Through years, through men, through nature fleet,
  Through love and thought, through power and dream.

Musketaquit, a goblin strong,
  Of shard and flint makes jewels gay;
They lose their grief who hear his song,
  And where he winds is the day of day.

So forth and brighter fares my stream:
  Who drink it shall not thirst again;
No darkness stains its equal gleam,
  And ages drop in it like rain.
      RALPH WALDO EMERSON.

A PEAL OF BELLS.

Strike the bells wantonly,
  Tinkle tinkle well;
Bring me wine, bring me flowers,
  Ring the silver bell.
All my lamps burn scented oil,
  Hung on laden orange trees,
Whose shadow'd foliage is the foil
  To golden lamps and oranges.
Heap my golden plates with fruit,
  Golden fruit, fresh plucked and ripe,
Strike the bells and breathe the pipe;
Shut out showers from summer hours—
Silence that complaining lute—
  Shut out thinking, shut out pain,
From hours that cannot come again.

Strike the bells solemnly,
  Ding dong deep:
My friend is passing to his bed,
  Fast asleep;
There's plaited linen round his head,
  While foremost go his feet—
His feet that cannot carry him.
My feast's a show, my lights are dim;
  Be still, your music is not sweet,—
There is no music more for him:
  His lights are out, his feast is done;
His bowl that sparkled to the brim
  Is drain'd, is broken, cannot hold;
My blood is chill, his blood is cold;
  His death is full, and mine begun.
      CHRISTINA GEORGINA ROSSETTI.

THOSE EVENING BELLS.

Those evening bells! those evening bells!
How many a tale their music tells
Of youth, and home, and that sweet time
When last I heard their soothing chime!

Those joyous hours are pass'd away;
And many a heart that then was gay
Within the tomb now darkly dwells,
And hears no more those evening bells.

And so 'twill be when I am gone,—
That tuneful peal will still ring on;
While other bards shall walk these dells,
And sing your praise, sweet evening bells.
      THOMAS MOORE.

THE BELLS.

I.

Hear the sledges with the bells,—
    Silver bells,—
What a world of merriment their melody
    foretells!
  How they tinkle, tinkle, tinkle,
    In the icy air of night!
  While the stars that oversprinkle
  All the heavens seem to twinkle
    With a crystalline delight,—
  Keeping time, time, time,
  In a sort of Runic rhyme,
To the tintinnabulation that so musically
    wells
  From the bells, bells, bells, bells,
    Bells, bells, bells,—
From the jingling and the tinkling of the
    bells.

II.

  Hear the mellow wedding-bells,—
    Golden bells!
What a world of happiness their harmony
    foretells!
  Through the balmy air of night
  How they ring out their delight!
    From the molten-golden notes,
      And all in tune,
    What a liquid ditty floats
To the turtle-dove that listens while she
    gloats
      On the moon!
  Oh, from out the sounding cells
What a gush of euphony voluminously
    wells!
      How it swells!
      How it dwells
    On the Future! how it tells
    Of the rapture that impels
    To the swinging and the ringing
    Of the bells, bells, bells,
    Of the bells, bells, bells, bells,
      Bells, bells, bells,—
To the rhyming and the chiming of the
    bells.

III.

  Hear the loud alarum-bells,—
    Brazen bells!
What a tale of terror, now, their turbu-
    lency tells!
  In the startled ear of night
  How they scream out their affright!
    Too much horrified to speak,
    They can only shriek, shriek,
      Out of tune,
In the clamorous appealing to the mercy
    of the fire,
In a mad expostulation with the deaf and
    frantic fire
  Leaping higher, higher, higher,
    With a desperate desire,
    And a resolute endeavor,
  Now—now to sit or never,
By the side of the pale-faced moon.
    Oh the bells, bells, bells,
    What a tale their terror tells
      Of despair!
  How they clang and clash and roar!
  What a horror they outpour
On the bosom of the palpitating air!
  Yet the ear it fully knows,
    By the twanging,
    And the clanging,
  How the danger ebbs and flows;
  Yet the ear distinctly tells,
    In the jangling,
    And the wrangling,
  How the danger sinks and swells,
By the sinking or the swelling in the anger
    of the bells,—
      Of the bells,—
  Of the bells, bells, bells, bells,
    Bells, bells, bells,—
In the clamor and the clangor of the bells!

IV.

  Hear the tolling of the bells,—
    Iron bells!
What a world of solemn thought their
    monody compels!
  In the silence of the night,
  How we shiver with affright
At the melancholy menace of their tone;
  For every sound that floats
  From the rust within their throats
    Is a groan.
  And the people,—ah, the people,—
  They that dwell up in the steeple,
    All alone,
  And who tolling, tolling, tolling,
    In that muffled monotone,

Feel a glory in so rolling
  On the human heart a stone—
They are neither man nor woman,—
They are neither brute nor human,—
  They are ghouls:
And their king it is who tolls;
And he rolls, rolls, rolls,
    Rolls,
  A pæan from the bells!
And his merry bosom swells
  With the pæan of the bells!
And he dances and he yells;
Keeping time, time, time,
In a sort of Runic rhyme,
  To the pæan of the bells,—
    Of the bells:
Keeping time, time, time,
In a sort of Runic rhyme,
  To the throbbing of the bells,—
Of the bells, bells, bells,—
  To the sobbing of the bells;
Keeping time, time, time,
  As he knells, knells, knells,
In a happy Runic rhyme,
  To the rolling of the bells,—
Of the bells, bells, bells,—
  To the tolling of the bells,
Of the bells, bells, bells, bells,—
    Bells, bells, bells,—
To the moaning and the groaning of the bells.
        EDGAR ALLAN POE.

WHY THUS LONGING?

WHY thus longing, thus for ever sighing,
  For the far-off, unattain'd and dim,
While the beautiful, all round thee lying,
  Offers up its low, perpetual hymn?

Wouldst thou listen to its gentle teaching,
  All thy restless yearnings it would still;
Leaf and flower and laden bee are preaching
  Thine own sphere, though humble, first to fill.

Poor indeed thou must be if around thee
  Thou no ray of light and joy canst throw—
If no silken cord of love hath bound thee
  To some little world through weal and woe;

If no dear eyes thy fond love can brighten—
  No fond voices answer to thine own;
If no brother's sorrow thou canst lighten,
  By daily sympathy and gentle tone.

Not by deeds that win the crowd's applauses,
  Not by works that give thee world-renown,
Not by martyrdom or vaunted crosses,
  Canst thou win and wear the immortal crown.

Daily struggling, though unloved and lonely,
  Every day a rich reward will give;
Thou wilt find, by hearty striving only,
  And truly loving, thou canst truly live.

Dost thou revel in the rosy morning,
  When all Nature hails the lord of light,
And his smile, the mountain-tops adorning,
  Robes yon fragrant fields in radiance bright?

Other hands may grasp the field and forest,
  Proud proprietors in pomp may shine;
But with fervent love if thou adorest,
  Thou art wealthier—all the world is thine.

Yet if through earth's wide domains thou rovest,
  Sighing that they are not thine alone,
Not those fair fields, but thyself thou lovest,
  And their beauty and thy wealth are gone.

Nature wears the color of the spirit;
  Sweetly to her worshipper she sings;
All the glow, the grace she doth inherit,
  Round her trusting child she fondly flings.
        HARRIET WINSLOW SEWALL.

A LAMENT.

O WORLD! O Life! O Time!
  On whose last steps I climb,
    Trembling at that where I had stood before;
When will return the glory of your prime?
  No more—oh never more!

Out of the day and night
A joy has taken flight:
  Fresh spring, and summer, and winter hoar
Move my faint heart with grief, but with delight
  No more—oh never more!
PERCY BYSSHE SHELLEY.

THE TRAVELLER; OR, A PROSPECT OF SOCIETY.

REMOTE, unfriended, melancholy, slow,
Or by the lazy Scheldt, or wandering Po,
Or onward, where the rude Carinthian boor
Against the houseless stranger shuts the door,
Or where Campania's plain forsaken lies,
A weary waste expanding to the skies;
Where'er I roam, whatever realms to see,
My heart untravell'd fondly turns to thee;
Still to my brother turns, with ceaseless pain,
And drags at each remove a lengthening chain.

  Eternal blessings crown my earliest friend,
And round his dwelling guardian saints attend!
Blest be that spot where cheerful guests retire
To pause from toil, and trim their evening fire!
Blest that abode where want and pain repair,
And every stranger finds a ready chair;
Blest be those feasts with simple plenty crown'd,
Where all the ruddy family around
Laugh at the jests or pranks that never fail,
Or sigh with pity at some mournful tale;
Or press the bashful stranger to his food,
And learn the luxury of doing good!

  But me, not destined such delights to share,
My prime of life in wandering spent, and care;
Impell'd, with steps unceasing, to pursue
Some fleeting good that mocks me with the view,
That, like the circle bounding earth and skies,
Allures from far, yet, as I follow, flies;
My fortune leads to traverse realms alone,
And find no spot of all the world my own.

E'en now, where Alpine solitudes ascend,
I sit me down a pensive hour to spend;
And, placed on high above the storm's career,
Look downward where a hundred realms appear:
Lakes, forests, cities, plains extending wide,
The pomp of kings, the shepherd's humbler pride.

  When thus creation's charms around combine,
Amidst the store should thankless pride repine?
Say, should the philosophic mind disdain
That good which makes each humbler bosom vain?
Let school-taught pride dissemble all it can,
These little things are great to little man;
And wiser he whose sympathetic mind
Exults in all the good of all mankind.
Ye glittering towns, with wealth and splendor crown'd;
Ye fields, where summer spreads profusion round;
Ye lakes, whose vessels catch the busy gale;
Ye bending swains, that dress the flowery vale,—
For me your tributary stores combine:
Creation's heir, the world—the world is mine!

  As some lone miser, visiting his store,
Bends at his treasure, counts, recounts it o'er,
Hoards after hoards his rising raptures fill,
Yet still he sighs, for hoards are wanting still:
Thus to my breast alternate passions rise,
Pleased with each good that Heaven to man supplies;

Yet oft a sigh prevails, and sorrows fall,
To see the hoard of human bliss so small:
And oft I wish, amidst the scene to find
Some spot to real happiness consign'd,
Where my worn soul, each wandering hope at rest,
May gather bliss to see my fellows blest.

But where to find that happiest spot below
Who can direct, when all pretend to know?
The shuddering tenant of the frigid zone
Boldly proclaims that happiest spot his own;
Extols the treasures of his stormy seas,
And his long nights of revelry and ease:
The naked negro, panting at the line,
Boasts of his golden sands and palmy wine,
Basks in the glare, or stems the tepid wave,
And thanks his gods for all the good they gave.
Such is the patriot's boast where'er we roam,
His first, best country, ever is at home.
And yet perhaps, if countries we compare,
And estimate the blessings which they share,
Though patriots flatter, still shall wisdom find
An equal portion dealt to all mankind;
As different good, by Art or Nature given,
To different nations, makes their blessings even.

Nature, a mother kind alike to all,
Still grants her bliss at Labor's earnest call;
With food as well the peasant is supplied
On Idra's cliffs as Arno's shelvy side,
And though the rocky-crested summits frown,
These rocks by custom turn to beds of down.
From Art more various are the blessings sent,—
Wealth, commerce, honor, liberty, content.
Yet these each other's power so strong contest,
That either seems destructive of the rest.
Where wealth and freedom reign, contentment fails,
And honor sinks where commerce long prevails.
Hence every state, to one loved blessing prone,
Conforms and models life to that alone.
Each to the favorite happiness attends,
And spurns the plan that aims at other ends,
Till, carried to excess in each domain,
This favorite good begets peculiar pain.

But let us try these truths with closer eyes,
And trace them through the prospect as it lies:
Here, for a while, my proper cares resign'd,
Here let me sit in sorrow for mankind;
Like yon neglected shrub at random cast,
That shades the steep, and sighs at every blast.

Far to the right, where Apennine ascends,
Bright as the summer, Italy extends;
Its uplands sloping deck the mountain's side,
Woods over woods, in gay theatric pride,
While oft some temple's mouldering tops between
With venerable grandeur mark the scene.

Could Nature's bounty satisfy the breast,
The sons of Italy were surely blest:
Whatever fruits in different climes are found,
That proudly rise, or humbly court the ground;
Whatever blooms in torrid tracts appear,
Whose bright succession decks the varied year;
Whatever sweets salute the northern sky
With vernal lives, that blossom but to die;
These here disporting own the kindred soil,
Nor ask luxuriance from the planter's toil;
While sea-born gales their gelid wings expand,
To winnow fragrance round the smiling land.

But small the bliss that sense alone bestows,
And sensual bliss is all the nation knows.
In florid beauty groves and fields appear,
Man seems the only growth that dwindles here.
Contrasted faults through all his manners reign:
Though poor, luxurious; though submissive, vain;
Though grave, yet trifling; zealous, yet untrue;
And e'en in penance planning sins anew.
All evils here contaminate the mind,
That opulence departed leaves behind;
For wealth was theirs, not far removed the date,
When commerce proudly flourish'd through the state.
At her command the palace learn'd to rise,
Again the long-fall'n column sought the skies,
The canvas glow'd beyond e'en Nature warm,
The pregnant quarry teem'd with human form;
Till, more unsteady than the southern gale,
Commerce on other shores display'd her sail;
While naught remained, of all that riches gave,
But towns unmann'd, and lords without a slave:
And late the nation found, with fruitless skill,
Its former strength was but plethoric ill.

Yet still the loss of wealth is here supplied
By arts, the splendid wrecks of former pride;
From these the feeble heart and long-fallen mind
An easy compensation seem to find.
Here may be seen, in bloodless pomp array'd,
The pasteboard triumph and the cavalcade;
Processions form'd for piety and love,
A mistress or a saint in every grove.

By sports like these are all their cares beguiled;
The sports of children satisfy the child:
Each nobler aim, repress'd by long control,
Now sinks at last, or feebly mans the soul;
While low delights, succeeding fast behind,
In happier meanness occupy the mind.
As in those domes where Cæsars once bore sway,
Defaced by time, and tottering in decay,
There in the ruin, heedless of the dead,
The shelter-seeking peasant builds his shed;
And, wondering man could want the larger pile,
Exults, and owns his cottage with a smile.

My soul, turn from them! turn me to survey,
Where rougher climes a nobler race display,
Where the bleak Swiss their stormy mansion tread,
And force a churlish soil for scanty bread:
No product here the barren hills afford
But man and steel, the soldier and his sword;
No vernal blooms their torpid rocks array,
But winter lingering chills the lap of May;
No zephyr fondly sues the mountain's breast,
But meteors glare, and stormy glooms invest.

Yet still, even here content can spread a charm,
Redress the clime, and all its rage disarm.
Though poor the peasant's hut, his feast though small,
He sees his little lot the lot of all;
Sees no contiguous palace rear its head,
To shame the meanness of his humble shed;
No costly lord the sumptuous banquet deal,
To make him loathe his vegetable meal;
But calm, and bred in ignorance and toil,
Each wish contracting, fits him to the soil.

Cheerful at morn he wakes from short repose,
Breasts the keen air, and carols as he goes;
With patient angle trolls the finny deep,
Or drives his vent'rous ploughshare to the steep;
Or seeks the den where snow-tracks mark the way,
And drags the struggling savage into day.
At night returning, every labor sped,
He sits him down the monarch of a shed;
Smiles by his cheerful fire, and round surveys
His children's looks that brighten at the blaze,
While his loved partner, boastful of her hoard,
Displays her cleanly platter on the board;
And haply too some pilgrim, thither led,
With many a tale repays the nightly bed.

Thus every good his native wilds impart
Imprints the patriot passion on his heart;
And e'en those ills that round his mansion rise
Enhance the bliss his scanty fund supplies.
Dear is that shed to which his soul conforms,
And dear that hill which lifts him to the storms;
And as a child, when scaring sounds molest,
Clings close and closer to the mother's breast,
So the loud torrent and the whirlwind's roar
But bind him to his native mountains more.

Such are the charms to barren states assign'd:
Their wants but few, their wishes all confined.
Yet let them only share the praises due,—
If few their wants, their pleasures are but few:
For every want that stimulates the breast
Becomes a source of pleasure when redress'd.

Whence from such lands each pleasing science flies,
That first excites desire, and then supplies;
Unknown to them, when sensual pleasures cloy,
To fill the languid pause with finer joy;
Unknown those powers that raise the soul to flame,
Catch every nerve, and vibrate through the frame.
Their level life is but a smouldering fire,
Unquench'd by want, unfann'd by strong desire;
Unfit for raptures, or, if raptures cheer
On some high festival of once a year,
In wild excess the vulgar breast takes fire,
Till, buried in debauch, the bliss expire.

But not their joys alone thus coarsely flow,—
Their morals, like their pleasures, are but low:
For, as refinement stops, from sire to son
Unalter'd, unimproved the manners run;
And love's and friendship's finely-pointed dart
Fall blunted from each indurated heart.
Some sterner virtues o'er the mountain's breast
May sit like falcons cowering on the nest;
But all the gentler morals,—such as play
Through life's more cultured walks, and charm the way,—
These, far dispersed, on timorous pinions fly,
To sport and flutter in a kinder sky.

To kinder skies, where gentler manners reign,
I turn, and France displays her bright domain.
Gay, sprightly land of mirth and social ease,
Pleased with thyself, whom all the world can please,
How often have I led thy sportive choir
With tuneless pipe beside the murmuring Loire?
Where shading elms along the margin grew,
And, freshen'd from the wave, the zephyr flew;
And haply, though my harsh touch, faltering still,
But mock'd all tune and marr'd the dancer's skill;

Yet would the village praise my wondrous power,
And dance, forgetful of the noontide hour.
Alike all ages: dames of ancient days
Have led their children through the mirthful maze;
And the gay grandsire, skill'd in gestic lore,
Has frisk'd beneath the burden of threescore.

So blest a life these thoughtless realms display,
Thus idly busy rolls their world away.
Theirs are those arts that mind to mind endear,
For honor forms the social temper here:
Honor, that praise which real merit gains,
Or e'en imaginary worth obtains,
Here passes current; paid from hand to hand,
It shifts in splendid traffic round the land;
From courts to camps, to cottages it strays,
And all are taught an avarice of praise:
They please, are pleased; they give to get esteem;
Till, seeming blest, they grow to what they seem.

But while this softer art their bliss supplies,
It gives their follies also room to rise;
For praise too dearly loved, or warmly sought,
Enfeebles all internal strength of thought;
And the weak soul, within itself unblest,
Leans for all pleasure on another's breast.
Hence ostentation here, with tawdry art,
Pants for the vulgar praise which fools impart;
Here Vanity assumes her pert grimace,
And trims her robes of frieze with copper lace;
Here beggar Pride defrauds her daily cheer,
To boast one splendid banquet once a year;
The mind still turns where shifting fashion draws,
Nor weighs the solid worth of self-applause.

To men of other minds my fancy flies,
Embosom'd in the deep where Holland lies.
Methinks her patient sons before me stand,
Where the broad ocean leans against the land,
And, sedulous to stop the coming tide,
Lift the tall rampire's artificial pride.
Onward, methinks, and diligently slow,
The firm connected bulwark seems to grow,
Spreads its long arms amidst the watery roar,
Scoops out an empire, and usurps the shore;
While the pent ocean, rising o'er the pile,
Sees an amphibious world beneath him smile;
The slow canal, the yellow-blossom'd vale,
The willow-tufted bank, the gliding sail,
The crowded mart, the cultivated plain,
A new creation rescued from his reign.

Thus while around the wave-subjected soil
Impels the native to repeated toil,
Industrious habits in each bosom reign,
And industry begets a love of gain.
Hence all the good from opulence that springs,
With all those ills superfluous treasure brings,
Are here displayed. Their much-loved wealth imparts
Convenience, plenty, elegance, and arts:
But view them closer, craft and fraud appear;
E'en liberty itself is barter'd here;
At gold's superior charms all freedom flies,
The needy sell it, and the rich man buys.
A land of tyrants, and a den of slaves,
Here wretches seek dishonorable graves,
And, calmly bent, to servitude conform,
Dull as their lakes that slumber in the storm.

Heavens! how unlike their Belgic sires of old!
Rough, poor, content, ungovernably bold,
War in each breast and freedom on each brow;
How much unlike the sons of Britain now!

Fired at the sound, my genius spreads her wing,
And flies where Britain courts the western spring;
Where lawns extend that scorn Arcadian pride,
And brighter streams than famed Hydaspes glide.
There all around the gentlest breezes stray,
There gentle music melts on every spray;
Creation's mildest charms are there combined,
Extremes are only in the master's mind.
Stern o'er each bosom reason holds her state,
With daring aims irregularly great;
Pride in their port, defiance in their eye,
I see the lords of humankind pass by:
Intent on high designs, a thoughtful band,
By forms unfashion'd, fresh from Nature's hand,
Fierce in their native hardiness of soul,
True to imagined right, above control,—
While e'en the peasant boasts these rights to scan,
And learns to venerate himself as man.

Thine, Freedom, thine the blessings pictured here,
Thine are those charms that dazzle and endear!
Too blest indeed were such without alloy;
But, fostered e'en by freedom, ills annoy;
That independence Britons prize too high
Keeps man from man, and breaks the social tie;
The self-dependent lordlings stand alone,
All claims that bind and sweeten life unknown:
Here, by the bonds of Nature feebly held,
Minds combat minds, repelling and repell'd;
Ferments arise, imprison'd factions roar,
Repress'd ambition struggles round her shore,
Till, overwrought, the general system feels
Its motions stop, or frenzy fire the wheels.

Nor this the worst: as Nature's ties decay,
As duty, love, and honor fail to sway,
Fictitious bonds, the bonds of wealth and law,
Still gather strength, and force unwilling awe.
Hence all obedience bows to these alone,
And talent sinks, and merit weeps unknown;
Till time may come when, stripp'd of all her charms,
The land of scholars and the nurse of arms,
Where noble stems transmit the patriot flame,
Where kings have toil'd and poets wrote for fame,
One sink of level avarice shall lie,
And scholars, soldiers, kings, unhonor'd die.

But think not, thus when Freedom's ills I state,
I mean to flatter kings or court the great;
Ye powers of truth, that bid my soul aspire,
Far from my bosom drive the low desire!
And thou, fair Freedom, taught alike to feel
The rabble's rage and tyrant's angry steel;
Thou transitory flower, alike undone
By proud contempt or favor's fostering sun,—
Still may thy blooms the changeful clime endure!
I only would repress them to secure.
For just experience tells, in every soil,
That those who think must govern those that toil;
And all that Freedom's highest aims can reach
Is but to lay proportion'd loads on each.
Hence, should one order disproportion'd grow,
Its double weight must ruin all below.

Oh then how blind to all that truth requires,
Who think it freedom when a part aspires!
Calm is my soul, nor apt to rise in arms,
Except when fast-approaching danger warms;

But when contending chiefs blockade the throne,
Contracting regal power to stretch their own;
When I behold a factious band agree
To call it freedom when themselves are free,
Each wanton judge new penal statutes draw,
Laws grind the poor, and rich men rule the law,
The wealth of climes where savage nations roam
Pillaged from slaves to purchase slaves at home,—
Fear, pity, justice, indignation, start,
Tear off reserve and bare my swelling heart;
Till, half a patriot, half a coward grown,
I fly from petty tyrants to the throne.

Yes, brother, curse with me that baleful hour
When first ambition struck at regal power;
And thus, polluting honor in its source,
Gave wealth to sway the mind with double force.
Have we not seen, round Britain's peopled shore,
Her useful sons exchanged for useless ore?
Seen all her triumphs but destruction haste,
Like flaring tapers brightening as they waste?
Seen opulence, her grandeur to maintain,
Lead stern depopulation in her train,
And over fields where scatter'd hamlets rose
In barren, solitary pomp repose?
Have we not seen, at pleasure's lordly call,
The smiling, long-frequented village fall?
Beheld the duteous son, the sire decay'd,
The modest matron, and the blushing maid,
Forced from their homes, a melancholy train,
To traverse climes beyond the western main,
Where wild Oswego spreads her swamps around,
And Niagara stuns with thundering sound?

E'en now, perhaps, as there some pilgrim strays
Through tangled forests and through dangerous ways,
Where beasts with man divided empire claim,
And the brown Indian marks with murderous aim;
There, while above the giddy tempest flies,
And all around distressful yells arise,
The pensive exile, bending with his woe,
To stop too fearful, and too faint to go,
Casts a long look where England's glories shine,
And bids his bosom sympathize with mine.

Vain, very vain, my weary search to find
That bliss which only centres in the mind;
Why have I stray'd from pleasure and repose
To seek a good each government bestows?
In every government, though terrors reign,
Though tyrant kings or tyrant laws restrain,
How small, of all that human hearts endure,
That part which laws or kings can cause or cure!
Still to ourselves in every place consign'd,
Our own felicity we make or find;
With secret course which no loud storms annoy
Glides the smooth current of domestic joy.
The lifted axe, the agonizing wheel,
Luke's iron crown, and Damiens' bed of steel,
To men remote from power but rarely known,
Leave reason, faith, and conscience all our own.
OLIVER GOLDSMITH.

FOOTSTEPS OF ANGELS.

WHEN the hours of day are number'd,
  And the voices of the night
Wake the better soul that slumber'd
  To a holy, calm delight;

Ere the evening lamps are lighted,
  And, like phantoms grim and tall,
Shadows from the fitful firelight
  Dance upon the parlor wall;

Then the forms of the departed
  Enter at the open door;
The belovèd, the true-hearted,
  Come to visit me once more.

He, the young and strong, who cherish'd
  Noble longings for the strife,
By the roadside fell and perish'd,
  Weary with the march of life!

They, the holy ones and weakly,
  Who the cross of suffering bore,
Folded their pale hands so meekly,
  Spake with us on earth no more!

And with them the Being Beauteous
  Who unto my youth was given,
More than all things else to love me,
  And is now a saint in Heaven.

With a slow and noiseless footstep
  Comes that messenger divine,
Takes the vacant chair beside me,
  Lays her gentle hand in mine.

And she sits and gazes at me
  With those deep and tender eyes,
Like the stars, so still and saint-like,
  Looking downward from the skies.

Utter'd not, yet comprehended,
  Is the spirit's voiceless prayer,
Soft rebukes, in blessings ended,
  Breathing from her lips of air.

Oh, though oft depress'd and lonely,
  All my fears are laid aside,
If I but remember only
  Such as these have lived and died!
        HENRY WADSWORTH LONGFELLOW.

A DREAM.

ALL yesterday I was spinning,
  Sitting alone in the sun;
And the dream that I spun was so lengthy,
  It lasted till day was done.

I heeded not cloud or shadow
  That flitted over the hill,
Or the humming-bees, or the swallows,
  Or the trickling of the rill.

I took the threads for my spinning,
  All of blue summer air,
And a flickering ray of sunlight
  Was woven in here and there.

The shadows grew longer and longer,
  The evening wind pass'd by,
And the purple splendor of sunset
  Was flooding the western sky.

But I could not leave my spinning,
  For so fair my dream had grown,
I heeded not, hour by hour,
  How the silent day had flown.

At last the gray shadows fell round me,
  And the night came dark and chill,
And I rose and ran down the valley,
  And left it all on the hill.

I went up the hill this morning,
  To the place where my spinning lay,—
There was nothing but glistening dewdrops
  Remain'd of my dream to-day.
        ADELAIDE ANNE PROCTER.

THE DAY IS DONE.

THE day is done, and the darkness
  Falls from the wings of Night,
As a feather is wafted downward
  From an eagle in his flight.

I see the lights of the village
  Gleam through the rain and the mist:
And a feeling of sadness comes o'er me,
  That my soul cannot resist:

A feeling of sadness and longing,
  That is not akin to pain,
And resembles sorrow only
  As the mist resembles the rain.

Come, read to me some poem,
  Some simple and heartfelt lay,
That shall soothe this restless feeling,
  And banish the thoughts of day.

Not from the grand old masters,
  Not from the bards sublime,
Whose distant footsteps echo
  Through the corridors of Time.

For, like strains of martial music,
  Their mighty thoughts suggest
Life's endless toil and endeavor;
  And to-night I long for rest.

Read from some humbler poet,
  Whose songs gush'd from his heart,
As showers from the clouds of summer,
  Or tears from the eyelids start;

Who, through long days of labor,
  And nights devoid of ease,
Still heard in his soul the music
  Of wonderful melodies.

Such songs have power to quiet
  The restless pulse of care,
And come like the benediction
  That follows after prayer.

Then read from the treasured volume
  The poem of thy choice;
And lend to the rhyme of the poet
  The beauty of thy voice.

And the night shall be fill'd with music,
  And the cares that infest the day
Shall fold their tents like the Arabs,
  And as silently steal away.
       HENRY WADSWORTH LONGFELLOW.

NIGHT.

THE crackling embers on the hearth are dead;
  The indoor note of industry is still;
  The latch is fast; upon the window-sill
The small birds wait not for their daily bread;
The voiceless flowers,—how quietly they shed
  Their nightly odors!—and the household rill
  Murmurs continuous dulcet sounds that fill
The vacant expectation, and the dread
Of listening night. And haply now she sleeps;
  For all the garrulous noises of the air
Are hush'd in peace; the soft dew silent weeps,
  Like hopeless lovers for a maid so fair:—
Oh, that I were the happy dream that creeps
  To her soft heart, to find my image there!
       HARTLEY COLERIDGE.

THE RAINY DAY.

THE day is cold, and dark and dreary;
It rains, and the wind is never weary;
The vine still clings to the mouldering wall,
But at every gust the dead leaves fall,
  And the day is dark and dreary.

My life is cold, and dark, and dreary.
It rains, and the wind is never weary;
My thoughts still cling to the mouldering Past,
But the hopes of youth fall thick in the blast,
  And the days are dark and dreary.

Be still, sad heart! and cease repining;
Behind the clouds is the sun still shining;
Thy fate is the common fate of all,
Into each life some rain must fall,
  Some days must be dark and dreary.
       HENRY WADSWORTH LONGFELLOW.

NIGHT.

WHEN I survey the bright
    Celestial sphere,
So rich with jewels hung that night
Doth like an Ethiop bride appear,

My soul her wings doth spread,
    And heavenward flies,
The Almighty's mysteries to read
    In the large volume of the skies.

For the bright firmament
    Shoots forth no flame
So silent but is eloquent
    In speaking the Creator's name.

No unregarded star
    Contracts its light
Into so small chara´cter,
    Removed far from our human sight,

But if we steadfast look,
    We shall discern
In it, as in some holy book,
    How man may heavenly knowledge learn.

It tells the conqueror
    That far-stretch'd power,
Which his proud dangers traffic for,
Is but the triumph of an hour,—

That from the farthest north
  Some nation may,
Yet undiscover'd, issue forth,
  And o'er his new-got conquest sway!

Some nation, yet shut in
  With hills of ice,
May be let out to scourge his sin,
  Till they shall equal him in vice.

And they likewise shall
  Their ruin have;
For as yourselves your empires fall,
  And every kingdom hath a grave

Thus those celestial fires,
  Though seeming mute,
The fallacy of our desires
  And all the pride of life confute.

For they have watch'd since first
  The world had birth,
And found sin in itself accursed,
  And nothing permanent on earth.
WILLIAM HABINGTON.

SONNET ON SLEEP.

CARE-CHARMER Sleep, son of the sable Night,
  Brother to Death, in silent darkness born,
Relieve my languish, and restore the light;
  With dark forgetting of my care return.
And let the day be time enough to mourn
  The shipwreck of my ill-adventured youth:
Let waking eyes suffice to wail their scorn,
  Without the torment of the night's untruth.
Cease, dreams, the images of day-desires,
  To model forth the passions of the morrow;
Never let rising sun approve you liars
  To add more grief to aggravate my sorrow:
Still let me sleep, embracing clouds in vain,
And never wake to feel the day's disdain.
SAMUEL DANIEL.

SONNET ON SLEEP.

COME sleep, O sleep! the certain knot of peace,
  The baiting-place of wit, the balm of woe;
The poor man's wealth, the prisoner's release,
  The indifferent judge between the high and low!
With shield of proof, shield me from out the prease
  Of those fierce darts Despair doth at me throw.
Oh make in me those civil wars to cease;
  I will good tribute pay if thou do so.
Take thou of me smooth pillows, sweetest bed,
  A chamber deaf to noise and blind to light,
A rosy garland and a weary head;
  And if these things, as being thine by right,
Move not thy heavy grace, thou shalt in me,
Livelier than elsewhere, Stella's image see.
SIR PHILIP SIDNEY.

ODE TO FEAR.

THOU, to whom the world unknown,
With all its shadowy shapes, is shown,
Who seest appall'd the unreal scene,
While Fancy lifts the veil between:
  Ah, Fear! ah, frantic Fear!
  I see—I see thee near.
I know thy hurried step, thy haggard eye!
Like thee I start, like thee disorder'd fly,
For, lo, what monsters in thy train appear!
Danger, whose limbs of giant mould
What mortal eye can fix'd behold?
Who stalks his round, a hideous form,
Howling amidst the midnight storm,
Or throws him on the ridgy steep
Of some loose-hanging rock to sleep:
And with him thousand phantoms join'd,
Who prompt to deeds accursed the mind:
And those, the fiends, who, near allied,
O'er Nature's wounds and wrecks preside;

Whilst Vengeance, in the lurid air,
Lifts her red arm, exposed and bare:
On whom that ravening brood of Fate,
Who lap the blood of Sorrow, wait;
Who, Fear, this ghastly train can see,
And look not madly wild, like thee?

EPODE.

In earliest Greece, to thee, with partial choice,
  The grief-full Muse addrest her infant tongue;
The maids and matrons, on her awful voice,
  Silent and pale, in wild amazement hung.

Yet he, the bard who first invoked thy name,
  Disdain'd in Marathon its power to feel:
For not alone he nursed the poet's flame,
  But reach'd from Virtue's hand the patriot's steel.

But who is he, whom later garlands grace,
  Who left a while o'er Hybla's dews to rove,
With trembling eyes thy dreary steps to trace,
  Where thou and Furies shared the baleful grove?

Wrapt in thy cloudy veil, the incestuous queen
  Sigh'd the sad call her son and husband heard:
When once alone it broke the silent scene,
  And he, the wretch of Thebes, no more appear'd.

O Fear, I know thee by my throbbing heart:
  Thy withering power inspired each mournful line:
Though gentle Pity claim her mingled part,
  Yet all the thunders of the scene are thine!

ANTISTROPHE.

Thou who such weary lengths hast past,
Where wilt thou rest, mad nymph, at last?
Say, wilt thou shroud in haunted cell,
Where gloomy Rape and Murder dwell?
Or, in some hollow'd seat
'Gainst which the big waves beat,
Hear drowning seamen's cries in tempests brought?
Dark power, with shuddering meek submitted thought,
Be mine to read the visions old
Which thy awakening bards have told:
And, lest thou meet my blasted view,
Hold each strange tale devoutly true;
Ne'er be I found, by thee o'erawed,
In that thrice-hallow'd eve, abroad,
When ghosts, as cottage-maids believe,
Their pebbled beds permitted leave,
And goblins haunt from fire, or fen,
Or mine, or flood, the walks of men!
O thou, whose spirit most possest
The sacred seat of Shakespeare's breast!
By all that from thy prophet broke,
In thy divine emotions spoke;
Hither again thy fury deal,
Teach me but once like him to feel:
His cypress wreath my meed decree,
And I, O Fear, will dwell with thee!
                    WILLIAM COLLINS.

HYMN TO ADVERSITY.

DAUGHTER of Jove, relentless power,
  Thou tamer of the human breast,
Whose iron scourge and torturing hour
  The bad affright, afflict the best!
Bound in thy adamantine chain
The proud are taught to taste of pain,
And purple tyrants vainly groan
With pangs unfelt before, unpitied and alone.

When first thy sire to send on earth
  Virtue, his darling child, design'd,
To thee he gave the heavenly birth,
  And bade to form her infant mind.
Stern, rugged nurse! thy rigid lore
With patience many a year she bore:
What sorrow was thou bad'st her know,
And from her own she learn'd to melt at others' woe.

Scared at thy frown terrific, fly
  Self-pleasing Folly's idle brood,

Wild Laughter, Noise and thoughtless
    Joy,
  And leave us leisure to be good.
Light they disperse, and with them go
The summer friend, the flattering foe;
By vain Prosperity received,
To her they vow their truth, and are again
    believed.

Wisdom in sable garb array'd,
  Immers'd in rapturous thought profound,
And Melancholy, silent maid,
  With leaden eye that loves the ground,
Still on thy solemn steps attend:
Warm Charity, the general friend,
With Justice, to herself severe,
And Pity dropping soft the sadly-pleasing
    tear.

Oh, gently on thy suppliant's head,
  Dread goddess, lay thy chastening
    hand!
Not in thy Gorgon terrors clad,
  Not circled with the vengeful band
(As by the impious thou art seen)
With thundering voice, and threatening
    mien,
With screaming Horror's funeral cry,
Despair, and fell Disease, and ghastly
    Poverty:

Thy form benign, O goddess, wear,
  Thy milder influence impart,
Thy philosophic train be there
  To soften, not to wound my heart.
The generous spark extinct revive,
Teach me to love and to forgive,
Exact my own defects to scan,
What others are to feel, and know myself
    a Man.
                        THOMAS GRAY.

WHILST AS FICKLE FORTUNE SMILED.

WHILST as fickle Fortune smiled,
Thou and I were both beguiled.
Every one that flatters thee
Is no friend in misery.
Words are easy, like the wind;
Faithful friends are hard to find.

Every man will be thy friend
Whilst thou hast wherewith to spend;
But, if stores of crowns be scant,
No man will supply thy want.
If that one be prodigal,
Bountiful they will him call;
And, with such-like flattering,
"Pity but he were a king."
If he be addict to vice,
Quickly him they will entice;
But if Fortune once do frown,
Then farewell his great renown!
They that fawn'd on him before
Use his company no more.
He that is thy friend indeed,
He will help thee in thy need;
If thou sorrow, he will weep,
If thou wake, he cannot sleep.
Thus, of every grief in heart,
He with thee doth bear a part.
These are certain signs to know
Faithful friend from flattering foe.
                        RICHARD BARNEFIELD.

TIMES GO BY TURNS.

THE loppèd tree in time may grow again;
  Most naked plants renew both fruit and
    flower;
The sorest wight may find release of
    pain,
  The driest soil suck in some moist'ning
    shower:
Times go by turns, and chances change
    by course,
From foul to fair, from better hap to
    worse.

The sea of Fortune doth not ever flow;
  She draws her favors to the lowest ebb;
Her tides have equal times to come and
    go;
  Her loom doth weave the fine and
    coarsest web:
No joy so great but runneth to an end,
No hap so hard but may in fine amend.

Not always fall of leaf, nor ever spring,
  No endless night, yet not eternal day;
The saddest birds a season find to sing,
  The roughest storm a calm may soon
    allay;

Thus with succeeding turns God tempereth all,
That man may hope to rise, yet fear to fall.

A chance may win that by mischance was lost;
  The well that holds no great, takes little fish;
In some things all, in all things none are cross'd;
  Few all they need, but none have all they wish;
Unmeddled joys here to no man befall;
Who least, hath some; who most, hath never all.
ROBERT SOUTHWELL.

SONG.

RARELY, rarely, comest thou,
  Spirit of Delight!
Wherefore hast thou left me now
  Many a day and night?
Many a weary night and day
'Tis since thou art fled away.

How shall ever one like me
  Win thee back again?
With the joyous and the free
  Thou wilt scoff at pain.
Spirit false! thou hast forgot
All but those who need thee not.

As a lizard with the shade
  Of a trembling leaf,
Thou with sorrow art dismay'd;
  Even the sighs of grief
Reproach thee, that thou art not near,
And reproach thou wilt not hear.

Let me set my mournful ditty
  To a merry measure;—
Thou wilt never come for pity,
  Thou wilt come for pleasure;—
Pity, then, will cut away
Those cruel wings, and thou wilt stay.

I love all that thou lovest,
  Spirit of Delight!
The fresh Earth in new leaves drest
  And the starry night;
Autumn evening, and the morn
When the golden mists are born.

I love snow and all the forms
  Of the radiant frost;
I love waves, and winds, and storms,
  Everything almost
Which is Nature's, and may be
Untainted by man's misery.

I love tranquil solitude,
  And such society
As is quiet, wise, and good;
  Between thee and me
What difference? But thou dost possess
The things I seek, not love them less.

I love Love—though he has wings,
  And like light can flee,
But above all other things,
  Spirit, I love thee—
Thou art love and life! Oh come!
Make once more my heart thy home!
PERCY BYSSHE SHELLEY.

TO LADY ANNE HAMILTON.

Too late I stay'd,—forgive the crime!
  Unheeded flew the hours;
How noiseless falls the foot of Time
  That only treads on flowers!

What eye with clear account remarks
  The ebbing of the glass,
When all its sands are diamond sparks,
  That dazzle as they pass?

Oh, who to sober measurement
  Time's happy swiftness brings,
When birds of paradise have lent
  Their plumage for his wings?
WILLIAM ROBERT SPENCER.

O FAIREST OF THE RURAL MAIDS!

O FAIREST of the rural maids!
Thy birth was in the forest shades;
Green boughs, and glimpses of the sky,
Were all that met thine infant eye.

Thy sports, thy wanderings, when a child
Were ever in the sylvan wild;
And all the beauty of the place
Is in thy heart and on thy face.

The twilight of the trees and rocks
Is in the light shade of thy locks;
Thy step is as the wind that weaves
Its playful way among the leaves.

Thine eyes are springs, in whose serene
And silent waters heaven is seen;
Their lashes are the herbs that look
On their young figures in the brook.

The forest depths, by foot unpress'd,
Are not more sinless than thy breast;
The holy peace that fills the air
Of those calm solitudes is there.
WILLIAM CULLEN BRYANT.

ON AN INTAGLIO HEAD OF MINERVA.

BENEATH the warrior's helm behold
    The flowing tresses of a woman!
Minerva—Pallas—what you will,—
    A winsome creature, Greek or Roman.

Minerva? No! 'tis some sly minx
    In cousin's helmet masquerading;
If not, then Wisdom was a dame
    For sonnets and for serenading.

I thought the goddess cold, austere,
    Not made for love's despairs and blisses:
Did Pallas wear her hair like that?
    Was Wisdom's mouth so shaped for kisses?

The nightingale should be her bird,
    And not the owl, big-eyed and solemn:
How very fresh she looks,—and yet
    She's older far than Trajan's Column!

The magic hand that carved this face,
    And set this vine-work round it running,
Perhaps ere mighty Phidias wrought
    Had lost its subtle skill and cunning.

Who was he? Was he glad or sad,
    Who knew to carve in such a fashion?
Perchance he 'graved the dainty head
    For some brown girl that scorn'd his passion.

Perchance, in some still garden-place,
    Where neither fount nor tree to-day is,
He flung the jewel at the feet
    Of Phryne, or perhaps 'twas Lais.

But he is dust; we may not know
    His happy or unhappy story:
Nameless, and dead these centuries,
    His work outlives him—there's his glory!

Both man and jewel lay in earth
    Beneath a lava-buried city;
The countless summers came and went
    With neither haste, nor hate, nor pity.

Years blotted out the man, but left
    The jewel fresh as any blossom,
Till some Visconti dug it up,
    To rise and fall on Mabel's bosom!

O nameless brother! see how Time
    Your gracious handiwork has guarded;
See how your loving, patient art
    Has come, at last, to be rewarded.

Who would not suffer slights of men,
    And pangs of hopeless passion also,
To have his carven agate-stone
    On such a bosom rise and fall so?
THOMAS BAILEY ALDRICH.

DOLCINO TO MARGARET.

THE world goes up and the world goes down,
    And the sunshine follows the rain;
And yesterday's sneer, and yesterday's frown
    Can never come over again,
        Sweet wife,
    No, never come over again.

For woman is warm, though man be cold,
    And the night will hallow the day;
Till the heart which at even was weary and old
    Can rise in the morning gay,
        Sweet wife,
    To its work in the morning gay.
CHARLES KINGSLEY.

SONNET.

SWEET is the rose, but grows upon a brere;
    Sweet is the juniper, but sharp his bough;

Sweet is the eglantine, but pricketh near,
　Sweet is the firbloom, but his branches rough;
Sweet is the cyprus, but his rind is tough;
　Sweet is the nut, but bitter is his pill;
Sweet is the broom-flower, but yet sour enough;
And sweet is moly, but his root is ill;
So, every sweet with sour is temper'd still,
　That maketh it be coveted the more:
For easy things that may be got at will
　Most sorts of men do set but little store.
Why then should I account of little pain
That endless pleasure shall unto me gain?
　　　　　　　　　　EDMUND SPENSER.

SONNET.

SCORN not the Sonnet; Critic, you have frown'd,
　Mindless of its just honors; with this Key
　Shakespeare unlocked his heart; the melody
Of this small Lute gave ease to Petrarch's wound,
A thousand times this Pipe did Tasso sound;
Camoens soothed with it an Exile's grief;
The Sonnet glitter'd a gay myrtle Leaf
Amid the cypress with which Dante crown'd
His visionary brow: a glow-worm Lamp,
　It cheer'd mild Spenser, call'd from Faery-land
To struggle through dark ways; and, when a damp
　Fell round the path of Milton, in his hand
The Thing became a Trumpet, whence he blew
Soul-animating strains—alas, too few!
　　　　　　　　　WILLIAM WORDSWORTH.

SONNET.

BECAUSE I oft in dark abstracted guise
　Seem most alone in greatest company,
　With dearth of words, or answers quite awry
To them that would make speech of speech arise,
They deem, and of their doom the rumor flies,
　That poison foul of bubbling Pride doth lie
So in my swelling breast, that only I
Fawn on myself, and others do despise.
Yet Pride, I think, doth not my soul possess,
　Which looks too oft in his unflattering glass;
But one worse fault Ambition I confess,
　That makes me oft my best friends overpass,
Unseen, unheard, while thought to highest place
Bends all his powers, even unto Stella's grace.
　　　　　　　　　SIR PHILIP SIDNEY.

FAREWELL TO THEE, ARABY'S DAUGHTER.

FAREWELL,—farewell to thee, Araby's daughter!
　(Thus warbled a Peri beneath the dark sea);
No pearl ever lay under Oman's green water
　More pure in its shell than thy spirit in thee.

Oh, fair as the sea-flower close to thee growing,
　How light was thy heart till love's witchery came,
Like the wind of the south o'er a summer lute blowing,
　And hush'd all its music and wither'd its frame!

But long upon Araby's green sunny highlands,
　Shall maids and their lovers remember the doom
Of her who lies sleeping among the Pearl Islands,
　With naught but the sea-star to light up her tomb.

And still, when the merry date-season is burning,
　And calls to the palm-groves the young and the old,

The happiest there, from their pastime re-
  turning
  At sunset, will weep when thy story is
    told.

The young village maid, when with flowers
    she dresses
  Her dark-flowing hair for some festival
    day,
Will think of thy fate till, neglecting her
    tresses,
  She mournfully turns from the mirror
    away.

Nor shall Iran, beloved of her hero! forget
    thee,—
  Though tyrants watch over her tears as
    they start,
Close, close by the side of that hero she'll
    set thee,
  Embalm'd in the innermost shrine of
    her heart.

Farewell!—be it ours to embellish thy
    pillow
  With everything beauteous that grows in
    the deep;
Each flower of the rock and each gem of
    the billow
  Shall sweeten thy bed and illumine thy
    sleep.

Around thee shall glisten the loveliest
    amber
  That ever the sorrowing sea-bird has
    wept;
With many a shell, in whose hollow-
    wreathed chamber
  We, Peris of Ocean, by moonlight have
    slept.

We'll dive where the gardens of coral lie
    darkling,
  And plant all the rosiest stems at thy
    head;
We'll seek where the sands of the Caspian
    are sparkling,
  And gather their gold to strew over thy
    bed.

Farewell!—farewell!—until Pity's sweet
    fountain
  Is lost in the hearts of the fair and the
    brave,

They'll weep for the Chieftain who died on
    that mountain,
They'll weep for the Maiden who sleeps
    in the wave.
                    THOMAS MOORE.

STANZAS.

THOUGHT is deeper than all speech,
  Feeling deeper than all thought;
Souls to souls can never teach
  What unto themselves was taught.

We are spirits clad in veils;
  Man by man was never seen;
All our deep communing fails
  To remove the shadowy screen.

Heart to heart was never known;
  Mind with mind did never meet;
We are columns left alone
  Of a temple once complete.

Like the stars that gem the sky,
  Far apart though seeming near,
In our light we scattered lie;
  All is thus but starlight here.

What is social company
  But a babbling summer stream?
What our wise philosophy
  But the glancing of a dream?

Only when the sun of love
  Melts the scattered stars of thought,
Only when we live above
  What the dim-eyed world hath taught,

Only when our souls are fed
  By the fount which gave them birth,
And by inspiration led
  Which they never drew from earth,

We, like parted drops of rain,
  Swelling till they meet and run,
Shall be all absorbed again,
  Melting, flowing into one.
              CHRISTOPHER PEARSE CRANCH.

THE MORNING STREET.

ALONE I walk the morning street,
Filled with the silence vague and sweet:
All seems as strange, as still, as dead,
As if unnumbered years had fled,

Letting the noisy Babel lie
Breathless and dumb against the sky;
The light wind walks with me alone
Where the hot day flame-like was blown,
Where the wheels roared, the dust was
    beat:
The dew is in the morning street.

Where are the restless throngs that pour
Along this mighty corridor
While the noon shines?—the hurrying
    crowd
Whose footsteps make the city loud,—
The myriad faces, hearts that beat
No more in the deserted street?
Those footsteps in their dreaming maze
Cross thresholds of forgotten days;
Those faces brighten from the years
In rising suns long set in tears;
Those hearts,—far in the Past they beat,
Unheard within the morning street.

A city of the world's gray prime,
Lost in some desert far from time,
Where noiseless ages, gliding through,
Have only sifted sand and dew,—
Yet a mysterious hand of man
Lying on all the haunted plan,
The passions of the human heart
Quickening the marble breast of Art,—
Were not more strange to one who first
Upon its ghostly silence burst
Than this vast quiet where the tide
Of life, upheaved on either side,
Hangs trembling, ready soon to beat
With human waves the morning street.

Ay, soon the glowing morning flood
Breaks through the charmèd solitude:
This silent stone, to music won,
Shall murmur to the rising sun;
The busy place, in dust and heat,
Shall rush with wheels and swarm with
    feet;
The Arachne-threads of Purpose stream
Unseen within the morning gleam;
The life shall move, the death be plain;
The bridal throng, the funeral train,
Together, face to face shall meet
And pass within the morning street.
            JOHN JAMES PIATT.

PRE-EXISTENCE.

WHILE sauntering through the crowded
    street,
Some half-remembered face I meet,

Albeit upon no mortal shore
That face, methinks, has smiled before

Lost in a gay and festal throng,
I tremble at some tender song,—

Set to an air whose golden bars
I must have heard in other stars.

In sacred aisles I pause to share
The blessings of a priestly prayer,—

When the whole scene which greets mine
    eyes
In some strange mode I recognize

As one whose every mystic part
I feel prefigured in my heart.

At sunset, as I calmly stand,
A stranger on an alien strand,

Familiar as my childhood's home
Seems the long stretch of wave and foam.

One sails toward me o'er the bay,
And what he comes to do and say

I can foretell. A prescient lore
Springs from some life outlived of yore.

O swift, instinctive, startling gleams
Of deep soul-knowledge! not as *dreams*

For aye ye vaguely dawn and die,
But oft with lightning certainty

Pierce through the dark, oblivious brain,
To make old thoughts and memories plain:

Thoughts which perchance must travel
    back
Across the wild, bewildering track

Of countless æons; memories far,
High-reaching as yon pallid star,

Unknown, scarce seen, whose flickering
    grace
Faints on the outmost rings of space!
            PAUL HAMILTON HAYNE.

SONNET ON PARTING WITH HIS BOOKS.

As one who destined from his friends to part
 Regrets his loss, but hopes again erewhile
 To share their converse and enjoy their smile,
And tempers, as he may, affliction's dart;
Thus, loved associates, chiefs of elder art,
 Teachers of wisdom, who could once beguile
 My tedious hours and lighten every toil,
I now resign you! Nor with fainting heart;
For pass a few short years, or days, or hours,
 And happier seasons may their dawn unfold,
 And all your sacred fellowship restore;
When, freed from earth, unlimited its powers,
 Mind shall with mind direct communion hold,
 And kindred spirits meet to part no more.
WILLIAM ROSCOE.

SIR MARMADUKE.

SIR MARMADUKE was a hearty knight;
 Good man! old man!
He's painted standing bolt upright,
 With his hose rolled over his knee;
His periwig's as white as chalk,
And on his fist he holds a hawk,
 And he looks like the head
  Of an ancient family.

His dining-room was long and wide;
 Good man! old man!
His spaniels lay by the fireside;
 And in other parts, d' ye see,
Cross-bows, tobacco-pipes, old hats,
A saddle, his wife, and a litter of cats;
 And he looked like the head
  Of an ancient family.

He never turned the poor from his gate;
 Good man! old man!
But was always ready to break the pate
 Of his country's enemy.
What knight could do a better thing
Than serve the poor and fight for his king?
 And so may every head
  Of an ancient family.
GEORGE COLMAN THE YOUNGER.

PRAXITELES AND PHRYNE.

A THOUSAND silent years ago,
 The twilight faint and pale
Was drawing o'er the sunset glow
 Its soft and shadowy veil;

When from his work the Sculptor stayed
 His hand, and turned to one
Who stood beside him, half in shade,
 Said, with a sigh, "'Tis done.

"Thus much is saved from chance and change,
 That waits for me and thee;
Thus much—how little!—from the range
 Of Death and Destiny.

"Phryne, thy human lips shall pale,
 Thy rounded limbs decay,—
Nor love nor prayers can aught avail
 To bid thy beauty stay;

"But there thy smile for centuries
 On marble lips shall live,—
For Art can grant what love denies,
 And fix the fugitive.

"Sad thought! nor age nor death shall fade
 The youth of this cold bust;
When this quick brain and hand that made,
 And thou and I are dust!

"When all our hopes and fears are dead,
 And both our hearts are cold,
And love is like a tune that's played,
 And Life a tale that's told,

"This senseless stone, so coldly fair,
 That love nor life can warm,
The same enchanting look shall wear,
 The same enchanting form.

"Its peace no sorrow shall destroy;
 Its beauty age shall spare
The bitterness of vanished joy,
 The wearing waste of care.

"And there upon that silent face
 Shall unborn ages see
Perennial youth, perennial grace,
 And sealed serenity.

"And strangers, when we sleep in peace,
 Shall say, not quite unmoved,
So smiled upon Praxiteles
 The Phryne whom he loved."
WILLIAM WETMORE STORY.

THE HOUSE IS DARK AND DREARY.

The house is dark and dreary,
  And my heart is full of gloom;
But out of doors, in the blessed air,
The sun is warm, the sky is fair,
  And the flowers are still in bloom.

A moment ago in the garden
  I scattered the shining dew:
The wind was soft in the swaying trees,
The morning-glories were full of bees,
  And straight in my face they flew!

Yet I left them unmolested,
  Draining their honey-wine,
And entered the weary house again,
To sit, as now, by a bed of pain,
  With a fevered hand in mine.
            RICHARD HENRY STODDARD.

EXCELSIOR.

The shades of night were falling fast,
As through an Alpine village pass'd
A youth, who bore, 'mid snow and ice,
A banner, with the strange device—
  Excelsior!

His brow was sad; his eye beneath
Flash'd like a falchion from its sheath;
And like a silver clarion rung
The accents of that unknown tongue—
  Excelsior!

In happy homes he saw the light
Of household fires gleam warm and bright:
Above, the spectral glaciers shone,
And from his lips escaped a groan—
  Excelsior!

"Try not the pass," the old man said:
"Dark lowers the tempest overhead;
The roaring torrent is deep and wide!"
And loud that clarion voice replied,
  Excelsior!

"Oh stay," the maiden said, "and rest
Thy weary head upon this breast!"
A tear stood in his bright blue eye,
But still he answer'd with a sigh,
  Excelsior!

"Beware the pine tree's wither'd branch!
Beware the awful avalanche!"
This was the peasant's last good-night:
A voice replied, far up the height,
  Excelsior!

At break of day, as heavenward
The pious monks of St. Bernard
Utter'd the oft-repeated prayer,
A voice cried through the startled air,
  Excelsior!

A traveller, by the faithful hound,
Half buried in the snow was found,
Still grasping in his hand of ice
That banner with the strange device,
  Excelsior!

There in the twilight cold and gray,
Lifeless, but beautiful, he lay,
And from the sky, serene and far,
A voice fell, like a falling star—
  Excelsior!
            HENRY WADSWORTH LONGFELLOW.

FATE.

"The sky is clouded, the rocks are bare,
The spray of the tempest is white in air,
The winds are out with the waves at play,
And I shall not tempt the sea to-day.

"The trail is narrow, the wood is dim,
The panther clings to the arching limb,
And the lion's whelps are abroad at play,
And I shall not join in the chase to-day."

But the ship sail'd safely over the sea,
And the hunters came from the chase in glee,
And the town that was builded upon a rock
Was swallow'd up in the earthquake shock.
            FRANCIS BRET HARTE.

THE WRETCH, CONDEMNED WITH LIFE TO PART.

The wretch, condemn'd with life to part,
  Still, still on hope relies,
And every pang that rends the heart
  Bids expectation rise.

Hope, like the glimm'ring taper's light,
   Adorns and cheers the way;
And still, as darker grows the night,
   Emits a brighter ray.
OLIVER GOLDSMITH.

WEEP NO MORE.

WEEP no more, nor sigh, nor groan,
Sorrow calls no time that's gone;
Violets pluck'd, the sweetest rain
Makes not fresh nor grow again;
Trim thy locks, look cheerfully,
Fate's hidden ends eyes cannot see;
Joys as wingèd dreams fly fast,
Why should sadness longer last?
Grief is but a wound to woe;
Gentlest fair one, mourn no mo.
JOHN FLETCHER.

AFTER THE BALL.

THEY sat and comb'd their beautiful hair,
   Their long, bright tresses, one by one,
As they laugh'd and talk'd in the chamber there,
   After the revel was done.

Idly they talk'd of waltz and quadrille,
   Idly they laugh'd, like other girls,
Who over the fire, when all is still,
   Comb out their braids and curls.

Robe of satin and Brussels lace,
   Knots of flowers and ribbons, too,
Scatter'd about in every place,
   For the revel is through.

And Maud and Madge in robes of white,
   The prettiest night-gowns under the sun,
Stockingless, slipperless, sit in the night,
   For the revel is done,—

Sit and comb their beautiful hair,
   Those wonderful waves of brown and gold,
Till the fire is out in the chamber there,
   And the little bare feet are cold.

Then out of the gathering winter chill,
   All out of the bitter St. Agnes weather,
While the fire is out and the house is still,
   Maud and Madge together,—

Maud and Madge in robes of white,
   The prettiest night-gowns under the sun,
Curtain'd away from the chilly night,
   After the revel is done,—

Float along in a splendid dream,
   To a golden gittern's tinkling tune,
While a thousand lustres shimmering stream
   In a palace's grand saloon.

Flashing of jewels and flutter of laces,
   Tropical odors sweeter than musk,
Men and women with beautiful faces,
   And eyes of tropical dusk;

And one face shining out like a star,
   One face haunting the dreams of each
And one voice, sweeter than others are,
   Breaking into silvery speech,—

Telling, through lips of bearded bloom,
   An old, old story over again,
As down the royal banner'd room,
   To the golden gittern's strain,

Two and two, they dreamily walk,
   While an unseen spirit walks beside,
And all unheard in the lovers' talk,
   He claimeth one for a bride.

O Maud and Madge, dream on together,
   With never a pang of jealous fear!
For, ere the bitter St. Agnes weather
   Shall whiten another year,

Robed for the bridal, and robed for the tomb,
   Braided brown hair and golden tress,
There'll be only one of you left for the bloom
   Of the bearded lips to press,—

Only one for the bridal pearls,
   The robe of satin and Brussels lace,—
Only one to blush through her curls
   At the sight of a lover's face.

O beautiful Madge, in your bridal white,
   For you the revel has just begun,
But for her who sleeps in your arms to-night
   The revel of Life is done!

But robed and crown'd with your saintly
    bliss,
  Queen of heaven and bride of the sun,
O beautiful Maud, you'll never miss
  The kisses another hath won.
                    NORA PERRY.

INDIAN REVELRY.

WE meet 'neath the sounding rafter,
  And the walls around are bare;
As they shout back our peals of laughter
  It seems that the dead are there.
Then stand to your glasses, steady!
  We drink in our comrades' eyes;
One cup to the dead already—
  Hurrah for the next that dies!

Not here are the goblets glowing,
  Not here is the vintage sweet;
'Tis cold, as our hearts are growing,
  And dark as the doom we meet.
But stand to your glasses, steady!
  And soon shall our pulses rise;
A cup to the dead already—
  Hurrah for the next that dies!

There's many a hand that's shaking,
  And many a cheek that's sunk;
But soon, though our hearts are breaking,
  They'll burn with the wine we've drunk.
Then stand to your glasses, steady!
  'Tis here the revival lies;
Quaff a cup to the dead already—
  Hurrah for the next that dies!

Time was when we laugh'd at others;
  We thought we were wiser then;
Ha! ha! let them think of their mothers,
  Who hope to see them again.
No! stand to your glasses, steady!
  The thoughtless is here the wise;
One cup to the dead already—
  Hurrah for the next that dies!

Not a sigh for the lot that darkles,
  Not a tear for the friends that sink;
We'll fall, 'midst the wine-cup's sparkles,
  As mute as the wine we drink.
Come stand to your glasses, steady!
  'Tis this that the respite buys;
A cup to the dead already—
  Hurrah for the next that dies!

There's a mist on the glass congealing,
  'Tis the hurricane's sultry breath;
And thus does the warmth of feeling
  Turn ice in the grasp of Death.
But stand to your glasses, steady!
  For a moment the vapor flies;
Quaff a cup to the dead already—
  Hurrah for the next that dies!

Who dreads to the dust returning?
  Who shrinks from the sable shore,
Where the high and haughty yearning
  Of the soul can sting no more?
No, stand to your glasses, steady!
  The world is a world of lies;
A cup to the dead already—
  And hurrah for the next that dies!

Cut off from the land that bore us,
  Betray'd by the land we find,
When the brightest have gone before us,
  And the dullest are most behind—
Stand, stand to your glasses, steady!
  'Tis all we have left to prize;
One cup to the dead already—
  Hurrah for the next that dies!
                BARTHOLOMEW DOWLING.

TITHONUS.

THE woods decay, the woods decay and
    fall,
The vapors weep their burthen to the
    ground,
Man comes and tills the field and lies
    beneath,
And after many a summer dies the swan.
Me only cruel immortality
Consumes: I wither slowly in thine
    arms,
Here at the quiet limit of the world,
A white-hair'd shadow roaming like a
    dream
The ever-silent spaces of the East,
Far-folded mists, and gleaming halls of
    morn.

Alas! for this gray shadow, once a man—
So glorious in his beauty and thy choice,
Who madest him thy chosen, that he
    seem'd
To his great heart none other than a god!

I ask'd thee, "Give me immortality."
Then didst thou grant mine asking with a
    smile,
Like wealthy men who care not how they
    give.
But thy strong Hours indignant work'd
    their wills,
And beat me down and marr'd and wasted
    me,
And tho' they could not end me, left me
    maim'd
To dwell in presence of immortal youth,
Immortal age beside immortal youth,
And all I was, in ashes. Can thy love,
Thy beauty, make amends, tho' even now,
Close over us, the silver star, thy guide,
Shines in those tremulous eyes that fill with
    tears
To hear me? Let me go: take back thy
    gift:
Why should a man desire in any way
To vary from the kindly race of men,
Or pass beyond the goal of ordinance
Where all should pause, as is most meet
    for all?

A soft air fans the cloud apart: there
    comes
A glimpse of that dark world where I was
    born.
Once more the old mysterious glimmer
    steals
From thy pure brows, and from thy shoul-
    ders pure,
And bosom beating with a heart re-
    new'd.
Thy cheek begins to redden thro' the
    gloom,
Thy sweet eyes brighten slowly close to
    mine,
Ere yet they blind the stars, and the wild
    team
Which love thee, yearning for thy yoke,
    arise,
And shake the darkness from their loos-
    en'd manes,
And beat the twilight into flakes of fire.

Lo! ever thus thou growest beautiful
In silence, then before thine answer
    given
Departest, and thy tears are on my cheek.

Why wilt thou ever scare me with thy
    tears,
And make me tremble lest a saying
    learnt,
In days far-off, on that dark earth, be
    true:
"The gods themselves cannot recall their
    gifts."
Ay me! ay me! with what another heart
In days far-off, and with what other eyes
I used to watch—if I be he that watch'd—
The lucid outline forming round thee,
    saw
The dim curls kindle into sunny rings,
Changed with thy mystic change, and felt
    my blood
Glow with the glow that slowly crimson'd
    all
Thy presence and thy portals, while I
    lay,
Mouth, forehead, eyelids, growing dewy-
    warm
With kisses balmier than half-opening
    buds
Of April, and could hear the lips that
    kiss'd
Whispering I knew not what of wild and
    sweet,
Like that strange song I heard Apollo
    sing,
While Ilion like a mist rose into towers.

Yet hold me not for ever in thine East:
How can my nature longer mix with
    thine?
Coldly thy rosy shadows bathe me, cold
Are all thy lights, and cold my wrinkled
    feet
Upon thy glimmering thresholds, when
    the steam
Floats up from those dim fields about the
    homes
Of happy men that have the power to die,
And grassy barrows of the happier dead.
Release me, and restore me to the ground;
Thou seest all things, thou wilt see my
    grave;
Thou wilt renew thy beauty morn by
    morn;
I earth in earth forget these empty
    courts,
And thee returning on thy silver wheels.
ALFRED TENNYSON.

SHIPS AT SEA.

I HAVE ships that went to sea
  More than fifty years ago:
None have yet come home to me,
  But keep sailing to and fro.
I have seen them, in my sleep,
Plunging through the shoreless deep,
With tattered sails and battered hulls,
While around them screamed the gulls,
  Flying low, flying low.

I have wondered why they stayed
  From me, sailing round the world;
And I've said, "I'm half afraid
  That their sails will ne'er be furled."
Great the treasures that they hold—
Silks and plumes, and bars of gold;
While the spices which they bear
Fill with fragrance all the air,
  As they sail, as they sail.

Every sailor in the port
  Knows that I have ships at sea,
Of the waves and winds the sport;
  And the sailors pity me.
Oft they come and with me walk,
Cheering me with hopeful talk,
Till I put my fears aside,
And contented watch the tide
  Rise and fall, rise and fall.

I have waited on the piers,
  Gazing for them down the bay,
Days and nights, for many years,
  Till I turned heart-sick away.
But the pilots, when they land,
Stop and take me by the hand,
Saying, "You will live to see
Your proud vessels come from sea,
  One and all, one and all."

So I never quite despair,
  Nor let hope or courage fail;
And some day when skies are fair,
  Up the bay my ship will sail.
I can buy then all I need—
Prints to look at, books to read,
Horses, wines, and works of art,
Everything except a heart:
  That is lost, that is lost.

Once when I was pure and young,
  Poorer, too, than I am now,
Ere a cloud was o'er me flung,
  Or a wrinkle creased my brow,
There was one whose heart was mine;
But she's something now divine,
And though come my ships from sea,
They can bring no heart to me,
  Evermore, evermore.

  R. B. COFFIN.

MY SHIP.

DOWN to the wharves, as the sun goes down,
  And the daylight's tumult and dust and din
Are dying away in the busy town,
  I go to see if my ship comes in.

I gaze far over the quiet sea,
  Rosy with sunset, like mellow wine,
Where ships, like lilies, lie tranquilly,
  Many and fair, but I see not mine.

I question the sailors every night
  Who over the bulwarks idly lean,
Noting the sails as they come in sight:
  "Have you seen my beautiful ship come in?"

"Whence does she come?" they ask of me;
  "Who is her master, and what her name?"
And they smile upon me pityingly
  When my answer is ever and ever the same.

Oh mine was a vessel of strength and truth,
  Her sails were white as a young lamb's fleece,
She sailed long since from the port of Youth,—
  Her master was Love, and her name was Peace.

And like all beloved and beauteous things,
  She faded in distance and doubt away,—
With only a tremble of snowy wings
  She floated, swan-like, adown the bay,

Carrying with her a precious freight,—
  All I had gathered by years of pain;
A tempting prize to the pirate Fate,—
  And still I watch for her back again—

Watch from the earliest morning light,
  Till the pale stars grieve o'er the dying day,
To catch the gleam of her canvas white
  Among the islands which gem the bay.

But she comes not yet—she will never come
    To gladden my eyes and my spirit more;
And my heart grows hopeless and faint and dumb,
    As I wait and wait on the lonesome shore,

Knowing that tempest and time and storm
    Have wrecked and shattered my beauteous bark;
Rank sea-weeds cover her wasting form,
    And her sails are tattered and stained and dark.

But the tide comes up, and the tide goes down,
    And the daylight follows the night's eclipse,—
And still with the sailors, tanned and brown,
    I wait on the wharves and watch the ships.

And still with a patience that is not hope,
    For vain and empty it long hath been,
I sit on the rough shore's rocky slope,
    And watch to see if my ship comes in.
               ELIZABETH AKERS ALLEN.

THE DREAM.

I.

OUR life is twofold: sleep hath its own world—
A boundary between the things misnamed
Death and existence: sleep hath its own world,
And a wide realm of wild reality;
And dreams in their development have breath,
And tears, and tortures, and the touch of joy;
They leave a weight upon our waking thoughts;
They take a weight from off our waking toils;
They do divide our being; they become
A portion of ourselves as of our time,
And look like heralds of eternity;
They pass like spirits of the past,—they speak
Like sibyls of the future; they have power—
The tyranny of pleasure and of pain;
They make us what we were not—what they will;
And shake us with the vision that's gone by,
The dread of vanished shadows—are they so?
Is not the past all shadow? What are they?
Creations of the mind?—the mind can make
Substance, and people planets of its own
With beings brighter than have been, and give
A breath to forms which can outlive all flesh.
I would recall a vision, which I dreamed
Perchance in sleep—for in itself a thought,
A slumbering thought, is capable of years,
And curdles a long life into one hour.

II.

I saw two beings in the hues of youth
Standing upon a hill, a gentle hill,
Green and of mild declivity; the last,
As 'twere the cape of a long ridge of such,
Save that there was no sea to lave its base,
But a most living landscape, and the wave
Of woods and cornfields, and the abodes of men
Scattered at intervals, and wreathing smoke
Arising from such rustic roofs;—the hill
Was crowned with a peculiar diadem
Of trees, in circular array—so fixed,
Not by the sport of nature, but of man.
These two, a maiden and a youth, were there
Gazing—the one on all that was beneath
Fair as herself—but the boy gazed on her;
And both were young, and one was beautiful;
And both were young—yet not alike in youth.
As the sweet moon on the horizon's verge,
The maid was on the eve of womanhood;
The boy had fewer summers; but his heart
Had far outgrown his years, and to his eye
There was but one beloved face on earth,
And that was shining on him; he had looked
Upon it till it could not pass away;
He had no breath, no being, but in hers;
She was his voice; he did not speak to her,
But trembled on her words; she was his sight,
For his eye followed hers, and saw with hers,

Which colored all his objects;—he had
    ceased
To live within himself; she was his life,
The ocean to the river of his thoughts,
Which terminated all; upon a tone,
A touch of hers, his blood would ebb and
    flow,
And his cheek change tempestuously—his
    heart
Unknowing of its cause of agony.
But she in these fond feelings had no share:
Her sighs were not for him; to her he was
Even as a brother—but no more; 'twas
    much;
For brotherless she was, save in the name
Her infant friendship had bestowed on him;
Herself the solitary scion left
Of a time-honored race.—It was a name
Which pleased him, and yet pleased him
    not—and why?
Time taught him a deep answer—when she
    loved
Another. Even now she loved another;
And on the summit of that hill she stood
Looking afar, if yet her lover's steed
Kept pace with her expectancy, and flew.

III.

A change came o'er the spirit of my dream:
There was an ancient mansion; and before
Its walls there was a steed caparisoned.
Within an antique oratory stood
The boy of whom I spake;—he was alone,
And pale, and pacing to and fro. Anon
He sate him down, and seized a pen and
    traced
Words which I could not guess of; then
    he leaned
His bowed head on his hands, and shook
    as 'twere
With a convulsion—then arose again;
And with his teeth and quivering hands
    did tear
What he had written; but he shed no tears.
And he did calm himself, and fix his brow
Into a kind of quiet. As he paused
The lady of his love re-entered there;
She was serene and smiling then; and yet
She knew she was by him beloved: she knew,
For quickly comes such knowledge, that
    his heart
Was darkened with her shadow, and she saw
That he was wretched; but she saw not all.

He rose, and with a cold and gentle grasp
He took her hand; a moment o'er his face
A tablet of unutterable thoughts
Was traced; and then it faded as it came.
He dropped the hand he held, and with
    slow steps
Retired; but not as bidding her adieu,
For they did part with mutual smiles. He
    passed
From out the massy gate of that old hall,
And, mounting on his steed, he went his
    way;
And ne'er repassed that hoary threshold
    more.

IV.

A change came o'er the spirit of my dream:
The boy was sprung to manhood. In the
    wilds
Of fiery climes he made himself a home,
And his soul drank their sunbeams; he
    was girt
With strange and dusky aspects; he was not
Himself like what he had been; on the sea
And on the shore he was a wanderer;
There was a mass of many images
Crowded like waves upon me, but he was
A part of all; and in the last he lay
Reposing from the noontide sultriness,
Couched among fallen columns, in the shade
Of ruined walls that had survived the names
Of those who reared them; by his sleeping
    side
Stood camels grazing, and some goodly
    steeds
Were fastened near a fountain; and a man
Clad in a flowing garb did watch the while,
While many of his tribe slumbered around:
And they were canopied by the blue sky,
So cloudless, clear, and purely beautiful,
That God alone was to be seen in heaven.

V.

A change came o'er the spirit of my dream:
The lady of his love was wed with one
Who did not love her better. In her home,
A thousand leagues from his,—her native
    home—
She dwelt, begirt with growing infancy,
Daughters and sons of beauty. But behold!
Upon her face there was the tint of grief,
The settled shadow of an inward strife,
And an unquiet drooping of the eye,
As if its lids were charged with unshed tears.

What could her grief be?—She had all she
    loved;
And he who had so loved her was not there
To trouble with bad hopes or evil wish,
Or ill-repressed affection, her pure thoughts.
What could her grief be?—she had loved
    him not,
Nor given him cause to deem himself be-
    loved;
Nor could he be a part of that which preyed
Upon her mind—a spectre of the past.

VI.

A change came o'er the spirit of my dream:
The wanderer was returned—I saw him
    stand
Before an altar, with a gentle bride;
Her face was fair; but was not that which
    made
The starlight of his boyhood. As he stood,
Even at the altar, o'er his brow there came
The self-same aspect, and the quivering
    shock
That in the antique oratory shook
His bosom in its solitude; and then—
As in that hour—a moment o'er his face
The tablet of unutterable thoughts
Was traced—and then it faded as it came;
And he stood calm and quiet; and he
    spoke
The fitting vows, but heard not his own
    words;
And all things reeled around him; he could
    see
Not that which was, nor that which should
    have been—
But the old mansion, and the accustomed
    hall,
And the remembered chambers, and the
    place,
The day, the hour, the sunshine, and the
    shade,
All things pertaining to that place and hour,
And her who was his destiny, came back
And thrust themselves between him and
    the light:
What business had they there at such a
    time?

VII.

A change came o'er the spirit of my dream:
The lady of his love—oh! she was changed,
As by the sickness of the soul; her mind
Had wandered from its dwelling; and her
    eyes,
They had not their own lustre, but the look
Which is not of the earth; she was become
The queen of a fantastic realm; her
    thoughts
Were combinations of disjointed things;
And forms impalpable and unperceived
Of others' sight familiar were to hers.
And this the world calls frenzy; but the
    wise
Have a far deeper madness, and the glance
Of melancholy is a fearful gift;
What is it but the telescope of truth?
Which strips the distance of its fantasies,
And brings life near in utter nakedness,
Making the cold reality too real!

VIII.

A change came o'er the spirit of my dream:
The wanderer was alone, as heretofore;
The beings which surrounded him were
    gone
Or were at war with him; he was a mark
For blight and desolation — compassed
    round
With hatred and contention; pain was
    mixed
In all which was served up to him; until,
Like to the Pontic monarch of old days,
He fed on poisons, and they had no power,
But were a kind of nutriment. He lived
Through that which had been death to
    many men,
And made him friends of mountains. With
    the stars,
And the quick Spirit of the Universe,
He held his dialogues, and they did teach
To him the magic of their mysteries;
To him the book of night was opened
    wide,
And voices from the deep abyss revealed
A marvel and a secret—Be it so.

IX.

My dream was past; it had no further
    change.
It was of a strange order, that the doom
Of these two creatures should be thus
    traced out
Almost like a reality—the one
To end in madness—both in misery.
                      LORD BYRON.

New forms may fold the speech, new lands
Arise within these ocean-portals,
But Music waves eternal wands,—
Enchantress of the souls of mortals!

Edmund Clarence Stedman

WEIRD AND FANTASTIC.

THE FAIRY QUEEN.

COME, follow, follow me—
You, fairy elves that be,
Which circle on the green—
Come, follow Mab, your queen!
Hand in hand let's dance around,
For this place is fairy ground.

When mortals are at rest,
And snoring in their nest,
Unheard and unespied,
Through keyholes we do glide;
Over tables, stools, and shelves,
We trip it with our fairy elves.

And if the house be foul
With platter, dish, or bowl,
Up stairs we nimbly creep,
And find the sluts asleep;
There we pinch their arms and thighs—
None escapes, nor none espies.

But if the house be swept,
And from uncleanness kept,
We praise the household maid,
And duly she is paid;
For we use, before we go,
To drop a tester in her shoe.

Upon a mushroom's head
Our tablecloth we spread;
A grain of rye or wheat
Is manchet, which we eat;
Pearly drops of dew we drink,
In acorn cups, fill'd to the brink.

The brains of nightingales,
With unctuous fat of snails,
Between two cockles stew'd,
Is meat that's easily chew'd;
Tails of worms, and marrow of mice,
Do make a dish that's wondrous nice.

The grasshopper, gnat, and fly,
Serve us for our minstrelsy;
Grace said, we dance a while,
And so the time beguile;
And if the moon doth hide her head,
The glow-worm lights us home to bed.

On tops of dewy grass
So nimbly do we pass,
The young and tender stalk
Ne'er bends when we do walk;
Yet in the morning may be seen
Where we the night before have been.
AUTHOR UNKNOWN.

SONG OF THE FAIRIES.

BY the moon we sport and play;
With the night begins our day:
As we dance the dew doth fall;
Trip it, little urchins, all.
Lightly as the little bee,
Two by two, and three by three,
And about go we, and about go we.
JOHN LYLY.

FAIRY SONG.

SHED no tear! oh, shed no tear!
The flower will bloom another year.
Weep no more! oh, weep no more!
Young buds sleep in the root's white core,
Dry your eyes! oh, dry your eyes!
For I was taught in Paradise
To ease my breast of melodies,—
    Shed no tear.

Overhead! look overhead!
'Mong the blossoms white and red,—
Look up, look up! I flutter now
On this fresh pomegranate bough.

See me! 'tis this silvery bill
Ever cures the good man's ill.
Shed no tear! oh, shed no tear!
The flower will bloom another year.
Adieu, adieu—I fly—adieu!
I vanish in the Heaven's blue,—
        Adieu, adieu!
            JOHN KEATS.

OVER HILL, OVER DALE.
FROM "A MIDSUMMER NIGHT'S DREAM."

OVER hill, over dale,
   Thorough bush, thorough brier,
Over park, over pale,
   Thorough flood, thorough fire,
I do wander everywhere,
Swifter than the moon's sphere;
And I serve the fairy queen,
To dew her orbs upon the green.
The cowslips tall her pensioners be!
In their gold coats spots you see;
Those be rubies, fairy favors,
In those freckles live their savors:
I must go seek some dewdrops here,
And hang a pearl in every cowslip's ear.
        WILLIAM SHAKESPEARE.

ARIEL'S SONGS.
FROM "THE TEMPEST."

I.

COME unto these yellow sands,
   And then take hands:
Court'sied when you have, and kiss'd,—
   The wild waves whist,—
Foot it featly here and there;
And, sweet sprites, the burden bear.
   Hark, hark!
     Bow, wow.
   The watch-dogs bark—
     Bow, wow.
Hark, hark! I hear
The strain of strutting chanticleer
Cry Cock-a-diddle-dow.

II.

Full fathom five thy father lies;
   Of his bones are coral made;
Those are pearls that were his eyes;
   Nothing of him that doth fade
But doth suffer a sea-change
Into something rich and strange.
Sea-nymphs hourly ring his knell:
      Ding-dong.
Hark! now I hear them—ding, dong, bell!

III.

Where the bee sucks there suck I;
In a cowslip's bell I lie;
There I couch when owls do cry;
On the bat's back I do fly
After summer merrily.
Merrily, merrily, shall I live now,
Under the blossom that hangs on the
   bough.
        WILLIAM SHAKESPEARE.

SONG OF FAIRIES.

WE the fairies, blithe and antic,
Of dimensions not gigantic,
Though the moonshine mostly keep us,
Oft in orchards frisk and peep us.
Stolen sweets are always sweeter;
Stolen kisses much completer;
Stolen looks are nice in chapels:
Stolen, stolen be your apples.
When to bed the world are bobbing,
Then's the time for orchard-robbing;
Yet the fruit were scarce worth peeling
Were it not for stealing, stealing.
        LEIGH HUNT.
   (From the Latin of THOMAS RANDOLPH.)

THE FAIRIES.
A CHILD'S SONG.

Up the airy mountain,
   Down the rushy glen,
We daren't go a-hunting
   For fear of little men;
Wee folk, good folk,
   Trooping all together;
Green jacket, red cap,
   And white owl's feather!

Down along the rocky shore
   Some make their home,
They live on crispy pancakes
   Of yellow tide-foam;

Some in the reeds
  Of the black mountain-lake,
With frogs for their watch-dogs,
  All night awake.

High on the hill-top
  The old King sits;
He is now so old and gray
  He's nigh lost his wits.
With a bridge of white mist
  Columbkill he crosses,
On his stately journeys
  From Slieveleague to Rosses;
Or going up with music
  On cold starry nights,
To sup with the Queen
  Of the gay Northern Lights.

They stole little Bridget
  For seven years long;
When she came down again
  Her friends were all gone.
They took her lightly back,
  Between the night and morrow,
They thought that she was fast asleep,
  But she was dead with sorrow.
They have kept her ever since
  Deep within the lakes,
On a bed of flag-leaves,
  Watching till she wakes.

By the craggy hill-side,
  Through the mosses bare,
They have planted thorn trees
  For pleasure here and there.
Is any man so daring
  As dig one up in spite,
He shall find the thornies set
  In his bed at night.

Up the airy mountain,
  Down the rushy glen,
We daren't go a-hunting
  For fear of little men;
Wee folk, good folk,
  Trooping all together;
Green jacket, red cap,
  And white owl's feather!
        WILLIAM ALLINGHAM.

THE RAPE OF THE LOCK.

AN HEROI-COMICAL POEM.

Nolueram, Belinda, tuos violare capillos;
Sed juvat hoc precibus me tribuisse tuis.—MART.

CANTO I.

WHAT dire offence from amorous causes
    springs,
What mighty contests rise from trivial
    things,
I sing—This verse to Caryl, muse! is due;
This, e'en Belinda may vouchsafe to view;
Slight is the subject, but not so the praise,
If she inspire, and he approve my lays.
  Say what strange motive, goddess! could
    compel
A well-bred lord t' assault a gentle belle?
Oh, say what stranger cause, yet unex-
    plored,
Could make a gentle belle reject a lord?
In tasks so bold can little men engage,
And in soft bosoms dwell such mighty rage?
  Sol through white curtains shot a timor-
    ous ray,
And oped those eyes that must eclipse the
    day.
Now lap-dogs give themselves the rousing
    shake,
And sleepless lovers just at twelve awake:
Thrice rung the bell, the slipper knock'd
    the ground,
And the press'd watch returned a silver
    sound.
Belinda still her downy pillow prest—
Her guardian sylph prolong'd the balmy
    rest;
'Twas he had summon'd to her silent bed
The morning-dream that hover'd o'er her
    head:
A youth more glittering than a birthnight
    beau
(That e'en in slumber caused her cheek to
    glow),
Seem'd to her ear his winning lips to lay,
And thus in whispers said, or seem'd to
    say:
  "Fairest of mortals, thou distinguish'd
    care
Of thousand bright inhabitants of air!
If e'er one vision touch'd thy infant thought,
Of all the nurse and all the priest have
    taught,

Of airy elves by moonlight shadows seen,
The silver token, and the circled green;
Or virgins visited by angel powers
With golden crowns and wreaths of heavenly flowers—
Hear and believe! thy own importance know,
Nor bound thy narrow views to things below.
Some secret truths, from learnèd pride concealed,
To maids alone and children are reveal'd:
What though no credit doubting wits may give?
The fair and innocent shall still believe.
Know, then, unnumber'd spirits round thee fly—
The light militia of the lower sky:
These, though unseen, are ever on the wing,
Hang o'er the box, and hover round the ring.
Think what an equipage thou hast in air,
And view with scorn two pages and a chair.
As now your own, our beings were of old,
And once enclosed in woman's beauteous mould;
Thence, by a soft transition, we repair
From earthly vehicles to these of air.
Think not, when woman's transient breath is fled,
That all her vanities at once are dead;
Succeeding vanities she still regards,
And, though she plays no more, o'erlooks the cards.
Her joy in gilded chariots, when alive,
And love of ombre, after death survive;
For when the fair in all their pride expire,
To their first elements their souls retire,
The sprites of fiery termagants in flame
Mount up, and take a salamander's name;
Soft yielding minds to water glide away,
And sip, with nymphs, their elemental tea;
The graver prude sinks downward to a gnome
In search of mischief still on earth to roam;
The light coquettes in sylphs aloft repair,
And sport and flutter in the fields of air.

"Know further yet; whoever fair and chaste
Rejects mankind, is by some sylph embraced:
For spirits, freed from mortal laws, with ease
Assume what sexes and what shapes they please.
What guards the purity of melting maids,
In courtly balls and midnight masquerades,
Safe from the treacherous friend, the daring spark,
The glance by day, the whisper in the dark—
When kind occasion prompts their warm desires,
When music softens, and when dancing fires?
'Tis but their sylph, the wise celestials know,
Though honor is the word with men below.
"Some nymphs there are, too conscious of their face,
For life predestined to the gnome's embrace;
These swell their prospects and exalt their pride,
When offers are disdain'd, and love denied;
Then gay ideas crowd the vacant brain,
While peers, and dukes, and all their sweeping train,
And garters, stars, and coronets appear,
And in soft sounds 'Your Grace' salutes their ear.
'Tis these that early taint the female soul,
Instruct the eyes of young coquettes to roll;
Teach infant cheeks a bidden blush to know,
And little hearts to flutter at a beau.
"Oft when the world imagine women stray,
The sylphs through mystic mazes guide their way;
Through all the giddy circle they pursue,
And old impertinence expel by new.
What tender maid but must a victim fall
To one man's treat, but for another's ball?

When Florio speaks, what virgin could withstand,
If gentle Damon did not squeeze her hand?
With varying vanities from every part
They shift the moving toy-shop of their heart,
Where wigs with wigs, with sword-knots sword-knots strive,
Beaux banish beaux, and coaches coaches drive.
This erring mortals levity may call—
Oh, blind to truth! the sylphs contrive it all.
"Of these am I, who thy protection claim;
A watchful sprite, and Ariel is my name.
Late, as I ranged the crystal wilds of air,
In the clear mirror of thy ruling star,
I saw, alas! some dread event impend,
Ere to the main this morning's sun descend;
But Heaven reveals not what, or how, or where:
Warn'd by the sylph, O pious maid, beware!
This to disclose is all thy guardian can;
Beware of all, but most beware of man!"
He said; when Shock, who thought she slept too long,
Leap'd up, and waked his mistress with his tongue.
'Twas then, Belinda, if report say true,
Thy eyes first open'd on a billet-doux;
Wounds, charms, and ardors, were no sooner read,
But all the vision vanish'd from thy head.
And now, unveil'd, the toilet stands display'd,
Each silver vase in mystic order laid.
First, robed in white, the nymph intent adores,
With head uncover'd, the cosmetic powers.
A heavenly image in the glass appears—
To that she bends, to that her eyes she rears;
Th' inferior priestess, at her altar's side,
Trembling begins the sacred rites of pride.
Unnumber'd treasures ope at once, and here
The various offerings of the world appear;
From each she nicely culls with curious toil,
And decks the goddess with the glittering spoil.
This casket India's glowing gems unlocks,
And all Arabia breathes from yonder box.
The tortoise here and elephant unite,
Transform'd to combs—the speckled, and the white.
Here files of pins extend their shining rows;
Puffs, powders, patches, Bibles, billet-doux.
Now awful beauty puts on all its arms;
The fair each moment rises in her charms,
Repairs her smiles, awakens every grace,
And calls forth all the wonders of her face;
Sees by degrees a purer blush arise,
And keener lightnings quicken in her eyes.
The busy sylphs surround their darling care,
These set the head, and these divide the hair;
Some fold the sleeve, whilst others plait the gown;
And Betty's praised for labors not her own.

CANTO II.

Not with more glories, in th' ethereal plain,
The sun first rises o'er the purpled main,
Than, issuing forth, the rival of his beams
Launch'd on the bosom of the silver Thames.
Fair nymphs and well-dress'd youths around her shone,
But every eye was fixed on her alone.
On her white breast a sparkling cross she wore,
Which Jews might kiss, and infidels adore;
Her lively looks a sprightly mind disclose—
Quick as her eyes, and as unfix'd as those;
Favors to none, to all she smiles extends;
Oft she rejects, but never once offends.
Bright as the sun, her eyes the gazers strike;
And, like the sun, they shine on all alike.

Yet graceful ease, and sweetness void of pride,
Might hide her faults, if belles had faults to hide:
If to her share some female errors fall,
Look on her face, and you'll forget them all.
  This nymph, to the destruction of mankind,
Nourish'd two locks, which graceful hung behind
In equal curls, and well conspired to deck
With shining ringlets the smooth, ivory neck.
Love in these labyrinths his slaves detains,
And mighty hearts are held in slender chains.
With hairy springes we the birds betray;
Slight lines of hair surprise the finny prey;
Fair tresses man's imperial race ensnare,
And beauty draws us with a single hair.
  Th' adventurous baron the bright locks admired;
He saw, he wish'd, and to the prize aspired.
Resolved to win, he meditates the way,
By force to ravish, or by fraud betray;
For when success a lover's toil attends,
Few ask if fraud or force attain'd his ends.
  For this, ere Phœbus rose, he had implored
Propitious Heaven, and every power adored;
But chiefly Love—to Love an altar built,
Of twelve vast French romances neatly gilt.
There lay three garters, half a pair of gloves,
And all the trophies of his former loves;
With tender billet-doux he lights the pyre,
And breathes three amorous sighs to raise the fire.
Then prostrate falls, and begs with ardent eyes
Soon to obtain, and long possess the prize.
The powers gave ear, and granted half his prayer;
The rest the winds dispersed in empty air.

But now secure the painted vessel glides,
The sunbeams trembling on the floating tides,
While melting music steals upon the sky,
And soften'd sounds along the waters die;
Smooth flow the waves, the zephyrs gently play,
Belinda smiled, and all the world was gay.
All but the sylph—with careful thoughts oppress'd,
Th' impending woe sat heavy on his breast.
He summons straight his denizens of air:
The lucid squadrons round the sails repair;
Soft o'er the shrouds aërial whispers breathe,
That seem'd but zephyrs to the train beneath.
Some to the sun their insect-wings unfold,
Waft on the breeze, or sink in clouds of gold,
Transparent forms, too fine for mortal sight,
Their fluid bodies half dissolved in light;
Loose to the wind their airy garments flew,
Thin, glittering textures of the filmy dew,
Dipp'd in the richest tincture of the skies,
Where light disports in ever-mingling dyes;
While every beam new transient colors flings,
Colors that change whene'er they wave their wings.
Amid the circle, on the gilded mast,
Superior by the head, was Ariel placed;
His purple pinions opening to the sun,
He raised his azure wand, and thus begun:
"Ye sylphs and sylphids, to your chief give ear!
Fays, fairies, genii, elves, and demons, hear!
Ye know the spheres and various tasks assign'd
By laws eternal to th' aërial kind:

Some in the fields of purest ether play,
And bask and whiten in the blaze of day;
Some guide the course of wandering orbs on high,
Or roll the planets through the boundless sky;
Some, less refined, beneath the moon's pale light
Pursue the stars that shoot athwart the night,
Or suck the mists in grosser air below,
Or dip their pinions in the painted bow,
Or brew fierce tempests on the wintry main,
Or o'er the glebe distil the kindly rain.
Others, on earth, o'er human race preside,
Watch all their ways, and all their actions guide:
Of these the chief the care of nations own,
And guard with arms divine the British throne.
 "Our humbler province is to tend the fair,
Not a less pleasing, though less glorious care;
To save the powder from too rude a gale,
Nor let th' imprison'd essences exhale;
To draw fresh colors from the vernal flowers;
To steal from rainbows, ere they drop in showers,
A brighter wash; to curl their waving hairs,
Assist their blushes, and inspire their airs;
Nay oft, in dreams, invention we bestow,
To change a flounce, or add a furbelow.
 "This day black omens threat the brightest fair
That e'er deserved a watchful spirit's care;
Some dire disaster, or by force or sleight;
But what, or where, the Fates have wrapp'd in night—
Whether the nymph shall break Diana's law,
Or some frail china jar receive a flaw;
Or stain her honor, or her new brocade;
Forget her prayers, or miss a masquerade;
Or lose her heart, or necklace, at a ball;
Or whether Heaven has doom'd that Shock must fall—
Haste, then, ye spirits! to your charge repair:
The fluttering fan be Zephyretta's care;
The drops to thee, Brillante, we consign;
And, Momentilla, let the watch be thine;
Do thou, Crispissa, tend her favorite lock;
Ariel himself shall be the guard of Shock.
 "To fifty chosen sylphs, of special note,
We trust th' important charge, the petticoat—
Oft have we known that seven-fold fence to fail,
Though stiff with hoops, and arm'd with ribs of whale—
Form a strong line about the silver bound,
And guard the wide circumference around.
 "Whatever spirit, careless of his charge,
His post neglects, or leaves the fair at large,
Shall feel sharp vengeance soon o'ertake his sins,
Be stopp'd in vials, or transfix'd with pins;
Or plunged in lakes of bitter washes lie,
Or wedged whole ages in a bodkin's eye;
Gums and pomatums shall his flight restrain,
While clogg'd he beats his silken wings in vain;
Or alum styptics with contracting power
Shrink his thin essence like a rivell'd flower;
Or, as Ixion fix'd, the wretch shall feel
The giddy motion of the whirling mill;
In fumes of burning chocolate shall glow,
And tremble at the sea that froths below!"
 He spoke; the spirits from the sails descend;
Some, orb in orb, around the nymph extend;
Some thread the mazy ringlets of her hair;
Some hang upon the pendants of her ear;
With beating hearts the dire event they wait,
Anxious, and trembling for the birth of fate.

CANTO III.

Close by those meads, for ever crown'd with flowers,
Where Thames with pride surveys his rising towers,
There stands a structure of majestic frame,
Which from the neighboring Hampton takes its name.
Here Britain's statesmen oft the fall foredoom
Of foreign tyrants, and of nymphs at home;
Here thou, great Anna! whom three realms obey,
Dost sometimes counsel take—and sometimes tea.

Hither the heroes and the nymphs resort,
To taste a while the pleasures of a court;
In various talk th' instructive hours they past:
Who gave the ball, or paid the visit last;
One speaks the glory of the British queen;
And one describes a charming Indian screen;
A third interprets motions, looks, and eyes—
At every word a reputation dies;
Snuff, or the fan, supply each pause of chat,
With singing, laughing, ogling, and all that.

Meanwhile, declining from the noon of day,
The sun obliquely shoots his burning ray;
The hungry judges soon the sentence sign,
And wretches hang that jurymen may dine;
The merchant from th' Exchange returns in peace,
And the long labors of the toilet cease.
Belinda now, whom thirst of fame invites,
Burns to encounter two adventurous knights
At ombre singly to decide their doom,
And swells her breast with conquests yet to come.

Straight the three bands prepare in arms to join,
Each band the number of the sacred Nine.
Soon as she spreads her hand, the aërial guard
Descend, and sit on each important card:
First Ariel perch'd upon a matadore,
Then each according to the rank they bore;
For sylphs, yet mindful of their ancient race,
Are, as when women, wondrous fond of place.

Behold; four kings in majesty revered,
With hoary whiskers and a forky beard;
And four fair queens, whose hands sustain a flower,
Th' expressive emblem of their softer power;
Four knaves, in garbs succinct, a trusty band,
Caps on their heads, and halberts in their hand;
And parti-colored troops, a shining train,
Draw forth to combat on the velvet plain.

The skilful nymph reviews her force with care;
"Let spades be trumps!" she said, and trumps they were.
Now move to war her sable matadores,
In show like leaders of the swarthy Moors.
Spadillio first, unconquerable lord!
Led off two captive trumps, and swept the board.
As many more Manillio forced to yield,
And march'd a victor from the verdant field.
Him Basto follow'd, but his fate more hard
Gain'd but one trump and one plebeian card.
With his broad sabre next, a chief in years,
The hoary majesty of spades appears,
Puts forth one manly leg, to sight reveal'd,
The rest his many-color'd robe conceal'd.
The rebel knave, who dares his prince engage,
Proves the just victim of his royal rage.

"AT EVERY WORD A REPUTATION DIES."

RAPE OF THE LOCK.
Line 16 Canto III

E'en mighty Pam, that kings and queens o'erthrew,
And mow'd down armies in the fights of loo,
Sad chance of war! now destitute of aid,
Falls undistinguish'd by the victor spade!
  Thus far both armies to Belinda yield;
Now to the baron fate inclines the field.
His warlike amazon her host invades,
Th' imperial consort of the crown of spades.
The club's black tyrant first her victim died,
Spite of his haughty mien and barbarous pride:
What boots the regal circle on his head,
His giant limbs, in state unwieldy spread—
That long behind he trails his pompous robe,
And, of all monarchs, only grasps the globe?
  The baron now his diamonds pours apace;
Th' embroider'd king who shows but half his face,
And his refulgent queen, with powers combined,
Of broken troops an easy conquest find.
Clubs, diamonds, hearts, in wild disorder seen,
With throngs promiscuous strew the level green.
Thus when dispersed a routed army runs,
Of Asia's troops, and Afric's sable sons—
With like confusion different nations fly,
Of various habit, and of various dye;
The pierced battalions disunited fall
In heaps on heaps—one fate o'erwhelms them all.
The knave of diamonds tries his wily arts,
And wins (oh, shameful chance!) the queen of hearts.
At this the blood the virgin's cheek forsook,
A livid paleness spreads o'er all her look;
She sees, and trembles at th' approaching ill,
Just in the jaws of ruin, and codille.
And now (as oft in some distemper'd state)
On one nice trick depends the general fate:

An ace of hearts steps forth: the king unseen
Lurk'd in her hand, and mourn'd his captive queen:
He springs to vengeance with an eager pace,
And falls like thunder on the prostrate ace.
The nymph, exulting, fills with shouts the sky;
The walls, the woods, and long canals reply.
  O thoughtless mortals! ever blind to fate,
Too soon dejected, and too soon elate!
Sudden these honors shall be snatch'd away,
And cursed for ever this victorious day.
  For lo! The board with cups and spoons is crown'd;
The berries crackle, and the mill turns round;
On shining altars of japan they raise
The silver lamp; the fiery spirits blaze;
From silver spouts the grateful liquors glide,
While China's earth receives the smoking tide.
At once they gratify their scent and taste,
And frequent cups prolong the rich repast.
Straight hover round the fair her airy band:
Some, as she sipp'd, the fuming liquor fann'd;
Some o'er her lap their careful plumes display'd,
Trembling, and conscious of the rich brocade.
Coffee (which makes the politician wise,
And see through all things with his halfshut eyes)
Sent up in vapors to the baron's brain
New stratagems, the radiant lock to gain.
Ah cease, rash youth! desist ere 'tis too late;
Fear the just gods, and think of Scylla's fate!
Changed to a bird, and sent to flit in air,
She dearly pays for Nisus' injured hair!
  But when to mischief mortals bend their will,
How soon they find fit instruments of ill!

Just then, Clarissa drew with tempting grace
A two-edged weapon from her shining case:
So ladies, in romance, assist their knight—
Present the spear and arm him for the fight.
He takes the gift with reverence, and extends
The little engine on his fingers' ends;
This just behind Belinda's neck he spread,
As o'er the fragrant steams she bends her head.
Swift to the lock a thousand sprites repair,
A thousand wings, by turns, blow back the hair;
And thrice they twitch'd the diamond in her ear;
Thrice she look'd back, and thrice the foe drew near.
Just in that instant, anxious Ariel sought
The close recesses of the virgin's thought:
As on the nosegay in her breast reclined,
He watch'd the ideas rising in her mind,
Sudden he view'd, in spite of all her art,
An earthly lover lurking at her heart.
Amazed, confused, he found his power expired,
Resign'd to fate, and with a sigh retired.
  The peer now spreads the glittering forfex wide,
T' enclose the lock; now joins it, to divide.
E'en then, before the fatal engine closed,
A wretched sylph too fondly interposed;
Fate urged the shears, and cut the sylph in twain
(But airy substance soon unites again);
The meeting points the sacred hair dissever
From the fair head, for ever, and for ever!
  Then flash'd the living lightning from her eyes,
And screams of horror rend th' affrighted skies.
Not louder shrieks to pitying Heaven are cast
When husbands, or when lapdogs, breathe their last;
Or when rich china vessels, fallen from high,
In glittering dust and painted fragments lie!

"Let wreaths of triumph now my temples twine,"
The victor cried, "the glorious prize is mine!
While fish in streams, or birds delight in air;
Or in a coach and six the British fair;
As long as Atalantis shall be read,
Or the small pillow grace a lady's bed;
While visits shall be paid on solemn days,
When numerous wax-lights in bright order blaze;
While nymphs take treats, or assignations give,
So long my honor, name, and praise shall live!
What time would spare, from steel receives its date;
And monuments, like men, submit to fate!
Steel could the labor of the gods destroy,
And strike to dust th' imperial towers of Troy;
Steel could the works of mortal pride confound,
And hew triumphal arches to the ground.
What wonder then, fair nymph! thy hairs should feel
The conquering force of unresisted steel?"

CANTO IV.

But anxious cares the pensive nymph opprest,
And secret passions labor'd in her breast.
Not youthful kings in battle seized alive;
Not scornful virgins who their charms survive;
Not ardent lovers robb'd of all their bliss;
Not ancient ladies when refused a kiss;
Not tyrants fierce that unrepenting die;
Not Cynthia when her manteau's pinn'd awry,
E'er felt such rage, resentment, and despair,
As thou, sad virgin! for thy ravish'd hair.
  For, that sad moment, when the sylphs withdrew,
And Ariel weeping from Belinda flew,
Umbriel, a dusky, melancholy sprite,
As ever sullied the fair face of light,

Down to the central earth, his proper scene,
Repair'd to search the gloomy cave of Spleen.
  Swift on his sooty pinions flits the gnome,
And in a vapor reach'd the dismal dome.
No cheerful breeze this sullen region knows;
The dreaded east is all the wind that blows.
Here in a grotto shelter'd close from air,
And screen'd in shades from day's detested glare,
She sighs for ever on her pensive bed,
Pain at her side, and Megrim at her head.
  Two handmaids wait the throne; alike in place,
But differing far in figure and in face.
Here stood Ill-nature, like an ancient maid,
Her wrinkled form in black and white array'd;
With store of prayers for mornings, nights, and noons,
Her hand is fill'd; her bosom with lampoons.
There Affectation with a sickly mien,
Shows in her cheek the roses of eighteen;
Practised to lisp, and hang the head aside,
Faints into airs, and languishes with pride;
On the rich quilt sinks with becoming woe,
Wrapt in a gown, for sickness, and for show.
The fair ones feel such maladies as these,
When each new night-dress gives a new disease.
  A constant vapor o'er the palace flies;
Strange phantoms rising as the mists arise—
Dreadful, as hermits' dreams in haunted shades,
Or bright, as visions of expiring maids.
Now glaring fiends, and snakes on rolling spires,
Pale spectres, gaping tombs, and purple fires;
Now lakes of liquid gold, Elysian scenes,
And crystal domes, and angels in machines.

Unnumber'd throngs on every side are seen,
Of bodies changed to various forms by Spleen.
Here living teapots stand, one arm held out,
One bent—the handle this, and that the spout;
A pipkin there, like Homer's tripod, walks;
Here sighs a jar, and there a goose-pie talks;
Men prove with child, as powerful fancy works;
And maids, turn'd bottles, call aloud for corks.
  Safe pass'd the gnome through this fantastic band,
A branch of healing spleenwort in his hand.
Then thus address'd the power—" Hail, wayward queen!
Who rule the sex to fifty from fifteen;
Parent of vapors and of female wit,
Who give th' hysteric or poetic fit,
On various tempers act by various ways,
Make some take physic, others scribble plays;
Who cause the proud their visits to delay,
And send the godly in a pet to pray;
A nymph there is that all your power disdains,
And thousands more in equal mirth maintains.
But oh! if e'er thy gnome could spoil a grace,
Or raise a pimple on a beauteous face,
Like citron-waters matrons' cheeks inflame,
Or change complexions at a losing game—
If e'er with airy horns I planted heads,
Or rumpled petticoats or tumbled beds,
Or caused suspicion when no soul was rude,
Or discomposed the head-dress of a prude,
Or e'er to costive lapdog gave disease,
Which not the tears of brightest eyes could ease—
Hear me, and touch Belinda with chagrin;
That single act gives half the world the spleen."
  The goddess, with a discontented air,
Seems to reject him, though she grants his prayer.

A wondrous bag with both her hands she
　　binds,
Like that where once Ulysses held the
　　winds;
There she collects the force of female
　　lungs,
Sighs, sobs, and passions, and the war of
　　tongues.
A vial next she fills with fainting fears,
Soft sorrows, melting griefs, and flowing
　　tears.
The gnome rejoicing bears her gifts away,
Spreads his black wings, and slowly mounts
　　to day.
　　Sunk in Thalestris' arms the nymph he
　　　found,
Her eyes dejected, and her hair unbound.
Full o'er their heads the swelling bag he
　　rent,
And all the furies issued at the vent.
Belinda burns with more than mortal ire,
And fierce Thalestris fans the rising fire.
"O wretched maid!" she spread her hands
　　and cried
(While Hampton's echoes, "Wretched
　　maid," replied),
"Was it for this you took such constant
　　care
The bodkin, comb, and essence to pre-
　　pare?
For this your locks in paper durance
　　bound?
For this with torturing irons wreathed
　　around?
For this with fillets strain'd your tender
　　head?
And bravely bore the double loads of
　　lead?
Gods! shall the ravisher display your
　　hair,
While the fops envy, and the ladies
　　stare?
Honor forbid! at whose unrivall'd shrine
Ease, pleasure, virtue, all our sex resign.
Methinks already I your tears survey,
Already hear the horrid things they say;
Already see you a degraded toast,
And all your honor in a whisper lost!
How shall I, then, your hapless fame de-
　　fend?
'Twill then be infamy to seem your
　　friend!

And shall this prize, th' inestimable
　　prize,
Exposed through crystal to the gazing
　　eyes,
And heighten'd by the diamond's circling
　　rays,
On that rapacious hand for ever blaze?
Sooner shall grass in Hyde Park circus
　　grow,
And wits take lodgings in the sound of
　　Bow;
Sooner let earth, air, sea, to chaos fall,
Men, monkeys, lapdogs, parrots, perish
　　all!"
　　She said; then raging to Sir Plume re-
　　　pairs,
And bids her beau demand the precious
　　hairs.
Sir Plume, of amber snuff-box justly vain,
And the nice conduct of a clouded cane,
With earnest eyes, and round, unthinking
　　face,
He first the snuff-box open'd, then the
　　case,
And thus broke out—"My lord, why, what
　　the devil!
Z—ds! damn the lock! 'fore Gad, you must
　　be civil!
Plague on't! 'tis past a jest—nay, prithee,
　　pox!
Give her the hair."—He spoke, and rapp'd
　　his box.
　"It grieves me much (replied the peer
　　again)
Who speaks so well should ever speak in
　　vain;
But by this lock, this sacred lock, I swear
(Which never more shall join its parted
　　hair;
Which never more its honors shall renew.
Clipp'd from the lovely head where late it
　　grew),
That, while my nostrils draw the vital air,
This hand, which won it, shall for ever
　　wear."
He spoke, and speaking, in proud triumph
　　spread
The long-contended honors of her head.
　　But Umbriel, hateful gnome, forbears
　　　not so;
He breaks the vial whence the sorrows
　　flow.

Then see! the nymph in beauteous grief appears,
Her eyes half languishing, half drown'd in tears;
On her heaved bosom hung her drooping head,
Which with a sigh she raised, and thus she said:
"For ever cursed be this detested day,
Which snatch'd my best, my favorite curl away;
Happy! ah, ten times happy had I been,
If Hampton Court these eyes had never seen!
Yet am not I the first mistaken maid
By love of courts to numerous ills betray'd.
Oh had I rather unadmired remain'd
In some lone isle, or distant northern land;
Where the gilt chariot never marks the way,
Where none learn ombre, none e'er taste bohea!
There kept my charms conceal'd from mortal eye,
Like roses, that in deserts bloom and die.
What moved my mind with youthful lords to roam?
Oh had I stay'd, and said my prayers at home!
'Twas this the morning omens seem'd to tell,
Thrice from my trembling hand the patch-box fell;
The tottering china shook without a wind,
Nay, Poll sat mute, and Shock was most unkind!
A sylph, too, warn'd me of the threats of fate,
In mystic visions, now believed too late!
See the poor remnants of these slighted hairs!
My hand shall rend what e'en thy rapine spares:
These in two sable ringlets taught to break,
Once gave new beauties to the snowy neck;
The sister-lock now sits uncouth, alone,
And in its fellow's fate foresees its own;
Uncurl'd it hangs, the fatal shears demands,
And tempts once more thy sacrilegious hands.
Oh hadst thou, cruel! been content to seize
Hairs less in sight, or any hairs but these!"

CANTO V.

She said: the pitying audience melt in tears;
But Fate and Jove had stopp'd the baron's ears.
In vain Thalestris with reproach assails,
For who can move when fair Belinda fails?
Not half so fix'd the Trojan could remain,
While Anna begg'd and Dido raged in vain.
Then grave Clarissa graceful waved her fan;
Silence ensued, and thus the nymph began:
"Say, why are beauties praised and honor'd most,
The wise man's passion, and the vain man's toast?
Why deck'd with all that land and sea afford?
Why angels call'd, and angel-like adored?
Why round our coaches crowd the white-gloved beaux?
Why bows the side-box from its inmost rows?
How vain are all these glories, all our pains,
Unless good sense preserve what beauty gains;
That men may say, when we the front box grace,
Behold the first in virtue as in face!
Oh! if to dance all night, and dress all day,
Charm'd the small-pox, or chased old age away,
Who would not scorn what housewife's cares produce,
Or who would learn one earthly thing of use?
To patch, nay ogle, might become a saint;
Nor could it, sure, be such a sin to paint.

But since, alas! frail beauty must decay;
Curl'd or uncurl'd, since locks will turn to gray;
Since painted, or not painted, all shall fade,
And she who scorns a man must die a maid;
What then remains, but well our power to use,
And keep good humor still, whate'er we lose?
And trust me, dear, good humor can prevail,
When airs, and flights, and screams, and scolding fail.
Beauties in vain their pretty eyes may roll—
Charms strike the sight, but merit wins the soul."
So spoke the dame, but no applause ensued;
Belinda frown'd, Thalestris call'd her prude.
"To arms, to arms!" the fierce virago cries,
And swift as lightning to the combat flies.
All side in parties, and begin th' attack;
Fans clap, silks rustle, and tough whalebones crack;
Heroes' and heroines' shouts confusedly rise,
And bass and treble voices strike the skies.
No common weapons in their hands are found—
Like gods they fight, nor dread a mortal wound.
So when bold Homer makes the gods engage,
And heavenly breasts with human passions rage;
'Gainst Pallas Mars; Latona Hermes arms;
And all Olympus rings with loud alarms:
Jove's thunder roars, Heaven trembles all around,
Blue Neptune storms, the bellowing deeps resound:
Earth shakes her nodding towers, the ground gives way,
And the pale ghosts start at the flash of day!

Triumphant Umbriel, on a sconce's height,
Clapp'd his glad wings, and sat to view the fight:
Propp'd on their bodkin-spears, the sprites survey
The growing combat, or assist the fray.
While through the press enraged Thalestris flies,
And scatters death around from both her eyes,
A beau and witling perish'd in the throng—
One died in metaphor, and one in song:
"O cruel nymph! a living death I bear,"
Cried Dapperwit, and sunk beside his chair.
A mournful glance Sir Fopling upward cast,
"Those eyes are made so killing"—was his last.
Thus on Mæander's flowery margin lies
Th' expiring swan, and as he sings he dies.
When bold Sir Plume had drawn Clarissa down,
Chloe stepp'd in, and kill'd him with a frown;
She smiled to see the doughty hero slain,
But at her smile the beau revived again.
Now Jove suspends his golden scales in air,
Weighs the men's wits against the lady's hair;
The doubtful beam long nods from side to side;
At length the wits mount up, the hairs subside.
See, fierce Belinda on the baron flies,
With more than usual lightning in her eyes:
Nor fear'd the chief th' unequal fight to try,
Who sought no more than on his foe to die.
But this bold lord, with manly strength endued,
She with one finger and a thumb subdued:
Just where the breath of life his nostrils drew,
A charge of snuff the wily virgin threw;
The gnomes direct, to every atom just,
The pungent grains of titillating dust.

Sudden, with starting tears each eye o'er-
flows,
And the high dome re-echoes to his nose.
"Now meet thy fate!" incensed Belinda
cried,
And drew a deadly bodkin from her side.
(The same, his ancient personage to deck,
Her great-great-grandsire wore about his
neck,
In three seal-rings; which after, melted
down,
Form'd a vast buckle for his widow's
gown;
Her infant grandame's whistle next it
grew;
The bells she jingled, and the whistle blew;
Then in a bodkin graced her mother's
hairs,
Which long she wore, and now Belinda
wears.)
"Boast not my fall (he cried), insulting
foe!
Thou by some other shalt be laid as low;
Nor think, to die dejects my lofty mind;
All that I dread is leaving you behind!
Rather than so, ah let me still survive,
And burn in Cupid's flames—but burn
alive."
"Restore the lock!" she cries; and all
around
"Restore the lock!" the vaulted roofs re-
bound.
Not fierce Othello in so loud a strain
Roar'd for the handkerchief that caused
his pain.
But see how oft ambitious aims are cross'd,
And chiefs contend till all the prize is lost!
The lock, obtain'd with guilt, and kept
with pain,
In every place is sought, but sought in
vain:
With such a prize no mortal must be blest,
So Heaven decrees! with Heaven who can
contest?
Some thought it mounted to the lunar
sphere,
Since all things lost on earth are treasured
there.
There heroes' wits are kept in ponderous
vases,
And beaux' in snuff-boxes and tweezer-
cases;
There broken vows, and deathbed alms are
found,
And lovers' hearts with ends of riband
bound,
The courtier's promises, and sick men's
prayers,
The smiles of harlots, and the tears of
heirs,
Cages for gnats, and chains to yoke a flea,
Dried butterflies, and tomes of casuistry.
But trust the Muse—she saw it upward
rise,
Though mark'd by none but quick poetic
eyes
(So Rome's great founder to the heavens
withdrew,
To Proculus alone confess'd in view);
A sudden star, it shot through liquid air,
And drew behind a radiant trail of hair.
Not Berenice's locks first rose so bright,
The heavens bespangling with dishevell'd
light.
The sylphs behold it kindling as it flies,
And, pleased, pursue its progress through
the skies.
This the beau monde shall from the
Mall survey,
And hail with music its propitious ray;
This the blest lover shall for Venus take,
And send up vows from Rosamonda's
lake;
This Partridge soon shall view in cloudless
skies
When next he looks through Galileo's
eyes;
And hence th' egregious wizard shall
foredoom
The fate of Louis, and the fall of Rome.
Then cease, bright nymph! to mourn
thy ravish'd hair,
Which adds new glory to the shining
sphere!
Not all the tresses that fair head can
boast
Shall draw such envy as the lock you lost.
For after all the murders of your eye,
When, after millions slain, yourself shall
die;
When those fair suns shall set, as set they
must,
And all those tresses shall be laid in
dust—

This lock the Muse shall consecrate to
    fame,
And 'midst the stars inscribe Belinda's
    name.
ALEXANDER POPE.

THE MERRY PRANKS OF ROBIN GOOD-FELLOW.

FROM Oberon, in fairy-land,
  The king of ghosts and shadowes there,
Mad Robin, I, at his command,
  Am sent to view the night-sports here.
      What revell rout
      Is kept about
    In every corner where I go,
      I will o'ersee,
      And merrie be,
  And make good sport with ho, ho, ho!

More swift than lightning can I flye
  About this aëry welkin soone,
And in a minute's space descrye
  Each thing that's done belowe the moone.
      There's not a hag
      Or ghost shall wag,
    Or cry 'Ware goblins! where I go;
      But Robin, I,
      Their feates will spy,
  And send them home with ho, ho, ho!

Whene'er such wanderers I meete,
  As from their night-sports they trudge home,
With counterfeiting voice I greete,
  And call them on with me to roame
      Thro' woods, thro' lakes,
      Thro' bogs, thro' brakes;
    Or else unseene, with them I go,
      All in the nicke
      To play some tricke,
  And frolick it with ho, ho, ho!

Sometimes I meete them like a man,
  Sometimes an ox, sometimes a hound,
And to a horse I turn me can,
  To trip and trot about them round;
      But if, to ride,
      My backe they stride,
    More swift than wind away I goe;
      O'er hedge and lands,
      Through pools and ponds,
  I whirry, laughing ho, ho, ho!

When lads and lasses merry be,
  With possets, and with junkets fine,
Unseene of all the company,
  I eat their cakes and sip their wine;
      And to make sport
      I fume and snort,
    And out the candles I do blow.
      The maids I kiss,—
      They shrieke, Who's this?
  I answer naught but ho, ho, ho!

Yet now and then, the maids to please,
  At midnight I card up their wooll,
And while they sleepe and take their ease,
  With wheel to threads their flax I pull.
      I grind at mill
      Their malt up still;
    I dress their hemp, I spin their tow.
      If any wake,
      And would me take,
  I wend me, laughing ho, ho, ho!

When house or hearth doth sluttish lye,
  I pinch the maidens black and blue;
The bedd-clothes from the bedd pull I,
  And lay them naked all to view.
      'Twixt sleepe and wake
      I do them take,
    And on the key-cold floor them throw;
      If out they cry,
      Then forth I fly,
  And loudly laugh out, ho, ho, ho!

When any need to borrow aught,
  We lend them what they do require,
And for the use demand we naught,—
  Our owne is all we do desire.
      If to repay
      They do delay,
    Abroad amongst them then I go;
      And night by night
      I them affright,
  With pinchings, dreams, and ho, ho, ho!

When lazie queans have naught to do
  But study how to cog and lye,
To make debate and mischief too,
  'Twixt one another secretly,
      I marke their gloze,
      And it disclose

To them whom they have wrongèd so.
    When I have done
    I get me gone,
And leave them scolding, ho, ho, ho!

When men do traps and engines set
  In loope holes, where the vermine creepe,
Who from their foldes and houses get
  Their duckes and geese, and lambes and sheepe,
    I spy the gin,
    And enter in,
And seeme a vermine taken so;
    But when they there
    Approach me neare,
I leap out, laughing ho, ho, ho!

By wells and rills, in meadowes greene,
  We nightly dance our hey-day guise,
And to our fairye kinge and queene
  We chant our moon-lighte minstrelsies.
    When larkes 'gin sing
    Away we fling,
And babes new-born steale as we go,
    And elfe in bed
    We leave instead,
And wend us, laughing ho, ho, ho!

From hag-bred Merlin's time have I
  Thus nightly revell'd to and fro,
And, for my prankes, men call me by
  The name of Robin Good-Fellow.
    Fiends, ghosts, and sprites
    Who haunt the nightes,
The hags and goblins, do me know;
    And beldames old
    My feates have told,—
So *vale, vale!* Ho, ho, ho!
AUTHOR UNKNOWN.

THE FAIRIES OF THE CALDON LOW.

A MIDSUMMER LEGEND.

"AND where have you been, my Mary,
  And where have you been from me?"
"I've been to the top of the Caldon Low,
  The midsummer night to see!"

"And what did you see, my Mary,
  All up on the Caldon Low?"
"I saw the glad sunshine come down,
  And I saw the merry winds blow."

"And what did you hear, my Mary,
  All up on the Caldon Hill?"
"I heard the drops of the water made,
  And the ears of the green corn fill."

"Oh! tell me all, my Mary—
  All, all that ever you know;
For you must have seen the fairies
  Last night on the Caldon Low."

"Then take me on your knee, mother;
  And listen, mother of mine:
A hundred fairies danced last night,
  And the harpers they were nine;

"And their harp-strings rung so merrily
  To their dancing feet so small;
But oh! the words of their talking
  Were merrier far than all."

"And what were the words, my Mary,
  That then you heard them say?"
"I'll tell you all, my mother;
  But let me have my way.

"Some of them play'd with the water,
  And roll'd it down the hill;
'And this,' they said, 'shall speedily turn
  The poor old miller's mill;

"'For there has been no water
  Ever since the first of May;
And a busy man will the miller be
  At dawning of the day.

"'Oh! the miller, how he will laugh
  When he sees the mill-dam rise!
The jolly old miller, how he will laugh
  Till the tears fill both his eyes!'

"And some they seized the little winds
  That sounded over the hill;
And each put a horn unto his mouth,
  And blew both loud and shrill;

"'And there,' they said, 'the merry winds go
  Away from every horn;
And they shall clear the mildew dank
  From the blind old widow's corn.

"'Oh! the poor, blind widow,
  Though she has been blind so long,
She'll be blithe enough when the mildew's gone,
  And the corn stands tall and strong.'

"And some they brought the brown lint-seed,
And flung it down from the Low;
And this,' they said, 'by the sunrise,
In the weaver's croft shall grow.

Oh! the poor, lame weaver,
How he will laugh outright
When he sees his dwindling flax-field
All full of flowers by night!'

"And then outspoke a brownie,
With a long beard on his chin;
'I have spun up all the tow,' said he,
And I want some more to spin.

"'I've spun a piece of hempen cloth,
And I want to spin another;
A little sheet for Mary's bed,
And an apron for her mother.

"With that I could not help but laugh,
And I laugh'd out loud and free;
And then on the top of the Caldon Low
There was no one left but me.

"And all on the top of the Caldon Low
The mists were cold and gray,
And nothing I saw but the mossy stones
That round about me lay.

"But, coming down from the hill-top,
I heard afar below,
How busy the jolly miller was,
And how the wheel did go.

"And I peep'd into the widow's field,
And, sure enough, were seen
The yellow ears of the mildew'd corn,
All standing stout and green.

"And down by the weaver's croft I stole,
To see if the flax were sprung;
And I met the weaver at his gate,
With the good news on his tongue.

"Now this is all I heard, mother,
And all that I did see;
So, pr'ythee, make my bed, mother,
For I'm tired as I can be."

MARY HOWITT.

THE CULPRIT FAY.

"My visual orbs are purged from film, and, lo!
Instead of Anster's turnip-bearing vales,
I see old fairyland's miraculous show:
Her trees of tinsel kiss'd by freakish gales,
Her ouphs that, cloak'd in leaf-gold, skim the breeze,
And fairies, swarming . . ."
TENNANT'S *Anster Fair.*

I.

'TIS the middle watch of a summer's night—
The earth is dark, but the heavens are bright;
Naught is seen in the vault on high
But the moon, and the stars, and the cloudless sky,
And the flood which rolls its milky hue,
A river of light on the welkin blue.
The moon looks down on old Cronest;
She mellows the shades on his shaggy breast,
And seems his huge gray form to throw
In a silver cone on the wave below;
His sides are broken by spots of shade,
By the walnut bough and the cedar made,
And through their clustering branches dark
Glimmers and dies the fire-fly's spark—
Like starry twinkles that momently break
Through the rifts of the gathering tempest's rack.

II.

The stars are on the moving stream,
And fling, as its ripples gently flow,
A burnish'd length of wavy beam
In an eel-like, spiral line below;
The winds are whist, and the owl is still;
The bat in the shelvy rock is hid;
And naught is heard on the lonely hill
But the cricket's chirp, and the answer shrill
Of the gauze-wing'd katy-did;
And the plaint of the wailing whip-poor-will,
Who moans unseen, and ceaseless sings,
Ever a note of wail and woe,
Till Morning spreads her rosy wings,
And earth and sky in her glances glow.

III.

'Tis the hour of fairy ban and spell:
The wood-tick has kept the minutes well;

He has counted them all with click and
   stroke
Deep in the heart of the mountain-oak,
And he has awaken'd the sentry elve
   Who sleeps with him in the haunted
      tree,
To bid him ring the hour of twelve,
   And call the fays to their revelry;
Twelve small strokes on his tinkling bell
('Twas made of the white snail's pearly
      shell)—
"Midnight comes, and all is well!
Hither, hither, wing your way!
'Tis the dawn of the fairy day."

IV.

They come from beds of lichen green,
They creep from the mullein's velvet
      screen;
   Some on the backs of beetles fly
From the silver tops of moon-touch'd
      trees,
   Where they swung in their cobweb ham-
      mocks high,
And rock'd about in the evening breeze;
Some from the hum-bird's downy nest—
They had driven him out by elfin power,
   And, pillow'd on plumes of his rainbow
      breast,
Had slumber'd there till the charmèd
      hour;
Some had lain in the scoop of the rock,
With glittering ising-stars inlaid;
And some had open'd the four-o'clock,
And stole within its purple shade.
   And now they throng the moonlight
      glade,
   Above—below—on every side,
   Their little minim forms array'd
In the tricksy pomp of fairy pride!

V.

They come not now to print the lea
In freak and dance around the tree,
Or at the mushroom board to sup,
And drink the dew from the buttercup;—
A scene of sorrow waits them now,
For an ouphe has broken his vestal vow;
He has loved an earthly maid,
And left for her his woodland shade;
He has lain upon her lip of dew,
And sunn'd him in her eye of blue,
Fann'd her cheek with his wing of air,
Play'd in the ringlets of her hair,
And, nestling on her snowy breast,
Forgot the lily-king's behest.
For this the shadowy tribes of air
   To the elfin court must haste away:—
And now they stand expectant there,
   To hear the doom of the culprit fay.

VI.

The throne was rear'd upon the grass,
Of spice-wood and the sassafras;
On pillars of mottled tortoise-shell
   Hung the burnish'd canopy—
And over it gorgeous curtains fell
   Of the tulip's crimson drapery.
The monarch sat on his judgment-seat,
   On his brow the crown imperial shone,
The prisoner fay was at his feet,
   And his peers were ranged around the
      throne.
He waved his sceptre in the air,
   He look'd around and calmly spoke;
His brow was grave and his eye severe,
   But his voice in a soften'd accent broke:

VII.

"Fairy! fairy! list and mark:
   Thou hast broke thine elfin chain;
Thy flame-wood lamp is quench'd and
      dark,
   And thy wings are dyed with a deadly
      stain—
Thou hast sullied thine elfin purity
   In the glance of a mortal maiden's
      eye;
Thou hast scorn'd our dread decree,
   And thou shouldst pay the forfeit high.
But well I know her sinless mind
   Is pure as the angel forms above,
Gentle and meek, and chaste and kind,
   Such as a spirit well might love;
Fairy! had she spot or taint,
Bitter had been thy punishment:
Tied to the hornet's shardy wings;
Toss'd on the pricks of nettle stings;
Or seven long ages doom'd to dwell
With the lazy worm in the walnut-shell;
Or every night to writhe and bleed
Beneath the tread of the centipede;
Or bound in a cobweb dungeon dim,
Your jailer a spider, huge and grim,

Amid the carrion bodies to lie
Of the worm, and the bug, and the murder'd fly:
These it had been your lot to bear,
Had a stain been found on the earthly fair.
Now list, and mark our mild decree—
Fairy, this your doom must be:

VIII.

"Thou shalt seek the beach of sand
Where the water bounds the elfin land;
Thou shalt watch the oozy brine
Till the sturgeon leaps in the bright moonshine,
Then dart the glistening arch below,
And catch a drop from his silver bow.
The water-sprites will wield their arms
 And dash around, with roar and rave,
And vain are the woodland spirits' charms;
 They are the imps that rule the wave.
Yet trust thee in thy single might:
If thy heart be pure and thy spirit right,
Thou shalt win the warlock fight.

IX.

"If the spray-bead gem be won,
 The stain of thy wing is wash'd away;
But another errand must be done
 Ere thy crime be lost for aye:
Thy flame-wood lamp is quench'd and dark,
Thou must reillume its spark.
Mount thy steed and spur him high
To the heaven's blue canopy;
And when thou seest a shooting star,
Follow it fast, and follow it far—
The last faint spark of its burning train
Shall light the elfin lamp again.
Thou hast heard our sentence, fay;
Hence! to the water-side, away!"

X.

The goblin mark'd his monarch well;
 He spake not, but he bow'd him low,
Then pluck'd a crimson colen-bell,
 And turn'd him round in act to go.
The way is long, he cannot fly,
 His soiled wing has lost its power,
And he winds adown the mountain high,
 For many a sore and weary hour.

Through dreary beds of tangled fern,
Through groves of nightshade dark and dern,
Over the grass and through the brake,
Where toils the ant and sleeps the snake,
 Now over the violet's azure flush
He skips along in lightsome mood;
 And now he thrids the bramble-bush,
Till its points are dyed in fairy blood.
He has leap'd the bog, he has pierced the brier,
He has swum the brook, and waded the mire,
Till his spirits sank, and his limbs grew weak,
And the red wax'd fainter in his cheek.
He had fallen to the ground outright,
 For rugged and dim was his onward track,
But there came a spotted toad in sight,
 And he laugh'd as he jump'd upon her back;
He bridled her mouth with a silkweed twist,
He lash'd her sides with an osier thong;
And now, through evening's dewy mist,
 With leap and spring they bound along,
Till the mountain's magic verge is past,
And the beach of sand is reach'd at last.

XI.

Soft and pale is the moony beam,
Moveless still the glassy stream;
The wave is clear, the beach is bright
 With snowy shells and sparkling stones:
The shore-surge comes in ripples light,
 In murmurings faint and distant moans;
And ever afar in the silence deep
Is heard the splash of the sturgeon's leap,
And the bend of his graceful bow is seen—
A glittering arch of silver sheen,
Spanning the wave of burnish'd blue,
And dripping with gems of the river-dew.

XII.

The elfin cast a glance around,
 As he lighted down from his courser toad;
Then round his breast his wings he wound,
 And close to the river's brink he strode;

He sprang on a rock, he breathed a prayer,
  Above his head his arms he threw,
Then toss'd a tiny curve in air,
  And headlong plunged in the waters blue.

XIII.

Up sprung the spirits of the waves
From the sea-silk beds in their coral caves;
With snail-plate armor snatch'd in haste,
They speed their way through the liquid waste;
Some are rapidly borne along
On the mailèd shrimp or the prickly prong;
Some on blood-red leeches glide,
Some on the stony star-fish ride,
Some on the back of the lancing squab,
Some on the sideling soldier-crab;
And some on the jellied quarl, that flings
At once a thousand streamy stings;
They cut the wave with the living oar,
And hurry on to the moonlight shore,
To guard their realms and chase away
The footsteps of the invading fay.

XIV.

Fearlessly he skims along,
  His hope is high, and his limbs are strong;
He spreads his arms like the swallow's wing,
And throws his feet with a frog-like fling;
His locks of gold on the waters shine,
  At his breast the tiny foam-beads rise,
His back gleams bright above the brine,
  And the wake-line foam behind him lies.
But the water-sprites are gathering near
  To check his course along the tide;
Their warriors come in swift career
  And hem him round on every side;
On his thigh the leech has fix'd his hold,
The quarl's long arms are round him roll'd,
The prickly prong has pierced his skin,
And the squab has thrown his javelin;
The gritty star has rubb'd him raw,
And the crab has struck with his giant claw;

He howls with rage, and he shrieks with pain;
He strikes around, but his blows are vain;
Hopeless is the unequal fight,
Fairy! naught is left but flight.

XV.

He turn'd him round, and fled amain
With hurry and dash to the beach again;
He twisted over from side to side,
And laid his cheek to the cleaving tide;
The strokes of his plunging arms are fleet,
And with all his might he flings his feet,
But the water-sprites are round him still,
To cross his path and work him ill.
They bade the waves before him rise;
They flung the sea-fire in his eyes;
And they stunn'd his ears with the scallop stroke,
With the porpoise heave and the drum-fish croak.
Oh! but a weary wight was he
When he reach'd the foot of the dogwood tree.
Gash'd and wounded, and stiff and sore,
He laid him down on the sandy shore;
He bless'd the force of the charmèd line,
  And he bann'd the water-goblins' spite,
For he saw around in the sweet moonshine
Their little wee faces above the brine,
  Giggling and laughing with all their might
At the piteous hap of the fairy wight.

XVI.

Soon he gather'd the balsam dew
  From the sorrel-leaf and the henbane-bud;
Over each wound the balm he drew,
  And with cobweb lint he stanch'd the blood.
The mild west wind was soft and low,
It cool'd the heat of his burning brow,
And he felt new life in his sinews shoot,
As he suck'd the juice of the calamus-root;
And now he treads the fatal shore
As fresh and vigorous as before.

XVII.

Wrapp'd in musing stands the sprite;
'Tis the middle wane of night;

His task is hard, his way is far,
But he must do his errand right
  Ere dawning mounts her beamy car,
  And rolls her chariot-wheels of light;
And vain are the spells of fairy-land,—
He must work with a human hand.

XVIII.

He cast a sadden'd look around,
  But he felt new joy his bosom swell,
When, glittering on the shadow'd ground,
  He saw a purple mussel-shell;
Thither he ran, and he bent him low,
He heaved at the stern and he heaved at
    the bow,
And he push'd her over the yielding sand,
Till he came to the verge of the haunted
    land.
She was as lovely a pleasure-boat
  As ever fairy had travell'd in,
For she glow'd with purple paint without,
  And shone with silvery pearl within;
A sculler's notch in the stern he made,
An oar he shaped of the bootle-blade;
Then sprung to his seat with a lightsome
    leap,
And launch'd afar on the calm, blue
    deep.

XIX.

The imps of the river yell and rave;
  They had no power above the wave;
But they heaved the billow before the prow,
  And they dash'd the surge against her
    side,
And they struck her keel with jerk and
    blow,
  Till the gunwale bent to the rocking
    tide.
She whimpled about to the pale moon-
    beam,
Like a feather that floats on a wind-toss'd
    stream;
And momently athwart her track
The quarl uprear'd his island back,
And the fluttering scallop behind would
    float,
  And spatter the water about the boat;
But he bail'd her out with his colen-bell,
  And he kept her trimm'd with a wary
    tread,
While on every side like lightning fell
  The heavy strokes of his bootle-blade.

XX.

Onward still he held his way,
  Till he came where the column of moon-
    shine lay,
And saw beneath the surface dim
The brown-back'd sturgeon slowly swim;
Around him were the goblin train,
But he scull'd with all his might and main,
And follow'd wherever the sturgeon led,
Till he saw him upward point his head;
Then he dropp'd his paddle blade,
And held his colen-goblet up
To catch the drop in its crimson cup.

XXI.

With sweeping tail and quivering fin
  Through the wave the sturgeon flew,
And, like the heaven-shot javelin,
  He sprung above the waters blue.
Instant as the star-fall light,
  He plunged him in the deep again,
But left an arch of silver bright,
  The rainbow of the moony main.
It was a strange and lovely sight
  To see the puny goblin there;
He seem'd an angel form of light,
  With azure wings and sunny hair,
  Throned on a cloud of purple fair,
Circled with blue and edged with white,
And sitting at the fall of even
Beneath the bow of summer heaven.

XXII.

A moment, and its lustre fell;
  But ere it met the billow blue,
He caught within his crimson bell
  A droplet of its sparkling dew—
Joy to thee, fay! thy task is done,
Thy wings are pure, for the gem is won—
Cheerly ply thy dripping oar,
And haste away to the elfin shore.

XXIII.

He turns, and, lo! on either side
The ripples on his path divide;
And the track o'er which his boat must
    pass
Is smooth as a sheet of polish'd glass.
Around, their limbs the sea-nymphs lave,
  With snowy arms half swelling out,
While on the gloss'd and gleamy wave
  Their sea-green ringlets loosely float;

They swim around with smile and song;
   They press the bark with pearly hand,
And gently urge her course along,
   Toward the beach of speckled sand;
And, as he lightly leap'd to land,
   They bade adieu with nod and bow;
Then gayly kiss'd each little hand,
   And dropp'd in the crystal deep below.

XXIV.

A moment stay'd the fairy there;
He kiss'd the beach and breathed a prayer;
Then spread his wings of gilded blue,
And on to the elfin court he flew:
As ever ye saw a bubble rise,
And shine with a thousand changing dyes,
Till, lessening far, through ether driven,
It mingles with the hues of heaven;
As, at the glimpse of morning pale,
The lance-fly spreads his silken sail,
And gleams with blendings soft and bright,
Till lost in the shades of fading night;
So rose from earth the lovely fay—
So vanish'd, far in heaven away!

*   *   *   *   *   *

Up, fairy! quit thy chickweed bower,
The cricket has call'd the second hour;
Twice again, and the lark will rise
To kiss the streakings of the skies—
Up! thy charmèd armor don,
Thou'lt need it ere the night be gone.

XXV.

He put his acorn helmet on;
It was plumed of the silk of the thistle-down;
The corslet-plate that guarded his breast
Was once the wild bee's golden vest;
His cloak, of a thousand mingled dyes,
Was form'd of the wings of butterflies;
His shield was the shell of a lady-bug queen,
Studs of gold on a ground of green;
And the quivering lance which he brandish'd bright
Was the sting of a wasp he had slain in fight.
Swift he bestrode his fire-fly steed;
   He bared his blade of the bent-grass blue;
He drove his spurs of the cockle-seed,
   And away like a glance of thought he flew,
To skim the heavens, and follow far
The fiery trail of the rocket-star.

XXVI.

The moth-fly, as he shot in air,
Crept under the leaf, and hid her there;
The katy-did forgot its lay,
The prowling gnat fled fast away,
The fell mosquito check'd his drone
And folded his wings till the fay was gone,
And the wily beetle dropp'd his head,
And fell on the ground as if he were dead;
They crouch'd them close in the darksome shade,
   They quaked all o'er with awe and fear,
For they had felt the blue-bent blade,
   And writhed at the prick of the elfin spear;
Many a time, on a summer's night,
When the sky was clear, and the moon was bright,
They had been roused from the haunted ground
By the yelp and bay of the fairy hound;
They had heard the tiny bugle-horn,
They had heard the twang of the maize-silk string,
When the vine-twig bows were tightly drawn,
And the nettle-shaft through the air was borne,
Feather'd with down of the hum-bird's wing.
And now they deem'd the courier ouphe
   Some hunter-sprite of the elfin ground;
And they watch'd till they saw him mount the roof
   That canopies the world around;
Then glad they left their covert lair,
And freak'd about in the midnight air.

XXVII.

Up to the vaulted firmament
His path the fire-fly courser bent,
And at every gallop on the wind,
He flung a glittering spark behind;

He flies like a feather in the blast
Till the first light cloud in heaven is past.
　But the shapes of air have begun their work,
　And a drizzly mist is round him cast;
　　He cannot see through the mantle murk;
He shivers with cold, but he urges fast;
　Through storm and darkness, sleet and shade,
He lashes his steed, and spurs amain—
For shadowy hands have twitch'd the rein,
　And flame-shot tongues around him play'd,
And near him many a fiendish eye
Glared with a fell malignity,
And yells of rage, and shrieks of fear,
Came screaming on his startled ear.

XXVIII.

His wings are wet around his breast,
The plume hangs dripping from his crest,
His eyes are blurr'd by the lightning's glare,
And his ears are stunn'd with the thunder's blare,
But he gave a shout, and his blade he drew,
　He thrust before and he struck behind,
Till he pierced their cloudy bodies through,
　And gash'd their shadowy limbs of wind;
Howling the misty spectres flew,
　They rend the air with frightful cries;
For he has gain'd the welkin blue,
　And the land of clouds beneath him lies.

XXIX.

Up to the cope careering swift,
　In breathless motion fast,
Fleet as the swallow cuts the drift,
　Or the sea-roc rides the blast,
The sapphire sheet of eve is shot,
　The spherèd moon is past,
The earth but seems a tiny blot
　On a sheet of azure cast.
Oh! it was sweet, in the clear moonlight,
　To tread the starry plain of even!
To meet the thousand eyes of night,
　And feel the cooling breath of heaven!
But the elfin made no stop or stay
Till he came to the bank of the milky-way;
Then he check'd his courser's foot,
And watch'd for the glimpse of the planet-shoot.

XXX.

Sudden along the snowy tide
　That swell'd to meet their footsteps' fall,
The sylphs of heaven were seen to glide,
　Attired in sunset's crimson pall;
Around the fay they weave the dance,
　They skip before him on the plain,
And one has taken his wasp-sting lance,
　And one upholds his bridle-rein;
With warblings wild they lead him on
　To where through clouds of amber seen,
Studded with stars, resplendent shone
　The palace of the sylphid queen.
Its spiral columns, gleaming bright,
Were streamers of the northern light;
Its curtain's light and lovely flush
Was of the morning's rosy blush;
And the ceiling fair, that rose aboon,
The white and feathery fleece of noon.

XXXI.

But, oh! how fair the shape that lay
　Beneath a rainbow bending bright;
She seem'd to the entrancèd fay
　The loveliest of the forms of light;
Her mantle was the purple roll'd
　At twilight in the west afar;
'Twas tied with threads of dawning gold,
　And button'd with a sparkling star.
Her face was like the lily roon
　That veils the vestal planet's hue;
Her eyes, two beamlets from the moon,
　Set floating in the welkin blue.
Her hair is like the sunny beam,
And the diamond gems which round it gleam
Are the pure drops of dewy even
That ne'er have left their native heaven.

XXXII.

She raised her eyes to the wondering sprite,
　And they leap'd with smiles; for well I ween

Never before in the bowers of light
   Had the form of an earthly fay been seen.
Long she look'd in his tiny face;
   Long with his butterfly cloak she play'd;
She smoothed his wings of azure lace,
   And handled the tassel of his blade;
And as he told in accents low
The story of his love and woe,
She felt new pains in her bosom rise,
And the tear-drop started in her eyes.
And " O sweet spirit of earth," she cried,
   "Return no more to your woodland height,
But ever here with me abide
   In the land of everlasting light!
Within the fleecy drift we'll lie,
   We'll hang upon the rainbow's rim;
And all the jewels of the sky
   Around thy brow shall brightly beam!
And thou shalt bathe thee in the stream
   That rolls its whitening foam aboon,
And ride upon the lightning's gleam,
   And dance upon the orbèd moon!
We'll sit within the Pleiad ring,
   We'll rest on Orion's starry belt,
And I will bid my sylphs to sing
   The song that makes the dew-mist melt;
Their harps are of the umber shade
   That hides the blush of waking day,
And every gleamy string is made
   Of silvery moonshine's lengthen'd ray;
And thou shalt pillow on my breast,
   While heavenly breathings float around,
And, with the sylphs of ether blest,
   Forget the joys of fairy ground."

XXXIII.

She was lovely and fair to see,
And the elfin's heart beat fitfully;
But lovelier far, and still more fair
The earthly form imprinted there;
Naught he saw in the heavens above
Was half so dear as his mortal love,
For he thought upon her look so meek,
And he thought of the light flush on her cheek;
Never again might he bask and lie
On that sweet cheek and moonlight eye;
But in his dreams her form to see,
To clasp her in his revery,
To think upon his virgin bride,
Was worth all heaven, and earth beside.

XXXIV.

"Lady," he cried, "I have sworn to-night,
On the word of a fairy-knight,
To do my sentence-task aright;
My honor scarce is free from stain—
I may not soil its snows again;
Betide me weal, betide me woe,
Its mandate must be answer'd now."
Her bosom heaved with many a sigh,
The tear was in her drooping eye;
But she led him to the palace-gate,
   And call'd the sylphs who hover'd there,
And bade them fly and bring him straight,
   Of clouds condensed, a sable car.
With charm and spell she bless'd it there,
   From all the fiends of upper air;
Then round him cast the shadowy shroud,
And tied his steed behind the cloud;
And press'd his hand as she bade him fly
Far to the verge of the northern sky,
For by its wan and wavering light
There was a star would fall to-night.

XXXV.

Borne afar on the wings of the blast,
Northward away he speeds him fast,
And his courser follows the cloudy wain
Till the hoof-strokes fall like pattering rain.
The clouds roll backward as he flies,
Each flickering star behind him lies,
And he has reach'd the northern plain
And back'd his fire-fly steed again,
Ready to follow in its flight
The streaming of the rocket-light.

XXXVI.

The star is yet in the vault of heaven,
   But it rocks in the summer gale;
And now 'tis fitful and uneven,
   And now 'tis deadly pale;
And now 'tis wrapp'd in sulphur-smoke,
   And quench'd is its rayless beam;
And now with a rattling thunder-stroke
   It bursts in flash and flame.
As swift as the glance of the arrowy lance
   That the storm-spirit flings from high,
The star-shot flew o'er the welkin blue,
   As it fell from the sheeted sky.

As swift as the wind in its train behind
  The elfin gallops along :
The fiends of the clouds are bellowing loud,
  But the sylphid charm is strong ;
He gallops unhurt in the shower of fire,
  While the cloud-fiends fly from the blaze ;
He watches each flake till its sparks expire,
  And rides in the light of its rays.
But he drove his steed to the lightning's speed,
  And caught a glimmering spark ;
Then wheel'd around to the fairy ground,
  And sped through the midnight dark.

*   *   *   *   *   *

Ouphe and goblin ! imp and sprite !
  Elf of eve ! and starry fay !
Ye that love the moon's soft light,
  Hither—hither wend your way ;
Twine ye in a jocund ring,
  Sing and trip it merrily,
Hand to hand, and wing to wing,
  Round the wild witch-hazel tree.

Hail the wanderer again
  With dance and song, and lute and lyre ;
Pure his wing and strong his chain,
  And doubly bright his fairy fire.
Twine ye in an airy round,
  Brush the dew and print the lea ;
Skip and gambol, hop and bound,
  Round the wild witch-hazel tree.

The beetle guards our holy ground,
  He flies about the haunted place,
And if mortal there be found,
  He hums in his ears and flaps his face ;
The leaf-harp sounds our roundelay,
  The owlet's eyes our lanterns be ;
Thus we sing and dance and play
  Round the wild witch-hazel tree.

XXXVII.

But hark ! from tower on tree-top high
  The sentry-elf his call has made ;
A streak is in the eastern sky,
  Shapes of moonlight ! flit and fade !
The hill-tops gleam in morning's spring,
The skylark shakes his dabbled wing,
The day-glimpse glimmers on the lawn,
The cock has crow'd, and the fays are gone.
          JOSEPH RODMAN DRAKE.

COMUS: A MASK.

THE FIRST SCENE DISCOVERS A WILD WOOD.

The ATTENDANT SPIRIT *descends or enters.*

BEFORE the starry threshold of Jove's court
My mansion is, where those immortal shapes
Of bright aërial spirits live inspher'd
In regions mild of calm and serene air,
Above the smoke and stir of this dim spot,
Which men call Earth ; and with low-thoughted care
Confined, and pester'd in this pinfold here,
Strive to keep up a frail and feverish being,
Unmindful of the crown that Virtue gives,
After this mortal change, to her true servants,
Amongst the enthroned gods on sainted seats.
Yet some there be that by due steps aspire
To lay their just hands on that golden key,
That opes the palace of eternity ;
To such my errand is ; and but for such,
I would not soil these pure ambrosial weeds
With the rank vapors of this sin-worn mould.
  But to my task. Neptune, besides the sway
Of every salt flood, and each ebbing stream,
Took in by lot 'twixt high and nether Jove
Imperial rule of all the sea-girt isles,
That like to rich and various gems inlay
The unadornèd bosom of the deep ;
Which he, to grace his tributary gods,
By course commits to several government,
And gives them leave to wear their sapphire crowns,
And wield their little tridents : but this Isle,
The greatest and the best of all the main,
He quarters to his blue-hair'd deities :
And all this tract that fronts the falling sun
A noble Peer of mickle trust and power

Has in his charge, with temper'd awe to guide
An old and haughty nation proud in arms:
Where his fair offspring, nursed in princely lore,
Are coming to attend their father's state,
And new-entrusted sceptre; but their way
Lies through the perplex'd paths of this drear wood,
The nodding horror of whose shady brows
Threats the forlorn and wandering passenger;
And here their tender age might suffer peril,
But that by quick command from sovereign Jove
I was despatch'd for their defence and guard;
And listen why, for I will tell you now
What never yet was heard in tale or song,
From old or modern bard, in hall or bower.
  Bacchus, that first from out the purple grape
Crush'd the sweet poison of misusèd wine,
After the Tuscan mariners transform'd,
Coasting the Tyrrhene shore, as the winds listed,
On Circe's island fell. (Who knows not Circe,
The daughter of the Sun, whose charmèd cup
Whoever tasted, lost his upright shape,
And downward fell into a grovelling swine?)
This Nymph that gazed upon his clust'ring locks,
With ivy berries wreathed, and his blithe youth,
Had by him, ere he parted thence, a son
Much like his father, but his mother more,
Whom therefore she brought up, and Comus named:
Who ripe, and frolic of his full-grown age,
Roving the Celtic and Iberian fields,
At last betakes him to this ominous wood,
And in thick shelter of black shades embower'd
Excels his mother at her mighty art,
Offering to every weary traveller
His orient liquor in a crystal glass,
To quench the drouth of Phœbus; which as they taste

(For most do taste through fond intemp'rate thirst),
Soon as the potion works, their human count'nance,
Th' express resemblance of the gods, is changed
Into some brutish form of wolf, or bear,
Or ounce, or tiger, hog, or bearded goat,
All other parts remaining as they were;
And they, so perfect is their misery,
Not once perceive their foul disfigurement,
But boast themselves more comely than before,
And all their friends and native home forget,
To roll with pleasure in a sensual sty.
Therefore, when any favor'd of high Jove
Chances to pass through this adventurous glade,
Swift as the sparkle of a glancing star
I shoot from heaven, to give him safe convoy,
As now I do: But first I must put off
These my sky robes spun out of Iris' woof,
And take the weeds and likeness of a swain,
That to the service of this house belongs,
Who with his soft pipe, and smooth-dittied song,
Well knows to still the wild winds when they roar,
And hush the waving woods; nor of less faith,
And in this office of his mountain-watch,
Likeliest, and nearest to the present aid
Of this occasion. But I hear the tread
Of hateful steps; I must be viewless now.

COMUS *enters with a charming-rod in one hand, his glass in the other; with him a rout of monsters, headed like sundry sorts of wild beasts, but otherwise like men and women, their apparel glistering; they come in making a riotous and unruly noise, with torches in their hands.*

  COMUS. The star that bids the shepherd fold
Now the top of heaven doth hold;
And the gilded car of day
His glowing axle doth allay

In the steep Atlantic stream;
And the slope sun his upward beam
Shoots against the dusky pole,
Pacing toward the other goal
Of his chamber in the east.
Meanwhile welcome joy, and feast,
Midnight shout and revelry,
Tipsy dance and jollity.
Braid your locks with rosy twine,
Dropping odors, dropping wine.
Rigor now is gone to bed,
And Advice with scrupulous head,
Strict Age, and sour Severity,
With their grave saws in slumber lie.
We that are of purer fire
Imitate the starry quire,
Who in their nightly watchful spheres
Lead in swift round the months and years.
The sounds and seas, with all their finny drove,
Now to the moon in wavering morrice move;
And on the tawny sands and shelves
Trip the pert fairies and the dapper elves.
By dimpled brook, and fountain brim,
The wood-nymphs, deck'd with daisies trim,
Their merry wakes and pastimes keep;
What hath night to do with sleep?
Night hath better sweets to prove,
Venus now wakes, and wakens Love.
Come, let us our rites begin,
'Tis only daylight that makes sin,
Which these dun shades will ne'er report.
Hail, goddess of nocturnal sport,
Dark-veil'd Cotytto! t' whom the secret flame
Of midnight torches burns; mysterious dame,
That ne'er art call'd, but when the dragon womb
Of Stygian darkness spets her thickest gloom,
And makes one blot of all the air;
Stay thy cloudy ebon chair,
Wherein thou rid'st with Hecat', and befriend
Us thy vow'd priests, till utmost end
Of all thy dues be done, and none left out,
Ere the babbling eastern scout,

The nice Morn on th' Indian steep,
From her cabin'd loophole peep,
And to the tell-tale Sun descry
Our conceal'd solemnity.
Come, knit hands, and beat the ground
In a light fantastic round.

The Measure.

Break off, break off, I feel the different pace
Of some chaste footing near about this ground.
Run to your shrouds, within these brakes and trees;
Our number may affright. Some virgin sure
(For so I can distinguish by mine art)
Benighted in these woods. Now to my charms,
And to my wily trains; I shall ere long
Be well stock'd with as fair a herd as grazed
About my mother Circe. Thus I hurl
My dazzling spells into the spongy air,
Of power to cheat the eye with blear illusion,
And give it false presentments, lest the place
And my quaint habits breed astonishment,
And put the damsel to suspicious flight,
Which must not be, for that's against my course:
I, under fair pretence of friendly ends,
And well-placed words of glozing courtesy,
Baited with reasons not unplausible,
Wind me into the easy-hearted man,
And hug him into snares. When once her eye
Hath met the virtue of this magic dust,
I shall appear some harmless villager,
Whom thrift keeps up about his country gear.
But here she comes; I fairly step aside,
And hearken, if I may, her business here.

The Lady enters.

This way the noise was, if mine ear be true,
My best guide now; methought it was the sound

Of riot and ill-managed merriment,
Such as the jocund flute or gamesome pipe
Stirs up among the loose unletter'd hinds,
When for their teeming flocks, and granges full,
In wanton dance, they praise the bounteous Pan,
And thank the gods amiss. I should be loath
To meet the rudeness, and swill'd insolence
Of such late wassailers; yet oh! where else
Shall I inform my unacquainted feet
In the blind mazes of this tangled wood?
My brothers, when they saw me wearied out
With this long way, resolving here to lodge
Under the spreading favor of these pines,
Stepp'd, as they said, to the next thicket-side
To bring me berries, or such cooling fruit
As the kind hospitable woods provide.
They left me then, when the gray-hooded Even,
Like a sad votarist in palmer's weed,
Rose from the hindmost wheels of Phœbus' wain.
But where they are, and why they came not back,
Is now the labor of my thoughts; 'tis likeliest
They had engaged their wand'ring steps too far;
And envious darkness, ere they could return,
Had stole them from me: else, O thievish Night,
Why shouldst thou, but for some felonious end,
In thy dark lantern thus close up the stars,
That Nature hung in heav'n, and fill'd their lamps
With everlasting oil, to give due light
To the misled and lonely traveller?
This is the place, as well as I may guess,
Whence even now the tumult of loud mirth
Was rife, and perfect in my list'ning ear,
Yet naught but single darkness do I find.
What might this be? A thousand fantasies
Begin to throng into my memory,
Of calling shapes, and beck'ning shadows dire,
And airy tongues, that syllable men's names
On sands, and shores, and desert wildernesses.
These thoughts may startle well, but not astound
The virtuous mind, that ever walks attended
By a strong-siding champion, Conscience.—
O welcome pure-eyed Faith, white-handed Hope,
Thou hovering Angel, girt with golden wings,
And thou, unblemish'd form of Chastity!
I see ye visibly, and now believe
That he, the Supreme Good, t' whom all things ill
Are but as slavish officers of vengeance,
Would send a glist'ring guardian, if need were,
To keep my life and honor unassail'd.
Was I deceived, or did a sable cloud
Turn forth her silver lining on the night?
I did not err, there does a sable cloud
Turn forth her silver lining on the night,
And casts a gleam over this tufted grove:
I cannot halloo to my brothers, but
Such noise as I can make to be heard farthest
I'll venture, for my new-enliven'd spirits
Prompt me; and they perhaps are not far off.

Song.

Sweet Echo, sweetest nymph, that liv'st unseen
  Within thy airy shell,
By slow Mæander's margent green,
And in the violet-embroider'd vale,
  Where the love-lorn nightingale
Nightly to thee her sad song mourneth well;
  Canst thou not tell me of a gentle pair
    That likest thy Narcissus are?
    Oh, if thou have
  Hid them in some flow'ry cave,
    Tell me but where,
Sweet Queen of Parley, Daughter of the Sphere!
So mayst thou be translated to the skies,
And give resounding grace to all Heav'n's harmonies.

Enter COMUS.

COM. Can any mortal mixture of earth's mould
Breathe such divine enchanting ravishment?
Sure something holy lodges in that breast,
And with these raptures moves the vocal air
To testify his hidden residence:
How sweetly did they float upon the wings
Of silence, through the empty-vaulted night,
At every fall smoothing the raven down
Of darkness till it smiled! I have oft heard
My mother Circe with the Sirens three,
Amidst the flow'ry-kirtled Naiades,
Culling their potent herbs, and baleful drugs,
Who, as they sung, would take the prison'd soul,
And lap it in Elysium; Scylla wept,
And chid her barking waves into attention,
And fell Charybdis murmur'd soft applause:
Yet they in pleasing slumber lull'd the sense,
And in sweet madness robb'd it of itself;
But such a sacred, and homefelt delight,
Such sober certainty of waking bliss,
I never heard till now. I'll speak to her,
And she shall be my queen. Hail, foreign wonder!
Whom certain these rough shades did never breed,
Unless the goddess that in rural shrine
Dwell'st here with Pan, or Sylvan, by blest song
Forbidding every bleak unkindly fog
To touch the prosperous growth of this tall wood.

LAD. Nay, gentle shepherd, ill is lost that praise
That is address'd to unattending ears;
Not any boast of skill, but extreme shift
How to regain my sever'd company,
Compell'd me to awake the courteous Echo
To give me answer from her mossy couch.

COM. What chance, good Lady, hath bereft you thus?

LAD. Dim darkness, and this leafy labyrinth.

COM. Could that divide you from near-ushering guides?

LAD. They left me weary on a grassy turf.

COM. By falsehood, or discourtesy, or why?

LAD. To seek i' th' valley some cool friendly spring.

COM. And left your fair side all unguarded, Lady?

LAD. They were but twain, and purposed quick return.

COM. Perhaps forestalling night prevented them.

LAD. How easy my misfortune is to hit!

COM. Imports their loss, beside the present need?

LAD. No less than if I should my brothers lose.

COM. Were they of manly prime, or youthful bloom?

LAD. As smooth as Hebe's their unrazor'd lips.

COM. Two such I saw, what time the labor'd ox
In his loose traces from the furrow came,
And the swink'd hedger at his supper sat;
I saw them under a green mantling vine
That crawls along the side of yon small hill,
Plucking ripe clusters from the tender shoots;
Their port was more than human, as they stood:
I took it for a faery vision
Of some gay creatures of the element,
That in the colors of the rainbow live,
And play i' th' plighted clouds. I was awestruck,
And as I pass'd, I worshipp'd; if those you seek,
It were a journey like the path to heaven,
To help you find them.

LAD. Gentle villager,
What readiest way would bring me to that place?

COM. Due west it rises from this shrubby point.

LAD. To find that out, good shepherd, I suppose,

In such a scant allowance of star-light,
Would overtask the best land-pilot's art,
Without the sure guess of well-practised
   feet.
   COM. I know each lane, and every alley
      green,
Dingle or bushy dell of this wild wood,
And every bosky bourn from side to side,
My daily walks and ancient neighbor-
   hood;
And if your stray attendants be yet lodged
Or shroud within these limits, I shall
   know
Ere morrow wake, or the low-roosted lark
From her thatch'd pallat rouse; if other-
   wise,
I can conduct you, Lady, to a low
But loyal cottage, where you may be safe
Till further quest.
   LAD. Shepherd, I take thy word,
And trust thy honest-offer'd courtesy,
Which oft is sooner found in lowly sheds
With smoky rafters, than in tap'stry halls
And courts of princes, where it first was
   named,
And yet is most pretended: in a place
Less warranted than this, or less secure,
I cannot be, that I should fear to change
   it.
Eye me, blest Providence, and square my
   trial
To my proportion'd strength. Shepherd,
   lead on.

Enter THE TWO BROTHERS.

   1 BR. Unmuffle, ye faint stars, and thou,
      fair moon,
That wont'st to love the traveller's benizon,
Stoop thy pale visage through an amber
   cloud,
And disinherit Chaos, that reigns here
In double night of darkness and of shades;
Or if your influence be quite damm'd up
With black usurping mists, some gentle
   taper,
Though a rush candle, from the wicker-
   hole
Of some clay habitation, visit us
With thy long-levell'd rule of streaming
   light;
And thou shalt be our star of Arcady,
Or Tyrian Cynosure.

   2 BR. Or if our eyes
Be barr'd that happiness, might we but
   hear
The folded flocks penn'd in their wattled
   cotes,
Or sound of past'ral reed with oaten
   stops,
Or whistle from the lodge, or village
   cock
Count the night watches to his feathery
   dames,
'Twould be some solace yet, some little
   cheering
In this close dungeon of innumerous
   boughs.
But oh, that hapless virgin, our lost
   sister!
Where may she wander now, whither be-
   take her
From the chill dew, among rude burs and
   thistles?
Perhaps some cold bank is her bolster
   now,
Or 'gainst the rugged bark of some broad
   elm
Leans her unpillow'd head, fraught with
   sad fears.
What, if in wild amazement, and affright,
Or, while we speak, within the direful
   grasp
Of savage hunger, or of savage heat?
   1 BR. Peace, brother, be not over ex-
      quisite
To cast the fashion of uncertain evils;
For grant they be so, while they rest un-
   known,
What need a man forestall his date of
   grief,
And run to meet what he would most
   avoid?
Or if they be but false alarms of fear,
How bitter is such self-delusion!
I do not think my sister so to seek,
Or so unprincipled in virtue's book,
And the sweet peace that goodness bosoms
   ever,
As that the single want of light and noise
(Not being in danger, as I trust she is
   not)
Could stir the constant mood of her calm
   thoughts,
And put them into misbecoming plight.

Virtue could see to do what virtue would
By her own radiant light, though sun and moon
Were in the flat sea sunk. And Wisdom's self
Oft seeks to sweet retired solitude,
Where, with her best nurse Contemplation,
She plumes her feathers, and lets grow her wings,
That in the various bustle of resort
Were all-to ruffled, and sometimes impair'd.
He that has light within his own clear breast,
May sit i' th' centre, and enjoy bright day:
But he that hides a dark soul, and foul thoughts,
Benighted walks under the mid-day sun;
Himself is his own dungeon.
    2 Br. 'Tis most true,
That musing meditation most affects
The pensive secrecy of desert cell,
Far from the cheerful haunt of men and herds,
And sits as safe as in a senate-house;
For who would rob a hermit of his weeds,
His few books, or his beads, or maple dish,
Or do his gray hairs any violence?
But beauty, like the fair Hesperian tree
Laden with blooming gold, had need the guard
Of dragon watch with unenchanted eye,
To save her blossoms, and defend her fruit
From the rash hand of bold incontinence.
You may as well spread out the unsunn'd heaps
Of miser's treasure by an outlaw's den,
And tell me it is safe, as bid me hope
Danger will wink on opportunity,
And let a single helpless maiden pass
Uninjured in this wild surrounding waste.
Of night, or loneliness, it recks me not;
I fear the dread events that dog them both,
Lest some ill-greeting touch attempt the person
Of our unownèd sister.
    1 Br. I do not, brother,
Infer, as if I thought my sister's state
Secure without all doubt, or controversy;
Yet where an equal poise of hope and fear
Does arbitrate th' event, my nature is
That I incline to hope, rather than fear,
And gladly banish squint suspicion.
My sister is not so defenceless left,
As you imagine; she has a hidden strength
Which you remember not.
    2 Br. What hidden strength,
Unless the strength of Heaven, if you mean that?
    1 Br. I mean that too, but yet a hidden strength,
Which, if Heav'n gave it, may be term'd her own;
'Tis chastity, my brother, chastity:
She that has that, is clad in complete steel,
And like a quiver'd nymph with arrows keen
May trace huge forests, and unharbor'd heaths,
Infamous hills, and sandy perilous wilds,
Where through the sacred rays of chastity,
No savage fierce, bandite, or mountaineer
Will dare to soil her virgin purity:
Yea there, where very desolation dwells,
By grots, and caverns shagg'd with horrid shades,
She may pass on with unblench'd majesty,
Be it not done in pride, or in presumption.
Some say no evil thing that walks by night,
In fog, or fire, by lake, or moorish fen,
Blue meagre hag, or stubborn unlaid ghost,
That breaks his magic chains at curfew-time,
No goblin, or swart faery of the mine,
Hath hurtful power o'er true virginity.
Do ye believe me yet, or shall I call
Antiquity from the old schools of Greece
To testify the arms of chastity?
Hence had the huntress Dian her dread bow,
Fair silver-shafted queen, for ever chaste,
Wherewith she tamed the brinded lioness

And spotted mountain-pard, and set at
    naught
The frivolous bolt of Cupid; gods and
    men
Fear'd her stern frown, and she was queen
    o' the woods.
What was that snaky-headed Gorgon
    shield,
That wise Minerva wore, unconquer'd
    virgin,
Wherewith she freezed her foes to con-
    geal'd stone,
But rigid looks of chaste austerity,
And noble grace that dash'd brute vio-
    lence
With sudden adoration and blank awe?
So dear to Heav'n is saintly chastity,
That when a soul is found sincerely so,
A thousand liveried angels lackey her,
Driving far off each thing of sin and
    guilt,
And in clear dream, and solemn vision,
Tell her of things that no gross ear can
    hear,
Till oft converse with heav'nly habitants
Begins to cast a beam on th' outward
    shape,
The unpolluted temple of the mind,
And turns it by degrees to the soul's es-
    sence,
Till all be made immortal: but when
    lust,
By unchaste looks, loose gestures, and foul
    talk,
But most by lewd and lavish act of sin,
Lets in defilement to the inward parts,
The soul grows clotted by contagion,
Embodies, and imbrutes, till she quite lose
The divine property of her first being.
Such are those thick and gloomy shadows
    damp
Oft seen in charnel vaults, and sepulchres,
Ling'ring and sitting by a new-made
    grave,
As loath to leave the body that it loved,
And link'd itself by carnal sensuality
To a degenerate and degraded state.
    2 Br. How charming is divine philos-
    ophy!
Not harsh, and crabbed, as dull fools sup-
    pose,
But musical as is Apollo's lute,

And a perpetual feast of nectar'd sweets,
Where no crude surfeit reigns.
    1 Br. List, list, I hear
Some far-off halloo break the silent air.
    2 Br. Methought so too; what should
    it be?
    1 Br. For certain
Either some one like us night-founder'd
    here,
Or else some neighbor woodman, or, at
    worst,
Some roving robber calling to his fellows.
    2 Br. Heaven keep my sister! Again,
    again, and near!
Best draw, and stand upon our guard.
    1 Br. I'll halloo;
If he be friendly, he comes well; if not,
Defence is a good cause, and Heav'n be
    for us.

Enter the ATTENDANT SPIRIT, *habited like
a shepherd.*

That halloo I should know, what are you?
    speak:
Come not too near, you fall on iron stakes
    else.
    Spir. What voice is that? my young
    Lord? speak again.
    2 Br. O brother, 'tis my father's shep-
    herd, sure.
    1 Br. Thyrsis! Whose artful strains
    have oft delay'd
The huddling brook to hear his madrigal,
And sweeten'd every musk-rose of the
    dale.
How cam'st thou here, good swain? hath
    any ram
Slipt from the fold, or young kid lost his
    dam,
Or straggling wether the pent flock for-
    sook?
How could'st thou find this dark seques-
    ter'd nook?
    Spir. O my loved master's heir, and his
    next joy,
I came not here on such a trivial toy
As a stray'd ewe, or to pursue the stealth
Of pilfering wolf; not all the fleecy
    wealth
That doth enrich these downs is worth a
    thought
To this my errand, and the care it brought.

But, oh my virgin Lady, where is she?
How chance she is not in your company?
  1 Br. To tell thee sadly, Shepherd, without blame,
Or our neglect, we lost her as we came.
  Spir. Aye me unhappy! then my fears are true.
  1 Br. What fears, good Thyrsis? Prithee briefly shew.
  Spir. I'll tell ye; 'tis not vain or fabulous,
Though so esteem'd by shallow ignorance,
What the sage poets, taught by th' heavenly Muse,
Storied of old in high immortal verse,
Of dire chimæras, and enchanted isles,
And rifted rocks whose entrance leads to Hell;
For such there be, but unbelief is blind.
  Within the navel of this hideous wood,
Immured in cypress shades a sorcerer dwells,
Of Bacchus and of Circe born, great Comus,
Deep skill'd in all his mother's witcheries;
And here to every thirsty wanderer
By sly enticement gives his baneful cup,
With many murmurs mix'd, whose pleasing poison
The visage quite transforms of him that drinks,
And the inglorious likeness of a beast
Fixes instead, unmoulding reason's mintage
Charácter'd in the face: this I have learnt
Tending my flocks hard by i' th' hilly crofts,
That brow this bottom-glade, whence, night by night,
He and his monstrous rout are heard to howl,
Like stabled wolves, or tigers at their prey,
Doing abhorrèd rites to Hecate
In their obscured haunts of inmost bowers.
Yet have they many baits, and guileful spells,
T' inveigle and invite th' unwary sense
Of them that pass unweeting by the way.
This evening late, by then the chewing flocks
Had ta'en their supper on the savory herb
Of knot-grass dew-besprent, and were in fold,
I sat me down to watch upon a bank
With ivy canopied, and interwove
With flaunting honeysuckle, and began,
Wrapt in a pleasing fit of melancholy,
To meditate my rural minstrelsy,
Till Fancy had her fill; but ere a close,
The wonted roar was up amidst the woods,
And fill'd the air with barbarous dissonance;
At which I ceased, and listen'd them a while,
Till an unusual stop of sudden silence
Gave respite to the drowsy frighted steeds,
That draw the litter of close-curtain'd sleep;
At last a soft and solemn-breathing sound
Rose like a steam of rich-distill'd perfumes,
And stole upon the air, that even Silence
Was took ere she was ware, and wish'd she might
Deny her nature, and be never more,
Still to be so displaced. I was all ear,
And took in strains that might create a soul
Under the ribs of death: but oh ere long
Too well I did perceive it was the voice
Of my most honor'd Lady, your dear sister.
Amazed I stood, harrow'd with grief and fear,
And O poor hapless nightingale, thought I,
How sweet thou sing'st, how near the deadly snare!
Then down the lawns I ran with headlong haste,
Through paths and turnings often trod by day,
Till guided by mine ear I found the place,
Where that damn'd wizard, hid in sly disguise
(For so by certain signs I knew), had met
Already, ere my best speed could prevent,
The aidless innocent lady his wish'd prey;
Who gently ask'd if he had seen such two,
Supposing him some neighbor villager.
Longer I durst not stay, but soon I guess'd
Ye were the two she meant; with that I sprung

Into swift flight, till I had found you here,
But further know I not.
  2 BR. O night and shades,
How are ye join'd with Hell in triple knot,
Against th' unarmèd weakness of one virgin,
Alone and helpless! Is this the confidence
You gave me, brother?
  1 BR. Yes, and keep it still,
Lean on it safely; not a period
Shall be unsaid for me: against the threats
Of malice or of sorcery, or that power
Which erring men call Chance, this I hold firm,
Virtue may be assail'd, but never hurt,
Surprised by unjust force, but not enthrall'd;
Yea even that which Mischief meant most harm,
Shall in the happy trial prove most glory:
But evil on itself shall back recoil,
And mix no more with goodness, when at last
Gather'd like scum, and settled to itself,
It shall be in eternal restless change
Self-fed, and self-consumed: if this fail,
The pillar'd firmament is rottenness,
And earth's base built on stubble. But come, let's on.
Against the opposing will and arm of Heaven
May never this just sword be lifted up;
But for that damn'd magician, let him be girt
With all the grisly legions that troop
Under the sooty flag of Acheron,
Harpies and Hydras, or all the monstrous forms
'Twixt Africa and Ind, I'll find him out,
And force him to restore his purchase back,
Or drag him by the curls to a foul death,
Cursed as his life.
  SPIR. Alas! good vent'rous youth,
I love thy courage yet, and bold emprise;
But here thy sword can do thee little stead;
Far other arms and other weapons must
Be those that quell the might of hellish charms:
He with his bare wand can unthread thy joints,
And crumble all thy sinews.
  1 BR. Why prithee, Shepherd,
How durst thou then thyself approach so near,
As to make this relation?
  SPIR. Care and utmost shifts
How to secure the lady from surprisal
Brought to my mind a certain shepherd lad,
Of small regard to see to, yet well skill'd
In every virtuous plant and healing herb,
That spreads her verdant leaf to th' morning ray:
He loved me well, and oft would beg me sing,
Which when I did, he on the tender grass
Would sit, and hearken e'en to ecstasy,
And in requital ope his leathern scrip,
And show me simples of a thousand names,
Telling their strange and vigorous faculties.
Amongst the rest a small unsightly root,
But of divine effect, he cull'd me out;
The leaf was darkish, and had prickles on it,
But in another country, as he said,
Bore a bright golden flow'r, but not in this soil:
Unknown, and like esteem'd, and the dull swain
Treads on it daily with his clouted shoon:
And yet more med'cinal is it than that moly
That Hermes once to wise Ulysses gave;
He call'd it Hæmony, and gave it me,
And bade me keep it as of sovereign use
'Gainst all enchantments, mildew, blast, or damp,
Or ghastly Furies' apparition.
I pursed it up, but little reck'ning made,
Till now that this extremity compell'd;
But now I find it true, for by this means
I knew the foul enchanter though disguised,
Enter'd the very lime-twigs of his spells,
And yet came off: if you have this about you
(As I will give you when we go), you may
Boldly assault the necromancer's hall;
Where if he be, with dauntless hardihood,
And brandish'd blade rush on him, break his glass,
And shed the luscious liquor on the ground,

But seize his wand; though he and his
  cursed crew
Fierce sign of battle make, and menace
  high,
Or like the sons of Vulcan vomit smoke,
Yet will they soon retire, if he but shrink.
  1 BR. Thyrsis, lead on apace, I'll fol-
    low thee,
And some good angel bear a shield before
  us.

*The scene changes to a stately palace, set out
with all manner of deliciousness; soft
music, tables spread with all dainties.
COMUS appears with his rabble, and the
LADY set in an enchanted chair, to whom
he offers his glass, which she puts by, and
goes about to rise.*

  COM. Nay, Lady, sit; if I but wave
    this wand,
Your nerves are all chain'd up in alabas-
  ter,
And you a statue, or as Daphne was,
Root-bound, that fled Apollo.
  LAD. Fool, do not boast,
Thou canst not touch the freedom of my
  mind
With all thy charms, although this cor-
  poral rind
Thou hast immanacled, while Heaven sees
  good.
  COM. Why are you vext, Lady? why
    do you frown?
Here dwell no frowns nor anger; from
  these gates
Sorrow flies far; see, here be all the
  pleasures
That fancy can beget on youthful thoughts,
When the fresh blood grows lively, and re-
  turns
Brisk as the April buds in primrose sea-
  son.
And first behold this cordial julep here,
That flames, and dances in his crystal
  bounds,
With spirits of balm, and fragrant syrups
  mix'd.
Not that Nepenthes, which the wife of
  Thone
In Egypt gave to Jove-born Helena,
Is of such pow'r to stir up joy as this,
To life so friendly, or so cool to thirst.

Why should you be so cruel to yourself,
And to those dainty limbs which Nature
  lent
For gentle usage, and soft delicacy?
But you invert the covenants of her trust
And harshly deal, like an ill borrower,
With that which you received on other
  terms;
Scorning the unexempt condition
By which all mortal frailty must subsist,
Refreshment after toil, ease after pain,
That have been tired all day without re-
  past,
And timely rest have wanted; but, fair
  virgin,
This will restore all soon.
  LAD. 'Twill not, false traitor,
'Twill not restore the truth and honesty
That thou hast banish'd from thy tongue
  with lies.
Was this the cottage, and the safe abode
Thou toldst me of? What grim aspects are
  these,
These ugly-headed monsters? Mercy guard
  me!
Hence with thy brew'd enchantments, foul
  deceiver!
Hast thou betray'd my credulous innocence
With visor'd falsehood and base forgery?
And would'st thou seek again to trap me
  here
With liquorish baits fit to ensnare a brute?
Were it a draft for Juno when she ban-
  quets,
I would not taste thy treasonous offer;
  none
But such as are good men can give good
  things,
And that which is not good, is not de-
  licious
To a well-govern'd and wise appetite.
  COM. O foolishness of men! that lend
    their ears
To those budge doctors of the Stoic fur,
And fetch their precepts from the Cynic
  tub,
Praising the lean and sallow Abstinence.
Wherefore did Nature pour her bounties
  forth,
With such a full and unwithdrawing hand,
Covering the earth with odors, fruits, and
  flocks,

Thronging the seas with spawn innumerable,
But all to please, and sate the curious taste?
And set to work millions of spinning worms,
That in their green shops weave the smooth-hair'd silk
To deck her sons; and that no corner might
Be vacant of her plenty, in her own loins
She hutch'd th' all-worshipp'd ore, and precious gems,
To store her children with: if all the world
Should in a pet of temperance feed on pulse,
Drink the clear stream, and nothing wear but frieze,
Th' All-giver would be unthank'd, would be unprais'd,
Not half his riches known, and yet despised;
And we should serve him as a grudging master,
As a penurious niggard of his wealth;
And live like Nature's bastards, not her sons,
Who would be quite surcharged with her own weight,
And strangled with her waste fertility;
Th' earth cumber'd, and the wingèd air dark'd with plumes,
The herds would over-multitude their lords,
The sea o'erfraught would swell, and th' unsought diamonds
Would so emblaze the forehead of the deep,
And so bestud with stars, that they below
Would grow inured to light, and come at last
To gaze upon the sun with shameless brows.
List, Lady, be not coy, and be not cozen'd
With that same vaunted name Virginity.
Beauty is Nature's coin, must not be hoarded,
But must be current, and the good thereof
Consists in mutual and partaken bliss,
Unsavory in th' enjoyment of itself;
If you let slip time, like a neglected rose
It withers on the stalk with languish'd head.
Beauty is Nature's brag, and must be shown
In courts, at feasts, and high solemnities,
Where most may wonder at the workmanship;
It is for homely features to keep home,
They had their name thence; coarse complexions,
And cheeks of sorry grain, will serve to ply
The sampler, and to tease the huswife's wool.
What need a vermeil-tinctured lip for that,
Love-darting eyes, or tresses like the morn?
There was another meaning in these gifts;
Think what, and be advised, you are but young yet.

LAD. I had not thought to have unlockt my lips
In this unhallow'd air, but that this juggler
Would think to charm my judgment, as mine eyes,
Obtruding false rules prank'd in reason's garb.
I hate when vice can bolt her arguments,
And virtue has no tongue to check her pride.
Impostor, do not charge most innocent Nature,
As if she would her children should be riotous
With her abundance; she, good cateress,
Means her provision only to the good,
That live according to her sober laws,
And holy dictate of spare temperance:
If every just man, that now pines with want,
Had but a moderate and beseeming share
Of that which lewdly-pamper'd luxury
Now heaps upon some few with vast excess,
Nature's full blessings would be well dispensed
In unsuperfluous even proportion,
And she no whit encumber'd with her store;
And then the Giver would be better thank'd,

His praise due paid; for swinish gluttony
Ne'er looks to Heav'n amidst his gorgeous feast,
But with besotted base ingratitude
Crams, and blasphemes his feeder. Shall I go on?
Or have I said enow? To him that dares
Arm his profane tongue with contemptuous words
Against the sun-clad power of Chastity,
Fain would I something say, yet to what end?
Thou hast nor ear, nor soul to apprehend
The sublime notion, and high mystery,
That must be utter'd to unfold the sage
And serious doctrine of Virginity,
And thou art worthy that thou shouldst not know
More happiness than this thy present lot.
Enjoy your dear wit, and gay rhetoric,
That hath so well been taught her dazzling fence;
Thou art not fit to hear thyself convinced;
Yet should I try, the uncontrollèd worth
Of this pure cause would kindle my rapt spirits
To such a flame of sacred vehemence,
That dumb things would be moved to sympathize,
And the brute earth would lend her nerves, and shake,
Till all thy magic structures rear'd so high,
Were shatter'd into heaps o'er thy false head.

Com. She fables not: I feel that I do fear
Her words set off by some superior power:
And though not mortal, yet a cold shudd'ring dew
Dips me all o'er, as when the wrath of Jove
Speaks thunder, and the chains of Erebus,
To some of Saturn's crew. I must dissemble,
And try her yet more strongly. Come, no more,
This is mere moral babble, and direct
Against the canon laws of our foundation;
I must not suffer this; yet 'tis but the lees
And settlings of a melancholy blood:
But this will cure all straight; one sip of this
Will bathe the drooping spirits in delight,
Beyond the bliss of dreams. Be wise, and taste.—

The BROTHERS *rush in with swords drawn, wrest his glass out of his hand, and break it against the ground; his rout make sign of resistance, but are all driven in. The* ATTENDANT SPIRIT *comes in.*

SPIR. What, have you let the false enchanter 'scape?
Oh ye mistook, ye should have snatch'd his wand,
And bound him fast; without his rod reversed,
And backward mutters of dissevering power,
We cannot free the Lady that sits here
In stony fetters fix'd, and motionless:
Yet stay, be not disturb'd: now I bethink me,
Some other means I have which may be used,
Which once of Meliboeus old I learnt,
The soothest shepherd that e'er piped on plains.
There is a gentle nymph not far from hence,
That with moist curb sways the smooth Severn stream,
Sabrina is her name, a virgin pure;
Whilom she was the daughter of Locrine,
That had the sceptre from his father Brute.
She, guiltless damsel, flying the mad pursuit
Of her enragèd stepdame Guendolen,
Commended her fair innocence to the flood,
That stay'd her flight with his cross-flowing course.
The water-nymphs that in the bottom play'd,
Held up their pearlèd wrists, and took her in,
Bearing her straight to aged Nereus' hall,
Who piteous of her woes, rear'd her lank head,
And gave her to his daughters to imbathe
In nectar'd lavers strow'd with asphodil,
And through the porch and inlet of each sense

Dropp'd in ambrosial oils, till she revived,
And underwent a quick immortal change,
Made Goddess of the river: still she retains
Her maiden gentleness, and oft at eve
Visits the herds along the twilight meadows,
Helping all urchin blasts, and ill-luck signs
That the shrewd meddling elf delights to make,
Which she with precious vial'd liquors heals;
For which the shepherds at their festivals
Carol her goodness loud in rustic lays,
And throw sweet garland wreaths into her stream
Of pansies, pinks, and gaudy daffodils.
And, as the old swain said, she can unlock
The clasping charm, and thaw the numbing spell,
If she be right invoked in warbled song;
For maidenhood she loves, and will be swift
To aid a virgin, such as was herself,
In hard-besetting need; this will I try,
And add the pow'r of some adjuring verse.

Song.

Sabrina fair,
   Listen where thou art sitting
Under the glassy, cool, translucent wave,
   In twisted braids of lilies knitting
The loose train of thy amber-dropping hair;
   Listen for dear honor's sake,
   Goddess of the silver lake,
     Listen and save.
Listen and appear to us
In name of great Oceanus,
By th' earth-shaking Neptune's mace,
And Tethys' grave majestic pace,
By hoary Nereus' wrinkled look,
And the Carpathian wizard's hook,
By scaly Triton's winding shell,
And old soothsaying Glaucus' spell,
By Leucothea's lovely hands,
And her son that rules the strands,
By Thetis' tinsel-slipper'd feet,
And the songs of sirens sweet,
By dead Parthenope's dear tomb,
And fair Ligea's golden comb,

Wherewith she sits on diamond rocks,
Sleeking her soft alluring locks,
By all the nymphs that nightly dance
Upon thy streams with wily glance,
Rise, rise, and heave thy rosy head
From thy coral-paven bed,
And bridle in thy headlong wave,
Till thou our summons answer'd have.
     Listen and save.

Sabrina *rises, attended by water-nymphs, and sings.*

By the rushy-fringèd bank,
Where grows the willow and the osier dank,
   My sliding chariot stays,
Thick set with agate, and the azurn sheen
Of turkis blue, and emerald green,
   That in the channel strays;
Whilst from off the waters fleet,
Thus I set my printless feet
O'er the cowslip's velvet head,
   That bends not as I tread;
Gentle Swain, at thy request
   I am here.
  Spir. Goddess dear,
We implore thy pow'rful hand
To undo the charmèd band
Of true virgin here distrest,
Through the force, and through the wile
Of unbless'd enchanter vile.
  Sabr. Shepherd, 'tis my office best
To help ensnarèd chastity:
Brightest Lady, look on me;
Thus I sprinkle on thy breast
Drops that from my fountain pure
I have kept of precious cure,
Thrice upon thy finger's tip,
Thrice upon thy rubied lip;
Next this marble venom'd seat,
Smear'd with gums of glutinous heat,
I touch with chaste palms moist and cold:
Now the spell hath lost his hold;
And I must haste ere morning hour
To wait in Amphitrite's bow'r.

Sabrina *descends, and the* Lady *rises out of her seat.*

  Spir. Virgin, daughter of Locrine,
Sprung of old Anchises' line,

May thy brimmèd waves for this
Their full tribute never miss
From a thousand petty rills,
That tumble down the snowy hills:
Summer drouth, or singèd air
Never scorch thy tresses fair,
Nor wet October's torrent flood
Thy molten crystal fill with mud;
May thy billows roll ashore
The beryl, and the golden ore;
May thy lofty head be crown'd
With many a tow'r and terrace round,
And here and there thy banks upon
With groves of myrrh and cinnamon.
  Come, Lady, while Heav'n lends us grace,
Let us fly this cursèd place,
Lest the sorcerer us entice
With some other new device.
Not a waste or needless sound
Till we come to holier ground;
I shall be your faithful guide
Through this gloomy covert wide,
And not many furlongs thence
Is your Father's residence,
Where this night are met in state
Many a friend to gratulate
His wish'd presence, and beside
All the swains that there abide,
With jigs and rural dance resort;
We shall catch them at their sport,
And our sudden coming there
Will double all their mirth and cheer;
Come let us haste, the stars grow high,
But night sits monarch yet in the mid sky.

The scene changes, presenting Ludlow town and the President's castle; then come in country dancers, after them the ATTENDANT SPIRIT, *with the Two* BROTHERS *and the* LADY.

SONG.

SPIR. Back, Shepherds, back, enough your play,
Till next sunshine holiday;
Here be without duck or nod
Other trippings to be trod
Of lighter toes, and such court guise
As Mercury did first devise,
With the mincing Dryades,
On the lawns, and on the leas.

This second Song presents them to their Father and Mother.

Noble Lord, and Lady bright,
I have brought ye new delight,
Here behold so goodly grown
Three fair branches of your own;
Heav'n hath timely tried their youth,
Their faith, their patience, and their truth,
And sent them here through hard assays
With a crown of deathless praise,
To triumph in victorious dance
O'er sensual folly, and intemperance.

The dances ended, the SPIRIT *epiloguizes.*

  SPIR. To the ocean now I fly,
And those happy climes that lie
Where day never shuts his eye,
Up in the broad fields of the sky:
There I suck the liquid air
All amidst the gardens fair
Of Hesperus, and his daughters three
That sing about the golden tree:
Along the crispèd shades and bowers
  Revels the spruce and jocund Spring,
The Graces, and the rosy-bosom'd Hours,
  Thither all their bounties bring;
There eternal Summer dwells,
  And west winds, with musky wing,
  About the cedarn alleys fling
Nard and cassia's balmy smells.
Iris there with humid bow
Waters the odorous banks, that blow
Flowers of more mingled hue
Than her purfled scarf can shew,
And drenches with Elysian dew
(List, mortals, if your ears be true),
Beds of hyacinth and roses,
Where young Adonis oft reposes,
Waxing well of his deep wound
In slumber soft, and on the ground
Sadly sits th' Assyrian queen;
But far above in spangled sheen
Celestial Cupid her famed son advanced,
Holds his dear Psyche sweet entranced,
After her wand'ring labors long,
Till free consent the Gods among
Make her his eternal bride,
And from her fair unspotted side
Two blissful twins are to be born,
Youth and Joy; so Jove hath sworn.
  But now my task is smoothly done,
I can fly, or I can run

Quickly to the green earth's end,
Where the bow'd welkin slow doth bend,
And from thence can soar as soon
To the corners of the moon.
  Mortals, that would follow me,
Love Virtue, she alone is free;
She can teach ye how to climb
Higher than the sphery chime:
Or, if Virtue feeble were,
Heav'n itself would stoop to her.
                    JOHN MILTON.

FAREWELL TO THE FAIRIES

FAREWELL rewards and Fairies!
  Good housewives now may say;
For now foule sluts in dairies
  Doe fare as well as they:
And though they sweepe their hearths no
      less
  Than mayds were wont to doe,
Yet who of late for cleanliness
  Finds sixe-pence in her shoe?

Lament, lament old Abbies,
  The fairies lost command;
They did but change priests babies,
  But some have changed your land:
And all your children stoln from thence
  Are now growne Puritanes,
Who live as changelings ever since,
  For love of your demaines.

At morning and at evening both
  You merry were and glad,
So little care of sleepe and sloth,
  These prettie ladies had.
When Tom came home from labour,
  Or Ciss to milking rose,
Then merrily went their tabour,
  And nimbly went their toes.

Witness those rings and roundelayes
  Of theirs, which yet remaine;
Were footed in Queene Maries dayes
  On many a grassy playne.
But since of late Elizabeth
  And later James came in;
They never danced on any heath,
  As when the time hath bin.

By which wee note the fairies
  Were of the old profession:
Their songs were *Ave Maries*,
  Their dances were procession.
But now, alas! they all are dead,
  Or gone beyond the seas,
Or farther for religion fled,
  Or else they take their ease.

A tell-tale in their company
  They never could endure;
And whoso kept not secretly
  Their mirth, was punish'd sure:
It was a just and Christian deed
  To pinch such blacke and blue:
Oh how the common-welth doth need
  Such justices as you!

Now they have left our quarters;
  A Register they have,
Who can preserve their charters;
  A man both wise and grave.
An hundred of their merry pranks,
  By one that I could name
Are kept in store; con twenty thanks
  To William for the same.

To William Churne of Staffordshire
  Give laud and praises due,
Who every meale can mend your cheare
  With tales both old and true:
To William all give audience,
  And pray yee for his noddle:
For all the fairies evidence
  Were lost, if it were addle.
                    RICHARD CORBET.

KILMENY.

BONNY Kilmeny gaed up the glen;
But it wasna to meet Duneira's men,
Nor the rosy monk of the isle to see,
For Kilmeny was pure as pure could be.
It was only to hear the Yorlin sing,
And pu' the cress-flower round the spring;
The scarlet hyppe, and the hindberry,
And the nut that hung frae the hazel
    tree;
For Kilmeny was pure as pure could be.
But lang may her minny look o'er the
    wa',
And lang may she seek i' the greenwood
    shaw;
Lang the laird of Duneira blame,
And lang, lang greet or Kilmeny come
    hame!

When many lang day had come and fled,
When grief grew calm, and hope was
   dead,
When mess for Kilmeny's soul had been
   sung,
When the bedes-man had prayed, and the
   deadbell rung:
Late, late in a gloamin when all was
   still,
When the fringe was red on the westlin
   hill,
The wood was sere, the moon i' the wane,
The reek o' the cot hung o'er the plain,
Like a little wee cloud in the world its
   lane;
When the ingle lowed with an eiry leme,
Late, late in the gloamin Kilmeny came
   hame!

"Kilmeny, Kilmeny, where have you
   been?
Lang hae we sought baith holt and dean;
By linn, by ford, and greenwood tree,
Yet you are halesome and fair to see.
Where gat you that joup o' the lily
   sheen?
That bonny snood o' the birk sae green?
And these roses the fairest that ever was
   seen?—
Kilmeny, Kilmeny, where have you
   been?"

Kilmeny looked up with a lovely grace,
But nae smile was seen on Kilmeny's
   face;
As still was her look, and as still was
   her ee,
As the stillness that lay on the emerant
   lea,
Or the mist that sleeps on a waveless
   sea.
For Kilmeny had been she ken'd not
   where,
And Kilmeny had seen what she could
   not declare;
Kilmeny had been where the cock never
   crew,
Where the rain never fell, and the wind
   never blew.
But it seemed as the harp of the sky had
   rung,
And the airs of heaven played round her
   tongue,
When she spake of the lovely forms she
   had seen,
And a land where sin had never been;
A land of love, and a land of light,
Withouten sun, or moon, or night;
Where the river swa'd a living stream,
And the light a pure and cloudless beam;
The land of vision it would seem,
A still, an everlasting dream.

In yon greenwood there is a waik,
And in that waik there is a wene,
And in that wene there is a maike,
That neither has flesh, nor blood, nor bane;
And down in yon greenwood he walks his
   lane.

In that green wene Kilmeny lay,
Her bosom happ'd wi' flowerets gay;
But the air was soft and the silence deep,
And bonny Kilmeny fell sound asleep.
She kenned nae mair, nor open'd her ee,
Till waked by the hymns of a far coun-
   trye.

She woke on a couch of the silk sae
   slim,
All striped wi' the bars of the rainbow's
   rim;
And lovely beings round were rife,
Who erst had travelled mortal life;
And aye they smiled, and 'gan to speer,
"What spirit has brought this mortal
   here?"

"Lang have I ranged the world wide,"
A meek and reverend fere replied;
"Baith night and day I have watched the
   fair
Eident a thousand years and mair.
Yes, I have watched o'er ilk degree,
Wherever blooms femenitye;
And sinless virgin, free of stain
In mind and body, fand I nane.
Never, since the banquet of time,
Found I a virgin in her prime,
Till late this bonnie maiden I saw,
As spotless as the morning snaw:
Full twenty years she has lived as free
As the spirits that sojourn in this coun-
   trye:
I have brought her away frae the snares of
   men,
That sin or death she never may ken."

They clasped her waist and her hands sae
 fair,
They kissed her cheek, and they kemed
 her hair;
And round came many a blooming fere,
Saying, "Bonny Kilmeny, ye're welcome
 here!
Women are freed of the littand scorn:—
O, blessed be the day Kilmeny was born!
Now shall the land of the spirits see,
Now shall it ken what a woman may be!
Many lang year in sorrow and pain,
Many lang year through the world we've
 gane,
Commissioned to watch fair womankind,
For it's they who nurse the immortal
 mind.
We have watched their steps as the dawn-
 ing shone,
And deep in the greenwood walks alone;
By lily bower and silken bed,
The viewless tears have o'er them shed;
Have soothed their ardent minds to sleep,
Or left the couch of love to weep.
We have seen! we have seen! but the time
 maun come,
And the angels will weep at the day of
 doom!

"O, would the fairest of mortal kind
Aye keep these holy truths in mind,
That kindred spirits their motions see,
Who watch their ways with anxious ee,
And grieve for the guilt of humanitye!
O, sweet to Heaven the maiden's prayer,
And the sigh that heaves a bosom sae fair!
And dear to Heaven the words of truth,
And the praise of virtue frae beauty's
 mouth!
And dear to the viewless forms of air,
The mind that kythes as the body fair!

"O bonny Kilmeny! free frae stain,
If ever you seek the world again,
That world of sin, of sorrow, and fear,
O, tell of the joys that are waiting here;
And tell of the signs you shall shortly see;
Of the times that are now, and the times
 that shall be."

They lifted Kilmeny, they led her away,
And she walked in the light of a sunless
 day:
The sky was a dome of crystal bright,
The fountain of vision, and fountain of
 light:
The emerant fields were of dazzling glow,
And the flowers of everlasting blow.
Then deep in the stream her body they
 laid,
That her youth and beauty never might
 fade;
And they smiled on heaven, when they
 saw her lie
In the stream of life that wandered by.
And she heard a song, she heard it sung,
She kend not where; but sae sweetly it
 rung,
It fell on her ear like a dream of the
 morn:—
"O, blest be the day Kilmeny was
 born!
Now shall the land of the spirits see,
Now shall it ken what a woman may be!
The sun that shines on the world sae
 bright,
A borrowed gleid frae the fountain of
 light;
And the moon that sleeks the sky sae dun,
Like a gouden bow, or a beamless sun,
Shall wear away and be seen nae mair,
And the angels shall miss them travelling
 the air.
But lang, lang after baith night and day,
When the sun and the world have fled
 away;
When the sinner has gane to his waesome
 doom,
Kilmeny shall smile in eternal bloom!"

They bore her away, she wist not how,
For she felt not arm nor rest below;
But so swift they wained her through the
 light,
'Twas like the motion of sound or sight;
They seemed to split the gales of air,
And yet nor gale nor breeze was there.
Unnumbered groves below them grew;
They came, they past, and backward
 flew,
Like floods of blossoms gliding on,
A moment seen, in a moment gone.
O, never vales to mortal view
Appeared like those o'er which they flew!
That land to human spirits given,
The lowermost vales of the storied heaven;

From thence they can view the world
    below,
And heaven's blue gates with sapphires
    glow,
More glory yet unmeet to know.

They bore her far to a mountain green,
To see what mortal never had seen;
And they seated her high on a purple
    sward,
And bade her heed what she saw and
    heard;
And note the changes the spirits wrought,
For now she lived in the land of
    thought.
She looked, and she saw nor sun nor skies,
But a crystal dome of a thousand dyes;
She looked, and she saw nae land aright,
But an endless whirl of glory and light:
And radiant beings went and came
Far swifter than wind, or the linkèd flame.
She hid her een frae the dazzling view;
She looked again, and the scene was new.

She saw a sun on a summer sky,
And clouds of amber sailing by;
A lovely land beneath her lay,
And that land had lakes and mountains
    gray;
And that land had valleys and hoary
    piles,
And marlèd seas and a thousand isles.
Its fields were speckled, its forests green,
And its lakes were all of the dazzling
    sheen,
Like magic mirrors, where slumbering lay
The sun and the sky, and the cloudlet
    gray;
Which heaved and trembled, and gently
    swung,
On every shore they seemed to be hung:
For there they were seen on their down-
    ward plain
A thousand times, and a thousand again;
In winding lake, and placid firth,
Little peaceful heavens in the bosom of
    earth.

Kilmeny sighed and seemed to grieve,
For she found her heart to that land did
    cleave;
She saw the corn wave on the vale,
She saw the deer run down the dale;
She saw the plaid and the broad claymore,
And the brows that the badge of freedom
    bore;—
And she thought she had seen the land be-
    fore.

She saw a lady sit on a throne,
The fairest that ever the sun shone on:
A lion licked her hand of milk,
And she held him in a leish of silk;
And a leifu' maiden stood at her knee,
With a silver wand and melting ee;
Her sovereign shield till love stole in,
And poisoned all the fount within.

Then a gruff untoward bedes-man came,
And hundit the lion on his dame;
And the guardian maid wi' the dauntless
    ee,
She dropped a tear, and left her knee;
And she saw till the queen frae the lion
    fled,
Till the bonniest flower of the world lay
    dead;
A coffin was set on a distant plain,
And she saw the red blood fall like rain:
Then bonny Kilmeny's heart grew sair,
And she turned away, and could look nae
    mair.

Then the gruff grim carle girnèd amain,
And they trampled him down, but he rose
    again;
And he baited the lion to deeds of weir,
Till he lapped the blood to the kingdom
    dear;
And weening his head was danger-preef,
When crowned with the rose and clover
    leaf,
He gowled at the carle, and chased him
    away
To feed wi' the deer on the mountain
    gray.
He gowled at the carle, and he gecked at
    Heaven;
But his mark was set, and his arles given.
Kilmeny a while her een withdrew;
She looked again, and the scene was new.

She saw below her fair unfurled
One half of all the glowing world,
Where oceans rolled, and rivers ran,
To bound the aims of sinful man.

She saw a people, fierce and fell,
Burst frae their bounds like fiends of hell;
There lilies grew, and the eagle flew,
And she herked on her ravening crew,
Till the cities and towers were wrapt in a blaze,
And the thunder it roared o'er the lands and the seas.
The widows they wailed, and the red blood ran,
And she threatened an end to the race of man:
She never lened, nor stood in awe,
Till caught by the lion's deadly paw.
Oh! then the eagle swinked for life,
And brainzelled up a mortal strife;
But flew she north, or flew she south,
She met wi' the gowl of the lion's mouth.

With a mooted wing and waefu' maen,
The eagle sought her eiry again;
But lang may she cower in her bloody nest,
And lang, lang sleek her wounded breast,
Before she sey another flight,
To play wi' the norland lion's might.

But to sing the sights Kilmeny saw,
So far surpassing nature's law,
The singer's voice wad sink away,
And the string of his harp wad cease to play.
But she saw till the sorrows of man were by,
And all was love and harmony;—
Till the stars of heaven fell calmly away,
Like the flakes of snaw on a winter's day.

Then Kilmeny begged again to see
The friends she had left in her own countrye,
To tell of the place where she had been,
And the glories that lay in the land unseen;
To warn the living maidens fair,
The loved of Heaven, the spirits' care,
That all whose minds unmeled remain
Shall bloom in beauty when time is gane.

With distant music, soft and deep,
They lulled Kilmeny sound asleep;
And when she awakened, she lay her lane,
All happed with flowers in the greenwood wene.

When seven lang years had come and fled;
When grief was calm, and hope was dead;
When scarce was remembered Kilmeny's name,
Late, late in a gloamin Kilmeny came hame.
And O, her beauty was fair to see,
But still and steadfast was her ee!
Such beauty bard may never declare,
For there was no pride nor passion there;
And the soft desire of maidens' een
In that mild face could never be seen.
Her seymar was the lily flower,
And her cheek the moss-rose in the shower;
And her voice like the distant melodye,
That floats along the twilight sea.
But she loved to raike the lanely glen,
And keep afar frae the haunts of men;
Her holy hymns unheard to sing,
To suck the flowers and drink the spring.
But wherever her peaceful form appeared,
The wild beasts of the hills were cheered;
The wolf played blythely round the field,
The lordly byson lowed and kneeled;
The dun deer wooed with manner bland,
And cowered aneath her lily hand.
And when at eve the woodlands rung,
When hymns of other worlds she sung
In ecstasy of sweet devotion,
O, then the glen was all in motion!
The wild beasts of the forest came,
Broke from their boughts and faulds the tame,
And goved around, charmed and amazed;
Even the dull cattle crooned and gazed,
And murmured and looked with anxious pain.
For something the mystery to explain.
The buzzard came with the throstle-cock;
The corby left her houf in the rock;
The blackbird alang wi' the eagle flew;
The hind came tripping o'er the dew;
The wolf and the kid their raike began,
And the tod, and the lamb, and the leveret ran;
The hawk and the hern attour them hung,
And the merl and the mavis forhooyed their young;
And all in a peaceful ring were hurled:—
It was like an eve in a sinless world!

When a month and day had come and
    gane,
Kilmeny sought the greenwood wene;
There laid her down on the leaves sae
    green,
And Kilmeny on earth was never mair
    seen.
But O, the words that fell from her
    mouth,
Were words of wonder and words of
    truth!
But all the land were in fear and dread,
For they kendna whether she was living
    or dead.
It wasna her hame, and she couldna re-
    main;
She left this world of sorrow and pain,
And returned to the land of thought again.
                  JAMES HOGG.

SONG

FROM "THE MERCHANT OF VENICE."

TELL me where is fancy bred,
  Or in the heart, or in the head?
How begot, how nourishèd?
  Reply, reply.

It is engender'd in the eyes,
  With gazing fed; and fancy dies
In the cradle where it lies:
  Let us all ring fancy's knell;
  I'll begin it,—Ding, dong, bell.
      Ding, dong, bell.
            WILLIAM SHAKESPEARE.

ALICE BRAND.

MERRY it is in the good greenwood,
  When the mavis and merle are sing-
    ing,
When the deer sweeps by, and the hounds
    are in cry,
  And the hunter's horn is ringing.

"O Alice Brand, my native land
  Is lost for love of you;
And we must hold by wood and wold,
  As outlaws wont to do.

"O Alice, 'twas all for thy locks so bright,
  And 'twas all for thine eyes so blue,
That on the night of our luckless flight,
  Thy brother bold I slew.

"Now must I teach to hew the beech,
  The hand that held the glaive,
For leaves to spread our lowly bed,
  And stakes to fence our cave.

"And for vest of pall, thy fingers small,
  That wont on harp to stray,
A cloak must shear from the slaughter'd
    deer,
  To keep the cold away."—

"O Richard! if my brother died,
  'Twas but a fatal chance;
For darkling was the battle tried,
  And fortune sped the lance.

"If pall and vair no more I wear,
  Nor thou the crimson sheen,
As warm, we'll say, is the russet gray,
  As gay the forest green.

"And, Richard, if our lot be hard,
  And lost thy native land,
Still Alice has her own Richard,
  And he his Alice Brand."

'Tis merry, 'tis merry, in good greenwood,
  So blithe Lady Alice is singing;
On the beech's pride, and oak's brown side,
  Lord Richard's axe is ringing.

Up spoke the moody Elfin King,
  Who wonn'd within the hill,—
Like wind in the porch of a ruin'd church,
  His voice was ghostly shrill.

"Why sounds yon stroke on beech and
    oak,
  Our moonlight circle's screen?
Or who comes here to chase the deer,
  Beloved of our Elfin Queen?
Or who may dare on wold to wear
  The fairie's fatal green?

"Up, Urgan, up! to yon mortal hie,
  For thou wert christen'd man;
For cross or sign thou wilt not fly,
  For mutter'd word or ban.

"Lay on him the curse of the wither'd
    heart,
  The curse of the sleepless eye;
Till he wish and pray that his life would
    part,
  Nor yet find leave to die."

'Tis merry, 'tis merry, in good greenwood,
　Though the birds have still'd their singing;
The evening blaze doth Alice raise,
　And Richard is fagots bringing.

Up Urgan starts, that hideous dwarf,
　Before Lord Richard stands,
And, as he cross'd and bless'd himself,
" I fear not sign," quoth the grisly elf,
　" That is made with bloody hands."

But out then spoke she, Alice Brand,
　That woman void of fear,—
"And if there's blood upon his hand,
　'Tis but the blood of deer.—"

" Now loud thou liest, thou bold of mood!
　It cleaves unto his hand,
The stain of thine own kindly blood,
　The blood of Ethert Brand."

Then forward stepp'd she, Alice Brand,
　And made the holy sign,—
"And if there's blood on Richard's hand,
　A spotless hand is mine.

"And I conjure thee, Demon elf,
　By Him whom Demons fear,
To show us whence thou art thyself,
　And what thine errand here?—"

" 'Tis merry, 'tis merry, in Fairy-land,
　When fairy birds are singing,
When the court doth ride by their monarch's side,
　With bit and bridle ringing:

"And gaily shines the Fairy-land—
　But all is glistening show,
Like the idle gleam that December's beam
　Can dart on ice and snow.

"And fading, like that varied gleam,
　Is our inconstant shape,
Who now like knight and lady seem,
　And now like dwarf and ape.

" It was between the night and day,
　When the Fairy King has power,
That I sunk down in a sinful fray,
And, 'twixt life and death, was snatch'd away
　To the joyless Elfin bower.

" But wist I of a woman bold,
　Who thrice my brow durst sign,
I might regain my mortal mold,
　As fair a form as thine."

She cross'd him once—she cross'd him twice—
　That lady was so brave;
The fouler grew his goblin hue,
　The darker grew the cave.

She cross'd him thrice, that lady bold;
　He rose beneath her hand
The fairest knight on Scottish mold,
　Her brother, Ethert Brand!

Merry it is in good greenwood,
　When the mavis and merle are singing,
But merrier were they in Dunfermline grey,
　When all the bells were ringing.
　　　　　　　　Sir Walter Scott.

THE BLESSED DAMOZEL.

The blessed damozel leaned out
　From the gold bar of Heaven;
Her eyes were deeper than the depth
　Of waters stilled at even;
She had three lilies in her hand,
　And the stars in her hair were seven.

Her robe, ungirt from clasp to hem,
　No wrought flowers did adorn,
But a white rose of Mary's gift,
　For service meetly worn;
Her hair that lay along her back
　Was yellow like ripe corn.

Her seemed she scarce had been a day
　One of God's choristers;
The wonder was not yet quite gone
　From that still look of hers;
Albeit, to them she left, her day
　Had counted as ten years.

(To one, it is ten years of years.
　. . . Yet now, and in this place,
Surely she leaned o'er me; her hair
　Fell all about my face. . . .
Nothing: the autumn fall of leaves.
　The whole year sets apace.)

It was the rampart of God's house
　That she was standing on;

By God built over the sheer depth
  The which is Space begun;
So high, that looking downward thence
  She scarce could see the sun.

It lies in Heaven, across the flood
  Of ether, as a bridge.
Beneath, the tides of day and night
  With flame and darkness ridge
The void, as low as where this earth
  Spins like a fretful midge.

Heard hardly, some of her new friends
  Amid their loving games
Spake evermore among themselves
  Their virginal chaste names;
And the souls mounting up to God
  Went by her like thin flames.

And still she bowed herself, and stooped
  Out of the circling charm;
Until her bosom must have made
  The bar she leaned on warm,
And the lilies lay as if asleep
  Along her bended arm.

From the fixed place of Heaven she saw
  Time like a pulse shake fierce
Through all the worlds. Her gaze still strove
  Within the gulf to pierce
Its path; and now she spoke as when
  The stars sang in their spheres.

The sun was gone now; the curlèd moon
  Was like a little feather
Fluttering far down the gulf; and now
  She spoke through the still weather.
Her voice was like the voice the stars
  Had when they sang together.

(Ah, sweet! Even now, in that bird's song,
  Strove not her accents there,
Fain to be hearken'd? When those bells
  Possessed the mid-day air,
Strove not her steps to reach my side
  Down all the echoing stair?)

" I wish that he were come to me,
  For he will come," she said.
" Have I not pray'd in heaven?—on earth,
  Lord, Lord, has he not pray'd?
Are not two prayers a perfect strength?
  And shall I feel afraid?

" When round his head the aureole clings
  And he is clothed in white,
I'll take his hand and go with him
  To the deep wells of light;
We will step down as to a stream,
  And bathe there in God's sight.

" We two will stand beside that shrine,
  Occult, withheld, untrod,
Whose lamps are stirred continually
  With prayer sent up to God;
And see our old prayers, granted, melt
  Each like a little cloud.

" We two will lie i' the shadow of
  That living mystic tree,
Within whose secret growth the Dove
  Is sometimes felt to be,
While every leaf that His plumes touch
  Saith His name audibly.

" And I myself will teach to him,
  I myself, lying so,
The songs I sing here; which his voice
  Shall pause in, hushed and slow,
And find some knowledge at each pause,
  Or some new thing to know."

(Alas! We two, we two, thou say'st!
  Yea, one wast thou with me
That once of old. But shall God lift
  To endless unity
The soul whose likeness with thy soul
  Was but its love for thee?)

" We two," she said, " will seek the groves
  Where the lady Mary is,
With her five handmaidens, whose names
  Are five sweet symphonies,
Cecily, Gertrude, Magdalen,
  Margaret and Rosalys.

" Circlewise sit they, with bound locks
  And foreheads garlanded;
Into the fine cloth white like flame,
  Weaving the golden thread,
To fashion the birth-robes for them
  Who are just born, being dead.

" He shall fear, haply, and be dumb:
  Then will I lay my cheek
To his, and tell about our love,
  Not once abash'd or weak:
And the dear Mother will approve
  My pride, and let me speak.

"Herself shall bring us, hand in hand,
  To Him round whom all souls
Kneel, the clear-ranged unnumbered heads
  Bowed with their aureoles:
And angels meeting us shall sing
  To their citherns and citoles.

"There will I ask of Christ the Lord
  Thus much for him and me:—
Only to live as once on earth
  With Love,—only to be,
And then a while, for ever now
  Together, I and he."

She gazed and listened, and then said,
  Less sad of speech than mild,—
"All this is when he comes." She ceased.
  The light thrill'd toward her, fill'd
With angels in strong level flight.
  Her eyes prayed, and she smiled.

(I saw her smile.) But soon their path
  Was vague in distant spheres;
And then she cast her arms along
  The golden barriers,
And laid her face between her hands,
  And wept. (I heard her tears.)
DANTE GABRIEL ROSSETTI.

CHRISTABEL.

PART I.

'TIS the middle of night by the castle
    clock,
And the owls have awakened the crowing
    cock;
Tu-whit!—Tu-whoo!
And hark, again! the crowing cock,
How drowsily it crew.

Sir Leoline, the Baron rich,
Hath a toothless mastiff bitch;
From her kennel beneath the rock
She maketh answer to the clock,
Four for the quarters, and twelve for the
    hour;
Ever and aye, by shine and shower,
Sixteen short howls, not over-loud;
Some say, she sees my lady's shroud.

Is the night chilly and dark?
The night is chilly, but not dark.
The thin gray cloud is spread on high,
It covers but not hides the sky.

The moon is behind, and at the full;
And yet she looks both small and dull.
The night is chill, the cloud is gray:
'Tis a month before the month of May,
And the Spring comes slowly up this way.

The lovely lady, Christabel,
Whom her father loves so well,
What makes her in the wood so late,
A furlong from the castle-gate?
She had dreams all yesternight
Of her own betrothèd knight;
And she in the midnight wood will pray
For the weal of her lover that's far away.

She stole along, she nothing spoke,
The sighs she heaved were soft and low,
And naught was green upon the oak,
But moss and rarest mistletoe:
She kneels beneath the huge oak tree,
And in silence prayeth she.

The lady sprang up suddenly,
The lovely lady, Christabel!
It moaned as near, as near can be,
But what it is, she cannot tell.—
On the other side it seems to be,
Of the huge, broad-breasted, old oak tree.

The night is chill; the forest bare;
Is it the wind that moaneth bleak?
There is not wind enough in the air
To move away the ringlet curl
From the lovely lady's cheek—
There is not wind enough to twirl
The one red leaf, the last of its clan,
That dances as often as dance it can,
Hanging so light, and hanging so high,
On the topmost twig that looks up at the
    sky.

Hush, beating heart of Christabel!
Jesu, Maria, shield her well!
She folded her arms beneath her cloak,
And stole to the other side of the oak.
    What sees she there?

There she sees a damsel bright,
Drest in a silken robe of white,
That shadowy in the moonlight shone:
The neck that made that white robe wan,
Her stately neck, and arms were bare;
Her blue-veined feet unsandall'd were,

And wildly glittered here and there
The gems entangled in her hair.
I guess, 'twas frightful there to see
A lady so richly clad as she,—
Beautiful exceedingly!

"Mary mother, save me now!"
(Said Christabel;) "And who art thou?"

The lady strange made answer meet,
And her voice was faint and sweet:—
"Have pity on my sore distress,
I scarce can speak for weariness."
"Stretch forth thy hand, and have no fear!"
Said Christabel, "how camest thou here?"
And the lady, whose voice was faint and sweet,
Did thus pursue her answer meet:—

"My sire is of a noble line,
And my name is Geraldine:
Five warriors seized me yestermorn,
Me, even me, a maid forlorn:
They choked my cries with force and fright,
And tied me on a palfrey white.
The palfrey was as fleet as wind,
And they rode furiously behind.
They spurred amain, their steeds were white:
And once we crossed the shade of night.
As sure as Heaven shall rescue me,
I have no thought what men they be;
Nor do I know how long it is
(For I have lain entranced I wis)
Since one, the tallest of the five,
Took me from the palfrey's back,
A weary woman, scarce alive.
Some muttered words his comrades spoke:
He placed me underneath this oak;
He swore they would return with haste;
Whither they went I cannot tell—
I thought I heard, some minutes past,
Sounds as of a castle bell.
Stretch forth thy hand" (thus ended she),
"And help a wretched maid to flee."

Then Christabel stretched forth her hand
And comforted fair Geraldine:
"Oh, well, bright dame! may you command
The service of Sir Leoline;
And gladly our stout chivalry
Will he send forth and friends withal
To guide and guard you safe and free
Home to your noble father's hall."

She rose: and forth with steps they passed
That strove to be, and were not, fast.
Her gracious stars the lady blest,
And thus spake on sweet Christabel:
"All our household are at rest,
The hall as silent as the cell;
Sir Leoline is weak in health,
And may not well awakened be,
But we will move as if in stealth,
And I beseech your courtesy,
This night, to share your couch with me."

They crossed the moat, and Christabel
Took the key that fitted well;
A little door she opened straight,
All in the middle of the gate;
The gate that was ironed within and without,
Where an army in battle array had marched out.
The lady sank, belike through pain,
And Christabel with might and main
Lifted her up, a weary weight,
Over the threshold of the gate:
Then the lady rose again,
And moved, as she were not in pain.

So free from danger, free from fear,
They crossed the court: right glad they were.
And Christabel devoutly cried
To the Lady by her side,
"Praise we the Virgin all divine
Who hath rescued thee from thy distress!"
"Alas, alas!" said Geraldine,
"I cannot speak for weariness."
So, free from danger, free from fear,
They cross'd the court: right glad thee were.

Outside her kennel the mastiff old
Lay fast asleep, in moonshine cold.
The mastiff old did not awake,
Yet she an angry moan did make!
And what can ail the mastiff bitch?
Never till now she uttered yell
Beneath the eye of Christabel.
Perhaps it is the owlet's scritch,
For what can ail the mastiff bitch?

They passed the hall, that echoes still,
Pass as lightly as you will!
The brands were flat, the brands were dying,
Amid their own white ashes lying;
But when the lady passed, there came
A tongue of light, a fit of flame;
And Christabel saw the lady's eye,
And nothing else saw she thereby,
Save the boss of the shield of Sir Leoline tall,
Which hung in a murky old niche in the wall.
"O, softly tread!" said Christabel,
"My father seldom sleepeth well."

Sweet Christabel her feet doth bare,
And, jealous of the listening air,
They steal their way from stair to stair,
Now in glimmer, and now in gloom,
And now they pass the Baron's room,
As still as death with stifled breath!
And now have reach'd her chamber door;
And now doth Geraldine press down
The rushes of the chamber floor.

The moon shines dim in the open air,
And not a moonbeam enters here.
But they without its light can see
The chamber carved so curiously,
Carved with figures strange and sweet,
All made out of the carver's brain,
For a lady's chamber meet:
The lamp with twofold silver chain
Is fastened to an angel's feet.
The silver lamp burns dead and dim;
But Christabel the lamp will trim.
She trimmed the lamp, and made it bright,
And left it swinging to and fro,
While Geraldine, in wretched plight,
Sank down upon the floor below.

"O weary lady, Geraldine,
I pray you, drink this cordial wine!
It is a wine of virtuous powers;
My mother made it of wild flowers."

"And will your mother pity me,
Who am a maiden most forlorn?"
Christabel answered—"Woe is me!
She died the hour that I was born.
I have heard the gray-haired friar tell,
How on her deathbed she did say,
That she should hear the castle-bell
Strike twelve upon my wedding day.
O mother dear! that thou wert here!"
"I would," said Geraldine, "she were!"
But soon with altered voice, said she—
"Off, wandering mother! Peak and pine!
I have power to bid thee flee."
Alas! what ails poor Geraldine?
Why stares she with unsettled eye?
Can she the bodiless dead espy?
And why with hollow voice cries she,
"Off, woman, off! this hour is mine—
Though thou her guardian spirit be,
Off, woman, off! 'tis given to me."

Then Christabel knelt by the lady's side,
And raised to heaven her eyes so blue—
"Alas!" said she, "this ghastly ride—
Dear lady! it hath wildered you!"
The lady wiped her moist cold brow,
And faintly said, "'tis over now!"

Again the wild-flower wine she drank:
Her fair large eyes 'gan glitter bright,
And from the floor whereon she sank,
The lofty lady stood upright;
She was most beautiful to see,
Like a lady of a far countrée.

And thus the lofty lady spake—
"All they, who live in the upper sky,
Do love you, holy Christabel!
And you love them, and for their sake
And for the good which me befell,
Even I in my degree will try,
Fair maiden, to requite you well.
But now unrobe yourself; for I
Must pray, ere yet in bed I lie."

Quoth Christabel, "So let it be!"
And as the lady bade, did she.
Her gentle limbs did she undress,
And lay down in her loveliness.

But through her brain of weal and woe
So many thoughts moved to and fro,
That vain it were her lids to close;
So halfway from the bed she rose,
And on her elbow did recline
To look at the Lady Geraldine.

Beneath the lamp the lady bowed,
And slowly rolled her eyes around;
Then drawing in her breath aloud
Like one that shuddered, she unbound
The cincture from beneath her breast:
Her silken robe, and inner vest,

Dropt to her feet, and full in view,
Behold! her bosom and half her side—
A sight to dream of, not to tell!
O shield her! shield sweet Christabel!

Yet Geraldine nor speaks nor stirs;
Ah! what a stricken look was hers!
Deep from within she seems half-way
To lift some weight with sick assay,
And eyes the maid and seeks delay;
Then suddenly as one defied
Collects herself in scorn and pride,
And lay down by the maiden's side!—
And in her arms the maid she took,
    Ah well-a-day!
And with low voice and doleful look
These words did say:
"In the touch of this bosom there worketh
    a spell,
Which is lord of thy utterance, Christabel!
Thou knowest to-night, and wilt know to-morrow
This mark of my shame, this seal of my
    sorrow;
    But vainly thou warrest,
    For this is alone in
    Thy power to declare,
    That in the dim forest
    Thou heard'st a low moaning,
And found'st a bright lady, surpassingly
    fair:
And didst bring her home with thee in love
    and in charity,
To shield her and shelter her from the damp
    air."

The Conclusion to Part I.

It was a lovely sight to see
The Lady Christabel, when she
Was praying at the old oak tree.
    Amid the jagged shadows
    Of mossy leafless boughs,
    Kneeling in the moonlight,
    To make her gentle vows;
Her slender palms together prest,
Heaving sometimes on her breast;
Her face resigned to bliss or bale—
Her face, oh call it fair not pale,
And both her blue eyes more bright than
    clear,
Each about to have a tear.

With open eyes (ah, woe is me!)
Asleep, and dreaming fearfully,
Fearfully dreaming, yet I wis,
Dreaming that alone which is—
O sorrow and shame! Can this be she,
The lady who knelt at the old oak tree?
And lo! the worker of these harms,
That holds the maiden in her arms,
Seems to slumber still and mild,
As a mother with her child.

A star hath set, a star hath risen,
O Geraldine! since arms of thine
Have been the lovely lady's prison.
O Geraldine! one hour was thine—
Thou'st had thy will! By tarn and rill,
The night-birds all that hour were still.
But now they are jubilant anew,
From cliff and tower, tu-whoo! tu-whoo!
Tu-whoo! tu-whoo! from wood and fell!
And see! the Lady Christabel
Gathers herself from out her trance;
Her limbs relax, her countenance
Grows sad and soft; the smooth thin lids
Close o'er her eyes; and tears she sheds—
Large tears that leave the lashes bright!
And oft the while she seems to smile
As infants at a sudden light!
Yea, she doth smile, and she doth weep,
Like a youthful hermitess,
Beauteous in a wilderness,
Who, praying always, prays in sleep.
And, if she move unquietly,
Perchance, 'tis but the blood so free,
Comes back and tingles in her feet.
No doubt, she hath a vision sweet.
What if her guardian spirit 'twere?
What if she knew her mother near?
But this she knows, in joys and woes,
That saints will aid if men will call:
For the blue sky bends over all!

Part II.

"Each matin bell," the Baron saith,
"Knells us back to a world of death."
These words Sir Leoline first said,
When he rose and found his lady dead:
These words Sir Leoline will say,
Many a morn to his dying day!

And hence the custom and law began,
That still at dawn the sacristan,

Who duly pulls the heavy bell,
Five and forty beads must tell
Between each stroke—a warning knell,
Which not a soul can choose but hear
From Bratha Head to Wyndermere.

Saith Bracy the bard, "So let it knell!
And let the drowsy sacristan
Still count as slowly as he can.
There is no lack of such, I ween,
As well fill up the space between.
In Langdale Pike and Witch's Lair,
And Dungeon-ghyll so foully rent,
With ropes of rock and bells of air
Three sinful sextons' ghosts are pent,
Who all give back, one after t'other,
The death-note to their living brother;
And oft too, by the knell offended,
Just as their one! two! three! is ended,
The devil mocks the doleful tale
With a merry peal from Borodale."

The air is still! through mist and cloud
That merry peal comes ringing loud;
And Geraldine shakes off her dread,
And rises lightly from the bed;
Puts on her silken vestments white,
And tricks her hair in lovely plight,
And, nothing doubting of her spell,
Awakens the Lady Christabel.
"Sleep you, sweet Lady Christabel?
I trust that you have rested well."

And Christabel awoke and spied
The same who lay down by her side—
O, rather say, the same whom she
Raised up beneath the old oak tree!
Nay, fairer yet! and yet more fair!
For she belike hath drunken deep
Of all the blessedness of sleep!
And while she spake, her looks, her air,
Such gentle thankfulness declare,
That (so it seemed) her girded vests
Grew tight beneath her heaving breasts.
"Sure I have sinned!" said Christabel,
"Now Heaven be praised if all be well!"
And in low faltering tones, yet sweet,
Did she the lofty lady greet
With such perplexity of mind
As dreams too lively leave behind.

So quickly she rose, and quickly arrayed
Her maiden limbs, and having prayed
That He, who on the cross did groan,
Might wash away her sins unknown,
She forthwith led fair Geraldine
To meet her sire, Sir Leoline.

The lovely maid and the lady tall
Are pacing both into the hall,
And pacing on through page and groom,
Enter the Baron's presence room.

The Baron rose, and while he prest
His gentle daughter to his breast,
With cheerful wonder in his eyes
The Lady Geraldine espies,
And gave such welcome to the same
As might beseem so bright a dame!

But when he heard the lady's tale,
And when she told her father's name,
Why waxed Sir Leoline so pale,
Murmuring o'er the name again,
Lord Roland de Vaux of Tryermaine?

Alas! they had been friends in youth;
But whispering tongues can poison truth;
And constancy lives in realms above;
And life is thorny; and youth is vain;
And to be wroth with one we love,
Doth work like madness in the brain.
And thus it chanced, as I divine,
With Roland and Sir Leoline.
Each spake words of high disdain
And insult to his heart's best brother:
They parted—ne'er to meet again!
But never either found another
To free the hollow heart from paining—
They stood aloof, the scars remaining,
Like cliffs which had been rent asunder;
A dreary sea now flows between;—
But neither heat, nor frost, nor thunder,
Shall wholly do away, I ween,
The marks of that which once hath been.

Sir Leoline, a moment's space,
Stood gazing on the damsel's face:
And the youthful Lord of Tryermaine
Came back upon his heart again.

O then the Baron forgot his age,
His noble heart swelled high with rage;
He swore by the wounds in Jesu's side,
He would proclaim it far and wide
With trump and solemn heraldry,
That they who thus had wronged the dame,

Were base as spotted infamy!
"And if they dare deny the same,
My herald shall appoint a week,
And let the recreant traitors seek
My tourney court—that there and then
I may dislodge their reptile souls
From the bodies and forms of men!"
He spake: his eye in lightning rolls!
For the lady was ruthlessly seized; and he kenned
In the beautiful lady the child of his friend!

And now the tears were on his face,
And fondly in his arms he took
Fair Geraldine, who met the embrace,
Prolonging it with joyous look.
Which when she viewed, a vision fell
Upon the soul of Christabel,
The vision of fear, the touch and pain!
She shrunk and shuddered, and saw again—
(Ah, woe is me! Was it for thee,
Thou gentle maid! such sights to see?)
Again she saw that bosom old,
Again she felt that bosom cold,
And drew in her breath with a hissing sound:
Whereat the Knight turned wildly round,
And nothing saw, but his own sweet maid
With eyes upraised, as one that prayed.

The touch, the sight, had passed away,
And in its stead that vision blest,
Which comforted her after-rest
While in the lady's arms she lay,
Had put a rapture in her breast,
And on her lips and o'er her eyes
Spread smiles like light!
With new surprise,
"What ails then my beloved child?"
The Baron said.—His daughter mild
Made answer, "All will yet be well!"
I ween, she had no power to tell
Aught else: so mighty was the spell.

Yet he, who saw this Geraldine,
Had deemed her sure a thing divine.
Such sorrow with such grace she blended,
As if she feared she had offended
Sweet Christabel, that gentle maid!
And with such lowly tones she prayed,
She might be sent without delay
Home to her father's mansion.
"Nay!

Nay, by my soul!" said Leoline.
"Ho! Bracy, the bard, the charge be thine!
Go thou, with music sweet and loud,
And take two steeds with trappings proud,
And take the youth whom thou lov'st best
To bear thy harp, and learn thy song,
And clothe you both in solemn vest,
And over the mountains haste along,
Lest wandering folk, that are abroad,
Detain you on the valley road.
And when he has crossed the Irthing flood,
My merry bard! he hastes, he hastes
Up Knorren Moor, through Halegarth Wood,
And reaches soon that castle good
Which stands and threatens Scotland's wastes.

"Bard Bracy! Bard Bracy! your horses are fleet,
Ye must ride up the hall, your music so sweet,
More loud than your horses' echoing feet!
And loud and loud to Lord Roland call,
Thy daughter is safe in Langdale hall!
Thy beautiful daughter is safe and free,—
Sir Leoline greets thee thus through me.
He bids thee come without delay
With all thy numerous array;
And take thy lovely daughter home:
And he will meet thee on the way
With all his numerous array
White with their panting palfreys' foam:
And by mine honor! I will say,
That I repent me of the day
When I spake words of fierce disdain
To Roland de Vaux of Tryermaine!—
For since that evil hour hath flown,
Many a summer's sun hath shone;
Yet ne'er found I a friend again
Like Roland de Vaux of Tryermaine."

The lady fell, and clasp'd his knees,
Her face upraised, her eyes o'erflowing;
And Bracy replied, with faltering voice,
His gracious hail on all bestowing!—
"Thy words, thou sire of Christabel,
Are sweeter than my harp can tell;
Yet might I gain a boon of thee,
This day my journey should not be,
So strange a dream hath come to me;
That I had vowed with music loud

To clear yon wood from thing unblest,
Warned by a vision in my rest!
For in my sleep I saw that dove,
That gentle bird, whom thou dost love,
And call'st by thy own daughter's name—
Sir Leoline! I saw the same
Fluttering, and uttering fearful moan,
Among the green herbs in the forest alone.
Which when I saw and when I heard,
I wonder'd what might ail the bird;
For nothing near it could I see,
Save the grass and green herbs underneath
    the old tree.

"And in my dream methought I went
To search out what might there be found;
And what the sweet bird's trouble meant,
That thus lay fluttering on the ground.
I went and peered and could descry
No cause for her distressful cry;
But yet for her dear lady's sake
I stooped, methought, the dove to take,
When lo! I saw a bright green snake
Coil'd around its wings and neck,
Green as the herbs on which it couched.
Close by the dove's its head it crouched;
And with the dove it heaves and stirs,
Swelling its neck as she swell'd hers!
I woke; it was the midnight hour,
The clock was echoing in the tower;
But though my slumber was gone by,
This dream it would not pass away—
It seems to live upon my eye!
And thence I vowed this selfsame day,
With music strong and saintly song
To wander through the forest bare,
Lest aught unholy loiter there."

Thus Bracy said: the Baron, the while,
Half listening heard him with a smile;
Then turned to Lady Geraldine,
His eyes made up of wonder and love,
And said in courtly accents fine,
"Sweet maid, Lord Roland's beauteous
    dove,
With arms more strong than harp or song,
Thy sire and I will crush the snake!"
He kissed her forehead as he spake,
And Geraldine, in maiden wise,
Casting down her large bright eyes,
With blushing cheek and courtesy fine
She turned her from Sir Leoline;

Softly gathering up her train,
That o'er her right arm fell again;
And folded her arms across her chest,
And couched her head upon her breast,
And looked askance at Christabel—
Jesu Maria, shield her well!

A snake's small eye blinks dull and
    shy,
And the lady's eyes they shrunk in her
    head,
Each shrunk up to a serpent's eye,
And with somewhat of malice, and more
    of dread,
At Christabel she look'd askance!—
One moment—and the sight was fled!
But Christabel, in dizzy trance
Stumbling on the unsteady ground,
Shuddered aloud, with a hissing sound:
And Geraldine again turned round,
And like a thing, that sought relief,
Full of wonder and full of grief,
She rolled her large bright eyes divine
Wildly on Sir Leoline.

The maid, alas! her thoughts are gone,
She nothing sees—no sight but one!
The maid, devoid of guile and sin,
I know not how, in fearful wise
So deeply had she drunken in
That look, those shrunken serpent eyes,
That all her features were resigned
To this sole image in her mind;
And passively did imitate
That look of dull and treacherous hate!
And thus she stood, in dizzy trance,
Still picturing that look askance
With forced unconscious sympathy
Full before her father's view—
As far as such a look could be,
In eyes so innocent and blue!
And when the trance was o'er, the maid
Paused a while, and inly pray'd:
Then falling at the Baron's feet,
"By my mother's soul do I entreat
That thou this woman send away!"
She said: and more she could not say:
For what she knew she could not tell,
O'er-mastered by the mighty spell.

Why is thy cheek so wan and wild,
Sir Leoline? Thy only child
Lies at thy feet, thy joy, thy pride,
So fair, so innocent, so mild;

The same for whom thy lady died!
O by the pangs of her dear mother
Think thou no evil of thy child!
For her, and thee, and for no other,
She prayed the moment ere she died,
Prayed that the babe for whom she died,
Might prove her dear lord's joy and pride!
　　That prayer her deadly pangs beguiled,
　　　　Sir Leoline!
　　And wouldst thou wrong thy only child,
　　　　Her child and thine?

Within the Baron's heart and brain,
If thoughts like these had any share,
They only swell'd his rage and pain,
And did but work confusion there.
His heart was cleft with pain and rage,
His cheeks they quivered, his eyes were wild.
Dishonored thus in his old age;
Dishonored by his only child,
And all his hospitality
To the wrong'd daughter of his friend,
By more than woman's jealousy
Brought thus to a disgraceful end.—
He roll'd his eyes with stern regard
Upon the gentle minstrel bard,
And said in tones abrupt, austere—
"Why, Bracy! dost thou loiter here?
I bade thee hence!" The bard obeyed;
And turning from his own sweet maid,
The aged knight, Sir Leoline,
Led forth the Lady Geraldine!

The Conclusion to Part II.

A little child, a limber elf,
Singing, dancing to itself,
A fairy thing with red round cheeks,
That always finds, and never seeks,
Makes such a vision to the sight
As fills a father's eyes with light;
And pleasures flow in so thick and fast
Upon his heart, that he at last
Must needs express his love's excess
With words of unmeant bitterness.
Perhaps 'tis pretty to force together
Thoughts so all unlike each other;
To mutter and mock a broken charm,
To dally with wrong that does no harm.
Perhaps 'tis tender too and pretty
At each wild word to feel within
A sweet recoil of love and pity.
And what if in a world of sin

(O sorrow and shame should this be true!)
Such giddiness of heart and brain
Comes seldom save from rage and pain,
So talks as it's most used to do.
　　　　　　SAMUEL TAYLOR COLERIDGE.

KUBLA KHAN.

IN Xanadu did Kubla Khan
　A stately pleasure-dome decree:
Where Alph, the sacred river, ran
Through caverns measureless to man
　Down to a sunless sea.
So twice five miles of fertile ground
With walls and towers were girdled round:
And there were gardens bright with sinuous rills
Where blossomed many an incense-bearing tree;
And here were forests ancient as the hills,
Enfolding sunny spots of greenery.

But oh! that deep romantic chasm which slanted
Down the green hill athwart a cedarn cover!
A savage place! as holy and enchanted
As e'er beneath a waning moon was haunted
By woman wailing for her demon-lover!
And from this chasm, with ceaseless turmoil seething,
As if this earth in fast thick pants were breathing,
A mighty fountain momently was forced:
Amid whose swift, half-intermitted burst
Huge fragments vaulted like rebounding hail,
Or chaffy grain beneath the thresher's flail:
And 'mid these dancing rocks at once and ever
It flung up momently the sacred river.
Five miles meandering with a mazy motion
Through wood and dale the sacred river ran,
Then reached the caverns measureless to man,
And sank in tumult to a lifeless ocean:
And 'mid this tumult Kubla heard from far
Ancestral voices prophesying war!

The shadow of the dome of pleasure
Floated midway on the waves;
Where was heard the mingled measure
From the fountain and the caves.
It was a miracle of rare device,
A sunny pleasure-dome with caves of ice!
  A damsel with a dulcimer
  In a vision once I saw;
  It was an Abyssinian maid,
  And on her dulcimer she played,
  Singing of Mount Abora.
  Could I revive within me
  Her symphony and song,
  To such a deep delight 'twould win me
That, with music loud and long,
I would build that dome in air,
That sunny dome! those caves of ice!
And all who heard should see them there,
And all should cry, Beware! beware
His flashing eyes, his floating hair!
Weave a circle round him thrice,
And close your eyes with holy dread,
For he on honey-dew hath fed,
And drunk the milk of Paradise.
SAMUEL TAYLOR COLERIDGE.

THE RAVEN.

ONCE upon a midnight dreary, while I pondered, weak and weary,
  Over many a quaint and curious volume of forgotten lore,
While I nodded, nearly napping, suddenly there came a tapping,
  As of some one gently rapping, rapping at my chamber-door.
"'Tis some visitor," I muttered, "tapping at my chamber-door—
  Only this, and nothing more."

Ah, distinctly I remember it was in the bleak December,
  And each separate dying ember wrought its ghost upon the floor.
Eagerly I wished the morrow;—vainly I had tried to borrow
  From my books surcease of sorrow—sorrow for the lost Lenore—
For the rare and radiant maiden whom the angels name Lenore,
  Nameless here for evermore.

And the silken sad uncertain rustling of each purple curtain
  Thrilled me,—filled me with fantastic terrors never felt before;
So that now, to still the beating of my heart, I stood repeating,
  "'Tis some visitor entreating entrance at my chamber-door,
Some late visitor entreating entrance at my chamber-door;
  This it is and nothing more."

Presently my soul grew stronger; hesitating then no longer,
  "Sir," said I, "or Madam, truly your forgiveness I implore;
But the fact is I was napping, and so gently you came rapping,
And so faintly you came tapping, tapping at my chamber-door,
  That I scarce was sure I heard you."—
Here I opened wide the door;—
  Darkness there and nothing more.

Deep into that darkness peering, long I stood there wondering, fearing,
  Doubting, dreaming dreams no mortal ever dared to dream before;
But the silence was unbroken, and the stillness gave no token,
  And the only word there spoken was the whispered word " Lenore!"
This I whispered, and an echo murmured back the word " Lenore!"—
  Merely this and nothing more.

Back into the chamber turning, all my soul within me burning,
  Soon again I heard a tapping, somewhat louder than before.
"Surely," said I, " surely that is something at my window-lattice;
Let me see, then, what thereat is, and this mystery explore,
Let my heart be still a moment, and this mystery explore;
  'Tis the wind, and nothing more!"

Open here I flung the shutter, when, with many a flirt and flutter,
  In there stepp'd a stately Raven of the saintly days of yore.

Not the least obeisance made he; not an
    instant stopped or stayed he;
But with mien of lord or lady, perched
    above my chamber-door,—
Perched upon a bust of Pallas, just
    above my chamber-door,—
Perched, and sat, and nothing more.

Then this ebony bird beguiling my sad
    fancy into smiling,
By the grave and stern decorum of the
    countenance it wore,
"Though thy crest be shorn and shaven,
    thou," I said, "art sure no craven,
Ghastly, grim, and ancient Raven, wandering from the Nightly shore,—
Tell me what thy lordly name is on the
    Night's Plutonian shore."
    Quoth the Raven, "Nevermore."

Much I marvelled this ungainly fowl to
    hear discourse so plainly,
Though its answer little meaning—little
    relevancy bore;
For we cannot help agreeing that no living
    human being
Ever yet was blest with seeing bird above
    his chamber-door—
Bird or beast upon the sculptured bust
    above his chamber-door,
    With such name as "Nevermore."

But the Raven, sitting lonely on the placid
    bust, spoke only
That one word, as if his soul in that one
    word he did outpour.
Nothing further then he uttered; not a
    feather then he fluttered—
Till I scarcely more than muttered,
    "Other friends have flown before—
On the morrow *he* will leave me, as my
    Hopes have flown before."
    Then the bird said, "Nevermore."

Startled at the stillness broken by reply so
    aptly spoken,
"Doubtless," said I, "what it utters is
    its only stock and store,
Caught from some unhappy master whom
    unmerciful Disaster
Followed fast and followed faster till his
    song one burden bore—
Till the dirges of his Hope that melancholy burden bore—
    Of 'Never'—'Nevermore.'"

But the Raven still beguiling all my sad
    soul into smiling,
Straight I wheel'd a cushion'd seat in
    front of bird, and bust, and door;
Then, upon the velvet sinking, I betook
    myself to linking
Fancy unto fancy, thinking what this
    ominous bird of yore—
What this grim, ungainly, ghastly,
    gaunt, and ominous bird of yore
    Meant in croaking "Nevermore."

This I sat engaged in guessing, but no
    syllable expressing
To the fowl whose fiery eyes now burned
    into my bosom's core;
This and more I sat divining, with my
    head at ease reclining
On the cushion's velvet lining that the
    lamplight gloated o'er,
But whose velvet violet lining with the
    lamplight gloating o'er—
    She shall press, ah, nevermore!

Then, methought the air grew denser, perfumed from an unseen censer
Swung by Seraphim whose footfalls
    tinkled on the tufted floor.
"Wretch," I cried, "thy God hath lent
    thee—by these angels he hath sent
    thee
Respite—respite and nepenthe from thy
    memories of Lenore!
Quaff, oh quaff this kind nepenthe, and
    forget this lost Lenore!"
    Quoth the Raven, "Nevermore."

"Prophet!" said I, "thing of evil! prophet still, if bird or devil!—
Whether Tempter sent, or whether tempest tossed thee here ashore,
Desolate, yet all undaunted, on this desert
    land enchanted—
On this home by Horror haunted—tell
    me truly, I implore—
Is there—*is* there balm in Gilead?—tell
    me, tell me, I implore!"
    Quoth the Raven, "Nevermore."

"Prophet!" said I, "thing of evil,—proph-
et still, if bird or devil!
By that Heaven that bends above us—
by that God we both adore—
Tell this soul with sorrow laden if, within
the distant Aidenn,
It shall clasp a sainted maiden whom
the angels name Lenore—
Clasp a rare and radiant maiden whom
the angels name Lenore."
Quoth the Raven. "Nevermore."

"Be that word our sign of parting, bird or
fiend!" I shrieked, upstarting—
"Get thee back into the tempest and the
Night's Plutonian shore!
Leave no black plume as a token of that
lie thy soul hath spoken!
Leave my loneliness unbroken! quit the
bust above my door!
Take thy beak from out my heart, and
take thy form from off my door!"
Quoth the Raven, "Nevermore."

And the Raven, never flitting, still is sit-
ting, still is sitting
On the pallid bust of Pallas just above
my chamber-door;
And his eyes have all the seeming of a
demon's that is dreaming,
And the lamplight o'er him streaming
throws his shadow on the floor;
And my soul from out that shadow that
lies floating on the floor,
Shall be lifted—nevermore!
EDGAR ALLAN POE.

THE PIED PIPER OF HAMELIN.

HAMELIN Town's in Brunswick,
By famous Hanover city;
The river Weser, deep and wide,
Washes its wall on the southern side;
A pleasanter spot you never spied;
But, when begins my ditty,
Almost five hundred years ago,
To see the townsfolk suffer so
From vermin was a pity.

Rats!
They fought the dogs, and kill'd the
cats,
And bit the babies in the cradles,
And ate the cheeses out of the vats,
And lick'd the soup from the cook's own
ladles,
Split open the kegs of salted sprats,
Made nests inside men's Sunday hats,
And even spoil'd the women's chats,
By drowning their speaking
With shrieking and squeaking
In fifty different sharps and flats.

At last the people in a body
To the Town Hall came flocking:
"'Tis clear," cried, they "our Mayor's a
noddy;
And as for our Corporation—shocking
To think we buy gowns lined with er-
mine
For dolts that can't or won't determine
What's best to rid us of our vermin!
You hope, because you're old and obese,
To find in the furry civic robe ease?
Rouse up, sirs! Give your brains a rack-
ing
To find the remedy we're lacking,
Or, sure as fate, we'll send you packing!"
At this the Mayor and Corporation
Quaked with a mighty consternation.

An hour they sate in counsel,
At length the Mayor broke silence:
"For a guilder I'd my ermine gown sell;
I wish I were a mile hence!
It's easy to bid one rack one's brain—
I'm sure my poor head aches again,
I've scratch'd it so, and all in vain.
Oh for a trap, a trap, a trap!"
Just as he said this, what should hap
At the chamber-door but a gentle tap?
"Bless us!" cried the Mayor, "what's
that?"
(With the Corporation as he sat,
Looking little though wondrous fat;
Nor brighter was his eye, nor moister
Than a too long-open'd oyster,
Save when at noon his paunch grew
mutinous
For a plate of turtle, green and glutin-
ous)
"Only a scraping of shoes on the mat?
Anything like the sound of a rat
Makes my heart go pit-a-pat!"

"Come in!"—the Mayor cried, looking
    bigger:
And in did come the strangest figure!
His queer long coat from heel to head
Was half of yellow and half of red;
And he himself was tall and thin,
With sharp blue eyes, each like a pin,
And light loose hair, yet swarthy skin,
No tuft on cheek nor beard on chin,
But lips where smiles went out and in—
There was no guessing his kith and kin!
And nobody could enough admire
The tall man and his quaint attire:
Quoth one: "It's as my great-grandsire,
Starting up at the Trump of Doom's
    tone,
Had walk'd this way from his painted
    tombstone!"

He advanced to the council-table:
And, "Please your honors," said he, "I'm
    able,
By means of a secret charm, to draw
All creatures living beneath the sun,
That creep, or swim, or fly, or run,
After me so as you never saw!
And I chiefly use my charm
On creatures that do people harm,
The mole, and toad, and newt, and viper;
And people call me the Pied Piper."
(And here they noticed round his neck
A scarf of red and yellow stripe,
To match with his coat of the selfsame
    check;
And at the scarf's end hung a pipe;
And his fingers, they noticed, were ever
    straying
As if impatient to be playing
Upon this pipe, as low it dangled
Over his vesture so old-fangled.)
"Yet," said he, "poor piper as I am,
In Tartary I freed the Cham,
Last June, from his huge swarm of gnats;
I eased in Asia the Nizam
Of a monstrous brood of vampyre bats;
And, as for what your brain bewilders—
If I can rid your town of rats,
Will you give me a thousand guilders?"
"One? fifty thousand!" was the exclama-
    tion
Of the astonish'd Mayor and Corpora-
    tion.

Into the street the piper stept,
    Smiling first a little smile,
As if he knew what magic slept
    In his quiet pipe the while;
Then, like a musical adept,
To blow the pipe his lips he wrinkled,
And green and blue his sharp eyes twink-
    led,
Like a candle-flame where salt is sprinkled;
And ere three shrill notes the pipe utter'd,
You heard as if an army mutter'd;
And the muttering grew to a grumbling;
And the grumbling grew to a mighty rum-
    bling;
And out of the houses the rats came tum-
    bling.
Great rats, small rats, lean rats, brawny
    rats,
Brown rats, black rats, gray rats, tawny
    rats,
Grave old plodders, gay young friskers,
    Fathers, mothers, uncles, cousins,
Cocking tails and pricking whiskers,
    Families by tens and dozens,
Brothers, sisters, husbands, wives—
Follow'd the piper for their lives.
From street to street he piped advancing,
And step for step they follow'd dancing,
Until they came to the river Weser,
Wherein all plunged and perish'd,
Save one who, stout as Julius Cæsar,
Swam across and lived to carry
(As the manuscript he cherish'd)
To Rat-land home his commentary,
Which was, "At the first shrill notes of
    the pipe,
I heard a sound as of scraping tripe,
And putting apples, wondrous ripe,
Into a cider press's gripe:
And a moving away of pickle-tub boards,
And a leaving ajar of conserve-cup-
    boards,
And a drawing the corks of train-oil
    flasks,
And a breaking the hoops of butter-casks;
And it seemed as if a voice
(Sweeter far than by harp or by psaltery
Is breathed) call'd out, O rats, rejoice!
The world is grown to one vast drysaltery!
So munch on, crunch on, take your nun-
    cheon,
Breakfast, supper, dinner, luncheon!

And just as a bulky sugar-puncheon,
All ready staved, like a great sun shone
Glorious scarce an inch before me,
Just as methought it said, Come, bore me!
I found the Weser rolling o'er me."

You should have heard the Hamelin people
Ringing the bells till they rock'd the steeple;
"Go," cried the Mayor, "and get long poles!
Poke out the nests and block up the holes!
Consult with carpenters and builders,
And leave in our town not even a trace
Of the rats!"—when suddenly up the face
Of the piper perk'd in the market-place,
With a, "First, if you please, my thousand guilders!"
A thousand guilders! The Mayor look'd blue;
So did the Corporation too.
For council dinners made rare havoc
With Claret, Moselle, Vin-de-Grave, Hock;
And half the money would replenish
Their cellar's biggest butt with Rhenish.
To pay this sum to a wandering fellow
With a gypsy coat of red and yellow!
"Beside," quoth the Mayor, with a knowing wink,
"Our business was done at the river's brink;
We saw with our eyes the vermin sink,
And what's dead can't come to life, I think.
So, friend, we're not the folks to shrink
From the duty of giving you something for drink,
And a matter of money to put in your poke;
But, as for the guilders, what we spoke
Of them, as you very well know, was in joke.
Beside, our losses have made us thrifty;
A thousand guilders! Come, take fifty!"

The piper's face fell and he cried,
"No trifling! I can't wait! beside,
I've promised to visit by dinner-time
Bagdat, and accept the prime
Of the Head Cook's pottage, all he's rich in,
For having left, in the Caliph's kitchen,
Of a nest of scorpions no survivor—
With him I proved no bargain-driver.
With you, don't think I'll bate a stiver!
And folks who put me in a passion
May find me pipe to another fashion."

"How?" cried the Mayor, "d'ye think I'll brook
Being worse treated than a Cook?
Insulted by a lazy ribald
With idle pipe and vesture piebald?
You threaten us, fellow? Do your worst,
Blow your pipe there till you burst!"

Once more he stept into the street;
    And to his lips again
Laid his long pipe of smooth straight cane;
    And ere he blew three notes (such sweet
Soft notes as yet musician's cunning
    Never gave the enraptured air)
There was a rustling, that seem'd like a bustling
Of merry crowds justling at pitching and hustling,
Small feet were pattering, wooden shoes clattering,
Little hands clapping, and little tongues chattering,
And, like fowls in a farm-yard when barley is scattering,
Out came the children running.
All the little boys and girls,
With rosy cheeks and flaxen curls,
And sparkling eyes and teeth like pearls,
Tripping and skipping, ran merrily after
The wonderful music with shouting and laughter.

The Mayor was dumb, and the Council stood
As if they were changed into blocks of wood,
Unable to move a step, or cry
To the children merrily skipping by—
And could only follow with the eye
That joyous crowd at the Piper's back.
But how the Mayor was on the rack,
And the wretched Council's bosoms beat,
As the Piper turn'd from the High Street
To where the Weser roll'd its waters
Right in the way of their sons and daughters!

However, he turned from south to west,
And to Koppelberg Hill his steps address'd,
And after him the children press'd;
Great was the joy in every breast.
"He never can cross that mighty top!
He's forced to let the piping drop,
And we shall see our children stop!"
When, lo, as they reach'd the mountain's side,
A wondrous portal open'd wide,
As if a cavern was suddenly hollow'd;
And the Piper advanced and the children follow'd,
And when all were in to the very last,
The door in the mountain-side shut fast.
Did I say all? No! one was lame,
And could not dance the whole of the way,
And in after years, if you would blame
His sadness, he was used to say,
"It's dull in our town since my playmates left!
I can't forget that I'm bereft
Of all the pleasant sights they see,
Which the Piper also promised me,
For he led us, he said, to a joyous land,
Joining the town and just at hand,
Where waters gush'd and fruit trees grew,
And flowers put forth a fairer hue,
And everything was strange and new;
The sparrows were brighter than peacocks here,
And their dogs outran our fallow deer,
And honey-bees had lost their stings,
And horses were born with eagles' wings;
And just as I became assured
My lame foot would be speedily cured,
The music stopp'd, and I stood still,
And found myself outside the Hill,
Left alone against my will,
To go now limping as before,
And never hear of that country more!"

Alas, alas for Hamelin!
  There came into many a burgher's pate
  A text which says that Heaven's Gate
  Opes to the rich at as easy rate
As the needle's eye takes a camel in!

The Mayor sent east, west, north, and south
To offer the Piper by word of mouth,
  Wherever it was men's lot to find him,
Silver and gold to his heart's content,
If he'd only return the way he went,
  And bring the children behind him.
But when they saw 'twas a lost endeavor,
And Piper and dancers were gone for ever,
They made a decree that lawyers never
  Should think their records dated duly
If, after the day of the month and year,
These words did not as well appear:
"And so long after what happen'd here
  On the twenty-second of July,
Thirteen hundred and Seventy-six;"
And the better in memory to fix
The place of the children's last retreat,
They call'd it the Pied Piper's Street,
Where any one playing on pipe or tabor
Was sure for the future to lose his labor.
Nor suffer'd they hostelry or tavern
  To shock with mirth a street so solemn,
But opposite the place of the cavern
  They wrote the story on a column,
And on the great church-window painted
The same, to make the world acquainted
How their children were stolen away,
And there it stands to this very day.
And I must not omit to say
That in Transylvania there's a tribe
Of alien people that ascribe
The outlandish ways and dress
On which their neighbors lay such stress,
To their fathers and mothers having risen
Out of some subterranean prison,
Into which they were trepann'd
Long time ago in a mighty band
Out of Hamelin town in Brunswick land,
But how or why, they don't understand.

So, Willy, let you and me be wipers
Of scores out with all men—especially pipers;
And, whether they pipe us free, from rats or from mice,
If we've promised them aught, let us keep our promise.
                  ROBERT BROWNING.

The Rime of the Ancient Mariner.

Part I.

An ancient mariner meeteth three gallants bidden to a wedding feast, and detaineth one.

It is an ancient mariner,
And he stoppeth one of three,
" By thy long gray beard and glittering eye,
Now wherefore stopp'st thou me?

" The Bridegroom's doors are opened wide,
And I am next of kin;
The guests are met, the feast is set:
May'st hear the merry din."

He holds him with his skinny hand,
"There was a ship," quoth he.
"Hold off! unhand me, gray-beard loon!"
Eftsoons his hand dropt he.

The weddingguest is spellbound by the eye of the old sea-faring man, and constrained to hear his tale.

He holds him with his glittering eye—
The wedding guest stood still,
And listens like a three years child:
The mariner hath his will.

The wedding guest sat on a stone:
He cannot choose but hear;
And thus spake on that ancient man,
The bright-eyed mariner.

The ship was cheer'd, the harbor clear'd,
Merrily did we drop
Below the kirk, below the hill,
Below the lighthouse top.

The mariner tells how the ship sailed southward with a good wind and fair weather, till it reached the line.

The sun came up upon the left,
Out of the sea came he!
And he shone bright, and on the right
Went down into the sea.

Higher and higher every day,
Till over the mast at noon—
The wedding guest here beat his breast,
For he heard the loud bassoon.

The bride hath paced into the hall,
Red as a rose is she;
Nodding their heads before her goes
The merry minstrelsy.

The weddingguest heareth the bridal music; but the mariner continueth his tale.

The wedding guest he beat his breast,
Yet he cannot choose but hear;
And thus spake on that ancient man,
The bright-eyed mariner.

And now the storm-blast came, and he
Was tyrannous and strong:
He struck with his o'ertaking wings,
And chased us south along.

The ship drawn by a storm toward the south pole.

With sloping masts and dipping prow,
As who pursued with yell and blow
Still treads the shadow of his foe
And forward bends his head,
The ship drove fast, loud roar'd the blast,
And southward aye we fled.

And now there came both mist and snow,
And it grew wondrous cold:
And ice, mast-high, came floating by,
As green as emerald.

And through the drifts the snowy clifts
Did send a dismal sheen:
Nor shapes of men nor beasts we ken—
The ice was all between.

The land of ice, and of fearful sounds, where no living thing was to be seen.

The ice was here, the ice was there,
The ice was all around:
It crack'd and growl'd, and roar'd and howl'd,
Like noises in a swound!

At length did cross an albatross,
Thorough the fog it came;
As if it had been a Christian soul,
We hail'd it in God's name.

Till a great sea-bird called the albatross came through the snow-fog, and was received with great joy and hospitality.

It ate the food it ne'er had eat,
And round and round it flew.
The ice did split with a thunder-fit;
The helmsman steer'd us through!

And lo! the albatross proveth a bird of good omen, and followeth the ship as it returned northward through fog and floating ice.

And a good south wind sprung up
 behind;
The albatross did follow,
And every day, for food or play,
Came to the mariners' hollo!

In mist or cloud, on mast or shroud,
It perch'd for vespers nine;
Whiles all the night, through fog-
 smoke white,
Glimmer'd the white moonshine.

The ancient mariner inhospitably killeth the pious bird of good omen.

"God save thee, ancient mariner!
From the fiends, that plague thee
 thus!—
Why look'st thou so?"—With my
 cross-bow
I shot the albatross.

PART II.

The Sun now rose upon the right:
Out of the sea came he,
Still hid in mist, and on the left
Went down into the sea.

And the good south wind still blew
 behind,
But no sweet bird did follow,
Nor any day, for food or play,
Came to the mariners' hollo!

His shipmates cry out against the ancient mariner, for killing the bird of good luck.

And I had done an hellish thing,
And it would work 'em woe:
For all averr'd, I had kill'd the bird
That made the breeze to blow.
Ah wretch! said they, the bird to
 slay,
That made the breeze to blow!

But when the fog cleared off, they justify the same, and thus make themselves accomplices in the crime.

Nor dim nor red, like God's own
 head
The glorious Sun uprist:
Then all averr'd, I had kill'd the
 bird
That brought the fog and mist.
'Twas right, said they, such birds
 to slay,
That bring the fog and mist.

The fair breeze blew, the white foam
 flew,
The furrow follow'd free;
We were the first that ever burst
Into that silent sea.

The fair breeze continues; the ship enters the Pacific Ocean, and sails northward, even till it reaches the line.

Down dropt the breeze, the sails
 dropt down,
'Twas sad as sad could be;
And we did speak only to break
The silence of the sea!

The ship hath been suddenly becalmed;

All in a hot and copper sky,
The bloody Sun, at noon,
Right up above the mast did
 stand,
No bigger than the Moon.

Day after day, day after day,
We stuck, nor breath nor mo-
 tion;
As idle as a painted ship
Upon a painted ocean.

Water, water, everywhere,
And all the boards did shrink;
Water, water, everywhere,
Nor any drop to drink.

And the albatross begins to be avenged.

The very deep did rot: O Christ!
That ever this should be!
Yea, slimy things did crawl with
 legs
Upon the slimy sea.

About, about, in reel and rout,
The death-fires danced at night,
The water, like a witch's oils,
Burnt green, and blue, and white.

And some in dreams assurèd were
Of the spirit that plagued us so;
Nine fathom deep he had follow'd
 us
From the land of mist and snow.

A spirit had followed them; one of the invisible inhabitants of this planet, neither departed souls nor angels; concerning whom the learned Jew Josephus, and the Platonic Constantinopolitan, Michael Psellus, may be consulted. They are very numerous, and there is no climate or element without one or more.

And every tongue, through utter drought,
Was wither'd at the root;
We could not speak, no more than if
We had been choked with soot.

The shipmates, in their sore distress, would fain throw the whole guilt Ah! well-a-day! what evil looks
Had I from old and young!
Instead of the cross, the albatross
About my neck was hung.

on the ancient mariner; in sign whereof they hang the dead sea-bird round his neck.

PART III.

There pass'd a weary time. Each throat
Was parch'd, and glazed each eye.
A weary time! a weary time!
How glazed each weary eye,
The ancient mariner beholdeth a sign in the element afar off. When looking westward, I beheld
A something in the sky.

At first it seem'd a little speck,
And then it seem'd a mist;
It moved and moved, and took at last
A certain shape I wist.

A speck, a mist, a shape, I wist;
And still it near'd and near'd;
As if it dodged a water-sprite,
It plunged and tack'd and veer'd.

At its nearer approach, it seemeth him to be a ship; and at a dear ransom he freeth his speech from the bonds of thirst. With throats unslaked, with black lips baked,
We could nor laugh nor wail;
Through utter drought all dumb we stood!
I bit my arm, I suck'd the blood,
And cried, A sail! a sail!

With throats unslaked, with black lips baked,
Agape they heard me call;
A flash of joy. Gramercy! they for joy did grin,
And all at once their breath drew in,
As they were drinking all.

See! see! (I cried), she tacks no more! *And horror follows. For can it be a ship that comes onward without wind or tide?*
Hither to work us weal;
Without a breeze, without a tide,
She steadies with upright keel!

The western wave was all aflame,
The day was well-nigh done!
Almost upon the western wave
Rested the broad bright Sun;
When that strange shape drove suddenly
Betwixt us and the Sun.

And straight the Sun was fleck'd with bars *It seemeth him but the skeleton of a ship.*
(Heaven's Mother send us grace!),
As if through a dungeon-grate he peer'd
With broad and burning face.

Alas! (thought I, and my heart beat loud),
How fast she nears and nears!
Are those *her* sails that glance in the Sun,
Like restless gossameres?

Are those *her* ribs through which the Sun *And its ribs are seen as bars on the face of the setting sun.*
Did peer, as through a grate?
And is that Woman all her crew?
Is that a Death? and are there two? *The spectre-woman and her deathmate, and no other, on board*
Is Death that woman's mate?

Her lips were red, *her* looks were free, *the skeleton-ship. Like vessel, like crew.*
Her locks were yellow as gold;
Her skin was as white as leprosy,
The night-mare Life-in-Death was she,
Who thicks man's blood with cold.

The naked hulk alongside came, *Death and Life-in-Death have diced for the ship's crew, and she (the latter)*
And the twain were casting dice;
"The game is done! I've won, I've won!"
Quoth she, and whistles thrice.
winneth the ancient mariner.

<small>No twilight within the courts of the Sun.</small>
The Sun's rim dips; the stars rush
   out;
At one stride comes the dark;
   With far-heard whisper, o'er the
     sea,
   Off shot the spectre-bark.

<small>At the rising of the moon,</small>
We listen'd and look'd sideways
   up!
Fear at my heart, as at a cup;
   My life-blood seem'd to sip!
The stars were dim, and thick the
     night,
   The steersman's face by his lamp
     gleam'd white;
From the sails the dew did drip—
   Till clombe above the eastern bar
The hornèd Moon, with one bright
     star
   Within the nether tip.

<small>One after another,</small>
One after one, by the star-dogg'd
     Moon,
   Too quick for groan or sigh,
Each turn'd his face with a ghastly
     pang,
   And cursed me with his eye.

<small>His shipmates drop down dead;</small>
Four times fifty living men
   (And I heard nor sigh nor groan),
With heavy thump, a lifeless lump,
   They dropp'd down one by one.

<small>But Life-in-Death begins her work on the ancient mariner.</small>
The souls did from their bodies
     fly,—
   They fled to bliss or woe!
And every soul, it pass'd me by,
   Like the whizz of my cross-bow!

PART IV.

<small>The wedding guest feareth that a spirit is talking to him;</small>
"I fear thee, ancient mariner!
   I fear thy skinny hand!
And thou art long, and lank, and
     brown,
   As is the ribb'd sea-sand.

"I fear thee and thy glittering eye,
   And thy skinny hand so brown."—

<small>But the ancient mariner assureth him of his bodily life, and proceedeth to relate his horrible penance.</small>
Fear not, fear not, thou wedding-
     guest!
This body dropt not down.

Alone, alone, all, all alone,
Alone on a wide, wide sea!
And never a saint took pity on
   My soul in agony.

The many men so beautiful! <small>He despiseth the creatures of the calm.</small>
And they all dead did lie:
And a thousand thousand slimy
     things
Lived on; and so did I.

I look'd upon the rotting sea, <small>And envieth that they should live, and so many lie dead.</small>
   And drew my eyes away;
I look'd upon the rotting deck,
   And there the dead men lay.

I look'd to heaven, and tried to
     pray;
But, or ever a prayer had gusht,
A wicked whisper came, and made
   My heart as dry as dust.

I closed my lids, and kept them
     close,
   And the balls like pulses beat;
For the sky and the sea, and the
     sea and the sky,
Lay like a load on my weary eye,
   And the dead were at my feet.

The cold sweat melted from their <small>But the curse liveth for him in the eye of the dead men.</small>
     limbs,
Nor rot nor reek did they:
The look with which they look'd
     on me
Had never pass'd away.

An orphan's curse would drag to
     hell
A spirit from on high;
But oh! more horrible than that
Is a curse in a dead man's eye!
Seven days, seven nights, I saw that
     curse,
And yet I could not die.

The moving Moon went up the sky, <small>In his loneliness and fixedness he yearneth towards the journeying moon, and the stars that still sojourn, yet still move onward; and everywhere the blue sky belongs to them, and is their appointed rest, and their native country, and their own natural homes, which they enter unannounced, as lords that are certainly expected, and yet there is a silent joy at their arrival.</small>
And nowhere did abide:
Softly she was going up,
And a star or two beside—

Her beams bemock'd the sultry main,
Like April hoar-frost spread;
But where the ship's huge shadow lay,
The charmèd water burnt alway
A still and awful red.

By the light of the moon he beholdeth God's creatures of the great calm.

Beyond the shadow of the ship,
I watch'd the water-snakes:
They moved in tracks of shining white,
And when they rear'd, the elfish light
Fell off in hoary flakes.

Within the shadow of the ship
I watch'd their rich attire:
Blue, glossy green, and velvet black,
They coil'd and swam; and every track
Was a flash of golden fire.

Their beauty and their happiness.

O happy living things! no tongue
Their beauty might declare:
A spring of love gush'd from my heart,

He blesseth them in his heart.

And I bless'd them unaware:
Sure my kind saint took pity on me,
And I bless'd them unaware.

The spell begins to break.

The selfsame moment I could pray;
And from my neck so free
The albatross fell off, and sank
Like lead into the sea.

PART V.

Oh sleep! it is a gentle thing,
Beloved from pole to pole!
To Mary Queen the praise be given!
She sent the gentle sleep from Heaven,
That slid into my soul.

By grace of the holy mother, the ancient mariner is refreshed with rain.

The silly buckets on the deck,
That had so long remain'd,
I dreamt that they were fill'd with dew;
And when I awoke, it rain'd.

My lips were wet, my throat was cold,
My garments all were dank;
Sure I had drunken in my dreams,
And still my body drank.

I moved, and could not feel my limbs:
I was so light—almost
I thought that I had died in sleep,
And was a blessed ghost.

And soon I heard a roaring wind:
It did not come anear;
But with its sound it shook the sails,
That were so thin and sere.

He heareth sounds, and seeth strange sights and commotions in the sky and the element.

The upper air burst into life!
And a hundred fire-flags sheen,
To and fro they were hurried about!
And to and fro, and in and out,
The wan stars danced between.

And the coming wind did roar more loud,
And the sails did sigh like sedge;
And the rain pour'd down from one black cloud;
The Moon was at its edge.

The thick black cloud was cleft, and still
The Moon was at its side:
Like waters shot from some high crag,
The lightning fell with never a jag,
A river steep and wide.

The loud wind never reach'd the ship,
Yet now the ship moved on!
Beneath the lightning and the Moon
The dead men gave a groan.

The bodies of the ship's crew are inspired, and the ship moves on;

They groan'd, they stirr'd, they all uprose,
Nor spake, nor moved their eyes;
It had been strange, even in a dream,
To have seen those dead men rise.

The helmsman steer'd, the ship moved on;
Yet never a breeze up blew;
The mariners all 'gan work the ropes,
Where they were wont to do;
They raised their limbs like lifeless tools—
We were a ghastly crew.

The body of my brother's son
Stood by me, knee to knee:
The body and I pull'd at one rope,
But he said naught to me.

But not by the souls of the men, nor by dæmons of earth or middle air, but by a blessed troop of angelic spirits, sent down by the invocation of the guardian saint.

"I fear thee, ancient mariner!"
Be calm, thou wedding guest!
'Twas not those souls that fled in pain,
Which to their corses came again,
But a troop of spirits blest:

For when it dawn'd—they dropp'd their arms,
And cluster'd round the mast;
Sweet sounds rose slowly through their mouths,
And from their bodies pass'd.

Around, around, flew each sweet sound,
Then darted to the Sun;
Slowly the sounds came back again,
Now mix'd, now one by one.

Sometimes a-dropping from the sky,
I heard the skylark sing;
Sometimes all little birds that are,
How they seem'd to fill the sea and air
With their sweet jargoning!

And now 'twas like all instruments,
Now like a lonely flute;
And now it is an angel's song
That makes the heavens be mute.

It ceased; yet still the sails made on
A pleasant noise till noon,
A noise like of a hidden brook
In the leafy month of June,
That to the sleeping woods all night
Singeth a quiet tune.

Till noon we quietly sail'd on,
Yet never a breeze did breathe:
Slowly and smoothly went the ship,
Moved onward from beneath.

Under the keel nine fathom deep,
From the land of mist and snow,
The spirit slid: and it was he
That made the ship to go.
The sails at noon left off their tune,
And the ship stood still also.

The lonesome spirit from the south pole carries on the ship as far as the line, in obedience to the angelic troop, but still requireth vengeance.

The Sun, right up above the mast,
Had fix'd her to the ocean:
But in a minute she 'gan stir,
With a short uneasy motion—
Backwards and forwards half her length
With a short uneasy motion.

Then like a pawing horse let go,
She made a sudden bound:
It flung the blood into my head
And I fell down in a swound.

How long in that same fit I lay,
I have not to declare;
But ere my living life return'd,
I heard, and in my soul discern'd
Two voices in the air.

"Is it he?" quoth one, "Is this the man?
By Him who died on cross,
With his cruel bow he laid full low
The harmless albatross.

"The spirit who bideth by himself
In the land of mist and snow,
He loved the bird that loved the man
Who shot him with his bow."

The Polar Spirit's fellow-dæmons, the invisible inhabitants of the element, take part in his wrong; and two of them relate, one to the other, that penance long and heavy for the ancient mariner hath been accorded to the Polar Spirit, who returneth southward.

The other was a softer voice,
As soft as honey-dew:
Quoth he, "The man hath penance done,
And penance more will do."

PART VI.

FIRST VOICE.

But tell me, tell me! speak again
Thy soft response renewing—
What makes that ship drive on so fast?
What is the ocean doing?

SECOND VOICE.

Still as a slave before his lord,
The ocean hath no blast;
His great bright eye most silently
Up to the Moon is cast—

If he may know which way to go;
For she guides him smooth or grim.
See, brother, see! how graciously
She looketh down on him.

FIRST VOICE.

<small>The mariner hath been cast into a trance: for the angelic power causeth the vessel to drive northward, faster than human life could endure.</small>

But why drives on that ship so fast,
Without or wave or wind?

SECOND VOICE.

The air is cut away before,
And closes from behind.

Fly, brother, fly! more high, more high!
Or we shall be belated:
For slow and slow that ship will go,
When the mariner's trance is abated.

<small>The supernatural motion is retarded; the mariner awakes, and his penance begins anew.</small>

I woke, and we were sailing on
As in a gentle weather:
'Twas night, calm night, the moon was high;
The dead men stood together.

All stood together on the deck,
For a charnel-dungeon fitter:
All fix'd on me their stony eyes
That in the Moon did glitter.

The pang, the curse, with which they died,
Had never pass'd away:
I could not draw my eyes from theirs,
Nor turn them up to pray.

And now this spell was snapt: once more <small>The curse is finally expiated;</small>
I view'd the ocean green,
And look'd far forth, yet little saw
Of what had else been seen—

Like one, that on a lonesome road
Doth walk in fear and dread,
And having once turn'd round walks on,
And turns no more his head;
Because he knows a frightful fiend
Doth close behind him tread.

But soon there breathed a wind on me,
Nor sound nor motion made:
Its path was not upon the sea,
In ripple or in shade.

It raised my hair, it fann'd my cheek
Like a meadow-gale of spring—
It mingled strangely with my fears,
Yet it felt like a welcoming.

Swiftly, swiftly flew the ship,
Yet she sail'd softly too:
Sweetly, sweetly blew the breeze—
On me alone it blew.

Oh! dream of joy! is this indeed <small>And the ancient mariner beholdeth his native country.</small>
The lighthouse top I see?
Is this the hill? is this the kirk?
Is this mine own countree?

We drifted o'er the harbor-bar,
And I with sobs did pray—
Oh let me be awake, my God!
Or let me sleep alway.

The harbor-bay was clear as glass,
So smoothly it was strewn!
And on the bay the moonlight lay,
And the shadow of the moon.

The rock shone bright, the kirk no less,
That stands above the rock:
The moonlight steep'd in silentness
The steady weathercock.

And the bay was white with silent
  light,
Till rising from the same,
Full many shapes, that shadows
  were,
In crimson colors came.

The angelic spirits leave the dead bodies,

A little distance from the prow
Those crimson shadows were:
I turn'd my eyes upon the deck—
O Christ! what saw I there!

And appear in their own forms of light.

Each corse lay flat, lifeless and flat,
And by the holy rood!
A man all light, a seraph man,
On every corse there stood.

This seraph-band, each waved his
  hand:
It was a heavenly sight!
They stood as signals to the land,
Each one a lovely light;

This seraph-band, each waved his
  hand,
No voice did they impart—
No voice; but oh! the silence sank
Like music on my heart.

But soon I heard the dash of oars,
I heard the pilot's cheer;
My head was turn'd perforce away,
And I saw a boat appear.

The pilot and the pilot's boy,
I heard them coming fast:
Dear Lord in Heaven! it was a joy
The dead men could not blast.

I saw a third—I heard his voice:
It is the hermit good!
He singeth loud his godly hymns
That he makes in the wood.
He'll shrieve my soul, he'll wash
  away
The albatross's blood.

PART VII.

The hermit of the wood.

This hermit good lives in that wood
Which slopes down to the sea.
How loudly his sweet voice he
  rears!
He loves to talk with marineres
  That come from a far countree.

He kneels at morn, and noon, and
  eve—
He hath a cushion plump:
It is the moss that wholly hides
The rotted old·oak-stump.

The skiff-boat near'd: I heard
  them talk,
"Why, this is strange, I trow!
Where are those lights so many and
  fair,
That signal made but now?"

"Strange, by my faith!" the hermit said—
"And they answer'd not our cheer!
The planks look'd warp'd! and see
  those sails
How thin they are and sere!
I never saw aught like to them,
Unless perchance it were

Approacheth the ship with wonder.

Brown skeletons of leaves that lag
My forest-brook along;
When the ivy-tod is heavy with
  snow,
And the owlet whoops to the wolf
  below,
That eats the she-wolf's young."

"Dear Lord! it hath a fiendish
  look
(The pilot made reply)—
I am a-fear'd."—"Push on, push
  on!"
Said the hermit cheerily.

The boat came closer to the ship,
But I nor spake nor stirr'd;
The boat came close beneath the
  ship,
And straight a sound was heard.

Under the water it rumbled on,
Still louder and more dread:
It reach'd the ship, it split the bay;
The ship went down like lead.

The ship suddenly sinketh.

Stunn'd by that loud and dreadful
  sound,
Which sky and ocean smote,
Like one that hath been seven days
  drown'd
My body lay afloat;
But swift as dreams, myself I found
Within the pilot's boat.

The ancient mariner is saved in the pilot's boat.

Upon the whirl, where sank the ship,
The boat spun round and round;
And all was still, save that the hill
Was telling of the sound.

I moved my lips—the pilot shriek'd
And fell down in a fit;
The holy hermit raised his eyes,
And pray'd where he did sit.

I took the oars: the pilot's boy,
Who now doth crazy go,
Laugh'd loud and long, and all the while
His eyes went to and fro.
"Ha! ha!" quoth he, "full plain I see,
The Devil knows how to row."

And now, all in my own countree,
I stood on the firm land!
The hermit stepp'd forth from the boat,
And scarcely he could stand.

<small>The ancient mariner earnestly entreateth the hermit to shrieve him; and the penance of life falls on him.</small>
"Oh shrieve me, shrieve me, holy man!"
The hermit cross'd his brow.
"Say quick," quoth he, "I bid thee say—
What manner of man art thou?"

Forthwith this frame of mine was wrench'd
With a woeful agony,
Which forced me to begin my tale;
And then it left me free.

<small>And ever and anon throughout his future life an agony constraineth him to travel from land to land.</small>
Since then, at an uncertain hour,
That agony returns:
And till my ghastly tale is told,
This heart within me burns.

I pass, like night, from land to land;
I have strange power of speech;
That moment that his face I see,
I know the man that must hear me;
To him my tale I teach.

What loud uproar bursts from that door!
The wedding-guests are there:
But in the garden-bower the bride
And bride-maids singing are:
And hark the little vesper-bell,
Which biddeth me to prayer!

O wedding-guest! this soul hath been
Alone on a wide wide sea:
So lonely 'twas, that God himself
Scarce seemèd there to be.

Oh sweeter than the marriage-feast,
'Tis sweeter far to me,
To walk together to the kirk
With a goodly company!—

To walk together to the kirk,
And all together pray,
While each to his great Father bends,
Old men, and babes, and loving friends,
And youths and maidens gay!

<small>And to teach, by his own example, love and reverence to all things that God made and loveth.</small>
Farewell, farewell! but this I tell
To thee, thou wedding-guest!
He prayeth well, who loveth well
Both man, and bird, and beast.

He prayeth best, who loveth best
All things both great and small;
For the dear God who loveth us,
He made and loveth all.

The mariner, whose eye is bright,
Whose beard with age is hoar,
Is gone; and now the wedding-guest
Turn'd from the bridegroom's door.

He went like one that hath been stunn'd,
And is of sense forlorn:
A sadder and a wiser man,
He rose the morrow morn.

SAMUEL TAYLOR COLERIDGE.

THE SKELETON IN ARMOR.

"Speak! speak! thou fearful guest!
  Who, with thy hollow breast
  Still in rude armor drest,
    Comest to daunt me!
  Wrapt not in Eastern balms,
  But with thy fleshless palms
  Stretch'd, as if asking alms;
    Why dost thou haunt me?"

Then, from those cavernous eyes
  Pale flashes seem'd to rise,
  As when the Northern skies
    Gleam in December;
  And, like the water's flow
  Under December's snow,
  Came a dull voice of woe
    From the heart's chamber.

"I was a Viking old!
  My deeds, though manifold,
  No Skald in song has told,
    No Saga taught thee!
  Take heed, that in thy verse
  Thou dost the tale rehearse,
  Else dread a dead man's curse;
    For this I sought thee.

"Far in the Northern land,
  By the wild Baltic's strand,
  I, with my childish hand,
    Tamed the ger-falcon;
  And, with my skates fast bound,
  Skimm'd the half-frozen sound,
  That the poor whimpering hound
    Trembled to walk on.

"Oft to his frozen lair
  Track'd I the grisly bear,
  While from my path the hare
    Fled like a shadow;
  Oft through the forest dark
  Follow'd the were-wolf's bark,
  Until the soaring lark
    Sang from the meadow.

"But when I older grew,
  Joining a corsair's crew,
  O'er the dark sea I flew
    With the marauders.
  Wild was the life we led;
  Many the souls that sped,
  Many the hearts that bled,
    By our stern orders.

"Many a wassail bout
  Wore the long winter out;
  Often our midnight shout
    Set the cocks crowing,
  As we the Berserk's tale
  Measured in cups of ale,
  Draining the oaken pail,
    Fill'd to o'erflowing.

"Once as I told in glee
  Tales of the stormy sea,
  Soft eyes did gaze on me,
    Burning, yet tender;
  And as the white stars shine
  On the dark Norway pine,
  On that dark heart of mine
    Fell their soft splendor.

"I woo'd the blue-eyed maid,
  Yielding, yet half afraid,
  And in the forest's shade
    Our vows were plighted.
  Under its loosen'd vest
  Flutter'd her little breast,
  Like birds within their nest
    By the hawk frighted.

"Bright in her father's hall
  Shields gleam'd upon the wall,
  Loud sang the minstrels all,
    Chanting his glory;
  When of old Hildebrand
  I ask'd his daughter's hand,
  Mute did the minstrels stand
    To hear my story.

"While the brown ale he quaff'd,
  Loud then the champion laugh'd,
  And as the wind-gusts waft
    The sea-foam brightly,
  So the loud laugh of scorn,
  Out of those lips unshorn,
  From the deep drinking-horn
    Blew the foam lightly.

"She was a prince's child,
  I but a Viking wild,
  And though she blush'd and smiled,
    I was discarded!
  Should not the dove so white
  Follow the sea-mew's flight?
  Why did they leave that night
    Her nest unguarded?

"Scarce had I put to sea,
  Bearing the maid with me,—
  Fairest of all was she
    Among the Norsemen!—
When on the white sea-strand,
Waving his armèd hand,
Saw we old Hildebrand,
    With twenty horsemen.

"Then launch'd they to the blast,
  Bent like a reed each mast,
  Yet we were gaining fast,
    When the wind fail'd us;
And with a sudden flaw
Came round the gusty Skaw,
So that our foe we saw
    Laugh as he hail'd us.

"And as to catch the gale
  Round veer'd the flapping sail,
  Death! was the helmsman's hail,
    Death without quarter!
Mid-ships with iron keel
Struck we her ribs of steel;
Down her black hulk did reel
    Through the black water!

"As with his wings aslant,
  Sails the fierce cormorant,
  Seeking some rocky haunt,
    With his prey laden,
So toward the open main,
Beating to sea again,
Through the wild hurricane
    Bore I the maiden.

"Three weeks we westward bore,
  And when the storm was o'er,
  Cloud-like we saw the shore
    Stretching to leeward;
There for my lady's bower
Built I the lofty tower,
Which, to this very hour,
    Stands looking seaward.

"There lived we many years;
  Time dried the maiden's tears;
  She had forgot her fears,
    She was a mother;
Death closed her mild blue eyes,
Under that tower she lies;
Ne'er shall the sun arise
    On such another!

"Still grew my bosom then,
  Still as a stagnant fen!
  Hateful to me were men,
    The sunlight hateful.
In the vast forest here,
Clad in my warlike gear,
Fell I upon my spear,
    Oh, death was grateful!

"Thus, seam'd with many scars,
  Bursting these prison-bars,
  Up to its native stars
    My soul ascended.
There, from the flowing bowl
Deep drinks the warrior's soul,
Skoal! to the Northland! skoal!"
    —Thus the tale ended.
        HENRY WADSWORTH LONGFELLOW.

LA BELLE DAME SANS MERCI.

OH what can ail thee, knight-at-arms!
  Alone and palely loitering?
The sedge has wither'd from the lake,
  And no birds sing.

Oh what can ail thee, knight-at-arms!
  So haggard and so woe-begone?
The squirrel's granary is full,
  And the harvest's done.

I see a lily on thy brow,
  With anguish moist and fever dew;
And on thy cheeks a fading rose
  Fast withereth too.

I met a lady in the mead—
  Full beautiful, a fairy's child;
Her hair was long, her foot was light,
  And her eyes were wild.

I made a garland for her head,
  And bracelets too, and fragrant zone;
She look'd at me as she did love,
  And made sweet moan.

I set her on my pacing steed,
  And nothing else saw all day long;
For sidelong would she bend, and sing
  A fairy song.

She found me roots of relish sweet,
  And honey wild, and manna dew;
And sure in language strange she said—
  "I love thee true."

She took me to her elfin grot,
   And there she wept, and sigh'd full sore;
And there I shut her wild, wild eyes
   With kisses four.

And there she lull'd me asleep;
   And there I dream'd—Ah! woe betide!
The latest dream I ever dream'd
   On the cold hill's side.

I saw pale kings and princes too—
   Pale warriors, death-pale were they all;
They cried—"La belle dame sans merci
   Hath thee in thrall!"

I saw their starved lips in the gloam,
   With horrid warning gapèd wide;
And I awoke, and found me here,
   On the cold hill's side.

And this is why I sojourn here,
   Alone and palely loitering,
Though the sedge is wither'd from the lake,
   And no birds sing.
                   JOHN KEATS.

THE HAUNTED HOUSE.

A ROMANCE.

"'A jolly place,' said he, 'in days of old,
But something ails it now; the spot is curst.'"
      HART-LEAP WELL, BY WORDSWORTH.

PART I.

SOME dreams we have are nothing else but dreams,
   Unnatural and full of contradictions,
Yet others of our most romantic schemes
   Are something more than fictions.

It might be only on enchanted ground,
   It might be merely by a thought's expansion,
But in the spirit, or the flesh, I found
   An old deserted mansion.

A residence for woman, child, and man,
   A dwelling-place,—and yet no habitation;
A house—but under some prodigious ban
   Of excommunication.

Unhinged the iron gates half open hung,
   Jarr'd by the gusty gales of many winters,
That from its crumbled pedestal had flung
   One marble globe in splinters.

No dog was at the threshold, great or small,
   No pigeon on the roof, no household creature,
No cat demurely dozing on the wall—
   Not one domestic feature.

No human figure stirr'd, to go or come,
   No face look'd forth from shut or open casement,
No chimney smoked—there was no sign of home
   From parapet to basement.

With shatter'd panes the grassy court was starr'd;
   The time-worn coping-stone had tumbled after,
And through the ragged roof the sky shone, barr'd
   With naked beam and rafter.

O'er all there hung a shadow and a fear,
   A sense of mystery the spirit daunted,
And said, as plain as whisper in the ear,
   The place is haunted!

The flow'r grew wild and rankly as the weed,
   Roses with thistles struggled for espial,
And vagrant plants of parasitic breed
   Had overgrown the dial.

But gay or gloomy, steadfast or infirm,
   No heart was there to heed the hour's duration;
All times and tides were lost in one long term
   Of stagnant desolation.

The wren had built within the porch; she found
   Its quiet loneliness so sure and thorough;
And on the lawn, within its turfy mound,
   The rabbit made his burrow.

The rabbit wild and gray, that flitted through
   The shrubby clumps, and frisk'd, and sat, and vanish'd,
But leisurely and bold, as if he knew
   His enemy was banish'd.

The wary crow, the pheasant from the
    woods,
  Lull'd by the still and everlasting same-
    ness,
Close to the mansion, like domestic broods,
  Fed with a "shocking tameness."

The coot was swimming in the reedy pond,
  Beside the water-hen, so soon affrighted,
And in the weedy moat the heron, fond
  Of solitude, alighted,—

The moping heron, motionless and stiff,
  That on a stone, as silently and stilly,
Stood, an apparent sentinel, as if
  To guard the water-lily.

No sound was heard except, from far away,
  The ringing of the witwall's shrilly
    laughter,
Or, now and then, the chatter of the jay,
  That Echo murmur'd after.

But Echo never mock'd the human tongue;
  Some weighty crime, that Heaven could
    not pardon,
A secret curse on that old building hung,
  And its deserted garden.

The beds were all untouch'd by hand or
    tool:
  No footstep mark'd the damp and mossy
    gravel,
Each walk as green as is the mantled pool,
  For want of human travel.

The vine unpruned, and the neglected
    peach,
  Droop'd from the wall with which they
    used to grapple;
And on the canker'd tree, in easy reach,
  Rotted the golden apple.

But awfully the truant shunn'd the ground,
  The vagrant kept aloof, and daring
    poacher;
In spite of gaps that through the fences
    round
  Invited the encroacher.

For over all there hung a cloud of fear,
  A sense of mystery the spirit daunted,
And said, as plain as whisper in the ear,
  The place is haunted!

The pear and quince lay squander'd on
    the grass;
  The mould was purple with unheeded
    showers
Of bloomy plums—a wilderness it was
  Of fruits, and weeds, and flowers!

The marigold amidst the nettles blew,
  The gourd embraced the rose-bush in
    its ramble,
The thistle and the stock together grew,
  The hollyhock and bramble.

The bearbine with the lilac interlaced,
  The sturdy burdock choked its slender
    neighbor,
The spicy pink. All tokens were effaced
  Of human care and labor.

The very yew formality had train'd
  To such a rigid pyramidal stature,
For want of trimming had almost regain'd
  The raggedness of nature.

The fountain was a-dry—neglect and
    time
  Had marr'd the work of artisan and
    mason,
And efts and croaking frogs, begot of
    slime,
  Sprawl'd in the ruin'd basin.

The statue, fallen from its marble base,
  Amidst the refuse leaves, and herbage
    rotten,
Lay like the idol of some bygone race,
  Its name and rites forgotten.

On ev'ry side the aspect was the same,
  All ruin'd, desolate, forlorn, and savage:
No hand or foot within the precinct came
  To rectify or ravage.

For over all there hung a cloud of fear,
  A sense of mystery the spirit daunted,
And said, as plain as whisper in the ear,
  The place is haunted!

PART II.

Oh, very gloomy is the house of Woe,
  Where tears are falling while the bell is
    knelling,
With all the dark solemnities which show
  That Death is in the dwelling!

Oh very, very dreary is the room
  Where Love, domestic Love, no longer nestles,
But, smitten by the common stroke of doom,
  The corpse lies on the trestles!

But House of Woe, and hearse, and sable pall,
  The narrow home of the departed mortal,
Ne'er looked so gloomy as that ghostly hall,
  With its deserted portal!

The centipede along the threshold crept,
  The cobweb hung across in mazy tangle,
And in its winding-sheet the maggot slept
  At every nook and angle.

The keyhole lodged the earwig and her brood,
  The emmets of the steps had old possession,
And march'd in search of their diurnal food
  In undisturb'd procession,—

As undisturb'd as the prehensile cell
  Of moth or maggot, or the spider's tissue,
For never foot upon that threshold fell,
  To enter or to issue.

O'er all there hung the shadow of a fear,
  A sense of mystery the spirit daunted,
And said, as plain as whisper in the ear,
  The place is haunted!

Howbeit, the door I push'd—or so I dream'd—
  Which slowly, slowly gaped—the hinges creaking
With such a rusty eloquence, it seem'd
  That Time himself was speaking.

But Time was dumb within that mansion old,
  Or left his tale to the heraldic banners
That hung from the corroded walls, and told
  Of former men and manners,—

Those tatter'd flags, that with the open'd door
  Seem'd the old wave of battle to remember,
While fallen fragments danced upon the floor
  Like dead leaves in December.

The startled bats flew out—bird after bird—
  The screech-owl overhead began to flutter,
And seem'd to mock the cry that she had heard
  Some dying victim utter!

A shriek that echo'd from the joisted roof,
  And up the stair, and further still and further,
Till in some ringing chamber far aloof
  It ceased its tale of murther!

Meanwhile the rusty armor rattled round,
  The banner shudder'd, and the ragged streamer;
All things the horrid tenor of the sound
  Acknowledged with a tremor.

The antlers, where the helmet hung and belt,
  Stirr'd as the tempest stirs the forest branches,
Or as the stag had trembled when he felt
  The bloodhound at his haunches.

The window jingled in its crumbled frame,
  And through its many gaps of destitution
Dolorous moans and hollow sighings came,
  Like those of dissolution.

The woodlouse dropp'd, and roll'd into a ball,
  Touch'd by some impulse occult or mechanic,
And nameless beetles ran along the wall
  In universal panic.

The subtle spider, that from overhead
  Hung like a spy on human guilt and error,
Suddenly turn'd, and up its slender thread
  Ran with a nimble terror.

The very stains and fractures on the wall,
  Assuming features solemn and terrific,
Hinted some tragedy of that old hall,
  Lock'd up in hieroglyphic,—

Some tale that might, perchance, have solved the doubt
  Wherefore, amongst those flags so dull and livid,
The banner of the Bloody Hand shone out so ominously vivid;

Some key to that inscrutable appeal,
  Which made the very frame of Nature quiver;
And every thrilling nerve and fibre feel
  So ague-like a shiver.

For over all there hung a cloud of fear,
  A sense of mystery the spirit daunted,
And said, as plain as whisper in the ear,
  The place is haunted!

If but a rat had linger'd in the house,
  To lure the thought into a social channel!
But not a rat remain'd, or tiny mouse,
  To squeak behind the panel.

Huge drops roll'd down the walls, as if they wept;
  And where the cricket used to chirp so shrilly,
The toad was squatting, and the lizard crept
  On that damp hearth and chilly.

For years no cheerful blaze had sparkled there,
  Or glanced on coat of buff or knightly metal;
The slug was crawling on the vacant chair,
  The snail upon the settle.

The floor was redolent of mould and must,
  The fungus in the rotten seams had quicken'd;
While on the oaken table coats of dust
  Perennially had thicken'd.

No mark of leathern jack or metal can,
  No cup—no horn—no hospitable token,—
All social ties between that board and man
  Had long ago been broken.

There was so foul a rumor in the air,
  The shadow of a presence so atrocious;
No human creature could have feasted there,
  Even the most ferocious!

For over all there hung a cloud of fear,
  A sense of mystery the spirit daunted,
And said, as plain as whisper in the ear,
  The place is haunted!

Part III.

'Tis hard for human actions to account,
  Whether from reason or from impulse only—
But some internal prompting bade me mount
  The gloomy stairs and lonely,—

Those gloomy stairs, so dark, and damp, and cold,
  With odors as from bones and relics carnal,
Deprived of rite, and consecrated mould,
  The chapel vault, or charnel;

Those dreary stairs, where with the sounding stress
  Of ev'ry step so many echoes blended,
The mind, with dark misgivings, fear'd to guess
  How many feet ascended.

The tempest with its spoils had drifted in,
  Till each unwholesome stone was darkly spotted,
As thickly as the leopard's dappled skin,
  With leaves that rankly rotted.

The air was thick—and in the upper gloom
  The bat—or something in its shape—was winging;
And on the wall, as chilly as a tomb,
  The Death's-head moth was clinging,—

That mystic moth, which, with a sense profound
  Of all unholy presence, augurs truly;
And with a grim significance flits round
  The taper burning bluely.

Such omens in the place there seem'd to be,
  At every crooked turn, or on the landing,
The straining eyeball was prepared to see
  Some apparition standing.

For over all there hung a cloud of fear,
  A sense of mystery the spirit daunted,
And said, as plain as whisper in the ear,
  The place is haunted!

Yet no portentous shape the sight amazed;
   Each object plain, and tangible, and valid;
But from their tarnish'd frames dark figures gazed,
   And faces spectre-pallid.

Not merely with the mimic life that lies
   Within the compass of Art's simulation:
Their souls were looking through their painted eyes
   With awful speculation.

On every lip a speechless horror dwelt;
   On every brow the burden of affliction;
The old ancestral spirits knew and felt
   The house's malediction.

Such earnest woe their features overcast,
   They might have stirr'd, or sigh'd, or wept, or spoken;
But, save the hollow moaning of the blast,
   The stillness was unbroken.

No other sound or stir of life was there,
   Except my steps in solitary clamber
From flight to flight, from humid stair to stair,
   From chamber into chamber.

Deserted rooms of luxury and state,
   That old magnificence had richly furnish'd
With pictures, cabinets of ancient date,
   And carvings gilt and burnish'd.

Rich hangings, storied by the needle's art
   With Scripture history, or classic fable;
But all had faded, save one ragged part,
   Where Cain was slaying Abel.

The silent waste of mildew and the moth
   Had marr'd the tissue with a partial ravage;
But undecaying frown'd upon the cloth
   Each feature stern and savage.

The sky was pale; the cloud a thing of doubt;
   Some hues were fresh, and some decay'd and duller;
But still the Bloody Hand shone strangely out
   With vehemence of color!—

The Bloody Hand that with a lurid stain
   Shone on the dusty floor, a dismal token,
Projected from the casement's painted pane,
   Where all beside was broken;

The Bloody Hand significant of crime,
   That, glaring on the old heraldic banner,
Had kept its crimson unimpair'd by time,
   In such a wondrous manner!

O'er all there hung the shadow of a fear,
   A sense of mystery the spirit daunted,
And said, as plain as whisper in the ear,
   The place is haunted!

The death-watch tick'd behind the panell'd oak,
   Inexplicable tremors shook the arras,
And echoes strange and mystical awoke,
   The fancy to embarrass.

Prophetic hints that fill'd the soul with dread,
   But through one gloomy entrance pointing mostly,
The while some secret inspiration said,
   That chamber is the ghostly!

Across the door no gossamer festoon
   Swung pendulous—no web—no dusty fringes,
No silky chrysalis or white cocoon,
   About its nooks and hinges.

The spider shunn'd the interdicted room,
   The moth, the beetle, and the fly were banish'd,
And where the sunbeam fell athwart the gloom
   The very midge had vanish'd.

One lonely ray that glanced upon a bed,
   As if with awful aim direct and certain,
To show the Bloody Hand in burning red
   Embroider'd on the curtain.

And yet no gory stain was on the quilt—
   The pillow in its place had slowly rotted:
The floor alone retain'd the trace of guilt,
   Those boards obscurely spotted,—

Obscurely spotted to the door, and thence
  With mazy doubles to the grated casement—
Oh what a tale they told of fear intense,
  Of horror and amazement!

What human creature in the dead of night
  Had coursed like hunted hare that cruel distance?
Had sought the door, the window, in his flight,
  Striving for dear existence?

What shrieking spirit in that bloody room
  Its mortal frame had violently quitted?—
Across the sunbeam, with a sudden gloom,
  A ghostly shadow flitted,—

Across the sunbeam, and along the wall,
  But painted on the air so very dimly,
It hardly veil'd the tapestry at all,
  Or portrait frowning grimly.

O'er all there hung the shadow of a fear,
  A sense of mystery the spirit daunted,
And said, as plain as whisper in the ear,
  The place is haunted!
    THOMAS HOOD.

THE HAUNTED PALACE.

IN the greenest of our valleys,
  By good angels tenanted,
Once a fair and stately palace
  (Radiant palace) rear'd its head.
In the monarch Thought's dominion
  It stood there!
Never seraph spread a pinion
  Over fabric half so fair.

Banners, yellow, glorious, golden,
  On its roof did float and flow
(This, all this, was in the olden
  Time, long ago);
And every gentle air that dallied
  In that sweet day,
Along the ramparts plumed and pallid,
  A wingèd odor went away.

Wanderers in that happy valley
  Through two luminous windows saw
Spirits moving musically
  To a lute's well-tunèd law;

Round about a throne, where, sitting
  (Porphyrogene!)
In state his glory well befitting,
  The ruler of the realm was seen.

And all with pearl and ruby glowing
  Was the fair palace-door,
Through which came flowing, flowing, flowing,
  And sparkling evermore,
A troop of echoes, whose sweet duty
  Was but to sing,
In voices of surpassing beauty,
  The wit and wisdom of their king.

But evil things, in robes of sorrow,
  Assail'd the monarch's high estate
(Ah! let us mourn, for never morrow
  Shall dawn upon him, desolate);
And round about his home the glory
  That blush'd and bloom'd
Is but a dim-remember'd story
  Of the old time entomb'd.

And travellers now, within that valley,
  Through the red-litten windows see
Vast forms that move fantastically
  To a discordant melody;
While, like a ghastly, rapid river,
  Through the pale door
A hideous throng rush out for ever,
  And laugh—but smile no more.
    EDGAR ALLAN POE.

ALONZO THE BRAVE AND THE FAIR IMOGINE.

A WARRIOR so bold, and a virgin so bright,
  Conversed as they sat on the green;
They gazed on each other with tender delight;
Alonzo the Brave was the name of the knight,
  The maiden's, the Fair Imogine.

"And oh!" said the youth, "since to-morrow I go
  To fight in a far-distant land,
Your tears for my absence soon ceasing to flow,
Some other will court you, and you will bestow
  On a wealthier suitor your hand."

"Oh, hush these suspicions," Fair Imogine said,
"Offensive to love and to me;
For if you be living, or if you be dead,
I swear by the Virgin that none in your stead
Shall husband of Imogine be.

"If e'er I, by lust or by wealth led aside,
Forget my Alonzo the Brave,
God grant that, to punish my falsehood and pride,
Your ghost at the marriage may sit by my side,
May tax me with perjury, claim me as bride,
And bear me away to the grave!"

To Palestine hasten'd the hero so bold;
His love she lamented him sore,
But scarce had a twelvemonth elapsed, when, behold!
A baron, all cover'd with jewels and gold,
Arrived at Fair Imogine's door.

His treasures, his presents, his spacious domain,
Soon made her untrue to her vows;
He dazzled her eyes, he bewilder'd her brain,
He caught her affections, so light and so vain,
And carried her home as his spouse.

And now had the marriage been bless'd by the priest,
The revelry now was begun,
The tables they groan'd with the weight of the feast,
Nor yet had the laughter and merriment ceased,
When the bell at the castle toll'd one.

Then first with amazement fair Imogine found
A stranger was placed by her side;
His air was terrific, he utter'd no sound,
He spake not, he moved not, he look'd not around,
But earnestly gazed on the bride.

His visor was closed, and gigantic his height,
His armor was sable to view;
All pleasure and laughter were hush'd at his sight;
The dogs, as they eyed him, drew back in affright;
The lights in the chamber burn'd blue!

His presence all bosoms appear'd to dismay;
The guests sat in silence and fear;
At length spake the bride—while she trembled—"I pray,
Sir Knight, that your helmet aside you would lay,
And deign to partake of our cheer."

The lady is silent; the stranger complies,
His visor he slowly unclosed;
O God! what a sight met fair Imogine's eyes!
What words can express her dismay and surprise
When a skeleton's head was exposed!

All present then utter'd a terrified shout,
All turn'd with disgust from the scene;
The worms they crept in, and the worms they crept out,
And sported his eyes and his temples about,
While the spectre address'd Imogine.

"Behold me, thou false one, behold me!" he cried,
"Remember Alonzo the Brave!
God grants that, to punish thy falsehood and pride,
My ghost at thy marriage should sit by thy side,
Should tax thee with perjury, claim thee as bride,
And bear thee away to the grave!"

Thus saying, his arms round the lady he wound,
While loudly she shriek'd in dismay;
Then sunk with his prey through the wide-yawning ground,
Nor ever again was Fair Imogine found,
Or the spectre that bore her away.

Not long lived the baron, and none, since that time,
To inhabit the castle presume,
For chronicles tell that, by order sublime,
There Imogine suffers the pain of her crime,
And mourns her deplorable doom.

At midnight, four times in each year, does
    her sprite,
When mortals in slumber are bound,
Array'd in her bridal apparel of white,
Appear in the hall with the skeleton
    knight,
And shriek as he whirls her around.

While they drink out of skulls newly torn
    from the grave,
    Dancing round them the spectres are
      seen;
Their liquor is blood, and this horrible
    stave
They howl: "To the health of Alonzo the
    Brave,
And his consort, the Fair Imogine!"
          MATTHEW GREGORY LEWIS.

TAM O'SHANTER.
A TALE.
"Of brownys and of bogilis full is this buke."—
          GAWIN DOUGLAS.

WHEN chapman billies leave the street,
And drouthy neebors neebors meet,
As market-days are wearing late,
An' folks begin to tak' the gate;
While we sit bousing at the nappy,
An' gettin' fou and unco happy,
We think na on the lang Scots miles,
The mosses, waters, slaps, and styles,
That lie between us and our hame,
Where sits our sulky sullen dame,
Gathering her brows like gathering storm,
Nursing her wrath to keep it warm.

This truth fand honest Tam O'Shanter,
As he frae Ayr ae night did canter
(Auld Ayr, wham ne'er a town surpasses,
For honest men and bonny lasses).
O Tam! hadst thou but been sae wise,
As ta'en thy ain wife Kate's advice!
She tauld thee weel thou was a skellum,
A blethering, blustering, drunken blellum;
That frae November till October,
Ae market-day thou was nae sober;
That ilka melder, wi' the miller,
Thou sat as lang as thou had siller;
That ev'ry naig was ca'd a shoe on,
The smith and thee gat roaring fou on;
That at the Lord's house, ev'n on Sunday,
Thou drank wi' Kirton Jean till Monday.

She prophesy'd, that late or soon,
Thou would be found deep drown'd in
    Doon;
Or catch'd wi' warlocks in the mirk,
By Alloway's auld haunted kirk.

Ah, gentle dames! it gars me greet,
To think how many counsels sweet,
How many lengthen'd sage advices,
The husband frae the wife despises!

But to our tale:—Ae market night,
Tam had got planted unco right;
Fast by an ingle, bleezing finely,
Wi' reaming swats, that drank divinely;
And at his elbow, Souter Johnny,
His ancient, trusty, drouthy crony;
Tam lo'ed him like a vera brither;
They had been fou for weeks thegither!
The night drave on wi' sangs an' clatter;
And ay the ale was growing better:
The landlady and Tam grew gracious;
Wi' favors secret, sweet, and precious;
The Souter tauld his queerest stories;
The landlord's laugh was ready chorus.
The storm without might rair and rustle—
Tam did na mind the storm a whistle.
Care, mad to see a man sae happy,
E'en drown'd himself amang the nappy!
As bees flee hame wi' lades o' treasure,
The minutes wing'd their way wi' pleasure:
Kings may be blest, but Tam was glorious,
O'er a' the ills of life victorious.

But pleasures are like poppies spread,
You seize the flow'r, its bloom is shed;
Or like the snow falls in the river,
A moment white—then melts for ever;
Or like the borealis race,
That flit ere you can point their place;
Or like the rainbow's lovely form
Evanishing amid the storm.
Nae man can tether time or tide;
The hour approaches Tam maun ride;
That hour, o' night's black arch the key-
    stane,
That dreary hour he mounts his beast in;
And sic a night he taks the road in
As ne'er poor sinner was abroad in.

The wind blew as 'twad blawn its last;
The rattling show'rs rose on the blast;
The speedy gleams the darkness swallow'd;
Loud, deep, and lang the thunder bellow'd;

That night, a child might understand,
The De'il had business on his hand.

Weel mounted on his gray mare, Meg,
  A better never lifted leg,
Tam skelpit on thro' dub and mire,
Despising wind, and rain, and fire;
Whiles holding fast his guid blue bonnet;
Whiles crooning o'er some auld Scots sonnet;
Whiles glow'ring round wi' prudent cares,
Lest bogles catch him unawares;
Kirk-Alloway was drawing nigh,
Where ghaists and houlets nightly cry.—
By this time he was cross the foord
Where in the snaw the chapman smoor'd;
And past the birks and meikle stane,
Where drunken Charlie brak's neck-bane;
And thro' the whins, and by the cairn,
Where hunters fand the murder'd bairn;
And near the thorn, aboon the well,
Where Mungo's mither hang'd hersel.
Before him Doon pours all his floods;
The doubling storm roars thro' the woods;
The lightnings flash from pole to pole;
Near and more near the thunders roll;
When, glimmering thro' the groaning trees,
Kirk-Alloway seem'd in a bleeze;
Thro' ilka bore the beams were glancing;
And loud resounded mirth and dancing.

Inspiring bold John Barleycorn!
What dangers thou canst make us scorn!
Wi' tippenny, we fear nae evil;
Wi' usquabae we'll face the devil!
The swats sae ream'd in Tammie's noddle,
Fair play, he cared nae deils a boddle.
But Maggie stood right sair astonish'd,
'Till, by the heel and hand admonish'd,
She ventured forward on the light;
And, wow! Tam saw an unco sight!
Warlocks and witches in a dance;
Nae cotillon brent new frae France,
But hornpipes, jigs, strathspeys, and reels,
Put life and mettle in their heels:
A winnock-bunker in the east,
There sat auld Nick, in shape o' beast;
A towzie tyke, black, grim, and large,
To gie them music was his charge;
He screw'd the pipes and gart them skirl,
Till roof and rafters a' did dirl.—
Coffins stood round, like open presses;
That shaw'd the dead in their last dresses;
And by some devilish cantrip slight
Each in its cauld hand held a light—
By which heroic Tam was able
To note upon the haly table,
A murderer's banes in gibbet airns;
Twa span-lang, wee unchristen'd bairns;
A thief, new-cutted frae a rape,
Wi' his last gasp his gab did gape;
Five tomahawks, wi' bluid red-rusted;
Five scimitars, wi' murder crusted;
A garter, which a babe had strangled;
A knife, a father's throat had mangled,
Whom his ain son o' life bereft,
The gray hairs yet stack to the heft:
Wi' mair o' horrible and awfu',
Which ev'n to name wad be unlawfu'.

As Tammie glowr'd, amazed, and curious,
The mirth and fun grew fast and furious:
The piper loud and louder blew;
The dancers quick and quicker flew;
They reel'd, they set, they cross'd, they cleekit,
'Till ilka carlin swat and reekit,
And coost her duddies to the wark,
And linket at it in her sark!

Now Tam, O Tam! had thae been queans
A' plump and strapping, in their teens;
Their sarks, instead o' creeshie flannen,
Been snaw-white seventeen-hunder linen,
Thir breeks o' mine, my only pair,
That ance were plush, o' guid blue hair,
I wad hae gi'en them off my hurdies,
For ae blink o' the bonnie burdies!

But wither'd beldams, auld and droll,
Rigwoodie hags, wad spean a foal,
Lowping an' flinging on a cummock,
I wonder didna turn thy stomach.

But Tam kenn'd what was what fu' brawlie,
There was a winsome wench and walie,
That night enlisted in the core
(Lang after kenn'd on Carrick shore;
For mony a beast to dead she shot,
And perish'd mony a bonnie boat,
And shook baith meikle corn and bear,
And kept the country-side in fear).
Her cutty sark, o' Paisley harn,
That while a lassie she had worn,
In longitude tho' sorely scanty,
It was her best, and she was vauntie.—

Ah! little kenn'd thy reverend grannie,
That sark she coft for her wee Nannie,
Wi' twa pund Scots ('twas a' her riches),
Wad ever graced a dance of witches!

But here my muse her wing maun cour;
Sic flights are far beyond her pow'r;
To sing how Nannie lap and flang
(A souple jade she was and strang),
And how Tam stood, like ane bewitch'd,
And thought his very een enrich'd;
Even Satan glowr'd, and fidged fu' fain,
And hotch'd and blew wi' might and
    main:
'Till first ae caper, syne anither,
Tam tint his reason a' thegither,
And roars out, " Weel done, Cutty-sark!"
And in an instant all was dark:
And scarcely had he Maggie rallied,
When out the hellish legion sallied.

As bees bizz out wi' angry fyke,
When plundering herds assail their byke;
As open pussie's mortal foes,
When, pop! she starts before their nose;
As eager runs the market-crowd,
When "Catch the thief!" resounds aloud;
So Maggie runs, the witches follow,
Wi' mony an eldritch screech and hollow.

Ah, Tam! ah, Tam! thou'll get thy
    fairin'!
In hell they'll roast thee like a herrin'!
In vain thy Kate awaits thy comin'!
Kate soon will be a woefu' woman!
Now do thy speedy utmost, Meg,
And win the key-stane of the brig;
There at them thou thy tail may toss,
A running stream they darena cross!
But ere the key-stane she could make,
The fient a tail she had to shake!
For Nannie, far before the rest,
Hard upon noble Maggie prest,
And flew at Tam wi' furious ettle;
But little wist she Maggie's mettle—
Ae spring brought off her master hale,
But left behind her ain gray tail:
The carlin claught her by the rump,
And left poor Maggie scarce a stump.

Now, wha this tale o' truth shall read,
Ilk man and mother's son, take heed:

Whene'er to drink you are inclined,
Or cutty-sarks run in your mind,
Think! ye may buy the joys o'er dear—
Remember Tam o' Shanter's mare.
                  ROBERT BURNS.

THE HAG.

THE hag is astride,
  This night for to ride—
The devil and she together;
  Through thick and through thin,
  Now out and then in,
Though ne'er so foul be the weather.

A thorn or a bur
  She takes for a spur;
With a lash of the bramble she rides now:
  Through brakes and through briers,
  O'er ditches and mires,
She follows the spirit that guides now.

No beast, for his food,
  Dares now range the wood,
But husht in his lair he lies lurking;
  While mischiefs, by these,
  On land and on seas,
At noon of night are a-working.

The storm will arise,
  And trouble the skies,
This night; and, more the wonder,
  The ghost from the tomb
  Affrighted shall come,
Call'd out by the clap of the thunder.
                  ROBERT HERRICK.

SISTER HELEN.

"WHY did you melt your waxen man,
    Sister Helen?
To-day is the third since you began."
" The time was long, yet the time ran,
    Little brother."
    (O Mother, Mary Mother,
Three days to-day, between hell and
    heaven!)

" But if you have done your work aright,
    Sister Helen,
You'll let me play, for you said I might."
" Be very still in your play to-night,
    Little brother."

(O Mother, Mary Mother,
Third night, to-night, between hell and
  heaven!)

"You said it must melt ere vesper-bell,
  Sister Helen,
If now it be molten, all is well."
"Even so,—nay, peace! you cannot tell,
  Little brother."
(O Mother, Mary Mother,
Oh what is this between hell and heaven?)

"Oh the waxen knave was plump to-day,
  Sister Helen;
How like dead folk he has dropp'd away!"
"Nay now, of the dead what can you say,
  Little brother?"
(O Mother, Mary Mother,
What of the dead, between hell and
  heaven?)

"See, see, the sunken pile of wood,
  Sister Helen,
Shines through the thinn'd wax red as
  blood!"
"Nay, now, when look'd you yet on blood,
  Little brother?"
(O Mother, Mary Mother,
How pale she is between hell and heaven!)

"Now close your eyes, for they're sick and
  sore,
  Sister Helen,
And I'll play without the gallery door."
"Ay, let me rest,—I'll lie on the floor,
  Little brother."
(O Mother, Mary Mother,
What rest to-night between hell and
  heaven?)

"Here high up in the balcony,
  Sister Helen,
The moon flies face to face with me."
"Ay, look and say whatever you see,
  Little brother."
(O Mother, Mary Mother,
What sight to-night, between hell and
  heaven?)

"Outside it's merry in the wind's wake,
  Sister Helen;
In the shaken trees the chill stars shake."
"Hush, heard you a horse-tread as you
  spake,
  Little brother?"
(O Mother, Mary Mother,
What sound to-night, between hell and
  heaven?)

"I hear a horse-tread, and I see,
  Sister Helen,
Three horsemen, that ride terribly."
"Little brother, whence come the three,
  Little brother?"
(O Mother, Mary Mother,
Whence should they come, between hell
  and heaven?)

"They come by the hill-verge from Boyne
  Bar,
  Sister Helen,
And one draws nigh, but two are afar."
"Look, look, do you know them who they
  are,
  Little brother?"
(O Mother, Mary Mother,
Who should they be between hell and
  heaven?)

"Oh, it's Keith of Eastholm rides so rast,
  Sister Helen,
For I know the white mane on the blast."
"The hour has come, has come at last,
  Little brother."
(O Mother, Mary Mother,
Her hour at last between hell and heaven!)

"He has made a sign and call'd, Halloo,
  Sister Helen,
And he says that he would speak with you."
"Oh tell him I fear the frozen dew,
  Little brother."
(O Mother, Mary Mother,
Why laughs she thus between hell and
  heaven?)

"The wind is loud, but I hear him cry,
  Sister Helen,
That Keith of Ewern's like to die."
"And he and thou, and thou and I,
  Little brother."
(O Mother, Mary Mother,
And they and we between hell and heaven.)

"For three days now he has lain abed,
  Sister Helen,
And he prays in torment to be dead."
"The thing may chance if he have pray'd

Little brother."
  (O Mother, Mary Mother,
If he have pray'd between hell and heaven!)

"But he has not ceased to cry to-day,
  Sister Helen,
That you should take your curse away."
"*My* prayer was heard—he need but pray,
  Little brother."
  (O Mother, Mary Mother,
Shall God not hear between hell and heaven?)

"But he says, till you take back your ban,
  Sister Helen,
His soul would pass, yet never can."
"Nay, then, shall I slay a living man,
  Little brother?"
  (O Mother, Mary Mother,
A living soul between hell and heaven!)

"But he calls for ever on your name,
  Sister Helen,
And says that he melts before a flame."
"My heart for his pleasure fared the same,
  Little brother."
  (O Mother, Mary Mother,
Fire at the heart between hell and heaven!)

"Here's Keith of Westholm riding fast,
  Sister Helen,
For I know the white plume on the blast."
"The hour, the sweet hour, I forecast,
  Little brother."
  (O Mother, Mary Mother,
Is the hour sweet between hell and heaven?)

"He stops to speak, and he stills his horse,
  Sister Helen;
But his words are drown'd in the wind's course."
"Nay, hear! nay, hear! you must hear perforce,
  Little brother!"
  (O Mother, Mary Mother,
A word ill heard between hell and heaven!)

"Oh, he says that Keith of Ewern's cry,
  Sister Helen,
Is ever to see you ere he die."
"He sees me in earth, in moon, and sky,
  Little brother."
  (O Mother, Mary Mother,
Earth, moon, and sky between hell and heaven!)

"He sends a ring and a broken coin,
  Sister Helen,
And bids you mind the banks of Boyne."
"What else he broke will he ever join,
  Little brother?"
  (O Mother, Mary Mother,
Oh never more between hell and heaven!)

"He yields you these and craves full fain,
  Sister Helen,
You pardon him in his mortal pain."
"What else he took will he give again,
  Little brother?"
  (O Mother, Mary Mother,
No more, no more, between hell and heaven!)

"He calls your name in an agony,
  Sister Helen,
That even dead Love must weep to see."
"Hate, born of Love, is blind as he,
  Little brother!"
  (O Mother, Mary Mother,
Love turn'd to hate between hell and heaven!)

"Oh, it's Keith of Keith now that rides fast,
  Sister Helen,
For I know the white hair on the blast."
"The short, short hour will soon be past,
  Little brother."
  (O Mother, Mary Mother,
Will soon be past, between hell and heaven!)

"He looks at me, and he tries to speak,
  Sister Helen,
But oh, his voice is sad and weak!"
"What here should the mighty Baron seek,
  Little brother?"
  (O Mother, Mary Mother,
Is this the end, between hell and heaven?)

"Oh, his son still cries if you forgive,
  Sister Helen,
The body dies, but the soul shall live."
"Fire shall forgive me as I forgive,
  Little brother."

(O Mother, Mary Mother,
As she forgives between hell and heaven!)

"Oh, he prays you as his heart would rive,
  Sister Helen,
To save his dear son's soul alive."
"Nay, flame cannot slay it; it shall thrive,
  Little brother."
(O Mother, Mary Mother,
Alas, alas, between hell and heaven!)

"He cries to you, kneeling in the road,
  Sister Helen,
To go with him for the love of God!"
"The way is long, to his son's abode,
  Little brother."
(O Mother, Mary Mother,
The way is long between hell and heaven!)

"O Sister Helen, you heard the bell,
  Sister Helen;
More loud than the vesper-chime it fell."
"No vesper-chime, but a dying knell,
  Little brother."
(O Mother, Mary Mother,
His dying knell, between hell and heaven!)

"Alas, but I fear the heavy sound,
  Sister Helen;
Is it in the sky or in the ground?"
"Say, have they turn'd their horses round,
  Little brother?"
(O Mother, Mary Mother,
What would she more, between hell and heaven?)

"They have raised the old man from his knee,
  Sister Helen,
And they ride in silence hastily."
"More fast the naked soul doth flee,
  Little brother."
(O Mother, Mary Mother,
The naked soul, between hell and heaven!)

"Oh, the wind is sad in the iron chill,
  Sister Helen,
And weary sad they look by the hill."
"But Keith of Ewern's sadder still,
  Little brother."
(O Mother, Mary Mother,
Most sad of all, between hell and heaven!)

"See, see, the wax has dropp'd from its place,
  Sister Helen,
And the flames are winning up apace."
"Yet here they burn but for a space,
  Little brother."
(O Mother, Mary Mother,
Here for a space, between hell and heaven!)

"Ah! what white thing at the door has cross'd,
  Sister Helen?
Ah! what is this that sighs in the frost?"
"A soul that's lost as mine is lost,
  Little brother."
(O Mother, Mary Mother,
Lost, lost, all lost, between hell and heaven!)
                    DANTE GABRIEL ROSSETTI.

THE ABBOT M'KINNON.

M'KINNON's tall mast salutes the day,
And beckons the breeze in Iona bay;
Plays lightly up in the morning sky,
And nods to the green wave rolling by;
The anchor upheaves, the sails unfurl,
The pennons of silk in the breezes curl;
But not one monk on holy ground
Knows whither the Abbot M'Kinnon is bound.

Well could that bark o'er the ocean glide,
Though monks and friars alone must guide;
For never man of other degree
On board that sacred ship might be.
On deck M'Kinnon walk'd soft and slow;
The haulers sung from the gilded prow;
The helmsman turn'd his brow to the sky,
Upraised his cowl and upraised his eye,
And away shot the bark on the wing of the wind,
Over billow and bay like an image of mind.

Aloft on the turret the monks appear,
To see where the bark of their abbot would bear;
They saw her sweep from Iona bay,
And turn her prow to the north away,
Still lessen to view in the hazy screen,
And vanish amid the islands green.

Then they turn'd their eyes to the female dome,
And thought of the nuns till the abbot came home.

Three times the night with aspect dull
Came stealing o'er the moors of Mull;
Three times the sea-gull left the deep,
To doze on the knob of the dizzy steep,
By the sound of the ocean lull'd to sleep;
And still the watch-lights sailors see
On the top of the spire, and the top of Dun-ye;
And the laugh rings through the sacred dome,
For still the abbot is not come home.

But the wolf that nightly swam the sound,
From Rosa's rude impervious bound,
On the ravenous burrowing race to feed,
That loved to haunt the home of the dead,
To him Saint Columb had left in trust
To guard the bones of the royal and just,
Of saints and of kings the sacred dust;
The savage was scared from his charnel of death,
And swam to his home in hunger and wrath,
For he momently saw, through the night so dun,
The cowering monk, and the veilèd nun,
Whispering, sighing, and stealing away
By cross dark alley and portal gray.
Oh, wise was the founder, and well said he,
"Where there are women, mischief must be."

No more the watch-fires gleam to the blast,
M'Kinnon and friends arrive at last.
A stranger youth to the isle they brought,
Modest of mien and deep of thought,
In costly sacred robes bedight,
And he lodged with the abbot by day and by night.

His breast was graceful, and round withal,
His leg was taper, his foot was small,
And his tread so light that it flung no sound
On listening ear or vault around.
His eye was the morning's brightest ray,
And his neck like the swan's in Iona bay;
His teeth the ivory polish'd new,
And his lip like the morel when gloss'd with dew,
While under his cowl's embroider'd fold
Were seen the curls of waving gold.
This comely youth, of beauty so bright,
Abode with the abbot by day and by night.

When arm in arm they walk'd the isle,
Young friars would beckon, and monks would smile;
But sires, in dread of sins unshriven,
Would shake their heads and look up to heaven,
Afraid the frown of the saint to see,
Who rear'd their temple amid the sea,
And pledged his soul to guard the dome,
Till Virtue should fly her western home.
But now a stranger of hidden degree,
Too fair, too gentle a man to be—
This stranger of beauty and step so light
Abode with the abbot by day and by night.

The months and the days flew lightly by,
The monks were kind and the nuns were shy;
But the gray-hair'd sires, in trembling mood,
Kneel'd at the altar and kiss'd the rood.

M'Kinnon he dream'd that the saint of the isle
Stood by his side, and with courteous smile,
Bade him arise from his guilty sleep,
And pay his respects to the God of the deep,
In temple that north in the main appear'd,
Which fire from bowels of ocean had sear'd,
Which the giant builders of heaven had rear'd,
To rival in grandeur the stately pile
Himself had uprear'd in Iona's isle;
For round them rose the mountains of sand,
The fishes had left the coasts of the land,
And so high ran the waves of the angry sea,
They had drizzled the cross on the top of Dun-ye.

The cycle was closed and the period run;
He had vow'd to the sea, he had vow'd to
 the sun,
If in that time rose trouble or pain,
Their homage to pay to the God of the
 main.
Then he bade him haste and the rites pre-
 pare,
Named all the monks should with him
 fare,
And promised again to see him there.

M'Kinnon awoke from his vision'd sleep,
He open'd his casement and look'd on the
 deep;
He look'd to the mountains, he look'd to
 the shore,
The vision amazed him and troubled him
 sore,
He never had heard of the rite before;
But all was so plain, he thought meet to
 obey,
He durst not decline, and he would not
 delay.

Uprose the abbot, uprose the morn,
Uprose the sun from the Bens of Lorn;
And the bark her course to the northward
 framed,
With all on board whom the saint had
 named.

The clouds were journeying east the sky,
The wind was low and the swell was high,
And the glossy sea was heaving bright
Like ridges and hills of liquid light;
While far on her lubrick bosom were seen
The magic dyes of purple and green.

How joy'd the bark her sides to lave!
She lean'd to the lee and she girdled the
 wave;
Aloft on the stayless verge she hung,
Light on the steep wave veer'd and swung,
And the crests of the billows before her
 flung.
Loud murmur'd the ocean with downward
 growl,
The seal swam aloof and the dark sea-
 fowl;
The pie-duck sought the depth of the
 main,
And rose in the wheel of her wake again;
And behind her far to the southward
 shone
A pathway of snow on the waste alone.

But now the dreadful strand they gain,
Where rose the sacred dome of the main;
Oft had they seen the place before,
And kept aloof from the dismal shore,
But now it rose before their prow,
And what they beheld they did not know.
The tall gray forms in close-set file,
Upholding the roof of that holy pile;
The sheets of foam and the clouds of
 spray,
And the groans that rush'd from the por-
 tals gray,
Appall'd their hearts and drove them
 away.

They wheel'd their bark to the east around,
And moor'd in basin, by rocks imbound;
Then, awed to silence, they trode the
 strand
Where furnaced pillars in order stand,
All framed of the liquid burning levin,
And bent like the bow that spans the
 heaven,
Or upright ranged in horrid array,
With purfle of green o'er the darksome
 gray.

Their path was on wondrous pavement of
 old,
Its blocks all cast in some giant mould,
Fair hewn and grooved by no mortal hand,
With countermure guarded by sea and by
 land.
The watcher Bushella frown'd over their
 way,
Enrobed in the sea-baize, and hooded with
 gray;
The warder that stands by that dome of
 the deep,
With spray-shower and rainbow, the en-
 trance to keep.
But when they drew nigh to the chancel
 of Ocean,
And saw her waves rush to their raving
 devotion,
Astounded and awed to the antes they
 clung,
And listen'd the hymns in her temple she
 sung.

The song of the cliffs, when the winter
    winds blow,
The thunder of heaven, the earthquake
    below,
Conjoin'd, like the voice of a maiden
    would be,
Compared with the anthem there sung by
    the sea.

The solemn rows in that darksome den
Were dimly seen like the forms of men,
Like giant monks in ages agone,
Whom the God of the ocean had sear'd to
    stone,
And bound in his temple for ever to lean,
In sackcloth of gray and visors of green,
An everlasting worship to keep,
And the big salt tears eternally weep.

So rapid the motion, the whirl and the
    boil,
So loud was the tumult, so fierce the tur-
    moil,
Appall'd from those portals of terror they
    turn,
On pillar of marble their incense to burn.
Around the holy flame they pray,
Then turning their faces all west away,
On angel pavement each bent his knee,
And sung this hymn to the God of the
    sea.

The Monks' Hymn.

Thou, who makest the ocean to flow,
Thou, who walkest the channels below;
To thee, to thee, this incense we heap,
Thou, who knowest not slumber nor sleep,
Great Spirit that mov'st on the face of the
    deep!
To thee, to thee, we sing to thee,
God of the western wind, God of the sea!

To thee, who bringest with thy right hand
The little fishes around our land;
To thee, who breath'st in the bosom'd sail,
Rulest the shark and the rolling whale,
Flingest the sinner to downward grave,
Lightest the gleam on the mane of the
    wave,
Bid'st the billows thy reign deform,
Laugh'st in the whirlwind, sing'st in the
    storm;

Or risest like mountain amid the sea,
Where mountain was never, and never
    will be,
And rearest thy proud and thy pale chap-
    eroon
'Mid walks of the angels and ways of the
    moon;
To thee, to thee, this wine we pour,
God of the western wind, God of the
    shower!

To thee, who bid'st those mountains of
    brine
Softly sink in the fair moonshine,
And spread'st thy couch of silver light,
To lure to thy bosom the queen of the
    night;
Who weavest the cloud of the ocean dew,
And the mist that sleeps on her breast so
    blue;
When the murmurs die at the base of the hill,
And the shadows lie rock'd and slumber-
    ing still,
And the solan's young, and the lines of
    foam,
Are scarcely heaved on thy peaceful home,
We pour this oil and this wine to thee,
God of the western wind, God of the sea!—
" Greater yet must the offering be."

The monks gazed round, the abbot grew
    wan,
For the closing notes were not sung by man.
They came from the rock, or they came
    from the air,
From voice they knew not, and knew not
    where;
But it sung with a mournful melody,
" Greater yet must the offering be."

In holy dread they pass'd away,
And they walk'd the ridge of that isle so
    gray,
And saw the white waves toil and fret,
An hundred fathoms below their feet;
They look'd to the countless isles that lie
From Barra to Mull, and from Jura to
    Skye;
They look'd to heaven, they look'd to the
    main,
They look'd at all with a silent pain,
As on places they were not to see again.

A little bay lies hid from sight,
O'erhung by cliffs of dreadful height;
When they drew nigh that airy steep,
They heard a voice rise from the deep,
And that voice was sweet as voice could be,
And they fear'd it came from the Maid of
   the Sea.

M'Kinnon lay stretch'd on the verge of
   the hill,
And peep'd from the height on the bay so
   still;
And he saw her sit on a weedy stone,
Laving her fair breast, and singing alone;
And aye she sank the wave within,
Till it gurgled around her lovely chin,
Then comb'd her locks of the pale sea-
   green,
And aye this song was heard between.

The Mermaid's Song.

Matilda of Skye
   Alone may lie,
And list to the wind that whistles by:
   Sad may she be,
   For deep in the sea,
Deep, deep, deep in the sea,
This night her lover shall sleep with me.
   She may turn and hide
   From the spirits that glide,
And the ghost that stands at her bedside:
But never a kiss the vow shall seal,
Nor warm embrace her bosom feel;
For far, far down in the floors below,
Moist as this rock-weed, cold as the snow,
With the eel, and the clam, and the pearl
   of the deep,
On soft sea-flowers her lover shall sleep;
And long and sound shall his slumber be,
In the coral bowers of the deep with me.

The trembling sun, far, far away,
Shall pour on his couch a soften'd ray,
And his mantle shall wave in the flowing
   tide,
And the little fishes shall turn aside;
But the waves and the tides of the sea
   shall cease,
Ere wakes her love from his bed of peace.
No home!—no kiss!—No, never! never!
His couch is spread for ever and ever.

The abbot arose in dumb dismay,
They turn'd and fled from the height
   away,
For dark and portentous was the day.
When they came in view of their rocking
   sail,
They saw an old man who sat on the wale;
His beard was long and silver-gray,
Like the rime that falls at the break of
   day;
His locks like wool and his color wan,
And he scarcely look'd like an earthly
   man.

They ask'd his errand, they ask'd his
   name,
Whereunto bound, and whence he came;
But a sullen, thoughtful silence he kept,
And turn'd his face to the sea and wept.
Some gave him welcome, and some gave
   him scorn,
But the abbot stood pale, with terror o'er-
   borne;
He tried to be jocund, but trembled the
   more,
For he thought he had seen the face be-
   fore.

Away went the ship with her canvas all
   spread,
So glad to escape from that island of
   dread;
And skimm'd the blue wave like a streamer
   of light,
Till fell the dim veil 'twixt the day and
   the night.
Then the old man arose and stood up on
   the prow,
And fix'd his dim eyes on the ocean be-
   low;
And they heard him saying, "Oh, woe is
   me!
But great as the sin must the sacrifice
   be."

Oh, mild was his eye, and his manner
   sublime,
When he look'd unto heaven, and said,
   "Now is the time."
He look'd to the weather, he look'd to the
   lee,
He look'd as for something he dreaded to
   see,

Then stretch'd his pale hand, and pointed his eye
To a gleam on the verge of the eastern sky.

The monks soon beheld, on the lofty Ben-More,
A sight which they never had seen before,
A belt of blue lightning around it was driven,
And its crown was encircled by morion of heaven;
And they heard a herald that loud did cry,
"Prepare the way for the abbot of I!"

Then a sound arose, they knew not where,
It came from the sea or it came from the air,
'Twas louder than tempest that ever blew,
And the sea-fowls scream'd, and in terror flew;
Some ran to the cords, some kneel'd at the shrine,
But all the wild elements seem'd to combine;
'Twas just but one moment of stir and commotion,
And down went the ship like a bird of the ocean!

This moment she sail'd all stately and fair,
The next, nor ship nor shadow was there,
But a boil that arose from the deep below;
A mountain-gurgling column of snow:
It sunk away with a murmuring moan—
The sea is calm, and the sinners are gone.
JAMES HOGG.

THE NECKAN.

IN summer, on the headlands,
 The Baltic Sea along,
Sits Neckan with his harp of gold,
 And sings his plaintive song.

Green rolls, beneath the headlands,
 Green rolls the Baltic Sea;
And there, below the Neckan's feet,
 His wife and children be.

He sings not of the ocean,
 Its shells and roses pale;
Of earth, of earth the Neckan sings—
 He hath no other tale.

He sits upon the headlands,
 And sings a mournful stave
Of all he saw and felt on earth,
 Far from the kind sea-wave.

Sings how, a knight, he wander'd
 By castle, field, and town—
But earthly knights have harder hearts
 Than the sea-children own.

Sings of his earthly bridal—
 Priest, knights, and ladies gay.
"—And who art thou," the priest began,
 "Sir Knight, who wedd'st to-day?"—

"—I am no knight," he answer'd;
 "From the sea-waves I come."—
The knights drew sword, the ladies scream'd,
 The surpliced priest stood dumb.

He sings how from the chapel
 He vanish'd with his bride,
And bore her down to the sea-halls,
 Beneath the salt sea-tide.

He sings how she sits weeping
 'Mid shells that round her lie.
"—False Neckan shares my bed," she weeps;
 "No Christian mate have I."—

He sings how through the billows
 He rose to earth again,
And sought a priest to sign the cross,
 That Neckan heaven might gain.

He sings how, on an evening,
 Beneath the birch trees cool,
He sate and play'd his harp of gold,
 Beside the river-pool.

Beside the pool sate Neckan—
 Tears fill'd his mild blue eye.
On his white mule, across the bridge,
 A cassock'd priest rode by.

"—Why sitt'st thou there, O Neckan,
 And play'st thy harp of gold?
Sooner shall this, my staff, bear leaves,
 Than thou shalt heaven behold."

But lo, the staff, it budded!
 It green'd, it branch'd, it waved.
"—O ruth of God," the priest cried out,
 "This lost sea-creature saved!"

The cassock'd priest rode onward,
  And vanish'd with his mule;
But Neckan in the twilight gray
  Wept by the river-pool.

He wept: "The earth hath kindness,
  The sea, the starry poles;
Earth, sea, and sky, and God above—
  But, ah, not human souls!"

In summer, on the headlands,
  The Baltic Sea along,
Sits Neckan with his harp of gold,
  And sings this plaintive song.
              MATTHEW ARNOLD.

HALLO, MY FANCY.

IN melancholic fancy,
  Out of myself,
In the vulcan dancy,
  All the world surveying,
  Nowhere staying,
    Just like a fairy elf;
Out o'er the tops of highest mountains skipping,
Out o'er the hills, the trees and valleys tripping,
Out o'er the ocean seas, without an oar or shipping.
Hallo, my fancy, whither wilt thou go?

  Amidst the misty vapors,
    Fain would I know
  What doth cause the tapers;
  Why the clouds benight us,
  And affright us
  While we travel here below.
Fain would I know what makes the roaring thunder,
And what these lightnings be that rend the clouds asunder,
And what these comets are on which we gaze and wonder.
Hallo, my fancy, whither wilt thou go?

  Fain would I know the reason
    Why the little ant,
  All the summer season,
  Layeth up provision,
  On condition
  To know no winter's want:
And how housewives, that are so good and painful,
Do unto their husbands prove so good and gainful,
And why the lazy drones to them do prove disdainful.
Hallo, my fancy, whither wilt thou go?

  Ships, ships, I will descry you
    Amidst the main;
  I will come and try you
  What you are protecting,
  And projecting,
    What's your end and aim.
One goes abroad for merchandise and trading,
Another stays to keep his country from invading,
A third is coming home with rich and wealth of lading.
Hallo, my fancy, whither wilt thou go?

  When I look before me,
    There I do behold
  There's none that sees or knows me;
  All the world's a-gadding,
  Running madding,
    None doth his station hold.
He that is below envieth him that riseth,
And he that is above, him that's below despiseth,
So every man his plot and counterplot deviseth.
Hallo, my fancy, whither wilt thou go?

  Look, look, what bustling
    Here I do espy;
  Each another jostling,
  Every one turmoiling,
  Th' other spoiling,
    As I did pass them by.
One sitteth musing in a dumpish passion,
Another hangs his head, because he's out of fashion,
A third is fully bent on sport and recreation.
Hallo, my fancy, whither wilt thou go?

  Amidst the foamy ocean,
    Fain would I know
  What doth cause the motion,
  And returning
  In its journeying,
    And doth so seldom swerve!

And how these little fishes, that swim
    beneath salt water,
Do never blind their eye; methinks it is a
    matter
An inch above the reach of old Erra
    Pater!
    Hallo, my fancy, whither wilt thou go?

    Fain would I be resolved
        How things are done;
    And where the bull was calved
        Of bloody Phalaris,
    And where the tailor is
        That works to the man i' the
            moon!
Fain would I know how Cupid aims so
    rightly;
And how these little fairies do dance and
    leap so lightly;
And where fair Cynthia makes her ambles
    nightly.
    Hallo, my fancy, whither wilt thou go?

    In conceit like Phaeton,
        I'll mount Phœbus' chair,
    Having ne'er a hat on,
    All my hair a-burning
        In my journeying,
    Hurrying through the air.
Fair would I hear his fiery horses neigh-
    ing,
And see how they on foamy bits are play-
    ing;
All the stars and planets I will be survey-
    ing!
    Hallo, my fancy, whither wilt thou go?

    Oh, from what ground of nature
        Doth the pelican,
    That self-devouring creature,
        Prove so froward
        And untoward,
    Her vitals for to strain?
And why the subtle fox, while in death's
    wounds is lying,
Doth not lament his pangs by howling and
    by crying;
And why the milk-white swan doth sing
    when she's a-dying.
    Hallo, my fancy, whither wilt thou go?

    Fain would I conclude this,
        At least make essay,
    What similitude is;
        Why fowls of a feather
        Flock and fly together,
    And lambs know beasts of prey:
How Nature's alchymists, these small
    laborious creatures,
Acknowledge still a prince in ordering
    their matters,
And suffer none to live, who slothing lose
    their features.
    Hallo, my fancy, whither wilt thou go?

    I'm rapt with admiration,
        When I do ruminate,
    Men of an occupation,
        How each one calls him brother,
        Yet each envieth other,
        And yet still intimate!
Yea, I admire to see some natures farther
    sund'red,
Than antipodes to us. Is it not to be
    wond'red,
In myriads ye'll find, of one mind scarce
    a hundred?
    Hallo, my fancy, whither wilt thou go?

    What multitude of notions
        Doth perturb my pate,
    Considering the motions,
        How the heavens are preserved,
        And this world served
    In moisture, light, and heat!
If one spirit sits the outmost circle turning,
Or one turns another, continuing in jour-
    neying,
If rapid circles' motion be that which
    they call burning!
    Hallo, my fancy, whither wilt thou go?

    Fain also would I prove this,
        By considering
    What that, which you call love, is:
        Whether it be a folly
        Or a melancholy,
        Or some heroic thing!
Fain I'd have it proved, by one whom love
    hath wounded,
And fully upon one his desire hath founded,
Whom nothing else could please though
    the world were rounded.
    Hallo, my fancy, whither wilt thou go?

To know this world's centre,
  Height, depth, breadth, and length,
Fain would I adventure
  To search the hid attractions
  Of magnetic actions,
    And adamantine strength.
Fain would I know, if in some lofty mountain,
Where the moon sojourns, if there be trees or fountain;
If there be beasts of prey, or yet be fields to hunt in.
Hallo, my fancy, whither wilt thou go?

  Fain would I have it tried
    By experiment,
  By none can be denied!
  If in this bulk of nature,
  There be voids less or greater,
    Or all remains complete.
Fain would I know if beasts have any reason;
If falcons killing eagles do commit a treason;
If fear of winter's want make swallows fly the season.
Hallo, my fancy, whither wilt thou go?

  Hallo, my fancy, hallo!
    Stay, stay at home with me,
  I can thee no longer follow,
  For thou hast betray'd me,
    And bewray'd me;
    It is too much for thee.
Stay, stay at home with me; leave off thy lofty soaring;
Stay thou at home with me, and on thy books be poring;
For he that goes abroad lays little up in storing:
Thou'rt welcome home, my fancy, welcome home to me.
                WILLIAM CLELAND.

PAN IN WALL STREET.
A. D. 1867.

JUST where the Treasury's marble front
  Looks over Wall Street's mingled nations;
Where Jews and Gentiles most are wont
  To throng for trade and last quotations;
Where, hour by hour, the rates of gold
  Outrival, in the ears of people,
The quarter-chimes, serenely tolled
  From Trinity's undaunted steeple,—

Even there I heard a strange, wild strain
  Sound high above the modern clamor,
Above the cries of greed and gain,
  The curbstone war, the auction's hammer;
And swift, on Music's misty ways,
  It led, from all this strife for millions,
To ancient, sweet do-nothing days
  Among the kirtle-robed Sicilians.

And as it stilled the multitude,
  And yet more joyous rose, and shriller,
I saw the minstrel, where he stood
  At ease against a Doric pillar:
One hand a droning organ played,
  The other held a Pan's pipe (fashioned
Like those of old) to lips that made
  The reeds give out that strain impassioned.

'Twas Pan himself had wandered here
  A-strolling through this sordid city,
And piping to the civic ear
  The prelude of some pastoral ditty!
The demigod had crossed the seas,—
  From haunts of shepherd, nymph, and satyr,
And Syracusan times,—to these
  Far shores and twenty centuries later.

A ragged cap was on his head;
  But—hidden thus—there was no doubting
That, all with crispy locks o'erspread,
  His gnarlèd horns were somewhere sprouting;
His club feet, cased in rusty shoes,
  Were crossed, as on some frieze you see them,
And trousers, patched of divers hues,
  Concealed his crooked shanks beneath them.

He filled the quivering reeds with sound,
  And o'er his mouth their changes shifted,
And with his goat's-eyes looked around
  Where'er the passing current drifted;
And soon, as on Trinacrian hills
  The nymphs and herdsmen ran to hear him,

Even now the tradesmen from their tills,
  With clerks and porters, crowded near him.

The bulls and bears together drew
  From Jauncey Court and New Street Alley,
As erst, if pastorals be true,
  Came beasts from every wooded valley;
The random passers stayed to list,—
  A boxer Ægon, rough and merry,
A Broadway Daphnis, on his tryst
  With Naís at the Brooklyn Ferry.

A one-eyed Cyclops halted long
  In tattered cloak of army pattern,
And Galatea joined the throng,—
  A blowsy, apple-vending slattern;
While old Silenus staggered out
  From some new-fangled lunch-house handy,
And bade the piper, with a shout,
  To strike up Yankee Doodle Dandy!

A news-boy and a peanut-girl
  Like little Fauns began to caper:
His hair was all in tangled curl,
  Her tawny legs were bare and taper;
And still the gathering larger grew,
  And gave its pence and crowded nigher,
While aye the shepherd-minstrel blew
  His pipe, and struck the gamut higher.

O heart of Nature, beating still
  With throbs her vernal passion taught her,—
Even here, as on the vineclad hill,
  Or by the Arethusan water!
New forms may fold the speech, new lands
  Arise within these ocean-portals,
But Music waves eternal wands,—
  Enchantress of the souls of mortals!

So thought I,—but among us trod
  A man in blue, with legal baton,
And scoffed the vagrant demigod,
  And pushed him from the step I sat on.
Doubting I mused upon the cry,
  "Great Pan is dead!"—and all the people
Went on their ways:—and clear and high
  The quarter sounded from the steeple.

      EDMUND CLARENCE STEDMAN.

HYMN TO NEPTUNE.

GOD of the mighty deep! wherever now
The waves beneath thy brazen axles bow—
Whether thy strong, proud steeds, wind-wing'd and wild,
Trample the storm-vex'd waters round them piled,
Swift as the lightning-flashes, that reveal
The quick gyrations of each brazen wheel;
While round and under thee, with hideous roar,
The broad Atlantic, with thy scourging sore,
Thundering, like antique Chaos in his spasms,
In heaving mountains and deep-yawning chasms
Fluctuates endlessly; while, through the gloom,
Their glossy sides and thick manes fleck'd with foam,
Career thy steeds, neighing with frantic glee
In fierce response to the tumultuous sea,—
Whether thy coursers now career below,
Where, amid storm-wrecks, hoary sea-plants grow,
Broad-leaved, and fanning with a ceaseless motion
The pale, cold tenants of the abysmal ocean—
Oh, come! our altars waiting for thee stand
Smoking with incense on the level strand!

Perhaps thou lettest now thy horses roam
Upon some quiet plain; no wind-toss'd foam
Is now upon their limbs, but leisurely
They tread with silver feet the sleeping sea,
Fanning the waves with slowly-floating manes,
Like mist in sunlight; haply, silver strains
From clamorous trumpets round thy chariot ring,
And green-robed sea-gods unto thee, their king,
Chant, loud in praise: Apollo now doth gaze
With loving looks upon thee, and his rays

Light up thy steeds' wild eyes: a pleasant
    warmth
Is felt upon the sea, where fierce, cold
    storm
Has just been rushing, and the noisy
    winds,
That Æolus now within their prison binds,
Flying with misty wings: perhaps, below
Thou liest in green caves, where bright
    things glow
With myriad colors—many a monster cumbers
The sand a-near thee, while old Triton
    slumbers
As idly as his wont, and bright eyes peep
Upon thee every way, as thou dost sleep.

Perhaps thou liest on some Indian isle,
Under a waving tree, where many a mile
Stretches a sunny shore, with golden sands
Heap'd up in many shapes by Naiads'
    hands,
And, blushing as the waves come rippling
    on,
Shaking the sunlight from them as they
    run
And curl upon the beach—like molten
    gold
Thick-set with jewelry most rare and
    old;
And sea-nymphs sit, and, with small, delicate shells,
Make thee sweet melody: as in deep dells
We hear, of summer nights, by fairies
    made,
The while they dance within some quiet
    shade,
Sounding their silver flutes most low and
    sweet,
In strange but beautiful tunes, that their
    light feet
May dance upon the bright and misty
    dew
In better time: all wanton airs that blew
But lately over spice trees, now are here,
Waving their wings, all odor-laden, near
The bright and laughing sea. Oh, wilt
    thou rise,
And come with them to our new sacrifice!
                        ALBERT PIKE.

THE LADY OF SHALOTT.
PART I.

On either side the river lie
Long fields of barley and of rye,
That clothe the wold and meet the sky;
And through the field the road runs by
    To many-tower'd Camelot;
And up and down the people go,
Gazing where the lilies blow
Round an island there below—
    The island of Shalott.

Willows whiten; aspens quiver;
Little breezes dusk and shiver
Through the wave that runs for ever
By the island in the river,
    Flowing down to Camelot.
Four gray walls, and four gray towers,
Overlook a space of flowers;
And the silent isle imbowers
    The Lady of Shalott.

By the margin, willow-veil'd,
Slide the heavy barges, trail'd
By slow horses; and, unhail'd,
The shallop flitteth, silken-sail'd—
    Skimming down to Camelot:
But who hath seen her wave her hand?
Or at the casement seen her stand?
Or is she known in all the land,
    The Lady of Shalott?

Only reapers, reaping early
In among the bearded barley,
Hear a song that echoes cheerly
From the river, winding clearly
    Down to tower'd Camelot:
And by the moon the reaper weary,
Piling sheaves in uplands airy,
Listening, whispers, "'T is the fairy
    Lady of Shalott."

PART II.

There she weaves by night and day
A magic web with colors gay.
She has heard a whisper say
A curse is on her if she stay
    To look down to Camelot.
She knows not what the curse may be;
And so she weaveth steadily,
And little other care hath she,
    The Lady of Shalott.

And, moving through a mirror clear
That hangs before her all the year,
Shadows of the world appear.
There she sees the highway near,
    Winding down to Camelot:
There the river-eddy whirls;
And there the surly village-churls,
And the red cloaks of market-girls,
    Pass onward from Shalott.

Sometimes a troop of damsels glad,
An abbot on an ambling pad—
Sometimes a curly shepherd-lad,
Or long-hair'd page, in crimson clad,
    Goes by to tower'd Camelot;
And sometimes through the mirror blue
The knights come riding, two and two:
She hath no loyal knight and true,
    The Lady of Shalott.

But in her web she still delights
To weave the mirror's magic sights;
For often, through the silent nights,
A funeral, with plumes and lights
    And music, went to Camelot:
Or, when the moon was overhead,
Came two young lovers lately wed;
"I am half sick of shadows," said
    The Lady of Shalott.

PART III.

A bow-shot from her bower-eaves
He rode between the barley sheaves;
The sun came dazzling through the leaves,
And flamed upon the brazen greaves
    Of bold Sir Lancelot.
A red-cross knight for ever kneel'd
To a lady in his shield,
That sparkled on the yellow field,
    Beside remote Shalott.

The gemmy bridle glitter'd free,
Like to some branch of stars we see
Hung in the golden galaxy.
The bridle bells rang merrily,
    As he rode down to Camelot:
And, from his blazon'd baldric slung,
A mighty silver bugle hung;
And as he rode his armor rung,
    Beside remote Shalott.

All in the blue unclouded weather
Thick-jewell'd shone the saddle-leather;
The helmet and the helmet-feather
Burn'd like one burning flame together,
    As he rode down to Camelot.
As often, through the purple night,
Below the starry clusters bright,
Some bearded meteor, trailing light,
    Moves over still Shalott.

His broad clear brow in sunlight glow'd;
On burnish'd hooves his war-horse trode;
From underneath his helmet flow'd
His coal-black curls as on he rode,
    As he rode down to Camelot.
From the bank and from the river
He flash'd into the crystal mirror:
"Tirra lirra," by the river,
    Sang Sir Lancelot.

She left the web, she left the loom;
She made three paces through the room;
She saw the water-lily bloom;
She saw the helmet and the plume;
    She look'd down to Camelot:
Out flew the web, and floated wide;
The mirror crack'd from side to side;
"The curse is come upon me," cried
    The Lady of Shalott.

PART IV.

In the stormy east-wind straining,
The pale yellow woods were waning,
The broad stream in his banks complaining,
Heavily the low sky raining
    Over tower'd Camelot;
Down she came, and found a boat
Beneath a willow left afloat;
And round about the prow she wrote
    The Lady of Shalott.

And down the river's dim expanse—
Like some bold seer in a trance,
Seeing all his own mischance—
With a glassy countenance
    Did she look to Camelot.
And at the closing of the day
She loosed the chain, and down she **lay**;
The broad stream bore her far away,
    The Lady of Shalott.

Lying robed in snowy white,
That loosely flew to left and right—
The leaves upon her falling light—
Throngh the noises of the night
    She floated down to Camelot.
And as the boat-head wound along,
The willowy hills and fields among,
They heard her singing her last song,
    The Lady of Shalott.

Heard a carol, mournful, holy,
Chanted loudly, chanted lowly,
Till her blood was frozen slowly,
And her eyes were darken'd wholly,
    Turn'd to tower'd Camelot.
For ere she reach'd, upon the tide,
The first house by the water-side,
Singing, in her song she died,
    The Lady of Shalott.

Under tower and balcony,
By garden-wall and gallery,
A gleaming shape she floated by,
Dead-pale between the houses high,
    Silent, into Camelot.
Out upon the wharfs they came,
Knight and burgher, lord and dame ;
And round the prow they read her name,
    The Lady of Shalott.

Who is this? and what is here?
And in the lighted palace near
Died the sound of royal cheer ;
And they cross'd themselves for fear,
    All the knights at Camelot:
But Lancelot mused a little space :
He said, "She has a lovely face ;
God in his mercy lend her grace,
    The Lady of Shalott."
ALFRED TENNYSON.

"PROUD MAISIE IS IN THE WOOD."

PROUD Maisie is in the wood,
    Walking so early ;
Sweet robin sits on the bush,
    Singing so rarely.

"Tell me, thou bonny bird,
    When shall I marry me ?"
"When six braw gentlemen
    Kirkward shall carry ye."

"Who makes the bridal bed,
    Birdie, say truly ?"
"The gray-headed sexton
    That delves the grave duly.

"The glow-worm o'er grave and stone
    Shall light thee steady ;
The owl from the steeple sing
    Welcome, proud lady !"
SIR WALTER SCOTT.

Side by Side. Though the King has his way,
Even the dead at last have their day.
Make you the moral. "Por el Rey"

— Bret Harte

HUMOROUS AND SATIRICAL.

THE COURTIN'.

God makes sech nights, all white an' still
  Fur'z you can look or listen,
Moonshine an' snow on field an' hill,
  All silence an' all glisten.

Zekle crep' up quite unbeknown,
  An' peek'd in thru the winder,
An' there sot Huldy all alone,
  'Ith no one nigh to hender.

A fireplace fill'd the room's one side,
  With half a cord o' wood in—
There warn't no stoves (tell comfort died)
  To bake ye to a puddin'.

The wa'nut logs shot sparkles out
  Towards the pootiest, bless her!
An' leetle flames danced all about
  The chiny on the dresser.

Agin the chimbley crook-necks hung,
  An' in amongst 'em rusted
The ole queen's-arm thet gran'ther Young
  Fetch'd back from Concord busted.

The very room, coz she was in,
  Seem'd warm from floor to ceilin',
An' she look'd full ez rosy agin
  Ez the apples she was peelin'.

'Twas kin' o' kingdom-come to look
  On sech a blessed cretur,
A dogrose blushin' to a brook
  Ain't modester nor sweeter.

He was six foot o' man, A, 1,
  Clean grit an' human natur';
None couldn't quicker pitch a ton,
  Nor dror a furrer straighter.

He'd spark'd it with full twenty gals,
  Hed squired 'em, danced 'em, druv 'em,
Fust this one, an' then thet, by spells—
  All is, he couldn't love 'em.

But long o' her his veins 'ould run
  All crinkly like curl'd maple,
The side she bresh'd felt full o' sun
  Ez a south slope in Ap'il.

She thought no v'ice hed sech a swing
  Ez hisn in the choir;
My! when he made Ole Hunderd ring,
  She *know'd* the Lord was nigher.

An' she'd blush scarlit, right in prayer,
  When her new meetin'-bunnet
Felt somehow thru its crown a pair
  O' blue eyes sot upon it.

Thet night, I tell ye, she look'd *some!*
  She seemed to've gut a new soul,
For she felt sartin-sure he'd come,
  Down to her very shoe-sole.

She heered a foot, an' know'd it tu,
  A-raspin' on the scraper,—
All ways to once her feelin's flew
  Like sparks in burnt-up paper,

He kin' o' l'iter'd on the mat,
  Some doubtfle o' the sekle,
His heart kep' goin' pity-pat,
  But hern went pity Zekle.

An' yit she gin her cheer a jerk,
  Ez though she wish'd him furder,
An' on her apples kep' to work,
  Parin' away like murder.

"You want to see my pa, I s'pose?"
  "Wal . . . . no . . . . I come dasign-
    in' "—
"To see my ma? She's sprinklin' clo'es
  Agin to-morrer's i'nin'."

To say why gals acts so or so,
  Or don't, 'ould be presumin';
Mebby to mean *yes* an' say *no*
  Comes natural to women.

He stood a spell on one foot fust,
  Then stood a spell on t'other,
An' on which one he felt the wust
  He couldn't ha' told ye nuther.

Says he, "I'd better call agin;"
  Says she, "Think likely, mister;"
Thet last word prick'd him like a pin,
  An' . . . . Wal, he up an' kist her.

When ma bimeby upon 'em slips,
  Huldy sot pale ez ashes,
All kin' o' smily roun' the lips
  An' teary roun' the lashes.

For she was jes' the quiet kind
  Whose naturs never vary,
Like streams that keep a summer mind
  Snow-hid in Jenooary.

The blood clost roun' her heart felt glued
  Too tight for all expressin',
Tell mother see how matters stood,
  An' gin 'em both her blessin'.

Then her red come back like the tide
  Down to the Bay o' Fundy,
An' all I know is they was cried
  In meetin' come nex' Sunday.
JAMES RUSSELL LOWELL.

THE LAIRD O' COCKPEN.

THE laird o' Cockpen he's proud and he's great,
His mind is ta'en up with the things o' the state;
He wanted a wife his braw house to keep,
But favor wi' wooin' was fashious to seek.

Down by the dyke-side a lady did dwell,
At his table-head he thought she'd look well;
M'Lish's ae daughter o' Claverse-ha' Lee,
A penniless lass wi' a lang pedigree.

His wig was weel pouther'd, and as gude as new;
His waistcoat was white, his coat it was blue;
He put on a ring, a sword, and cock'd hat,
And wha could refuse the Laird wi' a' that?

He took the gray mare, and rade cannily—
And rapp'd at the yett o' Claverse-ha' Lee:
"'Gae tell Mistress Jean to come speedily ben,
She's wanted to speak to the Laird o' Cockpen."

Mistress Jean was makin' the elder-flower wine:
"And what brings the Laird at sic a like time?"
She put aff her apron, and on her silk gown,
Her mutch wi' red ribbons, and gaed awa' down.

And when she cam' ben, he bow'd fu' low,
And what was his errand he soon let her know;
Amazed was the Laird when the lady said "Na;"
And wi' a laigh curtsey she turnèd awa'.

Dumfounder'd he was—nae sigh did he gie;
He mounted his mare—he rade cannily;
And aften he thought, as he gaed through the glen,
She's daft to refuse the Laird o' Cockpen.

And now that the Laird his exit had made,
Mistress Jean she reflected on what she had said;
"Oh! for ane I'll get better, it's waur I'll get ten,
I was daft to refuse the Laird o' Cockpen."

Next time that the Laird and the lady were seen,
They were gaun arm-in-arm to the kirk on the green.
Now she sits in the ha' like a weel-tappit hen—
But as yet there's nae chickens appear'd at Cockpen.
LADY CAROLINA NAIRNE.

THE WHISKERS.

THE kings who ruled mankind with haughty sway,
The prouder pope, whom even kings obey—

Love, at whose shrine both popes and monarchs fall,
And e'en self-interest, that controls them all—
Possess a petty power, when all combined,
Compared with fashion's influence on mankind:
For love itself will oft to fashion bow:
The following story will convince you how:

A petit maître woo'd a fair,
Of virtue, wealth, and graces rare;
But vainly had preferr'd his claim,
The maiden own'd no answering flame;
At length by doubt and anguish torn,
Suspense too painful to be borne,
Low at her feet he humbly kneel'd,
And thus his ardent flame reveal'd:

"Pity my grief, angelic fair,
Behold my anguish and despair;
For you this heart must ever burn—
Oh bless me with a kind return;
My love no language can express,
Reward it, then, with happiness;
Nothing on earth but you I prize,
All else is trifling in my eyes;
And cheerfully would I resign
The wealth of worlds to call you mine.
But, if another gain your hand,
Far distant from my native land,
Far hence from you and hope I'll fly,
And in some foreign region die."

The virgin heard, and thus replied:
"If my consent to be your bride
Will make you happy, then be blest;
But grant me, first, one small request;
A sacrifice I must demand,
And in return will give my hand."

"A sacrifice! Oh speak its name,
For you I'd forfeit wealth and fame;
Take my whole fortune—every cent—"

"'Twas something more than wealth I meant."

"Must I the realms of Neptune trace?
Oh speak the word—where'er the place,
For you, the idol of my soul,
I'd e'en explore the frozen pole;
Arabia's sandy deserts tread,
Or trace the Tigris to its head."

"Oh no, dear sir, I do not ask
So long a voyage, so hard a task;
You must—but ah! the boon I want,
I have no hope that you will grant."

"Shall I, like Bonaparte, aspire
To be the world's imperial sire?
Express the wish, and here I vow,
To place a crown upon your brow."

"Sir, these are trifles," she replied—
"But, if you wish me for your bride,
You must—but still I fear to speak—
You'll never grant the boon I seek."

"O say," he cried—"dear angel, say—
What must I do, and I obey;
No longer rack me with suspense,
Speak your commands, and send me hence."

"Well, then, dear generous youth!" she cries,
"If thus my heart you really prize,
And wish to link your fate with mine,
On one condition I am thine;
'Twill then become my pleasing duty
To contemplate a husband's beauty;
And, gazing on your manly face,
His feelings and his wishes trace;
To banish thence each mark of care,
And light a smile of pleasure there.
Oh let me, then, 'tis all I ask,
Commence at once the pleasing task;
Oh let me, as becomes my place,
Cut those huge whiskers from your face."

She said—but oh what strange surprise
Was pictured in her lover's eyes!
Like lightning from the ground he sprung,
While wild amazement tied his tongue :
A statue, motionless, he gazed,
Astonished, horror-struck, amazed.
So look'd the gallant Perseus, when
Medusa's visage met his ken;
So look'd Macbeth, whose guilty eye
Discern'd an "air-drawn dagger" nigh;
And so the Prince of Denmark stared,
When first his father's ghost appear'd.

At length our hero silence broke,
And thus in wildest accents spoke:

"Cut off my whiskers! O ye gods!
 I'd sooner lose my ears by odds;
Madam, I'd not be so disgraced,
 So lost to fashion and to taste,
To win an empress to my arms,
 Though blest with more than mortal
  charms.
My whiskers! zounds!" He said no
  more,
But quick retreated through the door,
And sought a less obdurate fair
To take the beau with all his hair.
                    SAMUEL WOODWORTH.

THE BUMBOAT WOMAN'S STORY.

I'M old, my dears, and shrivell'd, with age,
  and work, and grief,
My eyes are gone, and my teeth have been
  drawn by Time, the thief!
For terrible sights I've seen, and dangers
  great I've run—
I'm nearly seventy now, and my work is
  almost done!

Ah! I've been young in my time, and I've
  play'd the deuce with men—
I'm speaking of ten years past—I was
  barely sixty then:
My cheeks were mellow and soft, and my
  eyes were large and sweet,
Poll Pineapple's eyes were the standing
  toast of the Royal Fleet.

A bumboat woman was I, and I faithfully
  served the ships
With apples and cakes, and fowls and beer,
  and halfpenny dips,
And beef for the generous mess, where the
  officers dine at nights,
And fine fresh peppermint drops for the
  rollicking midshipmites.

Of all the kind commanders who anchor'd
  in Portsmouth Bay,
By far the sweetest of all was kind Lieu-
  tenant Belaye.
Lieutenant Belaye commanded the gun-
  boat Hot Cross Bun,
She was seven-and-thirty feet in length,
  and she carried a gun.

With the laudable view of enhancing his
  country's naval pride,
When people inquired her size, Lieutenant
  Belaye replied,
"Oh, my ship? my ship is the first of the
  Hundred and seventy-ones!"
Which meant her tonnage, but people im-
  agined it meant her guns.

Whenever I went on board he would
  beckon me down below:
"Come down, Little Buttercup, come!"
  (for he loved to call me so).
And he'd tell of the fights at sea in which
  he'd taken a part,
And so Lieutenant Belaye won poor Poll
  Pineapple's heart!

But at length his orders came, and he said
  one day, said he,
"I'm order'd to sail with the Hot Cross
  Bun to the German Sea."
And the Portsmouth maidens wept when
  they learnt the evil day,
For every Portsmouth maid loved good
  Lieutenant Belaye.

And I went to a back, back street, with
  plenty of cheap, cheap shops,
And I bought an oilskin hat, and a second-
  hand suit of slops,
And I went to Lieutenant Belaye (and he
  never suspected *me*),
And I enter'd myself as a chap as wanted
  to go to sea.

We sail'd that afternoon at the mystic
  hour of one,—
Remarkably nice young men were the crew
  of the Hot Cross Bun,
I'm sorry to say that I've heard that sailors
  sometimes swear,
But I never yet heard a Bun say anything
  wrong, I declare.

When Jack Tars meet, they meet with a
  "Messmate, ho! what cheer?"
But here, on the Hot Cross Bun; it was
  "How do you do, my dear?"
When Jack Tars growl, I believe they
  growl with a big big D—
But the strongest oath of the Hot Cross
  Buns was a mild "Dear me!"

Yet, though they were all well-bred, you
    could hardly call them slick:
Whenever a sea was on, they were all
    extremely sick;
And whenever the weather was calm, and
    the wind was light and fair,
They spent more time than a sailor should
    on his back, back hair.

They certainly shiver'd and shook when
    order'd aloft to run,
And they scream'd when Lieutenant Belaye
    discharged his only gun.
And as he was proud of his gun—such
    pride is hardly wrong—
The lieutenant was blazing away at inter-
    vals all day long.

They all agreed very well, though at times
    you heard it said
That Bill had a way of his own of making
    his lips look red—
That Joe look'd quite his age—or some-
    body might declare
That Barnacle's long pig-tail was never his
    own, own hair.

Belaye would admit that his men were of
    no great use to him,
"But then," he would say, "there is little
    to do on a gun-boat trim.
I can hand, and reef, and steer, and fire my
    big gun too—
And it *is* such a treat to sail with a gentle,
    well-bred crew."

I saw him every day! How the happy
    moments sped!
Reef topsails! Make all taut! There's
    dirty weather ahead!
(I do not mean that tempests threaten'd
    the Hot Cross Bun:
In *that* case I don't know whatever we
    should have done!)

After a fortnight's cruise, we put into port
    one day,
And off on leave for a week went kind
    Lieutenant Belaye,
And after a long, long week had pass'd
    (and it seem'd like a life)
Lieutenant Belaye return'd to his ship
    with a fair young wife!

He up and he says, says he, "O crew of
    the Hot Cross Bun,
Here is the wife of my heart, for the
    church has made us one."
And as he utter'd the word, the crew went
    out of their wits,
And all fell down in so many separate
    fainting fits.

And then their hair came down, or off, as
    the case might be,
And lo! the rest of the crew were simple
    girls, like me,
Who all had fled from their homes in a
    sailor's blue array,
To follow the shifting fate of kind Lieuten-
    ant Belaye.

*   *   *   *   *   *

It's strange to think *I* should ever have
    loved young men,
But I'm speaking of ten years past—I was
    barely sixty then,
And now my cheeks are furrow'd with
    grief and age, I trow!
And poor Poll Pineapple's eyes have lost
    their lustre now!

                      WILLIAM S. GILBERT.

THE SORROWS OF WERTHER.

WERTHER had a love for Charlotte,
    Such as words could never utter;
Would you know how first he met her?
    She was cutting bread and butter

Charlotte was a married lady,
    And a moral man was Werther,
And for all the wealth of Indies
    Would do nothing for to hurt her.

So he sigh'd and pined and ogled,
    And his passion boil'd and bubbled,
Till he blew his silly brains out,
    And no more was by it troubled.

Charlotte, having seen his body
    Borne before her on a shutter,
Like a well-conducted person,
    Went on cutting bread and butter.

                 WILLIAM MAKEPEACE THACKERAY.

THE IRISHMAN.

There was a lady lived at Leith,
　A lady very stylish, man,
And yet, in spite of all her teeth,
　She fell in love with an Irishman,—
　　A nasty, ugly Irishman,
　　A wild, tremendous Irishman,
A tearing, swearing, thumping, bumping,
　　ramping, roaring Irishman.

His face was no ways beautiful,
　For with small-pox 'twas scarr'd across,
And the shoulders of the ugly dog
　Were almost double a yard across.
　　Oh, the lump of an Irishman,
　　The whiskey-devouring Irishman,
The great he-rogue, with his wonderful
　brogue, the fighting, rioting Irishman!

One of his eyes was bottle-green,
　And the other eye was out, my dear,
And the calves of his wicked-looking
　　legs
　Were more than two feet about, my dear.
　　Oh, the great big Irishman,
　　The rattling, battling Irishman,
The stamping, ramping, swaggering, staggering, leathering swash of an Irishman!

He took so much of Lundy-Foot
　That he used to snort and snuffle, oh!
And in shape and size the fellow's neck
　Was as bad as the neck of a buffalo.
　　Oh, the horrible Irishman,
　　The thundering, blundering, Irishman,
The slashing, dashing, smashing, lashing,
　　thrashing, hashing Irishman!

His name was a terrible name indeed,
　Being Timothy Thady Mulligan;
And whenever he emptied his tumbler
　　of punch
　He'd not rest till he fill'd it full again.
　　The boozing, bruising Irishman,
　　The 'toxicated Irishman,
The whisky, frisky, rummy, gummy, brandy, no-dandy Irishman!

This was the lad the lady loved,
　Like all the girls of quality,
And he broke the skulls of the men of
　　Leith,
　Just by the way of jollity.
　　Oh, the leathering Irishman,
　　The barbarous, savage Irishman!
The hearts of the maids, and the gentlemen's heads, were bother'd, I'm sure, by this Irishman.
　　　　　　　　　WILLIAM MAGINN.

FAITHLESS NELLY GRAY.

A PATHETIC BALLAD.

Ben Battle was a soldier bold,
　And used to war's alarms:
But a cannon-ball took off his legs,
　So he laid down his arms!

Now as they bore him off the field,
　Said he, "Let others shoot,
For here I leave my second leg,
　And the Forty-second Foot!"

The army-surgeons made him limbs:
　Said he, "They're only pegs;
But there's as wooden Members quite,
　As represent my legs!"

Now, Ben he loved a pretty maid,
　Her name was Nelly Gray;
So he went to pay her his devours
　When he'd devour'd his pay!

But when he called on Nelly Gray,
　She made him quite a scoff;
And when she saw his wooden legs
　Began to take them off!

"O Nelly Gray! O Nelly Gray!
　Is this your love so warm?
The love that loves a scarlet coat
　Should be more uniform!"

Said she, "I loved a soldier once,
　For he was blithe and brave;
But I will never have a man
　With both legs in the grave!

"Before you had those timber toes,
　Your love I did allow;
But then, you know, you stand upon
　Another footing now!"

"O Nelly Gray! O Nelly Gray!
  For all your jeering speeches,
At duty's call, I left my legs,
  In Badajos's *breaches!*"

"Why, then," said she, "you've lost the feet
  Of legs in war's alarms,
And now you cannot wear your shoes
  Upon your feats of arms!"

"O false and fickle Nelly Gray!
  I know why you refuse:—
Though I've no feet—some other man
  Is standing in my shoes!

"I wish I ne'er had seen your face;
  But now a long farewell!
For you will be my death;—alas!
  You will not be my *Nell!*"

Now when he went from Nelly Gray,
  His heart so heavy got,
And life was such a burden grown,
  It made him take a knot!

So round his melancholy neck,
  A rope he did entwine,
And, for his second time in life,
  Enlisted in the Line.

One end he tied around a beam,
  And then removed his pegs,
And, as his legs were off—of course
  He soon was off his legs!

And there he hung, till he was dead
  As any nail in town,—
For, though distress had cut him up,
  It could not cut him down!

A dozen men sat on his corpse,
  To find out why he died—
And they buried Ben in four cross-roads,
  With a *stake* in his inside!
                        THOMAS HOOD.

FAITHLESS SALLY BROWN.

AN OLD BALLAD.

YOUNG BEN he was a nice young man,
  A carpenter by trade;
And he fell in love with Sally Brown,
  That was a lady's maid.

But as they fetch'd a walk one day,
  They met a press-gang crew;
And Sally she did faint away,
  Whilst Ben he was brought to.

The boatswain swore with wicked words,
  Enough to shock a saint,
That though she did seem in a fit,
  'Twas nothing but a feint.

"Come, girl," said he, "hold up your head,
  He'll be as good as me;
For when your swain is in our boat,
  A boatswain he will be."

So when they'd made their game of her,
  And taken off her elf,
She roused, and found she only was
  A-coming to herself.

"And is he gone? and is he gone?"
  She cried, and wept outright:
"Then I will to the waterside,
  And see him out of sight."

A waterman came up to her—
  "Now, young woman," said he,
"If you weep on so, you will make
  Eye-water in the sea."

"Alas! they've taken my beau Ben
  To sail with old Benbow;"
And her woe began to run afresh,
  As if she'd said, Gee woe!

Says he, "They've only taken him
  To the Tender ship, you see."
"The Tender ship!" cried Sally Brown,
  "What a hard-ship that must be!

"Oh! would I were a mermaid now,
  For then I'd follow him;
But oh!—I'm not a fish-woman,
  And so I cannot swim.

"Alas! I was not born beneath
  The Virgin and the Scales,
So I must curse my cruel stars,
  And walk about in Wales."

Now Ben had sail'd to many a place
  That's underneath the world,
But in two years the ship came home,
  And all her sails were furl'd.

But when he call'd on Sally Brown,
  To see how she got on,
He found she'd got another Ben,
  Whose Christian name was John.

"O Sally Brown! O Sally Brown!
  How could you serve me so?
I've met with many a breeze before,
  But never such a blow."

Then reading on his 'bacco-box,
  He heaved a bitter sigh,
And then began to eye his pipe,
  And then to pipe his eye.

And then he tried to sing "All's well,"
  But could not, though he tried;
His head was turn'd, and so he chew'd
  His pigtail till he died.

His death, which happen'd in his berth,
  At forty-odd befell:
They went and told the sexton, and
  The sexton toll'd the bell.
            THOMAS HOOD.

THE WELL OF ST. KEYNE.

A WELL there is in the west country,
  And a clearer one never was seen;
There is not a wife in the west country
  But has heard of the well of St. Keyne.

An oak and an elm tree stand beside,
  And behind doth an ash tree grow,
And a willow from the bank above
  Droops to the water below.

A traveller came to the well of St. Keyne;
  Joyfully he drew nigh,
For from cock-crow he had been travelling,
  And there was not a cloud in the sky.

He drank of the water so cool and clear,
  For thirsty and hot was he;
And he sat down upon the bank
  Under the willow tree.

There came a man from the house hard by
  At the well to fill his pail;
On the well-side he rested it,
  And he bade the stranger hail.

"Now, art thou a bachelor, stranger?"
    quoth he;
"For an if thou hast a wife,
The happiest draught thou hast drank this
    day
That ever thou didst in thy life.

"Or has thy good woman, if one thou hast,
  Ever here in Cornwall been?
For an if she have, I'll venture my life,
  She has drank of the well of St. Keyne."

"I have left a good woman who never was
    here,"
  The stranger he made reply;
"But that my draught should be the better
    for that,
  I pray you answer me why."

"St. Keyne," quoth the Cornish-man,
    "many a time
Drank of this crystal well;
And before the angel summon'd her,
  She laid on the water a spell.

"If the husband of this gifted well
  Shall drink before his wife,
A happy man thenceforth is he,
  For he shall be master for life.

"But if the wife should drink of it first,—
  God help the husband then!"
The stranger stoopt to the well of St. Keyne,
  And drank of the water again.

"You drank of the well, I warrant, be-
    times?"
  He to the Cornish-man said;
But the Cornish-man smiled as the stranger
    spake,
  And sheepishly shook his head.

"I hasten'd as soon as the wedding was
    done,
  And left my wife in the porch;
But i' faith she had been wiser than me,
  For she took a bottle to church."
            ROBERT SOUTHEY.

WHERE ARE YOU GOING, MY PRETTY MAID?

"WHERE are you going, my pretty maid?"
"I am going a-milking, sir," she said.

"THEN I CAN'T MARRY YOU, MY PRETTY MAID."
"NOBODY ASKED YOU, SIR!" SHE SAID.

"May I go with you, my pretty maid?"
"You're kindly welcome, sir," she said.
"What is your father, my pretty maid?"
"My father's a farmer, sir," she said.
"What is your fortune, my pretty maid?"
"My face is my fortune, sir," she said.
"Then I can't marry you, my pretty maid?"
"Nobody asked you, sir," she said.
AUTHOR UNKNOWN.

THE OLD MAN DREAMS.

OH for one hour of youthful joy!
  Give back my twentieth spring!
I'd rather laugh a bright-hair'd boy
  Than reign a gray-beard king!

Off with the spoils of wrinkled age!
  Away with learning's crown!
Tear out life's wisdom-written page,
  And dash its trophies down!

One moment let my life-blood stream
  From boyhood's fount of flame!
Give me one giddy, reeling dream
  Of life all love and fame!

My listening angel heard the prayer,
  And, calmly smiling, said,
"If I but touch thy silver'd hair,
  Thy hasty wish hath sped.

"But is there nothing in thy track
  To bid thee fondly stay,
While the swift seasons hurry back
  To find the wish'd-for day?"

Ah! truest soul of womankind!
  Without thee what were life?
One bliss I cannot leave behind:
  I'll take—my—precious—wife!

The angel took a sapphire pen
  And wrote in rainbow dew,
"The man would be a boy again,
  And be a husband, too!"

"And is there nothing yet unsaid
  Before the change appears?
Remember, all their gifts have fled
  With those dissolving years!"

"Why, yes; for memory would recall
  My fond paternal joys;
I could not bear to leave them all:
  I'll take—my—girl—and—boys!"

The smiling angel dropp'd his pen—
  "Why, this will never do;
The man would be a boy again,
  And be a father, too!"

And so I laugh'd—my laughter woke
  The household with its noise—
And wrote my dream, when morning broke,
  To please the gray-hair'd boys.
OLIVER WENDELL HOLMES.

BAUCIS AND PHILEMON.

IN ancient times, as story tells,
The saints would often leave their cells,
And stroll about, but hide their quality,
To try good people's hospitality.
  It happen'd on a winter night,
As authors of the legend write,
Two brother hermits, saints by trade,
Taking their tour in masquerade,
Disguised in tatter'd habits, went
To a small village down in Kent;
Where, in the strollers' canting strain,
They begg'd from door to door in vain,
Tried every tone might pity win;
But not a soul would let them in.
  Our wandering saints, in woeful state,
Treated at this ungodly rate,
Having through all the village past,
To a small cottage came at last
Where dwelt a good old honest ye'man,
Call'd in the neighborhood Philemon;
Who kindly did these saints invite
In his poor hut to pass the night;
And then the hospitable sire
Bid Goody Baucis mend the fire;
While he from out the chimney took
A flitch of bacon off the hook,
And freely from the fattest side
Cut out large slices to be fried;
Then stepp'd aside to fetch them drink,
Fill'd a large jug up to the brink,
And saw it fairly twice go round;
Yet (what was wonderful) they found
'Twas still replenish'd to the top,
As if they ne'er had touch'd a drop.

The good old couple were amazed,
And often on each other gazed;
For both were frighten'd to the heart,
And just began to cry "What ar't?"
Then softly turn'd aside to view
Whether the lights were burning blue.
The gentle pilgrims, soon aware on't,
Told them their calling and their errand:
"Good folks, you need not be afraid,
We are but saints," the hermits said;
"No hurt shall come to you or yours:
But for that pack of churlish boors,
Not fit to live on Christian ground,
They and their houses shall be drown'd;
While you shall see your cottage rise,
And grow a church before your eyes."
    They scarce had spoke, when fair and soft,
The roof began to mount aloft;
Aloft rose every beam and rafter;
The heavy wall climb'd slowly after.
    The chimney widen'd, and grew higher,
Became a steeple with a spire.
    The kettle to the top was hoist,
And there stood fasten'd to a joist,
But with the up side down, to show
Its inclination for below:
In vain; for a superior force
Applied at bottom stops its course:
Doom'd ever in suspense to dwell,
'Tis now no kettle, but a bell.
    A wooden jack, which had almost
Lost by disuse the art to roast,
A sudden alteration feels,
Increased by new intestine wheels;
And, what exalts the wonder more,
The number made the motion slower.
The flier, though it had leaden feet,
Turn'd round so quick you scarce could see't;
But, slacken'd by some secret power,
Now hardly moves an inch an hour.
The jack and chimney, near allied,
Had never left each other's side;
The chimney to a steeple grown,
The jack would not be left alone;
But, up against the steeple rear'd,
Became a clock, and still adhered;
And still its love to household cares,
By a shrill voice at noon, declares,
Warning the cook-maid not to burn
That roast meat which it cannot turn.

    The groaning chair began to crawl,
Like a huge snail, along the wall;
There stuck aloft in public view,
And with small change, a pulpit grew.
    The porringers, that in a row
Hung high, and made a glittering show
To a less noble substance changed,
Were now but leathern buckets ranged.
    The ballads pasted on the wall,
Of Joan of France, and English Moll,
Fair Rosamond, and Robin Hood,
The little Children in the Wood,
Now seem'd to look abundance better,
Improved in picture, size, and letter:
And, high in order placed, describe
The heraldry of every tribe.
    A bedstead of the antique mode,
Compact of timber many a load,
Such as our ancestors did use,
Was metamorphosed into pews;
Which still their ancient nature keep
By lodging folks disposed to sleep.
    The cottage, by such feats as these,
Grown to a church by just degrees,
The hermits then desired their host
To ask for what he fancied most.
Philemon, having paused a while,
Return'd them thanks in homely style;
Then said, "My house is grown so fine,
Methinks, I still would call it mine.
I'm old, and fain would live at ease;
Make me the parson if you please."
    He spoke, and presently he feels
His grazier's coat fall down his heels:
He sees, yet hardly can believe,
About each arm a pudding sleeve;
His waistcoat to a cassock grew,
And both assumed a sable hue;
But, being old, continued just
As threadbare, and as full of dust.
His talk was now of tithes and dues:
He smoked his pipe, and read the news;
Knew how to preach old sermons next,
Vamp'd in the preface and the text;
At christenings well could act his part,
And had the service all by heart;
Wish'd women might have children fast,
And thought whose sow had farrow'd last;
Against dissenters would repine,
And stood up firm for "right divine;"
Found his head fill'd with many a system;
But classic authors,—he ne'er miss'd 'em.

Thus having furbish'd up a parson,
Dame Baucis next they play'd their farce on.
Instead of homespun coifs, were seen
Good pinners edged with colberteen;
Her petticoat, transform'd apace,
Became black satin, flounced with lace.
"Plain Goody" would no longer down,
'Twas "Madame," in her grogram gown
Philemon was in great surprise,
And hardly could believe his eyes.
Amazed to see her look so prim,
And she admired as much at him.

Thus happy in their change of life,
Were several years this man and wife:
When on a day, which proved their last,
Discoursing o'er old stories past,
They went by chance, amid their talk,
To the churchyard to take a walk;
When Baucis hastily cried out,
"My dear, I see your forehead sprout!"—
"Sprout!" quoth the man; "What's this you tell us?
I hope you don't believe me jealous!
But yet, methinks I feel it true,—
And really yours is budding too—
Nay,—now I cannot stir my foot;
It feels as if 'twere taking root."
Description would but tire my Muse,
In short, they both were turn'd to yews.
Old Goodman Dobson of the green
Remembers he the trees has seen;
He'll talk of them from noon till night,
And goes with folks to show the sight;
On Sundays after evening prayer,
He gathers all the parish there;
Points out the place of either yew,
Here Baucis, there Philemon grew:
Till once a parson of our town,
To mend his barn, cut Baucis down;
At which, 'tis hard to be believed
How much the other tree was grieved,
Grew scrubbed, died a-top, was stunted.
So the next parson stubb'd and burnt it.
JONATHAN SWIFT.

TAKE THY OLD CLOAK ABOUT THEE.

THIS winters weather itt waxeth cold,
  And frost doth freese on every hill,
And Boreas blowes his blasts soe bold,
  That all our cattell are like to spill;
Bell my wiffe, who loves noe strife,
  Shee sayd unto me quietlye;
Rise up, and save cow Cumbockes liffe,
  Man, put thine old cloake about thee.

HE.

O Bell, why dost thou flyte "and scorne?"
  Thou kenst my cloak is very thin:
Itt is soe bare and overworne
  A cricke he theron cannot renn:
Then Ile no longer borrowe nor lend,
  "For once Ile new appareld bee,
To-morrow Ile to towne and spend,"
  For Ile have a new cloake about mee.

SHE.

Cow Cumbocke is a very good cowe,
  Shee ha beene alwayes true to the payle,
Shee has helpt us to butter and cheese, I trow,
  And other things shee will not fayle;
I wold be loth to see her pine,
  Good husband, councell take of mee,
It is not for us to go soe fine,
  Man, take thine old cloake about thee.

HE.

My cloake it was a very good cloake,
  Itt hath been always true to the weare,
But now it is not worth a groat;
  I have had it four and forty yeere;
Sometime itt was of cloth in graine,
  'Tis now but a sigh clout as you may see,
It will neither hold out winde nor raine;
  And Ile have a new cloake about mee.

SHE.

It is four and fortye yeeres agoe
  Since the one of us the other did ken,
And we have had betwixt us towe
  Of children either nine or ten;
Wee have brought them up to women and men;
  In the feare of God I trow they bee;
And why wilt thou thyselfe misken?
  Man, take thine old cloake about thee.

HE.

O Bell my wiffe, why dost thou "floute?"
  Now is nowe and then was then:
Seeke now all the world throughout,
  Thou kenst not clownes from gentlemen

They are clad in blacke, greene, yellow, or
    gray,
  Soe far above their owne degree:
  Once in my life Ile " doe as they,"
    For Ile have a new cloake about mee.

She.

King Stephen was a worthy peere,
  His breeches cost him but a crowne,
He held them sixpence all too deere;
  Therefore he called the taylor Lowne.
He was a wight of high renowne,
  And thouse but of a low degree:
Itt's pride that putts this countrye downe,
  Man, take thine old cloake about thee.

He.

" Bell my wife she loves not strife,
  Yet she will lead me if she can;
And oft, to live a quiet life,
  I am forced to yield, though Ime goodman ;"
Itt's not for a man with a woman to threape,
  Unlesse he first gave oer the plea:
As wee began wee now will leave,
  And Ile take mine old cloake about mee.
        AUTHOR UNKNOWN.

THE BACHELOR'S DREAM.

My pipe is lit, my grog is mix'd,
  My curtains drawn and all is snug;
Old Puss is in her elbow-chair,
  And Tray is sitting on the rug.
Last night I had a curious dream,
  Miss Susan Bates was Mistress Mog—
What d'ye think of that, my cat?
  What d'ye think of that, my dog?

She look'd so fair, she sang so well,
  I could but woo, and she was won;
Myself in blue, the bride in white,
  The ring was placed, the deed was done!
Away we went in chaise-and-four,
  As fast as grinning boys could flog—
What d'ye think of that, my cat,
  What d'ye think of that, my dog?

What loving *tête-à-têtes* to come!
  But *tête-à-têtes* must still defer!
When Susan came to live with *me*,
  Her mother came to live with *her*!

With Sister Belle she couldn't part,
  But all *my* ties had leave to jog—
What d'ye think of that, my cat?
  What d'ye think of that, my dog?

The mother brought a pretty Poll—
  A monkey, too, what work he made!
The sister introduced a beau,
  My Susan brought a favorite maid.
She had a tabby of her own,—
  A snappish mongrel christen'd Gog,—
What d'ye think of that, my cat?
  What d'ye think of that, my dog?

The monkey bit, the parrot scream'd,
  All day the sister strumm'd and sung;
The petted maid was such a scold!
  My Susan learn'd to use her tongue;
Her mother had such wretched health,
  She sate and croak'd like any frog—
What d'ye think of that, my cat?
  What d'ye think of that, my dog?

No longer Deary, Duck, and Love,
  I soon came down to simple " M !"
The very servants cross'd my wish,
  My Susan let me down to them.
The poker hardly seem'd my own,
  I might as well have been a log—
What d'ye think of that, my cat?
  What d'ye think of that, my dog?

My clothes they were the queerest shape!
  Such coats and hats she never met!
My ways they were the oddest ways!
  My friends were such a vulgar set!
Poor Tompkinson was snubb'd and huff'd
  She could not bear that Mister Blogg—
What d'ye think of that, my cat?
  What d'ye think of that, my dog?

At times we had a spar, and then
  Mamma must mingle in the song—
The sister took a sister's part—
  The maid declared her master wrong—
The parrot learn'd to call me " Fool !"
  My life was like a London fog—
What d'ye think of that, my cat?
  What d'ye think of that, my dog?

My Susan's taste was superfine,
  As proved by bills that had no end;
I never had a decent coat—
  I never had a coin to spend!

She forced me to resign my club,
　Lay down my pipe, retrench my grog—
What d'ye think of that, my cat?
　What d'ye think of that, my dog?

Each Sunday night we gave a rout
　To fops and flirts, a pretty list;
And when I tried to steal away,
　I found my study full of whist!
Then, first to come and last to go,
　There always was a Captain Hogg—
What d'ye think of that, my cat?
　What d'ye think of that, my dog?

Now was not that an awful dream
　For one who single is and snug,
With Pussy in the elbow-chair,
　And Tray reposing on the rug?—
If I must totter down the hill,
　'Tis safest done without a clog—
What d'ye think of that, my cat?
　What d'ye think of that, my dog?
　　　　　　　　　　THOMAS HOOD.

A SERENADE.

"LULLABY, O, lullaby!"
　Thus I heard a father cry.
"Lullaby, O, lullaby!
　The brat will never shut an eye;
Hither come, some power divine!
　Close his lids, or open mine!"

"Lullaby, O, lullaby!
　What the devil makes him cry?
Lullaby, O, lullaby!
　Still he stares—I wonder why,
Why are not the sons of earth
　Blind, like puppies, from their birth?"

"Lullaby, O, lullaby!"
　Thus I heard the father cry;
"Lullaby, O, lullaby!
　Mary, you must come and try!—
Hush, oh, hush, for mercy's sake—
　The more I sing, the more you wake!"

"Lullaby, O, lullaby!
　Fie, you little creature, fie!
Lullaby, O, lullaby!
　Is no poppy-syrup nigh?
Give him some, or give him all,
　I am nodding to his fall!"

"Lullaby, O, lullaby!
　Two such nights and I shall die!
Lullaby, O, lullaby!
　He'll be bruised, and so shall I—
How can I from bedposts keep,
　When I'm walking in my sleep?"

"Lullaby, O, lullaby!
　Sleep his very looks deny—
Lullaby, O, lullaby!
　Nature soon will stupefy—
My nerves relax—my eyes grow dim—
　Who's that fallen—me or him?"
　　　　　　　　　　THOMAS HOOD.

ODE TO MY LITTLE SON.

THOU happy, happy elf!
(But stop—first let me kiss away that tear)—
Thou tiny image of myself!
(My love, he's poking peas into his ear!)
Thou merry, laughing sprite!
　With spirits feather-light,
Untouch'd by sorrow, and unsoil'd by sin—
(Good heavens! the child is swallowing a pin!)

Thou little tricksy Puck!
With antic toys so funnily bestuck,
Light as the singing bird that wings the air—
(The door! the door! he'll tumble down the stair!)
Thou darling of thy sire!
(Why, Jane, he'll set his pinafore afire!)
Thou imp of mirth and joy!
In Love's dear chain so strong and bright a link,
Thou idol of thy parents—(Drat the boy! There goes my ink!)

Thou cherub—but of earth;
Fit playfellow for Fays, by moonlight pale,
　In harmless sport and mirth—
(That dog will bite him if he pulls its tail!)
Thou human humming-bee, extracting honey
From every blossom in the world that blows,
　Singing in youth's elysium ever sunny—
(Another tumble!—that's his precious nose!)

Thy father's pride and hope!
(He'll break the mirror with that skipping-rope!)
With pure heart newly stamp'd from Nature's mint—
(Where did he learn that squint?)
Thou young domestic dove!
(He'll have that jug off, with another shove!)
Dear nursling of the Hymeneal nest!
(Are those torn clothes his best?)
Little epitome of man!
(He'll climb upon the table, that's his plan!)
Touch'd with the beauteous tints of dawning life—
(He's got a knife!)

Thou enviable being!
No storms, no clouds, in thy blue sky foreseeing,
Play on, play on,
My elfin John!
Toss the light ball—bestride the stick—
(I knew so many cakes would make him sick!)
With fancies, buoyant as the thistle-down,
Prompting the face grotesque, and antic brisk,
With many a lamb-like frisk—
(He's got the scissors, snipping at your gown!)

Thou pretty opening rose!
(Go to your mother, child, and wipe your nose!)
Balmy and breathing music like the south—
(He really brings my heart into my mouth!)
Fresh as the morn, and brilliant as its star—
(I wish that window had an iron bar!)
Bold as the hawk, yet gentle as the dove—
(I'll tell you what, my love,
I cannot write, unless he's sent above!)

THOMAS HOOD.

THE LOST HEIR.

"Oh where, and oh where,
Is my bonny laddie gone?"—OLD SONG.

ONE day, as I was going by
That part of Holborn christen'd High,
I heard a loud and sudden cry
That chill'd my very blood;
And lo! from out a dirty alley,
Where pigs and Irish wont to rally,
I saw a crazy woman sally,
Bedaub'd with grease and mud.
She turn'd her east, she turn'd her west,
Staring like Pythoness possest,
With streaming hair and heaving breast,
As one stark mad with grief.
This way and that she wildly ran,
Jostling with woman and with man—
Her right hand held a frying-pan,
The left a lump of beef.
At last her frenzy seem'd to reach
A point just capable of speech,
And with a tone almost a screech,
As wild as ocean birds,
Or female Ranter moved to preach,
She gave her "sorrow words:"

"O Lord! O dear! my heart will break, I shall go stick stark staring wild!
Has ever a one seen anything about the streets like a crying lost-looking child?
Lawk help me, I don't know where to look, or to run, if I only knew which way—
A Child as is lost about London streets, and especially Seven Dials, is a needle in a bottle of hay.
I am all in a quiver—get out of my sight, do, you wretch, you little Kitty M'Nab!
You promised to have half an eye to him, you know you did, you dirty deceitful young drab.
The last time as ever I see him, poor thing, was with my own blessed Motherly eyes,
Sitting as good as gold in the gutter, a-playing at making little dirt pies.
I wonder he left the court where he was better off than all the other young boys,
With two bricks, an old shoe, nine oyster-shells, and a dead kitten by way of toys.
When his Father comes home—and he always comes home as sure as ever the clock strikes one—
He'll be rampant, he will, at his child being lost; and the beef and the inguns not done!

La bless you, good folks, mind your own consarns, and don't be making a mob in the street;
O Sergeant M'Farland! you have not come across my poor little boy, have you in your beat?
Do, good people, move on! don't stand staring at me like a parcel of stupid stuck pigs;
Saints forbid! but he's p'r'aps been inviggled away up a court for the sake of his clothes by the prigs;
He'd a very good jacket, for certain, for I bought it myself for a shilling one day in Rag Fair,
And his trowsers considering not very much patch'd, and red plush, they was once his Father's best pair.
His shirt, it's very lucky I'd got washing in the tub, or that might have gone with the rest;
But he'd got on a very good pinafore with only two slits and a burn on the breast.
He'd a goodish sort of hat, if the crown was sew'd in, and not quite so much jagg'd at the brim.
With one shoe on, and the other shoe is a boot, and not a fit, and you'll know by that if it's him.
Except being so well dress'd, my mind would misgive, some old beggar woman, in want of an orphan,
Had borrow'd the child to go a-begging with, but I'd rather see him laid out in his coffin!
Do, good people, move on, such a rabble of boys! I'll break every bone of 'em I come near,
Go home—you're spilling the porter—go home—Tommy Jones, go along home with your beer.
This day is the sorrowfullest day of my life, ever since my name was Betty Morgan,
Them vile Savoyards! they lost him once before all along of following a Monkey and an Organ:
O my Billy—my head will turn right round—if he's got kiddynapp'd with them Italians,
They'll make him a plaster parish image boy, they will, the outlandish tatterdemalions.

Billy—where are you, Billy?—I'm as hoarse as a crow with screaming for ye, you young sorrow!
And sha'n't have half a voice, no more I sha'n't, for crying fresh herrings to-morrow.
O Billy, you're bursting my heart in two, and my life won't be of no more vally,
If I'm to see other folks' darlins, and none of mine, playing like angels in our alley;
And what shall I do but cry out my eyes, when I looks at the old three-legged chair
As Billy used to make coach and horses of, and there ain't no Billy there?
I would run all the wide world over to find him, if I only know'd where to run.
Little Murphy, now I remember, was once lost for a month through stealing a penny bun,—
The Lord forbid of any child of mine! I think it would kill me raily
To find my Bill holdin' up his little innocent hand at the Old Bailey.
For though I say it as oughtn't, yet I will say, you may search for miles and mileses
And not find one better brought up, and more pretty behaved, from one end to t'other of St. Giles's.
And if I call'd him a beauty, it's no lie, but only as a mother ought to speak;
You never set eyes on a more handsomer face, only it hasn't been wash'd for a week;
As for hair, tho' it's red, it's the most nicest hair when I've time to just show it the comb;
I'll owe 'em five pounds, and a blessing besides, as will only bring him safe and sound home.
He's blue eyes, and not to be call'd a squint, though a little cast he's certainly got;
And his nose is still a good un, tho' the bridge is broke by his falling on a pewter pint pot;
He's got the most elegant wide mouth in the world, and very large teeth for his age;
And quite as fit as Mrs. Murdockson's child to play Cupid on the Drury Lane stage.

And then he has got such dear winning
  ways—but oh I never, never shall
  see him no more!
Oh dear! to think of losing him just after
  nussing him back from death's door!
Only the very last month when the windfalls,
  hang 'em, was at twenty a penny!
And the threepence he'd got by grottoing
  was spent in plums, and sixty for a
  child is too many.
And the Cholera man came and white-
  wash'd us all, and, drat him, made
  a seize of our hog.—
It's no use to send the Crier to cry him
  about, he's such a blunderin' drunk-
  en old dog;
The last time he was fetch'd to find a lost
  child, he was guzzling with his bell
  at the Crown,
And went and cried a boy instead of a girl,
  for a distracted mother and father
  about town.
Billy—where are you, Billy, I say? come,
  Billy, come home, to your best of
  mothers!
I'm scared when I think of them Cabroleys,
  they drive so, they'd run over their
  own sisters and brothers.
Or may be he's stole by some chimbly-
  sweeping wretch, to stick fast in
  narrow flues, and what not,
And be poked up behind with a pick'd
  pointed pole, when the soot has
  ketch'd, and the chimbly's red hot.
Oh I'd give the whole wide world, if the
  world was mine, to clap my two
  longin' eyes on his face,
For he's my darlin of darlins, and if he
  don't soon come back, you'll see
  me drop stone dead on the place.
I only wish I'd got him safe in these two
  Motherly arms, and wouldn't I hug
  him and kiss him!
Lauk! I never knew what a precious he
  was—but a child don't not feel like
  a child till you miss him.
Why, there he is! Punch and Judy hunt-
  ing, the young wretch, it's that Billy
  as sartin as sin!
But let me get him home, with a good grip
  of his hair, and I'm blest if he shall
  have a whole bone in his skin!
  THOMAS HOOD.

THE TWINS.

IN form and feature, face and limb,
  I grew so like my brother,
That folks got taking me for him,
  And each for one another.
It puzzled all our kith and kin,
  It reach'd a fearful pitch;
For one of us was born a twin,
  And not a soul knew which.

One day, to make the matter worse,
  Before our names were fix'd,
As we were being wash'd by nurse,
  We got completely mix'd;
And thus, you see, by Fate's decree,
  Or rather nurse's whim,
My brother John got christen'd me,
  And I got christen'd him.

This fatal likeness ever dogg'd
  My footsteps when at school,
And I was always getting flogg'd
  When John turn'd out a fool.
I put this question, fruitlessly,
  To every one I knew,
"What would you do, if you were me,
  To prove that you were you?"

Our close resemblance turned the tide
  Of my domestic life,
For somehow, my intended bride
  Became my brother's wife.
In fact, year after year the same
  Absurd mistakes went on,
And when I died, the neighbors came
  And buried brother John.
  HENRY S. LEIGH.

THE KING OF BRENTFORD'S TESTAMENT.

THE noble king of Brentford
  Was old and very sick;
He summon'd his physicians
  To wait upon him quick;
They stepp'd into their coaches,
  And brought their best physic.

They cramm'd their gracious master
  With potion and with pill;
They drench'd him and they bled him:
  They could not cure his ill.
"Go fetch," says he, "my lawyer;
  I'd better make my will."

The monarch's royal mandate
   The lawyer did obey;
The thought of six-and-eightpence
   Did make his heart full gay.
"What is't," says he, "Your Majesty
   Would wish of me to-day?"

"The doctors have belabor'd me
   With potion and with pill:
My hours of life are counted,
   O man of tape and quill!
Sit down and mend a pen or two,
   I want to make my will.

"O'er all the land of Brentford
   I'm lord, and eke of Kew:
I've three per cents. and five per cents.;
   My debts are but a few;
And to inherit after me
   I have but children two.

"Prince Thomas is my eldest son,
   A sober prince is he;
And from the day we breech'd him,
   Till now he's twenty-three,
He never caused disquiet
   To his poor mamma or me.

"At school they never flogg'd him;
   At college, though not fast,
Yet his little go and great go
   He creditably pass'd,
And made his year's allowance
   For eighteen months to last.

"He never owed a shilling,
   Went never drunk to bed,
He has not two ideas
   Within his honest head;
In all respects he differs
   From my second son, Prince Ned.

"When Tom has half his income
   Laid by at the year's end,
Poor Ned has ne'er a stiver
   That rightly he may spend,
But sponges on a tradesman,
   Or borrows from a friend.

"While Tom his legal studies
   Most soberly pursues,
Poor Ned must pass his mornings
   A-dawdling with the Muse;
While Tom frequents his banker,
   Young Ned frequents the Jews.

"Ned drives about in buggies,
   Tom sometimes takes a 'bus;
Ah, cruel Fate! why made you
   My children differ thus?
Why make of Tom a *dullard*,
   And Ned a *genius?*"

"You'll cut him with a shilling,"
   Exclaim'd the man of wits:
"I'll leave my wealth," said Brentford,
   "Sir Lawyer, as befits,
And portion both their fortunes
   Unto their several wits."

"Your Grace knows best," the lawyer said,
   "On your commands I wait."
"Be silent, sir," says Brentford;
   "A plague upon your prate!
Come, take your pen and paper,
   And write as I dictate."

The will, as Brentford spoke it,
   Was writ, and sign'd, and closed;
He bade the lawyer leave him,
   And turn'd him round and dozed;
And next week in the churchyard
   The good old king reposed.

Tom, dress'd in crape and hatband,
   Of mourners was the chief;
In bitter self-upbraidings
   Poor Edward show'd his grief;
Tom hid his fat, white countenance
   In his pocket handkerchief.

Ned's eyes were full of weeping,
   He falter'd in his walk;
Tom never shed a tear,
   But onward he did stalk,
As pompous, black, and solemn
   As any catafalque.

And when the bones of Brentford—
   That gentle king and just—
With bell, and book, and candle
   Were duly laid in dust,
"Now, gentlemen," says Thomas,
   "Let business be discuss'd.

"When late our sire beloved,
   Was taken deadly ill,
Sir Lawyer, you attended him
   (I mean to tax your bill);
And, as you sign'd and wrote it,
   I prithee read the will."

The lawyer wiped his spectacles,
   And drew the parchment out;
And all the Brentford family
   Sat eager round about:
Poor Ned was somewhat anxious,
   But Tom had ne'er a doubt.

"My son, as I make ready
   To seek my last long home,
Some cares I have for Neddy,
   But none for thee, my Tom:
Sobriety and order
   You ne'er departed from.

"Ned hath a brilliant genius,
   And thou a plodding brain;
On thee I think with pleasure,
   On him with doubt and pain."
("You see, good Ned," says Thomas,
   "What he thought about us twain.")

"Though small was your allowance,
   You saved a little store;
And those who save a little
   Shall get a plenty more."
As the lawyer read this compliment,
   Tom's eyes were running o'er.

"The tortoise and the hare, Tom,
   Set out, at each his pace;
The hare it was the fleeter,
   The tortoise won the race;
And since the world's beginning
   This ever was the case.

"Ned's genius, blithe and singing,
   Steps gayly o'er the ground;
As steadily you trudge it,
   He clears it with a bound;
But dulness has stout legs, Tom,
   And wind that's wondrous sound.

"O'er fruits and flowers alike, Tom,
   You pass with plodding feet;
You heed not one nor t'other,
   But onward go your beat,
While Genius stops to loiter
   With all that he may meet;

"And ever, as he wanders,
   Will have a pretext fine
For sleeping in the morning,
   Or loitering to dine,
Or dozing in the shade,
   Or basking in the shine.

"Your little steady eyes, Tom,
   Though not so bright as those
That restless round about him
   His flashing genius throws,
Are excellently suited
   To look before your nose.

"Thank Heaven, then, for the blinkers
   It placed before your eyes;
The stupidest are weakest,
   The witty are not wise;
Oh bless your good stupidity,
   It is your dearest prize!

"And though my lands are wide,
   And plenty is my gold,
Still better gifts from Nature,
   My Thomas, do you hold—
A brain that's thick and heavy,
   A heart that's dull and cold;

"Too dull to feel depression,
   Too hard to heed distress,
Too cold to yield to passion
   Or silly tenderness.
March on—your road is open
   To wealth, Tom, and success.

"Ned sinneth in extravagance,
   And you in greedy lust."
"I' faith," says Ned, "our father
   Is less polite than just."
"In you, son Tom, I've confidence,
   But Ned I cannot trust.

"Wherefore, my lease and copyholds,
   My lands and tenements,
My parks, my farms, and orchards,
   My houses and my rents,
My Dutch stock, and my Spanish stock,
   My five and three per cents.,

"I leave to you, my Thomas"—
   ("What, all?" poor Edward said;
"Well, well, I should have spent them,
   And Tom's a prudent head")—
"I leave to you, my Thomas,—
   To you, IN TRUST for Ned."

The wrath and consternation
   What poet e'er could trace
That at this fatal passage
   Came o'er Prince Tom his face;
The wonder of the company,
   And honest Ned's amaze!

"''Tis surely some mistake,"
  Good-naturedly cries Ned;
The lawyer answer'd gravely,
  "'Tis even as I said;
'Twas thus His Gracious Majesty
  Ordain'd on his deathbed.

"See, here the will is witness'd,
  And here's his autograph."
"In truth, our father's writing,"
  Says Edward, with a laugh;
"But thou shalt not be a loser, Tom,
  We'll share it half and half."

"Alas! my kind young gentleman,
  This sharing cannot be;
'Tis written in the testament
  That Brentford spoke to me,
'I do forbid Prince Ned to give
  Prince Tom a halfpenny.

"'He hath a store of money,
  But ne'er was known to lend it;
He never help'd his brother;
  The poor he ne'er befriended;
He hath no need of property
  Who knows not how to spend it.

"'Poor Edward knows but how to spend,
  And thrifty Tom to hoard;
Let Thomas be the steward then,
  And Edward be the lord;
And as the honest laborer
  Is worthy his reward,

"'I pray Prince Ned, my second son,
  And my successor dear,
To pay to his intendant
  Five hundred pounds a year;
And to think of his old father,
  And live and make good cheer.'"

Such was old Brentford's honest testament;
  He did devise his moneys for the best,
  And lies in Brentford church in peaceful rest.
Prince Edward lived, and money made and spent;
  But his good sire was wrong, it is confess'd,
To say his son, young Thomas, never lent.
  He did. Young Thomas lent at interest,
And nobly took his twenty-five per cent.

Long time the famous reign of Ned endured
  O'er Chiswick, Fulham, Brentford, Putney, Kew;
But of extravagance he ne'er was cured;
  And when both died, as mortal men will do,
'Twas commonly reported that the steward
Was very much the richer of the two.
                WILLIAM MAKEPEACE THACKERAY.

LITTLE BILLEE.

THERE were three sailors of Bristol City
  Who took a boat and went to sea,
But first with beef and captain's biscuits
  And pickled pork they loaded she.

There was gorging Jack and guzzling Jimmy,
  And the youngest he was little Billee;
Now when they'd got as far as the Equator
  They'd nothing left but one split pea.

Says gorging Jack to guzzling Jimmy,
  "I am extremely hungaree."
To gorging Jack says guzzling Jimmy,
  "We've nothing left, us must eat we."

Says gorging Jack to guzzling Jimmy,
  "With one another we shouldn't agree!
There's little Bill, he's young and tender,
  We're old and tough, so let's eat he."

"O Billy! we're going to kill and eat you,
  So undo the button of your chemie."
When Bill received this information,
  He used his pocket-handkerchie.

"First let me say my catechism
  Which my poor mammy taught to me."
"Make haste! make haste!" says guzzling Jimmy,
  While Jack pull'd out his snickersnee.

So Billy went up to the main-top-gallant mast,
  And down he fell on his bended knee;
He scarce had come to the twelfth commandment,
  When up he jumps—"There's land I see!

"Jerusalem and Madagascar
  And North and South Amerikee;
There's the British flag a-riding at anchor,
  With Admiral Napier, K. C. B."

So when they got aboard of the Admiral's,
  He hang'd fat Jack and flogg'd Jimmee,
But as for little Bill, he made him
  The captain of a Seventy-three.
WILLIAM MAKEPEACE THACKERAY.

THE YARN OF THE "NANCY BELL."

'TWAS on the shores that round our coast
  From Deal to Ramsgate span,
That I found alone, on a piece of stone,
  An elderly naval man.

His hair was weedy, his beard was long,
  And weedy and long was he;
And I heard this wight on the shore recite,
  In a singular minor key:—

"Oh, I am a cook and a captain bold,
  And the mate of the Nancy brig,
And a bo'sun tight, and a midshipmite,
  And the crew of the captain's gig."

And he shook his fists and he tore his hair,
  Till I really felt afraid,
For I couldn't help thinking the man had been drinking,
  And so I simply said:—

"O elderly man, it's little I know
  Of the duties of men of the sea,
And I'll eat my hand if I understand
  How ever you can be

"At once a cook and a captain bold,
  And the mate of the Nancy brig,
And a bo'sun tight, and a midshipmite,
  And the crew of the captain's gig!"

Then he gave a hitch to his trowsers, which
  Is a trick all seamen larn,
And having got rid of a thumping quid,
  He spun this painful yarn:—

"'Twas in the good ship Nancy Bell
  That we sail'd to the Indian sea,
And there on a reef we come to grief,
  Which has often occurr'd to me.

"And pretty nigh all o' the crew was drown'd
  (There was seventy-seven o' soul);
And only ten of the Nancy's men
  Said 'Here!' to the muster-roll.

"There was me, and the cook, and the captain bold,
  And the mate of the Nancy brig,
And the bo'sun tight and a midshipmite,
  And the crew of the captain's gig.

"For a month we'd neither wittles nor drink,
  Till a-hungry we did feel,
So we draw'd a lot, and, accordin', shot
  The captain for our meal.

"The next lot fell to the Nancy's mate,
  And a delicate dish he made;
Then our appetite with the midshipmite
  We seven survivors stay'd.

"And then we murder'd the bo'sun tight,
  And he much resembled pig;
Then we wittled free, did the cook and me,
  On the crew of the captain's gig.

"Then only the cook and me was left,
  And the delicate question, 'Which
Of us two goes to the kettle?' arose,
  And we argued it out as sich.

"For I loved that cook as a brother, I did,
  And the cook he worshipp'd me;
But we'd both be blow'd if we'd either be stow'd
  In the other chap's hold, you see.

"'I'll be eat if you dines off me,' says Tom.
  'Yes, that,' says I, 'you'll be.
I'm boil'd if I die, my friend,' quoth I;
  And 'Exactly so,' quoth he.

"Says he: 'Dear James, to murder me
  Were a foolish thing to do,
For don't you see that you can't cook *me*,
  While I can—and will—cook *you*?'

"So he boils the water, and takes the salt
  And the pepper in portions true
(Which he never forgot), and some chopp'd shalot,
  And some sage and parsley too.

"'Come here,' says he, with a proper pride,
  Which his smiling features tell;
''Twill soothing be if I let you see
  How extremely nice you'll smell.'

"And he stirr'd it round and round and
  round,
And he sniff'd at the foaming froth;
When I ups with his heels, and smothers
    his squeals
  In the scum of the boiling broth.

"And I eat that cook in a week or less,
  And as I eating be
The last of his chops, why I almost drops,
  For a wessel in sight I see.

*   *   *   *   *   *

"And I never larf, and I never smile,
  And I never lark nor play;
But I sit and croak, and a single joke
  I have—which is to say:

"Oh, I am a cook and a captain bold,
  And the mate of the Nancy brig,
And a bo'sun tight, and a midshipmite,
  And the crew of the captain's gig!"
                            WILLIAM S. GILBERT.

QUINCE.

NEAR a small village in the West,
  Where many very worthy people
Eat, drink, play whist, and do their best
  To guard from evil church and steeple,
There stood—alas! it stands no more!—
  A tenement of brick and plaster,
Of which, for forty years and four,
  My good friend Quince was lord and
    master.

Welcome was he in hut and hall
  To maids and matrons, peers and peasants;
He won the sympathies of all
  By making puns and making presents.
Though all the parish were at strife,
  He kept his counsel and his carriage,
And laugh'd, and loved a quiet life,
  And shrank from chancery suits and
    marriage.

Sound was his claret—and his head;
  Warm was his double ale—and feelings;
His partners at the whist-club said
  That he was faultless in his dealings:
He went to church but once a week;
  Yet Dr. Poundtext always found him
An upright man who studied Greek,
  And liked to see his friends around him.

Asylums, hospitals, and schools,
  He used to swear were made to cozen;
All who subscribed to them were fools,—
  And he subscribed to half a dozen:
It was his doctrine that the poor
  Were always able, never willing;
And so the beggar at his door
  Had first abuse, and then a shilling.

Some public principles he had,
  But was no flatterer nor fretter;
He rapp'd his box when things were bad,
  And said, "I cannot make them better!"
And much he loathed the patriot's snort,
  And much he scorn'd the placeman's
    snuffle;
And cut the fiercest quarrels short
  With "Patience, gentlemen, and shuffle!"

For full ten years his pointer Speed
  Had couch'd beneath her master's table;
For twice ten years his old white steed
  Had fatten'd in his master's stable;
Old Quince averr'd, upon his troth,
  They were the ugliest beasts in Devon;
And none knew why he fed them both
  With his own hands six days in seven.

Whene'er they heard his ring or knock,
  Quicker than thought the village slatterns
Flung down the novel, smoothed the frock,
  And took up Mrs. Glasse and patterns;
Adine was studying baker's bills;
  Louisa look'd the queen of knitters;
Jane happen'd to be hemming frills,
  And Bell by chance was making fritters.

But all was vain; and while decay
  Came like a tranquil moonlight o'er him,
And found him gouty still and gay,
  With no fair nurse to bless or bore him,
His rugged smile and easy-chair,
  His dread of matrimonial lectures,
His wig, his stick, his powder'd hair,
  Were themes for very strange conjectures.

Some sages thought the stars above
  Had crazed him with excess of knowledge;
Some heard he had been crost in love
  Before he came away from college;

Some darkly hinted that His Grace
  Did nothing great or small without him;
Some whisper'd with a solemn face
  That there was "something odd about him!"

I found him, at threescore and ten,
  A single man, but bent quite double;
Sickness was coming on him then,
  To take him from a world of trouble:
He prosed of slipping down the hill,
  Discover'd he grew older daily:
One frosty day he made his will,
  The next he sent for Doctor Bailey.

And so he lived, and so he died!—
  When last I sat beside his pillow,
He shook my hand, and "Ah!" he cried,
  "Penelope must wear the willow.
Tell her I hugg'd her rosy chain
  While life was flickering in the socket;
And say that when I call again,
  I'll bring a license in my pocket.

"I've left my house and grounds to Fag,
  I hope his master's shoes will suit him;
And I've bequeathed to you my nag,
  To feed him for my sake, or shoot him.
The vicar's wife will take old Fox,
  She'll find him an uncommon mouser;
And let her husband have my box,
  My Bible, and my Assmanshauser.

"Whether I ought to die or not,
  My doctors cannot quite determine;
It's only clear that I shall rot,
  And be like Priam food for vermin.
My debts are paid; but Nature's debt
  Almost escaped my recollection:
Tom! we shall meet again; and yet
  I cannot leave you my direction."

        WINTHROP MACKWORTH PRAED.

AN ELEGY ON THAT GLORY OF HER SEX, MRS. MARY BLAIZE.

GOOD people all, with one accord
  Lament for Madame Blaize,
Who never wanted a good word—
  From those who spoke her praise.

The needy seldom pass'd her door,
  And always found her kind;
She freely lent to all the poor—
  Who left a pledge behind.

She strove the neighborhood to please
  With manners wondrous winning;
And never follow'd wicked ways—
  Unless when she was sinning.

At church, in silks and satins new,
  With hoop of monstrous size,
She never slumber'd in her pew—
  But when she shut her eyes.

Her love was sought, I do aver
  By twenty beaux and more;
The king himself has follow'd her—
  When she has walk'd before.

But now, her wealth and finery fled,
  Her hangers-on cut short all,
The doctors found when she was dead—
  Her last disorder mortal.

Let us lament in sorrow sore,
  For Kent street well may say,
That had she lived a twelvemonth more,
  She had not died to-day.

        OLIVER GOLDSMITH.

OLD GRIMES.

OLD Grimes is dead; that good old man;—
  We ne'er shall see him more:
He used to wear a long black coat,
  All button'd down before.

His heart was open as the day,
  His feelings all were true;
His hair was some inclined to gray,
  He wore it in a queue.

Whene'er he heard the voice of pain,
  His breast with pity burn'd;
The large, round head upon his cane
  From ivory was turn'd.

Kind words he ever had for all;
  He knew no base design:
His eyes were dark and rather small,
  His nose was aquiline.

He lived at peace with all mankind,
  In friendship he was true:
His coat had pocket-holes behind,
  His pantaloons were blue.

Unharm'd, the sin which earth pollutes
  He pass'd securely o'er;
And never wore a pair of boots
  For thirty years or more.

But good old Grimes is now at rest,
  Nor fears misfortune's frown;
He wore a double-breasted vest;
  The stripes ran up and down.

He modest merit sought to find,
  And pay it its desert;
He had no malice in his mind,
  No ruffles on his shirt.

His neighbors he did not abuse,
  Was sociable and gay;
He wore large buckles on his shoes,
  And changed them every day.

His knowledge, hid from public gaze,
  He did not bring to view—
Nor make a noise town-meeting days,
  As many people do.

His worldly goods he never threw
  In trust to Fortune's chances;
But lived (as all his brothers do)
  In easy circumstances.

Thus, undisturb'd by anxious cares,
  His peaceful moments ran;
And everybody said he was
  A fine old gentleman.
                ALBERT G. GREENE.

THE VICAR.

SOME years ago, ere time and taste
  Had turn'd our parish topsy-turvy,
When Darnel Park was Darnel Waste,
  And roads as little known as scurvy,
The man who lost his way between
  St. Mary's Hill and Sandy Thicket
Was always shown across the green,
  And guided to the parson's wicket.

Back flew the bolt of lissom lath;
  Fair Margaret, in her tidy kirtle,
Led the lorn traveller up the path,
  Through clean-clipp'd rows of box and myrtle;
And Don and Sancho, Tramp and Tray,
  Upon the parlor steps collected,
Wagg'd all their tails, and seem'd to say,
  "Our master knows you; you're expected."

Up rose the reverend Doctor Brown,
  Up rose the doctor's "winsome marrow;"
The lady laid her knitting down,
  Her husband clasp'd his ponderous Barrow.
Whate'er the stranger's caste or creed,
  Pundit or papist, saint or sinner,
He found a stable for his steed,
  And welcome for himself, and dinner.

If, when he reach'd his journey's end,
  And warm'd himself in court or college,
He had not gain'd an honest friend,
  And twenty curious scraps of knowledge;
If he departed as he came,
  With no new light on love or liquor,
Good sooth, the traveller was to blame,
  And not the vicarage nor the vicar.

His talk was like a stream which runs
  With rapid change from rocks to roses;
It slipp'd from politics to puns,
  It pass'd from Mahomet to Moses,
Beginning with the laws which keep
  The planets in their radiant courses,
And ending with some precept deep
  For dressing eels or shoeing horses.

He was a shrewd and sound divine,
  Of loud dissent the mortal terror,
And when, by dint of page and line,
  He 'stablish'd truth or startled error,
The Baptist found him far too deep,
  The Deist sigh'd with saving sorrow,
And the lean Levite went to sleep,
  And dream'd of tasting pork to-morrow.

His sermons never said or show'd
  That earth is foul, that heaven is gracious,
Without refreshment on the road,
  From Jerome or from Athanasius;

And sure a righteous zeal inspired
  The hand and head that penn'd and
      plann'd them,
For all who understood admired,
  And some who did not understand
      them.

He wrote too, in a quiet way,
  Small treatises, and smaller verses,
And sage remarks on chalk and clay,
  And hints to noble lords and nurses;
True histories of last year's ghost;
  Lines to a ringlet or a turban,
And trifles for the "Morning Post,"
  And nothings for Sylvanus Urban.

He did not think all mischief fair,
  Although he had a knack of joking;
He did not make himself a bear,
  Although he had a taste for smoking;
And when religious sects ran mad,
  He held, in spite of all his learning,
That if a man's belief is bad,
  It will not be improved by burning.

And he was kind, and loved to sit
  In the low hut or garnish'd cottage,
And praise the farmer's homely wit,
  And share the widow's homelier pottage.
At his approach complaint grew mild,
  And when his hand unbarr'd the shutter,
The clammy lips of fever smiled
  The welcome which they could not utter.

He always had a tale for me
  Of Julius Cæsar or of Venus;
From him I learnt the rule of three,
  Cat's cradle, leap-frog, and *Quæ genus.*
I used to singe his powder'd wig,
  To steal the staff he put such trust in,
And make the puppy dance a jig
  When he began to quote Augustine.

Alack, the change! In vain I look
  For haunts in which my boyhood trifled,
The level lawn, the trickling brook,
  The trees I climb'd, the beds I rifled!
The church is larger than before,
  You reach it by a carriage entry;
It holds three hundred people more,
  And pews are fitted up for gentry.

Sit in the vicar's seat; you'll hear
  The doctrine of a gentle Johnian,
Whose hand is white, whose tone is
      clear,
  Whose phrase is very Ciceronian.
Where is the old man laid? Look down
  And construe on the slab before you—
"*Hic jacet Gvlielmvs Brown,
  Vir nullâ non donandus lauru.*"
      WINTHROP MACKWORTH PRAED.

THE VICAR OF BRAY.

IN good King Charles's golden days,
  When loyalty no harm meant,
A zealous high-churchman was I,
  And so I got preferment.
To teach my flock I never miss'd:
  Kings were by God appointed,
And lost are those that dare resist
  Or touch the Lord's anointed.
    And this is law that I'll maintain
      Until my dying day, sir,
    That whatsoever king shall reign,
      Still I'll be the vicar of Bray, sir.

When royal James possess'd the crown
  And popery grew in fashion,
The penal laws I hooted down,
  And read the declaration;
The Church of Rome I found would fit
  Full well my constitution;
And I had been a Jesuit,
  But for the revolution.
    And this is law that I'll maintain
      Until my dying day, sir,
    That whatsoever king shall reign,
      Still I'll be the vicar of Bray, sir.

When William was our king declared,
  To ease the nation's grievance;
With this new wind about I steer'd,
  And swore to him allegiance;
Old principles I did revoke,
  Set conscience at a distance;
Passive obedience was a joke,
  A jest was non-resistance.
    And this is law that I'll maintain
      Until my dying day, sir,
    That whatsoever king shall reign,
      Still I'll be the vicar of Bray, sir.

When royal Anne became our queen,
  The Church of England's glory,
Another face of things was seen,
  And I became a Tory;
Occasional conformists base,
  I blamed their moderation;
And thought the Church in danger was
  By such prevarication.
    And this is law that I'll maintain
      Until my dying day, sir,
    That whatsoever king shall reign,
      Still I'll be the vicar of Bray, sir,

When George in pudding-time came o'er,
  And moderate men look'd big, sir,
My principles I changed once more,
  And so became a Whig, sir;
And thus preferment I procured
  From our new Faith's defender,
And almost every day abjured
  The pope and the Pretender.
    And this is law that I'll maintain
      Until my dying day, sir,
    That whatsoever king shall reign,
      Still I'll be the vicar of Bray, sir.

Th' illustrious house of Hanover
  And Protestant succession,
To these I do allegiance swear—
  While they can keep possession:
For in my faith and loyalty
  I never more will falter,
And George my lawful king shall be—
  Until the times do alter.
    And this is law that I'll maintain
      Until my dying day, sir,
    That whatsoever king shall reign,
      Still I'll be the vicar of Bray, sir.
                AUTHOR UNKNOWN.

ST. ANTHONY'S SERMON TO THE FISHES.

ST. ANTHONY at church
Was left in the lurch,
So he went to the ditches
And preached to the fishes;
They wriggled their tails,
In the sun glanced their scales.

The carps, with their spawn,
Are all hither drawn;
Have open'd their jaws,
Eager for each clause.
  No sermon beside
  Had the carps so edified.

Sharp-snouted pikes,
Who keep fighting like tikes,
Now swam up harmonious
To hear St. Antonius.
  No sermon beside
  Had the pikes so edified.

And that very odd fish,
Who loves fast days, the cod-fish,—
The stock-fish, I mean,—
At the sermon was seen.
  No sermon beside
  Had the cods so edified.

Good eels and sturgeon,
Which aldermen gorge on,
Went out of their way
To hear preaching that day.
  No sermon beside
  Had the eels so edified.

Crabs and turtles also,
Who always move slow,
Made haste from the bottom,
As if the devil had got 'em.
  No sermon beside
  Had the crabs so edified.

Fish great and fish small,
Lords, lackeys, and all,
Each look'd at the preacher
Like a reasonable creature:
  At God's word,
  They Anthony heard.

The sermon now ended,
Each turned and descended;
The pikes went on stealing,
The eels went on eeling;
  Much delighted were they,
  But preferr'd the old way.

The crabs are backsliders,
The stock-fish thick-siders,
The carps are sharp-set,
All the sermon forget;
  Much delighted were they,
  But preferr'd the old way.
            AUTHOR UNKNOWN.

THE JESTER'S SERMON.

The Jester shook his hood and bells, and leap'd upon a chair,
The pages laugh'd, the women scream'd, and toss'd their scented hair;
The falcon whistled, staghounds bay'd, the lapdog bark'd without,
The scullion dropp'd the pitcher brown, the cook rail'd at the lout;
The steward, counting out his gold, let pouch and money fall,
And why? because the Jester rose to say grace in the hall!

The page play'd with the heron's plume, the steward with his chain,
The butler drumm'd upon the board, and laugh'd with might and main;
The grooms beat on their metal cans, and roar'd till they were red,
But still the Jester shut his eyes and roll'd his witty head;
And when they grew a little still, read half a yard of text,
And, waving hand, struck on the desk, then frown'd like one perplex'd.

"Dear sinners all," the Fool began, "man's life is but a jest,
A dream, a shadow, bubble, air, a vapor at the best.
In a thousand pounds of law I find not a single ounce of love;
A blind man kill'd the parson's cow in shooting at the dove;
The fool that eats till he is sick must fast till he is well;
The wooer who can flatter most will bear away the belle.

"Let no man halloo he is safe till he is through the wood;
He who will not when he may, must tarry when he should;
He who laughs at crookèd men should need walk very straight;
Oh, he who once has won a name may lie abed till eight!
Make haste to purchase house and land, be very slow to wed;
True coral needs no painter's brush, nor need be daub'd with red.

"The friar, preaching, cursed the thief (the pudding in his sleeve),
To fish for sprats with golden hooks is foolish, by your leave,—
To travel well—an ass's ears, ape's face, hog's mouth, and ostrich legs,
He does not care a pin for thieves who limps about and begs.
Be always first man at a feast and last man at a fray;
The short way round, in spite of all, is still the longest way.
When the hungry curate licks the knife, there's not much for the clerk;
When the pilot, turning pale and sick, looks up,—the storm grows dark."

Then loud they laugh'd, the fat cook's tears ran down into the pan:
The steward shook, that he was forced to drop the brimming can;
And then again the women scream'd, and every staghound bay'd,—
And why? because the motley Fool so wise a sermon made.

GEORGE WALTER THORNBURY.

I AM A FRIAR OF ORDERS GRAY.

I am a friar of orders gray,
And down in the valleys I take my way;
I pull not blackberry, haw, or hip—
Good store of venison fills my scrip;
My long bead-roll I merrily chant;
Where'er I walk no money I want;
And why I'm so plump the reason I tell—
Who leads a good life is sure to live well.
    What baron or squire,
    Or knight of the shire,
Lives half so well as a holy friar?

After supper, of heaven I dream,
But that is a pullet and clouted cream;
Myself, by denial, I mortify—
With a dainty bit of a warden pie;
I'm clothed in sackcloth for my sin—
With old sack wine I'm lined within;
A chirping cup is my matin song,
And the vesper's bell is my bowl, ding dong
    What baron or squire,
    Or knight of the shire,
Lives half so well as a holy friar?

JOHN O'KEEFE.

THE DEVIL'S THOUGHTS.

FROM his brimstone bed at break of day
 A-walking the Devil is gone,
To visit his snug little farm the Earth,
 And see how his stock goes on.

Over the hill and over the dale,
 And he went over the plain,
And backward and forward he switch'd
   his long tail,
 As a gentleman switches his cane.

And how then was the Devil drest?
Oh! he was in his Sunday's best:
His jacket was red and his breeches were
   blue,
And there was a hole where the tail came
   through.

He saw a Lawyer killing a viper
 On a dunghill hard by his own stable;
And the Devil smiled, for it put him in mind
 Of Cain and his brother, Abel.

He saw an Apothecary on a white horse
 Ride by on his vocations,
And the Devil thought of his old friend
 Death in the Revelations.

He saw a cottage with a double coach-house,
 A cottage of gentility;
And the Devil did grin, for his darling sin
 Is pride that apes humility.

He peep'd into a rich bookseller's shop;
 Quoth he, "We are both of one college!
For I sate myself like a cormorant, once,
 Hard by the tree of knowledge."

Down the river did glide, with wind and
   tide,
 A pig with vast celerity,
And the Devil look'd wise as he saw how,
   the while,
It cut its own throat. "There!" quoth he
   with a smile,
 "Goes England's commercial prosperity."

As he went through Coldbath Fields he
   saw
 A solitary cell;
And the Devil was pleased, for it gave him
   a hint
 For improving his prisons in Hell.

He saw a Turnkey in a trice
 Fetter a troublesome blade;
"Nimbly," quoth he, "do the fingers
   move
 If a man be but used to his trade."

He saw the same Turnkey unfetter a man
 With but little expedition;
Which put him in mind of the long
   debate
 On the Slave-trade abolition.

He saw an old acquaintance
 As he pass'd by a Methodist meeting;
She holds a consecrated key,
 And the Devil nods her a greeting.

She turn'd up her nose, and said,
 "Avaunt!—my name's Religion!"
And she look'd to Mr. ———,
 And leer'd like a love-sick pigeon.

He saw a certain minister,
 A minister to his mind,
Go up into a certain House,
 With a majority behind;

The Devil quoted Genesis,
 Like a very learnèd clerk,
How "Noah and his creeping things
 Went up into the Ark."

He took from the poor,
 And he gave to the rich,
And he shook hands with a Scotchman,
 For he was not afraid of the ———.

  *   *   *   *   *

General ———'s burning face
 He saw with consternation,
And back to Hell his way did he take—
For the Devil thought by a slight mistake
 It was a general conflagration.
SAMUEL TAYLOR COLERIDGE.

JOLLY GOOD ALE AND OLD.

I CANNOT eat but little meat—
 My stomach is not good;
But sure I think that I can drink
 With him that wears a hood.
Though I go bare, take ye no care;
 I am nothing a-cold,
I stuff my skin so full within
 Of jolly good ale and old.

Back and side go bare, go bare;
  Both foot and hand go cold;
But, belly, God send thee good ale enough,
  Whether it be new or old!

I love no roast but a nut-brown toast,
  And a crab laid in the fire;
And little bread shall do me stead—
  Much bread I nought desire.
No frost, no snow, no wind, I trow,
  Can hurt me if I wold—
I am so wrapt, and thorowly lapt
  Of jolly good ale and old.
Back and side go bare, go bare;
  Both foot and hand go cold;
But, belly, God send thee good ale enough,
  Whether it be new or old!

And Tyb, my wife, that as her life
  Loveth well good ale to seek,
Full oft drinks she, till you may see
  The tears run down her cheek;
Then doth she trowl to me the bowl,
  Even as a malt-worm shold;
And saith "Sweetheart, I took my part
  Of this jolly good ale and old."
Back and side go bare, go bare;
  Both foot and hand go cold;
But, belly, God send thee good ale enough,
  Whether it be new or old!

Now let them drink till they nod and wink,
  Even as good fellows should do;
They shall not miss to have the bliss
  Good ale doth bring men to;
And all poor souls that have scour'd bowls,
  Or have them lustily trowl'd,
God save the lives of them and their wives,
  Whether they be young or old!
Back and side go bare, go bare;
  Both foot and hand go cold;
But, belly, God send thee good ale enough,
  Whether it be new or old!
                    JOHN STILL.

THE JOVIAL BEGGAR.

THERE was a jovial beggar,
  He had a wooden leg,
Lame from his cradle,
  And forced for to beg.
    And a-begging we will go,
      Will go, will go,
    And a-begging we will go.

A bag for his oatmeal,
  Another for his salt,
And a long pair of crutches,
  To show that he can halt.
    And a-begging we will go
      Will go, will go,
    And a-begging we will go.

A bag for his wheat,
  Another for his rye,
And a little bottle by his side,
  To drink when he's a-dry.
    And a-begging we will go,
      Will go, will go,
    And a-begging we will go.

Seven years I begg'd
  For my old master Wilde,
He taught me how to beg
  When I was but a child.
    And a-begging we will go,
      Will go, will go,
    And a-begging we will go.

I begg'd for my master,
  And got him store of pelf,
But, Goodness now be praised,
  I'm begging for myself.
    And a-begging we will go,
      Will go, will go,
    And a-begging we will go.

In a hollow tree
  I live, and pay no rent,
Providence provides for me,
  And I am well content.
    And a-begging we will go,
      Will go, will go,
    And a-begging we will go.

Of all the occupations,
  A beggar's is the best,
For whenever he's a-weary,
  He can lay him down to rest.
    And a-begging we will go,
      Will go, will go,
    And a-begging we will go.

I fear no plots against me,
  I live in open cell;
Then who would be a king, lads,
  When the beggar lives so well?
    And a-begging we will go,
      Will go, will go,
    And a-begging we will go.
                  AUTHOR UNKNOWN.

A FAREWELL TO TOBACCO.

MAY the Babylonish curse
Straight confound my stammering verse,
If I can a passage see
In this word-perplexity,
Or a fit expression find,
Or a language to my mind
(Still the phrase is wide or scant),
To take leave of thee, Great Plant!
Or in any terms relate
Half my love, or half my hate:
For I hate, yet love thee so,
That whichever thing I show,
The plain truth will seem to be
A constrain'd hyperbole,
And the passion to proceed
More from a mistress than a weed.

Sooty retainer to the vine,
Bacchus' black servant, negro fine;
Sorcerer, that mak'st us dote upon
Thy begrimed complexion,
And, for thy pernicious sake,
More and greater oaths to break
Than reclaimèd lovers take
'Gainst women: thou thy siege dost lay
Much too in the female way,
While thou suck'st the lab'ring breath
Faster than kisses, or than death.

Thou in such a cloud dost bind us
That our worst foes cannot find us,
And ill-fortune, that would thwart us,
Shoots at rovers, shooting at us;
While each man, through thy height'ning steam,
Does like a smoking Etna seem,
And all about us does express
(Fancy and wit in richest dress)
A Sicilian fruitfulness.

Thou through such a mist dost show us,
That our best friends do not know us,
And for those allowèd features,
Due to reasonable creatures,
Liken'st us to fell chimeras,
Monsters that, who see us, fear us:
Worse than Cerberus or Geryon,
Or, who first loved a cloud, Ixion.

Bacchus we know, and we allow
His tipsy rites. But what art thou,
That but by reflex canst show
What his deity can do,
As the false Egyptian spell
Aped the true Hebrew miracle?
Some few vapors thou may'st raise,
The weak brain may serve to amaze,
But to the reins and nobler heart
Canst nor life nor heat impart.

Brother of Bacchus, later born,
The old world was sure forlorn,
Wanting thee, that aidest more
The god's victories than before
All his panthers, and the brawls
Of his piping Bacchanals.
These, as stale, we disallow,
Or judge of *thee* meant: only thou
His true Indian conquest art;
And for ivy round his dart,
The reformèd god now weaves
A finer thyrsus of thy leaves.

Scent to match thy rich perfume
Chemic art did ne'er presume
Through her quaint alembic strain,
None so sov'reign to the brain:
Nature, that did in thee excel,
Framed again no second smell.
Roses, violets, but toys
For the smaller sort of boys;
Or for greener damsels meant;
Thou art the only manly scent.

Stinking'st of the stinking kind,
Filth of the mouth, and fog of the mind,
Africa, that brags her foison,
Breeds no such prodigious poison;
Henbane, nightshade, both together,
Hemlock, aconite——
                Nay, rather,
Plant divine, of rarest virtue;
Blisters on the tongue would hurt you.
'Twas but in a sort I blamed thee;
None e'er prosper'd who defamed thee;
Irony all, and feign'd abuse,
Such as perplex'd lovers use
At a need, when in despair,
To paint forth their fairest fair,
Or in part but to express
That exceeding comeliness
Which their fancies doth so strike,
They borrow language of dislike;

And, instead of Dearest Miss,
Jewel, Honey, Sweetheart, Bliss,
And those forms of old admiring,
Call her Cockatrice and Siren,
Basilisk, and all that's evil,
Witch, Hyena, Mermaid, Devil,
Ethiop, Wench, and Blackamoor,
Monkey, Ape, and twenty more;
Friendly Trait'ress, loving Foe—
Not that she is truly so,
But no other way they know
A contentment to express,
Borders so upon excess,
That they do not rightly wot
Whether it be pain or not.

Or as men, constrain'd to part
With what's nearest to their heart,
While their sorrow's at the height,
Lose discrimination quite,
And their hasty wrath let fall,
To appease their frantic gall
On the darling thing whatever
Whence they feel it death to sever,
Though it be, as they, perforce,
Guiltless of the sad divorce.
For I must (nor let it grieve thee,
Friendliest of plants, that I must) leave thee.
For thy sake, Tobacco, I
Would do anything but die,
And but seek to extend my days
Long enough to sing thy praise.
But as she, who once hath been
A king's consort, is a queen
Ever after, nor will bate
Any tittle of her state,
Though a widow, or divorced,
So I, from thy converse forced,
The old name and style retain,
A right Katherine of Spain;
And a seat, too, 'mongst the joys
Of the blest Tobacco Boys;
Where, though I, by sour physician,
Am debarr'd the full fruition
Of thy favors, I may catch
Some collateral sweets, and snatch
Sidelong odors, that give life
Like glances from a neighbor's wife;
And still live in the by-places
And the suburbs of thy graces;
And in thy borders take delight,
An unconquer'd Canaanite.
Charles Lamb.

THE BRIEFLESS BARRISTER.

An Attorney was taking a turn,
  In shabby habiliments dress'd;
His coat it was shockingly worn,
  And the rust had invested his vest.

His breeches had suffer'd a breach,
  His linen and worsted were worse;
He had scarce a whole crown in his hat,
  And not half a crown in his purse.

And thus as he wander'd along,
  A cheerless and comfortless elf,
He sought for relief in a song,
  Or complainingly talk'd to himself:—

" Unfortunate man that I am!
  I've never a client but grief:
The case is, I've no case at all,
  And in brief, I've ne'er had a brief!

" I've waited and waited in vain,
  Expecting an 'opening' to find,
Where an honest young lawyer might gain
  Some reward for toil of his mind.

" 'Tis not that I'm wanting in law,
  Or lack an intelligent face,
That others have cases to plead,
  While I have to plead for a case.

" Oh, how can a modest young man
  E'er hope for the smallest progression—
The profession's already so full
  Of lawyers so full of profession!"

While thus he was strolling around,
  His eye accidentally fell
On a very deep hole in the ground,
  And he sigh'd to himself, "It is well!"

To curb his emotions, he sat
  On the curbstone the space of a minute,
Then cried, "Here's an opening at last!"
  And in less than a jiffy was in it!

Next morning twelve citizens came
  ('Twas the coroner bade them attend),
To the end that it might be determined
  How the man had determined his end!

" The man was a lawyer, I hear,"
  Quoth the foreman who sat on the corse.
" A lawyer? Alas!" said another,
  " Undoubtedly died of remorse!"

A third said, "He knew the deceased,
  An attorney well versed in the laws,
And as to the cause of his death,
  'Twas no doubt for the want of a cause."

The jury decided at length,
  After solemnly weighing the matter,
"That the lawyer was drown*d*ed, because
  He could not keep his head above water!"
JOHN G. SAXE.

MONODY ON THE DEATH OF AN ONLY CLIENT.

OH! take away my wig and gown,
  Their sight is mockery now to me:
I pace my chambers up and down,
  Reiterating, "Where is *he*?"

Alas! wild Echo, with a moan,
  Murmurs above my feeble head:
In the wide world I am alone;
  Ha! ha! my only client's—dead!

In vain the robing-room I seek;
  The very waiters scarcely bow;
Their looks contemptuously speak,
  "He's lost his only client now."

E'en the mild usher, who, of yore,
  Would hasten when his name I said,
To hand in motions, comes no more;
  He knows my only client's dead.

Ne'er shall I, rising up in court,
  Open the pleadings of a suit:
Ne'er shall the judges cut me short
  While moving them for a compute.

No more with a consenting brief
  Shall I politely bow my head;
Where shall I run to hide my grief?
  Alas! my only client's dead.

Imagination's magic power
  Brings back, as clear as clear can be,
The spot, the day, the very hour,
  When first I sign'd my maiden plea.

In the Exchequer's hindmost row
  I sat, and some one touch'd my head;
He tender'd ten-and-six, but oh!
  That only client now is dead.

In vain I try to sing—I'm hoarse:
  In vain I try to play the flute;
A phantom seems to flit across—
  It is the ghost of a compute.

I try to read,—but all in vain;
  My chamber listlessly I tread;
Be still, my heart; throb less, my brain;
  Ho! ho! my only client's dead.

I think I hear a double knock:
  I did—alas! it is a dun.
Tailor—avaunt! my sense you shock;
  He's dead! you know I had but one.

What's this they thrust into my hand?
  A bill return'd!—ten pounds for bread!
My butcher's got a large demand;
  I'm mad! my only client's dead.
LONDON PUNCH.

TO Q. H. F.

SUGGESTED BY A CHAPTER IN THEODORE MARTIN'S "HORACE."

"HORATIUS FLACCUS, B. C. 8,"
There's not a doubt about the date,—
  You're dead and buried:
As you remarked, the seasons roll,
And 'cross the Styx full many a soul
  Has Charon ferried,
Since, mourned of men and Muses nine,
They laid you on the Esquiline.

And that was centuries ago!
You'd think we'd learned enough, I know,
  To help refine us,
Since last you trod the Sacred Street,
And tacked from mortal fear to meet
  The bore Crispinus;
Or, by your cold Digentia, set
The web of winter birding-net.

Ours is so far-advanced an age!
Sensation tales, a classic stage,
  Commodious villas!
We boast high art, an Albert Hall,
Australian meats, and men who call
  Their sires gorillas!
We have a thousand things, you see,
Not dreamt in your philosophy.

And yet, how strange! our "world," to-day,
Tried in the scale, would scarce outweigh
    Your Roman cronies;
Walk in the Park, you'll seldom fail
To find a Sybaris on the rail
    By Lydia's ponies;
Or hap on Barrus, wigged and stayed,
Ogling some unsuspecting maid.

The great Gargilius then behold!
His "long-bow" hunting tales of old
    Are now but duller;
Fair Neobule, too! Is not
One Hebrus here—from Aldershot?
    Aha, you color!
Be wise! There old Canidia sits;
No doubt she's tearing you to bits.

And look, dyspeptic, brave, and kind,
Comes dear Mæcenas, half behind
    Terentia's skirting;
Here's Pyrrha, "golden-haired" at will;
Prig Damasippus, preaching still;
    Asterie flirting,—
Radiant, of course. We'll make her black:
Ask her when Gyges' ship comes back.

So with the rest. Who will may trace
Behind the new each elder face
    Defined as clearly;
Science proceeds, and man stands still;
Our "world" to-day's as good or ill,—
    As cultured (nearly),
As yours was, Horace! You alone,
Unmatched, unmet, we have not known.
                  AUSTIN DOBSON.

THE MODERN BELLE.

SHE sits in a fashionable parlor,
    And rocks in her easy-chair;
She is clad in silks and satins,
    And jewels are in her hair;
She winks and giggles and simpers,
    And simpers and giggles and winks;
And though she talks but little,
    'Tis a good deal more than she thinks.

She lies abed in the morning
    Till near the hour of noon,
Then comes down snapping and snarling
    Because she was called so soon;
Her hair is still in papers,
    Her cheeks still fresh with paint,—
Remains of her last night's blushes,
    Before she intended to faint.

She dotes upon men unshaven,
    And men with "flowing hair;"
She's eloquent over moustaches,
    They give such a foreign air.
She talks of Italian music,
    And falls in love with the moon;
And, if a mouse were to meet her,
    She would sink away in a swoon.

Her feet are so very little,
    Her hands are so very white,
Her jewels so very heavy,
    And her head so very light;
Her color is made of cosmetics
    (Though this she will never own),
Her body is made mostly of cotton,
    Her heart is made wholly of stone.

She falls in love with a fellow
    Who swells with a foreign air;
He marries her for her money,
    She marries him for his hair!
One of the very best matches,—
    Both are well mated in life;
She's got a fool for a husband,
    He's got a fool for a wife!
                  STARK.

WHAT MR. ROBINSON THINKS.

GUVENER B. is a sensible man;
    He stays to his home an' looks arter his
      folks;
He draws his furrer ez straight ez he can,
    An' into nobody's tater-patch pokes;
      But John P.
        Robinson, he
    Sez he wun't vote fer Guvener B.

My! ain't it terrible! Wut shall we du?
    We can't never choose him, o' course,—
      thet's flat;
Guess we shall hev to come round (don't
      you?)
    An' go in fer thunder an' guns, an' all
      that;
      Fer John P.
        Robinson, he
    Sez he wun't vote fer Guvener B.

Gineral C. is a dreffle smart man:
  He's ben on all sides thet give places
    or pelf;
But consistency still wuz a part of his
    plan,—
  He's ben true to *one* party,—an' thet is
    himself;—
      So John P.
      Robinson, he
  Sez he shall vote fer Gineral C.

Gineral C. he goes in fer the war;
  He don't vally principle more'n an old
    cud;
Wut did God make us raytional creeturs fer,
  But glory an' gunpowder, plunder an'
    blood?
      So John P.
      Robinson, he
  Sez he shall vote fer Gineral C.

We were gittin' on nicely up here to our
    village,
  With good old ideas o' wut's right an'
    wut ain't,
We kind o' thought Christ went agin war
    an' pillage,
  An' thet eppyletts worn't the best mark
    of a saint;
      But John P.
      Robinson, he
  Sez this kind o' thing's an exploded
    idee.

The side of our country must ollers be
    took,
  An' Presidunt Polk, you know, *he* is
    our country.
An' the angel thet writes all our sin in a
    book,
  Puts the debit to him, an' to us the per
    contry;
      An' John P.
      Robinson, he
  Sez this is his view o' the thing to a T.

Parson Wilbur he calls all these argimunts
    lies;
  Sez they're nothin' on airth but jest fee,
    faw, fum:
An' thet all this big talk of our destinies
  Is half on it ign'ance, an' t'other half
    rum;

      But John P.
      Robinson, he
  Sez it ain't no sech thing; an', of
    course, so must we.

Parson Wilbur sez *he* never heerd in his
    life
  Thet th' apostles rigg'd out in their
    swaller-tail coats,
An' march'd round in front of a drum an'
    a fife,
  To git some on 'em office, an' some on
    'em votes;
      But John P.
      Robinson, he
  Sez they didn't know everythin' down
    in Judee.

Wal, it's a marcy we've gut folks to tell us
  The rights and the wrongs o' these mat-
    ters, I vow,—
God sends country lawyers, an' other wise
    fellers,
  To start the world's team when it gits in
    a slough;
      Fer John P.
      Robinson, he
  Sez the world'll go right ef he hollers
    out Gee!
                JAMES RUSSELL LOWELL.

PARODY ON POPE.

WHY has not man a collar and a log?
For this plain reason,—man is not a dog.
Why is not man served up with sauce in
    dish?
For this plain reason,—man is not a fish.
                SYDNEY SMITH.

THE SMACK IN SCHOOL.

A DISTRICT school, not far away,
'Mid Berkshire hills, one winter's day,
Was humming with its wonted noise
Of threescore mingled girls and boys;
Some few upon their tasks intent,
But more on furtive mischief bent,
The while the master's downward look
Was fastened on a copy-book.
When suddenly, behind his back,
Rose sharp and clear a rousing smack!

As 'twere a battery of bliss
Let off in one tremendous kiss.
"What's that?" the startled master cries;
"That, thir," a little imp replies,
"Wath William Willith, if you pleathe,—
I thaw him kith Thuthanna Peathe!"
With frown to make a statue thrill,
The master thundered, "Hither, Will!"
Like wretch o'ertaken in his track,
With stolen chattels on his back,
Will hung his head in fear and shame,
And to the awful presence came,—
A great, green, bashful simpleton,
The butt of all good-natured fun.
With smile suppressed, and birch upraised,
The threatener faltered,—"I'm amazed
That you, my biggest pupil, should
Be guilty of an act so rude!
Before the whole set school to boot,—
What evil genius put you to't?"
"'Twas she herself, sir," sobbed the lad.
"I did not mean to be so bad;
But when Susanna shook her curls,
And whispered, I was 'fraid of girls
And dursn't kiss a baby's doll,
I couldn't stand it, sir, at all,
But up and kissed her on the spot!
I know—boo-hoo—I ought to not,
But, somehow, from her looks — boo-hoo—
I thought she kind o' wished me to!"
WILLIAM PITT PALMER.

ST. PATRICK WAS A GENTLEMAN.

OH, St. Patrick was a gentleman,
Who come of decent people;
He built a church in Dublin town,
And on it put a steeple.
His father was a Gallagher;
His mother was a Brady;
His aunt was an O'Shaughnessy,
His uncle an O'Grady.
   So, success attend St. Patrick's fist,
   For he's a saint so clever;
   Oh, he gave the snakes and toads a twist,
   And bothered them for ever!

The Wicklow hills are very high,
And so's the Hill of Howth, sir;
But there's a hill much bigger still,
Much higher nor them both, sir.
'Twas on the top of this high hill
St. Patrick preached his sarmint,
That drove the frogs into the bogs
And banished all the varmint.
   So, success attend St. Patrick's fist,
   For he's a saint so clever;
   Oh, he gave the snakes and toads a twist,
   And bothered them for ever!

There's not a mile in Ireland's isle
Where dirty varmint musters,
But there he put his dear fore foot
And murdered them in clusters.
The toads went pop, the frogs went hop,
Slap-dash into the water;
And the snakes committed suicide
To save themselves from slaughter.
   So, success attend St. Patrick's fist,
   For he's a saint so clever;
   Oh, he gave the snakes and toads a twist,
   And bothered them for ever!

Nine hundred thousand reptiles blue
He charmed with sweet discourses,
And dined on them at Killalloe
In soups and second courses.
Where blind-worms crawling in the grass
Disgusted all the nation,
He gave them a rise, which opened their eyes
To a sense of their situation.
   So, success attend St. Patrick's fist,
   For he's a saint so clever;
   Oh, he gave the snakes and toads a twist,
   And bothered them for ever!

No wonder that those Irish lads
Should be so gay and frisky,
For sure St. Pat he taught them that,
As well as making whiskey;
No wonder that the saint himself
Should understand distilling,

Since his mother kept a shebeen shop
  In the town of Enniskillen.
    So, success attend St. Patrick's
      fist,
    For he's a saint so clever;
    Oh, he gave the snakes and toads a
      twist,
    And bothered them for ever!

Oh, was I but so fortunate
  As to be back in Munster,
'Tis I'd be bound that from that ground
  I never more would once stir.
For there St. Patrick planted turf,
  And plenty of the praties,
With pigs galore, ma gra, ma 'store,
  And cabbages—and ladies!
    Then my blessing on St. Patrick's
      fist,
    For he's the darling saint, O!
    Oh, he gave the snakes and toads a
      twist;
    He's a beauty without paint, O!
          HENRY BENNETT.

ETIQUETTE.

THE "Ballyshannon" foundered off the coast of Cariboo,
And down in fathoms many went the captain and the crew;
Down went the owners—greedy men whom hope of gain allured:
Oh, dry the starting tear, for they were heavily insured.

Besides the captain and the mate, the owners and the crew,
The passengers were also drowned, excepting only two:
Young Peter Gray, who tasted teas for Baker, Croop & Co.,
And Somers, who from Eastern shores imported indigo.

These passengers, by reason of their clinging to a mast,
Upon a desert island were eventually cast.
They hunted for their meals, as Alexander Selkirk used,
But they couldn't chat together—they had not been introduced.

For Peter Gray, and Somers too, though certainly in trade,
Were properly particular about the friends they made;
And somehow thus they settled it, without a word of mouth—
That Gray should take the northern half, while Somers took the south.

On Peter's portion oysters grew—a delicacy rare,
But oysters were a delicacy Peter couldn't bear.
On Somers' side was turtle, on the shingle lying thick,
Which Somers couldn't eat, because it always made him sick.

Gray gnashed his teeth with envy as he saw a mighty store
Of turtle unmolested on his fellow-creature's shore.
The oysters at his feet aside impatiently he shoved,
For turtle and his mother were the only things he loved.

And Somers sighed in sorrow as he settled in the south,
For the thought of Peter's oysters brought the water to his mouth.
He longed to lay him down upon the shelly bed, and stuff:
He had often eaten oysters, but had never had enough.

How they wished an introduction to each other they had had
When on board the "Ballyshannon"! And it drove them nearly mad
To think how very friendly with each other they might get
If it wasn't for the arbitrary rule of etiquette!

One day, when out a-hunting for the *mus ridiculus,*
Gray overheard his fellow-man soliloquizing thus:
"I wonder how the playmates of my youth are getting on,
McConnell, S. B. Walters, Paddy Byles, and Robinson?"

These simple words made Peter as delighted
  as could be,
Old chummies at the Charter-house were
  Robinson and he!
He walked straight up to Somers, then he
  turned extremely red,
Hesitated, hummed and hawed a bit, then
  cleared his throat, and said:

"I beg your pardon—pray forgive me if I
  seem too bold,
But you have breathed a name I knew fa-
  miliarly of old.
You spoke aloud of Robinson—I happened
  to be by.
You know him?" "Yes, extremely well."
  "Allow me; so do I."

It was enough: they felt they could more
  pleasantly get on,
For (ah, the magic of the fact!) they each
  knew Robinson!
And Mr. Somers' turtle was at Peter's ser-
  vice quite,
And Mr. Somers punished Peter's oyster-
  beds all night.

They soon became like brothers from com-
  munity of wrongs:
They wrote each other little odes and sang
  each other songs;
They told each other anecdotes disparaging
  their wives;
On several occasions, too, they saved each
  other's lives.

They felt quite melancholy when they part-
  ed for the night,
And got up in the morning soon as ever it
  was light;
Each other's pleasant company they reck-
  oned so upon,
And all because it happened that they both
  knew Robinson!

They lived for many years on that inhos-
  pitable shore,
And day by day they learned to love each
  other more and more.
At last, to their astonishment, on getting
  up one day,
They saw a frigate anchored in the offing
  of the bay.

To Peter an idea occurred: "Suppose we
  cross the main?
So good an opportunity may not be found
  again."
And Somers thought a minute, then ejac-
  ulated, "Done!
I wonder how my business in the city's get-
  ting on?"

"But stay," said Mr. Peter: "when in Eng-
  land, as you know,
I earned a living tasting teas for Baker,
  Croop & Co.,
I may be superseded—my employers think
  me dead!"
"Then come with me," said Somers, "and
  taste indigo instead."

But all their plans were scattered in a mo-
  ment when they found
The vessel was a convict ship from Port-
  land, outward bound:
When a boat came off to fetch them, though
  they felt it very kind,
To go on board they firmly but respectfully
  declined.

As both the happy settlers roared with
  laughter at the joke,
They recognized a gentlemanly fellow pull-
  ing stroke:
'Twas Robinson—a convict, in an unbecom-
  ing frock!
Condemned to seven years for misappropri-
  ating stock!

They laughed no more, for Somers thought
  he had been rather rash
In knowing one whose friend had misap-
  propriated cash;
And Peter thought a foolish tack he must
  have gone upon
In making the acquaintance of a friend of
  Robinson.

At first they didn't quarrel very openly,
  I've heard;
They nodded when they met, and now and
  then exchanged a word:
The word grew rare, and rarer still the nod-
  ding of the head,
And when they meet each other now, they
  cut each other dead.

To allocate the island they agreed by word
  of mouth,
And Peter takes the north again, and Som-
  ers takes the south;
And Peter has the oysters, which he hates,
  in layers thick,
And Somers has the turtle—turtle always
  makes him sick.
W. S. GILBERT.

THE NANTUCKET SKIPPER.

MANY a long, long year ago,
  Nantucket skippers had a plan
Of finding out, though "lying low,"
  How near New York their schooners ran.

They greased the lead before it fell,
  And then by sounding through the night,
Knowing the soil that stuck so well,
  They always guessed their reckoning
    right.

A skipper gray, whose eyes were dim,
  Could tell, by tasting, just the spot,
And so below he'd "douse the glim,"—
  After, of course, his "something hot."

Snug in his berth, at eight o'clock
  This ancient skipper might be found;
No matter how his craft would rock,
  He slept,—for skippers' naps are sound.

The watch on deck would now and then
  Run down and wake him, with the lead;
He'd up and taste, and tell the men
  How many miles they went ahead.

One night 'twas Jotham Marden's watch,
  A curious wag,—the peddler's son;
And so he mused (the wanton wretch!),
  "To-night I'll have a grain of fun.

"We're all a set of stupid fools,
  To think the skipper knows, by tasting,
What ground he's on; Nantucket schools
  Don't teach such stuff, with all their bast-
    ing!"

And so he took the well-greased lead,
  And rubbed it o'er a box of earth
That stood on deck,—a parsnip-bed,—
  And then he sought the skipper's berth.

"Where are we now, sir? Please to taste."
  The skipper yawned, put out his tongue,
Opened his eyes in wondrous haste,
  And then upon the floor he sprung.

The skipper stormed, and tore his hair,
  Hauled on his boots, and roared to Mar-
    den,
"Nantucket's sunk, and here we are
  Right over old Marm Hackett's garden!"
JAMES THOMAS FIELDS.

THE JOLLY OLD PEDAGOGUE.

'TWAS a jolly old pedagogue, long ago,
  Tall and slender, and sallow and dry;
His form was bent, and his gait was slow,
His long, thin hair was as white as snow,
  But a wonderful twinkle shone in his
    eye;
And he sang every night as he went to bed,
  "Let us be happy down here below;
The living should live, though the dead be
    dead,"
  Said the jolly old pedagogue, long ago.

He taught his scholars the rule of three,
  Writing, and reading, and history, too;
He took the little ones up on his knee,
For a kind old heart in his breast had he,
  And the wants of the littlest child he
    knew:
"Learn while you're young," he often said;
  "There is much to enjoy down here be-
    low;
Life for the living, and rest for the dead!"
  Said the jolly old pedagogue, long ago.

With the stupidest boys he was kind and
    cool,
  Speaking only in gentlest tones;
The rod was hardly known in his school; . . .
  Whipping, to him, was a barbarous rule,
    And too hard work for his poor old
      bones;
Besides, it was painful, he sometimes said:
  "We should make life pleasant down
    here below;

The living need charity more than the
    dead,"
Said the jolly old pedagogue, long ago.

He lived in the house by the hawthorn lane,
    With roses and woodbine over the door;
His rooms were quiet, and neat, and plain,
But a spirit of comfort there held reign,
    And made him forget he was old and
        poor;
"I need so little," he often said;
    "And my friends and relatives here be-
        low
Won't litigate over me when I am dead,"
Said the jolly old pedagogue, long ago.

But the pleasantest times that he had, of
    all,
    Were the sociable hours he used to pass,
With his chair tipped back to a neighbor's
    wall,
Making an unceremonious call,
    Over a pipe and a friendly glass:
This was the finest pleasure, he said,
    Of the many he tasted here below;
"Who has no cronies had better be dead!"
Said the jolly old pedagogue, long ago.

Then the jolly old pedagogue's wrinkled
    face
    Melted all over in sunshiny smiles;
He stirred his glass with an old-school
    grace,
Chuckled, and sipped, and prattled apace,
    Till the house grew merry from cellar to
        tiles:
"I'm a pretty old man," he gently said;
    "I have lingered a long while here be-
        low;
But my heart is fresh, if my youth is fled!"
Said the jolly old pedagogue, long ago.

He smoked his pipe in the balmy air
    Every night when the sun went down,
While the soft wind played in his silvery
    hair,
Leaving its tenderest kisses there,
    On the jolly old pedagogue's jolly old
        crown:
And, feeling the kisses, he smiled, and said,
    'Twas a glorious world down here below;
"Why wait for happiness till we are dead?"
Said the jolly old pedagogue, long ago.

He sat in his door one midsummer night,
    After the sun had sunk in the west,
And the lingering beams of golden light
Made his kindly old face look warm and
    bright,
    While the odorous night-wind whispered,
        "Rest!"
Gently, gently he bowed his head. . . .
    There were angels waiting for him, I
        know.
He was sure of happiness, living or
    dead
This jolly old pedagogue, long ago!
                        GEORGE ARNOLD.

COLOGNE.

IN Köln, a town of monks and bones,
And pavements fang'd with murderous
    stones,
And rags and hags and hideous wenches—
I counted two-and-seventy stenches,
All well-defined and several stinks!
Ye nymphs that reign o'er sewers and
    sinks!
The river Rhine, it is well known,
Doth wash your city of Cologne;
But tell me, nymphs! what power divine
Shall henceforth wash the river Rhine?
                SAMUEL TAYLOR COLERIDGE.

ELEGY ON THE DEATH OF A MAD DOG.

GOOD people all, of every sort,
    Give ear unto my song;
And if you find it wond'rous short
    It cannot hold you long.

In Islington there was a man,
    Of whom the world might say
That still a godly race he ran
    Whene'er he went to pray.

A kind and gentle heart he had,
    To comfort friends and foes;
The naked every day he clad
    When he put on his clothes.

And in that town a dog was found,
    As many dogs there be,
Both mongrel, puppy, whelp, and hound,
    And curs of low degree.

This dog and man at first were friends:
  But when a pique began,
The dog, to gain some private ends,
  Went mad, and bit the man.

Around from all the neighboring streets
  The wondering neighbors ran,
And swore the dog had lost his wits,
  To bite so good a man.

The wound it seem'd both sore and sad
  To every Christian eye:
And while they swore the dog was mad,
  They swore the man would die.

But soon a wonder came to light,
  That show'd the rogues they lied:
The man recover'd of the bite,
  The dog it was that died.
              OLIVER GOLDSMITH.

THE DIVERTING HISTORY OF JOHN GILPIN.

SHOWING HOW HE WENT FARTHER THAN HE INTENDED, AND CAME SAFE HOME AGAIN.

JOHN GILPIN was a citizen
  Of credit and renown;
A trainband captain eke was he
  Of famous London town.

John Gilpin's spouse said to her dear—
  "Tho' wedded we have been
These twice ten tedious years, yet we
  No holiday have seen.

"To-morrow is our wedding-day,
  And we will then repair
Unto the Bell at Edmonton
  All in a chaise and pair.

" My sister and my sister's child,
  Myself and children three,
Will fill the chaise; so you must ride
  On horseback after we."

He soon replied, "I do admire
  Of womankind but one,
And you are she, my dearest dear:
  Therefore it shall be done.

"I am a linendraper bold,
  As all the world doth know;
And my good friend, the calender,
  Will lend his horse to go."

Quoth Mrs. Gilpin, "That's well said;
  And, for that wine is dear,
We will be furnish'd with our own,
  Which is both bright and clear."

John Gilpin kiss'd his loving wife;
  O'erjoy'd was he to find
That, though on pleasure she was bent,
  She had a frugal mind.

The morning came, the chaise was brought,
  But yet was not allow'd
To drive up to the door, lest all
  Should say that she was proud.

So three doors off the chaise was stay'd,
  Where they did all get in—
Six precious souls, and all agog
  To dash through thick and thin.

Smack went the whip, round went the wheel—
  Were never folks so glad;
The stones did rattle underneath,
  As if Cheapside were mad.

John Gilpin at his horse's side
  Seized fast the flowing mane,
And up he got, in haste to ride—
  But soon came down again:

For saddletree scarce reach'd had he,
  His journey to begin,
When, turning round his head, he saw
  Three customers come in.

So down he came: for loss of time,
  Although it grieved him sore,
Yet loss of pence, full well he knew,
  Would trouble him much more.

'Twas long before the customers
  Were suited to their mind;
When Betty, screaming, came down stairs—
  "The wine is left behind!"

"Good lack!" quoth he—"yet bring it me,
  My leathern belt likewise,
In which I bear my trusty sword
  When I do exercise."

Now Mistress Gilpin (careful soul!)
  Had two stone bottles found,
To hold the liquor that she loved,
  And keep it safe and sound.

Each bottle had a curling ear,
    Through which the belt he drew,
And hung a bottle on each side,
    To make his balance true.

Then over all, that he might be
    Equipp'd from top to toe,
His long red cloak, well brush'd and neat,
    He manfully did throw.

Now see him mounted once again
    Upon his nimble steed,
Full slowly pacing o'er the stones,
    With caution and good heed.

But finding soon a smoother road
    Beneath his well-shod feet,
The snorting beast began to trot,
    Which gall'd him in his seat.

So, " Fair and softly," John he cried,
    But John he cried in vain;
That trot became a gallop soon,
    In spite of curb and rein.

So stooping down, as needs he must
    Who cannot sit upright,
He grasp'd the mane with both his hands,
    And eke with all his might.

His horse, who never in that sort
    Had handled been before,
What thing upon his back had got
    Did wonder more and more.

Away went Gilpin, neck or naught;
    Away went hat and wig;
He little dreamt, when he set out,
    Of running such a rig.

The wind did blow—the cloak did fly,
    Like streamer long and gay;
Till, loop and button failing both,
    At last it flew away.

Then might all people well discern
    The bottles he had slung—
A bottle swinging at each side,
    As hath been said or sung.

The dogs did bark, the children scream'd,
    Up flew the windows all;
And every soul cried out, " Well done!"
    As loud as he could bawl.

Away went Gilpin—who but he?
    His fame soon spread around—
" He carries weight! he rides a race!
    'Tis for a thousand pound!"

And still as fast as he drew near,
    'Twas wonderful to view
How in a trice the turnpike-men
    Their gates wide open threw.

And now, as he went bowing down
    His reeking head full low,
The bottles twain behind his back
    Were shatter'd at a blow.

Down ran the wine into the road,
    Most piteous to be seen,
Which made his horse's flanks to smoke
    As they had basted been.

But still he seem'd to carry weight,
    With leathern girdle braced;
For all might see the bottle-necks
    Still dangling at his waist.

Thus all through merry Islington
    These gambols he did play,
Until he came unto the Wash
    Of Edmonton so gay;

And there he threw the wash about
    On both sides of the way,
Just like unto a trundling mop,
    Or a wild goose at play.

At Edmonton his loving wife
    From the balcony spied
Her tender husband, wondering much
    To see how he did ride.

" Stop, stop, John Gilpin! here's the house,"
    They all at once did cry;
" The dinner waits, and we are tired:"
    Said Gilpin—" So am I!"

But yet his horse was not a whit
    Inclined to tarry there;
For why?—his owner had a house
    Full ten miles off, at Ware.

So like an arrow swift he flew,
    Shot by an archer strong;
So did he fly—which brings me to
    The middle of my song.

Away went Gilpin out of breath,
   And sore against his will,
Till at his friend's the calender's
   His horse at last stood still.

The calender, amazed to see
   His neighbor in such trim,
Laid down his pipe, flew to the gate,
   And thus accosted him:

"What news? what news? your tidings tell;
   Tell me you must and shall—
Say why bareheaded you are come,
   Or why you come at all?"

Now Gilpin had a pleasant wit,
   And loved a timely joke;
And thus unto the calender
   In merry guise he spoke:

"I came because your horse would come;
   And, if I well forbode,
My hat and wig will soon be here,
   They are upon the road."

The calender, right glad to find
   His friend in merry pin,
Return'd him not a single word,
   But to the house went in;

Whence straight he came with hat and wig
   A wig that flow'd behind,
A hat not much the worse for wear—
   Each comely in its kind.

He held them up, and in his turn
   Thus show'd his ready wit—
"My head is twice as big as yours,
   They therefore needs must fit.

"But let me scrape the dirt away
   That hangs upon your face;
And stop and eat, for well you may
   Be in a hungry case."

Said John, "It is my wedding-day,
   And all the world would stare
If wife should dine at Edmonton,
   And I should dine at Ware."

So turning to his horse, he said,
   "I am in haste to dine;
'Twas for your pleasure you came here—
   You shall go back for mine."

Ah, luckless speech and bootless boast,
   For which he paid full dear!
For, while he spake, a braying ass
   Did sing most loud and clear;

Whereat his horse did snort, as he
   Had heard a lion roar,
And gallop'd off with all his might,
   As he had done before.

Away went Gilpin, and away
   Went Gilpin's hat and wig:
He lost them sooner than at first,
   For why?—they were too big.

Now Mistress Gilpin, when she saw
   Her husband posting down
Into the country far away,
   She pull'd out half a crown;

And thus unto the youth she said
   That drove them to the Bell,
"This shall be yours when you bring back
   My husband safe and well."

The youth did ride, and soon did meet
   John coming back amain—
Whom in a trice he tried to stop,
   By catching at his rein;

But not performing what he meant,
   And gladly would have done,
The frighted steed he frighted more,
   And made him faster run.

Away went Gilpin, and away
   Went post-boy at his heels,
The post-boy's horse right glad to miss
   The lumbering of the wheels.

Six gentlemen upon the road,
   Thus seeing Gilpin fly,
With post-boy scampering in the rear,
   They raised the hue and cry:

"Stop thief! stop thief!—a highwayman!"
   Not one of them was mute;
And all and each that pass'd that way
   Did join in the pursuit.

And now the turnpike-gates again
   Flew open in short space:
The toll-men thinking as before,
   That Gilpin rode a race.

And so he did, and won it too,
    For he got first to town;
Nor stopp'd till where he had got up
    He did again get down.

Now let us sing, Long live the king!
    And Gilpin, long live he;
And when he next doth ride abroad,
    May I be there to see!
                WILLIAM COWPER.

THE DEACON'S MASTERPIECE, OR THE WONDERFUL "ONE-HOSS SHAY."

A LOGICAL STORY.

HAVE you heard of the wonderful one-hoss shay,
That was built in such a logical way,
It ran a hundred years to a day,
And then, of a sudden, it— Ah, but stay,
I'll tell you what happen'd without delay,
Scaring the parson into fits,
Frightening people out of their wits,
Have you ever heard of that, I say?

Seventeen hundred and fifty-five.
Georgius Secundus was then alive,—
Snuffy old drone from the German hive.
That was the year when Lisbon-town
Saw the earth open and gulp her down,
And Braddock's army was done so brown,
Left without a scalp to its crown.
It was on the terrible Earthquake-day
That the Deacon finish'd the one-hoss shay.

Now in building of chaises, I tell you what,
There is always *somewhere* a weakest spot,—
In hub, tire, felloe, in spring or thill,
In panel, or cross-bar, or floor, or sill,
In screw, bolt, thoroughbrace,—lurking still
Find it somewhere you must and will,—
Above, or below, or within or without,—
And that's the reason, beyond a doubt,
That a chaise *breaks down*, but doesn't *wear out*.

But the Deacon *swore* (as Deacons do,
With an " I dew vum," or an " I tell *yeou* ")
He would build one shay to beat the taown
'N' the keounty 'n' all the kentry raoun';
It should be so built that it *couldn't* break daown:

" Fur," said the Deacon, "'t's mighty plain
Thut the weakes' place mus' stan' the strain;
'N' the wayt' fix it, uz I maintain,
    Is only jest
T' make that place uz strong uz the rest."

So the Deacon inquired of the village folk
Where he could find the strongest oak,
That couldn't be split nor bent nor broke,—
That was for spokes and floor and sills;
He sent for lancewood to make the thills;
The cross-bars were ash, from the straightest trees;
The panels of white-wood, that cuts like cheese,
But lasts like iron for things like these;
The hubs of logs from the "Settler's ellum,"—
Last of its timber—they couldn't sell 'em,
Never an axe had seen their chips,
And the wedges flew from between their lips,
Their blunt ends frizzled like celery-tips;
Step and prop-iron, bolt and screw,
Spring, tire, axle, and linchpin too,
Steel of the finest, bright and blue;
Thoroughbrace bison-skin, thick and wide;
Boot, top, dasher, from tough old hide
Found in the pit when the tanner died.
That was the way he " put her through."—
" There!" said the Deacon, " naow she'll dew."

Do! I tell you, I rather guess
She was a wonder, and nothing less!
Colts grew horses, beards turn'd gray,
Deacon and deaconess dropp'd away,
Children and grandchildren—where were they?
But there stood the stout old one-hoss shay,
As fresh as on Lisbon-earthquake-day!

Eighteen Hundred;—it came and found
The Deacon's masterpiece strong and sound.
Eighteen hundred increased by ten;
" Hahnsum kerridge " they call'd it then.
Eighteen hundred and twenty came;—
Running as usual; much the same.
Thirty and forty at last arrive,
And then come fifty, and fifty-five.

Little of all we value here
Wakes on the morn of its hundredth year
Without both feeling and looking queer.
In fact, there's nothing that keeps its youth,
So far as I know, but a tree and truth.
(This is a moral that runs at large;
Take it.—You're welcome.—No extra charge.)

First of November,—the Earthquake-day,—
There are traces of age in the one-hoss shay,
A general flavor of mild decay,—
But nothing local, as one may say.
There couldn't be,—for the Deacon's art
Had made it so like in every part
That there wasn't a chance for one to start.
For the wheels were just as strong as the thills,
And the floor was just as strong as the sills,
And the panels just as strong as the floor,
And the whippletree neither less nor more,
And the back crossbar as strong as the fore,
And spring and axle and hub *encore*.
And yet, *as a whole*, it is past a doubt,
In another hour it will be *worn out!*

First of November, 'Fifty-five!
This morning the parson takes a drive.
Now, small boys, get out of the way!
Here comes the wonderful one-hoss shay,
Drawn by a rat-tail'd, ewe-neck'd bay.
"Huddup!" said the parson.—Off went they.

The parson was working his Sunday's text,—
Had got to *fifthly*, and stopp'd perplex'd
At what the—Moses—was coming next.
All at once the horse stood still,
Close by the meet'n'-house on the hill.
—First a shiver, and then a thrill,
Then something decidedly like a spill,—
And the parson was sitting upon a rock,
At half-past nine by the meet'n'-house clock,—
Just the hour of the earthquake shock!

What do you think the parson found
When he got up and stared around?
The poor old chaise in a heap or mound,
As if it had been to the mill and ground!
You see, of course, if you're not a dunce,
How it went to pieces all at once,—
All at once, and nothing first,—
Just as bubbles do when they burst.—

End of the wonderful one-hoss shay.
Logic is *logic*. That's all I say.
OLIVER WENDELL HOLMES.

PLAIN LANGUAGE FROM TRUTHFUL JAMES.

WHICH I wish to remark,—
   And my language is plain,—
That for ways that are dark,
   And for tricks that are vain,
The heathen Chinee is peculiar,
Which the same I would rise to explain.

Ah Sin was his name;
   And I shall not deny
In regard to the same
   What that name might imply,
But his smile it was pensive and child-like,
As I frequent remark'd to Bill Nye.

It was August the third,
   And quite soft was the skies;
Which it might be inferr'd
   That Ah Sin was likewise;
Yet he play'd it that day upon William
And me in a way I despise.

Which we had a small game,
   And Ah Sin took a hand:
It was euchre. The same
   He did not understand;
But he smiled as he sat by the table,
With a smile that was child-like and bland.

Yet the cards they were stock'd
   In a way that I grieve,
And my feelings were shock'd
   At the state of Nye's sleeve,
Which was stuff'd full of aces and bowers,
And the same with intent to deceive.

But the hands that were play'd
   By that heathen Chinee,
And the points that he made,
   Were quite frightful to see,—
Till at last he put down a right bower,
Which the same Nye had dealt unto me.

Then I look'd up at Nye,
   And he gazed upon me;
And he rose with a sigh,
   And said, "Can this be?
We are ruin'd by Chinese cheap labor;"
And he went for that heathen Chinee.

In the scene that ensued
   I did not take a hand,
But the floor it was strew'd
   Like the leaves on the strand
With the cards that Ah Sin had been hiding,
In the game he "did not understand."

In his sleeves, which were long,
   He had twenty-four packs,—
Which was coming it strong,
   Yet I state but the facts;
And we found on his nails, which were taper,
What is frequent in tapers,— that's wax.

Which is why I remark,—
   And my language is plain, —
That for ways that are dark,
   And for tricks that are vain,
The heathen Chinee is peculiar,—
Which the same I am free to maintain.
              FRANCIS BRET HARTE.

MASSACRE OF THE MACPHERSON.

FHAIRSHON swore a feud
   Against the clan M'Tavish—
March'd into their land
   To murder and to rafish;
For he did resolve
   To extirpate the vipers,
With four-and-twenty men,
   And five-and-thirty pipers.

But when he had gone
   Half-way down Strath-Canaan,
Of his fighting tail
   Just three were remainin'.

They were all he had
   To back him in ta battle;
All the rest had gone
   Off to drive ta cattle.

"Fery coot!" cried Fhairshon—
   "So my clan disgraced is;
Lads, we'll need to fight
   Pefore we touch the peasties.
Here's Mhic-Mac-Methusaleh
   Coming wi' his fassals—
Gillies seventy-three,
   And sixty Dhuinéwassails!"

"Coot tay to you, sir!
   Are not you ta Fhairshon?
Was you coming here
   To visit any person?
You are a plackguard, sir!
   It is now six hundred
Coot long years, and more,
   Since my glen was plunder'd."

"Fat is tat you say?
   Dar you cock your peaver?
I will teach you, sir,
   Fat is coot pehavior!
You shall not exist
   For another day more;
I will shot you, sir,
   Or stap you with my claymore!"

"I am fery glad
   To learn what you mention,
Since I can prevent
   Any such intention."
So Mhic-Mac-Methusaleh
   Gave some warlike howls,
Trew his skhian-dhu,
   An' stuck it in his powels.

In this fery way
   Tied ta faliant Fhairshon,
Who was always thought
   A superior person.
Fhairshon had a son,
   Who married Noah's daughter,
And nearly spoil'd ta flood
   By trinking up ta water—

Which he would have done,
   I at least believe it,
Had ta mixture peen
   Only half Glenlivet.

This is all my tale:
Sirs, I hope 'tis new t'ye!
Here's your fery good healths,
And tamn ta whusky tuty!
WILLIAM EDMONDSTOUNE AYTOUN.

THE FRIEND OF HUMANITY AND THE KNIFE-GRINDER.

FRIEND OF HUMANITY.

"NEEDY knife-grinder, whither are you going?
Rough is the road, your wheel is out of order—
Bleak blows the blast, your hat has got a hole in't,
So have your breeches!

"Weary knife-grinder, little think the proud ones,
Who in their coaches roll along the turnpike-
Road, what hard work 'tis crying all day
' Knives and
Scissors to grind, oh!'

"Tell me, knife-grinder, how came you to grind knives?
Did some rich man tyrannically use you?
Was it the squire? or parson of the parish?
Or the attorney?

"Was it the squire, for killing of his game, or
Covetous parson, for his tithes distraining?
Or roguish lawyer, made you lose your little
All in a lawsuit?

"(Have you not read the *Rights of Man*, by Tom Paine?)
Drops of compassion tremble on my eyelids,
Ready to fall, as soon as you have told your
Pitiful story."

KNIFE-GRINDER.

"Story! God bless you, I have none to tell, sir;
Only last night a-drinking at the Chequers,
This poor old hat and breeches, as you see, were
Torn in a scuffle.

"Constables came up, for to take me into
Custody; they took me before the justice;
Justice Oldmixon put me in the parish
Stocks for a vagrant.

"I should be glad to drink your honor's health in
A pot of beer, if you will give me sixpence;
But for my part, I never love to meddle
With politics, sir."

FRIEND OF HUMANITY.

"*I* give thee sixpence! I will see the damn'd first—
Wretch! whom no sense of wrongs can rouse to vengeance—
Sordid, unfeeling, reprobate, degraded,
Spiritless outcast!"

[Kicks the knife-grinder, overturns his wheel, and exit in a transport of republican enthusiasm and universal philanthropy.]
GEORGE CANNING.

SONG.

SUNG BY ROGERO IN THE BURLESQUE PLAY OF "THE ROVER."

WHENE'ER with haggard eyes I view
This dungeon that I'm rotting in,
I think of those companions true
Who studied with me at the U-
—niversity of Gottingen—
—niversity of Gottingen.

[Weeps, and pulls out a blue kerchief, with which he wipes his eyes; gazing tenderly at it, he proceeds—]

Sweet kerchief, check'd with heavenly blue,
Which once my love sat knotting in! —
Alas! Matilda *then* was true!
At least I thought so at the U-
—niversity of Gottingen—
—niversity of Gottingen.

[At the repetition of this line *Rogero* clanks his chains in cadence.]

Barbs! barbs! alas! how swift you flew
Her neat post-wagon trotting in!
Ye bore Matilda from my view;
Forlorn I languish'd at the U-
—niversity of Gottingen—
—niversity of Gottingen.

This faded form! this pallid hue!
  This blood my veins is clotting in,
My years are many—they were few
When first I entered at the U-
      —niversity of Gottingen—
      —niversity of Gottingen.

There first for thee my passion grew,
  Sweet, sweet Matilda Pottingen!
Thou wast the daughter of my tu-
—tor, law professor at the U-
      —niversity of Gottingen—
      —niversity of Gottingen.

Sun, moon, and thou, vain world, adieu,
  That kings and priests are plotting in;
Here doom'd to starve on water gru-
—el, never shall I see the U-
      —niversity of Gottingen—
      —niversity of Gottingen.

[During the last stanza *Rogero* dashes his head repeatedly against the walls of his prison, and, finally, so hard as to produce a visible contusion; he then throws himself on the floor in an agony. The curtain drops, the music still continuing to play till it is wholly fallen.]
                    GEORGE CANNING.

A TALE OF DRURY LANE.

[To be spoken by Mr. Kemble, in a suit of the Black Prince's Armor, borrowed from the Tower.]

SURVEY this shield, all bossy bright—
  These cuisses twin behold!
Look on my form in armor dight
  Of steel inlaid with gold;
My knees are stiff in iron buckles,
Stiff spikes of steel protect my knuckles.
These once belonged to sable prince,
Who never did in battle wince;
With valor tart as pungent quince,
  He slew the vaunting Gaul.
Rest there a while, my bearded lance,
While from green curtain I advance
To yon footlights, no trivial dance,
And tell the town what sad mischance
  Did Drury Lane befall.

THE NIGHT.

On fair Augusta's towers and trees
Flitter'd the silent midnight breeze,
Curling the foliage as it past,
Which from the moon-tipp'd plumage cast
A spangled light, like dancing spray,
Then reassumed its still array;
When, as night's lamp unclouded hung,
And down its full effulgence flung,
It shed such soft and balmy power
That cot and castle, hall and bower,
And spire and dome, and turret height,
Appear'd to slumber in the light.
From Henry's Chapel, Rufus' Hall,
To Savoy, Temple, and St. Paul,
From Knightsbridge, Pancras, Camden
    Town,
To Redriff, Shadwell, Horsleydown,
No voice was heard, no eye unclosed,
But all in deepest sleep reposed.
They might have thought, who gazed
    around
Amid a silence so profound,
  It made the senses thrill,
That 'twas no place inhabited,
But some vast city of the dead—
  All was so hush'd and still.

THE BURNING.

As Chaos, which, by heavenly doom,
Had slept in everlasting gloom,
Started with terror and surprise
When light first flash'd upon her eyes—
So London's sons in night-cap woke,
  In bed-gown woke her dames;
For shouts were heard 'mid fire and
    smoke,
And twice ten hundred voices spoke—
  "The playhouse is in flames!"
And lo! where Catharine street extends,
A fiery tail its lustre lends
  To every window-pane;
Blushes each spout in Martlet Court,
And Barbican, moth-eaten fort,
And Covent Garden kennels sport
  A bright ensanguined drain;
Meux's new brewhouse shows the light,
Rowland Hill's chapel, and the height
Where patent shot they sell.
The Tennis-Court, so fair and tall,
Partakes the ray with Surgeons' Hall,
The ticket-porters' house of call,
Old Bedlam, close by London Wall,
Wright's shrimp and oyster shop withal,
  And Richardson's Hotel.
Nor these alone, but far and wide,
Across red Thames's gleaming tide,

To distant fields the blaze was borne,
And daisy white and hoary thorn
In borrow'd lustre seemed to sham
The rose of red sweet Wil-li-am.
To those who on the hills around
Beheld the flames from Drury's mound,
   As from a lofty altar rise,
It seem'd that nations did conspire
To offer to the god of fire
   Some vast stupendous sacrifice!
The summon'd firemen woke at call,
And hied them to their stations all:
Starting from short and broken snooze,
Each sought his pond'rous hobnail'd shoes,
But first his worsted hosen plied,
Plush breeches next, in crimson dyed,
   His nether bulk embraced;
Then jacket thick, of red or blue,
Whose massy shoulder gave to view
The badge of each respective crew,
   In tin or copper traced.
The engines thunder'd through the street,
Fire-hook, pipe, bucket, all complete,
And torches glared, and clattering feet
   Along the pavement paced.
And one, the leader of the band,
From Charing Cross along the Strand,
Like stag by beagles hunted hard,
Ran till he stopp'd at Vin'gar Yard.
The burning badge his shoulder bore,
The belt and oil-skin hat he wore,
The cane he had, his men to bang,
Show'd foreman of the British gang—
His name was Higginbottom. Now
   'Tis meet that I should tell you how
      The others came in view:
The Hand-in-Hand the race begun,
Then came the Phœnix and the Sun,
Th' Exchange, where old insurers run,
   The Eagle, where the new;
With these came Rumford, Bumford, Cole,
Robins from Hockley-in-the-Hole,
Lawson and Dawson, cheek by jowl,
   Crump from St. Giles's Pound;
Whitford and Mitford join'd the train,
Huggins and Muggins from Chick Lane,
And Clutterbuck, who got a sprain
   Before the plug was found.
Hobson and Jobson did not sleep,
But ah! no trophy could they reap,
For both were in the Donjon Keep
   Of Bridewell's gloomy mound!

E'en Higginbottom now was posed,
For sadder scene was ne'er disclosed.
Without, within, in hideous show,
Devouring flames resistless glow,
And blazing rafters downward go,
And never halloo "Heads below!"
   Nor notice give at all.
The firemen, terrified, are slow
To bid the pumping torrent flow,
   For fear the roof would fall.
Back, Robins, back! Crump, stand aloof!
   Whitford, keep near the walls!
Huggins, regard your own behoof,
For lo! the blazing, rocking roof
   Down, down, in thunder falls!
An awful pause succeeds the stroke,
And o'er the ruins volumed smoke,
Rolling around its pitchy shroud,
Conceal'd them from th' astonish'd crowd.
At length the mist a while was clear'd,
When, lo! amid the wreck uprear'd,
Gradually a moving head appear'd,
   And Eagle firemen knew
'Twas Joseph Muggins, name revered,
   The foreman of their crew.
Loud shouted all in signs of woe,
"A Muggins! to the rescue, ho!"
   And pour'd the hissing tide:
Meanwhile the Muggins fought amain,
And strove and struggled all in vain,
For, rallying but to fall again,
   He totter'd, sunk, and died!

Did none attempt, before he fell,
To succor one they loved so well?
Yes, Higginbottom did aspire
(His fireman's soul was all on fire)
   His brother chief to save;
But ah! his reckless generous ire
   Served but to share his grave!
'Mid blazing beams and scalding streams,
Through fire and smoke he dauntless
   broke,
   Where Muggins broke before.
But sulphury stench and boiling drench,
Destroying sight, o'erwhelm'd him quite,
   He sunk to rise no more.
Still o'er his head, while Fate he braved,
His whizzing water-pipe he waved;
"Whitford and Mitford, ply your pumps,
You, Clutterbuck, come, stir your stumps

Why are you in such doleful dumps?
A fireman and afraid of bumps!—
What are they fear'd on? fools! 'od rot
    'em!"
Were the last words of Higginbottom.

THE REVIVAL.

Peace to his soul! new prospects bloom,
And toil rebuilds what fires consume!
Eat we, and drink we, be our ditty,
" Joy to the managing committee!"
Eat we and drink we, join to rum
Roast beef and pudding of the plum;
Forth from thy nook, John Horner,
    come,
With bread of ginger brown thy thumb,
    For this is Drury's gay day:
Roll, roll thy hoop, and twirl thy tops,
And buy, to glad thy smiling chops,
Crisp parliament with lollypops,
    And fingers of the Lady.
Didst mark how toil'd the busy train
From morn to eve, till Drury Lane
Leap'd like a roebuck from the plain?
Ropes rose and sunk, and rose again,
    And nimble workmen trod;
To realize bold Wyatt's plan
Rush'd many a howling Irishman;
Loud clatter'd many a porter-can,
And many a ragamuffin clan,
    With trowel and with hod.
Drury revives! her rounded pate
Is blue, is heavenly blue, with slate;
She "wings the midway air," elate
    As magpie, crow, or chough;
White paint her modish visage smears,
Yellow and pointed are her ears.
No pendent portico appears
Dangling beneath, for Whitbread's shears
    Have cut the bauble off.
Yes, she exalts her stately head;
And, but that solid bulk outspread
Opposed you on your onward tread,
And posts and pillars warranted
That all was true that Wyatt said,
You might have deem'd her walls so thick
Were not composed of stone or brick,
But all a phantom, all a trick,
Of brain disturb'd and fancy-sick,
So high she soars, so vast, so quick!
                    HORACE SMITH.

THE THEATRE.

Interior of a Theatre described.—Pit gradually fills.—
The Check-taker.—Pit full.—The Orchestra tuned.—
One Fiddle rather dilatory.—Is reproved, and re-
pents.—Evolutions of a Play-bill.—Its final Settle-
ment on the Spikes.—The Gods taken to task—and
why.—Motley Group of Play-goers.—Holywell
street, St. Pancras.—Emanuel Jennings binds his
Son apprentice—not in London—and why.—Episode
of the Hat.

'TIS sweet to view, from half-past five to
    six,
Our long wax-candles, with short cotton
    wicks,
Touch'd by the lamplighter's Promethean
    art,
Start into light, and make the lighter
    start;
To see red Phœbus through the gallery-
    pane
Tinge with his beams the beams of Drury
    Lane;
While gradual parties fill our widen'd
    pit,
And gape, and gaze, and wonder, ere they
    sit.

At first, while vacant seats give choice
    and ease,
Distant or near, they settle where they
    please;
But when the multitude contracts the
    span,
And seats are rare, they settle where they
    can.

Now the full benches to late comers
    doom
No room for standing, miscall'd *standing-
    room*.

Hark! the check-taker moody silence
    breaks,
And bawling "Pit full!" gives the checks
    he takes;
Yet onward still the gathering numbers
    cram,
Contending crowders shout the frequent
    damn,
And all is bustle, squeeze, row, jabbering,
    and jam.

See, to their desks Apollo's sons re-
    pair—
Swift rides the rosin o'er the horse's hair!

In unison their various tones to tune,
Murmurs the hautboy, growls the coarse bassoon;
In soft vibration sighs the whispering lute;
Tang goes the harpsichord, too-too the flute,
Brays the loud trumpet, squeaks the fiddle sharp,
Winds the French horn, and twangs the tingling harp;
Till, like great Jove, the leader, fingering in,
Attunes to order the chaotic din.
Now all seems hush'd—but, no, one fiddle will
Give, half ashamed, a tiny flourish still.
Foil'd in his clash, the leader of the clan
Reproves with frowns the dilatory man:
Then on his candlestick thrice taps his bow,
Nods a new signal, and away they go.

Perchance, while pit and gallery cry "Hats off!"
And awed Consumption checks his chided cough,
Some giggling daughter of the Queen of Love
Drops, 'reft of pin, her play-bill from above:
Like Icarus, while laughing galleries clap,
Soars, ducks, and dives in air the printed scrap;
But, wiser far than he, combustion fears,
And, as it flies, eludes the chandeliers;
Till, sinking gradual, with repeated twirl,
It settles, curling, on a fiddler's curl;
Who from his powder'd pate the intruder strikes,
And, for mere malice, sticks it on the spikes.

Say, why these Babel strains from Babel tongues?
Who's that calls "Silence!" with such leathern lungs?
He who, in quest of quiet, "Silence!" hoots,
Is apt to make the hubbub he imputes.

What various swains our motley walls contain!
Fashion from Moorfields, honor from Chick Lane;
Bankers from Paper Buildings here resort,
Bankrupts from Golden Square and Riches court;
From the Haymarket canting rogues in grain,
Gulls from the Poultry, sots from Water Lane;
The lottery cormorant, the auction shark,
The full-price master, and the half-price clerk;
Boys who long linger at the gallery-door,
With pence twice five—they want but twopence more;
Till some Samaritan the twopence spares,
And sends them jumping up the gallery-stairs.

Critics we boast who ne'er their malice balk,
But talk their minds: we wish they'd mind their talk:
Big-worded bullies, who by quarrels live—
Who give the lie, and tell the lie they give;
Jews from St. Mary's Axe, for jobs so wary
That for old clothes they'd even ax St. Mary;
And bucks with pockets empty as their pate,
Lax in their gaiters, laxer in their gait;
Who oft, when we our house lock up, carouse
With tippling tipstaves in a lock-up house.

Yet here, as elsewhere, Chance can joy bestow,
Where scowling fortune seem'd to threaten woe.

John Richard William Alexander Dwyer
Was footman to Justinian Stubbs, Esquire;
But when John Dwyer 'listed in the Blues,
Emanuel Jennings polish'd Stubbs's shoes.
Emanuel Jennings brought his youngest boy
Up as a corn-cutter—a safe employ;

In Holywell street, St. Pancras, he was
    bred
(At number twenty-seven, it is said),
Facing the pump, and near the Granby's
    Head:
He would have bound him to some shop
    in town,
But with a premium he could not come
    down.
Pat was the urchin's name—a red-hair'd
    youth,
Fonder of purl and skittle-grounds than
    truth.

  Silence, ye gods! to keep your tongue
    in awe,
The Muse shall tell an accident she saw.

Pat Jennings in the upper gallery sat,
But, leaning forward, Jennings lost his
    hat:
Down from the gallery the beaver flew,
And spurn'd the one to settle in the two.
How shall he act? Pay at the gallery-
    door
Two shillings for what cost, when new,
    but four?
Or till half-price, to save his shilling,
    wait,
And gain his hat again at half-past eight?
Now, while his fears anticipate a thief,
John Mullins whispers, "Take my hand-
    kerchief."
"Thank you," cries Pat; "but one won't
    make a line."
"Take mine," cries Wilson; and cries
    Stokes, "Take mine."
A motley cable soon Pat Jennings ties,
Where Spitalfields with real India vies.
Like Iris' bow, down darts the painted
    clew,
Starr'd, striped, and spotted, yellow, red,
    and blue,
Old calico, torn silk and muslin new.
George Green below, with palpitating
    hand
Loops the last 'kerchief to the beaver's
    band—
Up soars the prize! The youth with joy
    unfeign'd,
Regain'd the felt, and felt the prize re-
    gain'd;

While to the applauding galleries grateful
    Pat
Made a low bow, and touch'd the ran-
    som'd hat.
JAMES SMITH.

THE BABY'S DÉBUT.

[Spoken in the character of Nancy Lake, a girl of eight years of age, who is drawn upon the stage in a child's chaise by Samuel Hughes, her uncle's porter.]

MY brother Jack was nine in May,
And I was eight on New Year's day;
  So in Kate Wilson's shop
Papa (he's my papa and Jack's)
Bought me, last week, a doll of wax,
  And brother Jack a top.
Jack's in the pouts, and this it is—
He thinks mine came to more than his;
  So to my drawer he goes,
Takes out the doll, and, oh, my stars!
He pokes her head between the bars,
  And melts off half her nose!

Quite cross, a bit of string I beg,
And tie it to his peg-top's peg,
  And bang, with might and main,
Its head against the parlor-door:
Off flies the head, and hits the floor,
  And breaks a window-pane.

This made him cry with rage and spite;
Well, let him cry, it serves him right.
  A pretty thing, forsooth!
If he's to melt, all scalding hot,
Half my doll's nose, and I am not
  To draw his peg-top's tooth!

Aunt Hannah heard the window break,
And cried, "O naughty Nancy Lake,
  Thus to distress your aunt!
No Drury Lane for you to-day!"
And while papa said, "Pooh, she may!"
  Mamma said, "No, she sha'n't!"

Well, after many a sad reproach,
They got into a hackney-coach,
  And trotted down the street.
I saw them go: one horse was blind,
The tails of both hung down behind,
  Their shoes were on their feet.

The chaise in which poor brother Bill
Used to be drawn to Pentonville,
  Stood in the lumber-room:
I wiped the dust from off the top,
While Mollie mopp'd it with a mop,
  And brush'd it with a broom.

My uncle's porter, Samuel Hughes,
Came in at six to black the shoes
  (I always talk to Sam):
So what does he, but takes, and drags
Me in the chaise along the flags,
  And leaves me where I am?

My father's walls are made of brick,
But not so tall and not so thick
  As these; and, goodness me!
My father's beams are made of wood,
But never, never half so good
  As those that now I see.

What a large floor! 'tis like a town!
The carpet, when they lay it down,
  Won't hide it, I'll be bound;
And there's a row of lamps!—my eye!
How they do blaze! I wonder why
  They keep them on the ground?

At first I caught hold of the wing,
And kept away; but Mr. Thing-
  umbob, the prompter-man,
Gave with his hand my chaise a shove,
And said, "Go on, my pretty love;
  Speak to 'em, little Nan.

"You've only got to curtsy, whisp-
  er, hold your chin up, laugh and lisp,
  And then you're sure to take:
I've known the day when brats, not
  quite
Thirteen, got fifty pounds a night;
  Then why not Nancy Lake?"

But while I'm speaking, where's papa?
And where's my aunt? and where's
  mamma?
  Where's Jack? Oh there they sit!
They smile, they nod; I'll go my ways,
And order round poor Billy's chaise,
  To join them in the pit.

And now, good gentlefolks, I go
To join mamma, and see the show;

So, bidding you adieu,
I curtsy like a pretty miss,
And if you'll blow to me a kiss,
  I'll blow a kiss to you.
      [Blows a kiss, and exit.]
              JAMES SMITH.

THE EXECUTION.

MY Lord Tomnoddy got up one day;
It was half after two; he had nothing to
  do,
So his lordship rang for his cabriolet.

  Tiger Tim was clean of limb,
  His boots were polish'd, his jacket was
    trim;
With a very smart tie in his smart cravat,
And a smart cockade on the top of his
  hat;
Tallest of boys, or shortest of men,
He stood in his stockings just four foot
  ten,
And he ask'd, as he held the door on the
  swing,
"Pray, did your lordship please to ring?"

My Lord Tomnoddy he raised his head,
And thus to Tiger Tim he said:
"Malibran's dead, Duvernay's fled,
Taglioni has not yet arrived in her stead;
Tiger Tim, come tell me true,
What may a nobleman find to do?"

Tim look'd up, and Tim look'd down,
He paused, and he put on a thoughtful
  frown,
And he held up his hat, and he peep'd in
  the crown;
He bit his lip, and he scratch'd his head,
He let go the handle, and thus he said,
As the door, released, behind him bang'd:
"An't please you, my lord, there's a man
  to be hang'd."

My Lord Tomnoddy jump'd up at the
  news:
"Run to M'Fuze and Lieutenant Tre-
  gooze,
And run to Sir Carnaby Jenks of the
  Blues.
Rope-dancers a score I've seen before—
Madame Sacchi, Antonio, and Master
  Blackmore;

But to see a man swing at the end of a string,
With his neck in a noose, will be quite a new thing.

My Lord Tomnoddy stepp'd into his cab—
Dark rifle green, with a lining of drab;
 Through street and through square,
 His high-trotting mare,
Like one of Ducrow's, goes pawing the air.
Adown Piccadilly and Waterloo Place
Went the high-trotting mare at a very quick pace;
 She produced some alarm, but did no great harm,
Save frightening a nurse with a child on her arm,
 Spattering with clay two urchins at play,
Knocking down—very much to the sweeper's dismay—
An old woman who wouldn't get out of the way,
 And upsetting a stall near Exeter Hall,
Which made all the pious church-mission folks squall.
But eastward afar, through Temple Bar,
My Lord Tomnoddy directs his car,
 Never heeding their squalls,
 Or their calls, or their bawls;
He passes by Waithman's emporium for shawls,
And, merely just catching a glimpse of St. Paul's,
 Turns down the Old Bailey,
 Where in front of the jail he
Pulls up at the door of the gin-shop, and gayly
Cries, "What must I fork out to-night, my trump,
For the whole first floor of the Magpie and Stump?"

The clock strikes twelve—it is dark midnight—
Yet the Magpie and Stump is one blaze of light,
 The parties are met, the tables are set,
There is " punch," " cold *without*," " hot *with*," heavy wet,
Ale-glasses and jugs, and rummers and mugs,
And sand on the floor, without carpets or rugs,
Cold fowl and cigars, pickled onions in jars,
Welsh rabbits and kidneys—rare work for the jaws—
And very large lobsters, with very large claws;
 And there is M'Fuze and Lieutenant Tregooze,
And there is Sir Carnaby Jenks of the Blues,
All come to see a man " die in his shoes."

The clock strikes one. Supper is done,
And Sir Carnaby Jenks is full of his fun,
Singing "Jolly companions every one."
 My Lord Tomnoddy is drinking gin-toddy,
And laughing at everything and everybody.

The clock strikes two, and the clock strikes three;
"Who so merry, so merry as we?"
 Save Captain M'Fuze, who is taking a snooze,
While Sir Carnaby Jenks is busy at work
Blacking his nose with a piece of burnt cork.

The clock strikes four: round the debtors' door
Are gather'd a couple of thousand or more;
 As many await at the press-yard gate,
Till slowly its folding doors open, and straight
The mob divides, and between their ranks
A wagon comes loaded with posts and with planks.

The clock strikes five. The sheriffs arrive,
And the crowd is so great that the street seems alive;
 But Sir Carnaby Jenks blinks and winks,
A candle burns down in the socket, and stinks.

Lieutenant Tregooze is dreaming of Jews,
And acceptances all the bill-brokers refuse;
   My Lord Tomnoddy has drunk all his toddy,
And just as the dawn is beginning to peep
The whole of the party are fast asleep.

Sweetly, oh sweetly the morning breaks,
   With roseate streaks,
Like the first faint blush on a maiden's cheeks;
Seem'd as that mild and clear blue sky
Smiled upon all things far and high,
On all—save the wretch condemn'd to die!
Alack! that ever so fair a sun
As that which its course has now begun,
Should rise on such a scene of misery!
Should gild with rays so light and free
That dismal, dark-frowning gallows-tree!

And hark!—a sound comes big with fate:
The clock from St. Sepulchre's tower strikes—eight!
List to that low funereal bell;
It is tolling, alas! a living man's knell!
And see! from forth that opening door
They come—HE steps that threshold o'er
Who never shall tread upon threshold more!
God! 'tis a fearsome thing to see
That pale wan man's mute agony,—
The glare of that wild, despairing eye,
Now bent on the crowd, now turn'd to the sky
As though 'twere scanning, in doubt and in fear,
The path of the spirit's unknown career.
Those pinion'd arms, those hands that ne'er
Shall be lifted again—not even in prayer;
That heaving chest! Enough; 'tis done!
The bolt has fallen, the spirit is gone,
For weal or for woe is known but to One!
Oh, 'twas a fearsome sight! Ah me!
A deed to shudder at,—not to see.

Again that clock! 'tis time, 'tis time!
The hour is past; with its earliest chime
The cord is sever'd, the lifeless clay
By "dungeon villains" is borne away;
Nine!—'twas the last concluding stroke,
And then my Lord Tomnoddy awoke.

And Tregooze and Sir Carnaby Jenks arose,
And Captain M'Fuze, with the black on his nose,
And they stared at each other, as much as to say,
   "Hollo! hollo! Here's a rum go!
Why, captain!—my lord!—Here's the devil to pay;
The fellow's been cut down and taken away!
   What's to be done? We've miss'd all the fun.
Why, they'll laugh at and quiz us all over the town,
We are all of us done so uncommonly brown!"

What *was* to be done? 'Twas perfectly plain
That they could not well hang the man over again;
What *was* to be done? The man was dead.
Naught *could* be done—naught could be said,
So my Lord Tomnoddy went home to bed!
                RICHARD HARRIS BARHAM.

THE BIRTH OF ST. PATRICK.

ON the eighth day of March it was, some people say,
That Saint Pathrick at midnight he first saw the day;
While others declare 'twas the ninth he was born,
And 'twas all a mistake between midnight and morn;
For mistakes will occur in a hurry and shock,
And some blamed the babby—and some blamed the clock—
Till with all their cross-questions sure no one could know
If the child was too fast, or the clock was too slow.

Now the first faction-fight in owld Ireland, they say,
Was all on account of Saint Pathrick's birthday:

Some fought for the eighth—for the ninth more would die,
And who wouldn't see right, sure they blacken'd his eye!
At last, both the factions so positive grew,
That each kept a birthday, so Pat then had two,
Till Father Mulcahy, who show'd them their sins,
Said, "No one could have two birthdays, but a twins."

Says he, "Boys, don't be fightin' for eight or for nine,
Don't be always dividin'—but sometimes combine;
Combine eight with nine, and seventeen is the mark,
So let that be his birthday,"—"Amen," says the clerk.
"If he wasn't a twins, sure our hist'ry will show
That, at least, he's worthy any two saints that we know!"
Then they all got blind dhrunk—which complated their bliss,
And we keep up the practice from that day to this.
SAMUEL LOVER.

THE SOCIETY UPON THE STANISLOW.

I RESIDE at Table Mountain, and my name is Truthful James;
I am not up to small deceit, or any sinful games;
And I'll tell in simple language what I know about the row
That broke up our society upon the Stanislow.

But first I would remark, that it is not a proper plan
For any scientific gent to whale his fellow-man,
And, if a member don't agree with his peculiar whim,
To lay for that same member for to "put a head" on him.

Now nothing could be finer or more beautiful to see
Than the first six months' proceedings of that same society,
Till Brown of Calaveras brought a lot of fossil bones
That he found within a tunnel near the tenement of Jones.

Then Brown he read a paper, and he reconstructed there,
From those same bones, an animal that was extremely rare;
And Jones then ask'd the chair for a suspension of the rules
Till he could prove that those same bones was one of his lost mules.

Then Brown he smiled a bitter smile, and said he was at fault.
It seemed he had been trespassing on Jones's family vault:
He was a most sarcastic man, this quiet Mr. Brown,
And on several occasions he had clean'd out the town.

Now I hold it is not decent for a scientific gent
To say another is an ass,—at least, to all intent;
Nor should the individual who happens to be meant
Reply by heaving rocks at him to any great extent.

Then Abner Dean of Angel's raised a point of order—when
A chunk of old red sandstone took him in the abdomen,
And he smiled a kind of sickly smile, and curl'd up on the floor,
And the subsequent proceedings interested him no more.

For, in less time than I write it, every member did engage
In a warfare with the remnants of a palæozoic age;
And the way they heaved those fossils in their anger was a sin,
Till the skull of an old Mammoth caved the head of Thompson in.

And this is all I have to say of these improper games,
For I live at Table Mountain, and my name is Truthful James;
And I've told in simple language what I know about the row
That broke up our society upon the Stanislow.

FRANCIS BRET HARTE.

MONSIEUR TONSON.

THERE lived, as Fame reports, in days of yore,
At least some fifty years ago or more,
  A pleasant wag on town, yclep'd Tom King;
A fellow that was clever at a joke,
Expert in all the arts, to tease and *smoke*,—
  In short, for strokes of humor quite the thing.

To many a jovial club this King was known,
With whom his active wit unrivall'd shone—
  Choice Spirit, grave Free-Mason, Buck, and Blood,
Would crowd, his stories and *bon-mots* to hear,
And none a disappointment e'er could fear,
  His humor flow'd in such a copious flood.

To him a frolic was a high delight—
A frolic he would hunt for day and night,
  Careless how Prudence on the sport might frown.
If e'er a pleasant mischief sprang to view,
At once o'er ditch and hedge away he flew,
  Nor left the game till he had run it down.

One night our hero, rambling with a friend,
Near famed St. Giles's chanced his course to bend,
  Just by that spot the Seven Dials hight,—
'Twas silence all around, and clear the coast,
The watch, as usual, dozing on his post,
  And scarce a lamp display'd a twinkling light.

Around this place there lived the num'rous clans
Of honest, plodding, foreign artisans,
  Known at that time by th' name of Refugees—
The rod of persecution from their home
Compell'd th' inoffensive race to roam,
  And here they lighted like a swarm of bees.

Well! our two friends were saunt'ring thro' the street,
In hopes some food for humor soon to meet,
  When in a window high a light they view,
And, though a dim and melancholy ray,
It seem'd the prologue to some merry play,
  So toward the gloomy dome our hero drew.

Straight at the door he gave a thund'ring knock
(The time, we may suppose, near two o'clock)—
  "I'll ask," says King, "if Thompson lodges here."
"Thompson!" cries t'other, "who the devil's he?"
"I know not," King replies, "but want to see
  What kind of animal will now appear."

After some time a little Frenchman came—
One hand display'd a rushlight's trembling flame,
  And from the other dangled his *culotte;*
An old striped woollen night-cap graced his head,
A tatter'd waistcoat o'er one shoulder spread;
  Scarce half awake, he heaved a yawning note.

Though thus untimely roused, he courteous smiled,
And soon address'd our wag in accents mild,

Bending his head obsequious to his
      knee,—
"Pray, sare, vat vant you, dat you come
      so late—
I beg your pardon, sare, to make you
      vait—
  Pray tell me, sare, vat your commands
      vit me?"

"Sir," answer'd King, "I merely thought
      to know,
As by your house I chanced this night to
      go,—
  But really I disturb'd your sleep I fear,—
I say, I thought that you perhaps could
      tell,
  Among the folks who in this street may
      dwell,
  If there's a Mr. Thompson lodges here?"

The shiv'ring Frenchman, though not
      pleased to find
The business of this unimportant kind,
  Too simple to suspect 'twas meant in
      jeer,
  Shrugg'd out a sigh, that thus his rest
      should break,
Then, with unalter'd courtesy, he spake—
  "No, sare, no Monsieur Tonson lodges
      here."

Our wag begg'd pardon, and toward home
      he sped,
While the poor Frenchman crawl'd again
      to bed;
  But King resolved not thus to drop the
      jest—
So the next night, with more of whim than
      grace,
Again he made a visit to the place,
  To break once more the poor old French-
      man's rest.

He knock'd—but waited longer than
      before,
No footstep seem'd approaching to the
      door,
  Our Frenchman lay in such a sleep pro-
      found—
King with the knocker thunder'd then
      again,
Firm on his post determined to remain,
  And oft, indeed, he made the door re-
      sound.

At last King hears him o'er the passage
      creep—
Wond'ring what fiend again disturb'd his
      sleep—
  The wag salutes him with a civil leer;
Thus drawling out, to heighten the sur-
      prise,
While the poor Frenchman rubb'd his
      heavy eyes,
  "Is there—a Mr. Thompson—lodging
      here?"

The Frenchman falter'd, with a kind of
      fright—
"Vy, sare, I'm sure, I toll you, sare, last
      night"
  (And here he labor'd with a sigh sincere)
"No Monsieur Tonson in de vorld I
      know—
No Monsieur Tonson here—I toll you so—
  Indeed, sare, dere no Monsieur Ton-
      son here."

Some more excuses tender'd, off King goes,
And the poor Frenchman sought once
      more repose.
  Our wag next night pursued his old
      career—
'Twas long, indeed, before the man came
      nigh,
And then he utter'd in a piteous cry,
  "Sare, 'pon my soul, no Monsieur Ton-
      son here."

Our sportive wight his usual visit paid,
And the next night came forth a prattling
      maid,
  Whose tongue, indeed, than any jack
      went faster—
Anxious she strove his errand to inquire;
He said, 'twas vain her pretty tongue to tire,
  He should not stir till he had seen her
      master.

The damsel then began, in doleful state,
The Frenchman's broken slumbers to re-
      late,
  And begg'd he'd call at proper time of
      day,—
King told her she must fetch her master
      down,
A chaise was ready, he was leaving town,
  But first had much of deep concern to
      say.

Thus urged, she went the snoring man to
   call,
And long, indeed, was she obliged to bawl
   Ere she could rouse the torpid lump of
      clay.
At last he wakes—he rises—and he
      swears—
But scarcely had he totter'd down the
      stairs,
   When King attacks him in his usual
      way.

The Frenchman now perceived 'twas all in
      vain
To this tormentor mildly to complain,
   And straight in rage began his crest to
      rear,—
"Sare, vat de devil make you treat me so?—
Sare, I inform you, sare, tree nights ago,
   Begar, I swear, no Monsieur Tonson
      here."

True as the night King went and heard a
      strife
Between the harass'd Frenchman and his
      wife,
   Which should descend to chase the fiend
      away;
At length to join their forces they agree,
And straight impetuously they turn the key,
   Prepared with mutual fury for the fray.

Our hero, with the firmness of a rock,
Collected to receive the mighty shock,
   Utt'ring his old inquiry, calmly stood,—
The *name* of Thompson raised the storm so
      high,
He deem'd it then the safest plan to fly,
   With "Well, I'll call when you're in
      gentler mood."

In short our hero, with the same intent,
Full many a night to plague the French-
      man went,
   So fond of mischief was the wicked wit;
They threw out water—for the watch they
      call,
But King, expecting, still escapes from all—
   Monsieur at last was forced his house to
      quit.

It happen'd that our wag, about this time,
On some fair prospect sought the Eastern
      clime;

Six ling'ring years were there his tedious
      lot:
At length, content amid his ripening store,
He treads again on Britain's happy shore,
   And his long absence is at once forgot.

To London with impatient hope he flies,
And the same night, as former freaks
      arise,
   He fain must stroll the well-known
      haunt to trace.
"Ah! here's the scene of frequent mirth,"
      he said;
"My poor old Frenchman, I suppose, is
      dead—
   Egad, I'll knock, and see who holds his
      place."

With rapid strokes he makes the mansion
      roar,
And while he eager eyes the op'ning door,
   Lo! who obeys the knocker's rattling
      peal?
Why, e'en our little Frenchman; strange
      to say,
He took his old abode that very day—
   Capricious turn of sportive Fortune's
      wheel!

Without one thought of the relentless
      foe,
Who, fiend-like, haunted him so long
      ago,
   Just in his former trim he now ap-
      pears;
The waistcoat and the night-cap seem'd
      the same,
With rushlight, as before he creeping
      came,
   And King's detested voice astonish'd
      hears.

As if some hideous spectre struck his
      sight,
His senses seem'd bewilder'd with affright;
   His face, indeed, bespoke a heart full
      sore—
Then starting, he exclaim'd in rueful
      strain,
"Begar! here's Monsieur Tonson come
      again!"
   Away he ran— and ne'er was heard of
      more.
                                        JOHN TAYLOR.

NONGTONGPAW.

John Bull for pastime took a prance,
Some time ago, to peep at France;
To talk of sciences and arts,
And knowledge gain'd in foreign parts.
Monsieur, obsequious, heard him speak,
And answer'd John in heathen Grèek:
To all he ask'd 'bout all he saw,
'Twas, "*Monsieur, je vous n'entends pas.*"

John to the Palais Royal come,
Its splendor almost struck him dumb:
"I say, whose house is that there here?"
"House! *Je vous n'entends pas, monsieur.*"
"What, Nongtongpaw again!" cries John,
"This fellow is some mighty Don:
No doubt he's plenty for the maw,
I'll breakfast with this Nongtongpaw."

John saw Versailles from Marle's height,
And cried, astonish'd at the sight,
"Whose fine estate is that there here?"
"State! *Je vous n'entends pas, monsieur.*"
"His? What! the land and houses too?
The fellow's richer than a Jew:
On *everything* he lays his claw;
I'd like to dine with Nongtongpaw."

Next tripping came a courtly fair,
John cried, enchanted with her air,
"What lovely wench is that there here?"
"Ventch! *Je vous n'entends pas, monsieur.*"
"What! he again? Upon my life!
A palace, lands, and then a wife
Sir Joshua might delight to draw;
I'd like to sup with Nongtongpaw."

"But hold! whose funeral's that?" cries John.
"*Je vous n'entends pas.*"—"What! is he gone?
Wealth, fame, and beauty could not save
Poor Nongtongpaw, then, from the grave?
His race is run, his game is up;—
I'd with him breakfast, dine, and sup;
But since he chooses to withdraw,
Good-night t'ye, Mounseer Nongtongpaw."
Charles Dibdin.

EPITAPH ON THE TOMBSTONE ERECTED OVER THE MARQUIS OF ANGLESEA'S LEG, LOST AT THE BATTLE OF WATERLOO.

Here rests, and let no saucy knave
Presume to sneer and laugh,
To learn that mouldering in the grave
Is laid a British Calf.

For he who writes these lines is sure,
That those who read the whole,
Will find such laugh was premature,
For here, too, lies a sole.

And here five little ones repose,
Twin born with other five,
Unheeded by their brother toes,
Who all are now alive.

A leg and foot, to speak more plain,
Rests here of one commanding;
Who, though his wits he might retain,
Lost half his understanding.

And when the guns, with thunder fraught,
Pour'd bullets thick as hail,
Could only in this way be taught
To give the foe leg-bail.

And now in England, just as gay
As in the battle brave,
Goes to a rout, review, or play,
With one foot in the grave.

Fortune in vain here show'd her spite,
For he will still be found,
Should England's sons engage in fight,
Resolved to stand his ground.

But Fortune's pardon I must beg;
She meant not to disarm,
For when she lopp'd the hero's leg,
She did not seek his harm.

And but indulged a harmless whim;
Since he could walk with one,
She saw two legs were lost on him,
Who never meant to run.
George Canning.

MALBROUCK.

Malbrouck, the prince of commanders,
Is gone to the war in Flanders;
His fame is like Alexander's;
But when will he come home?

Perhaps at Trinity feast; or
Perhaps he may come at Easter.
Egad! he had better make haste, or
   We fear he may never come.

For Trinity feast is over,
And has brought no news from Dover;
And Easter is past, moreover,
   And Malbrouck still delays.

Milady in her watch-tower
Spends many a pensive hour,
Not knowing why or how her
   Dear lord from England stays.

While sitting quite forlorn in
That tower, she spies returning
A page clad in deep mourning,
   With fainting steps and slow.

"O page, prythee, come faster!
What news do you bring of your master?
I fear there is some disaster—
   Your looks are so full of woe."

"The news I bring, fair lady,"
With sorrowful accent said he,
"Is one you are not ready
   So soon, alas! to hear.

"But since to speak I'm hurried,"
Added this page quite flurried,
"Malbrouck is dead and buried!"
   —And here he shed a tear.

"He's dead! he's dead as a herring!
For I beheld his berring,
And four officers transferring
   His corpse away from the field.

"One officer carried his sabre;
And he carried it not without labor,
Much envying his next neighbor,
   Who only bore a shield.

"The third was helmet-bearer—
That helmet which on its wearer
Fill'd all who saw with terror,
   And cover'd a hero's brains.

"Now, having got so far, I
Find that—by the Lord Harry!—
The fourth is left nothing to carry;—
   So there the thing remains."
      FRANCIS MAHONY ("Father Prout.")
        (From the French.)

THE MARCH TO MOSCOW.

THE Emperor Nap he would set off
   On a summer excursion to Moscow;
The fields were green, and the sky was blue,
     Morbleu! Parbleu!
What a pleasant excursion to Moscow!

Four hundred thousand men and more
   Must go with him to Moscow:
There were Marshals by the dozen,
   And Dukes by the score;
Princes a few, and Kings one or two;
While the fields are so green, and the sky
   so blue.
     Morbleu! Parbleu!
What a pleasant excursion to Moscow!

There was Junot and Augereau,
   Heigh-ho for Moscow!
Dombrowsky and Poniatowsky,
   Marshal Ney, lack-a-day!
General Rapp and the Emperor Nap;
   Nothing would do,
While the fields were so green, and the sky
   so blue,
     Morbleu! Parbleu!
   Nothing would do
For the whole of this crew,
But they must be marching to Moscow.

The Emperor Nap he talk'd so big
   That he frighten'd Mr. Roscoe.
John Bull, he cries, if you'll be wise,
   Ask the Emperor Nap if he will please
To grant you peace upon your knees,
   Because he is going to Moscow!
He'll make all the Poles come out of
   their holes,
   And beat the Russians, and eat the
     Prussians;
For the fields are green, and the sky is blue,
     Morbleu! Parbleu!
And he'll certainly march to Moscow!

And Counsellor Brougham was all in a
   fume
At the thought of the march to Moscow:
The Russians, he said, they were un-
   done,
   And the great Fee-Faw-Fum
   Would presently come,
With a hop, step, and jump, unto
   London;

For, as for his conquering Russia,
However some persons might scoff
    it,
Do it he could, and do it he would,
And from doing it nothing would come
    but good,
And nothing could call him off it,
Mr. Jeffrey said so, who must certainly
    know,
For he was the Edinburgh Prophet.
They all of them knew Mr. Jeffrey's
    Review,
Which with Holy Writ ought to be
    reckon'd :
It was, through thick and thin, to its
    party true ;
    Its back was buff, and its sides were
        blue,
        Morbleu! Parbleu!
    It served them for Law and for Gos-
        pel too.

But the Russians stoutly they turn'd
    to
    Upon the road to Moscow.
Nap had to fight his way all
    through ;
They could fight, though they could not
    parlez-vous ;
But the fields were green, and the sky was
    blue,
    Morbleu! Parbleu!
And so he got to Moscow.

He found the place too warm for him,
For they set fire to Moscow.
To get there had cost him much ado,
And then no better course he knew,
While the fields were green, and the sky
    was blue,
    Morbleu! Parbleu!
But to march back again from Moscow.

The Russians they stuck close to him
    All on the road from Moscow.
There was Tormazow and Jemalow,
And all the others that end in ow ;
Milarodovitch and Jaladovitch,
    And Karatschkowitch,
And all the others that end in itch ;
    Schamscheff, Souchosaneff ;
        And Schepaleff,
And all the others that end in eff ;
    Wasiltchikoff, Kostomaroff,
        And Tchoglokoff,
And all the others that end in off ;
    Rajeffsky, and Novereffsky,
        And Rieffsky,
And all the others that end in effsky ;
    Oscharoffsky and Rostoffsky,
And all the others that end in offsky ;
    And Platoff he play'd them off,
And Shouvaloff he shovell'd them off,
    And Markoff he mark'd them off,
    And Krosnoff he cross'd them off,
    And Touchkoff he touch'd them off,
    And Boroskoff he bored them off,
    And Kutousoff he cut them off,
    And Parenzoff he pared them off,
    And Worronzoff he worried them off,
    And Doctoroff he doctor'd them off,
    And Rodionoff he flogg'd them off,
    And, last of all, an Admiral
        came,
    A terrible man with a terrible
        name,
A name which you all know by sight very
    well,
But which no one can speak, and no one
    can spell.
They stuck close to Nap with all their
    might ;
    They were on the left and on the
        right,
    Behind and before, and by day and by
        night ;
    He would rather parlez-vous than
        fight ;
But he look'd white, and he look'd blue,
    Morbleu! Parbleu!
When parlez-vous no more would
    do ;
For they remember'd Moscow.

And then came on the frost and
    snow,
    All on the road from Moscow.
The wind and the weather he found, in
    that hour,
Cared nothing for him, nor for all his
    power—
For him who, while Europe crouch'd under
    his rod,
Put his trust in his Fortune, and not in
    his God.

Worse and worse every day the elements grew,
The fields were so white, and the sky so blue,
Sacrebleu! Ventrebleu!
What a horrible journey from Moscow!

What then thought the Emperor Nap
Upon the road from Moscow?
Why, I ween he thought it small delight
To fight all day, and to freeze all night;
And he was besides in a very great fright,
For a whole skin he liked to be in;
And so, not knowing what else to do,
When the fields were so white, and the sky so blue
Morbleu! Parbleu!
He stole away,—I tell you true,—
Upon the road from Moscow.
'Tis myself, quoth he, I must mind most;
So the Devil may take the hindmost.

Too cold upon the road was he;
Too hot had he been at Moscow;
But colder and hotter he may be,
For the grave is colder than Muscovy;
And a place there is to be kept in view,
Where the fire is red, and the brimstone blue,
Morbleu! Parbleu!
Which he must go to,
If the Pope say true,
If he does not in time look about him;
Where his namesake almost
He may have for his host;
He has reckon'd too long without him;
If that host get him in Purgatory,
He won't leave him there alone with his glory;
But there he must stay for a very long day,
For from thence there is no stealing away,
As there was on the road from Moscow.
    ROBERT SOUTHEY.

THE LAWYER'S INVOCATION TO SPRING.

WHEREAS, on certain boughs and sprays,
  Now divers birds are heard to sing,
And sundry flowers their heads upraise,
  Hail to the coming on of Spring!

The songs of those said birds arouse
  The memory of our youthful hours,
As green as those said sprays and boughs,
  As fresh and sweet as those said flowers.

The birds aforesaid—happy pairs!—
  Love, 'mid the aforesaid boughs, inshrines
In freehold nests; themselves, their heirs,
  Administrators, and assigns.

O busiest term of Cupid's court,
  Where tender plaintiffs actions bring,—
Season of frolic and of sport,
  Hail, as aforesaid, coming Spring!
      HENRY P. HOWARD BROWNELL.

THE ART OF BOOK-KEEPING.

How hard, when those who do not wish
  To lend, thus lose, their books,
Are snared by anglers—folks that fish
  With literary hooks—
Who call and take some favorite tome,
  But never read it through;
They thus complete their set at home
  By making one at you.

I, of my " Spenser " quite bereft,
  Last winter sore was shaken;
Of " Lamb " I've but a quarter left,
  Nor could I save my " Bacon;"
And then I saw my " Crabbe " at last,
  Like Hamlet, backward go,
And, as the tide was ebbing fast,
  Of course I lost my " Rowe."

My " Mallet " served to knock me down,
  Which makes me thus a talker,
And once, when I was out of town,
  My " Johnson " proved a " Walker."
While studying o'er the fire one day
  My " Hobbes " amidst the smoke,
They bore my " Colman " clean away,
  And carried off my " Coke."

They pick'd my " Locke," to me far more
 Than Bramah's patent worth,
And now my losses I deplore,
 Without a " Home " on earth.
If once a book you let them lift,
 Another they conceal,
For though I caught them stealing " Swift,"
 As swiftly went my " Steele."

Hope " is not now upon my shelf,
 Where late he stood elated,
But, what is strange, my " Pope " himself
 Is excommunicated.
My little " Suckling " in the grave
 Is sunk to swell the ravage,
And what was Crusoe's fate to save,
 'Twas mine to lose—a " Savage."

Even " Glover's " works I cannot put
 My frozen hands upon,
Though ever since I lost my " Foote "
 My " Bunyan " has been gone.
My " Hoyle " with " Cotton " went oppress'd,
 My " Taylor," too, must fail,
To save my " Goldsmith " from arrest,
 In vain I offer'd " Bayle."

I " Prior " sought, but could not see
 The " Hood " so late in front,
And when I turn'd to hunt for " Lee,"
 Oh, where was my " Leigh Hunt "?
I tried to laugh, old Care to tickle,
 Yet could not " Tickell " touch,
And then, alack! I miss'd my " Mickle,"
 And surely mickle's much.

'Tis quite enough my griefs to feed,
 My sorrows to excuse,
To think I cannot read my " Reid,"
 Nor even use my " Hughes."
My classics would not quiet lie,—
 A thing so fondly hoped;
Like Dr. Primrose, I may cry,
 My " Livy " has eloped.

My life is ebbing fast away;
 I suffer from these shocks;
And though I fix'd a lock on " Gray,"
 There's gray upon my locks.
I'm far from " Young," am growing pale,
 I see my " Butler " fly,
And when they ask about my ail,
 'Tis " Burton " I reply.

They still have made me slight returns,
 And thus my griefs divide;
For oh, they cured me of my " Burns,"
 And eased my " Akenside."
But all I think I shall not say,
 Nor let my anger burn,
For, as they never found me " Gay,"
 They have not left me " Sterne."
                              THOMAS HOOD.

EPICUREAN REMINISCENCES OF A SENTIMENTALIST.

"My *Tables! Meat* it is, *I set it* down!"—HAMLET.

I THINK it was Spring—but not certain I am—
 When my passion began first to work;
But I know we were certainly looking for lamb,
 And the season was over for pork.

'Twas at Christmas, I think, when I met with Miss Chase,
 Yes—for Morris had ask'd me to dine—
And I thought I had never beheld such a face,
 Or so noble a turkey and chine.

Placed close by her side, it made others quite wild
 With sheer envy, to witness my luck;
How she blush'd as I gave her some turtle, and smiled
 As I afterward offer'd some duck.

I look'd and I languish'd, alas! to my cost,
 Through three courses of dishes and meats;
Getting deeper in love—but my heart was quite lost
 When it came to the trifle and sweets.

With a rent-roll that told of my houses and land,
 To her parents I told my designs—
And then to herself I presented my hand,
 With a very fine pottle of pines!

I ask'd her to have me for weal or for woe,
 And she did not object in the least;—
I can't tell the date—but we married I know
 Just in time to have game at the feast.

We went to———, it certainly was the sea-
　　side;
　For the next, the most blessed of morns,
I remember how fondly I gazed at my
　　bride
　Sitting down to a plateful of prawns.

Oh never may memory lose sight of that
　　year,
　But still hallow the time as it ought!
That season the "grass" was remarkably
　　dear,
　And the peas at a guinea a quart.

So happy, like hours, all our days seem'd
　　to haste,
　A fond pair, such as poets have drawn,
So united in heart—so congenial in taste—
　We were both of us partial to brawn!

A long life I look'd for of bliss with my
　　bride,
　But then Death—I ne'er dreamt about
　　that!
Oh there's nothing is certain in life, as I
　　cried
　When my turbot eloped with the cat.

My dearest took ill at the turn of the year,
　But the cause no physician could nab;
But something, it seemed like consumption,
　　I fear—
　It was just after supping on crab.

In vain she was doctor'd, in vain she was
　　dosed,
　Still her strength and her appetite pined;
She lost relish for what she had relish'd
　　the most,
　Even salmon she deeply declined!

For months still I linger'd in hope and in
　　doubt,
　While her form it grew wasted and thin;
But the last dying spark of existence went
　　out,
　As the oysters were just coming in!

She died, and she left me the saddest of
　　men,
　To indulge in a widower's moan;
Oh! I felt all the power of solitude then,
　As I ate my first "natives" alone!

But when I beheld Virtue's friends in their
　　cloaks,
　And with sorrowful crape on their hats,
Oh my grief pour'd a flood! and the out-of-
　　door folks
　Were all crying—I think it was sprats!
　　　　　　　　　　　Thomas Hood.

ADDRESS TO THE TOOTHACHE.

Written when the Author was griev-
ously Tormented by that Disorder.

My curse upon thy venom'd stang,
That shoots my tortured gums alang;
And thro' my lugs gies mony a twang,
　　Wi' gnawing vengeance;
Tearing my nerves wi' bitter pang,
　　Like racking engines!

When fevers burn, or ague freezes,
Rheumatics gnaw, or colic squeezes,
Our neighbors' sympathy may ease us,
　　Wi' pitying moan;
But thee—thou hell o' a' diseases,
　　Aye mocks our groan!

Adown my beard the slavers trickle!
I kick the wee stools o'er the mickle,
As round the fire the giglets keckle,
　　To see me loup;
While, raving mad, I wish a heckle
　　Were in their doup.

O' a' the num'rous human dools,
Ill har'sts, daft bargains, cutty-stools,
Or worthy friends raked i' the mools,
　　Sad sight to see!
The tricks o' knaves, or fash o' fools,
　　Thou bear'st the gree.

Where'er that place be priests ca' hell,
Whence a' the tones o' mis'ry yell,
And rankèd plagues their numbers tell,
　　In dreadfu' raw,
Thou, Toothache, surely bear'st the bell,
　　Among them a';

O thou grim mischief-making chiel,
That gars the notes of discord squeal,
'Till daft mankind aft dance a reel
　　In gore a shoe-thick!—
Gie a' the faes o' Scotland's weal
　　A towmond's Toothache!
　　　　　　　　　　　Robert Burns.

UNFORTUNATE MISS BAILEY.
(AN EXPERIMENT.)

WHEN he whispers, "O Miss Bailey,
  Thou art brightest of the throng"—
She makes murmur, softly-gayly—
  "Alfred, I have loved thee long,"

Then he drops upon his knees, a
  Proof his heart is soft as wax:
She's—I don't know who, but he's a
  Captain bold from Halifax.

Though so loving, such another
  Artless bride was never seen,
Coachee thinks that she's his mother
  —Till they get to Gretna Green.

There they stand, by him attended,
  Hear the sable smith rehearse
That which links them, when 'tis ended,
  Tight for better—or for worse.

Now her heart rejoices—ugly
  Troubles need disturb her less—
Now the Happy Pair are snugly
  Seated in the night express.

So they go with fond emotion,
  So they journey through the night—
London is their land of Goshen—
  See, its suburbs are in sight!

Hark! the sound of life is swelling,
  Pacing up, and racing down,
Soon they reach her simple dwelling—
  Burley Street, by Somers Town.

What is there to so astound them?
  She cries "Oh!" for he cries "Hah!"
When five brats emerge—confound them!—
  Shouting out, "Mamma!—Papa!"

While at this he wonders blindly,
  Nor their meaning can divine,
Proud she turns them round, and kindly,
  "All of these are mine and thine!"
      *   *   *   *   *
Here he pines and grows dyspeptic,
  Losing heart, he loses pith—
Hints that Bishop Tait's a sceptic—
  Swears that Moses was a myth.

Sees no evidence in Paley—
  Takes to drinking ratifia;
Shies the muffins at Miss Bailey
  While she's pouring out the tea.

One day, knocking up his quarters,
  Poor Miss Bailey found him dead,
Hanging in his knotted garters,
  Which she knitted ere they wed.
              FREDERICK LOCKER.

CAPTAIN REECE.

OF all the ships upon the blue,
No ship contain'd a better crew
Than that of worthy Captain Reece,
Commanding of The Mantelpiece.

He was adored by all his men,
For worthy Captain Reece, R. N.,
Did all that lay within him to
Promote the comfort of his crew.

If ever they were dull or sad,
Their captain danced to them like mad,
Or told, to make the time pass by,
Droll legends of his infancy.

A feather bed had every man,
Warm slippers and hot-water can,
Brown windsor from the captain's store,
A valet, too, to every four.

Did they with thirst in summer burn,
Lo, seltzogenes at every turn,
And on all very sultry days
Cream ices handed round on trays.

Then currant wine and ginger pops
Stood handily on all the "tops:"
And, also, with amusement rife,
A "Zoetrope, or Wheel of Life."

New volumes came across the sea
From Mister Mudie's libraree;
The Times and Saturday Review
Beguiled the leisure of the crew.

Kind-hearted Captain Reece, R. N.,
Was quite devoted to his men;
In point of fact, good Captain Reece
Beatified The Mantelpiece.

One summer eve, at half-past ten,
　He said (addressing all his men):
"Come, tell me, please, what I can do
　To please and gratify my crew.

"By any reasonable plan
　I'll make you happy if I can;
My own convenience count as *nil;*
　It is my duty, and I will."

Then up and answer'd William Lee
(The kindly captain's coxswain he,
A nervous, shy, low-spoken man);
He cleared his throat, and thus began:

"You have a daughter, Captain Reece,
　Ten female cousins and a niece,
A ma, if what I'm told is true,
　Six sisters, and an aunt or two.

"Now, somehow, sir, it seems to me,
　More friendly-like we all should be,
If you united of 'em to
　Unmarried members of the crew.

"If you'd ameliorate our life,
　Let each select from them a wife;
And as for nervous me, old pal,
　Give me your own enchanting gal!"

Good Captain Reece, that worthy man,
　Debated on his coxswain's plan:
"I quite agree," he said, "O Bill;
　It is my duty, and I will.

"My daughter, that enchanting gurl,
　Has just been promised to an earl,
And all my other familee
　To peers of various degree.

"But what are dukes and viscounts to
　The happiness of all my crew?
The word I gave you I'll fulfil;
　It is my duty, and I will.

"As you desire it shall befall,
　I'll settle thousands on you all,
And I shall be, despite my hoard,
　The only bachelor on board."

The boatswain of The Mantelpiece,
　He blush'd and spoke to Captain Reece:
"I beg your honor's leave," he said,
"If you would wish to go and wed,

"I have a widow'd mother who
　Would be the very thing for you—
She long has loved you from afar,
　She washes for you, Captain R."

The captain saw the dame that day—
　Address'd her in his playful way—
"And did it want a wedding-ring?
　It was a tempting ickle sing!

"Well, well, the chaplain I will seek,
　We'll all be married this day week
At yonder church upon the hill;
　It is my duty, and I will!"

The sisters, cousins, aunts, and niece,
　And widow'd ma of Captain Reece,
Attended there as they were bid;
　It was their duty, and they did.
　　　　　　　　　　WILLIAM S. GILBERT.

MR. MOLONY'S ACCOUNT OF THE BALL

GIVEN TO THE NEPAULESE AMBASSADOR BY THE PENINSULAR AND ORIENTAL COMPANY.

OH will ye choose to hear the news?
　Bedad, I cannot pass it o'er:
I'll tell you all about the ball
　To the Naypaulase ambassador.
Begor! this fête all balls does bate
　At which I've worn a pump, and I
Must here relate the splendthor great
　Of th' Oriental Company.

These men of sinse dispoised expinse,
　To fête these black Achilleses.
"We'll show the blacks," says they, "Almack's,
　And take the rooms at Willis's."
With flags and shawls, for these Nepauls,
　They hung the rooms of Willis up,
And deck'd the walls, and stairs, and halls,
　With roses and with lilies up.

And Jullien's band it tuck its stand
　So sweetly in the middle there,
And soft bassoons play'd heavenly chunes,
　And violins did fiddle there.
And when the coort was tired of spoort,
　I'd lave you, boys, to think there was
A nate buffet before them set,
　Where lashins of good dhrink there was!

At ten, before the ball-room door
   His moighty Excellency was;
He smoiled and bow'd to all the crowd—
   So gorgeous and immense he was.
His dusky shuit, sublime and mute,
   Into the doorway follow'd him;
And oh the noise of the blackguard boys,
   As they hurrood and hollow'd him!

The noble Chair stud at the stair,
   And bade the dhrums to thump; and he
Did thus evince to that Black Prince
   The welcome of his Company.
Oh fair the girls, and rich the curls,
   And bright the oyes you saw there, was;
And fixed each oye, ye there could spoi,
   On Gineral Jung Bahawther was!

This Gineral great then tuck his sate,
   With all the other ginerals
(Bedad, his troat, his belt, his coat,
   All bleezed with precious minerals);
And as he there, with princely air,
   Recloinin' on his cushion was,
All round about his royal chair
   The squeezin' and the pushin' was.

O Pat, such girls, such jukes and earls,
   Such fashion and nobilitee!
Just think of Tim, and fancy him
   Amidst the hoigh gentilitee!
There was Lord De L'Huys, and the Portygeese
   Ministher and his lady there;
And I reckonized, with much surprise,
   Our messmate, Bob O'Grady, there.

There was Baroness Brunow, that look'd like Juno,
   And Baroness Rehausen there,
And Countess Roullier, that looked peculiar
   Well in her robes of gauze, in there.
There was Lord Crowhurst (I knew him first
   When only Mr. Pips he was),
And Mick O'Toole, the great big fool,
   That after supper tipsy was.

There was Lord Fingall and his ladies all,
   And Lords Killeen and Dufferin,
And Paddy Fife, with his fat wife—
   I wondther how he could stuff her in.
There was Lord Belfast, that by me past,
   And seem'd to ask how should *I* go there;

And the widow Macrae, and Lord A. Hay,
   And the marchioness of Sligo there.

Yes, jukes and earls, and diamonds and pearls,
   And pretty girls, was spoorting there;
And some beside (the rogues!) I spied
   Behind the windies, coorting there.
Oh, there's one I know, bedad, would show
   As beautiful as any there;
And I'd like to hear the pipers blow,
   And shake a fut with Fanny there!
        WILLIAM MAKEPEACE THACKERAY.

MR. BARNEY MAGUIRE'S ACCOUNT OF THE CORONATION.

OCH! the Coronation! what celebration
   For emulation can with it compare?
When to Westminster the Royal Spinster,
   And the Duke of Leinster, all in order did repair!
'Twas there you'd see the new Polishemen
   Making a skrimmage at half-after four,
And the Lords and Ladies, and the Miss O'Gradys,
   All standing round before the Abbey door.

Their pillows scorning, that self-same morning
   Themselves adorning, all by the candle-light,
With roses and lilies and daffy-down dillies,
   And gould, and jewels, and rich di'monds bright.
And then approaches five hundred coaches,
   With Giniral Dullbeak. Och! 'twas mighty fine
To see how asy bould Corporal Casey,
   With his sword drawn, prancing, made them kape the line.

Then the Guns' alarums, and the King of Arums,
   All in his Garters and his Clarence shoes,
Opening the massy doors to the bould Ambassydors,
   The Prince of Potboys and great haythen Jews;
'Twould have made you crazy to see Esterhazy
   All joo'ls from his jasey to his di'mond boots,

With Alderman Harmer and that swate charmer,
  The famale heiress, Miss Anja-ly Coutts.

And Wellington, walking with his swoord drawn, talking
  To Hill and Hardinge, haroes of great fame:
And Sir De Lacy and the Duke Dalmasey
  (They call'd him Sowlt afore he changed his name),
Themselves presading Lord Melbourne, lading
  The Queen, the darling, to her royal chair,
And that fine ould fellow, the Duke of Pell-Mello,
  The Queen of Portingal's Chargy-de-fair.

Then the noble Prussians, likewise the Russians,
  In fine laced jackets with their goulden cuffs,
And the Bavarians, and the proud Hungarians,
  And Everythingarians all in furs and muffs.
Then Misthur Spaker, with Misthur Pays the Quaker,
  All in the Gallery you might persave;
But Lord Brougham was missing, and gone a-fishing,
  Ounly crass Lord Essex would not give him lave.

There was Baron Alten himself exalting,
  And Prince Von Schwartzenburg, and many more,
Och! I'd be bother'd and entirely smother'd
  To tell the half of 'em was to the fore;
With the swate Peeresses, in their crowns and dresses,
  And Aldermanesses, and the Boord of Works;
But Mehemet Ali said, quite gintaly,
  "I'd be proud to see the likes among the Turks!"

Then the Queen, Heaven bless her! och! they did dress her
  In her purple garaments and her goulden crown;
Like Venus or Hebe, or the Queen of Sheby,
  With eight young ladies houlding up her gown.
Sure 'twas grand to see her, also for to he-ar
  The big drums bating and the trumpets blow,
And Sir George Smart! oh! he play'd a Consarto,
  With his four-and-twenty fiddlers all on a row.

Then the Lord Archbishop held a goulden dish up
  For to resave her bounty and great wealth,
Saying, "Plase your Glory, great Queen Vic-tory!
  Ye'll give the Clargy lave to dhrink your health!"
Then his Riverence, retrating, discoorsed the mating;
  "Boys, here's your Queen! deny it if you can!
And if any bould traitour or infarior craythur
  Sneezes at that, I'd like to see the man!"

Then the Nobles kneeling to the Pow'rs appealing,
  "Heaven send your Majesty a glorious reign!"
And Sir Claudius Hunter he did confront her,
  All in his scarlet gown and goulden chain.
The great Lord May'r, too, sat in his chair, too,
  But mighty sarious, looking fit to cry,
For the Earl of Surrey, all in his hurry,
  Throwing the thirteens, hit him in his eye.

Then there was preaching, and good store of speeching,
  With Dukes and Marquises on bended knee:
And they did splash her with raal Macasshur,
  And the Queen said, "Ah! then thank ye all for me!"
Then the trumpets braying and the organ playing,
  And sweet trombones with their silver tones;

But Lord Rolle was rolling;—'twas mighty
    consoling
  To think that his Lordship did not break
    his bones!

Then the crames and custard, and the beef
    and mustard,
  All on the tombstones like a poultherer's
    shop;
With lobsters and white-bait, and other
    swatemeats,
  And wine, and nagus, and Imperial Pop!
There was cakes and apples in all the
    Chapels,
  With fine polonies, and rich mellow
    pears,—
Och! the Count Von Strogonoff, sure he
    got prog enough,
  The sly ould Divil, undernathe the stairs.

Then the cannons thunder'd, and the people
    wonder'd,
  Crying, "God save Victoria, our Royal
    Queen!"
—Och! if myself should live to be a hun-
    dred,
  Sure it's the proudest day that I'll have
    seen!
And now I've ended, what I pretended,
  This narration splendid in swate poe-
    thry,
Ye dear bewitcher, just hand the pitcher,
  Faith, it's myself that's getting mighty
    dhry!
                RICHARD HARRIS BARHAM.

A VIRTUOSO.

BE seated, pray. "A grave appeal"?
  The sufferers by the war, of course;
Ah, what a sight for us who feel,—
  This monstrous *mélodrame* of Force!
We, sir, we connoisseurs, should know
  On whom its heaviest burden falls;
Collections shattered at a blow,
  Museums turned to hospitals!

"And worse," you say; "the wide distress!"
  Alas, 'tis true distress exists,
Though, let me add, our worthy Press
  Have no mean skill as colorists;—
Speaking of color, next your seat
  There hangs a sketch from Vernet's hand;

Some Moscow fancy, incomplete,
  Yet not indifferently planned;

Note specially the gray old Guard,
  Who tears his tattered coat to wrap
A closer bandage round the scarred
  And frozen comrade in his lap;—
But, as regards the present war,—
  Now, don't you think our pride of pence
Goes—may I say it?—somewhat far
  For objects of benevolence?

You hesitate. For my part, I—
  Though ranking Paris next to Rome,
Æsthetically—still reply
  That "Charity begins at home."
The words remind me. Did you catch
  My so-named "Hunt"? The girl's a gem;
And look how those lean rascals snatch
  The pile of scraps she brings to them!

"But your appeal's for home," you say,
  "For home, and English poor!" Indeed
I thought Philanthropy to-day
  Was blind to mere domestic need—
However sore—yet though one grants
  That home should have the foremost
    claims,
At least these Continental wants
  Assume intelligible names;

While here with us—Ah! who could hope
  To verify the varied pleas,
Or from his private means to cope
  With all our shrill necessities?
Impossible! One might as well
  Attempt comparison of creeds;
Or fill that huge Malayan shell
  With these half-dozen Indian beads.

Moreover, add that every one
  So well exalts his pet distress,
'Tis—Give to all, or give to none,
  If you'd avoid invidiousness.
Your case, I feel, is sad as A's,
  The same applies to B's and C's;
By my selection I should raise
  An alphabet of rivalries;

And life is short,—I see you look
  At yonder dish, a priceless bit;
You'll find it etched in Jacquemart's book,
  They say that Raphael painted it;—
And life is short, you understand;
  So, If I only hold you out

An open though an empty hand,
  Why, you'll forgive me, I've no doubt.

Nay, do not rise. You seem amused;
  One can but be consistent, sir!
'Twas on these grounds I just refused
  Some gushing lady-almoner,—
Believe me, on these very grounds.
  Good-bye, then. Ah, a rarity!
That cost me quite three hundred pounds,
  That Dürer figure,—"Charity."
                                AUSTIN DOBSON.

A RECIPE FOR A SALAD.

To make this condiment, your poet begs
The pounded yellow of two hard-boil'd eggs;
Two boil'd potatoes, pass'd through kitchen sieve,
Smoothness and softness to the salad give;
Let onion atoms lurk within the bowl,
And, half suspected, animate the whole;
Of mordant mustard add a single spoon,
Distrust the condiment that bites so soon;
But deem it not, thou man of herbs, a fault
To add a double quantity of salt;
Four times the spoon with oil from Lucca crown,
And twice with vinegar procured from town;
And, lastly o'er the flavor'd compound toss
A magic soupçon of anchovy sauce.
Oh, green and glorious! oh, herbaceous treat!
'Twould tempt a dying anchorite to eat:
Back to the world he'd turn his fleeting soul,
And plunge his fingers in the salad-bowl!
Serenely full, the epicure would say,
"Fate cannot harm me, I have dined to-day!"
                                SYDNEY SMITH.

EPIGRAM.

SLY Beelzebub took all occasions
To try Job's constancy and patience.
He took his honor, took his health,
He took his children, took his wealth,
His servants, oxen, horses, cows—
But cunning Satan did *not* take his spouse.

But Heaven, that brings out good from evil,
And loves to disappoint the devil,
Had predetermined to restore
Twofold all he had before;
His servants, horses, oxen, cows—
Short-sighted devil, *not* to take his spouse!
                        SAMUEL TAYLOR COLERIDGE.

A NOCTURNAL SKETCH.

EVEN is come; and from the dark Park, hark,
The signal of the setting sun—one gun!
And six is sounding from the chime, prime time
To go and see the Drury-Lane Dane slain,
Or hear Othello's jealous doubt spout out,
Or Macbeth raving at that shade-made blade,
Denying to his frantic clutch much touch;—
Or else to see Ducrow with wide stride ride
Four horses as no other man can span;
Or in the small Olympic Pit, sit split
Laughing at Liston, while you quiz his phiz.

Anon Night comes, and with her wings brings things
Such as, with his poetic tongue, Young sung;
The gas up-blazes with its bright white light,
And paralytic watchmen prowl, howl, growl,
About the streets and take up Pall-Mall Sal,
Who, hasting to her nightly jobs, robs fobs.
Now thieves to enter for your cash, smash, crash,
Past drowsy Charley, in a deep sleep, creep,
But frightened by Policeman B. 3, flee,
And, while they're going, whisper low, "No go!"

Now puss, while folks are in their beds, treads leads,
And sleepers waking grumble, "Drat that cat!"
Who in the gutter caterwauls, squalls, mauls
Some feline foe, and screams in shrill ill-will.

Now Bulls of Bashan, of a prize size, rise
In childish dreams, and with a roar gore poor

Georgy, or Charley, or Billy, willy-nilly;—
But Nursemaid in a nightmare rest, chest-pressed,
Dreameth of one of her old flames, James Games,
And that she hears—what faith is man's!—Ann's banns
And his, from Reverend Mr. Rice, twice, thrice:
White ribbons flourish, and a stout shout out,
That upward goes, shows Rose knows those bows' woes!
THOMAS HOOD.

THE SIEGE OF BELGRADE.

An Austrian army, awfully arrayed,
Boldly by battery besieged Belgrade.
Cossack commanders cannonading come,
Dealing destruction's devastating doom.
Every endeavor engineers essay,
For fame, for fortune fighting,—furious fray!
Generals 'gainst generals grapple — gracious God!
How honors Heaven heroic hardihood!
Infuriate, indiscriminate in ill,
Kindred kill kinsmen, kinsmen kindred kill.
Labor low levels longest, loftiest lines;
Men march mid mounds, mid moles, mid murderous mines;
Now noxious, noisy numbers nothing, naught
Of outward obstacles, opposing ought;
Poor patriots, partly purchased, partly pressed,
Quite quaking, quickly "Quarter! Quarter!" quest.
Reason returns, religious right redounds,
Suwarrow stops such sanguinary sounds.
Truce to thee, Turkey! Triumph to thy train,
Unwise, unjust, unmerciful Ukraine!
Vanish, vain victory! vanish, victory vain!
Why wish we warfare? Wherefore welcome were
Xerxes, Ximenes, Xanthus, Xavier?
Yield, yield, ye youths! ye yeomen, yield your yell!
Zeus's, Zarpater's, Zoroaster's zeal,
Attracting all, arms against acts appeal!
AUTHOR UNKNOWN.

BACHELOR'S HALL.

BACHELOR'S HALL! what a quare-lookin' place it is!
Kape me from sich all the days of my life!
Sure, but I think what a burnin' disgrace it is
Niver at all to be gettin' a wife.

See the old bachelor, gloomy and sad enough,
Placing his taykettle over the fire;
Soon it tips over—St. Patrick! he's mad enough
(If he were present) to fight wid the squire.

Then, like a hog in a mortar-bed wallowing,
Awkward enough, see him knading his dough;
Troth! if the bread he could ate widout swallowing,
How it would favor his palate, you know!

His dishcloth is missing: the pigs are devouring it;
In the pursuit he has battered his shin;
A plate wanted washing: Grimalkin is scouring it;
Thunder and turf! what a pickle he's in!

His meal being over, the table's left setting so;
Dishes, take care of yourselves, if you can!
But hunger returns; then he's fuming and fretting so!
Och! let him alone for a baste of a man.

Pots, dishes, pans, and such grasy commodities,
Ashes and prata-skins, kiver the floor;
His cupboard's a storehouse of comical oddities
Sich as had niver been neighbors before.

Late in the night, then, he goes to bed shiverin';
Niver the bit is the bed made at all;
He crapes, like a tarrapin, under the kiverin'—
Bad luck to the picter of Bachelor's Hall.
JOHN FINLEY.

NOTES

Explanatory and Corroborative.

NOTES
EXPLANATORY AND CORROBORATIVE.

Page 1.—HOME, SWEET HOME!—The following additional verses to the song of "Home, Sweet Home!" Mr. Payne affixed to the sheet music, and presented them to Mrs. Bates in London, a relative of his, and the wife of a rich banker:

To *us*, in despite of the absence of years,
How sweet the remembrance of *home* still appears!
From allurements abroad, which but flatter the eye,
The unsatisfied heart turns, and says with a sigh,
    "Home, home, sweet, sweet home!
    There's no place like home!
    There's no place like home!"

Your exile is blest with all fate can bestow;
But *mine* has been checkered with many a woe!
Yet, tho' different our fortunes, our thoughts are the same,
And both, as we think of Columbia, exclaim,
    "Home, home, sweet, sweet home!
    There's no place like home!
    There's no place like home!"

—*Life and Writings of John Howard Payne*, 4to, Albany, 1875.

Page 3.—THE COTTER'S SATURDAY NIGHT.—The house of William Burns was the scene of this fine, devout, and tranquil drama, and William himself was the saint, the father, and the husband who gives life and sentiment to the whole. "Robert had frequently remarked to me," says Gilbert Burns, "that he thought there was something peculiarly venerable in the phrase, 'Let us worship God!' used by a decent, sober head of a family, introducing family worship." To this sentiment of the author the world is indebted for the "Cotter's Saturday Night." He owed some little, however, of the inspiration to Fergusson's "Farmer's Ingle," a poem of great merit.
—*Burns's Poetical Works*, 8vo ed., Philada.

Page 7.—MATRIMONIAL HAPPINESS.—Lapraik was a very worthy facetious old fellow, late of Dalfram near Muirkirk, which little property he was obliged to sell in consequence of some connection as security for some persons concerned in that villainous bubble, "The Ayr Bank." He has often told me that he composed this song one day when his wife had been fretting over their misfortunes.—*Robert Burns.*

Page 10.—THE MARINER'S WIFE.—This most felicitous song is better known as "There's nae Luck about the House." It first appeared on the streets about the middle of the last century, and was included in Herd's *Collection*, 1776. The authorship is a matter of doubt. A copy of it, like a first draught, was found among the papers of William Julius Mickle, and the song has hence been believed to be his, notwithstanding that he did not include it in his own works. On the other hand, there has been some plausible argument to show that it must have been the work of a Mrs. Jane Adams, who kept a school at Crawford's Dyke, near Greenock; it is not, however, included in her volume of *Miscellany Poems*, published as early as 1734. Jane Adams gave Shakespearian readings to her pupils, and so admired Richardson's *Clarissa Harlowe* that she walked to London to see the author. Toward the close of her life she became a wandering beggar, died in the poorhouse of Glasgow on April 3, 1765, and was "buried at the house expense."—*Notes and Queries*, Third Series, vol. x.

Notwithstanding the weighty authority of *Notes and Queries*, I am inclined to ascribe its authorship to Jean Adam (not Jane Adams). Mickle never lived near a seaport, and never wrote anything as good as this poem. The remarkable statement that the poem does not appear in any of the published works of either claimant is, as far as it goes, an argument in favor of Miss Adam. She was poor, and probably published but one edition of her poems, which had a sale so small that the industrious Allibone does not mention her name in his *Dictionary of Authors*, while the scholarly translator of the *Lusiad* published many volumes of poems, some of which ran into several editions; and the fact that he never included "The Mariner's Wife" in any of them should determine the question of its authorship in her favor.

Page 11.—THE EXILE TO HIS WIFE.—Joseph Brennan (b. 1829, d. 1857) was a native of the north of Ireland. He joined the Young Ireland party in 1848, and was one of the conductors of the *Irish Felon*. He was imprisoned for nine months in Dublin, afterward edited the *Irishman*, and in October, 1849, being implicated in an insurrectionary movement in Tipperary, fled to America. He was for three years connected with the New Orleans *Delta*, and died in that city in May, 1857.—*Single Famous Poems.*

Page 21.—LADY ANNE BOTHWELL'S LAMENT.— The subject of this pathetic ballad the editor once thought might possibly relate to the Earl of Bothwell, and his desertion of his wife, Lady Jean Gordon, to make room for his marriage with the Queen of Scots. But this opinion he now believes to be groundless; indeed, Earl Bothwell's age, who was upward of sixty at the time of that marriage, renders it unlikely that he should be the object of so warm a passion as this elegy supposes. He has been since informed that it entirely refers to a private story. A young lady of the name of Bothwell—or rather Boswell—having been, together with her child, deserted by her husband or lover, composed these affecting lines herself.—*Percy's Reliques.*

Page 22.—THE ANGELS' WHISPER.—A superstition of great beauty prevails in Ireland, that when a child smiles in its sleep it is "talking with the angels."—*Lover's Lyrics of Ireland.*

Page 27.—GOLDEN TRESSÈD ADELAIDE.—The gifted child of the poet, Adelaide Anne Procter.

Page 34.—THE MITHERLESS BAIRN.—An Inverary correspondent writes: "Thom gave me the following narrative as to the origin of 'The Mitherless Bairn;' I quote his own words: 'When I was livin' in Aberdeen, I was limping roun' the house to my garret, when I heard the greetin' o' a wean. A lassie was thumpin' a bairn, when out cam' a big dame, bellowin', "Ye hussie! will ye lick a mitherless bairn?" I hobbled up the stair and wrote the sang afore sleepin'.'"

Page 41.—THE CHILDREN IN THE WOOD.—The subject of this very popular ballad (which has been set in so favorable a light by *The Spectator*, No. 85) seems to be taken from an old play, entitled "Two Lamentable Tragedies; the one of the murder of Maister Beech, a chandler in Thames-streete, etc. The other of a young child murthered in a wood by two ruffians, with the consent of his unkle. By Rob. Yarrington, 1601, 4to." Our ballad-maker has strictly followed the play in the description of the father's and mother's dying charge; in the uncle's promise to take care of their issue; his hiring two ruffians to destroy his wards, under pretence of sending them to school; their choosing a wood to perpetrate the murder in; one of the ruffians relenting and a battle ensuing, etc. In other respects he has departed from the play. In the latter the scene is laid in Padua; there is but one child, which is murdered by a sudden stab of the unrelenting ruffian; he is slain himself by his less bloody companion, but ere he dies he gives the other a mortal wound, the latter living just long enough to impeach the uncle, who, in consequence of this impeachment, is arraigned and executed by the hand of justice, etc. Whoever compares the play with the ballad will have no doubt but the former is the original: the language is far more obsolete, and such a vein of simplicity runs through the whole performance that, had the ballad been written first, there is no doubt but every circumstance of it would have been received into the drama; whereas this was probably built on some Italian novel. Printed from two ancient copies, one of them in black-letter in the *Pepys Collection*. Its title at large is, *The Children in the Wood, or The Norfolk Gentleman's Last Will and Testament*, to the tune of Rogero, etc.—*Percy's Reliques.*

Page 75.—WOODMAN, SPARE THAT TREE.—This song owes its existence to the following incident: The author some years since was riding out with a friend in the suburbs of New York City, and when near Bloomingdale they observed a cottager in the act of sharpening his axe under the shadow of a noble ancestral tree. His friend, who was once the proprietor of the estate on which the tree stood, suspected that the woodman intended to cut it down, remonstrated against the act, and, accompanying the protest with a ten-dollar note, succeeded in preserving from destruction this legendary memorial of his earlier and better days. —*Frederick Saunders's Festival of Song.*

Page 81.—AULD LANG SYNE.—Of the two versions of this song, we adopt for our text that supplied to Johnson in preference to the copy made for George Thomson. The arrangement of the verses is more natural; it wants the redundant syllable in the fourth line of stanza first; and the spelling of the Scotch words is more correct. The poet transcribed the song for Mrs. Dunlop in his letter to her dated 17th December, 1788, and it is unfortunate that Dr. Currie did not print a verbatim copy of it, along with that letter, instead of simply referring his reader to the Thomson correspondence for it. Thomson's closing verse stands *second* in Johnson, where it seems in its proper place, as having manifest reference to the earlier stages of the interview between the long-separated friends. Many of our readers must have observed that when a social company unites in singing the song before dispersing, it is the custom for the singers to join hands in a circle at the words, "And there's a hand," etc. This ought to conclude the song, with the chorus sung rapidly and emphatically thereafter. But how awkwardly and out of place does the slow singing of Thomson's closing verse come in after that excitement!—"And surely ye'll be your pint stowp," etc. No, no! The play is over; no more pint stowps!—*Burns's Poems*, William Scott Douglas's edition.

Page 87.—ODE TO AN INDIAN GOLD COIN.—This remarkable poem was written in Cherical, Malabar, the author having left his native land, Scotland, in quest of a fortune in India. He died shortly afterward in Java.—*Frederick Saunders's Festival of Song.*

Page 103.—WALY, WALY, BUT LOVE BE BONNY.—Nothing is known with certainty as to the authorship of this exquisite song, one of the most affecting of the many that Scotland can boast. It had been supposed to refer to an incident in the life of Lady Barbara Erskine, wife of the second Marquis of Douglas; but the allusions are evidently to the deeper woes of one not a wife —who "loved not wisely, but too well."—*Illustrated Book of Scottish Song.*

Page 112.—THE NUT-BROWN MAID.—Henry, Lord Clifford, first Earl of Cumberland, and Lady Margaret Percy his wife, are the originals of this ballad. Lord Clifford had a miserly father and ill-natured stepmother, so he left home and became the head of a band of robbers. The ballad was written in 1502, and says that the "Notbrowne Mayd" was wooed and won by a knight who gave out that he was a banished man. After describing the hardships she would have to undergo if she married him, and finding her love true to the test, he revealed himself to be an earl's son, with large hereditary estates in Westmoreland.— *Percy's Reliques* (Series II.).

Page 120.— HIGHLAND MARY. — "Highland Mary," says the Hon. A. Erskine in a letter to Mr. George Thomson, "is most enchantingly pathetic." Burns says of it himself, in a letter to Mr. Thomson: "The foregoing song pleases myself; I think it is in my happiest manner; you will see at first glance that it suits the air. The subject of the song is one of the most interesting passages of my youthful days; and I own that I should be much flattered to see the verses set to an air which would ensure celebrity. Perhaps, after all, 'tis the still-glowing prejudice of my heart that throws a borrowed lustre over the merits of the composition."—*Illustrated Book of Scottish Song.*

The history of this humble maiden is now known to all the world, and will continue to be remembered as long as Scottish song exists. Her name was Mary Campbell, and her parents resided at Campbelltown, in Argyleshire. At the time Burns became acquainted with her she was servant at Coilsfield House, the seat of Colonel Montgomery, afterward Earl of Eglinton. In notes to the *Museum*, Burns says of the present song: "This was a composition of mine before I was known at all to the world. My Highland lassie was a warm-hearted, charming young creature as ever blessed a man with generous love. After a pretty long trial of the most ardent reciprocal attachment, we met by appointment on the second Sunday of May in a sequestered spot on the banks of the Ayr, where we spent the day in taking a farewell before she should embark for the West Highlands to arrange matters among her friends for our projected change of life. At the close of the autumn following she crossed the sea to meet me at Greenock, where she had scarce landed when she was seized with a malignant fever, which hurried my dear girl to her grave in a few days, before I could even hear of her illness." Cromek adds a few particulars of the final interview of the youthful lovers: "This adieu was performed with all those simple and striking ceremonials which rustic sentiment has devised to prolong tender emotion and to inspire awe. The lovers stood on each side of a small purling brook, they laved their hands in the limpid stream, and, holding a Bible between them, they pronounced their vows to be faithful to each other. They parted never to meet again." Cromek's account of this parting interview was considered somewhat apocryphal till, a good many years ago, a pocket Bible in two volumes, presented by Burns to Mary Campbell, was discovered in the possession of her sister at Ardrossan. This Bible afterward found its way to Canada, whither the family had removed; and having excited the interest of some Scotchmen at Montreal, they purchased it (for its possessors were unfortunately in reduced circumstances), and had it conveyed back to Scotland, with the view of being permanently placed in the monument at Ayr. On its arrival at Glasgow, Mr. Weir, stationer, Queen street (through the instrumentality of whose son, we believe, the precious relic was mainly procured), kindly announced that he would willingly show it for a few days at his shop to any person who might choose to see it. The result was, that thousands flocked to obtain a view of this interesting memorial, and the ladies in particular displayed an unwonted eagerness regarding it, some of them being even moved to tears on beholding an object which appealed so largely to female sympathies. On the anniversary of the poet in 1841, the Bible, enclosed in an oaken glass case, was deposited among other relics in the monument at Ayr. On the boards of one of the volumes is inscribed in Burns's handwriting, "And ye shall not swear by my name falsely, I am the Lord," Levit., chap. xix. v. 12; and on the other, "Thou shalt not forswear thyself, but shalt perform unto the Lord thine oath," St. Matt., chap. v. v. 33; and on the blank leaves of both volumes, "Robert Burns, Mossgiel."—*Burns's Works*, Blackie & Son's ed.

Page 120.—SALLY IN OUR ALLEY.—Carey says the occasion of his ballad was this: "A shoemaker's apprentice, making holiday with his sweetheart, treated her with a sight of Bedlam, the puppet-shows, the flying chain, and all the elegancies of Moorfields; from whence proceeding to the Farthing Piehouse, he gave her a collation of buns, cheese-cakes, gammon of bacon, stuffed beef and bottle ale; through all which scenes the author dodged them (charmed with the simplicity of their courtship), from whence he drew this little sketch of nature." The song, he adds, made its way into the polite world, and was more than once mentioned with approbation by "the divine Addison."—*Chambers's Cyclopædia of English Literature.*

Page 124.—To ALTHEA, FROM PRISON.—This excellent sonnet, which possessed a high degree of fame among the old Cavaliers, was written by Colonel Richard Lovelace during his confinement in the Gate-house, Westminster, to which he was committed by the House of Commons in April, 1642, for presenting a petition from the county of Kent, requesting them to restore the king to his rights and to settle the government. See Wood's *Athenæ*, vol. ii., p. 228, and Lysons's *Environs of London*, vol. i., p. 109, where may be seen at large the affecting story of this elegant writer, who after having been distinguished for every gallant and polite accomplishment, the pattern of his own sex and the darling of the ladies, died in the lowest wretchedness, obscurity, and want in 1658.—*Percy's Reliques.*

Page 126.—JEAN.—This song was written in celebration of the charms of Jean Armour, afterward the poet's wife.

" Of a' the Airts the Wind can Blaw" was the most universally popular of all Burns's songs, at least in the west of Scotland, and it is still a great favorite. The air is by Mr. Marshall, who in Burns's time was butler to the Duke of Gordon, and who composed several other fine airs. Only the first two stanzas were written by Burns. The last two have been ascribed to John Hamilton, music-seller, Edinburgh.—*Burns's Works*, Blackie & Son's ed.

Page 127.—THE EVE OF ST. AGNES.—The Feast of St. Agnes was formerly held as in a special degree a holiday for women. It was thought possible for a girl, on the eve of St. Agnes, to obtain by divination a knowledge of her future husband. She might take a row of pins, and, plucking them out one after another, stick them in her sleeve, singing the whilst a Paternoster, and thus ensure that her dreams would that night present the person in question. Or, passing into a different country from that of her ordinary residence, and taking her right-leg stocking, she might knit the left garter round it, repeating:

" I knit this knot, this knot I knit,
To know the thing I know not yet,
That I may see
The man that shall my husband be,
Not in his best or worst array,
But what he weareth every day;
That I to-morrow may him ken
From among all other men."

Lying down on her back that night with her hands under her head, the anxious maiden was led to expect that her future spouse would appear in a dream and salute her with a kiss.—*Chambers's Book of Days.*

Page 136.—LOCHINVAR.—The ballad of Lochinvar is in a very slight degree founded on a ballad called " Katharine Janfarie." (*See Note to Katharine Janfarie.*)

Page 137.—AULD ROBIN GRAY.—This beautiful ballad, of which the authorship was long a mystery, was written by Lady Anne Lindsay, daughter of the Earl of Balcarras, and afterward Lady Barnard. It appears to have been composed at the commencement of the year 1772, when the author was yet a young girl. It was published anonymously, and acquired great popularity. No one, however, came forward to lay claim to the laurels lavished upon it, and a literary controversy sprang up to decide the authorship. Many conjectured that it was as old as the days of David Rizzio, if not composed by that unfortunate minstrel himself, while others considered it of much later date. The real author was, however, suspected; and ultimately, when her ladyship was an old woman, Sir Walter Scott received a letter from Lady Anne herself openly avowing that she had written it. She stated that she had been long suspected by her more intimate friends, and often questioned with respect to the mysterious ballad, but that she had always managed to keep her secret to herself without a direct and absolute denial. She was induced to write the song by a desire to see an old plaintive Scottish air ("The Bridegroom Grat when the Sun gaed down") which was a favorite with her fitted with words more suitable to its character than the ribald verses which had always hitherto, for want of better, been sung to it. She had previously been endeavoring to beguile the tedium occasioned by her sister's marriage and departure for London by the composition of verses; but of all she had written, either before or since, none have reached the merit of this admirable little poem. It struck her that some tale of virtuous distress in humble life would be most suitable to the plaintive character of her favorite air; and she accordingly set about such an attempt, taking the name of "Auld Robin Gray" from an ancient herd at Balcarras. When she had written two or three of the verses she called to her junior sister (afterward Lady Hardwicke), who was the only person near her, and thus addressed her: "I have been writing a ballad, my dear; I am oppressing my heroine with many misfortunes; I have already sent her Jamie to sea, and broken her father's arm, and made her mother fall sick, and given her Auld Robin Gray for her lover: but I wish to load her with a fifth sorrow within the four lines—poor thing! Help me to one." "Steal the cow, sister Anne," said the little Elizabeth. "The cow," adds Lady Anne in her letter, "was immediately *lifted* by me, and the song completed."—*Illustrated Book of Scottish Song*.

Page 137.—TO MARY IN HEAVEN.—"At Ellisland," says Professor Wilson, "Burns wrote many of his finest strains, and, above all, that immortal burst of passion, 'To Mary in Heaven.' This celebrated poem was composed in September, 1789, on the anniversary of the day in which he heard of the death of his early love, Mary Campbell. According to Mrs. Burns, he spent that day, though laboring under cold, in the usual work of his harvest, and apparently in excellent spirits; but as the twilight deepened he appeared to grow very sad about something, and at length wandered out to the barnyard, to which his wife, in her anxiety for his health, followed him, entreating him in vain to observe that the frost had set in, and to return to the fireside. On being again and again requested to do so, he always promised compliance, but still remained where he was, striding up and down slowly and contemplating the sky, which was singularly clear and starry. At last Mrs. Burns found him stretched on a mass of straw, with his eyes fixed on a beautiful planet 'that shone like another moon,' and prevailed on him to come in. He immediately on entering the house called for his desk, and wrote as they now stand, with all the ease of one copying from memory, these sublime and pathetic verses."—*John Gibson Lockhart*.

Page 140.—THE MILKMAID'S SONG.—This song and "The Milkmaid's Mother's Answer" have been ascribed by some editors to Shakespeare, but there is very little doubt but that they were written respectively by Marlowe and Raleigh. Izaak Walton says, in *The Compleat Angler:* "As I left this place and entered into the next field a second pleasure entertained me. 'Twas a handsome milkmaid, that had not yet attained so much age and wisdom as to load her mind with any fears of many things that will never be, as too many men too often do; but she cast away all care, and sung like a nightingale. Her voice was good, and the ditty suited for it. 'Twas that smooth song which was made by *Kit Marlow* now at least fifty years ago; and the milkmaid's mother sung an answer to it, which was made by *Sir Walter Raleigh* in his younger days. They were old-fashioned poetry, but choicely good; I think much better than the strong lines that are now in fashion in this critical age. Look yonder! On my word, yonder they both be a-milking again! I will give her the chub, and persuade them to sing those two songs to us."

Page 145.—MAID OF ATHENS.—Our servant, who had gone before to procure accommodation, met us at the gate and conducted us to Theodora Macri, the Consulina's, where we at present live. This lady is the widow of the consul, and has three lovely daughters; the eldest celebrated for her beauty, and said to be the subject of those stanzas by Lord Byron—

"Maid of Athens, ere we part,
Give, oh, give me back my heart!" etc.

Theresa, the Maid of Athens, Catinco, and Mariana, are of middle stature. On the crown of the head of each is a red Albanian skull-cap, with a blue tassel spread out and fastened down like a star. Near the edge or bottom of the skull-cap is a handkerchief of various colors bound around their temples. The youngest wears her hair loose, falling on her shoulders—the hair behind descending down the back nearly to the waist, and, as usual, mixed with silk. The two eldest generally have their hair bound, and fastened under the handkerchief. Their upper robe is a pelisse edged with fur, hanging loose down to the ankles; below is a handkerchief of muslin covering the bosom and terminating at the waist, which is short; under that, a gown of striped silk or muslin, with a gore round the swell of the loins, falling in front in graceful negligence; white stockings and yellow slippers complete their attire. The two eldest have black or dark hair and eyes; their visage oval and complexion somewhat pale, with teeth of dazzling whiteness. Their cheeks are rounded and nose straight, rather inclined to aquiline. The youngest, Mariana, is very fair, her face not so finely rounded, but has a gayer expression than her sisters', whose countenances, except when the conversation has something of mirth in it, may be said to be rather pensive. Their persons are elegant and their manners pleasing and lady-like, such as would be fascinating in any country. They possess very considerable powers of conversation, and their minds seem to be more instructed than those of the Greek women in general. With such attractions it would, indeed, be remarkable if they did not meet with great attention from the travellers who occasionally are resident in Athens. They sit in the Eastern style, a little reclined, with their limbs gathered under them on the divan, and without shoes. Their employments are the needle, tambourine, and reading.—*Travels in Italy, Greece, etc.*, by H. W. Williams, Esq.

Page 145.—BONNIE LESLEY.—The poet, in a letter to Mrs. Dunlop dated August, 1792, describes the influence which the beauty of Miss Lesley Baillie exercised over his imagination. "Know, then," said he, "that the heartstruck awe, the distant, humble approach, the delight we should have in gazing upon and listening to a messenger of heaven, appearing in all the unspotted purity of his celestial home among the coarse, polluted, far inferior sons of men, to deliver to them tidings that make their hearts swim in joy and their imaginations soar in transport,— such, so delighting and so pure, were the emotions of my soul on meeting the other day with Miss Lesley Baillie, your neighbor. Mr. Baillie with his two daughters, accompanied by Mr. H. of G., passing through Dumfries a few days ago on their way to England, did me the honor of calling on me, on which I took my horse (though God knows I could ill spare the time!) and accompanied them fourteen or fifteen miles, and dined and spent the day with them. 'Twas about nine, I think, when I left them, and riding home I composed the following ballad."—*Burns's Poems.*

Page 155.—THE LASS O' PATIE'S MILL.— "'The Lass o' Patie's Mill,'" says Burns, "is one of Ramsay's best songs. The following anecdote was told by the late John, Earl of Loudon: Allan Ramsay was residing at Loudon Castle with the then earl, father to Earl John, and one afternoon, riding or walking out together, his lordship and Allan passed a sweet romantic spot on Irwine Water, still called 'Patie's Mill,' where a bonnie lass was 'tedding hay bareheaded on the green.' My lord observed to Allan that it would be a fine theme for a song. Ramsay took the hint, and lingering behind he composed the first sketch of it, which he produced at dinner."—*Illustrated Book of Scottish Song.*

Page 166.—JESSY.—The Jessy of this and several other songs was Jessy Lewars, sister of a fellow-exciseman of Burns in Dumfries. She was distinguished from many of his contemporarary admirers by the affectionate sympathy which she always had for him and for his wife, and which during his last illness took the form of a daughter's watchful care. This is the last song Burns ever wrote.—*Mary Carlyle Aitken.*

Page 167.—WHEN THE KYE COMES HAME.—In the title and chorus of this favorite little pastoral I choose rather to violate a rule in grammar than a Scottish phrase so common that when it is altered into the proper way every shepherd and shepherd's sweetheart accounts it nonsense. I was once singing it at a wedding with great glee the latter way ("When the kye come hame"), when a tailor, scratching his head, said, "It was a terrible affected way, that!" I stood corrected, and have never sung it so again.— *Hogg's Poems.*

Page 173.—A PASTORAL.—The Phœbe of this admired pastoral was Joanna, the daughter of the very learned Dr. Richard Bentley, archdeacon and prebendary of Ely, regius professor and master of Trinity College, Cambridge, who died in 1742. She was afterward married to Dr. Dennison Cumberland, bishop of Clonfert in Killaloe in Ireland, and grandson of Dr. Richard Cumberland, bishop of Peterborough.—*Spectator*, No. 603, note.

Page 179.—CASTARA.—Castara was a daughter of William Herbert, first Lord Percy, and became the wife of the poet. There are no purer and few more graceful records of a noble attachment than that which is contained in the poems to which Habington has given the name of the lady of his happy love.—*Richard Chenevix Trench.*

Page 185.—GO, LOVELY ROSE.—A lady of Cambridge lent Waller's poems to Henry Kirke White, and when he returned them to her she discovered this additional stanza written by him at the end of this poem:

"Yet, though thou fade,
From thy dead leaves let fragrance rise;
And teach the maid
That Goodness Time's rude hand defies,
That Virtue lives when Beauty dies."
—*Henry Kirke White's Poems.*

Page 185.—TO HIS MISTRESS, THE QUEEN OF BOHEMIA.—On that amiable princess, Elizabeth, daughter of James I. and wife of the Elector Palatine, who was chosen King of Bohemia September 5, 1619. The consequences of this fatal election are well known. Sir Henry Wotton, who in that and the following year was employed in several embassies in Germany in behalf of this unfortunate lady, seems to have had an uncommon attachment to her merit and fortunes; for he gave away a jewel that was worth a thousand pounds, that was presented to him by the emperor, "because it came from an enemy to his royal mistress the Queen of Bohemia" ("for so," says Walton in

The *Life of Wotton,* "she was pleased he should always call her ").—*Bellew's Poets' Corner.*

Page 186.—JENNY KISSED ME.—These lines are said to be due to the following incident: Leigh Hunt called on Carlyle to inform him of some very pleasant piece of news. Mrs. Carlyle, who was in the room at the time, was so delighted that she jumped up and kissed him. On his return home he wrote this pretty little compliment.

Page 199.—ANNIE LAURIE.—
MAXWELTON BANKS.

Maxwelton banks are bonnie,
  Where early fa's the dew:
Where me and Annie Laurie
  Made up the promise true;
Made up the promise true,
  And never forget will I;
And for bonnie Annie Laurie
  I'll lay me doun and die.

She's backit like the peacock,
  She's breistit like the swan,
She's jimp about the middle,
  Her waist ye weel micht span;
Her waist ye weel micht span,
  And she has a rolling eye;
And for bonnie Annie Laurie
  I'll lay me doun and die.

"These two verses," as we are informed by Mr. Robert Chambers, "were written by Mr. Douglas of Finland upon Annie, one of the four daughters of Sir Robert Laurie, first baronet of Maxwelton, by his second wife, who was a daughter of Riddell of Minto. As Sir Robert was created a baronet in the year 1685, it is probable that the verses were composed about the end of the seventeenth or the beginning of the eighteenth century. It is painful to record that, notwithstanding the ardent and chivalrous affection displayed by Mr. Douglas in his poem, he did not obtain the heroine for a wife; she was married to Mr. Ferguson of Craigdarroch." The first four lines of the second stanza are taken from the old and indecent ballad of "John Anderson, my Jo," a fact which Mr. Chambers has not mentioned. The ballad of "John Anderson," as it was sung before it was rendered decent by Robert Burns, appeared in a very scarce volume of English songs, with music, entitled *The Convivial Songster,* published in 1782. —*Illustrated Book of Scottish Song.*

Page 201.—THE LORD OF BURLEIGH.—Henry Cecil, eleventh Baron Burleigh, tenth Earl of Exeter and first Marquis of Exeter, was born at Brussels in 1754, and for many years in his early life was M. P. for Stamford. His lordship was married three times: first, to Emma, only daughter and heiress of Thomas Vernon, Esq., of Han- bury, from whom he was divorced in 1791, after having issue by her one son, who died young; secondly, to Sarah, daughter to Thomas Hoggins, of Bolas, Shropshire, by whom he had issue four children—namely, the Lady Sophia Cecil, married to the Hon. Henry Manvers Pierrepoint (whose daughter married Lord Charles Wellesley, second son of the first Duke of Wellington, and was mother of the present heir-presumptive to that dukedom); Lord Henry Cecil, who died young; Lord Brownlow Cecil, who became second Marquis of Exeter; and Lord Thomas Cecil, who married Lady Sophia Georgiana Lennox; and, thirdly, to Elizabeth, Duchess Hamilton, by whom he had no issue. The second of these three marriages has supplied a theme to many novelists and dramatists. They have used the poet's license somewhat, but it is certain that the bride and her family had no idea of the rank of the wooer until the Lord of Burleigh had wedded the peasant girl. Thus Moore pictures Ellen, the "hamlet's pride," loving in poverty, leaving her home to seek uncertain fortune. Stopping at the entrance to a lordly mansion, blowing the horn with a chieftain's air, while the porter bowed as he passed the gate, "she believed him wild" when he said, "This castle is thine, and these dark woods all;" but "his words were truth," and "Ellen was Lady of Rosna Hall."—*The Stately Homes of England,* Second Series.

Page 202.—LUCY'S FLITTIN'.—The author of this sweet little poem was Scott's valued friend and steward. On Scott's return to Abbotsford from Naples, after having travelled from London in a state of utter prostration and semi-unconsciousness, seeing Laidlaw at his bedside, he said, his eyes brightening, "Is that you, Willie? I ken I'm hame noo."—*Mary Carlyle Aitken.*

Page 221.—THE GRAVE OF MACAURA.—At Callan, a pass on an unfrequented road leading from Glanerought (the Vale of the Roughty) to Bantry, the country-people point out a flat stone by the pathway which they name as the burial-place of Daniel MacCarthy, who fell there in an engagement with the Fitzgeralds in 1261. The stone still preserves the traces of characters, which are, however, illegible. From the scanty records of the period it would appear that this battle was no inconsiderable one. The Geraldines were defeated, and their leader, Thomas Fitzgerald, and his son, eighteen barons, fifteen knights, and many others of his adherents, slain. But the honor and advantage of victory were dearly purchased by the exulting natives, owing to the death of their brave and noble chieftain. The name MacCarthy, as spelt in Irish, would be (represented in Roman characters) MacCartha. But it would be pronounced MacCaura, the *th,* or dotted *t,* having, in the Irish tongue, the soft sound of *h*.—*Lover's Lyrics of Ireland.*

Page 223.—THE GOOD LORD CLIFFORD.—Mr. Southey, describing the mountain-scenery of the Lake region, says: "The story of the shepherd Lord Clifford, which was known only to a few antiquarians till it was told so beautifully in verse by Wordsworth, gives a romantic history to Blencathara." Henry, Lord Clifford, was the son of John, Lord Clifford, who was slain at Towton, which battle placed the House of York upon the throne. His family could expect no mercy from the conqueror, for he was the man who slew the younger brother of Edward IV. in the battle of Wakefield—a deed of cruelty in a cruel age. The hero of this poem fled from his paternal home, and lived for twenty-four years as a shepherd. He was restored to his rank and estates by Henry VII. The following narrative is from an old MS. quoted by Mr. Southey:

"So in the condition of a shepherd's boy at Lonsborrow, where his mother then lived for the most part, did this Lord Clifford spend his youth, till he was about fourteen years of age, about which time his mother's father, Henry Bromflett, Lord Vesey, deceased. But a little after his death it came to be rumored, at the court, that his daughter's two sons were alive, about which their mother was examined; but her answer was, that she had given directions to send them both beyond seas, to be bred there, and she did not know whether they were dead or alive.

"And as this Henry, Lord Clifford, did grow to more years, he was still the more capable of his danger, if he had been discovered. And therefore presently after his grandfather, the Lord Vesey, was dead, the said rumor of his being alive being more and more whispered at the court, made his said loving mother, by the means of her second husband, Sir Launcelot Threlkeld, to send him away with the said shepherds and their wives into Cumberland, to be kept as a shepherd there, sometimes at Threlkeld, and amongst his father-in-law's kindred, and sometimes upon the borders of Scotland, where they took lands purposely for these shepherds that had the custody of him; where many times his father-in-law came purposely to visit him, and sometimes his mother, though very secretly. By which mean kind of breeding this inconvenience befell him, that he could neither write nor read; for they durst not bring him up in any kind of learning, lest by it his birth should be discovered. Yet, after he came to his lands and honors, he learnt to write his name only.

"Notwithstanding which disadvantage, after he came to be possessed again, and restored to the enjoyment of his father's estate, he came to be a very wise man, and a very good manager of his estate and fortunes.

"This Henry, Lord Clifford, after he came to be possessed of his said estate, was a great builder and repairer of all his castles in the North, which had gone to decay when he came to enjoy them; for they had been in strangers' hands about twenty-four or twenty-five years. Skipton Castle, and the lands about it, had been given to William Stanley by King Edward IV., which William Stanley's head was cut off about the tenth year of King Henry VII.; and Westmoreland was given by Edward IV. to his brother Richard, Duke of Gloucester, who was afterward king of England, and was slain in battle, the 22d of August, 1485.

"This Henry, Lord Clifford, did, after he came to his estate, exceedingly delight in astronomy and the contemplation of the course of the stars, which it is likely he was seasoned in during the course of his shepherd's life. He built a great part of Barden Tower (which is now much decayed), and there he lived much; which it is thought he did the rather because in that place he had furnished himself with instruments for that study.

"He was a plain man, and lived for the most part a country life, and came seldom either to the court or London but when he was called thither to sit in them as a peer of the realm, in which parliament, it is reported, he behaved himself wisely, and nobly, and like a good Englishman."—*Knight's Half Hours with the Best Authors.*

Page 233.—EPITAPH ON THE COUNTESS OF PEMBROKE.—The accomplished sister of Sir Philip Sidney, who dedicated to her his *Arcadia.* The countess of Pembroke wrote some graceful poems, translated the tragedy of *Antony* from the French, and joined her brother in a translation of the Psalms. Spenser speaks of her as

"Most resembling, both in shape and spirit,
Her brother dear."

She died in 1621. The above epitaph was first introduced into the collected works of Ben Jonson by Whalley, on the ground that it was "universally assigned to him." Jonson's claim to it, however, is by no means certain.—*Bellew's Poets' Corner.*

Page 233.—ON LUCY, COUNTESS OF BEDFORD.—Lucy, the lady of Edward, third Earl of Bedford, and daughter of John, Lord Harrington. She was a munificent patron of genius, and seems to have been peculiarly kind to Jonson. One of the most exquisite compliments that ever was offered to talents, beauty, and goodness was paid by the graceful poet to this lady The biographers are never weary of repeating after one another that she was "the friend of Donne and Daniel, who wrote verses on her," but of Jonson, who wrote more than both, they preserve a rigid silence.—*Jonson's Works,* vol. vii.

Page 234.—SONNET TO CYRIAC SKINNER.—Cyriac Skinner was one of the principal members of Harrington's political club. Wood says that he was "an ingenious young gentleman and scholar to John Milton."

Page 235.—MILTON'S PRAYER OF PATIENCE.—This poem, so Miltonic in its purity and force of expression, was at first attributed to the great poet himself, and was actually published in an English edition of his works as a recently-discovered poem by him.

Page 235.—TO THE LADY MARGARET LEY.—The daughter of Sir James Ley, whose singular learning and abilities raised him through all the great posts of the law till he came to be made Earl of Marlborough, Lord High Treasurer, and Lord President of the Council to King James I. He died at an advanced age, and Milton attributes his death to *the breaking of the Parliament;* and it is true that the Parliament was dissolved the 10th of March, 162⅔, and he died on the 14th of the same month.

Page 235.—LYCIDAS.—The name under which Milton celebrates the untimely death of Edward King, Fellow of Christ College, Cambridge, who was drowned in his passage from Chester to Ireland, August 10th, 1637. He was the son of Sir John King, Secretary for Ireland.—*Brewer's Dictionary of Phrase and Fable.*

Page 238.—AN HORATIAN ODE.—This ode was written in the summer of 1650, after Cromwell's return from the campaign in Ireland, and after he had been designated for the expedition to Scotland, but while as yet the "laureat wreath" of Dunbar Field was unwon.

Page 245.—ON THE DEATH OF DR. LEVETT.—In one of his (Johnson's) memorandum-books in my possession is the following entry: "January 20, Sunday, 1782, Robert Levett was buried in the churchyard of Bridewell between one and two in the afternoon. He died on Thursday, 17, about seven in the morning, by an instantaneous death. He was an old and faithful friend. I have known him from about 1746. *Commendavi.* May God have mercy on him! May He have mercy on me!" Boswell quotes as follows from "Critical Remarks" by Nathan Drake, M. D.: "The stanzas on the death of this man of great but humble utility are beyond all praise. The wonderful powers of Johnson were never shown to greater advantage than on this occasion, where the subject, from its obscurity and mediocrity, seemed to bid defiance to poetical efforts; it is, in fact, warm from the heart, and is the only poem from the pen of Johnson that has been bathed with tears. Would to God that on every medical man who attends the poor such encomiums could be justly passed!"—*Boswell's Life of Johnson.*

Page 247.—ELEGY ON CAPTAIN MATTHEW HENDERSON.—Captain Matthew Henderson, a gentleman of very agreeable manners and great propriety of character, usually lived in Edinburgh, dined constantly at Fortune's Tavern, and was a member of the Capillaire Club, which was composed of all who desired to be thought witty or joyous. He died in 1789. Burns, in a note to the poem, says: "I loved the man much, and have not flattered his memory." Henderson seems, indeed, to have been universally liked. "In our travelling party," says Sir James Campbell of Ardkinglass, "was Matthew Henderson, then (1759) and afterward well known and much esteemed in the town of Edinburgh, at that time an officer in the Twenty-fifth regiment of foot, and, like myself, on his way to join the army; and I may say with truth that in the course of a long life I have never known a more estimable character than Matthew Henderson."—*Memoirs of Campbell of Ardkinglass.*

Page 252.—BURIAL OF SIR JOHN MOORE.—Sir John Moore often said that if he were killed in battle he wished to be buried where he fell. The body was removed at midnight to the citadel of Corunna. A grave was dug for him on the rampart there by a body of the Ninth regiment, the aides-de-camp attending by turns. No coffin could be procured, and the officers of his staff wrapped the body, dressed as it was, in a military cloak and blanket. The interment was hastened, for about eight in the morning some firing was heard, and the officers feared that if a serious attack were made they should be ordered away and not suffered to pay him their last duty. The officers of his family bore him to the grave, the funeral service was read by the chaplain, and the corpse was covered with earth.—*Edinburgh Annual Register* (1808).

Page 252.—OH, BREATHE NOT HIS NAME.—This poem refers to Robert Emmett, an eloquent Irish enthusiast, born in Cork in 1780. He was an ardent but misguided partisan of Irish independence, and appears to have been a sincere patriot. He was one of the chiefs of the "United Irishmen." In July, 1803, he rashly put himself at the head of a party of insurgents consisting of the rabble of Dublin, who murdered the chief-justice, Lord Kilwarden, and others, but were quickly dispersed by the military. Emmett was arrested, was tried, and after an eloquent and impassioned speech in vindication of his course, suffered with intrepid courage a felon's death, September, 1803.—*Thomas's Biographical Dictionary.*

Page 263.—THE LOST LEADER.—In his earlier years, Wordsworth, who had travelled in France during the French Revolution, was very democratic in his opinions, but afterward grew more conservative, which some of his old associates attributed to his having received from the English government the office of poet-laureate.

Page 267.—ICHABOD.—"And she named the child Ichabod, saying, The glory is departed from Israel." 1 Samuel iv. 21. This poem was written upon receipt of the intelligence of Daniel Webster's speech in the U. S. Senate, March 7, 1850, in defence of the Compromise measures, and especially of the Fugitive Slave Law.

Page 273.—LINES WRITTEN ON THE NIGHT OF THE 30TH OF JULY, 1847.—The contest was short, but sharp. For ten days the city was white with broadsides, and the narrow courts off the High street rang with the dismal strains of innumerable ballad-singers. The opposition was nominally directed against both the sitting members, but from the first it was evident that all the scurrility was meant exclusively for Macaulay. He came scathless even out of that ordeal. The vague charge of being too much of an essayist and too little of a politician was the worst that either saint or sinner could find to say of him. The burden of half the election songs was to the effect that he had written poetry, and that one who knew so much of ancient Rome could not possibly be the man for modern England. The day of nomination was the 29th of July. The space in front of the hustings had been packed by the advocates of cheap whiskey. Professor Aytoun, who stooped to second Mr. Blackburn, was applauded to his heart's content, while Macaulay was treated with a brutality the details of which are painful to read and would be worse than useless to record. The polling took place on the morrow. A considerable number of the Tories, instead of plumping for Blackburn or dividing their favors with the sitting members (who were both of them moderate Whigs and supporters of the Establishment), thought fit to give their second votes to Mr. Cowan, an avowed Voluntaryist in church matters and the accepted champion of the Radical party.

"I waited with Mr. Macaulay," says Mr. Adam Black, "in a room of the Merchants' Hall to receive at every hour the numbers who had polled in all the districts. At 10 o'clock we were confounded to find that he was 150 below Cowan, but still had faint hopes that the next hour might turn the scale. The next hour came, and a darker prospect. At 12 o'clock he was 340 below Cowan. It was obvious now that the field was lost, but we were left from hour to hour under the torture of a sinking poll, till at 4 o'clock it stood thus: Cowan, 2063; Craig, 1854; Macaulay, 1477; Blackburn, 980."

That same night, while the town was still alive with jubilation over a triumph that soon lost its gloss even in the eyes of those who had won it, Macaulay, in the grateful silence of his chamber, was weaving his perturbed thoughts into those exquisite lines which tell within the compass of a score of stanzas the essential secret of the life whose outward aspect these volumes have endeavored to portray.—*Macaulay's Life and Letters.*

Page 291.—HARMOZAN.—After a noble defence, Harmozan, the prince or satrap of Ahwaz and Susa, was compelled to surrender his person and his state to the discretion of the caliph; and their interview exhibits a portrait of the Arabian manners. In the presence and by the command of Omar the gay barbarian was despoiled of his silken robes embroidered with gold, and of his tiara bedecked with rubies and emeralds. "Are you not sensible," said the conqueror to his naked captive—"are you not sensible of the judgment of God, and of the different rewards of infidelity and obedience?"—"Alas!" replied Harmozan, "I feel them too deeply. In the days of our common ignorance we fought with the weapons of the flesh, and my nation was superior. God was then neuter; since He has espoused your quarrel you have subverted our kingdom and religion." Oppressed by this painful dialogue, the Persian complained of intolerable thirst, but discovered some apprehension lest he should be killed whilst he was drinking a cup of water. "Be of good courage," said the caliph; "your life is safe till you have drunk this water." The crafty satrap accepted the assurance, and instantly dashed the vase against the ground. Omar would have avenged the deceit, but his companions represented the sanctity of an oath; and the speedy conversion of Harmozan entitled him not only to a free pardon, but even to a stipend of two thousand pieces of gold.—*Gibbon's Rome,* chap. li.

Page 292.—CRESCENTIUS.—Crescentius was consul of the Romans in the reign of the Emperor Otho III. He attempted to shake off the Saxon yoke, and was besieged by Otho in the Mole of Hadrian (long called the Tower of Crescentius). He was betrayed and beheaded.—*Bellew's Poets' Corner.*

Page 292.—THE VENGEANCE OF MUDARA.—Gonçalo Bustos de Salas de Lara, a Castilian hero of the eleventh century, had seven sons. His brother, Rodrigo Velasquez, married a Moorish lady, and these seven nephews were invited to the feast. A fray took place in which one of the seven slew a Moor, and the bride demanded vengeance. Rodrigo, to please his bride, waylaid his brother Gonçalo, and kept him in durance in a dungeon of Cordova, and the seven boys were betrayed into a ravine where they were cruelly murdered. While in the dungeon the daughter of the Moorish king fell in love with Gonçalo and became the mother of Mudara, who avenged the death of Lara's seven sons by slaying Rodrigo. —*Brewer's Dictionary of Phrase and Fable.*

Page 293.—THE BARD.—This ode is founded on a tradition current in Wales, that Edward I., when he completed the conquest of that country, ordered all the Bards that fell into his hands to be put to death. The original argument of this ode, as Mr. Gray had set it down in one of the pages of his commonplace book, was as follows: The army of Edward I., as they march through a deep valley, are suddenly stopped by the appearance of a venerable figure seated on the summit of an inaccessible rock, who, with a voice more than human, reproaches the king with all the misery and desolation which he had brought on his country; foretells the misfortunes of the Norman race, and with prophetic spirit declares that all his cruelty shall never extinguish the noble ardor of poetic genius in this island; and that men shall never be wanting to celebrate true virtue and valor in immortal strains, to expose vice and infamous pleasure, and boldly censure tyranny and oppression. His song ended, he precipitates himself from the mountain, and is swallowed up by the river that rolls at its foot.—*Gray's Poems.*

Page 295.—A VERY MOURNFUL BALLAD.—The effect of the original ballad (which existed both in Spanish and Arabic) was such that it was forbidden to be sung by the Moors, on pain of death, within Granada.—*Byron's Poems.*

Page 296.—THE LORD OF BUTRAGO.—The incident to which this ballad relates is supposed to have occurred on the famous field of Aljubarrota, where King Juan I. of Castile was defeated by the Portuguese. The king, who was at the time in a feeble state of health, exposed himself very much during the action, and, being wounded, had great difficulty in making his escape. The battle was fought A. D. 1385.—*Lockhart's Spanish Ballads.*

Page 297.—MAKE WAY FOR LIBERTY!—This poem is founded on the heroic achievement of Arnold de Winkelried at the battle of Sempach, which was fought on the 9th of July, 1386. In this battle the Swiss gained a great victory over Leopold, Duke of Austria, and secured the liberty of their country, which had been grossly oppressed by Austria.

Page 298.—THE BALLAD OF AGINCOURT.—In the battle of Agincourt, fought on the 25th of October, 1415, Henry V. of England, with an army of about ten thousand men, totally defeated the French under the Constable d'Albret. The French army consisted of about sixty thousand men.

Page 299.—THE BALLAD OF CHEVY CHACE.— There had long been a rivalry between the families of Percy and Douglas, which showed itself by incessant raids into each other's territory. Percy of Northumberland one day vowed he would hunt for three days in the Scottish border without condescending to ask leave of Earl Douglas. The Scottish warden said in his anger, "Tell this vaunter he shall find one day more than sufficient." The ballad called "Chevy Chace" mixes up this hunt with the battle of Otterburn, which, Dr. Percy justly observes, was "a very different event." Chevy Chace means the chase or hunt among the "Chyviat hyls."— *Brewer's Dictionary of Phrase and Fable.*

Page 302.—EDINBURGH AFTER FLODDEN.—The great battle of Flodden was fought upon the 9th of September, 1513. The defeat of the Scottish army, resulting mainly from the fantastic ideas of chivalry entertained by James IV., and his refusal to avail himself of the natural advantages of his position, was by far the most disastrous of any recounted in the history of the northern wars. The whole strength of the kingdom, both Lowland and Highland, was assembled, and the contest was one of the sternest and most desperate upon record. For several hours the issue seemed doubtful. On the left the Scots obtained a decided advantage; on the right they were broken and overthrown; and at last the whole weight of the battle was brought into the centre, where King James and the Earl of Surrey commanded in person. The determined valor of James, imprudent as it was, had the effect of rousing to a pitch of desperation the courage of the meanest soldiers; and the ground becoming soft and slippery from blood, they pulled off their boots and shoes, and secured a firmer footing by fighting in their hose. Both parties did wonders, but none performed more than the king. He would fight not only in person, but on foot. At first he had abundance of success; but at length his battalion was surrounded, and the Scots formed themselves into a ring, and, being resolved to die nobly with their sovereign, who scorned to ask quarter, were altogether cut off. The loss of the Scots was about ten thousand men. The loss to Edinburgh was peculiarly great. All the magistrates and able-bodied citizens had followed their king to Flodden, whence very few of them returned. The news of the overthrow on the field of Flodden overwhelmed the inhabitants with grief and confusion. The streets were crowded with women seeking intelligence about their friends, clamoring and weeping. The city banner referred to in the poem is a standard still held in great honor by the burghers, having been presented to them by James III. in return for their loyal service in 1482. This banner, still conspicuous in the library of the Faculty of Advocates, was honorably brought back from Flodden, and could certainly never have been displayed on a more memorable field. No event in Scottish history ever took a more lasting hold on the public mind than the "woeful fight" of Flodden; and even now the songs and traditions which are current on the Border recall the memory of a contest unsullied by disgrace, though terminating in disaster and defeat.—*Harper's Magazine.*

Page 306.—THE FLOWERS OF THE FOREST.— The "Flowers of the Forest" are the young men of the districts of Selkirkshire and Peeblesshire, anciently known as "the Forest." The song is founded by the author upon an older composition of the same name, deploring the loss of the Scotch at Flodden Field, of which all has been lost except two or three lines.— *Illustrated Book of Scottish Song.*

Page 307. — IVRY. — Henry IV., on his accession to the French throne, was opposed by a large part of his subjects under the Duke of Mayenne, with the assistance of Spain and Savoy, and from the union of these several nations their army was called the "Army of the League." In March, 1590, he gained a decisive victory over that party at Ivry, a small town in France. Before the battle he said to his troops, "My children, if you lose sight of your colors, rally to my white plume; you will always find it in the path to honor and glory." His conduct was answerable to his promise. Nothing could resist his impetuous valor, and the Leaguers underwent a total and bloody defeat. In the midst of the rout Henry followed, crying, "Save the French!" and his clemency added a number of the enemy to his own army.

Page 309.— THE SACK OF BALTIMORE. — Baltimore is a small seaport in the barony of Carbery in South Munster. It grew up round a castle of O'Driscoll's, and was after his ruin colonized by the English. On the 20th of June, 1631, the crews of two Algerine galleys landed in the dead of the night, sacked the town, and bore off into slavery all who were not too old, or too young, or too fierce for their purpose. The pirates were steered up the intricate channel by one Hackett, a Dungarvan fisherman, whom they had taken at sea for the purpose. Two years after, he was convicted and executed for the crime. Baltimore never recovered this. To the artist, the antiquary, and the naturalist its neighborhood is most interesting. (See *The Ancient and Present State of the County and City of Cork*, by Charles Smith, M. D., second edition, Dublin, 1774. Note by Thomas Osborne Davis.)

Page 311.—NASEBY.—The battle of Naseby was fought June 14, 1645, between the royal forces, commanded by Charles I., and the Parliamentary party, nicknamed "Roundheads," under Lord Fairfax. The forces on both sides were about equal, Fairfax having rather the choice of position. At first, Prince Rupert, who commanded the right wing of the royal army, made such an impetuous attack upon the left wing of the Parliamentarians that it was broken and put to flight, and Ireton, its commander, wounded and taken prisoner; but finally Cromwell, who commanded the right wing of Fairfax's army, routed the left wing of the opposing army, and came to the relief of the Parliamentary centre, commanded by Fairfax and Skippon, when the royal army was defeated, and Charles fled from the bloody field, leaving 800 killed, 4500 prisoners, besides his artillery, ammunition, and several thousand stand of arms. The battle virtually decided the war.

Page 313.—WHEN THE ASSAULT WAS INTENDED TO THE CITY. — This sonnet, the first of those which refer to English public affairs, was written in November, 1642, and probably on Saturday, the 12th of that month. The Civil War had then begun, and Milton, already known as a vehement anti-Episcopal pamphleteer and Parliamentarian, was living, with two young nephews whom he was educating, in his house in Aldersgate street, a surburban thoroughfare just beyond one of the city gates of London. After some of the first actions of the war, including the indecisive battle of Edgehill (Oct. 23), the king's army, advancing out of the Midlands, with the king and Prince Rupert present in it, had come as near to London as Hounslow and Brentford, and was threatening a further march to crush the Londoners and the Parliament at once. They were at their nearest on Saturday, the 12th of November; and all that day and the next there was immense excitement in London in expectation of an assault—chains put up across streets, houses barred, etc. It was not till the evening of the 13th that the citizens were reassured by the retreat of the king's army, which had been checked from a closer advance by a rapid march-out of the trained bands under Essex and Skippon. Milton, we are to fancy, had shared the common alarm. His was one of the houses which, if the Cavaliers had been let loose, it would have given them particular pleasure to sack. Knowing this, the only precaution he takes is, hàlf in jest, and yet perhaps with some anxiety, to write a sonnet addressed to the imaginary Royalist captain, colonel, or knight who may command the Aldersgate street sacking-party. "*On his dore when ye citty expected an assault*" is the original heading of the sonnet in the copy of it, by an amanuensis, among the Cambridge MSS., as if the sonnet had actually been pasted or nailed up on the outside of Milton's door. This title was afterward deleted by Milton himself, and the other title substituted in his own hand; but the sonnet appeared without any title at all in the editions of 1645 and 1673.—*Milton*, Masson's edition.

Page 313.—ON THE LATE MASSACRE IN PIEDMONT.—This, the most powerful of Milton's sonnets, was written in 1655, and refers to the persecutions instituted, in the early part of that year, by Charles Emmanuel II., Duke of Savoy and Prince of Piedmont, against his Protestant subjects of the valleys of the Cottian Alps. This Protestant community, half French and half Italian, and known as the Waldenses or Vaudois, were believed to have kept up the tradition of a primitive Christianity from the time of the apostles. There had been various persecutions of them since the Reformation, but that of 1655 surpassed all. By an edict of the duke they were required to part with their property and leave their habitations within twenty days, or else to become Roman Catholics. On their resistance, forces were sent into their valleys, and the most dreadful atrocities followed. Many were butchered, others were taken away in chains, and hundreds of families were driven for refuge to the mountains covered with snow, to live there miserably or perish with cold and hunger. Among the Protestant nations of Europe, and especially in England, the indignation was immediate and violent. Cromwell, who was then Protector, took up the matter with his whole strength. He caused Latin letters, couched in the strongest terms, to be immediately sent, not only to the offending Duke of Savoy, but also to the chief princes and powers of Europe. These letters were drawn up by Milton, and may be read among his Letters of State. An ambassador was also sent to collect information; a Fast Day was appointed; a subscription of £40,000 was raised for the sufferers; and altogether Cromwell's remonstrances were such that, backed as they would have been, if necessary, by armed force, the cruel edict was withdrawn, and a convention made with the Vaudois, allowing them the exercise of their worship. Milton's sonnet is his private and more tremendous expression in verse of the feeling he expressed publicly, in Cromwell's name, in his Latin State Letters.—*Milton*, Masson's edition.

Page 313.—THE EXECUTION OF MONTROSE.— James Graham, Marquis of Montrose, was born at Edinburgh in 1612. Having finished his studies in France, after his return to Scotland he served for a time in the Presbyterian army, but subsequently went over to the royalists. He was appointed by Charles I., in 1644, Marquis of Montrose and commander-in-chief of the Scottish forces. He signally defeated the Covenanters at Tippermuir in 1644, also at Inverlochy and at Kilsyth in 1645; but his army was surprised and totally defeated by General Leslie at Philiphaugh in September, 1645. Montrose soon after went to Germany, where he was received with great distinction by the Austrian emperor and made a marshal of the Empire. Having collected a small but ill-organized force, he returned to Scotland in 1650, but was soon after defeated and taken prisoner. He was executed, without a trial, at Edinburgh, in May, 1650.—*Thomas's Biographical Dictionary.*

Page 316.—THE BONNETS OF BONNIE DUNDEE.— Dundee, enraged at his enemies, and still more at his friends, resolved to retire to the Highlands, and to make preparations for civil war, but with secrecy, for he had been ordered by James to make no public insurrection until assistance should be sent him from Ireland.

Whilst Dundee was in this temper, information was brought him—whether true or false is uncertain—that some of the Covenanters had associated themselves to assassinate him, in revenge for his former severities against their party. He flew to the Convention and demanded justice. The Duke of Hamilton, who wished to get rid of a troublesome adversary, treated his complaint with neglect, and, in order to sting him in the tenderest part, reflected upon that courage which could be alarmed by imaginary dangers. Dundee left the house in a rage, mounted his horse, and with a troop of fifty horsemen, who had deserted to him from his regiment in England, galloped through the city. Being asked by one of his friends, who stopped him, "Where he was going?" he waved his hat, and is reported to have answered, "Wherever the spirit of Montrose shall direct me." In passing under the walls of the Castle, he stopped, scrambled up the precipice at a place difficult and dangerous, and held a conference with the Duke of Gordon at a postern-gate, the marks of which are still to be seen, though the gate itself is built up. Hoping, in vain, to infuse the vigor of his own spirit into the duke, he pressed him to retire with him into the Highlands, raise his vassals there, who were numerous, brave, and faithful, and leave the command of the Castle to Winram, the lieutenant-governor, an officer on whom Dundee could rely. The duke concealed his timidity under the excuse of a soldier. "A soldier," said he, "cannot in honor quit the post that is assigned him." The novelty of the sight drew numbers to the foot of the rock upon which the conference was held. These numbers every minute increased, and, in the end, were mistaken for Dundee's adherents. The Convention was then sitting; news was carried thither that Dundee was at the gates with an army, and had prevailed upon the governor of the Castle to fire upon the town. The Duke of Hamilton, whose intelligence was better, had the presence of mind, by improving the moment of agitation, to overwhelm the one party, and provoke the other, by their fears. He ordered the doors of the house to be shut, and the keys to be laid on the table before him. He cried out, "That there was danger within as well as without doors; that traitors must be held in confinement until the present danger was over; but that the friends of liberty had nothing to fear, for that thousands were ready to start up in their defence at the stamp of his foot." He ordered the drums to be beat and the trumpets to sound through the city. In an instant vast swarms of those who had been brought into town by him and Sir John Dalrymple from the western counties, and who had been hitherto hid in garrets and cellars, showed themselves in the streets; not, indeed, in the proper habiliments of war, but in arms, and with looks fierce and sullen, as if they felt disdain at their former concealment. This unexpected sight increased the noise and tumult of the town, which grew loudest in the square adjoining the house where the members were confined, and appeared still louder to those who were within, because they were ignorant of the cause from which the tumult arose, and caught contagion from the anxious looks of each other. After some hours the doors were thrown open, and the Whig members, as they went out, were received with acclamations, and those of the opposite party with the threats and curses of a *prepared* populace. Terrified by the prospect of future alarms, many of the adherents of James quitted the Convention and retired to the country; most of them changed sides; only a very few of the most resolute continued their attendance.—*Dalrymple's Memoirs.*

Page 317.—THE BURIAL MARCH OF DUNDEE.—John Graham, Viscount Dundee, was born in 1643. He served in the French army from 1668 to 1672, and next entered the Dutch service as cornet in the Prince of Orange's horse-guards, and is reported to have saved the life of the prince at the battle of Seneffe in 1674. Returning to Scotland, he took a prominent part in the persecution of the Covenanters and in the attempt to force Episcopacy on the people of that country. In 1688, on the eve of the Revolution, he was raised to the peerage by James II. as Viscount Dundee and Lord Graham of Claverhouse. When James was driven from the throne, Dundee remained faithful to the fallen monarch. He was joined by the Jacobite Highland clans and by auxiliaries from Ireland, and raised the standard of rebellion against the government of William and Mary. After various movements in the North, he advanced upon Blair in Athol, and General Mackay, commanding the government forces, hastened to meet him. The two armies confronted each other at the Pass of Killiecrankie, July 27, 1689. Mackay's force was about four thousand men; Dundee's, twenty-five hundred foot, with one troop of horse. A few minutes decided the contest. After both armies had exchanged fire, the Highlanders rushed on with their swords, and the enemy instantly scattered and gave way. Mackay lost by death and capture two thousand five hundred men; the victors, nine hundred. Dundee fell by a musket-shot while waving on one of his battalions to advance. He was carried off the field to Urrard House, or Blair Castle, and there expired.

Page 321.—FONTENOY.—The battle of Fontenoy was fought between the French, under Marshal Saxe, and the English, Dutch, and Austrians, under the Duke of Cumberland, May 11, 1745. The fortunes of war were at first in favor of the French, who were posted on a hill behind Fontenoy, when Cumberland, heading a column of fourteen thousand British and Hanoverian infantry, with fixed bayonets, plunged down the ravine separating the two armies, and gained the hill, carrying everything before him. The day was apparently lost to the French, and Marshal Saxe in vain urged the king to fly. At this critical moment the Irish brigade charged on the English flank, and changed the apparent defeat into a decisive victory.

Page 323.—LOCHIEL'S WARNING.—Lochiel, the chief of the warlike clan of the Camerons, and descended from ancestors distinguished in their narrow sphere for great personal prowess, was a man worthy of a better cause and fate than that in which he embarked--the enterprise of the Stuarts in 1745. His memory is still fondly cherished among the Highlanders by the appellation of the "gentle Lochiel," for he was famed for his social virtues as much as his martial and magnanimous (though mistaken) loyalty. His influence was so important among the Highland chiefs, that it depended on his joining with his clan whether the standard of Charles should be raised or not in 1745. Lochiel was himself too wise a man to be blind to the consequences of so hopeless an enterprise, but his sensibility to the point of honor overruled his wisdom. Lochiel, with many arguments, but in vain, pressed the Pretender to return to France and reserve himself and his friends for a more favorable occasion, as he had come, by his own acknowledgment, without arms, or money, or adherents; or, at all events, to remain concealed till his friends should meet and deliberate what was best to be done. Charles, whose mind was wound up to the utmost impatience, paid no regard to his proposal, but answered that he was determined to put all to the hazard. "In a few days," said he, "I will erect the royal standard, and will proclaim to the people of Great Britain that Charles Stuart is come over to claim the crown of his ancestors, and to win it or perish in the attempt. Lochiel, who my father has often told me was our firmest friend, may stay at home and learn from the newspapers the fate of his prince." "No," said Lochiel, "I will share the fate of my prince, and so shall every man over whom nature or fortune hath given me any power."—*Campbell's Poems*, note.

Page 327.—THE TEARS OF SCOTLAND.—Written on the barbarities committed in the Highlands by the English forces under the command of the Duke of Cumberland after the battle of Culloden, 1746. It is said that Smollett originally finished the poem in six stanzas, when some one representing that such a diatribe against government might injure his prospects, he sat down and added the still more pointed invective of the seventh stanza. —*Chambers's Cyclopædia of English Literature.*

Page 328.—LOUIS XV.—The story of the king's meeting a coffin was in everybody's mouth. No one here had heard it. So Jerome told that the king was fond of asking questions of strangers, and particularly about disease, death, and churchyards, because he thought his gay attendants did not like to hear of such things. One day he was hunting in the forest of Senard when he met a man on horseback carrying a coffin. "Where are you carrying that coffin?" asked the king. "To the village yonder." "Is it for a man or a woman?" "For a man." "What did he die of?" "Of hunger." The king clapped spurs to his horse and rode away.—*The Peasant and the Prince*, by Harriet Martineau.

Page 329.—PAUL REVERE'S RIDE.—Paul Revere was one of the four engravers in America at the time of the Revolution, and one of the most active participants in the political movements immediately preceding the breaking out of the war. He was prominent in the destruction of the tea in Boston harbor, and was sent to Philadelphia and New York to convey the news of that event; and again visited those cities to enlist their sympathy and co-operation when the decree for closing the port of Boston was passed. On the night of April 18th, 1775, Dr. Joseph Warren sent him and William Dawes to Lexington and Concord to give notice of General Gage's intended expedition to destroy the Provincial military stores and cannon at Concord. Dawes went by way of Roxborough to Lexington, while Revere went through Charlestown. After the latter had crossed the Charles River orders were sent from the British head-quarters to arrest him, but, eluding the British sentinels, he rowed across the Charles River five minutes before the order was received, and galloped through the country to Lexington, arousing the inhabitants as he went along. The two messengers passed through Lexington a little after midnight, and aroused Hancock and Adams, who were lodging at the house of the Rev. Jonas Clark, and then hurried on to Concord. They were afterward taken prisoners, and brought as far as Lexington, but were released in the confusion of the battle.

Page 331.—SONG OF MARION'S MEN.—The exploits of General Francis Marion, the famous partisan warrior of South Carolina, form an interesting chapter in the annals of the American Revolution. The British troops were so harassed by the irregular and successful warfare which he kept up at the head of a few daring followers, that they sent an officer to remonstrate with him for not coming into the open field and fighting "like a gentleman and a Christian."—*Notes to Bryant's Poems.*

Page 340.—HOHENLINDEN.—During his tour in Germany, Campbell saw a battle from a convent near Ratisbon, and he saw the field of Ingolstadt after a battle. From such experiences he derived his poem on the battle in which the French defeated the Austrians at Hohenlinden on the 3d of December, 1800. Ten thousand Austrians were killed or wounded, and as many were made prisoners.—*Morley's Shorter English Poems.*

Page 341.—BATTLE OF THE BALTIC.—In December, 1800, a maritime alliance was formed between Russia, Prussia, Denmark, and Sweden in regard to the rights of neutral nations in war. For the purpose of breaking up this confederacy a fleet of 52 sail was sent in March, 1801, to the Baltic under Sir Hyde Parker, Nelson consenting to act as second in command. The squadron passed the Sound on the 30th, and entered the harbor of Copenhagen. To Nelson, at the head of 12 ships of the line and smaller vessels, making 36 in all, was assigned the attack; against him were opposed 18 vessels mounting 628 guns, moored in a line a mile in length and flanked by two batteries. The action began about 10 A. M., April 2, and lasted five hours. About 1 o'clock Sir Hyde Parker made the signal for discontinuing. Nelson ordered it to be acknowledged, but, putting the glass to his blind eye, exclaimed, "I really don't see the signal. Keep mine for closer battle still flying. That's the way I answer such signals. Nail mine to the mast." By 2 o'clock, the Danish fleet being almost entirely taken or destroyed, he wrote to the crown prince the following note: "Vice-Admiral Nelson has been commanded to spare Denmark when she no longer resists. The line of defence which covered her shores has struck to the British flag; but if the firing is continued on the part of Denmark, he must set on fire all the prizes he has taken, without having the power of saving the men who have so nobly defended them. The brave Danes are the brothers, and should never be the enemies, of the English." An armistice of fourteen weeks was agreed to, and in the mean time the accession of Alexander to the throne of Russia broke up the confederacy and left matters on their old footing. For this battle, which Nelson said was the most terrible of all in which he had ever been engaged, he was raised to the rank of viscount.—*Appleton's Cyclopædia.*

Page 344. — CASABIANCA. — Young Casabianca, a boy about thirteen years old, son of the admiral of the Orient, remained at his post (in the battle of the Nile) after the ship had taken fire and all the guns had been abandoned, and perished in the explosion of the vessel when the flames had reached the powder.—*Hemans's Poems.*

Page 344.—THE ANGELS OF BUENA VISTA.—At the terrible fight of Buena Vista, Mexican women were seen hovering near the field of death for the purpose of giving aid and succor to the wounded. One poor woman was found surrounded by the maimed and suffering of both armies, ministering to the wants of Americans as well as Mexicans with impartial tenderness.

Page 346.—MARCO BOZZARIS.—Marco Bozzaris was one of the bravest and best of the modern Greek chieftains. He fell in a night-attack upon the Turkish camp at Laspi, the site of the ancient Platæa, August 20, 1823, and expired in the moment of victory.—*Halleck's Poems.*

Page 347.—ON THE EXTINCTION OF THE VENETIAN REPUBLIC. — During the revolutionary movements of 1848, Venice in March revolted against the Austrian rule and proclaimed the restoration of the republic; but after enduring a long siege and a terrible bombardment, she capitulated on August 23, 1849, and on the 30th Radetzky entered the city, which was not released from the state of siege until May 1, 1854.—*Appleton's Cyclopædia.*

Page 347.—THE CHARGE OF THE LIGHT BRIGADE.—The battle of Balaklava was fought October, 1854, between the allied English, French, and Turkish forces, under Lord Raglan, Omar Pacha, and Marshal St. Arnaud, and the Russian armies; the fighting being principally by the English and Russians. The brilliant but useless charge of the Light Brigade has made this battle famous in song and story, but it really did little toward deciding the result of the war.

Page 353.—THE STAR-SPANGLED BANNER.—This song was composed under the following circumstances: A gentleman had left Baltimore with a flag of truce for the purpose of getting released from the British fleet a friend of his, who had been captured at Marlborough. He went as far as the mouth of the Patuxent, and was not permitted to return, lest the intended attack on Baltimore should be disclosed. He was therefore brought up the bay to the mouth of the Patapsco, where the flag-vessel was kept under the guns of a frigate; and he was compelled to witness the bombardment of Fort McHenry, which the admiral had boasted he would carry in a few hours, and that the city must fall. He watched the flag at the fort through the whole day, with anxiety that can be better felt than described, until the night prevented him from seeing it. In the night he watched the bomb-shells, and at early dawn his eye was again greeted by the flag of his country.—*McCarty's National Songs.*

Page 359.—PIBROCH OF DONUIL DHU.—This is a very ancient pibroch belonging to Clan MacDonald, and supposed to refer to the expedition of Donald Balloch, who, in 1431, launched from the Isles with a considerable force, invaded Lochaber, and at Inverlochy defeated and put to flight the Earls of Mar and Caithness, though at the head of an army superior to his own.—*Scott's Poems,* Abbotsford ed.

Page 362.—THE HARP THAT ONCE THROUGH TARA'S HALLS.—Tara, or Tarah, was from the earliest times the capital of Ireland. Each province appears to have had its own king, but he was subject to the monarch who ruled in person over the central district of Meath and resided at Tarah. There is now preserved in the old museum of Trinity College, at Dublin, an old harp which is said to have been owned by one of these old monarchs of Ireland at Tara. It is made of willow and oak, and ornamented with brass and silver and various carvings. Only one of its twenty-eight strings remains. The following history is told of it: It was at one time the property of Brian Borumha or Brien Boroimhe, monarch of Ireland, about the year A. D. 1000. After his death, at the battle of Clontarf, in 1014, it was presented by his son to the pope. After remaining in the Vatican for several centuries it was given by Pope Leo X. to Henry VIII. of England, who transmitted it to the first earl of Clanricarde. It passed from the possession of one family to that of another, until at the end of the last century the marquis of Conyngham gave it to the museum of Trinity College, where it now can be seen.—*Literary World, Boston.*

Page *367.*—SIR PATRICK SPENS.—The name of Sir Patrick Spens is not mentioned in history, but I am able to state that tradition has preserved it. In the little island of Papa Stronsay, one of the Orcadian group, lying over against Norway, there is a large grave, or *tumulus,* which has been known to the inhabitants, from time immemorial, as "the grave of Sir Patrick Spens." . . . The people know nothing beyond the traditional appellation of the spot, and they have no legend to tell. Spens is a Scottish, not a Scandinavian name. Is it, then, a forced conjecture that the shipwreck took place off the iron-bound coast of the northern islands, which did not then belong to the crown of Scotland?—*Aytoun (Noted Names of Fiction).*

Page *372.*—HOW THEY BROUGHT THE GOOD NEWS.—The following is an extract from a private note of Robert Browning, dated London, Jan. 23, 1881: "There is no sort of historical foundation for the poem about 'Good News to Ghent.' I wrote it under the bulwark of a vessel, off the African coast, after I had been at sea long enough to appreciate even the fancy of a gallop on the back of a certain good horse 'York,' then in my stable at home. It was written in pencil on the fly-leaf of Bartoli's *Simboli,* I remember."—*Literary World, Boston.*

Page *374.*—THE WANDERING JEW.—The story of the "Wandering Jew" is of considerable antiquity. It had obtained full credit in this part of the world before the year 1228, as we learn from Matthew Paris; for in that year, it seems, there came an Armenian archbishop into England to visit the shrines and reliques preserved in our churches; who, being entertained at the monastery of St. Albans, was asked several questions relating to his country, etc. Among the rest, a monk who sat near him inquired "if he had ever seen or heard of the famous person named Joseph, that was so much talked of, who was present at our Lord's crucifixion and conversed with him, and who was still alive, in confirmation of the Christian faith." The archbishop answered that the fact was true; and afterward one of his train, who was well known to a servant of the abbot's, interpreting his master's words, told them in French " that his lord knew the person they spoke of very well; that he had dined at his table but a little while before he left the East; that he had been Pontius Pilate's porter, by name Cartaphilus, who, when they were dragging Jesus out of the door of the judgment-hall, struck him with his fist on the back, saying, 'Go faster, Jesus, go faster! why dost thou linger?' Upon which Jesus looked at him with a frown and said, 'I indeed am going, but thou shalt tarry till I come.' Soon after he was converted, and baptized by the name of Joseph. He lives for ever, but at the end of every hundred years falls into an incurable illness, and at length into a fit or ecstasy, out of which, when he recovers, he returns to the same state of youth he was in when Jesus suffered, being then about thirty years of age. He remembers all the circumstances of the death and resurrection of Christ, the saints that arose with him, the composing of the apostles' creed, their preaching and dispersion, and is himself a very grave and holy person." This is the substance of Matthew Paris's account, who was himself a monk of St. Albans, and was living at the time when the Armenian archbishop made the above relation.

Since his time several impostors have appeared at intervals under the name and character of the "Wandering Jew," whose several histories may be seen in Calmet's *Dictionary of the Bible.* See also *The Turkish Spy,* vol. ii., book 3, let. 1. The story that is copied in the following ballad is of one who appeared at Hamburg in 1547, and pretended he had been a Jewish shoemaker at the time of Christ's crucifixion. The ballad, however, seems to be of a later date.—*Percy's Reliques.*

Page *375.*—THE DREAM OF EUGENE ARAM.— Eugene Aram, the son of a poor gardener, but who by the most indefatigable industry and unswerving perseverance in the face of the greatest difficulties had won for himself the reputation of extensive scholarship, was a schoolmaster in Knaresborough. In 1745 he was implicated in a robbery committed by Daniel Clark, a shoemaker of that place, but was acquitted for want of evidence. Nevertheless, he left Knaresborough and went to London, while at the same time Clark mysteriously disappeared. Nothing was known of the matter until February, 1759, nearly fourteen years afterward, when a skeleton was dug up near Knaresborough which was suspected to be that of the shoemaker. At the time of this discovery Aram was an usher at an academy in Lynn, pursuing his favorite studies of heraldry, botany, the Chaldee, Arabic, Welsh, and Irish languages, and was just engaged in compiling a comparative lexicon of the English, Latin, Greek, Hebrew, and Celtic languages, when he was suddenly arrested on the charge of murder. At the trial he conducted his own defence with wonderful ability and ingenuity, but the evidence of his crime was overwhelming, and he was found guilty. After his condemnation he confessed his guilt and attempted to commit suicide, but was discovered before he had bled to death, and expiated his crime on the gallows.

Page 378. — Inchcape Rock. — An old writer mentions a curious tradition which may be worth quoting. "By east the Isle of May," says he, "twelve miles from all land, in the German seas, lyes a great hidden rock, called Inchcape, very dangerous for navigators, because it is overflowed everie tide. It is reported, in old times upon the saide rock there was a bell, fixed upon a tree or timber, which rang continually, being moved by the sea, giving notice to the saylers of the danger. This bell or clocke was put there and maintained by the abbot of Aberbrothok, and being taken down by a sea-pirate, a yeare thereafter he perished upon the same rocke, with ship and goodes, in the righteous judgment of God." — *Stoddart's Remarks on Scotland.*

Page 379. — CUMNOR HALL. — The death of Lord Dudley's deserted wife at this critical juncture, under peculiarly suspicious circumstances, gave rise to dark rumors that she had been put out of the way to enable him to accept the willing hand of a royal bride. Several days before the tragedy was perpetrated at Cumnor Hall, it had been reported in the court that she was very ill and not expected to recover, although at that time in perfect health. The Spanish ambassador, De Quadra, writes to the Duchess of Parma: "The queen, on her return from hunting, told me that Lord Robert's wife was dead, or nearly so, and begged me to say nothing about it. Assuredly it is a matter full of shame and infamy. Since this was written," His Excellency adds, "the death of Lord Robert's wife has been given out publicly." The queen said in Italian, "She had broken her neck; she was found dead at the foot of a staircase at Cumnor Hall." There was certainly a great lack of feminine feeling in the brief, hard terms in which Elizabeth announced the tragic fate of the unfortunate lady, from whom she had alienated a husband's love. Lever, one of the popular preachers of the day, wrote to Cecil, "that the country was full of dangerous suspicion and muttering of the death of her that was Lord Robert Dudley's wife, and entreated that there might be an earnest investigation, with punishment if any were found guilty; for if the matter were hushed up or passed over, the displeasure of God, the dishonor of the queen, and the danger of the whole realm were to be feared." Lord Robert caused a coroner's inquest to sit on the body of his deceased wife, but we detect him in correspondence with the foreman of the jury; and, although a verdict of accidental death was returned, Lord Robert continued to be burdened with the suspicion of having contrived the murder, or, to use Cecil's more expressive words, "was infamed by the death of his wife." Throckmorton, the English ambassador at Paris, was so thoroughly mortified at the light in which this affair was regarded on the Continent that he wrote to Cecil: "The bruits be so *brim*, and so maliciously reported here, touching the marriage of the Lord Robert and the death of his wife, that I know not where to turn me nor what countenance to bear."—*Strickland's Queens of England.*

Page 381.—THE DOWIE DENS OF YARROW.— This ballad was first published in the *Minstrelsy of the Scottish Border;* but other versions of it were previously in circulation, and it is stated by Sir Walter Scott to have been "a very great favorite among the inhabitants of Ettrick Forest," where it is universally believed to be founded on fact. Sir Walter, indeed, "found it easy to collect a variety of copies;" and from them he collated the present edition—avowedly for the purpose of "suiting the tastes of these more light and giddy-paced times." A copy is contained in Motherwell's *Minstrelsy, Ancient and Modern;* another in Buchan's *Ballads and Songs of the North of Scotland;* it no doubt originated the popular composition beginning—

"Busk ye, busk ye, my bonny, bonny bride,"

by Hamilton of Bangour, first published in Ramsay's *Tea-Table Miscellany,* and suggested the ballad "The Braes of Yarrow," by the Rev. John Logan. In Herd's *Collection,* in Ritson's *Scottish Songs,* and in the *Tea-Table Miscellany* are to be found fragments of another ballad, entitled "Willie's drowned in Yarrow," of which this is the concluding stanza:

"She sought him east, she sought him west,
  She sought him braid and narrow;
Syne in the cleaving of a craig,
  She found him drowned in Yarrow."

Indeed, "Yarrow stream" has been a fertile source of poetry, and seems to have inspired the poets; the very sound is seductive: and, as Mr. Buchan remarks, "All who have attempted to sing its praise or celebrate the actions of those who have been its visitors have almost universally succeeded in their attempts."

That the several versions of the story scattered among the people and preserved by them in some form or other had one common origin there can be little doubt. "Tradition," according to Sir Walter Scott, "places the event recorded in the song very early, and it is probable the ballad was composed soon afterward, although the language has been modernized in the course of its transmission to us through the inaccurate channel of oral tradition." "The hero of the ballad," he adds, "was a knight of great bravery, called Scott;" and he believes it refers to a duel fought at Deucharswyre, of which Annan's Treat is a part, betwixt John Scott of Tushielaw and his brother-in-law Walter Scott, third son of Robert of Thirlstane, in which the latter was slain. Annan's Treat is a low muir on the banks of the Yarrow, lying to the west of Yarrow kirk. Two tall unhewn masses of stone are erected about eighty yards distant from each other, and the least child, that can herd a cow, will tell the passenger that there lie "the two lords who were slain in single combat." Sir Walter also informs us that, according to tradition, the murderer was the brother of either the wife or the betrothed bride of the murdered, and that the alleged cause of quarrel was the lady's father having proposed to endow her with half of his property upon her marriage with a warrior of such renown. The name of the murderer is said to have been Annan, hence the place of combat is still called Annan's Treat.—*Percy's Reliques.*

Page 387.—HARTLEAP WELL.—Hartleap Well is a small spring of water about five miles from Richmond in Yorkshire, and near the side of the road that leads from Richmond to Askrigg. Its name is derived from a remarkable chase, the memory of which is preserved by the monuments spoken of in the second part of the following poem, which monuments do now exist as I have there described them.—*Wordsworth,* 8vo ed.

Page 393. — KATHARINE JANFARIE. — Of this ballad—first published in the *Minstrelsy of the Scottish Border*—the editor informs us that it is "given from several recited copies." It has obviously undergone some alteration, yet much of the rugged character of the original has been retained. The scenery of the ballad is said by tradition to lie upon the banks of the Caddenwater, "a small rill which joins the Tweed (from the north) betwixt Inverleithen and Clovenford." It is also traditionally stated that Katharine Janfarie "lived high up in the glen"—a beautiful and sequestered vale connected with Traquair, and situated about three miles above Traquair House. The recited copies, from which it is probable Sir Walter Scott collected the verses he has here brought together, exist in Buchan's *Ancient Ballads and Songs,* and in Motherwell's *Minstrelsy, Ancient and Modern.* It derives interest and importance, however, less from its intrinsic merit than from the circumstance of its having given to Scott the hint upon which he founded one of the most brilliant and spirit-stirring of his compositions — the famous and favorite ballad of "Young Lochinvar."—*Percy's Reliques.*

Page 395.—O'CONNOR'S CHILD.—The poem of "O'Connor's Child" is an exquisitely finished and pathetic tale. The rugged and ferocious features of ancient feudal manners and family pride are there displayed in connection with female suffering, love, and beauty, and with the romantic and warlike coloring suited to the country and times. It is full of antique grace and passionate energy —the mingled light and gloom of the wild Celtic character. — *Chambers's Cyclopædia of English Literature.*

Page 398.—PRISONER OF CHILLON. — François de Bonnivard was born in Seyssel, in the department of Ain, in 1496. Having adopted republican opinions, he took sides with the Genevese against Duke Charles III. of Savoy; but he had the misfortune in 1530 to fall into the power of the latter, who confined him six years in the castle of Chillon. The Château de Chillon is situated between Clarens and Villeneuve, which last is at one extremity of the Lake of Geneva. On its left are the entrances of the Rhone, and opposite are the heights of Meillerie and the range of the Alps above Boveret and St. Gingo. Near it, on a hill behind, is a torrent; below it, washing its walls, the lake has been fathomed to the depth of eight hundred feet (French measure); within it are a range of dungeons, in which the early Reformers, and subsequently prisoners of state, were confined. Across one of the vaults is a beam black with age, on which we were informed that the condemned were formerly executed. In the cells are seven pillars, or rather eight, one being half merged in the wall; in some of these are rings for the fetters and fettered; in the pavement the steps of Bonnivard have left their traces.

Page 402.—FAIR HELEN.—The story upon which this ballad is founded is thus related in the first edition of the *Statistics of Scotland*: "In the burial-ground of Kirkconnell are still to be seen the tombstones of Fair Helen and her favorite lover, Adam Fleeming. She was a daughter of the family of Kirkconnell, and fell a victim to the jealousy of a lover. Being courted by two young gentlemen at the same time, the one of whom, thinking himself slighted, vowed to sacrifice the other to his resentment when he again discovered him in her company. An opportunity soon presented itself when the faithful pair, walking along the romantic banks of the Kirtle, were discovered from the opposite banks by the assassin. Helen, perceiving him lurking among the bushes, and dreading the fatal resolution, rushed to her lover's bosom to rescue him from the danger, and thus receiving the wound intended for another, sank and expired in her favorite's arms. He immediately avenged her death and slew her murderer. The inconsolable Adam Fleeming, now sinking under the pressure of grief, went abroad and served under the banners of Spain against the infidels. The impression, however, was too strong to be obliterated. The image of woe attended him thither, and the pleasing remembrance of the tender scenes that were past, with the melancholy reflection that they could never return, harassed his soul and deprived his mind of repose. He soon returned, and stretching himself on her grave, expired, and was buried by her side. Upon the tombstone are engraven a sword and cross, with 'Hic jacet Adamus Fleeming.'"—*Burns's Works*, Blackie and Son's edition.

Page 408.—BULL-FIGHT OF GAZUL.—Gazul is the name of one of the Moorish heroes who figure in the *Historia de las Guerras Civiles de Granada*. The following ballad is one of the very many in which the dexterity of the Moorish cavaliers in the bull-fight is described. The reader will observe that the shape, activity, and resolution of the unhappy animal destined to furnish the amusement of the spectators are enlarged upon, just as the qualities of a modern race-horse might be among ourselves; nor is the bull without his *name*. The day of the Baptist is a festival among the Mussulmans as well as among Christians.—*Lockhart's Spanish Ballads*.

Page 409.—GOD'S JUDGMENT ON A WICKED BISHOP.—It hapned in the year 914, that there was an exceeding great famine in Germany, at what time Otho, surnamed the Great was Emperor, and one Hatto, once Abbot of Fulda, was Archbishop of Mentz, of the Bishops after Crescens and Crescentius the two and thirtieth, of the Archbishops after St. Bonifacius the thirteenth. This Hatto in the time of this great famine afore-mentioned, when he saw the poor people of the country exceedingly oppressed with famine, assembled a great company of them together into a Barne, and, like a most accursed and mercilesse caitiffe, burnt up those poor innocent souls, that were so far from doubting any such matter, that they rather hoped to receive some comfort and relief at his hands. The reason that moved the prelat to commit that execrable impiety was, because he thought the famine would the sooner cease, if those unprofitable beggars, that consumed more bread than they were worthy to eat, were dispatched out of the world. For he said that those poor folks were like to Mice, that were good for nothing but to devour corne. But God Almighty, the just avenger of the poor folks quarrel, did not long suffer this hainous tyranny, this most detestable fact, unpunished. For he mustered up an army of Mice against the Archbishop, and sent them to persecute him as his furious Alastors, so that they afflicted him both day and night, and would not suffer him to take his rest in any place. Whereupon the Prelate, thinking he should be secure from the injury of Mice if he were in a certain tower, that standeth in the Rhine near to the towne, betook himself unto the said tower as to a safe refuge and sanctuary from his enemies, and locked himself in. But the innumerable troupes of Mice chased him continually very eagerly, and swumme unto him upon the top of the water to execute the just judgment of God, and so at last he was most miserably devoured by those sillie creatures; who pursued him with such bitter hostility, that it is recorded they scraped and knawed out his very name from the walls and tapistry wherein it was written, after they had so cruelly devoured his body. Wherefore the tower wherein he was eaten up by the Mice is shewn to this day, for a perpetual monument to all succeeding ages of the barbarous and inhuman tyranny of this impious Prelate, being situate in a little green Island in the midst of the Rhine near to the towne of Bingen, and is commonly called in the German Tongue the Mowse-turn.—*Coryat's Crudities*.

Page 417.—BARBARA ALLEN'S CRUELTY.—There are several versions of this popular ballad, and we have chosen the one adopted by Mr. Allingham in his *Ballad Book*. Allingham says: "No doubt, however, those who have been bred up, as it were, in a particular form of a ballad will be apt, at least at first, to mislike any other form. One who has had impressed upon his youthful mind—

'It was in or about the Martinmas time,
  When the green leaves were a-fallin',
That Sir John Graeme in the west countrie
  Fell in love with Barbara Allen,'—

may very likely be ill-content to find name of person and season of year altered, as they are in this equally authentic version. But let him not, therefore, fall foul of the editor, who was bound to choose without prejudice between Autumn and Spring, Jemmy Grove and Sir John."

Page 417.—LAMENT OF THE BORDER WIDOW.—This fragment, obtained from recitation in the Forest of Ettrick, is said to relate to the execution of Cockburne of Henderland, a Border freebooter hanged over the gate of his own tower by James V. in the course of that memorable expedition in 1529 which was fatal to Johnie Armstrong, Adam Scott of Tushielaw, and many other marauders.—*Sir Walter Scott*.

Page 421.—A SONG OF THE NORTH.—In May, 1845, Sir John Franklin sailed from England with the two ships Erebus and Terror, to discover a north-west passage through the Arctic seas. Not returning, several expeditions were sent out in search, among which was the celebrated one headed by the late Dr. E. K. Kane, Lady Franklin, especially, being indefatigable in her endeavors to ascertain his fate, but without any success until 1854, when Dr. Rae found some relics, and in 1859, Captain McClintock discovered on the shore of King William's Land a record deposited in a cairn by the survivors of Franklin's company. This document was dated April 25, 1848, and stated that Sir John died June 11, 1847—that the Erebus and Terror were abandoned April 22, 1848, when the survivors, 105 in number, started for the Great Fish River. Many relics were also found of this party, who perished on their journey, probably soon after leaving the vessels. It appears also that Sir John really did discover the long-sought-for north-west passage, but the knowledge of its whereabouts perished with him, although subsequent expeditions have been sent out to find it.

Page 456.—THE DEATH OF THE FLOWERS.—The verse beginning—

"And then I think of one who in her youthful beauty died,"

is an allusion to the memory of the poet's sister, who died of consumption in 1824.—*Duyckinck's Cyclopædia of American Literature.*

Page 504.—LINES ON THE MERMAID TAVERN.—The Mermaid Tavern was the resort of Ben Jonson and his literary friends, members of a club established by Sir Walter Raleigh in 1603, and numbering among them Shakespeare, Beaumont, Fletcher, Donne, Selden, and the noblest names in English authorship. Truly might Beaumont, in his poetical epistle to Jonson, exclaim—

"What things have seen
  Done at the Mermaid; heard words that have been
So nimble, and so full of subtle flame,
As if that every one from whom they came
Had mean'd to put his whole wit in a jest!"
 —*Chambers's Book of Days.*

Page 513.—ALNWICK CASTLE.—Alnwick Castle is one of the finest in England. It is built of freestone, in the Gothic style, and covers five acres of ground, and was restored in 1830 at an outlay of $1,000,000. It belongs to the Duke of Northumberland, a descendant of the Percys so famed in ancient ballads, and especially for their feuds with their neighbors on the other side of the border, the noble Douglases. One of the Percys was an emperor of Constantinople, another was a major in the British army, and "fought for King George at Lexington" and at the battle of the Brandywine.

Page 514.— HELLVELLYN. — In the spring of 1805 a young gentleman of talents, and of a most amiable disposition, perished by losing his way on the mountain Hellvellyn. His remains were not discovered till three months afterward, when they were found guarded by a faithful terrier bitch, his constant attendant during frequent solitary rambles through the wilds of Cumberland and Westmoreland.—*Scott's Poems.*

Page 517.—THE MEETING OF THE WATERS.—"The Meeting of the Waters" forms a part of that beautiful scenery which lies between Rathdrum and Arklow, in the county of Wicklow, and these lines were suggested by a visit to this romantic spot in the summer of the year 1807.—*Moore's Works,* 8vo.

Page 522.—THE LAKE OF THE DISMAL SWAMP.—Moore's "Lake of the Dismal Swamp," written at Norfolk, in Virginia, is founded on the following legend: "A young man who lost his mind upon the death of a girl he loved, and who, suddenly disappearing from his friends, was never afterward heard of. As he had frequently said in his ravings that the girl was not dead, but gone to the *Dismal Swamp,* it is supposed he had wandered into that dreary wilderness, and had died of hunger or had been lost in some of its dreadful morasses."—*Frederick Saunders's Festival of Song.*

Page 523.—ON THE MORNING OF CHRIST'S NATIVITY.—This magnificent ode, called by Hallam "perhaps the finest in the English language," was composed, as we learn from Milton's own heading of it in the edition of 1645, in the year 1629. Milton was then twenty-one years of age, in the sixth academic year at Cambridge, and a B. A. of a year's standing. There is an interesting allusion to the ode by Milton himself, when he was in the act of composing it, in the sixth of his Latin elegies. In that elegy, addressed to his friend Charles Diodati, residing in the country, in answer to a friendly epistle which Diodati had sent to him on the 13th of December, 1629, there is a distinct description of the "Ode on the Nativity" as then finished, or nearly so, and ready to be shown to Diodati, together with the express information that it was begun on Christmas Day, 1629.—*Milton,* Masson's ed.

Page 549.—EMIGRANTS IN THE BERMUDAS.—Representative government was introduced into the Bermudas in 1620, and in 1621 the Bermuda Company of London issued a sort of charter to the colony, including rights and liberties—among them liberty of worship—that attracted many of those English emigrants whose feeling Marvell has here fashioned into song.—*Morley's Shorter Poems of the English Language.*

Page 550.—REBECCA'S HYMN.—It was in the twilight of the day when her trial—if it could be called such—had taken place, that a low knock was heard at the door of Rebecca's prison-chamber. It disturbed not the inmate, who was then engaged in the evening prayer recommended by her religion, and which concluded with a hymn which we have ventured thus to translate into English.—*Ivanhoe.*

Page 593.—I Would Not Live Alway.—This hymn was written without the remotest idea that any portion of it would ever be employed in the devotions of the Church. Whatever service it has done in that way is owing to the late Bishop of Pennsylvania, then the rector of St. Ann's Church, Brooklyn, who made the selection of verses out of the whole which constitutes the present hymn, and offered it to the Committee on Hymns appointed by the General Convention of ——. The hymn was at first rejected by the committee, of which the unknown author was a member, who, upon a satirical criticism being made upon it, earnestly voted against its adoption. It was admitted on the importunate application of Dr. Onderdonk to the bishops on the committee.—*Duyckinck's Cyclopædia of American Literature.*

Page 630.—Elegy Written in a Country Churchyard.—As he was floating down the river to attack Quebec, General Wolfe read the "Elegy" in low tones to his officers, and upon its conclusion said: "I had rather be the author of that poem than take Quebec"—a remark which has perhaps done as much to perpetuate Wolfe's name as the capture of Quebec, great as that achievement was.

Page 637.—Stanzas.—These beautiful lines were composed by Hood on his death-bed.

Page 642.—To a Skeleton.—The manuscript of this poem was found near a skeleton in the London Royal College of Surgeons about 1820. The author has never been found, though a reward of fifty guineas was offered for his discovery.—*Single Famous Poems.*

Page 655.—The Lie.—This celebrated poem has been attributed to Joshua Sylvester. In a note of Mr. Peter Cunningham's to his edition of Campbell's *Lives of the Poets*, referring to the passage in which Campbell says, "We would willingly ascribe the 'Soul's Errand' to him (Raleigh)," we read, "'The Lie' is ascribed to Sir Walter Raleigh in an *answer to it written at the time,* and recently discovered in the Cheetham Library at Manchester. That it was written by Raleigh is now almost past a doubt."—*Bellew's Poets' Corner.*

Page 656.—Armstrong's Good-Night.—These verses are said to have been composed by one of the Armstrongs, executed for the murder of Sir John Carmichael of Edrom, Warden of the Middle Marches. Whether these are the original words will admit of a doubt.—*Sir Walter Scott.*

This is one of the songs which so touched Goldsmith in his youth that nothing he heard sung in after years had an equal charm for him. "The music of the finest singer," he wrote in the *Bee*, October 13, 1759, "is dissonance to what I felt when our old dairymaid sung me into tears with 'Johnny Armstrong's Last Good-Night' or the 'Cruelty of Barbara Allen;'" and in a letter to his Irish friend Hodson, December 27, 1757, he says: "If I go to the opera where Signora Columba pours out all the mazes of melody, I sit and sigh for 'Lishoy's Fireside' and 'Johnny Armstrong's Last Good-Night,' from Peggy Golden."—*Mary Carlyle Aitken.*

Page 672.—The Old and Young Courtier.—The whole of the sixteenth century was marked by important changes of every kind—political, religious, and social. The wars with France and the internal contests of the Roses were over, and the energy of the nation was directed to new objects. Trade and commerce were extended; fresh sources of wealth were developed; and new classes of society sprang up into importance whose riches enabled them to outvie the old landed gentry, but who had few of their hereditary tastes and habits. Hence the innovation of old customs and the decay of ancient manners to which the gentry themselves were compelled to conform. This old song, which is printed in the *Percy Reliques* from an ancient black-letter copy in the *Pepys Collection*, is a lament over the changes which had taken place in the early part of the seventeenth century, as compared with the days of Queen Elizabeth.—*Knight's Half Hours with the Best Authors.*

Page 677.—Battle of Blenheim.—The battle of Blenheim or Hochstadt was fought August 13, 1704, between the English and Austrians, under the Duke of Marlborough and Prince Eugene, and the French and Bavarians, under Marshal Tallard, Marson, and the Elector of Bavaria. The latter army, being badly handled and huddled together in the village of Blenheim, was suddenly attacked by Marlborough and completely defeated, losing 30,000 in killed, wounded, and prisoners. Marlborough's loss was but 11,000. This victory completely shattered the French prestige which Louis XIV. had struggled so hard to obtain.

Page 688.—Lines Written by One in the Tower.—Chidiock Tychborn shared in Babington's conspiracy, and was executed with him in 1586. (For a fuller account see Disraeli's *Curiosities of Literature.*)

Page 704.—HONEST POVERTY.—A great critic (Aikin) on songs says that love and wine are the exclusive themes for song-writing. The following is on neither subject, and consequently is no song, but will be allowed, I think, to be two or three pretty good prose thoughts inverted into rhyme.—*In a Letter from Burns to G. Thomson.*

Page 724.—ALEXANDER'S FEAST.—St. Cecilia is said to have been a Roman lady born about A. D. 295, bred in the Christian faith, and married to a Pagan nobleman, Valerianus. She told her husband that she was visited nightly by an angel, whom he was allowed to see after his own conversion. The celestial youth had brought from paradise two wreaths, which he gave to them. One was of the lilies of heaven, the other of its roses. They both suffered martyrdom at the beginning of the third century, in the reign of Septimius Severus. The angel by whom Cecilia was visited is referred to in the closing lines of Dryden's "Ode," coupled with a tradition that he had been drawn down to her from heaven by her melodies. In the earliest traditions of Cecilia there is no mention of her skill in music. This part of her story seems to have been developed by a little play of fancy over her relations with the angel, and the great Italian painters—Raffaelle, Domenichino, and others—fixed her position as the patron saint of music by representing her always with symbols of harmony, a harp or organ-pipes. Then came the suggestion adopted in Dryden's "Ode," that the organ was invented by St. Cecilia. The practice of holding musical festivals on St. Cecilia's Day, the 22d of November, began to prevail in England at the close of the seventeenth century. The earliest piece composed for such a meeting was produced in 1683, and was by Henry Purcell. From that date to about 1740 there was an annual Cecilian festival in London, and the fashion spread into the provinces. Poets—Dryden and Pope among them—were applied to for odes which were to celebrate the power of music, and to be set to music for performance as a special feature of the anniversary.—*Morley's Shorter Poems.*

Page 735.—A CANADIAN BOAT-SONG.—I wrote these words to an air which our boatmen sung to us frequently. The wind was so unfavorable that they were obliged to row all the way, and we were five days in descending the river from Kingston to Montreal, exposed to an intense sun during the day, and at night forced to take shelter from the dews in any miserable hut upon the banks that would receive us. But the magnificent scenery of the St. Lawrence repays all such difficulties.

Our *voyageurs* had good voices, and sung perfectly in tune together. The original words of the air to which I adapted these stanzas appeared to be a long, incoherent story, of which I could understand but little, from the barbarous pronunciation of the Canadians. It begins—

Dans mon chemin j'ai rencontré
Deux cavaliers très-bien montés;

and the *refrain* to every verse was—

A l'ombre d'un bois je m'en vais jouer,
A l'ombre d'un bois je m'en vais danser.

I ventured to harmonize this air, and have published it. Without that charm which association gives to every little memorial of scenes or feelings that are past, the melody may perhaps be thought common and trifling; but I remember when we have entered, at sunset, upon one of those beautiful lakes into which the St. Lawrence so grandly and unexpectedly opens, I have heard this simple air with a pleasure which the finest compositions of the first masters have never given me; and now there is not a note of it which does not recall to my memory the dip of our oars in the St. Lawrence, the flight of our boat down the rapids, and all those new and fanciful impressions to which my heart was alive during the whole of this very interesting voyage.—*Moore's Poems*, note.

Page 739.—A VISION UPON THIS CONCEIT OF THE FAERIE QUEENE.—This sonnet is the first among the commendatory poems prefixed to the earliest edition of *The Faerie Queene*. As original in conception as it is grand in execution, it is about the finest compliment which was ever paid by poet to poet, such as it became Raleigh to indite and Spenser to receive. Yet it labors under a serious defect. The great poets of the past lose no whit of their glory because later poets are found worthy to share it. Petrarch in his lesser, and Homer in his greater sphere, are just as illustrious since Spenser appeared as before.—*Richard Chenevix Trench.*

Page 756.—THE DESERTED VILLAGE.—Lissoy, near Ballymahon, where the poet's brother, a clergyman, had his living, claims the honor of being the spot from which the localities of "The Deserted Village" were derived. The church which tops the neighboring hill, the mill, and the brook, are still pointed out; and a hawthorn has suffered the penalty of poetical celebrity, being cut to pieces by those admirers of the bard who desired to have classical toothpick-cases and tobacco-stoppers. Much of this supposed locality may be fanciful, but it is a pleasing tribute to the poet in the land of his fathers.—*Sir Walter Scott.*

Page 787.—INDIAN REVELRY.—This remarkable poem appeared originally, it is believed, in the *St. Helena Magazine*, and was afterward copied in the *London Spectator* and other journals. It relates to the early service of English officers in India when the army was mowed down by pestilence. When Macaulay's account of the effects of smallpox in England is remembered, as it describes the separation of brothers, sisters, and lovers, it will be seen that this poem gives with wonderful effect what is far nobler, however painful—the very poetry of military despair, but still the dying together of brothers in arms.

Page 787.—TITHONUS.—Tithonus was a beautiful Trojan, beloved by Aurora. He begged the goddess to grant him immortality, which request she granted; but as he had forgotten to ask for youth and vigor, he soon grew old, infirm, and ugly. When life became insupportable, he prayed Aurora to remove him from the world; this, however, she could not do, but she changed him into a grasshopper.—*Brewer's Dictionary of Phrase and Fable.*

Page 795.— THE RAPE OF THE LOCK.— The stealing of Miss Belle Fermor's hair (by Lord Petre) was taken too seriously, and caused an estrangement between the two families, though they had lived so long in great friendship before. A common acquaintance and well-wisher to both desired me to write a poem, to make a jest of it and laugh them together again. It was with this view that I wrote "The Rape of the Lock," which was well received, and had its effect in the two families. Nobody but Sir George Brown was angry, and he was a good deal so, and for a long time. He could not bear that Sir Plume should talk nothing but nonsense. The machinery was added afterward.—*Pope's Letter to Spence.*

Page 810.—THE CULPRIT FAY.—This exquisite poem was composed hastily among the highlands of the Hudson in the summer of 1819. The author was walking with some friends on a warm moonlight evening, when one of the party remarked that it would be difficult to write a faery poem, purely imaginative, without the aid of human characters. The party was reassembled two or three days afterward, and "The Culprit Fay" was read to them, nearly as it is now printed.— *Introduction to the "Culprit Fay."*

Page 818.—COMUS.—"Comus" was presented at Ludlow Castle in 1634, before the Earl of Bridgewater, then President of Wales. This drama was founded on an actual occurrence. The Earl of Bridgewater then resided at Ludlow Castle; his sons, Lord Brackley and Mr. Egerton, and Lady Alice Egerton, his daughter, passing through Haywood Forest in Herefordshire, on their way to Ludlow, were benighted, and the lady was for a short time lost. This accident being related to their father upon their arrival at his castle, Milton —at the request of his friend, Henry Lawes—wrote the musician, who taught music in the family—wrote the masque. Lawes set it to music, and it was acted on Michaelmas Night, 1634, the two brothers, the young lady, and Lawes himself, bearing each a part in the representation.

Page 833.—KILMENY.—Besides the old tradition on which this ballad is founded, there are some modern incidents of a similar nature which cannot well be accounted for, yet are as well attested as any occurrence that has taken place in the present age. The relation may be amusing to some readers:

A man in the parish of Traquair and county of Peebles was busied one day casting turf in a large modern field opposite the mansion-house—the spot is well known, and is still pointed out as rather unsafe; his daughter, a child seven years of age, was playing beside him and amusing him with her prattle. Chancing to ask a question of her, he was surprised at receiving no answer, and, looking behind him, he perceived that his child was not there. He always averred that, as far as he could remember, she had been talking to him about half a minute before; he was certain it was not above a whole one at most. It was in vain that he ran searching all about like one distracted, calling her name; no trace of her remained. He went home in a state of mind that may be better conceived than expressed, and raised the people of the parish, who searched for her several days with the same success. Every pool in the river, every bush and den on the mountains around, was searched in vain. It was remarked that the father never much encouraged the search, being thoroughly persuaded that she had been carried away by some invisible being, else she could not have vanished so suddenly. As a last resource, he applied to the minister of Inverleithen, a neighboring divine of exemplary piety and zeal in religious matters, who enjoined him to cause prayers to be offered to God for her in seven Christian churches next Sabbath at the same instant of time; "And then," said he, "if she is dead, God will forgive our sin in praying for the dead, as we do it through ignorance; and if she is still alive, I will answer for it that all the devils in hell shall be unable to keep her." The injunction was punctually attended to. She was remembered in the prayers of all the neighboring congregations next Sunday at the same hour, and never were there such prayers for fervor heard before. There was one clergyman in particular, Mr. Davidson, who prayed in such a manner that all the hearers trembled. As the old divine foreboded, so it fell out. On that very day, and within an hour of the time on which these prayers were offered, the girl was found in the Plora wood, sitting picking the bark from a tree. She could give no perfect account of the circumstances which had befallen to her, but she said she did not want plenty of meat, for that her mother came and fed her with milk and bread several times a day, and sung her to sleep at night. Her skin had acquired a bluish cast, which gradually wore off in the course of a few weeks. Her name was Jane Brown; she lived to a very advanced age, and was known to many still alive. Every circumstance of this story is truth, if the father's report of the suddenness of her disappearance may be relied on.

Another circumstance, though it happened still later, is not less remarkable. A shepherd of Tushilaw, in the parish of Ettrick, whose name was Walter Dalgleish, went out to the heights of that farm one Sabbath morning to herd the young sheep of his son and let him go to church. He took his own dinner along with him, and his son's breakfast. When the sermon was over, the lad went straight home, and did not return to his father. Night came, but nothing of the old shepherd appeared. When it grew very late his dog came home—seemed terrified, and refused to take any meat. The family were ill at ease during the night, especially as they had never known his dog leave him before; and early next morning the lad arose and went to the height to look after his father and his flock. He found his sheep all scattered, and his father's dinner unbroken, lying on the same spot where they had parted the day before. At the distance of twenty yards from the spot the plaid which the old man wore was lying as if it had been flung from him, and a little farther on, in the same direction, his bonnet was found, but nothing of himself. The country people, as on all such occasions, rose in great numbers and searched for him many days. My father and several old men still alive were of the party. He could not be found or heard of, neither dead nor alive, and at length they gave up all thoughts of ever seeing him more. On the twentieth day after his disappearance, a shepherd's wife, at a place called Berrybush, came in as the family were sitting down to dinner and said that if it were possible to believe that Walter Dalgleish was still in existence, she would say yonder was he coming down the hill. They all ran out to watch the phenomenon, and as the person approached nigher they perceived that it was actually he, walking without his plaid and his bonnet. The place where he was first descried is not a mile distant from that where he was last seen, and there is neither brake, bog, nor bush. When he came into the house he shook hands with them all —asked for his family, and spoke as if he had been absent for years, and as if convinced something had befallen them. As they perceived something singular in his looks and manner, they unfortunately forbore asking him any questions at first, but desired him to sit and share their dinner. This he readily complied with, and began to sup some broth with seeming eagerness. He had only taken one or two spoonfuls when he suddenly stopped, a kind of rattling sound was heard in his breast, and he sank back in a faint. They put him to bed, and from that time forth he never spoke another word that any person could make sense of. He was removed to his own home, where he lingered a few weeks and died. What befell him remains to this day a mystery, and for ever must.—*Hogg's Poems.*

Page 841.—CHRISTABEL.— Coleridge's friend, Mr. Gilman, with whom he spent much of the latter part of his life, and who began his biography, tells us that "the following relation was to have occupied a third and fourth canto, and to have closed the tale: 'Over the mountains the Bard, as directed by Sir Leoline, hastes with his disciple, but in consequence of one of those inundations supposed to be common to this country, the spot only where the castle once stood is discovered, the edifice being washed away. He determines to return. Geraldine, being acquainted with all that is passing, like the Weird Sisters in *Macbeth*, vanishes. Reappearing, however, she waits the return of the Bard, exciting, in the mean time, by her wily arts, all the anger she could rouse in the baron's breast, as well as that jealousy of which he is described to have been susceptible. The old Bard and the youth at length arrive, and therefore she can no longer personate the character of Geraldine, the daughter of Lord Roland de Vaux, but changes her appearance to that of the accepted, though absent, lover of Christabel. Next ensues a courtship most distressing to Christabel, who feels— she knows not why—great disgust for her once-favored knight. This coldness is very painful to the baron, who has no more conception than herself of the supernatural transformation. She at last yields to her father's entreaties, and consents to approach the altar with this hated suitor. The real lover, returning, enters at this moment, and produces the ring which she had once given him in sign of her betrothment. Thus defeated, the supernatural being, Geraldine, disappears. As predicted, the castle-bell tolls, the mother's voice is heard, and, to the exceeding great joy of the parties, the rightful marriage takes place, after which follow a reconciliation and explanation between the father and daughter.'"—*Morley's Shorter Poems.*

Page 848.—KUBLA KHAN.—In the summer of the year 1797 the author, then in ill health, had retired to a lonely farm-house between Porlock and Linton, on the Exmoor confines of Somerset and Devonshire. In consequence of a slight indisposition, an anodyne had been prescribed, from the effect of which he fell asleep in his chair at the moment that he was reading the following sentence, or words of the same substance, in *Purchas's Pilgrimage:* "Here the Khan Kubla commanded a palace to be built, and a stately garden thereunto, and thus ten miles of fertile ground were enclosed with a wall." The author continued for about three hours in a profound sleep, at least of the external senses, during which time he has the most vivid confidence that he could not have composed less than from two to three hundred lines, if that, indeed, can be called composition in which all the images rose up before him as things, with a parallel production of the correspondent expressions, without any sensation or consciousness of effort. On awaking he appeared to himself to have a distinct recollection of the whole, and taking his pen, ink, and paper, instantly and eagerly wrote down the lines that are here preserved. At this moment he was unfortunately called out by a person on business from Porlock, and detained by him above an hour, and on his return to his room found, to his no small surprise and mortification, that though he still retained some vague and dim recollection of the general purport of the vision, yet, with the exception of some eight or ten scattered lines and images, all the rest had passed away like the images on the surface of a stream into which a stone had been cast, but alas! without the after-restoration of the latter.—*Coleridge's Poems.*

Page 851.—THE PIED PIPER OF HAMELIN.— The story of the Pied Piper—that first by his pipe gathered together all the rats and mice and drowned them in the river, and afterward, being defrauded of his reward, which the town promised him if he could deliver them from the plague of those vermin, took his opportunity and by the same pipe made the children of the town follow him, and leading them into a hill that opened, buried them there all alive—has so evident proof of it in the town of Hammel where it was done, that it ought not at all to be discredited. For the fact is very religiously kept among their ancient records, painted out also in their church-windows, and is an epoch joined with the year of our Lord in their bills and indentures and other law instruments.—*Henry Moore's Philosophy.*

Page 855.—THE RIME OF THE ANCIENT MARINER.—Wordsworth has given the following account of the origin of "The Ancient Mariner." "It arose," he says, "out of the want of five pounds which Coleridge and I needed to make a tour together in Devonshire. We agreed to write jointly a poem, the subject of which Coleridge took from a dream, which a friend of his had once dreamt, concerning a person suffering under a dire curse from the commission of some crime. I supplied the crime, the shooting of the albatross, from an incident I had met with in one of Shelvocke's voyages. We tried the poem conjointly for a day or two, but we pulled different ways, and only a few lines of it are mine."—*Frederick Saunders's Festival of Song.*

Page 878.—THE ABBOT M'KINNON.—To describe the astonishing scenes to which this romantic tale relates, Icolmkill and Staffa, would only be multiplying pages to no purpose. By the Temple of the Ocean is meant the Isle of Staffa, and by its chancel the Cave of Fingal.

St. Columba placed the nuns in an island at a little distance from Iona, where he would not suffer either a cow or a woman; "for where there are cows," said he, "there must be women; and where there are women, there must be mischief." —*Hogg's Poems.*

Page 892.—THE LAIRD O' COCKPEN.—Miss Ferrier, who wrote *Marriage Destiny,* etc., added the last two verses.

Page 899.—BAUCIS AND PHILEMON.—The original tale here playfully modernized is in the Eighth Book of Ovid's *Metamorphoses,* where Jove and Mercury are the originals of the two brother hermits. Finding hospitality only in the thatched cottage of the poor old couple, Baucis and Philemon, the gods after their entertainment took the old couple to the top of the hill, whence they saw the houses and lands of their uncharitable neighbors all swallowed in a lake. Only their little home remained, which expanded to a temple. In this they served as the priests of Jove until they were changed into companion trees, hung over with fresh garlands by their worshippers.—*Morley's Shorter Poems.*

Page 914.—THE VICAR OF BRAY.—The Vicar of Bray, in Berkshire, was a Papist under the reign of Henry VIII., and a Protestant under Edward VI.; he was a Papist again under Mary, and once more became a Protestant in the reign of Elizabeth. When this scandal to the gown was reproached for his versatility of religious creeds, and taxed for being a turncoat and an inconstant changeling, as Fuller expresses it, he replied, "Not so, neither; for if I changed my religion, I am sure I kept true to my principle; which is, to live and die the Vicar of Bray."

This vivacious and reverend hero has given birth to a proverb peculiar to this county: "The Vicar of Bray will be Vicar of Bray still." But how has it happened that this *vicar* should be so notorious, and one in much higher rank, acting the same part, should have escaped notice? Dr. Kitchen, Bishop of Llandaff, from an idle abbot under Henry VIII. was made a busy bishop;

Protestant under Edward, he returned to his old master under Mary; and at last took the oath of supremacy under Elizabeth, and finished as a Parliament Protestant. A pun spread the odium of his name, for they said that he had always loved the *Kitchen* better than the *Church.—Disraeli's Curiosities of Literature.*

Page 922.—WHAT MR. ROBINSON THINKS.—This satire was written to ridicule the habit of comparatively obscure personages writing long letters to the newspapers supporting this or that candidate. The General C. mentioned in the poem is Gen. Caleb Cushing, afterward Attorney-General of the United States. During his absence at the head of his troops in the Mexican war he was nominated for Governor of Massachusetts, but was not elected.

Page 929.—THE DIVERTING HISTORY OF JOHN GILPIN.—Mr. Beyer, an eminent linen-draper at the end of Paternoster Row, where it adjoins to Cheapside—who died on the 11th of May, 1791, at the ripe age of ninety-eight—is reported upon tolerable authority to have undergone in his earlier days the adventure which Cowper has depicted in his ballad of "John Gilpin." It appears from Southey's life of the poet that, among the efforts which Lady Austen from time to time made to dispel the melancholy of Cowper, was her recital of a story told to her in her childhood of an attempted but unlucky pleasure-party of a London linen-draper, ending in his being carried past his point both in going and returning, and finally brought home by his contrarious beast, without ever having come in contact with his longing family at Edmonton. Cowper is said to have been extremely amused by the story, and kept awake by it the great part of the ensuing night, during which he probably laid the foundations of his ballad embodying the incidents. This was in October, 1782.

Southey's account of the origin of the ballad may be consistent with truth; but any one who candidly reads the marriage adventure of Commodore Trunnion, in *Peregrine Pickle,* will be forced to own that what is effective in the narration previously existed there.—*Chambers's Book of Days.*

Page 935.—THE FRIEND OF HUMANITY AND THE KNIFE-GRINDER.—In this poem Canning ridicules the youthful Jacobin effusions of Southey, in which, he says, it was sedulously inculcated that there was a natural and eternal warfare between the poor and the rich. The Sapphic rhymes of Southey afforded a tempting subject for ludicrous parody, and Canning quotes the following stanza, lest he should be suspected of painting from fancy, and not from life:

" Cold was the night-wind: drifting fast the snows fell;
Wide were the downs, and shelterless and naked;
When a poor wanderer struggled on her journey,
        Weary and waysore."

Page 935.—SONG, BY ROGERO.—*The Rovers; or, The Double Arrangement,* was a caricature of the sentimental drama, and was levelled at Schiller's *Robbers* and Goethe's *Stella.* The following extract will throw some light on the song. The soliloquy is by Frere, the song by Canning and Ellis:

SCENE FROM "THE ROVERS."

(*Scene changes to a subterranean vault in the Abbey of Quedlinburgh, with coffins, 'scutcheons, Death's heads, and cross-bones.—Toads and other loathsome reptiles are seen traversing the obscurer parts of the stage.—Rogero appears in chains, in a suit of rusty armor, with his beard grown and a cap of a grotesque form upon his head.—Beside him a crock or pitcher, supposed to contain his daily allowance of sustenance.—A long silence, during which the wind is heard to whistle through the caverns.—Rogero rises and comes slowly forward, with his arms folded.*)

Rog. Eleven years ! It is now eleven years since I was first immured in this living sepulchre—the cruelty of a minister—the perfidy of a monk—yes, Matilda! for thy sake—alive amidst the dead —chained—coffined—confined—cut off from the converse of my fellow-men. Soft! what have we here? (*Stumbles over a bundle of sticks.*) This cavern is so dark that I can scarcely distinguish the objects under my feet. Oh!—the register of my captivity—let me see, how stands the account? (*Takes up the sticks and turns them over with a melancholy air; then stands silent for a few moments, as if absorbed in calculation.*) Eleven years and fifteen days!—Ha! the twenty-eighth of August! How does the recollection of it vibrate on my heart! It was on this day that I took my last leave of my Matilda. It was a summer evening; her melting hand seemed to dissolve in mine as I pressed it to my bosom—some demon whispered me that I should never see her more. I stood gazing on the hated vehicle which was conveying her away for ever. The tears were petrified under my eyelids. My heart was crystallized with agony. Anon, I looked along the road. The diligence seemed to diminish every instant. I felt my heart beat against its prison as if anxious to leap out and overtake it. My soul whirled round as I watched the rotation of the hinder wheels. A long trail of glory followed after her, and mingled with the dust; it was the emanation of divinity, luminous with love and beauty like the splendor of the setting sun, but it told me that the sun of my joys was sunk for ever. Yes, here in the depths of an eternal dungeon—in the nursing-cradle of hell—the suburbs of perdition—in a nest of demons, where despair in vain sits brooding over the putrid eggs of hope; where agony woos the embrace of death; where patience, beside the bottomless pool of despondency, sits angling for impossibilities—yet even *here* to behold her, to embrace her!—yes, Matilda, whether in this dark abode, amidst toads and spiders, or in a royal palace, amidst the more loathsome reptiles of a court, would be indifferent to me. Angels would shower down their hymns of gratulation upon our heads, while fiends would envy the eternity of suffering love. . . . Soft, what air was that? It seemed a sound of more than human warblings. Again (*listens attentively for some minutes*). Only the wind. It is well, however—it reminds me of that melancholy air which has so often solaced the hours of my captivity. Let me see whether the damps of this dungeon have not yet injured my guitar. (*Takes his guitar, tunes it, and begins the song with a full accompaniment of violins from the orchestra.*)—*Morley's Shorter Poems.*

Page 936.—A TALE OF DRURY LANE.—The opening of Drury Lane Theatre in 1802, after having been burnt and rebuilt, and the offering of a prize of fifty pounds by the manager for the best opening address, were the circumstances which suggested the production of the *Rejected Addresses*. The idea of the work was suddenly conceived, and it was executed in six weeks. Of the examples of the *Rejected Addresses* given in this book, "A Tale of Drury Lane" is a burlesque imitation of Sir Walter Scott's poems, "The Theatre" of Crabbe's, and "The Baby's Début" of Wordsworth's.

Page 948.—MALBROUCK.—"Malbrouck" does not date from the battle of Malplaquet (1709), but from the time of the Crusades, six hundred years before. According to a tradition discovered by M. de Chateaubriand, the air came from the Arabs, and the tale is a legend of Mambrou, a crusader. It was brought into fashion during the Revolution by Mme. Poitrine, who used to sing it to her royal foster-child, the son of Louis XVI. M. Arago tells us that when M. Monge, at Cairo, sang this air to an Egyptian audience, they all knew it, and joined in it. Certainly the song has nothing to do with the Duke of Marlborough, as it is all about feudal castles and Eastern wars. We are told also that the band of Captain Cook, in 1770, was playing the air one day on the east coast of Australia, when the natives evidently recognized it, and seemed enchanted.—*Moniteur de l'Armée.*—*Brewer's Dictionary of Phrase and Fable.*

INDEX OF FIRST LINES.

	PAGE
A Baby was sleeping	33
Abide with me! fast falls the eventide	557
Abou Ben Adhem (may his tribe increase!)	644
Above the pines the moon was slowly drifting	282
A chieftain to the Highlands bound	381
A cloud lay cradled near the setting sun	442
A country life is sweet!	692
A dewdrop came with a spark of flame	459
A district school, not far away	923
Ae fond kiss and then we sever!	154
Afar in the desert I love to ride	490
Again at Christmas did we weave	689
Again the Lord of Life and Light	536
A good that never satisfies the mind	656
A good wife rose from her bed one morn	24
A happy bit hame this auld world would be	706
Ah, Chloris! could I now but sit	189
Ah! County Guy, the hour is nigh	189
Ah, how sweet it is to love!	97
Ah me! full sorely is my heart forlorn	57
Ah! my heart is weary waiting	429
Ah! then how sweetly closed those crowded days!	53
Ah! what a weary race my feet have run	508
Ah! what is love? It is a pretty thing	142
Airy, fairy Lilian	203
A life on the ocean wave	695
A little child beneath a tree	55
A little pause in life while daylight lingers	683
Allen-a-Dale has no fagot for burning	186
All hail the power of Jesus' name!	536
All in the Downs the fleet was moor'd	119
All in the merry month of May	417
All praise to Thee, my God, this night	555
"All quiet along the Potomac," they say	349
All thoughts, all passions, all delights	100
All worldly shapes shall melt in gloom	643
All yesterday I was spinning	774
All ye woods, and trees, and bowers	425
Aloft upon an old basaltic crag	276
Alone I walk the morning street	782
Although I enter not	211
A man there came, whence none could tell	665
A monk, when his rites sacerdotal were o'er	665
An attorney was taking a turn	920
An Austrian army, awfully arrayed	960
And are ye sure the news is true?	10

	PAGE
And hast thou sought thy heavenly home	39
And is this Yarrow?—this the stream	510
And this is thy grave, Macaura	221
And thou art dead, as young and fair	742
And thou hast walked about (how strange a story!)	744
"And wherefore do the poor complain?"	714
"And where have you been, my Mary"	809
And ye sall walk in silk attire	147
An old song made by an aged old pate	672
A poor wayfaring man of grief	541
Arethusa arose	460
Ariel to Miranda:—Take	732
Art thou pale for weariness	446
Art thou poor, yet hast thou golden slumbers?	660
Art thou weary, art thou languid	577
As, by some tyrant's stern command	738
As by the shore at break of day	363
As I gaed down by yon house-en'	412
A simple child	51
As it fell upon a day	480
As Julia once a-slumbering lay	209
Ask me no more: the moon may draw the sea	192
Ask me no more where Jove bestows	192
Ask me why I send you here	214
A slanting ray of evening light	671
A soldier of the Legion lay dying in Algiers	83
As one who destined from his friends to part	784
A song of a boat	21
As ships becalm'd at eve, that lay	744
A steed! a steed of matchlesse speed	311
As thro' the land at eve we went	39
A street there is in Paris famous	89
A sweet disorder in the dress	740
A thousand miles from land are we	470
A thousand silent years ago	784
At midnight in his guarded tent	347
At Paris hard by the Maine barriers	334
At Paris it was, at the opera there	180
At setting day and rising morn	195
At the close of the day, when the hamlet is still	648
At the gate of old Granada, when all its bolts are barr'd	373
At the king's gate the subtle noon	702
Avenge, O Lord! thy slaughter'd saints, whose bones	313
Awake, Æolian lyre, awake	728

INDEX OF FIRST LINES.

	PAGE
Awake, awake, my lyre!	121
Awake, my soul, and with the sun	553
Awake thee, my lady-love	178
A warrior so bold, and a virgin so bright	871
"Away! away!" cried the stout Sir John	421
Away, away o'er the feathery crest	696
Away! let naught to love displeasing	7
A weary weed, toss'd to and fro	463
A wee bird came to our ha'-door	326
A well there is in the west country	898
A wet sheet and a flowing sea	695
Ay, I saw her, we have met	195
Ay, this is freedom! these pure skies	494
BACHELOR's Hall! what a quare-lookin' place it is!	960
Backward, turn backward, O Time, in your flight	74
Balow, my babe, lye stil and sleipe!	32
Bards of passion and of mirth	740
Beat on, proud billows; Boreas blow	241
Beautiful Evelyn Hope is dead!	196
Because I oft in dark abstracted guise	781
Before I trust my fate to thee	187
Before Jehovah's awful throne	546
Before the beginning of years	744
Before the starry threshold of Jove's court	818
Behold	615
Behold the sun, that seem'd but now	556
Behold this ruin! 'Twas a skull	642
Be it ryght, or wrong, these men among	112
Believe me, if all those endearing young charms	162
Ben Battle was a soldier bold	896
Beneath the warrior's helm behold	780
Be seated pray. "A grave appeal?"	958
Best and brightest, come away!	499
Better trust all and be deceived	679
Between the broad fields of wheat and corn	75
Between the dark and the daylight	45
Beyond the smiling and the weeping	595
Bird of the wilderness	473
Blame not my Lute! for he must sound	190
Blest as the immortal gods is he	192
Blest be Thy love, dear Lord	548
Blossom of the almond trees	457
Blow, blow, thou winter wind	438
Blue-bird! on yon leafless tree	475
Bonny Kilmeny gaed up the glen	833
Born in yon blaze of orient sky	431
Bound upon th' accursèd tree	535
Break, break, break	88
Brightest and best of the sons of the morning	534
Bright flower, whose home is everywhere	454
Bright shadows of true rest! some shoots of blisse	560
Brothers, the day declines	552
Brother, thou art gone before us; and thy saintly soul is flown	595
Burly, dozing humble-bee!	482
Bury the Great Duke	270
Busk ye, busk ye, my bonny, bonny bride	382
Busy, curious, thirsty fly	483
By cool Siloam's shady rill	575
By Nebo's lonely mountain	580
By our camp-fires rose a murmur	322
By the moon we sport and play	793
CALL for the robin redbreast and the wren	638
Calm me, my God, and keep me calm	565
Cam ye by Athol, lad wi' the philabeg	326
Can I see another's woe	589
Can I, who have for others oft compiled	226
Captain, or colonel, or knight in arms	313
Care-charmer Sleep, son of the sable Night	776
Carol, carol, Christians	530
Cheeks as soft as July peaches	29
Cherry-ripe, ripe, ripe, I cry	214
Child, amidst the flowers at play	564
Child of the sun! pursue thy rapturous flight	482
Children are what the mothers are	36
Children of the heavenly King	574
Christians, awake, salute the happy morn	531
Christ the Lord is risen to-day	535
Christ will gather in his own	609
Clear and cool, clear and cool	461
Clear the brown path to meet his coulter's gleam!	692
Close his eyes, his work is done	279
Come, all ye jolly shepherds	167
Come away, come away, Death	197
Come, follow, follow me	793
Come from my first, ay, come!	264
Come hither, Evan Cameron	313
Come, Holy Ghost, our souls inspire	542
Come, Holy Spirit, heavenly Dove	542
Come in the evening, or come in the morning	158
Come into the garden, Maud	177
Come listen to me, you gallants so free	390
Come live with me, and be my love	140
Come, oh come! in pious lays	551
Come, O thou Traveller unknown	571
Come, rest in this bosom, my own stricken deer	147
Come, see the Dolphin's anchor forged! 'tis at a white heat now	693
Come sleep, O sleep! the certain knot of peace	776
Come, Thou Fount of every blessing	585
Come to me, dearest, I'm lonely without thee	11
Come unto these yellow sands	794
Come. ye lofty, come, ye lowly	530
Come, ye thankful people, come	558
Comfort thee, O thou mourner, yet a while	273
Comrades, leave me here a little, while as yet 'tis early morn	149

INDEX OF FIRST LINES.

	PAGE
Condemn'd to hope's delusive mine	245
Consider the sea's listless chime	462
Contemplate all this work of Time	690
Could ye come back to me, Douglas, Douglas.	17
Crabbèd age and youth	756
Creator Spirit, by whose aid	543
Cromwell, our chief of men, who through a cloud	234
Cupid and my Campaspe play'd	99
Cyriac, this three years day these eyes, tho' clear	234
DAUGHTER of Jove, relentless power	777
Daughter to that good earl, once President	235
Day, in melting purple dying	170
Day of vengeance, without morrow!	611
Day of wrath! O day of mourning!	610
Day-stars! that ope your frownless eyes to twinkle	451
Dazzled thus with height of place	230
Dead! One of them shot by the sea in the East.	26
Dear Chloe, while the busy crowd	2
Dear chorister, who from those shadows sends.	478
Dear is my little native vale	498
Dear my friend and fellow-student, I would lean my spirit o'er you	104
Deathless principle, arise!	596
Deep in the wave is a coral grove	464
Deep on the convent-roof the snows	546
Descend, ye Nine! descend and sing	727
Did Christ o'er sinners weep?	535
Dies Iræ, Dies Illa!	609
Does the road wind up-hill all the way?	578
Do not beguile my heart	585
Down the dimpled green-sward dancing	53
Down to the wharves, as the sun goes down	789
Downward sinks the setting sun	688
Do ye hear the children weeping, O my brothers	63
Drink to me only with thine eyes	195
Drop, drop, slow tears	544
Duncan Gray cam here to woo	144
EARTH has not anything to show more fair	503
Earth, with its dark and dreadful ills	629
E'en such is time; which takes on trust	230
Eternal source of every joy	559
Eternal Spirit of the chainless Mind!	398
Ethereal Minstrel! Pilgrim of the sky!	473
Even is come; and from the dark Park, hark.	959
Ever let the Fancy roam	500
Every wedding, says the proverb	183
Eyes which can but ill define	749
FAINTLY as tolls the evening chime	735
Fair as the dawn of the fairest day	466
Fair Daffodils, we weep to see	453

	PAGE
Fair pledges of a fruitful tree	457
Fair stood the wind for France	298
False world, thou ly'st; thou canst not lend...	654
Fare thee well! and if for ever	15
Farewell! but whenever you welcome the hour	85
Farewell,—farewell to thee, Araby's daughter!	781
Farewell, life! my senses swim	637
Farewell, rewards and fairies	833
Farewell, thou busy world, and may	495
Farewell to Lochaber, and farewell, my Jean.	195
Far from the world, O Lord, I flee	582
Far in a wild, unknown to public view	666
Father, I know that all my life	567
Father of all! in every age	545
Fear no more the heat o' the sun	637
Fhairshon swore a feud	934
First time he kiss'd me, he but only kiss'd	135
Flee fro the pres, and duelle with sothfastnesse	688
Flower of the waste! the heathfowl shuns	447
Flow gently, sweet Afton, among thy green braes	515
Follow a shadow, it still flies you	124
For ever with the Lord!	597
Fountain of mercy! God of Love!	563
Friend after friend departs!	638
From all that dwell below the skies	552
From beauteous Windsor's high and storied halls	504
From gold to gray	675
From Greenland's icy mountains	580
From harmony, from heavenly harmony	726
From his brimstone bed at break of day	917
From Oberon, in fairy-land	808
From out the grave of one whose budding years	740
From Stirling Castle we had seen	510
Full fathom five thy father lies	794
From the desert I come to thee	177
Full knee-deep lies the winter snow	438
Full many a glorious morning have I seen	439
GAMARRA is a dainty steed	488
Gane were but the winter cauld	638
Gather ye rosebuds while ye may	123
Genteel in personage	210
Gently, Lord, oh, gently lead us	543
Get up, get up, for shame! the blooming morn.	428
Gin a body meet a body	214
Give me my scallop-shell of quiet	578
Give place, ye lovers, here before	154
"Give us a song!" the soldiers cried	216
Glories, pleasures, pomps, delights, and ease.	203
Glorious things of thee are spoken	598
God bless the king!—I mean the Faith's Defender	310
God is love! His mercy brightens	544

	PAGE
God makes sech nights, all white an' still	891
God might have bade the earth bring forth	455
God moves in a mysterious way	543
God of the mighty deep! wherever now	887
God prosper long our noble king	299
God rest ye, merry gentlemen; let nothing you dismay	533
God rest you, merry gentlemen	531
God save our gracious king!	355
Golden slumbers kiss your eyes	32
Go, lovely rose!	185
Good-bye, good-bye to Summer!	477
Good-bye, proud world! I'm going home	657
Good-morrow to thy sable beak	481
Good-night to all the world! there's none	618
Good people all, of every sort	928
Good people all, with one accord	912
Go patter to lubbers and swabs, do ye see	698
Go, soul, the body's guest	655
Go to dark Gethsemane	534
Go where glory waits thee	95
Go, youth beloved, in distant glades	94
Graceful may seem the fairy form	24
Green be the turf above thee	253
Green little vaulter in the sunny grass	482
Grown to man's stature! O my little child!	682
Guide me, O Thou great Jehovah!	573
Guvener B. is a sensible man	922
HAIL, beauteous stranger of the grove!	481
Hail, Thou once-despisèd Jesus	538
Hail to the Chief, who in triumph advances	364
Hail to thee, blithe spirit	474
Hail to the Lord's Anointed	537
Half a league, half a league	348
Hamelin Town's in Brunswick	851
Happy me! O happy sheep	562
Happy the man, whose wish and care	755
Happy those early days, when I	92
Hark! ah, the nightingale!	472
Hark! hark! my soul! angelic songs are swelling	600
Hark—hark! the lark at heaven's gate sings	439
Hark! how all the welkin rings!	532
Hark, my soul! it is the Lord	541
Hark, the glad sound! the Saviour comes	533
Has sorrow thy young days shaded	742
Has there any old fellow got mix'd with the boys?	80
Hast thou a charm to stay the morning-star	518
Have you heard of the wonderful one-hoss shay	932
Have you not heard the poets tell	30
Having this day my horse, my hand, my lance	192
Hear my prayer, O heavenly Father	564
Hear the sledges with the bells	765
Hear ye, ladies that despise	169
He came too late! neglect had tried	102

	PAGE
He first deceased; she for a little tried	228
Heigh-ho! daisies and buttercups	20
He is gone on the mountain	625
Hence, all you vain delights	656
Hence away, thou Siren; leave me	153
Hence, loathèd Melancholy	733
Hence, vain deluding joys	735
Here, a sheer hulk, lies poor Tom Bowling	639
Here, passenger, beneath this shed	226
Here rests, and let no saucy knave	948
Here's a health to ane I lo'e dear	166
Here's to thee, my Scottish lassie! here's a hearty health to thee!	214
Her eyes the glow-worme lend thee	127
Her hair was tawny with gold, her eyes with purple were dark	361
Her suffering ended with the day	625
He sendeth sun, he sendeth shower	544
He that loves a rosy cheek	180
He that of such a height hath built his mind	230
He who died at Azan sends	681
Hie upon Hielands	419
High in the breathless hall the minstrel sate	223
His golden locks time hath to silver turn'd	751
His steed was old, his armor worn	404
Ho! city of the gay!	268
Holy, holy, holy, Lord God Almighty	546
Home of the Percy's high-born race	513
Home they brought her warrior dead	56
Ho, pretty page with the dimpled chin	87
"Horatius Flaccus, B. C. 8"	921
"Ho, sailor of the sea!"	67
How are Thy servants blest, O Lord!	558
How blest has my time been, what joys have I known	2
How calmly sinks the parting sun!	441
How dear to this heart are the scenes of my childhood	74
"How does the water	508
How do I love thee? let me count the ways	135
How fresh, O Lord, how sweet and clean	579
How happy is he born and taught	661
How hard, when those who do not wish	951
How little recks it where men die	680
How much the heart may bear, and yet not break!	617
Ho! why dost thou shiver and shake	715
How many summers, love	14
How many times do I love thee, dear?	102
How seldom, friend, a good great man inherits	662
How sleep the Brave who sink to rest	363
How soon hath time, the subtle thief of youth	226
How sweet it were, if without feeble fright	743
How sweet the Name of Jesus sounds	541
How sweet thy modest light to view	447
How vainly men themselves amaze	497
Hush, my dear! Lie still and slumber!	34

INDEX OF FIRST LINES.

	Page
I am a friar of orders gray	916
I am as I am, and so will I be	191
I am content, I do not care	660
I am dying, Egypt, dying	290
I am monarch of all I survey	679
I am old and blind!	235
I am! yet what I am who cares, or knows?	618
Ianthe! you are call'd to cross the sea!	213
I arise from dreams of thee	103
I bring fresh showers for the thirsting flowers.	444
I cannot eat but little meat	917
I cannot make him dead	48
I care not though it be	179
I climb'd the dark brow of the mighty Hellvellyn	514
I come from haunts of coot and hern	460
I do confess thou'rt smooth and fair	148
I do not ask, O Lord, that life may be	537
I dream'd that as I wander'd by the way	459
I envy not, in any moods	689
If all the world and love were young	140
If aught of oaten stop or pastoral song	440
If doughty deeds my lady please	161
If, dumb too long, the drooping Muse hath stay'd	242
I feel a newer life in every gale	432
If I leave all for thee, wilt thou exchange	135
If I live to grow old, as I find I go down	754
I fill this cup to one made up	178
If life's pleasures cheer thee	577
If this fair rose offend thy sight	214
If thou must love me, let it be for naught	134
If thou shouldst ever come by choice or chance	406
If thou wert by my side, my love	9
If to be absent were to be	125
If women could be fair, and yet not fond	190
If you become a nun, dear	171
I give immortal praise	546
I hae naebody now, I hae naebody now	83
I hae seen great anes, and sat in great ha's	1
I have a son, a little son, a boy just five years old	50
I have had playmates, I have had companions	77
I have ships that went to sea	789
I hear thee speak of the better land	598
I held it truth, with him who sings	689
I in these flowery meads would be	467
I knew by the smoke that so gracefully curl'd	763
I know not that the men of old	747
I lay in sorrow, deep distress'd	687
I lean'd out of window, I smelt the white clover	20
I like a church, I like a cowl	663
I look'd upon his brow; no sign	292
I love, and have some cause to love, the earth.	576
I loved him not; and yet now he is gone	141

	Page
I loved thee long and dearly.	171
I loved thee once; I'll love no more	141
I love it, I love it; and who shall dare	73
I love thy kingdom, Lord	574
I love to look on a scene like this	77
I made a posy, while the day ran by	756
I mind me of a pleasant time	93
I'm in love with you, Baby Louise!	29
I'm old, my dears, and shrivell'd with age, and work, and grief	894
I mourn no more my vanish'd years	613
I'm sitting alone by the fire	207
I'm sittin' on the stile, Mary	86
I'm wearin' awa', Jean	636
In all the land, range up, range down	203
In ancient times, as story tells	899
In Clementina's artless mien	214
In eddying course when leaves began to fly	502
I never gave a lock of hair away	134
In form and feature, face and limb	906
In good King Charles's golden days	914
In her ear he whispers gayly	201
In Köln, a town of monks and bones	928
In May, when sea-winds pierced our solitudes.	455
In melancholic fancy	884
In slumbers of midnight the sailor-boy lay	696
In such a night, when every louder wind	434
In summer, on the headlands	883
In the down-hill of life, when I find I'm declining	674
In the fair land o'erwatch'd by Ischia's mountains	277
In the greenest of our valleys	871
In their ragged regimentals	331
In the merrie moneth of Maye	145
In the ranks of the Austrian you found him	364
In the silent midnight watches	575
In token that thou shalt not fear	563
Into the Devil Tavern	309
In vain men tell us time can alter	741
In Xanadu did Kubla Khan	848
In yonder grave a Druid lies	244
I prithee send me back my heart	171
I remember, I remember	73
I reside at Table Mountain, and my name is Truthful James	944
I saw him last on this terrace proud	342
I saw him once before	755
I saw the young bride in her beauty and pride	589
I saw two clouds at morning	220
I say to thee, do thou repeat	662
Is it come? they said on the banks of the Nile.	748
I sleep and rest, my heart makes moan	21
I sprang to the stirrup, and Joris, and he	372
Is there for honest poverty	704
Is there, where the winds are singing	52
Is this a fast—to keep	587

63

INDEX OF FIRST LINES.

	PAGE
It came upon the midnight clear	532
I think it was spring—but not certain I am	952
It is a beauteous evening, calm and free	441
It is an ancient mariner	855
It is a place where poets crown'd may feel the heart's decaying	246
It is not beauty I demand	139
It is the miller's daughter	155
It's hame, and it's hame, hame fain wad I be	357
It was a friar of orders gray	117
It was a summer evening	677
It was a time of sadness, and my heart	590
It was many and many a year ago	410
It was the calm and silent night!	529
It was the time when lilies blow	138
I've a letter from thy sire	25
I've heard them lilting at our ewe-milking	306
I've wander'd east, I've wander'd west	118
I've wander'd to the village, Tom, I've sat beneath the tree	78
I wander'd by the brookside	169
I wander'd lonely as a cloud	452
I was a young fair tree	458
I was thy Neighbor once, thou rugged Pile!	505
I weep for Adonais—he is dead!	253
I weigh not fortune's frown or smile	660
I will not let you say a woman's part	188
I will not say that thou wast true	213
I wish I were where Helen lies	402
I wish I were where Helen lies	403
I worship thee, sweet Will of God!	566
I would have gone; God bade me stay	591
I would I were an excellent divine	552
I would not live alway—live alway below!	593
JENNY kiss'd me when we met	186
Jesu, lover of my soul	540
Jesu, my strength, my hope	579
Jesus, I my cross have taken	539
John Anderson, my jo, John	8
John Brown of Ossawatomie spake on his dying day	279
John Bull for pastime took a prance	948
John Gilpin was a citizen	929
Joy to the world! the Lord is come	549
Just as I am, without one plea	568
Just for a handful of silver he left us	263
Just where the Treasury's marble front	886
KENTISH Sir Byng stood for his king	310
Ken ye aught of brave Lochiel?	325
King Almanzor of Granada, he hath bid the trumpets sound	408
King Francis was a hearty king, and loved a royal sport	411
LADY Clara Vere de Vere	210
Laid in my quiet bed	657
Lars Porsena of Clusium	283
Late at e'en, drinking the wine	381
Lay a garland on my hearse	212
Lead, kindly Light, amid th' encircling gloom	569
Leaves have their time to fall	630
Let me move slowly through the street	647
Let me not to the marriage of true minds	218
Let Observation, with extensive view	649
Let us go, lassie, go	498
Life! I know not what thou art	613
Like as the culver, on the barèd bough	190
Like as the damask rose you see	626
Like as the waves make toward the pebbled shore	753
Like the violet, which alone	179
Like to the clear in highest sphere	123
Like to the falling of a star	688
Listen, my children, and you shall hear	329
Lithe and listen, gentlemen	368
Little Ellie sits alone	47
Little thinks, in the field, yon red-cloak'd clown	707
"Live while you live!" the epicure would say	574
Lochiel, Lochiel! beware of the day	323
Lo! He comes with clouds descending	611
Lo! here a little volume, but great book	586
Lone upon a mountain, the pine trees wailing round him	172
Long did I toil, and knew no earthly rest	569
Look at me with thy large brown eyes	30
Look out, bright eyes, and bless the air!	184
Lord, dismiss us with thy blessing	612
Lord, it belongs not to my care	566
Lord John stood in his stable-door	412
Lord Lovel he stood at his castle-gate	198
Lord, shall thy children come to Thee?	582
Lord, thou hast given me a cell	559
Lord, with glowing heart I'd praise Thee	548
Loud is the summer's busy song	432
Love in my bosom, like a bee	98
Love is a sickness full of woes	98
Love is the blossom where there blows	98
Lovely, lasting peace of mind!	659
Love not, love not! ye hapless sons of clay!	187
Love not me for comely grace	139
Love still hath something of the sea	99
Love thy mother, little one!	35
Lo! where the rosy-bosom'd Hours	427
"Lullaby, O, lullaby!"	903
MAGNIFICENT thy fate!	350
Maiden! with the meek brown eyes	66
Maid of Athens, ere we part	145
Maid of my love, sweet Genevieve	155
"Make way for liberty!"—he cried	297
Malbrouck, the prince of commanders	948
Many a long, long year ago	927
March, march, Ettrick and Teviotdale	338

INDEX OF FIRST LINES. 995

	PAGE
Martial, the things that do attain	616
Mary! I want a lyre with other strings	245
Matron! the children of whose love	682
Maud Muller, on a summer's day	167
Maxwelton braes are bonnie	199
May! queen of blossoms	428
May the Babylonish curse	919
M'Kinnon's tall mast salutes the day	878
Men of England! who inherit	356
Merry it is in the good greenwood	838
Merry Margaret	225
Methinks it is good to be here	633
Methought I saw the grave where Laura lay	739
Midnight past! Not a sound of aught	199
'Mid pleasures and palaces though we may roam	1
Mild offspring of a dark and sullen sire!	452
Milton! thou shouldst be living at this hour	240
Mine be a cot beside the hill	6
Mine eyes have seen the glory of the coming of the Lord	354
Miss Flora M'Flimsey, of Madison Square	708
Mortality, behold and fear	504
Mourn, hapless Caledonia, mourn	327
Much have I travell'd in the realms of gold	739
Music, when soft voices die	185
My beautiful! my beautiful! that standest meekly by	492
My brother Jack was nine in May	940
My coachman, in the moonlight there	707
My country, 'tis of thee	354
My curse upon thy venom'd stang	953
My days among the dead are pass'd	737
My days pass pleasantly away	751
My dear and only love, I pray	193
My earrings! my earrings! they've dropp'd into the well	183
My fairest child, I have no song to give you	72
My faith looks up to Thee	538
My God and Father, while I stray	566
My God, now I from sleep awake	557
My heart aches, and a drowsy numbness pains	478
My heart leaps up when I behold	444
My heart's in the Highlands, my heart is not here	358
My letters! all dead paper, . . . mute and white!	135
My life is like the summer rose	616
My life, which was so straight and plain	617
My little love, do you remember	85
My Lord Tomnoddy got up one day	941
My lov'd, my honor'd, much-respected friend	3
My love and I for kisses play'd	156
My love he built me a bonny bower	417
My lute, be as thou wert when thou didst grow	734
My luve is like a red, red rose	157
My minde to me a kingdom is	737

	PAGE
My mother bore me in the southern wild	37
My pipe is lit, my grog is mix'd	902
My prime of youth is but a frost of cares	688
My sheep I neglected, I broke my sheep-hook	200
My soul to-day	465
Mysterious night! when our first parent knew	441
My time, O ye Muses, was happily spent	173
My true-love hath my heart, and I have his	127
Nae shoon to hide her tiny taes	41
Naked on parent's knees, a new-born child	50
Near a small village in the West	911
Nearer, my God, to Thee	564
"Needy knife-grinder, whither are you going?	935
Never any more	211
News of battle!—news of battle!	302
Night is the time for rest	687
Nobles and heralds, by your leave	241
No longer mourn for me when I am dead	219
No stir in the air, no stir in the sea	378
Not a drum was heard, not a funeral note	252
Not as all other women are	208
Nothing but leaves; the Spirit grieves	578
Not marble, nor the gilded monuments	752
Not ours the vows of such as plight	101
Now gentle sleep hath closèd up those eyes	156
Now glory to the Lord of Hosts, from whom all glories are!	307
Now ponder well, you parents deare	53
Now poor Tom Dunstan's cold	702
Now the bright morning star, day's harbinger	427
Now there's peace on the shore, now there's calm on the sea	357
Now the third and fatal conflict for the Persian throne was done	291
O blithe new-comer! I have heard	480
O day most calm, most bright!	560
Och! the Coronation! what celebration	956
O Death! thou tyrant fell and bloody!	247
O'er a low couch the setting sun	621
O faint, delicious, spring-time violet!	453
O fair and stately maid, whose eyes	217
O fairest of the rural maids!	779
Of all the girls that are so smart	120
Of all the rides since the birth of time	371
Of all the ships upon the blue	954
Of all the thoughts of God that are	622
Of a' the airts the wind can blaw	126
Of Leinster, famed for maidens fair	197
Of Nelson and the North	341
Oft has it been my lot to mark	686
Oft I had heard of Lucy Gray	56
Oft in the stilly night	77
O God of Bethel, by whose hand	587
O God! whose thunder shakes the sky	565
Oh! a dainty plant is the ivy green	456

	PAGE		PAGE
O happy soul that lives on high	575	Old girl that has borne me far and fast	493
O happy Thames that didst my Stella bear!	191	Old Grimes is dead; that good old man	912
Oh, breathe not his name! let it sleep in the shade	252	Old letters! wipe away the tear	88
		Old wine to drink!	749
Oh, Brignall banks are wild and fair	176	O Lord, another day is flown	568
Oh, England is a pleasant place for them that's rich and high	419	O lovely Mary Donnelly, it's you I love the best!	122
Oh, ever skill'd to wear the form we love!	663	O Mary, at thy window be!	147
Oh, for a closer walk with God	564	O melancholy bird! a winter's day	472
Oh for one hour of youthful joy!	899	O mistress mine, where are you roaming?	163
Oh, hadst thou never shared my fate	9	O moon that shinest on this heathy wild	446
Oh, had we some bright little isle of our own	194	O mother dear, Jerusalem	602
Oh, happy is the man who hears	575	O Mother Earth! upon thy lap	262
Oh, how kindly hast Thou led me	570	On a day, alack the day!	141
Oh, how much more doth beauty beauteous seem	753	On a hill there grows a flower	182
		O Nanny, wilt thou go with me	161
Oh! it is great for our country to die where the ranks are contending	365	Once did she hold the gorgeous East in fee	348
		Once, in the flight of ages past	618
Oh, it is hard to work for God	572	Once this soft turf, this rivulet's sands	676
Oh, it is pleasant, with a heart at ease	446	Once upon a midnight dreary, while I pondered, weak and weary	849
Oh listen, listen, ladies gay!	403	
"Oh, Mary, go and call the cattle home	417	One by one the sands are flowing	683
Oh, my love's like the steadfast sun	18	One day, as I was going by	904
Oh, never talk again to me	146	On either side the river lie	888
Oh no, no,—let me lie	677	One more Unfortunate	719
Oh! once the harp of Innisfail	395	One sweetly solemn thought	587
Oh saw ye bonnie Lesley	145	One time my soul was pierced as with a sword	43
Oh, saw ye not fair Ines	102	
Oh, say, can you see by the dawn's early light	353	One word is too often profaned	148
		O nightingale, that on yon bloomy spray	478
Oh, say what is that thing call'd Light	67	On Leven's banks, while free to rove	515
Oh, sing unto my roundelay!	147	On Linden, when the sun was low	340
Oh! snatch'd away in beauty's bloom	743	Only waiting till the shadows	639
Oh, St. Patrick was a gentleman	924	On the eighth day of March it was, some people say	943
Oh! take away my wig and gown	921	
Oh, talk not to me of a name great in story	157	On the sea and at the Hogue, sixteen hundred ninety-two	319
Oh that those lips had language! Life has pass'd	15	
		On thy fair bosom, silver lake	521
Oh, the gallant fisher's life!	468	On yonder hill a castle standes	385
Oh! the pleasant days of old, which so often people praise!	747	O Paradise! O Paradise!	601
		O reader! hast thou ever stood to see	458
Oh! the snow, the beautiful snow	720	Orpheus with his lute made trees	732
Oh, the sweet contentment	496	O stream descending to the sea	614
Oh, timely happy, timely wise	553	O Thou, from whom all goodness flows	584
Oh waly waly up the bank	103	O Thou, the contrite sinners' friend	539
Oh, weel may the boatie row	701	O Time, who know'st a lenient hand to lay	686
Oh welcome, bat and owlet gray	481	Our band is few, but true and tried	331
Oh what can ail thee, knight-at-arms!	865	Our bugles sang truce, for the night-cloud had lower'd	83
Oh, what will a' the lads do	161	
Oh wha will shoe my fair foot	394	Our God, our help in ages past	549
Oh, wherefore come ye forth in triumph from the north	311	Our good steeds snuff the evening air	366
		Our life is twofold: sleep hath its own world	790
Oh, why left I my hame?	362	Our wean's the most wonderfu' wean e'er I saw	42
Oh, why should the spirit of mortal be proud?	627	
Oh, will ye choose to hear the news?	955	Out and in the river is winding	680
Oh yet we trust that somehow good	689	Out of the church she follow'd them	188
Oh, young Lochinvar is come out of the West	136	Over hill, over dale	794
O Jesu, thou art standing	550	Over the mountains	97

INDEX OF FIRST LINES.

	PAGE
Over the river they beckon to me	629
O wild West Wind, thou breath of autumn's being	436
O World! O Life! O Time!	766
PACK, clouds, away, and welcome, day	215
Passions are likened best to floods and streams	182
Pause not to dream of the future before us	691
Peace in the clover-scented air	365
Pibroch of Donuil Dhu	359
Piped the blackbird on the beechwood spray	38
Piping down the valleys wild	68
Pity the sorrows of a poor old man	717
Pleasant are Thy courts above	600
Poor lone Hannah	698
Poor Soul, the centre of my sinful earth	753
"Praise God from whom all blessings flow"	583
Praise to God, immortal praise	548
Prayer is the soul's sincere desire	563
Prithee tell me, Dimple-Chin	163
Proud Maisie is in the wood	890
QUEEN and huntress, chaste and fair	446
Quhy dois zour brand sae drop wi' bluid	380
Quivering fears, heart-tearing cares	467
RARELY, rarely, comest thou	779
Remote, unfriended, melancholy, slow	767
Restless forms of living light	469
Ride on, ride on in majesty!	534
Ring out, wild bells, to the wild sky	690
Rise, my soul, and stretch thy wings	570
"Rise up, rise up, Xarifa! lay the golden cushion down	209
Rock of Ages, cleft for me	540
"Ruin seize thee, ruthless King!"	293
SAD is our youth, for it is ever going	614
Saint Augustine! well hast thou said	679
Saviour, when in dust to Thee	539
Saviour, who Thy flock art feeding	540
Saw ye my wee thing, saw ye my ain thing	164
Say over again, and yet once over again	134
Scorn not the Sonnet; Critic, you have frown'd	781
Scots, wha hae wi' Wallace bled	295
Season of mists and mellow fruitfulness!	435
See, from this counterfeit of him	221
See the chariot at hand here of Love!	160
See the course throng'd with gazers, the sports are begun	488
See with what simplicity	240
Shall I compare thee to a summer's day?	220
Shall I tell you whom I love?	123
Shall I, wasting in despair	169
Shed no tear! oh, shed no tear!	793
She dwelt among the untrodden ways	49
She is a winsome wee thing	9

	PAGE
She is far from the land where her young hero sleeps	275
She is my only girl	41
She is not fair to outward view	172
Shepherds all, and maidens fair	495
She's gane to dwall in heaven, my lassie	218
She sits in a fashionable parlor	922
She smiles and smiles, and will not sigh	216
She stood breast-high amid the corn	144
She walks in beauty like the night	741
She was a Phantom of delight	10
Should auld acquaintance be forgot	81
Shout the glad tidings, exultingly sing	533
Sigh no more, ladies, sigh no more	187
Silence, in truth, would speak my sorrow best	228
Silent nymph, with curious eye!	506
Since I did leave the presence of my love	190
Since there's no help, come, let us kiss and part	170
Since Thou hast added now, O God!	554
Sing, I pray, a little song	39
Sing, sweet thrushes, forth and sing!	469
Sir Marmaduke was a hearty knight	784
Slave of the dark and dirty mine!	87
Sleep, baby, sleep!	32
Sleep breathes at last from out thee	36
Sleep on, baby on the floor	33
Slowly England's sun was setting o'er the hill-tops far away	404
Sly Beelzebub on all occasions	959
So cruel prison how could betide, alas!	222
So fallen! so lost! the light withdrawn	267
Softly	638
Softly now the light of day	552
Soldier, rest! thy warfare o'er	700
Some dreams we have are nothing else but dreams	866
Some murmur when their sky is clear	658
Sometimes a light surprises	573
Somewhat back from the village street	76
Some years ago, ere time and taste	913
Songs of praise the angels sang	588
Souls of poets dead and gone	504
Sound fife, and cry the slogan	317
Sound the loud timbrel o'er Egypt's dark sea!	550
Spake full well, in language quaint and olden	448
Speak and tell us, our Ximena, looking northward far away	345
Speak low! tread softly through these halls	738
"Speak! speak! thou fearful guest!"	864
Spirit that breathest through my lattice; thou	442
Spring, the sweet spring, is the year's pleasant king	427
Spring, with that nameless pathos in the air	431
St. Agnes' Eve—Ah, bitter chill it was!	127
Stand! the ground's your own, my braves!	329
Stand the omnipotent decree!	585
St. Anthony at church	915
Star that bringest home the bee	447

	PAGE
Stay, lady, stay, for mercy's sake	46
Stern Daughter of the Voice of God!	664
Still to be neat, still to be drest	740
Still young and fine, but what is still in view.	443
Strike the bells wantonly	764
Such was old Chaucer: such the placid mien.	225
Sun of my soul, Thou Saviour dear	555
Survey this shield, all bossy bright	936
Sweet and low, sweet and low	31
Sweet are the charms of her I love	154
Sweet are the thoughts that savor of content.	660
Sweet Auburn! loveliest village of the plain.	756
Sweet baby, sleep! what ails my dear?	34
Sweet, be not proud of those two eyes	210
Sweet bird! that sing'st away the early hours	477
Sweet day, so cool, so calm, so bright	662
Sweet Highland Girl, a very shower	65
Sweet Innisfallen, fare thee well	517
Sweet is the rose, but grows upon a brere	780
Sweet is the scene when virtue dies	618
Sweet is the voice that calls	434
Sweetly breathing, vernal air	431
Sweet nurslings of the vernal skies	448
Sweet poet of the woods—a long adieu!	480
Sweet Saviour! bless us ere we go	556
Sweet Spring! thou turn'st with all thy goodly train	425
Swiftly walk over the western wave	442
TAKE, oh take those lips away	184
Tasteful illumination of the night	483
Teach me, my God and King	544
Tears, idle tears, I know not what they mean.	91
Tell me not in mournful numbers	615
Tell me not, sweet, I am unkinde	124
Tell me where is fancy bred	838
Ternissa, you are fled	196
That day of wrath, that dreadful day	610
That time of year thou may'st in me behold...	219
That way look, my Infant, lo!	485
That which her slender waist confined	185
The Assyrian came down like the wolf on the fold	283
The baby wept	45
The "Ballyshannon" foundered off the coast of Cariboo	925
The blessed damozel leaned out	839
The bonnie, bonnie bairn, who sits poking in the ase	37
The boy stood on the burning deck	345
The breaking waves dash'd high	308
The castle-clock had toll'd midnight	312
The child leans on its parent's breast	573
The chimes, the chimes of Motherland	503
The crackling embers on the hearth are dead.	775
The curfew tolls the knell of parting day	630
The day is cold and dark and dreary	775

	PAGE
The day is done and the darkness	774
The day of tumult, strife, defeat, was o'er....	273
The dews of summer night did fall	379
The dew was falling fast, the stars began to blink	487
The doubt which we misdeem, fair love, is vain	101
The dule's i' this bonnet o' mine	166
The dusky night rides down the sky	493
Thee finds me in the garden, Hannah,—come in! 'Tis kind of thee	22
"Thee, Mary, with this ring I wed"	10
The Emperor Nap he would set off	949
The farmer sat in his easy-chair	6
The farmer's wife sat at the door	699
The forward youth that would appear	238
The fountains mingle with the river	97
The fourteenth of July had come	332
The gallant youth who may have gain'd	511
The glories of our blood and state	623
The God of Abraham praise	583
The groves of Blarney they look so charming.	516
The hag is astride	875
The harp that once through Tara's halls	362
The heath this night must be my bed	186
The hosts of Don Rodrigo were scatter'd in dismay	290
The house is dark and dreary	785
The isles of Greece! the isles of Greece!	360
The Jester shook his hood and bells, and leap'd upon a chair	916
The king can drink the best of wine	705
The king sits in Dunfermline town	367
The kings who ruled mankind with haughty sway	892
The king with all his kingly train	328
The Knight had ridden down from Wensley Moor	387
The lady lay in her bed	714
The laird o' Cockpen he's proud and he's great.	892
The lark now leaves his watery nest	472
The lass of Patie's mill	155
The little gate was reach'd at last	217
The loppèd tree in time may grow again	778
The Lord my pasture shall prepare	561
The melancholy days are come, the saddest of the year	456
The midges dance aboon the burn	440
The mighty sun had just gone down	268
The Moorish king rides up and down	295
The Muse, disgusted at an age and clime	723
The night has a thousand eyes	180
The night is come; like to the day	556
The night is dark, and the winter winds	12
The night was made for cooling shade	465
The noble king of Brentford	906
The old mayor climb'd the belfry-tower	415
The Ordeal's fatal trumpet sounded	145

	PAGE
The pines were dark on Ramoth hill	82
The play is done, the curtain drops	673
The poetry of earth is never dead	482
There are gains for all our losses	764
There be none of Beauty's daughters	157
There be those who sow beside	617
There came to the beach a poor exile of Erin	359
There is a calm for those who weep	641
There is a dwelling-place above	599
There is a garden in her face	185
There is a happy land	599
There is a land of pure delight	599
There is no flock, however watch'd and tended	646
There is not in the wide world a valley so sweet	517
There lived, as Fame reports, in days of yore	945
There's a good time coming, boys	750
There's a grim one-horse hearse in a jolly round trot	722
There's music in the morning air	561
There's no dew left on the daisies and clover	19
There's not a joy the world can give like that it takes away	656
There was a jovial beggar	918
There was a lady lived at Leith	896
There was a may, and a weel-fared may	393
There was a time when meadow, grove, and stream	644
There was once a gentle time	156
There were ninety and nine that safely lay	581
There were three ravens sat on a tree	411
There were three sailors of Bristol City	909
There were two sisters sat in a bour	418
The rich man's son inherits land	705
The roses grew so thickly	456
These, as they change, Almighty Father, these	423
The sea! the sea! the open sea!	462
These to His memory—since he held them dear	280
The shades of night were falling fast	785
The shivering column of the moonlight lies	518
"The sky is clouded, the rocks are bare	785
The snow had begun in the gloaming	437
The soote season, that bud and bloom forth brings	425
The spacious firmament on high	545
The Spearmen heard the bugle sound	392
The splendor falls on castle-walls	502
The stars above will make thee known	225
The stately Homes of England	1
The summer and autumn had been so wet	409
The Summer, the divinest Summer burns	433
The sun has gane down o'er the lofty Ben-lomond	163
The sun is warm, the sky is clear	261
The sun rises bright in France	358
The tempest has darken'd the face of the skies	462
The thirsty earth soaks up the rain	446

	PAGE
The thoughts are strange that crowd into my brain	520
The tree of deepest root is found	619
The twentieth year is well-nigh past	245
The wanton troopers, riding by	501
The warm sun is failing, the bleak wind is wailing	436
The wife sat thoughtfully turning over	12
The wisest of the wise	751
The woods decay, the woods decay and fall	787
The world goes up and the world goes down	780
The world is very evil	604
The World's a bubble, and the Life of Man	613
The wretch, condemn'd with life to part	785
They are all gone into the world of light	597
They come! the merry summer months of beauty, song, and flowers	430
They grew in beauty, side by side	28
"They made her a grave too cold and damp	422
The young May moon is beaming, love	162
They sat and comb'd their beautiful hair	786
They say that God lives very high	44
They that have power to hurt, and will do none	754
This ancient silver bowl of mine,—it tells of good old times	90
This figure, that thou here seest put	230
This is the Arsenal. From floor to ceiling	521
This is the month, and this the happy morn	523
This is the ship of pearl, which, poets feign	470
This morning, timely rapt with holy fire	233
This night is my departing night	656
This only grant me, that my means may lie	233
This was the ruler of the land	289
This winter's weather itt waxeth cold	901
Those evening bells! those evening bells!	764
Thou art gone to the grave; but we will not deplore thee	594
Thou art, O God! the life and light	551
Thou blossom, bright with autumn dew	455
Thou chronicle of crimes! I read no more	352
Thought is deeper than all speech	782
Thou happy, happy elf!	903
Thou hast made me, and shall Thy work decay?	565
Thou hast sworn by thy God, my Jeanie	157
Thou lingering star, with lessening ray	137
Thou little bird, thou dweller by the sea	471
Thou still unravish'd bride of quietness!	746
Thou, to whom the world unknown	776
Thou unrelenting Past!	91
Three fishers went sailing away to the west	699
Three Poets, in three distant ages born	240
Threescore o' nobles rade up the king's ha'	406
Three years she grew in sun and shower	49
Thrice, at the huts of Fontenoy, the English column fail'd	321
Thrice happy he, who by some shady grove	658

INDEX OF FIRST LINES.

	PAGE
Thy braes were bonny, Yarrow stream	384
Thy cheek is o' the rose's hue	202
Thy goodness, Lord, our souls confess	562
Thy summer voice, Musketaquit	764
Thy voice is heard thro' rolling drums	743
Tiger! tiger! burning bright	494
Timely blossom, infant fair	35
Time wasteth years, and months, and hours	172
Tired with all these, for restful death I cry	219
'Tis midnight's holy hour, and silence now	95
'Tis Morn :—the sea-breeze seems to bring	14
'Tis sweet to hear the merry lark	472
'Tis sweet to view, from half-past five to six	938
'Tis the last rose of Summer	456
'Tis the middle of the night by the castle-clock	841
'Tis the middle watch of a summer's night	810
'Tis time this heart should be unmoved	88
'Tis twenty years, and something more	79
To battle! to battle!	310
To bear, to nurse, to rear	21
To draw no envy (Shakespeare) on thy name	228
To fair Fidele's grassy tomb	637
To him who in the love of Nature holds	624
Toiling in the naked fields	702
To live in hell, and heaven to behold	212
To make this condiment, your poet begs	959
To me, fair friend, you never can be old	752
Too late I stay'd,—forgive the crime.!	779
To one who has been long in city pent	499
To praise thy life, or waile thy worthie death	227
To sigh, yet feel no pain	182
To the chase goes Rodrigo, with hound and with hawk	292
To the lords of convention 'twas Claverhouse who spoke	316
T'other day, as I was twining	103
To these, whom death again did wed	635
To the sound of timbrels sweet	220
To thy lover	126
To Thy temple I repair	561
Touch us gently, Time!	751
To wake the soul by tender strokes of art	242
Tread softly,—bow the head	721
Triumphal arch that fill'st the sky	444
Trust not, sweet soul, those curlèd waves of gold	741
"Turn, gentle hermit of the dale	159
Turn I my looks unto the skies	156
'Twas a jolly old pedagogue, long ago	927
'Twas at the royal feast for Persia won	724
'Twas at the silent solemn hour	175
'Twas in the prime of summer-time	375
'Twas morn, and beauteous on the mountain's brow	518
'Twas morn—but not the ray which falls the summer boughs among	264
'Twas on a Monday morning	325
'Twas on the shores that round our coast	910
'Twas the night before Christmas, when all through the house	67
'Twas when the seas were roaring	125
'Twas when the wan leaf frae the birk tree was fa'in	202
Twelve years ago I made a mock	79
"Two hands upon the breast	620
Tying her bonnet under her chin	217
UNDER a spreading chestnut tree	693
Under my window, under my window	53
Underneath this sable hearse	233
Under the greenwood tree	457
Under yonder beech tree standing on the green sward	142
Up from the meadows rich with corn	350
Up from the south, at break of day	351
Up! quit thy bower; late wears the hour	499
Up the airy mountain	794
Up the dale and down the bourne	433
Up to the hills I lift mine eyes	583
Up with me! up with me into the clouds!	473
VAIN world, what is in thee?	592
Versailles!—Up the chestnut alley	327
Verse, a breeze 'mid blossoms straying	94
Victorious men of earth, no more	623
Vital spark of heavenly flame	596
WANTON droll, whose harmless play	484
Was it the chime of a tiny bell	628
Watchman, tell us of the night	523
Way down upon de Swannee Ribber	18
We are all here	17
We are born; we laugh; we weep	615
We are the sweet Flowers	449
We are two travellers, Roger and I	717
We count the broken lyres that rest	626
Wee, modest, crimson-tippèd flower	454
Weep no more, nor sigh, nor groan	786
Weep with me, all you that read	232
Wee, sleekit, cow'rin', tim'rous beastie	483
Wee Willie Winkie rins through the town	41
We hail this morn	250
Welcome, welcome, do I sing	125
We meet 'neath the sounding rafter	787
We parted in silence, we parted by night	85
Were I as base as is the lowly plain	99
Werther had a love for Charlotte	895
We see not, know not; all our way	568
We sing the praise of Him who died	535
We the fairies, blithe and antic	794
We watch'd her breathing through the night	625
We were crowded in the cabin	38
We were not many—we who stood	348
We wreathed about our darling's head	49
What ails this heart o' mine?	199
What an image of peace and rest	522
What are these in bright array	598

INDEX OF FIRST LINES.

	PAGE
What beck'ning ghost, along the moonlight shade	635
What bird so sings, yet so does wail?	480
What constitutes a state?	363
What dire offence from amorous causes springs.	795
What hid'st thou in thy treasure-caves and cells	463
What I shall leave thee, none can tell	233
What is the meaning of the song	146
What need my Shakespeare for his honor'd bones	230
What shall I do with all the days and hours..	101
What's hallow'd ground? Has earth a clod..	633
What state of life can be so blest..	213
What was he doing, the great god Pan	723
When a deed is done for Freedom, through the broad earth's aching breast	343
When age hath made me what I am not now.	755
When a' ither bairnies are hush'd to their hame.	46
When all is done and said	658
When all Thy mercies, O my God	547
When as in faire Jerusalem	374
When Britain first, at Heaven's command	355
Whence comes my love? O, heart, disclose...	124
When chapman billies leave the street	873
When coldness wraps this suffering clay	625
Whene'er with haggard eyes I view	935
When first I saw sweet Peggy	165
When Freedom from her mountain-height	353
When gathering clouds around I view	569
When God at first made Man	662
When he whispers, "O Miss Bailey	954
When hope lies dead within the heart	685
When icicles hang by the wall	438
When I consider how my light is spent	234
When I do count the clock that tells the time.	752
When in disgrace with fortune and men's eyes.	219
When in the chronicle of wasted time	220
When Israel, of the Lord beloved	550
When I survey the bright	775
When I survey the wondrous cross	547
When I upon thy bosom lean	7
When lovely woman stoops to folly	687
When Love, with unconfinèd wings	124
When maidens such as Hester die	741
When marshall'd on the nightly plain	577
When May is in his prime, and youthful Spring	428
When midnight o'er the moonless skies	94
When Music, heavenly maid, was young	730
When o'er the mountain steeps	433
When on my ear your loss was knell'd	638
When our heads are bow'd with woe	582
When silent time wi' lightly foot	93
When stars are in the quiet skies	218
When that the fields put on their gay attire...	477
When the fields were white with harvest, and the laborers were few	684
When the hounds of spring are on winter's traces	426
When the hours of day are number'd.	773
When the lessons and tasks are all ended	62
When the sheep are in the fauld, when the kye's come hame	137
When to the sessions of sweet silent thought.	753
When troubled in spirit, when weary of life...	489
When we for age could neither read nor write.	688
When we two parted	86
When winter's cold tempests and snows are no more	475
Where are the swallows fled?	684
Where are you going, my pretty maid?	898
Whereas on certain boughs and sprays	951
Where did you come from, baby dear?	31
Where dost thou careless lie	225
Where is the grave of Sir Arthur O'Kellyn?..	626
Where lies the land to which the ship would go?	466
Where shall the lover rest	176
Where the bee sucks, there suck I	794
Where the remote Bermudas ride	549
Wherever I wander, up and about	7
Which I wish to remark	933
Which shall it be? Which shall it be?	45
While sauntering through the crowded street.	783
While shepherds watch'd their flocks by night.	529
Whilst as fickle Fortune smiled	778
Whilst in this cold and blustering clime	467
Whilst Thee I seek, protecting Power	572
Whither, 'midst falling dew	471
Whoe'er she be.	121
Who finds a woman good and wise	24
Who is Sylvia? what is she	217
Who'll press for gold this crowded street	675
Who loves not Knowledge? Who shall rail.	690
"'Who's dead?' Ye want to know	704
Why, Damon, with the forward day	637
"Why did you melt your waxen man	875
Why do ye weep, sweet babes? Can tears.	452
Why has not man a collar and a log?	923
Why so pale and wan, fond lover?	104
Why thus longing, thus for ever sighing	766
"Why weep ye by the tide, ladie?	134
Wild rose of Alloway! my thanks	249
With a glancing eye and curving mane	493
With deep affection	516
With fingers weary and worn	716
With how sad steps, O Moon, thou climb'st the skies!	118
Within a thick and spreading hawthorn bush.	476
Within his sober realm of leafless trees	640
Within the midnight of her hair	700
With little here to do or see	453
With one consent let all the earth	545
With silent awe I hail the sacred morn	439
Woodman, spare that tree!	75

	Page		Page
Word was brought to the Danish king	420	"Yes," I answered you last night	138
Worship, honor, glory, blessing	601	Yet once more, O ye laurels, and once more	235
Wouldst thou heare what man can say	233	You are old, Father William, the young man cried	674
Ye banks, and braes, and streams around	120	You bells in the steeple, ring, ring out your changes	19
Ye banks and braes o' bonnie Doon	170	You know we French storm'd Ratisbon	341
Ye clouds! that far above me float and pause	333	You lay a wreath on murder'd Lincoln's bier	280
Ye distant spires, ye antique towers	504	You may give over plough, boys	620
Ye gentlemen of England	701	You meaner beauties of the night	185
Ye golden lamps of heaven, farewell	588	You must wake and call me early, call me early, mother dear	69
Ye little birds, that sit and sing	162	Young Ben he was a nice young man	897
Ye Mariners of England	356	Young Rory O'More courted Kathleen bawn	165
Ye nymphs of Solyma! begin the song	527	Your horse is faint, my King—my Lord! your gallant horse is sick	296
Ye say they all have passed away	520		
Yes! from mine eyes the tears unbidden start	356		
Ye shepherds so cheerful and gay	205		

Ref.
821.008
C652
c.2

98883

For Reference

Not to be taken from this room

$32.51